ninth edition

STRATEGIC MANAGEMENT and BUSINESS POLICY

Thomas L. Wheelen
University of South Florida

J. David Hunger
Iowa State University

PEARSON

Prentice Hall

Upper Saddle River, New Jersey 07458

Library of Congress Cataloging-in-Publication Data

Wheelen, Thomas L.
    Strategic management and business policy / Thomas L. Wheelen, J. David Hunger.--9th ed.
        p. cm.
    Various multi-media instructional aids, including a Web site, are available to supplement
the text.
    Includes bibliographical references and index.
    ISBN 0-13-142179-4
        1. Strategic planning. 2. Strategic planning--Case studies. I. Hunger, J. David.
    Title.

HD30.28.W43 2004
658.4'012--dc21

Senior Managing Editor (Editorial): Jennifer Glennon
Editor-in-Chief: Jeff Shelstad
Assistant Editor: Melanie Olsen
Editorial Assistant: Kelly Wendrychowicz
Media Project Manager: Jessica Sabloff
Executive Marketing Manager: Shannon Moore
Marketing Assistant: Patrick Danzuso
Senior Managing Editor (Production): Judy Leale
Production Editor: Cindy Spreder
Permissions Supervisor: Suzanne Grappi
Associate Director, Manufacturing: Vincent Scelta
Production Manager: Arnold Vila
Buyer: Diane Peirano
Design Manager: Maria Lange
Designer: Steve Frim
Interior Design: Lee Goldstein
Cover Design: Steve Frim
Cover Illustration/Photo: Hermann/Starke—CORBIS
Illustrator (Interior): UG / GGS Information Services, Inc.
Manager, Print Production: Christy Mahon
Print Production Liaison: Ashley Scattergood
Composition: UG / GGS Information Services, Inc.
Full-Service Project Management: UG / GGS Information Services, Inc.
Printer/Binder: Courier-Kendallville

Credits and acknowledgments borrowed from other sources and reproduced, with permission, in this textbook appear on appropriate page within text.

Pearson Education LTD   Pearson Education Australia PTY, Limited
Pearson Education Singapore, Pte. Ltd   Pearson Education North Asia Ltd
Pearson Education, Canada, Ltd   Pearson Educación de Mexico, S.A. de C.V.
Pearson Education–Japan   Pearson Education Malaysia, Pte. Ltd

10 9 8 7 6 5 4 3 2 1
ISBN 013-142179-4

Dedicated to

Kathy
Richard
Tom

Betty
Kari, Jeff, Maddie, and Megan
Suzi, Nick, and Summer
Lori
Merry
Smokey

And to the Prentice Hall sales representatives who work so hard to promote this book, we thank you!

Tara Algeo	Kate Derrick	Dave Hill
Peter Ancona	George Devenny	Kristen Hodge
Geralyn Applegate	Sue Dikun	Brett Holmes
Larry Armstrong	Dana Duncan	Carole Horton
Tracy Augustine	Beverly Dunn	David Hough
Jonathan Axelrod	Scott Dustan	Jody Ipsen
Hal Balmer	Susan Fackert	David Jackson
Cordelia Barrera	Trey Feigle	Susan Jackson
Kelly Bell	Marissa Feliberty	Connie James
William Beville	Dennis Fernandes	Vince Jansen
Jennifer Blackburn	Mary Fernandez	Leah Johnson
Joan Blasco-Paul	John Fishback	Susan Joseph
Melissa Blum	Sean Fisher	Curtis Ketterman
Sara Bredbenner	Jonathan Fitting	Stacy Keyser
Jeanne Bronson	Steve Foster	Romayne Kilde
Julie Burgmeier	Mary Gallagher	Sally Kissel
Shauna Burgmeier	Cheryle Gehrlich	Tammy Knight
Ruth Cardiff	Sybil Geraud	Susan Koller
Darrin Carr	Carolyn Chazi-Tehrani	Eric Krassow
Michael Carrigg	David Gillespie	Daniel Krauss
Andrea Catullo	Chip Gillikin	Steven Ladd
Meredith Chandler	Eric Gilmore	Kelly Lambing
Natalie Cherry	Evan Girard	Sharon Lavoy
Krista Christenson	Kevin Glynn	Kristen Lindley
Matt Christopherson	Keri Goldberg-Leonard	Stacie Lipten
Catherine Colucci	Katherine Grassi	Tricia Liscio
Thayne Conrad	Lisa Greer	Tracy Long
Cyndi Crimmins	Doug Greive	David Lopez
Meilynn D'Alessandro	Edith Hall	Jennifer Lucking
Sarah Davis	Melissa Hallett	Kimberly Manzi
Matthew DeGroat	Alison Harvey	Meredith Margraf
Matt Denham	Julie Hildebrand	Patrick Mast

Jennifer Matty
Joshua McClary
Eileen McClay
Regina McCray
Brian McGarry
Milton McGowen
Irene McGuinness
Lou McGuire
Ryan McHenry
Jeff McIlroy
Sally McPherson
Mary Meyer
Laura Middleton
Sue Miller
Ashley Millinor
Paul Misselwitz
Becky Mitchell
Kate Moore
Karen Moreau
Julie Morel
Katie Morgan
Joseph Murray
Pete Nasta
Celeste Nossiter
Meghan O'Donnell
Kevin O'Sullivan
Tori Olson Alves
Nancy Palmer

Deborah Patterson
Emilia Pawlowski
Antoinette Payne
Mick Pfaff
Carol Pharo
Andrew Pollard
David Ramsey
Allison Rauch
Karen Reifsteck
Leann Reisinger
Julie Resler
Mary Rhodes
Anne Riddick
Molly Riggs
Dan Rinn
Dorothy Rosene
Richard Rowe
Brad Sallmen
Corrina Schultz
Terra Schultz
Steven Shapiro
Brent Sheppard
Mark Sibla
Wayne Siegert
Phyllis Simon
Donald Smith
Ann Sorenson
Beth Spencer

Richard Spencer
Joe Sturino
Cindy Sullivan
Dan Sullivan
Chuck Synovec
Moira Tarpy
Mark Templeman
Devorah Tharp
David Theisen
Derek Thibodeau
Frank Timoney
Catherine Traywick
Nugent Tyra
Karen Villagomez
David Visser
Jennifer Walters
Michael Ward
Mary Weatherly
LeDawn Webb
Ann Weiss
Eric Weiss
Jim West
Hannah Whitlock
Read Wickham
Alissa Wilmoth
Jennifer Woodle
Sharon Young

Brief Contents

Contents

and JetBlue in profitability. After a $2.8 million loss in 2001, AirTran's management hoped to return the firm to profitability by moving into regional short-haul markets.

new

(Contributor: Maryanne M. Rouse)

Tyson produces and distributes beef, chicken, and pork products in the United States. It recently acquired IBP, a major competitor, but has been the subject of lawsuits by its employees and the EPA. How should management deal with its poor public relations and position the company to gain and sustain competitive advantage in an industry characterized by increasing consolidation and intense competition?

new

(Contributor: Maryanne M. Rouse)

A leading pharmaceutical company, Eli Lilly produces a wide variety of ethical drugs and animal health products. Despite an array of new products, industry analysts were concerned after the firm lost its patent protection for Prozac in 2001. The FDA found quality problems at several of the company's manufacturing sites—resulting in a delay in new product approvals.

Additional Internet Research Mini-Cases Are Available on the Companion Website at www.prenhall.com/wheelen

Southwest Airlines Company

new

(Contributor: Maryanne M. Rouse)

The fourth largest U.S. airline in terms of passengers carried and second largest in scheduled domestic departures, Southwest was the only domestic airline to remain profitable in 2001. Emphasizing high-frequency, short-haul, point-to-point, and low-fare service, the airline had the lowest cost per available seat mile flown of any U.S. major passenger carrier. Can Southwest continue to be successful as competitors increasingly imitate its competitive strategy?

Stryker Corporation

new

(Contributor: Maryanne M. Rouse)

Stryker is a leading maker of specialty medical and surgical products. It markets its products directly to hospitals and physicians in the United States and 100 other countries. Given the decline in the number of hospitals due to consolidation and cost containment efforts by government programs and health care insurers, the industry expects continued downward pressure on prices. How can Stryker effectively deal with these developments to continue its growth?

H. J. Heinz Company

new

(Contributor: Maryanne M. Rouse)

Heinz, a manufacturer and marketer of processed food products, pursued global growth via market penetration and acquisitions. Unfortunately, its modest sales growth was primarily from its acquisitions. Now that the firm is divesting Del Monte Foods, analysts wonder how a 20% smaller Heinz will grow its profits.

Williams-Sonoma

new

(Contributor: Maryanne M. Rouse)

Williams-Sonoma is a specialty retailer of home products. Following a related diversification growth strategy, the company operates 415 Williams-Sonoma, Pottery Barn, and Hold Everything retail stores throughout North America. Its direct sales segment includes six retail catalogues and three e-commerce sites. The company must deal with increasing competition in this fragmented industry characterized by low entry barriers.

Pfizer, Inc.

new

(Contributor: Maryanne M. Rouse)

With its acquisition in 2000 of rival pharmaceutical firm, Warner-Lambert, for its Lipitor prescription drug, Pfizer became the world's largest ethical pharmaceutical company in terms of sales. Already the leading company in the United States, Pfizer's purchase of Pharmacia in 2002 moved Pfizer from fourth to first place in Europe. Will large size hurt or help the company's future growth and profitability in an industry facing increasing scrutiny?

Preface

We wrote *Strategic Management and Business Policy* to introduce you to strategic management—a field of inquiry that focuses on the organization as a whole and its interactions with its environment. The corporate world is in the process of transformation driven by information technology (in particular the Internet) and globalization. Strategic management takes a panoramic view of this changing corporate terrain and attempts to show how large and small firms can be more effective and efficient not only in today's world, but in tomorrow's as well.

Both the text and the cases have been class-tested in strategy courses and revised based on feedback from students and instructors. For the most part, the text is unchanged from the eighth edition. The only changes are the additions of Enron, Tyco, and Worldcom examples in Chapter 2 and the inclusion of a glossary of key terms at the back of the book. The first 10 chapters are organized around a strategic management model that prefaces each chapter and provides a structure for both content and case analysis. We emphasize those concepts that have proven to be most useful in understanding strategic decision-making and in conducting case analysis. Our goal was to make the text as comprehensive as possible without getting bogged down in any one area. Endnote references are provided for those who wish to learn more about any particular topic. The primary changes from the eighth edition are the selection of cases. We included new versions of eight popular full-length cases and five entirely new cases. We also added a special category of ten experiential cases called Internet Research Mini-Cases. All of the cases are about actual organizations. The firms range in size from large, established multinationals to small, entrepreneurial ventures, and cover a broad variety of issues. As an aid to case analysis, we propose the strategic audit as an analytical technique.

Objectives

This book focuses on the following objectives, typically found in most strategic management and business policy courses:

- To develop an understanding of strategic management concepts, research, and theories.

- To develop a framework of analysis to enable a student to identify central issues and problems in complex, comprehensive cases; to suggest alternative courses of action; and to present well-supported recommendations for future action.

- To develop conceptual skills so that a student is able to integrate previously learned aspects of corporations.

- To develop an understanding of the global economy and the Internet and their current and potential impact on business activities in any location.

- To develop an understanding of the role of corporate governance in strategic management.

- To develop the ability to analyze and evaluate, both quantitatively and qualitatively, the performance of the people responsible for strategic decisions.

- To bridge the gap between theory and practice by developing an understanding of when and how to apply concepts and techniques learned in earlier courses on marketing, accounting, finance, management, operations, and information systems.

- To improve research capabilities necessary to gather and interpret key environmental data.
- To develop a better understanding of the present and future environments in which corporations must function.
- To develop analytical and decision-making skills for dealing with complex conceptual problems in an ethical manner.

This book achieves these objectives by presenting and explaining concepts and theories useful in understanding the strategic management process. It critically analyzes studies in the field of strategy to acquaint the student with the literature of this area and to help develop the student's research capabilities. It also suggests a model of strategic management. It recommends the strategic audit as one approach to the systematic analysis of complex organization-wide issues. Through a series of special issue and comprehensive cases, it provides the student with an opportunity to apply concepts, skills, and techniques to real-world corporate problems. The book focuses on the business corporation because of its crucial position in the economic system of the world and in the material development of any society.

Time-Tested Features

This edition contains many of the same features and content that helped make previous editions successful. Some of the features are the following:

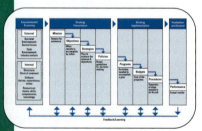

- A **strategic management model** runs throughout the first 10 chapters as a unifying concept. (Explained in Chapter 1)

chapter 2

Corporate Governance and Social Responsibility

- **Corporate governance** is examined in terms of the roles, responsibilities, and interactions of top management and the board of directors. (Chapter 2) Most of the cases contain information about the company's board of directors and top management.

2.3 Social Responsibilities of Strategic Decision Makers

Should strategic decision makers be responsible only to shareholders, or do they have broader responsibilities? The concept of **social responsibility** proposes that a private corporation has responsibilities to society that extend beyond making a profit. Strategic decisions often affect more than just the corporation. A decision to retrench by closing some plants and discontinuing product lines, for example, affects not only the firm's workforce, but also the communities where the plants are located and the customers that have no other source for the discontinued product. Such situations raise questions of the appropriateness of certain missions, objectives, and strategies of business corporations. Managers must be able to deal with these conflicting interests in an ethical manner to formulate a viable strategic plan.

RESPONSIBILITIES OF A BUSINESS FIRM

What are the responsibilities of a business firm, and how many of them must be fulfilled? Milton Friedman and Archie Carroll offer two contrasting views of the responsibilities of business firms to society.

- **Social responsibility and managerial ethics** are examined in detail in terms of how they affect strategic decision making. (Chapter 2)

- Equal emphasis is placed on **environmental scanning** of the societal environment as well as on the task environment. Topics include forecasting and Miles and Snow's typology in addition to Porter's industry analysis. (Chapter 3) ▶

- **Core and distinctive competencies** are examined within the framework of the resource-based view of the firm. (Chapter 4)

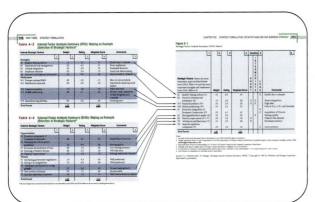

- Internal and external strategic factors are emphasized through the use of specially-designed **EFAS, IFAS,** and **SFAS tables.** (Chapters 3, 4, and 5)

◀

- Two chapters deal with issues in **strategy implementation**, such as organizational and job design plus strategy-manager fit, action planning, and corporate culture. (Chapters 8 and 9)

- A separate chapter on **evaluation and control** explains the importance of measurement and incentives to organizational performance. (Chapter 10)

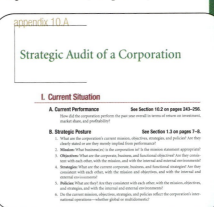

- The **strategic audit**, a way to operationalize the strategic decision-making process, provides a tested methodology in case analysis. (Chapter 10) ▶

- Special chapters deal with strategic issues in **managing technology and innovation, entrepreneurial ventures and small businesses,** and **not-for-profit organizations.** (Chapters 11, 12, and 13, respectively) These issues are often ignored by other strategy textbooks.

chapter 14

PART SIX
Introduction to Case Analysis

**Suggestions
for Case Analysis**

A few years ago, AlliedSignal's free cash flow measure turned negative. Although the company reported a 16% gain in net income for the second quarter, the free cash flow was a negative $90 million. Top management dismissed the cash flow situation as only temporary, arguing that capital spending and increasing inventory during the first part of the year was needed to fuel the company's sales growth expected later in the year. A company spokesman predicted that the free cash flow for the year should hit $300 million and concluded, "There's no problem with cash flow here."

"Not so!" responded Jeffrey Forta, President of Boston's Ernst Institutional Research. Forta contended that Allied's growing sales and earnings masked a serious problem in the company. Over the past year, Allied's push to boost sales had caused it difficulty in meeting its cash needs from operations. "They're growing too fast and not getting the returns from capital investments they used to get. Allied peaked in mid 1995, and returns have been deteriorating since." Forta predicted that without major changes, AlliedSignal would have increasing difficulty continuing its double-digit sales growth."

This is an example of how one analyst used a performance measure to assess the overall health of a company. You can do the same type of in-depth analysis on a comprehensive strategic management case. This chapter provides you with various analytical techniques and suggestions for conducting this kind of case analysis.

341

- **Suggestions for in-depth case analysis** provide a complete listing of financial ratios, recommendations for oral and written analysis, and ideas for further research. (Chapter 14)

◄

- The **Strategic Audit Worksheet** is based on the time-tested strategic audit and is designed to help students organize and structure daily case preparation in a brief period of time. The worksheet works exceedingly well for checking the level of daily student case preparation—especially for open class discussions of cases. (Chapter 14)   ►

- **Key Theory As It Applies Capsules** in various chapters explain key theories underlying strategic management. This feature adds emphasis to the theories, but does not interrupt the flow of the text material.

Projections for the 21st Century

- From 1994 to 2010, the world population will grow from 5.607 billion to 7.32 billion.
- From 1994 to 2010, the number of nations will increase from 192 to 202.[67]

- **Projections for the 21st Century** end each chapter by forecasting what the world will be like in 2010.

◄

Strategic Practice Exercise

How far should people in a business firm go in gathering competitive intelligence? Where do you draw the line?

Evaluate each of the following approaches that a business firm could use to gather information about competition. For each approach, mark your feeling about its appropriateness: 1 (definitely not appropriate), 2 (probably not appropriate), 3 (undecided), 4 (probably appropriate), or 5 (definitely appropriate).

The business firm should try to get useful information about competitors by:

_____ Carefully studying trade journals.

_____ Wiretapping the telephones of competitors.

_____ Posing as a potential customer to competitors.

_____ Getting loyal customers to put out a phony "request for proposal" to solicit competitors' bids.

_____ Buying competitors' products and taking them apart.

_____ Hiring management consultants who have worked for competitors.

_____ Rewarding competitors' employees for useful "tips."

_____ Questioning competitors' customers and/or suppliers.

_____ Buying and analyzing competitors' garbage.

_____ Advertising and interviewing for nonexistent jobs.

_____ Taking public tours of competitors' facilities.

_____ Releasing false information about the company in order to confuse competitors.

_____ Questioning competitors' technical people at trade shows and conferences.

_____ Hiring key people away from competitors.

_____ Analyzing competitors' labor union contracts.

_____ Having employees date persons who work for competitors.

_____ Studying aerial photographs of competitors' facilities.

After you mark each of the preceding approaches, compare your responses to those of other people in your class. For each approach, the people marking 4 or 5 should say why they thought this particular act would be appropriate. Those who marked 1 or 2 should then state why they thought this act would be inappropriate.

What does this tell you about ethics and socially responsible behavior?

Source: Developed from W. A. Jones, Jr., and N. B. Bryan, Jr., "Business Ethics and Business Intelligence: An Empirical Study of Information-Gathering Alternatives," *International Journal of Management* (June 1995), pp. 204–208. For actual examples of some of these activities, see J. Kerstetter, P. Burrows, J. Greene, G. Smith, and M. Conlin, "The Dark Side of the Valley," *Business Week* (July 17, 2000), pp. 42–43.

- An **experiential exercise** focusing on the material covered in each chapter helps the reader to apply strategic concepts to an actual situation.   ►

- A list of **key terms** and the pages in which they are discussed enable the reader to keep track of important concepts as they are introduced in each chapter.

- **Timely, well-researched, and class-tested cases** deal with interesting companies and industries. Many of the cases are about well-known, publicly held corporations—ideal subjects for further research by students wishing to "update" the cases.

- An **Industry Note for use in industry analysis** of the major home appliance industry is included for use by itself or with the Maytag case.

Features New to This 9th Edition

TEXT

We have incorporated information from some of the recent scandals in corporate governance and business ethics in Chapter 2, Corporate Governance and Social Responsibility. The opening vignette to the chapter now deals with governance issues at Tyco International. A special boxed feature highlights the "whistle blowers" who brought to light the unethical and even criminal practices at Enron and Worldcom.

NEW! We have added a Glossary to the back of the book listing the many key terms and their definitions used within the chapters. Rather than paging through the book to find a particular term, the reader can go to one spot to find the definition and the page location of any important concept and technique.

NEW CASES

We have added five new cases dealing with contemporary issues and industries.

- A new case on corporate governance: McKesson Makes a Deal
- Two new technology cases: Palm Computing and Handspring
- A new entrepreneurial venture: Adrenaline Air Sports
- A new airline case: American Airlines

NEW VERSIONS OF POPULAR CASES

We have updated eight of our most popular cases to make them even more relevant in the classroom.

- Harley-Davidson
- Carnival Cruise Lines
- Reebok
- U. S. Major Home Appliance Industry
- Maytag Corporation
- Kmart
- Wal-Mart
- Arm & Hammer

We have added the address, phone numbers, Web site and stock market symbol for each case of a publicly-held company. This table appears on pages xlvi and xlvii of this book.

NEW! INTERNET RESEARCH MINI-CASES

We have added a new exciting section of Internet Research Mini-Cases to be used as exercises for researching and analyzing companies for class discussion and presentation. These are mini-cases that introduce a particular company, but leave it to the reader to research the company on the Internet to obtain further information. It is then up to the student to analyze the company on the basis of information that has been found. These exercises are very useful to those instructors who like to assign cases for students to update and analyze. All of these cases are new and up-to-date as of 2002.

Five mini-cases are included in the book.

- eBay
- Hershey Foods
- AirTran
- Tyson Foods
- Eli Lilly

Five more mini-cases are on Prentice Hall's Website at www.prenhall.com/wheelen.

- Southwest Airlines
- Stryker
- Heinz
- Williams-Sonoma
- Pfizer

CUSTOMIZE!

Want to customize your Wheelen/Hunger cases?
This program is intended for professors who wish to build a custom casebook or custom course pack. You can either use a portion of a Prentice Hall business casebook or you can mix and match materials from several Prentice Hall books. In addition, you can add your own materials or outside cases; up to 20 percent of the text can come from outside Prentice Hall Custom Business Resources. This material can range from professor-produced material such as a syllabus and class notes to articles from business periodicals such as *The Economist, Business Week,* and many more. **It's just a click away. Visit www.prenhall.com/custombusiness.**

Supplements

Supplemental materials are available to the instructor from the publisher. These include both Text and Case Instructor Manuals, an Instructor's Resource CD-ROM containing testing software and PowerPoints, videos, a book specific Web site, and transparency acetates in color.

INSTRUCTOR'S MANUALS

Two comprehensive Instructor's Manuals have been carefully constructed to accompany this book. The first one accompanies the text chapters; the second one accompanies the cases.

Text Instructor's Manual

To aid in discussing the 14 chapters dealing with strategic management concepts, the Text Instructor's Manual includes:

(1) *Suggestions for Teaching Strategic Management*—discusses various teaching methods and includes suggested course syllabi.

(2) *Chapter Notes*—includes summaries of each chapter, suggested answers to discussion questions, suggestions for using end of chapter cases exercises, plus additional discussion questions (with answers) and lecture modules.

(3) *Multiple-Choice Test Questions*—contains approximately 100 questions for each of the 14 chapters for a total of over 1,400 questions!

(4) *Video Guide*—includes teaching notes for the Newbury Comics video.

Case Instructor's Manual

The Case Instructor's Manual has been fully updated for this edition. To aid in case method teaching, the Case Instructor's Manual includes detailed suggestions for use, teaching objectives, and examples of student analyses for each of the 34 complete cases, plus information about using the ten Internet Research Mini-Cases. This is the most comprehensive instructor's manual available in strategic management. A standardized format is provided for each case:

(1) Case Abstract

(2) Case Issues and Subjects

(3) Steps Covered in the Strategic Decision-Making Process

(4) Case Objectives

(5) Suggested Classroom Approaches

(6) Discussion Questions

(7) Case Author's Teaching Note

(8) Student-Written Strategic Audit or Paper

(9) EFAS, IFAS, SFAS Exhibits

(10) Financial Analysis—ratios and common-size income statements

INSTRUCTOR'S RESOURCE CD-ROM

The Instructor's Resource CD-ROM contains tools to facilitate the instructor's lectures and examinations. These include PowerPoint Electronic Transparency Masters, a collection of about 150 figures and tables from the text. PowerPoints for the cases in the text are also available. The instructor may customize these presentations and can present individual slides for student handouts. The CD also contains a computerized test bank of all the multiple-choice questions (over 1,400) listed in the Text Instructor's Manual. The Instructor's Manuals have also been added to the Instructor's Resource CD-ROM, as well as the video case notes for Newbury Comics.

VIDEO: NEWBURY COMICS

This videotape features part-ending segments shot at Newbury Comics, an exciting and current popular culture retail chain. Beginning life as a store buying and selling used CDs, Newbury Comics has been expanding its product line and locations. Segments address key issues such as the company's basic model, mission and vision, and decision-making models. Accompanying case information can be found at the end of the parts in the concepts and full-volume text, and a video guide is included in the Text Instructor's Manual.

POWERPOINTS

The PowerPoint transparencies, a comprehensive package of text outlines and figures corresponding to the text and cases, are designed to aid the educator and supplement in-class lectures. The PPTs can be found on the Instructor's CD, as well as on the text Web site, located at **www.prenhall.com/wheelen.**

MY COMPANION WEBSITE

The new MyCompanion Website provides professors with a customized course Website including new communication tools, one-click navigation of chapter content, and In the News articles provided by XanEdu. It also features an online Study Guide for students and download files of both Instructor's Manuals and the PowerPoints for Instructors. **www.prenhall.com/wheelen**

ONLINE COURSES

Courses are available in *Blackboard, Course Compass,* and *WebCT*. These courses feature Companion Website and Test Item File Content in an easy-to-use system. Developed by educators for educators and their students, this online content and tools feature the most advanced educational technology and instructional design available today. The rich set of materials, communication tools, and course management resources can be easily customized to either enhance a traditional course or create the entire course online.

MASTERING STRATEGY

Mastering Strategy is the first product in the *Mastering Business* series. It offers students an interactive, multimedia experience as they follow the people and issues of CanGo, Inc., a small Internet startup. The text, video, and interactive exercises provide students an opportunity to simulate the strategic planning experience and chart the future activities for CanGo.

FINANCIAL TIMES STUDENT SUBSCRIPTION

Participating students qualify for a $10.00, 15-week subscription to the *Financial Times*. **How It Works:** Wheelen/Hunger text + subscription package will contain a 16-page full-color *Financial Times* student guide shrink-wrapped to the text. Bound inside the student guide will be a postcard which entitles the student to claim a pre-paid 15-week subscription to the *Financial Times*. Free subscription for professors who choose to use this package! Contact your local Prentice Hall representative for more information.

ACKNOWLEDGMENTS

We thank the many people at Prentice Hall who helped to make this edition possible. We are especially grateful to Jennifer Glennon, Cindy Spreder, Jessica Sabloff, Melanie Olsen, and Sandra Krausman, who took the book through the production process.

We are also very grateful to Kathy Wheelen for her first-rate administrative support and to Betty Hunger for her preparation of the subject and name indexes and the glossary. We are especially thankful to the many students who tried out the cases we chose to include in the combined book and the case book. Their comments helped us find any flaws in the cases before the book went to the printer.

In addition, we express our appreciation to Dr. Labh Hira, Dean, and Dr. Russ Laczniac, Management Department Chair, of Iowa State University's College of Business, for their support and provision of the resources so necessary to produce a textbook. We also recognize Dr. Robert L. Anderson, Dean, and Dr. Alan Balfour, Management Department Chair of the College of Business of the University of South Florida. Both of us acknowledge our debt to Dr. William Shenkir and Dr. Frank S. Kaulback, former Deans of the McIntire School of Commerce of the University of Virginia for the provision of a work climate most supportive to the original development of this book.

Lastly, to the many strategy/policy instructors and students who have expressed their problems with the strategy/policy course: we have tried to respond to your concerns as best we could by providing a comprehensive yet usable text coupled with recent and complex cases. To you, the people who work hard in the strategy/policy trenches, we acknowledge our debt. This book is yours.

T. L. W.
Tampa, Florida

J. D. H.
Ames, Iowa

About the Contributors

Moustafa H. Abdelsamad, D.B.A. (George Washington University), is Dean of the College of Business at Texas A&M University–Corpus Christi. He previously served as Dean of the College of Business and Industry at University of Massachusetts–Dartmouth and as Professor of Finance and Associate Dean of Graduate Studies in Business at Virginia Commonwealth University. He is Editor-in-Chief of SAM *Advanced Management Journal* and International President of the Society for Advancement of Management. He is author of *A Guide to Capital Expenditure Analysis* and two chapters in the *Dow Jones–Irwin Capital Budgeting Handbook.* He is the author and coauthor of numerous articles in various publications.

Hitesh (John) P. Adhia, CPA, is currently the money manager for Adhia Twenty Fund and Adhia Investment Advisors, Inc. He resides in Tampa, Florida.

Larry D. Alexander, Ph.D., M.S. (UCLA) and B.S. (California State University at Fresno), is Associate Professor of Management at Pamplin College of Business at Virginia Polytechnic Institute and State University.

Stephen E. Barndt, Ph.D. (Ohio State University), is retired Professor of Management at the School of Business, Pacific Lutheran University. Formerly, he was head of a department in the Graduate Education Division of the Air Force Institute of Technology's School of Systems and Logistics and taught at Central Michigan University. He has over 15 years of line and staff experience in operations and research and development. He has coauthored two fundamentals texts, *Managing by Project Management* and *Operations Management Concepts and Practices,* as well as numerous papers, articles, chapters, and cases addressing such subjects as organizational communication, project management, and strategic management. He serves on the Editorial Review Board of the *Business Case Journal.*

Ben M. Bensaou, Ph.D. (MIT Sloan School of Management), M.A. (Hitosubashi University, Tokyo), M.S. in Civil Engineering and D.E.A. in Mechanical Engineering from, respectively, Ecole National des TPE, Lyon and Institute National Polytechnique de Grenble, two Grandes Ecoles in France. In 1998–1999 he was Visiting Professor at Harvard Business School. He was also a Visiting Professor in 1994 and 1997 at Aoyama Gakuin University in Tokyo. Dr. Bensaou is an Associate Professor of Technology Management and Asian Business at INSEAD, Fountainbleu, France. His publications include papers in *Management Science, Information Systems Research, Strategic Management Journal, Harvard Business Review,* the *European Journal of Information Systems,* book chapters, and conference proceedings. He has been consulting for Asian, European, and U.S. corporations since 1993. Professor Bensaou grew up in France and was educated in Japan. He and his wife, Masako, live in Belmont, Massachusetts, with their three sons.

Peter M. Bergevin, Ph.D. (Arizona State University), is a Professor of Accounting and Finance at Valdosta State University. He served as the Head of the Department of Accounting and Finance at the Langdale College of Business Administration from 1995 through 2001. Dr. Bergevin teaches finanical statement analysis, financial reporting, auditing, and international accounting. Prior to joining the faculty at Valdosta State University in 1995, Dr. Bergevin was an Associate Professor of World Business at Thunderbird—The American Graduate School of International Management and an Assistant Professor of Accounting at the University of Las Vegas. His textbook, *Financial Statement Analysis: An Integrated Approach,* which emphasizes a comprehensive case approach to financial analysis, was published by Prentice Hall in 2002, along with the accompanying *Instructor's Guide, Solutions Manual,* and *Test Bank* volumes. He has published over 60 research maunuscripts, which have appeared in such journals as *Case Research Journal, Business Case Journal, Journal of Accounting Education, The Journal of Lending & Credit Risk Management, The Journal of Commercial Bank Lending, The International Executive,* and *The Journal of Accounting and Finance Research.*

James W. Camerius, M.S. (University of North Dakota), is Professor of Marketing at Northern Michigan University. He has served as President of the Society for Case Research, Marketing Track Chair of the North American Case Research Association, and Workshop and Colloquium Director of the World Association for Case Method Research. He is a research grant recipient of the Walker L. Cisler College of Business at Northern Michigan University and also a 1995 recipient of the Distinguished Faculty Award of the Michigan Association of Governing Boards of State Universities. His cases appear in over 90 management, marketing, and retailing textbooks in addition to *Annual Advances in Business Cases,* a publication of the Society for Case Research. His studies of corporate situations include Kmart Corporation; Tanner Companies, Inc.; Mary Kay Cosmetics, Inc.; Sasco Products, Inc.; The Fuller Brush Company; Wal-Mart Stores, Inc.; Longaberger Marketing, Inc.; Encyclopaedia Britannica International; RWC, Inc.; and several others. His writings include several studies of the case method of instruction. He is an award and grant recipient of the Direct Selling Educational Foundation, Washington, D.C., and is listed in *Who's Who in the World, America, Midwest, American Education,* and *Finance and Industry.*

Roy A. Cook, D.B.A. (Mississippi State University), is Associate Dean of the School of Business Administration and Professor of Management, Fort Lewis College, Durango, Colorado. He has written a best-selling textbook, *Tourism: The Business of Travel,* now in its second edition, and has two forthcoming textbooks: *Cases and Experiential Exercises in Human Resource Management* and *Guide to Business Etiquette.* He has authored numerous articles, cases, and papers based on his extensive experience in the hospitality industry and research interests in the areas of strategy, small business management, human resource management, and communications. Dr. Cook is the Director of Colorado's Center for Tourism Research®, Editor of *The Annual Advances in Business Cases,* and also serves on the editorial boards of the *Business Case Journal,* the *Journal of Business Strategies,* and the *Journal of Teaching and Tourism.* He is a member of the Academy of Management, Society for Case Research (past President), and the International Society of Travel and Tourism Educators. Dr. Cook teaches courses in Strategic Management, Small Business Management, Tourism and Resort Management, and Human Resource Management.

Laura W. Cooke, M.B.A. (University of Michigan), B.A. (Wittenberg University), is a Business Director at Metatec International, a disc manufacturing and supply chain solutions company located in Columbus, Ohio. Her responsibilities include sales, customer support, and marketing for the publishing/media business unit. Prior to Metatec, Laura was President and Founder of Millennium Multimedia Publishing, a CD-ROM publishing company. Laura also serves on the Board of Trustees at the Wellington School, an independent K-12 school.

Richard A. Cosier, Ph.D. (University of Iowa), is Dean and Leeds Professor of Management at Purdue University. He formerly was Dean and Fred B. Brown Chair at the University of Oklahoma and was Associate Dean for Academics and Professor of Business Administration at Indiana University. He served as Chairperson of the Department of Management at Indiana for seven years prior to assuming his current position. He was formerly a Planning Engineer with Western Electric Company and Instructor of Management and Quantitative Methods at the University of Notre Dame. Dr. Cosier is interested in researching the managerial decision-making process, organization responses to external forces, and participative management. He has published in *Behavior Science, Academy of Management Journal, Academy of Management Review, Organizational Behavior and Human Performance,*

Management Science, Strategic Management Journal, Business Horizons, Decision Sciences, Personnel Psychology, Journal of Creative Behavior, International Journal of Management, The Business Quarterly, Public Administration Quarterly, Human Relations, and other journals. In addition, Dr. Cosier has presented numerous papers at professional meetings and has coauthored a management text. He has been active in many executive development programs and has acted as management-education consultant for several organizations. Dr. Cosier is the recipient of Teaching Excellence Awards in the M.B.A. Program at Indiana and a Richard D. Irwin Fellowship. He belongs to the Institute of Management Consults, Inc., Beta Gamma Sigma, the Academy of Management, Sigma Iota Epsilon, and the Decision Sciences Institute.

Andrew James Croll, B.A. (Appalachian State University), is currently teaching 4th grade in Boone, North Carolina. He previously resided in Charlottesville, Virginia.

David B. Croll, Ph.D. (Pennsylvania State University), is a retired Professor of Accounting at the McIntire School of Commerce, the University of Virginia. He was Visiting Associate Professor at the Graduate Business School, the University of Michigan. He is on the editorial board of *SAM Advanced Management Journal.* He has published in the *Accounting Review* and the *Case Research Journal.* His cases appear in twelve accounting and management textbooks.

Gordon Paul Croll, B.A. (University of Alabama), is currently the Executive Vice President of Cavalier Reporting and the President of Cavalier Videography. He resides in Charlottesville, Virginia.

Dan R. Dalton, Ph.D. (University of California, Irvine), is the Dean of the Graduate School of Business, Indiana University, and Harold A. Polipl Chair of Strategic Management. He was formerly with General Telephone & Electronics for 13 years. Widely published in business and psychology periodicals, his articles have appeared in the *Academy of Management Journal, Journal of Applied Psychology, Personnel Psychology, Academy of Management Review,* and *Strategic Management Journal.*

Cathy A. Enz, Ph.D. (Ohio State University), is the Lewis G. Schaeneman Jr. Professor of Innovation and Dynamic Management at Cornell University's School of Hotel Administration where she is also the Executive Director of the Center for Hospitality Research. Her doctoral degree is in organization theory and behavior. Professor Enz has written numerous articles, cases, and books on corporate culture, value sharing, change management, and strategic human resource management effects on performance. Professor Enz consults extensively in the service sector and serves on the Board of Directors for two hospitality related organizations.

Ellie A. Fogarty, M.L.S. (University of Pittsburgh), M.B.A. (Temple University), is Executive Assistant to the Provost and was formerly Business and Economics Librarian at the College of New Jersey. She is active in the American Library Association, where she serves on the Business Reference Committee; the Special Libraries Association, where she is President of the Princeton-Trenton chapter; and the New Jersey Library Association.

Gamewell D. Gantt, JD, CPA, is Professor of Accounting and Management in the College of Business at Idaho State University in Pocatello, Idaho, where he teaches a variety of legal studies courses. He is a past President of the Rocky Mountain Academy of Legal Studies in Business and a past Chair of the Idaho Endowment Investment Fund Board. His published articles and papers have appeared in journals including *Midwest Law Review, Business Law Review, Copyright World,* and *Intellectual Property World.* His published cases have appeared in several textbooks and in *Annual Advances in Business Cases.*

Norman J. Gierlasinski, D.B.A., CPA, C.F.E., C.I.A., is Professor of Accounting at Central Washington University. He served as Chairman of the Small Business Division of the Midwest Business Administration Association. He has authored and coauthored cases for professional associations and the Harvard Case Study Series. He has authored various articles in professional journals as well as serving as a contributing author for textbooks and as a consultant to many organizations. He has also served as a reviewer for various publications.

Loizos Heracleous, Ph.D. (University of Cambridge), is Associate Professor of Business Policy at the National University of Singapore. His research has been published in the *Academy of Management Journal, Human Relations, Journal of Applied Behavioral Science, Long Range Planning, Asia Pacific Journal of Management, Organization Development Journal, European Management Journal,* and several other journals. He serves on the Editorial Board of the *Asia Pacific Journal of Management.*

Nicole Herskowitz, M.B.A. (University of Michigan), B.A. (University of Texas at Austin), spent three years working as a business consultant for Arthur Anderson focusing on the telecommunications industry. She then returned to school to pursue an M.B.A. from the University of Michigan. After graduating, Nicole went to work for Agillion in CRM software solutions for small/mid-size businesses, as a Product Marketing Manager.

Tom Hinthorne, Ph.D. (University of Oregon), is a Professor of Management, Montana State University–Billings. He has published in the *Case Research Journal, Industrial Management,* the *Strategic Management Journal,* and Thompson & Strickland's textbook *Strategic Management: Concepts and Cases,* 10th Edition. He has 15 years of management experience with a large multinational forest products company and has worked as a consultant, expert witness, and corporate director.

Alan N. Hoffman, D.B.A. (Indiana University), is Associate Professor of Strategic Management at Bentley College in Waltham, Massachusetts. Major areas of interest include strategic management, high technology investment strategy, and global competition. Co-author of *The Strategic Management Casebook* and *Skill Builder.* Recent publications have appeared in the *Academy of Management Journal, Human Relations,* the *Journal of Business Ethics,* the *Journal of Business Research,* and *Business Horizons.* He is the author of fifteen strategic management cases including: "The Boston YWCA", "Ryka, Inc.", "Liz Claiborne", "Ben & Jerry's Homemade", "Cognex", and "Harley Davidson, Inc." He has taught at Bentley College since 1988.

Phyllis G. Holland, Ph.D. (University of Georgia), is Associate Professor of Management at Valdosta State University and Acting Head of the Management Department. Her research has appeared in *Journal of Business and Entrepreneurship, Business Horizons* and others. She coauthored *Strategic Management: Concepts and Experiences* and has published cases in more than 20 strategic management and marketing textbooks. She is a member of the editorial review board of *Entrepreneurship: Theory and Practice.*

Elizabeth B. Hovey, M.B.A. (University of Michigan), B.A. (College University), is an Associate Brand Manager at Kraft Foods North America. Her work at Kraft has included experiences managing the Toblerone and Milka Chocolate brands as well as the Ready to Eat Jell-O products as a part of these brand teams. Prior to joining Kraft, Elizabeth was the National Sales Manager for Safety 1st, Inc., a manufacturer of childcare products.

Fred Howard, M.B.A. (University of Michigan), B.S. (Yale University). Following Yale, Fred spent five years in the financial world primarily in consulting with Merrill Lynch. Fred is currently a Senior Consultant with DiamondCluster International. His consulting experiences have included the development of an overarching e-commerce strategy for a major international pharmaceutical company as well as the development of a corporate perspective on the wireless Internet market.

J. David Hunger, Ph.D. (Ohio State University), is Professor of Strategic Management at Iowa State University. He previously taught at George Mason University, the University of Virginia, and Baldwin-Wallace College. His research interests lie in strategic management, corporate governance, and entrepreneurship. He served as Academic Director of the Pappajohn Center for Entrepreneurship at Iowa State University. He worked in brand management at Procter & Gamble Company, as a selling supervisor at Lazarus Department Store, and served as a Captain in U.S. Army Military Intelligence. He has been active as consultant and trainer to business corporations, as well as to state and federal government agencies. He has written numerous articles and cases that have appeared in the *Academy of Management Journal, International Journal of Management, Human Resource Management, Journal of Business Strategies, Case Research Journal, Business Case Journal, Handbook of Business Strategy, Journal of Management Case Studies, Annual Advances in Business Cases, Journal of Retail Banking, SAM Advanced Management Journal,* and *Journal of Management,* among others. Dr. Hunger is a member of the Academy of Management North American Case Research Association (NACRA), Society for Case Research (SCR), North American Management Society, World Association for Case Method Research and Application (WACRA), Textbook and Academic Authors Association, and the Strategic Management Society. He is past President of the Society for Case Research and the Iowa State University Board of Directors. He also served as Vice President of the U.S. Association for Small Business and Entrepreneurship (USASBE). He is currently serving as President of the North American Case Research Association and on the editorial review boards of SAM *Advanced Management Journal, Journal of Business Strategies, Business Case Journal* and *Current Issues in Management.* He is also a member of the Board of Directors of the North American Case Research Association and the Society for Case Research. He is coauthor with Thomas L. Wheelen of *Strategic Management and Business Policy, Essentials of Strategic Management, Cases in Strategic Management and Business Policy,* as well as *Concepts in Strategic Management and Business Policy,* and a monograph assessing undergraduate business education in the United States. His textbook *Strategic Management and Business Policy* received the McGuffey Award for Excellence and Longevity in 1999 from the Text and Academic Authors Association. Dr. Hunger received the *Best Case Award* given by the McGraw-Hill Publishing Company and the Society for Case Research in 1991 for outstanding case development. He is listed in various versions of *Who's Who,* including *Who's Who in the World.* He was also recognized in 1999 by the Iowa State University College of Business with its Innovation in Teaching Award and was elected a Fellow of the Teaching and Academic Authors Association in 2001.

George A. Johnson, Ph.D., is Professor of Management and Director of the Idaho State University M.B.A. program. He has published in the fields of management education, ethics, project management, and simulation. He is also active in developing and publishing case material for educational purposes. His industry experience includes several years as a Project Manager in the development and procurement of aircraft systems.

Michael J. Keeffe, Ph.D. (University of Arkansas), is Associate Professor of Management at Southwest Texas State University. He has served as Chair of the Department of Management and Marketing, Co-Director of AACSB—International Accreditation at SWT, authored numerous cases in the field of strategic management, published in several journals, and served as an independent consultant since 1982. He currently teaches and conducts research in the fields of strategic management and human resource management.

John A. Kilpatrick, Ph.D. (University of Iowa), is Professor of Management and International Business, Idaho State University. He has taught in the areas of business and business ethics for over 25 years. He served as Co-Chair of the management track of the Institute for Behavioral and Applied Management from its inception and continues as a board member for that organization. He is author of *The Labor Content of American Foreign Trade,* and coauthor of *Issues in International Business.* His cases have appeared in a number of organizational behavior and strategy texts and casebooks, and in *Annual Advances in Business Cases.*

Hyung T. Kim, M.D., M.B.A., B.A. (Johns Hopkins University, University of Michigan and Johns Hopkins University, respectively), is a consultant in the Detroit Office of McKinsey & Company, Inc., where his work has included post-merger management and strategy in banking, new economy, transportation, and healthcare. Prior to joining McKinsey, Kim was a

Clinical Instructor of Internal Medicine at the University of Michigan Medical School where he taught and performed patient care. He earned an M.B.A. with High Distinction from the University of Michigan Business School; an M.D. from the Johns Hopkins University School of Medicine, where he was a Hartford Foundation Clinical Scholar in Geriatric Medicine; and a B.A. from Johns Hopkins in Natural Sciences with a concentration in the History of Science.

Eric G. Kirby, Ph.D. (University of Kentucky), is Assistant Professor of Strategic Management at Southwest Texas State University. He previously held a joint appointment on the faculties of the Colleges of Business Administration and Medicine at Texas Tech University. He has received numerous awards for his research in the areas of health care administration and sport management. He has published over a dozen articles in scholarly journals and presented many more at academic conferences. Most of his research examines how businesses understand and respond to their external environment. Prior to becoming an academic, he was a building contractor, technical writer, and information system manager. He can be contacted online at <www.EricKirby.com>.

Donald F. Kuratko is the Stoops Distinguished Professor of Entrepreneurship and Founding Director of the Entrepreneurship Program, College of Business, Ball State University. In addition, he is Executive Director of the Midwest Entrepreneurial Education Center. He has published 18 books, including the leading entrepreneurship book in American universities today, *Entrepreneurship: A Contemporary Approach,* 5th ed. (Harcourt College Publishers, 2001), as well as *Strategic Entrepreneurial Growth* (Harcourt College Publishers, 2001), and *Effective Small Management,* 7th ed. (Harcourt College Publishers, 2001). He has published over 150 articles on aspects of entrepreneurship, new venture development, and corporate entrepreneurship. His work has been published in journals such as *Strategic Management Journal, Academy of Management Executive, Journal of Business Venturing, Entrepreneurship Theory & Practice, Journal of Small Business Management, Journal of Small Business Strategy, Family Business Review,* and *Advanced Management Journal.* In addition, Dr. Kuratko has been consultant on Corporate Intrapreneurship and Entrepreneurial Strategies to a number of major corporations such as Anthem Blue Cross/Blue Shield, AT&T, United Technologies, Ameritech, The Associated Group (Acordia), Union Carbide Corporation, ServiceMaster, and TruServ.

The academic program in entrepreneurship that Kuratko developed at Ball State University has continually earned national ranking including: *Top 20 in Business Week* and *Success* magazines; *Top 10 Business Schools for Entrepreneurship Research Over the Last 10 Years* (MIT study); and *Top 5* in *U.S. News & World Report's* elite ranking (including the No. 1 State University for Entrepreneurship). The program has also been honored with the NFIB Entrepreneurship Excellence Award (1993); The National Model Entrepreneurship Undergraduate Program Award (1990); The National Model Entrepreneurship Graduate Program Award (1998); and the National Model Innovative Pedagogy Award for Entrepreneurship (2001). In addition to earning the Ball State University College Business Teaching Award for 15 consecutive years, Kuratko holds the distinction of being the *only* professor in the history of Ball State University to achieve all four of the university's major lifetime awards, which include: Ball State University's *Outstanding Young Faculty* (1987); *Outstanding Teaching Award* (1990); *Outstanding Faculty Award* (1996); and *Outstanding Researcher Award* (1999). In 2000, he was honored with the Thomas W. Binford Memorial Award for Outstanding Contribution to Entrepreneurial Development by the Indiana Health Industry Forum. In 2001 Dr. Kuratko was named a *21st Century Entrepreneurship Research Fellow* by the National Consortium of Entrepreneurship Centers.

Geok Theng Lau, Ph.D. (Ivey School of Business, University of Western Ontario), is Associate Professor of Marketing at the National University of Singapore. His research interests are in B2B Marketing and Purchasing Management. His research has appeared in international journals such as *Industrial Marketing Management, Journal of Supply Chain Management,* and *European Journal of Purchasing and Supply Management.*

Janet Mehlhop, M.B.A. (University of Michigan), B.A. (UCLA), has worked and lived in Europe and Asia and specializes in International Business Development with focus on multilingual communications. She spent four years at the San Francisco Chamber of Commerce and three years working for a multilingual communications agency, based in New York. After business school, Janet joined Charles Schwab & Co., Inc. in a management training rotation program, focusing on affinity marketing and business development. In her spare time, Janet directs a Bay Area singing group called Global Voices.

Bill J. Middlebrook, Ph.D. (University of North Texas), is Professor of Management at Southwest Texas State University. He has served as Acting Chair of the Department of Management and Marketing, published in numerous journals, served as a consultant in industry, and is currently teaching and researching in the fields of Strategic Management and Human Resources.

Lisa-Marie Mulkern, M.B.A. (Bentley College), is the Director of Public Affairs and Development at the New Hampshire Veterans Home in Tilton, New Hampshire. She received her Bachelor of Arts degree in International Relations from St. Joseph's University. Prior to joining the New Hampshire Veterans Home, she was the Investor Relations Manager for Aavid Thermal Technologies, Inc. located in Concord, New Hampshire.

Nathan Nebbe, M.B.A. and M.A. (Iowa State University), has significant interests in the indigenous peoples of the Americas. With an undergraduate degree in Animal Ecology, he served as a Peace Corps Volunteer in Honduras, where he worked at the Honduran national forestry school ESNACIFORE (Escuela Nacional de Ciencias Forestales). After the Peace Corps, Nathan worked for a year on a recycling project for the Town of Ignacio and the Southern Ute Indian Tribe in southwestern Colorado. Following his experience in Colorado, Nathan returned to Iowa State University where he obtained his M.B.A. followed by an M.A. in Anthropology. He is currently studying how globalization of the Chilean forestry industry is affecting the culture of the indigenous Mapuche people of south central Chile.

John E. Oliver, Ph.D. (Georgia State University), is a Professor of Management at Valdosta State University in Valdosta, Georgia. He was formerly Head of the Department of Management and Director of the MBA Programs for the Langdale College of Business Administration. He has served on the Editorial Review Board of the *Case Research Journal* and the *Journal of Business Strategies* and has been an active member, case writer, and reviewer for the North American Case Research Association and the Southeast Case Research Association. He has published over 100 articles, cases, and chapters in several books and journals including the *Academy of Management Journal, Case Research Journal, Industrial Marketing Management, Industrial Management,* and many others.

Thomas M. Patrick, Ph.D. (University of Kentucky), is Professor of Finance at The College of New Jersey. He has also taught at Rider University and the University of Notre Dame. He has published widely in the areas of commercial banking and small business finance. His research appears in such journals as *Journal of Consumer Finance, Journal of International Business Studies, Journal of Small Business Management,* and *Banker's Monthly.* He also serves on the editorial review boards of a number of academic journals.

Paul Rakouski, M.B.A. (University of Michigan), B.S. (John Carroll University), is a Manager in the Strategy and Business Architecture service line in the Boston office of Accenture. His primary focus is the communications and high-technology industry where he works with clients in the areas of e-business strategy, marketing and channel strategy, new business development, and brand portfolio analysis. Prior to joining Accenture, Paul spent over five years at IBM Global Services and a software startup that developed enterprise applications for small to medium businesses.

John K. Ross, III, Ph.D. (University of North Texas), is Associate Professor of Management at Southwest Texas State University. He has served as SBI Director, Associate Dean, Chair of the Department of Management and Marketing, published in numerous journals, and is currently teaching and researching in the fields of strategic management and human resources.

Maryanne M. Rouse, CPA, M.B.A. (University of South Florida), B.A. in English, Romance Languages, and Political Science (Syracuse University). She is a Certified Public Accountant (Florida). She joined the faculty of the College of Business Administration at the University of South Florida in 1971. She served as the College's Assistant Dean from 1974 to 1976 and as Director of Executive Education and Management Development from 1981 to 1994. Ms. Rouse's current teaching assignments include Strategic Management, the undergraduate capstone course, Measuring Organizational Performance in the Graduate Leadership Program, Integrative Business Applications II in the MBA, and Managerial Accounting in the Executive MBA and the MBA Program for Physicians. She has also taught in the USF/EDC French Executive MBA Program in Paris. The recipient of a number of MBA teaching awards, including "MVP" by the Physicians MBA class and Outstanding Professor for the Executive MBA, she is a frequent program speaker and continuing education faculty member. A consultant in strategic planning and accounting in several industries including the not-for-profit sector and health care, she served as one of four international accreditation fellows for the Accreditation Commission for Education in Health Services Administration (ACEHSA.) Maryanne is a member of the Board of Directors and Vice Chair of the Tampa Economic Development Corporation, a CDC, and serves on the board of the University's Small Business Development Center, and chairs the college's Undergraduate Programs Committee.

Patricia A. Ryan, Ph.D. (University of South Florida), is an Associate Professor of Finance at Colorado State University. She has published cases and articles in the *Business Case Journal, Journal of Accounting and Finance Research, Journal of Finance and Strategic Decisions, Educational and Psychological Measurement, Journal of Research in Finance, American Business Review,* and *Annual Advances in Business Cases.* Her work has also appeared in *Strategic Management and Business Policy, 6th, 7th, and 8th editions,* as well as *Research and Cases in Strategic Management.* She has served on multiple review boards and finance association program committees. She served as Track Chair for the Midwest Finance Association's 2002 meeting. Dr. Ryan is past Editor of *Annual Advances in Business Cases,* a publication of the Society for Case Research.

Richard C. Scamehorn, M.B.A. (Indiana University), B.S. in Aeronautical and Aerospace Engineering (University of Michigan), is Executive in Residence Emeritus at Ohio University's College of Business. Prior to Ohio University, he was with Diamond Power Specialty Company, where he served as President, Vice President of Marketing, and Vice President of Manufacturing. He has conducted business and traveled in 52 countries and served on boards of directors of companies in Australia, Canada, China, Finland, Korea, Mexico, South Africa, Sweden, and the United Kingdom. He is listed in *Who's Who in Finance and Industry in America* and the *International Businessmen's Who's Who.*

Kulwant Singh, Ph.D. (University of Michigan), is Associate Professor of Business Policy at the National University of Singapore. He is Chief Editor of the *Asia Pacific Journal of Management* and serves on the Editorial Board of *Strategic Management Journal.* His research has been published in *Strategic Management Journal, Academy of Management Journal, Organization Science, Industrial and Corporate Change, Journal of Economic Behavior and Organization,* and other journals. He is coauthor of *Business Strategy in Asia: A Casebook* and *Surviving the New Millennium, Lessons from the Asian Crisis.* His cases have been published in the *Asian Case Research Journal* and in other case collections.

Pilar Speer, M.B.A. (University of Michigan), B.A. (University of Colorado), is a Senior Consultant in Cap Gemini, Ernst & Young's Strategy & Transformation practice. While at the

University of Colorado, she gained five years of advertising and sales experience in small business retail and print media. She then received her M.B.A. from the University of Michigan Business School with emphases in Corporate Strategy, Marketing, and Organizational Behavior and Design. Mrs. Speer also has business development, marketing and e-commerce experience. Within CGEY, she has worked in Consumer Products, High Tech for Middle Market clients, Mergers & Acquisitions in the energy sector, and B2B Private Exchange Strategy Evaluation.

Kenneth L. Stanley, Ph.D. (Purdue University), M.B.A. (Emory University), B.A. (Rhodes College), Dr. Stanley has served as Dean and Professor of Finance at Valdosta State University's Harley Langdale, Jr. College of Business Administration since 1984. Prior to his appointment at VSU, he was on the faculty and served as Director of the MBA Program at Emory University's School of Business Administration. In addition to his current duties at VSU's Langdale College of Business Administration, Dr. Stanley serves as Executive Director of the South Georgia Institute (SGI). Started in 1988, the SGI provides support for economic and regional development throughout south Georgia. Dr. Stanley also serves as the Lead Dean for Georgia's WebMBA Consortium, a five-school collaborative program offering an online MBA program.

Laurence J. Stybel, Ed.D. (Harvard University), is Cofounder of Stybel Peabody Lincolnshire, a Boston-based management consulting firm devoted to enhancing career effectiveness of executives who report to boards of directors. Services include search, outplacement, outplacement avoidance, and valued executive career consulting. Stybel Peabody Lincolnshire was voted "Best Outplacement Firm" by the readers of *Massachusetts Lawyers Weekly.* Its programs are the only ones officially endorsed by the Massachusetts Hospital Association and the Financial Executives Institute. He serves on the Board of Directors of the New England Chapter of the National Association of Corporate Directors and of the Boston Human Resources Association. His home page can be found at <www.stybelpeabody.com>. The "Your Career" department of the home page contains downloadable back issues of his monthly *Boston Business Journal* column, "Your Career."

Paul M. Swiercz, M.S., Ph.D. (Virginia Polytechnic Institute and State University), M.P.H. (University of Michigan), served on the faculty at Saginaw Valley State University from 1982 to 1984, where he was elected Chairman of the Department of Management/ Marketing. From 1984 to 1986 he was a Visiting Professor at the Graduate School of Labor and Industrial Relations at Michigan State University. In 1986 he joined the faculty at Georgia State University, where he was a member of the Department of Management and a Senior Research Associate in the W.T. Beebe Institute of Personnel and Employment Relations. In 1992 he joined the faculty at George Washington University as an Associate Professor of Human Systems and Employment Relations Policy. Dr. Swiercz is the Founder and Principal in the firm Executive Development Services International (EDSI). In his capacity as a consultant and trainer, he has directed workshops for AT&T, General Motors, Management Science Associates, the State of Georgia, the Pentagon, and others. He has been a principal investigator on a number of research projects, including those sponsored by the State of Georgia, the Hewlett Foundation, and the Society for Human Resource Planning. Dr. Swiercz has published more than 30 referred articles; his case studies on *Home Depot* and *Delta Airlines* have appeared in the six best-selling strategy textbooks; and he has been interviewed by numerous news organizations, including CNN. He currently serves as Editor of the journal *Human Resource Planning* and is Director of the Strategic HRM Partnership Project at George Washington University.

Cynthia J. Tonucci received her B.S. in Finance from Northeastern University and her M.B.A. from Bentley College.

Joyce P. Vincelette, D.B.A. (Indiana University), is Professor of Management and Division Head of Management, Marketing, Information Systems Management, and General Business at

The College of New Jersey. She was previously a faculty member at the University of South Florida. She has published articles, professional papers, chapters, and cases in management journals and strategic management textbooks. She is also active as a consultant and trainer for a number of local and national business organizations as well as for a variety of not-for-profit and government agencies.

Kathryn E. Wheelen, B.A. (University of Tampa), has worked as an administrative assistant for case and textbook development with the Thomas Wheelen Company (circa 1879). She is currently developing her own company, Kathryn E. Wheelen, Inc.

Richard D. Wheelen, B.S. (University of South Florida), has worked as a case research assistant. He is currently a buyer at Microserv, Inc., in Seattle.

Thomas L. Wheelen II, B.A. (Boston College), has worked as a case research assistant.

Thomas L. Wheelen, D.B.A., M.B.A., B.S. Cum Laude (George Washington University, Babson College, and Boston College, respectively), **Teaching Experience:** Visiting Professor, Trinity College–University of Dublin (Fall 1999); Professor of Strategic Management, University of South Florida (1983–present); Ralph A. Beeton Professor of Free Enterprise, University of Virginia–McIntire School of Commerce (1985–1981); Professor (1981–1974); Associate Professor (1974–1971); and Assistant Professor (1971–1968); Visiting Professor—University of Arizona (1980–1979) and Northeastern University (Summer 1979, 1977, and 1975). **Academic, Industry, and Military Experience:** University of Virginia College of Continuing Education: (1) Coordinator for Business Education (1983–1978, 1976–1971)—approved all undergraduate courses offered at seven Regional Centers and approved faculty; (2) Liaison Faculty and Consultant to the National Academy of the FBI Academy (1983–1972); and (3) developed, sold, and conducted over 200 seminars for local, state, and national governments, and companies for McIntire School of Commerce and Continuing Education. *General Electric Company*—various management positions (1965–1961); *U.S. Navy Supply Corps* (SC)—Lt. (SC) USNR—Assistant Supply Officer Aboard Nuclear Support Tender (1960–1957). Publications: (1) *Monograph—An Assessment of Undergraduate Business Education in the United States* (with J. D. Hunger), 1980; (2) *Books*—coauthor with J. D. Hunger—five active books: *Strategic Management and Business Policy,* 9th ed. (2004); *Cases in Strategic Management and Business Policy,* 9th ed. (2004); *Concepts in Strategic Management and Business Policy,* 9th ed. (2004); *Strategic Management,* 8th ed. (2002); *Strategic Management and Business Policy,* 8th ed., *International Edition* (2002); and *Essentials of Strategic Management,* 3rd ed. (2003). (3) *Coeditor—Developments in Information Systems* (1974) *and Collective Bargaining in the Public Sector* (1977) and (4) *Codeveloper of software—* STrategic Financial ANalyzer (ST. FAN) (1993, 1990, 1989—different versions); (5) *Articles*—authored over 40 articles that have appeared in such journals as the *Journal of Management, Business Quarterly, Personnel Journal, SAM Advanced Management Journal, Journal of Retailing, International Journal of Management,* and the *Handbook of Business Strategy.* (6) *Cases*—about 200 cases appearing in over 65 text and case books, as well as the *Business Case Journal, Journal of Management Case Studies, International Journal of Case Studies and Research* and *Case Research Journal.* Awards: (1) *Fellow* elected by the Society for Advancement of Management in 2002; (2) *Fellow* elected by North American Case Research Association in 2000; (3) *Fellow* elected by Text and Academic Authors Association in 2000; *(4) 1999 Phil Carroll Advancement of Management Award in Strategic Management* from the Society for Advancement of Management; (5) 1999 McGuffey Award for Excellence and Longevity for Strategic Management and Business Policy—6th Edition from the Text and Academic Authors Association; (6) 1996/97 Teaching Incentive Program Award for teaching undergraduate strategic management; (7) Fulbright, 1996–97, to Ireland but had to turn it down; (8) Endowed Chair, Ralph A. Beeton Professor, at University of Virginia (1981–1985); (9) Sesquicentennial Associateship research grant from the Center for Advanced Studies at the

University of Virginia, 1979–80; (10) <u>Small Business Administration</u> (Small Business Institute) supervised undergraduate team that won <u>District, Regional III, and Honorable Mention Awards</u>; and (11) awards for two articles. <u>Associations:</u> Dr. Wheelen currently serves on the Board of Directors of Adhia Mutual Fund, Society for Advancement of Management, and on the Editorial Board and the Associate Editor of *SAM Advanced Management Journal.* He served on the Board of Directors of Lazer Surgical Software, Inc, and Southern Management Association and on the Editorial Boards of the *Journal of Management* and *Journal of Management Case Studies, Journal of Retail Banking, Case Research Journal,* and *Business Case Journal.* He was Vice President of *Strategic Management* for the *Society for the Advancement of Management,* and President of the *North American Case Research Association.* Dr. Wheelen is a member of the *Academy of Management, Beta Gamma Sigma, Southern Management Association, North American Case Research Association, Society for Advancement of Management, Society for Case Research, Strategic Management Association,* and *World Association for Case Method Research and Application.* He has been listed in *Who's Who in Finance and Industry, Who's Who in the South and Southwest,* and *Who's Who in American Education.*

Other Contributors:
Michael Iverson
Eric Pfaffman
Bobby Cockrell
Jonathan Charlton

Strategic Management and Busines Policy Case Companies

Case Number	Case Title	Web Page Address	Telephone Number	Headquarters Address	Stock Symbol	Stock Exchange
Case 1	Byte Products, Inc	N/A	N/A	N/A	N/A	N/A
Case 2	The Wallace Group	N/A	N/A	N/A	N/A	N/A
Case 3	The Audit	N/A	N/A	N/A	N/A	N/A
Case 4	McKesson	www.mckesson.com	(415)983-8300	One Post Street San Francisco, CA 94104	MCK	NYSE
Case 5	Singapore Telecom	www.singtel.com	N/A	N/A	SGX	Singapore Exchange
Case 6	Hewlett-Packard	www.hewlett-packard.com	(650)857-1501	3000 Hanover Street Palo Alto, CA 94304	HPQ	NYSE
Case 7	The Body Shop International	www.thebodyshop.com	(919)554-4900	5036 One World Way Wake Forest, NC 27587	BOS	FTSE London Stock Exchange
Case 8	Waterford Crystal, PLC.	www.waterford-usa.com	(800)955-1550	1330 Campus Parkway Neptune, NJ	WTFU	Irish Exchange
Case 9	Oracle	www.oracle.com	(650)506-7000	500 Oracle Parkway Redwood Shores, CA 94065	ORCL	NASDAQ
Case 10	Palm	www.palm.com	(408)503-7000	400 N. McCarthy Blvd. Milpitas, CA 95035	PALM	NASDAQ
Case 11	Handspring	www.handspring.com	(650)230-5000	189 Bernardo Avenue Mountain View, CA 94043	HAND	NASDAQ
Case 12	Apple	www.apple.com	(408)996-1010	1 Infinite Loop Cupertino, CA 95014	APPL	NASDAQ
Case 13	WingspanBank.com	www.bankone.com	(877)226-5663	1 Bank One Plaza Chicago, IL 60670	ONE	NYSE
Case 14	drkoop.com	www.drkoop.com	N/A	N/A	N/A	N/A
Case 15	Harley-Davidson	www.harley-davidson.com	(877)HDSTOCK	3700 W. Juneau Avenue Milwaukee, Wisconsin 53208	HDI	NYSE
Case 16	Carnival	www.carnivalcorp.com	(800)438-6744	3655 N.W. 87th Avenue Miami, FL 33178	CCL	NYSE
Case 17	Reebok	www.reebok.com	(781)401-5000	100 Technology Center Dr. Stroughton, MA 02072	RBK	NYSE
Case 18	U.S. Major Home Appliance Industry	N/A	N/A	N/A	N/A	N/A
Case 19	Maytag	www.maytag.com	(641)792-7000	403 West Fourth Street North P.O. Box 39 Newton, Iowa 50208-0039	MYG	NYSE
Case 20	Kmart	www.kmart.com	(248)463-1040	3100 W. Big Beaver Road Troy, MI 48084-3163	KMRTQ	OTC
Case 21	Wal-mart	www.wal-mart.com	(501)273-4000 (501)277-6921	702 SW Eighth St Bentonville, Arkansas 72716-8611	WMT	NYSE

Case Number	Case Title	Telephone Number	Web Page Address	Headquarters Address	Stock Symbol	Stock Exchange
Case 22	Home Depot	(800)553-3199	www.homedepot.com	2455 Paces Ferry Road Atlanta, GA 30339	HD	NYSE
Case 23	Gardner Distribution Co	N/A	N/A	N/A	N/A	N/A
Case 24	Adrenaline Air Sports	(540)296-1100	www.air-sports.com	405 West Main Street Christianburg, VA 24073	N/A	N/A
Case 25	Inner-City Paint Corporation	N/A	N/A	N/A	N/A	N/A
Case 26	Guajilote Cooperativo Forestal: Honduras	N/A	N/A	N/A	N/A	N/A
Case 27	Vermont Teddy Bear Co.	(802)985-3001	www.vermontteddybear.com	6655 Shelburne Road Shelburne, VT 05482	BEAR	NASDAQ
Case 28	The Carey Plant	N/A	N/A	N/A	N/A	N/A
Case 29	Arm & Hammer	(609)683-5900	www.churchdwight.com	469 North Harrison Street Princeton, NJ 08543-5297	CHD	NYSE
Case 30	Redhook Ale Brewery	(425)483-3232	www.redhook.com	14300 NE 145th Street Suite 210 Woodville, WA 98072	HOOK	NASDAQ
Case 31	American Airlines	(817)963-1234	www.amrcorp.com	4333 Amon Carter Blvd. Fort Worth, TX 76155	AMR	NYSE
Case 32	Boeing Commercial Group	(206)655-2121	www.boeing.com	7755 E. Marginal Way S Seattle, WA 98108	BA	NYSE
Case 33	Mercedes-Benz	(800)367-6372	www.mercedes-benz.com	3 Paragon Drive Montvale, NJ 07645	BOS	NYSE
Case 34	A.W.A.R.E.	N/A	N/A	N/A	N/A	N/A
Case 35	eBay	(408)558-7400	www.ebay.com	2005 Hamilton Ave San Jose, CA 95125	EBAY	NASDAQ
Case 36	Hershey Foods Corporation	(717)534-6799	www.hersheys.com	100 Crystal Drive Hershey, PA 17033	HSY	NYSE
Case 37	AirTran Holding, Inc.	(407)251-5600	www.airtran.com	9955 Airtran Boulevard Orlando, FL 32827	AAI	NYSE
Case 38	Tyson Foods, Inc.	(479)290-4316	www.tysonfoods.com	P.O. Box 2020 Springdale, AR 72765-2020	TSN	NYSE
Case 39	Eli Lilly & Company	(317)276-2000	www.lilly.com	Lilly Corporate Center Indianapolis, IN 46285	LLY	NYSE
Web	Southwest Airlines Company	(214)792-4908	www.iflyswa.com www.southwest.com	2702 Love Field Dallas, TX 75235	LUV	NYSE
	Stryker Corporation	(616)385-2600	www.strykercorp.com	2775 Fairfield Road Kalamazoo, MI 49002	SYK	NYSE
	H.J. Heinz Company	(717)534-6799	www.heinz.com	600 Grant Street Pittsburg, PA 15219	HSY	NYSE
	William-Sonoma	(415)421-7900	www.william-sonoma.com	3250 Van Ness Ave San Francisco, CA 94109	WSM	NYSE
	Pfizer, Inc.	(212)733-2323	www.pfizer.com	235 East 42nd Street New York, NY 10017	PFE	NYSE

chapter 1

Basic Concepts of Strategic Management

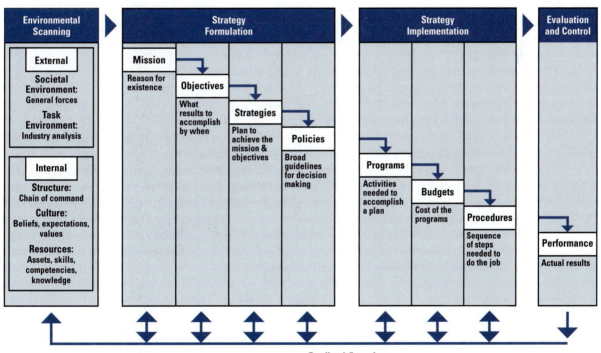

How does a company become successful and stay successful? Certainly not by playing it safe and following the traditional ways of doing business! Even a company like General Electric, an established, old-line *Fortune* 500 company with operations throughout the world, must constantly renew itself or else be outmaneuvered by aggressive newcomers. Realizing the potential impact of the Internet on all industries, Jack Welch, Chairman of the Board, issued a challenge at a March 1999 meeting to managers of the firm's business units to, in effect, replace their own product lines before competitors could do so. They also needed to learn how to conduct their business on the Internet. Welch had witnessed his own family and colleagues complete most or all of their Christmas shopping online and decided that the company had to enter the Internet age with a vengeance. Welch directed the top 600 managers to find an internal "Internet mentor" who would tutor them in the World Wide Web. According to Welch, "There's no such thing as an 'old economy.' Commerce is the same as it was 500 years ago. People sell and people buy—whether it's from a wagon or the Internet."[1]

In early February 2000, General Electric quietly launched the General Electric Financial Network ⟨gefn.com⟩, its first financial Web site for consumers. After having already invested over $10 million in developing the new business, GE heavily advertised its Web site in the televised summer Olympics. Gefn.com was marketed as the Web site where consumers could go to simplify their investment lives and find everything from a bank account to life insurance and GE mutual funds. According to Michael Frazier, head of the GE Capital consumer unit in charge of creating gefn.com, "Make no mistake, we want to be as well known to consumers for financial security as we are for light bulbs and appliances."[2] Knowing that many of the 50+ "baby boomers" were in the market for financial services as a way to save for their retirement, gefn.com entered a market already crowded with strong competitors.

Acknowledging GE's thrust as a bold strategic move, a number of industry analysts questioned if gefn.com had what was needed to be a major competitor in this business. For example, even though the Web site allowed customers to do online banking and obtain GE insurance and loans, it did not provide the ability to trade stocks or buy non-GE mutual funds. They also wondered if gefn.com could achieve its objectives with only an Internet presence and no "bricks and mortar" branch offices in which customers and loan officers could interact. E*Trade, in contrast, had realized the limited growth potential of its online brokerage and banking businesses and had begun opening E*Trade Zone retail offices and automated teller machines.[3]

Realizing these to be important issues, GE executives claimed, nevertheless, that gefn.com would be an important new distribution channel for GE's existing financial services units. One of the fastest growing units was GE Financial Assurance (GEFA), a provider of insurance, mutual funds, and 401(k) retirement plans in 17 countries. GE planned to put links to gefn.com on the intranets of those companies that already had a relationship with GE through their insurance or retirement plans. GE executives were seriously examining the alternative of a "carefully crafted alliance" over an acquisition to enter the electronic brokerage business. Referring to GE's well-known companywide policy that a business unit must be either number one or two in market share or have the potential to achieve it, Michael Frazier argued that "being number one or number two is not as important as being big enough to control your own destiny." General Electric, as a late entrant, clearly had the resources to make an impact on this competitive and fragmented market, but did it have what was needed to become a major player in the financial services industry?

1.1 The Study of Strategic Management

Strategic management is that set of managerial decisions and actions that determines the long-run performance of a corporation. It includes environmental scanning (both external and internal), strategy formulation (strategic or long-range planning), strategy implementation, and evaluation and control. The study of strategic management, therefore, emphasizes the monitoring and evaluating of external opportunities and threats in light of a corporation's strengths and weaknesses. Originally called business policy, strategic management incorporates such topics as long-range planning and strategy. **Business policy**, in contrast, has a general management orientation and tends primarily to look inward with its concern for properly integrating the corporation's many functional activities. Strategic management, as a field of study, incorporates the integrative concerns of business policy with a heavier environmental and strategic emphasis. Therefore, strategic management has tended to replace business policy as the preferred name of the field.[4]

PHASES OF STRATEGIC MANAGEMENT

Many of the concepts and techniques dealing with strategic management have been developed and used successfully by business corporations such as General Electric and the Boston Consulting Group. Over time, business practitioners and academic researchers have expanded and refined these concepts. Initially strategic management was of most use to large corporations operating in multiple industries. Increasing risks of error, costly mistakes, and even economic ruin are causing today's professional managers in all organizations to take strategic management seriously in order to keep their company competitive in an increasingly volatile environment.

As managers attempt to better deal with their changing world, a firm generally evolves through the following four **phases of strategic management**:[5]

Phase 1.   *Basic financial planning:* Managers initiate serious planning when they are requested to propose next year's budget. Projects are proposed on the basis of very little analysis, with most information coming from within the firm. The sales force usually provides the small amount of environmental information. Such simplistic operational planning only pretends to be strategic management, yet it is quite time consuming. Normal company activities are often suspended for weeks while managers try to cram ideas into the proposed budget. The time horizon is usually one year.

Phase 2.   *Forecast-based planning:* As annual budgets become less useful at stimulating long-term planning, managers attempt to propose five-year plans. They now consider projects that may take more than one year. In addition to internal information, managers gather any available environmental data—usually on an ad hoc basis—and extrapolate current trends five years into the future. This phase is also time consuming, often involving a full month of managerial activity to make sure all the proposed budgets fit together. The process gets very political as managers compete for larger shares of funds. Endless meetings take place to evaluate proposals and justify assumptions. The time horizon is usually three to five years.

Phase 3.   *Externally oriented planning (strategic planning):* Frustrated with highly political, yet ineffectual five-year plans, top management takes control of the planning process by initiating strategic planning. The company seeks to increase its responsiveness to changing markets and competition by thinking strategically. Planning is taken out of the hands of lower level managers and concentrated in a planning staff whose task is to develop strategic plans for the corporation. Consultants often provide the sophisticated and innovative techniques that the planning staff uses to gather information and forecast future trends. Ex-military experts develop competitive intelligence units. Upper level managers meet once a year at a resort "retreat" led by key members of the planning staff to evaluate and update the current strategic plan. Such top-down planning emphasizes formal strategy formulation and leaves the implementation issues to lower management levels. Top management typically develops five-year plans with help from consultants but minimal input from lower levels.

Phase 4.   *Strategic management:* Realizing that even the best strategic plans are worthless without the input and commitment of lower level managers, top management forms planning groups of managers and key employees at many levels from various departments and work groups. They develop and integrate a series of strategic plans aimed at achieving the company's primary objectives. Strategic plans now detail the implementation, evaluation, and control issues. Rather than attempting to perfectly forecast the future, the plans emphasize probable scenarios and contingency strategies. The sophisticated annual five-year strategic plan is replaced with strategic thinking at all levels of the organization throughout the year. Strategic information, previously available only centrally to top management, is available via local area networks and intranets to people throughout the organization. Instead of a large centralized planning staff, internal and external planning consultants are available to help guide group strategy discussions. Although top management may still initiate the strategic planning process, the resulting strategies may come from anywhere in the organization. Planning is typically interactive across levels and is no longer top down. People at all levels are now involved.

General Electric, one of the pioneers of strategic planning, led the transition from strategic planning to strategic management during the 1980s.[6] By the 1990s, most corporations around the world had also begun the conversion to strategic management.

Until 1978, Maytag Corporation, the major home appliance manufacturer, could be characterized as being in Phase one of strategic management. Maytag's CEO, Daniel Krum, formed a strategic planning task force to answer the question: "If we keep doing what we're doing now, what will the Maytag Corporation look like in five years?" The answer to this question served as the impetus for the firm's subsequent expansion into a full line of major home appliances and its entry into the world market through the purchase of Hoover.

BENEFITS OF STRATEGIC MANAGEMENT

Research has revealed that organizations that engage in strategic management generally outperform those that do not.[7] The attainment of an appropriate match or "fit" between an organization's environment and its strategy, structure, and processes has positive effects on the organization's performance.[8] For example, a study of the impact of deregulation on U.S. railroads found that those railroads that changed their strategy as their environment changed outperformed those railroads that did not change their strategy.[9]

A survey of nearly 50 corporations in a variety of countries and industries found the three most highly rated benefits of strategic management to be:

- Clearer sense of strategic vision for the firm
- Sharper focus on what is strategically important
- Improved understanding of a rapidly changing environment[10]

To be effective, however, strategic management need not always be a formal process. As occurred at Maytag, it can begin with a few simple questions:

1. **Where is the organization now? (Not where do we hope it is!)**
2. **If no changes are made, where will the organization be in 1 year? 2 years? 5 years? 10 years? Are the answers acceptable?**
3. **If the answers are not acceptable, what specific actions should management undertake? What are the risks and payoffs involved?**

A survey by Bain & Company revealed the most popular management tools to be strategic planning and developing mission and vision statements—essential parts of strategic management.[11] Studies of the planning practices of actual organizations suggest that the real value of strategic planning may be more in the future orientation of the planning process itself than in any written strategic plan. Small companies, in particular, may plan informally and irregularly. Nevertheless, studies of small businesses reveal that even though the degree of formality in strategic planning may have only a small to moderate impact on a firm's profitability, formal planners have significantly greater growth in sales than do informal planners.[12]

Planning the strategy of large, multidivisional corporations can become complex and time consuming. It often takes slightly more than a year for a large company to move from situation assessment to a final decision agreement. Because of the relatively large number of people affected by a strategic decision in such a firm, a formalized, more sophisticated system is needed to ensure that strategic planning leads to successful performance. Otherwise, top management becomes isolated from developments in the business units, and lower level managers lose sight of the corporate mission and objectives.

1.2 Globalization and Electronic Commerce: Challenges to Strategic Management

Not too long ago, a business corporation could be successful by focusing only on making and selling goods and services within its national boundaries. International considerations were minimal. Profits earned from exporting products to foreign lands were considered frosting on the cake but not really essential to corporate success. During the 1960s, for example, most U.S. companies organized themselves around a number of product divisions that made and sold goods only in the United States. All manufacturing and sales outside the United States were typically managed through one international division. An international assignment was usually considered a message that the person was no longer promotable and should be looking for another job.

Similarly, until the mid-1990s, a business firm could be very successful without using the Internet for anything more than a public relations Web site. Most business was done through a sales force and a network of distributors with the eventual sale to the consumer being made through retail outlets. Few executives used a personal computer, let alone "surfed" the World Wide Web. The Internet may have been useful for research, but until recently it was not seriously viewed as a means to actually conduct normal business transactions.

IMPACT OF GLOBALIZATION

Today, everything has changed. **Globalization**, the internationalization of markets and corporations, has changed the way modern corporations do business. To reach the economies of scale necessary to achieve the low costs, and thus the low prices, needed to be competitive, companies are now thinking of a global (worldwide) market instead of a national market. Nike and Reebok, for example, manufacture their athletic shoes in various countries throughout Asia for sale on every continent. Instead of using one international division to manage everything outside the home country, large corporations are now using matrix structures in which product units are interwoven with country or regional units. International assignments are now considered key for anyone interested in reaching top management.

As more industries become global, strategic management is becoming an increasingly important way to keep track of international developments and position the company for long-term competitive advantage. For example, Maytag Corporation purchased Hoover not so much for its vacuum cleaner business, but for its European laundry, cooking, and refrigeration business. Maytag's management realized that a company without a manufacturing presence in the European Union (EU) would be at a competitive disadvantage in the changing major home appliance industry. See the 🌐 **Global Issue** feature to learn how regional trade associations are changing how international business is conducted. Similar international considerations have led to the strategic alliance between British Airways and American Airlines and to the merger between Daimler-Benz and Chrysler Corporation.

IMPACT OF ELECTRONIC COMMERCE

Electronic commerce refers to the use of the Internet to conduct business transactions. A 1999 survey conducted by Booz-Allen & Hamilton and the Economist Intelligence Unit of more than 525 top executives from a wide range of industries revealed that the Internet is reshaping the global marketplace and that it will continue to do so for many years. More than 90% of the executives believed that the Internet would transform or have a major impact on their corporate strategy within two years. According to Matthew Barrett, Chairman and CEO of the Bank of Montreal, "We are only standing at the threshold of a New World. It is as if we had just invented printing or the steam engine."[13] Not only is the Internet changing the way customers, suppliers, and companies interact, it is changing the way companies work internally.

Global Issue

Regional Trade Associations Replace National Trade Barriers

Previously known as the Common Market and the European Community, the **European Union (EU)** is the most significant trade association in the world. The goal of the EU is the complete economic integration of its 15 member countries—Austria, Belgium, Denmark, Finland, France, Germany, Greece, Ireland, Italy, Luxembourg, the Netherlands, Portugal, Spain, Sweden, and the United Kingdom—so that goods made in one part of Western Europe can move freely without ever stopping for a customs inspection. One currency, the euro, is being used throughout the region as members integrate their monetary systems. The steady elimination of barriers to free trade is providing the impetus for a series of mergers, acquisitions, and joint ventures among business corporations. The requirement of at least 60% local content to avoid tariffs has forced many American and Asian companies to abandon exporting in favor of a strong local presence in Europe. The EU has agreed to expand its membership to include the Czech Republic, Hungary, Estonia, Poland, Malta, Cyprus, and Slovenia by 2004; Latvia, Lithuania, and Slovakia by 2006; and Bulgaria and Romania by 2010. Turkey is being considered for admission in 2011.

Canada, the United States, and Mexico are affiliated economically under the **North American Free Trade Agreement (NAFTA)**. The goal of NAFTA is improved trade among the three member countries rather than complete economic integration. Launched in 1994, the agreement requires all three members to remove all tariffs among themselves over 15 years, but they are allowed to have their own tariff arrangements with nonmember countries. Cars and trucks must have 62.5% North American content to qualify for duty-free status.

Transportation restrictions and other regulations are being significantly reduced. Some Asian and European corporations are locating operations in one of the countries to obtain access to the entire North American region. Vicente Fox, President of Mexico, is proposing that NAFTA become more like the European Union in that both people and goods would have unlimited access across borders from Mexico to Canada. In addition, there have been some discussions of extending NAFTA southward to include Chile, but thus far nothing formal has been proposed.

South American countries are also working to harmonize their trading relationships with each other and to form trade associations. The establishment of the **Mercosur** (**Mercosul** in Portuguese) free-trade area among Argentina, Brazil, Uruguay, and Paraguay means that a manufacturing presence within these countries is becoming essential to avoid tariffs for nonmember countries. Claiming to be NAFTA's southern counterpart, Mercosur has extended free-trade agreements to Bolivia and Venezuela. With Chile and Argentina cooperating to build a tunnel through the Andes to connect both countries, it is likely that Chile may soon form some economic relationship with Mercosur.

Asia has yet no comparable regional trade association to match the potential economic power of either NAFTA or the EU. Japan, South Korea, China, and India generally operate as independent economic powers. Nevertheless, the **Association of South East Asian Nations (ASEAN)**—composed of Brunei, Indonesia, Malaysia, the Philippines, Singapore, Thailand, and Vietnam—is attempting to link its members into a borderless economic zone. Increasingly referred to as ASEAN+3, it is already including China, Japan, and South Korea in its annual summit meetings. The ASEAN nations are negotiating the linkage of the ASEAN Free-Trade Area (AFTA) with the existing FTA of Australia and New Zealand. With the EU extending eastward and NAFTA extending southward to someday connect with Mercosur, pressure is already building on the independent Asian nations to soon form an expanded version of ASEAN.

In just the few years since its introduction, it has profoundly affected the basis of competition in many industries. Instead of the traditional focus on product features and costs, the Internet is shifting the basis for competition to a more strategic level in which the traditional value chain of an industry is drastically altered. A 1999 report by AMR Research indicated that industry leaders are in the process of moving 60 to 100% of their business to business (B2B) transactions to the Internet. The net B2B marketplace includes (a) Trading Exchange Platforms like VerticalNet and i2 Technologies's TradeMatrix, which support trading communities in multiple markets; (b) Industry-Sponsored Exchanges, such as the one being built by major automakers; and (c) Net Market Makers, like e-Steel, NECX, and BuildPoint, which focus on a specific industry's value chain or business processes to mediate multiple transactions among businesses. The Garner Group predicts that the worldwide B2B market will grow from $145 billion in 1999 to $7.29 trillion in 2004, at which time it will represent 7% of the total global sales transactions.[14]

The previously mentioned survey of top executives identified the following seven trends, due at least in part, to the rise of the Internet:[15]

1. **The Internet is forcing companies to transform themselves.** The concept of electronically networking customers, suppliers, and partners is now a reality.

2. **New channels are changing market access and branding, causing the *disintermediation* (breaking down) of traditional distribution channels.** By working directly with the customers, companies are able to avoid the usual distributors, thus forming closer relationships with the end users, improving service, and reducing costs.

3. **The balance of power is shifting to the consumer.** Now having unlimited access to information on the Internet, customers are much more demanding than their "nonwired" predecessors.

4. **Competition is changing.** New technology-driven firms plus older traditional competitors are exploiting the Internet to become more innovative and efficient.

5. **The pace of business is increasing drastically.** Planning horizons, information needs, and customer/supplier expectations are reflecting the immediacy of the Internet. Because of this turbulent environment, time is compressed into "dog years" in which one year feels like seven years.

6. **The Internet is pushing corporations out of their traditional boundaries.** The traditional separation between suppliers, manufacturers, and customers is becoming blurred with the development and expansion of extranets, in which cooperating firms have access to each other's internal operating plans and processes. For example, Lockheed Martin, the aerospace company, has an extranet linking Lockheed to Boeing, a project partner, and to the U.S. Defense Department, a key customer.

7. **Knowledge is becoming a key asset and a source of competitive advantage.** For example, physical assets accounted for 62.8% of the total market value of U.S. manufacturing firms in 1980 but only 37.9% in 1991. The remainder of the market value is composed of intangible assets, primarily intellectual capital.[16]

1.3 Theories of Organizational Adaptation

Globalization and electronic commerce present real challenges to the strategic management of business corporations. How can any one company keep track of all the changing technological, economic, political-legal, and sociocultural trends around the world and make the necessary adjustments? This is not an easy task. Various theories have been proposed to account for how organizations obtain fit with their environment. The theory of **population ecology**, for example, proposes that once an organization is successfully established in a particular environmental niche, it is unable to adapt to changing conditions. Too much inertia prevents the organization from changing. The company is thus replaced (bought out or goes bankrupt) by other organizations more suited to the new environment. Although popular in sociology, research fails to support the arguments of population ecology.[17] **Institution theory**, in contrast, proposes that organizations can and do adapt to changing conditions by imitating other successful organizations. To its credit, many examples can be found of companies that have adapted to changing circumstances by imitating another firm's strategies. The theory does not, however, explain how or by whom successful new strategies are developed in the first place. The **strategic choice perspective** goes one step further by proposing that not only do organizations adapt to a changing environment, but that they also have the opportunity and power to reshape their environment. Because of its emphasis on managers making rational strategic decisions, the strategic choice perspective is the dominant one taken in strategic management. Its argument that adaptation is a dynamic process fits with the view of **organizational learning theory** that organizations adjust defensively to a changing environment and use knowledge offensively to improve the fit between the organization and its environment. This perspective expands the strategic choice perspective to include people at all levels becoming involved in providing input into strategic decisions.[18]

In agreement with the concepts of organizational learning theory, an increasing number of companies are realizing that they must shift from a vertically organized, top-down type of organization to a more horizontally managed, interactive organization. They are attempting to adapt more quickly to changing conditions by becoming "learning organizations."

1.4 Creating a Learning Organization

Strategic management has now evolved to the point that its primary value is in helping the organization operate successfully in a dynamic, complex environment. Inland Steel Company, for example, uses strategic planning as a tool to drive organizational change. Managers at all levels are expected to continually analyze the changing steel industry in order to create or modify strategic plans throughout the year.[19] To be competitive in dynamic environments, corporations are having to become less bureaucratic and more flexible. In stable environments such as have existed in years past, a competitive strategy simply involved defining a competitive position and then defending it. As it takes less and less time for one product or technology to replace another, companies are finding that there is no such thing as a permanent competitive advantage. Many agree with Richard D'Aveni (in his book *Hypercompetition*) that any sustainable competitive advantage lies not in doggedly following a centrally managed five-year plan, but in stringing together a series of strategic short-term thrusts (as Intel does by cutting into the sales of its own offerings with periodic introductions of new products).[20] This means that corporations must develop strategic flexibility—the ability to shift from one dominant strategy to another.[21]

Strategic flexibility demands a long-term commitment to the development and nurturing of critical resources. It also demands that the company become a **learning organization**—an organization skilled at creating, acquiring, and transferring knowledge, and at modifying its behavior to reflect new knowledge and insights. Organizational learning is a critical component of competitiveness in a dynamic environment. It is particularly important to innovation and new product development.[22] For example, Hewlett-Packard uses an extensive network of informal committees to transfer knowledge among its cross-functional teams and to help spread new sources of knowledge quickly.[23] Learning organizations are skilled at 4 main activities:

- Solving problems systematically
- Experimenting with new approaches
- Learning from their own experiences and past history as well as from the experiences of others
- Transferring knowledge quickly and efficiently throughout the organization[24]

Learning organizations avoid stability through continuous self-examination and experimentation. People at all levels, not just top management, need to be involved in strategic management—helping to scan the environment for critical information; suggesting changes to strategies and programs to take advantage of environmental shifts; and working with others to continuously improve work methods, procedures, and evaluation techniques. Motorola, for example, developed an action learning format in which people from marketing, product development, and manufacturing meet to argue and reach agreement about the needs of the market, the best new product, and the schedules of each group producing it. This action learning approach overcame the problems that arose previously when the three departments met and formally agreed on plans but continued with their work as if nothing had happened.[25]

Organizations that are willing to experiment and are able to learn from their experiences are more successful than those that do not. For example, in a study of U.S. manufacturers of diagnostic imaging equipment, the most successful firms were those that improved products sold in the United States by incorporating some of what they had learned from their manufacturing and sales experiences in other nations. The less successful firms used the foreign operations primarily as sales outlets, not as important sources of technical knowledge.[26]

1.5 Basic Model of Strategic Management

Strategic management consists of four basic elements:

- **Environmental scanning**
- **Strategy formulation**
- **Strategy implementation**
- **Evaluation and control**

Figure 1–1 shows simply how these elements interact; **Figure 1–2** expands each of these elements and serves as the model for this book.[27] The terms used in **Figure 1–2** are explained in the following pages.

ENVIRONMENTAL SCANNING

Environmental scanning is the monitoring, evaluating, and disseminating of information from the external and internal environments to key people within the corporation. Its purpose is to identify **strategic factors**—those external and internal elements that will determine the future of the corporation. The simplest way to conduct environmental scanning is through **SWOT analysis**. SWOT is an acronym used to describe those particular **S**trengths, **W**eaknesses, **O**pportunities, and **T**hreats that are strategic factors for a specific company. The **external environment** consists of variables (**O**pportunities and **T**hreats) that are outside the organization and not typically within the short-run control of top management. These

Figure 1–1

Basic Elements of the Strategic Management Process

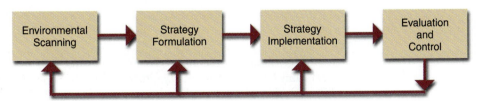

Figure 1–2
Strategic Management Model

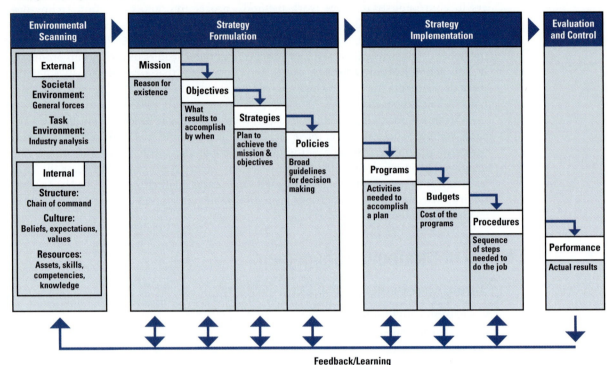

variables form the context within which the corporation exists. **Figure 1–3** depicts key environmental variables. They may be general forces and trends within the overall societal environment or specific factors that operate within an organization's specific task environment—often called its industry. (These external variables are defined and discussed in more detail in **Chapter 3**.)

The **internal environment** of a corporation consists of variables (**S**trengths and **W**eaknesses) that are within the organization itself and are not usually within the short-run control of top management. These variables form the context in which work is done. They include the corporation's structure, culture, and resources. Key strengths form a set of core competencies that the corporation can use to gain competitive advantage. (These internal variables and core competencies are defined and discussed in more detail in **Chapter 4**.)

STRATEGY FORMULATION

Strategy formulation is the development of long-range plans for the effective management of environmental opportunities and threats, in light of corporate strengths and weaknesses. It includes defining the corporate mission, specifying achievable objectives, developing strategies, and setting policy guidelines.

Mission

An organization's **mission** is the purpose or reason for the organization's existence. It tells what the company is providing to society, either a service like housecleaning or a product like automobiles. A well-conceived mission statement defines the fundamental, unique purpose

Figure 1–3
Environmental Variables

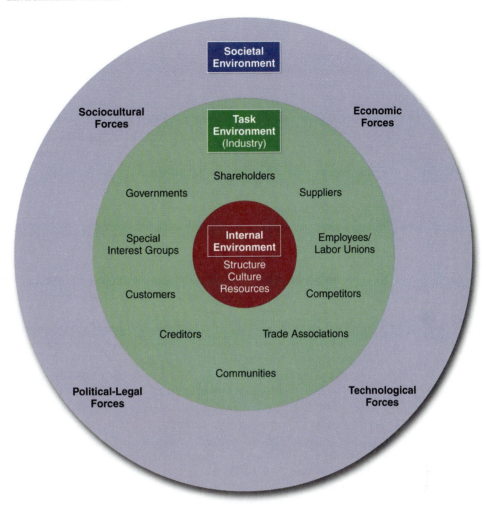

that sets a company apart from other firms of its type and identifies the scope of the company's operations in terms of products (including services) offered and markets served. It may also include the firm's philosophy about how it does business and treats its employees. It puts into words not only what the company is now, but also what it wants to become—management's strategic vision of the firm's future. (Some people like to consider vision and mission as two different concepts: A mission statement describes what the organization is now; a vision statement describes what the organization would like to become. We prefer to combine these ideas into a single mission statement.)[28] The mission statement promotes a sense of shared expectations in employees and communicates a public image to important stakeholder groups in the company's task environment. *It tells who we are and what we do as well as what we'd like to become.*

One example of a mission statement is that of Maytag Corporation:

To improve the quality of home life by designing, building, marketing, and servicing the best appliances in the world.

Another classic example is that etched in bronze at Newport News Shipbuilding, unchanged since its founding in 1886:

We shall build good ships here—at a profit if we can—at a loss if we must—but always good ships.[29]

A mission may be defined narrowly or broadly in scope. An example of a **broad** mission statement is that used by many corporations: Serve the best interests of shareowners, customers, and employees. A broadly defined mission statement such as this keeps the company from restricting itself to one field or product line, but it fails to clearly identify either what it makes or which product/markets it plans to emphasize. Because this broad statement is so general, a **narrow** mission statement, such as the preceding one by Maytag emphasizing appliances, is more useful. A narrow mission very clearly states the organization's primary business, but it may limit the scope of the firm's activities in terms of product or service offered, the technology used, and the market served. Instead of just stating it is a "railroad," a company might be better calling itself a "transportation company."

Objectives

Objectives are the end results of planned activity. They state what is to be accomplished by when and should be quantified if possible. The achievement of corporate objectives should result in the fulfillment of a corporation's mission. In effect, this is what society gives back to the corporation when the corporation does a good job of fulfilling its mission. Robert Lane, Chairman of Deere & Company, the world's largest maker of farm equipment, uses the phrase "double and double again" to express ambitious objectives for the company. "It gives us a sense that we're on the move," explained Lane. For example, one of Deere's current objectives is to double the market value (number of shares multiplied by stock price) of the company ($8 billion in 2000) to $16 billion and then to double it again to $32 billion over 10 years. Similarly, the sales objective is to have sales ($13 billion in 2000) double and double again over the next 10 years.[30]

The term "goal" is often used interchangeably with the term "objective." In this book, we prefer to differentiate the two terms. In contrast to an objective, we consider a **goal** as an open-ended statement of what one wants to accomplish with no quantification of what is to be achieved and no time criteria for completion. For example, a simple statement of "increased profitability" is thus a goal, not an objective, because it does not state how much profit the firm wants to make the next year. An objective would say something like, "increase profits 10% over last year."

Some of the areas in which a corporation might establish its goals and objectives are:

- Profitability (net profits)
- Efficiency (low costs, etc.)
- Growth (increase in total assets, sales, etc.)
- Shareholder wealth (dividends plus stock price appreciation)
- Utilization of resources (return on investment or equity)
- Reputation (being considered a "top" firm)
- Contributions to employees (employment security, wages, diversity)
- Contributions to society (taxes paid, participation in charities, providing a needed product or service)
- Market leadership (market share)
- Technological leadership (innovations, creativity)
- Survival (avoiding bankruptcy)
- Personal needs of top management (using the firm for personal purposes, such as providing jobs for relatives)

Strategies

A **strategy** of a corporation forms a comprehensive master plan stating how the corporation will achieve its mission and objectives. It maximizes competitive advantage and minimizes competitive disadvantage. For example, after Rockwell International Corporation realized that it could no longer achieve its objectives by continuing with its strategy of diversification into multiple lines of businesses, it sold its aerospace and defense units to Boeing. Rockwell instead chose to concentrate on commercial electronics, an area that management felt had greater opportunities for growth.

The typical business firm usually considers three types of strategy: corporate, business, and functional.

1. **Corporate strategy** describes a company's overall direction in terms of its general attitude toward growth and the management of its various businesses and product lines. Corporate strategies typically fit within the three main categories of stability, growth, and retrenchment. For example, Maytag Corporation followed a corporate growth strategy by acquiring other appliance companies in order to have a full line of major home appliances.

2. **Business strategy** usually occurs at the business unit or product level, and it emphasizes improvement of the competitive position of a corporation's products or services in the specific industry or market segment served by that business unit. Business strategies may fit within the two overall categories of *competitive* or *cooperative* strategies. For example, Apple Computer uses a differentiation competitive strategy that emphasizes innovative products with creative design. The distinctive design and colors of its iMac line of personal computers (when contrasted with the usual beige of the competitor's products) has successfully boosted the company's market share and profits. In contrast, British Airways followed a cooperative strategy by forming an alliance with American Airlines in order to provide global service.

3. **Functional strategy** is the approach taken by a functional area to achieve corporate and business unit objectives and strategies by maximizing resource productivity. It is concerned with developing and nurturing a *distinctive competence* (see **Chapter 4**) to provide a company or business unit with a competitive advantage. Examples of R&D functional strategies are technological followership (imitate the products of other companies) and technological leadership (pioneer an innovation). For years, Magic Chef had been a successful appliance maker by spending little on R&D but by quickly imitating the innovations of other competitors. This helped the company to keep its costs lower than its competitors and consequently to compete with lower prices. In terms of marketing functional strategies, Procter & Gamble is a master of marketing "pull"—the process of spending huge amounts on advertising in order to create customer demand. This supports P&G's competitive strategy of differentiating its products from its competitors.

Business firms use all three types of strategy simultaneously. A **hierarchy of strategy** is the grouping of strategy types by level in the organization. This hierarchy of strategy is a nesting of one strategy within another so that they complement and support one another. (See **Figure 1–4.**) Functional strategies support business strategies, which, in turn, support the corporate strategy(ies).

Just as many firms often have no formally stated objectives, many firms have unstated, incremental, or intuitive strategies that have never been articulated or analyzed. Often the only way to spot a corporation's implicit strategies is to look not at what management says, but at what it does. Implicit strategies can be derived from corporate policies, programs approved

Figure 1–4
Hierarchy of Strategy

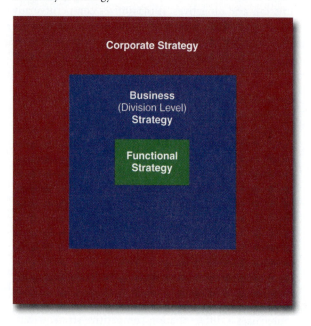

(and disapproved), and authorized budgets. Programs and divisions favored by budget increases and staffed by managers who are considered to be on the fast promotion track reveal where the corporation is putting its money and its energy.

Policies

A **policy** is a broad guideline for decision making that links the formulation of strategy with its implementation. Companies use policies to make sure that employees throughout the firm make decisions and take actions that support the corporation's mission, objectives, and strategies. For example, consider the following company policies:

- **Maytag Company:** Maytag will not approve any cost reduction proposal if it reduces product quality in any way. (This policy supports Maytag's strategy for Maytag brands to compete on quality rather than on price.)
- **3M:** Researchers should spend 15% of their time working on something other than their primary project. (This supports 3M's strong product development strategy.)
- **Intel:** Cannibalize your product line (undercut the sales of your current products) with better products before a competitor does it to you. (This supports Intel's objective of market leadership.)
- **General Electric:** GE must be number one or two wherever it competes. (This supports GE's objective to be number one in market capitalization.)
- **Nordstrom:** A "no questions asked" merchandise return policy, because the customer is always right. (This supports Nordstrom's competitive strategy of differentiation through excellent service.)

Policies like these provide clear guidance to managers throughout the organization. (Strategy formulation is discussed in greater detail in **Chapters 5**, **6**, and **7**.)

STRATEGY IMPLEMENTATION

Strategy implementation is the process by which strategies and policies are put into action through the development of programs, budgets, and procedures. This process might involve changes within the overall culture, structure, and/or management system of the entire organization. Except when such drastic corporate-wide changes are needed, however, the implementation of strategy is typically conducted by middle and lower level managers with review by top management. Sometimes referred to as operational planning, strategy implementation often involves day-to-day decisions in resource allocation.

Programs

A **program** is a statement of the activities or steps needed to accomplish a single-use plan. It makes the strategy action oriented. It may involve restructuring the corporation, changing the company's internal culture, or beginning a new research effort. For example, consider Intel Corporation, the microprocessor manufacturer. Realizing that Intel would not be able to continue its corporate growth strategy without the continuous development of new generations of microprocessors, management decided to implement a series of programs:

- They formed an alliance with Hewlett-Packard to develop the successor to the Pentium Pro chip.
- They assembled an elite team of engineers and scientists to do long-term, original research into computer chip design.

Another example is FedEx Corporation's program to install a sophisticated information system to enable its customers to track their shipments at any point in time. FedEx thus installed computer terminals at 100,000 customers and gave proprietary software to another 650,000 so shippers could label much of their own packages.[31]

Budgets

A **budget** is a statement of a corporation's programs in terms of dollars. Used in planning and control, a budget lists the detailed cost of each program. Many corporations demand a certain percentage return on investment, often called a "hurdle rate," before management will approve a new program. This ensures that the new program will significantly add to the corporation's profit performance and thus build shareholder value. The budget thus not only serves as a detailed plan of the new strategy in action, but also specifies through pro forma financial statements the expected impact on the firm's financial future.

For example, General Motors budgeted $4.3 billion during 2000 through 2004 to update and expand its Cadillac line of automobiles. With this money, the company is increasing the number of models from five to nine, and offering more powerful engines, sportier handling, and edgier styling. The company hopes to reverse its declining market share by appealing to a younger market. (The average Cadillac buyer was 67 years old in 2000.)[32]

Procedures

Procedures, sometimes termed *Standard Operating Procedures* (*SOP*), are a system of sequential steps or techniques that describe in detail how a particular task or job is to be done. They typically detail the various activities that must be carried out in order to complete the corporation's programs. For example, Delta Airlines used various procedures to cut costs. To reduce the number of employees, Delta asked technical experts in hydraulics, metal working, avionics, and other trades to design cross-functional work teams. To cut marketing expenses, Delta instituted a cap on travel agent commissions and emphasized sales to bigger accounts. Delta also changed its purchasing and food service procedures. (Strategy implementation is discussed in more detail in **Chapters 8** and **9**.)

EVALUATION AND CONTROL

Evaluation and control is the process in which corporate activities and performance results are monitored so that actual performance can be compared with desired performance. Managers at all levels use the resulting information to take corrective action and resolve problems. Although evaluation and control is the final major element of strategic management, it also can pinpoint weaknesses in previously implemented strategic plans and thus stimulate the entire process to begin again.

Performance is the end result of activities.[33] It includes the actual outcomes of the strategic management process. The practice of strategic management is justified in terms of its ability to improve an organization's performance, typically measured in terms of profits and return on investment. For evaluation and control to be effective, managers must obtain clear, prompt, and unbiased information from the people below them in the corporation's hierarchy. Using this information, managers compare what is actually happening with what was originally planned in the formulation stage. For example, the success of Delta Airline's turnaround strategy was evaluated in terms of the amount spent on each airplane seat per mile of flight. Before the "Leadership 7.5" program was instituted, the cost per seat was 9.76¢. The program needed to reach 7.5¢ to achieve the company's objective of reducing annual expenses by $2.1 billion.

The evaluation and control of performance completes the strategic management model. Based on performance results, management may need to make adjustments in its strategy formulation, in implementation, or in both. (Evaluation and control is discussed in more detail in **Chapter 10**.)

FEEDBACK/LEARNING PROCESS

Note that the strategic management model depicted in **Figure 1–2** includes a feedback/learning process. Arrows are drawn coming out of each part of the model and taking information to each of the previous parts of the model. As a firm or business unit develops strategies, programs, and the like, it often must go back to revise or correct decisions made earlier in the model. For example, poor performance (as measured in evaluation and control) usually indicates that something has gone wrong with either strategy formulation or implementation. It could also mean that a key variable, such as a new competitor, was ignored during environmental scanning and assessment.

1.6 Initiation of Strategy: Triggering Events

After much research, Henry Mintzberg discovered that strategy formulation is typically not a regular, continuous process: "It is most often an irregular, discontinuous process, proceeding in fits and starts. There are periods of stability in strategy development, but also there are periods of flux, of groping, of piecemeal change, and of global change."[34] This view of strategy formulation as an irregular process can be explained by the very human tendency to continue on a particular course of action until something goes wrong or a person is forced to question his or her actions. This period of "strategic drift" may simply result from inertia on the part of the organization or may simply reflect management's belief that the current strategy is still appropriate and needs only some "fine-tuning." Most large organizations tend to follow a particular strategic orientation for about 15 to 20 years before making a significant change in direction.[35] After this rather long period of fine-tuning an existing strategy, some sort of shock to the system is needed to motivate management to seriously reassess the corporation's situation.

A **triggering event** is something that acts as a stimulus for a change in strategy. Some possible triggering events are:

- **New CEO:** By asking a series of embarrassing questions, the new CEO cuts through the veil of complacency and forces people to question the very reason for the corporation's existence.

- **External Intervention:** The firm's bank refuses to approve a new loan or suddenly demands payment in full on an old one. A customer complains about a serious product defect.

- **Threat of a Change in Ownership:** Another firm may initiate a takeover by buying the company's common stock.

- **Performance Gap:** A performance gap exists when performance does not meet expectations. Sales and profits either are no longer increasing or may even be falling.

- **Strategic Inflection Point:** Coined by Andy Grove, Chairman of the Board of Intel Corporation, this represents what happens to a business when a major change takes place due to the introduction of new technologies, a different regulatory environment, a change in customer's values, or a change in what customers prefer.[36]

Sun Microsystems is an example of one company in which a triggering event forced its management to radically rethink what it was doing. See the **Internet Issue** feature to learn how one phone call to Sun's president stimulated a change in strategy at Sun.

Internet Issue

TRIGGERING EVENT AT SUN MICROSYSTEMS

Sun Microsystems President Edward Zander received a personal phone call in June 2000 directly from Margaret Whitman, CEO of eBay, Inc., the Internet auction firm. After a string of small computer crashes, eBay had just suffered a 22-hour outage of its Web site. Whitman called Zander to report that there was a bug in Sun's top-of-the-line server and that Sun had better fix it immediately or else lose eBay's business. A series of around-the-clock meetings at Sun revealed that the problem was that Sun's customers had no idea of how to maintain a $1 million+ computer. eBay had failed to provide sufficient air conditioning to keep the machine cool. Even though Sun had issued a software patch to fix a problem many months earlier, eBay had neglected to install it. The list went on and on. Sun soon realized that the problem was bigger than just eBay. Over 40% of the servers that manage most Web sites were made by Sun.

As more firms were expanding their business to include the Internet, this market for Sun's servers was expected to boom. Nevertheless, many of these firms were too new and small to have the proper technology infrastructure. "It suddenly hit me," said Zander. "How many future eBays are buying their first computer from us this very minute?" According to Scott McNealy, CEO of Sun, "That's when we realized that it wasn't eBay's fault. It was our fault."

Since that realization, Sun's management team has been rebuilding the company to make its servers as reliable as the telephone system. In a drastic strategic change, management decided to expand beyond simply selling servers to providing many of the technologies required to make Web servers completely reliable. It now provides storage products, e-business software, and consultants who not only supply the hardware, but also work directly with the customers to ensure that the servers are operated properly. Just as high-tech mainframe managers used to say that "No one gets fired for choosing IBM," Zander aims to have the same said of Sun Microsystems. "I want to be the sage bet for companies that need the most innovative technology," added Sun's president.

Source: P. Burrows, "Sun's Bid to Rule the Web," *Business Week E.Biz* (July 24, 2000), pp. EB 31–42.

1.7 Strategic Decision Making

The distinguishing characteristic of strategic management is its emphasis on strategic decision making. As organizations grow larger and more complex with more uncertain environments, decisions become increasingly complicated and difficult to make. In agreement with the strategic choice perspective mentioned earlier, this book proposes a strategic decision-making framework that can help people make these decisions regardless of their level and function in the corporation.

WHAT MAKES A DECISION STRATEGIC

Unlike many other decisions, **strategic decisions** deal with the long-run future of the entire organization and have three characteristics:

1. **Rare:** Strategic decisions are unusual and typically have no precedent to follow.

2. **Consequential:** Strategic decisions commit substantial resources and demand a great deal of commitment from people at all levels.

3. **Directive:** Strategic decisions set precedents for lesser decisions and future actions throughout the organization.[37]

One example of a strategic decision was that made by Monsanto to move away from being a chemical company emphasizing fertilizers and herbicides to becoming a "life sciences" enterprise, devoted to improving human health by seeking synergies in biotech, pharmaceutical research, and food products. Management decided to sell its slow-growing chemical business and invest $4 billion into R&D and a series of acquisitions. Realizing that the planet couldn't survive an expected doubling of its population without serious environmental degradation, Monsanto decided to develop genetically engineered seeds to double crop yields using less fertilizer and poisons.[38]

MINTZBERG'S MODES OF STRATEGIC DECISION MAKING

Some strategic decisions are made in a flash by one person (often an entrepreneur or a powerful chief executive officer) who has a brilliant insight and is quickly able to convince others to adopt his or her idea. Other strategic decisions seem to develop out of a series of small incremental choices that over time push the organization more in one direction than another. According to Henry Mintzberg, the three most typical approaches, or modes, of strategic decision making are entrepreneurial, adaptive, and planning.[39] A fourth mode, logical incrementalism, was added later by Quinn.

- **Entrepreneurial Mode:** Strategy is made by one powerful individual. The focus is on opportunities; problems are secondary. Strategy is guided by the founder's own vision of direction and is exemplified by large, bold decisions. The dominant goal is growth of the corporation. America Online, founded by Steve Case, is an example of this mode of strategic decision making. The company reflects his vision of the Internet provider industry. Although AOL's clear growth strategy is certainly an advantage of the entrepreneurial mode, its tendency to market its products before the company is able to support them is a significant disadvantage.

- **Adaptive Mode:** Sometimes referred to as "muddling through," this decision-making mode is characterized by reactive solutions to existing problems, rather than a proactive search for new opportunities. Much bargaining goes on concerning priorities of objectives. Strategy is fragmented and is developed to move the corporation forward incrementally. This mode is typical of most universities, many large hospitals, a large number of governmental agencies, and a surprising number of large corporations. Encyclopaedia Britannica, Inc., operated successfully for many years in this mode. It continued to rely on the door-to-door selling of its prestigious books long after dual career couples made this marketing approach obsolete. Only after it was acquired in 1996 did the company change its marketing strategy to television advertising and Internet marketing. (See ⟨www.eb.com⟩.) It now offers an online version of the encyclopedia in addition to the printed volumes.

- **Planning Mode:** This decision-making mode involves the systematic gathering of appropriate information for situation analysis, the generation of feasible alternative strategies, and the rational selection of the most appropriate strategy. It includes both the proactive search for new opportunities and the reactive solution of existing problems. Hewlett-Packard (HP) is an example of the planning mode. After a careful study of trends in the computer and communications industries, management noted that the company needed to stop thinking of itself as a collection of stand-alone products with a primary focus on instrumentation and computer hardware. Led by its new CEO, Carly Fiorina, top management felt that the company needed to become a customer-focused and integrated provider of information appliances, highly reliable information technology infrastructure, and electronic commerce services. Consequently, products were merged into packages for electronic services solutions, such as software for building internal company portals and "e-speak," a software platform that can quickly create and combine different kinds of online services. HP also sold its venerable test and measurement unit—the business in which the company had begun. HP's research labs also received significant support and were encouraged to quit focusing on incremental improvements so that they could develop "disruptive technologies," such as molecular computing, a technology to build integrated circuits using molecules.[40]

- **Logical Incrementalism:** A fourth decision-making mode, which can be viewed as a synthesis of the planning, adaptive, and, to a lesser extent, the entrepreneurial modes, was proposed by Quinn. In this mode, top management has a reasonably clear idea of the corporation's mission and objectives, but, in its development of strategies, it chooses to use "an interactive process in which the organization probes the future, experiments and learns from a series of partial (incremental) commitments rather than through global formulations of total strategies."[41] Thus, although the mission and objectives are set, the strategy is allowed to emerge out of debate, discussion, and experimentation. This approach appears to be useful when the environment is changing rapidly and when it is important to build consensus and develop needed resources before committing the entire corporation to a specific strategy.

STRATEGIC DECISION-MAKING PROCESS: AID TO BETTER DECISIONS

Good arguments can be made for using either the entrepreneurial or adaptive modes (or logical incrementalism) in certain situations. This book proposes, however, that in most situations the planning mode, which includes the basic elements of the strategic management process, is a more rational and thus better way of making strategic decisions. Research indicates that the planning mode is not only more analytical and less political than are the other modes, but it is also more appropriate for dealing with complex, changing environments.[42]

Figure 1–5
Strategic Decision-Making Process

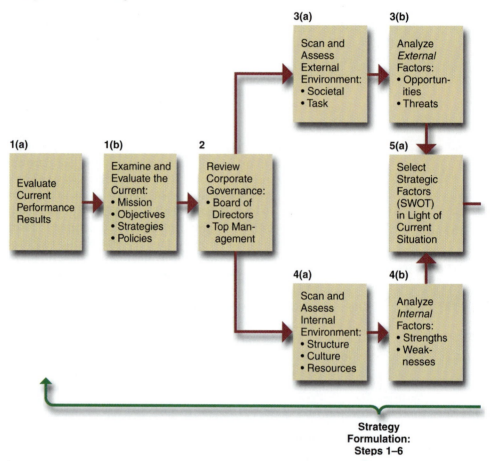

Source: T. L. Wheelen and J. D. Hunger, "Strategic Decision-Making Process," Copyright © 1994 and 1997 by Wheelen and Hunger Associates. Reprinted by permission.

We therefore propose the following eight-step **strategic decision-making process** to improve the making of strategic decisions (see **Figure 1–5**):

1. **Evaluate current performance results** in terms of (a) return on investment, profitability, and so forth, and (b) the current mission, objectives, strategies, and policies.

2. **Review corporate governance**, that is, the performance of the firm's board of directors and top management.

3. **Scan and assess the external environment** to determine the strategic factors that pose **O**pportunities and Threats.

4. **Scan and assess the internal corporate environment** to determine the strategic factors that are **S**trengths (especially core competencies) and **W**eaknesses.

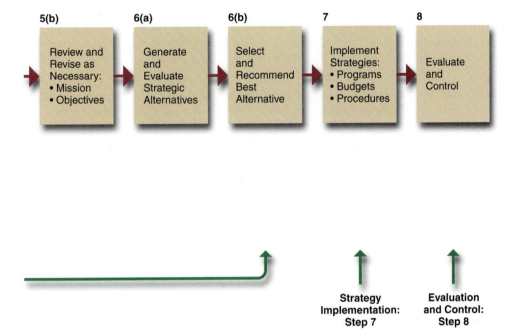

5(b)

Review and
Revise as
Necessary:
• Mission
• Objectives

6(a)

Generate
and
Evaluate
Strategic
Alternatives

6(b)

Select
and
Recommend
Best
Alternative

7

Implement
Strategies:
• Programs
• Budgets
• Procedures

8

Evaluate
and
Control

**Strategy
Implementation:
Step 7**

**Evaluation
and Control:
Step 8**

5. **Analyze strategic (SWOT) factors** to (a) pinpoint problem areas, and (b) review and revise the corporate mission and objectives as necessary.

6. **Generate, evaluate, and select the best alternative strategy** in light of the analysis conducted in Step 5.

7. **Implement selected strategies** via programs, budgets, and procedures.

8. **Evaluate implemented strategies** via feedback systems and the control of activities to ensure their minimum deviation from plans.

This rational approach to strategic decision making has been used successfully by corporations like Warner-Lambert, Dayton Hudson, General Electric, Avon Products, Bechtel Group, Inc., and Taisei Corporation. **It is also the basis for the Strategic Audit found in Chapter 10.**

1.8 Impact of the Internet on Strategic Management

Few innovations in history provide as many potential benefits to the strategic management of a corporation as does electronic commerce (e-commerce) via the Internet. The global nature of the technology, low cost, opportunity to reach millions of people, interactive nature, and variety of possibilities result in many potential benefits to strategic managers. E-commerce provides the following benefits to the strategic management of corporations.

- Expands the marketplace to national and international markets. All anyone now needs is a computer to connect buyers and sellers.

- Decreases the cost of creating, processing, distributing, storing, and retrieving information. The cost of electronic payment is $.02, whereas the cost of a paper check is $.43.

- Enables people to create new, highly specialized business ventures. Very narrow market niches can now be reached via special interest chat rooms and Internet search engines.

- Allows smaller inventories, just-in-time manufacturing, and less overhead expenses by facilitating pull-type supply chain management. Dell Computer orders the parts it needs as soon as it receives an order from a customer.

- Enables the customization of products and services to better suit customer needs. Customers are encouraged to select options and styles for the auto of their choice on the BMW Web site ⟨www.bmw.com⟩.

- Provides the stimulus to rethink a firm's strategy and to initiate reengineering projects. The arrival of Amazon.com forced Barnes and Noble to rethink its pure "bricks and mortar" strategy of retail book stores and to begin selling books over its own Web site.

- Increases flexibility, compresses cycle and delivery time, and provides easy access to information on customers, suppliers, and competitors.[43]

Projections for the 21st Century

- From 1994 to 2010, the world economy will grow from $26 trillion to $48 trillion.
- From 1994 to 2010, world trade will increase from $4 trillion to $16.6 trillion.[44]

Discussion Questions

1. Why has strategic management become so important to today's corporations?

2. How does strategic management typically evolve in a corporation?

3. What is a learning organization? Is this approach to strategic management better than the more traditional top-down approach?

4. Why are strategic decisions different from other kinds of decisions?

5. When is the planning mode of strategic decision making superior to the entrepreneurial and adaptive modes?

Strategic Practice Exercise

Mission statements vary widely from one company to another. Why is one mission statement better than another? Develop some criteria for evaluating a mission statement. Then, do one or both of the following exercises:

1. Evaluate the following mission statement of Celestial Seasonings:

   Our mission is to grow and dominate the U.S. specialty tea market by exceeding consumer expectations with the best tasting, 100% natural hot and iced teas, packaged with Celestial art and philosophy, creating the most valued tea experience. Through leadership, inno-

vation, focus, and teamwork, we are dedicated to continuously improving value to our consumers, customers, employees, and stakeholders with a quality-first organization.[45]

2. Using the Internet, find the mission statements of three different organizations, which can be business or not-for-profit. (*Hint*: Check annual reports and 10k forms. They can often be found via a link on a company's Web page or through Hoovers.com.) Which mission statement is best? Why?

Key Terms

adaptive mode (pp. 18–19)
Association of South East Asian Nations (ASEAN) (p. 6)
budget (p. 15)
business policy (p. 2)
business strategy (p. 13)
corporate strategy (p. 13)
electronic commerce (p. 15)
entrepreneurial mode (p. 18)
environmental scanning (p. 9)
European Union (EU) (p. 6)
evaluation and control (p. 16)
external environment (pp. 9–10)
functional strategy (p. 13)
globalization (p. 5)
goal (p. 12)

hierarchy of strategy (p. 13)
institution theory (p. 7)
internal environment (p. 10)
learning organization (p. 8)
logical incrementalism (p. 19)
mission (p. 10)
Mercosur/Mercosul (p. 6)
North American Free Trade Agreement (NAFTA) (p. 6)
objectives (p. 12)
organizational learning theory (p. 8)
performance (p. 16)
performance gap (p. 17)
phases of strategic management (p. 3)
planning mode (p. 19)

policy (p. 14)
population ecology (p. 7)
procedures (p. 15)
program (p. 15)
strategic choice perspective (p. 8)
strategic decision-making process (p. 20)
strategic decisions (p. 18)
strategic factors (p. 9)
strategic inflection point (p. 17)
strategic management (p. 2)
strategy (p. 13)
strategy formulation (p. 10)
strategy implementation (p. 15)
SWOT analysis (p. 9)
triggering event (p. 17)

Notes

1. E. Corcoran, "The E Gang," *Fortune* (July 24, 2000), p. 146.
2. P. L. Moore and G. Smith, "GE Catches Online Fever," *Business Week* (August 14, 2000), pp. 122–123.
3. L. Lee, "Not Just Clicks Anymore," *Business Week* (August 28, 2000), pp. 226–227.
4. For an excellent description of the evolution of business policy into strategic management, see R. E. Hoskisson, M. A. Hitt, W. P. Wan, and D. Yiu, "Theory and Research in Strategic Management: Swings of the Pendulum," *Journal of Management*, Vol. 25, No. 3 (1999), pp. 417–456.
5. F. W. Gluck, S. P. Kaufman, and A. S. Walleck, "The Four Phases of Strategic Management," *Journal of Business Strategy* (Winter 1982), pp. 9–21.
6. M. R. Vaghefi and A. B. Huellmantel, "Strategic Leadership at General Electric," *Long Range Planning* (April 1998), pp. 280–294.
7. T. J. Andersen, "Strategic Planning, Autonomous Actions and Corporate Performance," *Long Range Planning* (April 2000), pp. 184–200; C. C. Miller and L. B. Cardinal, "Strategic Planning and

Firm Performance: A Synthesis of More Than Two Decades of Research," *Academy of Management Journal* (December 1994), pp. 1649–1665; P. Pekar, Jr., and S. Abraham, "Is Strategic Management Living Up to Its Promise?" *Long Range Planning* (October 1995), pp. 32–44.
8. E. J. Zajac, M. S. Kraatz, and R. F. Bresser, "Modeling the Dynamics of Strategic Fit: A Normative Approach to Strategic Change," *Strategic Management Journal* (April 2000), pp. 429–453.
9. K. G. Smith and C. M. Grimm, "Environmental Variation, Strategic Change and Firm Performance: A Study of Railroad Deregulation," *Strategic Management Journal* (July–August 1987), pp. 363–376.
10. I. Wilson, "Strategic Planning Isn't Dead—It Changed," *Long Range Planning* (August 1994), p. 20.
11. R. M. Grant, "Transforming Uncertainty Into Success: Strategic Leadership Forum 1999," *Strategy & Leadership* (July/August/ September, 1999), p. 33.

12. L. W. Rue and N. A. Ibrahim, "The Relationship Between Planning Sophistication and Performance in Small Businesses," *Journal of Small Business Management* (October 1998), pp. 24–32; M. A. Lyles, I. S. Baird, J. B. Orris, and D. F. Kuratko, "Formalized Planning in Small Business: Increasing Strategic Choices," *Journal of Small Business Management* (April 1993), pp. 38–50.

13. C. V. Callahan and B. A. Pasternack, "Corporate Strategy in the Digital Age," *Strategy and Business*, Issue 15 (2nd Quarter 1999), pp. 2–6.

14. J. Bowles, "How Digital Marketplaces Are Shaping the Future of B2B Commerce," Special Advertising Section on e Marketmakers, *Forbes* (July 23, 2000).

15. C. V. Callahan and B. A. Pasternack, "Corporate Strategy in the Digital Age," *Strategy & Business*, Issue 15 (2nd Quarter 1999), p. 3.

16. R. M. Kanter, "Managing the Extended Enterprise in a Globally Connected World," *Organizational Dynamics* (Summer 1999), pp. 7–23; C. Havens and E. Knapp, "Easing into Knowledge Management," *Strategy & Leadership* (March/April 1999), pp. 4–9.

17. J. A. C. Baum, "Organizational Ecology," in *Handbook of Organization Studies*, edited by S. R. Clegg, C. Handy, and W. Nord (London: Sage, 1996), pp. 77–114.

18. For more information on these theories, see A. Y. Lewin and H. W. Voloberda, "Prolegomena on Coevolution: A Framework for Research on Strategy and New Organizational Forms," *Organization Science* (October 1999), pp. 519–534, and H. Aldrich, *Organizations Evolving* (London: Sage, 1999), pp. 43–74.

19. C. Gebelein, "Strategic Planning: The Engine of Change," *Planning Review* (September/October 1993), pp. 17–19.

20. R. A. D'Aveni, *Hypercompetition* (New York: Free Press, 1994). Hypercompetition is discussed in more detail in Chapter 3.

21. R. S. M. Lau, "Strategic Flexibility: A New Reality for World-Class Manufacturing," *SAM Advanced Management Journal* (Spring 1996), pp. 11–15.

22. M. A. Hitt, B. W. Keats, and S. M. DeMarie, "Navigating in the New Competitive Landscape: Building Strategic Flexibility and Competitive Advantage in the 21st Century," *Academy of Management Executive* (November 1998), pp. 22–42.

23. D. Lei, J. W. Slocum, and R. A. Pitts, "Designing Organizations for Competitive Advantage: The Power of Unlearning and Learning," *Organizational Dynamics* (Winter 1999), pp. 24–38.

24. D. A. Garvin, "Building a Learning Organization," *Harvard Business Review* (July/August 1993), p. 80. See also P. M. Senge, *The Fifth Discipline: The Art and Practice of the Learning Organization* (New York: Doubleday, 1990).

25. T. T. Baldwin, C. Danielson, and W. Wiggenhorn, "The Evolution of Learning Strategies in Organizations: From Employee Development to Business Redefinition," *Academy of Management Executive* (November 1997), pp. 47–58.

26. W. Mitchell, J. M. Shaver, and B. Yeung, "Getting There in a Global Industry: Impacts on Performance of Changing International Presence," *Strategic Management Journal* (September 1992), pp. 419–432.

27. Research supports the use of this model in examining firm strategies. See J. A. Smith, "Strategies for Start-Ups," *Long Range Planning* (December 1998), pp. 857–872.

28. See A. Campbell and S. Yeung, "Brief Case: Mission, Vision, and Strategic Intent," *Long Range Planning* (August 1991), pp. 145–147; S. Cummings and J. Davies, "Mission, Vision, Fusion," *Long Range Planning* (December 1994), pp. 147–150.

29. J. Cosco, "Down to the Sea in Ships," *Journal of Business Strategy* (November/December 1995), p. 48.

30. W. Ryberg, "Deere Chief Takes 'Double' Aim," *Des Moines Register* (September 9, 2000), p. D1.

31. L. Grant, "Why FedEx Is Flying High," *Fortune* (November 10, 1997), pp. 156–160.

32. D. Welch, "Cadillac Hits the Gas," *Business Week* (September 4, 2000), p. 50.

33. H. A. Simon, *Administrative Behavior*, 2nd edition (NY: Free Press, 1957), p. 231.

34. H. Mintzberg, "Planning on the Left Side and Managing on the Right," *Harvard Business Review* (July–August 1976), p. 56.

35. This phenomenon of "punctuated equilibrium" describes corporations as evolving through relatively long periods of stability (equilibrium periods) punctuated by relatively short bursts of fundamental change (revolutionary periods). See E. Romanelli and M. L. Tushman, "Organizational Transformation as Punctuated Equilibrium: An Empirical Test," *Academy of Management Journal* (October 1994), pp. 1141–1166.

36. Speech to the 1998 Academy of Management. Reported by S. M. Puffer, "Global Executive: Intel's Andrew Grove on Competitiveness," *Academy of Management Executive* (February 1999), pp. 15–24.

37. D. J. Hickson, R. J. Butler, D. Cray, G. R. Mallory, and D. C. Wilson, *Top Decisions: Strategic Decision-Making in Organizations* (San Francisco: Jossey-Bass, 1986), pp. 26–42.

38. L. Grant, "Monsanto's Bet: There's Gold in Going Green," *Fortune* (April 14, 1997), pp. 116–118.

39. H. Mintzberg, "Strategy-Making in Three Modes," *California Management Review* (Winter 1973), pp. 44–53.

40. "Rebuilding the Garage," *Economist* (July 15, 2000), pp. 59–61.

41. J. B. Quinn, *Strategies for Change: Logical Incrementalism* (Homewood, Ill.: Irwin, 1980), p. 58.

42. I. Gold and A. M. A. Rasheed, "Rational Decision-Making and Firm Performance: The Moderating Role of the Environment," *Strategic Management Journal* (August 1997), pp. 583–591; R. L. Priem, A. M. A. Rasheed, and A. G. Kotulic, "Rationality in Strategic Decision Processes, Environmental Dynamism and Firm Performance," *Journal of Management*, Vol. 21, No. 5 (1995), pp. 913–929; J. W. Dean, Jr., and M. P. Sharfman, "Does Decision Process Matter? A Study of Strategic Decision-Making Effectiveness," *Academy of Management Journal* (April 1996), pp. 368–396.

43. E. Turban, J. Lee, D. King, and H. M. Chung, *Electronic Commerce: A Managerial Perspective* (Upper Saddle River, NJ: Prentice Hall, 2000), p. 15. See also M. J. Shaw, "Electronic Commerce: State of the Art," in M. J. Shaw, R. Blanning, T. Strader, and A. Whinston (eds.), *Handbook on Electronic Commerce* (Berlin: Springer, 2000), pp. 3–24.

44. J. Warner, "21st Century Capitalism: Snapshot of the Next Century," *Business Week* (November 18, 1994), p. 194.

45. P. Jones and L. Kahaner, *Say It & Live It: 50 Corporate Mission Statements That Hit the Mark* (New York: Currency Doubleday, 1995), p. 53.

chapter 2

Corporate Governance and Social Responsibility

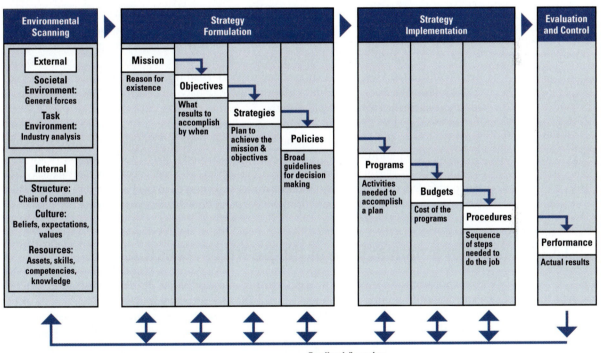

| Environmental Scanning | Strategy Formulation | Strategy Implementation | Evaluation and Control |

External

Societal Environment: General forces

Task Environment: Industry analysis

Internal

Structure: Chain of command

Culture: Beliefs, expectations, values

Resources: Assets, skills, competencies, knowledge

Mission

Reason for existence

Objectives

What results to accomplish by when

Strategies

Plan to achieve the mission & objectives

Policies

Broad guidelines for decision making

Programs

Activities needed to accomplish a plan

Budgets

Cost of the programs

Procedures

Sequence of steps needed to do the job

Performance

Actual results

Feedback/Learning

T yco International Ltd. is a diversified manufacturing and service company that operates in more than 100 countries and has annual revenues of over $36 billion. Taking over as CEO in 1992, Dennis Kozlowski transformed Tyco from an obscure U.S. manufacturer into the world's largest provider of undersea telecommunications systems, fire protection systems, and electronic security services. In doing so, Kozlowski treated Tyco as his own personal empire, lavishing hundreds of millions of dollars in unauthorized loans and exorbitant gifts on himself and his top managers. Even though his annual compensation jumped from $8.8 million in 1996 to $136.1 million in 1999, Kozlowski regularly took loans from the company worth hundreds of millions of dollars. Among his purchases were a $2.1 million birthday celebration for his wife plus a $6,000 shower curtain and a $15,000 dog umbrella stand for his $16.8 million New York apartment. By operating without a second-in-command and by hand-picking top mangers who were "smart, poor, and want-to-be-rich," he kept personal control of the corporation. He hand-picked members of the board of directors and filtered all information, such as internal audits, that went to the board. Without board approval, Kozlowski gave $56 million in bonuses to 51 Tyco employees to effectively cancel loans they had earlier taken from the company.

In the wake of the recent Enron scandal, the U.S. Securities and Exchange Commission (SEC), the Internal Revenue Service, and the State of New Hampshire began investigating Tyco for accounting irregularities and its CPA firm for failing to report the questionable practices. Kozlowski resigned as CEO just before being indicted on tax evasion. Subsequent investigation revealed why the board of directors had been so silent during this period of top management excess: Of the company's 10 directors, 3 were Tyco executives who had serious conflicts of interest. Even though board member Joshua Berman had been serving as a Tyco executive since 1997, the company continued to pay millions of dollars in legal fees to his former law firm. John Fort, the Tyco executive who was named the company's interim CEO upon Kozlowski's resignation, had been an investor in a buyout fund that made an $810 million purchase of Tyco operations in 1999, while Fort served as a board member. Tyco's CFO, Mark Swartz, also served as a board member when he received $6.5 million in loans from the company.

In addition, the nonmanagement, or "outside," directors had such deep ties to the company that it raised questions about the board's ability to oversee management. Michael Ashcroft, for example, had previously worked for the company until 1997. Another board member, Stephen Foss, leased an airplane to Tyco. Lead director Frank Walsh, Jr., received $200 million for his services in helping to arrange Tyco's disastrous 2001 acquisition of commercial-finance company CIT Group.

In October 2001, Tyco agreed to pay $5 million to the State of New Hampshire to reimburse shareholders and the public, who had been hurt by the financial misconduct of its former officers. In addition, Tyco's auditing firm was investigated for its failure to identify accounting irregularities. According to Lyn Turner, former chief accountant for the SEC, $41 million of a $96 million loan forgiveness scheme was charged to the balance sheet for "accrued federal income tax." Said Turner, "I can't understand how they missed that one."[1]

2.1 Corporate Governance: Role of the Board of Directors

A **corporation** is a mechanism established to allow different parties to contribute capital, expertise, and labor for their mutual benefit. The investor/shareholder participates in the profits of the enterprise without taking responsibility for the operations. Management runs the company without being responsible for personally providing the funds. To make this possible, laws have been passed so that shareholders have limited liability and, correspondingly, limited involvement in a corporation's activities. That involvement does include, however, the right to elect directors who have a legal duty to represent the shareholders and protect their interests. As representatives of the shareholders, directors have both the authority and the responsibility to establish basic corporate policies and to ensure that they are followed.[2]

The board of directors has, therefore, an obligation to approve all decisions that might affect the long-run performance of the corporation. This means that the corporation is fundamentally governed by the board of directors overseeing top management, with the concurrence of the shareholder. The term **corporate governance** refers to the relationship among these three groups in determining the direction and performance of the corporation.[3]

Over the past decade, shareholders and various interest groups have seriously questioned the role of the board of directors in corporations. They are concerned that inside board members may use their position to feather their own nests and that outside board members often lack sufficient knowledge, involvement, and enthusiasm to do an adequate job of monitoring and providing guidance to top management. Instances of widespread corruption and questionable accounting practices at Enron, Global Crossing, WorldCom, Tyco, and Qwest, among others, seem to justify their concerns. Tyco's board, for example, seemed more interested in keeping CEO Kozlowski happy than in safeguarding shareholder interests. The very passivity of the board (in addition to questionable financial dealings) was one reason the Kozlowski-era directors were forced to resign in 2003.[4]

The general public has not only become more aware and more critical of many boards' apparent lack of responsibility for corporate activities, it has begun to push government to demand accountability. As a result, the board as a rubber stamp of the CEO or as a bastion of the "old-boy" selection system is being replaced by more active, more professional boards.

RESPONSIBILITIES OF THE BOARD

Laws and standards defining the responsibilities of boards of directors vary from country to country. For example, board members in Ontario, Canada, face more than 100 provincial and federal laws governing director liability. The United States, however, has no clear national standards or federal laws. Specific requirements of directors vary, depending on the state in which the corporate charter is issued. There is, nevertheless, a developing worldwide consensus concerning the major responsibilities of a board. Interviews with 200 directors from eight countries (Canada, France, Germany, Finland, Switzerland, The Netherlands, the United Kingdom, and Venezuela) revealed strong agreement on the following five **board of directors responsibilities**, listed in order of importance:

1. Setting corporate strategy, overall direction, mission, or vision
2. Hiring and firing the CEO and top management
3. Controlling, monitoring, or supervising top management
4. Reviewing and approving the use of resources
5. Caring for shareholder interests[5]

Directors in the United States must make certain, in addition to the duties just listed, that the corporation is managed in accordance with the laws of the state in which it is incorporated. They must also ensure management's adherence to laws and regulations, such as those dealing with the issuance of securities, insider trading, and other conflict-of-interest situations. They must also be aware of the needs and demands of constituent groups so that they can achieve a judicious balance among the interests of these diverse groups while ensuring the continued functioning of the corporation.

In a legal sense, the board is required to direct the affairs of the corporation but not to manage them. It is charged by law to act with **due care**. If a director or the board as a whole fails to act with due care and, as a result, the corporation is in some way harmed, the careless director or directors can be held personally liable for the harm done. This is no small concern, given that one survey of outside directors revealed that more than 40% had been named as part of lawsuits against the corporations.[6]

Role of the Board in Strategic Management

How does a board of directors fulfill these many responsibilities? The **role of the board of directors in strategic management** is to carry out three basic tasks:

- **Monitor:** By acting through its committees, a board can keep abreast of developments inside and outside the corporation, bringing to management's attention developments it might have overlooked. A board should at least carry out this task.

- **Evaluate and influence:** A board can examine management's proposals, decisions, and actions; agree or disagree with them; give advice and offer suggestions; and outline alternatives. Active boards perform this task in addition to the monitoring one.

- **Initiate and determine:** A board can delineate a corporation's mission and specify strategic options to its management. Only the most active boards take on this task in addition to the two previous ones.

Board of Directors Continuum

A board of directors is involved in strategic management to the extent that it carries out the three tasks of monitoring, evaluating and influencing, and initiating and determining. The **board of directors continuum** shown in **Figure 2–1** shows the possible degree of involvement (from low to high) in the strategic management process. As types, boards can range from phantom boards with no real involvement to catalyst boards with very high degrees of involvement. Research suggests that active board involvement in strategic management is positively related to corporate financial performance.[7]

Highly involved boards tend to be very active. They take their tasks of monitoring, evaluating, and influencing, plus initiating and determining, very seriously; they provide advice when necessary and keep management alert. As depicted in **Figure 2–1**, their heavy involvement in the strategic management process places them in the active participation or even catalyst positions. For example, in a survey of directors of large U.S. corporations conducted by Korn/Ferry International, more than 60% indicated that they were deeply involved in the strategy-setting process. In the same survey, 54% of the respondents indicated that their boards participate in annual retreats or special planning sessions to discuss company strategy. Nevertheless, only slightly more than 32% of the boards help develop the strategy. More than two-thirds of the boards review strategy only after it has been first developed by management. Another 1% admit playing no role at all in strategy.[8] These and other studies suggest that most large publicly owned corporations have boards that operate at some point between nominal

Figure 2–1
Board of Directors Continuum

DEGREE OF INVOLVEMENT IN STRATEGIC MANAGEMENT

Low (Passive) ← → **High** (Active)

Phantom	Rubber Stamp	Minimal Review	Nominal Participation	Active Participation	Catalyst
Never knows what to do, if anything; no degree of involvement.	Permits officers to make all decisions. It votes as the officers recommend on action issues.	Formally reviews selected issues that officers bring to its attention.	Involoved to a limited degree in the performance or review of selected key decisions, indicators, or programs of management.	Approves, questions, and makes final decisions on mission, strategy, policies, and objectives. Has active board committees. Performs fiscal and management audits.	Takes the leading role in establishing and modifying the mission, objectives, strategy, and policies. It has a very active strategy committee.

Source: T. L. Wheelen and J. D. Hunger, "Board of Directors Continuum." Copyright © 1994 by Wheelen and Hunger Associates. Reprinted by permission.

and active participation. Some corporations that have actively participating boards are Mead Corporation, Rolm and Haas, Whirlpool, 3M, Apria Healthcare, General Electric, Pfizer, and Texas Instruments.[9]

As a board becomes less involved in the affairs of the corporation, it moves farther to the left on the continuum shown in **Figure 2–1**. On the far left are passive phantom or rubber-stamp boards that typically do not initiate or determine strategy (for example, Tyco) unless a crisis occurs. In these situations, the CEO also serves as Chairman of the Board, personally nominates all directors, and works to keep board members under his or her control by giving them the "mushroom treatment"—throw manure on them and keep them in the dark!

Generally, the smaller the corporation, the less active its board of directors. In an entre-preneurial venture, for example, the privately held corporation may be 100% owned by the founders, who also manage the company. In this case, there is no need for an active board to protect the interests of the owner-manager shareholders—the interests of the owners and the managers are identical. In this instance, a board is really unnecessary and meets only to satisfy legal requirements. If stock is sold to outsiders to finance growth, however, the board becomes more active. Key investors want seats on the board so they can oversee their investment. To the extent that they still control most of the stock, however, the founders dominate the board. Friends, family members, and key shareholders usually become members, but the board acts primarily as a rubber stamp for any proposals put forward by the owner-managers. This cozy relationship between the board and management should change, however, when the corporation goes public and stock is more widely dispersed. The founders, who are still acting as management, may sometimes make decisions that conflict with the needs of the other shareholders (especially if the founders own less than 50% of the common stock). In this instance, problems could occur if the board failed to become more active in terms of its roles and responsibilities.

MEMBERS OF A BOARD OF DIRECTORS

The boards of most publicly owned corporations are composed of both inside and outside directors. **Inside directors** (sometimes called management directors) are typically officers or executives employed by the corporation. **Outside directors** (sometimes called nonmanage-ment directors) may be executives of other firms but are not employees of the board's corporation. Although there is no clear evidence indicating that a high proportion of outsiders on a board results in improved corporate performance, there is a trend in the United States to increase the number of outsiders on boards. The typical large U.S. corporation has an average of 11 directors, of whom 2 are insiders.[10] Even though outsiders account for slightly more than 80% of the board members in these large U.S. corporations (approximately the same as in Canada), they only account for about 42% of board membership in small U.S. companies.[11] People who favor a high proportion of outsiders state that outside directors are less biased and more likely to evaluate management's performance objectively than are inside directors. This is the main reason the New York Stock Exchange requires that each company listed on the exchange have an audit committee composed entirely of independent, outside members. This view is in agreement with **agency theory**, which states that problems arise in corporations because the agents (top management) are not willing to bear responsibility for their decisions unless they own a substantial amount of stock in the corporation. The theory suggests that a majority of a board needs to be from outside the firm so that top management is prevented from acting selfishly, to the detriment of the shareholders. See the **Theory As It Applies** feature for a discussion of agency theory contrasted with **stewardship theory**.

In contrast, those who prefer inside over outside directors contend that outside directors are less effective than are insiders because the outsiders are less likely to have the necessary interest, availability, or competency. Directors may sometimes serve on so many boards that

Theory As It Applies

Agency Theory Versus Stewardship Theory in Corporate Governance

Managers of large, modern publicly held corporations are typically not the owners. In fact, most of today's top managers own only nominal amounts of stock in the corporations they manage. The real owners (shareholders) elect boards of directors who hire managers as their agents to run the firm's day-to-day activities. Once hired, how trustworthy are these executives? Do they put themselves or the firm first?

Agency Theory

As suggested in the classic study by Berle and Means, top managers are, in effect, "hired hands" who may very likely be more interested in their personal welfare than in that of the shareholders. For example, management might emphasize strategies, such as acquisitions, that increase the size of the firm (to become more powerful and to demand increased pay and benefits) or that diversify the firm into unrelated businesses (to reduce short-term risk and to allow them to put less effort into a core product line that may be facing difficulty) but that result in a reduction in dividends and/or stock price.

Agency theory is concerned with analyzing and resolving two problems that occur in relationships between principals (owners/shareholders) and their agents (top management):

1. The agency problem that arises when (a) the desires or objectives of the owners and the agents conflict or (b) it is difficult or expensive for the owners to verify what the agent is actually doing. One example is when top management is more interested in raising its own salary than in increasing stock dividends.

2. The risk-sharing problem that arises when the owners and agents have different attitudes toward risk. Executives may not select risky strategies because they fear losing their jobs if the strategy fails.

According to agency theory, the likelihood that these problems will occur increases when stock is widely held (no one shareholder owns more than a small percentage of the total common stock), when the board of directors is composed of people who know little of the company or who are personal friends of top management, and when a high percentage of board members are inside (management) directors.

To better align the interests of the agents with those of the owners and to increase the corporation's overall performance, agency theory suggests that top management have a significant degree of ownership in the firm and/or have a strong financial stake in its long-term performance. In support of this argument, research indicates a positive relationship between corporate performance and the amount of stock owned by directors.

Stewardship Theory

In contrast to agency theory, stewardship theory suggests that executives tend to be more motivated to act in the best interests of the corporation than in their own self-interests. Whereas agency theory focuses on extrinsic rewards that serve the lower-level needs, such as pay and security, stewardship theory focuses on the higher-order needs, such as achievement and self-actualization. Stewardship theory argues that senior executives over time tend to view the corporation as an extension of themselves. Rather than use the firm for their own ends, these executives are most interested in guaranteeing the continued life and success of the corporation. The relationship between the board and top management is thus one of principal and steward, not principal and agent ("hired hand"). Stewardship theory notes that in a widely held corporation, the shareholder is free to sell her or his stock at any time. A diversified investor may care little about risk at the company level, preferring that management assume extraordinary risk so long as the return is adequate. Because executives in a firm cannot so easily leave their jobs when in difficulty, they are more interested in a merely satisfactory return and put heavy emphasis on the firm's continued survival. Thus, stewardship theory would argue that in many instances top management may care more about a company's long-term success than do more short-term–oriented shareholders.

Note: For more information about agency theory and stewardship theory, see J. H. Davis, F. D. Schoorman, and L. Donaldson, "Toward a Stewardship Theory of Management," *Academy of Management Review* (January 1997), pp. 20–47. See also P. J. Lane, A. A. Cannella, Jr., and M. H. Lubatkin, "Agency Problems As Antecedents to Unrelated Mergers and Diversification: Amihud and Lev Reconsidered," *Strategic Management Journal* (June 1998), pp. 555–578, and M. L. Hayward and D. C. Hambrick, "Explaining the Premiums Paid for Large Acquisitions: Evidence of CEO Hubris," *Administrative Science Quarterly* (March 1997), pp. 103–127. For background, refer to A. A. Berle, Jr. and G. C. Means, *The Modern Corporation and Private Property* (New York: Macmillan, 1932).

they spread their time and interest too thin to actively fulfill their responsibilities. They could also point out that the term "outsider" is too simplistic—some outsiders are not truly objective and should be considered more as insiders than as outsiders. For example, there can be:

1. **Affiliated directors** who, though not really employed by the corporation, handle the legal or insurance work for the company or are important suppliers (thus dependent on the current management for a key part of their business). These outsiders face a conflict of interest and are not likely to be objective. The number of affiliated directors on Tyco's board was one of the reasons the board was so strongly criticized.

2. **Retired directors** who used to work for the company, such as the past CEO (who is partly responsible for much of the corporation's current strategy and who probably groomed the current CEO as his or her replacement). Many boards of large firms keep the firm's recently retired CEO on the board for one or two years after retirement as a courtesy, especially if he or she performed well as the CEO. It is almost certain, however, that this person will not be able to objectively evaluate the corporation's performance. Nevertheless, a survey by Korn/Ferry International found that only 29% of directors surveyed indicated that their boards required the former CEO to leave the board upon retirement.[12]

3. **Family directors** who are descendants of the founder and own significant blocks of stock (with personal agendas based on a family relationship with the current CEO). The Schlitz Brewing Company, for example, was unable to complete its turnaround strategy with a nonfamily CEO because family members serving on the board wanted their money out of the company, forcing it to be sold.[13]

The majority of outside directors are active or retired CEOs and COOs of other corporations. Others are major investors/shareholders, academicians, attorneys, consultants, former government officials, and bankers. Given that approximately 60% of the outstanding stock in the largest U.S. and U.K. corporations is now owned by institutional investors, such as mutual funds and pension plans, these investors are taking an increasingly active role in board membership and activities.[14] In Germany, bankers are represented on almost every board—primarily because they own large blocks of stock in German corporations. In Denmark, Sweden, Belgium, and Italy, however, investment companies assume this role. For example, the investment company Investor AB casts 42.5% of the Electrolux AB shareholder votes, thus guaranteeing itself positions on the Electrolux board. Surveys of large U.S. corporations found that 73% of the boards have at least one woman director, with 25% having two female directors. Boards having at least one minority member increased from 9% in 1973 to 60% today (African American: 39%; Hispanic: 12%; Asian: 9%).[15]

The globalization of business is having an impact on board membership. By 1998, 10% of all directors of companies surveyed internationally by The Conference Board's Global Corporate Governance Research Center were nonnationals, up from 6% three years earlier. Europe is the most "globalized" region of the world, with 71% of companies reporting having one or more nonnational directors, followed by North America, where the figure was 60% in 1998. Asian and Latin American boards are still predominantly staffed by nationals.[16]

Outside directors serving on the boards of large U.S. corporations annually earned on average (median) $33,000. Almost 90% of large U.S. corporations also provided some form of payment through stock options or grants, raising the median annual total compensation to $43,700.[17] Directors serving on the boards of small companies usually received much less (around $10,000). One study found directors to hold on average 3% of their corporations' outstanding stock.[18]

The vast majority of inside directors are the CEO, COO, and Presidents or Vice Presidents of key operating divisions or functional units. Few, if any, inside directors receive any extra compensation for assuming this extra duty. Very rarely does a U.S. board include any lower-level operating employees.

Codetermination: Should Employees Serve on Boards?

Codetermination, the inclusion of a corporation's workers on its board, began only recently in the United States. Corporations such as Chrysler, Northwest Airlines, United Airlines (UAL), and Wheeling-Pittsburgh Steel have added representatives from employee associations to their boards as part of union agreements or employee stock ownership plans (ESOPs). For example, UAL workers traded 15% in pay cuts for 55% of the company (through an ESOP) and 3 of the firm's 12 board seats. In this instance, workers represent themselves on the board not so much as employees, but primarily as owners. At Chrysler, however, the United Auto Workers union obtained a temporary seat on the board as part of a union contract agreement in exchange for changes in work rules and reductions in benefits. In situations like this, when a director represents an internal stakeholder, critics raise the issue of conflict of interest. Can a member of the board, who is privy to confidential managerial information, function, for example, as a union leader whose primary duty is to fight for the best benefits for his or her members? Although the movement to place employees on the boards of directors of U.S. companies shows little likelihood of increasing (except through employee stock ownership), the European experience reveals an increasing acceptance of worker participation (without ownership) on corporate boards.

Germany pioneered codetermination during the 1950s, with a two-tiered system: a supervisory board elected by shareholders and employees to approve or decide corporate strategy and a policy and management board (composed primarily of top management) appointed by the supervisory board to manage the company's activities. Most other Western European countries have either passed similar codetermination legislation (for example, Sweden, Denmark, Norway, Austria) or use worker councils to work closely with management (for example, Belgium, Luxembourg, France, Italy, Ireland, The Netherlands).

Interlocking Directorates

CEOs often nominate chief executives (as well as board members) from other firms to membership on their own boards in order to create an **interlocking directorate**. A *direct* interlocking directorate occurs when two firms share a director or when an executive of one firm sits on the board of a second firm. An *indirect* interlock occurs when two corporations have directors who also serve on the board of a third firm, such as a bank. Both inside and outside directors at the largest U.S. companies serve on an average of three boards.

Although the Clayton Act and the Banking Act of 1933 prohibit interlocking directorates by U.S. companies competing in the same industry, interlocking continues to occur in almost all corporations, especially large ones. Interlocking occurs because large firms have a large impact on other corporations; these other corporations, in turn, have some control over the firm's inputs and marketplace. For example, most large corporations in the United States, Japan, and Germany are interlocked either directly or indirectly with financial institutions.[19] Interlocking directorates are also a useful method for gaining both inside information about an uncertain environment and objective expertise about potential strategies and tactics. For example, Kleiner Perkins, the high-tech venture capital firm, not only has seats on the boards of the companies in which it invests, but it also has executives (whom Kleiner Perkins hired) from one entrepreneurial venture serve as directors on others. Kleiner Perkins refers to its network of interlocked firms as its *keiretsu*.[20] Family-owned corporations, however, are less likely to have interlocking directorates than are corporations with highly dispersed stock ownership, probably because family-owned corporations do not like to dilute their corporate control by adding outsiders to boardroom discussions. Nevertheless, some evidence indicates that well-interlocked corporations are better able than others to survive in a highly competitive environment.[21]

NOMINATION AND ELECTION OF BOARD MEMBERS

Traditionally the CEO of a corporation decided whom to invite to board membership and merely asked the shareholders for approval in the annual proxy statement. All nominees were usually elected. There are some dangers, however, in allowing the CEO free rein in nominating directors. The CEO might select only board members who, in the CEO's opinion, will not disturb the company's policies and functioning. Given that the average length of service of a U.S. board member is for five 4-year terms, CEO-friendly, passive boards are likely to result. This is especially likely given that 92% of surveyed directors indicated that their company did not have term limits for board members. Directors selected by the CEO often feel that they should go along with any proposal the CEO makes. Thus board members find themselves accountable to the very management they are charged to oversee. Because this is likely to happen, more boards are using a nominating committee to nominate new outside board members for the shareholders to elect. Approximately 74% of large U.S. corporations now use nominating committees to identify potential directors.[22]

Virtually every corporation whose directors serve terms of more than one year divides the board into classes and staggers elections so that only a portion of the board stands for election each year. This is called a **staggered board**. Arguments in favor of this practice are that it provides continuity by reducing the chance of an abrupt turnover in its membership and that it reduces the likelihood of electing people who are unfriendly to management (who might be interested in a hostile takeover) through cumulative voting. An argument against staggered boards is that they make it more difficult for concerned shareholders to curb a CEO's power, especially when that CEO is also Chairman of the Board. For example, out of dissatisfaction with the company's poor performance and their perception that the board was inactive, two unions supported a shareholder proposal in 1996 to cancel Kmart's staggered board so that the entire board would be elected annually.

A survey of directors of U.S. corporations revealed the following criteria for selecting a good director:

- Is willing to challenge management when necessary (95%)
- Has special expertise important to the company (67%)
- Is available outside meetings to advise management (57%)
- Has expertise on global business issues (41%)
- Understands firm's key technologies and processes (39%)
- Brings external contacts that are potentially valuable to the firm (33%)
- Has detailed knowledge of the firm's industry (31%)
- Is highly visible in his or her field (31%)
- Is accomplished at representing the firm to stakeholders (18%)[23]

ORGANIZATION OF THE BOARD

The size of a board in the United States is determined by the corporation's charter and its bylaws, in compliance with state laws. Although some states require a minimum number of board members, most corporations have quite a bit of discretion in determining board size. The average large, publicly held firm has around 11 directors. The average small/medium-size privately held company has approximately seven to eight members.

Sixty-seven percent of the top executives of large U.S. publicly held corporations hold the dual designation of Chairman and CEO. (The percentage of firms having the Chair/CEO position combined in Canada and the United Kingdom is 43% and 20%, respectively.)[24] The combined Chair/CEO position is being increasingly criticized because of the potential for conflict of interest. The CEO is supposed to concentrate on strategy, planning, external relations, and responsibility to the board. The Chairman's responsibility is to ensure that the board and its committees perform their functions as stated in the board's charter. Further, the Chairman schedules board meetings and presides over the annual shareholders' meeting. Critics of combining the two offices in one person ask how the board can properly oversee top management if the Chairman is also top management. For this reason, the Chairman and CEO roles are separated by law in Germany, The Netherlands, and Finland. A similar law has been considered in Britain and Australia. Although research does not clearly indicate either a definite positive or negative effect of combined positions on corporate performance, the stock market does respond negatively to announcements of CEOs also assuming the Chairman position.[25]

Many of those who prefer that the Chairman and CEO positions be combined agree that the outside directors should elect a **lead director**. This person would be consulted by the Chair/CEO regarding board affairs and would coordinate the annual evaluation of the CEO.[26] The lead director position is very popular in the United Kingdom, where it originated. Of those U.S. companies combining the Chair and CEO positions, 30% currently have lead directors.[27] This is one way to give the board more power without undermining the power of the Chair/CEO.

The most effective boards accomplish much of their work through committees. Although they do not usually have legal duties, most committees are granted full power to act with the authority of the board between board meetings. Typical standing committees (in order of prevalence) are the audit (100%), compensation (99%), nominating (74%), and executive (60%) committees. The executive committee is usually composed of two inside and two nearby outside directors who can meet between board meetings to attend to matters that must be settled quickly. This committee acts as an extension of the board and, consequently, may have almost unrestricted authority in certain areas. The audit, compensation, and nominating committees are usually composed only of outside directors.

TRENDS IN CORPORATE GOVERNANCE

The role of the board of directors in the strategic management of the corporation is likely to be more active in the future. Although neither the composition of boards nor the board leadership structure has been consistently linked to firm financial performance, a McKinsey survey reveals that investors are willing to pay 16% more for a corporation's stock if it is known to have good corporate governance. The investors explained that they would pay more because, in their opinion, (1) good governance leads to better performance over time, (2) good governance reduces the risk of the company getting into trouble, and (3) governance is a major strategic issue.[28]

Some of today's **trends in governance** (particularly prevalent in the United States and the United Kingdom) that are likely to continue include the following:[29]

- Boards are getting more involved not only in reviewing and evaluating company strategy but also in shaping it.
- Institutional investors, such as pension funds, mutual funds, and insurance companies, are becoming active on boards and are putting increasing pressure on top management to improve corporate performance. For example, the California Public Employees' Retirement System (CalPERS), the largest pension system in the United States, annually publishes a list of poorly performing companies, hoping to embarrass management into taking remedial action.
- Shareholders are demanding that directors and top managers own more than token amounts of stock in the corporation. Stock is increasingly being used as part of a director's compensation.
- Nonaffiliated outside (nonmanagement) directors are increasing their numbers and power in publicly held corporations as CEOs loosen their grips on boards. Outside members are taking charge of annual CEO evaluations.
- Boards are getting smaller, partially because of the reduction in the number of insiders but also because boards desire new directors to have specialized knowledge and expertise instead of general experience.

- Boards continue to take more control of board functions by either splitting the combined Chair/CEO position into two separate positions or establishing a lead outside director position.

- As corporations become more global, they are increasingly looking for international experience in their board members.

- Society, in the form of special interest groups, increasingly expects boards of directors to balance the economic goal of profitability with the social needs of society. Issues dealing with workforce diversity and the environment are now reaching the board level. For example, the board of Chase Manhattan Corporation recently questioned top management about its efforts to improve the sparse number of women and minorities in senior management.[30]

2.2 Corporate Governance: The Role of Top Management

The top management function is usually conducted by the CEO of the corporation in coordination with the COO or President, Executive Vice President, and Vice Presidents of divisions and functional areas. Even though strategic management involves everyone in the organization, the board of directors holds top management primarily responsible for the strategic management of the firm.[31]

RESPONSIBILITIES OF TOP MANAGEMENT

Top management responsibilities, especially those of the CEO, involve getting things accomplished through and with others in order to meet the corporate objectives. Top management's job is thus multidimensional and is oriented toward the welfare of the total organization. Specific top management tasks vary from firm to firm and are developed from an analysis of the mission, objectives, strategies, and key activities of the corporation. Tasks are typically divided among the members of the top management team. A diversity of skills can thus be very important. Research indicates that top management teams with a diversity of functional and educational backgrounds and length of time with the company tend to be significantly related to improvements in corporate market share and profitability.[32] Nevertheless, the CEO, with the support of the rest of the top management team, must successfully handle two primary responsibilities that are crucial to the effective strategic management of the corporation: (1) provide executive leadership and a strategic vision and (2) manage the strategic planning process.

Provide Executive Leadership and Strategic Vision

Executive leadership is the directing of activities toward the accomplishment of corporate objectives. Executive leadership is important because it sets the tone for the entire corporation. A **strategic vision** is a description of what the company is capable of becoming. It is often communicated in the mission statement. People in an organization want to have a sense of mission, but only top management is in the position to specify and communicate this strategic vision to the general workforce. Top management's enthusiasm (or lack of it) about the corporation tends to be contagious. Entrepreneurs are noted for having a strong passion for their company and for their ability to communicate it to others. The importance of executive leadership is illustrated by John Welch, Jr., the successful Chairman and CEO of General Electric Company (GE). According to Welch, "Good business leaders create a vision, articulate the vision, passionately own the vision, and relentlessly drive it to completion."[33]

CEOs with clear strategic vision are often perceived as dynamic and charismatic leaders. For instance, the positive attitude characterizing many well-known industrial leaders—such as Bill Gates at Microsoft, Anita Roddick at The Body Shop, Ted Turner at CNN, Steve Jobs at Apple Computer, Herb Kelleher at Southwest Airlines, and Andy Grove at Intel—has energized their respective corporations. They are able to command respect and to influence strategy formulation and implementation because they tend to have three key characteristics:

1. **The CEO articulates a strategic vision** for the corporation. The CEO envisions the company not as it currently is, but as it can become. The new perspective that the CEO's vision brings to activities and conflicts gives renewed meaning to everyone's work and enables employees to see beyond the details of their own jobs to the functioning of the total corporation. In a survey of 1,500 senior executives from 20 different countries, when asked the most important behavioral trait a CEO must have, 98% responded that the CEO must convey "a strong sense of vision."[34]

2. **The CEO presents a role** for others to identify with and to follow. The leader sets an example in terms of behavior and dress. The CEO's attitudes and values concerning the corporation's purpose and activities are clear-cut and constantly communicated in words and deeds. People know what to expect and have trust in their CEO. Research indicates that businesses in which the general manager has the trust of the employees have higher sales and profits with lower turnover than do businesses in which there is a lower amount of trust.[35]

3. **The CEO communicates high performance standards and also shows confidence in the followers' abilities** to meet these standards. No leader ever improved performance by setting easily attainable goals that provided no challenge. The CEO must be willing to follow through by coaching people. Selected the "Best CEO" of 2000, John Chambers of Cisco Systems has this characteristic. According to his subordinates, "John treats us like peers. . . . He asks our advice. He gives us power and resources, then sets the sales targets incredibly high, which keeps us challenged. He is an adhesive force keeping us working together and not flying apart."[36]

Manage the Strategic Planning Process

As business corporations adopt more of the characteristics of the learning organization, strategic planning initiatives can now come from any part of an organization. A survey of 90 U.S. global corporations revealed that, in 90% of the firms, strategies are first proposed in the subsidiaries and sent to headquarters for approval.[37] However, unless top management encourages and supports the planning process, strategic management is not likely to result. In most corporations, top management must initiate and manage the strategic planning process. It may do so by first asking business units and functional areas to propose strategic plans for themselves, or it may begin by drafting an overall corporate plan within which the units can then build their own plans. Research suggests that bottom-up strategic planning may be most appropriate in multidivisional corporations operating in relatively stable environments but that top-down strategic planning may be most appropriate for firms operating in turbulent environments.[38] Other organizations engage in concurrent strategic planning, in which all the organization's units draft plans for themselves after they have been provided with the organization's overall mission and objectives.

Regardless of the approach taken, the typical board of directors expects top management to manage the overall strategic planning process so that the plans of all the units and functional areas fit together into an overall corporate plan. Top management's job therefore includes the tasks of evaluating unit plans and providing feedback. To do this, top management may require each unit to justify its proposed objectives, strategies, and programs in terms of how well they satisfy the organization's overall objectives in light of available resources.[39]

Many large organizations have a **strategic planning staff** charged with supporting both top management and the business units in the strategic planning process. This planning staff typically consists of just under 10 people, headed by a Senior Vice President or Director of Corporate Planning. The staff's major responsibilities are to:

1. Identify and analyze companywide strategic issues and suggest corporate strategic alternatives to top management.

2. Work as facilitators with business units to guide them through the strategic planning process.

2.3 Social Responsibilities of Strategic Decision Makers

Should strategic decision makers be responsible only to shareholders, or do they have broader responsibilities? The concept of **social responsibility** proposes that a private corporation has responsibilities to society that extend beyond making a profit. Strategic decisions often affect more than just the corporation. A decision to retrench by closing some plants and discontinuing product lines, for example, affects not only the firm's workforce, but also the communities where the plants are located and the customers that have no other source for the discontinued product. Such situations raise questions of the appropriateness of certain missions, objectives, and strategies of business corporations. Managers must be able to deal with these conflicting interests in an ethical manner to formulate a viable strategic plan.

RESPONSIBILITIES OF A BUSINESS FIRM

What are the responsibilities of a business firm, and how many of them must be fulfilled? Milton Friedman and Archie Carroll offer two contrasting views of the responsibilities of business firms to society.

Friedman's Traditional View of Business Responsibility

Urging a return to a laissez-faire worldwide economy with a minimum of government regulation, Friedman argues against the concept of social responsibility. A business person who acts "responsibly" by cutting the price of the firm's product to prevent inflation or by making expenditures to reduce pollution, or by hiring the hard-core unemployed, according to Friedman, is spending the shareholder's money for a general social interest. Even if the business person has shareholder permission or encouragement to do so, he or she is still acting from motives other than economic and may, in the long run, harm the very society the firm is trying to help. By taking on the burden of these social costs, the business becomes less efficient—either prices go up to pay for the increased costs or investment in new activities and research is postponed. These results negatively affect—perhaps fatally—the long-term efficiency of a business. Friedman thus referred to the social responsibility of business as a "fundamentally subversive doctrine" and stated that:

> There is one and only one social responsibility of business—to use its resources and engage in activities designed to increase its profits so long as it stays within the rules of the game, which is to say, engages in open and free competition without deception or fraud.[40]

Carroll's Four Responsibilities of Business

As shown in Figure 2–2, Archie Carroll proposes that the managers of business organizations have four **responsibilities**:[41]

1. **Economic** responsibilities of a business organization's management are to produce goods and services of value to society so that the firm can repay its creditors and shareholders.

2. **Legal** responsibilities are defined by governments in laws that management is expected to obey. For example, U.S. business firms are required to hire and promote people based on their credentials rather than to discriminate based on non-job-related characteristics such as race, gender, or religion.

3. **Ethical** responsibilities of an organization's management are to follow the generally held beliefs about behavior in a society. For example, society generally expects firms to work with the employees and the community in planning for layoffs, even though no law may require this. The affected people can get very upset if an organization's management fails to act according to generally prevailing ethical values.

4. **Discretionary** responsibilities are the purely voluntary obligations a corporation assumes. Examples are philanthropic contributions, training the hard-core unemployed, and providing day care centers. The difference between ethical and discretionary responsibilities is that few people expect an organization to fulfill discretionary responsibilities, whereas many expect an organization to fulfill ethical ones.[42]

Carroll lists these four responsibilities *in order of priority*. A business firm must first make a profit to satisfy its economic responsibilities. To continue in existence, the firm must follow the laws, thus fulfilling its legal responsibilities. There is evidence that companies found guilty of violating laws have lower profits and sales growth after conviction.[43] To this point Carroll and Friedman are in agreement. Carroll, however, argues that business managers have responsibilities beyond the economic and legal ones.

Having satisfied the two basic responsibilities, according to Carroll, the firm should look to fulfilling its social responsibilities. Social responsibility, therefore, *includes both ethical and discretionary, but not economic and legal, responsibilities*. A firm can fulfill its ethical responsibilities by taking actions that society tends to value but has not yet put into law. When ethical responsibilities are satisfied, a firm can focus on discretionary responsibilities—purely voluntary actions that society has not yet decided are important.

The discretionary responsibilities of today may become the ethical responsibilities of tomorrow. The provision of day care facilities is, for example, moving rapidly from being a discretionary to an ethical responsibility. Carroll suggests that to the extent that business corporations fail to acknowledge discretionary or ethical responsibilities, society, through government, will act, making them legal responsibilities. Government may do this, moreover, without regard to an organization's economic responsibilities. As a result, the organization may have greater difficulty earning a profit than it would have had if it had voluntarily assumed some ethical and discretionary responsibilities.

Both Friedman and Carroll argue their positions based on the impact of socially responsible actions on a firm's profits. Friedman says that socially responsible actions hurt a firm's

Figure 2–2

Responsibilities of Business

Source: Adapted from A. B. Carroll, "A Three Dimensional Conceptual Model of Corporate Performance," *Academy of Management Review* (October 1979), p. 499. Reprinted with permission.

efficiency. Carroll proposes that a lack of social responsibility results in increased government regulations, which reduce a firm's efficiency.

Research is mixed regarding the effect of social responsibility on a corporation's financial performance. Although a number of research studies find no significant relationship,[44] an increasing number are finding a positive relationship.[45]

Being known as a socially responsible firm may provide a company a competitive advantage. For example, companies that take the lead in being environmentally friendly, such as by using recycled materials, preempt attacks from environmental groups and enhance their corporate image. Programs to reduce pollution, for example, can actually reduce waste and maximize resource productivity. One study that examined 70 ecological initiatives taken by 43 companies found the average payback period to be 18 months.[46] Other examples of benefits received from being socially responsible are:

- Their environmental concerns may enable them to charge premium prices and gain brand loyalty (Ben & Jerry's Homemade, Inc.).
- Their trustworthiness may help them generate enduring relationships with suppliers and distributors without needing to spend a lot of time and money policing contracts (Maytag).
- They can attract outstanding employees who prefer working for a responsible firm (Procter & Gamble).
- They are more likely to be welcomed into a foreign country (Levi Strauss).
- They can utilize the goodwill of public officials for support in difficult times (for example, Minnesota supported Dayton-Hudson's fight to avoid being acquired by Dart Industries of Maryland).
- They are more likely to attract capital infusions from investors who view reputable companies as desirable long-term investments (Rubbermaid).[47]

CORPORATE STAKEHOLDERS

The concept that business must be socially responsible sounds appealing until we ask, "Responsible to whom?" A corporation's task environment includes a large number of groups with interest in a business organization's activities. These groups are referred to as **corporate stakeholders** because they affect or are affected by the achievement of the firm's objectives.[48] Should a corporation be responsible only to some of these groups, or does business have an equal responsibility to all of them?

Recent surveys suggest that the U.S. general public is worried that business is becoming too concerned with profits. A recent survey conducted by Harris Poll found that 66% either strongly or somewhat agreed that large profits are more important to big business than developing safe, reliable, quality products for consumers. Recent revelations of tainted milk in Japan (Snow Brand), flawed child strollers in the United States (Cosco), and unsafe tires globally (Firestone) only add to the public concern that business is ignoring its stakeholders and may be operating unethically or even illegally. According to Harris Poll, 73% of U.S. adults agreed that the compensation of top officers of large U.S. companies is "too much." The survey also found that 95% felt that U.S. corporations owe something to their workers and the communities in which they operate and that they should sometimes sacrifice some profit for the sake of making things better for their workers and communities.[49] Such attitudes become grist for populist politicians who make business people into villains during election campaigns.

In any one strategic decision, the interests of one stakeholder group can conflict with those of another. For example, a business firm's decision to use only recycled materials in its manufacturing process may have a positive effect on environmental groups but a negative effect on shareholder dividends. In another example, Maytag Corporation's top management decided to move dishwasher production from Iowa to a lower-wage location in Tennessee. On the one hand, shareholders were generally pleased with the decision because it would lower costs. On the other hand, Iowa officials and local union people were very unhappy at what they called "community cannibalism." Which group's interests should have priority?

Given the wide range of interests and concerns present in any organization's task environment, one or more groups, at any one time, probably will be dissatisfied with an organization's activities—even if management is trying to be socially responsible. A company may have some stakeholders of which it is only marginally aware. Therefore, before making a strategic decision, strategic managers should consider how each alternative will affect various stakeholder groups. What seems at first to be the best decision because it appears to be the most profitable may actually result in the worst set of consequences to the corporation.

2.4 Ethical Decision Making

Some people joke that there is no such thing as "business ethics." They call it an oxymoron—a concept that combines opposite or contradictory ideas. Unfortunately there is some truth to this sarcastic comment. For example, a survey by the Ethics Resource Center of 1,324 employees of 747 U.S. companies found that 48% of employees surveyed said that they had engaged in one or more unethical and/or illegal actions during the past year. The most common questionable behavior involved cutting corners on quality (16%), covering up incidents (14%), abusing or lying about sick days (11%), and lying to or deceiving customers (9%). Some 56% of workers reported pressure to act unethically or illegally on the job.[50] See the **Global Issue** feature for examples of unethical practices at Enron and WorldCom.

Global Issue

Unethical Practices at Enron and WorldCom Exposed by "Whistleblowers"

Corporate scandals at Enron, WorldCom, and Tyco, among other international companies, have caused people around the world to seriously question the ethics of business executives. Enron, in particular, has become infamous for the questionable actions of its top executives in the form of (1) off-balance sheet partnerships used to hide the company's deteriorating finances, (2) revenue from long-term contracts being recorded in its first year instead of being spread over multiple years, (3) financial reports being falsified to inflate executive bonuses, and (4) manipulation of the electricity market, leading to a California energy crisis. Only Sherron Watkins, an Enron accountant, was willing to speak out regarding the questionable nature of these practices. In a now-famous memo to then-CEO Kenneth Lay, Watkins warned:

I realize that we have had a lot of smart people looking at this and a lot of accountants including AA & Co. (Arthur Anderson) have blessed the accounting treatment. None of that will protect Enron if these transactions are ever disclosed in the bright light of day.

At WorldCom, Cynthia Cooper, an internal auditor, noted that some of the company's capital expenditures should have been listed on the second-quarter financial statements as expenses. When she mentioned this to both WorldCom's Controller and its CFO, she was told to stop what she was doing and to delay the audit until the third quarter (when expensing the transactions would not be noticed). Instead, Cooper informed the board of directors' audit committee. Two weeks later, WorldCom announced that it was reducing earnings by $3.9 billion, the largest restatement in history.

Sources: G. Colvin, "Wonder Women of Whistleblowing," *Fortune* (August 12, 2002), p. 56; W. Zellner, "The Deadly Sins of Enron," *Business Week* (October 14, 2002, pp. 26–28, and M. J. Mandel, "And the Enron Award Goes to . . . Enron," *Business Week* (May 20, 2002), p. 46.

SOME REASONS FOR UNETHICAL BEHAVIOR

Why are many business people perceived to be acting unethically? It may be that the involved people are not even aware that they are taking questionable actions. There is no worldwide standard of conduct for business people. Cultural norms and values vary between countries and even between different geographic regions and ethnic groups within a country. For example, what is considered in one country to be a bribe to expedite service is sometimes considered in another country to be normal business practice.

Another possible reason for what is often perceived to be unethical behavior lies in differences in values between business people and key stakeholders. Some business people may believe profit maximization is the key goal of their firm, whereas concerned interest groups may have other priorities, such as the hiring of minorities and women or the safety of their neighborhoods. Of the six values measured by the Allport-Vernon-Lindzey Study of Values test (aesthetic, economic, political, religious, social, and theoretical), both U.S. and British executives consistently score highest on economic and political values and lowest on social and religious ones. This is similar to the value profile of managers from Japan, Korea, India, and Australia, as well as those of U.S. business school students. U.S. Protestant ministers, in contrast, score highest on religious and social values and very low on economic values.[51]

This difference in values can make it difficult for one group of people to understand another's actions. For example, even though some people feel that the advertising of cigarettes (especially to youth) is unethical, the people managing these companies respond that they are simply offering a product; "Let the buyer beware" is a traditional saying in free market capitalism. They argue that customers in a free market democracy have the right to choose how they spend their money and live their lives. Social progressives may contend that business people working in tobacco, alcoholic beverages, and gambling industries are acting unethically by making and advertising products with potentially dangerous and expensive side effects, such as cancer, alcoholism, and addiction. People working in those industries could respond by asking if it is ethical for people who don't smoke, drink, or gamble to reject another person's right to do so.

Moral Relativism

Some people justify their seemingly unethical positions by arguing that there is no one absolute code of ethics and that morality is relative. Simply put, **moral relativism** claims that morality is relative to some personal, social, or cultural standard and that there is no method for deciding whether one decision is better than another.

Adherents of moral relativism may believe that all moral decisions are deeply personal and that individuals have the right to run their own lives; each person should be allowed to interpret situations and act on his or her own moral values. They may also argue that social roles carry with them certain obligations to those roles only. A manager in charge of a department, for example, must put aside his or her personal beliefs and do instead what the role requires—that is, act in the best interests of the department. They could also argue that a decision is legitimate if it is common practice, regardless of other considerations ("Everyone's doing it"). Some propose that morality itself is relative to a particular culture, society, or community. People should therefore understand the practices of other countries but not judge them. If the citizens of another country share certain norms and customs, what right does an outsider have to criticize them?

Although these arguments make some sense, moral relativism could enable a person to justify almost any sort of decision or action, so long as it is not declared illegal.

Kohlberg's Levels of Moral Development

Another reason some business people might be seen as unethical is that they may have no well-developed personal sense of ethics. A person's ethical behavior is affected by his or her level of moral development, certain personality variables, and such situational factors as the job itself, the supervisor, and the organizational culture.[52] Kohlberg proposes that a person progresses through three **levels of moral development**.[53] Similar in some ways to Maslow's hierarchy of needs, Kohlberg's levels of moral development have the individual move from total self-centeredness to a concern for universal values. Kohlberg's three levels are as follows:

1. **The preconventional level** is characterized by a concern for self. Small children and others who have not progressed beyond this stage evaluate behaviors on the basis of personal interest—avoiding punishment or quid pro quo.
2. **The conventional level** is characterized by considerations of society's laws and norms. Actions are justified by an external code of conduct.
3. **The principled level** is characterized by a person's adherence to an internal moral code. The individual at this level looks beyond norms or laws to find universal values or principles.

Kohlberg places most people in the conventional level, with fewer than 20% of U.S. adults in the principled level of development.[54]

ENCOURAGING ETHICAL BEHAVIOR

According to Carroll's work, if business people do not act ethically, government will be forced to pass laws regulating their actions—and usually increasing their costs. For self-interest, if for no other reason, managers should be more ethical in their decision making. One way to do that is by encouraging codes of ethics. Another is by providing guidelines for ethical behavior.

Codes of Ethics

Codes of ethics specify how an organization expects its employees to behave while on the job. Developing codes of ethics can be a useful way to promote ethical behavior, especially for people who are operating at Kohlberg's conventional level of moral development. Such codes are currently being used by about half of U.S. business corporations. According to a report by the Business Roundtable, an association of CEOs from 200 major U.S. corporations, the importance of a code of ethics is that it (1) clarifies company expectations of employee conduct in various situations and (2) makes clear that the company expects its people to recognize the ethical dimensions in decisions and actions.[55]

Various studies indicate that an increasing number of companies are developing codes of ethics and implementing ethics training workshops and seminars. However, research also indicates that when faced with a question of ethics, managers tend to ignore codes of ethics and try to solve their dilemmas on their own.[56] To combat this tendency, the management of a company that wants to improve its employees' ethical behavior should not only develop a comprehensive code of ethics but also communicate the code in its training programs, in its performance appraisal system, its policies and procedures, and through its own actions. It may also want to do the same for the companies with which it does business. For example, Reebok International has developed a set of production standards for the manufacturers that supply the company with its athletic shoes on a contract basis. In response to a report commissioned by Reebok (at a cost of $50,000) that found health and safety problems at two subcontractor plants in Indonesia, the two suppliers were forced to spend $500,000 in factory improvements in order to keep Reebok's business.[57]

Guidelines for Ethical Behavior

Ethics is defined as the consensually accepted standards of behavior for an occupation, a trade, or a profession. **Morality**, in contrast, is the precepts of personal behavior that are based on religious or philosophical grounds. **Law** refers to formal codes that permit or forbid certain behaviors and may or may not enforce ethics or morality.[58] Given these definitions, how do we arrive at a comprehensive statement of ethics to use in making decisions in a specific occupation, trade, or profession? A starting point for such a code of ethics is to consider the three basic approaches to ethical behavior:[59]

1. **Utilitarian approach:** This approach proposes that actions and plans should be judged by their consequences. People should therefore behave in a way that will produce the greatest benefit to society and produce the least harm or the lowest cost. A problem with this approach is the difficulty in recognizing all the benefits and the costs of any particular decision. Research has revealed that only the stakeholders having the most *power* (ability to affect the company), *legitimacy* (legal or moral claim on company resources), and *urgency* (demand for immediate attention) are given priority by CEOs.[60] It is therefore likely that only the most obvious stakeholders will be considered, while others will be ignored.

2. **Individual rights approach:** This approach proposes that human beings have certain fundamental rights that should be respected in all decisions. A particular decision or behavior should be avoided if it interferes with the rights of others. A problem with this approach is in defining "fundamental rights." The U.S. Constitution includes a Bill of Rights that may or may not be accepted throughout the world. This approach can also encourage selfish behavior when a person defines a personal need or want as a right.

3. **Justice approach:** This approach proposes that decision makers be equitable, fair, and impartial in the distribution of costs and benefits to individuals and groups. It follows the principles of *distributive justice* (people who are similar on relevant dimensions such as job seniority should be treated in the same way) and *fairness* (liberty should be equal for all persons). The justice approach can also include the concepts of *retributive justice* (punishment should be proportional to the "crime") and *compensatory justice* (wrongs should be compensated in proportion to the offense). Affirmative action issues such as reverse discrimination are examples of conflicts between distributive and compensatory justice.

Cavanagh proposes that we solve ethical problems by asking the following three questions regarding an act or a decision:[61]

1. **Utility:** Does it optimize the satisfactions of all stakeholders?
2. **Rights:** Does it respect the rights of the individuals involved?
3. **Justice:** Is it consistent with the canons of justice?

For example, is padding an expense account ethical? Using the utility criterion, this action increases the company's costs and thus does not optimize benefits for shareholders or customers. Using the rights approach, a person has no right to the money (otherwise we wouldn't call it "padding"). Using the justice criterion, salary and commissions constitute ordinary compensation, but expense accounts compensate a person only for expenses incurred in doing his or her job—expenses that the person would not normally incur except in doing this job.

Another approach to resolving ethical dilemmas is by applying the logic of the philosopher Immanual Kant. Kant presents two principles (called **categorical imperatives**) to guide our actions:[62]

1. A person's action is ethical only if that person is willing for that same action to be taken by everyone who is in a similar situation. This is the same as the *Golden Rule*: Treat others as you would like them to treat you. For example, padding an expense account would be considered ethical if the person were also willing for everyone to do the same if he or she were the boss. Because it is very doubtful that any manager would be pleased with expense account padding, the action must be considered unethical.

2. A person should never treat another human being simply as a means, but always as an end. This means that an action is morally wrong for a person if that person uses others merely as means for advancing his or her own interests. To be moral, the act should not restrict other people's actions so that they are left disadvantaged in some way.

2.5 Impact of the Internet on Corporate Governance and Social Responsibility

Electronic commerce is offering a great deal of benefits, but it is also raising a number of issues related to social responsibility and stakeholders. Thus far, the Internet has generally been unregulated by governments. To the extent that groups of people find the Internet to have negative effects, government will eventually be called upon to intervene. Europeans are concerned with a user's privacy. Middle Easterners are concerned with decency standards. Americans are concerned with con artists using Web sites and e-mail to take money without providing a service.

In Russia, for example, a recently passed law allows the Federal Security Bureau (FSB) to monitor all Internet, cellular telephone, and pager communication traffic. Directives require all Russian internet service providers (ISPs) to equip their networks with FSB monitors and connect them via high-speed fiber-optic links to FSB headquarters.[63]

A number of problems may make it difficult to keep the Internet unregulated. Some of these are:

- **Cybersquatting:** This occurs when a private speculator purchases the right to a valuable corporate brand name domain, such as businessweek.com, and then sells it to the company at an exorbitant price. Because Web addresses are critical to online branding, companies want to establish a rule that they are entitled to domain names that use their trademarks. In response, consumer advocates say that such a rule would unfairly restrict the rights of schools, museums, religions, and clubs. They argue that an astronomy club should be able to register Saturn.com if the domain is available—and not later lose it to a car company.[64]

- **Fraud:** The Internet is an excellent source of information—information that can be used to defraud innocent people by temporarily stealing their identity. Thanks to personal Web sites and other publicly available information, the Internet can provide all that is needed to charge purchases to someone else's credit cards and to transfer funds out of their bank accounts.

- **Taxation:** In international trade, goods tend to be subject to tariffs, whereas services are not. The Internet is making this distinction difficult. For example, a compact disc (CD) sent from one country to another is a good and thus incurs a tariff as it crosses a border. But what if the music on the CD is sent electronically from a computer in one country to a computer in another country? Because customized data and software, which can also be put on a CD, are usually treated as services, is the music a good or a service?[65]

- **Public interest:** Because most societies have some sort of restrictions on children's access to pornography, should pornographic Web sites also be restricted? If so, by whom? Given that government is often expected to protect its citizens from fraudulent investment schemes and from quack medical treatments, what should it do when these things are offered on the Internet? Governments could impose trade restrictions requiring that financial firms selling on the Internet to residents of a country must also have an office in that country. See the ▓ **Internet Issue** feature for examples of governmental attempts to regulate the Internet.

In addition, the Internet is providing a fast way to communicate a company's mistakes and any unethical or illegal actions to interested people throughout the world. This is making it increasingly difficult for companies undertaking questionable activities to keep things quiet while they cover up the problem with public relations campaigns. Fueled by passion and technical expertise, activists of all kinds have launched sophisticated Web sites that attack individual companies regarding their environmental or labor practices and other issues. For example, the Web site www.corporatewatch.org.uk is operated by Corporate Watch and contains articles on the risks of genetic modification of plants, with case studies targeting leading biotech companies. Interestingly, some companies are beginning to respond by upgrading their Web sites to reflect their shift to a more open dialogue with a wide range of stakeholders. In response to Greenpeace's Shareholders Against New Exploration (SANE) campaign, BP Amoco has added links to environmental information and to its animated explanation of its solar energy research.[66]

Internet Issue

Governments Act to Protect Society by Regulating the Internet

November 20, 2000, a French court ordered Yahoo! to find some way of banning French users from seeing the Nazi memorabilia posted on its U.S. Web sites or face a daily fine of FF100,000 ($13,000). Although Yahoo! appealed the court's decision, it stopped listing sales of Nazi memorabilia on any of its Web sites. France is not alone in regulating the Internet. Myanmar (formerly known as Burma) bans access to the Internet. South Korea outlawed access to gambling Web sites. The United States passed a law requiring schools and libraries that received federal funds for Internet connections to install software on their computers to block material deemed harmful to children. Under a new European Union (EU) law, European consumers can now sue EU-based Internet sites in their own countries. There is some pressure to extend the rule internationally. The United States has endorsed the Council of

Europe's cyber-crime treaty, which aims to harmonize international laws against hacking, Internet fraud, and child pornography.

Two tools that can be used to "protect" Internet users are filtering and Internet Protocol (IP) address identification software. Filtering software can be installed on a computer, on an Internet provider's servers, or on gateways that link one country with another. This software acts to block access to certain Web sites. China, for example, has installed this software nationwide to block access to Internet sites that have unwanted content. China has also passed laws requiring Internet companies to apply for licenses and for them to be held accountable for illegal content carried on their Web sites. Web sites can also block users by tracking an Internet server's IP address, the number that identifies computers on the Internet and often reveals where a user is located. A controversial version of IP, called IP/6, was designed by the Internet Engineering Task Force (IETF) to expand the IP address to include the unique serial number of each computer's network connection software. Every data packet would thus contain a user's electronic "fingerprints."

Source: "Stop Signs on the Web," *The Economist* (January 13, 2001), pp. 21–25.

Projections for the 21st Century

- From 1994 to 2010, the world population will grow from 5.607 billion to 7.32 billion.
- From 1994 to 2010, the number of nations will increase from 192 to 202.[67]

Discussion Questions

1. Does a corporation really need a board of directors?

2. What recommendations would you make to improve the effectiveness of today's boards of directors?

3. What is the relationship between corporate governance and social responsibility?

4. What is your opinion of Reebok's production standards of human rights for its suppliers? What would Milton Friedman say? Contrast his view with Archie Carroll's view.

5. Does a company have to act selflessly to be considered socially responsible? For example, when building a new plant, a corporation voluntarily invested in additional equipment that enabled it to reduce its pollution emissions beyond the requirements of any current laws. Knowing that it would be very expensive for its competitors to do the same, the firm lobbied the government to make pollution regulations more restrictive on the entire industry. Is this company socially responsible? Were its managers acting ethically?

Strategic Practice Exercise

How far should people in a business firm go in gathering competitive intelligence? Where do you draw the line?

Evaluate each of the following approaches that a business firm could use to gather information about competition. For each approach, mark your feeling about its appropriateness: 1 (definitely not appropriate), 2 (probably not appropriate), 3 (undecided), 4 (probably appropriate), or 5 (definitely appropriate).

The business firm should try to get useful information about competitors by:

_____ Carefully studying trade journals.

_____ Wiretapping the telephones of competitors.

_____ Posing as a potential customer to competitors.

_____ Getting loyal customers to put out a phony "request for proposal" to solicit competitors' bids.

_____ Buying competitors' products and taking them apart.

_____ Hiring management consultants who have worked for competitors.

_____ Rewarding competitors' employees for useful "tips."

_____ Questioning competitors' customers and/or suppliers.

_____ Buying and analyzing competitors' garbage.

_____ Advertising and interviewing for nonexistent jobs.

_____ Taking public tours of competitors' facilities.

_____ Releasing false information about the company in order to confuse competitors.

_____ Questioning competitors' technical people at trade shows and conferences.

_____ Hiring key people away from competitors.

_____ Analyzing competitors' labor union contracts.

_____ Having employees date persons who work for competitors.

_____ Studying aerial photographs of competitors' facilities.

After you mark each of the preceding approaches, compare your responses to those of other people in your class. For each approach, the people marking 4 or 5 should say why they thought this particular act would be appropriate. Those who marked 1 or 2 should then state why they thought this act would be inappropriate.

What does this tell you about ethics and socially responsible behavior?

Source: Developed from W. A. Jones, Jr., and N. B. Bryan, Jr., "Business Ethics and Business Intelligence: An Empirical Study of Information-Gathering Alternatives," *International Journal of Management* (June 1995), pp. 204–208. For actual examples of some of these activities, see J. Kerstetter, P. Burrows, J. Greene, G. Smith, and M. Conlin, "The Dark Side of the Valley," *Business Week* (July 17, 2000), pp. 42–43.

Key Terms

affiliated directors (p. 31)

agency theory (p. 29)

board of directors continuum (p. 28)

board of directors responsibilities (p. 27)

categorical imperatives (p. 43)

codes of ethics (p. 42)

codetermination (p. 32)

corporate governance (p. 26)

corporate stakeholders (p. 39)

corporation (p. 26)

due care (p. 27)

ethics (p. 42)

executive leadership (p. 35)

family directors (p. 31)

individual rights approach (p. 43)

inside directors (p. 29)

interlocking directorate (p. 32)

justice approach (p. 43)

law (p. 42)

lead director (p. 34)

levels of moral development (p. 42)

moral relativism (p. 41)

morality (p. 42)

outside directors (p. 29)

responsibilities of business (p. 37)

retired directors (p. 31)

role of the board of directors in strategic management (p. 27)

social responsibility (p. 37)

staggered board (p. 33)

stewardship theory (p. 29)

strategic planning staff (p. 37)

strategic vision (p. 35)

top management responsibilities (p. 35)

trends in governance (p. 34)

utilitarian approach (p. 43)

Notes

1. N. Byrnes and W. C. Symonds, "Is the Avalanche Headed for PriceWaterhouse?" *Business Week* (October 14, 2002), pp. 45–46; W. C. Symonds, "Tyco: How Did They Miss a Scam So Big?" *Business Week* (September 30, 2002), pp. 40–42; H. R. Weber, "Questions Arise About Board Reviewing Tyco's Finances," *The* (Ames, IA) *Tribune* (July 6, 2002), p. C8; N. Varchaver, "The Big Kozlowski," *Fortune* (November 18, 2002), pp. 123–126; H. R. Weber, "The King Is Gone," *Des Moines Register* (September 18, 2002), p. D1; "Tyco Settles," *Des Moines Register* (October 24, 2002), p. 3D.

2. A. G. Monks and N. Minow, *Corporate Governance* (Cambridge, MA: Blackwell Business, 1995), pp. 8–32.

3. Ibid., p. 1.

4. W. Symonds, "Tyco: The Vise Grows Ever-Tighter," *Business Week* (October 7, 2002), pp. 48–49.

5. A. Demb and F. F. Neubauer, "The Corporate Board: Confronting the Paradoxes," *Long Range Planning* (June 1992), p. 13. These results are supported by a 1995 Korn/Ferry International survey in which chairmen and directors agreed that strategy and management succession, in that order, are the most important issues the board expects to face.

6. L. Light, "Why Outside Directors Have Nightmares," *Business Week* (October 23, 1996), p. 6.

7. W. Q. Judge, Jr., and C. P. Zeithaml, "Institutional and Strategic Choice Perspectives on Board Involvement in the Strategic Choice Process," *Academy of Management Journal* (October 1992), 766–794; J. A. Pearce II and S. A. Zahra, "Effective Power-Sharing Between the Board of Directors and the CEO," *Handbook of Business Strategy*, 1992/93 Yearbook (Boston: Warren, Gorham, and Lamont, 1992), pp. 1.1–1.16.

8. *26th Annual Board of Directors Study*, Korn/Ferry International (1999), p. 7.

9. L. Lavelle, "The Best and Worst Boards," *Business Week* (October 7, 2002), pp. 104–114.

10. Statistics on boards of directors are taken from *26th Annual Board of Directors Survey* (New York: Korn/Ferry International, 1999) and *Directors' Compensation and Board Practices in 1999* (New York: Conference Board, 1999).

11. L. L. Carr, "Strategic Determinants of Executive Compensation in Small Publicly Traded Firms," *Journal of Small Business Management* (April 1997), pp. 1–12.

12. *26th Annual Board of Directors Study*, Korn/Ferry International (1999), p. 8.

13. S. Finkelstein and D. C. Hambrick, *Strategic Leadership: Top Executives and Their Impact on Organizations* (St. Paul, MN: West, 1996), p. 213.

14. R. A. G. Monks, "What Will Be the Impact of Acting Shareholders? A Practical Recipe for Constructive Change," *Long Range Planning* (February 1999), p. 20.

15. *26th Annual Board of Directors Study*, Korn/Ferry International (1999), pp. 11–12.

16. *Globalizing the Board of Directors: Trends and Strategies* (New York: The Conference Board, 1999).

17. For additional information on average board retainers, fees, and stock compensation, see *Directors' Compensation and Board Practices in 1999* (New York: The Conference Board, 1999).

18. R. W. Pouder and R. S. Cantrell, "Corporate Governance Reform: Influence on Shareholder Wealth," *Journal of Business Strategies* (Spring 1999), pp. 48–66.

19. M. L. Gerlach, "The Japanese Corporate Network: A Blockmodel Analysis," *Administrative Science Quarterly* (March 1992), pp. 105–139.

20. M. Warner, "Inside the Silicon Valley Money Machine," *Fortune* (October 26, 1998), pp. 128–140.

21. J. A. C. Baum and C. Oliver, "Institutional Linkages and Organizational Mortality," *Administrative Science Quarterly* (June 1991) pp. 187–218; J. P. Sheppard, "Strategy and Bankruptcy: An Exploration into Organizational Death," *Journal of Management* (Winter 1994), pp. 795–833.

22. *26th Annual Board of Directors Study* (New York: Korn/Ferry International, 1999), pp. 7–13.

23. *26th Annual Board of Directors Study* (New York: Korn/Ferry International, 1999), p. 30.

24. The Conference Board reports that although 21% of U.S. firms had outsiders as chairs, 12% had other employees as chair in 1999.

25. D. Harris and C. E. Helfat, "CEO Duality, Succession, Capabilities and Agency Theory: Commentary and Research Agenda," *Strategic Management Journal* (September 1998), pp. 901–904; C. M. Daily and D. R. Dalton, "CEO and Board Chair Roles Held Jointly or Separately: Much Ado About Nothing," *Academy of Management Executive* (August 1997), pp. 11–20; D. L. Worrell, C. Nemec, and W. N. Davidson III, "One Hat Too Many: Key Executive Plurality and Shareholder Wealth," *Strategic Management Journal* (June 1997), pp. 499–507; J. W. Coles and W. S. Hesterly, "Independence of the Chairman and Board Composition: Firm Choices and Shareholder Value," *Journal of Management*, Vol. 26, No. 2 (2000), pp. 195–214.

26. M. Lipton and J. W. Lorsch, "The Lead Director," *Directors & Boards* (Spring 1993), pp. 28–31.

27. The Korn/Ferry and Conference Board reports for 1999 provide different figures regarding combined CEO/Chair positions and lead directors. For example, the Conference Board reported that only 4% of firms had lead directors when the Chairman is also CEO. Korn/Ferry stated that 91% of the firms had a combined CEO/Chair position.

28. D. R. Dalton, C. M. Daily, A. E. Ellstrand, and J. L. Johnson, "Meta-Analytic Reviews of Board Composition, Leadership Structure, and Financial Performance," *Strategic Management Journal* (March 1998), pp. 269–290; G. Beaver, "Competitive Advantage and Corporate Governance—Shop Soiled and Needing Attention!" *Strategic Change* (September–October 1999), p. 330.

29. For governance trends in Europe, see A. Cadbury, "What Are the Trends in Corporate Governance? How Will They Impact Your Company?" *Long Range Planning* (February 1999), pp. 12–19.

30. J. S. Lublin, "Texaco Case Causes a Stir in Boardrooms," *Wall Street Journal* (November 22, 1996), p. B1.

31. S. Finkelstein and D. C. Hambrick, *Strategic Leadership: Top Executives and Their Impact on Organizations* (St. Louis: West, 1996).

32. D. C. Hambrick, T. S. Cho, and M-J Chen, "The Influence of Top Management Team Heterogeneity on Firms' Competitive Moves," *Administrative Science Quarterly* (December 1996), pp. 659–684.

33. N. Tichy and R. Charan, "Speed, Simplicity, Self-Confidence: An Interview with Jack Welch," *Harvard Business Review* (September–October 1989), p. 113.

34. M. Lipton, "Demystifying the Development of an Organizational Vision," *Sloan Management Review* (Summer 1996), p. 84.

35. J. H. David, F. D. Schoorman, R. Mayer, and H. H. Tan, "The Trusted General Manager and Business Unit Performance: Empirical Evidence of a Competitive Advantage," *Strategic Management Journal* (May 2000), pp. 563–576.

36. R. X. Cringely, "The Best CEOs," *Worth* (May 2000), p. 128.

37. M-S. Chae and J. S. Hill, "The Hazards of Strategic Planning for Global Markets," *Long Range Planning* (December 1996), pp. 880–891.

38. T. R. Eisenmann and J. L. Bower, "The Entrepreneurial M-Form: Strategic Integration in Global Media Firms," *Organization Science* (May–June 2000), pp. 348–355.

39. For an in-depth guide to conducting the strategic planning process, see C. D. Fogg, *Team-Based Strategic Planning* (New York: AMACOM, 1994).

40. M. Friedman, "The Social Responsibility of Business Is to Increase Its Profits," *New York Times Magazine* (September 13, 1970), pp. 30, 126–127; M. Friedman, *Capitalism and Freedom* (Chicago: University of Chicago Press, 1963), p. 133.

41. A. B. Carroll, "A Three-Dimensional Conceptual Model of Corporate Performance," *Academy of Management Review* (October 1979), pp. 497–505.

42. Carroll refers to discretionary responsibilities as philanthropic responsibilities in A. B. Carroll, "The Pyramid of Corporate Social Responsibility: Toward the Moral Management of Organizational Stakeholders," *Business Horizons* (July–August 1991), pp. 39–48.

43. M. S. Baucus and D. A. Baucus, "Paying the Piper: An Empirical Examination of Longer-Term Financial Consequences of Illegal Corporate Behavior," *Academy of Management Journal* (February 1997), pp. 129–151.

44. A. McWilliams and D. Siegel, "Corporate Social Responsibility and Financial Performance: Correlation or Misspecification?" *Strategic Management Journal* (May 2000), pp. 603–609; P. Rechner and K. Roth, "Social Responsibility and Financial Performance: A Structural Equation Methodology," *International Journal of Management* (December 1990), pp. 382–391; K. E. Aupperle, A. B. Carroll, and J. D. Hatfield, "An Empirical Examination of the Relationship Between Corporate Social Responsibility and Profitability," *Academy of Management Journal* (June 1985), p. 459.

45. S. A. Waddock and S. B. Graves, "The Corporate Social Performance–Financial Performance Link," *Strategic Management Journal* (April 1997), pp. 303–319; M. V. Russo and P. A. Fouts, "Resource-Based Perspective on Corporate Environmental Performance and Profitability," *Academy of Management Journal* (June 1997), pp. 534–559; H. Meyer, "The Greening of Corporate America," *Journal of Business Strategy* (January/February 2000), pp. 38–43.

46. C. L. Harman and E. R. Stafford, "Green Alliances: Building New Business with Environmental Groups" *Long Range Planning* (April 1997), pp. 184–196.

47. D. B. Turner and D. W. Greening, "Corporate Social Performance and Organizational Attractiveness to Prospective Employees," *Academy of Management Journal* (July 1997), pp. 658–672; S. Preece, C. Fleisher, and J. Toccacelli, "Building a Reputation Along the Value Chain at Levi Strauss," *Long Range Planning* (December 1995), pp. 88–98; J. B. Barney and M. H. Hansen, "Trustworthiness As a Source of Competitive Advantage," *Strategic Management Journal* (Special Winter Issue, 1994), pp. 175–190.

48. R. E. Freeman and D. R. Gilbert, *Corporate Strategy and the Search for Ethics* (Upper Saddle River, NJ: Prentice Hall, 1988), p. 6.

49. M. Arndt, W. Zellner, and P. Coy, "Too Much Corporate Power?" *Business Week* (September 11, 2000), pp. 144–158.

50. "Nearly Half of Workers Take Unethical Actions—Survey," *Des Moines Register* (April 7, 1997), p. 18B.

51. K. Kumar, "Ethical Orientation of Future American Executives: What the Value Profiles of Business School Students Portend," *SAM Advanced Management Journal* (Autumn 1995), pp. 32–36, 47; M. Gable and P. Arlow, "A Comparative Examination of the Value Orientations of British and American Executives," *International Journal of Management* (September 1986), pp. 97–106; W. D. Guth and R. Tagiuri, "Personal Values and Corporate Strategy," *Harvard Business Review* (September–October 1965), pp. 126–127; G. W. England, "Managers and Their Value Systems: A Five Country Comparative Study," *Columbia Journal of World Business* (Summer 1978), p. 35.

52. L. K. Trevino, "Ethical Decision Making in Organizations: A Person-Situation Interactionist Model," *Academy of Management Review* (July 1986), pp. 601–617.

53. L. Kohlberg, "Moral Stage and Moralization: The Cognitive-Development Approach," in *Moral Development and Behavior*, edited by T. Lickona (New York: Holt, Rinehart & Winston, 1976).

54. Trevino, p. 606.

55. J. Keogh, ed., *Corporate Ethics: A Prime Business Asset* (New York: The Business Roundtable, 1988), p. 5.

56. G. F. Kohut and S. E. Corriher, "The Relationship of Age, Gender, Experience and Awareness of Written Ethics Policies to Business Decision Making," *SAM Advanced Management Journal* (Winter 1994), pp. 32–39.

57. "Reebok Finds Bad Conditions in Two Factories," *Des Moines Register* (October 19, 1999), p. 8S.

58. T. J. Von der Embse and R. A. Wagley, "Managerial Ethics: Hard Decisions on Soft Criteria," *SAM Advanced Management Journal* (Winter 1988), p. 6.

59. G. F. Cavanagh, *American Business Values*, 3rd ed. (Upper Saddle River, NJ: Prentice Hall, 1990), pp. 186–199.

60. B. R. Agle, R. K. Mitchell, and J. A. Sonnenfeld, "Who Matters Most to CEOs? An Investigation of Stakeholder Attributes and Salience, Corporate Performance, and CEO Values," *Academy of Management Journal* (October 1999), pp. 507–525.

61. G. F. Cavanagh, pp. 195–196.

62. I. Kant, "The Foundations of the Metaphysic of Morals," in *Ethical Theory: Classical and Contemporary Readings*, 2nd ed., by L. P. Pojman (Belmont, CA: Wadsworth Publishing, 1995), pp. 255–279.

63. M. Coker, "Russia's Stealth Monitoring of Web Traffic," The (Ames, IA) *Daily Tribune* (September 11, 2000), p. C8.

64. M. France, "The Net: How to Head Off Big-Time Regulation," *Business Week* (May 10, 1999), p. 89.

65. "The Wired Trade Organization." *The Economist: Survey of World Trade* (October 3, 1998), p. 16.

66. S. Berkeley, "Web Attack," *Harvard Business Review* (September–October 2000), p. 20.

67. J. Warner, "21st Century Capitalism: Snapshot of the Next Century," *Business Week* (November 18, 1994), p. 194.

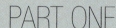

Newbury Comics, Inc.

STRATEGY BASICS

Newbury Comics was founded in 1978 by MIT roommates, Mike Dreese and John Brusger. With $2,000 and a comic book collection they converted a Newbury Street studio apartment in Boston's trendy Back Bay into the second organized comic book shop in the area. In 1979, Newbury Comics began selling punk and new wave music and quickly became the region's leading specialist in alternative music. By 1982, with a second store open in Harvard Square, the company's revenues were being generated mostly from cutting-edge music and rock-related merchandise.

Newbury Comics consists of 22 stores spanning the New England region and is known to be the place to shop for everything from the best of the underground/independent scene to major label superstars. The chain also stocks a wide variety of non-music related items such as T-shirts, Dr. (doc) Martens shoes, posters, jewelry, cosmetics, books, magazines, and other trendy items.

The video features Cofounders Mike Dreese and John Brusger, as well as Jan Johannet, Manager of one of the New Hampshire stores, talking about the entrepreneurial beginning of Newbury Comics. They point out that the company wants its customers and its employees to "have a good time" in the store. Newbury Comics hires good people who like working in the store. The company attracts creative people because it is different from other retailers. Mike Dreese thinks of the company as expanding out of a comic book retailer into a lifestyle store emphasizing popular culture. He wants Newbury Comics to dominate its product categories and to be the retailer customers seek out in order to obtain what they want. He refers to an expression used throughout the company: "If you can't dominate it, don't do it." He wants the company to grow by looking for "incredible opportunities" (elephant hunting). This approach seems to work at Newbury Comics. The company sustained an annual growth rate of about 80% over the past 7 years resulting in 1000% overall growth.

With some input from others at corporate headquarters, Mike Dreese develops the overall plan for the company by looking at where he would like the company to be in 3, 5, or 10 years. He analyzes the external environment in terms of competition, trends, and customer preferences. John Brusger then puts Mike's plan into action. The company identifies product growth areas by conducting dozens of experiments each month to learn what the customer wants.

Concepts Illustrated in the Video

- The Learning Organization
- Theories of Organizational Adaptation
- Model of Strategic Management
- Modes of Strategic Decision Making
- Strategic Decision Making Process
- Executive Leadership
- Strategic Vision

Study Questions

1. How is Newbury Comics an example of a learning organization?
2. What is the process of strategic management at Newbury Comics? Who is involved in each part?
3. What do you think might be the company's (a) current mission/vision, (b) objectives, (c) strategies, and (d) policies? Give an example of each from the video.
4. What theory of organizational adaptation is being followed by Mike Dreese?
5. Newbury Comics illustrates what mode of strategic decision making? Is it appropriate?

chapter 3

Environmental Scanning and Industry Analysis

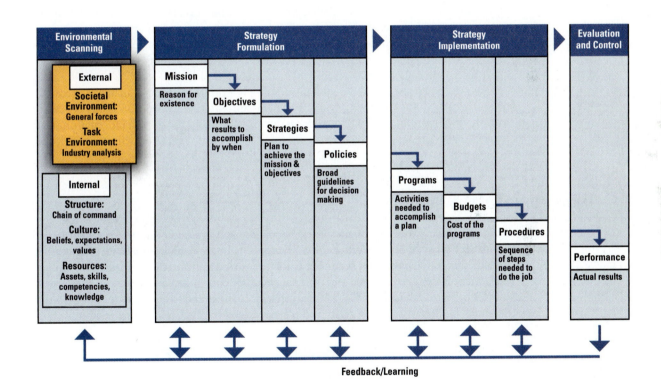

Feedback/Learning

Chefs Unlimited was founded by Dodd and Michelle Aldred of Raleigh, North Carolina. As husband and wife veterans of the restaurant industry, they knew how difficult it was to work long hours and still allow time to prepare home-cooked meals. That was one reason why people were spending more at restaurants. (The percentage of food dollars spent away from home had increased from 36% in 1980 to 44% by the mid-1990s.) The Aldreds felt that many people were beginning to tire of eating out and would be willing to pay for a quality meal eaten in their own home. They offered people the opportunity to order entrees for either a one- or two-week period. Doing their own cooking in a 3,000 square foot commercial kitchen, the Aldreds delivered meals to customers for subsequent reheating. Although more expensive, these meals were of higher quality than the typical frozen dinner. In just four years Chefs Unlimited was so successful catering to modern families that the Aldreds were planning to air express their meals to a nationwide audience the next year. Meanwhile, the U.S. Personal Chef Association was predicting a five-fold increase in the number of personal chef entrepreneurs in the United States and Canada.[1]

Pioneering companies have gone out of business because of their failure to adapt to environmental change or, even worse, by failing to create change. For example, Baldwin Locomotive, the major manufacturer of steam locomotives, was very slow in making the switch to diesel locomotives. General Electric and General Motors soon dominated the diesel locomotive business. The dominant manufacturers of vacuum tubes failed to make the change to transistors and consequently lost this market. Failure to adapt is, however, only one side of the coin. The aforementioned Chefs Unlimited example shows how a changing environment can create new opportunities at the same time it destroys old ones. The lesson is simple: To be successful over time, an organization needs to be in tune with its external environment. There must be a strategic fit between what the environment wants and what the corporation has to offer, as well as between what the corporation needs and what the environment can provide.

Current predictions are that the environment for all organizations will become even more uncertain with every passing year. What is **environmental uncertainty**? It is the *degree of complexity* plus the *degree of change* existing in an organization's external environment. As more and more markets become global, the number of factors a company must consider in any decision become huge—more complex. With new technologies being discovered every year, markets change and products must change with them.

On the one hand, environmental uncertainty is a threat to strategic managers because it hampers their ability to develop long-range plans and to make strategic decisions to keep the corporation in equilibrium with its external environment. On the other hand, environmental uncertainty is an opportunity because it creates a new playing field in which creativity and innovation can have a major part in strategic decisions.

3.1 Environmental Scanning

Before an organization can begin strategy formulation, it must scan the external environment to identify possible opportunities and threats and its internal environment for strengths and weaknesses. **Environmental scanning** is the monitoring, evaluating, and disseminating of information from the external and internal environments to key people within the corporation. A corporation uses this tool to avoid strategic surprise and to ensure its long-term health. Research has found a positive relationship between environmental scanning and profits.[2]

IDENTIFYING EXTERNAL ENVIRONMENTAL VARIABLES

In undertaking environmental scanning, strategic managers must first be aware of the many variables within a corporation's societal and task environments. The **societal environment** includes general forces that do not directly touch on the short-run activities of the organization but that can, and often do, influence its long-run decisions. These, shown in **Figure 1–3**, are as follows:

- **Economic** forces that regulate the exchange of materials, money, energy, and information
- **Technological** forces that generate problem-solving inventions
- **Political-legal** forces that allocate power and provide constraining and protecting laws and regulations
- **Sociocultural** forces that regulate the values, mores, and customs of society

The **task environment** includes those elements or groups that directly affect the corporation and, in turn, are affected by it. These are governments, local communities, suppliers, competitors, customers, creditors, employees/labor unions, special-interest groups, and trade associations. A corporation's task environment is typically the industry within which that firm operates. **Industry analysis** refers to an in-depth examination of key factors within a corporation's task environment. Both the societal and task environments must be monitored to detect the strategic factors that are likely to have a strong impact on corporate success or failure.

Scanning the Societal Environment

The number of possible strategic factors in the societal environment is very high. The number becomes enormous when we realize that, generally speaking, each country in the world can be represented by its own unique set of societal forces—some of which are very similar to neighboring countries and some of which are very different.

For example, even though Korea and China share Asia's Pacific Rim area with Thailand, Taiwan, and Hong Kong (sharing many similar cultural values), they have very different views about the role of business in society. It is generally believed in Korea and China (and to a lesser extent in Japan) that the role of business is primarily to contribute to national development; whereas in Hong Kong, Taiwan, and Thailand (and to a lesser extent in the Philippines, Indonesia, Singapore, and Malaysia), the role of business is primarily to make profits for the shareholders.[3] Such differences may translate into different trade regulations and varying difficulty in the **repatriation of profits** (transferring profits from a foreign subsidiary to a corporation's headquarters) from one group of Pacific Rim countries to another.

Monitoring Societal Trends   As noted in **Table 3–1**, large corporations categorize the societal environment in any one geographic region into four areas and focus their scanning in each area on trends with corporatewide relevance. Obviously trends in any 1 area may be very important to the firms in one industry but of lesser importance to firms in other industries.

Table 3–1   Some Important Variables in the Societal Environment

Economic	Technological	Political-Legal	Sociocultural
GDP trends	Total government spending for R&D	Antitrust regulations	Lifestyle changes
Interest rates	Total industry spending for R&D	Environmental protection laws	Career expectations
Money supply	Focus of technological efforts	Tax laws	Consumer activism
Inflation rates	Patent protection	Special incentives	Rate of family formation
Unemployment levels	New products	Foreign trade regulations	Growth rate of population
Wage/price controls	New developments in technology transfer from lab to marketplace	Attitudes toward foreign companies	Age distribution of population
Devaluation/revaluation	Productivity improvements through automation	Laws on hiring and promotion	Regional shifts in population
Energy availability and cost	Internet availability	Stability of government	Life expectancies
Disposable and discretionary income	Telecommunication infrastructure		Birth rates

Trends in the *economic* part of the societal environment can have an obvious impact on business activity. For example, an increase in interest rates means fewer sales of major home appliances. Why? A rising interest rate tends to be reflected in higher mortgage rates. Because higher mortgage rates increase the cost of buying a house, the demand for new and used houses tends to fall. Because most major home appliances are sold when people change houses, a reduction in house sales soon translates into a decline in sales of refrigerators, stoves, and dishwashers and reduced profits for everyone in that industry.

Changes in the *technological* part of the societal environment can also have a great impact on multiple industries. For example, improvements in computer microprocessors have not only led to the widespread use of home computers, but also to better automobile engine performance in terms of power and fuel economy through the use of microprocessors to monitor fuel injection. Researchers at George Washington University have identified a number of breakthrough developments in technology, which they forecast will have a significant impact during the decade from 2000 to 2010:

- **Portable Information Devices and Electronic Networking:** Combining the computing power of the personal computer, the networking of the Internet, the images of the television, and the convenience of the telephone, these appliances will soon be used by over 30% of the population of industrialized nations to make phone calls, send e-mail, and transmit data and documents. Even now, homes, autos, and offices are being connected (via wires and wireless) into intelligent networks that interact with one another. The traditional stand-alone desktop computer may soon join the manual typewriter as a historical curiosity.

- **Fuel Cells and Alternative Energy Sources:** The use of wind, geothermal, hydroelectric, solar, biomass, and other alternative energy sources should increase from their present level of 10% to about 30% by the end of the decade. Once used exclusively to power spacecraft, fuel cells offer the prospect of pollution-free electrical power. Fuel cells chemically combine hydrogen and oxygen to produce electricity with water as a byproduct. Although it will take a number of years before fuel cells replace gas-powered engines or vast power generation plants, this technology is already providing an alternate source of power for large buildings.

- **Precision Farming:** The computerized management of crops to suit variations in land characteristics will make farming more efficient. Farm equipment dealers, such as Case and Deere, add this equipment to tractors for an additional $6,000. It enables farmers to reduce costs, increase yields, and decrease environmental impact. The old system of small, low-tech farming will become less viable as large corporate farms are able to increase crop yields on limited farmland for a growing population.

- **Virtual Personal Assistants:** Very smart computer programs that monitor e-mail, faxes, and phone calls will be able to take over routine tasks, such as writing a letter, retrieving a file, making a phone call, or screening requests. Acting like a secretary, a person's virtual assistant (VA) could substitute for a person at meetings or in dealing with routine actions.

- **Genetically Altered Organisms:** A convergence of biotechnology and agriculture is creating a new field of life sciences. Plant seeds can be genetically modified to produce more needed vitamins or to be less attractive to pests and more able to survive. Animals (and people) could be similarly modified for desirable characteristics and to eliminate genetic disabilities and diseases.

- **Smart, Mobile Robots:** Robot development has been limited by a lack of sensory devices and sophisticated artificial intelligence systems. Improvements in these areas mean that robots will be performing more sophisticated factory work, run errands, do household chores, and assist the handicapped.[4]

Trends in the *political-legal* part of the societal environment have a significant impact not only on the level of competition within an industry, but also on which strategies might be successful.[5] For example, periods of strict enforcement of U.S. antitrust laws directly affect corporate growth strategy. As large companies find it more difficult to acquire another firm in the same or in a related industry, they are typically driven to diversify into unrelated industries.[6] In Europe, the formation of the European Union has led to an increase in merger activity across national boundaries.

Demographic trends are part of the *sociocultural* aspect of the societal environment. The demographic bulge in the U.S. population caused by the "baby boom" in the 1950s strongly affects market demand in many industries. For example, between 1995 and 2005, an average of 4,400 Americans turns 50 every day. This over-50 age group has become the fastest growing age group in all developed countries. Companies with an eye on the future can find many opportunities offering products and services to the growing number of "woofies" (well-off old folks)—defined as people over 50 with money to spend.[7] These people are very likely to purchase recreational vehicles, take ocean cruises, and enjoy leisure sports such as boating, fishing, and bowling, in addition to needing financial services and health care.

This trend can mean increasing sales for firms like Winnebago (RVs), Carnival Cruise Lines, and Brunswick (sports equipment), among others. To attract older customers, retailers will need to place seats in their larger stores so aging shoppers can rest. Washrooms need to be more accessible. Signs need to be larger. Restaurants need to raise the level of lighting so people can read their menus. Home appliances need simpler and larger controls. Already, the market for road bikes is declining as sales for tread mills and massagers for aching muscles increase.

Seven sociocultural trends in the United States that are helping to define what North America and the world will soon look like are:

1. **Increasing environmental awareness:** Recycling and conservation are becoming more than slogans. Busch Gardens, for example, eliminated the use of disposable styrofoam trays in favor of washing and reusing plastic trays.

2. **Growth of the seniors market:** As their numbers increase, people over age 55 will become an even more important market. Already some companies are segmenting the senior population into Young Matures, Older Matures, and the Elderly—each having a different set of attitudes and interests.

3. **Impact of Generation Y boomlet:** Born after 1980 to the boomer and X generations, this cohort may end up being as large as the boomer generation. In 1957, the peak year of the postwar boom, 4.3 million babies were born. In 1990, there were 4.2 million births. By the mid-1990s, elementary schools were becoming overcrowded.[8] As a result, both Republican and Democratic candidates in the 2000 presidential election made "education" a primary issue. The U.S. census bureau projects Generation Y to crest at 30.8 million births by 2005. Expect this cohort to have a strong impact on future products and services.

4. **Decline of the mass market:** Niche markets are beginning to define the marketers' environment. People want products and services that are adapted more to their personal needs. For example, Estee Lauder's "All Skin" and Maybelline's "Shades of You" lines of cosmetic products are specifically made for African American women. "Mass customization"—the making and marketing of products tailored to a person's requirements (e.g., Dell and Gateway Computers)—is replacing the mass production and marketing of the same product in some markets.

5. **Changing pace and location of life:** Instant communication via fax machines, cell phones, and overnight mail enhances efficiency, but it also puts more pressure on people.

Merging the personal computer with the communication and entertainment industry through telephone lines, satellite dishes, and cable television increases consumers' choices and allows workers to leave overcrowded urban areas for small towns and "telecommute" via personal computers and modems.

6. **Changing household composition:** Single-person households could become the most common household type in the United States after the year 2005. By 2005, only households composed of married couples with no children will be larger.[9] Although the Y generation baby boomlet may alter this estimate, a household clearly is no longer the same as it was once portrayed in *The Brady Bunch* in the 1970s or even *The Cosby Show* in the 1980s.

7. **Increasing diversity of workforce and markets:** Minority groups are increasing as a percentage of the total U.S. population. From 1996 to 2050, group percentages are expected by the U.S. Census Bureau to change as follows: whites—from 83% to 75%; African Americans—from 13% to 15%; Asian—from 4% to 9%; American Indian—slight increase. Hispanics, who can be of any race, are projected to grow from 10% to 25% during this time period.[10] Traditional minority groups are increasing their numbers in the workforce and are being identified as desirable target markets. For example, the South Dekalb Mall in Atlanta, Georgia, restyled itself as an "Afrocentric retail center" in response to the rapid growth of the African American 18-to-34 age group.[11]

International Societal Considerations

Each country or group of countries in which a company operates presents a whole new societal environment with a different set of economic, technological, political-legal, and sociocultural variables for the company to face. International societal environments vary so widely that a corporation's internal environment and strategic management process must be very flexible. Cultural trends in Germany, for example, have resulted in the inclusion of worker representatives in corporate strategic planning. Differences in societal environments strongly affect the ways in which a **multinational corporation (MNC)**, a company with significant assets and activities in multiple countries, conducts its marketing, financial, manufacturing, and other functional activities. For example, the existence of regional associations like the European Union, the North American Free Trade Zone, and Mercosur in South America has a significant impact on the competitive "rules of the game" both for those MNCs operating within and for those MNCs wanting to enter these areas.

To account for the many differences among societal environments from one country to another, consider **Table 3–2**. It includes a list of economic, technological, political-legal, and sociocultural variables for any particular country or region. For example, an important economic variable for any firm investing in a foreign country is currency convertibility. Without convertibility, a company operating in Russia cannot convert its profits from rubles to dollars. In terms of sociocultural variables, many Asian cultures (especially China) are less concerned with the value of human rights than are European and North American cultures. Some Asians actually contend that American companies are trying to impose Western human rights requirements on them in an attempt to make Asian products less competitive by raising their costs.[12]

Before planning its strategy for a particular international location, a company must scan the particular country environment(s) in question for opportunities and threats, and compare these with its own organizational strengths and weaknesses. For example, to operate successfully in a global industry such as automobiles, tires, electronics, or watches, a company must be prepared to establish a significant presence in the three developed areas of the world known collectively as the **Triad**. This term was coined by the Japanese management expert, Kenichi Ohmae, and it refers to the three developed markets of Japan, North America, and Western Europe, which now form a single market with common needs.[13] Focusing on the Triad is

Table 3-2   Some Important Variables in *International* Societal Environments

Economic	Technological	Political-Legal	Sociocultural
Economic development	Regulations on technology transfer	Form of government	Customs, norms, values
Per capita income	Energy availability/cost	Political ideology	Language
Climate	Natural resource availability	Tax laws	Demographics
GDP trends	Transportation network	Stability of government	Life expectancies
Monetary and fiscal policies	Skill level of work force	Government attitude toward foreign companies	Social institutions
Unemployment level	Patent-trademark protection		Status symbols
Currency convertibility	Internet availability	Regulations on foreign ownership of assets	Lifestyle
Wage levels	Telecommunication infrastructure	Strength of opposition groups	Religious beliefs
Nature of competition		Trade regulations	Attitudes toward foreigners
Membership in regional economic associations		Protectionist sentiment	Literacy level
		Foreign policies	Human rights
		Terrorist activity	Environmentalism
		Legal system	

essential for an MNC pursuing success in a global industry, according to Ohmae, because close to 90% of all high-value-added, high-technology manufactured goods are produced and consumed in North America, Western Europe, and Japan. Ideally a company should have a significant presence in each of these regions so that it can develop, produce, and market its products simultaneously in all three areas. Otherwise, it will lose competitive advantage to Triad-oriented MNCs. No longer can an MNC develop and market a new product in one part of the world before it exports it to other developed countries.

Focusing only on the developed nations, however, causes a corporation to miss important market opportunities in the developing nations of the world. Although these nations may not have developed to the point that they have significant demand for a broad spectrum of products, they may very likely be on the threshold of rapid growth in the demand for specific products. This would be the ideal time for a company to enter this market—before competition is established. The key is to be able to identify the "trigger point" when demand for a particular product or service is ready to boom. See the 🌐 **Global Issue** feature for an in-depth explanation of a technique to identify the optimum time to enter a particular market in a developing nation.

Scanning the Task Environment

As shown in **Figure 3-1**, a corporation's scanning of the environment will include analyses of all the relevant elements in the task environment. These analyses take the form of individual reports written by various people in different parts of the firm. At Procter & Gamble (P&G), for example, people from each of the brand management teams work with key people from the sales and market research departments to research and write a "competitive activity report" each quarter on each of the product categories in which P&G competes. People in purchasing also write similar reports concerning new developments in the industries that supply P&G. These and other reports are then summarized and transmitted up the corporate hierarchy for top management to use in strategic decision making. If a new development is reported regarding a particular product category, top management may then send memos asking peo-

Global Issue

Identifying Potential Markets in Developing Nations

Research by the Deloitte & Touche Consulting Group reveals that the demand for a specific product increases exponentially at certain points in a country's development. Identifying this trigger point of demand is thus critical to entering emerging markets at the best time. A **trigger point** is the time when enough people have enough money to buy what a company has to sell, but before competition is established. This can be done by using the concept of **purchasing power parity (PPP)**, which measures the cost in dollars of the U.S.–produced equivalent volume of goods that an economy produces.

PPP offers an estimate of the material wealth a nation can purchase, rather than the financial wealth it creates as typically measured by Gross Domestic Product (GDP). As a result, restating a nation's GDP in PPP terms reveals much greater spending power than market exchange rates would suggest. For example, a shoe shine costing $5 to $10 in New York City can be purchased for 50¢ in Mexico City. Consequently the

people of Mexico City can enjoy the same standard of living (with respect to shoe shines) as people in New York City with only 5% to 10% of the money. Correcting for PPP restates all Mexican shoe shines at their U.S. purchase value of $5. If one million shoe shines were purchased in Mexico last year, using the PPP model would effectively increase Mexican GDP by $5 million to $10 million. Using PPP, China becomes the world's second largest economy after the United States, with Brazil, Mexico, and India moving ahead of Canada into the top 10 world markets.

Trigger points identify when demand for a particular product is about to rapidly increase in a country. This can be a very useful technique to identify when to enter a new market in a developing nation. Trigger points vary for different products. For example, an apparent trigger point for long-distance telephone services is at $7,500 in GDP per capita—a point when demand for telecommunications services increases rapidly. Once national wealth surpasses $15,000 per capita, demand increases at a much slower rate with further increases in wealth. The trigger point for life insurance is around $8,000 in GDP per capita. At this point, the demand for life insurance increases between 200% and 300% above those countries with GDP per capita below the trigger point.

Source: Summarized from D. Fraser and M. Raynor, "The Power of Parity," *Forecast* (May/June, 1996), pp. 8–12.

Figure 3–1

Scanning the External Environment

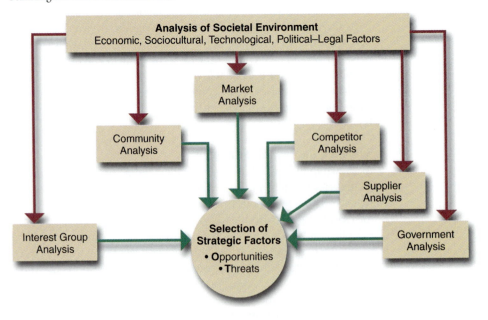

ple throughout the organization to watch for and report on developments in related product areas. The many reports resulting from these scanning efforts, when boiled down to their essentials, act as a detailed list of external strategic factors.

IDENTIFYING EXTERNAL STRATEGIC FACTORS

Why do companies often respond differently to the same environmental changes? One reason is because of differences in the ability of managers to recognize and understand external strategic issues and factors. No firm can successfully monitor all external factors. Choices must be made regarding which factors are important and which are not. Even though managers agree that strategic importance determines what variables are consistently tracked, they sometimes miss or choose to ignore crucial new developments.[14] Personal values and functional experiences of a corporation's managers as well as the success of current strategies are likely to bias both their perception of what is important to monitor in the external environment and their interpretations of what they perceive.[15]

This willingness to reject unfamiliar as well as negative information is called **strategic myopia**.[16] If a firm needs to change its strategy, it might not be gathering the appropriate external information to change strategies successfully.

One way to identify and analyze developments in the external environment is to use the **issues priority matrix** (**Figure 3–2**) as follows:

1. Identify a number of likely trends emerging in the societal and task environments. These are strategic environmental issues—those important trends that, if they occur, determine what the industry or the world will look like in the near future.

2. Assess the probability of these trends actually occurring from low to high.

3. Attempt to ascertain the likely impact (from low to high) of each of these trends on the corporation being examined.

Figure 3–2
Issues Priority Matrix

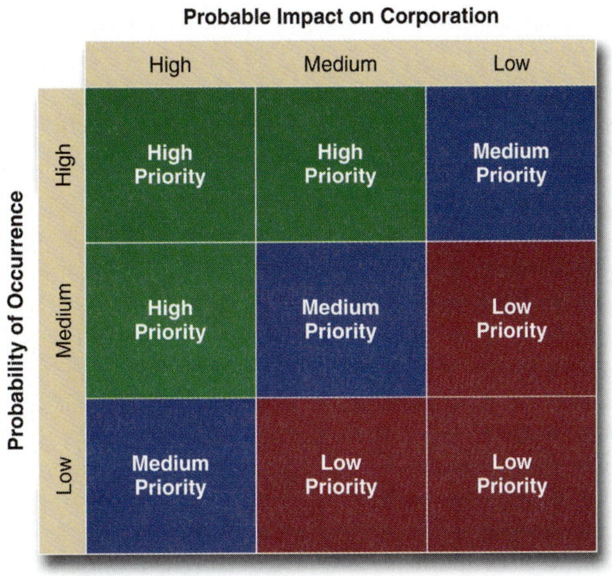

Source: Reprinted from L. L. Lederman, "Foresight Activities in the U.S.A.: Time for a Re-Assessment?" *Long-Range Planning* (June 1984), p. 46. Copyright © 1984. Reprinted with permission from Elsevier Science.

A corporation's **external strategic factors** are those key environmental trends that are judged to have both a medium to high probability of occurrence and a medium to high probability of impact on the corporation. The issues priority matrix can then be used to help managers decide which environmental trends should be merely scanned (low priority) and which should be monitored as strategic factors (high priority). Those environmental trends judged to be a corporation's strategic factors are then categorized as opportunities and threats and are included in strategy formulation.

3.2 Industry Analysis: Analyzing the Task Environment

An **industry** is a group of firms producing a similar product or service, such as soft drinks or financial services. An examination of the important stakeholder groups, such as suppliers and customers, in a particular corporation's task environment is a part of industry analysis.

PORTER'S APPROACH TO INDUSTRY ANALYSIS

Michael Porter, an authority on competitive strategy, contends that a corporation is most concerned with the intensity of competition within its industry. The level of this intensity is determined by basic competitive forces, which are depicted in **Figure 3–3**. "The collective strength of these forces," he contends, "determines the ultimate profit potential in the industry, where profit potential is measured in terms of long-run return on invested capital."[17] In carefully scanning its industry, the corporation must assess the importance to its success of each of the six forces: threat of new entrants, rivalry among existing firms, threat of substitute products or services, bargaining power of buyers, bargaining power of suppliers, and relative power of other stakeholders.[18] The stronger each of these forces, the more limited companies are in their ability to raise prices and earn greater profits. Although Porter mentions only five forces, a sixth—other stakeholders—is added here to reflect the power that governments, local communities, and other groups from the task environment wield over industry activities.

Using the model in **Figure 3–3**, a high force can be regarded as a threat because it is likely to reduce profits. A low force, in contrast, can be viewed as an opportunity because it may allow the company to earn greater profits. In the short run, these forces act as constraints on a company's activities. In the long run, however, it may be possible for a company, through its choice of strategy, to change the strength of one or more of the forces to the company's advantage. For example, in order to pressure its customers (PC makers) to purchase more of Intel's latest microprocessors for use in their PCs, Intel supported the development of sophisticated software needing increasingly larger amounts of processing power. In the mid-1990s Intel began selling 3D graphics chips—not because it wanted to be in that business, but because 3D chips needed large amounts of processing power (provided of course by Intel). Intel also introduced software that made it easier for network administrators to manage PCs on their networks, which Intel believed would help sell more PCs and neutralize a threat from network computers.[19]

A strategist can analyze any industry by rating each competitive force as **high, medium**, or **low** in strength. For example, the athletic shoe industry could be currently rated as follows: rivalry is high (Nike, Reebok, Adidas, and Converse are strong competitors worldwide); threat of potential entrants is low (industry has reached maturity; sales growth rate has slowed); threat of substitutes is low (other shoes don't provide support for sports activities); bargaining power of suppliers is medium but rising (suppliers in Asian countries are increasing in size and ability); bargaining power of buyers is medium, but increasing (athletic shoes are dropping in popularity as brown shoes gain); threat of other stakeholders is medium to high (government regulations and human rights concerns are growing). Based on current trends in each of these competitive forces, the industry appears to be increasing in its level of competitive intensity, meaning profit margins will be falling for the industry as a whole.

Figure 3–3
Forces Driving Industry Competition

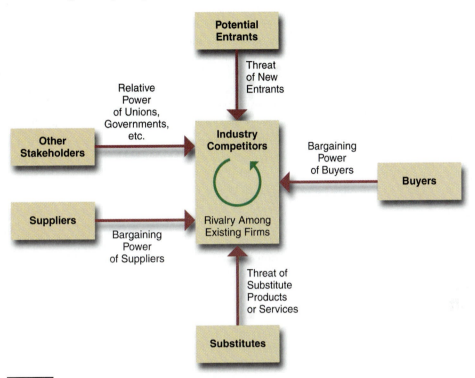

Source: Adapted with permission of The Free Press, a Division of Simon & Schuster, from *Competitive Strategy: Techniques for Analyzing Industries and Competitors* by Michael E. Porter. Copyright © 1980, 1988 by The Free Press.

Threat of New Entrants

New entrants to an industry typically bring to it new capacity, a desire to gain market share, and substantial resources. They are, therefore, threats to an established corporation. The threat of entry depends on the presence of entry barriers and the reaction that can be expected from existing competitors. An **entry barrier** is an obstruction that makes it difficult for a company to enter an industry. For example, no new domestic automobile companies have been successfully established in the United States since the 1930s because of the high capital requirements to build production facilities and to develop a dealer distribution network. Some of the possible barriers to entry are:

- **Economies of Scale:** Scale economies in the production and sale of microprocessors, for example, gave Intel a significant cost advantage over any new rival.

- **Product Differentiation:** Corporations like Procter & Gamble and General Mills, which manufacture products like Tide and Cheerios, create high entry barriers through their high levels of advertising and promotion.

- **Capital Requirements:** The need to invest huge financial resources in manufacturing facilities in order to produce large commercial airplanes creates a significant barrier to entry to any competitor for Boeing and Airbus.

- **Switching Costs:** Once a software program like Excel or Word becomes established in an office, office managers are very reluctant to switch to a new program because of the high training costs.

- **Access to Distribution Channels:** Small entrepreneurs often have difficulty obtaining supermarket shelf space for their goods because large retailers charge for space on their shelves and give priority to the established firms who can pay for the advertising needed to generate high customer demand.

- **Cost Disadvantages Independent of Size:** Once a new product earns sufficient market share to be accepted as the *standard* for that type of product, the maker has a key advantage. Microsoft's development of the first widely adopted operating system (MS-DOS) for the IBM-type personal computer gave it a significant competitive advantage over potential competitors. Its introduction of Windows helped to cement that advantage so that the Microsoft operating system is now on over 90% of personal computers worldwide.

- **Government Policy:** Governments can limit entry into an industry through licensing requirements by restricting access to raw materials, such as oil-drilling sites in protected areas.

Rivalry Among Existing Firms

In most industries, corporations are mutually dependent. A competitive move by one firm can be expected to have a noticeable effect on its competitors and thus may cause retaliation or counterefforts. For example, the entry by mail order companies such as Dell and Gateway into a PC industry previously dominated by IBM, Apple, and Compaq increased the level of competitive activity to such an extent that any price reduction or new product introduction is now quickly followed by similar moves from other PC makers. The same is true of prices in the U.S. airline industry. According to Porter, intense rivalry is related to the presence of several factors, including:

- **Number of Competitors:** When competitors are few and roughly equal in size, such as in the U.S. auto and major home appliance industries, they watch each other carefully to make sure that any move by another firm is matched by an equal countermove.

- **Rate of Industry Growth:** Any slowing in passenger traffic tends to set off price wars in the airline industry because the only path to growth is to take sales away from a competitor.

- **Product or Service Characteristics:** Many people choose a videotape rental store based on location, variety of selection, and pricing because they view videotapes as a commodity—a product whose characteristics are the same regardless of who sells it.

- **Amount of Fixed Costs:** Because airlines must fly their planes on a schedule regardless of the number of paying passengers for any one flight, they offer cheap standby fares whenever a plane has empty seats.

- **Capacity:** If the only way a manufacturer can increase capacity is in a large increment by building a new plant (as in the paper industry), it will run that new plant at full capacity to keep its unit costs as low as possible—thus producing so much that the selling price falls throughout the industry.

- **Height of Exit Barriers: Exit barriers** keep a company from leaving an industry. The brewing industry, for example, has a low percentage of companies that voluntarily leave the industry because breweries are specialized assets with few uses except for making beer.

- **Diversity of Rivals:** Rivals that have very different ideas of how to compete are likely to cross paths often and unknowingly challenge each other's position. This happens often in the retail clothing industry when a number of retailers open outlets in the same location—thus taking sales away from each other.

Threat of Substitute Products or Services

Substitute products are those products that appear to be different but can satisfy the same need as another product. For example, fax machines are a substitute for FedEx, Nutrasweet is a substitute for sugar, and bottled water is a substitute for a cola. According to Porter,

"Substitutes limit the potential returns of an industry by placing a ceiling on the prices firms in the industry can profitably charge."[20] To the extent that switching costs are low, substitutes may have a strong effect on an industry. Tea can be considered a substitute for coffee. If the price of coffee goes up high enough, coffee drinkers will slowly begin switching to tea. The price of tea thus puts a price ceiling on the price of coffee. Identifying possible substitute products or services is sometimes a difficult task. It means searching for products or services that can perform the same function, even though they have a different appearance and may not appear to be easily substitutable.

Bargaining Power of Buyers

Buyers affect an industry through their ability to force down prices, bargain for higher quality or more services, and play competitors against each other. A buyer or a group of buyers is powerful if some of the following factors hold true:

- A buyer purchases a large proportion of the seller's product or service (for example, oil filters purchased by a major auto maker).

- A buyer has the potential to integrate backward by producing the product itself (for example, a newspaper chain could make its own paper).

- Alternative suppliers are plentiful because the product is standard or undifferentiated (for example, motorists can choose among many gas stations).

- Changing suppliers costs very little (for example, office supplies are easy to find).

- The purchased product represents a high percentage of a buyer's costs, thus providing an incentive to shop around for a lower price (for example, gasoline purchased for resale by convenience stores makes up half their total costs).

- A buyer earns low profits and is thus very sensitive to costs and service differences (for example, grocery stores have very small margins).

- The purchased product is unimportant to the final quality or price of a buyer's products or services and thus can be easily substituted without affecting the final product adversely (for example, electric wire bought for use in lamps).

Bargaining Power of Suppliers

Suppliers can affect an industry through their ability to raise prices or reduce the quality of purchased goods and services. A supplier or supplier group is powerful if some of the following factors apply:

- The supplier industry is dominated by a few companies, but it sells to many (for example, the petroleum industry).

- Its product or service is unique and/or it has built up switching costs (for example, word processing software).

- Substitutes are not readily available (for example, electricity).

- Suppliers are able to integrate forward and compete directly with their present customers (for example, a microprocessor producer like Intel can make PCs).

- A purchasing industry buys only a small portion of the supplier group's goods and services and is thus unimportant to the supplier (for example, sales of lawn mower tires are less important to the tire industry than are sales of auto tires).

Relative Power of Other Stakeholders

A sixth force should be added to Porter's list to include a variety of stakeholder groups from the task environment. Some of these groups are governments (if not explicitly included elsewhere), local communities, creditors (if not included with suppliers), trade associations, special-interest groups, unions (if not included with suppliers), shareholders, and complementors. According to Andy Grove, ex-CEO of Intel, a **complementor** is a company (e.g., Microsoft) or an industry whose product works well with another industry's or a firm's (e.g., Intel's) product and without which the product would lose much of its value.[21] Another example is the tire and automobile industries.

The importance of these stakeholders varies by industry. For example, environmental groups in Maine, Michigan, Oregon, and Iowa successfully fought to pass bills outlawing disposable bottles and cans, and thus deposits for most drink containers are now required. This effectively raised costs across the board, with the most impact on the marginal producers who could not internally absorb all of these costs. The traditionally strong power of national unions in the U.S. auto and railroad industries has effectively raised costs throughout these industries but are of little importance in computer software.

INDUSTRY EVOLUTION

Over time most industries evolve through a series of stages from growth through maturity to eventual decline. The strength of each of the six forces mentioned earlier varies according to the stage of industry evolution. The industry life cycle is useful for explaining and predicting trends among the six forces driving industry competition. For example, when an industry is new, people often buy the product regardless of price because it fulfills a unique need. This is probably a **fragmented industry**—no firm has large market share and each firm serves only a small piece of the total market in competition with others (for example, Chinese restaurants and cleaning services). As new competitors enter the industry, prices drop as a result of competition. Companies use the experience curve (to be discussed in Chapter 4) and economies of scale to reduce costs faster than the competition. Companies integrate to reduce costs even further by acquiring their suppliers and distributors. Competitors try to differentiate their products from one another's in order to avoid the fierce price competition common to a maturing industry.

By the time an industry enters maturity, products tend to become more like commodities. This is now a **consolidated industry**—dominated by a few large firms, each of which struggles to differentiate its products from the competition. As buyers become more sophisticated over time, purchasing decisions are based on better information. Price becomes a dominant concern, given a minimum level of quality and features. One example of this trend is the videocassette recorder industry. By the 1990s, VCRs had reached the point where there were few major differences among them. Consumers realized that because slight improvements cost significantly more money, it made little sense to pay more than the minimum for a VCR. The same is true of gasoline.

As an industry moves through maturity toward possible decline, its products' growth rate of sales slows and may even begin to decrease. To the extent that exit barriers are low, firms will begin converting their facilities to alternate uses or will sell them to another firm. The industry tends to consolidate around fewer but larger competitors. In the case of the U.S. major home appliance industry, the industry changed from being a fragmented industry (pure competition) composed of hundreds of appliance manufacturers in the industry's early years to a consolidated industry (mature oligopoly) composed of five companies controlling over 98% of U.S. appliance sales. A similar consolidation is occurring now in European major home appliances.

CATEGORIZING INTERNATIONAL INDUSTRIES

According to Porter, world industries vary on a continuum from multidomestic to global (see **Figure 3–4**).[22] **Multidomestic industries** are specific to each country or group of countries. This type of international industry is a collection of essentially domestic industries, like retail-

Figure 3–4

Continuum of International Industries

Multidomestic ←————————————————————————→ **Global**

Industry in which companies tailor
their products to the specific needs
of consumers in a particular country.
• Retailing
• Insurance
• Banking

Industry in which companies manufacture
and sell the same products, with only minor
adjustments made for individual countries
around the world.
• Automobiles
• Tires
• Television sets

ing and insurance. The activities in a subsidiary of a multinational corporation (MNC) in this type of industry are essentially independent of the activities of the MNC's subsidiaries in other countries. Within each country, it has a manufacturing facility to produce goods for sale within that country. The MNC is thus able to tailor its products or services to the very specific needs of consumers in a particular country or group of countries having similar societal environments.

Global industries, in contrast, operate worldwide, with MNCs making only small adjustments for country-specific circumstances. A global industry is one in which an MNC's activities in one country are significantly affected by its activities in other countries. MNCs produce products or services in various locations throughout the world and sell them, making only minor adjustments for specific country requirements. Examples of global industries are commercial aircraft, television sets, semiconductors, copiers, automobiles, watches, and tires. The largest industrial corporations in the world in terms of dollar sales are, for the most part, multinational corporations operating in global industries.

The factors that tend to determine whether an industry will be primarily multidomestic or primarily global are:

1. *Pressure for coordination* within the multinational corporations operating in that industry
2. *Pressure for local responsiveness* on the part of individual country markets

To the extent that the pressure for coordination is strong and the pressure for local responsiveness is weak for multinational corporations within a particular industry, that industry will tend to become global. In contrast, when the pressure for local responsiveness is strong and the pressure for coordination is weak for multinational corporations in an industry, that industry will tend to be multidomestic. Between these two extremes lie a number of industries with varying characteristics of both multidomestic and global industries. The dynamic tension between these two factors is contained in the phrase: *Think globally, but act locally.*

INTERNATIONAL RISK ASSESSMENT

Some firms, such as American Can Company and Mitsubishi Trading Company, develop elaborate information networks and computerized systems to evaluate and rank investment risks. Small companies can hire outside consultants such as Chicago's Associated Consultants International or Boston's Arthur D. Little, Inc., to provide political-risk assessments. Among the many systems that exist to assess political and economic risks are the Political System Stability Index, the Business Environment Risk Index, Business International's Country Assessment Service, and Frost and Sullivan's World Political Risk Forecasts.[23] Business International provides subscribers with continuously updated information on conditions in 63 countries. A Boston company called International Strategies offers an Export Hotline (800 USA-XPORT) that faxes information to callers for only the cost of the call. (Contact

⟨ExportHotline.com⟩ for a free membership.) Regardless of the source of data, a firm must develop its own method of assessing risk. It must decide on its most important risk factors and then assign weights to each.

STRATEGIC GROUPS

A **strategic group** is a set of business units or firms that "pursue similar strategies with similar resources."[24] Categorizing firms in any one industry into a set of strategic groups is very useful as a way of better understanding the competitive environment.[25] Because a corporation's structure and culture tend to reflect the kinds of strategies it follows, companies or business units belonging to a particular strategic group within the same industry tend to be strong rivals and tend to be more similar to each other than to competitors in other strategic groups within the same industry.

For example, although McDonald's and Olive Garden are a part of the same restaurant industry, they have different missions, objectives, and strategies, and thus belong to different strategic groups. They generally have very little in common and pay little attention to each other when planning competitive actions. Burger King and Hardee's, however, have a great deal in common with McDonald's in terms of their similar strategy of producing a high volume of low-priced meals targeted for sale to the average family. Consequently they are strong rivals and are organized to operate similarly.

Strategic groups in a particular industry can be mapped by plotting the market positions of industry competitors on a two-dimensional graph using two strategic variables as the vertical and horizontal axes. (See **Figure 3–5.**)

1. Select two broad characteristics, such as price and menu, that differentiate the companies in an industry from one another.

2. Plot the firms using these two characteristics as the dimensions.

3. Draw a circle around those companies that are closest to one another as one strategic group, varying the size of the circle in proportion to the group's share of total industry sales. (You could also name each strategic group in the restaurant industry with an identifying title, such as quick fast food or buffet style service.)

Other dimensions, such as quality, service, location, or degree of vertical integration, can also be used in additional graphs of the restaurant industry to gain a better understanding of how the various firms in the industry compete. Keep in mind, however, that when choosing the two dimensions, they should not be highly correlated; otherwise, the circles on the map will simply lie along the diagonal, providing very little new information other than the obvious.

STRATEGIC TYPES

In analyzing the level of competitive intensity within a particular industry or strategic group, it is useful to characterize the various competitors for predictive purposes. A **strategic type** is a category of firms based on a common strategic orientation and a combination of structure, culture, and processes consistent with that strategy. According to Miles and Snow, competing firms within a single industry can be categorized on the basis of their general strategic orientation into one of four basic types.[26] This distinction helps explain why companies facing similar situations behave differently and why they continue to do so over a long period of time. These general types have the following characteristics:

- **Defenders** are companies with a limited product line that *focus on improving the efficiency of their existing operations.* This cost orientation makes them unlikely to innovate in new areas.

Figure 3–5

Mapping Strategic Groups in the U.S. Restaurant Chain Industry

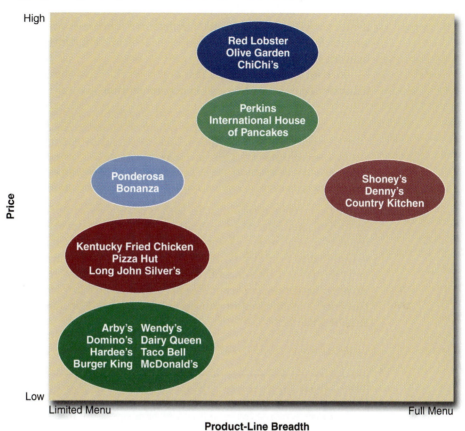

- **Prospectors** are companies with fairly broad product lines that *focus on product innovation and market opportunities*. This sales orientation makes them somewhat inefficient. They tend to emphasize creativity over efficiency.

- **Analyzers** are corporations that *operate in at least two different product–market areas*, one stable and one variable. In the stable areas, efficiency is emphasized. In the variable areas, innovation is emphasized.

- **Reactors** are corporations that *lack a consistent strategy–structure–culture relationship*. Their (often ineffective) responses to environmental pressures tend to be piecemeal strategic changes.

Dividing the competition into these four categories enables the strategic manager not only to monitor the effectiveness of certain strategic orientations, but also to develop scenarios of future industry developments (discussed later in this chapter).

HYPERCOMPETITION

Most industries today are facing an ever-increasing level of environmental uncertainty. They are becoming more complex and more dynamic. Industries that used to be multidomestic are becoming global. New flexible, aggressive, innovative competitors are moving into established markets to erode rapidly the advantages of large previously dominant firms. Distribution channels vary from country to country and are being altered daily through the use of sophisticated information systems. Closer relationships with suppliers are being forged to reduce costs, increase quality, and gain access to new technology. Companies learn to quickly imitate the successful strategies of market leaders, and it becomes harder to sustain any competitive advantage for very long. Consequently, the level of competitive intensity is increasing in most industries.

Richard D'Aveni contends that as this type of environmental turbulence reaches more industries, competition becomes **hypercompetition**. According to D'Aveni:

> *In hypercompetition the frequency, boldness, and aggressiveness of dynamic movement by the players accelerates to create a condition of constant disequilibrium and change. Market stability is threatened by short product life cycles, short product design cycles, new technologies, frequent entry by unexpected outsiders, repositioning by incumbents, and tactical redefinitions of market boundaries as diverse industries merge. In other words, environments escalate toward higher and higher levels of uncertainty, dynamism, heterogeneity of the players and hostility.[27]*

In hypercompetitive industries such as computers, competitive advantage comes from an up-to-date knowledge of environmental trends and competitive activity coupled with a willingness to risk a current advantage for a possible new advantage. Companies must be willing to **cannibalize** their own products (replacing popular products before competitors do so) in order to sustain their competitive advantage. As a result, industry or competitive intelligence has never been more important. See the boxed example to learn how Microsoft is operating in the hypercompetitive industry of computer software. (Hypercompetition is discussed in more detail in **Chapter 5**.)

Microsoft Operates in a Hypercompetitive Industry

Microsoft is a hypercompetitive firm operating in a hypercompetitive industry. It has used its dominance in operating systems (DOS and Windows) to move into a very strong position in application programs like word processing and spreadsheets (Word and Excel). Even though Microsoft held 90% of the market for personal computer operating systems in 1992, it still invested millions in developing the next generation—Windows 95 and Windows NT. Instead of trying to protect its advantage in the profitable DOS operating system, Microsoft actively sought to replace DOS with various versions of Windows. Before hypercompetition, most experts argued against *cannibalization* of a company's own product line because it destroys a very profitable product instead of harvesting it like a "cash cow." According to this line of thought, a company would be better off defending its older products. New products would be introduced only if it could be proven that they would not take sales away from current products. Microsoft was one of the first companies to disprove this argument against cannibalization.

Bill Gates, Microsoft's Cofounder, Chairman, and CEO, realized that if his company didn't replace its own DOS product line with a better product, someone else would (such as IBM with OS/2 Warp). He knew that success in the software industry depends not so much on company size but on moving aggressively to the next competitive advantage before a competitor does. "This is a hypercompetitive market," explained Gates. "Scale is not all positive in this business. Cleverness is the position in this business." By 2000, Microsoft still controlled over 90% of operating systems software and had achieved a dominant position in applications software as well.

Source: R. A. D'Aveni, *Hypercompetition* (New York: Free Press, 1994), p. 2.

Table 3–3   Industry Matrix

Key Success Factors	Weight	Company A Rating	Company A Weighted Score	Company B Rating	Company B Weighted Score
1	2	3	4	5	6
Total	1.00				

Source: T. L. Wheelen and J. D. Hunger, "Industry Matrix." Copyright © 2001 by Wheelen and Hunger Associates. Reprinted by permission.

USING KEY SUCCESS FACTORS TO CREATE AN INDUSTRY MATRIX

Within any industry there usually are certain variables—key success factors—that a company's management must understand in order to be successful. **Key success factors** are those variables that can affect significantly the overall competitive positions of all companies within any particular industry. They typically vary from industry to industry and are crucial to determining a company's ability to succeed within that industry. They are usually determined by the economic and technological characteristics of the industry and by the competitive weapons on which the firms in the industry have built their strategies.[28] For example, in the major home appliance industry, a firm must achieve low costs, typically by building large manufacturing facilities dedicated to making multiple versions of one type of appliance, such as washing machines. Since 60% of major home appliances in the United States are sold through "power retailers" like Sears and Best Buy, a firm must have a strong presence in the mass merchandiser distribution channel. It must offer a full line of appliances and provide a just-in-time delivery system to keep store inventory and ordering costs to a minimum. Because the consumer expects reliability and durability in an appliance, a firm must have excellent process R&D. Any appliance manufacturer that is unable to deal successfully with these key success factors will not long survive in the U.S. market.

Key success factors are different from strategic factors. *Key success factors* deal with an entire industry; whereas, *strategic factors* deal with a particular company.

An **industry matrix** summarizes the key success factors within a particular industry. As shown in **Table 3–3**, the matrix gives a weight for each factor based on how important that factor is for success within the industry. The matrix also specifies how well various competitors in the industry are responding to each factor. To generate an industry matrix using two industry competitors (called A and B), complete the following steps for the industry being analyzed:

1. In **Column 1** (Key Success Factors) list the 8 to 10 factors that appear to determine current and expected success in the industry.

2. In **Column 2** (Weight) assign a weight to each factor from **1.0** (Most Important) to **0.0** (Not Important) based on that factor's probable impact on the overall industry's current and future success. (**All weights must sum to 1.0 regardless of the number of strategic factors.**)

3. In **Column 3** (Company A Rating) examine a particular company within the industry—for example, Company A. Assign a rating to each factor from **5.0** (Outstanding) to **1.0** (Poor) based on Company A's current response to that particular factor. Each rating is a judgment regarding how well that company is currently dealing with each key success factor.

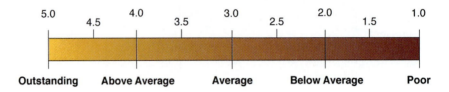

4. In **Column 4** (Company A Weighted Score) multiply the weight in **Column 2** for each factor times its rating in **Column 3** to obtain that factor's weighted score for Company A. This results in a weighted score for each key success factor ranging from **5.0** (Outstanding) to **1.0** (Poor) with **3.0** as the average.

5. In **Column 5** (Company B Rating) examine a second company within the industry—in this case, Company B. Assign a rating to each key success factor from **5.0** (Outstanding) to **1.0** (Poor) based on Company B's current response to each particular factor.

6. In **Column 6** (Company B Weighted Score) multiply the weight in **Column 2** for each factor times its rating in **Column 5** to obtain that factor's weighted score for Company B.

Finally, add the weighted scores for all the factors in **Columns 4** and **6** to determine the total weighted scores for companies A and B. The total weighted score indicates how well each company is responding to current and expected key success factors in the industry's environment. The industry matrix can be expanded to include all the major competitors within an industry simply by adding two additional columns for each additional competitor.

3.3 Competitive Intelligence

Much external environmental scanning is done on an informal and individual basis. Information is obtained from a variety of sources—suppliers, customers, industry publications, employees, industry experts, industry conferences, and the Internet.[29] For example, scientists and engineers working in a firm's R&D lab can learn about new products and competitors' ideas at professional meetings; someone from the purchasing department, speaking with supplier-representatives' personnel, may also uncover valuable bits of information about a competitor. A study of product innovation found that 77% of all product innovations in the scientific instruments and 67% in semiconductors and printed circuit boards were initiated by the customer in the form of inquiries and complaints.[30] In these industries, the sales force and service departments must be especially vigilant.

Competitive intelligence is a formal program of gathering information on a company's competitors. Until recently, few U.S. corporations had fully developed competitive intelligence programs. In contrast, all Japanese corporations involved in international business and most large European companies have active intelligence programs.[31] This situation is changing, however. Competitive intelligence is now one of the fastest growing fields within strategic management.[32] At General Mills, for example, all employees have been trained to recognize and tap sources of competitive information. Janitors no longer simply place orders with suppliers of cleaning materials, they also ask about relevant practices at competing firms! A recent survey of large U.S. corporations revealed that 78% of them reported competitive intelligence activities within their firm.[33]

Most corporations rely on outside organizations to provide them with environmental data. Firms such as A. C. Nielsen Co. provide subscribers with bimonthly data on brand share, retail prices, percentages of stores stocking an item, and percentages of stock-out stores. Strategists can use this data to spot regional and national trends as well as to assess market share. Information on market conditions, government regulations, competitors, and new products can be bought from "information brokers" such as Marketresearch.com and Finsbury Data Services. Company and industry profiles are generally available from the Hoover's Online site on the Internet 〈www.hoovers.com〉. Many business corporations have established their own in-house libraries and computerized information systems to deal with the growing mass of available information.

Some companies, however, choose to use industrial espionage or other intelligence-gathering techniques to get their information straight from their competitors. According to the American Society of Industrial Security, there were more than 1,100 documented incidents of illegal economic espionage in 1997 alone.[34] Using current or former competitors' employees and by using private contractors, some firms attempt to steal trade secrets, technology, business plans, and pricing strategies. For example, Avon Products hired private investigators to retrieve from a public dumpster documents (some of them shredded) that Mary Kay Corporation had thrown away. Even Procter & Gamble, which defends itself like a fortress from information leaks, is vulnerable. A competitor was able to learn the precise launch date of a concentrated laundry detergent in Europe when one of its people visited the factory where machinery was being made. Simply asking a few questions about what a certain machine did, whom it was for, and when it would be delivered was all that was necessary.

To combat the increasing theft of company secrets, the U.S. government passed the Economic Espionage Act in 1996. The law makes it illegal (with fines up to $5 million and 10 years in jail) to steal any material that a business has taken "reasonable efforts" to keep secret and if the material derives its value from not being known.[35] The Society of Competitive Intelligence Professionals 〈www.scip.org〉 urges strategists to stay within the law and to act ethically when searching for information. The society states that illegal activities are foolish because the vast majority of worthwhile competitive intelligence is available publicly via annual reports, Web sites, and public libraries.

3.4 Forecasting

Environmental scanning provides reasonably hard data on the present situation and current trends, but intuition and luck are needed to predict accurately if these trends will continue. The resulting forecasts are, however, usually based on a set of assumptions that may or may not be valid.

DANGER OF ASSUMPTIONS

Faulty underlying assumptions are the most frequent cause of forecasting errors. Nevertheless many managers who formulate and implement strategic plans rarely consider that their success is based on a series of assumptions. Many long-range plans are simply based on projections of the current situation.

One example of what can happen when a corporate strategy rests on the very questionable assumption that the future will simply be an extension of the present is that of Tupperware, the company that originated air-tight, easy-to-use plastic food storage containers. Much of the company's success had been based on Tupperware parties in the 1950s when housewives gathered in each other's homes to socialize and play games while the local Tupperware lady demonstrated and sold new products. Management assumed during the following decades that Tupperware parties would continue being an excellent distribution channel. Its faith in this assumption blinded it to information about America's changing lifestyle (two-career families) and its likely impact on sales. Even in the 1990s, when Tupperware executives realized that their sales forecasts were no longer justified, they were unable to improve their forecasting techniques until they changed their assumption that the best way to sell Tupperware was at a Tupperware party. Consequently, Rubbermaid and other competitors, who chose to market their containers in grocery and discount stores continued to grow at the expense of Tupperware.[36]

USEFUL FORECASTING TECHNIQUES

Various techniques are used to forecast future situations. Each has its proponents and critics. A study of nearly 500 of the world's largest corporations revealed trend **extrapolation** to be the most widely practiced form of forecasting—over 70% use this technique either occasionally or frequently.[37] Simply stated, extrapolation is the extension of present trends into the future. It rests on the assumption that the world is reasonably consistent and changes slowly in the short run. Time-series methods are approaches of this type; they attempt to carry a series of historical events forward into the future. The basic problem with extrapolation is that a historical trend is based on a series of patterns or relationships among so many different variables that a change in any one can drastically alter the future direction of the trend. As a rule of thumb, the further back into the past you can find relevant data supporting the trend, the more confidence you can have in the prediction.

Brainstorming, expert opinion, and statistical modeling are also very popular forecasting techniques. **Brainstorming** is a nonquantitative approach requiring simply the presence of people with some knowledge of the situation to be predicted. The basic ground rule is to propose ideas without first mentally screening them. No criticism is allowed. Ideas tend to build on previous ideas until a consensus is reached. This is a good technique to use with operating managers who have more faith in "gut feel" than in more quantitative "number crunching" techniques. **Expert opinion** is a nonquantitative technique in which experts in a particular area attempt to forecast likely developments. This type of forecast is based on the ability of a knowledgeable person(s) to construct probable future developments based on the interaction of key variables. One application is the **Delphi technique** in which separated experts independently assess the likelihoods of specified events. These assessments are combined and sent back to each expert for fine tuning until an agreement is reached. **Statistical modeling** is a quantitative technique that attempts to discover causal or at least explanatory factors that link two or more time series together. Examples of statistical modeling are regression analysis and other econometric methods. Although very useful for grasping historic trends, statistical modeling, like trend extrapolation, is based on historical data. As the patterns of relationships change, the accuracy of the forecast deteriorates. Other forecasting techniques, such as *cross-impact analysis (CIA)* and *trend-impact analysis (TIA)*, have not established themselves successfully as regularly employed tools.

Scenario writing appears to be the most widely used forecasting technique after trend extrapolation. Originated by Royal Dutch Shell, scenarios are focused descriptions of different likely futures presented in a narrative fashion. The scenario thus may be merely a written description of some future state, in terms of key variables and issues, or it may be generated in combination with other forecasting techniques.

An **industry scenario** is a forecasted description of a particular industry's likely future. Such a scenario is developed by analyzing the probable impact of future societal forces on key groups in a particular industry. The process may operate as follows.[38]

1. Examine possible shifts in the societal variables globally.

2. Identify uncertainties in each of the six forces of the task environment (for example, potential entrants, competitors, likely substitutes, buyers, suppliers, and other key stakeholders).

3. Make a range of plausible assumptions about future trends.

4. Combine assumptions about individual trends into internally consistent scenarios.

5. Analyze the industry situation that would prevail under each scenario.

6. Determine the sources of competitive advantage under each scenario.

7. Predict competitors' behavior under each scenario.

8. Select the scenarios that are either most likely to occur or most likely to have a strong impact on the future of the company. Use these scenarios in strategy formulation.

3.5 Synthesis of External Factors—EFAS

After strategic managers have scanned the societal and task environments and identified a number of likely external factors for their particular corporation, they may want to refine their analysis of these factors using a form such as that given in **Table 3–4**. The **EFAS (External Factors Analysis Summary) Table** is one way to organize the external factors into the generally accepted categories of opportunities and threats as well as to analyze how well a particular company's management (rating) is responding to these specific factors in light of the perceived importance (weight) of these factors to the company. To generate an EFAS Table for the company being analyzed, complete the following steps:

- In **Column 1** (External Factors), list the 8 to 10 most important opportunities and threats facing the company.

- In **Column 2** (Weight), assign a weight to each factor from **1.0** (Most Important) to **0.0** (Not Important) based on that factor's probable impact on a particular company's current strategic position. The higher the weight, the more important is this factor to the current and future success of the company. (**All weights must sum to 1.0 regardless of the number of factors.**)

- In **Column 3** (Rating), assign a rating to each factor from **5.0** (Outstanding) to **1.0** (Poor) based on management's current response to that particular factor. Each rating is a judgment on how well the company's management is currently dealing with each specific external factor.

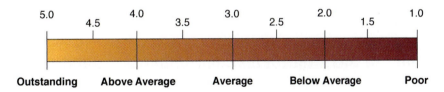

- In **Column 4** (Weighted Score), multiply the weight in **Column 2** for each factor times its rating in **Column 3** to obtain each factor's weighted score. This results in a weighted score for each factor ranging from **5.0** (Outstanding) to **1.0** (Poor) with **3.0** as average.

- In **Column 5** (Comments), note why a particular factor was selected and/or how its weight and rating were estimated.

Finally, add the individual weighted scores for all the external factors in **Column 4** to determine the total weighted score for that particular company. The total weighted **score** indicates how well a particular company is responding to current and expected factors in its external environment. The score can be used to compare that firm to other firms in its industry. The total weighted score for an average firm in an industry is always 3.0.

Table 3–4 External Factor Analysis Summary (EFAS Table): Maytag as Example

External Factors	Weight	Rating	Weighted Score	Comments
	1	2	3	4	5
Opportunities				
• Economic integration of European Community	.20	4.1	.82	Acquisition of Hoover
• Demographics favor quality appliances	.10	5.0	.50	Maytag quality
• Economic development of Asia	.05	1.0	.05	Low Maytag presence
• Opening of Eastern Europe	.05	2.0	.10	Will take time
• Trend to "Super Stores"	.10	1.8	.18	Maytag weak in this channel
Threats				
• Increasing government regulations	.10	4.3	.43	Well positioned
• Strong U.S. competition	.10	4.0	.40	Well positioned
• Whirlpool and Electrolux strong globally	.15	3.0	.45	Hoover weak globally
• New product advances	.05	1.2	.06	Questionable
• Japanese appliance companies	.10	1.6	.16	Only Asian presence is Australia
Total Scores	**1.00**		**3.15**	

Notes:
1. List opportunities and threats (8–10) in column 1.
2. Weight each factor from 1.0 (Most Important) to 0.0 (Not Important) in Column 2 based on that factor's probable impact on the company's strategic position. **The total weights must sum to 1.00**.
3. Rate each factor from 5.0 (Outstanding) to 1.0 (Poor) in Column 3 based on the company's response to that factor.
4. Multiply each factor's weight times its rating to obtain each factor's weighted score in Column 4.
5. Use Column 5 (comments) for rationale used for each factor.
6. Add the individual weighted scores to obtain the total weighted score for the company in Column 4. This tells how well the company is responding to the strategic factors in its external environment.

Source: T. L. Wheelen and J. D. Hunger, "External Factors Analysis Summary (EFAS)." Copyright © 1991 by Wheelen and Hunger Associates. Reprinted by permission.

As an example of this procedure, **Table 3–4** includes a number of external factors for Maytag Corporation with corresponding weights, ratings, and weighted scores provided. This table is appropriate for 1995 before Maytag sold its European and Australian operations. Note that Maytag's total weight is 3.15, meaning that the corporation was slightly above average in the major home appliance industry at that time.

3.6 Impact of the Internet on Environmental Scanning and Industry Analysis

The Internet has changed the way the strategist engages in environmental scanning. It provides the quickest means to obtain data on almost any subject. A recent joint study of 77 companies by the American Productivity & Quality Center and the Society of Competitive Intelligence Professionals reveals that 73% of the firms ranked the Internet as being used to a "great" or "very great" extent. Other mentioned sources of information were competitor offerings & products (66%), industry experts (62%), personal industry contacts (60%), online databases (56%), market research (55%), and the sales force (54%).[39] Although the scope and quality of Internet information is increasing geometrically, it is also littered with "noise," misinformation, and utter nonsense. For example, a number of corporate Web sites are sending unwanted guests to specially constructed bogus Web sites![40]

Unlike the library, the Internet lacks the tight bibliographic control standards that exist in the print world. There is no ISBN or Dewey Decimal System to identify, search, and retrieve a document. Many Web documents lack the name of the author and the date of publication. A Web page providing useful information may be accessible on the Web one day and gone the next! Unhappy ex-employees, far-out environmentalists, and prank-prone hackers create Web sites to attack and discredit an otherwise reputable corporation. Rumors with no basis in fact are spread via chat rooms and personal Web sites. This creates a serious problem for the researcher. How can one evaluate the information found on the Internet?

A basic rule in intelligence gathering is that before a piece of information can be used in any report or briefing, it must first be evaluated in two ways. *First, the source of the information should be judged in terms of its truthfulness and reliability.* How trustworthy is the source? How well can a researcher rely upon it for truthful and correct information? One approach is to rank the reliability of the source on a scale from A (extremely reliable), B (reliable), C (unknown reliability), D (probably unreliable), to E (very questionable reliability). The reliability of a source can be judged on the basis of the author's credentials, the organization sponsoring the information, and past performance, among other factors. *Second, the information or data should be judged in terms of its likelihood of being correct.* The correctness of the data may be ranked on a scale from 1 (correct), 2 (probably correct), 3 (unknown), 4 (doubtful), to 5 (extremely doubtful). The correctness of a piece of data or information can be judged on the basis of its agreement with other bits of separately obtained information or with a general trend supported by previous data. For every piece of information found on the Internet, list not only the Web address of the Web page, but also the evaluation of the information from A1 (good stuff) to E5 (bad doodoo). Information found through library research in sources such as *Moody's Industrials*, *Standard & Poor's*, or *Value Line* can generally be evaluated as having a reliability of A. The correctness of the data can still range anywhere from 1 to 5, but in most instances is likely to be either 1 or 2, but probably no worse than 3 or 4. Other sources may be less reliable.

Sites such as those sponsored by the U.S. Securities and Exchange Commission ⟨www.sec.gov⟩ or Hoovers Online ⟨www.hoovers.com⟩ are extremely reliable. Company sponsored Web sites are generally reliable but are not the place to go for trade secrets, strategic plans, or proprietary information. For one thing, many firms think of their Web sites primarily in terms of marketing, and they provide little data aside from product descriptions and distribution channels. Other companies provide their latest financial statements and links to other useful Web sites. Nevertheless, some companies in very competitive industries may install software on their Web site to ascertain a visitor's Web address. Visitors from a competitor's domain name are thus screened before they are allowed to access certain Web sites. They may not be allowed beyond the product information page or they may be sent to a bogus Web site containing misinformation. Cisco Systems, for example, uses its Web site to send visitors from other high-tech firms to a special Web page asking if they would like to apply for a job at Cisco!

Time searching the Internet can be saved by using search engines—Web sites that search the Internet for names and products typed in by the user. The search engines most used by competitive intelligence professionals are AltaVista (50%), Yahoo! (25%), and Lycos (15%). Others are WebCrawler (7.5%), Switchboard (7.5%), Infoseek (5%), and Metacrawler (5%).[41]

Although information about publicly held corporations is widely available, it is much harder to obtain information on privately held companies. For a comparison of the type of information generally available on publicly and privately held companies, see the **Internet Issue** feature for competitor information available on the Internet.

Internet Issue

Competitor Information Available on the Internet

Type of Information	Likelihood of Finding Data on the Net for Publicly Held Company	Likelihood of Finding Data on the Net for Privately Held Company
Total Annual Sales	Very high	Very low
Sales and Profitability by Product Line or Distribution Channel	Very low	Very low
Market Sizes in Segments of Interest	Depends on the market: High for large companies, low for small "niche" firms	Same as for publicly held
Trends in Marketing, Technology, Distribution	Same as above	Same as for publicly held
Prices, Including the Lowest Prices to Best Customers	Very low	Very low
Marketing Strategy	Some information available from trade articles and analyst reports, but incomplete and dated	Even less than for publicly held
Sales and Technical Literature on Products	Strong likelihood, but often incomplete; less chance for detailed technical information	Even less than for publicly held
Number of Employees Working on Certain Products or in Particular Departments	Highly unlikely	Highly unlikely
Compensation Levels	Top management generally available; others unlikely	Will not be found
Customer Opinions Regarding Strengths and Weaknesses	Available from trade articles and industry reports; at best, may be incomplete and dated	Less likely than for publicly held
Feedback on Firm's Own Products and Services	Will not be found; look for independent user chat rooms	Same as for publicly held

Source: Adapted from C. Klein, "Overcoming 'Net Disease,'" *Competitive Intelligence Magazine* (July–September 1999), p. 31.

Projections for the 21st Century

- From 1994 to 2010, the number of people living in poverty will increase from 3.7 billion to 3.9 billion.
- From 1994 to 2010, the average number of children per woman will decrease from 3.2 to 2.7.[42]

Discussion Questions

1. Discuss how a development in a corporation's societal environment can affect the corporation through its task environment.

2. According to Porter, what determines the level of competitive intensity in an industry?

3. According to Porter's discussion of industry analysis, is Pepsi-Cola a substitute for Coca-Cola?

4. How can a decision maker identify strategic factors in the corporation's external international environment?

5. Compare and contrast trend extrapolation with the writing of scenarios as forecasting techniques.

Strategic Practice Exercise

What are the forces driving industry competition in the airline industry? Read the following paragraphs. Using Porter's approach to industry analysis, evaluate each of the six forces to ascertain what drives the level of competitive intensity in this industry.

In recent years, the airline industry has become increasingly competitive. Since being deregulated during the 1970s in the United States, long established airlines such as Pan American and Eastern have gone out of business as new upstarts like Midwest Express and Southwest have successfully entered the market. It appeared that almost anyone could buy a few used planes to serve the smaller cities that the larger airlines no longer wanted to serve. These low-cost, small-capacity commuter planes were able to make healthy profits in these markets where it was too expensive to land large jets. Rail and bus transportation either did not exist or was undesirable in many locations. Eventually the low-cost local commuter airlines expanded service to major cities and grabbed market share from the majors by offering cheaper fares with no-frills service. In order to be competitive with these lower cost upstarts, United Airlines and Northwest Airlines offered stock in the company and seats on the Board of Directors to their unionized employees in exchange for wage and benefit reductions. Delta and American Airlines, among other major carriers, reduced their costs by instituting a cap on travel agent commissions. Travel agencies were livid at this cut in their livelihood, but they needed the airlines' business in order to offer customers a total travel package.

Globally it seemed as though every nation had to have its own airline for national prestige. These state-owned airlines were expensive, but the governments subsidized them with money and supporting regulations. For example, a foreign airline was normally allowed to fly only into one of a country's airports, forcing travelers to switch to the national airline to go to other cities. During the 1980s and 1990s, however, many countries began privatizing their airlines as governments tried to improve their budgets. To be viable in an increasingly global industry, national or regional airlines were forced to form alliances and even purchase an airline in another country or region. For example, the Dutch KLM Airline acquired half interest in the U.S Northwest Airlines in order to obtain not only U.S. destinations, but also Northwest's Asian travel routes, thus making it one of the few global airlines.

Costs were still relatively high for all of the world's major airlines because of the high cost of new airplanes. Just one new jet plane costs anywhere from $25 million to $100 million. By 2001, only two airplane manufacturers provided almost all of the large commercial airliners: Boeing and Airbus. Major airlines were forced to purchase new planes because they were more fuel efficient, safer, and easier to maintain. Airlines that chose to stay with an older fleet of planes had to deal with higher fuel and maintenance costs—factors that often made it cheaper to buy new planes.

1. Evaluate each of the forces currently driving competition in the airline industry:

Threat of New Entrants	High, Medium, or Low? _____
Rivalry Among Existing Firms	High, Medium, or Low? _____
Threat of Substitutes	High, Medium, or Low? _____
Bargaining Power of Buyers/Distributors	High, Medium, or Low? _____
Bargaining Power of Suppliers	High, Medium, or Low? _____
Relative Power of Other Stakeholders	High, Medium, or Low? _____

Such as_____

2. Which of these forces is changing? What will this mean to the overall level of competitive intensity in the airline industry in the future? Would you invest or look for a job in this industry?

Key Terms

brainstorming (p. 72)

cannibalize (p. 68)

competitive intelligence (p. 70)

complementor (p. 64)

consolidated industry (p. 64)

Delphi technique (p. 72)

EFAS Table (p. 73)

entry barrier (p. 61)

environmental scanning (p. 52)

environmental uncertainty (p. 52)

exit barriers (p. 62)

expert opinion (p. 72)

external strategic factors (p. 60)

extrapolation (p. 72)

fragmented industry (p. 64)

global industry (p. 65)

hypercompetition (p. 68)

industry (p. 60)

industry analysis (p. 53)

industry matrix (p. 69)

industry scenario (p. 72)

issues priority matrix (p. 59)

key success factors (p. 69)

multidomestic industry (p. 64)

multinational corporation (MNC) (p. 56)

new entrants (p. 61)

purchasing power parity (PPP) (p. 58)

repatriation of profits (p. 53)

scenario writing (p. 72)

societal environment (p. 52)

statistical modeling (p. 72)

strategic group (p. 66)

strategic myopia (p. 59)

strategic type (p. 66)

substitute products (p. 62)

task environment (p. 53)

Triad (p. 56)

trigger point (p. 58)

Notes

1. D. Phillips, "Special Delivery," *Entrepreneur* (September 1996), pp. 98–100; B. Saporito, "What's for Dinner?" *Fortune* (May 15, 1995), pp. 50–64.

2. J. B. Thomas, S. M. Clark, and D. A. Gioia, "Strategic Sensemaking and Organizational Performance: Linkages Among Scanning, Interpretation, Action, Outcomes," *Academy of Management Journal* (April 1993), pp. 239–270; J. A. Smith, "Strategies for Start-Ups," *Long Range Planning* (December 1998), pp. 857–872.

3. P. Lasserre and J. Probert, "Competing on the Pacific Rim: High Risks and High Returns," *Long Range Planning* (April 1994), pp. 12–35.

4. W. E. Halal, "The Top 10 Emerging Technologies," *Special Report* (World Future Society, 2000).

5. F. Dobbin and T. J. Dowd, "How Policy Shapes Competition: Early Railroad Foundings in Massachusetts," *Administrative Science Quarterly* (September 1997), pp. 501–529.

6. A. Shleifer and R. W. Viskny, "Takeovers in the 1960s and the 1980s: Evidence and Implications," in *Fundamental Issues in Strategy: A Research Agenda*, edited by R. P. Rumelt, D. E. Schendel, and D. J. Teece (Boston: Harvard Business School Press, 1994), pp. 403–418.

7. J. Wyatt, "Playing the Woofie Card," *Fortune* (February 6, 1995), pp. 130–132.

8. J. Greco, "Meet Generation Y," *Forecast* (May/June, 1996), pp. 48–54; J. Fletcher, "A Generation Asks: 'Can the Boom Last?'" *Wall Street Journal* (June 14, 1996), p. B10.

9. "Alone in America," *Futurist* (September–October 1995), pp. 56–57.

10. "Population Growth Slowing as Nation Ages," (Ames, IA) *Daily Tribune* (March 14, 1996), p. A7.

11. L. M. Grossman, "After Demographic Shift, Atlanta Mall Restyles Itself as Black Shopping Center," *Wall Street Journal* (February 26, 1992), p. B1.

12. J. Naisbitt, *Megatrends Asia* (New York: Simon & Schuster, 1996), p. 79.

13. K. Ohmae, "The Triad World View," *Journal of Business Strategy* (Spring 1987), pp. 8–19.

14. B. K. Boyd and J. Fulk, "Executive Scanning and Perceived Uncertainty: A Multidimensional Model," *Journal of Management*, Vol. 22, No. 1 (1996), pp. 1–21.

15. R. A. Bettis and C. K. Prahalad, "The Dominant Logic: Retrospective and Extension," *Strategic Management Journal* (January 1995), pp. 5–14; J. M. Stofford and C. W. F. Baden-Fuller, "Creating Corporate Entrepreneurship," *Strategic Management Journal* (September 1994), pp. 521–536; J. M. Beyer, P. Chattopadhyay, E. George, W. H. Glick, D. Pugliese, "The Selective Perception of Managers Revisited," *Academy of Management Journal* (June 1997), pp. 716–737.

16. H. I. Ansoff, "Strategic Management in a Historical Perspective," in *International Review of Strategic Management*, Vol. 2, No. 1 (1991), edited by D. E. Hussey (Chichester, England: Wiley, 1991), p. 61.

17. M. E. Porter, *Competitive Strategy* (New York: Free Press, 1980), p. 3.

18. This summary of the forces driving competitive intensity is taken from Porter, *Competitive Strategy*, pp. 7–29.

19. P. N. Avakian, "Political Realities in Strategy," *Strategy & Leadership* (October, November, December 1999), pp. 42–48.

20. Porter, *Competitive Strategy*, p. 23.

21. A. S. Grove, "Surviving a 10x Force," *Strategy & Leadership* (January/February 1997), pp. 35–37.

22. M. E. Porter, "Changing Patterns of International Competition," *California Management Review* (Winter 1986), pp. 9–40.

23. T. N. Gladwin, "Assessing the Multinational Environment for Corporate Opportunity," in *Handbook of Business Strategy*, edited by W. D. Guth (Boston: Warren, Gorham and Lamont, 1985), pp. 7.28–7.41.

24. K. J. Hatten and M. L. Hatten, "Strategic Groups, Asymmetrical Mobility Barriers, and Contestability," *Strategic Management Journal* (July–August 1987), p. 329.

25. A. Fiegenbaum and H. Thomas, "Strategic Groups as Reference Groups: Theory, Modeling and Empirical Examination of Industry and Competitive Strategy," *Strategic Management Journal* (September 1995), pp. 461–476; H. R. Greve, "Managerial Cognition and the Mimetic Adoption of Market Positions: What You See Is What You Do," *Strategic Management Journal* (October 1998), pp. 967–988.

26. R. E. Miles and C. C. Snow, *Organizational Strategy, Structure, and Process* (New York: McGraw-Hill, 1978).

27. R. A. D'Aveni, *Hypercompetition* (New York: The Free Press, 1994), pp. xiii–xiv.

28. C. W. Hofer and D. Schendel, *Strategy Formulation: Analytical Concepts* (St. Paul, MN: West Publishing Co., 1978), p. 77.

29. "Information Overload," *Journal of Business Strategy* (January–February 1998), p. 4.

30. E. Von Hipple, *Sources of Innovation* (New York: Oxford University Press, 1988), p. 4.

31. L. Kahaner, *Competitive Intelligence* (New York: Simon & Schuster, 1996).

32. S. M. Shaker and M. P. Gembicki, *WarRoom Guide to Competitive Intelligence* (New York: McGraw-Hill, 1999), p. 10.

33. R. G. Vedder, "CEO and CIO Attitudes about Competitive Intelligence," *Competitive Intelligence Magazine* (October–December 1999), pp. 39–41.

34. S. M. Shaker and M. P. Gembicki, *WarRoom Guide to Competitive Intelligence* (New York: McGraw-Hill, 1999), p. 202.

35. B. Flora, "Ethical Business Intelligence Is NOT Mission Impossible," *Strategy & Leadership* (January/February 1998), pp. 40–41.

36. L. M. Grossman, "Families Have Changed But Tupperware Keeps Holding Its Parties," *Wall Street Journal* (July 21, 1992), pp. A1, A13.

37. H. E. Klein and R. E. Linneman, "Environmental Assessment: An International Study of Corporate Practices," *Journal of Business Strategy* (Summer 1984), p. 72.

38. This process of scenario development is adapted from M. E. Porter, *Competitive Advantage* (New York: Free Press, 1985), pp. 448–470.

39. S. H. Miller, "Developing a Successful CI Program: Preliminary Study Results," *Competitive Intelligence Magazine* (October–December 1999), p. 9.

40. S. H. Miller, "Beware Rival's Web Site Subterfuge," *Competitive Intelligence Magazine* (January–March 2000), p. 8.

41. S. M. Shaker and M. P. Gembicki, *WarRoom Guide to Competitive Intelligence* (New York: McGraw-Hill, 1999), pp. 113–115.

42. J. Warner, "21st Century Capitalism: Snapshot of the Next Century," *Business Week* (November 18, 1994), p. 194

chapter 4

Internal Scanning: Organizational Analysis

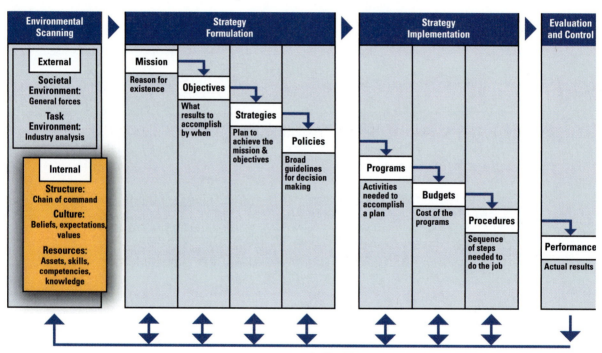

On November 17, 2000, United Airlines increased domestic fares by $50 for trips of less than 1,500 miles and $100 for flights over 1,500 miles. Continental, Delta, and American Airlines quickly followed with their own fare increases. Northwest Airlines and TWA stated that they were considering fare hikes. In contrast (and as usual), Dallas-based Southwest Airlines ignored the increase. "We are aware of it, but we are not taking any action," stated Southwest's spokesman Ed Stewart. He added that management hoped that the price increases by other airlines would drive more traffic to Southwest.[1]

Southwest is the undisputed master of the low fare. It is America's most efficient and profitable airline. Other airlines have tried many times to match or beat Southwest's low fares but have failed. For example, United Airlines used to dominate the California market before Southwest replaced it in the 1990s. To regain this lucrative market, United launched its own low-cost carrier, Shuttle by United. It tried to imitate what it thought were Southwest's advantages. It used a fleet of Boeing 737s, the same plane Southwest used at that time. It was able to obtain looser union work rules and a lower wage scale from those at its United Airlines' parent. To compete effectively, the Shuttle aimed to reduce United's cost of flying from the main airline's 10.5¢ to 7.4¢ per passenger mile. It planned to fly planes longer, speed up passenger boarding and takeoffs, and reduce idle time on the ground. Sixteen months later, however, Shuttle by United had been able to reduce its costs only to 8¢ per passenger mile contrasted with Southwest's 7.1¢ in California. (Southwest's overall cost-per-passenger mile was the lowest in the industry at 6.43¢ compared to American Airlines' 12.95¢ per passenger mile—the highest in the industry.)[2] To keep from losing money, Shuttle by United was forced to raise fares and to pull out of all routes that did not connect with the carrier's hubs in San Francisco and Los Angeles. Even United's most loyal customers were taking Southwest for shorter flights. United's fare from San Francisco to Southern California was often $30 more than Southwest's rate of $69. Southwest had not only regained traffic it had lost initially to the Shuttle, it had actually increased its share of the California market!

In addition to Southwest's reputation for having the lowest costs in the industry, it has a well-earned reputation for flying passengers safely to their destination on time. What gave Southwest Airlines this kind of advantage in a very competitive industry? So far no U.S. airline seems able to copy the secret of its success.

4.1 A Resource-Based Approach to Organizational Analysis

Scanning and analyzing the external environment for opportunities and threats is not enough to provide an organization a competitive advantage. Analysts must also look within the corporation itself to identify **internal strategic factors**—those critical strengths and weaknesses that are likely to determine if the firm will be able to take advantage of opportunities while avoiding threats. This internal scanning is often referred to as **organizational analysis** and is concerned with identifying and developing an organization's resources.

A **resource** is an asset, competency, process, skill, or knowledge controlled by the corporation. A resource is a strength if it provides a company with a competitive advantage. It is something the firm does or has the potential to do particularly well relative to the abilities of existing or potential competitors. A resource is a weakness if it is something the corporation does poorly or doesn't have the capacity to do although its competitors have that capacity. Barney, in his **VRIO framework** of analysis, proposes 4 questions to evaluate each of a firm's key resources:

1. **Value:** Does it provide competitive advantage?
2. **Rareness:** Do other competitors possess it?
3. **Imitability**: Is it costly for others to imitate?
4. **Organization**: Is the firm organized to exploit the resource?

If the answer to these questions is "yes" for a particular resource, that resource is considered a strength and a distinctive competence.[3]

Evaluate the importance of these resources to ascertain if they are internal strategic factors—those particular strengths and weaknesses that will help determine the future of the company. This can be done by comparing measures of these resources with measures of (1) the company's past performance, (2) the company's key competitors, and (3) the industry as a whole. To the extent that a resource (such as a firm's financial situation) is significantly different from the firm's own past, its key competitors, or the industry average, the resource is likely to be a strategic factor and should be considered in strategic decisions.

USING RESOURCES TO GAIN COMPETITIVE ADVANTAGE

Proposing that a company's sustained competitive advantage is primarily determined by its resource endowments, Grant proposes a five-step, resource-based approach to strategy analysis.

1. Identify and classify the firm's resources in terms of strengths and weaknesses.

2. Combine the firm's strengths into specific capabilities. **Corporate capabilities** (often called **core competencies**) are the things that a corporation can do exceedingly well. When these capabilities/competencies are superior to those of competitors, they are often called **distinctive competencies**.

3. Appraise the profit potential of these resources and capabilities in terms of their potential for sustainable competitive advantage and the ability to harvest the profits resulting from the use of these resources and capabilities.

4. Select the strategy that best exploits the firm's resources and capabilities relative to external opportunities.

5. Identify resource gaps and invest in upgrading weaknesses.[4]

As indicated in Step 2, when an organization's resources are combined, they form a number of capabilities. In the earlier example, Southwest Airlines has two identifiable capabilities: low costs per passenger mile, and the capability of energizing its people to provide safe, on-time flight service. To ensure highly motivated employees, Southwest spends an inordinate amount of time and money on hiring and promoting, using a system to identify prospective employees who will fit into the company's corporate culture while retaining their individualism.[5]

DETERMINING THE SUSTAINABILITY OF AN ADVANTAGE

Just because a firm is able to use its resources and capabilities to develop a competitive advantage does not mean it will be able to sustain it. Two characteristics determine the sustainability of a firm's distinctive competency(ies): durability and imitability.

Durability is the rate at which a firm's underlying resources and capabilities (core competencies) depreciate or become obsolete. New technology can make a company's core competency obsolete or irrelevant. For example, Intel's skills in using basic technology developed by others to manufacture and market quality microprocessors was a crucial capability until management realized that the firm had taken current technology as far as possible with the Pentium chip. Without basic R&D of its own, it would slowly lose its competitive advantage to others.

Imitability is the rate at which a firm's underlying resources and capabilities (core competencies) can be duplicated by others. To the extent that a firm's distinctive competency gives it competitive advantage in the marketplace, competitors will do what they can to learn and imitate that set of skills and capabilities. Competitors' efforts may range from **reverse engineering** (taking apart a competitor's product in order to find out how it works), to hiring employees from the competitor, to outright patent infringement. A core competency can be easily imitated to the extent that it is transparent, transferable, and replicable.

- **Transparency** is the speed with which other firms can understand the relationship of resources and capabilities supporting a successful firm's strategy. For example, Gillette has always supported its dominance in the marketing of razors with excellent R&D. A competitor could never understand how the Sensor or Mach 3 razor was produced simply by taking one apart. Gillette's Sensor razor design, in particular, was very difficult to copy, partially because the manufacturing equipment needed to produce it was so expensive and complicated.

- **Transferability** is the ability of competitors to gather the resources and capabilities necessary to support a competitive challenge. For example, it may be very difficult for a wine maker to duplicate a French winery's key resources of land and climate, especially if the imitator is located in Iowa.

- **Replicability** is the ability of competitors to use duplicated resources and capabilities to imitate the other firm's success. For example, even though many companies have tried to imitate Procter & Gamble's success with brand management by hiring brand managers away from P&G, they have often failed to duplicate P&G's success. The competitors failed to identify less visible P&G coordination mechanisms or to realize that P&G's brand management style conflicted with the competitor's own corporate culture. Another example is Wal-Mart's sophisticated cross-docking system, which provides the company a substantial cost advantage by improving its ability to reduce shipping and handling costs. While Wal-Mart has the same resources in terms of retail space, employee skills, and equipment as many other discount chains, it has the unique capability to manage its resources for maximum productivity.[6]

It is relatively easy to learn and imitate another company's core competency or capability if it comes from **explicit knowledge**, that is, knowledge that can be easily articulated and communicated. This is the type of knowledge that competitive intelligence activities can quickly identify and communicate. **Tacit knowledge**, in contrast, is knowledge that is *not* easily communicated because it is deeply rooted in employee experience or in a corporation's culture.[7] Tacit knowledge is more valuable and more likely to lead to a sustainable competitive advantage than is explicit knowledge because it is much harder for competitors to imitate. The knowledge may be complex and combined with other types of knowledge in an unclear fashion in such a way that even management cannot clearly explain the competency.[8] Because Procter & Gamble's successful approach to brand management is primarily composed of tacit knowledge, the firm's top management is very reluctant to make any significant modifications to it, fearing that they might destroy the very thing they are trying to improve!

An organization's resources and capabilities can be placed on a continuum to the extent they are durable and can't be imitated (that is, aren't transparent, transferable, or replicable) by another firm. This **continuum of sustainability** is depicted in **Figure 4–1**. At one extreme are slow-cycle resources, which are sustainable because they are shielded by patents, geography, strong brand names, or tacit knowledge. These resources and capabilities are distinctive competencies because they provide a sustainable competitive advantage. Gillette's Sensor

Figure 4–1

Continuum of Resource Sustainability

Level of Resource Sustainability

High
(Hard to Imitate)

Low
(Easy to Imitate)

Slow-Cycle Resources	Standard-Cycle Resources	Fast-Cycle Resources
• Strongly shielded • Patents, brand name • Gilette: Sensor razor	• Standardized mass production • Economies of scale Complicated processes • Chrysler: Minivan	• Easily duplicated • Idea driven • Sony: Walkman

Source: Suggested by J. R. Williams, "How Sustainable Is Your Competitive Advantage?" *California Management Review* (Spring 1992), p. 33. Copyright © 1992 by the Regents of the University of California. Reprinted by permission of the Regents.

razor is a good example of a product built around slow-cycle resources. The other extreme includes fast-cycle resources, which face the highest imitation pressures because they are based on a concept or technology that can be easily duplicated, such as Sony's Walkman. To the extent that a company has fast-cycle resources, the primary way it can compete successfully is through increased speed from lab to marketplace. Otherwise, it has no real sustainable competitive advantage.

With its low-cost position, reputation for safe, on-time flights, and its dedicated workforce, Southwest Airlines has successfully built a sustainable competitive advantage based on relatively slow-cycle resources—resources that are durable and can't be easily imitated because they lack transparency, transferability, and replicability.

4.2 Value Chain Analysis

A good way to begin an organizational analysis is to ascertain where a firm's products are located in the overall value chain. A **value chain** is a linked set of value-creating activities beginning with basic raw materials coming from suppliers, moving on to a series of value-added activities involved in producing and marketing a product or service, and ending with distributors getting the final goods into the hands of the ultimate consumer. See **Figure 4–2** for an example of a typical value chain for a manufactured product. The focus of value chain analysis is to examine the corporation in the context of the overall chain of value-creating activities, of which the firm may be only a small part.

Very few corporations include a product's entire value chain. Ford Motor Company did when it was managed by its founder, Henry Ford I. During the 1920s and 1930s, the company owned its own iron mines, ore-carrying ships, and a small rail line to bring ore to its mile-long River Rouge plant in Detroit. Visitors to the plant would walk along an elevated walkway where they could watch iron ore being dumped from the rail cars into huge furnaces. The resulting steel was poured and rolled out onto a moving belt to be fabricated into auto frames and parts while the visitors watched in awe. As a group of visitors walked along the walkway, they observed an automobile being built piece by piece. Reaching the end of the moving line, the finished automobile was driven out of the plant into a vast adjoining parking lot. Ford trucks would then load the cars for delivery to dealers. Although the Ford dealers were not employees of the company, they had almost no power in the arrangement. Dealerships were awarded by the company and taken away if a dealer was at all disloyal. Ford Motor Company at that time was completely vertically integrated, that is, it controlled (usually by ownership) every stage of the value chain from the iron mines to the retailers.

INDUSTRY VALUE CHAIN ANALYSIS

The value chains of most industries can be split into two segments, *upstream* and *downstream* halves. In the petroleum industry, for example, upstream refers to oil exploration, drilling, and moving the crude oil to the refinery, and downstream refers to refining the oil plus the trans-

Figure 4–2
Typical Value Chain for a Manufactured Product

Source: Suggested by J. R. Galbraith, "Strategy and Organization Planning," in *The Strategy Process: Concepts, Contexts, Cases,* 2nd ed., edited by H. Mintzberg and J. B. Quinn (Upper Saddle River, NJ: Prentice Hall, 1991), p. 316. Reprinted by permission of Pearson Education, Inc., Upper Saddle River, NJ.

porting and marketing of gasoline and refined oil to distributors and gas station retailers. Even though most large oil companies are completely integrated, they often vary in the amount of expertise they have at each part of the value chain. Texaco, for example, has its greatest expertise downstream in marketing and retailing. Others, such as British Petroleum (now BP Amoco), are more dominant in upstream activities like exploration.

An industry can be analyzed in terms of the profit margin available at any one point along the value chain. For example, the U.S. auto industry's revenues and profits are divided among many value chain activities, including manufacturing, new and used car sales, gasoline retailing, insurance, after-sales service and parts, and lease financing. From a revenue standpoint, auto manufacturers dominate the industry, accounting for almost 60% of total industry revenues. Profits are, however, a different matter. Auto leasing is the most profitable activity in the value chain, followed by insurance and auto loans. The core activities of manufacturing and distribution, however, earn significantly smaller shares of the total industry profits than they do of total revenues. For example, since auto sales have become marginally profitable, dealerships are now emphasizing service and repair. As a result of various differences along the industry value chain, manufacturers have moved aggressively into auto financing. Ford, for example, generates nearly half its profits from financing, even though financing accounts for less than 20% of the company's revenues.[9]

In analyzing the complete value chain of a product, note that even if a firm operates up and down the entire industry chain, it usually has an area of primary expertise where its primary activities lie. A company's **center of gravity** is the part of the chain that is most important to the company and the point where its greatest expertise and capabilities lie—its core competencies. According to Galbraith, a company's center of gravity is usually the point at which the company started. After a firm successfully establishes itself at this point by obtaining a competitive advantage, one of its first strategic moves is to move forward or backward along the value chain in order to reduce costs, guarantee access to key raw materials, or to guarantee distribution.[10] This process is called *vertical integration* and is discussed in more detail in Chapter 6.

In the paper industry, for example, Weyerhauser's center of gravity is in the raw materials and primary manufacturing parts of the value chain in **Figure 4–2**. Weyerhauser's expertise is in lumbering and pulp mills, which is where the company started. It integrated forward by using its wood pulp to make paper and boxes, but its greatest capability still lay in getting the greatest return from its lumbering activities. In contrast, Procter & Gamble is primarily a consumer products company that also owned timberland and operated pulp mills. Its expertise is in the product producer and marketer distributor parts of the **Figure 4–2** value chain. P&G purchased these assets to guarantee access to the large quantities of wood pulp it needed to expand its disposable diaper, toilet tissue, and napkin products. P&G's strongest capabilities have always been in the downstream activities of product development, marketing, and brand management. It has never been as efficient in upstream paper activities as Weyerhauser. It had no real distinctive competence on that part of the value chain. When paper supplies became more plentiful (and competition got rougher), P&G gladly sold its land and mills to focus more on that part of the value chain where it could provide the greatest value at the lowest cost—creating and marketing innovative consumer products.

CORPORATE VALUE CHAIN ANALYSIS

Each corporation has its own internal value chain of activities. See **Figure 4–3** for an example of a corporate value chain. Porter proposes that a manufacturing firm's **primary activities** usually begin with inbound logistics (raw materials handling and warehousing), go through an operations process in which a product is manufactured, and continue on to outbound logistics (warehousing and distribution), marketing and sales, and finally to service (installa-

Figure 4–3

A Corporation's Value Chain

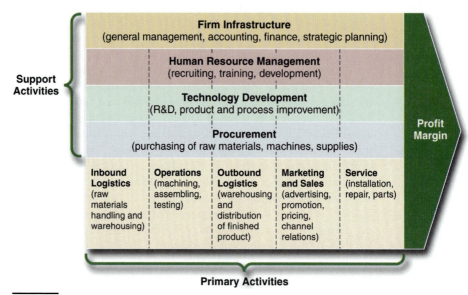

Source: Adapted/reprinted with the permission of The Free Press, an imprint of Simon & Schuster, from *Competitive Advantage: Creating and Sustaining Superior Performance* by Michael E. Porter, p. 37. Copyright © 1985, 1988 by Michael E. Porter.

tion, repair, and sale of parts). Several **support activities**, such as procurement (purchasing), technology development (R&D), human resource management, and firm infrastructure (accounting, finance, strategic planning), ensure that the primary value-chain activities operate effectively and efficiently. Each of a company's product lines has its own distinctive value chain. Because most corporations make several different products or services, an internal analysis of the firm involves analyzing a series of different value chains.

The systematic examination of individual value activities can lead to a better understanding of a corporation's strengths and weaknesses. According to Porter, "Differences among competitor value chains are a key source of competitive advantage."[11] Corporate value chain analysis involves the following three steps:

1. *Examine each product line's value chain in terms of the various activities involved in producing that product or service.* Which activities can be considered strengths (core competencies) or weaknesses (core deficiencies)? Do any of the strengths provide competitive advantage and can thus be labeled distinctive competencies?

2. *Examine the "linkages" within each product line's value chain.* **Linkages** are the connections between the way one value activity (for example, marketing) is performed and the cost of performance of another activity (for example, quality control). In seeking ways for a corporation to gain competitive advantage in the marketplace, the same function can be performed in different ways with different results. For example, quality inspection of 100% of output by the workers themselves instead of the usual 10% by quality control inspectors might increase production costs, but that increase could be more than offset by the savings obtained from reducing the number of repair people needed to fix defective products and increasing the amount of salespeople's time devoted to selling instead of exchanging already-sold, but defective, products.

3. *Examine the potential synergies among the value chains of different product lines or business units.* Each value element, such as advertising or manufacturing, has an inherent economy of scale in which activities are conducted at their lowest possible cost per unit of output. If a particular product is not being produced at a high enough level to reach economies of scale in distribution, another product could be used to share the same distribution channel. This is an example of **economies of scope**, which result when the value chains of two separate products or services share activities, such as the same marketing channels or manufacturing facilities. For example, the cost of joint production of multiple products can be less than the cost of separate production.

4.3 Scanning Functional Resources

The simplest way to begin an analysis of a corporation's value chain is by carefully examining its traditional functional areas for potential strengths and weaknesses. Functional resources include not only the financial, physical, and human assets in each area, but also the ability of the people in each area to formulate and implement the necessary functional objectives, strategies, and policies. The resources include the knowledge of analytical concepts and procedural techniques common to each area as well as the ability of the people in each area to use them effectively. If used properly, these resources serve as strengths to carry out value-added activities and support strategic decisions. In addition to the usual business functions of marketing, finance, R&D, operations, human resources, and information systems, we also discuss structure and culture as key parts of a business corporation's value chain.

BASIC ORGANIZATIONAL STRUCTURES

Although there is an almost infinite variety of structural forms, certain basic types predominate in modern complex organizations. **Figure 4–4** illustrates three basic **organizational structures**. The conglomerate structure is a variant of divisional structure and is thus not depicted as a fourth structure. Generally speaking, each structure tends to support some corporate strategies over others.

- **Simple structure** has no functional or product categories and is appropriate for a small, entrepreneur-dominated company with one or two product lines that operates in a reasonably small, easily identifiable market niche. Employees tend to be generalists and jacks-of-all-trades.

- **Functional structure** is appropriate for a medium-sized firm with several related product lines in one industry. Employees tend to be specialists in the business functions important to that industry, such as manufacturing, marketing, finance, and human resources.

- **Divisional structure** is appropriate for a large corporation with many product lines in several related industries. Employees tend to be functional specialists organized according to product/market distinctions. General Motors, for example, groups its various auto lines into the separate divisions of Chevrolet, Pontiac, Saturn, Oldsmobile, Buick, and Cadillac. Management attempts to find some synergy among divisional activities through the use of committees and horizontal linkages.

- **Strategic business units** (SBUs) are a recent modification to the divisional structure. Strategic business units are divisions or groups of divisions composed of independent product-market segments that are given primary responsibility and authority for the management of their own functional areas. *An SBU may be of any size or level, but it must have (1) a unique mission, (2) identifiable competitors, (3) an external market focus, and (4) control of its business functions.*[12] The idea is to decentralize on the basis of strategic elements rather than on the basis of size, product characteristics, or span of control and to create

Figure 4–4

Basic Organizational Structures

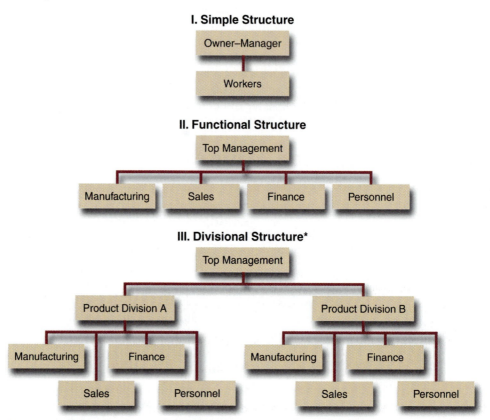

*Conglomerate structure is a variant of the divisional structure.

horizontal linkages among units previously kept separate. For example, rather than organize products on the basis of packaging technology like frozen foods, canned foods, and
bagged foods, General Foods organized its products into SBUs on the basis of consumer-
oriented menu segments: breakfast food, beverage, main meal, dessert, and pet foods.

- **Conglomerate structure** is appropriate for a large corporation with many product lines in
several unrelated industries. A variant of the divisional structure, the conglomerate structure (sometimes called a holding company) is typically an assemblage of legally independent firms (subsidiaries) operating under one corporate umbrella but controlled through
the subsidiaries' boards of directors. The unrelated nature of the subsidiaries prevents any
attempt at gaining synergy among them.

If the current basic structure of a corporation does not easily support a strategy under
consideration, top management must decide if the proposed strategy is feasible or if the structure should be changed to a more advanced structure such as the matrix or network.
(Advanced structural designs such as the matrix and network are discussed in Chapter 7.)

CORPORATE CULTURE: THE COMPANY WAY

There is an oft-told story of a person new to a company asking an experienced coworker what
an employee should do when a customer calls. The old-timer responded: "There are three
ways to do any job—the right way, the wrong way, and the company way. Around here, we

always do things the company way." In most organizations, the "company way" is derived from the corporation's culture. **Corporate culture** is the collection of beliefs, expectations, and values learned and shared by a corporation's members and transmitted from one generation of employees to another. The corporate culture generally reflects the values of the founder(s) and the mission of the firm.[13] It gives a company a sense of identity: *This is who we are. This is what we do. This is what we stand for.* The culture includes the dominant orientation of the company, such as research and development at Hewlett-Packard, customer service at Nordstrom, or product quality at Maytag. It often includes a number of informal work rules (forming the "company way") that employees follow without question. These work practices over time become part of a company's unquestioned tradition.

Corporate culture has two distinct attributes, intensity and integration.[14] **Cultural intensity** is the degree to which members of a unit accept the norms, values, or other culture content associated with the unit. This shows the culture's depth. Organizations with strong norms promoting a particular value, such as quality at Maytag, have intensive cultures, whereas new firms (or those in transition) have weaker, less intensive cultures. Employees in an intensive culture tend to exhibit consistent behavior, that is, they tend to act similarly over time. **Cultural integration** is the extent to which units throughout an organization share a common culture. This is the culture's breadth. Organizations with a pervasive dominant culture may be hierarchically controlled and power oriented, such as a military unit, and have highly integrated cultures. All employees tend to hold the same cultural values and norms. In contrast, a company that is structured into diverse units by functions or divisions usually exhibits some strong subcultures (for example, R&D versus manufacturing) and a less integrated corporate culture.

Corporate culture fulfills several important functions in an organization:

1. Conveys a sense of identity for employees
2. Helps generate employee commitment to something greater than themselves
3. Adds to the stability of the organization as a social system
4. Serves as a frame of reference for employees to use to make sense out of organizational activities and to use as a guide for appropriate behavior[15]

Corporate culture shapes the behavior of people in the corporation. Because these cultures have a powerful influence on the behavior of people at all levels, they can strongly affect a corporation's ability to shift its strategic direction. A strong culture should not only promote survival, but it should also create the basis for a superior competitive position. For example, a culture emphasizing constant renewal may help a company adapt to a changing, hypercompetitive environment.[16] To the extent that a corporation's distinctive competence is embedded in an organization's culture, it will be a form of tacit knowledge and very difficult for a competitor to imitate.[17] See the ⊕ **Global Issue** feature to see how the Swiss company ABB Asea Brown Boveri AG uses its corporate culture to obtain competitive advantage in a global industry.

A change in mission, objectives, strategies, or policies is not likely to be successful if it is in opposition to the accepted culture of the firm. Foot-dragging and even sabotage may result as employees fight to resist a radical change in corporate philosophy. Like structure, if an organization's culture is compatible with a new strategy, it is an internal strength. But if the corporate culture is not compatible with the proposed strategy, it is a serious weakness.

STRATEGIC MARKETING ISSUES

The marketing manager is the company's primary link to the customer and the competition. The manager, therefore, must be especially concerned with the market position and marketing mix of the firm.

Global Issue

ABB Uses Corporate Culture as a Competitive Advantage

Zurich-based ABB Asea Brown Boveri AG is a world-wide builder of power plants, electrical equipment, and industrial factories in 140 countries. By establishing one set of values throughout its global operations, ABB's management believes that the company will gain an advantage over its rivals Siemens AG of Germany, France's Alcatel-Alsthom NV, and the United State's General Electric Company.

Percy Barnevik, Swedish Chairman of ABB, managed the merger that created ABB from Sweden's Asea AB and Switzerland's BBC Brown Boveri Ltd. At that time both companies were far behind the world leaders in electrical equipment and engineering. Barnevik introduced his concept of a company with no geographic base—one that had many "home" markets that could draw on expertise from around the globe. To do

this, he created a set of 500 global managers who could adapt to local cultures while executing ABB's global strategies. These people are multilingual and move around each of ABB's 5,000 profit centers in 140 countries. Their assignment is to cut costs, improve efficiency, and integrate local businesses with the ABB world view.

ABB requires local business units, such as Mexico's motor factory, to report both to one of ABB's traveling global managers and to a business area manager who sets global motor strategy for ABB. When the goals of the local factory conflict with worldwide priorities, it is up to the global manager to resolve it.

Few multinational corporations are as successful as ABB in getting global strategies to work with local operations. In agreement with the resource-based view of the firm, Barnevik states, "Our strength comes from pulling together. . . . If you can make this work real well, then you get a competitive edge out of the organization which is very, very difficult to copy."

Source: J. Guyon, "ABB Fuses Units with One Set of Values," *Wall Street Journal* (October 2, 1996), p. A15. Copyright © 1996 by the *Wall Street Journal.* Reprinted by permission of the *Wall Street Journal* via the Copyright Clearance Center.

Market Position and Segmentation

Market position deals with the question, "Who are our customers?" It refers to the selection of specific areas for marketing concentration and can be expressed in terms of market, product, and geographical locations. Through market research, corporations are able to practice **market segmentation** with various products or services so that managers can discover what niches to seek, which new types of products to develop, and how to ensure that a company's many products do not directly compete with one another.

Marketing Mix

The **marketing mix** refers to the particular combination of key variables under the corporation's control that can be used to affect demand and to gain competitive advantage. These variables are product, place, promotion, and price. Within each of these four variables are several subvariables, listed in **Table 4–1**, that should be analyzed in terms of their effects on divisional and corporate performance.

Product Life Cycle

One of the most useful concepts in marketing, insofar as strategic management is concerned, is that of the **product life cycle.** As depicted in **Figure 4–5**, the product life cycle is a graph showing time plotted against the dollar sales of a product as it moves from introduction through growth and maturity to decline. This concept enables a marketing manager to examine the marketing mix of a particular product or group of products in terms of its position in its life cycle.

Table 4-1   Marketing Mix Variables

Product	Place	Promotion	Price
Quality	Channels	Advertising	List price
Features	Coverage	Personal selling	Discounts
Options	Locations	Sales promotion	Allowances
Style	Inventory	Publicity	Payment periods
Brand name	Transport		Credit items
Packaging			
Sizes			
Services			
Warranties			
Returns			

Source: Philip Kotler, *Marketing Management: Analysis, Planning, and Control*, 4th ed. (Upper Saddle River, NJ: Prentice Hall, 1980), p. 89. Copyright © 1980. Reprinted by permission of Pearson Education, Inc., Upper Saddle River, NJ.

STRATEGIC FINANCIAL ISSUES

The financial manager must ascertain the best sources of funds, uses of funds, and control of funds. Cash must be raised from internal or external (local and global) sources and allocated for different uses. The flow of funds in the operations of the organization must be monitored. To the extent that a corporation is involved in international activities, currency fluctuations must be dealt with to ensure that profits aren't wiped out by the rise or fall of the dollar versus the yen, euro, or other currencies. Benefits in the form of returns, repayments, or products and services must be given to the sources of outside financing. All these tasks must be handled in a way that complements and supports overall corporate strategy. A firm's capital structure (amounts of debt and equity) can influence its strategic choices. For example, increased debt tends to increase risk aversion and decrease the willingness of management to invest in R&D.[18]

Figure 4-5
Product Life Cycle

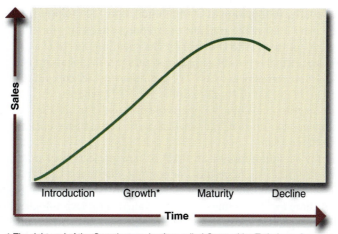

Introduction   Growth*   Maturity   Decline

Sales

Time

* The right end of the Growth stage is often called Competitive Turbulence because of price and distribution competition that shakes out the weaker competitors. For further information, see C.R. Wasson, *Dynamic Competitive Strategy and Product Life Cycles,* 3rd ed. (Austin, TX: Austin Press, 1978).

Financial Leverage

The mix of externally generated short-term and long-term funds in relation to the amount and timing of internally generated funds should be appropriate to the corporate objectives, strategies, and policies. The concept of **financial leverage** (the ratio of total debt to total assets) is helpful in describing how debt is used to increase the earnings available to common shareholders. When the company finances its activities by sales of bonds or notes instead of through stock, the earnings per share are boosted: The interest paid on the debt reduces taxable income, but fewer shareholders share the profits than if the company had sold more stock to finance its activities. The debt, however, does raise the firm's break-even point above what it would have been if the firm had financed from internally generated funds only. High leverage may therefore be perceived as a corporate strength in times of prosperity and ever-increasing sales, or as a weakness in times of a recession and falling sales. This is because leverage acts to magnify the effect on earnings per share of an increase or decrease in dollar sales. Research indicates that greater leverage has a positive impact on performance for firms in stable environments, but a negative impact for firms in dynamic environments.[19]

Capital Budgeting

Capital budgeting is the analyzing and ranking of possible investments in fixed assets such as land, buildings, and equipment in terms of the additional outlays and additional receipts that will result from each investment. A good finance department will be able to prepare such capital budgets and to rank them on the basis of some accepted criteria or hurdle rate (for example, years to pay back investment, rate of return, or time to break-even point) for the purpose of strategic decision making. Most firms have more than one hurdle rate and vary it as a function of the type of project being considered. Projects with high strategic significance, such as entering new markets or defending market share, will often have low hurdle rates.[20]

STRATEGIC RESEARCH AND DEVELOPMENT (R&D) ISSUES

The R&D manager is responsible for suggesting and implementing a company's technological strategy in light of its corporate objectives and policies. The manager's job, therefore, involves (1) choosing among alternative new technologies to use within the corporation, (2) developing methods of embodying the new technology in new products and processes, and (3) deploying resources so that the new technology can be successfully implemented.

R&D Intensity, Technological Competence, and Technology Transfer

The company must make available the resources necessary for effective research and development. A company's **R&D intensity** (its spending on R&D as a percentage of sales revenue) is a principal means of gaining market share in global competition. The amount spent on R&D often varies by industry. For example, the U.S. computer software industry spends an average of 13.5% of its sales dollar for R&D, whereas the paper and forest products industry spends only 1.0%.[21] A good rule of thumb for R&D spending is that a corporation should spend at a "normal" rate for that particular industry unless its strategic plan calls for unusual expenditures.

Simply spending money on R&D or new projects does not mean, however, that the money will produce useful results. For example, Pharmacia Upjohn spent more of its revenues on research than any other company in any industry (18%), but it was ranked low in innovation.[22] A company's R&D unit should be evaluated for **technological competence** in both the development and the use of innovative technology. Not only should the corporation make a consistent research effort (as measured by reasonably constant corporate expenditures that result in usable innovations), it should also be proficient in managing research personnel and integrating their innovations into its day-to-day operations. If a company is not proficient in

technology transfer, the process of taking a new technology from the laboratory to the marketplace, it will not gain much advantage from new technological advances. For example, Xerox Corporation has been criticized for failing to take advantage of various innovations (such as the mouse and the graphical user interface for personal computers) developed originally in its sophisticated Palo Alto Research Center. See the **boxed example** for a classic example of how Apple Computer's ability to imitate a core competency of Xerox gave it a competitive advantage (sustainable until Microsoft launched Windows 95).

R&D Mix

Basic R&D is conducted by scientists in well-equipped laboratories where the focus is on theoretical problem areas. The best indicators of a company's capability in this area are its patents and research publications. **Product R&D** concentrates on marketing and is concerned with product or product-packaging improvements. The best measurements of ability in this area are the number of successful new products introduced and the percentage of total sales and profits coming from products introduced within the past five years. **Engineering (or process) R&D** is concerned with engineering, concentrating on quality control and the development of design specifications and improved production equipment. A company's capability in this area can be measured by consistent reductions in unit manufacturing costs and by the number of product defects.

Most corporations will have a mix of basic, product, and process R&D, which varies by industry, company, and product line. The balance of these types of research is known as the **R&D mix** and should be appropriate to the strategy being considered and to each product's life cycle. For example, it is generally accepted that product R&D normally dominates the early stages of a product's life cycle (when the product's optimal form and features are still being debated), whereas process R&D becomes especially important in the later stages (when the product's design is solidified and the emphasis is on reducing costs and improving quality).

A Problem of Technology Transfer at Xerox Corporation

In the mid-1970s, Xerox Corporation's Palo Alto Research Center (PARC) had developed Alto, a new type of computer with some innovative features. Although Alto was supposed to serve as a research prototype, it became so popular among PARC personnel that some researchers began to develop Alto as a commercial product. Unfortunately this put PARC into direct conflict with Xerox's product development group, which was at the same time developing a rival machine called the Star. Because the Star was in line with the company's expressed product development strategy, top management, who placed all its emphasis on the Star, ignored Alto.

In 1979, Steve Jobs, Cofounder of Apple Computer, Inc., made a now-legendary tour of the normally very secretive PARC. Researchers gave Jobs a demonstration of the Alto. Unlike the computers that Apple was then building, Alto had the power of a minicomputer. Its user-friendly software generated crisp text and bright graphics. Jobs fell in love with the machine. He promptly asked Apple's engineers to duplicate the look and feel of Alto. The result was the Macintosh—a personal computer that soon revolutionized the industry.

Note: See the 1999 motion picture, *The Pirates of Silicon Valley,* for the full story of how Apple Computer imitated the features of the Alto and how Microsoft, in turn, imitated the "look and feel" of Apple's Macintosh.

Impact of Technological Discontinuity on Strategy

The R&D manager must determine when to abandon present technology and when to develop or adopt new technology. Richard Foster of McKinsey and Company states that the displacement of one technology by another (**technological discontinuity**) is a frequent and strategically important phenomenon. Such a discontinuity occurs when a new technology cannot simply be used to enhance the current technology but actually substitutes for that technology to yield better performance. For each technology within a given field or industry, according to Foster, the plotting of product performance against research effort/expenditures on a graph results in an S-shaped curve. He describes the process depicted in **Figure 4–6**:

> Early in the development of the technology a knowledge base is being built and progress requires a relatively large amount of effort. Later, progress comes more easily. And then, as the limits of that technology are approached, progress becomes slow and expensive. That is when R&D dollars should be allocated to technology with more potential. That is also—not so incidentally—when a competitor who has bet on a new technology can sweep away your business or topple an entire industry.[23]

Computerized information technology is currently on the steep upward slope of its S-curve in which relatively small increments in R&D effort result in significant improvement in performance. This is an example of Moore's Law, which states that silicon chips (microprocessors) double in complexity every 18 months. Proposed by Gordon Moore, Cofounder of Intel, in 1965, the law originally stated that processor complexity would double in one year, but Moore soon changed it to two years. Others changed it to 18 months—the number now generally accepted. In 1965, 16 components could be placed on a silicon chip. By 2000, that number had grown exponentially to 10 million. According to Moore, "Moore's Law has been the name given to everything that changes exponentially in the industry."[24]

Figure 4–6
Technological Discontinuity

What the S-Curves Reveal

Product Performance

Mature Technology

New Technology

Research Effort/Expenditure

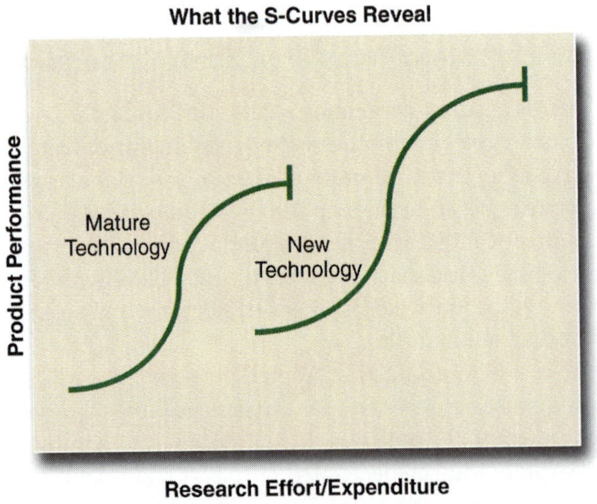

In the corporate planning process, it is generally assumed that incremental progress in technology will occur. But past developments in a given technology cannot be extrapolated into the future because every technology has its limits. The key to competitiveness is to determine when to shift resources to a technology with more potential.

Source: P. Pascarella, "Are You Investing in the Wrong Technology?" *Industry Week* (July 25, 1983), p. 38. Copyright © 1983 Penton Media, Inc., Cleveland, OH. All rights reserved. Reprinted with permission from *Industry Week.*

The presence of a technological discontinuity in the world's steel industry during the 1960s explains why the large capital expenditures by U.S. steel companies failed to keep them competitive with the Japanese firms that adopted the new technologies. As Foster points out, "History has shown that as one technology nears the end of its S-curve, competitive leadership in a market generally changes hands."[25]

Christensen explains in *The Innovator's Dilemma* why this transition occurs when a "disruptive technology" enters an industry. In a study of computer disk drive manufacturers, he explains that established market leaders are typically reluctant to move in a timely manner to a new technology. This reluctance to switch technologies (even when the firm is aware of the new technology and may have even invented it!) is because the resource allocation process in most companies gives priority to those projects (typically based on the old technology) with the greatest likelihood of generating a good return on investment—those projects appealing to the firm's current customers (whose products are also based on the characteristics of the old technology). For example, in the 1980s a disk drive manufacturer's customers (PC manufacturers) wanted a better (faster) 5¼″ drive with greater capacity. These PC makers were not interested in the new 3½″ drives based on the new technology because (at that time) the smaller drives were slower and had less capacity. Smaller size was irrelevant since these companies primarily made desktop personal computers that were designed to hold large drives.

The new technology is generally riskier and of little appeal to the current customers of established firms. Products derived from the new technology are more expensive and do not meet the customers' requirements, which are based on the old technology. New entrepreneurial firms are typically more interested in the new technology because it is one way to appeal to a developing market niche in a market currently dominated by established companies. Even though the new technology may be more expensive to develop, it offers performance improvements in areas that are attractive to this small niche, but of no consequence to the customers of the established competitors.

This was the case with the entrepreneurial manufacturers of 3½″ disk drives. These smaller drives appealed to the PC makers who were trying to increase their small PC market share by offering laptop computers. Size and weight were more important to these customers than were capacity and speed. By the time the new technology was developed to the point that the 3½″ drive matched and even surpassed the 5¼″ drive in terms of speed and capacity (in addition to size and weight), it was too late for the established 5¼″ disk drive firms to switch to the new technology. Once their customers begin demanding smaller products using the new technology, the established firms were unable to respond quickly and lost their leadership position in the industry. They were able to remain in the industry (with a much reduced market share) only if they were able to utilize the new technology to be competitive in the new product line.[26]

STRATEGIC OPERATIONS ISSUES

The primary task of the operations (manufacturing or service) manager is to develop and operate a system that will produce the required number of products or services, with a certain quality, at a given cost, within an allotted time. Many of the key concepts and techniques popularly used in manufacturing can be applied to service businesses.

In very general terms, manufacturing can be intermittent or continuous. In **intermittent systems** (job shops), the item is normally processed sequentially, but the work and sequence of the process vary. An example is an auto body repair shop. At each location, the tasks determine the details of processing and the time required for them. These job shops can be very labor intensive. For example, a job shop usually has little automated machinery and thus a small amount of fixed costs. It has a fairly low break-even point, but its variable cost line (composed of wages and costs of special parts) has a relatively steep slope. Because most of the costs associated with the product are variable (many employees earn piece-rate wages), a job shop's variable costs are higher than those of automated firms. Its advantage over other firms is that it can operate at low levels and still be profitable. After a job shop's sales reach breakeven, however, the huge variable costs as a percentage of total costs keep the profit per unit at a relatively low level. In terms of strategy, this firm should look for a niche in the marketplace for which it can produce and sell a reasonably small quantity of goods.

In contrast, **continuous systems** are those laid out as lines on which products can be continuously assembled or processed. An example is an automobile assembly line. A firm using continuous systems invests heavily in fixed investments such as automated processes and highly sophisticated machinery. Its labor force, relatively small but highly skilled, earns salaries rather than piece-rate wages. Consequently this firm has a high amount of fixed costs. It also has a relatively high break-even point, but its variable cost line rises slowly. This is an example of **operating leverage**, the impact of a specific change in sales volume on net operating income. The advantage of high operating leverage is that once the firm reaches breakeven, its profits rise faster than do those of less automated firms having lower operating leverage. Continuous systems reap benefits from economies of scale. In terms of strategy, this firm needs to find a high-demand niche in the marketplace for which it can produce and sell a large quantity of goods. However, a firm with high operating leverage is likely to suffer huge losses during a recession. During an economic downturn, the firm with less automation and thus less leverage is more likely to survive comfortably because a drop in sales primarily affects variable costs. It is often easier to lay off labor than to sell off specialized plants and machines.

Experience Curve

A conceptual framework that many large corporations have used successfully is the experience curve (originally called the learning curve). The **experience curve** suggests that unit production costs decline by some fixed percentage (commonly 20% to 30%) each time the total accumulated volume of production in units doubles. The actual percentage varies by industry and is based on many variables: the amount of time it takes a person to learn a new task, scale economies, product and process improvements, and lower raw materials costs, among others. For example, in an industry with an 85% experience curve, a corporation might expect a 15% reduction in unit costs for every doubling of volume. The total costs per unit can be expected to drop from $100 when the total production is 10 units, to $85 ($100 × 85%) when production increases to 20 units, and to $72.25 ($85 × 85%) when it reaches 40 units. Achieving these results often means investing in R&D and fixed assets; higher fixed costs and less flexibility thus result. Nevertheless the manufacturing strategy is one of building capacity ahead of demand in order to achieve the lower unit costs that develop from the experience curve. On the basis of some future point on the experience curve, the corporation should price the product or service very low to preempt competition and increase market demand. The resulting high number of units sold and high market share should result in high profits, based on the low unit costs.

Management commonly uses the experience curve in estimating the production costs of (1) a product never before made with the present techniques and processes or (2) current products produced by newly introduced techniques or processes. The concept was first applied in the airframe industry and can be applied in the service industry as well. For example, a cleaning company can reduce its costs per employee by having its workers use the same equipment and techniques to clean many adjacent offices in one office building rather than just cleaning a few offices in multiple buildings. Although many firms have used experience curves extensively, an unquestioning acceptance of the industry norm (such as 80% for the airframe industry or 70% for integrated circuits) is very risky. The experience curve of the industry as a whole might not hold true for a particular company for a variety of reasons.

Flexible Manufacturing for Mass Customization

Recently the use of large, continuous, mass-production facilities to take advantage of experience-curve economies has been criticized. The use of Computer-Assisted Design and Computer-Assisted Manufacturing (CAD/CAM) and robot technology means that learning times are shorter and products can be economically manufactured in small, customized batches in a process called **mass customization**—the low-cost production of individually customized goods and services.[27] **Economies of scope** (in which common parts of the manufacturing activities of various products are combined to gain economies even though small numbers of each product are made) replace **economies of scale** (in which unit costs are reduced by making large numbers of the same product) in flexible manufacturing. **Flexible manufacturing** permits the low-volume output of custom-tailored products at relatively low unit costs through economies of scope. It is thus possible to have the cost advantages of continuous systems with the customer-oriented advantages of intermittent systems.

STRATEGIC HUMAN RESOURCE MANAGEMENT (HRM) ISSUES

The primary task of the manager of human resources is to improve the match between individuals and jobs. A good HRM department should know how to use attitude surveys and other feedback devices to assess employees' satisfaction with their jobs and with the corporation as a whole. HRM managers should also use job analysis to obtain job description information about what each job needs to accomplish in terms of quality and quantity. Up-to-date job descriptions are essential not only for proper employee selection, appraisal, training, and development for wage and salary administration, and for labor negotiations, but also for summarizing the corporatewide human resources in terms of employee-skill categories. Just as a company must know the number, type, and quality of its manufacturing facilities, it must also know the kinds of people it employs and the skills they possess. The best strategies are meaningless if employees do not have the skills to carry them out or if jobs cannot be designed to accommodate the available workers. Hewlett-Packard, for example, uses employee profiles to ensure that it has the right mix of talents to implement its planned strategies.

Use of Teams

Management is beginning to realize that it must be more flexible in its utilization of employees in order for human resources to be a strength. Human resource managers, therefore, need to be knowledgeable about work options such as part-time work, job sharing, flex-time, extended leaves, contract work, and especially about the proper use of teams. Over two-thirds of large U.S. companies are successfully using **autonomous (self-managing) work teams** in which a group of people work together without a supervisor to plan, coordinate, and evaluate their own work.[28] Northern Telecom found productivity and quality to increase with work teams to such an extent that it was able to reduce the number of quality inspectors by 40%.[29]

As a way to move a product more quickly through its development stage, companies like Motorola, Chrysler, NCR, Boeing, and General Electric are using **cross-functional work teams**. Instead of developing products in a series of steps—beginning with a request from sales, which leads to design, then to engineering and on to purchasing, and finally to manufacturing (and often resulting in a costly product rejected by the customer)—companies are tearing down the traditional walls separating the departments so that people from each discipline can get involved in projects early on. In a process called **concurrent engineering**, the once-isolated specialists now work side by side and compare notes constantly in an effort to design cost-effective products with features customers want. Taking this approach enabled Chrysler Corporation to reduce its product development cycle from 60 to 36 months.[30] For such cross-functional work teams to be successful, the groups must receive training and coaching.

Otherwise, poorly implemented teams may worsen morale, create divisiveness, and raise the level of cynicism among workers.[31]

Union Relations and Temporary Workers

If the corporation is unionized, a good human resource manager should be able to work closely with the union. Union membership in the United States has dropped to 13.9% overall and to less than 12% of private sector workers in the mid 1990s from more than one-third a few decades earlier.[32] To save jobs, U.S. unions are increasingly willing to support employee involvement programs designed to increase worker participation in decision making.

Outside the United States, the average proportion of unionized workers among major industrialized nations is around 50%. European unions tend to be militant, politically oriented, and much less interested in working with management to increase efficiency. Nationwide strikes can occur quickly. Japanese unions are typically tied to individual companies and are usually supportive of management. These differences among countries have significant implications for the management of multinational corporations.

To increase flexibility, avoid layoffs, and reduce labor costs, corporations are using more temporary workers. From the 1980s to the 1990s, the employment of temporary (also known as contingent) workers in the U.S. increased 250% compared to a 20% increase in overall employment. Ninety percent of U.S. firms use temporary workers in some capacity; 43% now use them in professional and technical functions. Approximately 10% of the U.S. workforce (over 12 million individuals) are now temporary workers.[33] The percentage is even higher in some European countries, such as France. Labor unions are concerned that companies use temps to avoid hiring costlier unionized workers. At United Parcel Service, for example, 80% of the jobs created from 1993 to 1997 were staffed by part-timers, whose pay rates hadn't changed since 1982. Fully 10% of the company's 128,000 part-timers work 30 hours or more per week, but are still paid at a lower rate than are full-time employees.[34] According to John Kinloch, vice-president of Communications Workers of America Local 1058, "Corporations are trying to create a disposable workforce with low wages and no benefits."[35]

Quality of Work Life and Human Diversity

Human resource departments have found that to reduce employee dissatisfaction and unionization efforts (or, conversely, to improve employee satisfaction and existing union relations), they must consider the **quality of work life** in the design of jobs. Partially a reaction to the traditionally heavy emphasis on technical and economic factors in job design, quality of work life emphasizes improving the human dimension of work. The knowledgeable human resource manager, therefore, should be able to improve the corporation's quality of work life by (1) introducing participative problem solving, (2) restructuring work, (3) introducing innovative reward systems, and (4) improving the work environment. It is hoped that these improvements will lead to a more participative corporate culture and thus higher productivity and quality products. Ford Motor Company, for example, is rebuilding and modernizing its famous River Rouge plant using flexible equipment and new processes. Employees will work in teams and use Internet-connected PCs on the shop floor to share their concerns instantly with suppliers or product engineers. Workstations are being redesigned to make them more ergonomic and to reduce repetitive-strain injuries. "If you feel good while you're working, I think quality and productivity will increase, and Ford thinks that too, otherwise, they wouldn't do this," observed Jerry Sullivan, President of United Auto Worker Local 600.[36]

Human diversity refers to the mix in the workplace of people from different races, cultures, and backgrounds. This is a hot issue in HRM. Realizing that the demographics are changing toward an increasing percentage of minorities and women in the U.S. workforce, companies are now concerned with hiring and promoting people without regard to ethnic background. According to a study reported by *Fortune* magazine, companies that pursue diversity outperform the S&P 500.[37] Good human resource managers should be working to ensure that people are treated fairly on the job and not harassed by prejudiced coworkers or managers. Otherwise, they may find themselves subject to lawsuits. Coca-Cola Company, for example, agreed to pay $192.5 million because of discrimination against African American salaried employees in pay, promotions, and evaluations from 1995 and 2000. According to Chairman and CEO Douglas Daft, "Sometimes things happen in an unintentional manner. And I've made it clear that can't happen anymore."[38]

An organization's human resources are especially important in today's world of global communication and transportation systems. For example, on a visit to China during Spring 2000, one of Coca-Cola Company's executives was challenged by Chinese reporters regarding the company's racial problems. Advances in technology are copied almost immediately by competitors around the world. People are not as willing to move to other companies in other countries. This means that the only long-term resource advantage remaining to corporations operating in the industrialized nations may lie in the area of skilled human resources. Research does reveal that competitive strategies are more successfully executed in those companies with a high level of commitment to their employees than in those firms with less commitment.[39]

STRATEGIC INFORMATION SYSTEMS/TECHNOLOGY ISSUES

The primary task of the manager of information systems/technology is to design and manage the flow of information in an organization in ways that improve productivity and decision making. Information must be collected, stored, and synthesized in such a manner that it will answer important operating and strategic questions. The growth of the global Internet economy is forcing corporations to make significant investments in this functional area. (See the **Internet Issue** feature.) Corporate investments in information systems/technology are growing 11% annually even though 70% of all investments are either not completed or exceed cost projections by nearly 200%.[40]

Internet Issue

The Growing Global Internet Economy

Electronic commerce is poised to grow rapidly throughout the world to a total of $6.9 trillion in Internet sales by 2004. According to a report by Forrester Research entitled, *Global eCommerce Approaches Hypergrowth*, Internet sales in the United States should increase to $3.2 trillion by 2004 and account for 46.4% of the global Internet economy. The Asia-Pacific region should grow to $1.6 trillion in sales and account for 23.2% of the total Internet sales. Western Europe should reach $1.5 trillion in sales (21.7% of the total) by 2004. After a slow start, Latin America's Internet sales should total $82.9 billion and account for 1.2% of total world Internet sales. Technologically, Latin America lags behind North America and Western Europe, but is being pushed by trading partners who are sophisticated Internet users to invest in crucial technology infrastructure such as phone lines, computers, Internet hosts, and cell phones. With Brazil and Argentina leading the way in liberalizing trade, the economic climate is rapidly improving. By 2004, Brazil should generate $64 billion on its own in online sales. Eastern Europe, Africa, and the Middle East are still facing the same problems that Latin America is now overcoming and will account for only $68.6 billion in sales, a mere 0.9% of the total world sales. The rest of the world's Internet sales will total $450 billion for the remaining 6.6% of total world sales.

Source: "Hypergrowth for E-Commerce?" *The Futurist* (September–October 2000), p. 15.

A corporation's information system can be a strength or a weakness in all elements of strategic management. It can not only aid in environmental scanning and in controlling a company's many activities, it can also be used as a strategic weapon in gaining competitive advantage. For example, American Hospital Supply (AHS), a leading manufacturer and distributor of a broad line of products for doctors, laboratories, and hospitals, developed an order entry distribution system that directly linked the majority of its customers to AHS computers. The system was successful because it simplified ordering processes for customers, reduced costs for both AHS and the customer, and allowed AHS to provide pricing incentives to the customer. As a result, customer loyalty was high and AHS's share of the market became large.

Information systems/technology offers four main contributions to corporate performance. *First* (beginning in the 1970s with main frame computers), it is used to automate existing back-office processes, such as payroll, human resource records, accounts payable and receivable, and to establish huge databases. *Second* (beginning in the 1980s), it is used to automate individual tasks, such as keeping track of clients and expenses, through the use of personal computers with word processing and spreadsheet software. Corporate databases are accessed to provide sufficient data to analyze the data and create what-if scenarios. These first two contributions tend to focus on reducing costs. *Third* (beginning in the 1990s), it is used to enhance key business functions, such as marketing and operations. This third contribution focuses on productivity improvements. The system provides customer support and help in distribution and logistics. For example, FedEx found that by allowing customers to directly access its package-tracking database via its Internet Web site instead of their having to ask a human operator, the company saved up to $2 million annually.[41] Business processes are analyzed to increase efficiency and productivity via reengineering. Enterprise resource planning application software, by firms such as SAP, PeopleSoft, Oracle, Baan, and J.D. Edwards, are used to integrate worldwide business activities so that employees need to enter information only once and that information is available to all corporate systems (including accounting) around the world. *Fourth* (beginning in 2000), it is used to develop competitive advantage. The focus is now on taking advantage of opportunities via supply chain management, electronic commerce, and knowledge management. Currently, most companies devote 85% of their IS/IT budget to the first two utility functions, 12% to productivity enhancement, and only 3% to efforts to gain competitive advantage.[42]

A current trend in corporate information systems is the increasing use of the Internet for marketing, intranets for internal communication, and extranets for logistics and distribution. An **intranet** is an information network within an organization that also has access to the external worldwide Internet. Intranets typically begin as ways to provide employees with company information such as lists of product prices, fringe benefits, and company policies. They are then converted into extranets for supply chain management. An **extranet** is an information network within an organization that is available to key suppliers and customers. The key issue in building an extranet is the creation of "fire walls" to block extranet users from accessing the firm's or other users' confidential data. Once this is accomplished, companies can allow employees, customers, and suppliers to access information and conduct business on the Internet in a completely automated manner. By connecting these groups, companies hope to obtain a competitive advantage by reducing the time needed to design and bring new products to market, slashing inventories, customizing manufacturing, and entering new markets.[43]

4.4 The Strategic Audit: A Checklist for Organizational Analysis

One way of conducting an organizational analysis to ascertain a company's strengths and weaknesses is by using the Strategic Audit found in **Appendix 10.A of Chapter 10**. The audit provides a checklist of questions by area of concern. For example, Part IV of the audit examines corporate structure, culture, and resources. It looks at resources in terms of the functional areas of marketing, finance, R&D, operations, human resources, and information systems, among others.

4.5 Synthesis of Internal Factors: IFAS

After strategists have scanned the internal organizational environment and identified factors for their particular corporation, they may want to summarize their analysis of these factors using a form such as that given in **Table 4–2**. This **IFAS** (**I**nternal **F**actor **A**nalysis **S**ummary) **Table** is one way to organize the internal factors into the generally accepted categories of strengths and weaknesses as well as to analyze how well a particular company's management is responding to these specific factors in light of the perceived importance of these factors to the company. Use the VRIO framework (**V**alue, **R**areness, **I**mitability, and **O**rganization) to assess the importance of each of the factors that might be considered strengths. Except for its internal orientation, this IFAS Table is built the same way as the EFAS Table described in **Chapter 3** (in **Table 3–4**). To use the IFAS Table, complete the following steps:

- In **Column 1** (Internal Factors), list the 8 to 10 most important strengths and weaknesses facing the company.

- In **Column 2** (Weight), assign a weight to each factor from **1.0** (Most Important) to **0.0** (Not Important) based on that factor's probable impact on a particular company's current strategic position. The higher the weight, the more important is this factor to the current and future success of the company. All weights must sum to 1.0 regardless of the number of factors.

- In **Column 3** (Rating), assign a rating to each factor from **5.0** (Outstanding) to **1.0** (Poor) based on management's current response to that particular factor. Each rating is a judgment regarding how well the company's management is currently dealing with each internal factor.

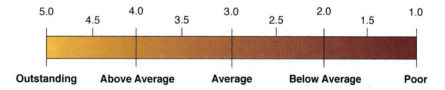

- In **Column 4** (Weighted Score), multiply the weight in **Column 2** for each factor times its rating in **Column 3** to obtain each factor's weighted score. This results in a weighted score for each factor ranging from **5.0** (Outstanding) to **1.0** (Poor) with **3.0** as Average.

- In **Column 5** (Comments), note why a particular factor was selected and/or how its weight and rating were estimated.

Finally, add the individual weighted scores for all the internal factors in **Column 4** to determine the total weighted score for that particular company. The **total weighted score** indicates how well a particular company is responding to current and expected factors in its internal environment. The score can be used to compare that firm to other firms in its industry. The total weighted score for an average firm in an industry is always 3.0.

As an example of this procedure, **Table 4–2** includes a number of internal factors for Maytag Corporation in 1995 (before Maytag sold its European and Australian operations) with corresponding weights, ratings, and weighted scores provided. Note that Maytag's total weighted score was 3.05, meaning that the corporation was about average compared to the strengths and weaknesses of others in the major home appliance industry at that time.

Table 4–2 **Internal Factor Analysis Summary (IFAS Table): Maytag as Example**

Internal Factors	Weight	Rating	Weighted Score	Comments
	1	2	3	4	5
Strengths				
• Quality Maytag culture	.15	5.0	.75	Quality key to success
• Experienced top management	.05	4.2	.21	Know appliances
• Vertical integration	.10	3.9	.39	Dedicated factories
• Employee relations	.05	3.0	.15	Good, but deteriorating
• Hoover's international orientation	.15	2.8	.42	Hoover name in cleaners
Weaknesses				
• Process-oriented R&D	.05	2.2	.11	Slow on new products
• Distribution channels	.05	2.0	.10	Superstores replacing small dealers
• Financial position	.15	2.0	.30	High debt load
• Global positioning	.20	2.1	.42	Hoover weak outside the United Kingdom and Australia
• Manufacturing facilities	.05	4.0	.20	Investing now
Total Scores	1.00		3.05	

Notes:
1. List strengths and weaknesses (8–10) in Column 1.
2. Weight each factor from 1.0 (Most Important) to 0.0 (Not Important) in Column 2 based on that factor's probable impact on the company's strategic position. **The total weights must sum to 1.00.**
3. Rate each factor from 5.0 (Outstanding) to 1.0 (Poor) in Column 3 based on the company's response to that factor.
4. Multiply each factor's weight times its rating to obtain each factor's weighted score in Column 4.
5. Use Column 5 (comments) for rationale used for each factor.
6. Add the individual weighted scores to obtain the total weighted score for the company in Column 4. This tells how well the company is responding to the strategic factors in its internal environment.

Source: T. L. Wheelen and J. D. Hunger, "Internal Factor Analysis Summary (IFAS)." Copyright © 1991 by Wheelen and Hunger Associates. Reprinted by permission.

4.6 Impact of the Internet on Internal Scanning and Organizational Analysis

The expansion of the marketing-oriented Internet into intranets and extranets is making significant contributions to organizational performance through supply chain management and virtual teams. **Supply chain management** is the forming of networks for sourcing raw materials, manufacturing products or creating services, storing and distributing the goods, and delivering them to customers and consumers.[44] Industry leaders are integrating modern information systems into their corporate value chains to harmonize companywide efforts and to achieve competitive advantage. For example, Heineken Beer distributors input actual depletion figures and replenishment orders to the Netherlands brewer through their linked Web pages. This interactive planning system generates time-phased orders based on actual usage rather than on projected demand. Distributors are then able to modify plans based on local conditions or changes in marketing. Heineken uses these modifications to adjust brewing and supply schedules. As a result of this system, lead times have been reduced from the traditional 10 to 12 weeks to 4 to 6 weeks. This time savings is especially useful in an industry competing on product freshness. In another example, Procter & Gamble participates in an information network to move the company's line of consumer products through Wal-Mart's many stores. As part of the network with Wal-Mart, P&G

knows by cash register and by store what products have passed through the system each day. The network is linked by satellite communications on a real-time basis. With actual point-of-sale information, products are replenished to meet current demand and minimize stockouts while maintaining exceptionally low inventories.[45]

Virtual teams are groups of geographically and/or organizationally dispersed coworkers that are assembled using a combination of telecommunications and information technologies to accomplish an organizational task.[46] Internet, intranet, and extranet systems are combining with other new technologies such as desktop videoconferencing and collaborative software to create a new workplace in which teams of workers are no longer restrained by geography, time, or organizational boundaries. As more companies outsource some of the activities previously conducted internally, the traditional organizational structure is being replaced by a series of virtual teams, which rarely, if ever, meet face-to-face. Such teams may be established as temporary groups to accomplish a specific task or may be more permanent to address continuing issues such as strategic planning. Membership on these teams is often fluid, depending upon the task to be accomplished. They may include not only employees from different functions within a company, but also members of various stakeholder groups, such as suppliers, customers, and law or consulting firms. The use of virtual teams to replace traditional face-to-face work groups is being driven by five trends:

1. Flatter organizational structures with increasing cross-functional coordination needs

2. Turbulent environments requiring more interorganizational cooperation

3. Increasing employee autonomy and participation in decision making

4. Higher knowledge requirements derived from a greater emphasis on service

5. Increasing globalization of trade and corporate activity[47]

Projections for the 21st Century

- From 1994 to 2010, the average income per capita in the developed nations will rise from $16,610 to $22,802.

- From 1994 to 2010, the average income per capita in the developing nations will increase from $950 to $2,563.[48]

Discussion Questions

1. What is the relevance of the resource-based view of the firm to strategic management in a global environment?

2. How can value-chain analysis help identify a company's strengths and weaknesses?

3. In what ways can a corporation's structure and culture be internal strengths or weaknesses?

4. What are the pros and cons of management's using the experience curve to determine strategy?

5. How might a firm's management decide whether it should continue to invest in current known technology or in new, but untested technology? What factors might encourage or discourage such a shift?

Strategic Practice Exercise

Can you analyze a corporation using the Internet? Try the following exercise.

1. Form teams of around five people. Find the Internet 100 Index from the latest copy of *USA Today*. (**Check this publisher's Web site for a recent listing of the** **Internet 100.**) The index is divided into the e-Commerce 50 and the e-Business 50. The e-Commerce 50 is composed of four subindustries: e-Retail, e-Finance, e-New Media, and e-Service Providers. The e-Business 50 is composed of three

subindustries: e-Infrastructure, e-Services/Solutions, and e-Advertising.

2. Each team selects four companies plus one assigned by the instructor. (The list of companies from which assignments will be made is Amazon.com, E-loan, Cisco Systems, AOL, Yahoo!, and DoubleClick.) Provide the instructor with your list.

3. Conduct research on each of your five companies *using the Internet only.*

4. Write a three to six page double-spaced typed report for each of the five companies. The report should include the following:

   a. Does the firm have any core competencies? Are any of these distinctive (better than the competition)

competencies? Does the firm have any competitive advantage? Provide a SWOT analysis using EFAS and IFAS Tables.

   b. What is the likely future of this firm? Will the company survive industry consolidation?

   c. Would you buy stock in this company? Assume that your team has $25,000 to invest. Allocate the money among your five companies. Be specific. List the five companies, the number of shares purchased of each, the cost of each share as of a given date, and the total cost for each purchase assuming a typical commission used by an Internet broker, such as E-Trade. (This part of your report will be common to all members of your team.)

Key Terms

autonomous (self-managing) work teams (p. 97)
basic R&D (p. 93)
capital budgeting (p. 92)
center of gravity (p. 85)
concurrent engineering (p. 97)
conglomerate structure (p. 88)
continuous systems (p. 96)
continuum of sustainability (p. 83)
core competencies (p. 82)
corporate capabilities (p. 82)
cross-functional work teams (p. 97)
corporate culture (p. 89)
cultural integration (p. 89)
cultural intensity (p. 89)
distinctive competencies (p. 82)
divisional structure (p. 87)
durability (p. 82)
economies of scale (p. 97)
economies of scope (p. 87)
engineering (or process) R&D (p. 93)
experience curve (p. 96)

explicit knowledge (p. 83)
extranet (p. 100)
financial leverage (p. 92)
flexible manufacturing (p. 97)
functional structure (p. 87)
human diversity (p. 98)
IFAS Table (p. 101)
imitability (p. 82)
intermittent systems (p. 95)
internal strategic factors (p. 81)
intranet (p. 100)
linkages (p. 86)
market position (p. 90)
market segmentation (p. 90)
marketing mix (p. 90)
mass customization (p. 97)
operating leverage (p. 96)
organizational analysis (p. 81)
organizational structures (p. 87)
primary activities (p. 85)
product life cycle (p. 90)
product R&D (p. 93)

quality of work life (p. 98)
R&D intensity (p. 92)
R&D mix (p. 93)
replicability (p. 83)
resource (p. 81)
reverse engineering (p. 82)
simple structure (p. 87)
strategic business units (SBUs) (p. 87)
support activities (p. 86)
supply chain management (p. 102)
tacit knowledge (p. 83)
technological competence (p. 92)
technological discontinuity (p. 94)
technology transfer (p. 93)
transferability (p. 82)
transparency (p. 82)
value chain (p. 84)
VRIO framework (p. 81)
virtual teams (p. 103)

Notes

1. M. Babineck, "United Airlines Increases Fares; Others Follow," *Des Moines Register* (November 18, 2000), p. 6D.
2. R. Roach & Associates, cited in *Air Transport World* (June 1996), p. 1.
3. J. B. Barney, *Gaining and Sustaining Competitive Advantage* (Reading, MA: Addison-Wesley, 1997), pp. 145–164.
4. R. M. Grant, "The Resource-Based Theory of Competitive Advantage: Implications for Strategy Formulation," *California Management Review* (Spring 1991), pp. 114–135.
5. M. Brellis, "Simple Strategy Makes Southwest Successful," (Ames) *Daily Tribune* (November 9, 2000), p. B7.
6. J. E. McGee and L. G. Love, "Sources of Competitive Advantage for Small Independent Retailers: Lessons from the Neighborhood Drugstore," *Association for Small Business & Entrepreneurship*, Houston, Texas (March 10–13, 1999), p. 2.
7. M. Polanyi, *The Tacit Dimension* (London: Routledge & Kegan Paul, 1966).

8. P. E. Bierly III, "Development of a Generic Knowledge Strategy Typology," *Journal of Business Strategies* (Spring 1999), p. 3.

9. O. Gadiesh and J. L. Gilbert, "Profit Pools: A Fresh Look at Strategy," *Harvard Business Review* (May–June, 1998), pp. 139–147.

10. J. R. Galbraith, "Strategy and Organization Planning," in *The Strategy Process: Concepts, Contexts, and Cases*, 2nd ed., edited by H. Mintzberg and J. B. Quinn (Upper Saddle River, NJ: Prentice Hall, 1991), pp. 315–324.

11. M. Porter, *Competitive Advantage: Creating and Sustaining Superior Performance* (New York: The Free Press, 1985), p. 36.

12. M. Leontiades, "A Diagnostic Framework for Planning," *Strategic Management Journal* (January–March 1983), p. 14.

13. E. H. Schein, *The Corporate Culture Survival Guide* (San Francisco: Jossey-Bass, 1999), p. 12; L. C. Harris and E. Ogbonna, "The Strategic Legacy of Company Founders," *Long Range Planning* (June 1999), pp. 333–343.

14. D. M. Rousseau, "Assessing Organizational Culture: The Case for Multiple Methods," in *Organizational Climate and Culture*, edited by B. Schneider (San Francisco: Jossey-Bass, 1990), pp. 153–192.

15. L. Smircich, "Concepts of Culture and Organizational Analysis," *Administrative Science Quarterly* (September 1983), pp. 345–346.

16. K. E. Aupperle, "Spontaneous Organizational Reconfiguration: A Historical Example Based on Xenophon's Anabasis," *Organization Science* (July–August 1996), pp. 445–460.

17. Barney, p. 155.

18. R. L. Simerly and M. Li, "Environmental Dynamism, Capital Structure and Performance: A Theoretical Integration and an Empirical Test," *Strategic Management Journal* (January 2000), pp. 31–49.

19. R. L. Simerly and M. Li, "Environmental Dynamism, Capital Structure and Performance: A Theoretical Integration and an Empirical Test," *Strategic Management Journal* (January 2000), pp. 31–49.

20. J. M. Poterba and L. H. Summers, "A CEO Survey of U.S. Companies' Time Horizons and Hurdle Rates," *Sloan Management Review* (Fall 1995), pp. 43–53.

21. "R&D Scoreboard," *Business Week* (June 27, 1994), pp. 81–103.

22. B. O'Reilly, "The Secrets of America's Most Admired Corporations: New Ideas and New Products," *Fortune* (March 3, 1997), p. 62.

23. P. Pascarella, "Are You Investing in the Wrong Technology?" *Industry Week* (July 25, 1983), p. 37.

24. D. J. Yang, "Leaving Moore's Law in the Dust," *U.S. News & World Report* (July 10, 2000), pp. 37–38; R. Fishburne and M. Malone, "Laying Down the Laws: Gordon Moore and Bob Metcalfe in Conversation," *Forbes ASAP* (February 21, 2000), pp. 97–100.

25. Pascarella., p. 38.

26. C. M. Christensen, *The Innovator's Dilemma* (Boston: Harvard Business School Press, 1997).

27. B. J. Pine, *Mass Customization: The New Frontier in Business Competition* (Boston: Harvard Business School Press, 1993).

28. E. E. Lawler, S. A. Mohrman, and G. E. Ledford, Jr., *Creating High Performance Organizations* (San Francisco: Jossey-Bass, 1995), p. 29.

29. A. Versteeg, "Self-Directed Work Teams Yield Long-Term Benefits," *Journal of Business Strategy* (November/December 1990), pp. 9–12.

30. R. Sanchez, "Strategic Flexibility in Product Competition," *Strategic Management Journal* (Summer 1995), p. 147.

31. A. R. Jassawalla and H. C. Sashittal, "Building Collaborative Cross-Functional New Product Teams," *Academy of Management Executive* (August 1999), pp. 50–63.

32. E. E. Lawler, S. A. Mohrman, and G. E. Ledford, Jr., *Creating High Performance Organizations* (San Francisco: Jossey-Bass, 1995), p. 123. The percentage of unionized government employees is 38.7%. See "Uncle Sam Gompers," *Wall Street Journal* (October 25, 1994), p. A20.

33. S. F. Matusik and C. W. L. Hill, "The Utilization of Contingent Work, Knowledge Creation, and Competitive Advantage," *Academy of Management Executive* (October 1998), pp. 680–697.

34. A. Bewrnstein, "At UPS, Part-Time Work Is a Full-Time Issue," *Business Week* (June 16, 1997), pp. 88–90.

35. D. L. Boroughs, "The New Migrant Workers," *U.S. News & World Report* (July 4, 1994), p. 53.

36. J. Muller, "A Ford Redesign," *Business Week* (November 13, 2000), Special Report.

37. G. Colvin, "The 50 Best Companies for Asians, Blacks, and Hispanics," *Fortune* (July 19, 1999), pp. 53–58.

38. J. Bachman, "Coke to Pay $192.5 Million to Settle Lawsuit," *The* (Ames) *Tribune* (November 20, 2000), p. D4.

39. J. Lee and D. Miller, "People Matter: Commitment to Employees, Strategy, and Performance in Korean Firms," *Strategic Management Journal* (June 1999), pp. 579–593.

40. B. Rosser, "Making IT Investments Cost Effective," *Executive Edge* (September 1998), pp. 50–54.

41. A. Cortese, "Here Comes the Intranet," *Business Week* (February 26, 1996), p. 76.

42. B. Rosser, "Making IT Investments Cost Effective," *Executive Edge* (September 1998), pp. 50–54.

43. D. Bartholomew, "Blue-Collar Computing," *InformationWeek* (June 19, 1995), pp. 34–43.

44. C. C. Poirier, *Advanced Supply Chain Management* (San Francisco: Berrett-Koehler Publishers, 1999), p. 2.

45. C. C. Poirer, pp. 3–5.

46. A. M. Townsend, S. M. DeMarie, and A. R. Hendrickson, "Virtual Teams" Technology and the Workplace of the Future," *Academy of Management Executive* (August 1998), pp. 17–29.

47. Townsend, DeMarie, and Hendrickson, p. 18.

48. J. Warner, "21st Century Capitalism: Snapshot of the Next Century," *Business Week* (November 18, 1994), p. 194.

Newbury Comics, Inc.

ENVIRONMENTAL SCANNING AND ORGANIZATIONAL ANALYSIS

Newbury Comics Cofounders, Mike Dreese and John Brusger, parlayed $2,000 and a comic book collection into a thriving chain of 22 stores spanning the New England region. Known to be *the* place to shop for everything from the best of the underground/independent scene to major label superstars, the chain also stocks a wide variety of non-music related items such as T-shirts, Dr. (doc) Martens shoes, posters, jewelry, cosmetics, books, magazines, and other trendy items.

In Part Two, "**Scanning the Environment**," the video case addresses the identification of external environmental variables, industry analysis, and organizational analysis. Newbury Comics, Inc., Cofounders Mike and John, and Jan Johannet, Store Manager for one of the New Hampshire stores, reveal more about the development of the company. They discuss factors contributing to the successful growth of Newbury Comics. They describe how their diverse customers plus the emergence of bootlegging (selling illegal copies) and burning discs (copying 1 CD onto another CD) led the company to begin offering used CDs in its stores.

Used CDs have become a very important business for Newbury Comics. Mike Dreese reports that used CDs account for $6 to 7 million in annual sales and $4 million in annual gross profits for the company. This fact is remarkable given that the firm's overall annual sales and pre-tax profits are $75 million and $8 million, respectively. According to John Brusger and Jan Johannet, the new CD market turned "soft" when the mass merchandisers like Target and Best Buy began offering CDs and Internet companies, such as Napster, offered the downloading of music. John and Mike wanted another product to supplement their sales of new CDs. They scanned their environment to learn if it made sense to enter this business.

They asked the owners of local specialty music stores for information. These "mom and pop" retailers had been buying and selling used CDs for years and were very familiar with this product. Mike refers to the local mom and pop retailers as his "strategic alliance of information sources." According to John, surveys of current customers revealed that a large number of Newbury Comics customers wanted the company to be in the used CD business. Management analyzed the competition for used CDs in Newbury Comics' market area. Used CDs appeared to have high sales potential. The immediate competition was composed of mom and pop specialty music retailers; no chain stores offered used CDs at that time. According to Mike Dreese, the local stores weren't doing a good job of marketing used CDs.

According to Mike and Jan, Newbury Comics has several internal strengths which uniquely fit the used CD market. The stores have a wide variety of customers and a staff with "knowledge of the street." The employees live the lifestyle of Newbury Comics' discriminating customers and are thus able to identify trends before the public at large learns of them. Consequently, the stores are able to purchase an excellent selection of underground music in addition to the usual top 50 and older CDs. Mike Dreese states that new entrant specialist shops into the used CD business are "not a threat to us." He is concerned that established chains such as Tower Records, Best Buy, and Music Land might someday enter the used CD business.

Concepts Illustrated in the Video

- Environmental Scanning
- Industry Analysis
- Organizational Analysis
- Identifying Societal Trends
- Rivalry Among Existing Firms

- Threat of New Entrants/Entry Barriers
- Threat of Substitute Products
- Industry Evolution
- Core and Distinctive Competencies
- Corporate Culture

Study Questions

1. How does Newbury Comics conduct environmental scanning? How well is it doing it?
2. Describe the competitors in Newbury Comics's market area. Do they form strategic groups? How do the actions of competitors affect Newbury Comics (and vice versa)?
3. What are the substitutes for CDs? Are they a threat or an opportunity for Newbury Comics?
4. What external factors played a role in the decision to enter the used CD business? What other businesses should the company consider entering?
5. What are the core competencies of Newbury Comics? Are they distinctive? Why?

chapter 5

PART THREE
Strategy Formulation

Strategy Formulation: Situation Analysis and Business Strategy

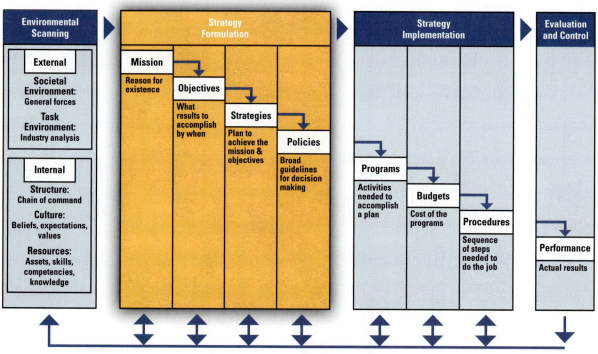

Environmental Scanning	Strategy Formulation				Strategy Implementation			Evaluation and Control

Environmental Scanning:
- **External**
  - **Societal Environment:** General forces
  - **Task Environment:** Industry analysis
- **Internal**
  - **Structure:** Chain of command
  - **Culture:** Beliefs, expectations, values
  - **Resources:** Assets, skills, competencies, knowledge

Strategy Formulation:
- **Mission** — Reason for existence
- **Objectives** — What results to accomplish by when
- **Strategies** — Plan to achieve the mission & objectives
- **Policies** — Broad guidelines for decision making

Strategy Implementation:
- **Programs** — Activities needed to accomplish a plan
- **Budgets** — Cost of the programs
- **Procedures** — Sequence of steps needed to do the job

Evaluation and Control:
- **Performance** — Actual results

Feedback/Learning

W hen Donald Lamberti incorporated Casey's General Stores in 1967 in Des Moines, Iowa, he formulated a strategy unknown at that time in the convenience store industry. Instead of targeting the large, growing metropolitan areas of the eastern, western, and southern United States where potential sales were high, he chose to focus on the small towns in the agricultural heartland of the Midwest. Contrary to all the conventional wisdom arguing against beginning a business in a declining market, Lamberti avoided direct competition with 7-Eleven and moved into these increasingly ignored small markets. The company expanded its offerings from just gasoline and basic groceries to include fast food and bakeries. In many small Midwestern towns, Casey's was now the only retail business left. These were towns too small for even Wal-Mart to covet. Like any convenience store, prices were somewhat higher than in larger, more specialized stores in the cities. But people from small towns did not want to have to drive 10 to 20 miles for a loaf of bread or a pizza.

By 2001, Casey's had opened over 1,100 stores in the upper midwestern United States. At a time when other convenience stores were struggling to show a profit and avoid bankruptcy, Casey's recorded continuing growth and profitability. (For further information, see <www.caseys.com>.)

Casey's General Stores is successful because its strategic managers formulated a new strategy designed to give it an advantage in a very competitive industry. Casey's is an example of a differentiation focus competitive strategy in which a company focuses on a particular market area to provide a differentiated product or service. This strategy is one of the business competitive strategies discussed in this chapter.

5.1 Situational Analysis: SWOT Analysis

Strategy formulation is often referred to as strategic planning or long-range planning and is concerned with developing a corporation's mission, objectives, strategies, and policies. It begins with situation analysis: the process of finding a strategic fit between external opportunities and internal strengths while working around external threats and internal weaknesses. As shown in the *Strategic Decision-Making Process* in **Figure 1–5** on pages 20–21, this is step 5(a): analyzing strategic factors in light of the current situation using SWOT analysis. **SWOT** is an acronym used to describe the particular **S**trengths, **W**eaknesses, **O**pportunities, and **T**hreats that are strategic factors for a specific company. SWOT analysis should not only result in the identification of a corporation's **distinctive competencies**—the particular capabilities and resources that a firm possesses and the superior way in which they are used—but also in the identification of opportunities that the firm is not currently able to take advantage of due to a lack of appropriate resources. Over the years, SWOT analysis has proven to be the most enduring analytical technique used in strategic management. For example, a survey of 113 manufacturing and service companies in the United Kingdom reported the five most-used tools and techniques in strategic analysis to be (1) spreadsheet "what if" analysis, (2) analysis of key or critical success factors, (3) financial analysis of competitors, (4) SWOT analysis, and (5) core capabilities analysis.[1] It is very likely that these have a similar rate of usage in the rest of the world.

It can be said that the essence of strategy is opportunity divided by capacity.[2] An opportunity by itself has no real value unless a company has the capacity (i.e., resources) to take advantage of that opportunity. This approach, however, considers only opportunities and strengths when considering alternative strategies. By itself, a distinctive competency in a key resource or capability is no guarantee of competitive advantage. Weaknesses in other resource areas can prevent a strategy from being successful. SWOT can thus be used to take a broader view of strategy through the formula SA = O/(S − W) (Strategic Alternative equals Opportunity divided by Strengths minus Weaknesses). This reflects an important issue facing strategic managers: *Should we invest more in our strengths to make them even stronger (a distinctive competence), or should we invest in our weaknesses to at least make them competitive?*

SWOT analysis, by itself, is not a panacea. Some of the primary **criticisms of SWOT** analysis are:

- It generates lengthy lists.
- It uses no weights to reflect priorities.
- It uses ambiguous words and phrases.
- The same factor can be placed in two categories (e.g., a strength may also be a weakness).
- There is no obligation to verify opinions with data or analysis.
- It requires only a single level of analysis.
- There is no logical link to strategy implementation.[3]

Table 4–2 Internal Factor Analysis Summary (IFAS): Maytag as Example (Selection of Strategic Factors)*

Internal Strategic Factors	Weight	Rating	Weighted Score	Comments
	1	2	3	4	5
Strengths				
S1 Quality Maytag culture	.15	5.0	.75	Quality key to success
S2 Experienced top management	.05	4.2	.21	Know appliances
S3 Vertical integration	.10	3.9	.39	Dedicated factories
S4 Employee relations	.05	3.0	.15	Good, but deteriorating
S5 Hoover's international orientation	.15	2.8	.42	Hoover name in cleaners
Weaknesses				
W1 Process-oriented R&D	.05	2.2	.11	Slow on new products
W2 Distribution channels	.05	2.0	.10	Superstores replacing small dealers
W3 Financial position	.15	2.0	.30	High debt load
W4 Global positioning	.20	2.1	.42	Hoover weak outside the United Kingdom and Australia
W5 Manufacturing facilities	.05	4.0	.20	Investing now
Total Scores	1.00		3.05	

Table 3–4 External Factor Analysis Summary (EFAS): Maytag as Example (Selection of Strategic Factors)*

External Strategic Factors	Weight	Rating	Weighted Score	Comments
	1	2	3	4	5
Opportunities				
O1 Economic integration of European Community	.20	4.1	.82	Acquisition of Hoover
O2 Demographics favor quality appliances	.10	5.0	.50	Maytag quality
O3 Economic development of Asia	.05	1.0	.05	Low Maytag presence
O4 Opening of Eastern Europe	.05	2.0	.10	Will take time
O5 Trend to "Super Stores"	.10	1.8	.18	Maytag weak in this channel
Threats				
T1 Increasing government regulations	.10	4.3	.43	Well positioned
T2 Strong U.S. competition	.10	4.0	.40	Well positioned
T3 Whirlpool and Electrolux strong globally	.15	3.0	.45	Hoover weak globally
T4 New product advances	.05	1.2	.06	Questionable
T5 Japanese appliance companies	.10	1.6	.16	Only Asian presence is Australia
Total Scores	1.00		3.15	

*The most important external and internal factors are identified in the EFAS and IFAS tables as shown here by shading these factors.

GENERATING A STRATEGIC FACTORS ANALYSIS SUMMARY (SFAS) MATRIX

The EFAS and IFAS Tables plus the SFAS Matrix have been developed to deal with the above criticisms of SWOT analysis. When used together, they are a powerful set of analytical tools for strategic analysis. The **SFAS (Strategic Factors Analysis Summary) Matrix** summarizes an organization's strategic factors by combining the external factors from the EFAS Table with the

Figure 5–1

Strategic Factor Analysis Summary (SFAS) Matrix

	1	2	3	4	Duration 5			6
Strategic Factors (Select the most important opportunities/threats from EFAS, Table 3–4 and the most important strengths and weaknesses from IFAS, Table 4–2)	**Weight**	**Rating**	**Weighted Score**	**S H O R T**	**I N T E R M E D I A T E**	**L O N G**	**Comments**
S1 Quality Maytag culture (S)	.10	5.0	.50			X	Quality key to success
S5 Hoover's international orientation (S)	.10	2.8	.28	X	X		Name recognition
W3 Financial position (W)	.10	2.0	.20	X	X		High debt
W4 Global positioning (W)	.15	2.2	.33			X	Only in N.A., U.K., and Australia
01 Economic integration of European Community (O)	.10	4.1	.41			X	Acquisition of Hoover
02 Demographics favor quality (O)	.10	5.0	.50		X		Maytag quality
05 Trend to super stores (O + T)	.10	1.8	.18	X			Weak in this channel
T3 Whirlpool and Electrolux (T)	.15	3.0	.45	X			Dominate industry
T5 Japanese appliance companies (T)	.10	1.6	.16			X	Asian presence
Total Scores	**1.00**		**3.01**				

Notes:
1. List each of the most important factors developed in your IFAS and EFAS tables in Column 1.
2. Weight each factor from 1.0 (Most Important) to 0.0 (Not Important) in Column 2 based on that factor's probable impact on the company's strategic position. **The total weights must sum to 1.00.**
3. Rate each factor from 5.0 (Outstanding) to 1.0 (Poor) in Column 3 based on the company's response to that factor.
4. Multiply each factor's weight times its rating to obtain each factor's weighted score in Column 4.
5. For duration in Column 5, check appropriate column (short term—less than 1 year; intermediate—1 to 3 years; long term—over 3 years).
6. Use Column 6 (comments) for rationale used for each factor.

Source: T. L. Wheelen and J. D. Hunger, "Strategic Factors Analysis Summary (SFAS)." Copyright © 1997 by Wheelen and Hunger Associates. Reprinted by permission.

internal factors from the IFAS Table. The EFAS and IFAS examples given of Maytag Corporation (as it was in 1995) in **Tables 3–4** and **4–2** list a total of 20 internal and external factors. These are too many factors for most people to use in strategy formulation. The SFAS Matrix requires the strategic decision maker to condense these strengths, weaknesses, opportunities, and threats into fewer than 10 strategic factors. This is done by reviewing and revising the weight given each factor. The revised weights reflect the priority of each factor as a determinant of the company's future success. The highest weighted EFAS and IFAS factors should appear in the SFAS Matrix.

As shown in **Figure 5–1**, you can create an SFAS Matrix by following these steps:

- In the **Strategic Factors** column (column 1), list the most important (in terms of weight) EFAS and IFAS items. After each factor, indicate whether it is a strength (S), weakness (W), opportunity (O), threat (T), or a combination.

- In the **Weight** column (column 2), enter the weights for all of the internal and external strategic factors. As with the EFAS and IFAS Tables, the **weight column must still total 1.00.** This means that the weights calculated for EFAS and IFAS will probably have to be adjusted.

- In the **Rating** column (column 3), enter the ratings of how the company's management is responding to each of the strategic factors. These ratings will probably (but not always) be the same as those listed in the EFAS and IFAS Tables.

- In the **Weighted Score** column (column 4), calculate the weighted scores as done earlier for EFAS and IFAS.

- In the new **Duration** column (column 5), depicted in **Figure 5–1**, indicate **short-term** *(less than 1 year)*, **intermediate-term** *(1 to 3 years)*, or **long-term** *(3 years and beyond)*.

- In the **Comments** column (column 6), repeat or revise your comments for each strategic factor from the EFAS and IFAS Tables.

The resulting SFAS Matrix is a listing of the firm's external and internal strategic factors in one table. The example given is that of Maytag Corporation in 1995 before the firm sold its European and Australian operations. The SFAS Matrix includes only the most important factors gathered from environmental scanning and thus provides the information essential for strategy formulation. The use of EFAS and IFAS Tables together with the SFAS Matrix deal with many of the criticisms of SWOT analysis.

FINDING A PROPITIOUS NICHE

One desired outcome of analyzing strategic factors is identifying a niche where an organization can use its core competencies to take advantage of a particular market opportunity. A niche is a need in the marketplace that is currently unsatisfied. The goal is to find a **propitious niche**—an extremely favorable niche—that is so well suited to the firm's internal and external environment that other corporations are not likely to challenge or dislodge it.[4] A niche is propitious to the extent that it currently is just large enough for one firm to satisfy its demand. After a firm has found and filled that niche, it is not worth a potential competitor's time or money to also go after the same niche.

Finding such a niche is not always easy. A firm's management must be always looking for a **strategic window**, that is, a unique market opportunity that is available only for a particular time. The first firm through a strategic window can occupy a propitious niche and discourage competition (if the firm has the required internal strengths). One company that has successfully found a propitious niche is Frank J. Zamboni & Company, the manufacturer of the machines that smooth the ice at ice skating rinks. Frank Zamboni invented the unique tractorlike machine in 1949 and no one has found a substitute for what it does. Before the machine was invented, people had to clean and scrape the ice by hand to prepare the surface for skating. Now hockey fans look forward to intermissions just to watch "the Zamboni" slowly drive up and down the ice rink turning rough, scraped ice into a smooth mirror surface—almost like magic. So long as Zamboni's company is able to produce the machines in the quantity and quality desired at a reasonable price, it's not worth another company's time to go after Frank Zamboni & Company's propitious niche.

As the niche grows, so can the company within that niche—by increasing its operations' capacity or through alliances with larger firms. The key is to identify a market opportunity in which the first firm to reach that market segment can obtain and keep dominant market share. For example, Church & Dwight was the first company in the United States to successfully market sodium bicarbonate for use in cooking. Its Arm & Hammer brand baking soda is still found in 95% of all U.S. households. The propitious niche concept is crucial to the software industry. Small initial demand in emerging markets allows new entrepreneurial ventures to go after niches too small to be noticed by established companies. When Microsoft developed its first disk operating system (DOS) in 1980 for IBM's personal computers, for example, the demand for such open systems software was very small—a small niche for a then very small Microsoft. The company was able to fill that niche and to successfully grow with it.

Niches can also change—sometimes faster than a firm can adapt to that change. A company's managers may discover in their situation analysis that they need to invest heavily in the firm's capabilities to keep them competitively strong in a changing niche. South African Breweries (SAB), for example, took this approach when management realized that the only way to keep competitors out of its market was to continuously invest in increased productivity and infrastructure in order to keep its prices very low. See the **Global Issue** feature to see how SAB was able to successfully defend its market niche during significant changes in its environment.

Global Issue

SAB Defends Its Propitious Niche

Out of 50 beers consumed by South Africans, 49 are brewed by South African Breweries (SAB). Founded more than a century ago, SAB controlled most of the local beer market by 1950 with brands like Castle and Lion. When the government repealed the ban on the sale of alcohol to blacks in the 1960s, SAB and other brewers competed for the rapidly growing market. SAB fought successfully to retain its dominance of the market. With the end of apartheid, foreign brewers have been tempted to break SAB's near-monopoly, but have been deterred by the entry barriers SAB has erected.

Entry Barrier #1

Every year for the past two decades SAB has reduced its prices. The "real" (adjusted for inflation) price of its beer is now half what it was during the 1970s. SAB has been able to achieve this through a continuous emphasis on productivity improvements—boosting production while cutting the workforce almost in half. Keeping prices low has been key to SAB's avoiding charges of abusing its monopoly.

Entry Barrier #2

In South Africa's poor and rural areas, roads are rough and electricity is undependable. SAB has long experience in transporting crates to remote villages along bad roads and making sure that distributors have refrigerators (and electricity generators if needed). Many of its distributors are former employees who have been helped by the company to start their own trucking businesses.

Entry Barrier #3

Most of the beer sold in South Africa is sold through unlicensed pubs called *shebeens*, most of which date back to apartheid when blacks were not allowed licenses. Although the current government of South Africa would be pleased to grant pub licenses to blacks, the shebeen-owners don't want them. They enjoy not paying any taxes. SAB cannot sell directly to the shebeens, but it does so indirectly through wholesalers. The government, in turn, ignores the situation, preferring that people drink SAB beer than potentially deadly moonshine.

To break into South Africa, a new entrant would have to build large breweries and a substantial distribution network. SAB would, in turn, probably reduce its prices still further to defend its market. The difficulties of operating in South Africa are too great, the market is growing too slowly, and (given SAB's low-cost position) the likely profit margin is too low to justify entering the market. Some foreign brewers, such as Heineken, would rather use SAB to distribute their products throughout South Africa. As a result, SAB is now the world's fifth largest brewer by volume. With its home market secure, SAB's management considered acquiring a global brewer such as Bass in June 2000, but decided against it because of the high price.

Source: "Big Lion, Small Cage," *The Economist* (August 12, 2000), p. 56. Reprinted with permission.

5.2 Review of Mission and Objectives

A reexamination of an organization's current mission and objectives must be made before alternative strategies can be generated and evaluated. Even when formulating strategy, decision makers tend to concentrate on the alternatives—the action possibilities—rather than on a mission to be fulfilled and objectives to be achieved. This tendency is so attractive because it is much easier to deal with alternative courses of action that exist right here and now than to really think about what you want to accomplish in the future. The end result is that we often choose strategies that set our objectives for us, rather than having our choices incorporate clear objectives and a mission statement.

Problems in performance can derive from an inappropriate statement of mission, which may be too narrow or too broad. If the mission does not provide a *common thread* (a unifying theme) for a corporation's businesses, managers may be unclear about where the company is heading. Objectives and strategies might be in conflict with each other. Divisions might be competing against one another, rather than against outside competition, to the detriment of the corporation as a whole.

A company's objectives can also be inappropriately stated. They can either focus too much on short-term operational goals or be so general that they provide little real guidance. There may be a gap between planned and achieved objectives. When such a gap occurs, either the strategies have to be changed to improve performance or the objectives need to be adjusted downward to be more realistic. Consequently, objectives should be constantly reviewed to ensure their usefulness. This is what happened at Toyota Motor Corporation when top management realized that its "Global 10" objective of aiming for 10% of the global vehicle market was no longer feasible. Emphasis was then shifted from market share to profits. Interestingly, at the same time that both Toyota and General Motors were de-emphasizing market share as a key corporate objective, Ford Motor Company was stating that it wanted to be Number 1 in sales worldwide. No longer content with being in second place, Alexander Trotman, Ford's Chairman of the Board, contends: "Have you ever seen a team run out on the field and say, 'We're going to be Number 2?'"[5]

5.3 Generating Alternative Strategies Using a TOWS Matrix

Thus far we have discussed how a firm uses SWOT analysis to assess its situation. SWOT can also be used to generate a number of possible alternative strategies. The **TOWS Matrix** (TOWS is just another way of saying SWOT) illustrates how the external opportunities and threats facing a particular corporation can be matched with that company's internal strengths and weaknesses to result in four sets of possible strategic alternatives. (See **Figure 5–2.**) This is a good way to use brainstorming to create alternative strategies that might not otherwise be considered. It forces strategic managers to create various kinds of growth as well as retrenchment strategies. It can be used to generate corporate as well as business strategies.

To generate a TOWS Matrix for Maytag Corporation in 1995, for example, use the *External Factor Analysis Summary* (EFAS) listed in **Table 3–4** from **Chapter 3** and the *Internal Factor Analysis Summary* (IFAS) listed in **Table 4–2** from **Chapter 4**. To build **Figure 5–3**, take the following steps:

1. In the **Opportunities (O)** block, list the external opportunities available in the company's or business unit's current and future environment from the EFAS Table (**Table 3–4**).

2. In the **Threats (T)** block, list the external threats facing the company or unit now and in the future from the EFAS Table (**Table 3–4**).

Figure 5–2
TOWS Matrix

INTERNAL FACTORS (IFAS) EXTERNAL FACTORS (EFAS)	Strengths (S) List 5 – 10 *internal* strengths here	Weaknesses (W) List 5 – 10 *internal* weaknesses here
Opportunities (O) List 5 – 10 *external* opportunities here	**SO Strategies** Generate strategies here that use **strengths** to take **advantage** of **opportunities**	**WO Strategies** Generate strategies here that take **advantage** of **opportunities** by **overcoming weaknesses**
Threats (T) List 5 – 10 *external* opportunities here	**ST Strategies** Generate strategies here that use **strengths** to **avoid threats**	**WT Strategies** Generate strategies here that **minimize weaknesses** and **avoid threats**

Source: Reprinted from *Long-Range Planning*, April 1982. H. Weihrich, "The TOWS Matrix—A Tool for Situational Analysis," p. 60. Copyright 1982, with permission from Elsevier Science.

3. In the **Strengths (S)** block, list the specific areas of current and future strength for the company or unit from the IFAS Table (**Table 4–2**).

4. In the **Weaknesses (W)** block, list the specific areas of current and future weakness for the company or unit from the IFAS Table (**Table 4–2**).

5. Generate a series of possible strategies for the company or business unit under consideration based on particular combinations of the four sets of factors:

   - **SO Strategies** are generated by thinking of ways in which a company or business unit could use its strengths to take advantage of opportunities.

   - **ST Strategies** consider a company's or unit's strengths as a way to avoid threats.

   - **WO Strategies** attempt to take advantage of opportunities by overcoming weaknesses.

   - **WT Strategies** are basically defensive and primarily act to minimize weaknesses and avoid threats.

The TOWS Matrix is very useful for generating a series of alternatives that the decision makers of a company or business unit might not otherwise have considered. It can be used for the corporation as a whole (as was done in **Figure 5–3** with Maytag Corporation before it sold Hoover Europe), or it can be used for a specific business unit within a corporation (like Hoover's floor-care products). Nevertheless the TOWS Matrix is only one of many ways to generate alternative strategies. Another approach is to evaluate each business unit within a corporation in terms of possible competitive and cooperative strategies.

5.4 Business Strategies

Business strategy focuses on improving the competitive position of a company's or business unit's products or services within the specific industry or market segment that the company or business unit serves. Business strategy can be competitive (battling against all competitors for

Table 4–2 **Internal Factor Analysis Summary (IFAS): Maytag as Example (Selection of Strategic Factors)***

Internal Strategic Factors	Weight	Rating	Weighted Score	Comments
	1	2	3	4	5
Strengths				
S1 Quality Maytag culture	.15	5.0	.75	Quality key to success
S2 Experienced top management	.05	4.2	.21	Know appliances
S3 Vertical integration	.10	3.9	.39	Dedicated factories
S4 Employee relations	.05	3.0	.15	Good, but deteriorating
S5 Hoover's international orientation	.15	2.8	.42	Hoover name in cleaners
Weaknesses				
W1 Process-oriented R&D	.05	2.2	.11	Slow on new products
W2 Distribution channels	.05	2.0	.10	Superstores replacing small dealers
W3 Financial position	.15	2.0	.30	High debt load
W4 Global positioning	.20	2.1	.42	Hoover weak outside the United Kingdom and Australia
W5 Manufacturing facilities	.05	4.0	.20	Investing now
Total Scores	**1.00**		**3.05**	

Table 3–4 **External Factor Analysis Summary (EFAS): Maytag as Example (Selection of Strategic Factors)***

External Strategic Factors	Weight	Rating	Weighted Score	Comments
	1	2	3	4	5
Opportunities				
01 Economic integration of European Community	.20	4.1	.82	Acquisition of Hoover
02 Demographics favor quality appliances	.10	5.0	.50	Maytag quality
03 Economic development of Asia	.05	1.0	.05	Low Maytag presence
04 Opening of Eastern Europe	.05	2.0	.10	Will take time
05 Trend to "Super Stores"	.10	1.8	.18	Maytag weak in this channel
Threats				
T1 Increasing government regulations	.10	4.3	.43	Well positioned
T2 Strong U.S. competition	.10	4.0	.40	Well positioned
T3 Whirlpool and Electrolux strong globally	.15	3.0	.45	Hoover weak globally
T4 New product advances	.05	1.2	.06	Questionable
T5 Japanese appliance companies	.10	1.6	.16	Only Asian presence is Australia
Total Scores	**1.00**		**3.15**	

*The most important external and internal factors are identified in the EFAS and IFAS tables as shown here by shading these factors.

Figure 5–3

Generating a TOWS Matrix for Maytag Corporation

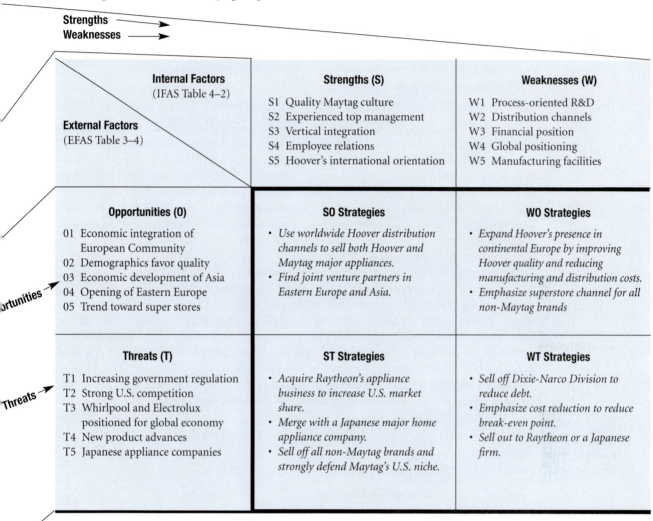

Internal Factors (IFAS Table 4–2)	**Strengths (S)**	**Weaknesses (W)**
External Factors (EFAS Table 3–4)	S1 Quality Maytag culture S2 Experienced top management S3 Vertical integration S4 Employee relations S5 Hoover's international orientation	W1 Process-oriented R&D W2 Distribution channels W3 Financial position W4 Global positioning W5 Manufacturing facilities
Opportunities (O) O1 Economic integration of European Community O2 Demographics favor quality O3 Economic development of Asia O4 Opening of Eastern Europe O5 Trend toward super stores	**SO Strategies** • *Use worldwide Hoover distribution channels to sell both Hoover and Maytag major appliances.* • *Find joint venture partners in Eastern Europe and Asia.*	**WO Strategies** • *Expand Hoover's presence in continental Europe by improving Hoover quality and reducing manufacturing and distribution costs.* • *Emphasize superstore channel for all non-Maytag brands*
Threats (T) T1 Increasing government regulation T2 Strong U.S. competition T3 Whirlpool and Electrolux positioned for global economy T4 New product advances T5 Japanese appliance companies	**ST Strategies** • *Acquire Raytheon's appliance business to increase U.S. market share.* • *Merge with a Japanese major home appliance company.* • *Sell off all non-Maytag brands and strongly defend Maytag's U.S. niche.*	**WT Strategies** • *Sell off Dixie-Narco Division to reduce debt.* • *Emphasize cost reduction to reduce break-even point.* • *Sell out to Raytheon or a Japanese firm.*

advantage) and/or cooperative (working with one or more competitors to gain advantage against other competitors). Just as corporate strategy asks what industry(ies) the company should be in, business strategy asks how the company or its units should compete or cooperate in each industry.

PORTER'S COMPETITIVE STRATEGIES

Competitive strategy raises the following questions:

■ Should we compete on the basis of low cost (and thus price), or should we differentiate our products or services on some basis other than cost, such as quality or service?

■ Should we compete head to head with our major competitors for the biggest but most sought-after share of the market, or should we focus on a niche in which we can satisfy a less sought-after but also profitable segment of the market?

Michael Porter proposes two "generic" competitive strategies for outperforming other corporations in a particular industry: lower cost and differentiation.[6] These strategies are called generic because they can be pursued by any type or size of business firm, even by not-for-profit organizations.

- **Lower cost strategy** is the ability of a company or a business unit to design, produce, and market a comparable product more efficiently than its competitors.

- **Differentiation strategy** is the ability to provide unique and superior value to the buyer in terms of product quality, special features, or after-sale service.

Porter further proposes that a firm's competitive advantage in an industry is determined by its **competitive scope**, that is, the breadth of the company's or business unit's target market. Before using one of the two generic competitive strategies (lower cost or differentiation), the firm or unit must choose the range of product varieties it will produce, the distribution channels it will employ, the types of buyers it will serve, the geographic areas in which it will sell, and the array of related industries in which it will also compete. This should reflect an understanding of the firm's unique resources. Simply put, a company or business unit can choose a broad target (that is, aim at the middle of the mass market) or a narrow target (that is, aim at a market niche). Combining these two types of target markets with the two competitive strategies results in the four variations of generic strategies depicted in **Figure 5–4**. When the lower cost and differentiation strategies have a broad mass market target, they are simply called *cost leadership* and *differentiation*. When they are focused on a market niche (narrow target), however, they are called *cost focus* and *differentiation focus*. Although research does indicate that established firms pursuing broad-scope strategies outperform firms following narrow-scope strategies in terms of ROA, new entrepreneurial firms have a better chance of surviving if they follow a narrow-scope over a broad-scope strategy.[7]

Cost leadership is a low-cost competitive strategy that aims at the broad mass market and requires "aggressive construction of efficient-scale facilities, vigorous pursuit of cost reduc-

Figure 5–4
Porter's Generic Competitive Strategies

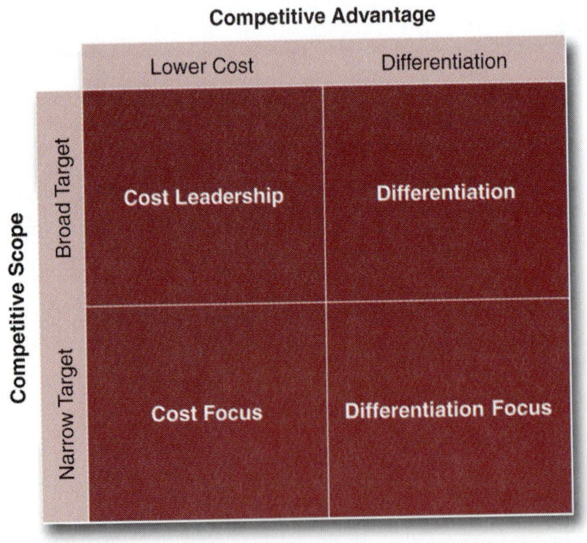

Source: Reprinted with permission of The Free Press, an imprint of Simon & Schuster, from *The Competitive Advantage of Nations* by Michael E. Porter, p. 39. Copyright © 1990 by Michael E. Porter.

tions from experience, tight cost and overhead control, avoidance of marginal customer accounts, and cost minimization in areas like R&D, service, sales force, advertising, and so on."[8] Because of its lower costs, the cost leader is able to charge a lower price for its products than its competitors and still make a satisfactory profit. Some companies successfully following this strategy are Wal-Mart, Alamo Rent-A-Car, Southwest Airlines, Timex, and Gateway 2000. Having a low-cost position also gives a company or business unit a defense against rivals. Its lower costs allow it to continue to earn profits during times of heavy competition. Its high market share means that it will have high bargaining power relative to its suppliers (because it buys in large quantities). Its low price will also serve as a barrier to entry because few new entrants will be able to match the leader's cost advantage. As a result, cost leaders are likely to earn above-average returns on investment.

Differentiation is aimed at the broad mass market and involves the creation of a product or service that is perceived throughout its industry as unique. The company or business unit may then charge a premium for its product. This specialty can be associated with design or brand image, technology, features, dealer network, or customer service. Differentiation is a viable strategy for earning above-average returns in a specific business because the resulting brand loyalty lowers customers' sensitivity to price. Increased costs can usually be passed on to the buyers. Buyer loyalty also serves as an entry barrier—new firms must develop their own distinctive competence to differentiate their products in some way in order to compete successfully. Examples of the successful use of a differentiation strategy are Walt Disney Productions, Maytag appliances, Nike athletic shoes, Apple Computer, and Mercedes-Benz automobiles. Research does suggest that a differentiation strategy is more likely to generate higher profits than is a low-cost strategy because differentiation creates a better entry barrier. A low-cost strategy is more likely, however, to generate increases in market share.[9]

Cost focus is a low-cost competitive strategy that focuses on a particular buyer group or geographic market and attempts to serve only this niche, to the exclusion of others. In using cost focus, the company or business unit seeks a cost advantage in its target segment. A good example of this strategy is Fadal Engineering. Fadal focuses its efforts on building and selling no-frills machine tools to small manufacturers. Fadal achieved cost focus by keeping overhead and R&D to a minimum and by focusing its marketing efforts strictly on its market niche. The cost focus strategy is valued by those who believe that a company or business unit that focuses its efforts is better able to serve its narrow strategic target more efficiently than can its competition. It does, however, require a tradeoff between profitability and overall market share.

Differentiation focus, like cost focus, concentrates on a particular buyer group, product line segment, or geographic market. This is the strategy successfully followed by Casey's General Stores, Morgan Motor Car Company (manufacturer of classic British sports cars), and local health food stores. In using differentiation focus, the company or business unit seeks differentiation in a targeted market segment. This strategy is valued by those who believe that a company or a unit that focuses its efforts is better able to serve the special needs of a narrow strategic target more effectively than can its competition. This is the strategy being effectively used by Inner City Entertainment (ICE), a company focusing on building new high quality movie theaters in inner-city locations aimed primarily at African Americans. Owned and managed by Alisa and Donzell Starks, ICE has successfully opened numerous theaters in Chicago's South Side. The company uses urban radio stations to promote its films and offers special screenings of films with high interest, such as *Amistad*. "I want to be the first black-owned theater chain," states Mr. Starks, the company's CEO. "No ifs, ands, or buts."[10]

Risks in Competitive Strategies

No one competitive strategy is guaranteed to achieve success, and some companies that have successfully implemented one of Porter's competitive strategies have found that they could not sustain the strategy. As shown in **Table 5–1**, each of the generic strategies has its risks. For

Table 5–1 Risks of Generic Competitive Strategies

Risks of Cost Leadership	Risks of Differentiation	Risks of Focus
Cost leadership is not sustained: • Competitors intimate. • Technology changes. • Other bases for cost leadership erode. Proximity in differentiation is lost.	Differentiation is not sustained: • Competitors imitate. • Bases for differentiation become less important to buyers. Cost proximity is lost.	The focus strategy is imitated. The target segment becomes structurally unattractive: • Structure erodes. • Demand disappears. Broadly targeted competitors overwhelm the segment: • The segment's differences from other segments narrow.
Cost focusers achieve even lower cost in segments.	Differentiation focusers achieve even greater differentiation in segments.	• The advantages of a broad line increase. New focusers subsegment the industry.

Source: Adapted/reprinted with permission of The Free Press, an imprint of Simon & Schuster, from *Competitive Advantage: Creating and Sustaining Superior Performance* by Michael E. Porter, p. 21. Copyright © 1985 by Michael E. Porter.

example, a company following a differentiation strategy must ensure that the higher price it charges for its higher quality is not priced too far above the competition, otherwise customers will not see the extra quality as worth the extra cost. This is what is meant in **Table 5–1** by the term **cost proximity**. Procter & Gamble's use of R&D and advertising to differentiate its products had been very successful for many years until customers in the value-conscious 1990s turned to cheaper private brands. As a result, P&G was forced to reduce costs until it could get prices back in line with customer expectations.

Issues in Competitive Strategies

Porter argues that to be successful, a company or business unit must achieve one of the preceding generic competitive strategies. It is especially difficult to move between a narrow target strategy and a broad target strategy. Otherwise, the company or business unit is **stuck in the middle** of the competitive marketplace with no competitive advantage and is doomed to below-average performance. An example of a business unit that may be stuck in the middle is Hewlett-Packard's (HP) personal computer division. For years, HP was a niche player following a differentiation focus strategy in personal computers. Its Vectra personal computers were cherished by engineers and scientists for their high quality and for HP's solid service support. The computers were also expensive. HP's management decided in the mid-1990s to leave the niche and to compete instead in the broad-target market. The objective became high market share. In order to compete with its lower cost rivals such as Dell and Gateway, HP reduced prices. The plan worked. With more than 40% sales growth in 2000, it even outpaced Dell, the industry leader. Nevertheless, HP's reputation for high quality and exceptional service support (as reported in *PC Magazine* and *PC World*) declined from the years when it was a quality niche player. HP's switch from a narrow-target to a broad-target competitive strategy had its down side. As of 2000, the computer unit generated 43% of HP's revenues, but only a 4.6% operating margin, the lowest of HP's business units. In contrast, the printer and imaging division, which also accounted for 43% of HP's annual revenues, generated a 12% operating margin.[11] In moving to the mass market, HP had not kept up its quality image (thus losing its differentiation) and had thus far failed to achieve the lower cost position.

Although it may be difficult to move from a narrow- to a broad-target scope strategy (and vice versa) successfully, research does not support the argument that a firm or unit must choose between differentiation and lower cost in order to have success.[12] What of companies that attempt to achieve *both* a low-cost and a high-differentiation position? The Japanese auto

Table 5–2   The Eight Dimensions of Quality

1. **Performance**	Primary operating characteristics, such as a washing machine's cleaning ability
2. **Features**	"Bells and whistles," like cruise control in a car, that supplement the basic functions
3. **Reliability**	Probability that the product will continue functioning without any significant maintenance
4. **Conformance**	Degree to which a product meets standards. When a customer buys a product out of the warehouse, it will perform identically to that viewed on the showroom floor.
5. **Durability**	Number of years of service a consumer can expect from a product before it significantly deteriorates. Differs from reliability in that a product can be durable, but still need a lot of maintenance.
6. **Serviceability**	Product's ease of repair
7. **Aesthetics**	How a product looks, feels, sounds, tastes, or smells
8. **Perceived Quality**	Product's overall reputation. Especially important if there are no objective, easily used measures of quality.

Source: Adapted from D. A. Garvin, *Managing Quality: The Strategic and Competitive Edge* (New York: Free Press, 1988).

companies of Toyota, Nissan, and Honda are often presented as examples of successful firms able to achieve both of these generic strategies. Thanks to advances in technology, a company may be able to design quality into a product or service in such a way that it can achieve both high quality and high market share, thus lowering costs.[13] Although Porter agrees that it is possible for a company or a business unit to achieve low cost and differentiation simultaneously, he continues to argue that this state is often temporary.[14] Porter does admit, however, that many different kinds of potentially profitable competitive strategies exist. Although there is generally room for only one company to successfully pursue the mass market cost leadership strategy (because it is so dependent on achieving dominant market share), there is room for an almost unlimited number of differentiation and focus strategies (depending on the range of possible desirable features and the number of identifiable market niches). Quality, alone, has 8 different dimensions—each with the potential of providing a product with a competitive advantage (see **Table 5–2**).

Most entrepreneurial ventures follow focus strategies. The successful ones differentiate their product from those of other competitors in the areas of quality and service, and they focus the product on customer needs in a segment of the market, thereby achieving a dominant share of that part of the market. Adopting guerrilla warfare tactics, these companies go after opportunities in market niches too small to justify retaliation from the market leaders. Veteran entrepreneur Norm Brodsky argues that it's often much easier for a small company to compete against a big company than against a well-run small company. "We beat the giants on service. We beat them on flexibility. We beat them on location and price."[15]

Industry Structure and Competitive Strategy

Although each of Porter's generic competitive strategies may be used in any industry, certain strategies are more likely to succeed than others in some instances. In a **fragmented industry**, for example, where many small- and medium-sized local companies compete for relatively small shares of the total market, focus strategies will likely predominate. Fragmented industries are typical for products in the early stages of their life cycle. If few economies are to be gained through size, no large firms will emerge and entry barriers will be low, allowing a stream of new entrants into the industry. Chinese restaurants, veterinary care, used-car sales, and funeral homes are examples. As recently as 1996, over 85% of funeral homes in the United States were independently owned.[16]

If a company is able to overcome the limitations of a fragmented market, however, it can reap the benefits of a broadly targeted cost leadership or differentiation strategy. Until Pizza Hut was able to use advertising to differentiate itself from local competitors, the pizza fast-food business was a fragmented industry composed primarily of locally owned pizza parlors, each with its own distinctive product and service offering. Subsequently Domino's used the cost leader strategy to achieve U.S. national market share.

As an industry matures, fragmentation is overcome and the industry tends to become a **consolidated industry** dominated by a few large companies. Although many industries begin fragmented, battles for market share and creative attempts to overcome local or niche market boundaries often increase the market share of a few companies. After product standards become established for minimum quality and features, competition shifts to a greater emphasis on cost and service. Slower growth, overcapacity, and knowledgeable buyers combine to put a premium on a firm's ability to achieve cost leadership or differentiation along the dimensions most desired by the market. Research and development shifts from product to process improvements. Overall product quality improves, and costs are reduced significantly.

The **strategic rollup** was developed in the mid-1990s as an efficient way to quickly consolidate a fragmented industry. With the aid of money from venture capitalists, an entrepreneur acquires hundreds of owner-operated small businesses. The resulting large firm creates economies of scale by building regional or national brands, applies best practices across all aspects of marketing and operations, and hires more sophisticated managers than the small businesses could previously afford. Rollups differ from conventional mergers and acquisitions in three ways: (1) They involve large numbers of firms, (2) the acquired firms are typically owner operated, and (3) the objective is not to gain incremental advantage, but to reinvent an entire industry.[17] Rollups are currently underway in the funeral industry led by Service Corporation International, Stewart Enterprises, the Loewen Group and in the veterinary care industries by Veterinary Centers of America. Of the 16,000 pet hospitals in the United States, Veterinary Centers of American had acquired around 160 by 1997 and was in the process of buying at least 25 more each year for the foreseeable future.[18]

Once consolidated, the industry has become one in which cost leadership and differentiation tend to be combined to various degrees. A firm can no longer gain high market share simply through low price. The buyers are more sophisticated and demand a certain minimum level of quality for price paid. The same is true for firms emphasizing high quality. Either the quality must be high enough and valued by the customer enough to justify the higher price or the price must be dropped (through lowering costs) to compete effectively with the lower priced products. This consolidation is taking place worldwide in the automobile, airline, and home appliance industries.

Hypercompetition and Competitive Strategy

In his book *Hypercompetition*, D'Aveni proposes that it is becoming increasingly difficult to sustain a competitive advantage for very long. "Market stability is threatened by short product life cycles, short product design cycles, new technologies, frequent entry by unexpected outsiders, repositioning by incumbents, and tactical redefinitions of market boundaries as diverse industries merge."[19] Consequently a company or business unit must constantly work to improve its competitive advantage. It is not enough to be just the lowest cost competitor. Through continuous improvement programs, competitors are usually working to lower their costs as well. Firms must find new ways not only to reduce costs further, but also to add value to the product or service being provided.

The same is true of a firm or unit that is following a differentiation strategy. Maytag Company (a unit of Maytag Corporation), for example, was successful for many years by offering the most durable brand in major home appliances. It was able to charge the highest prices for Maytag brand washing machines. When other competitors improved the quality of their products, however, it became increasingly harder for customers to justify Maytag's significantly higher price. Consequently Maytag Company was forced not only to add new features to its products, but also to reduce costs through improved manufacturing processes so that its prices were no longer out of line with those of the competition.

D'Aveni contends that when industries become **hypercompetitive**, they tend to go through escalating stages of competition. Firms initially compete on cost and quality until an abundance of high-quality, low-priced goods result. This occurred in the U.S. major home appliance industry by 1980. In a second stage of competition, the competitors move into untapped markets. Others usually imitate these moves until the moves become too risky or expensive. This epitomized the major home appliance industry during the 1980s and 1990s as firms moved first to Europe and then into Asia and South America.

According to D'Aveni, firms then raise entry barriers to limit competitors. Economies of scale, distribution agreements, and strategic alliances made it all but impossible for a new firm to enter the major home appliance industry by the end of the 20th century. After the established players have entered and consolidated all new markets, the next stage is for the remaining firms to attack and destroy the strongholds of other firms. Maytag's 1995 decision to divest its European division and concentrate on improving its position in North America could be a prelude to building a North American stronghold while Whirlpool, GE, and Electrolux are distracted by European and worldwide investments. Eventually, according to D'Aveni, the remaining large global competitors work their way to a situation of perfect competition in which no one has any advantage and profits are minimal.

Before hypercompetition, strategic initiatives provided competitive advantage for many years, perhaps for decades. This is no longer the case. According to D'Aveni, as industries become hypercompetitive, there is no such thing as a sustainable competitive advantage. Successful strategic initiatives in this type of industry typically last only months to a few years. According to D'Aveni, the only way a firm in this kind of dynamic industry can sustain any competitive advantage is through a continuous series of multiple short-term initiatives aimed at replacing a firm's current successful products with the next generation of products before the competitors can do so. Intel and Microsoft are taking this approach in the hypercompetitive computer industry.

Hypercompetition views competition, in effect, as a distinct series of ocean waves on what used to be a fairly calm stretch of water. As industry competition becomes more intense, the waves grow higher and require more dexterity to handle. Although a strategy is still needed to sail from point A to point B, more turbulent water means that a craft must continually adjust course to suit each new large wave. One danger of D'Aveni's concept of hypercompetition, however, is that it may lead to an overemphasis on short-term tactics (to be discussed in the next section) over long-term strategy. Too much of an orientation on the individual waves of hypercompetition could cause a company to focus too much on short-term temporary advantage and not enough on achieving its long-term objectives through building sustainable competitive advantage.

Which Competitive Strategy Is Best?

Before selecting one of Porter's generic competitive strategies for a company or business unit, management should assess its feasibility in terms of company or business unit resources and capabilities. Porter lists some of the commonly required skills and resources as well as organizational requirements, in **Table 5–3**.

Competitive Tactics

Studies of decision making report that half the decisions made in organizations fail because of poor tactics.[20] A **tactic** is a specific operating plan detailing how a strategy is to be implemented in terms of when and where it is to be put into action. By their nature, tactics are nar-

Table 5–3   Requirements for Generic Competitive Strategies

Generic Strategy	Commonly Required Skills and Resources	Common Organizational Requirements
Overall Cost Leadership	• Sustained capital investment and access to capital • Process engineering skills • Intense supervision of labor • Products designed for ease of manufacture • Low-cost distribution system	• Tight cost control • Frequent, detailed control reports • Structured organization and responsibilities • Incentives based on meeting strict quantitative targets
Differentiation	• Strong marketing abilities • Product engineering • Creative flair • Strong capability in basic research • Corporate reputation for quality or technological leadership • Long tradition in the industry or unique combination of skills drawn from other businesses • Strong cooperation from channels	• Strong coordination among functions in R&D, product development, and marketing • Subjective measurement and incentives instead of quantitative measures • Amenities to attract highly skilled labor, scientists, or creative people
Focus	• Combination of the above policies directed at the particular strategic target	• Combination of the above policies directed at the particular strategic target

Source: Adapted/reprinted with permission of The Free Press, an imprint of Simon & Schuster, from *Competitive Strategy: Techniques for Analyzing Industries and Competitors* by Michael E. Porter, pp. 40–41. Copyright © 1980, 1988 by The Free Press.

rower in their scope and shorter in their time horizon than are strategies. Tactics, therefore, may be viewed (like policies) as a link between the formulation and implementation of strategy. Some of the tactics available to implement competitive strategies are **timing tactics** (when) and **market location tactics** (where).

Timing Tactics: When to Compete

The first company to manufacture and sell a new product or service is called the **first mover** (or **pioneer**). Some of the advantages of being a first mover are that the company is able to establish a reputation as an industry leader, move down the learning curve to assume the cost leader position, and earn temporarily high profits from buyers who value the product or service very highly. A successful first mover can also set the standard for all subsequent products in the industry. A company that sets the standard "locks in" customers and is then able to offer further products based on that standard.[21] Microsoft was able to do this in software with its Windows operating system, and Netscape garnered over 80% share of the Internet browser market by being first to commercialize the product successfully. Research does indicate that moving first or second into a new industry or foreign country results in greater market share and shareholder wealth than does moving later.[22] This is only true, however, if the first mover has sufficient resources to both exploit the new market and to defend its position against later arrivals with greater resources.[23]

Being a first mover does, however, have its disadvantages. These disadvantages can be, conversely, advantages enjoyed by late mover firms. **Late movers** may be able to imitate the technological advances of others (and thus keep R&D costs low), keep risks down by waiting until a new market is established, and take advantage of the first mover's natural inclination to ignore market segments.[24] Once Netscape had established itself as the standard for Internet browsers, Microsoft used its huge resources to directly attack Netscape's position. It did not want Netscape to also set the standard in the developing and highly lucrative intranet market inside corporations. Nevertheless, research suggests that the advantages and disadvantages of first and late movers may not always generalize across industries because of differences in entry barriers and the resources of the specific competitors.[25]

Market Location Tactics: Where to Compete

A company or business unit can implement a competitive strategy either offensively or defensively. An **offensive tactic** usually takes place in an established competitor's market location. A **defensive tactic** usually takes place in the firm's own current market position as a defense against possible attack by a rival.[26]

Offensive Tactics   Some of the methods used to attack a competitor's position are:

- **Frontal Assault:** The attacking firm goes head to head with its competitor. It matches the competitor in every category from price to promotion to distribution channel. To be successful, the attacker must not only have superior resources, but also the willingness to persevere. This is generally a very expensive tactic and may serve to awaken a sleeping giant (as MCI and Sprint did to AT&T in long-distance telephone service), depressing profits for the whole industry.

- **Flanking Maneuver:** Rather than going straight for a competitor's position of strength with a frontal assault, a firm may attack a part of the market where the competitor is weak. Cyrix Corporation followed this tactic with its entry into the microprocessor market—a market then almost totally dominated by Intel. Rather than going directly after Intel's microprocessor business, Cyrix developed a math co-processor for Intel's 386 chip that would run 20 times faster than Intel's microprocessor. To be successful, the flanker must be patient and willing to carefully expand out of the relatively undefended market niche or else face retaliation by an established competitor.

- **Bypass Attack:** Rather than directly attacking the established competitor frontally or on its flanks, a company or business unit may choose to change the rules of the game. This tactic attempts to cut the market out from under the established defender by offering a new type of product that makes the competitor's product unnecessary. For example, instead of competing directly against Microsoft's Windows 95 operating system, Netscape chose to use Java "applets" in its Internet browser so that an operating system and specialized programs were no longer necessary to run applications on a personal computer.

- **Encirclement:** Usually evolving out of a frontal assault or flanking maneuver, encirclement occurs as an attacking company or unit encircles the competitor's position in terms of products or markets or both. The encircler has greater product variety (a complete product line ranging from low to high price) and/or serves more markets (it dominates every secondary market). As a late mover into Internet browsers, Microsoft followed this tactic when it attacked Netscape's business with its "embrace and extend" strategy. By embracing Netscape's use of cross-platform Internet applets and quickly extending it into multiple applications, Microsoft worked to dominate the browser market.

- **Guerrilla Warfare:** Instead of a continual and extensive resource-expensive attack on a competitor, a firm or business unit may choose to "hit and run." Guerrilla warfare is characterized by the use of small, intermittent assaults on different market segments held by the competitor. In this way, a new entrant or small firm can make some gains without seriously threatening a large, established competitor and evoking some form of retaliation. To be successful, the firm or unit conducting guerrilla warfare must be patient enough to accept small gains and to avoid pushing the established competitor to the point that it must respond or else lose face. Microbreweries, which make beer for sale to local customers, use this tactic against national brewers like Anheuser-Busch.

Defensive Tactics   According to Porter, defensive tactics aim to lower the probability of attack, divert attacks to less threatening avenues, or lessen the intensity of an attack. Instead of increasing competitive advantage per se, they make a company's or business unit's competitive advantage more sustainable by causing a challenger to conclude that an attack is unattractive. These tactics deliberately reduce short-term profitability to ensure long-term profitability.[27]

- **Raise Structural Barriers**: Entry barriers act to block a challenger's logical avenues of attack. Some of the most important according to Porter are to:
  1. Offer a full line of products in every profitable market segment to close off any entry points (for example, Coca-Cola offers unprofitable noncarbonated beverages to keep competitors off store shelves).
  2. Block channel access by signing exclusive agreements with distributors.
  3. Raise buyer switching costs by offering low-cost training to users.
  4. Raise the cost of gaining trial users by keeping prices low on items new users are most likely to purchase.
  5. Increase scale economies to reduce unit costs.
  6. Foreclose alternative technologies through patenting or licensing.
  7. Limit outside access to facilities and personnel.
  8. Tie up suppliers by obtaining exclusive contracts or purchasing key locations.
  9. Avoid suppliers that also serve competitors.
  10. Encourage the government to raise barriers such as safety and pollution standards or favorable trade policies.

- **Increase Expected Retaliation**: This tactic is any action that increases the perceived threat of retaliation for an attack. For example, management may strongly defend any erosion of market share by drastically cutting prices or matching a challenger's promotion through a policy of accepting any price-reduction coupons for a competitor's product. This counter-attack is especially important in markets that are very important to the defending company or business unit. For example, when Clorox Company challenged Procter & Gamble Company in the detergent market with Clorox Super Detergent, P&G retaliated by test marketing its liquid bleach, Lemon Fresh Comet, in an attempt to scare Clorox into retreating from the detergent market.

- **Lower the Inducement for Attack**: A third type of defensive tactic is to reduce a challenger's expectations of future profits in the industry. Like Southwest Airlines, a company can deliberately keep prices low and constantly invest in cost-reducing measures. With prices kept very low, there is little profit incentive for a new entrant.

COOPERATIVE STRATEGIES

Competitive strategies and tactics are used to gain competitive advantage within an industry by battling against other firms. These are not, however, the only business strategy options available to a company or business unit for competing successfully within an industry. **Cooperative strategies** can also be used to gain competitive advantage within an industry by working with other firms.

Collusion

The two general types of cooperative strategies are collusion and strategic alliances. **Collusion** is the active cooperation of firms within an industry to reduce output and raise prices in order to get around the normal economic law of supply and demand. Collusion may be explicit, in which firms cooperate through direct communication and negotiation, or tacit, in which firms cooperate indirectly through an informal system of signals. Explicit collusion is illegal in most countries. For example, Archer Daniels Midland (ADM), the large U.S. agricultural products firm, has been accused of conspiring with its competitors to limit the sales volume and raise the price of the food additive lysine. Executives from three Japanese and South Korean lysine manufacturers admitted meeting in hotels in major cities throughout the world to form a "lysine trade association." The three companies were fined more than $20 million by the U.S. federal government. Although ADM had earlier agreed to pay $25 million to settle a lawsuit on behalf of 600 lysine customers, U.S. federal prosecutors pursued a grand jury indictment of the company and two of its senior executives.[28]

Collusion can also be tacit, in which there is no direct communication among competing firms. According to Barney, tacit collusion in an industry is most likely to be successful if (1) there are a small number of identifiable competitors, (2) costs are similar among firms, (3) one firm tends to act as the "price leader," (4) there is a common industry culture that accepts cooperation, (5) sales are characterized by a high frequency of small orders, (6) large inventories and order backlogs are normal ways of dealing with fluctuations in demand, and (7) there are high entry barriers to keep out new competitors.[29]

Even tacit collusion can, however, be illegal. For example, when General Electric wanted to ease price competition in the steam turbine industry, it widely advertised its prices and publicly committed not to sell below these prices. Customers were even told that if GE reduced turbine prices in the future, it would give customers a refund equal to the price reduction. GE's message was not lost on Westinghouse, the major competitor in steam turbines. Both prices and profit margins remained stable for the next 10 years in this industry. The U.S. Department of Justice then sued both firms for engaging in "conscious parallelism" (following each other's lead to reduce the level of competition) in order to reduce competition.

Strategic Alliances

A **strategic alliance** is a partnership of two or more corporations or business units to achieve strategically significant objectives that are mutually beneficial.[30] Alliances between companies or business units have become a fact of life in modern business. More than 20,000 alliances occurred between 1992 and 1997, quadruple the total five years earlier.[31] Some alliances are very short term, only lasting long enough for one partner to establish a beachhead in a new market. Over time, conflicts over objectives and control often develop among the partners. For these and other reasons, between 30% and 50% of all alliances perform unsatisfactorily.[32] Others are more long lasting and may even be the prelude to a full merger between two companies. A study by Cooper and Lybrand found that firms involved in strategic alliances had 11% higher revenue and 20% higher growth rate than did companies not involved in alliances.[33]

Companies or business units may form a strategic alliance for a number of reasons, including:

1. **To obtain technology and/or manufacturing capabilities**: For example, Intel formed a partnership with Hewlett-Packard to use HP's capabilities in RISC technology in order to develop the successor to Intel's Pentium microprocessor.

2. **To obtain access to specific markets**: Rather than buy a foreign company or build breweries of its own in other countries, Anheuser-Busch chose to license the right to brew and market Budweiser to other brewers, such as Labatt in Canada, Modelo in Mexico, and Kirin in Japan.

3. **To reduce financial risk**: For example, because the costs of developing a new large jet airplane were becoming too high for any one manufacturer, Boeing, Aerospatiale of France, British Aerospace, Construcciones Aeronáuticas of Spain, and Deutsche Aerospace of Germany planned a joint venture to design such a plane.

4. **To reduce political risk**: To gain access to China while ensuring a positive relationship with the often restrictive Chinese government, Maytag Corporation formed a joint venture with the Chinese appliance maker, RSD.

5. **To achieve or ensure competitive advantage**: General Motors and Toyota formed Nummi Corporation as a joint venture to provide Toyota a manufacturing facility in the United States and GM access to Toyota's low-cost, high-quality manufacturing expertise.[34]

Cooperative arrangements between companies and business units fall along a continuum from weak and distant to strong and close. (See **Figure 5–5**.) The types of alliances range from mutual service consortia to joint ventures and licensing arrangements to value-chain partnerships.[35]

Mutual Service Consortia   A **mutual service consortium** is a partnership of similar companies in similar industries who pool their resources to gain a benefit that is too expensive to develop alone, such as access to advanced technology. For example, IBM of the United States, Toshiba of Japan, and Siemens of Germany formed a consortium to develop new generations of computer chips. As part of this alliance, IBM offered Toshiba its expertise in chemical mechanical polishing to help develop a new manufacturing process using ultraviolet lithography to etch tiny circuits in silicon chips. IBM then transferred the new technology to a facility in the United States.[36] The mutual service consortia is a fairly weak and distant alliance— appropriate for partners who wish to work together but not share their core competencies. There is very little interaction or communication among the partners.

Joint Venture   A **joint venture** is a "cooperative business activity, formed by two or more separate organizations for strategic purposes, that creates an independent business entity and allocates ownership, operational responsibilities, and financial risks and rewards to each member, while preserving their separate identity/autonomy."[37] Along with licensing arrangements, joint ventures lay at the midpoint of the continuum and are formed to pursue an opportunity that needs a capability from two companies or business units, such as the technology of one and the distribution channels of another.

Joint ventures are the most popular form of strategic alliance. They often occur because the companies involved do not want to or cannot legally merge permanently. Joint ventures provide a way to temporarily combine the different strengths of partners to achieve an outcome of value to both. For example, Toys "R" Us and Amazon.com formed a joint venture in August 2000 called Toysrus.com to act as an online toy store. Amazon was to include the joint venture on its Web site, ship the products, and handle customer service. In turn, Toys "R" Us was to choose and buy the toys, using its parent's purchasing power to get the most desired toys at the best price.[38]

Figure 5–5
Continuum of Strategic Alliances

Mutual Service Consortia	Joint Venture, Licensing Arrangement	Value-Chain Partnership

Weak and Distant   **Strong and Close**

Source: Suggested by R. M. Kanter, "Collaborative Advantage: The Art of Alliances," *Harvard Business Review* (July–August 1994), pp. 96–108. Copyright © 2001 by the President and Fellows of Harvard College, all rights reserved.

Extremely popular in international undertakings because of financial and political-legal constraints, joint ventures are a convenient way for corporations to work together without losing their independence. Disadvantages of joint ventures include loss of control, lower profits, probability of conflicts with partners, and the likely transfer of technological advantage to the partner. Joint ventures are often meant to be temporary, especially by some companies who may view them as a way to rectify a competitive weakness until they can achieve long-term dominance in the partnership. Partially for this reason, joint ventures have a high failure rate. Research does indicate, however, that joint ventures tend to be more successful when both partners have equal ownership in the venture and are mutually dependent on each other for results.[39]

Licensing Arrangement   A **licensing arrangement** is an agreement in which the licensing firm grants rights to another firm in another country or market to produce and/or sell a product. The licensee pays compensation to the licensing firm in return for technical expertise. Licensing is an especially useful strategy if the trademark or brand name is well known, but the MNC does not have sufficient funds to finance its entering the country directly. Anheuser-Busch uses this strategy to produce and market Budweiser beer in the United Kingdom, Japan, Israel, Australia, Korea, and the Philippines. This strategy also becomes important if the country makes entry via investment either difficult or impossible. The danger always exists, however, that the licensee might develop its competence to the point that it becomes a competitor to the licensing firm. Therefore, a company should never license its distinctive competence, even for some short-run advantage.

Value-Chain Partnership   The **value-chain partnership** is a strong and close alliance in which one company or unit forms a long-term arrangement with a key supplier or distributor for mutual advantage. To improve the quality of parts it purchases, companies in the U.S. auto industry, for example, have decided to work more closely with fewer suppliers and to involve them more in product design decisions. Activities that had been previously done internally by an auto maker are being outsourced to suppliers specializing in those activities.

Such partnerships are also a way for a firm to acquire new technology to use in its own products. For example, Maytag Company was approached by one of its suppliers, Honeywell's Microswitch Division, which offered its expertise in fuzzy logic technology—a technology Maytag did not have at that time. The resulting partnership in product development resulted in Maytag's new IntelliSense™ dishwasher. Unlike previous dishwashers that the operator had to set, Maytag's fuzzy logic dishwasher automatically selected the proper cleaning cycle based on a series of factors such as the amount of dirt and presence of detergent. According to Paul Ludwig, business development manager for Honeywell's Microswitch division, "Had Maytag not included us on the design team, we don't believe the two companies would have achieved the same innovative solution, nor would we have completed the project in such a short amount of time."[40] The benefits of such relationships do not just accrue to the purchasing firm. Research suggests that suppliers who engage in long-term relationships are more profitable than suppliers with multiple short-term contracts.[41] For an example of an Internet value-chain partnership between Cisco Systems and its suppliers, see the 🖳 **Internet Issue** feature.

All forms of strategic alliances are filled with uncertainty. There are many issues that need to be dealt with when the alliance is initially formed and others that emerge later. Many problems revolve around the fact that a firm's alliance partners may also be its competitors, either now or in the future. According to Peter Lorange, an authority in strategy, one thorny issue in any strategic alliance is how to cooperate without giving away the company or business unit's core competence. "Particularly when advanced technology is involved, it can be difficult for partners in an alliance to cooperate and openly share strategic know-how, but it is mandatory if the joint venture is to succeed."[42] It is therefore important that a company or business unit that is interested in joining or forming a strategic alliance consider the strategic alliance success factors listed in **Table 5–4**.

Internet Issue

Business to Business at Cisco Systems

Every day Cisco Systems, successful manufacturer of Internet servers, posts its requirements for components on an extranet, the dedicated Internet-based network connecting the company to 32 manufacturing plants. Although Cisco does not own these plants, each plant has completed a lengthy process of certification ensuring that each meets Cisco's quality and other standards. Within hours of the posting, these suppliers respond with a price, a delivery time, and a record of their recent performance in terms of reliability and product quality. Cisco then chooses which bid to select and the deal is finalized.

This process has replaced 50 purchasing agents who used to assemble the same information using telephones and faxes. The operation, which used to take three to four days, now takes only hours. The purchasing agents are instead managing the quality of the components.

Three aspects of Cisco's supply system are especially significant. *One* is the use of the electronic market to set prices. This is characteristic of online auctions and of business to business (B2B) value chain relationships. A *second* is the exchange of information between buyer and seller. The Internet allows the inexpensive flow of information in a way never before realized. *Third* is the extent to which Cisco outsources activities that many other companies do internally. The ability of the Internet to connect multiple departments together with suppliers and distributors in other companies makes outsourcing both effective and efficient.

Source: "Trying to Connect You," *The Economist E-Management Survey* (November 11, 2000), p. 28. Reprinted with permission.

Table 5–4 Strategic Alliance Success Factors

- Have a clear strategic purpose. Integrate the alliance with each partner's strategy. Ensure that mutual value is created for all partners.
- Find a fitting partner with compatible goals and complementary capabilities.
- Identify likely partnering risks and deal with them when the alliance is formed.
- Allocate tasks and responsibilities so that each partner can specialize in what it does best.
- Create incentives for cooperation to minimize differences in corporate culture or organization fit.
- Minimize conflicts among the partners by clarifying objectives and avoiding direct competition in the marketplace.
- If an international alliance, ensure that those managing it should have comprehensive cross-cultural knowledge.
- Exchange human resources to maintain communication and trust. Don't allow individual egos to dominate.
- Operate with long-term time horizons. The expectation of future gains can minimize short-term conflicts.
- Develop multiple joint projects so that any failures are counterbalanced by successes.
- Agree upon a monitoring process. Share information to build trust and keep projects on target. Monitor customer responses and service complaints.
- Be flexible in terms of willingness to renegotiate the relationship in terms of environmental changes and new opportunities.
- Agree upon an exit strategy for when the partners' objectives are achieved or the alliance is judged a failure.

Sources: Compiled from B. Gomes-Casseres, "Do You Really Have an Alliance Strategy?" *Strategy & Leadership* (September/October 1998), pp. 6–11; L. Segil, "Strategic Alliances for the 21st Century," *Strategy & Leadership* (September/October 1998), pp. 12–16; A. C. Inkpen and K-Q Li, "Joint Venture Formation: Planning and Knowledge Gathering for Success," *Organizational Dynamics* (Spring 1999), pp. 33–47. Inkpen and Li provide a checklist of 17 questions on p. 46.

5.5 Impact of the Internet on Business Strategy

The initial impact of the Internet was on marketing. **Business to consumer (B2C)** described the many dot-com start-ups selling items directly to consumers via their Web sites. The most well-known of these first entrants or pioneers was Amazon.com, the successful marketer of books and related merchandise. Not wanting to be disadvantaged late entrants, established manufacturers became active participants on the Internet. They supplemented their current distribution network with direct selling through their own Internet site or formed marketing alliances with technologically competent Web-based businesses. One such alliance is the joint venture between Toys "R" Us and Amazon.com to form Toysrus.com.

Business to business (B2B) describes the launching of Web portals aimed at electronically connecting buyers with suppliers, strengthening collective purchasing activities, and auctioning inventory. Dick Hunter, head of Dell Computer's supply chain management, states that one purpose of B2B is for information to replace inventory. For example, the companies supplying Dell with metal and plastic boxes for Dell's computers are located within 90 miles of Dell's assembly plant. They have access to Dell's real-time information on its use of their products. On the basis of Dell's usage of their parts, they make more and ship them as needed to Dell's plant. In turn, the suppliers keep only a day's worth of finished stock on hand. "If our information was 100% right," asserts Hunter, "the only inventory that would exist would be in transit."[43]

The B2B consortium is a recent example of the use of cooperative strategies to obtain competitive advantage. Traditional competitors are forming Internet consortia to centralize many activities, such as purchasing, which had been previously done internally. General Motors, Ford, and Chrysler have established an auto parts exchange called Covisint. Boeing, Lockheed Martin, Raytheon, and BAE Systems have formed the Global Aerospace & Defense Trading Exchange. Hewlett-Packard, Compaq, and 10 other computer makers have created Ehitex.com. Goodyear, Michelin, Bridgestone, and 4 other tire makers have formed Rubbernetwork.com. Although these consortia are being formed with great expectations, the reality has problems. For example, Covisint has three project leaders (one for each auto maker) who are battling over what to charge and how much trading data to allow users to access. The U. S. Federal Trade Commission is reviewing these consortia among erstwhile competitors for antitrust issues. Since Covisint's owners collectively dominate the North American automobile market, there could easily be collusion. According to Dana Corporation, an auto components supplier, "We're concerned about how big this gorilla is going to be. There's only so much room to squeeze prices."[44]

Although B2B is still in its initial stages, Hau Lee, director of the Global Supply Chain Management Forum at Stanford University proposes that business-to-business commerce will move through 4 stages of development.

Stage 1: *Information, such as demand forecasts and sales data, is exchanged.* Companies work to define common standards for inventory and point-of-sale to allow better planning.

Stage 2: *Companies move beyond data transfer to exchanging information.* For example, when Wal-Mart's Florida stores ran out of mosquito repellant during a heat wave, the company discovered that Warner Lambert, its supplier, was able to track weather forecasts to predict future peaks in demand. The sharing of this information enabled both companies to do better.

Stage 3: *Companies exchange the right to make decisions.* For example, since Wal-Mart sells disposable diapers made by P&G, which use sticky tape made by 3M, the three companies are experimenting with a system allowing one person instead of three to make the ordering decision for all three companies.

Stage 4: *Companies exchange work and roles.* The manufacturer becomes a retailer and the retailer moves to a support role. For example, companies such as VooDooCycles and Cannondale, makers of sport bicycles, are increasingly taking customers' orders directly and only then building the bicycles. Since a high quality bike needs last minute adjustments before it is ready for the customer, bicycle retailers are needed to perform this crucial service as well as to offer last minute purchases of helmets or other paraphernalia.[45]

Projections for the 21st Century

- From 1994 to 2010, the average life expectancy for women will rise from 67 to 71 and for men will increase from 63 to 67.
- From 1994 to 2010, the number of AIDS cases worldwide will increase from 20 million to 38 million.[46]

Discussion Questions

1. What industry forces might cause a propitious niche to disappear?

2. Is it possible for a company or business unit to follow a cost leadership strategy and a differentiation strategy simultaneously? Why or why not?

3. Is it possible for a company to have a sustainable competitive advantage when its industry becomes hyper-competitive?

4. What are the advantages and disadvantages of being a first mover in an industry? Give some examples of first mover and late mover firms. Were they successful?

5. Why are many strategic alliances temporary?

Strategic Practice Exercise

Following is an Internet case focusing upon strategic alliances. To begin the exercise, you will need a computer with Internet access. The rest is up to you!

Amy's Bread at Chelsea Market: A Web Discovery Case

CATHLEEN S. BURNS, UNIVERSITY OF MISSOURI, AND PAULA S. WEBER, ST. CLOUD STATE UNIVERSITY

COMPANY BACKGROUND AND HISTORY

In 1992, Amy Scherber opened her own business, "Amy's Bread." Amy's Bread is a retail and wholesale bakery in the Hell's Kitchen area of Manhattan. Amy's Bread has now expanded to a second Manhattan location in Chelsea Market, an innovative mall full of other entrepreneurs selling both food and nonfood items.

AMY'S DILEMMA

While Amy's Bread is doing well in Chelsea Market, profits are less than desired and the bakery has excess capacity. Amy is trying to decide what strategic alliances with other tenants in the mall would help her boost profits and absorb excess production capacity. You will help formulate Amy's emerging marketing strategy during your Web-based search process.

First Activity: Get familiar with Internet searches (if you are not already).

1. Check out a Web site that provides information on search engines and searching:
   - ⟨www.pbs.org/uti/begin.html⟩
   - ⟨www.microsoft.com/insider/internet/default.htm⟩
   - ⟨www.itrc.ucf.edu⟩ [search "search engines"]
   - ⟨www.zdnet.com/pccomp/features/fea1096/sub2.html⟩

- ⟨www.cl.ais.net/egsmlib/crawler.html⟩
- ⟨www.hamline.edu/library/bush/handouts/worms.html⟩

2. Search the Internet for Amy's Bread using at least three search engines:
   - ⟨yahoo.com⟩
   - ⟨altavista.com⟩
   - ⟨excite.com⟩
   - ⟨infoseek.com⟩
   - your choice

3. Search the Internet for Amy's Bread using one mega-search engine:
   - ⟨askjeeves.com⟩
   - ⟨metacrawler.com⟩

4. **Class discussion opportunity**: Share with the class (or your team) what you discovered about how search engines search the Internet. What differences exist in the data accessed by each search engine?

Second Activity: Get familiar with Amy's Bread's homepage.

   Class discussion opportunity: Share with the class (or your team) what information is included in Amy's Bread's Web site.
   - ⟨amysbread.com/sitemap.htm⟩

Third Activity: Prepare a brief Strengths/Weaknesses/Opportunities/Threats (SWOT) analysis for Amy's Bread.

1. **The Owner**: How did Amy prepare herself to be an entrepreneur?
   - ⟨amysbread.com/bio/htm⟩

2. **The Products**: How does Amy differentiate her bread products from low cost breads?
   - ⟨amysbread.com/chelsea.htm⟩

3. **The Media**: How does the media differentiate Amy's bread products from other bakeries' products?
   - ⟨amysbread.com/news.htm⟩

4. **The Locations**: How many Amy's Bread locations are there and how are they different or the same?
   - ⟨amysbread.com/locate.htm⟩
   - ⟨library.northernlight.com/SG19990714170000046.html?cb=13&sc=0⟩
   [The Web site above has some interesting history on Oreo cookies and the Chelsea Market location.]

5. **The Competition**: How many competitors does Amy's Bread have in the Manhattan area?
   - ⟨go-newyork.city.com/food/index.html⟩
   - ⟨www.womenshands.com/artisans/chelsea_market/related_story.htm⟩
   - ⟨www.womenshands.com/artisans/chelsea_market⟩

- ⟨store.yahoo.com/cmb/aboutcm.html⟩
- ⟨www.chelseamarketbaskets.com⟩
- ⟨www.elizabar.com⟩

6. **The Customers**: What can you discover about Chelsea Market customers? What do you think pedestrian traffic is like in that area? What are some of the demographics of New York City citizens that would affect their bakery purchases? For example, New Yorkers tend to walk or use public transportation; how does this impact their grocery shopping? New Yorkers tend to live in small apartments or condos; how does this impact their interest in dining out? What options exist for dining out in New York as opposed to a medium-sized city in your area?
   - ⟨www.demographia.com/dm-nyc.htm⟩ [Population density in NYC]
   - ⟨stats.bls.gov/csxmsa.htm⟩ [Consumer Expenditure Data by Metropolitan Statistical Area]

Fourth Activity: Consider strategic alliances that would be appropriate for Amy's Bread to pursue.

1. Using the textbook or Web resources, define what is meant by "strategic alliances." What are the advantages and disadvantages of strategic alliances?
   - ⟨www.e-marketing.com.au/documents/strategicalliances.htm⟩

2. On a macro level, what businesses has the developer, Irwin Cohen, included in the Chelsea Market commercial development?
   - ⟨store.yahoo.cmb/aboutcm.html⟩
   - ⟨westvillage.about.com/cities/midatlanticus/westvillage/ library/weekly/aa050499.htm⟩
   - ⟨www.womenshands.com/artisans/chelsea_market/related_story.htm⟩

3. Use the information in #2 above and your creativity to answer this question. On a more micro level, which of the Chelsea Market tenants appear to have potential for strategic alliances with Amy's Bread? Why?

4. Using the information in #2 above and your creativity, what other businesses (non-Chelsea Market tenants) can you imagine would have potential for strategic alliances with Amy's Bread? Why?

5. If the Chelsea Market developer asked you, Amy Scherber, for input on potential new mall tenants, what mall tenants would you recommend that the developer add to the mall? Why? What would be some of the decision factors the developer would consider in selecting tenants?

Source: This exercise was written as a case by Cathleen S. Burns of the University of Missouri, Columbia, and Paula S. Weber of St. Cloud State University and presented to the North American Research Association, October 2000. Copyright © 2000 by Cathleen S. Burns and Paula S. Weber. Reprinted by permission.

Key Terms

business strategy (p. 115)
business to business (B2B) (p. 131)
business to consumer (B2C) (p. 131)
collusion (p. 126)
competitive scope (p. 118)
competitive strategy (p. 117)
consolidated industry (p. 122)
cooperative strategies (p. 126)
cost focus (p. 119)
cost leadership (p. 118)
cost proximity (p. 120)
criticism of SWOT (p. 109)
differentiation (p. 119)

differentiation focus (p. 119)
differentiation strategy (p. 118)
distinctive competencies (p. 109)
first movers (p. 124)
fragmented industry (p. 121)
hypercompetitive (p. 123)
joint venture (p. 128)
late movers (p. 124)
licensing arrangement (p. 129)
lower cost strategy (p. 118)
market location tactics (p. 124)
mutual service consortium (p. 128)
offensive tactic (p. 125)
pioneer (p. 124)

propitious niche (p. 112)
SFAS (Strategic Factors Analysis
    Summary) Matrix (p. 110)
SO, ST, WO, WT Strategies (p. 115)
strategic alliance (p. 127)
strategic rollup (p. 122)
strategic window (p. 112)
stuck in the middle (p. 120)
SWOT (p. 109)
tactic (p. 123)
timing tactics (p. 124)
TOWS Matrix (p. 114)
value-chain partnership (p. 129)

Notes

1. K. W. Glaister and J. R. Falshaw, "Strategic Planning: Still Going Strong?" *Long Range Planning* (February 1999), pp. 107–116.
2. T. Brown, "The Essence of Strategy," *Management Review* (April 1997), pp. 8–13.
3. T. Hill and R. Westbrook, "SWOT Analysis: It's Time for a Product Recall," *Long Range Planning* (February 1997), pp. 46–52.
4. W. H. Newman, "Shaping the Master Strategy of Your Firm," *California Management Review*, Vol. 9, No. 3 (1967), pp. 77–88.
5. R. L. Simpson and O. Suris, "Alex Trotman's Goal: To Make Ford No. 1 in World Auto Sales," *Wall Street Journal* (July 18, 1995), p. A5.
6. M. E. Porter, *Competitive Strategy* (New York: The Free Press, 1980), pp. 34–41 as revised in M. E. Porter, *The Competitive Advantage of Nations* (New York: The Free Press, 1990), pp. 37–40.
7. J. O. DeCastro and J. J. Chrisman, "Narrow-Scope Strategies and Firm Performance: An Empirical Investigation," *Journal of Business Strategies* (Spring 1998), pp. 1–16; T. M. Stearns, N. M. Carter, P. D. Reynolds, and M. L. Williams, "New Firm Survival: Industry, Strategy, and Location," *Journal of Business Venturing* (January 1995), pp. 23–42.
8. Porter, *Competitive Strategy*, p. 35.
9. R. E. Caves and P. Ghemawat, "Identifying Mobility Barriers," *Strategic Management Journal* (January 1992), pp. 1–12.
10. R. O. Crockett, "They're Lining Up for Flicks in the 'Hood," *Business Week* (June 8, 1998), pp. 75–76.
11. D. P. Hamilton, "H-P's First Breakdown of Profit Shows Under 25% Is from Computer Business," *Wall Street Journal* (November 28, 2000), p. B8; P. Burrows, "Can Fiorina Reboot HP?" *Business Week* (November 27, 2000), p. 59.
12. C. Campbell-Hunt, "What Have We Learned About Generic Competitive Strategy? A Meta Analysis," *Strategic Management Journal* (February 2000), pp. 127–154.
13. M. Kroll, P. Wright, and R. A. Heiens, "The Contribution of Product Quality to Competitive Advantage: Impacts on Systematic Variance and Unexplained Variance in Returns," *Strategic Management Journal* (April 1999), pp. 375–384.
14. R. M. Hodgetts, "A Conversation with Michael E. Porter: A 'Significant Extension' Toward Operational Improvement and Positioning," *Organizational Dynamics* (Summer 1999), pp. 24–33.

15. N. Brodsky, "Size Matters," *INC.* (September 1998), pp. 31–32.
16. R. Tomsho, "Funeral Parlors Become Big Business," *Wall Street Journal* (September 18, 1996), pp. B1, B4.
17. P. F. Kocourek, S. Y. Chung, and M. G. McKenna, "Strategic Rollups: Overhauling the Multi-Merger Machine," *Strategy + Business* (2nd Qtr 2000), pp. 45–53.
18. J. A. Tannenbaum, "Acquisitive Companies Set Out to 'Roll Up' Fragmented Industries," *Wall Street Journal* (March 3, 1997), pp. P. A1, A6.
19. R. A. D'Aveni, *Hypercompetition* (New York: The Free Press, 1994), pp. xiii–xiv.
20. P. C. Nutt, "Surprising But True: Half the Decisions in Organizations Fail," *Academy of Management Executive* (November 1999), pp. 75–90.
21. Some refer to this as the economic concept of "increasing returns." Instead of reaching a point of diminishing returns when a product saturates a market and the curve levels off, the curve continues to go up as the company takes advantage of setting the standard to spin off new products that use the new standard to achieve higher performance than competitors. See J. Alley, "The Theory That Made Microsoft," *Fortune* (April 29, 1996), pp. 65–66.
22. H. Lee, K. G. Smith, C. M. Grimm, and A. Schomburg, "Timing, Order and Durability of New Product Advantages with Imitation," *Strategic Management Journal* (January 2000), pp. 23–30; Y. Pan and P. C. K. Chi, "Financial Performance and Survival of Multinational Corporations in China," *Strategic Management Journal* (April 1999), pp. 359–374; R. Makadok, "Can First-Mover and Early-Mover Advantages Be Sustained in an Industry with Low Barriers to Entry/Imitation?" *Strategic Management Journal* (July 1998), pp. 683–696; B. Mascarenhas, "The Order and Size of Entry Into International Markets," *Journal of Business Venturing* (July 1997), pp. 287–299.
23. G. J. Tellis and P. N. Golder, "First to Market, First to Fail? Real Causes of Enduring Market Leadership," *Sloan Management Review* (Winter 1996), pp. 65–75.
24. For an in-depth discussion of first and late mover advantages and disadvantages, see D-S. Cho, D-J. Kim, and D. K. Rhee, "Latecomer Strategies: Evidence from the Semiconductor Industry in Japan and Korea," *Organization Science* (July–August 1998), pp. 489–505.

25. T. S. Schoenecker and A. C. Cooper, "The Role of Firm Resources and Organizational Attributes in Determining Entry Timing: A Cross-Industry Study," *Strategic Management Journal* (December 1998), pp. 1127–1143.

26. Summarized from various articles by L. Fahey in *The Strategic Management Reader*, edited by L. Fahey (Englewood Cliffs, N.J.: Prentice-Hall, 1989), pp. 178–205.

27. This information on defensive tactics is summarized from M. E. Porter, *Competitive Advantage* (New York: Free Press, 1985), pp. 482–512.

28. T. M. Burton, "Archer-Daniels Faces a Potential Blow as Three Firms Admit Price-Fixing Plot," *Wall Street Journal* (August 28, 1996), pp. A3, A6; R. Henkoff, "The ADM Tale Gets Even Stranger," *Fortune* (May 13, 1996), pp. 113–120.

29. Much of the content on cooperative strategies was summarized from J. B. Barney, *Gaining and Sustaining Competitive Advantage* (Reading, Mass.: Addison-Wesley, 1997), pp. 255–278.

30. E. A. Murray, Jr., "Strategic Alliances: Gateway to the New Europe?" *Long Range Planning* (August 1993), p. 103.

31. H. Meyer, "My Enemy, My Friend," *Journal of Business Strategy* (September–October 1998), pp. 42–46.

32. T. K. Das and B-S Teng, "Instabilities of Strategic Alliances: An Internal Tensions Perspective," *Organization Science* (January–February 2000), pp. 77–101.

33. L. Segil, "Strategic Alliances for the 21st Century," *Strategy & Leadership* (September/October 1998), pp. 12–16.

34. E. A. Murray, Jr., and J. F. Mahon, "Strategic Alliances: Gateway to the New Europe?" *Long Range Planning* (August 1993), pp. 105–106.

35. R. M. Kanter, "Collaborative Advantage: The Art of Alliances," *Harvard Business Review* (July–August 1994), pp. 96–108.

36. B. Bremner, Z. Schiller, T. Smart, and W. J. Holstein, "Keiretsu Connections," *Business Week* (July 22, 1996), pp. 52–54.

37. R. P. Lynch, *The Practical Guide to Joint Ventures and Corporate Alliances* (New York: John Wiley and Sons, 1989), p. 7.

38. H. Green, "Double Play," *Business Week E-Biz* (October 23, 2000), pp. EB42–EB46.

39. L. L. Blodgett, "Factors in the Instability of International Joint Ventures: An Event History Analysis," *Strategic Management Journal* (September 1992), pp. 475–481; J. Bleeke and D. Ernst, "The Way to Win in Cross-Border Alliances," *Harvard Business Review* (November–December 1991), pp. 127–135; J. M. Geringer, "Partner Selection Criteria for Developed Country Joint Ventures," in *International Management Behavior*, 2nd ed., edited by H. W. Lane, and J. J. DiStephano (Boston: PWS-Kent, 1992), pp. 206–216.

40. S. Stevens, "Speeding the Signals of Change," *Appliance* (February 1995), p. 7.

41. K. Z. Andrews, "Manufacturer/Supplier Relationships: The Supplier Payoff," *Harvard Business Review* (September–October 1995), pp. 14–15.

42. P. Lorange, "Black-Box Protection of Your Core Competencies in Strategic Alliances," in *Cooperative Strategies: European Perspectives*, edited by P. W. Beamish and J. P. Killing (San Francisco: The New Lexington Press, 1997), pp. 59–99.

43. "Enter the Eco-System," *The Economist E-Management Survey* (November 11, 2000), p. 30.

44. N. Weinberg, "Herding Cats," *Forbes* (July 24, 2000), pp. 108–110.

45. "Enter the Eco-System," *The Economist E-Management Survey* (November 11, 2000), p. 34.

46. J. Warner, "21st Century Capitalism: Snapshot of the Next Century," *Business Week* (November 18, 1994), p. 194.

chapter 6

Strategy Formulation: Corporate Strategy

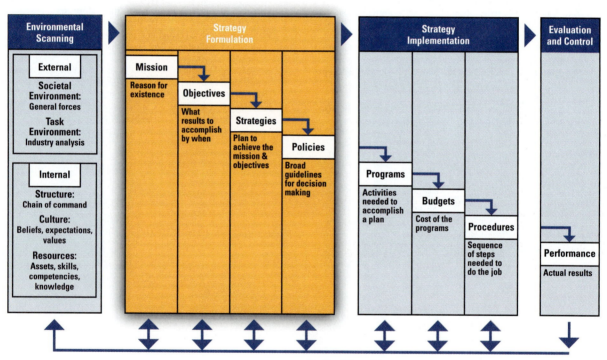

Environmental Scanning	Strategy Formulation	Strategy Implementation	Evaluation and Control

Feedback/Learning

eregulation and antitrust decisions by the U.S. federal government forced American Telephone and Telegraph (AT&T) to sell its local telephone business. This presented AT&T with some serious problems. For one thing, it no longer had any direct access to the individual households. It could no longer sell local service to its long-distance customers. The so-called "Baby Bells," such as US West and Bell South, controlled the telephone lines as well as the local phone business. Thanks to deregulation, upstarts like MCI and Sprint entered the long-distance business and began a price war to cut into AT&T's dominance of this market. As if this wasn't bad enough, the Baby Bells began talking about also entering the long-distance business. AT&T's market research revealed that consumers preferred to buy local and long-distance service from one source and get just one bill. The company had to either create a way to offer local phone service or watch its current long-distance customers be taken by competitors.

AT&T's top management established a new objective to obtain local access for its long-distance customers. How could it achieve this objective? One possibility, becoming a wholesaler by reselling local Bell service, didn't allow the company to control its costs or provide innovative services. The firm still needed its own local lines. It could buy a local phone system, such as Bell South, but for financial and antitrust reasons it could not purchase all of the Baby Bells. In a drastic change to the company's corporate strategy, AT&T chose to acquire the country's biggest cable operators, TCI and Media One, for $110 billion. With cable modems offering faster service than standard modems using phone lines, these acquisitions put AT&T directly into the booming Internet business. This was a significant advantage of the strategy. Unfortunately, the cable companies served only about half of AT&T's long-distance customers. To achieve its corporate objective, should the company purchase more cable companies (very expensive), form strategic alliances with cable companies (many cable companies were not interested), or should it try something different?[1]

AT&T's solution was to offer the tens of millions of U.S. households not served by AT&T Cable Services a new technology called "fixed wireless." This new technology would be able to beam both phone and Internet service from existing AT&T cell phone towers. This would enable the company to offer not only local and long-distance services, but also digital television, interactive TV, and high-speed Internet access. The hope was that this new strategy would provide AT&T with significant growth potential and sizable profits for many years to come.

6.1 Corporate Strategy

The vignette about AT&T illustrates the importance of corporate strategy to a firm's survival and success. **Corporate strategy** deals with three key issues facing the corporation as a whole:

1. The firm's overall orientation toward growth, stability, or retrenchment (*directional strategy*)
2. The industries or markets in which the firm competes through its products and business units (*portfolio strategy*)
3. The manner in which management coordinates activities, transfers resources, and cultivates capabilities among product lines and business units (*parenting strategy*)

Corporate strategy is primarily about the choice of direction for the firm as a whole.[2] This is true whether the firm is a small, one-product company or a large multinational corporation. In a large multibusiness company, however, corporate strategy is also about managing various product lines and business units for maximum value. In this instance, corporate headquarters must play the role of the organizational "parent," in that it must deal with various product and business unit "children." Even though each product line or business unit has its own competitive or cooperative strategy that it uses to obtain its own competitive advantage in the marketplace, the corporation must coordinate these different business strategies so that the corporation as a whole succeeds as a "family."[3]

Corporate strategy, therefore, includes decisions regarding the flow of financial and other resources to and from a company's product lines and business units. Through a series of coordinating devices, a company transfers skills and capabilities developed in one unit to other units that need such resources. In this way, it attempts to obtain synergies among numerous product lines and business units so that the corporate whole is greater than the sum of its individual business unit parts.[4] All corporations, from the smallest company offering one product in only one industry to the largest conglomerate operating in many industries with many products must, at one time or another, consider one or more of these issues.

To deal with each of the key issues, this chapter is organized into three parts that examine corporate strategy in terms of *directional strategy* (orientation toward growth), *portfolio analysis* (coordination of cash flow among units), and *corporate parenting* (building corporate synergies through resource sharing and development).

6.2 Directional Strategy

Just as every product or business unit must follow a business strategy to improve its competitive position, every corporation must decide its orientation toward growth by asking the following three questions:

1. Should we expand, cut back, or continue our operations unchanged?
2. Should we concentrate our activities within our current industry or should we diversify into other industries?
3. If we want to grow and expand nationally and/or globally, should we do so through internal development or through external acquisitions, mergers, or strategic alliances?

A corporation's **directional strategy** is composed of three general orientations (sometimes called grand strategies):

- **Growth strategies** expand the company's activities.
- **Stability strategies** make no change to the company's current activities.
- **Retrenchment strategies** reduce the company's level of activities.

Having chosen the general orientation (such as growth), a company's managers can select from several more specific corporate strategies such as concentration within one product line/industry or diversification into other products/industries. (See **Figure 6–1.**) These strategies are useful both to corporations operating in only one industry with one product line and to those operating in many industries with many product lines.

GROWTH STRATEGIES

By far the most widely pursued corporate directional strategies are those designed to achieve growth in sales, assets, profits, or some combination. Companies that do business in expanding industries must grow to survive. Continuing growth means increasing sales and a chance to take advantage of the experience curve to reduce the per-unit cost of products sold, thereby increasing profits. This cost reduction becomes extremely important if a corporation's industry is growing quickly and competitors are engaging in price wars in attempts to increase their shares of the market. Firms that have not reached "critical mass" (that is, gained the necessary economy of large-scale production) will face large losses unless they can find and fill a small,

Figure 6–1
Corporate Directional Strategies

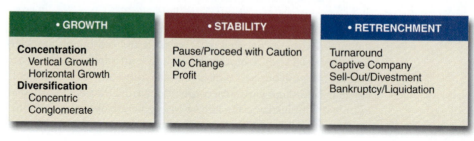

• GROWTH	• STABILITY	• RETRENCHMENT
Concentration Vertical Growth Horizontal Growth **Diversification** Concentric Conglomerate	Pause/Proceed with Caution No Change Profit	Turnaround Captive Company Sell-Out/Divestment Bankruptcy/Liquidation

but profitable, niche where higher prices can be offset by special product or service features. That is why Motorola, Inc., continued to spend large sums on the product development of cellular phones, pagers, and two-way radios, despite a serious drop in market share and profits. According to Motorola's Chairman George Fisher, "What's at stake here is leadership." Even though the industry was changing quickly, the company was working to avoid the erosion of its market share by jumping into new wireless markets as quickly as possible. Being one of the market leaders in this industry would almost guarantee Motorola enormous future returns.

A corporation can grow internally by expanding its operations both globally and domestically, or it can grow externally through mergers, acquisitions, and strategic alliances. A **merger** is a transaction involving two or more corporations in which stock is exchanged, but from which only one corporation survives. Mergers usually occur between firms of somewhat similar size and are usually "friendly." The resulting firm is likely to have a name derived from its composite firms. One example is the merging of Allied Corporation and Signal Companies to form Allied Signal. An **acquisition** is the purchase of a company that is completely absorbed as an operating subsidiary or division of the acquiring corporation. Examples are Procter & Gamble's acquisition of Richardson-Vicks, known for its Oil of Olay and Vidal Sassoon brands, and Noxell Corporation, known for Noxzema and Cover Girl.

Acquisitions usually occur between firms of different sizes and can be either friendly or hostile. Hostile acquisitions are often called takeovers. A **strategic alliance** is a partnership of two or more corporations or business units to achieve strategically significant objectives that are mutually beneficial. See **Chapter 5** for a detailed discussion of strategic alliances.

Growth is a very attractive strategy for two key reasons:

- Growth based on increasing market demand may mask flaws in a company—flaws that would be immediately evident in a stable or declining market. A growing flow of revenue into a highly leveraged corporation can create a large amount of **organization slack** (unused resources) that can be used to quickly resolve problems and conflicts between departments and divisions. Growth also provides a big cushion for a turnaround in case a strategic error is made. Larger firms also have more bargaining power than do small firms and are more likely to obtain support from key stakeholders in case of difficulty.

- A growing firm offers more opportunities for advancement, promotion, and interesting jobs. Growth itself is exciting and ego-enhancing for CEOs. The marketplace and potential investors tend to view a growing corporation as a "winner" or "on the move." Executive compensation tends to get bigger as an organization increases in size. Large firms are also more difficult to acquire than are smaller ones; thus an executive's job is more secure.

The two basic growth strategies are **concentration** on the current product line(s) in one industry and **diversification** into other product lines in other industries.

Concentration

If a company's current product lines have real growth potential, concentration of resources on those product lines makes sense as a strategy for growth. The two basic concentration strategies are vertical growth and horizontal growth. Growing firms in a growing industry tend to choose these strategies before they try diversification.

Vertical Growth   **Vertical growth** can be achieved by taking over a function previously provided by a supplier or by a distributor. The company, in effect, grows by making its own supplies and/or by distributing its own products. This may be done in order to reduce costs, gain control over a scarce resource, guarantee quality of a key input, or obtain access to potential customers. This growth can be achieved either internally by expanding current operations or externally through acquisitions. Henry Ford, for example, used internal company resources to build his River Rouge Plant outside Detroit. The manufacturing process was integrated to the point that iron ore entered one end of the long plant and finished automobiles rolled out the other end into a huge parking lot. In contrast, Cisco Systems, the maker of Internet hardware, chose the external route to vertical growth by purchasing Radiata, Inc., a maker of chip sets for wireless networks. This acquisition gave Cisco access to technology permitting wireless communications at speeds previously possible only with wired connections.[5]

Vertical growth results in **vertical integration**—the degree to which a firm operates vertically in multiple locations on an industry's value chain from extracting raw materials to manufacturing to retailing. More specifically, assuming a function previously provided by a supplier is called **backward integration** (going backward on an industry's value chain). The purchase of Carroll's Foods for its hog-growing facilities by Smithfield Foods, the world's largest pork processor, is an example of backward integration.[6] Assuming a function previously provided by a distributor is labeled **forward integration** (going forward on an industry's value chain). Micron, for example, used forward integration when it expanded out of its successful memory manufacturing business to make and market its own personal computers.

Vertical growth is a logical strategy for a corporation or business unit with a strong competitive position in a highly attractive industry—especially when technology is predictable and markets are growing.[7] To keep and even improve its competitive position, the company may use backward integration to minimize resource acquisition costs and inefficient operations as well as forward integration to gain more control over product distribution. The firm, in effect, builds on its distinctive competence by expanding along the industry's value chain to gain greater competitive advantage.

Although backward integration is usually more profitable than forward integration, it can reduce a corporation's strategic flexibility. The resulting encumbrance of expensive assets that might be hard to sell could create an *exit barrier*, preventing the corporation from leaving that particular industry. When sales of its autos were declining, General Motors, for example, resorted to offering outside parts suppliers the use of its idle factories and workers.

Transaction cost economics proposes that vertical integration is more efficient than contracting for goods and services in the marketplace when the transaction costs of buying goods on the open market become too great. When highly vertically integrated firms become excessively large and bureaucratic, however, the costs of managing the internal transactions may become greater than simply purchasing the needed goods externally, thus justifying outsourcing over vertical integration. See the **Theory As It Applies** feature on how transaction cost economics helps explain why firms vertically integrate.

Harrigan proposes that a company's degree of vertical integration can range from total ownership of the value chain needed to make and sell a product to no ownership at all.[8] (**See Figure 6–2.**) Under **full integration**, a firm internally makes 100% of its key supplies and completely controls its distributors. Large oil companies, such as BP Amoco and Royal Dutch Shell, are fully integrated. They own the oil rigs that pump the oil out of the ground, the ships and pipelines that transport the oil, the refineries that convert the oil to gasoline, and the trucks that deliver the gasoline to company-owned and franchised gas stations. If a corporation does not want the disadvantages of full vertical integration, it may choose either taper or

Figure 6–2
Vertical Integration Continuum

Full Integration	Taper Integration	Quasi-Integration	Long-Term Contract

Source: Suggested by K. R. Harrigan, *Strategies for Vertical Integration* (Lexington, MA: Lexington Books, D.C. Heath, 1983), pp. 16–21.

Theory As It Applies

Transaction Cost Economics Analyzes Vertical Growth Strategy

Why do corporations use vertical growth to permanently own suppliers or distributors when they could simply purchase individual items when needed on the open market? Transaction cost economics is a branch of institutional economics that attempts to answer this question. Beginning with work by Coase and extended by Williamson, transaction cost economics proposes that ownership of resources through vertical growth is more efficient than contracting for goods and services in the marketplace when the transaction costs of buying goods on the open market become too great. Transaction costs include the basic costs of drafting, negotiating, and safeguarding a market agreement (a contract) as well as the later managerial costs when the agreement is creating problems (goods aren't being delivered on time or quality is lower than needed), renegotiation costs (costs of meetings and phone calls), and the costs of settling disputes (lawyers' fees and court costs).

According to Williamson, three conditions must be met before a corporation will prefer internalizing a vertical transaction through ownership over contracting for the transaction in the marketplace: (1) a high level of uncertainty must surround the transaction, (2) assets involved in the transaction must be highly specialized to the transaction, and (3) the transaction must occur frequently. If there is a high level of uncertainty, it will be impossible to write a contract covering all contingencies and it is likely that the contractor will act opportunistically to exploit any gaps in the written agreement, thus creating problems and increasing costs. If the assets

being contracted for are highly specialized (goods or services with few alternate uses), there are likely to be few alternative suppliers, thus allowing the contractor to take advantage of the situation and increase costs. The more frequent the transactions, the more opportunity for the contractor to demand special treatment and thus increase costs further.

Vertical integration is not always more efficient than the marketplace, however. When highly vertically integrated firms become excessively large and bureaucratic, the costs of managing the internal transactions may become greater than simply purchasing the needed goods externally, thus justifying outsourcing over ownership. The usually hidden management costs (excessive layers of management, endless committee meetings needed for interdepartmental coordination, and delayed decision making due to excessively detailed rules and policies) add to the internal transaction costs, thus reducing the effectiveness and efficiency of vertical integration. The decision to own or to contract is, therefore, based on the particular situation surrounding the transaction and the ability of the corporation to manage the transaction internally both effectively and efficiently.

Sources: O. E. Williamson and S. G. Winter, eds., *The Nature of the Firm: Origins, Evolution, and Development* (New York: Oxford University Press, 1991); E. Mosakowski, "Organizational Boundaries and Economic Performance: An Empirical Study of Entrepreneurial Computer Firms," *Strategic Management Journal* (February 1991), pp. 115–133; P. S. Ring and A. H. Van De Ven, "Structuring Cooperative Relationships Between Organizations," *Strategic Management Journal* (October 1992), pp. 483–498.

quasi-integration strategies. With **taper integration**, a firm internally produces less than half of its own requirements and buys the rest from outside suppliers. In case of Smithfield Foods, its purchase of Carroll's allows it to produce 27% of the hogs it needs to process into pork. In terms of distributors, a firm sells part of its goods through company-owned stores and the rest through general wholesalers. Both Xerox and IBM have experimented (unsuccessfully) with selling their products through their own stores. With **quasi-integration**, a company does not make any of its key supplies but purchases most of its requirements from outside suppliers that are under its partial control. For example, by purchasing 20% of the common stock of a key supplier, In Focus Systems, Motorola guaranteed its access to In Focus' technology and enabled Motorola to establish a joint venture with In Focus to manufacture flat-panel video displays.[9] An example of forward quasi-integration would be a large pharmaceutical firm that acquires part interest in a drugstore chain in order to guarantee that its drugs have access to the distribution channel. Purchasing part interest in a key supplier or distributor usually provides a company with a seat on the other firm's board of directors, thus guaranteeing the acquiring firm both information and control. A company may not want to invest in suppliers or distributors, but it still wants to guarantee access to needed supplies or distribution channels. In this case, it may use contractual agreements. **Long-term contracts** are agreements between two separate firms to provide agreed-upon goods and services to each other for a specified period of time. This cannot really be considered to be vertical integration unless the contract specifies that the supplier or distributor cannot have a similar relationship with a competitive firm. In this case, the supplier or distributor is really a *captive company* that, although officially independent, does most of its business with the contracted firm and is formally tied to the other company through a long-term contract.

Recently there has been a movement away from vertical growth strategies (and thus vertical integration) toward cooperative contractual relationships with suppliers and even with competitors. These relationships range from **outsourcing**, in which resources are purchased from outsiders through long-term contracts instead of being made in-house (for example, Hewlett-Packard buys all its laser engines from Canon for HP's laser jet printers), to strategic alliances, in which partnerships, technology licensing agreements, and joint ventures supplement a firm's capabilities (for example, Toshiba has used strategic alliances with GE, Siemens, Motorola, and Ericsson to become one of the world's leading electronic companies).[10]

Horizontal Growth **Horizontal growth** can be achieved by expanding the firm's products into other geographic locations and/or by increasing the range of products and services offered to current markets. In this case, the company expands sideways at the same location on the industry's value chain. For example, Dell Computers followed a horizontal growth strategy when it extended its mail order business to Europe and to China. A company can grow horizontally through internal development or externally through acquisitions or strategic alliances with another firm in the same industry.

Horizontal growth results in **horizontal integration**—the degree to which a firm operates in multiple geographic locations at the same point in an industry's value chain. Horizontal integration for a firm may range from full to partial ownership to long-term contracts. For example, KLM, the Dutch airline, purchased a controlling stake (partial ownership) in Northwest Airlines to obtain access to American and Asian markets. KLM was unable to acquire all of Northwest's stock because of U.S. government regulations forbidding foreign ownership of a domestic airline (for defense reasons). Many small commuter airlines engage in long-term contracts with major airlines in order to offer a complete arrangement for travelers. For example, Mesa Airlines arranged a five-year agreement with United Airlines to be listed on United's computer reservations as United Express through the Denver airport.

Diversification Strategies

When an industry consolidates and becomes mature, most of the surviving firms have reached the limits of growth using vertical and horizontal growth strategies. Unless the competitors are able to expand internationally into less mature markets, they may have no choice but to diversify into different industries if they want to continue growing. The two basic diversification strategies are concentric and conglomerate.

Concentric (Related) Diversification Growth through **concentric diversification** into a related industry may be a very appropriate corporate strategy when a firm has a strong competitive position but industry attractiveness is low. By focusing on the characteristics that have given the company its distinctive competence, the company uses those very strengths as its means of diversification. The firm attempts to secure strategic fit in a new industry where the firm's product knowledge, its manufacturing capabilities, and the marketing skills it used so effectively in the original industry can be put to good use.[11] The corporation's products or processes are related in some way: They possess some common thread. The search is for **synergy**, the concept that two businesses will generate more profits together than they could separately. The point of commonality may be similar technology, customer usage, distribution, managerial skills, or product similarity.

This is the rationale taken by Toro Company when it diversified out of lawn mowers into snow blowers, recycling products, and irrigation equipment. According to CEO Kendrick Melrose, the company is changing from a lawn mower company to "an outdoor environmental problem-solver."[12]

The firm may choose to diversify concentrically through either internal or external means. American Airlines, for example, has diversified both internally and externally out of the unpredictable airline business into a series of related businesses run by the parent company, AMR Corporation. Building on the expertise of its SABRE Travel Information Network, it built a computerized reservations system for the French high-speed rail network and for the tunnel under the English Channel.

Conglomerate (Unrelated) Diversification   When management realizes that the current industry is unattractive and that the firm lacks outstanding abilities or skills that it could easily transfer to related products or services in other industries, the most likely strategy is **conglomerate diversification**—diversifying into an industry unrelated to its current one. Rather than maintaining a common thread throughout their organization, strategic managers who adopt this strategy are primarily concerned with financial considerations of cash flow or risk reduction.

The emphasis in conglomerate diversification is on financial considerations rather than on the product–market synergy common to concentric diversification. A cash-rich company with few opportunities for growth in its industry might, for example, move into another industry where opportunities are great but cash is hard to find. Another instance of conglomerate diversification might be when a company with a seasonal and, therefore, uneven cash flow purchases a firm in an unrelated industry with complementing seasonal sales that will level out the cash flow. CSX management considered the purchase of a natural gas transmission business (Texas Gas Resources) by CSX Corporation (a railroad-dominated transportation company) to be a good fit because most of the gas transmission revenue was realized in the winter months—the railroads' lean period.

INTERNATIONAL ENTRY OPTIONS

In today's world, growth usually has international implications. Research indicates that going international is positively associated with firm profitability.[13] A corporation can select from several strategic options the most appropriate method for it to use in entering a foreign market or establishing manufacturing facilities in another country. The options vary from simple exporting to acquisitions to management contracts. As in the case of KLM's purchase of stock in Northwest Airlines, this can be a part of the corporate strategies previously discussed. See the   **Global Issue** feature to see how Wal-Mart is using international entry options in a horizontal growth strategy to expand in Europe. Some of the more popular options for international entry are as follows:

- **Exporting**: A good way to minimize risk and experiment with a specific product is **exporting**, shipping goods produced in the company's home country to other countries for marketing. The company could choose to handle all critical functions itself, or it could contract these functions to an export management company. Exporting is becoming increasingly popular for small businesses because of the Internet, fax machines, 800 numbers, and overnight air express services, which reduce the once formidable costs of going international.

Global Issue

Wal-Mart Enters International Markets

How can Wal-Mart continue to grow? From its humble beginnings in Bentonville, Arkansas, the company has successfully grown such that its discount stores can now be found in most every corner of the United States. Wal-Mart long ago surpassed Sears as the largest retailer in the country. Over the next few years most of the company's growth will likely continue to come from expansion within the U.S., but an increasing percentage will be coming from international markets. The company's first attempts to expand outside the country in the early 1990s had flopped miserably. It offered the wrong products, such as tennis balls that wouldn't bounce in high-altitude Mexico City and 110-volt appliances in Argentina where 220 volts is the norm. Learning from those early attempts, Wal-Mart opened profitable stores in Canada, Mexico, China, Brazil, and Britain. Of the company's total 1998 sales, 9% came from international operations. Management wanted to raise that amount to 20% by 2001.

After closing a losing operation in Indonesia, management altered its strategy to focus on becoming a major retailer in Europe. In December 1997, Wal-Mart purchased the 21-store German Tertkauf chain. A year later, it strengthened its hold in Germany by acquiring 74 Interspar stores. It took months of remodeling the stores with wider aisles, better lighting, and more check-out counters before the stores were rechristened Wal-Mart. In 1999, Wal-Mart bought Britain's 229-store Asda Group, the country's third largest grocery chain. Nevertheless, according to Hubertus Pellengahr of the Association of German Retailers, "They will have to grow a lot to gain critical mass."

Not content to grow by acquisition, Wal-Mart's management announced in July 2000 a three-year plan to open 50 new locations in Germany and to double its share of the European discount market to 20%. Given difficulties in obtaining building permits from the German bureaucracy, management negotiated with Germany's largest retailer, Metro AG, to swap subsidiaries. This would give Wal-Mart two additional German chains. Given that nonunionized Wal-Mart was now dealing with German unions, analysts wondered if management could turn the money-losing German operation into a profitable one.

Sources: L. Kim, "Crossing the Rhine," *U.S. News & World Report* (August 14, 2000; "Wal-Mart to Buy British Food Chain," *Des Moines Register* (June 15, 1999), p. 9S; P. Geitner, "Wal-Mart Rises in Germany," *Des Moines Register* (December 11, 1999), p. 12S; *Money* (December, 1999), p. 162.

- **Licensing:** Under a **licensing** agreement, the licensing firm grants rights to another firm in the host country to produce and/or sell a product. The licensee pays compensation to the licensing firm in return for technical expertise. This is an especially useful strategy if the trademark or brand name is well known, but the company does not have sufficient funds to finance its entering the country directly. Anheuser-Busch uses this strategy to produce and market Budweiser beer in the United Kingdom, Japan, Israel, Australia, Korea, and the Philippines. This strategy also becomes important if the country makes entry via investment either difficult or impossible. The danger always exists, however, that the licensee might develop its competence to the point that it becomes a competitor to the licensing firm. Therefore, a company should never license its distinctive competence, even for some short-run advantage.

- **Franchising:** Under a **franchising** agreement, the franchiser grants rights to another company to open a retail store using the franchiser's name and operating system. In exchange, the franchisee pays the franchiser a percentage of its sales as a royalty. Franchising provides an opportunity for firms to establish a presence in countries where the population or per capita spending is not sufficient to support a major expansion effort.[14] Franchising accounts for 40% of total U.S. retail sales. Approximately 44% of U.S. franchisers, such as Toys "R" Us, are currently franchising internationally while an additional 31% are planning to do so.[15]

- **Joint Ventures:** The rate of **joint venture** formation between U.S. companies and international partners has been growing 27% annually since 1985.[16] It is the most popular strategy used to enter a new country.[17] Companies often form joint ventures to combine the resources and expertise needed to develop new products or technologies. It also enables a firm to enter a country that restricts foreign ownership. The corporation can enter another country with fewer assets at stake and thus lower risk. For example, when Mexico privatized its railroads in 1996 (two years after the North American Trade Agreement was ratified), the Kansas City Southern (KCS) saw an opportunity to form one complete railroad from Mexico's industrialized northeast to Canada. KCS jointly bid with the Mexican shipping line Transportacion Maritima Mexicana (with whom it would jointly operate the Mexican rail system) to purchase 80% of Grupo Transportacion Ferroviaria Mexicana (TFM). KCS then formed an alliance with Canadian National Railway to complete the route.[18] A joint venture may be an association between a company and a firm in the host country or a government agency in that country. A quick method of obtaining local management, it also reduces the risks of expropriation and harassment by host country officials.

- **Acquisitions:** A relatively quick way to move into an international area is through **acquisitions**—purchasing another company already operating in that area. Synergistic benefits can result if the company acquires a firm with strong complementary product lines and a good distribution network. Maytag Corporation's acquisition of Hoover gave it entry into Europe through Hoover's strength in home appliances in the United Kingdom and in its vacuum cleaner distribution centers on the European continent. To expand into North America, the Swedish appliance maker, A.B. Electrolux, purchased the major home appliance operations of White Consolidated Industries and renamed the unit Frigidaire. Research does suggest that wholly owned subsidiaries are more successful in international undertakings than are strategic alliances, such as joint ventures.[19] This is one reason why firms more experienced in international markets take a higher ownership position when making a foreign investment.[20] In some countries, however, acquisitions can be difficult to arrange because of a lack of available information about potential candidates. Government restrictions on ownership, such as the U.S. requirement that limits foreign ownership of U.S. airlines to 49% of nonvoting and 25% of voting stock, can also discourage acquisitions.

- **Green-Field Development:** If a company doesn't want to purchase another company's problems along with its assets (as Japan's Bridgestone did when it acquired Firestone in the United States) it may choose **green-field development**—building its own manufacturing plant and distribution system. This is usually a far more complicated and expensive operation than acquisition, but it allows a company more freedom in designing the plant, choosing suppliers, and hiring a workforce. For example, Nissan, Honda, and Toyota built auto factories in rural areas of Great Britain and then hired a young workforce with no experience in the industry.

- **Production Sharing:** Coined by Peter Drucker, the term **production sharing** means the process of combining the higher labor skills and technology available in the developed countries with the lower cost labor available in developing countries. The current trend is to move data processing and programming activities "offshore" to places such as Ireland, India, Barbados, Jamaica, the Philippines, and Singapore where wages are lower, English is spoken, and telecommunications are in place.

- **Turnkey Operations: Turnkey operations** are typically contracts for the construction of operating facilities in exchange for a fee. The facilities are transferred to the host country or firm when they are complete. The customer is usually a government agency of, for example, a Middle Eastern country that has decreed that a particular product must be produced locally and under its control. For example, Fiat built an auto plant in Russia to produce an older model of Fiat under a Russian brand name. MNCs that perform turnkey operations are frequently industrial equipment manufacturers that supply some of their own equipment for the project and that commonly sell replacement parts and maintenance services to the host country. They thereby create customers as well as future competitors.

- **BOT Concept:** The **BOT** (**B**uild, **O**perate, **T**ransfer) **concept** is a variation of the turnkey operation. Instead of turning the facility (usually a power plant or toll road) over to the host country when completed, the company operates the facility for a fixed period of time during which it earns back its investment, plus a profit. It then turns the facility over to the government at little or no cost to the host country.[21]

- **Management Contracts:** A large corporation operating throughout the world is likely to have a large amount of management talent at its disposal. **Management contracts** offer a means through which a corporation may use some of its personnel to assist a firm in a host country for a specified fee and period of time. Management contracts are common when a host government expropriates part or all of a foreign-owned company's holdings in its country. The contracts allow the firm to continue to earn some income from its investment and keep the operations going until local management is trained.

CONTROVERSIES IN DIRECTIONAL GROWTH STRATEGIES

Is vertical growth better than horizontal growth? Is concentric diversification better than conglomerate diversification? Although the research is not in complete agreement, growth into areas related to a company's current product lines is generally more successful than is growth into completely unrelated areas.[22] For example, one study of various growth projects examined how many were considered successful, that is, still in existence after 22 years. The results were: vertical growth, 80%; horizontal growth, 50%; concentric diversification, 35%; and conglomerate diversification, 28%.[23]

In terms of diversification strategies, research suggests that the relationship between relatedness and performance is curvilinear in the shape of an inverted U-shaped curve. If a new business is very similar to that of the acquiring firm, it adds little new to the corporation and only marginally improves performance. If the new business is completely different from the acquiring company's businesses, there may be very little potential for any synergy. If, however, the new business provides new resources and capabilities in a different, but similar, business, the likelihood of a significant performance improvement is high.[24]

Is internal growth better than external growth? Corporations can follow the growth strategies of either concentration or diversification through the internal development of new products and services or through external acquisitions, mergers, and strategic alliances. The value of global acquisitions and mergers has steadily increased from around $300,000 billion in 1991 to $3.5 trillion in 2000.[25] Although not yet conclusive, the research indicates that firms that grow through acquisitions do not perform financially as well as firms that grow through internal means.[26] Studies do reveal that over two-thirds of acquisitions are failures primarily because the premiums paid were too high for them to earn their cost of capital.[27] Other research indicates, however, that acquisitions have a higher survival rate than do new internally generated business ventures.[28] It is likely that neither strategy is best by itself and that some combination of internal and external growth strategies is better than using one or the other exclusively.[29]

STABILITY STRATEGIES

A corporation may choose stability over growth by continuing its current activities without any significant change in direction. Although sometimes viewed as a lack of strategy, the stability family of corporate strategies can be appropriate for a successful corporation operating in a reasonably predictable environment.[30] They are very popular with small business owners who have found a niche and are happy with their success and the manageable size of their firms. Stability strategies can be very useful in the short run, but they can be dangerous if followed for too long (as many small-town businesses discovered when Wal-Mart came to town). Some of the more popular of these strategies are the pause/proceed with caution, no change, and profit strategies.

Pause/Proceed with Caution Strategy

A **pause/proceed with caution strategy** is, in effect, a timeout—an opportunity to rest before continuing a growth or retrenchment strategy. It is a very deliberate attempt to make only incremental improvements until a particular environmental situation changes. It is typically conceived as a temporary strategy to be used until the environment becomes more hospitable or to enable a company to consolidate its resources after prolonged rapid growth. This was the strategy Dell Computer Corporation followed in 1993 after its growth strategy had resulted in more growth than it could handle. Explained CEO Michael Dell, "We grew 285% in two years, and we're having some growing pains." Selling personal computers by mail enabled it to underprice Compaq Computer and IBM, but it could not keep up with the needs of the $2 billion, 5,600-employee company selling PCs in 95 countries. Dell did not give up on its growth strategy; it merely put it temporarily in limbo until the company was able to hire new managers, improve the structure, and build new facilities.

No Change Strategy

A **no change strategy** is a decision to do nothing new—a choice to continue current operations and policies for the foreseeable future. Rarely articulated as a definite strategy, a no change strategy's success depends on a lack of significant change in a corporation's situation. The relative stability created by the firm's modest competitive position in an industry facing little or no growth encourages the company to continue on its current course, making only small adjustments for inflation in its sales and profit objectives. There are no obvious opportunities or threats nor much in the way of significant strengths or weaknesses. Few aggressive new competitors are likely to enter such an industry. The corporation has probably found a reasonably profitable and stable niche for its products. Unless the industry is undergoing consolidation, the relative comfort a company in this situation experiences is likely to encourage the company to follow a no change strategy in which the future is expected to continue as an extension of the present. Most small-town businesses probably follow this strategy before Wal-Mart moves into their areas.

Profit Strategy

A **profit strategy** is a decision to do nothing new in a worsening situation but instead to act as though the company's problems are only temporary. The profit strategy is an attempt to artificially support profits when a company's sales are declining by reducing investment and short-term discretionary expenditures. Rather than announcing the company's poor position to shareholders and the investment community at large, top management may be tempted to follow this very seductive strategy. Blaming the company's problems on a hostile environment (such as antibusiness government policies, unethical competitors, finicky customers, and/or greedy lenders), management defers investments and/or cuts expenses (such as R&D, maintenance, and advertising) to stabilize profits during this period. It may even sell one of its product lines for the cash flow benefits. Obviously the profit strategy is useful only to help a company get through a temporary difficulty. Unfortunately the strategy is seductive and if continued long enough will lead to a serious deterioration in a corporation's competitive position. The profit strategy is thus usually top management's passive, short-term, and often self-serving response to the situation.

RETRENCHMENT STRATEGIES

A company may pursue retrenchment strategies when it has a weak competitive position in some or all of its product lines resulting in poor performance—sales are down and profits are becoming losses. These strategies impose a great deal of pressure to improve performance. In an attempt to eliminate the weaknesses that are dragging the company down, management may follow one of several retrenchment strategies ranging from turnaround or becoming a captive company to selling out, bankruptcy, or liquidation.

Turnaround Strategy

The **turnaround strategy** emphasizes the improvement of operational efficiency and is probably most appropriate when a corporation's problems are pervasive but not yet critical. Analogous to a weight reduction diet, the two basic phases of a turnaround strategy are contraction and consolidation.[31]

Contraction is the initial effort to quickly "stop the bleeding" with a general across-the-board cutback in size and costs. The second phase, **consolidation**, implements a program to stabilize the now-leaner corporation. To streamline the company, plans are developed to reduce unnecessary overhead and to make functional activities cost-justified. This is a crucial time for the organization. If the consolidation phase is not conducted in a positive manner, many of the best people leave the organization. An overemphasis on downsizing and cutting costs coupled with a heavy hand by top management is usually counterproductive and can actually hurt performance.[32] If, however, all employees are encouraged to get involved in productivity improvements, the firm is likely to emerge from this retrenchment period a much stronger and better organized company. It has improved its competitive position and is able once again to expand the business. See the **boxed feature** for a description of IBM's effective use of the turnaround strategy.

Captive Company Strategy

A **captive company strategy** is the giving up of independence in exchange for security. A company with a weak competitive position may not be able to engage in a full-blown turnaround strategy. The industry may not be sufficiently attractive to justify such an effort from either the current management or from investors. Nevertheless a company in this situation faces poor sales and increasing losses unless it takes some action. Management desperately searches for an "angel" by offering to be a captive company to one of its larger customers in order to guarantee the company's continued existence with a long-term contract. In this way, the corporation may be able to reduce the scope of some of its functional activities, such as marketing, thus reducing costs significantly. The weaker company gains certainty of sales and production in return for becoming heavily dependent on one firm for at least 75% of its sales. For example, to become the sole supplier of an auto part to General Motors, Simpson Industries of Birmingham, Michigan, agreed to let a special team from GM inspect its engine parts facilities and books and interview its employees. In return, nearly 80% of the company's production was sold to GM through long-term contracts.[33]

Sell-Out/Divestment Strategy

If a corporation with a weak competitive position in its industry is unable either to pull itself up by its bootstraps or to find a customer to which it can become a captive company, it may have no choice but to **sell out**. The sell-out strategy makes sense if management can still obtain a good price for its shareholders and the employees can keep their jobs by selling the entire company to another firm. The hope is that another company will have the necessary resources and determination to return the company to profitability. This is why Rover, the venerable British car manufacturer, was sold to BMW (Bayerische Motoren Werke AG) for $1.2 billion in 1994.

Chapter 5 dealt with how individual product lines and business units can gain competitive advantage in the marketplace by using competitive and cooperative strategies. Companies with multiple product lines or business units must also ask themselves how these various products and business units should be managed to boost overall corporate performance.

- How much of our time and money should we spend on our best products and business units to ensure that they continue to be successful?

- How much of our time and money should we spend developing new costly products, most of which will never be successful?

One of the most popular aids to developing corporate strategy in a multibusiness corporation is portfolio analysis. Although its popularity has dropped since the 1970s and 1980s, when over half of the largest business corporations used portfolio analysis, it is still used by around 27% of *Fortune 500* firms in corporate strategy formulation.[38] Portfolio analysis puts corporate headquarters into the role of an internal banker. In **portfolio analysis**, top management views its product lines and business units as a series of investments from which it expects a profitable return. The product lines/business units form a portfolio of investments that top management must constantly juggle to ensure the best return on the corporation's invested money. Two of the most popular approaches are the BCG Growth-Share Matrix and GE Business Screen. This concept can also be used to develop strategies for international markets.

BCG GROWTH-SHARE MATRIX

The **BCG (Boston Consulting Group) Growth-Share Matrix** depicted in **Figure 6–3** is the simplest way to portray a corporation's portfolio of investments. Each of the corporation's product lines or business units is plotted on the matrix according to both the growth rate of the industry in which it competes and its relative market share. A unit's relative competitive position is defined as its market share in the industry divided by that of the largest other competitor. By this calculation, a relative market share above 1.0 belongs to the market leader. The business growth rate is the percentage of market growth, that is, the percentage by which sales of a particular business unit classification of products have increased. The matrix assumes that, other things being equal, a growing market is attractive.

The line separating areas of high and low relative competitive position is set at 1.5 times. A product line or business unit must have relative strengths of this magnitude to ensure that it will have the dominant position needed to be a "star" or "cash cow." On the other hand, a product line or unit having a relative competitive position less than 1.0 has "dog" status.[39] Each product or unit is represented in **Figure 6–3** by a circle. The area of the circle represents the relative significance of each business unit or product line to the corporation in terms of assets used or sales generated.

The BCG Growth-Share Matrix has a lot in common with the product life cycle. As a product moves through its life cycle, it is categorized into one of four types for the purpose of funding decisions:

- **Question marks** (sometimes called "problem children" or "wildcats") are new products with the potential for success, but they need a lot of cash for development. If such a product is to gain enough market share to become a market leader and thus a star, money must be taken from more mature products and spent on a question mark.

- **Stars** are market leaders typically at the peak of their product life cycle and are usually able to generate enough cash to maintain their high share of the market. When their market growth rate slows, stars become cash cows.

Figure 6–3

BCG Growth-Share Matrix

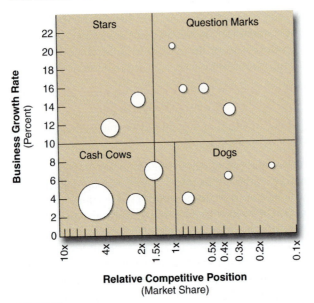

Source: B. Hedley, "Strategy and the Business Portfolio," *Long Range Planning* (February 1977), p. 12. Reprinted with permission from Elsevier Science.

- **Cash cows** typically bring in far more money than is needed to maintain their market share. In this declining stage of their life cycle, these products are "milked" for cash that will be invested in new question marks.

- **Dogs** have low market share and do not have the potential (because they are in an unattractive industry) to bring in much cash. Question marks unable to obtain a dominant market share (and thus become stars) by the time the industry growth rate inevitably slows become dogs. According to the BCG Growth-Share Matrix, dogs should be either sold off or managed carefully for the small amount of cash they can generate.

Underlying the BCG Growth-Share Matrix is the concept of the experience curve (discussed in **Chapter 4**). The key to success is assumed to be market share. Firms with the highest market share tend to have a cost leadership position based on economies of scale, among other things. If a company is able to use the experience curve to its advantage, it should be able to manufacture and sell new products at a price low enough to garner early market share leadership (assuming no successful imitation by competitors). Once the product becomes a star, it is destined to be very profitable, considering its inevitable future as a cash cow.

Having plotted the current positions of its product lines or business units on a matrix, a company can project their future positions, assuming no change in strategy. Present and projected matrixes can thus be used to help identify major strategic issues facing the organization. The goal of any company is to maintain a balanced portfolio so it can be self-sufficient in cash and always working to harvest mature products in declining industries to support new ones in growing industries.

The BCG Growth-Share Matrix is a very well-known portfolio concept with some clear *advantages.* It is quantifiable and easy to use. Cash cows, dogs, and stars are an easy-to-remember way to refer to a corporation's business units or products. Unfortunately the BCG Growth-Share Matrix also has some serious *limitations*:

- The use of highs and lows to form four categories is too simplistic.
- The link between market share and profitability is questionable.[40] Low-share businesses can also be profitable. For example, Olivetti is still profitably selling manual typewriters through mail order catalogues.
- Growth rate is only one aspect of industry attractiveness.
- Product lines or business units are considered only in relation to one competitor: the market leader. Small competitors with fast-growing market shares are ignored.
- Market share is only one aspect of overall competitive position.

GE BUSINESS SCREEN

General Electric, with the assistance of the McKinsey and Company consulting firm, developed a more complicated matrix. As depicted in **Figure 6–4**, the **GE Business Screen** includes 9 cells based on long-term industry attractiveness and business strength/competitive position. The GE Business Screen, in contrast to the BCG Growth-Share Matrix, includes much more data in its 2 key factors than just business growth rate and comparable market share. For example, at GE, industry attractiveness includes market growth rate, industry profitability, size, and pricing practices, among other possible opportunities and threats. Business strength or competitive position includes market share as well as technological position, profitability, and size, among other possible strengths and weaknesses.[41]

Figure 6–4

General Electric's Business Screen

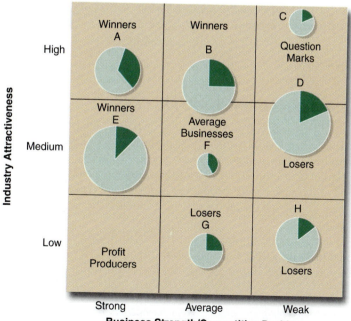

Source: Adapted from *Strategic Management in GE*, Corporate Planning and Development, General Electric Corporation. Used by permission of General Electric Company.

The individual product lines or business units are identified by a letter and plotted as circles on the GE Business Screen. The area of each circle is in proportion to the size of the industry in terms of sales. The pie slices within the circles depict the market share of each product line or business unit.

To plot product lines or business units on the GE Business Screen, follow these 4 steps:

Step 1: Select criteria to rate the industry for each product line or business unit. Assess overall industry attractiveness for each product line or business unit on a scale from 1 (very unattractive) to 5 (very attractive).

Step 2: Select the key factors needed for success in each product line or business unit. Assess business strength/competitive position for each product line or business unit on a scale of 1 (very weak) to 5 (very strong).

Step 3: Plot each product line's or business unit's current position on a matrix like that depicted in **Figure 6–4**.

Step 4: Plot the firm's future portfolio assuming that present corporate and business strategies remain unchanged. Is there a performance gap between projected and desired portfolios? If so, this gap should serve as a stimulus to seriously review the corporation's current mission, objectives, strategies, and policies.

Overall the nine-cell GE Business Screen is an improvement over the BCG Growth-Share Matrix. The GE Business Screen considers many more variables and does not lead to such simplistic conclusions. It recognizes, for example, that the attractiveness of an industry can be assessed in many different ways (other than simply using growth rate), and it thus allows users to select whatever criteria they feel are most appropriate to their situation. This portfolio matrix, however, does have some *shortcomings*:

- It can get quite complicated and cumbersome.
- The numerical estimates of industry attractiveness and business strength/competitive position give the appearance of objectivity, but they are in reality subjective judgments that may vary from one person to another.
- It cannot effectively depict the positions of new products or business units in developing industries.

INTERNATIONAL PORTFOLIO ANALYSIS

To aid international strategic planning, portfolio analysis can be applied to international markets.[42] Two factors form the axes of the matrix in **Figure 6–5**. A **country's attractiveness** is composed of its market size, the market rate of growth, the extent and type of government regulation, and economic and political factors. A **product's competitive strength** is composed of its market share, product fit, contribution margin, and market support. Depending on where a product fits on the matrix, it should either receive more funding or be harvested for cash.

Portfolio analysis might not be useful, however, to corporations operating in a global industry rather than a multidomestic one. In discussing the importance of global industries, Porter argues against the use of portfolio analysis on a country-by-country basis:

> *In a global industry, however, managing international activities like a portfolio will undermine the possibility of achieving competitive advantage. In a global industry, a firm must in some way integrate its activities on a worldwide basis to capture the linkage among countries.*[43]

Figure 6–5
Portfolio Matrix for Plotting Products by Country

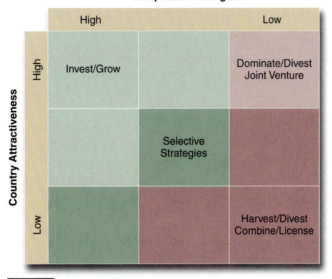

Source: G. D. Harrell and R. O. Kiefer, "Multinational Strategic Market Portfolios," *MSU Business Topics* (Winter 1981), p. 7. Reprinted by permission.

ADVANTAGES AND LIMITATIONS OF PORTFOLIO ANALYSIS

Portfolio analysis is commonly used in strategy formulation because it offers certain *advantages*:

- It encourages top management to evaluate each of the corporation's businesses individually and to set objectives and allocate resources for each.
- It stimulates the use of externally oriented data to supplement management's judgment.
- It raises the issue of cash flow availability for use in expansion and growth.
- Its graphic depiction facilitates communication.

Portfolio analysis does, however, have some very real *limitations* that have caused some companies to reduce their use of this approach:

- It is not easy to define product/market segments.
- It suggests the use of standard strategies that can miss opportunities or be impractical.
- It provides an illusion of scientific rigor when in reality positions are based on subjective judgments.
- Its value-laden terms like cash cow and dog can lead to self-fulfilling prophecies.
- It is not always clear what makes an industry attractive or where a product is in its life cycle.
- Naively following the prescriptions of a portfolio model may actually reduce corporate profits if they are used inappropriately. For example, General Mills' Chief Executive H. Brewster Atwater cites his company's Bisquick brand of flour as a product that would have been written off years ago based on portfolio analysis. "This product is 57 years old. By all rights it should have been overtaken by newer products. But with the proper research to improve the product and promotion to keep customers excited, it's doing very well."[44]

6.4 **Corporate Parenting**

Campbell, Goold, and Alexander, authors of *Corporate-Level Strategy: Creating Value in the Multibusiness Company*, contend that corporate strategists must address two crucial questions:

- What businesses should this company own and why?
- What organizational structure, management processes, and philosophy will foster superior performance from the company's business units?[45]

Portfolio analysis attempts to answer these questions by examining the attractiveness of various industries and by managing business units for cash flow, that is, by using cash generated from mature units to build new product lines. Unfortunately portfolio analysis fails to deal with the question of what industries a corporation should enter or with how a corporation can attain synergy among its product lines and business units. As suggested by its name, portfolio analysis tends to primarily view matters financially, regarding business units and product lines as separate and independent investments.

Corporate parenting, in contrast, views the corporation in terms of resources and capabilities that can be used to build business unit value as well as generate synergies across business units. According to Campbell, Goold, and Alexander:

> *Multibusiness companies create value by influencing—or parenting—the businesses they own. The best parent companies create more value than any of their rivals would if they owned the same businesses. Those companies have what we call parenting advantage.*[46]

Corporate parenting generates corporate strategy by focusing on the core competencies of the parent corporation and on the value created from the relationship between the parent and its businesses. In the form of corporate headquarters, the parent has a great deal of power in this relationship. If there is a good fit between the parent's skills and resources and the needs and opportunities of the business units, the corporation is likely to create value. If, however, there is not a good fit, the corporation is likely to destroy value.[47] This approach to corporate strategy is useful not only in deciding what new businesses to acquire, but also in choosing how each existing business unit should be best managed. This appears to be the secret to the success of General Electric under CEO Jack Welch. According to one analyst, ". . . he and his managers really add value by imposing tough standards of profitability and by disseminating knowledge and best practice quickly around the GE empire. If some manufacturing trick cuts costs in GE's aero-engine repair shops in Wales, he insists it be applied across the group."[48]

The primary job of corporate headquarters is, therefore, to obtain synergy among the business units by providing needed resources to units, transferring skills and capabilities among the units, and by coordinating the activities of shared unit functions to attain economies of scope (as in centralized purchasing).[49] This is in agreement with the concept of the learning organization discussed in Chapter 1 in which the role of the large firm is to facilitate and transfer the knowledge assets and services throughout the corporation.[50] This is especially important given that ¾ of a modern company's market value stems from its intangible assets—the organization's knowledge.[51]

DEVELOPING A CORPORATE PARENTING STRATEGY

Campbell, Goold, and Alexander recommend that the search for appropriate corporate strategy involves three analytical steps.

First, examine each business unit (or target firm in the case of acquisition) in terms of its strategic factors. People in the business units probably identified the strategic factors when they were generating business strategies for their units.

Second, examine each business unit (or target firm) in terms of areas in which performance can be improved. These are considered to be parenting opportunities. For example, two business units might be able to gain economies of scope by combining their sales forces. In another instance, a unit may have good, but not great, manufacturing and logistics skills. A parent company having world-class expertise in these areas can improve that unit's performance. The corporate parent could also transfer some people from one business unit having the desired skills to another unit in need of those skills. People at corporate headquarters may, because of their experience in many industries, spot areas where improvements are possible that even people in the business unit may not have noticed. Unless specific areas are significantly weaker than the competition, people in the business units may not even be aware that these areas could be improved, especially if each business unit only monitors its own particular industry.

Third, analyze how well the parent corporation fits with the business unit (or target firm). Corporate headquarters must be aware of its own strengths and weaknesses in terms of resources, skills, and capabilities. To do this, the corporate parent must ask if it has the characteristics that fit the parenting opportunities in each business unit. It must also ask if there is a misfit between the parent's characteristics and the critical success factors of each business unit.

PARENTING-FIT MATRIX

Campbell, Goold, and Alexander further recommend the use of a **parenting-fit matrix** that summarizes the various judgments regarding corporate/business unit fit for the corporation as a whole. Instead of describing business units in terms of their growth potential, competitive position, or industry structure, such a matrix emphasizes their fit with the corporate parent. As shown in **Figure 6–6**, the parenting-fit matrix is composed of two dimensions: the positive contributions that the parent can make and the negative effects the parent can make. The combination of these two dimensions creates five different positions—each with its own implications for corporate strategy.

Figure 6–6

Parenting-Fit Matrix

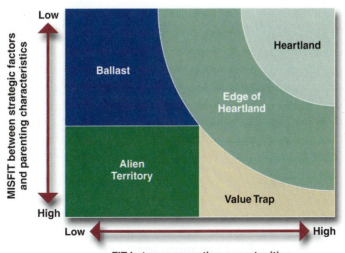

Source: Adapted from M. Alexander, A. Campbell, and M. Goold, "A New Model for Reforming the Planning Review Process," *Planning Review* (January/ February 1995), p. 17. Copyright © MCB University Press Ltd. Reprinted with permission.

Heartland Businesses

According to Campbell, Goold, and Alexander, business units that lie in the top right corner of the matrix should be at the heart of the corporation's future. These **heartland businesses** have opportunities for improvement by the parent, and the parent understands their strategic factors well. These businesses should have priority for all corporate activities.

Edge-of-Heartland Businesses

For **edge-of-heartland businesses**, some parenting characteristics fit the business, but others do not. The parent may not have all the characteristics needed by a unit, or the parent may not really understand all of the unit's strategic factors. For example, a unit in this area may be very strong in creating its own image through advertising—a critical success factor in its industry (such as in perfumes). The corporate parent may, however, not have this strength and tends to leave this to its advertising agency. If the parent forced the unit to abandon its own creative efforts in favor of using the corporation's favorite ad agency, the unit may flounder. Such business units are likely to consume much of the parent's attention, as the parent tries to understand them better and transform them into heartland businesses. In this instance, the parent needs to know when to interfere in business unit activities and strategies and when to keep at arm's length.

Ballast Businesses

Ballast businesses fit very comfortably with the parent corporation but contain very few opportunities to be improved by the parent. This is likely to be the case in units that have been with the corporation for many years and have been very successful. The parent may have added value in the past, but it can no longer find further parenting opportunities. Like cash cows, ballast businesses may be important sources of stability and earnings. They can, however, also be a drag on the corporation as a whole by slowing growth and distracting the parent from more productive activities. Some analysts might put IBM's mainframe business units in this category. Because there is always a danger that environmental changes could move a ballast business unit into alien territory, corporate decision makers should consider divesting this unit as soon as they can get a price that exceeds the expected value of future cash flows.

Alien Territory Businesses

Alien territory businesses have little opportunity to be improved by the corporate parent, and a misfit exists between the parenting characteristics and the units' strategic factors. There is little potential for value creation but high potential for value destruction on the part of the parent. These units are usually small and are often remnants of past experiments with diversification, businesses acquired as part of a larger purchase, or pet projects of senior managers. Even though corporate headquarters may admit that there is little fit, there may be reasons for keeping a unit: It is currently profitable, there are few buyers, the parent has made commitments to the unit's managers, or it is a favorite of the chairman. Because the corporate parent is probably destroying value in its attempts to improve fit, Campbell, Goold, and Alexander recommend that the corporation divest this unit while it still has value.

Value Trap Businesses

Value trap businesses fit well with parenting opportunities, but they are a misfit with the parent's understanding of the units' strategic factors. This is where corporate headquarters can make its biggest error. It mistakes what it sees as opportunities for ways to improve the business unit's profitability or competitive position. For example, in its zeal to make the unit a world-class manufacturer (because the parent has world-class manufacturing skills), it may not notice that the unit is primarily successful because of its unique product development and niche marketing expertise. The potential for possible gain blinds the parent to the downside risks of doing the wrong thing and destroying the unit's core competencies.

HORIZONTAL STRATEGY AND MULTIPOINT COMPETITION

A **horizontal strategy** is a corporate strategy that cuts across business unit boundaries to build synergy across business units and to improve the competitive position of one or more business units. When used to build synergy, it acts like a parenting strategy. When used to improve the competitive position of one or more business units, it can be thought of as a corporate competitive strategy. In **multipoint competition**, large multibusiness corporations compete against other large multibusiness firms in a number of markets. These multipoint competitors are firms that compete with each other not only in one business unit, but also in a number of business units. At one time or another, a cash-rich competitor may choose to build its own market share in a particular market to the disadvantage of another corporation's business unit. Although each business unit has primary responsibility for its own business strategy, it may sometimes need some help from its corporate parent, especially if the competitor business unit is getting heavy financial support from its corporate parent. In this instance, corporate headquarters develops a horizontal strategy to coordinate the various goals and strategies of related business units.[52]

For example, Procter & Gamble, Kimberly-Clark, Scott Paper, and Johnson and Johnson compete with one another in varying combinations of consumer paper products, from disposable diapers to facial tissue. If (purely hypothetically) Johnson and Johnson had just developed a toilet tissue with which it chose to challenge Procter & Gamble's high-share Charmin brand in a particular district, it might charge a low price for its new brand to build sales quickly. Procter & Gamble might not choose to respond to this attack on its share by cutting prices on Charmin. Because of Charmin's high market share, Procter & Gamble would lose significantly more sales dollars in a price war than Johnson and Johnson would with its initially low-share brand. To retaliate, Procter & Gamble might thus challenge Johnson and Johnson's high-share baby shampoo with Procter & Gamble's own low-share brand of baby shampoo in a different district. Once Johnson and Johnson had perceived Procter & Gamble's response, it might choose to stop challenging Charmin so that Procter & Gamble would stop challenging Johnson and Johnson's baby shampoo.

Multipoint competition and the resulting use of horizontal strategy may actually slow the development of hypercompetition in an industry. The realization that an attack on a market leader's position could result in a response in another market leads to mutual forbearance in which managers behave more conservatively toward multimarket rivals and competitive rivalry is reduced.[53] In one industry, for example, multipoint competition resulted in firms being less likely to exit a market. "Live and let live" replaced strong competitive rivalry.[54] Multipoint competition is likely to become even more prevalent in the future as corporations become global competitors and expand into more markets through strategic alliances.[55]

6.5 Impact of the Internet on Corporate Strategy

One impact of the growth of the Internet is that corporations are rethinking what businesses they should be in. For example, Emerson Electric, the 110-year-old St. Louis manufacturer of electrical motors, refrigeration components, and industrial tools, is now positioning itself in power backup systems for computers. In January 2000, Emerson purchased Jordan Industries Inc.'s telecommunications-products business. Three months later, Emerson bought the power supply division of Swedish phone maker Ericsson. With the power grid reaching its capacity, electrical outages are becoming more commonplace in the United States. For example, the state of California suffered under "rolling blackouts" in 2001 because of insufficient power generation capacity.

Emerson's acquisitions mean that the company could now provide reliable power backup capability for its customers. When the power goes out, Emerson's components act to switch the power from one source to another and regulate the voltage. Emerson provides the generators and fuel cells to generate the temporary electricity. These products have become crucial for any company that relies on the Internet for conducting business. Intira Corp., a St. Louis Web-hosting company, suffered a seven-hour outage due to a malfunctioning transformer but was able to stay online thanks to Emerson equipment. According to John Steensen, Intira's chief technology officer, "All of our affected customers would have gotten a month of free service if we had gone down, costing us hundreds of thousands of dollars." The acquisitions significantly increased Emerson's sales and made the power unit the largest and fastest growing of Emerson's five SBUs. Cisco Systems, WorldCom, and Intel are Emerson customers. Emerson's management is estimating that its high-tech power-systems business will grow at 15% to 20% annually for the foreseeable future.[56]

Any company considering entering international markets must consider the impact of the Internet. Simply creating a Web site is likely to result in inquiries from people in foreign countries where the company may have no experience. (See the **Internet Issue** feature for Internet usage by country and by language.) A few years ago, The Doll Collection was a barely profitable neighborhood retail shop in Louisville, Kentucky, with a staff of three people. Looking for an inexpensive way to boost its sales, one of the employees, Jason Walters, suggested putting a Web page ⟨www.dollpage.com⟩ on the Internet. After spending two weeks learning the Internet computer language, html, Walters designed a simple site showcasing well-known dolls like Barbie and Madam Alexander to attract buyers. Employees of The Doll Collection were amazed by the response—much of which came from outside North America. Sales jumped 375%. In one year the shop had become a global retailer, marketing Barbie and Madam Alexander dolls to people in almost every country, including Japan, China, and Australia.[57]

Internet Issue

Global Online Population

Country	Internet Users (in thousands)
3. United Kingdom	13,156
4. Canada	12,277
5. Germany	12,285
6. Australia	6,837
7. Brazil	6,790
8. China	6,308
9. France	5,696
10. South Korea	5,688

By 2002, 490 million people throughout the world will have achieved Internet access. For every 1,000 people, 80 will be using the Web. By the end of 2005, the number is expected to rise to 118 per 1,000 people. Fifteen countries will account for nearly 82% of these worldwide Internet users. The United States in 2000 accounted for 43% of the total 259 million worldwide. This percentage will drop to 33% in 2002 and only 27% in 2005. The top 10 nations with the most Internet users in 2000 were:

Country	Internet Users (in thousands)
1. United States	110,825
2. Japan	18,156

Given that 4 of the top 10 countries using the Internet speak English, it is no surprise that English has become the dominant language of the Internet. In 1996, it was the first language of 80% of Internet users. As other countries become active in the Internet, that figure is changing. By 2000, only 49.9% of Internet users had English as their first language. Chinese was second with 7.6%, followed by Japanese at 7.2%, German at 5.9%, and Spanish at 5%.

Source: J. Kirchner, "Global Online Population," *PC Magazine* (June 6, 2000), p. 23; R. O. Crockett, "Surfing in Tongues," *Business Week E.Biz* (December 11, 2000), p. EB 18.

Projections for the 21st Century

- From 1994 to 2010, the number of wired telephone lines in the world will increase from 607 million to 1.4 billion.
- From 1994 to 2010, the number of wireless telephone lines in the world will increase from 34 million to 1.3 billion.[58]

Discussion Questions

1. How does horizontal growth differ from vertical growth as a corporate strategy? From concentric diversification?

2. What are the tradeoffs between an internal and an external growth strategy? Which approach is best as an international entry strategy?

3. Is stability really a strategy or just a term for no strategy?

4. Compare and contrast SWOT analysis with portfolio analysis.

5. How is corporate parenting different from portfolio analysis? How is it alike? Is it a useful concept in a global industry?

Strategic Practice Exercise

On March 14, 2000, Stephen King, the horror writer, published his new book, *Riding the Bullet*, on the Internet before it appeared in print. Within 24 hours, around 400,000 people had downloaded the book—even though most of them needed to download the software in order to read the book. The unexpected demand crashed servers. According to Jack Romanos, President of Simon & Schuster, "I don't think anybody could have anticipated how many people were out there who are willing to accept the written word in a paperless format." To many, this announced the coming of the electronic novel. Environmentalists applauded that e-books would soon replace paper books and newspapers, thus reducing pollution coming from paper mills and landfills. The King book was easy to download and took less time than a trip to the bookstore. Critics argued that the King book used the Internet because at 66 pages, it was too short to be a standard printed novel. It was also free, so there was nothing to discourage natural curiosity. Some people in the industry remarked that 75% of those who downloaded the book did not read it.[59]

1. Form into small groups in the class to discuss the future of Internet publishing.

2. Consider the following questions as discussion guides:
   - What are the *pros* and *cons* of electronic publishing?
   - Should newspaper and book publishers convert to electronic publishing over paper?
   - The *Wall Street Journal* and others publish in both paper and electronic formats. Has this been a success?
   - Would you prefer this textbook and others in an electronic format?
   - How would publishers distribute books and textbooks?

3. Present your group's conclusions to the class.

Key Terms

acquisition (pp. 139, 145)
alien territory businesses (p. 158)
backward integration (p. 140)
ballast businesses (p. 158)
bankruptcy (p. 150)
BCG (Boston Consulting Group) Growth-Share Matrix (p. 151)
BOT concept (p. 146)
captive company strategy (p. 148)
cash cows (p. 152)

concentration (p. 139)
concentric diversification (p. 142)
conglomerate diversification (p. 143)
consolidation (p. 148)
contraction (p. 148)
corporate parenting (p. 156)
corporate strategy (p. 137)
country's attractiveness (p. 154)
directional strategy (p. 138)
diversification (p. 139)

divestment (p. 150)
dogs (p. 152)
edge-of-heartland businesses (p. 158)
exporting (p. 143)
forward integration (p. 140)
franchising (p. 144)
full integration (p. 140)
GE Business Screen (p. 153)
green-field development (p. 145)
growth strategies (p. 138)

Notes

1. J. Guyon, "AT&T's Big Bet Keeps Getting Dicier," *Fortune* (January 10, 2000): 126–129.

2. R. P. Rumelt, D. E. Schendel, and D. J. Teece, "Fundamental Issues in Strategy," in *Fundamental Issues in Strategy: A Research Agenda*, edited by R. P. Rumelt, D. E. Schendel, and D. J. Teece (Boston: HBS Press, 1994), p. 42.

3. This analogy of corporate parent and business unit children was initially proposed by A. Campbell, M. Goold, and M. Alexander. See "Corporate Strategy: The Quest for Parenting Advantage," *Harvard Business Review* (March–April, 1995), pp. 120–132.

4. M. E. Porter, "From Competitive Strategy to Corporate Strategy," in *International Review of Strategic Management*, Vol. 1, edited by D. E. Husey (Chicester, England: John Wiley & Sons, 1990), p. 29.

5. "Cisco Buys Wireless Chip-Set Maker," *The (Ames) Tribune* (November 11, 2000), p. B7.

6. J. Perkins, "It's a Hog Predicament," *Des Moines Register* (April 11, 1999), pp. J1–J2.

7. J. W. Slocum, Jr., M. McGill, and D. T. Lei, "The New Learning Strategy: Anytime, Anything, Anywhere," *Organizational Dynamics* (Autumn 1994), p. 36.

8. K. R. Harrigan, *Strategies for Vertical Integration* (Lexington, MA: Lexington Books, D. C. Heath, 1983), pp. 16–21.

9. L. Grant, "Partners in Profit," *U. S. News and World Report* (September 20, 1993), pp. 65–66.

10. For a discussion of the pros and cons of contracting versus vertical integration, see J. T. Mahoney, "The Choice of Organizational Form: Vertical Financial Ownership Versus Other Methods of Vertical Integration," *Strategic Management Journal* (November 1992), pp. 559–584.

11. A. Y. Ilinich and C. P. Zeithaml, "Operationalizing and Testing Galbraith's Center of Gravity Theory," *Strategic Management Journal* (June 1995), pp. 401–410.

12. R. Gibson, "Toro Charges into Greener Fields with New Products," *Wall Street Journal* (July 22, 1997), p. B4.

13. A. Delios and P. W. Beamish, "Geographic Scope, Product Diversification, and the Corporate Performance of Japanese Firms," *Strategic Management Journal* (August 1999), pp. 711–727.

14. E. Elango and V. H. Fried, "Franchising Research: A Literature Review and Synthesis," *Journal of Small Business Management* (July 1997), pp. 68–81.

15. T. Thilgen, "Corporate Clout Replaces 'Small Is Beautiful,'" *Wall Street Journal* (March 27, 1997), p. B14.

16. S. Sherman, "Are Strategic Alliances Working?" *Fortune* (September 21, 1992), p. 77.

17. J. E. McCann, III, "The Growth of Acquisitions in Services," *Long Range Planning* (December 1996), pp. 835–841.

18. P. Gogoi and G. Smith, "The Way to Run a Railroad," *Business Week* (October 23, 2000), pp. 106–110.

19. B. Voss, "Strategic Federations Frequently Falter in Far East," *Journal of Business Strategy* (July/August 1993), p. 6; S. Douma, "Success and Failure in New Ventures," *Long Range Planning* (April 1991), pp. 54–60.

20. A. Delios and P. W. Beamish, "Ownership Strategy of Japanese Firms: Transactional, Institutional, and Experience Approaches," *Strategic Management Journal* (October 1999), pp. 915–933.

21. J. Naisbitt, *Megatrends Asia* (New York: Simon & Schuster, 1996), p. 143.

22. K. Ramaswamy, "The Performance Impact of Strategic Similarity in Horizontal Mergers: Evidence from the U.S. Banking Industry," *Academy of Management Journal* (July 1997), pp. 697–715; D. J. Flanagan, "Announcements of Purely Related and Purely Unrelated Mergers and Shareholder Returns: Reconciling the Relatedness Paradox," *Journal of Management*, Vol. 22, No. 6 (1996), pp. 823–835; D. D. Bergh, "Predicting Diversification of Unrelated Acquisitions: An Integrated Model of Ex Ante Conditions," *Strategic Management Journal* (October 1997), pp. 715–731.

23. J. M. Pennings, H. Barkema, and S. Douma, "Organizational Learning and Diversification," *Academy of Management Journal* (June 1994), pp. 608–640.

24. L. E. Palich, L. B. Cardinal, and C. C. Miller, "Curvilinearity in the Diversification-Performance Linkage: An Examination of Over Three Decades of Research," *Strategic Management Journal* (February 2000), pp. 155–174.

25. "The Great Merger Wave Breaks," *The Economist* (January 27, 2001), pp. 59–60.

26. W. B. Carper, "Corporate Acquisitions and Shareholder Wealth: A Review and Exploratory Analysis, "*Journal of Management* (December 1990), pp. 807–823; P. G. Simmonds, "Using Diversification as a Tool for Effective Performance," *Handbook of Business Strategy, 1992/93 Yearbook*, edited by H. E. Glass and M. A. Hovde (Boston: Warren, Gorham & Lamont, 1992), pp. 3.1–3.7; B. T. Lamont and C. A. Anderson, "Mode of Corporate Diversification and Economic Performance," *Academy of Management Journal* (December 1985), pp. 926–936.

27. M. L. Sirower, *The Synergy Trap* (NY: Free Press, 1997); B. Jensen, "Make It Simple! How Simplicity Could Become Your Ultimate Strategy," *Strategy & Leadership* (March/April 1997), p. 35.

28. J. M. Pennings, H. Barkema, and S. Douma, "Organizational Learning and Diversification," *Academy of Management Journal* (June 1994), pp. 608–640.

29. E. C. Busija, H. M. O'Neill, and C. P. Zeithaml, "Diversification Strategy, Entry Mode, and Performance: Evidence of Choice and Constraints," *Strategic Management Journal* (April 1997), pp. 321–327; A. Sharma, "Mode of Entry and Ex-Post Performance," *Strategic Management Journal* (September 1998), pp. 879–900.

30. A. Inkpen and N. Choudhury, "The Seeking of Strategy Where It Is Not: Towards a Theory of Strategy Absence," *Strategic Management Journal* (May 1995), pp. 313–323.

31. J. A. Pearce II and D. K. Robbins, "Retrenchment Remains the Foundation of Business Turnaround," *Strategic Management Journal* (June 1994), pp. 407–417.

32. J. R. Morris, W. F. Cascio, and C. E. Young, "Downsizing After All These Years," *Organizational Dynamics* (Winter 1999), pp. 78–87; P. H. Mirvis, "Human Resource Management: Leaders, Laggards, and Followers," *Academy of Management Executive* (May 1997), pp. 43–56; J. K. DeDee and D. W. Vorhies, "Retrenchment Activities of Small Firms During Economic Downturn: An Empirical Investigation," *Journal of Small Business Management* (July 1998), pp. 46–61.

33. J. B. Treece, "U.S. Parts Makers Just Won't Say 'Uncle,'" *Business Week* (August 10, 1987), pp. 76–77.

34. S. Miller and M. Champion, "BMW Sells Rover Cars to Phoenix Group of U.K.," *Wall Street Journal* (May 10, 2000), p. A23.

35. "Quaker Oats Gives Up on Snapple, Sells It at a $1.4 Billion Loss," *Des Moines Register* (March 28, 1997), p. 8S.

36. S. P. Dinnen, "Common Shareholders Lose in Bankruptcy of L. A. Gear," *Des Moines Register* (June 18, 2000), p. 1D.

37. K. L. McQuaid, "Packaging Company Diss-ked by AOL," *INC.* (September 1997), p. 31.

38. B. C. Reimann and A. Reichert, "Portfolio Planning Methods for Strategic Capital Allocation: A Survey of Fortune 500 Firms," *International Journal of Management* (March 1996), pp. 84–93; D. K. Sinha, "Strategic Planning in the Fortune 500," *Handbook of Business Strategy, 1991/92 Yearbook*, edited by H. E. Glass and M. A. Hovde (Boston: Warren Gorham & Lamont, 1991), p. 9.6.

39. B. Hedley, "Strategy and the Business Portfolio," *Long Range Planning* (February 1977), p. 9.

40. C. Anterasian, J. L. Graham, and R. B. Money, "Are U.S. Managers Superstitious About Market Share," *Sloan Management Review* (Summer 1996), pp. 67–77.

41. R. G. Hamermesh, *Making Strategy Work* (New York: John Wiley & Sons, 1986), p. 14.

42. G. D. Harrell and R. O. Kiefer, "Multinational Strategic Market Portfolios," *MSU Business Topics* (Winter 1981), p. 5.

43. M. E. Porter, "Changing Patterns of International Competition," *California Management Review* (Winter 1986), p. 12.

44. J. J. Curran, "Companies That Rob the Future," *Fortune* (July 4, 1988), p. 84.

45. A. Campbell, M. Goold, and M. Alexander, *Corporate-Level Strategy: Creating Value in the Multibusiness Company* (New York: John Wiley & Sons, 1994). See also M. Goold, A. Campbell, and M. Alexander, "Corporate Strategy and Parenting Theory," *Long Range Planning* (April 1998), pp. 308–318

46. A. Campbell, M. Goold, and M. Alexander, "Corporate Strategy: The Quest for Parenting Advantage," *Harvard Business Review* (March–April 1995), p. 121.

47. Campbell, Goold, and Alexander, p. 122.

48. "Jack's Gamble," *The Economist* (October 28, 2000), pp. 13–14.

49. D. J. Collis, "Corporate Strategy in Multibusiness Firms," *Long Range Planning* (June 1996), pp. 416–418; D. Lei, M. A. Hitt, and R. Bettis, "Dynamic Core Competencies Through Meta-Learning and Strategic Context," *Journal of Management*, Vol. 22, No. 4 (1996), pp. 549–569.

50. D. J. Teece, "Strategies for Managing Knowledge Assets: The Role of Firm Structure and Industrial Context," *Long Range Planning* (February 2000), pp. 35–54.

51. C. Havens and E. Knapp, "Easing into Knowledge Management," *Strategy & Leadership* (March/April 1999), pp. 4–9.

52. M. E. Porter, *Competitive Advantage* (New York: Free Press, 1985), pp. 317–382.

53. J. Gimeno and C. Y. Woo, "Hypercompetition in a Multimarket Environment: The Role of Strategic Similarity and Multimarket Contact in Competitive De-Escalation," *Organization Science* (May/June 1996), pp. 322–341.

54. W. Boeker, J. Goodstein, J. Stephan, and J. P. Murmann, "Competition in a Multimarket Environment: The Case of Market Exit," *Organization Science* (March/April 1997), pp. 126–142.

55. J. Gimeno and C. Y. Woo, "Multimarket Contact, Economies of Scope, and Firm Performance," *Academy of Management Journal* (June 1999), pp. 239–259.

56. D. Little, "Emerson Electric Jump-Starts Itself," *Business Week* (July 24, 2000), pp. 78–80.

57. L. Beresford, "Global Smarts, Toy Story," *Entrepreneur* (February 1997), p. 38.

58. J. Warner, "21st Century Capitalism: Snapshot of the Next Century," *Business Week* (November 18, 1994), p. 194.

59. "Learning to E-Read," *The Economist Survey E-Entertainment* (October 7, 2000), p. 22.

chapter 7

Strategy Formulation: Functional Strategy and Strategic Choice

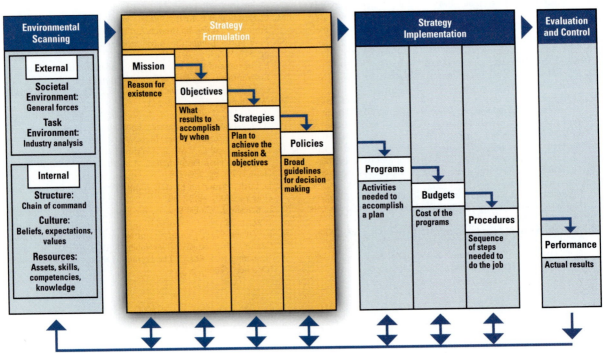

Feedback/Learning

For almost 150 years, the Church & Dwight Company has been building market share on a brand name whose products are in 95% of all U.S. households. Yet if you asked the average person what products this company made, few would know. Although Church & Dwight may not be a household name, the company's ubiquitous orange box of Arm & Hammer[1] brand baking soda is cherished throughout North America. Church & Dwight is a classic example of a marketing functional strategy called product development. Shortly after its introduction in 1878, Arm & Hammer Baking Soda became a fundamental item on the pantry shelf as people found many uses for sodium bicarbonate other than baking, such as cleaning, deodorizing, and tooth brushing. Hearing of the many uses people were finding for its product, the company advertised that its baking soda was good not only for baking, but also for deodorizing refrigerators—simply by leaving an open box in the refrigerator. In a brilliant marketing move, the firm then suggested that consumers buy the product and throw it away—deodorize a kitchen sink by dumping Arm & Hammer baking soda down the drain! The company did not stop here. It looked for other uses of its sodium bicarbonate in new products. Church & Dwight has achieved consistent growth in sales and earnings through the use of "line extensions"—putting the Arm & Hammer brand first on baking soda, then on laundry detergents, toothpaste, and deodorants. By the beginning of the 21st century, Church & Dwight had become a significant competitor in markets previously dominated only by giants like Procter & Gamble, Lever Brothers, and Colgate, using only one brand name. Was there a limit to this growth? Was there a point at which these continuous line extensions would begin to eat away at the integrity of the Arm & Hammer name?

7.1 Functional Strategy

Functional strategy is the approach a functional area takes to achieve corporate and business unit objectives and strategies by maximizing resource productivity. It is concerned with developing and nurturing a distinctive competence to provide a company or business unit with a competitive advantage. Just as a multidivisional corporation has several business units, each with its own business strategy, each business unit has its own set of departments, each with its own functional strategy.

The orientation of the functional strategy is dictated by its parent business unit's strategy. For example, a business unit following a competitive strategy of differentiation through high quality needs a manufacturing functional strategy that emphasizes expensive, quality assurance processes over cheaper, high-volume production; a human resource functional strategy that emphasizes the hiring and training of a highly skilled, but costly, workforce; and a marketing functional strategy that emphasizes distribution channel "pull" using advertising to increase consumer demand over "push" using promotional allowances to retailers. If a business unit were to follow a low-cost competitive strategy, however, a different set of functional strategies would be needed to support the business strategy.

Just as a competitive strategy may need to vary from one region of the world to another, functional strategies may need to vary from region to region. When Mr. Donut expanded into Japan, for example, it had to market donuts not as breakfast, but as snack food. Because the Japanese had no breakfast coffee-and-donut custom, they preferred to eat the donuts in the afternoon or evening. Mr. Donut restaurants were thus located near railroad stations and supermarkets. All signs were in English to appeal to the Western interests of the Japanese.

CORE COMPETENCIES

As defined earlier in **Chapter 4**, a **core competency** is something that a corporation can do exceedingly well. It is a key strength. It may also be called a **core capability** because it includes a number of constituent skills. For example, a core competency of Avon Products is its expertise in door-to-door selling. FedEx has a core competency in information technology. A company must continually reinvest in its core competencies or risk losing them.[2] When these competencies or capabilities are superior to those of the competition, they are called **distinctive competencies**. Although it is typically not an asset in the accounting sense, a core competency is a very valuable resource—it does not "wear out." In general, the more core competencies are used, the more refined they get and the more valuable they become. To be considered a *distinctive competency*, the competency must meet three tests:

1. **Customer Value**: It must make a disproportionate contribution to customer-perceived value.

2. **Competitor Unique**: It must be unique and superior to competitor capabilities.

3. **Extendibility:** It must be something that can be used to develop new products/services or enter new markets.[3]

Even though a distinctive competency is certainly considered a corporation's key strength, a key strength may not always be a distinctive competency. As competitors attempt to imitate another company's competence in a particular functional area, what was once a distinctive competency becomes a minimum requirement to compete in the industry.[4] Even though the competency may still be a core competency and thus a strength, it is no longer unique. For example, when Maytag Company alone had high-quality products, Maytag's ability to make exceedingly reliable and durable washing machines was a distinctive competency. As other appliance makers imitated its quality control and design processes, this continued to be a key strength (that is, a core competency) of Maytag, but it was less and less a distinctive competency.

Where do these competencies come from? A corporation can gain access to a distinctive competency in four ways:

- It may be an asset endowment, such as a key patent, coming from the founding of the company—Xerox grew on the basis of its original copying patent.

- It may be acquired from someone else—Whirlpool bought a worldwide distribution system when it purchased Philips's appliance division.

- It may be shared with another business unit or alliance partner—Apple Computer worked with a design firm to create the special appeal of its Apple II and Mac computers.

- It may be carefully built and accumulated over time within the company—Honda carefully extended its expertise in small motor manufacturing from motorcycles to autos and lawn-mowers.[5]

For core competencies to be distinctive competencies, they must be superior to those of the competition. As more industries become hypercompetitive (discussed in **Chapter 3**), it will be increasingly difficult to keep a core competence distinctive. These resources are likely either to be imitated or made obsolete by new technologies.

For a functional strategy to have the best chance of success, it should be built on a distinctive competency residing within that functional area. If a corporation does not have a distinctive competency in a particular functional area, that functional area could be a candidate for outsourcing.

THE SOURCING DECISION: WHERE SHOULD FUNCTIONS BE HOUSED?

Where should a function be housed? Should it be integrated within the organization or purchased from an outside contractor? **Outsourcing** is purchasing from someone else a product or service that had been previously provided internally. For example, DuPont contracted out project engineering and design to Morrison Knudsen; AT&T outsourced its credit card processing to Total System Services; and Northern Telecom outsourced its electronic component manufacturing to Comptronix. Outsourcing is becoming an increasingly important part of strategic decision making and an important way to increase efficiency and often quality. Firms competing in global industries must in particular search worldwide for the most appropriate suppliers.

In a study of 30 firms, outsourcing resulted on average in a 9% reduction in costs and a 15% increase in capacity and quality.[6] For example, Motorola sold its factories in Iowa and Ireland to Celestica, Inc., for $70 million. Motorola then agreed to pay Celestica more than $1 billion over three years to make handsets, pagers, two-way radios, and other accessories for Motorola. Celestica, which was once a factory of IBM in Toronto, Canada, offered jobs to many of Motorola's employees in Iowa and Ireland. Motorola then shifted manufacturing from its plant in Florida to the Ireland plant it just sold Celestica so that its Florida facility could concentrate on software design and administration. According to Motorola's management, this was part of a broad effort to make the corporation's supply chain more efficient, consolidate its manufacturing operations, and improve financial performance.[7]

According to an American Management Association survey of member companies, 94% of the firms outsource at least one activity. The outsourced activities are general and administrative (78%), human resources (77%), transportation and distribution (66%), information systems (63%), manufacturing (56%), marketing (51%), and finance and accounting (18%). The survey also reveals that 25% of the respondents have been disappointed in their outsourcing results. Fifty-one percent of the firms reported bringing an outsourced activity back in-house. Nevertheless, authorities expect the number of companies engaging in outsourcing to not only increase, but also to outsource an increasing number of functions, especially in customer service, bookkeeping, financial clerical, sales/telemarketing, and mailroom.[8]

Sophisticated strategists, according to Quinn, are no longer thinking just of market share or vertical integration as the keys to strategic planning:

> *Instead they concentrate on identifying those few core service activities where the company has or can develop: (1) a continuing strategic edge and (2) long-term streams of new products to satisfy future customer demands. They develop these competencies in greater depth than anyone else in the world. Then they seek to eliminate, minimize, or outsource activities where the company cannot be preeminent, unless those activities are essential to support or protect the chosen areas of strategic focus.[9]*

The key to outsourcing is to purchase from outside only those activities that are not key to the company's distinctive competencies. Otherwise, the company may give up the very capabilities that made it successful in the first place—thus putting itself on the road to eventual decline. Therefore, in determining functional strategy, the strategist must:

- Identify the company's or business unit's core competencies.
- Ensure that the competencies are continually being strengthened.
- Manage the competencies in such a way that best preserves the competitive advantage they create.

An outsourcing decision depends on the fraction of total value added that the activity under consideration represents and by the amount of potential competitive advantage in that activity for the company or business unit. See the outsourcing matrix in **Figure 7-1**. A firm should consider outsourcing any activity or function that has low potential for competitive advantage. If that activity constitutes only a small part of the total value of the firm's products or services, it should be purchased on the open market (assuming that quality providers of the activity are plentiful). If, however, the activity contributes highly to the company's products or services, the firm should purchase it through long-term contracts with trusted suppliers or distributors. A firm should always produce at least some of the activity or function (taper vertical integration) if that activity has the potential for providing the company some competitive advantage. Full vertical integration should only be considered, however, when that activity or function adds significant value to the company's products or services in addition to providing competitive advantage.

Outsourcing does, however, have some disadvantages. For example, GE's introduction of a new washing machine was delayed three weeks by production problems at a supplier's company to whom it had contracted out key work. Some companies have found themselves locked into long-term contracts with outside suppliers that are no longer competitive.[10] Some authorities propose that the cumulative effects of continued outsourcing steadily reduces a firm's ability to learn new skills and to develop new core competencies.[11] A study of 30 firms

Figure 7–1
Proposed Outsourcing Matrix

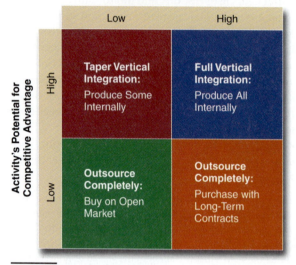

with outsourcing experience revealed that *unsuccessful* outsourcing efforts had three common characteristics:

- The firms' finance and legal departments and their vendors dominated the decision process.
- Vendors were not prequalified based on total capabilities.
- Short-term benefits dominated decision making.[12]

Outsourcing has become an important issue in all industries, especially in global industries such as automobiles where cost competition is fierce. General Motors, for example, was faced with a strike by its Canadian unions when it wanted to outsource some operations. The Canadian unions were very concerned that such outsourcing would reduce union employment and increase the number of low-paying jobs. Expect this issue to continue in importance throughout the world as more industries become global.

MARKETING STRATEGY

Marketing strategy deals with pricing, selling, and distributing a product. Using a **market development** strategy, a company or business unit can (1) capture a larger share of an existing market for current products through market saturation and market penetration or (2) develop new markets for current products. Consumer product giants such as Procter & Gamble, Colgate-Palmolive, and Unilever are experts at using advertising and promotion to implement a market saturation/penetration strategy to gain the dominant market share in a product category. As seeming masters of the product life cycle, these companies are able to extend product life almost indefinitely through "new and improved" variations of product and packaging that appeal to most market niches. These companies also follow the second market development strategy by taking a successful product they market in one part of the world and marketing it elsewhere. Noting the success of their presoak detergents in Europe, for example, both P&G and Colgate successfully introduced this type of laundry product to North America under the trade names of Biz and Axion.

Using the **product development** strategy, a company or unit can (1) develop new products for *existing markets* or (2) develop new products for *new markets*. Church & Dwight has had great success following the first product development strategy by developing new products to sell to its current customers. Acknowledging the widespread appeal of its Arm & Hammer brand baking soda, the company generated new uses for its sodium bicarbonate by reformulating it as toothpaste, deodorant, and detergent. Using a successful brand name to market other products is called *line extension* and is a good way to appeal to a company's current customers. Sara Lee Corporation (famous for its frozen cheesecake) is taking the same approach by putting the Sara Lee name on various new food products, such as premium meats and fresh baked goods. Arm & Hammer successfully followed the second product development strategy by developing new pollution reduction products (using sodium bicarbonate compounds) for sale to coal-fired electric utility plants—a very different market from grocery stores.

There are numerous other marketing strategies. For advertising and promotion, for example, a company or business unit can choose between a "push" or a "pull" marketing strategy. Many large food and consumer products companies in the United States and Canada have followed a **push strategy** by spending a large amount of money on trade promotion in order to gain or hold shelf space in retail outlets. Trade promotion includes discounts, in-store special offers, and advertising allowances designed to "push" products through the distribution system. The Kellogg Company recently decided to change its emphasis from a push to a **pull strategy**, in which advertising "pulls" the products through the distribution channels. The company now spends more money on consumer advertising designed to build brand awareness so that shoppers will ask for the products. Research has indicated that a high level of advertising (a key part of a pull strategy) is most beneficial to leading brands in a market.[13]

Other marketing strategies deal with distribution and pricing. Should a company use distributors and dealers to sell its products or should it sell directly to mass merchandisers? Using both channels simultaneously can lead to problems. In order to increase the sales of its lawn tractors and mowers, for example, John Deere decided to sell the products not only through its current dealer network, but also through mass merchandisers like Home Depot. Deere's dealers, however, were furious. They considered Home Depot to be a key competitor. The dealers were concerned that Home Depot's ability to underprice them would eventually lead to their becoming little more than repair facilities for their competition and left with insufficient sales to stay in business.[14]

When pricing a new product, a company or business unit can follow one of two strategies. For new-product pioneers, **skim pricing** offers the opportunity to "skim the cream" from the top of the demand curve with a high price while the product is novel and competitors are few. **Penetration pricing**, in contrast, attempts to hasten market development and offers the pioneer the opportunity to use the experience curve to gain market share with a low price and dominate the industry. Depending on corporate and business unit objectives and strategies, either of these choices may be desirable to a particular company or unit. Penetration pricing is, however, more likely than skim pricing to raise a unit's operating profit in the long term.[15]

FINANCIAL STRATEGY

Financial strategy examines the financial implications of corporate and business-level strategic options and identifies the best financial course of action. It can also provide competitive advantage through a lower cost of funds and a flexible ability to raise capital to support a business strategy. Financial strategy usually attempts to maximize the financial value of the firm.

The tradeoff between achieving the desired debt-to-equity ratio and relying on internal long-term financing via cash flow is a key issue in financial strategy. Many small- and medium-sized companies such as Urschel Laboratories try to avoid all external sources of funds in order to avoid outside entanglements and to keep control of the company within the family. Many financial analysts believe, however, that only by financing through long-term debt can a corporation use financial leverage to boost earnings per share, thus raising stock price and the overall value of the company. Research indicates that higher debt levels not only deter takeover by other firms (by making the company less attractive), but also leads to improved productivity and improved cash flows by forcing management to focus on core businesses.[16]

Research reveals that a firm's financial strategy is influenced by its corporate diversification strategy. Equity financing, for example, is preferred for related diversification while debt financing is preferred for unrelated diversification.[17] The recent trend away from unrelated to related acquisitions explains why the number of acquisitions being paid for entirely with stock increased from only 2% in 1988 to 50% in 1998.[18]

A very popular financial strategy is the leveraged buy out (LBO). In a **leveraged buy out**, a company is acquired in a transaction financed largely by debt—usually obtained from a third party, such as an insurance company or an investment banker. Ultimately the debt is paid with money generated from the acquired company's operations or by sales of its assets. The acquired company, in effect, pays for its own acquisition! Management of the LBO is then under tremendous pressure to keep the highly leveraged company profitable. Unfortunately the huge amount of debt on the acquired company's books may actually cause its eventual decline by focusing management's attention on short-term matters. One study of LBOs (also called MBOs—**M**anagement **B**uy **O**uts) revealed that the financial performance of the typical LBO usually falls below the industry average in the fourth year after the buy out. The firm declines because of inflated expectations, utilization of all slack, management burnout, and a lack of strategic management.[19] Often the only solution is to go public once again by selling stock to finance growth.

The management of dividends to shareholders is an important part of a corporation's financial strategy. Corporations in fast-growing industries such as computers and computer software often do not declare dividends. They use the money they might have spent on dividends to finance rapid growth. If the company is successful, its growth in sales and profits is reflected in a higher stock price—eventually resulting in a hefty capital gain when shareholders sell their common stock. Other corporations that do not face rapid growth must support the value of their stock by offering generous and consistent dividends.

A recent financial strategy being used by large established corporations to highlight a high-growth business unit in a popular sector of the stock market is to establish a tracking stock. A **tracking stock** is a type of common stock tied to one portion of a corporation's business. This strategy allows established companies to highlight a high-growth business unit without selling the business. By keeping the unit as a subsidiary with its common stock separately identified, the corporation is able to keep control of the subsidiary and yet allow the subsidiary the ability to fund its own growth with outside money. It goes public as an IPO and pays dividends based on the unit's performance. Because the tracking stock is actually an equity interest in the parent company (not the subsidiary), another company cannot acquire the subsidiary by buying its shares. Examples of corporations using tracking stocks as part of their financial strategy are AT&T (AT&T Wireless), Sprint (Sprint PCS), J.C. Penney (Eckerd Drugs), and Staples (Staples.com).[20]

RESEARCH AND DEVELOPMENT (R&D) STRATEGY

R&D strategy deals with product and process innovation and improvement. It also deals with the appropriate mix of different types of R&D (basic, product, or process) and with the question of how new technology should be accessed—internal development, external acquisition, or through strategic alliances.

Table 7–1 Research and Development Strategy and Competitive Advantage

	Technological Leadership	Technological Followership
Cost Advantage	Pioneer the lowest cost product design. Be the first firm down the learning curve. Create low-cost ways of performing value activities.	Lower the cost of the product or value activities by learning from the leader's experience. Avoid R&D costs through imitation.
Differentiation	Pioneer a unique product that increases buyer value. Innovate in other activities to increase buyer value.	Adapt the product or delivery system more closely to buyer needs by learning from the leader's experience.

Source: Adapted/reprinted with the permission of The Free Press, an imprint of Simon & Schuster, from *Competitive Advantage: Creating and Sustaining Superior Performance* by Michael E. Porter, p. 181. Copyright © 1985 by Michael E. Porter.

One of the R&D choices is to be either a **technological leader** in which one pioneers an innovation or a **technological follower** in which one imitates the products of competitors. Porter suggests that deciding to become a technological leader or follower can be a way of achieving either overall low cost or differentiation. (See **Table 7–1**.)

One example of an effective use of the *leader* R&D functional strategy to achieve a differentiation competitive advantage is Nike, Inc. Nike spends more than most in the industry on R&D to differentiate the performance of its athletic shoes from that of its competitors. As a result, its products have become the favorite of the serious athlete. An example of the use of the *follower* R&D functional strategy to achieve a low-cost competitive advantage is Dean Foods Company. "We're able to have the customer come to us and say, 'If you can produce X, Y, and Z product for the same quality and service, but at a lower price and without that expensive label on it, you can have the business,'" says Howard Dean, President of the company.[21]

An increasing number of companies are working with their suppliers to help them keep up with changing technology. They are beginning to realize that a firm cannot be competitive technologically only through internal development. For example, Chrysler Corporation's skillful use of parts suppliers to design everything from car seats to drive shafts has enabled it to spend consistently less money than its competitors to develop new car models. Strategic technology alliances are one way to combine the R&D capabilities of two companies. Maytag Company worked with one of its suppliers to apply fuzzy logic technology to its new IntelliSense™ dishwasher. The partnership enabled Maytag to complete the project in a shorter amount of time than if it had tried to do it alone.[22]

OPERATIONS STRATEGY

Operations strategy determines how and where a product or service is to be manufactured, the level of vertical integration in the production process, and the deployment of physical resources. It should also deal with the optimum level of technology the firm should use in its operations processes. See the **Global Issue** feature to see how differences in national conditions can lead to differences in product design and manufacturing facilities from one country to another.

Advanced **M**anufacturing **T**echnology (AMT) is revolutionizing operations worldwide and should continue to have a major impact as corporations strive to integrate diverse business activities using computer-integrated design and manufacturing (CAD/CAM) principles. The use of CAD/CAM, flexible manufacturing systems, computer numerically controlled systems, automatically guided vehicles, robotics, manufacturing resource planning (MRP II), optimized production technology, and just-in-time contribute to increased flexibility, quick response time, and higher productivity. Such investments also act to increase the company's

Global Issue

International Differences Alter Whirlpool's Operations Strategy

To better penetrate the growing markets in developing nations, Whirlpool decided to build a "world washer." This new type of washing machine was to be produced in Brazil, Mexico, and India. Lightweight, with substantially fewer parts than its U.S. counterpart, its performance was to be equal to or better than anything on the world market while being competitive in price with the most popular models in these markets. The goal was to develop a complete product, process, and facility design package that could be used in different countries with low initial investment. Originally the plan had been to make the same low-cost washer in identical plants in each of the three countries.

Significant differences in each of the three countries forced Whirlpool to change its product design to suit each nation's situation. According to Lawrence Kremer, Senior Vice-President of Global Technology and Operations, "Our Mexican affiliate, Vitromatic, has

porcelain and glassmaking capabilities. Porcelain baskets made sense for them. Stainless steel became the preferred material for the others." Costs also affected decisions. "In India, for example, material costs may run as much as 200% to 800% higher than elsewhere, while labor and overhead costs are comparatively minimal," added Kremer. Another consideration were the garments to be washed in each country. For example, saris—the 18-foot lengths of cotton or silk with which Indian women drape themselves—needed special treatment in an Indian washing machine, forcing additional modifications.

Manufacturing facilities also varied from country to country. Brastemp, Whirlpool's Brazilian partner, built its plant of precast concrete to address the problems of high humidity. In India, however, the construction crew cast the concrete, allowed it to cure, and then using chain, block, and tackle, five or six men raised each three-ton slab into place. Instead of using one building, Mexican operations used two, one housing the flexible assembly lines and stamping operations and an adjacent facility housing the injection molding and extrusion processes.

Source: A. A. Ullmann, "Whirlpool Corporation, 1993: A Metamorphosis," in Wheelen and Hunger, *Strategic Management and Business Policy*, 5th ed. (Reading, MA: Addison-Wesley, 1995), pp. 713–715.

fixed costs and could cause significant problems if the company is unable to achieve economies of scale or scope.

A firm's manufacturing strategy is often affected by a product's life cycle. As the sales of a product increase, there will be an increase in production volume ranging from lot sizes as low as one in a **job shop** (one-of-a-kind production using skilled labor) through **connected line batch flow** (components are standardized; each machine functions like a job shop but is positioned in the same order as the parts are processed) to lot sizes as high as 100,000 or more per year for **flexible manufacturing systems** (parts are grouped into manufacturing families to produce a wide variety of mass-produced items) and **dedicated transfer lines** (highly automated assembly lines making one mass-produced product using little human labor). According to this concept, the product becomes standardized into a commodity over time in conjunction with increasing demand. Flexibility thus gives way to efficiency.[23]

Increasing competitive intensity in many industries has forced companies to switch from traditional mass production using dedicated transfer lines to a continuous improvement production strategy. A **mass production** system was an excellent method to produce a large amount of low-cost, standard goods and services. Employees worked on narrowly defined, repetitious tasks under close supervision in a bureaucratic and hierarchical structure. Quality, however, often tended to be fairly low. Learning how to do something better was the prerogative of management; workers were expected only to learn what was assigned to them. This system tended to dominate manufacturing until the 1970s. Under the **continuous improvement** system developed by Japanese firms, empowered cross-functional teams strive constantly to improve production processes. Managers become more like coaches. The result is a large quantity of low-cost, standard goods and services, but with high quality. The key to continuous improvement is the acknowledgment that workers' experience and knowledge can help managers solve production problems and contribute toward tightening variances and reducing errors. Because continuous improvement enables firms to use the same low-cost competitive strategy as do mass production firms but at a significantly higher level of quality, it is rapidly replacing mass production as an operations strategy.

The automobile industry is currently experimenting with the strategy of **modular manufacturing** in which preassembled subassemblies are delivered as they are needed *(Just-in-Time)* to a company's assembly line workers, who quickly piece the modules together into a finished product. For example, General Motors built a new automotive complex in Brazil to make its new subcompact, the Celta. Sixteen of the 17 buildings are occupied by suppliers, including Delphi, Lear, and Goodyear. These suppliers deliver preassembled modules (which comprise 85% of the final value of each car) to GM's building for assembly. In a process new to the industry, the suppliers act as a team to build a single module comprising the motor, transmission, fuel lines, rear axle, brake-fluid lines, and exhaust system, which is then installed as one piece. GM is hoping that this manufacturing strategy will enable it to produce 100 vehicles annually per worker compared to standard rate of 30 to 50 autos.[24] Ford and Chrysler have also opened similar modular facilities in Brazil.

The concept of a product's life cycle eventually leading to one-size-fits-all mass production is being increasingly challenged by the new concept of mass customization. Appropriate for an ever-changing environment, **mass customization** requires that people, processes, units, and technology reconfigure themselves to give customers exactly what they want, when they want it. In contrast to continuous improvement, mass customization requires flexibility and quick responsiveness. Managers coordinate independent, capable individuals. An efficient linkage system is crucial. The result is low-cost, high-quality, customized goods and services. Mass customization is having a significant impact on product development. Under a true mass customization system, no one knows exactly what the next customer will want. Therefore, no one can know exactly what product the company will be creating/producing next. Because it is becoming increasingly difficult to predict what product–market opportunity will open up next, it is harder to create a long-term vision of the company's products.

One example of mass customization is the "Personal Pair" system Levi Strauss introduced to combat the growing competition from private label jeans. The customer is measured at one of the company's Personal Pair outlets, the measurements are sent to Levi's by computer, and the made-to-order jeans arrive a few days later. The jeans cost more than an off-the-shelf pair. Levi Strauss then launched Original Spin, offering more options plus men's jeans. More choices are now available to the customer without any increase in store inventory. For example, a fully stocked Levi's store carries approximately 130 pairs of jeans for any given waist and inseam. That number virtually increases to 430 with Personal Pair and to 750 with Original Spin. Lands' End is currently working to develop special body scanning booths that will create an electronic 3D model of a person's body that will sit in memory at a Web site. Mattel is hoping to soon allow people to customize the manufacturing of their own Barbie doll. According to Mattel's marketing vice president, Anne Parducci, "We are going to build a database of children's names to develop a one-to-one relationship with these girls."[25]

PURCHASING STRATEGY

Purchasing strategy deals with obtaining the raw materials, parts, and supplies needed to perform the operations function. The basic purchasing choices are multiple, sole, and parallel sourcing. Under **multiple sourcing**, the purchasing company orders a particular part from several vendors. Multiple sourcing has traditionally been considered superior to other purchasing approaches because (1) it forces suppliers to compete for the business of an important buyer, thus reducing purchasing costs; and (2) if one supplier could not deliver, another usually could, thus guaranteeing that parts and supplies would always be on hand when needed. Multiple sourcing was one way a purchasing firm could control the relationship with its suppliers. So long as suppliers could provide evidence that they could meet the product specifications, they were kept on the purchaser's list of acceptable vendors for specific parts and supplies. Unfortunately the common practice of accepting the lowest bid often compromised quality.

W. Edward Deming, a well-known management consultant, strongly recommended **sole sourcing** as the only manageable way to obtain high supplier quality. Sole sourcing relies on only one supplier for a particular part. Given his concern with designing quality into a product in its early stages of development, Deming argued that the buyer should work closely with the supplier at all stages. This reduces both cost and time spent on product design as well as improving quality. It can also simplify the purchasing company's production process by using the **Just-In-Time (JIT)** concept of the purchased parts arriving at the plant just when they are needed rather than keeping inventories. The concept of sole sourcing is being taken one step further in JIT II, in which vendor sales representatives actually have desks next to the purchasing company's factory floor, attend production status meetings, visit the R&D lab, and analyze the purchasing company's sales forecasts. These in-house suppliers then write sales orders for which the purchasing company is billed. Developed by Lance Dixon at Bose Corporation, JIT II is also being used at IBM, Honeywell, and Ingersoll-Rand. Karen Dale, Purchasing Manager for Honeywell's office supplies, said she was very concerned about confidentiality when JIT II was first suggested to her. Now she has 5 suppliers working with her 20 buyers and reports few problems.[26]

Sole sourcing reduces transaction costs and builds quality by having purchaser and supplier work together as partners rather than as adversaries. Sole sourcing means that more companies are going to have longer relationships with fewer suppliers. Sole sourcing does, however, have its limitations. If a supplier is unable to deliver a part, the purchaser has no alternative but to delay production. Multiple suppliers can provide the purchaser with better information about new technology and performance capabilities. The limitations of sole sourcing have led to the development of parallel sourcing. In **parallel sourcing**, two suppliers are the sole suppliers of two different parts, but they are also backup suppliers for each other's parts. In case one vendor cannot supply all of its parts on time, the other vendor would be asked to make up the difference.[27]

The Internet is being increasingly used both to find new sources of supply and to keep inventories replenished. For example, Hewlett-Packard introduced a Web-based procurement system to enable its 84,000 employees to buy office supplies from a standard set of suppliers. The new system enabled the company to save $60 to $100 million annually in purchasing costs.[28] See the 📶 **Internet Issue** feature to learn how David Crosier, Vice President for supply-chain management at Staples, uses the Internet to keep the retailer in Post-it notes and Scotch tape from 3M.

LOGISTICS STRATEGY

Logistics strategy deals with the flow of products into and out of the manufacturing process. Three trends are evident: centralization, outsourcing, and the use of the Internet. To gain logistical synergies across business units, corporations began centralizing logistics in the headquarters group. This centralized logistics group usually contains specialists with expertise in different transportation modes such as rail or trucking. They work to aggregate shipping volumes across the entire corporation to gain better contracts with shippers. Companies like Amoco Chemical, Georgia-Pacific, Marriott, and Union Carbide view the logistics function as an important way to differentiate themselves from the competition, to add value, and to reduce costs.

Internet Issue

Staples Uses Internet to Replenish Inventory from 3M

David Crosier was mad. As the Vice President for supply-chain management for Staples, the office supplies retailer, Crosier couldn't even find a Post-it Note to write down the complaint that his stores were consistently low on 3M products. Crosier would send an order to the Minnesota Mining & Manufacturing Company (3M) for 10,000 rolls of Scotch tape and receive only 8,000. Even worse, the supplies from 3M often arrived late causing "stock outs" of popular products. Crosier then discovered 3M's new online ordering system for office supplies. The Web site enabled 3M to reduce customer frustration caused by paper forms and last minute phone calls by eliminating error-prone steps in purchasing. Since using 3M's Web site, Staples' Crosier reports that 3M's fill rate has improved by 20% and that its on-time performance has almost doubled. "The technology takes a lot of inefficiencies out of the supply-chain process," says Crosier.

This improvement at 3M was initiated by Allen Messerli, Information Manager at 3M, over a five-year period. Since 1997, 3M has invested $30 million in the project. Ongoing maintenance costs of keeping the system current are $2.6 million. Previous to implementing this online system, 3M had serious problems with its finished goods inventory, distribution, and customer service. For example, nearly 40% of its customer records (in the United States alone) have invalid addresses. Bloated finished goods inventory in 1998 caused a 45% drop in earnings. With more than 70,000 employees around the world, 3M had difficulty linking employees, managers, and customers because of incompatible networks. With its new Global Enterprise Data Warehouse, 3M is now delivering customer, product, sales, inventory, and financial data directly to its employees and partners, who can access the information via the Internet ⟨www.3m.com⟩. The company reports saving $10 million annually in maintenance and customer-service costs. More accurate and current sales reporting is saving an additional $2.5 million per year. The new technology improved productivity, boosting global sales. Supply-chain managers like David Crosier at Staples are pleased with making the Internet an important part of their purchasing strategy.

Source: D. Little, "3M: Glued to the Web," *Business Week E.Biz* (November 2000), pp. EB65–EB70. Reprinted by special permission, copyright © 2000 by The McGraw-Hill Companies, Inc.

Many companies have found that outsourcing of logistics reduces costs and improves delivery time. For example, Hewlett-Packard (HP) contracted with Roadway Logistics to manage its inbound raw materials warehousing in Vancouver, Canada. Nearly 140 Roadway employees replaced 250 HP workers, who were transferred to other HP activities.[29]

Many companies are using the Internet to simplify their logistical system. For example, Ace Hardware created an online system for its retailers and suppliers. An individual hardware store can now see on the Web site that ordering 210 cases of wrenches is cheaper than ordering 200 cases. Since a full pallet is composed of 210 cases of wrenches, an order for a full pallet means that the supplier doesn't have to pull 10 cases off a pallet and repackage them for storage. There is less chance for loose cases to be lost in delivery and the paperwork doesn't have to be redone. As a result, Ace's transportation costs are down 18% and warehouse costs have been cut 28%.[30] As shown in the 🔲 **Internet Issue** feature, 3M's new system enabled it to save $10 million annually in maintenance and customer-service costs.

HUMAN RESOURCE MANAGEMENT (HRM) STRATEGY

HRM strategy, among other things, addresses the issue of whether a company or business unit should hire a large number of low-skilled employees who receive low pay, perform repetitive jobs, and most likely quit after a short time (the McDonald's restaurant strategy) or hire skilled employees who receive relatively high pay and are cross-trained to participate in *self-managing work teams.* As work increases in complexity, the more suited it is for teams, especially in the case of innovative product development efforts. Multinational corporations are increasingly using self-managing work teams in their foreign affiliates as well as in home country operations.[31] Research indicates that the use of work teams leads to increased quality and productivity as well as to higher employee satisfaction and commitment.[32]

Many North American and European companies are not only using an increasing amount of part-time and temporary employees, they are also experimenting with leasing *temporary employees* from employee leasing companies. The percentage of the U.S. workforce employed by personnel supply agencies has increased from half a percent in 1980 to almost 3%—more than 3 million people—by 2000. An additional 10% of the U.S. workforce are either independent contractors or temporary workers hired directly by companies.[33] Around 90% of U.S. corporations use temporary workers in some capacity—even as managers. Temporary managers accounted for $2.8 billion of the total temporary worker payroll of $43.4 billion in 1998.[34]

The number of employees who work only part-time is steadily increasing. Part-timers are attractive to a company because the firm does not need to pay fringe benefits, such as health insurance and pension plans. In the United States, the percentage of part-time regular employees (defined as those working for less than 35 hours per week) has risen from 10.2% in 1955 to 17.7% in 2000.[35] In the European Union, the number of part-time workers increased from 13.3% in 1990 to 16.4% in 1999. At the same time, overall part-time employment in all the developed (OECD) countries of the world increased from 14.3% to 15.8%.[36]

Companies are finding that having a *diverse workforce* can be a competitive advantage. Research reveals that firms with a high degree of racial diversity following a growth strategy have higher productivity than do firms with less racial diversity.[37] Avon Company, for example, was able to turn around its unprofitable inner-city markets by putting African American and Hispanic managers in charge of marketing to these markets.[38] Diversity in terms of age and national origin also offers benefits. DuPont's use of multinational teams has helped the company develop and market products internationally. McDonald's has discovered that older workers perform as well as, if not better than, younger employees. According to Edward Rensi, CEO of McDonald's USA: "We find these people to be particularly well motivated, with a sort of discipline and work habits hard to find in younger employees."[39]

INFORMATION SYSTEMS STRATEGY

Corporations are increasingly adopting **information systems strategies** in that they are turning to information systems technology to provide business units with competitive advantage. When FedEx first provided its customers with *PowerShip* computer software to store addresses, print shipping labels, and track package location, its sales jumped significantly. UPS soon followed with its own *MaxiShips* software. Viewing its information system as a distinctive competency, FedEx continued to push for further advantage against UPS by using its Web site to enable customers to track their packages. FedEx uses this competency in its advertisements by showing how customers can track the progress of their shipments.

Multinational corporations are finding that the use of a sophisticated intranet for the use of its employees allows them to practice *follow-the-sun management*, in which project team members living in one country can pass their work to team members in another country in which the work day is just beginning. Thus, night shifts are no longer needed.[40] The development of instant translation software is also enabling workers to have online communication with coworkers in other countries who use a different language. Lotus Translation Services for Sametime is a Java-based application that can deliver translated text during a chat session or an instant message in 17 languages. Another software, e-lingo ⟨www.e-lingo.com⟩ offers a multilingual search function and Web surfing as well as text and e-mail translation.[41]

Many companies are also attempting to use information systems to form closer relationships with both their customers and suppliers through sophisticated extranets. For example,

General Electric's Trading Process Network allows suppliers to electronically download GE's requests for proposals, view diagrams of parts specifications, and communicate with GE purchasing managers. According to Robert Livingston, GE's head of worldwide sourcing for the Lighting Division, going on the Web reduces processing time by one-third.[42]

7.2 Strategies to Avoid

Several strategies, which could be considered corporate, business, or functional, are very dangerous. Managers who have made a poor analysis or lack creativity may be trapped into considering some of the following **strategies to avoid**:

- **Follow the Leader:** Imitating a leading competitor's strategy might seem to be a good idea, but it ignores a firm's particular strengths and weaknesses and the possibility that the leader may be wrong. Fujitsu Ltd., the world's second-largest computer maker, was driven since the 1960s by the sole ambition of catching up to IBM. Like IBM, Fujitsu competed primarily as a mainframe computer maker. So devoted was it to catching IBM, however, that it failed to notice that the mainframe business had reached maturity by 1990 and was no longer growing.

- **Hit Another Home Run:** If a company is successful because it pioneered an extremely successful product, it tends to search for another super product that will ensure growth and prosperity. Like betting on long shots at the horse races, the probability of finding a second winner is slight. Polaroid spent a lot of money developing an "instant" movie camera, but the public ignored it in favor of the camcorder.

- **Arms Race:** Entering into a spirited battle with another firm for increased market share might increase sales revenue, but that increase will probably be more than offset by increases in advertising, promotion, R&D, and manufacturing costs. Since the deregulation of airlines, price wars and rate "specials" have contributed to the low profit margins or bankruptcy of many major airlines such as Eastern and Continental.

- **Do Everything:** When faced with several interesting opportunities, management might tend to leap at all of them. At first, a corporation might have enough resources to develop each idea into a project, but money, time, and energy are soon exhausted as the many projects demand large infusions of resources. The Walt Disney Company's expertise in the entertainment industry led it to acquire the ABC network. As the company churned out new motion pictures and television programs like *Who Wants To Be a Millionaire*, it spent $750 million to build new theme parks and buy a cruise line (as well as a hockey team). By 2000, even though corporate sales continued to increase, net income was falling.[43]

- **Losing Hand:** A corporation might have invested so much in a particular strategy that top management is unwilling to accept its failure. Believing that it has too much invested to quit, the corporation continues to throw "good money after bad." Pan American Airlines, for example, chose to sell its Pan Am Building and Intercontinental Hotels, the most profitable parts of the corporation, to keep its money-losing airline flying. Continuing to suffer losses, the company followed this strategy of shedding assets for cash, until it had sold off everything and went bankrupt.

7.3 Strategic Choice: Selection of the Best Strategy

After the pros and cons of the potential strategic alternatives have been identified and evaluated, one must be selected for implementation. By now, it is likely that many feasible alternatives will have emerged. How is the best strategy determined?

Perhaps the most important criterion is the ability of the proposed strategy to deal with the specific strategic factors developed earlier in the SWOT analysis. If the alternative doesn't take advantage of environmental opportunities and corporate strengths/competencies, and lead away from environmental threats and corporate weaknesses, it will probably fail.

Another important consideration in the selection of a strategy is the ability of each alternative to satisfy agreed-on objectives with the least resources and the fewest negative side effects. It is, therefore, important to develop a tentative implementation plan so that the difficulties that management is likely to face are addressed. This should be done in light of societal trends, the industry, and the company's situation based on the construction of scenarios.

CONSTRUCTING CORPORATE SCENARIOS

Corporate scenarios are *pro forma* balance sheets and income statements that forecast the effect each alternative strategy and its various programs will likely have on division and corporate return on investment. In a survey of *Fortune* 500 firms, 84% reported using computer simulation models in strategic planning. Most of these were simply spreadsheet-based simulation models dealing with "what if" questions.[44]

The recommended scenarios are simply extensions of the industry scenarios discussed in **Chapter 3**. If, for example, industry scenarios suggest the probable emergence of a strong market demand in a specific country for certain products, a series of alternative strategy scenarios can be developed. The alternative of acquiring another firm having these products in that country can be compared with the alternative of a green-field development (building new operations in that country). Using three sets of estimated sales figures (optimistic, pessimistic, and most likely) for the new products over the next five years, the two alternatives can be evaluated in terms of their effect on future company performance as reflected in its probable future financial statements. Pro forma (estimated future) balance sheets and income statements can be generated with spreadsheet software, such as Lotus 1-2-3 or Excel, on a personal computer.

To construct a scenario, follow these steps:

- **First**, *use industry scenarios* (discussed earlier in **Chapter 3**) to develop a set of assumptions about the task environment (in the specific country under consideration). For example, 3M requires the general manager of each business unit to describe annually what his or her industry will look like in 15 years. List *optimistic, pessimistic,* and *most likely* assumptions for key economic factors such as the GDP (Gross Domestic Product), CPI (Consumer Price Index), and prime interest rate, and for other key external strategic factors such as governmental regulation and industry trends. *This should be done for every country/region in which the corporation has significant operations that will be affected by each strategic alternative.* These same underlying assumptions should be listed for each of the alternative scenarios to be developed.

- **Second**, *develop common-size financial statements* (to be discussed in **Chapter 10**) for the company's or business unit's previous years, to serve as the basis for the trend analysis projections of **pro forma financial statements**. Use the *Scenario Box* form in **Table 7–2**.
  - **a.** Use the historical common-size percentages to estimate the level of revenues, expenses, and other categories in pro forma statements for future years.
  - **b.** Develop for each strategic alternative a set of *optimistic, pessimistic,* and *most likely* assumptions about the impact of key variables on the company's future financial statements.
  - **c.** Forecast three sets of sales and cost of goods sold figures for at least five years into the future.
  - **d.** Analyze historical data and make adjustments based on the environmental assumptions listed earlier. Do the same for other figures that can vary significantly.

Table 7-2   Scenario Box for Use in Generating Financial Pro Forma Statements

Factor	Last Year	Historical Average	Trend Analysis	Projections[1] 200- O	200- P	200- ML	200- O	200- P	200- ML	200- O	200- P	200- ML	Comments
GDP													
CPI													
Other													
Sales units													
Dollars													
COGS													
Advertising and marketing													
Interest expense													
Plant expansion													
Dividends													
Net profits													
EPS													
ROI													
ROE													
Other													

Note:
1. **O** = Optimistic; **P** = Pessimistic; **ML** = Most Likely.

Source: T. L. Wheelen and J. D. Hunger. Copyright © 1993 by Wheelen and Hunger Associates. Reprinted by permission.

e. Assume for other figures that they will continue in their historical relationship to sales or some other key determining factor. Plug in expected inventory levels, accounts receivable, accounts payable, R&D expenses, advertising and promotion expenses, capital expenditures, and debt payments (assuming that debt is used to finance the strategy), among others.

f. Consider not only historical trends, but also programs that might be needed to implement each alternative strategy (such as building a new manufacturing facility or expanding the sales force).

- **Third**, *construct detailed pro forma financial statements* for each strategic alternative.

    a. List the actual figures from this year's financial statements in the left column of the spreadsheet.

    b. List to the right of this column the optimistic figures for years one through five.

    c. Go through this same process with the same strategic alternative, but now list the pessimistic figures for the next five years.

    d. Do the same with the most likely figures.

    e. Develop a similar set of *optimistic* (O), *pessimistic* (P), and *most likely* (ML) pro forma statements for the second strategic alternative. This process generates six different pro forma scenarios reflecting three different situations (O, P, and ML) for two strategic alternatives.

    f. Calculate financial ratios and common-size income statements, and balance sheets to accompany the pro forma statements.

    g. Compare the assumptions underlying the scenarios with these financial statements and ratios to determine the feasibility of the scenarios. For example, if cost of goods sold drops from 70% to 50% of total sales revenue in the pro forma income statements, this drop should result from a change in the production process or a shift to cheaper raw materials or labor costs, rather than from a failure to keep the cost of goods sold in its usual percentage relationship to sales revenue when the predicted statement was developed.

The result of this detailed scenario construction should be anticipated net profits, cash flow, and net working capital for each of three versions of the two alternatives for five years into the future. A strategist might want to go further into the future if the strategy is expected to have a major impact on the company's financial statements beyond five years. The result of this work should provide sufficient information on which forecasts of the likely feasibility and probable profitability of each of the strategic alternatives could be based.

Obviously these scenarios can quickly become very complicated, especially if three sets of acquisition prices and development costs are calculated. Nevertheless this sort of detailed "what if" analysis is needed to realistically compare the projected outcome of each reasonable alternative strategy and its attendant programs, budgets, and procedures. Regardless of the quantifiable pros and cons of each alternative, the actual decision will probably be influenced by several subjective factors like those described in the following sections.

Management's Attitude Toward Risk

The attractiveness of a particular strategic alternative is partially a function of the amount of risk it entails. **Risk** is composed not only of the *probability* that the strategy will be effective, but also of the *amount of assets* the corporation must allocate to that strategy and the *length of time* the assets will be unavailable for other uses. Because of variation among countries in terms of customs, regulations, and resources, companies operating in global industries must deal with a greater amount of risk than firms operating only in one country. The greater the assets involved and the longer they are committed, the more likely top management is to demand a high probability of success. Do not expect managers with no ownership position in a company to have much interest in putting their jobs in danger with a risky decision. Research does indicate that managers who own a significant amount of stock in their firms are more likely to engage in risk-taking actions than are managers with no stock.[45]

A high level of risk was why Intel's Board of Directors found it difficult to vote for a proposal in the early 1990s to commit $5 billion to making the Pentium microprocessor chip—five times the amount needed for its previous chip. In looking back on that board meeting, then-CEO Andy Grove remarked, "I remember people's eyes looking at that chart and getting big. I wasn't even sure I believed those numbers at the time." The proposal committed the company to building new factories, something Intel had been reluctant to do. A wrong decision would mean that the company would end up with a killing amount of overcapacity. Based on Grove's presentation, the board decided to take the gamble. Intel's resulting manufacturing expansion eventually cost $10 billion, but resulted in Intel's obtaining 75% of the microprocessor business and huge cash profits.[46]

Risk might be one reason that significant innovations occur more often in small firms than in large, established corporations. The small firm managed by an entrepreneur is willing to accept greater risk than would a large firm of diversified ownership run by professional managers.[47] It is one thing to take a chance if you are the primary shareholder and are not concerned with periodic changes in the value of the company's common stock. It is something else if the corporation's stock is widely held and acquisition-hungry competitors or takeover artists surround the company like sharks every time the company's stock price falls below some external assessment of the firm's value!

A new approach to evaluating alternatives under conditions of high environmental uncertainty is to use real-options theory. According to the **real options** approach, when the future is highly uncertain, it pays to have a broad range of options open. This is in contrast to using **net present value** (npv) to calculate the value of a project by predicting its payouts, adjusting them for risk, and subtracting the amount invested. By boiling everything down to one scenario, npv doesn't provide any flexibility in case circumstances change. Npv is also difficult to apply to projects in which the potential payoffs are currently unknown. The real options approach, however, deals with these issues by breaking the investment into stages. Management allocates a small amount of funding to initiate multiple projects, monitors their development, and then cancels the projects that aren't successful and funds those that are doing well. This approach is very similar to the way venture capitalists fund an entrepreneurial venture in stages of funding based upon the venture's performance. Corporations using the real options approach are Chevron for bidding on petroleum reserves, Airbus for calculating the costs of airlines changing their orders at the last minute, and the Tennessee Valley Authority for outsourcing electricity generation instead of building its own plant. Because of its complexity, the real options approach is not worthwhile for minor decisions or for projects requiring a full commitment at the beginning.[48]

Pressures from Stakeholders

The attractiveness of a strategic alternative is affected by its perceived compatibility with the key stakeholders in a corporation's task environment. Creditors want to be paid on time. Unions exert pressure for comparable wage and employment security. Governments and interest groups demand social responsibility. Shareholders want dividends. All of these pressures must be given some consideration in the selection of the best alternative.

Stakeholders can be categorized in terms of their (1) interest in the corporation's activities and (2) relative power to influence the corporation's activities.[49] Using the **Stakeholder Priority Matrix** depicted in **Figure 7-2**, each stakeholder group may be placed in one of the nine cells.

Strategic managers should ask four questions to assess the importance of stakeholder concerns in a particular decision:

1. How will this decision affect each stakeholder, especially those given high and medium priority?
2. How much of what each stakeholder wants are they likely to get under this alternative?
3. What are they likely to do if they don't get what they want?
4. What is the probability that they will do it?

Strategy makers should be better able to choose strategic alternatives that minimize external pressures and maximize the probability of gaining stakeholder support. In addition, top management can propose a **political strategy** to influence its key stakeholders. Some of the most commonly used political strategies are constituency building, political action committee contributions, advocacy advertising, lobbying, and coalition building.

Pressures from the Corporate Culture

If a strategy is incompatible with the corporate culture, the likelihood of its success is very low. Foot-dragging and even sabotage will result as employees fight to resist a radical change in corporate philosophy. Precedents from the past tend to restrict the kinds of objectives and strategies that can be seriously considered.[50] The "aura" of the founders of a corporation can linger long past their lifetimes because their values have been imprinted on a corporation's members.

Figure 7–2
Stakeholder Priority Matrix

	Low Power	Medium Power	High Power
High Interest	Medium Priority	High Priority	High Priority
Medium Interest	Low Priority	Medium Priority	High Priority
Low Interest	Low Priority	Low Priority	Medium Priority

Source: Suggested by C. Anderson, "Values-Based Management," *Academy of Management Executive* (November 1997), p, 31. Reprinted by permission of *Academy of Management Executive* via the Copyright Clearance Center.

In evaluating a strategic alternative, the strategy makers must consider **corporate culture pressures** and assess the strategy's compatibility with the corporate culture. If there is little fit, management must decide if it should:

- Take a chance on ignoring the culture.
- Manage around the culture and change the implementation plan.
- Try to change the culture to fit the strategy.
- Change the strategy to fit the culture.

Further, a decision to proceed with a particular strategy without a commitment to change the culture or manage around the culture (both very tricky and time consuming) is dangerous. Nevertheless restricting a corporation to only those strategies that are completely compatible with its culture might eliminate from consideration the most profitable alternatives. (See **Chapter 9** for more information on managing corporate culture.)

Needs and Desires of Key Managers
Even the most attractive alternative might not be selected if it is contrary to the needs and desires of important top managers. Personal characteristics and experience do affect a person's assessment of an alternative's attractiveness.[51] A person's ego may be tied to a particular proposal to the extent that all other alternatives are strongly lobbied against. As a result, he or she may have unfavorable forecasts altered so that they are more in agreement with the desired alternative.[52] A key executive might influence other people in top management to favor a par-

ticular alternative so that objections to it are ignored. For example, Nextel's CEO, Daniel Akerson, decided that the best place to locate the corporation's 500-person national headquarters would be the Washington, DC, area, close to his own home.[53]

Industry and cultural backgrounds affect strategic choice. For example, executives with strong ties within an industry tend to choose strategies commonly used in that industry. Other executives who have come to the firm from another industry and have strong ties outside the industry tend to choose different strategies from what is being currently used in their industry.[54] Research reveals that executives from Korea, the United States, Japan, and Germany tend to make different strategic choices in similar situations because they use different decision criteria and weights. For example, Korean executives emphasize industry attractiveness, sales, and market share in their decisions; whereas, U.S. executives emphasize projected demand, discounted cash flow, and ROI.[55]

There is a tendency to maintain the status quo, which means that decision makers continue with existing goals and plans beyond the point when an objective observer would recommend a change in course. Some executives show a self-serving tendency to attribute the firm's problems not to their own poor decisions, but to environmental events out of their control such as government policies or a poor economic climate.[56] Negative information about a particular course of action to which a person is committed may be ignored because of a desire to appear competent or because of strongly held values regarding consistency. It may take a crisis or an unlikely event to cause strategic decision makers to seriously consider an alternative they had previously ignored or discounted.[57] For example, it wasn't until the CEO of ConAgra, a multinational food products company, had a heart attack that ConAgra started producing the Healthy Choice line of low-fat, low-cholesterol, low-sodium frozen-food entrees.

PROCESS OF STRATEGIC CHOICE

There is an old story at General Motors:

> *At a meeting with his key executives, CEO Alfred Sloan proposed a controversial strategic decision. When asked for comments, each executive responded with supportive comments and praise. After announcing that they were all in apparent agreement, Sloan stated that they were not going to proceed with the decision. Either his executives didn't know enough to point out potential downsides of the decision, or they were agreeing to avoid upsetting the boss and disrupting the cohesion of the group. The decision was delayed until a debate could occur over the pros and cons.[58]*

Strategic choice is the evaluation of alternative strategies and selection of the best alternative. There is mounting evidence that when an organization is facing a dynamic environment, the best strategic decisions are not arrived at through **consensus** when everyone agrees on one alternative. They actually involve a certain amount of heated disagreement and even conflict. This is certainly the case for firms operating in a global industry. Because unmanaged conflict often carries a high emotional cost, authorities in decision making propose that strategic managers use "programmed conflict" to raise different opinions regardless of the personal feelings of the people involved.[59] Two techniques help strategic managers avoid the consensus trap that Alfred Sloan found:

1. **Devil's Advocate:** The devil's advocate originated in the medieval Roman Catholic Church as a way of ensuring that impostors were not canonized as saints. One trusted person was selected to find and present all reasons why the person should not be canonized. When applied to strategic decision making, the **devil's advocate** (who may be an individual or a group) is assigned to identify potential pitfalls and problems with a proposed alternative strategy in a formal presentation.

2. **Dialectical Inquiry:** The dialectic philosophy, which can be traced back to Plato and Aristotle and more recently to Hegel, involves combining two conflicting views—the thesis and the antithesis—into a synthesis. When applied to strategic decision making, **dialectical inquiry** requires that two proposals using different assumptions be generated for each alternative strategy under consideration. After advocates of each position present and debate the merits of their arguments before key decision makers, either one of the alternatives or a new compromise alternative is selected as the strategy to be implemented.

Research generally supports the conclusion that both the devil's advocate and dialectical inquiry are equally superior to consensus in decision making, especially when the firm's environment is dynamic. The debate itself, rather than its particular format, appears to improve the quality of decisions by formalizing and legitimizing constructive conflict and by encouraging critical evaluation. Both lead to better assumptions and recommendations and to a higher level of critical thinking among the people involved.[60]

Another approach to generating a series of diverse and creative strategic alternatives is to use a **strategy shadow committee.** At Anheuser-Busch, top management established such a committee composed of employees at least two to three echelons below the executive-level strategy committee. Members of the shadow committee serve for two years. During that time they see all materials and attend all meetings of the executive strategy committee. One year the shadow committee was taken off site and asked what was wrong with management and to propose what the company should be doing differently. The group's report was then given to the Board of Directors.[61]

Regardless of the process used to generate strategic alternatives, each resulting alternative must be rigorously evaluated in terms of its ability to meet four criteria:

1. **Mutual Exclusivity:** Doing any one would preclude doing any other.
2. **Success:** It must be doable and have a good probability of success.
3. **Completeness:** It must take into account all the key strategic issues.
4. **Internal Consistency:** It must make sense on its own as a strategic decision for the entire firm and not contradict key goals, policies, and strategies currently being pursued by the firm or its units.[62]

7.4 Development of Policies

The selection of the best strategic alternative is not the end of strategy formulation. The organization must now engage in **developing policies**. Policies define the broad guidelines for implementation. Flowing from the selected strategy, policies provide guidance for decision making and actions throughout the organization. At General Electric, for example, Chairman Jack Welch initiated the policy that any GE business unit be number one or number two wherever it competes. This policy gives clear guidance to managers throughout the organization. Another example of such a policy is Casey's General Stores' policy that a new service or product line may be added to its stores only when the product or service can be justified in terms of increasing store traffic.

Policies tend to be rather long lived and can even outlast the particular strategy that created them. Interestingly these general policies—such as "The customer is always right" or "Research and development should get first priority on all budget requests"—can become, in time, part of a corporation's culture. Such policies can make the implementation of specific strategies easier. They can also restrict top management's strategic options in the future. Thus a change in strategy should be followed quickly by a change in policies. Managing policy is one way to manage the corporate culture.

7.5 Impact of the Internet on Functional Strategy

Every time a person clicks on a banner or views a product on the Internet, Web site operators add this information to that person's digital trail. The user doesn't have to purchase anything because a decision not to buy is almost as important as a decision to buy. The data is used to answer questions such as, "Why did the customer visit our site but not buy our products? Is our checkout process too long? Did the customer come from an affiliate site? Should we have offered this person a discount or special offer?" The answers to these questions can strongly influence a company's marketing functional strategy.

Tracking potential online customers is the rationale for **electronic customer relationship management (e-CRM) software**. Divided into the three areas of marketing, services, and sales, e-CRM is the fastest growing area of the software industry. The marketing part of e-CRM is growing at a rate of 50% annually and is divided into the fields of analytics, e-marketing, and personalization. According to Phil Fernandez, Executive Vice President of E.piphany, an e-CRM developer, "*Analytics* helps you to understand the customer. *E-marketing* helps structure how you reach out to that customer, and *personalization* is about using all that knowledge to create a personalized experience."

Analytics software creates information from data gathered from a number of customer *touch points*, both online and off-line. Combining demographic data with sales information from customer records can indicate how purchases vary by demographic group. Online activity records can tell what particular groups of customers buy, what Web pages they tend to visit, and their tastes. Companies such as Accrue, digiMine, Coremetrics, NetGenesis, Personify, and MicroStrategy offer software that can analyze customer data and turn it into usable reports. Hoover's Online used analytics software to analyze Web site traffic, create customer profiles, and classify users by market segment. According to Craig Lakey, vice president of marketing for Hoover's Online, "Using Personify's technology, we were able to analyze where people were going and promote areas that they were ignoring. We were able to cross-promote other aspects of the site. Just by virtue of analyzing what we found, we tripled the traffic on the business travel channel."

E-marketing software is used to keep track of which marketing campaigns succeed and which fail as well as to plan future marketing programs. The analytics stage answers questions such as "Of the people who bought Gucci bags, how many also bought Calvin Klein shirts?" In the e-marketing stage, companies use the answers to allow a firm to offer discounts on Gucci bags via e-mail to customers who bought Calvin Klein shirts. Companies offering e-marketing software are Annuncio, Broadbase Software, E.piphany, and Responsys.com.

Personalization software allows businesses to offer products uniquely relevant to the individual visitor to a Web site by creating a Web experience tailored to that individual's taste. Amazon.com uses this software to inform people who purchase a book or CD that people who previously bought that book or CD also bought books by another author/artist. Like Amazon.com, statistical correlation techniques are used to find other Web site visitors with similar patterns of behavior and use the behavior of these like-minded people to make recommendations for further purchases. Personalization software also uses neural network-based artificial intelligence to model Web site visitors on the basis of their "clickstream" (a sequence of Web pages selected by a visitor) and purchase behavior. Personalization is superior to blindly e-mailing coupons to potential customers because it is more closely connected to that person's interests. Personalization software is still in the development stage but has a lot of appeal to companies with an Internet presence. Some of the companies offering personalization software are Net Perceptions,

Angara, the Art Technology Group, Blaze Software, and BroadVision. According to Lynne Harvey, Senior Consultant with the Patricia Seybold Group, "The number of touch points is expanding, so there will be an increased demand by the customers for companies to be more responsive, as opposed to the old way, where you had a predefined offer and you hoped that someone would be attracted enough to buy it."[63]

Thanks to e-CRM software, firms are now able to practice *dynamic pricing*, a controversial pricing practice in which different customers pay different prices for the same product or service. Tried by Amazon.com, the company uses a customer's address, record of previous purchases, sites visited, and other information to decide if the customer is price-sensitive. If the software puts the customer in a price-sensitive category, the customer is offered a low price. Otherwise, the customer pays a premium. Other firms practice *dynamic service*, in which they offer varying levels of service for the same price. Customers are coded based on the profitability of their business. Using a customer's code, phone centers or Web sites route customers to different queues. The most profitable customers have fees waived and receive special offers the typical customer doesn't know exist.[64] Gambling casinos have used this marketing strategy for years to encourage "high rollers" who are prone to spend (and lose) a large amount of money in gambling establishments.

Projections for the 21st Century

- From 1994 to 2010, the number of desktop PCs worldwide will double from 132 million to 278 million.
- From 1994 to 2010, the number of mobile PCs worldwide will increase from 18 million to 47 million.[63]

Discussion Questions

1. How can a corporation identify its core competencies? Its distinctive competencies?

2. When should a corporation or business unit outsource a function or activity?

3. Why is penetration pricing more likely than skim pricing to raise a company's or a business unit's operating profit in the long run?

4. How does mass customization support a business unit's competitive strategy?

5. What is the relationship of policies to strategies?

Strategic Practice Exercise

Wal-Mart is a very successful mass marketing retailer with stores throughout North America and an increasing presence in Europe, South America, and Asia. The company is known for its distinctive competency in information systems and distribution logistics. According to Michael Campbell, CEO of Campbell Software, "Wal-Mart is so far ahead of the (technology) curve because they were the first ones to embrace the fact that they are in the information business."[66]

In 1996, management decided to establish a position for the company on the Internet. During this period of time when its brick and mortar stores were registering double-digit sales and earnings growth, its virtual store on the Internet had continual problems. For example, in 1999 the company was forced to warn Web customers that it couldn't guarantee Christmas delivery of goods ordered after December 14. A redesigned and expanded Web site debuted in February 2000 but was criticized for its cumbersome design, slow downloading time, and poor search engine. In September 2000, it was ranked 47th out of 50 retail sites by Media Metrix.[67]

Timothy Mullaney, a columnist for *Business Week's* e-biz section, compared Wal-Mart's Web site during September 2000 with that of Amazon.com. He found that Wal-Mart's Web site didn't measure up to its own brick and mortar stores, much less to Amazon. He rated Walmart.com a failure on content, convenience, and fun. Among its faults were the following: Walmart.com settled for taking orders rather than enticing visitors (as Amazon did) to consider things they hadn't thought of buying. Compared to Amazon.com, he found the site boring. Its home page was composed of a long list of categories. The site provided basic data on each product offered but failed to provide any reviews of the products or show them in use. In contrast, Amazon.com's Web site provided reviews by both Amazon and 33 users supplemented by a table that let the user compare the features of one CD player with those of other players. Simple one-click boxes referred the user to accessories and batteries. Amazon.com tailored its recommendations to the visitor's tastes and interests; whereas, Walmart.com made generic suggestions that fit few visitors. Walmart.com's navigation features were poor. The site contained a number of broken or poorly designed links. For example, a request for romantic comedies starring Tom Hanks led to *Nightmare at 43 Hillcrest*, a Hanks' drama about drug-dealing. Prices and shipping costs were, however, about the same at both sites. The columnist summed up his experience with the statement, "Right now, Amazon.com is a very good store, and Walmart.com is still learning the online fundamentals."[68]

Reacting to the poor performance of its Web site, Wal-Mart's management hired Jeanne Jackson as the new CEO of Walmart.com Hired during the Spring of 2000 from Banana Republic where she had been CEO as well as head of the company's catalogue and Web operations, Jackson vowed to make the largest brick and mortar retailer into a successful virtual retailer. She closed the Web site in late September for remodeling and opened it a few weeks later as a much leaner site without personalized promotions or 3D graphics. Although the site had a more streamlined and intuitive layout in 2001, critics found it dull. CEO Jackson continued to be optimistic. The online efforts of Sears, Kmart, and Target were still in their infancy. Jackson commented, "This is a marathon. It's not a sprint."

1. Given that Wal-Mart has a distinctive competence in information technology, why has it done so poorly on the Internet?

2. Considering that as of early 2001, almost no dot.com retailer (including Amazon.com) had yet to show a profit, why all the fuss about Internet retailing?

3. Is the marriage of "bricks" and "clicks" the right formula for marketing success on the Internet?

4. Should Wal-Mart be investing in the Internet at a time when it has so many alternative growth opportunities throughout the world?

5. What advice would you give Jeanne Jackson regarding Walmart.com?

Key Terms

connected line batch flow (p. 172)

consensus (p. 183)

continuous improvement (p. 172)

core capability (p. 165)

core competency (p. 165)

corporate culture pressures (p. 182)

corporate scenarios (p. 178)

dedicated transfer lines (p. 172)

developing policies (p. 184)

devil's advocate (p. 183)

dialectical inquiry (p. 184)

distinctive competency (p. 165)

electronic customer relationship management (e-CRM) software (p. 185)

financial strategy (p. 169)

flexible manufacturing systems (p. 172)

functional strategy (p. 165)

HRM strategy (p. 175)

information systems strategy (p. 176)

job shop (p. 172)

Just-In-Time (p. 174)

leveraged buy out (p. 170)

logistics strategy (p. 174)

market development (p. 168)

marketing strategy (p. 168)

mass customization (p. 173)

mass production (p. 172)

modular manufacturing (p. 173)

multiple sourcing (p. 173)

net present value (p. 181)

operations strategy (p. 171)

outsourcing (p. 166)

parallel sourcing (p. 174)

penetration pricing (p. 169)

political strategy (p. 181)

pro forma financial statements (p. 178)

product development (p. 169)

pull strategy (p. 169)

purchasing strategy (p. 173)

push strategy (p. 169)

R&D strategy (p. 170)

real options (p. 181)

risk (p. 180)

skim pricing (p. 169)

sole sourcing (p. 174)

stakeholder priority matrix (p. 181)

strategic choice (p. 183)

strategies to avoid (p. 177)

strategy shadow committee (p. 184)

technological follower (p. 171)

technological leader (p. 171)

tracking stock (p. 170)

Notes

1. Arm & Hammer is a registered trademark of Church & Dwight Company, Inc.

2. M. A. Hitt, B. W. Keats, and S. M. DeMarie, "Navigating in the New Competitive Landscape: Building Strategic Flexibility and Competitive Advantage in the 21st Century," *Academy of Management Executive* (November 1998), pp. 22–42. According to the authors, failure to reinvest in a core competency will result in its becoming a "core rigidity."

3. G. Hamel and S. K. Prahalad, *Competing for the Future* (Boston: Harvard Business School Press, 1994), pp. 202–207.

4. Ibid, p. 211.

5. P. J. Verdin and P. J. Williamson, "Core Competencies, Competitive Advantage and Market Analysis: Forging the Links," in *Competence-Based Competition*, edited by G. Hamel and A. Heene (New York: John Wiley and Sons, 1994), pp. 83–84.

6. B. Kelley, "Outsourcing Marches On," *Journal of Business Strategy* (July/August 1995), p. 40.

7. BridgeNews, "Motorola Will Cut 2,870 Jobs in Outsourcing Deal," *The (Ames) Tribune* (December 11, 2000), p. D4.

8. J. Greco, "Outsourcing: The New Partnership," *Journal of Business Strategy* (July/August 1997), pp. 48–54.

9. J. B. Quinn, "The Intelligent Enterprise: A New Paradigm," *Academy of Management Executive* (November 1992), pp. 48–63.

10. J. A. Byrne, "Has Outsourcing Gone Too Far?" *Business Week* (April 1, 1996), pp. 26–28.

11. D. Lei and M. A. Hitt, "Strategic Restructuring and Outsourcing: The Effect of Mergers and Acquisitions and LBOs on Building Firm Skills and Capabilities," *Journal of Management*, Vol. 21, No. 5 (1995), pp. 835–859.

12. Kelley, "Outsourcing Marches On," p. 40.

13. S. M. Oster, *Modern Competitive Analysis*, 2d ed. (New York: Oxford University Press, 1994), p. 93.

14. M. Springer, "Plowed Under," *Forbes* (February 21, 2000), p. 56.

15. W. Redmond, "The Strategic Pricing of Innovative Products," *Handbook of Business Strategy, 1992/1993 Yearbook*, edited by H. E. Glass and M. A. Hovde (Boston: Warren, Gorham and Lamont, 1992), pp. 16.1–16.13.

16. A. Safieddine and S. Titman in April 1999 *Journal of Finance* as summarized by D. Champion, "The Joy of Leverage," *Harvard Business Review* (July–August 1999), pp. 19–22.

17. R. Kochhar and M. A. Hitt, "Linking Corporate Strategy to Capital Structure: Diversification Strategy, Type and Source of Financing," *Strategic Management Journal* (June 1998), pp. 601–610.

18. A. Rappaport and M. L. Sirower, "Stock or Cash?" *Harvard Business Review* (November–December 1999), pp. 147–158.

19. D. Angwin and I. Contardo, "Unleashing Cerberus: Don't Let Your MBOs Turn on Themselves," *Long Range Strategy* (October 1999), pp. 494–504.

20. S. Scherreik, "Tread Carefully When You Buy Tracking Stocks," *Business Week* (March 6, 2000), pp. 182–184.

21. T. Due, "Dean Foods Thrives on Regional Off-Brand Products," *Wall Street Journal* (September 17, 1987), p. A6.

22. S. Stevens, "Speeding the Signals of Change," *Appliance* (February 1995), p. 7.

23. J. R. Williams and R. S. Novak, "Aligning CIM Strategies to Different Markets," *Long Range Planning* (February 1990), pp. 126–135.

24. J. Wheatley, "Super Factory—or Super Headache," *Business Week* (July 31, 2000), p. 66.

25. G. Hamel, "Strategy as Revolution," *Harvard Business Review* (July–August, 1996), p. 73 and E. Schonfeld, "The Customized, Digitized, Have-It-Your-Way Economy," *Fortune* (September 28, 1998), pp. 115–124.

26. F. R. Bleakley, "Some Companies Let Supplier Work on Site and Even Place Orders," *Wall Street Journal* (January 13, 1995), pp. A1, A6.

27. J. Richardson, "Parallel Sourcing and Supplier Performance in the Japanese Automobile Industry," *Strategic Management Journal* (July 1993), pp. 339–350.

28. S. Roberts-Witt, "Procurement: The HP Way," *PC Magazine* (November 21, 2000), pp. iBiz 21–22.

29. J. Bigness, "In Today's Economy, There Is Big Money to Be Made in Logistics," *Wall Street Journal* (September 6, 1995), pp. A1, A9.

30. F. Keenan, "Logistics Gets a Little Respect," *Business Week* (November 20, 2000), pp. E.Biz 112–116.

31. B. L. Kirkman and D. L. Shapiro, "The Impact of Cultural Values on Employee Resistance to Teams: Toward a Model of Globalized Self-Managing Work Team Effectiveness," *Academy of Management Review* (July 1997), pp. 730–757.

32. R. D. Banker, J. M. Field, R. G. Schroeder, and K. K. Sinha, "Impact of Work Teams on Manufacturing Performance: A Longitudinal Field Study," *Academy of Management Journal* (August 1996), pp. 867–890; B. L. Kirkman and B. Rosen, "Beyond Self-Management: Antecedents and Consequences of Team Empowerment," *Academy of Management Journal* (February 1999), pp. 58–74.

33. M. J. Mandel, "The Risk that Boom Will Turn to Bust," *Business Week* (February 14, 2000), pp. 120–122; "Economic Indicators," *The Economist* (June 24, 2000), p. 120.

34. P. Johnson, "Temporary Executives Score Big," *Des Moines Register* (October 30, 2000), pp. 1D, 4D.

35. P. Brimelow, "Part-Time U.S.A.," *Forbes* (January 22, 2001), p. 81.

36. "Economic Indicators," *The Economist* (June 24, 2000), p. 120.

37. O. C. Richard, "Racial Diversity, Business Strategy, and Firm Performance: A Resource-Based View," *Academy of Management Journal* (April 2000), pp. 164–177.

38. G. Robinson and K. Dechant, "Building a Business Case for Diversity," *Academy of Management Executive* (August 1997), pp. 21–31.

39. K. Labich, "Making Diversity Pay," *Fortune* (September 9, 1996), pp. 177–180.

40. J. Greco, "Good Day Sunshine," *Journal of Business Strategy* (July/August 1998), pp. 4–5.

41. W. Howard, "Translate Now," *PC Magazine* (September 19, 2000), p. 81.

42. T. Smart, "Jack Welch's Cyber-Czar," *Business Week* (August 5, 1996), p. 83.

43. R. Grover and D. Polek, "Millionaire Buys Disney Time," *Business Week* (June 26, 2000), pp. 141–144.

44. D. K. Sinha, "Strategic Planning in the Fortune 500," *Handbook of Business Strategy, 1991/1992 Yearbook*, edited by H. E. Glass and M. A. Hovde (Boston: Warren, Gorham and Lamont, 1991), pp. 9.6–9.8.

45. T. B. Palmer and R. M. Wiseman, "Decoupling Risk Taking from Income Stream Uncertainty: A Holistic Model of Risk," *Strategic Management Journal* (November 1999), pp. 1037–1062.

46. D. Clark, "All the Chips: A Big Bet Made Intel What It Is Today; Now It Wagers Again," *Wall Street Journal* (June 6, 1995), pp. A1, A5.

47. L. W. Busenitz and J. B. Barney, "Differences Between Entrepreneurs and Managers in Large Organizations: Biases and Heuristics in Strategic Decision-Making," *Journal of Business Venturing* (January 1997), pp. 9–30.

48. P. Coy, "Exploiting Uncertainty," *Business Week* (June 7, 1999), pp. 118–124. For further information on real options, see M. Amram and N. Kulatilaka, "Uncertainty: The New Rules for Strategy," *Journal of Business Strategy* (May/June 1999), pp. 25–29; M. Amram and N. Kulatilaka, "Disciplined Decisions: Aligning Strategy with the Financial Markets," *Harvard Business Review* (January–February 1999), pp. 95–104; T. A. Luehrman, "Strategy

as a Portfolio of Real Options," *Harvard Business Review* (September–October 1998), pp. 89–99; T. A. Luehrman, "Investment Opportunities as Real Options: Getting Started with the Numbers," *Harvard Business Review* (July-August 1998), pp. 51–67; R. G. McGrath, "Falling Forward: Real Options Reasoning and Entrepreneurial Failure," *Academy of Management Review* (January 1999), pp. 13–30.

49. C. Anderson, "Values-Based Management," *Academy of Management Executive* (November 1997), pp. 25–46.

50. H. M. O'Neill, R. W. Pouder, and A. K. Buchholtz, "Patterns in the Diffusion of Strategies Across Organizations: Insights from the Innovation Diffusion Literature," *Academy of Management Executive* (January 1998), pp. 98–114.

51. B. B. Tyler and H. K. Steensma, "Evaluating Technological Collaborative Opportunities: A Cognitive Modeling Perspective," *Strategic Management Journal* (Summer 1995), pp. 43–70; D. Duchan, D. P. Ashman, and M. Nathan, "Mavericks, Visionaries, Protestors, and Sages: Toward a Typology of Cognitive Structures for Decision Making in Organizations," *Journal of Business Strategies* (Fall 1997), pp. 106–125; P. Chattopadhyay, W. H. Glick, C. C. Miller, and G. P. Huber, "Determinants of Executive Beliefs: Comparing Functional Conditioning and Social Influence," *Strategic Management Journal* (August 1999), pp. 763–789; B. Katey and G. G. Meredith, "Relationship Among Owner/Manager Personal Values, Business Strategies, and Enterprise Performance," *Journal of Small Business Management* (April 1997), pp. 37–64.

52. C. S. Galbraith and G. B. Merrill, "The Politics of Forecasting: Managing the Truth," *California Management Review* (Winter 1996), pp. 29–43.

53. M. Leuchter, "The Rules of the Game," *Forecast* (May/June 1996), pp. 16–23.

54. M. A. Geletkanycz and D. C. Hambrick, "The External Ties of Top Executives: Implications for Strategic Choice and Performance," *Administrative Science Quarterly* (December 1997), pp. 654–681.

55. M. A. Hitt, M. T. Dacin, B. B. Tyler, and D. Park, "Understanding the Differences in Korean and U.S. Executives' Strategic Orientation," *Strategic Management Journal* (February 1997), pp. 159–167; L. G. Thomas III and G. Waring, "Competing Capitalisms: Capital Investment in American, German, and Japanese Firms," *Strategic Management Journal* (August 1999), pp. 729–748.

56. J. A. Wagner III and R. Z. Gooding, "Equivocal Information and Attribution: An Investigation of Patterns of Managerial Sensemaking," *Strategic Management Journal* (April 1997), pp. 275–286.

57. J. Ross and B. M. Staw, "Organizational Escalation and Exit: Lessons from the Shoreham Nuclear Power Plant," *Academy of Management Journal* (August 1993), pp. 701–732; P. W. Mulvey, J. F. Veiga, and P. M. Elsass, "When Teammates Raise a White Flag," *Academy of Management Executive* (February 1996), pp. 40–49.

58. R. A. Cosier and C. R. Schwenk, "Agreement and Thinking Alike: Ingredients for Poor Decisions," *Academy of Management Executive* (February 1990), p. 69.

59. A. C. Amason, "Distinguishing the Effects of Functional and Dysfunctional Conflict on Strategic Decision Making: Resolving a Paradox for Top Management Teams," *Academy of Management Journal* (February 1996), pp. 123–148; A. C. Amason and H. J. Sapienza, "The Effects of Top Management Team Size and Interaction Norms on Cognitive and Affective Conflict," *Journal of Management*, Vol. 23, No. 4 (1997), pp. 495–516.

60. D. M. Schweiger, W. R. Sandberg, and P. L. Rechner, "Experiential Effects of Dialectical Inquiry, Devil's Advocacy, and Consensus Approaches to Strategic Decision Making," *Academy of Management Journal* (December 1989), pp. 745–772; G. Whyte, "Decision Failures: Why They Occur and How to Prevent Them," *Academy of Management Executive* (August 1991), pp. 23–31; R. L. Priem, D. A. Harrison, and N. K. Muir, "Structured Conflict and Consensus Outcomes in Group Decision Making," *Journal of Management*, Vol. 21, No. 4 (1995), pp. 691–710.

61. G. Hamel, "Turning Your Business Upside Down," *Fortune* (June 23, 1997), p. 87.

62. S. C. Abraham, "Using Bundles to Find the Best Strategy," *Strategy & Leadership* (July/August/September 1999), pp. 53–55.

63. C. Medford, "Know Who I Am," *PC Magazine* (January 16, 2001), pp. 136–148; S. L. Roberts-Witt, "Personalization: Is It Worth It?" *PC Magazine* (December 19, 2000), pp. iBiz 8–12.

64. P. Krugman, "The Cost of Convenience," *The (Ames) Tribune* (October 5, 2000), p. A6; D. Brady, "Customer Service?" *Business Week* (October 23, 2000), pp. 119–128.

65. J. Warner, "21st Century Capitalism: Snapshot of the Next Century," *Business Week* (November 18, 1994), p. 194.

66. J. Jordan and D. Svetcov, "Data-Crunching Santa," *U.S. News & World Report* (December 21, 1998), pp. 44–48.

67. W. Zellner, "Will Walmart.com Get It Right This Time?" *Business Week* (November 6, 2000), pp. 104–112.

68. T. J. Mullaney, "This Race Isn't Even Close," *Business Week* (December 18, 2000), pp. 208–210.

Newbury Comics, Inc.

STRATEGY FORMULATION

Newbury Comics Cofounders, Mike Dreese and John Brusger parlayed $2,000 and a comic book collection into a thriving chain of 22 stores spanning the New England region, known to be *the* place to shop for everything from the best of the underground/independent scene to major label superstars. The chain also stocks a wide variety of non-music related items such as T-shirts, Dr. (doc) Martens shoes, posters, jewelry, cosmetics, books, magazines, and other trendy items.

In Part Three, **"Strategy Formulation,"** the video addresses strategy formulation in terms of situation analysis, business, corporate, and functional strategy. Mike, John, and Jan conduct a SWOT analysis of Newbury Comics in terms of Strengths, Weaknesses, Opportunities and Threats and how strategy is formulated. They are very much aware of how the company's core competencies provide competitive advantage.

Mike explains that he dislikes setting three-year revenue targets (objectives), but prefers to formulate strategy on an experimental basis. Note that even when discussing strategy formulation, Mike talks about implementation. He tells how he assigned the development of the used CD implementation plan to Duncan Brown, Senior Vice President. Brown was to look for long-run roadblocks in case the strategy was successful in the short run.

Newbury Comics is a good example of the value of SWOT analysis when formulating strategy. Most of the information, such as the employees' knowledge and competition, was presented in the earlier video dealing with environmental scanning. Some of the threats, however, are mentioned for the first time. Mike notes that the vendor community (suppliers of new CDs) may decide to make it difficult for any retailer to buy new CDs if that retailer sells used ones. He also notes that in four to five years, Napster-type operators who deal in digit-to-digit downloads instead of CDs may dominate the business of music distribution.

The management of Newbury Comics definitely believes that the company has a competitive advantage (edge) in its market. Jan states that the company's prices are cheaper than the mall music stores plus it offers used CDs. Even when competitors like Best Buy have similar prices, Newbury Comics has a better selection plus used CDs. Mike again points out that the company's corporate culture attracts employees with a "knowledge of the street." One-third of the employees play in bands. John adds that Newbury Comics offers hard-to-find material that is sold in "onesies" and "twosies" to the discriminating buyer.

Concepts Illustrated in the Video

- Strategy Formulation
- SWOT Analysis
- Propitious Niche
- Competitive Strategy
- Competitive Tactics (timing)

- Corporate Growth Strategy
- Marketing Strategy
- Human Resource Management Strategy
- Information Systems Strategy
- Management's Attitude Toward Risk

Study Questions

1. Has Newbury Comics found a "propitious niche"?
2. Conduct a SWOT analysis of Newbury Comics. Did you list anything that management failed to list?
3. The video casually mentions mission and objectives for the company. Formulate a mission statement for Newbury Comics.
4. What competitive strategy is being followed by Newbury Comics?
5. What corporate strategy is being followed by Newbury Comics?

Strategy Implementation: Organizing for Action

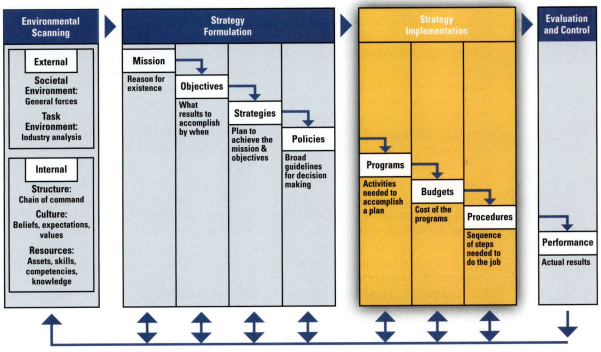

In 1998, Fingerhut Company had been a thriving mail order retailer with annual revenues of $2 billion. It was making a successful transition to electronic commerce. This venerable catalogue company was rapidly opening Internet Web sites and buying equity stakes in other online retailers. With its expertise in filling and shipping catalogue orders, Fingerhut successfully marketed its order-fulfillment competency on a contract basis to other companies, such as eToys and Wal-Mart. Business analysts were impressed by Fingerhut's diversification strategy. *Fortune* magazine declared Fingerhut one of the "10 companies that get it." Impressed with the company's performance, Federated Department Stores acquired Fingerhut in February

1999 for $1.7 billion. Federated's management confidently predicted that the corporation's overall Internet sales would reach $2 to $3 billion by 2004 with the addition of Fingerhut.

Twenty months after purchasing Fingerhut, Federated discovered that its Internet sales had reached only $180 million and were not likely to go much higher anytime soon. Management found that while Fingerhut had an excellent strategy for the Internet and its catalogue businesses, its implementation of that strategy had been dismal. Fingerhut's fulfillment contracts had dropped from 22 to 8 after allegations of poor service and a very visible dispute with eToys. The company had also mismanaged its plan to provide additional credit to its catalogue customers. The result was a number of special charges and layoffs totaling $795 million in expenses plus losses from unpaid credit card bills totaling around $400 million in 2000. As a result, Federated's stock dropped 35% in value. What went wrong?

According to a former Fingerhut executive, "The infrastructure was always a step-and-a-half behind." The company didn't have sufficient knowledge of the technology needed to operate successfully as an Internet retailer. With growth, its operations had become sluggish, and management failed to hire enough competent people to run its Web sites and fulfillment software. For example, Fingerhut found it too difficult to modify its existing software to communicate with fulfillment customers and its warehouse. Instead, the company created another version of the software to handle orders from other companies. Unfortunately, the software was so buggy that notices of a customer's purchase would get lost between the company's central computers and its warehouses, causing days of delay. At other times, the software lost track of inventory so Fingerhut didn't have an accurate measure of what was in stock at a warehouse. Its fulfillment customers, like eToys and Children's Place, complained that Fingerhut was, in some cases, sending out partial orders, forcing them to pay for two separate shipments instead of one. In other instances, Fingerhut took so long to assemble orders that the customer had to pay for express shipments. According to Mark Amodio, head of e-commerce at Children's Place, because of Fingerhut's inability to track shipments, his company was forced to cancel orders and try again!

Fingerhut failed to properly manage its credits and collections. To boost sales, the company offered credit cards to its current (generally low income) customers who had been previously purchasing Fingerhut products on the installment plan. It offered large lines of credit to even its riskier customers. Many of these customers ran up large bills but were unable to pay them. The company also failed to think through its acquisitions. After the company had purchased the Popular Club catalogue, it moved the catalogue's operations from New Jersey to its Minnesota facility. On the surface this move made sense. Nevertheless, the move tripled the time it took to get mailings to Popular Club's mainly Northeast-based customers, causing sales to plummet. Fingerhut was eventually forced to move the operation back to New Jersey.

Federated's management was furious. It closed five of Fingerhut's eight Web sites and stopped investing in a sixth site, Garage.com, a clearance retailer. It also cut 550 positions, 24% of the Fingerhut workforce. Management stated that Federated would no longer invest in e-commerce companies and that it will stop pursuing new third party fulfillment contracts.[1]

8.1 Strategy Implementation

Strategy implementation is the sum total of the activities and choices required for the execution of a strategic plan. It is the process by which strategies and policies are put into action through the development of programs, budgets, and procedures. Although implementation is usually considered after strategy has been formulated, implementation is a key part of strategic management. Strategy formulation and strategy implementation should thus be considered as two sides of the same coin. Poor implementation has been blamed for a number of strategic failures. For example, studies show that half of all acquisitions fail to achieve what was expected of them, and one out of four international ventures do not succeed.[2] A study by KPMG of the 700 largest mergers from 1996 to 1998 found that 83% of the mergers failed to increase the acquirer's shareholder value within a year of completing the merger.[3] Fingerhut Company is one example of how a good strategy can result in a disaster through poor strategy implementation.

To begin the implementation process, strategy makers must consider these questions:

- *Who* are the people who will carry out the strategic plan?
- *What* must be done to align the company's operations in the new intended direction?
- *How* is everyone going to work together to do what is needed?

These questions and similar ones should have been addressed initially when the pros and cons of strategic alternatives were analyzed. They must also be addressed again before appropriate implementation plans can be made. Unless top management can answer these basic questions satisfactorily, even the best planned strategy is unlikely to provide the desired outcome.

A survey of 93 *Fortune* 500 U.S. firms revealed that over half of the corporations experienced the following 10 problems when they attempted to implement a strategic change. These problems are listed in order of frequency.

1. Implementation took more time than originally planned.
2. Unanticipated major problems arose.
3. Activities were ineffectively coordinated.
4. Competing activities and crises took attention away from implementation.
5. The involved employees had insufficient capabilities to perform their jobs.
6. Lower-level employees were inadequately trained.
7. Uncontrollable external environmental factors created problems.
8. Departmental managers provided inadequate leadership and direction.
9. Key implementation tasks and activities were poorly defined.
10. The information system inadequately monitored activities.[4]

Fingerhut experienced almost all of these problems in its Internet expansion—all except the first one. Fingerhut's President, William Lansing, had been hired in the spring of 1998 to remake the catalogue company into an e-commerce player. Within months he started so many Web initiatives that the firm was soon unable to keep up with them. He started new Web sites and catalogues and acquired others. He offered unused warehouse space plus packaging and shipping services to other catalogue and Web companies. To boost sales faster, Lansing pushed giving credit cards to four million low-income customers over a two-year period instead of the originally planned three-year period.

8.2 Who Implements Strategy?

Depending on how the corporation is organized, those who implement strategy will probably be a much more diverse set of people than those who formulate it. In most large, multi-industry corporations, the implementers are everyone in the organization. Vice presidents of functional areas and directors of divisions or SBUs work with their subordinates to put together large-scale implementation plans. Plant managers, project managers, and unit heads put together plans for their specific plants, departments, and units. Therefore, every operational manager down to the first-line supervisor and every employee is involved in some way in implementing corporate, business, and functional strategies.

Many of the people in the organization who are crucial to successful strategy implementation probably have little to do with the development of the corporate and even business strategy. Therefore, they might be entirely ignorant of the vast amount of data and work that went into the formulation process. Unless changes in mission, objectives, strategies, and policies and their importance to the company are communicated clearly to all operational managers, there can be a lot of resistance and foot-dragging. Managers might hope to influence top management into abandoning its new plans and returning to its old ways. This is one reason why involving people from all organizational levels in the formulation and in the implementation of strategy tends to result in better organizational performance.

8.3 What Must Be Done?

The managers of divisions and functional areas work with their fellow managers to develop programs, budgets, and procedures for the implementation of strategy. They also work to achieve synergy among the divisions and functional areas in order to establish and maintain a company's distinctive competence.

DEVELOPING PROGRAMS, BUDGETS, AND PROCEDURES

Strategy implementation is composed of establishing programs to create a series of new organizational activities, budgets to allocate funds to the new activities, and procedures to handle the day-to-day details.

Programs

The purpose of a **program** is to make the strategy action-oriented. For example, PepsiCo recently made a strategic decision to grow in areas where the company could dominate. Instead of competing with Coca-Cola in every market, PepsiCo decided to concentrate on supermarkets where Pepsi had its greatest sales. To implement this strategy, the company developed a program called the "Power of One." The purpose of the strategy was to move Pepsi soft drinks next to Frito-Lay chips so that shoppers would be tempted to pick up both when they chose one. Since PepsiCo products accounted for 3% of total supermarket sales, 29% of supermarket cash flow, and offered 9% operating margins compared to the usual 2% margin for other goods, the supermarket managers were happy to put the PepsiCo's products together—especially since PepsiCo people delivered and stocked the shelves for them. As a result of this program, Frito-Lay increased its market share from 54% to 56% and Pepsi-Cola's volumes rose 0.6%. PepsiCo expanded the program into Mexico where its Sabritas brand had an 81% market share of the salty snack market. Management planned to initiate the program in other developing nations from India to China.[5]

One way to examine the likely impact new programs will have on an existing organization is to compare proposed programs and activities with current programs and activities. Brynjolfsson, Renshaw, and Van Alstyne propose a **matrix of change** to help managers decide how quickly change should proceed, in what order changes should take place, whether to start at a new site, and whether the proposed systems are stable and coherent. As shown in **Figure 8–1**, target practices (new programs) for a manufacturing plant are drawn on the vertical axis and existing practices (current activities) are drawn on the horizontal axis. As shown, any new strategy will likely involve a sequence of new programs and activities. Any one of these may conflict with existing practices/activities, creating implementation problems. Use the following steps to create the matrix:

1. Compare each of the new programs/target practices with each other to see if they are complementary (+), interfering (−), or have no effect on each other (leave blank).

2. Examine existing practices/activities for their interactions with each other using the same symbols.

3. Compare each new program/target practice with each existing practice/activity for any interaction effects. Place the appropriate symbols in the cells in the lower right part of the matrix.

4. Evaluate each program/activity in terms of its relative importance to achieving the strategy or getting the job accomplished.

5. Examine the overall matrix to identify problem areas where proposed programs are likely to either interfere with each other or with existing practices/activities. Note in **Figure 8–1** that the proposed program of installing flexible equipment interferes with the proposed program of assembly line rationalization. The two new programs need to be changed so that they no longer conflict with each other. Note also that the amount of change necessary to carry out the proposed implementation programs (target practices) is a function of the number of times each program interferes with existing practices/activities. That is, the more minus signs and the less plus signs exist in the matrix, the more implementation problems can be expected.

Figure 8–1
The Matrix of Change

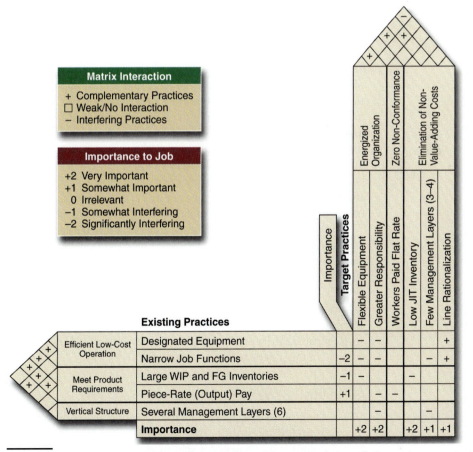

The matrix of change can be used to address the following types of questions:

- **Feasibility:** Do the proposed programs and activities constitute a coherent, stable system? Are the current activities coherent and stable? Is the transition likely to be difficult?
- **Sequence of Execution:** Where should the change begin? How does the sequence affect success? Are there reasonable stopping points?
- **Location:** Are we better off instituting the new programs at a new site or can we reorganize the existing facilities at a reasonable cost?
- **Pace and Nature of Change:** Should the change be slow or fast, incremental or radical? Which blocks of current activities must be changed at the same time?
- **Stakeholder Evaluations:** Have we overlooked any important activities or interactions? Should we get further input from interested stakeholders? Which new programs and current activities offer the greatest sources of value?

The matrix offers useful guidelines on where, when, and how fast to implement change.[6] A matrix of change could have been very useful for Fingerhut's William Lansing in developing his implementation programs of creating new Web sites, changing credit policies, offering fulfillment contracts, and acquiring other companies.

Budgets

After programs have been developed, the **budget** process begins. Planning a budget is the last real check a corporation has on the feasibility of its selected strategy. An ideal strategy might be found to be completely impractical only after specific implementation programs are costed in detail.

Procedures

After the program, divisional, and corporate budgets are approved, **procedures** must be developed. Often called **Standard Operating Procedures (SOPs)**, they typically detail the various activities that must be carried out to complete a corporation's programs. Once in place, they must be updated to reflect any changes in technology as well as in strategy. These procedures ensure that the day-to-day operations will be consistent over time (that is, next week's work activities will be the same as this week's) and consistent among locations (that is, each retail store will operate in the same manner as the others). For example, to ensure that its policies are carried out to the letter in every one of its fast-food retail outlets, McDonald's has done an excellent job of developing very detailed procedures (and policing them!).

In the case of PepsiCo's "Power of One" program, the company's sales people developed a set of procedures to persuade supermarket managers to add shelf space and displays in poorer performing locations, display snack foods with soft drinks, and to bring the two products together at end-of-aisle displays. They wrote a series of procedures to ensure the ideal display of snack foods and soft drinks in supermarkets given various types of store layouts. These procedures were incorporated in sales aids and information sheets given to the sales force and explained in monthly sales meetings. Logistics people developed procedures for the truck drivers to ensure that PepsiCo products were actually placed on the shelves as needed, not just dropped in the supermarket's back room.

ACHIEVING SYNERGY

One of the goals to be achieved in strategy implementation is synergy between and among functions and business units. This is the reason why corporations commonly reorganize after an acquisition. **Synergy** is said to exist for a divisional corporation if the return on investment (ROI) of each division is greater than what the return would be if each division were an independent business. According to Goold and Campbell, synergy can take place in one of six forms:

- **Shared Know-How:** Combined units often benefit from sharing knowledge or skills. This is a leveraging of core competencies.

- **Coordinated Strategies:** Aligning the business strategies of two or more business units may provide a corporation significant advantage by reducing interunit competition and developing a coordinated response to common competitors (horizontal strategy).

- **Shared Tangible Resources:** Combined units can sometimes save money by sharing resources, such as a common manufacturing facility or R&D lab.

- **Economies of Scale or Scope:** Coordinating the flow of products or services of one unit with that of another unit can reduce inventory, increase capacity utilization, and improve market access.

- **Pooled Negotiating Power:** Combined units can combine their purchasing to gain bargaining power over common suppliers to reduce costs and improve quality. The same can be done with common distributors.

- **New Business Creation:** Exchanging knowledge and skills can facilitate new products or services by extracting discrete activities from various units and combining them in a new unit or by establishing joint ventures among internal business units.[7]

For example, Federated Department Stores' purchase of Fingerhut was justified on the basis that Fingerhut would help Federated bolster its own Internet and catalogue operations. Since the acquisition, Fingerhut has successfully taken over control of Federated's order-fulfillment center and was starting to handle some of Federated's catalogue and Internet sales from its own warehouses.

8.4 How Is Strategy to Be Implemented? Organizing for Action

Before plans can lead to actual performance, a corporation should be appropriately organized, programs should be adequately staffed, and activities should be directed toward achieving desired objectives. (Organizing activities are reviewed briefly in this chapter; staffing, directing, and control activities are covered in **Chapters 9** and **10**.)

Any change in corporate strategy is very likely to require some sort of change in the way an organization is structured and in the kind of skills needed in particular positions. Managers must, therefore, closely examine the way their company is structured in order to decide what, if any, changes should be made in the way work is accomplished. Should activities be grouped differently? Should the authority to make key decisions be centralized at headquarters or decentralized to managers in distant locations? Should the company be managed like a "tight ship" with many rules and controls, or "loosely" with few rules and controls? Should the corporation be organized into a "tall" structure with many layers of managers, each having a narrow span of control (that is, few employees per supervisor) to better control his or her subordinates; or should it be organized into a "flat" structure with fewer layers of managers, each having a wide span of control (that is, more employees per supervisor) to give more freedom to his or her subordinates?

STRUCTURE FOLLOWS STRATEGY

In a classic study of large U.S. corporations such as DuPont, General Motors, Sears, and Standard Oil, Alfred Chandler concluded that **structure follows strategy**—that is, changes in corporate strategy lead to changes in organizational structure.[8] He also concluded that organizations follow a pattern of development from one kind of structural arrangement to another as they expand. According to Chandler, these structural changes occur because the old structure, having been pushed too far, has caused inefficiencies that have become too obviously detrimental to bear. Chandler, therefore, proposed the following as the sequence of what occurs:

1. New strategy is created.
2. New administrative problems emerge.
3. Economic performance declines.
4. New appropriate structure is invented.
5. Profit returns to its previous level.

Chandler found that in their early years, corporations such as DuPont tend to have a centralized functional organizational structure that is well suited to producing and selling a limited range of products. As they add new product lines, purchase their own sources of supply, and create their own distribution networks, they become too complex for highly centralized structures. To remain successful, this type of organization needs to shift to a decentralized structure with several semiautonomous divisions (referred to in **Chapter 4** as divisional structure).

Alfred P. Sloan, past CEO of General Motors, detailed how GM conducted such structural changes in the 1920s.[9] He saw decentralization of structure as "centralized policy determination coupled with decentralized operating management." After top management had developed a strategy for the total corporation, the individual divisions (Chevrolet, Buick, and so on) were free to choose how to implement that strategy. Patterned after DuPont, GM found the decentralized multidivisional structure to be extremely effective in allowing the maximum amount of freedom for product development. Return on investment (ROI) was used as a financial control. (*ROI is discussed in more detail in* **Chapter 10**.)

Research generally supports Chandler's proposition that structure follows strategy (as well as the reverse proposition that structure influences strategy).[10] As mentioned earlier, changes in the environment tend to be reflected in changes in a corporation's strategy, thus leading to changes in a corporation's structure. Strategy, structure, and the environment need to be closely aligned; otherwise, organizational performance will likely suffer.[11] For example, a business unit following a differentiation strategy needs more freedom from headquarters to be successful than does another unit following a low-cost strategy.[12]

Although it is agreed that organizational structure must vary with different environmental conditions, which, in turn, affect an organization's strategy, there is no agreement about an optimal organizational design. What was appropriate for DuPont and General Motors in the 1920s might not be appropriate today. Firms in the same industry do, however, tend to organize themselves similarly. For example, automobile manufacturers tend to emulate General Motors' divisional concept, whereas consumer-goods producers tend to emulate the brand-management concept (a type of matrix structure) pioneered by Procter & Gamble Company. The general conclusion seems to be that firms following similar strategies in similar industries tend to adopt similar structures.

STAGES OF CORPORATE DEVELOPMENT

Successful corporations tend to follow a pattern of structural development as they grow and expand. Beginning with the simple structure of the entrepreneurial firm (in which everybody does everything), they usually (if they are successful) get larger and organize along functional lines with marketing, production, and finance departments. With continuing success, the company adds new product lines in different industries and organizes itself into interconnected divisions. The differences among these three structural **stages of corporate development** in terms of typical problems, objectives, strategies, reward systems and other characteristics are specified in detail in **Table 8–1**.

Table 8–1   Factors Differentiating Stage I, II, and III Companies

Function	Stage I	Stage II	Stage III
1. Sizing up: Major problems	Survival and growth dealing with short-term operating problems.	Growth, rationalization, and expansion of resources, providing for adequate attention to product problems.	Trusteeship in management and investment and control of large, increasing, and diversified resources. Also, important to diagnose and take action on problems at division level.
2. Objectives	Personal and subjective.	Profits and meeting functionally oriented budgets and performance targets.	ROI, profits, earnings per share.
3. Strategy	Implicit and personal; exploitation of immediate opportunities seen by owner-manager.	Functionally oriented moves restricted to "one product" scope; exploitation of one basic product or service field.	Growth and product diversification; exploitation of general business opportunities.
4. Organization: Major characteristic of structure	One unit, "one-man show."	One unit, functionally specialized group.	Multiunit general staff office and decentralized operating divisions.
5. (a) Measurement and control	Personal, subjective control based on simple accounting system and daily communication and observation.	Control grows beyond one person; assessment of functional operations necessary; structured control systems evolve.	Complex formal system geared to comparative assessment of performance measures, indicating problems and opportunities and assessing management ability of division managers.
5. (b) Key performance indicators	Personal criteria, relationships with owner, operating efficiency, ability to solve operating problems.	Functional and internal criteria such as sales, performance compared to budget, size of empire, status in group, personal relationships, etc.	More impersonal application of comparisons such as profits, ROI, P/E ratio, sales, market share, productivity, product leadership, personnel development, employee attitudes, public responsibility.
6. Reward-punishment system	Informal, personal, subjective; used to maintain control and divide small pool of resources to provide personal incentives for key performers.	More structured; usually based to a greater extent on agreed policies as opposed to personal opinion and relationships.	Allotment by "due process" of a wide variety of different rewards and punishments on a formal and systematic basis. Companywide policies usually apply to many different classes of managers and workers with few major exceptions for individual cases.

Source: D. H. Thain, "Stages of Corporate Development," *Ivey Business Journal* (formerly *Ivey Business Quarterly*), (Winter 1969), p. 37. Copyright © 1969 by Ivey Management Services.

Stage I: Simple Structure

Stage I is typified by the entrepreneur, who founds the company to promote an idea (product or service). The entrepreneur tends to make all the important decisions personally and is involved in every detail and phase of the organization. The Stage I company has little formal structure, which allows the entrepreneur to directly supervise the activities of every employee (see **Figure 4–4** for an illustration of the simple, functional, and divisional structures). Planning is usually short range or reactive. The typical managerial functions of planning, organizing, directing, staffing, and controlling are usually performed to a very limited degree, if at all. The greatest strengths of a Stage I corporation are its flexibility and dynamism. The drive of the entrepreneur energizes the organization in its struggle for growth. Its greatest weakness is its extreme reliance on the entrepreneur to decide general strategies as well as detailed procedures. If the entrepreneur falters, the company usually flounders. This is labeled by Greiner as a **crisis of leadership**.[13]

Stage I describes Oracle Corporation, the computer software firm, under the management of its Cofounder and CEO Lawrence Ellison. The company adopted a pioneering approach to retrieving data called structured query language (SQL). When IBM made SQL its standard, Oracle's success was assured. Unfortunately Ellison's technical wizardry was not sufficient to manage the company. Often working at home, he lost sight of details outside his technical interests. Although the company's sales were rapidly increasing, its financial controls were so weak that management had to restate an entire year's results to rectify irregularities. After the company recorded its first loss, Ellison hired a set of functional managers to run the company while he retreated to focus on new product development.

Stage II: Functional Structure

Stage II is the point when the entrepreneur is replaced by a team of managers who have functional specializations. The transition to this stage requires a substantial managerial style change for the chief officer of the company, especially if he or she was the Stage I entrepreneur. He or she must learn to delegate; otherwise, having additional staff members yields no benefits to the organization. The previous example of Ellison's retreat from top management at Oracle Corporation to new product development manager is one way that technically brilliant founders are able to get out of the way of the newly empowered functional managers. Once into Stage II, the corporate strategy favors protectionism through dominance of the industry, often through vertical and horizontal growth. The great strength of a Stage II corporation lies in its concentration and specialization in one industry. Its great weakness is that all of its eggs are in one basket.

By concentrating on one industry while that industry remains attractive, a Stage II company, like Oracle Corporation in computer software, can be very successful. Once a functionally structured firm diversifies into other products in different industries, however, the advantages of the functional structure break down. A **crisis of autonomy** can now develop in which people managing diversified product lines need more decision-making freedom than top management is willing to delegate to them. The company needs to move to a different structure.

Stage III: Divisional Structure

Stage III is typified by the corporation's managing diverse product lines in numerous industries; it decentralizes the decision-making authority. These organizations grow by diversifying their product lines and expanding to cover wider geographical areas. They move to a divisional structure with a central headquarters and decentralized operating divisions—each division or business unit is a functionally organized Stage II company. They may also use a conglomerate structure if top management chooses to keep its collection of Stage II subsidiaries operating autonomously. A **crisis of control** can now develop in which the various units act to optimize their own sales and profits without regard to the overall corporation, whose headquarters seems so far away and almost irrelevant.

Recently divisions have been evolving into Strategic Business Units (SBUs) to better reflect product–market considerations. Headquarters attempts to coordinate the activities of its operating divisions or SBUs through performance- and results-oriented control and reporting systems, and by stressing corporate planning techniques. The units are not tightly controlled but are held responsible for their own performance results. Therefore, to be effective, the company has to have a decentralized decision process. The greatest strength of a Stage III corporation is its almost unlimited resources. Its most significant weakness is that it is usually so large and complex that it tends to become relatively inflexible. General Electric, DuPont, and General Motors are Stage III corporations.

Stage IV: Beyond SBUs

Even with its evolution into strategic business units during the 1970s and 1980s, the divisional form is not the last word in organization structure. The use of SBUs may result in a **red tape crisis** in which the corporation has grown too large and complex to be managed through formal programs and rigid systems and procedures take precedence over problem-solving. Under conditions of (1) increasing environmental uncertainty, (2) greater use of sophisticated technological production methods and information systems, (3) the increasing size and scope of worldwide business corporations, (4) a greater emphasis on multi-industry competitive strategy, and (5) a more educated cadre of managers and employees, new advanced forms of organizational structure have emerged and are continuing to emerge. These structures attempt to emphasize collaboration over competition in the managing of an organization's multiple overlapping projects and developing businesses.

The *matrix* and the *network* are two possible candidates for a fourth stage in corporate development—a stage that not only emphasizes horizontal over vertical connections between people and groups, but also organizes work around temporary projects in which sophisticated information systems support collaborative activities. According to Greiner, it is likely that this stage of development will have its own crisis as well—a sort of **pressure-cooker crisis**. He predicts that employees in these collaborative organizations will eventually grow emotionally and physically exhausted from the intensity of teamwork and the heavy pressure for innovative solutions.[14]

Blocks to Changing Stages

Corporations often find themselves in difficulty because they are blocked from moving into the next logical stage of development. Blocks to development may be internal (such as lack of resources, lack of ability, or a refusal of top management to delegate decision making to others) or they may be external (such as economic conditions, labor shortages, and lack of market growth). For example, Chandler noted in his study that the successful founder/CEO in one stage was rarely the person who created the new structure to fit the new strategy, and that, as a result, the transition from one stage to another was often painful. This was true of General Motors Corporation under the management of William Durant, Ford Motor Company under Henry Ford I, Polaroid Corporation under Edwin Land, Apple Computer under Steven Jobs, and Hayes Microcomputer Products under Dennis Hayes. (See the 🖳 **Internet Issue** feature for what happened to the company founded by the inventor of the modern modem.)

This difficulty in moving to a new stage is compounded by the founder's tendency to maneuver around the need to delegate by carefully hiring, training, and grooming his or her own team of managers. The team tends to maintain the founder's influence throughout the organization long after the founder is gone. This is what happened at Walt Disney Productions when the family continued to emphasize Walt's policies and plans long after he was dead. Although this may often be an organization's strength, it may also be a weakness—to the extent that the culture supports the status quo and blocks needed change.

ORGANIZATIONAL LIFE CYCLE

Instead of considering stages of development in terms of structure, the organizational life cycle approach places the primary emphasis on the dominant issue facing the corporation. Organizational structure is only a secondary concern. The **organizational life cycle** describes

Internet Issue

The Founder of the Modem Blocks Transition to Stage II

Would there be an Internet without the modem? Although most large organizations now rent digital T1 lines for fast Internet access, most individuals and small business owners still access the World Wide Web using the same type of modem and command set invented by Dennis Hayes.

Dennis Hayes is legendary not only for inventing the personal computer modem, but also for driving his company into bankruptcy—not once but twice. Hayes and retired partner Dale Heatherington founded Hayes Microcomputer Products 20 years ago when they invented a device called the Hayes Smartmodem, which allowed personal computers to communicate with each other through telephone lines via the Hayes Standard AT Command Set. The modem was needed to convert voice analogue data into the digital data needed by computers. Modem sales boomed from $4.8 million in 1981 to $150 million in 1985. When competitors developed low-cost modems, Hayes delayed until the early 1990s to respond with its own low-priced version. Sales and profits plummeted. Hayes lost its dominant position to U.S. Robotics. Management problems mounted. Creditors and potential investors looking into the company's books and operations found them a shambles. According to one investment banker, "The factory was in complete disarray." The company reported its first

loss in 1994, by which time the company had nearly $70 million in debt. In November 1994, Hayes applied for protection from creditors under Chapter 11 of the U.S. Bankruptcy Code.

Under the leadership of its founder, the company underwent a turnaround during 1995. Still in second place with a 9.3% market share of modem sales in North America, Dennis Hayes put his company up for sale. He turned down a bid of $140 million from rival Diamond Multimedia Systems and instead accepted only $30 million for 49% of the company from Asian investors. Although the offer required Mr. Hayes to relinquish the title of CEO, Hayes would still be Chairman of the Board. He explained his decision as deriving from his unwillingness to completely let go of his baby. "I'll be able to have input, through the board and as chairman, that will best use my abilities. What I was concerned about was that someone would come in and . . . slash a part of the company without understanding how it fit in."

The company, renamed Hayes Corporation, continued to suffer losses. On October 9, 1998, the company declared Chapter 11 bankruptcy for the last time. Unable to find further financing to turn things around, the company was forced to sell its brands, manufacturing facilities, and distribution offices to the Canadian firm, Zoom Telephonics ⟨www.zoomtel.com⟩, for $5.3 million. It sold its Web site domain name, Hayes.com, service center, and spare parts inventories to Modem Express ⟨www.modemexpress.com⟩, a seller of refurbished "orphan" products. The company founded by Dennis Hayes now exists only as a division of another company.

Sources: D. McDermott, "Asians Rejuvenate Hayes Microcomputer," *Wall Street Journal* (May 6, 1996), p. A10 plus information gathered from company Web sites and Hayes Company documents within the SEC's Edgar database.

how organizations grow, develop, and eventually decline. It is the organizational equivalent of the product life cycle in marketing. These stages are Birth (Stage I), Growth (Stage II), Maturity (Stage III), Decline (Stage IV), and Death (Stage V). The impact of these stages on corporate strategy and structure is summarized in **Table 8–2**. Note that the first three stages of the organizational life cycle are similar to the three commonly accepted stages of corporate development mentioned previously. The only significant difference is the addition of Decline and Death stages to complete the cycle. Even though a company's strategy may still be sound, its aging structure, culture, and processes may be such that they prevent the strategy from being executed properly. Its core competencies become core rigidities no longer able to adapt to changing conditions—thus the company moves into Decline.[15]

Movement from Growth to Maturity to Decline and finally to Death is not, however, inevitable. A Revival phase may occur sometime during the Maturity or Decline stages. The corporation's life cycle can be extended by managerial and product innovations.[16] Revival often occurs during the implementation of a turnaround strategy. This is what happened at Lionel, the maker of toy electric trains. Founded by Joshua Lionel Cowen in 1900 to make

Table 8–2   Organizational Life Cycle

	Stage I	Stage II	Stage III*	Stage IV	Stage V
Dominant Issue	Birth	Growth	Maturity	Decline	Death
Popular Stategies	Concentration in a niche	Horizontal and vertical growth	Concentric and conglomerate diversification	Profit strategy followed by retrenchment	Liquidation or bankruptcy
Likely Structure	Entrepreneur-dominated	Functional management emphasized	Decentralization into profit or investment centers	Structural surgery	Dismemberment of structure

Note: *An organization may enter a *Revival Phase* either during the Maturity or Decline Stages and thus extend the organization's life.

electrical devices, Lionel came to define the toy "electric train." In 1953, Lionel sold three million engines and freight cars, making it the biggest toy manufacturer in the world. By the mid-1960s, the company was in decline. Electric trains were becoming a historical curiosity. Slot cars and space toys were in demand. Train hobbyists preferred the smaller HO gauge electric train over Lionel's larger train because HO gauge trains were more realistic and used less space. The company barely managed to remain in business over the next three decades. In 1999, Lionel's new owners hired Richard Maddox, a lifelong train enthusiast and an executive close to retirement at toy company Bachmann Industries. Maddox and his executive team worked to update Lionel's trains with new models and the latest technology. He improved the catalogue and established dozens of licensing agreements. "We're trying to excel in things whimsical, clever," says Maddox. The unofficial Lionel historian, Todd Wagner, discovered long-forgotten blueprints of trains from the 1920s and 1930s that were gathering dust in old Lionel storerooms. The company is now using those plans to build more authentic historical models. The reinvigorated company's sales increased 15% in 2000 and were expected to increase by the same amount in 2001.[17]

Unless a company is able to resolve the critical issues facing it in the Decline stage, it is likely to move into Stage V, corporate death—also known as bankruptcy. This is what happened to Montgomery Ward, Pan American Airlines, Macy's Department Stores, Baldwin-United, Eastern Airlines, Colt's Manufacturing, Orion Pictures, and Wheeling-Pittsburgh Steel, as well as to many other firms. So many Internet ventures went bankrupt during 2000 that *Fortune* magazine listed 135 Internet companies on its "Dot-Com Deathwatch."[18] As in the cases of Johns-Manville, International Harvester, and Macy's—all of which went bankrupt—a corporation might nevertheless rise like a phoenix from its own ashes and live again under the same or a different name. The company may be reorganized or liquidated, depending on individual circumstances. For example, Fashionmall.com spent $4,000 for all rights to Boo.com, which had gone bankrupt in May 2000 (and listed on Fortune's Dot-Com Deathwatch), and relaunched it five months later as a high-fashion Web site with links to the hottest stores throughout the world.[19] Unfortunately fewer than 20% of firms entering Chapter 11 bankruptcy in the United States emerge as going concerns; the rest are forced into liquidation.[20]

Few corporations will move through these five stages in order. Some corporations, for example, might never move past Stage II. Others, like General Motors, might go directly from Stage I to Stage III. A large number of entrepreneurial ventures jump from Stage I or II directly into Stage IV or V. Hayes Microcomputer Products, for example, went from the Growth to Decline stage under its founder Dennis Hayes. The key is to be able to identify indications that a firm is in the process of changing stages and to make the appropriate strategic and structural adjustments to ensure that corporate performance is maintained or even improved. This is what the successful Internet auction firm eBay did when it hired Meg Whitman from Hasbro as CEO to professionalize its management and to improve its marketing.

Table 8-3 Changing Structural Characteristics of Modern Corporations

Old Organizational Design	New Organizational Design
One large corporation	Minibusiness units and cooperative relationships
Vertical communication	Horizontal communication
Centralized top-down decision making	Decentralized participative decision making
Vertical integration	Outsourcing and virtual organizations
Work/quality teams	Autonomous work teams
Functional work teams	Cross-functional work teams
Minimal training	Extensive training
Specialized job design focused on individual	Value-chain team-focused job design

Source: Adapted from B. Macy and H. Izumi, "Organizational Change, Design, and Work Innovation: A Meta-Analysis of 131 North American Field Studies—1961–1991," in Woodman: *Research in Organizational Change and Development*, Vol. 7, JAI Press (1993), p. 298. Copyright © 1993 with permission from Elsevier Science.

ADVANCED TYPES OF ORGANIZATIONAL STRUCTURES

The basic structures (simple, functional, divisional, and conglomerate) were discussed earlier in **Chapter 4** and summarized under the first three stages of corporate development. A new strategy may require more flexible characteristics than the traditional functional or divisional structure can offer. Today's business organizations are becoming less centralized with a greater use of cross-functional work teams. **Table 8–3** depicts some of the changing structural characteristics of modern corporations. Although many variations and hybrid structures contain these characteristics, two forms stand out: the matrix structure and the network structure.

Matrix Structure

Most organizations find that organizing around either functions (in the functional structure) or around products and geography (in the divisional structure) provides an appropriate organizational structure. The matrix structure, in contrast, may be very appropriate when organizations conclude that neither functional nor divisional forms, even when combined with horizontal linking mechanisms like strategic business units, are right for their situations. In **matrix structures**, functional and product forms are combined simultaneously at the same level of the organization. (See **Figure 8–2**.) Employees have two superiors, a product or project manager and a functional manager. The "home" department—that is, engineering, manufacturing, or sales—is usually functional and is reasonably permanent. People from these functional units are often assigned temporarily to one or more product units or projects. The product units or projects are usually temporary and act like divisions in that they are differentiated on a product–market basis.

Pioneered in the aerospace industry, the matrix structure was developed to combine the stability of the functional structure with the flexibility of the product form. The matrix structure is very useful when the external environment (especially its technological and market aspects) is very complex and changeable. It does, however, produce conflicts revolving around duties, authority, and resource allocation. To the extent that the goals to be achieved are vague and the technology used is poorly understood, a continuous battle for power between product and functional managers is likely. The matrix structure is often found in an organization or within an SBU when the following three conditions exist:

- Ideas need to be cross-fertilized across projects or products.

- Resources are scarce.

- Abilities to process information and to make decisions need to be improved.[21]

Figure 8–2

Matrix and Network Structures

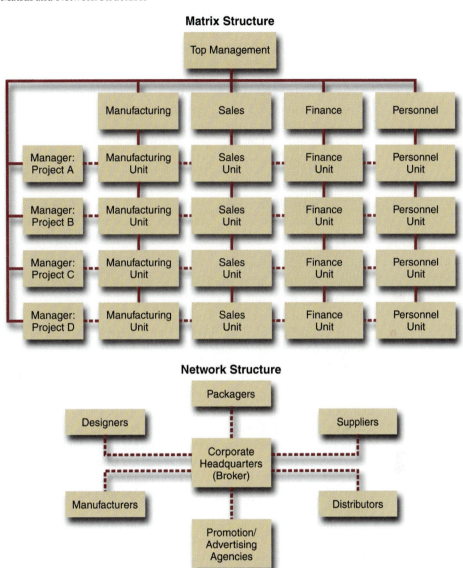

Davis and Lawrence, authorities on the matrix form of organization, propose that *three distinct phases* exist in the development of the matrix structure.[22]

1. **Temporary Cross-Functional Task Forces:** These are initially used when a new product line is being introduced. A project manager is in charge as the key horizontal link. Chrysler has extensively used this approach in product development.

2. **Product/Brand Management:** If the cross-functional task forces become more permanent, the project manager becomes a product or brand manager and a second phase begins. In this arrangement, function is still the primary organizational structure, but product or brand managers act as the integrators of semipermanent products or brands. Considered by many a key to the success of Procter & Gamble, brand management has been widely imitated by other consumer products firms around the world.

3. **Mature Matrix:** The third and final phase of matrix development involves a true dual-authority structure. Both the functional and product structures are permanent. All employees are connected to both a vertical functional superior and a horizontal product manager. Functional and product managers have equal authority and must work well together to resolve disagreements over resources and priorities. Boeing and TRW Systems are example of companies that use a mature matrix.

Network Structure—The Virtual Organization

A newer and somewhat more radical organizational design, the **network structure** (see **Figure 8–2**) is an example of what could be termed a "nonstructure" by its virtual elimination of in-house business functions. Many activities are outsourced. A corporation organized in this manner is often called a **virtual organization** because it is composed of a series of project groups or collaborations linked by constantly changing nonhierarchical, cobweblike networks.[23]

The network structure becomes most useful when the environment of a firm is unstable and is expected to remain so. Under such conditions, there is usually a strong need for innovation and quick response. Instead of having salaried employees, it may contract with people for a specific project or length of time. Long-term contracts with suppliers and distributors replace services that the company could provide for itself through vertical integration. Electronic markets and sophisticated information systems reduce the transaction costs of the marketplace, thus justifying a "buy" over a "make" decision. Rather than being located in a single building or area, an organization's business functions are scattered worldwide. The organization is, in effect, only a shell, with a small headquarters acting as a "broker," electronically connected to some completely owned divisions, partially owned subsidiaries, and other independent companies. In its ultimate form, the network organization is a series of independent firms or business units linked together by computers in an information system that designs, produces, and markets a product or service.[24]

An example of a complete network organization is Just Toys. The New York City company licenses characters like Disney's Little Mermaid, Hanna-Barbera's Flintstones, and Marvel Entertainment's Spiderman to make bendable polyvinyl chloride figures called Bend-Ems. The manufacturing and administrative work for Bend-Ems is contracted out. The company has only 30 employees. If a toy isn't selling well, production can be reduced and shipments stopped almost immediately. It would take Mattel and Hasbro months to react in a similar situation.

Other companies like Nike, Reebok, and Benetton use the network structure in their operations function by subcontracting manufacturing to other companies in low-cost locations around the world. For control purposes, the Italian-based Benetton maintains what it calls an "umbilical cord" by assuring production planning for all its subcontractors, planning materials requirements for them, and providing them with bills of labor and standard prices and costs, as well as technical assistance to make sure their quality is up to Benetton's standards.

The network organization structure provides an organization with increased flexibility and adaptability to cope with rapid technological change and shifting patterns of international trade and competition. It allows a company to concentrate on its distinctive competencies, while gathering efficiencies from other firms who are concentrating their efforts in their areas of expertise. The network does, however, have disadvantages. Some believe that the network is really only a transitional structure because it is inherently unstable and subject to tensions.[25] The availability of numerous potential partners can be a source of trouble. Contracting out functions to separate suppliers/distributors may keep the firm from discovering any synergies by combining activities. If a particular firm overspecializes on only a few functions, it runs the risk of choosing the wrong functions and thus becoming noncompetitive.

Cellular Organization: A New Type of Structure?

Miles and Snow et al. propose that the evolution of organizational forms is leading from the matrix and the network to the cellular. According to them, "a **cellular organization** is composed of cells (self-managing teams, autonomous business units, etc.) that can operate alone but that can interact with other cells to produce a more potent and competent business mechanism." It is this combination of independence and interdependence that allows the cellular organizational form to generate and share the knowledge and expertise to produce continuous innovation. The cellular form includes the dispersed entrepreneurship of the divisional structure, customer responsiveness of the matrix, and self-organizing knowledge and asset sharing of the network.[26] As proposed, the cellular structure is similar to a current trend in industry of using internal joint ventures to temporarily combine specialized expertise and skills within a corporation to accomplish a task individual units alone could not accomplish.[27]

According to the authors of the cellular organization, the impetus for such a new structure is the pressure for a continuous process of innovation in all industries. Each cell has an entrepreneurial responsibility to the larger organization. Beyond knowledge creation and sharing, the cellular form adds value by keeping the firm's total knowledge assets more fully in use than any other type of structure. It is beginning to appear in those firms focused on rapid product and service innovation—providing unique or state-of-the-art offerings.

REENGINEERING AND STRATEGY IMPLEMENTATION

Reengineering is the radical redesign of business processes to achieve major gains in cost, service, or time. It is not in itself a type of structure, but it is an effective way to implement a turnaround strategy.

Reengineering strives to break away from the old rules and procedures that develop and become ingrained in every organization over the years. These may be a combination of policies, rules, and procedures that have never been seriously questioned because they were established years earlier. These may range from "Credit decisions are made by the credit department" to "Local inventory is needed for good customer service." These rules of organization and work design were based on assumptions about technology, people, and organizational goals that may no longer be relevant. Rather than attempting to fix existing problems through minor adjustments and fine-tuning existing processes, the key to reengineering is to ask "If this were a new company, how would we run this place?"

Michael Hammer, who popularized the concept, suggests the following principles for reengineering:

- **Organize around outcomes, not tasks.** Design a person's or a department's job around an objective or outcome instead of a single task or series of tasks.

- **Have those who use the output of the process perform the process.** With computer-based information systems, processes can now be reengineered so that the people who need the result of the process can do it themselves.

- **Subsume information-processing work into the real work that produces the information.** People or departments that produce information can also process it for use instead of just sending raw data to others in the organization to interpret.

- **Treat geographically dispersed resources as though they were centralized.** With modern information systems, companies can provide flexible service locally while keeping the actual resources in a centralized location for coordination purposes.

- **Link parallel activities instead of integrating their results.** Instead of having separate units perform different activities that must eventually come together, have them communicate while they work so that they can do the integrating.

- **Put the decision point where the work is performed, and build control into the process.** The people who do the work should make the decisions and be self-controlling.
- **Capture information once and at the source.** Instead of having each unit develop its own database and information processing activities, the information can be put on a network so that all can access it.[28]

Studies of the performance of reengineering programs show mixed results. Several companies have had success with reengineering. For example, the Mossville Engine Center, a business unit of Caterpillar, Inc., used reengineering to decrease process cycle times by 50%, reduce the number of process steps by 45%, reduce manpower by 8%, and improve cross-divisional interactions and overall employee decision making.[29] One study of North American financial firms found: "The average reengineering project took 15 months, consumed 66 person-months of effort, and delivered cost savings of 24%."[30] In a survey of 782 corporations using reengineering, 75% of the executives said their companies had succeeded in reducing operating expenses and increasing productivity. Although only 47% stated that their companies had succeeded in generating revenue growth and 37% at raising market share, 70% of the respondents stated that their companies planned to use reengineering in the future.[31] Nevertheless, other studies report that anywhere from 50% to 70% of reengineering programs fail to achieve their objectives.[32]

DESIGNING JOBS TO IMPLEMENT STRATEGY

Organizing a company's activities and people to implement strategy involves more than simply redesigning a corporation's overall structure; it also involves redesigning the way jobs are done. With the increasing emphasis on reengineering, many companies are beginning to rethink their work processes with an eye toward phasing unnecessary people and activities out of the process. Process steps that had traditionally been performed sequentially can be improved by performing them concurrently using cross-functional work teams. Harley-Davidson, for example, has managed to reduce total plant employment by 25% while reducing by 50% the time needed to build a motorcycle. Restructuring through fewer people requires broadening the scope of jobs and encouraging teamwork. The design of jobs and subsequent job performance are, therefore, increasingly being considered as sources of competitive advantage.

Job design refers to the design of individual tasks in an attempt to make them more relevant to the company and to the employee(s). To minimize some of the adverse consequences of task specialization, corporations have turned to new job design techniques: **job enlargement** (combining tasks to give a worker more of the same type of duties to perform), **job rotation** (moving workers through several jobs to increase variety), and **job enrichment** (altering the jobs by giving the worker more autonomy and control over activities). The job characteristics model is a good example of job enrichment. (See the **Theory As It Applies** feature.) Although each of these methods has its adherents, no one method seems to work in all situations.

A good example of modern job design is the introduction of team-based production by Corning, Inc., the glass manufacturer, in its Blacksburg, Virginia, plant. With union approval, Corning reduced job classifications from 47 to 4 to enable production workers to rotate jobs after learning new skills. The workers were divided into 14-member teams that, in effect, managed themselves. The plant had only two levels of management: Plant Manager Robert Hoover and two line leaders who only advised the teams. Employees worked demanding 12½ hour shifts, alternating three-day and four-day weeks. The teams made managerial decisions, imposed discipline on fellow workers, and were required to learn three "skill modules" within two years or else lose their jobs. As a result of this new job design, a Blacksburg team, made up of workers with interchangeable skills, can retool a line to produce a different type of filter in only 10 minutes—six times faster than workers in a traditionally designed filter plant. The Blacksburg plant earned

Theory As It Applies

Designing Jobs with the Job Characteristics Model

The **job characteristics model** is an advanced approach to job design based on the belief that tasks can be described in terms of certain objective characteristics and that these characteristics affect employee motivation. In order for the job to be motivating, (1) the worker needs to feel a sense of responsibility, feel the task to be meaningful, and receive useful feedback on his or her performance; and (2) the job has to satisfy needs that are important to the worker. The model proposes that managers follow five principles for redesigning work:

1. Combine tasks to increase task variety and to enable workers to identify with what they are doing.

2. Form natural work units to make a worker more responsible and accountable for the performance of the job.

3. Establish client relationships so the worker will know what performance is required and why.

4. Vertically load the job by giving workers increased authority and responsibility over their activities.

5. Open feedback channels by providing workers with information on how they are performing.

Research supports the job characteristics model as a way to improve job performance through job enrichment. Although there are several other approaches to job design, practicing managers seem increasingly to follow the prescriptions of this model as a way of improving productivity and product quality.

Sources: J. R. Hackman and G. R. Oldham, *Work Redesign* (Reading, MA: Addison-Wesley, 1980), pp. 135–141; G. Johns, J. L. Xie, and Y. Fang, "Mediating and Moderating Effects in Job Design," *Journal of Management* (December 1992), pp. 657–676; R. W. Griffin, "Effects of Work Redesign on Employee Perceptions, Attitudes, and Behaviors: A Long-Term Investigation," *Academy of Management Journal* (June 1991), pp. 425–435.

a $2 million profit in its first eight months of production, instead of losing the $2.3 million projected for the start-up period. The plant performed so well that Corning's top management acted to convert the company's 27 other factories to team-based production.[33]

8.5 International Issues in Strategy Implementation

An international company is one that engages in any combination of activities, from exporting/importing to full-scale manufacturing, in foreign countries. The **multinational corporation (MNC)**, in contrast, is a highly developed international company with a deep involvement throughout the world, plus a worldwide perspective in its management and decision making. For a multinational corporation to be considered global, it must manage its worldwide operations as if they were totally interconnected. This approach works best when the industry has moved from being *multidomestic* (each country's industry is essentially separate from the same industry in other countries; an example is retailing) to *global* (each country is a part of one worldwide industry; an example is consumer electronics).

Strategic alliances, such as joint ventures and licensing agreements, between a multinational company (MNC) and a local partner in a host country are becoming increasingly popular as a means by which a corporation can gain entry into other countries, especially less developed countries. The key to the successful implementation of these strategies is the selection of the local partner. Each party needs to assess not only the strategic fit of each company's project strategy, but also the fit of each company's respective resources. A successful joint venture may require as much as two years of prior contacts between both parties.

The design of an organization's structure is strongly affected by the company's stage of development in international activities and the types of industries in which the company is involved. The issue of centralization versus decentralization becomes especially important for a multinational corporation operating in both multidomestic and global industries.

STAGES OF INTERNATIONAL DEVELOPMENT

Corporations operating internationally tend to evolve through five common stages, both in their relationships with widely dispersed geographic markets and in the manner in which they structure their operations and programs. These **stages of international development** are:

- **Stage 1 (Domestic Company):** The primarily domestic company exports some of its products through local dealers and distributors in the foreign countries. The impact on the organization's structure is minimal because an export department at corporate headquarters handles everything.

- **Stage 2 (Domestic Company with Export Division):** Success in Stage 1 leads the company to establish its own sales company with offices in other countries to eliminate the middlemen and to better control marketing. Because exports have now become more important, the company establishes an export division to oversee foreign sales offices.

- **Stage 3 (Primarily Domestic Company with International Division):** Success in earlier stages leads the company to establish manufacturing facilities in addition to sales and service offices in key countries. The company now adds an international division with responsibilities for most of the business functions conducted in other countries.

- **Stage 4 (Multinational Corporation with Multidomestic Emphasis):** Now a full-fledged multinational corporation, the company increases its investments in other countries. The company establishes a local operating division or company in the host country, such as Ford of Britain, to better serve the market. The product line is expanded, and local manufacturing capacity is established. Managerial functions (product development, finance, marketing, and so on) are organized locally. Over time, the parent company acquires other related businesses, broadening the base of the local operating division. As the subsidiary in the host country successfully develops a strong regional presence, it achieves greater autonomy and self-sufficiency. The operations in each country are, nevertheless, managed separately as if each is a domestic company.

- **Stage 5 (Multinational Corporation with Global Emphasis):** The most successful multinational corporations move into a fifth stage in which they have worldwide personnel, R&D, and financing strategies. Typically operating in a global industry, the MNC denationalizes its operations and plans product design, manufacturing, and marketing around worldwide considerations. Global considerations now dominate organizational design. The global MNC structures itself in a matrix form around some combination of geographic areas, product lines, and functions. All managers are now responsible for dealing with international as well as domestic issues.

Research provides some support for the stages of international development concept, but it does not necessarily support the preceding sequence of stages. For example, a company may initiate production and sales in multiple countries without having gone through the steps of exporting or having local sales subsidiaries. In addition, any one corporation can be at different stages simultaneously with different products in different markets at different levels. Firms may also leapfrog across stages to a global emphasis. Developments in information technology are changing the way business is being done internationally. See the [globe icon] **Global Issue** feature to see how FedEx is using its expertise in information technology to help customers sidestep the building of a costly logistical infrastructure to take advantage of global markets. Nevertheless the stages concept provides a useful way to illustrate some of the structural changes corporations undergo when they increase their involvement in international activities.

CENTRALIZATION VERSUS DECENTRALIZATION

A basic dilemma a multinational corporation faces is how to organize authority centrally so that it operates as a vast interlocking system that achieves synergy, and at the same time decentralize authority so that local managers can make the decisions necessary to meet the demands

Global Issue

FedEx Provides the Infrastructure for Companies to Become Global

Globalization is becoming a permanent and irreversible part of economic life. A key reason is the use of information system technology to connect operations around the world. The Internet via e-mail, chat rooms, and Web sites in multiple languages provides instantaneous communication 24 hours a day. *Enterprise resource planning (ERP) systems,* such as SAP's R/3 software, can manage all of a corporation's internal operations (including international) in a single powerful network. ERP is able to unite customers and suppliers so that they can transact business with each other online. Retailers like Wal-Mart are going global and are pressuring suppliers to have global sourcing and pricing.

FedEx is a key force behind globalization, but not just because it delivers 2.8 million packages in 210 countries each day. It is using information technology to remake its clients' worldwide supply and distribution systems. FedEx is becoming the global logistical backbone for many of its customers. Using its technology, FedEx man-

ages its customers' worldwide inventory, warehousing, distribution, and customs clearance. It can help a customer assemble and make products by securing supplies globally in a reliable and cost-effective manner. It is able to do this because it is able to electronically track any of its shipments at any point in time. This provides FedEx with a distinctive competency, which it is able to use to provide valuable service to others. With a guarantee of on-time delivery, customers are able to reduce costly inventories and institute just-in-time systems. According to CEO and Chairman Frederick Smith, "We decided years ago that the most important element in this business is information technology, and we have geared everything to that philosophy—recruitment, training, and compensation. Fail-safe precision is the key to it all."

Dell Computer Corporation eliminated its costly distribution infrastructure in favor of using FedEx to coordinate the assembly of computers and their customs clearance and shipping from a manufacturing center in Malaysia to customers in Japan and Taiwan. By managing National Semiconductor Corporation's global warehousing and distribution systems, FedEx was able to reduce its customer's total costs of logistics from 3% to 1.9% of revenues.

Source: J. E. Garten, "Why the Global Economy Is Here to Stay," *Business Week* (March 23, 1998), p. 21. By special permission, copyright © 1998 by The McGraw-Hill Companies, Inc.

---

of the local market or host government.[34] To deal with this problem, MNCs tend to structure themselves either along product groups or geographic areas. They may even combine both in a matrix structure—the design chosen by 3M Corporation and Asea Brown Boveri (ABB), among others.[35] One side of 3M's matrix represents the company's product divisions; the other side includes the company's international country and regional subsidiaries.

Two examples of the usual international structures are Nestlé and American Cyanamid. Nestlé's structure is one in which significant power and authority have been decentralized to geographic entities. This structure is similar to that depicted in **Figure 8–3**, in which each geographic set of operating companies has a different group of products. In contrast, American Cyanamid has a series of centralized product groups with worldwide responsibilities. To depict Cyanamid's structure, the geographical entities in **Figure 8–3** would have to be replaced by product groups or strategic business units.

The **product-group structure** of American Cyanamid enables the company to introduce and manage a similar line of products around the world. This enables the corporation to centralize decision making along product lines and to reduce costs. The **geographic-area structure** of Nestlé, in contrast, allows the company to tailor products to regional differences and to achieve regional coordination. This decentralizes decision making to the local subsidiaries. As industries move from being multidomestic to more globally integrated, multinational corporations are increasingly switching from the geographic-area to the product-group structure. Texaco, Inc., for example, changed to a product-group structure by consolidating its international, U.S., and new business opportunities under each line of business at its White Plains,

Figure 8–3
Geographic Area Structure for a Multinational Corporation

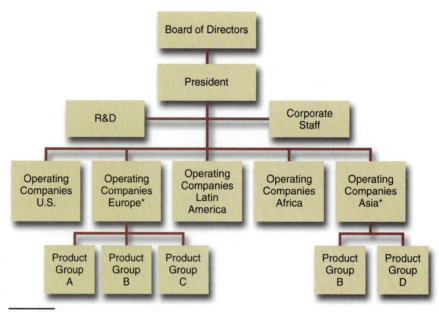

*Note: Because of space limitations, product groups for only Europe and Asia are shown here.

New York, headquarters. According to Chairman Peter Bijur, "By placing groups which will perform similar work in the same location, they will be able to share information, ideas, and resources more readily—and move critical information throughout the organization."[36]

Simultaneous pressures for decentralization to be locally responsive and centralization to be maximally efficient are causing interesting structural adjustments in most large corporations. Companies are attempting to decentralize those operations that are culturally oriented and closest to the customers—manufacturing, marketing, and human resources. At the same time, the companies are consolidating less visible internal functions, such as research and development, finance, and information systems, where there can be significant economies of scale.

8.6 Impact of the Internet on Organizational Design and Structure

The Cluetrain Manifesto written by Levine, Locke, Searls, and Weinberger, proposes 95 theses about how the Internet is changing the world and the way it does business. Many of today's companies are still stuck in traditional, conservative mindsets, creating virtual barriers between themselves and the people they hope to reach. The book argues that the Internet has "something special" about it, which the **Cluetrain Manifesto** calls "voice" that sets it apart from any other medium. The Internet connects people to each other allowing them to have conversations and comment on things in a forum that joins a wealth of knowledge from different resources. The **hyperlinked organization** is a new type of developing organization, which provides all employees easy access to one another and to people outside the organization in a rich variety of ways from e-mail to personal Web sites. Workers and markets speak the same language.

According to Levine et al., bringing the Internet into a corporation changes things in unpredictable ways. The new hyperlinked organization contains several major themes.

- **Hyperlinked and Decentralized:** There is no central authority on the Web; it consists of hundreds of millions of pages linked together by the author of each individual page. Organizations become hyperlinked when they decentralize their teams, committees, task forces, and individuals. Official structure is set aside in favor of networks of trusted colleagues.

- **Hypertime:** With the Internet, people can look for information and connections at their own pace and under their own control any time of the day or week without having to search for a parking place and obtaining a library card. In a hyperlinked organization, schedules are driven locally, not centrally, created by local groups and individuals. Traditional deadlines are replaced by a team's motivation to help a customer or coworker.

- **Directly Accessible:** The Internet provides direct access to everyone on the planet to every piece of information made available. Hyperlinked organizations replace the old mindset of hoarding information with new, wide-open policies that encourage collaboration over intranets, moving individual tasks to group tasks, and bringing in people because they have the necessary skills and shared interests, not because of their position in the hierarchy.

- **Full of Rich Data:** The currency of the Internet is pages of information. The various types of Internet communication (especially e-mail) allow the hyperlinked organization to link staff, management, and customers who can tell stories, create valuable narratives, and explore the many ways to translate ideas using each participant's distinctive voice.

- **Broken:** Because the Internet is a large, complex network controlled by no one, it will always be somewhat "broken." Any search of the Internet is bound to find many dead links and dead ends (those "sticky" sites that refuse to allow the visitor to use the browser to go back to a previous Web page). While the traditional hierarchy demanded predictability and consistency, the hyperlinked organization looks for innovation and expects mistakes and slightly broken systems and structures, which are always in a state of repair and rebuilding.

- **Borderless:** Traditional organizations and networks were concerned as much with security as with access. They were usually very clear where one department ended and another began—even within the same company. People had access to important information only if they "had a need to know." In contrast, the Internet was designed so that one page could be linked to another without obtaining the author's permission. Because of the way links work, it is often hard to tell if one is still on the same Web page or on another page located in another part of the world. Hyperlinked organizations accept that borders between units are permeable and changing. Intranets and extranets allow companies to share previously unknown processes with customers and to solicit ideas and suggestions from them. They also allow internal communications to flow easier, replacing closed meeting rooms with e-mail discussion groups and group intranet sites. As the hurdles to membership lower, the boundaries begin to blur.[37]

According to *The Cluetrain Manifesto*, the structures of corporations must change if they are to be effective in a changing, global, Internet-linked environment. This suggests that traditional organization structures must adopt more of the characteristics of the matrix, the network, and the cellular forms of organization.

Projections for the 21st Century

- From 1994 to 2010, the number of automobiles produced in the developed countries will increase from 20 million to 30 million vehicles.

- From 1994 to 2010, the number of automobiles produced in the emerging market nations will jump from 8 million to 30 million vehicles.[38]

Discussion Questions

1. How should a corporation attempt to achieve synergy among functions and business units?

2. How should an owner-manager prepare a company for its movement from Stage I to Stage II?

3. How can a corporation keep from sliding into the Decline stage of the organizational life cycle?

4. Is reengineering just another management fad or does it offer something of lasting value?

5. How is the cellular organization different from the network structure?

Strategic Practice Exercise

The Synergy Game

Yolanda Sarason and Catherine Banbury

SETUP
Put three to five chairs on either side of a room facing each other in the front of the class. Put a table in the middle with a bell in the middle of the table.

PROCEDURE
The instructor/moderator divides the class into teams of three to five people. Each team selects a name for itself. The instructor/moderator lists the team names on the board. The first two teams come to the front and sit in the chairs facing each other. The instructor/moderator reads a list of products or services being provided by an actual company. The winning team must identify (1) possible sources of synergy and (2) the actual company being described. For example, if the products/services listed are family restaurants, airline catering, hotels, and retirement centers, the synergy is **standardized food service and hospitality settings** and the company is **The Marriott Corporation**. The first team to successfully name the company *and* the synergy wins the round.

After one practice session, the game begins. Each of the teams is free to discuss the question with other team members. Once one of the two teams thinks that it has the answer to both parts of the question, it must be the first to ring the bell in order to announce their answer. If it gives the correct answer, it is deemed the winner of round one. Both parts of the answer must be given for a team to have the correct answer. If a team correctly provides only one part, that answer is still wrong—no partial credit. The instructor/moderator does not say which part of the answer, if either,

was correct. The second team then has the opportunity to state the answer. If the second team is wrong, both teams may try once more. If neither chooses to try again, the instructor/moderator may (1) declare no round winner and both teams sit down, (2) allow the next two teams to provide the answer to round one, or (3) go on to the next round with the same two teams. Two new teams then come to the front for the next round. Once all groups have played once, the winning teams play each other. Rounds continue until there is a grand champion. The instructor should provide a suitable prize, such as candy bars, for the winning team.

Source: This exercise was developed by Professors Yolanda Sarason of Colorado State University and Catherine Banbury of St. Mary's College and Purdue University and presented at the Organizational Behavior Teaching Conference, June 1999. Copyright © 1999 by Yolanda Sarason and Catherine Banbury. Adapted with permission.

Note from Wheelen and Hunger
The *Instructors' Manual* for this book contains a list of products and services with their synergy and the name of the company. In case your instructor does not use this exercise, try the following examples.

1. Motorcycles, autos, lawn mowers, generators

2. Athletic footwear, Rockport shoes, Greg Norman clothing, sportswear

Did you guess the company providing these products/services and the synergy obtained? The answers are printed here upside down:

1. *Engine technology by Honda*

2. *Marketing and distribution for athletic conscious by Reebok*

Key Terms

budget (p. 196)
cellular organization (p. 207)
Cluetrain Manifesto (p. 212)
crisis of autonomy (p. 200)
crisis of control (p. 200)
crisis of leadership (p. 200)
geographic-area structure (p. 211)
hyperlinked organization (p. 212)
job characteristics model (p. 209)
job design (p. 208)
job enlargement (p. 208)
job enrichment (p. 208)

job rotation (p. 208)
matrix of change (p. 194)
matrix structure (p. 204)
multinational corporation (MNC) (p. 209)
network structure (p. 206)
organizational life cycle (p. 201)
pressure-cooker crisis (p. 201)
procedures (p. 196)
product-group structure (p. 211)
program (p. 194)
red tape crises (p. 201)

reengineering (p. 207)
stages of corporate development (p. 198)
stages of international development (p. 210)
standard operating procedures (SOPs) (p. 196)
strategy implementation (p. 192)
structure follows strategy (p. 197)
synergy (p. 196)
virtual organization (p. 206)

Notes

1. C. Edwards, "Federated's Fingerhut Fiasco," *Business Week* (December 18, 2000), pp. 198–202.
2. J. W. Gadella, "Avoiding Expensive Mistakes in Capital Investment," *Long Range Planning* (April 1994), pp. 103–110; B. Voss, "World Market Is Not for Everyone," *Journal of Business Strategy* (July/August 1993), p. 4.
3. J. I. Rigdon, "The Integration Game," *Red Herring* (July 2000), pp. 356–366.
4. L. D. Alexander, "Strategy Implementation: Nature of the Problem," *International Review of Strategic Management*, Vol. 2, No. 1, edited by D. E. Hussey (New York: John Wiley & Sons, 1991), pp. 73–113.
5. J. A. Byrne, "PepsiCo's New Formula," *Business Week* (April 10, 2000), pp. 172–184.
6. E. Brynjolfsson, A. A. Renshaw, and M. Van Alstyne, "The Matrix of Change," *Sloan Management Review* (Winter 1997), pp. 37–54.
7. M. Goold and A. Campbell, "Desperately Seeking Synergy," *Harvard Business Review* (September–October 1998), pp. 131–143.
8. A. D. Chandler, *Strategy and Structure* (Cambridge, MA: MIT Press, 1962).
9. A. P. Sloan, Jr., *My Years with General Motors* (Garden City, NY: Doubleday, 1964).
10. T. L. Amburgey and T. Dacin, "As the Left Foot Follows the Right? The Dynamics of Strategic and Structural Change," *Academy of Management Journal* (December 1994), pp. 1427–1452; M. Ollinger, "The Limits of Growth of the Multidivisional Firm: A Case Study of the U.S. Oil Industry from 1930–90," *Strategic Management Journal* (September 1994), pp. 503–520.
11. D. F. Jennings and S. L. Seaman, "High and Low Levels of Organizational Adaptation: An Empirical Analysis of Strategy, Structure, and Performance," *Strategic Management Journal* (July 1994), pp. 459–475; L. Donaldson, "The Normal Science of Structured Contingency Theory," in *Handbook of Organization Studies*, edited by S. R. Clegg, C. Hardy, and W. R. Nord (London: Sage Publications, 1996), pp. 57–76.
12. A. K. Gupta, "SBU Strategies, Corporate-SBU Relations, and SBU Effectiveness in Strategy Implementation," *Academy of Management Journal* (September 1987), pp. 477–500.
13. L. E. Greiner, "Evolution and Revolution as Organizations Grow," *Harvard Business Review* (May–June 1998), pp. 55–67. This is an updated version of Greiner's classic 1972 article.

14. Greiner, p. 64. Although Greiner simply labeled this as the "?" crisis, the term "pressure-cooker" seems apt.
15. W. P. Barnett, "The Dynamics of Competitive Intensity," *Administrative Science Quarterly* (March 1997), pp. 128–160; D. Miller, *The Icarus Paradox: How Exceptional Companies Bring About Their Own Downfall* (New York: Harper Business, 1990).
16. D. Miller and P. H. Friesen, "A Longitudinal Study of the Corporate Life Cycle," *Management Science* (October 1984), pp. 1161–1183.
17. J. Green, "The Toy-Train Company that Thinks It Can," *Business Week* (December 4, 2000), pp. 64–69.
18. G. David, F. Garcia, and I. Gashurov, "Welcome to the Valley of the Damned.Com," *Fortune* (January 22, 2001), p. 52.
19. "First Dot-Com Casualty Is Back," *The (Ames) Tribune* (November 29, 2000), p. B7.
20. H. Tavakolian, "Bankruptcy: An Emerging Corporate Strategy," *SAM Advanced Management Journal* (Spring 1995), p. 19.
21. L. G. Hrebiniak and W. F. Joyce, *Implementing Strategy* (New York: Macmillan, 1984), pp. 85–86.
22. S. M. Davis and P. R. Lawrence, *Matrix* (Reading, MA: Addison-Wesley, 1977), pp. 11–24.
23. J. G. March, "The Future Disposable Organizations and the Rigidities of Imagination," *Organization* (August/November 1995), p. 434.
24. M. P. Koza and A. Y. Lewin, "The Coevolution of Network Alliances: A Longitudinal Analysis of an International Professional Service Network," *Organization Science* (September/October 1999), pp. 638–653.
25. For more information on managing a network organization, see G. Lorenzoni and C. Baden-Fuller, "Creating a Strategic Center to Manage a Web of Partners," *California Management Review* (Spring 1995), pp. 146–163.
26. R. E. Miles, C. C. Snow, J. A. Mathews, G. Miles, and H. J. Coleman, Jr., "Organizing in the Knowledge Age: Anticipating the Cellular Form," *Academy of Management Executive* (November 1997), pp. 7–24.
27. J. Naylor and M. Lewis, "Internal Alliances: Using Joint Ventures in a Diversified Company," *Long Range Planning* (October 1997), pp. 678–688.
28. Summarized from M. Hammer, "Reengineering Work: Don't Automate, Obliterate," *Harvard Business Review* (July–August 1990), pp. 104–112.

29. D. Paper, "BPR: Creating the Conditions for Success," *Long Range Planning* (June 1998), pp. 426–435.

30. S. Drew, "BPR in Financial Services: Factors for Success," *Long Range Planning* (October 1994), pp. 25–41.

31. "Do as I Say, Not as I Do," *Journal of Business Strategy* (May/June 1997), pp. 3–4.

32. K. Grint, Reengineering History: Social Resonances and Business Process Reengineering," *Organization* ((July 1994), pp. 179–201; A. Kleiner, "Revisiting Reengineering," *Strategy + Business* (3rd Quarter 2000), pp. 27–31.

33. J. Hoerr, "Sharpening Minds for a Competitive Edge," *Business Week* (December 17, 1990), pp. 72–78.

34. J. H. Taggart, "Strategy Shifts in MNC Subsidiaries," *Strategic Management Journal* (July 1998), pp. 663–681.

35. C. A. Bartlett and S. Ghoshal, "Beyond the M-Form: Toward a Managerial Theory of the Firm," *Strategic Management Journal* (Winter 1993), pp. 23–46.

36. A. Sullivan, "Texaco Revamps Executive Structure to Focus on Business, Not Geography," *Wall Street Journal* (October 3, 1996), p. B15.

37. R. Levine, C. Locke, D. Searls, and D. Weinberger, *The Cluetrain Manifesto* (Cambridge, MA: Perseus Books, 2000). Originally posted on a Web site ⟨www.cluetrain.com⟩, *The Cluetrain Manifesto* has now reached the status of a cult book within the Internet community.

38. J. Warner, "21st Century Capitalism: Snapshot of the Next Century," *Business Week* (November 18, 1994), p. 194.

chapter 9

Strategy Implementation: Staffing and Directing

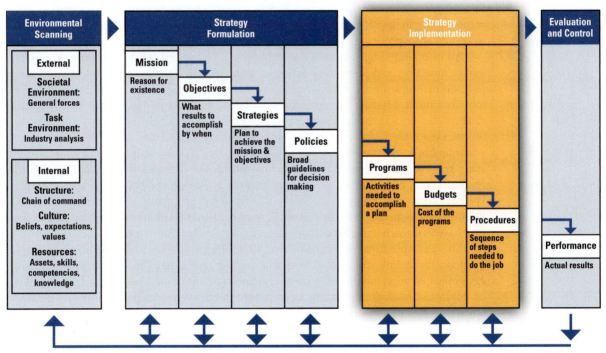

Environmental Scanning	Strategy Formulation	Strategy Implementation	Evaluation and Control

External

Societal Environment: General forces

Task Environment: Industry analysis

Internal

Structure: Chain of command

Culture: Beliefs, expectations, values

Resources: Assets, skills, competencies, knowledge

Mission

Reason for existence

Objectives

What results to accomplish by when

Strategies

Plan to achieve the mission & objectives

Policies

Broad guidelines for decision making

Programs

Activities needed to accomplish a plan

Budgets

Cost of the programs

Procedures

Sequence of steps needed to do the job

Performance

Actual results

Feedback/Learning

Have you heard of Enterprise Rent-A-Car? You won't find it at the airport with Hertz, Avis, or National car rental operations. Yet Enterprise owns more cars and operates in more locations than Hertz. The company accounts for over 20% of the $15 billion per year U.S. car rental market compared to 17% for Hertz and 12% for Avis. In ignoring the highly competitive airport market, Enterprise has chosen a differentiation competitive strategy by marketing to people in need of a spare car. Instead of locating many cars at a few high-priced locations at airports, Enterprise sets up inexpensive offices throughout metropolitan areas. As a result, cars are rented for 30% less than they cost at airports. As soon as one branch office grows to about 150 cars, the company opens another rental office a few miles away. People are increasingly renting from Enterprise even when their current car works fine. According to CEO Andy

Taylor, "We call it a 'virtual car.' Small-business people who have to pick up clients call us when they want something better than their own car." Why is Enterprise able to follow this competitive strategy so successfully without attracting Hertz and Avis into its market?

The secret to Enterprise's success is its well-executed strategy implementation. Clearly laid out programs, budgets, and procedures support the company's competitive strategy by making Enterprise stand out in the mind of the consumer. When a new rental office opens, employees spend time developing relationships with the service managers of every auto dealership and body shop in the area. Enterprise employees bring pizza and doughnuts to workers at the auto garages across the country. Enterprise forms agreements with dealers to provide replacements for cars brought in for service. At major accounts, the company actually staffs an office at the dealership and has cars parked outside so customers don't have to go to an Enterprise office to complete paperwork.

One key to implementation at Enterprise is staffing—through hiring and promoting a certain kind of person. Virtually every Enterprise employee is a college graduate, usually from the bottom half of the class. According to COO Donald Ross, "We hire from the half of the college class that makes the upper half possible. We want athletes, fraternity types—especially fraternity presidents and social directors. People people." These new employees begin as management trainees in the $20,000 to $25,000 salary range. Instead of regular raises, their pay is tied to branch office profits.

Another key to implementation at Enterprise is leading—through specifying clear performance objectives and promoting a team-oriented corporate culture. The company stresses promotion from within. Every Enterprise employee, including top executives, starts at the bottom. As a result, a bond of shared experience connects all employees and managers. To reinforce a cohesive culture of camaraderie, senior executives routinely do "grunt work" at branch offices. Even Andy Taylor, the CEO, joins the work. "We were visiting an office in Berkeley and it was mobbed, so I started cleaning cars," says Taylor. "As it was happening, I wondered if it was a good use of my time, but the effect on morale was tremendous." Because the financial results of every branch office and every region are available to all, the collegial culture stimulates good-natured competition. "We're this close to beating out Middlesex," grins Woody Erhardt, an area manager in New Jersey. "I want to pound them into the ground. If they lose, they have to throw a party for us, and we get to decide what they wear."[1]

This example from Enterprise Rent-A-Car illustrates how a strategy must be implemented with carefully considered programs in order to succeed. This chapter discusses strategy implementation in terms of staffing and leading. *Staffing* focuses on the selection and use of employees. *Leading* emphasizes the use of programs to better align employee interests and attitudes with a new strategy.

9.1 Staffing

The implementation of new strategies and policies often calls for new human resource management priorities and a different use of personnel. Such **staffing** issues can involve hiring new people with new skills, firing people with inappropriate or substandard skills, and/or training existing employees to learn new skills.

If growth strategies are to be implemented, new people may need to be hired and trained. Experienced people with the necessary skills need to be found for promotion to newly created managerial positions. When a corporation follows a growth through acquisition strategy, it may find that it needs to replace several managers in the acquired company. The percentage of an acquired company's top management team that either quit or was asked to leave is around 25% after the first year, 35% after the second year, 48% after the third year, 55% after the fourth year, and 61% after five years.[2] It is one thing to lose excess employees after a merger, but it is something else to lose highly skilled people who are difficult to replace. To deal with problems such as this, some companies are appointing special integration managers to shepherd companies through the implementation process of an acquisition. To be a successful integration manager, a person should have (1) a deep knowledge of the acquiring company, (2) a flexible management style, (3) an ability to work in cross-functional project teams, (4) a willingness to work independently, and (5) sufficient emotional and cultural intelligence to work well with people from all backgrounds.[3]

If a corporation adopts a retrenchment strategy, however, a large number of people may need to be laid off or fired; and top management, as well as the divisional managers, needs to specify the criteria to be used in making these personnel decisions. Should employees be fired on the basis of low seniority or on the basis of poor performance? Sometimes corporations find it easier to close or sell off an entire division than to choose which individuals to fire.

STAFFING FOLLOWS STRATEGY

As in the case of structure, staffing requirements are likely to follow a change in strategy. For example, promotions should be based not only on current job performance, but also on whether a person has the skills and abilities to do what is needed to implement the new strategy.

Hiring and Training Requirements Change

Having formulated a new strategy, a corporation may find that it needs to either hire different people or retrain current employees to implement the new strategy. Consider the introduction of team-based production at Corning's filter plant mentioned earlier in **Chapter 8**. Employee selection and training were crucial to the success of the new manufacturing strategy. Plant Manager Robert Hoover sorted through 8,000 job applications before hiring 150 people with the best problem-solving ability and a willingness to work in a team setting. Those selected received extensive training in technical and interpersonal skills. During the first year of production, 25% of all hours worked were devoted to training at a cost of $750,000.[4]

One way to implement a company's business strategy, such as overall low cost, is through training and development. A study of 51 corporations in the United Kingdom found that 71% of "leading" companies rated staff learning and training as important or very important compared to 62% of the other companies.[5] Another study of 155 U.S. manufacturing firms revealed that those with training programs had 19% higher productivity than did those without such a program. Another study found that a doubling of formal training per employee resulted in a 7% reduction in scrap.[6] Training is especially important for a differentiation strategy emphasizing quality or customer service. For example, Motorola, with annual sales of $17 billion, spends 4% of its payroll on training by providing at least 40 hours of training a year to each employee. There is a very strong connection between strategy and training at Motorola. For example, after setting a goal to reduce product development cycle time, Motorola created a two-week course to teach its employees how to accomplish that goal. It brought together marketing, product development, and manufacturing managers to create an action learning format in which the managers worked together instead of separately. The company is especially concerned with attaining the highest quality possible in all its operations. Realizing that it couldn't hit quality targets with poor parts, Motorola developed a class for its suppliers on statistical process control. The company estimates that every $1 it spends on training delivers $30 in productivity gains within three years.[7]

Training is also important when implementing a retrenchment strategy. As suggested earlier, successful downsizing means that the company has to invest in its remaining employees. General Electric's Aircraft Engine Group used training to maintain its share of the market even though it had cut its workforce from 42,000 to 33,000 in the 1990s.[8]

Matching the Manager to the Strategy

The most appropriate type of general manager needed to effectively implement a new corporate or business strategy depends on the desired strategic direction of that firm or business unit. Executives with a particular mix of skills and experiences may be classified as an **executive type** and paired with a specific corporate strategy. For example, a corporation following a concentration strategy emphasizing vertical or horizontal growth would probably want an aggressive new chief executive with a great deal of experience in that particular industry—a *dynamic industry expert*. A diversification strategy, in contrast, might call for someone with an analytical mind who is highly knowledgeable in other industries and can manage diverse product lines—an *analytical portfolio manager*. A corporation choosing to follow a stability strategy would probably want as its CEO a *cautious profit planner*, a person with a conservative style, a production or engineering background, and experience with controlling budgets, capital expenditures, inventories, and standardization procedures. Weak companies in a relatively attractive industry tend to turn to a type of challenge-oriented executive known as the **turnaround specialist** to save the company. Albert J. Dunlap, known as "Chainsaw Al" or "Rambo in Pinstripes," was a premier example of a turnaround "artist" who saved troubled corporations by trimming expenses and downsizing the workforce. After restoring Scott Paper to profitability, Dunlap successfully did the same to Sunbeam Corporation. Unfortunately, Dunlap was unable to build a company once he had turned it around, so he chose to acquire three companies—each showing losses and needing to be "turned around." Dunlap was soon fired by the board in favor of an executive with a less mercurial management style who could regain the confidence of both investors and the employees.[9]

If a company cannot be saved, a *professional liquidator* might be called on by a bankruptcy court to close the firm and liquidate its assets. This is what happened to Montgomery Ward, Inc., the nation's first catalogue retailer, which closed its stores for good in 2001 after declaring bankruptcy for the second time. Research tends to support the conclusion that as a firm's environment changes, it tends to change the type of top executive to implement a new strategy.[10] For example, during the 1990s when the emphasis was on growth in a company's core products/services, the most desired background for a U.S. CEO was either in marketing or international, contrasted with finance during the 1980s when conglomerate diversification was popular.[11]

This approach is in agreement with Chandler, who proposed in **Chapter 8** that the most appropriate CEO of a company changes as a firm moves from one stage of development to another. Because priorities certainly change over an organization's life, successful corporations need to select managers who have skills and characteristics appropriate to the organization's particular stage of development and position in its life cycle. For example, founders of firms tend to have functional backgrounds in technological specialties; whereas successors tend to have backgrounds in marketing and administration.[12] A change in the environment leading to a change in a company's strategy also leads to a change in the top management team. For example, a change in the U.S. utility industry's environment in 1992 supporting internally focused, efficiency-oriented strategies, led to the top management teams being dominated by older managers with longer company and industry tenure with efficiency-oriented backgrounds in operations, engineering, and accounting.[13]

Other studies have found a link between the type of CEO and the firm's overall strategic type. (Strategic types were presented in **Chapter 3**.) For example, successful prospector firms tend to be headed by CEOs from research/engineering and general management backgrounds. High performance defenders tend to have CEOs with accounting/finance, manufacturing/production, and general management experience. Analyzers tend to have CEOs with a marketing/sales background.[14]

A study of 173 firms over a 25-year period revealed that CEOs in these companies tended to have the same functional specialization as the former CEO, especially when the past CEO's strategy continued to be successful. This may be a pattern for successful corporations.[15] In particular, it explains why so many prosperous companies tend to recruit their top executives from one particular area. At Procter & Gamble (a good example of an analyzer firm), the route to the CEO's position has traditionally been through brand management with a strong emphasis on marketing—and more recently international experience. In other firms, the route may be through manufacturing, marketing, accounting, or finance, depending on what the corporation has always considered its key area (and its overall strategic orientation).

SELECTION AND MANAGEMENT DEVELOPMENT

Selection and development are important not only to ensure that people with the right mix of skills and experiences are initially hired, but also to help them grow on the job so that they might be prepared for future promotions.

Executive Succession: Insiders Versus Outsiders

Executive succession is the process of replacing a key top manager. Given that two-thirds of all major corporations worldwide have replaced their CEO at least once between 1995 and 2000, it is important that the firm plan for this eventuality.[16] It is especially important for a company that usually promotes from within to prepare its current managers for promotion. Companies known for being excellent training grounds for executive talent are AlliedSignal, Bain & Company, Bankers Trust, Bristol Myers Squibb, Cititcorp, General Electric, Hewlett-Packard, McDonalds, McKinsey & Company, Microsoft, Nike, PepsiCo, Pfizer, and Procter & Gamble. For example, approximately 10,000 of GE's 276,000 employees take at least one class at the company's famous Leadership Development Center in Crotonville, New York.[17] Some of the best practices for top management succession are encouraging boards to help the CEO create a succession plan, identifying succession candidates below the top layer, measuring internal candidates against outside candidates to ensure the development of a comprehensive set of skills, and providing appropriate financial incentives.[18] See the **boxed feature** to see how Hewlett-Packard identifies those with potential for executive leadership positions.

Prosperous firms tend to look outside for CEO candidates only if they have no obvious internal candidates. Firms in trouble, however, tend to choose outsiders to lead them.[19] For example, one study of 22 firms undertaking a turnaround strategy over a 13-year period found that the CEO was replaced in all but two companies. Of 27 changes of CEO (several firms had more than one CEO during this period), only 7 were insiders—20 were outsiders.[20] The probability of an outsider being chosen to lead a firm in difficulty increases if there is no internal heir apparent, the last CEO was fired, and if the board of directors is composed of a large percentage of outsiders.[21] Boards realize that the best way to force a change in strategy is to hire a new CEO with no connections to the current strategy.[22]

Identifying Abilities and Potential

A company can identify and prepare its people for important positions in several ways. One approach is to establish a sound **performance appraisal system** to identify good performers with promotion potential. A survey of 34 corporate planners and human resource executives from 24 large U.S. corporations revealed that approximately 80% made some attempt to identify managers' talents and behavioral tendencies so that they could place a manager with a likely fit to a given competitive strategy.[23] A company should examine its human resource system to ensure not only that people are being hired without regard to their racial, ethnic, or religious background, but also that they are being identified for training and promotion in the same manner. Management diversity could be a competitive advantage in a multiethnic world. With more women in the workplace, an increasing number are moving into top management. Recent studies are suggesting that female executives score higher than men on motivating oth-

---

How Hewlett-Packard Identifies Potential Executives

Hewlett-Packard identifies those with high potential for executive leadership by looking for six broad competencies that the company believes are necessary.

1. *Practice the HP way* by building trust and respect, focusing on achievement, demonstrating integrity, being innovative with customers, contributing to the community, and developing organizational decision making.

2. *Lead change and learning* by recognizing and acting on signals for change, leading organizational change, learning from organizational experience, removing barriers to change, developing self, and challenging and developing others.

3. *Know the internal and external environments* by anticipating global trends, acting on trends, and learning from others.

4. *Lead strategy setting* by inspiring breakthrough business strategy, leading the strategy-making process, committing to business vision, creating long-range strategies, building financial strategies, and defining a business-planning system.

5. *Align the organization* by working across boundaries, implementing competitive cost structures, developing alliances and partnerships, planning and managing core business, and designing the organization.

6. *Achieve results* by building a track record, establishing accountability, supporting calculated risks, making tough individual decisions, and resolving performance problems.

Source: R. M. Fulmer, P. A. Gibbs, and M. Goldsmith, "The New HP Way: Leveraging Strategy with Diversity, Leadership Development and Decentralization," *Strategy & Leadership* (October/November/December, 1999), pp. 21–29.

---

ers, fostering communication, producing high-quality work, and listening to others, while there is no difference in strategic planning or in analyzing issues.[24]

Many large organizations are using **assessment centers** to evaluate a person's suitability for an advanced position. Corporations such as AT&T, Standard Oil, IBM, Sears, and GE have successfully used assessment centers. Because each is specifically tailored to its corporation, these assessment centers are unique. They use special interviews, management games, in-basket exercises, leaderless group discussions, case analyses, decision-making exercises, and oral presentations to assess the potential of employees for specific positions. Promotions into these positions are based on performance levels in the assessment center. Many assessment centers have been able to accurately predict subsequent job performance.

Job rotation—moving people from one job to another—is also used in many large corporations to ensure that employees are gaining the appropriate mix of experiences to prepare them for future responsibilities. Rotating people among divisions is one way that the corporation can improve the level of organizational learning. For example, companies that pursue related diversification strategies through internal development make greater use of interdivisional transfers of people than do companies that grow through unrelated acquisitions. Apparently the companies that grow internally attempt to transfer important knowledge and skills throughout the corporation in order to achieve some sort of synergy.[25]

PROBLEMS IN RETRENCHMENT

Downsizing (sometimes called "rightsizing") refers to the planned elimination of positions or jobs. This program is often used to implement retrenchment strategies. Because the financial community is likely to react favorably to announcements of downsizing from a company in difficulty, such a program may provide some short-term benefits such as raising the company's stock price. If not done properly, however, downsizing may result in less, rather than more, productivity. One study found that a 10% reduction in people resulted in only a 1.5% reduction in costs, profits increased in only half the firms downsizing, and that the stock price of downsized firms increased over three years, but not as much as did that of firms which did not downsize.[26] Why were the results so marginal? Another study of downsizing revealed that at 20 out of 30 automobile-related U.S. industrial companies, either the wrong jobs were eliminated or blanket offers of early retirement prompted managers, even those considered invaluable, to leave. After the layoffs, the remaining employees had to do not only their work, but also the work of the people who had gone. Because the survivors often didn't know how to do the departeds' work, morale and productivity plummeted.[27] Creativity drops significantly (affecting new product development) and it becomes very difficult to keep high performers from leaving the company.[28] In addition, cost-conscious executives tend to defer maintenance, skimp on training, delay new product introductions, and avoid risky new businesses—all of which leads to lower sales and eventually to lower profits.

A good retrenchment strategy can thus be implemented well in terms of organizing but poorly in terms of staffing. A situation can develop in which retrenchment feeds on itself and acts to further weaken instead of strengthening the company. Research indicates that companies undertaking cost-cutting programs are four times more likely than others to cut costs again, typically by reducing staff.[29] This happened at Eastman Kodak and Xerox during the 1990s, but the companies were still having difficulty in 2001. In contrast, successful downsizing firms undertake a strategic reorientation, not just a bloodletting of employees. Research shows that when companies use downsizing as part of a larger restructuring program to narrow company focus, they enjoy better performance.[30]

Consider the following guidelines that have been proposed for successful downsizing:

- **Eliminate unnecessary work instead of making across-the-board cuts.** Spend the time to research where money is going and eliminate the task, not the workers, if it doesn't add value to what the firm is producing. Reduce the number of administrative levels rather than the number of individual positions. Look for interdependent relationships before eliminating activities. Identify and protect core competencies.

- **Contract out work that others can do cheaper.** For example, Bankers Trust of New York has contracted out its mail room and printing services and some of its payroll and accounts payable activities to a division of Xerox. Outsourcing may be cheaper than vertical integration.

- **Plan for long-run efficiencies.** Don't simply eliminate all postponable expenses, such as maintenance, R&D, and advertising, in the unjustifiable hope that the environment will become more supportive. Continue to hire, grow, and develop—particularly in critical areas.

- **Communicate the reasons for actions.** Tell employees not only why the company is downsizing, but also what the company is trying to achieve. Promote educational programs.

- **Invest in the remaining employees.** Because most "survivors" in a corporate downsizing will probably be doing different tasks from what they were doing before the change, firms need to draft new job specifications, performance standards, appraisal techniques, and compensation packages. Additional training is needed to ensure that everyone has the proper skills to deal with expanded jobs and responsibilities. Empower key individuals/groups and emphasize team building. Identify, protect, and mentor people with leadership talent.

- **Develop value-added jobs to balance out job elimination.** When no other jobs are currently available within the organization to transfer employees to, management must consider other staffing alternatives. Harley-Davidson, for example, worked with the company's unions to find other work for surplus employees by moving work into Harley plants that was previously done by suppliers.[31]

INTERNATIONAL ISSUES IN STAFFING

Implementing a strategy of international expansion takes a lot of planning and can be very expensive. Nearly 80% of midsize and larger companies send their employees abroad and 45% plan to increase the number they have on foreign assignment. A complete package for one executive working in another country costs from $300,000 to $1 million annually. Nevertheless, between 10% and 20% of all U.S. managers sent abroad returned early because of job dissatisfaction or difficulties in adjusting to a foreign country. Of those who stayed for the duration of their assignment, nearly one-third did not perform as well as expected. One-fourth of those completing an assignment left their company within one year of returning home—often leaving to join a competitor.[32] One common mistake is failing to educate the person about the customs in other countries.

Because of cultural differences, managerial style and human resource practices must be tailored to fit the particular situations in other countries. Since only 11% of human resource managers have ever worked abroad, most have little understanding of a global assignment's unique personal and professional challenges and thus fail to develop the training necessary for such an assignment.[33] Ninety percent of companies select employees for an international assignment based on their technical expertise while ignoring other areas.[34] This situation is, however, improving. Multinational corporations are now putting more emphasis on intercultural training for those managers being sent on an assignment to a foreign country. This training is one of the commonly cited reasons for the lower expatriate failure rates—6% or less—for European and Japanese MNCs, which have emphasized cross-cultural experiences, compared with a 35% failure rate for U.S.-based MNCs.[35]

To improve organizational learning, many multinational corporations are providing their managers with international assignments lasting as long as five years. Upon their return to headquarters, these expatriates have an in-depth understanding of the company's operations in another part of the world. This has value to the extent that these employees communicate this understanding to others in decision-making positions. Unfortunately, not all corporations appropriately manage international assignments. While out of the country, a person may be overlooked for an important promotion (out of sight, out of mind). Upon his or her return to the home country, coworkers may deprecate the out-of-country experience as a waste of time.

Out of their study of 750 U.S., Japanese, and European companies, Black and Gregersen found that the companies that do a good job of managing foreign assignments follow three general practices.

- When making international assignments, they focus on transferring knowledge and developing global leadership.
- They make foreign assignments to people whose technical skills are matched or exceeded by their cross-cultural abilities.
- They end foreign assignments with a deliberate repatriation process with career guidance and jobs where the employees can apply what they learned in their assignments.[36]

Once a corporation has established itself in another country, it hires and promotes people from the host country into higher level positions. For example, most large multinational corporations (MNCs) attempt to fill managerial positions in their subsidiaries with well-qualified citizens of the host countries. Unilever and IBM take this approach to international staffing. This policy serves to placate nationalistic governments and to better attune management practices to the host country's culture. The danger in using primarily foreign nationals to staff managerial positions in subsidiaries is the increased likelihood of suboptimization (the local subsidiary ignores the needs of the larger parent corporation). This makes it difficult for a multinational corporation to meet its long-term, worldwide objectives. To a local national in an MNC subsidiary, the corporation as a whole is an abstraction. Communication and coordination across subsidiaries become more difficult. As it becomes harder to coordinate the activities of several international subsidiaries, an MNC will have serious problems operating in a global industry.

Another approach to staffing the managerial positions of multinational corporations is to use people with an "international" orientation, regardless of their country of origin or host country assignment. This is a widespread practice among European firms. For example, Electrolux, a Swedish firm, had a French director in its Singapore factory. Using third-country "nationals" can allow for more opportunities for promotion than does Unilever's policy of hiring local people, but it can also result in more misunderstandings and conflicts with the local employees and with the host country's government.

Some U.S. corporations take advantage of immigrants and their children to staff key positions when negotiating entry into another country and when selecting an executive to manage the company's new foreign operations. For example, when General Motors wanted to learn more about business opportunities in China, it turned to Shirley Young, a Vice-President of Marketing at GM. Born in Shanghai and fluent in Chinese language and customs, Young was instrumental in helping GM negotiate a $1 billion joint venture with Shanghai Automotive to build a Buick plant in China. With other Chinese Americans, Young formed a committee to advise GM on relations with China. Although just a part of a larger team of GM employees working on the joint venture, Young coached GM employees on Chinese customs and traditions.[37]

Multinational corporations with a high level of international interdependence among activities need to provide their managers with significant international assignments and experiences as part of their training and development. Such assignments provide future corporate leaders with a series of valuable international contacts in addition to a better personal understanding of international issues and global linkages among corporate activities.[38] Executive recruiters report that more major corporations are now requiring candidates to have international experience.[39]

9.2 Leading

Implementation also involves **leading** people to use their abilities and skills most effectively and efficiently to achieve organizational objectives. Without direction, people tend to do their work according to their personal view of what tasks should be done, how, and in what order. They may approach their work as they have in the past or emphasize those tasks that they most enjoy—regardless of the corporation's priorities. This can create real problems, particularly if the company is operating internationally and must adjust to customs and traditions in other countries. This direction may take the form of management leadership, communicated norms of behavior from the corporate culture, or agreements among workers in autonomous work groups. It may also be accomplished more formally through action planning or through programs such as Management By Objectives and Total Quality Management.

MANAGING CORPORATE CULTURE

Because an organization's culture can exert a powerful influence on the behavior of all employees, it can strongly affect a company's ability to shift its strategic direction. A problem for a strong culture is that a change in mission, objectives, strategies, or policies is not likely to be successful if it is in opposition to the accepted culture of the company. Corporate culture has a strong tendency to resist change because its very reason for existence often rests on preserving stable relationships and patterns of behavior. For example, the male-dominated, Japanese-centered corporate culture of the giant Mitsubishi Corporation created problems for the company when it implemented its growth strategy in North America. The alleged sexual harassment of its female employees by male supervisors resulted in a lawsuit by the U.S. Equal Employment Opportunity Commission and a boycott of the company's automobiles by the National Organization for Women.[40]

Figure 9–1

Assessing Strategy–Culture Compatibility

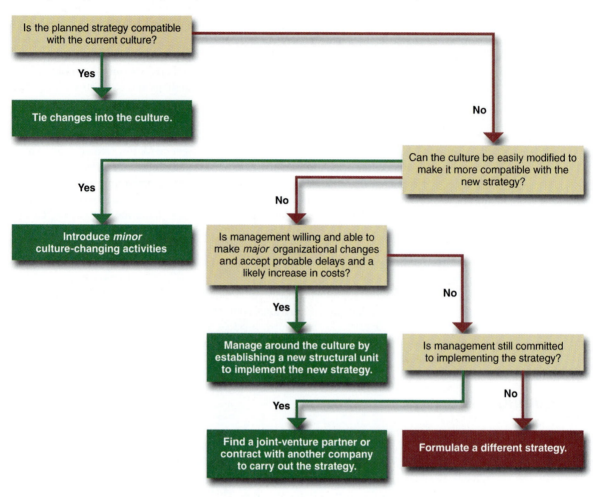

There is no one best corporate culture. An optimal culture is one that best supports the mission and strategy of the company of which it is a part. This means that, like structure and staffing, *corporate culture should support the strategy.* Unless strategy is in complete agreement with the culture, any significant change in strategy should be followed by a modification of the organization's culture. Although corporate culture can be changed, it may often take a long time and it requires much effort. A key job of management involves **managing corporate culture.** In doing so, management must evaluate what a particular change in strategy means to the corporate culture, assess if a change in culture is needed, and decide if an attempt to change the culture is worth the likely costs.

Assessing Strategy-Culture Compatibility

When implementing a new strategy, a company should take the time to assess **strategy–culture compatibility.** (See **Figure 9–1.**) Consider the following questions regarding the corporation's culture:

1. **Is the planned strategy compatible with the company's current culture?** *If yes,* full steam ahead. Tie organizational changes into the company's culture by identifying how the new strategy will achieve the mission better than the current strategy does. *If not . . .*

2. **Can the culture be easily modified to make it more compatible with the new strategy?** *If yes,* move forward carefully by introducing a set of culture-changing activities such as minor structural modifications, training and development activities, and/or hiring new managers who are more compatible with the new strategy. When Procter & Gamble's top management decided to implement a strategy aimed at reducing costs, for example, it made some changes in how things were done, but it did not eliminate its brand-management system. The culture adapted to these modifications over a couple years and productivity increased. *If not . . .*

3. **Is management willing and able to make major organizational changes and accept probable delays and a likely increase in costs?** *If yes,* manage around the culture by establishing a new structural unit to implement the new strategy. At General Motors, for example, top management realized the company had to make some radical changes to be more competitive. Because the current structure, culture, and procedures were very inflexible, management decided to establish a completely new division (GM's first new division since 1918) called Saturn to build its new auto. In cooperation with the United Auto Workers, an entirely new labor agreement was developed, based on decisions reached by consensus. Carefully selected employees received from 100 to 750 hours of training, and a whole new culture was built piece by piece. *If not . . .*

4. **Is management still committed to implementing the strategy?** *If yes,* find a joint-venture partner or contract with another company to carry out the strategy. *If not,* formulate a different strategy.

Managing Cultural Change Through Communication

Communication is key to the effective management of change. Rationale for strategic changes should be communicated to workers not only in newsletters and speeches, but also in training and development programs. Companies in which major cultural changes have taken place successfully had the following characteristics in common:

- The CEO and other top managers had a strategic vision of what the company could become and communicated this vision to employees at all levels. The current performance of the company was compared to that of its competition and constantly updated.

- The vision was translated into the key elements necessary to accomplish that vision. For example, if the vision called for the company to become a leader in quality or service, aspects of quality and service were pinpointed for improvement and appropriate measurement systems were developed to monitor them. These measures were communicated widely through contests, formal and informal recognition, and monetary rewards, among other devices.[41]

Managing Diverse Cultures Following an Acquisition

When merging with or acquiring another company, top management must give some consideration to a potential clash of corporate cultures. According to a Hewitt Associates survey of 218 major U.S. corporations, integrating culture was a top challenge for 69% of the reporting companies.[42] It's dangerous to assume that the firms can simply be integrated into the same reporting structure. The greater the gap between the cultures of the acquired firm and the acquiring firm, the faster executives in the acquired firm quit their jobs and valuable talent is lost.

There are four general methods of managing two different cultures. (See **Figure 9–2.**) The choice of which method to use should be based on (1) *how much members of the acquired firm value preserving their own culture* and (2) *how attractive they perceive the culture of the acquirer to be.*[43]

1. **Integration** involves a relatively balanced give-and-take of cultural and managerial practices between the merger partners, and no strong imposition of cultural change on either company. It merges the two cultures in such a way that the separate cultures of both firms

Figure 9–2

Methods of Managing the Culture of an Acquired Firm

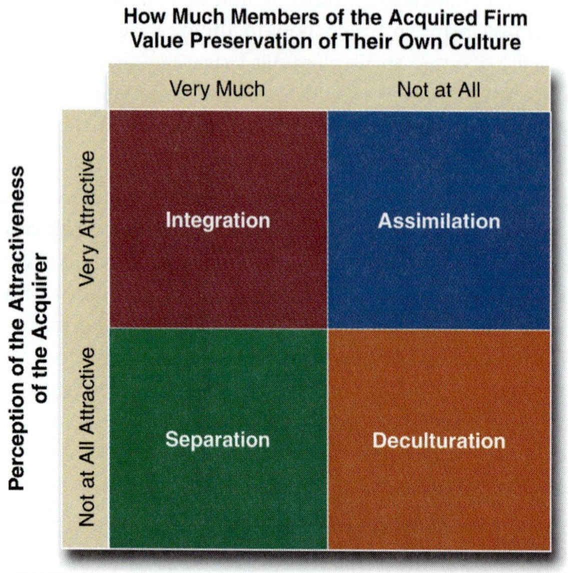

How Much Members of the Acquired Firm Value Preservation of Their Own Culture

Source: A. Nahavardi and A. R. Malekzadeh, "Acculturation in Mergers and Acquisitions," *Academy of Management Review* (January 1988), p. 83. Copyright © 1988 by the Academy of Management. Reprinted by permission of Academy of Management via the Copyright Clearance Center.

are preserved in the resulting culture. This is what occurred when the Seaboard and Chesapeake & Ohio railroads merged to form CSX Corporation. The top executives were so concerned that both cultures be equally respected that they kept referring to the company as a "partnership of equals."

2. **Assimilation** involves the domination of one organization over the other. The domination is not forced, but it is welcomed by members of the acquired firm, who may feel for many reasons that their culture and managerial practices have not produced success. The acquired firm surrenders its culture and adopts the culture of the acquiring company. See the **boxed feature** describing this method of acculturation when Admiral was acquired by Maytag Corporation.

3. **Separation** is characterized by a separation of the two companies' cultures. They are structurally separated, without cultural exchange. In the Shearson-American Express merger, both parties agreed to keep the fast-paced Shearson completely separate from the planning-oriented American Express. This approach allowed American Express to easily divest Shearson once it discovered that the merger was not working.

4. **Deculturation** involves the disintegration of one company's culture resulting from unwanted and extreme pressure from the other to impose its culture and practices. This is the most common and most destructive method of dealing with two different cultures. It is often accompanied by much confusion, conflict, resentment, and stress. This is a primary reason why so many executives tend to leave after their firm is acquired.[44] Such a merger typically results in poor performance by the acquired company and its eventual divestment. This is what happened when AT&T acquired NCR Corporation in 1990 for its computer business. It replaced NCR managers with an AT&T management team, reor-

Admiral Assimilates Maytag's Culture

Maytag's corporate culture had been dominated almost from the beginning of the company by the concept of quality. Maytag employees took great pride in being known as the "dependability people." Over the years, Maytag Company consistently advertised that their repairmen were "lonely" because Maytag products rarely, if ever, needed repair.

Admiral's history had, however, been quite different. Prior to Maytag's purchase of Magic Chef (and thus Admiral) in 1986, Admiral had been owned by three different corporations. Its manufacturing plant in Galesburg, Illinois, had deteriorated to a dismal level by the time Maytag acquired it. Refrigerators sometimes rolled off the assembly line with screws driven in crooked and temperature balances askew!

Maytag's management had always wanted to have its own Maytag brand refrigerator. That was one reason why it purchased Admiral. But it was worried that Admiral might not be able to produce a quality product to Maytag's specifications. To improve Admiral's quality, Maytag's top management decided to integrate Admiral directly into Maytag Company operations. As a result, all Admiral functional departments, except marketing, reported directly to the Maytag Company president.

Under the direction of Leonard Hadley, while he was serving as Maytag Company President, a project was initiated to design and manufacture a refrigerator for the Maytag brand at the Admiral plant. When Hadley first visited Admiral's facilities to discuss the design of a Maytag line of refrigerators, Admiral personnel asked Hadley when the name on their plant's water tower would be changed from Admiral to Maytag. Hadley (acknowledging Maytag's cultural concerns regarding quality) responded: "*When you earn it.*"

The refrigerator resulting from the Maytag–Admiral collaboration was a huge success. The project crystallized corporate management's philosophy for forging synergies among the Maytag companies while simultaneously allowing the individual expertise of those units to flourish. Admiral's employees were willing to accept the dominance of Maytag's strong quality-oriented culture because they respected it. In turn, they expected to be treated with some respect for their tradition of skill in refrigeration technology.

ganized sales, forced employees to adhere to the AT&T code of values (called the "Common Bond"), and even dropped the proud NCR name (successor to National Cash Register) in favor of a sterile GIS (Global Information Solutions) nonidentity. By 1995, AT&T was forced to take a $1.2 billion loss and lay off 10,000 people.[45] The NCR unit was put up for sale in 1996.

ACTION PLANNING

Activities can be directed toward accomplishing strategic goals through action planning. At a minimum, an **action plan** states what actions are going to be taken, by whom, during what timeframe, and with what expected results. After a program has been selected to implement a particular strategy, an action plan should be developed to put the program in place.

Take the example of a company choosing forward vertical integration through the acquisition of a retailing chain as its growth strategy. Now that it owns its own retail outlets, it must integrate the stores into the company. One of the many programs it would have to develop is a new advertising program for the stores. See **Table 9–1** for an example of an action plan for a

Table 9–1 Example of an Action Plan

Action Plan for Jan Lewis, Advertising Manager, and Rick Carter, Advertising Assistant, Ajax Continental

Program Objective: To Run a New Advertising and Promotion Campaign for the Combined Jones Surplus/Ajax Continental Retail Stores for the Coming Christmas Season Within a Budget of $XX.

Program Activities:
1. Identify three Best Ad Agencies for New Campaign.
2. Ask three Ad Agencies to Submit a Proposal for a New Advertising and Promotion Campaign for Combined Stores.
3. Agencies Present Proposals to Marketing Manager.
4. Select Best Proposal and Inform Agencies of Decision.
5. Agency Presents Winning Proposal to Top Management.
6. Ads Air on TV and Promotions Appear in Stores.
7. Measure Results of Campaign in Terms of Viewer Recall and Increase in Store Sales.

Action Steps	Responsibility	Start–End
1. A. Review previous programs	Lewis & Carter	1/1–2/1
B. Discuss with boss	Lewis & Smith	2/1–2/3
C. Decide on three agencies	Lewis	2/4
2. A. Write specifications for ad	Lewis	1/15–1/20
B. Assistant writes ad request	Carter	1/20–1/30
C. Contact ad agencies	Lewis	2/5–2/8
D. Send request to three agencies	Carter	2/10
E. Meet with agency acct. execs	Lewis & Carter	2/16–2/20
3. A. Agencies work on proposals	Acct. Execs	2/23–5/1
B. Agencies present proposals	Carter	5/1–5/15
4. A. Select best proposal	Lewis	5/15–5/20
B. Meet with winning agency	Lewis	5/22–5/30
C. Inform losers	Carter	6/1
5. A. Fine-tune proposal	Acct. Exec	6/1–7/1
B. Presentation to management	Lewis	7/1–7/3
6. A. Ads air on TV	Lewis	9/1–12/24
B. Floor displays in stores	Carter	8/20–8/30
7. A. Gather recall measures of ads	Carter	9/1–12/24
B. Evaluate sales data	Carter	1/1–1/10
C. Prepare analysis of campaign	Carter	1/10–2/15

new advertising and promotion program. The resulting action plan to develop a new advertising program should include much of the following information:

1. **Specific actions to be taken to make the program operational:** One action might be to contact three reputable advertising agencies and ask them to prepare a proposal for a new radio and newspaper ad campaign based on the theme "Jones Surplus is now a part of Ajax Continental. Prices are lower. Selection is better."

2. **Dates to begin and end each action:** Time would have to be allotted not only to select and contact three agencies, but also to allow them sufficient time to prepare a detailed proposal. For example, allow one week to select and contact the agencies plus three months for them to prepare detailed proposals to present to the company's marketing director. Also allow some time to decide which proposal to accept.

3. **Person (identified by name and title) responsible for carrying out each action:** List someone—such as Jan Lewis, advertising manager, or Rick Carter, advertising assistant—who can be put in charge of each action.

4. **Person responsible for monitoring the timeliness and effectiveness of each action:** Indicate that Jan Lewis is responsible for ensuring that the proposals are of good quality and are priced within the planned program budget. She will be the primary company contact for the ad agencies and will report on the progress of the program once a week to the company's marketing director.

5. **Expected financial and physical consequences of each action:** Estimate when a completed ad campaign will be ready to show top management and how long it will take after approval to begin to air the ads. Estimate also the expected increase in store sales over the six-month period after the ads are first aired. Indicate if "recall" measures will be used to help assess the ad campaign's effectiveness plus how, when, and by whom the recall data will be collected and analyzed.

6. **Contingency plans:** Indicate how long it will take to get an acceptable ad campaign to show top management if none of the initial proposals is acceptable.

Action plans are important for several reasons. First, action plans serve as a link between strategy formulation and evaluation and control. Second, the action plan specifies what needs to be done differently from the way operations are currently carried out. Third, during the evaluation and control process that comes later, an action plan helps in both the appraisal of performance and in the identification of any remedial actions, as needed. In addition, the explicit assignment of responsibilities for implementing and monitoring the programs may contribute to better motivation.

MANAGEMENT BY OBJECTIVES

Management By Objectives (MBO) is an organization-wide approach to help ensure purposeful action toward desired objectives. MBO links organizational objectives and the behavior of individuals. Because it is a system that links plans with performance, it is a powerful implementation technique.

The MBO process involves:

1. Establishing and communicating organizational objectives

2. Setting individual objectives (through superior-subordinate interaction) that help implement organizational ones

3. Developing an action plan of activities needed to achieve the objectives

4. Periodically (at least quarterly) reviewing performance as it relates to the objectives and including the results in the annual performance appraisal

MBO provides an opportunity for the corporation to connect the objectives of people at each level to those at the next higher level. MBO, therefore, acts to tie together corporate, business, and functional objectives, as well as the strategies developed to achieve them.

One of the real benefits of MBO is that it can reduce the amount of internal politics operating within a large corporation. Political actions within a firm can cause conflict and create divisions between the very people and groups who should be working together to implement strategy. People are less likely to jockey for position if the company's mission and objectives are clear and they know that the reward system is based not on game playing, but on achieving clearly communicated, measurable objectives.

TOTAL QUALITY MANAGEMENT

Total Quality Management (TQM) is an operational philosophy committed to *customer satisfaction* and *continuous improvement.* TQM is committed to quality/excellence and to being the best in all functions. Because TQM aims to reduce costs and improve quality, it can be used as a program to implement both an overall low-cost or a differentiation business strategy. About 92% of manufacturing companies and 69% of service firms have implemented some form of quality management practices.[46] Nevertheless, a report by McKinsey & Company reported that two-thirds of the TQM programs it examined had failed to produce expected improvements. An analysis of the successes and failures of TQM concluded that the key is top management. Successful TQM programs occur in those companies in which "top managers move beyond defensive and tactical orientations to embrace a developmental orientation."[47]

TQM has four objectives:

1. Better, less variable quality of the product and service
2. Quicker, less variable response in processes to customer needs
3. Greater flexibility in adjusting to customers' shifting requirements
4. Lower cost through quality improvement and elimination of non–value-adding work[48]

According to TQM, faulty processes, not poorly motivated employees, are the cause of defects in quality. The program involves a significant change in corporate culture, requiring strong leadership from top management, employee training, empowerment of lower level employees (giving people more control over their work), and teamwork for it to succeed in a company. TQM emphasizes prevention, not correction. Inspection for quality still takes place, but the emphasis is on improving the process to prevent errors and deficiencies. Thus quality circles or quality improvement teams are formed to identify problems and to suggest how to improve the processes that may be causing the problems.

TQM's *essential ingredients* are:

- **An intense focus on customer satisfaction:** Everyone (not just people in the sales and marketing departments) understands that their jobs exist only because of customer needs. Thus all jobs must be approached in terms of how it will affect customer satisfaction.

- **Internal as well as external customers:** An employee in the shipping department may be the internal customer of another employee who completes the assembly of a product, just as a person who buys the product is a customer of the entire company. An employee must be just as concerned with pleasing the internal customer as in satisfying the external customer.

- **Accurate measurement of every critical variable in a company's operations:** This means that employees have to be trained in what to measure, how to measure, and how to interpret the data. A rule of TQM is "you only improve what you measure."

- **Continuous improvement of products and services:** Everyone realizes that operations need to be continuously monitored to find ways to improve products and services.

- **New work relationships based on trust and teamwork:** Important is the idea of empowerment—giving employees wide latitude in how they go about achieving the company's goals. Research indicates that the key to TQM success lies in executive commitment, an open organizational culture, and employee empowerment.[49]

INTERNATIONAL CONSIDERATIONS IN LEADING

In a study of 53 different national cultures, Hofstede found that each nation's unique culture could be identified using five dimensions. He found that national culture is so influential that it tends to overwhelm even a strong corporate culture. In measuring the differences among these **dimensions of national culture** from country to country, he was able to explain why a certain management practice might be successful in one nation, but fail in another.[50]

1. **Power distance (PD)** is the *extent to which a society accepts an unequal distribution of power* in organizations. Malaysia and Mexico scored highest, whereas Germany and Austria scored lowest. People in those countries scoring high on this dimension tend to prefer autocratic to more participative managers.

2. **Uncertainty avoidance (UA)** is the *extent to which a society feels threatened by uncertain and ambiguous situations.* Greece and Japan scored highest on disliking ambiguity, whereas the United States and Singapore scored lowest. People in those nations scoring high on this dimension tend to want career stability, formal rules, and clear-cut measures of performance.

3. **Individualism–collectivism (I–C)** is the *extent to which a society values individual freedom and independence of action compared with a tight social framework and loyalty to the group.* The United States and Canada scored highest on individualism, whereas Mexico and Guatemala scored lowest. People in those nations scoring high on individualism tend to value individual success through competition, whereas people scoring low on individualism (thus high on collectivism) tend to value group success through collective cooperation.

4. **Masculinity–femininity (M–F)** is the *extent to which society is oriented toward money and things* (which Hofstede labels masculine) *or toward people* (which Hofstede labels feminine). Japan and Mexico scored highest on masculinity, whereas France and Sweden scored lowest (thus highest on femininity). People in those nations scoring high on masculinity tend to value clearly defined sex roles where men dominate and to emphasize performance and independence, whereas people scoring low on masculinity (and thus high on femininity) tend to value equality of the sexes where power is shared and to emphasize the quality of life and interdependence.

5. **Long-term orientation (LT)** is the *extent to which society is oriented toward the long versus the short term.* Hong Kong and Japan scored highest on long-term orientation, whereas Pakistan scored the lowest. A long-term time orientation emphasizes the importance of hard work, education, and persistence as well as the importance of thrift. Nations with a long-term time orientation should value strategic planning and other management techniques with a long-term payback.

These dimensions of national culture may help to explain why some management practices work well in some countries, but not in others. For example, Management By Objectives (MBO), which originated in the United States, has succeeded in Germany, according to Hofstede, because the idea of replacing the arbitrary authority of the boss with the impersonal authority of mutually agreed-upon objectives fits the low power distance that is a dimension of the German culture. It has failed in France, however, because the French are used to high power distances—to accepting orders from a highly personalized authority. In addition, some of the difficulties experienced by U.S. companies in using Japanese-style quality circles in TQM may stem from the extremely high value U.S. culture places on individualism. The differences between the U.S and Mexico on power distance (Mexico 104 versus U.S. 46) and individualism–collectivism (U.S. 91 versus Mexico 30) dimensions may help explain why some companies operating in both countries have difficulty adapting to the differences in customs.[51]

When one successful company in one country merges with another successful company in another country, the clash of corporate cultures is compounded by the clash of national cultures. With the value of cross-border mergers and acquisitions totaling $720 billion in 1999, the management of cultures is becoming a key issue in strategy implementation.[52]

See the **Global Issue** feature to learn how differences in national and corporate cultures created conflict when Upjohn Company of the United States and Pharmacia AB of Sweden merged.

Multinational corporations must pay attention to the many differences in cultural dimensions around the world and adjust their management practices accordingly. Cultural differences can easily go unrecognized by a headquarters staff that may interpret these differences as personality defects, whether the people in the subsidiaries are locals or expatriates. When conducting strategic planning in a multinational corporation, top management must be aware that the process will vary based upon the national culture where a subsidiary is located. For example, in one MNC, the French expect concepts and key questions and answers. North American managers provide heavy financial analysis. Germans give precise dates and financial analysis. Information is usually late from Spanish and Moroccan operations and quotas are typically inflated. It is up to management to adapt to the differences.[53] Hofstede and Bond conclude: "Whether they like it or not, the headquarters of multinationals are in the business of multicultural management."[54]

Global Issue

Cultural Differences Create Implementation Problems in Merger

When Upjohn Pharmaceuticals of Kalamazoo, Michigan, and Pharmacia AB of Stockholm, Sweden, merged in 1995, employees of both sides were optimistic for the newly formed Pharmacia & Upjohn, Inc. Both companies were second-tier competitors fighting for survival in a global industry. Together, the firms would create a global company that could compete scientifically with its bigger rivals.

Because Pharmacia had acquired an Italian firm in 1993, it also had a large operation in Milan. American executives scheduled meetings throughout the summer of 1996, only to cancel them when their European counterparts could not attend. Although it was common knowledge in Europe that most Swedes take the entire month of July for vacation and that Italians take off all of August, this was not common knowledge in Michigan. Differences in management styles became a special irritant. Swedes were used to an open system with autonomous work teams. Executives sought the whole group's approval before making an important decision. Upjohn executives followed the more traditional American top-down approach. Upon taking command of the newly merged firm, Dr. Zabriskie (who had been Upjohn's CEO), divided the company into departments reporting to the new London headquarters. He required frequent reports, budgets, and staffing updates. The Swedes reacted negatively to this top-down management hierarchical style. "It was degrading," said Stener Kvinnsland, head of Pharmacia's cancer research in Italy before he quit the new company.

The Italian operations baffled the Americans, even though the Italians felt comfortable with a hierarchical management style. Italy's laws and unions made layoffs difficult. Italian data and accounting were often inaccurate. Because the Americans didn't trust the data, they were constantly asking for verification. In turn, the Italians were concerned that the Americans were trying to take over Italian operations. At Upjohn, all workers were subject to testing for drug and alcohol abuse. Upjohn also banned smoking. At Pharmacia's Italian business center, however, waiters poured wine freely every afternoon in the company dining room. Pharmacia's boardrooms were stocked with humidors for executives who smoked cigars during long meetings. After a brief attempt to enforce Upjohn's policies, the company dropped both of the no-drinking and no-smoking policies for European workers.

Although the combined company had cut annual costs by $200 million, overall costs of the merger reached $800 million, some $200 million more than projected. Nevertheless, Jan Eckberg, CEO of Pharmacia before the merger, remained confident of the new company's ability to succeed. He admitted, however, that "we have to make some smaller changes to release the full power of the two companies."

Source: R. Frank and T. M. Burton, "Cross-Border Merger Results in Headaches for a Drug Company," *Wall Street Journal* (February 4, 1997), pp. A1, A12. Copyright © 1997 by the *Wall Street Journal*. Reprinted by permission of the *Wall Street Journal* via the Copyright Clearance Center.

9.3 Impact of the Internet on Staffing and Leading in Organizations

The widespread acceptance of the Internet has created demand for the development of intranets in most large organizations. An **intranet** is an *internal Internet created for the use of a corporation's employees.* The availability of the World Wide Web, servers, chat rooms, bulletin boards, and electronic mail allows companies to use their existing technologies to build intranets without needing additional investment in hardware or software. Intranets support the development of virtual teams, disseminate information about the company's products and services, provide information about internal job openings and health benefits, plus offer e-mail and file transfer services so that people can transfer project information from one personal computer to another. Unlike the Internet, an intranet is owned entirely by the corporation. Information posted on them cannot be accessed by the general public without being provided explicit access privileges. Intranets are protected from unauthorized entry through "firewalls," software programs that check and verify the credentials of potential users. Unlike other technologies, intranets don't need standard hardware platforms, such as IBM or Macintosh, on which an application resides. The vast majority of companies report a positive return from their intranet investment.[55]

Intranets can be either *static* (updated periodically) or *dynamic* (updated continuously). Examples of static information are phone directories, internal job openings, employee benefits information, company news releases, corporate events, technical documents, and company policies and procedures. Examples of dynamic information are sales, inventory, and expense account transactions.

Static Intranet Applications

The primary goal of static intranet applications is to provide information when and if people need it. For example, a number of large corporations are installing internal *Yellow Pages* in which an employee can type key skills, knowledge, or experience into the computer and get back the names and resumes of other employees within the firm who have those skills, knowledge, or experiences. Deere & Company uses a "People Who Know" database to help people with questions find people with answers. Bruce Boardman, head of metals research at Deere, states that the cost of the system is "less than the salary of one engineer—it pays for itself at least half a dozen times a year," especially when the production line stops and someone needs help immediately.

When Bechtel Corporation created a new division called Bechtel Systems & Infrastructure (BSII), it developed a Yellow Pages for the unit. The division was a combination of all Bechtel's work for governments around the world and included 6,000 people. According to Mary O'Donnell of BSII's human resource department, "We didn't know all the skills we had." The Yellow Pages, based on Lotus Notes, contains employee resumes listing a person's skills, current project and when it will be completed, past projects, military, international, and supervisory experience, and other information. Together with online Notes forums called "twigs" (technical working groups), the system provides a way to find answers to technical questions. It also enables the division to staff jobs more quickly.

NatWest Markets, the investment banking division of Britain's NatWest Group, developed a Green Book containing the names of 800 people arranged by area of expertise within the five categories of financial products, industry sectors, geography, support, and business intelligence. About 100 of the people are "knowledge coordinators" who have volunteered to direct other people not only to other people, but to legal documents or files. Interestingly, the people are not listed by titles. According to Victoria Ward, NatWest

Markets Chief Knowledge Officer: "I'm not interested in titles. It might turn out that one of our best experts in securitization works in the equities unit, not in the debt unit. This is about function, not form."[56]

Dynamic Intranet Applications

Intranets can also be used effectively to process and exchange dynamic information by linking employees with company databases and proprietary transaction systems such as inventory and purchasing systems. Software, such as HotOffice, allows project coworkers to access folders and read posted documents. The HotOffice system includes a bulletin board, group calendar, personal calendars, virtual meeting rooms for real-time discussions, and private e-mail. For real-time collaboration over a LAN (local area network), Lotus Sametime is a software package that includes text chat and whiteboard applications as well as application sharing.[57] (See the **Internet Issue** feature for an example of how business people use the net to interact over long distances.)

Ford Motor Company's intranet connects 120,000 workstations at offices and factories worldwide to thousands of Ford Web sites containing proprietary information like market research, analyses of competitors' components, and rankings of the most efficient suppliers of parts. Its product development system allows engineers, designers, and suppliers to work from the same data. Every vehicle team has a Web site where team members can post questions and progress reports, note bottlenecks, and resolve issues. According to Paul Blumberg, Director of Product Development, sharing such information widely has helped Ford reduce the time to get new models into production from 36 to 24 months. The company links its dealers into the intranet so they can order vehicles from the assembly plant, check on production status, and change orders up to seven days before a car is finished. The dealers are then able to offer custom ordering and delivery on every car or truck.[58]

Internet Issue

Virtual Teams Use the Net to Operate at Long Distance

Christine Martin, President and CEO of TLCi, tells how her company uses the net for both the internal and external transaction of business.

My company is a virtual company in three ways:

First, our CFO and Ops Director works from eastern Canada, while the company is headquartered in Southern California. We meet every morning over the Internet, employing a videocam along with audio. If the Internet connection is not satisfactory, we work over the telephone. We regularly address our strategic plan and work on our various client projects together. This is a highly productive and beneficial arrangement.

Second, TLCi has various strategic partners with whom we are connected virtually. We use e-mail on a regular basis. We send important links and information, and exchange drafts and final documents (such as business plans) over the Internet. We find e-mail to be the best vehicle for exchanging working documents, saving time and ensuring accuracy.

Third, to ensure ourselves against catastrophe, we regularly update our virus-protection software and back up files religiously. We also manage our own Web site, to make sure that company information is always current. Future projects include videoconferencing with clients worldwide.

Source: C. Martin, "Virtual Companies: A Reality," *EntreWorld Discussion ListServe* (December 18, 2000). Reprinted by permission.

Advantages and Disadvantages of Intranets

Intranets have many *advantages*. Among them are:

- **Speed, effectiveness, and relatively low cost:** Less time and money is spent on printing reams of paper and disseminating it to employees who often just dump it in the trash.

- **Elimination of time and space barriers:** People can find answers to their questions regardless of the time or the location.

- **Can use existing infrastructure:** Once a firm has the hardware in place to use the Internet, it is very easy to create an intranet.

- **Ease of use:** Accessing information on an intranet is much simpler and faster than digging into file cabinets to find policy folders or calling friends to find an expert on a particular problem.

- **Enhances productivity:** The time spent in searching for information is significantly reduced.

Intranets also have some *disadvantages*. Among them are:

- **Information and hyperlinks need to be continually updated.** Nothing is more frustrating than being sent to a site that is no longer operating or one that contains out-of-date information. Employees need to be periodically reminded to update their resumes.

- **Technology is continually changing and must be updated often.** The increasing use of virtual work teams is pushing the development of video and voice systems on computers, requiring investments in newer, more powerful, and faster personal computers and workstations.

- **Technical support is needed to maintain the system.** People must be trained on how to use it. Someone must monitor what people put on the intranet, such as resumes, to ensure that the information is correct.

- **Security is a critical issue.** Even well-constructed firewalls cannot keep out serious hackers who like to meddle with confidential documents. Industrial espionage is always a concern for companies in highly competitive or defense-related industries.

- **Access is an issue.** Unless all employees have access to the intranet, many of the advantages may be lost.[59]

Projections for the 21st Century

- From 1994 to 2010, movie screens will increase in the United States from 25,105 to 74,114.
- From 1994 to 2010, movie screens will grow worldwide from 86,902 to 162,766.[60]

Discussion Questions

1. What skills should a person have for managing a business unit following a differentiation strategy? Why? What should a company do if no one is available internally and the company has a policy of promotion from within?

2. When should someone from outside the company be hired to manage the company or one of its business units?

3. What are some ways to implement a retrenchment strategy without creating a lot of resentment and conflict with labor unions?

4. How can corporate culture be changed?

5. Why is an understanding of national cultures important in strategic management?

Strategic Practice Exercise

Staffing involves finding the person with the right blend of characteristics, such as personality, training, and experience, to implement a particular strategy. The Keirsey Temperament Sorter is designed to identify different kinds of personality temperament. It is similar to other instruments derived from Carl Jung's theory of psychological types, such as the Myers-Briggs, the Singer-Loomis, and the Grey-Wheelright. The questionnaire identifies four temperament types: **Guardian (SJ), Artisan (SP), Idealist (NF),** and **Rational (NT).** *Guardians* have natural talent in managing goods and services. They are dependable and trustworthy. *Artisans* have keen senses and are at home with tools, instruments, and vehicles. They are risk-takers and like action. *Idealists* are concerned with growth and development and like to work with people. They prefer friendly cooperation over confrontation and conflict. *Rationalists* are problem solvers who like to know how things work. They work tirelessly to accomplish their goals. Each of these four types has four variants.[61]

Keirsey challenges the assumption that people are basically the same in the ways that we think, feel, and approach problems. Keirsey argues that it is far less desirable to attempt to change others (because it has little likelihood of success) than to attempt to understand, work with, and take advantage of normal differences. Companies can use this type of questionnaire to help team members understand how each person can contribute to team performance. For example, Lucent Technology used the Myers-Briggs Type Indicator to help build trust and understanding among 500 engineers in 13 time zones and 3 continents in a distributed development project.

1. Access the Keirsey Temperament Sorter using your Internet browser. Type in the following url:

   ⟨www.keirsey.com/cgi-bin/keirsey/newkts.cgi⟩.

2. Once you complete and score the questionnaire, print the description of your personality type.

3. Read the information on the Web site about each personality type. Become familiar with each.

4. Bring to class a sheet of paper containing your name and your personality type: Guardian, Artisan, Idealist, or Rational. Your instructor will either put you into a group containing people with the same predominant style or into a group with representatives from each type. She or he may then give each group a number. The instructor will then give the teams a project to accomplish. Each group will have approximately 30 minutes to do the project. It may be to solve a problem, analyze a short case, or propose a new entrepreneurial venture. The instructor will provide you with very little guidance other than to form and number the groups, give them the project, and keep track of time. He or she may move from group to group to sit in on each team's progress. When the time is up, the instructor will ask a spokesperson from each group to (1) describe the process the group went through and (2) present orally each group's ideas. After each group makes its presentation, the instructor may choose one or more of the following:

   - On a sheet of paper, each person in the class identifies his or her personality type and votes which team did the best on the project.

   - The class as a whole tries to identify each group's dominant decision-making style in terms of how they did their assignment. See how many people vote for one of the four types for each team.

   - Each member of a group guesses if she or he was put into a team composed of the same personality types or in one composed of all four personality types.

Key Terms

Notes

1. B. O'Reilly, "The Rent-A-Car Jocks Who Made Enterprise #1," *Fortune* (October 28, 1996), pp. 125–128.
2. The numbers are approximate averages from 3 separate studies of top management turnover after mergers. See M. Lubatkin, D. Schweiger, and Y. Weber, "Top Management Turnover in Related M&Ss: An Additional Test of the Theory of Relative Standing," *Journal of Management* 25, 1 (1999), pp. 55–73.
3. R. N. Ashkenas and S. C. Francis, "Integration Managers: Special Leaders for Special Times," *Harvard Business Review* (November–December 2000), pp. 108–116.
4. J. Hoerr, "Sharpening Minds for a Competitive Edge," *Business Week* (December 17, 1990), pp. 72–78.
5. "Training and Human Resources," *Business Strategy News Review* (July 2000), p. 6.
6. *High Performance Work Practices and Firm Performance* (Washington, DC: U.S. Department of Labor, Office of the American Workplace, 1993), pp. i, 4.
7. T. T. Baldwin, C. Danielson, and W. Wiggenhorn, "The Evolution of Learning Strategies in Organizations: From Employee Development to Business Redefinition," *Academy of Management Executive* (November 1997), pp. 47–58; K. Kelly, "Motorola: Training for the Millennium," *Business Week* (March 28, 1996), pp. 158–161.
8. R. Henkoff, "Companies That Train Best," *Fortune* (March 22, 1993), pp. 62–75.
9. For further details, see J. A. Byrne, *Chainsaw: The Notorious Career of Al Dunlap in the Era of Profit-at-Any-Price* (NY: HarperBusiness, 1999).
10. D. K. Datta and N. Rajagopalan, "Industry Structure and CEO Characteristics: An Empirical Study of Succession Events," *Strategic Management Journal* (September 1998), pp. 833–852; A. S. Thomas and K. Ramaswamy, "Environmental Change and Management Staffing: A Comment," *Journal of Management* (Winter 1993), pp. 877–887; J. P. Guthrie, C. M. Grimm, and K. G. Smith, "Environmental Change and Management Staffing: An Empirical Study," *Journal of Management* (December 1991), pp. 735–748.
11. J. Greco, "The Search Goes On," *Journal of Business Strategy* (September/October 1997), pp. 22–25; W. Ocasio and H. Kim, "The Circulation of Corporate Control: Selection of Functional Backgrounds on New CEOs in Large U.S. Manufacturing Firms, 1981–1992," *Administrative Science Quarterly* (September 1999), pp. 532–562.
12. R. Drazin and R. K. Kazanjian, "Applying the Del Technique to the Analysis of Cross-Classification Data: A Test of CEO Succession and Top Management Team Development," *Academy of Management Journal* (December 1993), pp. 1374–1399; W. E. Rothschild, "A Portfolio of Strategic Leaders," *Planning Review* (January/February 1996), pp. 16–19.
13. R. Subramanian and C. M. Sanchez, "Environmental Change and Management Staffing: An Empirical Examination of the Electric Utilities Industry," *Journal of Business Strategies* (Spring 1998), pp. 17–34.
14. J. A. Parnell, "Functional Background and Business Strategy: The Impact of Executive-Strategy Fit on Performance," *Journal of Business Strategies* (Spring 1994), pp. 49–62.
15. M. Smith and M. C. White, "Strategy, CEO Specialization, and Succession," *Administrative Science Quarterly* (June 1987), pp. 263–280.
16. A. Bianco, L. Lavelle, J. Merrit, and A. Barrett, "The CEO Trap," *Business Week* (December 11, 2000), pp. 86–92.
17. M. Leuchter, "Management Farm Teams," *Journal of Business Strategy* (May/June 1998), pp. 29–32.
18. D. C. Carey and D. Ogden, *CEO Succession: A Window on How Boards Do It Right When Choosing a New Chief Executive* (NY: Oxford University Press, 2000).
19. A. A. Buchko and D. DiVerde, "Antecedents, Moderators, and Consequences of CEO Turnover: A Review and Reconceptualization," Paper presented to *Midwest Academy of Management* (Lincoln, NE: 1997), p. 10; W. Ocasio, "Institutionalized Action and Corporate Governance: The Reliance on Rules of CEO Succession," *Administrative Science Quarterly* (June 1999), pp. 384–416.
20. C. Gopinath, "Turnaround: Recognizing Decline and Initiating Intervention," *Long Range Planning* (December 1991), pp. 96–101.
21. K. B. Schwartz and K. Menon, "Executive Succession in Failing Firms," *Academy of Management Journal* (September 1985), pp. 680–686; A. A. Cannella, Jr., and M. Lubatkin, "Succession as a Sociopolitical Process: Internal Impediments to Outsider Selection," *Academy of Management Journal* (August 1993), pp. 763–793; W. Boeker and J. Goodstein, "Performance and Succession Choice: The Moderating Effects of Governance and Ownership," *Academy of Management Journal* (February 1993), pp. 172–186.
22. W. Boeker, "Executive Migration and Strategic Change: The Effect of Top Manager Movement on Product-Market Entry," *Administrative Science Quarterly* (June 1997), pp. 213–236.
23. P. Lorange and D. Murphy, "Bringing Human Resources Into Strategic Planning: System Design Characteristics," in *Strategic Human Resource Management*, edited by C. J. Fombrun, N. M. Tichy, and M. A. Devanna (New York: John Wiley & Sons, 1984), pp. 281–283.
24. R. Sharpe, "As Leaders, Women Rule," *Business Week* (November 20, 2000), pp. 75–84.
25. R. A. Pitts, "Strategies and Structures for Diversification," *Academy of Management Journal* (June 1997), pp. 197–208.
26. K. E. Mishra, G. M. Spreitzer, and A. K. Mishra, "Preserving Employee Morale During Downsizing," *Sloan Management Review* (Winter 1998), pp. 83–95.
27. B. O'Reilly, "Is Your Company Asking Too Much?" *Fortune* (March 12, 1990), p. 41. For more information on the emotional reactions of survivors of downsizing, see C. R. Stoner and R. I. Hartman, "Organizational Therapy: Building Survivor Health & Competitiveness," *SAM Advanced Management Journal* (Summer 1997), pp. 15–31, 41.
28. T. M. Amabile and R. Conti, "Changes in the Work Environment for Creativity During Downsizing," *Academy of Management Journal* (December 1999), pp. 630–640; A. G. Bedeian and A. A. Armenakis, "The Cesspool Syndrome: How Dreck Floats to the Top of Declining Organizations," *Academy of Management Executive* (February 1998), pp. 58–67.
29. *Wall Street Journal* (December 22, 1992), p. B1.
30. G. D. Bruton, J. K. Keels, and C. L. Shook, "Downsizing the Firm: Answering the Strategic Questions," *Academy of Management Executive* (May 1996), pp. 38–45.
31. M. A. Hitt, B. W. Keats, H. F. Harback, and R. D. Nixon, "Rightsizing: Building and Maintaining Strategic Leadership and Long-Term Competitiveness," *Organizational Dynamics* (Autumn 1994), pp. 18–32. For additional suggestions, see T. Mroczkowski and M. Hanaoka, "Effective Rightsizing Strategies in Japan and America: Is There a Convergence of Employment Practices?" *Academy of Management Executive* (May 1997), pp. 57–67.
32. J. S. Black and H. B. Gregersen, "The Right Way to Manage Expats," *Harvard Business Review* (March–April 1999), pp. 52–61.
33. Black and Gregersen, p. 54.
34. J. I. Sanchez, P. E. Spector, and C. L. Cooper, "Adapting to a Boundaryless World: A Developmental Expatriate Model," *Academy of Management Executive* (May 2000), pp. 96–106.

35. R. L. Tung, *The New Expatriates* (Cambridge, MA: Ballinger, 1988); J. S. Black, M. Mendenhall, and G. Oddou, "Toward a Comprehensive Model of International Adjustment: An Integration of Multiple Theoretical Perspectives," *Academy of Management Review* (April 1991), pp. 291–317.

36. Black and Gregersen, p. 54.

37. G. Stern, "GM Executive's Ties to Native Country Help Auto Maker Clinch Deal in China," *Wall Street Journal* (November 2, 1995), p. B7.

38. K. Roth, "Managing International Interdependence: CEO Characteristics in a Resource-Based Framework," *Academy of Management Journal* (February 1995), pp. 200–231.

39. J. S. Lublin, "An Overseas Stint Can Be a Ticket to the Top," *Wall Street Journal* (January 29, 1996), pp. B1, B2.

40. P. Elstrom and S. V. Brull, "Mitsubishi's Morass," *Business Week* (June 3, 1996), p. 35.

41. G. G. Gordon, "The Relationship of Corporate Culture to Industry Sector and Corporate Performance," in *Gaining Control of the Corporate Culture,* edited by R. H. Kilmann, M. J. Saxton, R. Serpa, and Associates (San Francisco: Jossey-Bass, 1985), p. 123; T. Kono, "Corporate Culture and Long-Range Planning," *Long Range Planning* (August 1990), pp. 9–19.

42. T. J. Tetenbaum, "Seven Key Practices that Improve the Chance for Expected Integration and Synergies," *Organizational Dynamics* (Autumn 1999), pp. 22–35.

43. A. R. Malekzadeh and A. Nahavandi, "Making Mergers Work by Managing Cultures," *Journal of Business Strategy* (May/June 1990), pp. 53–57; A. Nahavandi and A. R. Malekzadeh, "Acculturation in Mergers and Acquisitions," *Academy of Management Review* (January 1988), pp. 79–90.

44. Lubatkin, Schweiger, and Weber, pp. 55–73.

45. J. J. Keller, "Why AT&T Takeover of NCR Hasn't Been a Real Bell Ringer," *Wall Street Journal* (September 19, 1995), pp. A1, A5.

46. S. S. Masterson and M. S. Taylor, "Total Quality Management and Performance Appraisal: An Integrative Perspective," *Journal of Quality Management 1,* No. 1 (1996), pp. 67–89.

47. T. Y. Choi and O. C. Behling, "Top Managers and TQM Success: One More Look After All These Years," *Academy of Management Executive* (February 1997), pp. 37–47.

48. R. J. Schonberger, "Total Quality Management Cuts a Broad Swath—Through Manufacturing and Beyond," *Organizational Dynamics* (Spring 1992), pp. 16–28.

49. T. C. Powell, "Total Quality Management as Competitive Advantage: A Review and Empirical Study," *Strategic Management Journal* (January 1995), pp. 15–37.

50. G. Hofstede, *Cultures and Organizations: Software of the Mind* (London: McGraw-Hill, 1991); G. Hofstede and M. H. Bond, "The Confucius Connection: From Cultural Roots to Economic Growth," *Organizational Dynamics* (Spring 1988), pp. 5–21; R. Hodgetts, "A Conversation with Geert Hofstede," *Organizational Dynamics* (Spring 1993), pp. 53–61.

51. See Hofstede and Bond, "The Confucius Connection," pp. 12–13.

52. "Emerging-Market Indicators," *The Economist* (October 7, 2000), p. 124.

53. T. T. Herbert, "Multinational Strategic Planning: Matching Central Expectations to Local Realities," *Long Range Planning* (February 1999), pp. 81–87.

54. Hofstede and Bond, "The Confucius Connection," p. 20.

55. U. G. Gupta and F. J. Hebert, "Is Your Company Ready for an Intranet?" *SAM Advanced Management Journal* (Autumn 1998), pp. 11–17, 26.

56. T. A. Stewart, "Does Anyone Around Here Know . . . ?" *Fortune* (September 29, 1997), pp. 279–280.

57. C. Metz, "Work Together," *PC Magazine* (July 2000), pp. 171–172.

58. M. J. Cronin, "Ford's Intranet Success," *Fortune* (March 30, 1998), p. 158.

59. Gupta and Hebert, p. 16.

60. J. Warner, "21st Century Capitalism: Snapshot of the Next Century," *Business Week* (November 18, 1994), p. 194.

61. D. Keirsey, *Please Understand Me II* (Del Mar, CA: Prometheus Nemesis Book Co., 1998).

chapter 10

Evaluation and Control

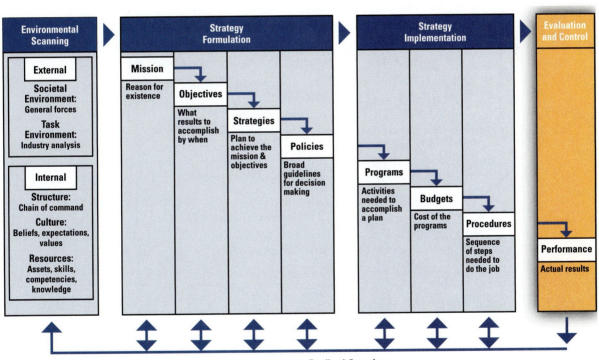

Environmental Scanning	Strategy Formulation	Strategy Implementation	Evaluation and Control

Feedback/Learning

Nucor Corporation, one of the most successful steel firms operating in the United States, keeps its evaluation and control process simple and easy to manage. According to Kenneth Iverson, Chairman of the Board:

We try to keep our focus on what really matters—bottom-line performance and long-term survival. That's what we want our people to be thinking about. Management takes care not to distract the company with a lot of talk about other issues. We don't clutter the picture with lofty vision statements or ask employees to pursue vague, intermediate objectives like "excellence" or burden them with complex business strategies. Our competitive strategy is to build manufacturing facilities

241

economically and to operate them efficiently. Period. Basically, we ask our employees to produce more product for less money. Then we reward them for doing that well.[1]

The **evaluation and control process** ensures that the company is achieving what it set out to accomplish. It compares performance with desired results and provides the feedback necessary for management to evaluate results and take corrective action, as needed. This process can be viewed as a five-step feedback model, as depicted in **Figure 10–1.**

1. **Determine what to measure**. Top managers and operational managers need to specify what implementation processes and results will be monitored and evaluated. The processes and results must be capable of being measured in a reasonably objective and consistent manner. The focus should be on the most significant elements in a process—the ones that account for the highest proportion of expense or the greatest number of problems. Measurements must be found for all important areas, regardless of difficulty.

2. **Establish standards of performance**. Standards used to measure performance are detailed expressions of strategic objectives. They are measures of acceptable performance results. Each standard usually includes a tolerance range, which defines acceptable deviations. Standards can be set not only for final output, but also for intermediate stages of production output.

3. **Measure actual performance**. Measurements must be made at predetermined times.

4. **Compare actual performance with the standard.** If actual performance results are within the desired tolerance range, the measurement process stops here.

5. **Take corrective action**. If actual results fall outside the desired tolerance range, action must be taken to correct the deviation. The following questions must be answered:
   a. Is the deviation only a chance fluctuation?
   b. Are the processes being carried out incorrectly?
   c. Are the processes appropriate to the achievement of the desired standard? Action must be taken that will not only correct the deviation, but will also prevent its happening again.
   d. Who is the best person to take corrective action?

Top management is often better at the first two steps of the control model than it is in the last three follow-through steps. It tends to establish a control system and then delegate the implementation to others. This can have unfortunate results. Nucor is unusual in its ability to deal with the entire evaluation and control process.

Figure 10–1
Evaluation and Control Process

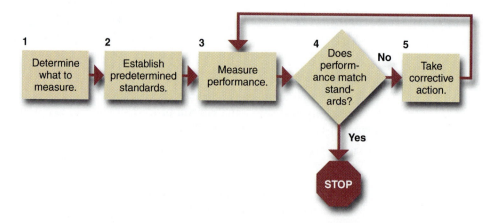

10.1 Evaluation and Control in Strategic Management

Evaluation and control information consists of performance data and activity reports (gathered in Step 3 of **Figure 10–1**). If undesired performance results because the strategic management processes were inappropriately used, operational managers must know about it so that they can correct the employee activity. Top management need not be involved. If, however, undesired performance results from the processes themselves, top managers, as well as operational managers, must know about it so that they can develop new implementation programs or procedures. Evaluation and control information must be relevant to what is being monitored. One of the obstacles to effective control is the difficulty in developing appropriate measures of important activities and outputs.

An application of the control process to strategic management is depicted in **Figure 10–2**. It provides strategic managers with a series of questions to use in evaluating an implemented strategy. Such a strategy review is usually initiated when a gap appears between a company's financial objectives and the expected results of current activities. After answering the proposed set of questions, a manager should have a good idea of where the problem originated and what must be done to correct the situation.

10.2 Measuring Performance

Performance is the end result of activity. Which measures to select to assess performance depends on the organizational unit to be appraised and the objectives to be achieved. The objectives that were established earlier in the strategy formulation part of the strategic management process (dealing with profitability, market share, and cost reduction, among others) should certainly be used to measure corporate performance once the strategies have been implemented.

APPROPRIATE MEASURES

Some measures, such as return on investment (ROI), are appropriate for evaluating the corporation's or division's ability to achieve a profitability objective. This type of measure, however, is inadequate for evaluating additional corporate objectives such as social responsibility or employee development. Even though profitability is a corporation's major objective, ROI can be computed only after profits are totaled for a period. It tells what happened after the fact— not what is happening or what will happen. A firm, therefore, needs to develop measures that predict likely profitability. These are referred to as **steering controls** because they measure variables that influence future profitability. One example of this type of control is the use of control charts in Statistical Process Control (SPC). In SPC, workers and managers maintain charts and graphs detailing quality and productivity on a daily basis. They are thus able to make adjustments to the system before it gets out of control.[2]

TYPES OF CONTROLS

Controls can be established to focus on actual performance results (output), the activities that generate the performance (behavior), or on resources that are used in performance (input). **Behavior controls** specify how something is to be done through policies, rules, standard operating procedures, and orders from a superior. **Output controls** specify what is to be accomplished by focusing on the end result of the behaviors through the use of objectives and performance targets or milestones. **Input controls** focus on resources, such as knowledge, skills, abilities, values, and motives of employees.[3]

Figure 10–2
Evaluating an Implemented Strategy

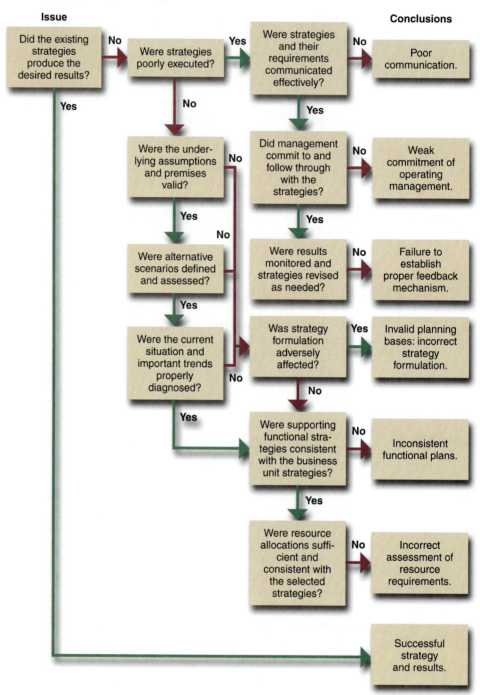

Behavior, output, and input controls are not interchangeable. Behavior controls (such as following company procedures, making sales calls to potential customers, and getting to work on time) are most appropriate when performance results are hard to measure but the cause–effect connection between activities and results is clear. Output controls (such as sales quotas, specific cost reduction or profit objectives, and surveys of customer satisfaction) are most appropriate when specific output measures have been agreed on but the cause–effect connection between activities and results is not clear. Input controls (such as number of years of education and experience) are most appropriate when output is difficult to measure and there is no clear cause–effect relationship between behavior and performance (such as in college teaching). Corporations following the strategy of conglomerate diversification tend to emphasize output controls with their divisions and subsidiaries (presumably because they are managed independently of each other); whereas, corporations following concentric diversification use all three types of controls (presumably because synergy is desired).[4] Even if all three types of control are used, one or two of them may be emphasized more than another depending on the circumstances. For example, Muralidharan and Hamilton propose that as a multinational corporation moves through its stages of development, its emphasis on control should shift from being primarily output at first, to behavioral, and finally to input control.[5]

One example of an increasingly popular behavior control is the **ISO 9000 Standards Series** on quality management and assurance developed by the International Standards Association of Geneva, Switzerland. The ISO 9000 series (composed of five sections from 9000 to 9004) is a way of objectively documenting a company's high level of quality operations. ISO 9000 and 9004 contain guidelines for use with the other sections; 9001 is the most comprehensive standard; 9002 is less stringent; 9003 is used only for inspecting and testing procedures. A company wanting certification would probably document its process for product introductions, among other things. ISO 9001 would require this firm to separately document design input, design process, design output, and design verification—a large amount of work. Although the average total cost for a company to be certified is close to $250,000, the annual savings are around $175,000 per company.[6]

Many corporations view ISO 9000 certification as assurance that a supplier sells quality products. Firms such as DuPont, Hewlett-Packard, and 3M have facilities registered to ISO standards. Companies in over 60 countries, including Canada, Mexico, Japan, the United States (including the entire U.S. auto industry), and the European Union (EU), are requiring ISO 9000 certification of their suppliers. By 1996, close to 100,000 firms were registered worldwide.[7] In one survey of manufacturing executives, 51% of the executives found that certification increased their international competitiveness. Other executives noted that it signaled their commitment to quality and gave them a strategic advantage over noncertified competitors.[8]

ACTIVITY-BASED COSTING

Activity-based costing (ABC) is a new accounting method for allocating indirect and fixed costs to individual products or product lines based on the value-added activities going into that product.[9] This accounting method is thus very useful in doing a value-chain analysis of a firm's activities for making outsourcing decisions. Traditional cost accounting, in contrast, focuses on valuing a company's inventory for financial reporting purposes. To obtain a unit's cost, cost accountants typically add direct labor to the cost of materials. Then they compute overhead from rent to R&D expenses, based on the number of direct labor hours it takes to make a product. To obtain unit cost, they divide the total by the number of items made during the period under consideration.

Traditional cost accounting is useful when direct labor accounts for most of total costs and a company produces just a few products requiring the same processes. This may have been true of companies during the early part of the twentieth century, but it is no longer relevant today when overhead may account for as much as 70% of manufacturing costs. According to Bob Van Der Linde, CEO of a contract manufacturing services firm in San Diego, California: "Overhead is 80% to 90% in our industry, so allocation errors lead to pricing errors, which could easily bankrupt the company."[10] The appropriate allocation of indirect costs and overhead has thus become crucial for decision making. The traditional volume-based cost-driven system systematically understates the cost per unit of products with low sales volumes and products with a high degree of complexity. Similarly, it overstates the cost per unit of products with high sales volumes and with a low degree of complexity.[11]

ABC accounting allows accountants to charge costs more accurately than the traditional method because it allocates overhead far more precisely. For example, imagine a production line in a pen factory where black pens are made in high volume and blue pens in low volume. Assume it takes eight hours to retool (reprogram the machinery) to shift production from one kind of pen to the other. The total costs include supplies (the same for both pens), the direct labor of the line workers, and factory overhead. In this instance, a very significant part of the overhead cost is the cost of reprogramming the machinery to switch from one pen to another. If the company produces 10 times as many black pens as blue pens, 10 times the cost of the reprogramming expenses will be allocated to the black pens as to the blue pens under traditional cost accounting methods. This approach underestimates, however, the true cost of making the blue pens.

ABC accounting, in contrast, first breaks down pen manufacturing into its activities. It is then very easy to see that it is the activity of changing pens that triggers the cost of retooling. The ABC accountant calculates an average cost of setting up the machinery and charges it against each batch of pens that requires retooling regardless of the size of the run. Thus a product carries only those costs for the overhead it actually consumes. Management is now able to discover that its blue pens cost almost twice as much as do the black pens. Unless the company is able to charge a higher price for its blue pens, it cannot make a profit on these pens. Unless there is a strategic reason why it must offer blue pens (such as a key customer who must have a small number of blue pens with every large order of black pens or a marketing trend away from black to blue pens), the company will earn significantly greater profits if it completely stops making blue pens.[12]

PRIMARY MEASURES OF CORPORATE PERFORMANCE

The days when simple financial measures such as ROI or EPS were used alone to assess overall corporate performance are coming to an end. Analysts now recommend a broad range of methods to evaluate the success or failure of a strategy. Some of these methods are stakeholder measures, shareholder value, and the balanced scorecard approach. Even though each of these methods has its supporters as well as detractors, the current trend is clearly toward more complicated financial measures and an increasing use of nonfinancial measures of corporate performance.[13] For example, research indicates that companies pursuing strategies founded on innovation and new product development now tend to favor nonfinancial over financial measures.[14]

Traditional Financial Measures

The most commonly used measure of corporate performance (in terms of profits) is **return on investment (ROI)**. It is simply the result of dividing net income before taxes by total assets. Although using ROI has several advantages, it also has several distinct limitations. (See **Table 10–1**.) Although ROI gives the impression of objectivity and precision, it can be easily manipulated.

Earnings per share (EPS), dividing net earnings by the number of shares of common stock issued, also has several deficiencies as an evaluation of past and future performance.

Table 10–1 Advantages and Limitations of Using ROI as a Measure of Corporate Performance

Advantages

1. ROI is a single comprehensive figure influenced by everything that happens.
2. It measures how well the division manager uses the property of the company to generate profits. It is also a good way to check on the accuracy of capital investment proposals.
3. It is a common denominator that can be compared with many entities.
4. It provides an incentive to use existing assets efficiently.
5. It provides an incentive to acquire new assets only when doing so would increase the return.

Limitations

1. ROI is very sensitive to depreciation policy. Depreciation write-off variances between divisions affect ROI performance. Accelerated depreciation techniques increase ROI, conflicting with capital budgeting discounted cash-flow analysis.
2. ROI is sensitive to book value. Older plants with more depreciated assets have relatively lower investment bases than newer plants (note also the effect of inflation), thus increasing ROI. Note that asset investment may be held down or assets disposed of in order to increase ROI performance.
3. In many firms that use ROI, one division sells to another. As a result, transfer pricing must occur. Expenses incurred affect profit. Since, in theory, the transfer price should be based on the total impact on firm profit, some investment center managers are bound to suffer. Equitable transfer prices are difficult to determine.
4. If one division operates in an industry that has favorable conditions and another division operates in an industry that has unfavorable conditions, the former division will automatically "look" better than the other.
5. The time span of concern here is short range. The performance of division managers should be measured in the long run. This is top management's timespan capacity.
6. The business cycle strongly affects ROI performance, often despite managerial performance.

Source: "Advantages and Limitations of ROI as a Measure of Corporate Performance" from *Organizational Policy and Strategic Management: Text and Cases*, 2nd ed. by James M. Higgins, copyright © 1983. Reproduced by permission of South-Western College Publishing, a division of Thomson Learning.

First, because alternative accounting principles are available, EPS can have several different but equally acceptable values, depending on the principle selected for its computation. Second, because EPS is based on accrual income, the conversion of income to cash can be near term or delayed. Therefore, EPS does not consider the time value of money. **Return on equity (ROE)**, dividing net income by total equity, also has its share of limitations because it is also derived from accounting-based data. In addition, EPS and ROE are often unrelated to a company's stock price. Because of these and other limitations, ROI, EPS and ROE by themselves are not adequate measures of corporate performance. Nevertheless, they are still better than the measures proposed by Internet startups during the 1990s. (See the ▓ **Internet Issue** feature for an example of how Amazon.com used "eyeballs" as its primary measure of performance.)

Stakeholder Measures

Each stakeholder has its own set of criteria to determine how well the corporation is performing. These criteria typically deal with the direct and indirect impact of corporate activities on stakeholder interests. Top management should establish one or more simple **stakeholder measures** for each stakeholder category so that it can keep track of stakeholder concerns. (See **Table 10–2**.)

Internet Issue

"Eyeballs" and "MUUs": Questionable Performance Measures

When Amazon.com's investor-relations team went to Denver in September, 2000, to seek funding from Marsico Capital Management, a mutual fund company, it presented its usual performance story. Even though the company had never shown a profit, the team told how Amazon.com had a "first to market" advantage and that its Web site received an extremely high number of "monthly unique visitors" and "eyeballs." Although such presentations had in the past raised millions of dollars for the company in stock purchases, it failed this time. Marsico was more concerned with when the company would become profitable. The Amazon.com team left empty-handed.

Until 2000, investors had been so enamored with new Internet firms that they made decisions based on novel measures of performance and firm valuation. They looked at measures such as "stickiness" (length of Web site visit), "eyeballs" (number of people who visit a Web site), and "mindshare" (brand awareness). Mergers and acquisitions were priced on multiples of "MUUs" (monthly unique users) or even on registered users. Since practically all the dot.com (Internet) firms failed to earn a profit, investors and analysts used these mea-

sures to estimate what the firms might be worth sometime in the future. By 2000, however, "the market concluded the (Net stock) valuations were insane," commented Charles Wolf, analyst with UBS Warburg.

With $2.1 billion in debt, Amazon.com's accumulated net loss from 1994 through 2000 was $1.75 billion. Its management had proposed that as the company grew in scale, its operations would become more efficient, and its gross margin per customer would improve. The question from investors was—when? For example, Amazon.com in 2000 averaged $160.01 annually in revenue from each of its 17 million customers for books and CDs. The annual cost of these books and CDs was $139.22, leaving a gross profit of $20.79 per customer. Annual marketing expenses amounted to $42.47 per customer. Using the traditional profit measure, Amazon.com was losing $21.68 per person. This didn't include an additional $19.83 per person for warehousing, shipping, customer service, and other operating expenses. The company did sell prominent positions on its Web site to firms such as drugstore.com for $105 million and car-dealer Greenlight.com for $145 million. With sufficient sales of space on its Web site, it could become profitable soon. Since Amazon.com realized an 80% margin from this sort of advertising, it was not so much an Internet retailer as a newspaper or television station existing off advertising.

Sources: E. Schonfeld, "How Much Are Your Eyeballs Worth?" *Fortune* (February 21, 2000), pp. 197–204; N. Byrnes, "Eyeballs, Bah! Figuring Dot-Coms' Real Worth," *Business Week* (October 30, 2000), p. 62; R. Barker, "Amazon: Cheaper—But Cheap Enough?" *Business Week* (December 4, 2000), p. 172.

Shareholder Value

Because of the belief that accounting-based numbers such as return on investment, return on equity, and earnings per share are not reliable indicators of a corporation's economic value, many corporations are using shareholder value as a better measure of corporate performance and strategic management effectiveness. **Shareholder value** can be defined as the present value of the anticipated future stream of cash flows from the business plus the value of the company if liquidated. Arguing that the purpose of a company is to increase shareholder wealth, shareholder value analysis concentrates on cash flow as the key measure of performance. The value of a corporation is thus the value of its cash flows discounted back to their present value, using the business's cost of capital as the discount rate. As long as the returns from a business exceed its cost of capital, the business will create value and be worth more than the capital invested in it.

The New York consulting firm Stern Stewart & Company devised and popularized two shareholder value measures: economic value added (EVA) and market value added (MVA). Well-known companies, such as Coca-Cola, General Electric, AT&T, Whirlpool, Quaker Oats, Eli Lilly, Georgia-Pacific, Polaroid, Sprint, Teledyne, and Tenneco have adopted MVA and/or

Table 10–2 A Sample Scorecard for "Keeping Score" with Stakeholders

Stakeholder Category	Possible Near-Term Measures	Possible Long-Term Measures
Customers	Sales ($ and volume) New customers Number of new customer needs met ("tries")	Growth in sales Turnover of customer base Ability to control price

Suppliers	Cost of raw material
	Delivery time
	Inventory
	Availability of raw material
		Growth rates of:
		  Raw material costs
		  Delivery time
		  Inventory
		New ideas from suppliers

Financial community	EPS Stock price Number of "buy" lists ROE	Ability to convince Wall Street of strategy Growth in ROE
Employees	Number of suggestions Productivity Number of grievances	Number of internal promotions Turnover
Congress	Number of new pieces of legislation that affect the firm Access to key members and staff	Number of new regulations that affect industry Ratio of "cooperative" vs. "competitive" encounters
Consumer advocate (CA)	Number of meetings Number of "hostile" encounters Number of times coalitions formed Number of legal actions	Number of changes in policy due to C.A. Number of C.A.-initiated "calls for help"
Environmentalists	Number of meetings Number of hostile encounters Number of times coalitions formed Number of EPA complaints Number of legal actions	Number of changes in policy due to environmentalists Number of environmentalist "calls for help"

Source: R. E. Freeman, *Strategic Management: A Stakeholder Approach* (Boston: Ballinger Publishing Company, 1984), p. 179. Copyright © 1984 by R. E. Freeman. Reprinted by permission.

EVA as the best yardstick for corporate performance. According to Sprint's CFO, Art Krause, "Unlike EPS, which measures accounting results, MVA gauges true economic performance."[15]

Economic value added (EVA) has become an extremely popular shareholder value method of measuring corporate and divisional performance and may be on its way to replacing ROI as the standard performance measure. EVA measures the difference between the pre-strategy and poststrategy value for the business. Simply put, EVA is after-tax operating income minus the total annual cost of capital. The formula to measure EVA is:

EVA = After tax operating income − (investment in assets × weighted average cost of capital)[16]

The cost of capital combines the cost of debt and equity. The annual cost of borrowed capital is the interest charged by the firm's banks and bondholders. To calculate the cost of equity, assume that shareholders generally earn about 6% more on stocks than on government bonds. If long-term treasury bills are selling at 7.5%, the firm's cost of equity should be 13.5%—more if the firm is in a risky industry. A corporation's overall cost of capital is the weighted-average cost of the firm's debt and equity capital. The investment in assets is the total the amount of capital invested in the business, including buildings, machines, computers, and investments in

R&D and training (allocating costs annually over their useful life). Since the typical balance sheet understates the investment made in a company, Stern Stewart has identified 150 possible adjustments, before EVA is calculated.[17] Multiply the firm's total investment in assets by the weighted-average cost of capital. Subtract that figure from after-tax operating income. If the difference is positive, the strategy (and the management employing it) is generating value for the shareholders. If it is negative, the strategy is destroying shareholder value.[18]

Roberto Goizueta, CEO of Coca-Cola, explains, "We raise capital to make concentrate, and sell it at an operating profit. Then we pay the cost of that capital. Shareholders pocket the difference."[19] Managers can improve their company's or business unit's EVA by: (1) earning more profit without using more capital, (2) using less capital, and (3) investing capital in high-return projects. Studies have found that companies using EVA outperform their median competitor by an average of 8.43% of total return annually.[20] EVA does, however, have some limitations. For one thing, it does not control for size differences across plants or divisions. Like ROI, managers can manipulate the numbers. Like ROI, EVA is an after-the-fact measure and cannot be used like a steering control.[21] Although proponents of EVA argue that EVA (unlike ROI, ROE, and/or ROS) has a strong relationship to stock price, other studies do not support this contention.[22]

Market value added (MVA) is the difference between the market value of a corporation and the capital contributed by shareholders and lenders. Like net present value, it measures the stock market's estimate of the net present value of a firm's past and expected capital investment projects. As such, MVA is the present value of future EVA.[23] To calculate MVA:

1. First add all the capital that has been put into a company—from shareholders, bondholders, and retained earnings.

2. Reclassify certain accounting expenses, such as R&D, to reflect that they are actually investments in future earnings. This provides the firm's total capital. So far, this is the same approach taken in calculating EVA.

3. Using the current stock price, total the value of all outstanding stock, adding it to the company's debt. This is the company's market value. If the company's market value is greater than all the capital invested in it, the firm has a positive MVA—meaning that management (and the strategy it is following) has created wealth. In some cases, however, the market value of the company is actually less than the capital put into it—shareholder wealth is being destroyed.

Microsoft, General Electric, Intel, and Coca-Cola tend to have high MVAs in the United States, whereas General Motors and RJR Nabisco have low ones.[24] Studies have shown that EVA is a predictor of MVA. Consecutive years of positive EVA generally lead to a soaring MVA.[25] Research also reveals that CEO turnover is significantly correlated with MVA and EVA, whereas ROA and ROE are not. This suggests that EVA and MVA may be more appropriate measures of the market's evaluation of a firm's strategy and its management than are the traditional measures of corporate performance.[26] Nevertheless, these measures consider only the financial interests of the shareholder and ignore other stakeholders, such as environmentalists and employees.

Balanced Scorecard Approach: Using Key Performance Measures

Rather than evaluate a corporation using a few financial measures, Kaplan and Norton argue for a "balanced scorecard," including nonfinancial as well as financial measures.[27] This approach is especially useful given that research indicates that nonfinancial assets explain 50% to 80% of a firm's value.[28] The **balanced scorecard** combines financial measures that tell the results of actions already taken with operational measures on customer satisfaction, internal processes, and the corporation's innovation and improvement activities—the drivers of future financial performance. Management should develop goals or objectives in each of four areas:

1. **Financial**: How do we appear to shareholders?
2. **Customer**: How do customers view us?
3. **Internal Business Perspective**: What must we excel at?
4. **Innovation and Learning**: Can we continue to improve and create value?

Each goal in each area (for example, avoiding bankruptcy in the financial area) is then assigned one or more measures, as well as a target and an initiative. These measures can be thought of as **key performance measures**—measures that are essential for achieving a desired strategic option.[29] For example, a company could include cash flow, quarterly sales growth, and ROE as measures for success in the financial area. It could include market share (competitive position goal) and percentage of new sales coming from new products (customer acceptance goal) as measures under the customer perspective. It could include cycle time and unit cost (manufacturing excellence goal) as measures under the internal business perspective. It could include time to develop next generation products (technology leadership objective) under the innovation and learning perspective.

Several companies are starting to use one or more variations of the scorecard and view it as complementary to its knowledge management activities. A study of the *Fortune 500* firms in the United States and the *Post 300* firms in Canada revealed the most popular nonfinancial measures to be customer satisfaction, customer service, product quality, market share, productivity, service quality, and core competencies. New product development, corporate culture, and market growth were not far behind.[30] CIGNA, for example, uses the balanced scorecard to determine employee bonuses. Moving cautiously, financial measures still account for half of the bonus at CIGNA.[31]

Evaluating Top Management

Through its strategy, audit, and compensation committees, a board of directors closely evaluates the job performance of the CEO and the top management team. Of course, it is concerned primarily with overall corporate profitability as measured quantitatively by return on investment, return on equity, earnings per share, and shareholder value. The absence of short-run profitability certainly contributes to the firing of any CEO. The board, however, is also concerned with other factors.

Members of the compensation committees of today's boards of directors generally agree that a CEO's ability to establish strategic direction, build a management team, and provide leadership are more critical in the long run than are a few quantitative measures. The board should evaluate top management not only on the typical output-oriented quantitative measures, but also on behavioral measures—factors relating to its strategic management practices. The specific items that a board uses to evaluate its top management should be derived from the objectives that both the board and top management agreed on earlier. If better relations with the local community and improved safety practices in work areas were selected as objectives for the year (or for five years), these items should be included in the evaluation. In addition, other factors that tend to lead to profitability might be included, such as market share, product quality, or investment intensity. Although the number of boards conducting systematic evaluations of their CEO are increasing in number, it is estimated that no more than half of the boards do so.

An increasing number of companies are using a 17-item questionnaire developed by Charan that focuses on the four key areas of company performance, leadership of the organization, team-building and management succession, and leadership of external constituencies.[32] After taking an hour to complete the questionnaire, the board of KeraVision, Inc., used it as a basis for a lengthy discussion with the CEO, Thomas Loarie. The board criticized Loarie for "not tempering enthusiasm with reality" and urged Loarie to develop a clear management succession plan. The evaluation caused Loarie to involve the board more closely in setting the company's primary objectives and discussing "where we are, where we want to go, and the operating environment."[33]

Management audits are very useful to boards of directors in evaluating management's handling of various corporate activities. Management audits have been developed to evaluate activities such as corporate social responsibility, functional areas such as the marketing department, and divisions such as the international division, as well as to evaluate the corporation itself in a strategic audit. The strategic audit is explained in detail later in this chapter.

PRIMARY MEASURES OF DIVISIONAL AND FUNCTIONAL PERFORMANCE

Companies use a variety of techniques to evaluate and control performance in divisions, SBUs, and functional areas. If a corporation is composed of SBUs or divisions, it will use many of the same performance measures (ROI or EVA, for instance) that it uses to assess overall corporate performance. To the extent that it can isolate specific functional units such as R&D, the corporation may develop responsibility centers. It will also use typical functional measures such as market share and sales per employee (marketing), unit costs and percentage of defects (operations), percentage of sales from new products and number of patents (R&D), and turnover and job satisfaction (HRM). For example, FedEx uses Enhanced Tracker software with its COSMOS database to track the progress of its 2.5 to 3.5 million shipments daily. As a courier is completing her or his day's activities, the Enhanced Tracker asks if the person's package count equals the Enhanced Tracker's count. If the count is off, the software helps reconcile the differences.[34]

During strategy formulation and implementation, top management approves a series of programs and supporting **operating budgets** from its business units. During evaluation and control, actual expenses are contrasted with planned expenditures and the degree of variance is assessed. This is typically done on a monthly basis. In addition, top management will probably require **periodic statistical reports** summarizing data on such key factors as the number of new customer contracts, volume of received orders, and productivity figures.

Responsibility Centers

Control systems can be established to monitor specific functions, projects, or divisions. Budgets are one type of control system that is typically used to control the financial indicators of performance. **Responsibility centers** are used to isolate a unit so that it can be evaluated separately from the rest of the corporation. Each responsibility center, therefore, has its own budget and is evaluated on its use of budgeted resources. It is headed by the manager responsible for the center's performance. The center uses resources (measured in terms of costs or expenses) to produce a service or a product (measured in terms of volume or revenues). There are five major types of responsibility centers. The type is determined by the way the corporation's control system measures these resources and services or products.

1. **Standard Cost Centers:** Primarily used in manufacturing facilities, standard (or expected) costs are computed for each operation on the basis of historical data. In evaluating the center's performance, its total standard costs are multiplied by the units produced. The result is the expected cost of production, which is then compared to the actual cost of production.

2. **Revenue Centers:** Production, usually in terms of unit or dollar sales, is measured without consideration of resource costs (for example, salaries). The center is thus judged in terms of effectiveness rather than efficiency. The effectiveness of a sales region, for exam-

ple, is determined by comparing its actual sales to its projected or previous year's sales. Profits are not considered because sales departments have very limited influence over the cost of the products they sell.

3. **Expense Centers:** Resources are measured in dollars without consideration for service or product costs. Thus budgets will have been prepared for *engineered expenses* (those costs that can be calculated) and for *discretionary expenses* (those costs that can be only estimated). Typical expense centers are administrative, service, and research departments. They cost an organization money, but they only indirectly contribute to revenues.

4. **Profit Centers:** Performance is measured in terms of the difference between revenues (which measure production) and expenditures (which measure resources). A profit center is typically established whenever an organizational unit has control over both its resources and its products or services. By having such centers, a company can be organized into divisions of separate product lines. The manager of each division is given autonomy to the extent that she or he is able to keep profits at a satisfactory (or better) level.

   Some organizational units that are not usually considered potentially autonomous can, for the purpose of profit center evaluations, be made so. A manufacturing department, for example, can be converted from a standard cost center (or expense center) into a profit center; it is allowed to charge a transfer price for each product it "sells" to the sales department. The difference between the manufacturing cost per unit and the agreed-upon transfer price is the unit's "profit."

   Transfer pricing is commonly used in vertically integrated corporations and can work well when a price can be easily determined for a designated amount of product. Even though most experts agree that market-based transfer prices are the best choice, only 30% to 40% of companies use market price to set the transfer price. (Of the rest, 50% use cost; 10% to 20% use negotiation.)[35] When a price cannot be set easily, however, the relative bargaining power of the centers, rather than strategic considerations, tends to influence the agreed-upon price. Top management has an obligation to make sure that these political considerations do not overwhelm the strategic ones. Otherwise, profit figures for each center will be biased and provide poor information for strategic decisions at both corporate and divisional levels.

5. **Investment Centers:** Because many divisions in large manufacturing corporations use significant assets to make their products, their asset base should be factored into their performance evaluation. Thus it is insufficient to focus only on profits, as in the case of profit centers. An investment center's performance is measured in terms of the difference between its resources and its services or products. For example, two divisions in a corporation made identical profits, but one division owns a $3 million plant, whereas the other owns a $1 million plant. Both make the same profits, but one is obviously more efficient; the smaller plant provides the shareholders with a better return on their investment. The most widely used measure of investment center performance is return on investment (ROI).

Most single-business corporations, such as Apple Computer, tend to use a combination of cost, expense, and revenue centers. In these corporations, most managers are functional specialists and manage against a budget. Total profitability is integrated at the corporate level. Multidivisional corporations with one dominating product line, such as Anheuser-Busch, which have diversified into a few businesses but that still depend on a single product line (such as beer) for most of their revenue and income, generally use a combination of cost, expense, revenue, plus profit centers. Multidivisional corporations, such as General Electric, tend to emphasize investment centers—although in various units throughout the corporation other types of responsibility centers are also used. One problem with using responsibility centers, however, is that the separation needed to measure and evaluate a division's performance can diminish the level of cooperation among divisions that is needed to attain synergy for the corporation as a whole. (This problem is discussed later in this chapter under "Suboptimization.")

Using Benchmarking to Evaluate Performance

According to Xerox Corporation, the company that pioneered this concept in the United States, **benchmarking** is "the continual process of measuring products, services, and practices against the toughest competitors or those companies recognized as industry leaders."[36] Benchmarking, an increasingly popular program, is based on the concept that it makes no sense to reinvent something that someone else is already using. It involves openly learning how others do something better than one's own company so that one not only can imitate, but perhaps even improve on their current techniques. The benchmarking process usually involves the following steps:

- **Identify the area or process to be examined.** It should be an activity that has the potential to determine a business unit's competitive advantage.

- **Find behavioral and output measures of the area or process and obtain measurements.**

- **Select an accessible set of competitors and best-in-class companies against which to benchmark.** These may very often be companies that are in completely different industries, but perform similar activities. For example, when Xerox wanted to improve its order fulfillment, it went to L. L. Bean, the successful mail-order firm, to learn how it achieved excellence in this area.

- **Calculate the differences among the company's performance measurements and those of the best-in-class and determine why the differences exist.**

- **Develop tactical programs for closing performance gaps.**

- **Implement the programs and then compare the resulting new measurements with those of the best-in-class companies.**

Benchmarking has been found to produce best results in companies that are already well managed. Apparently poorer performing firms tend to be overwhelmed by the discrepancy between their performance and the benchmark, and they tend to view the benchmark as too difficult to reach.[37] Nevertheless, a survey by Bain & Company of 460 companies of various sizes across all U.S. industries indicated that over 70% were using benchmarking in either a major or limited manner.[38] Cost reductions range from 15% to 45%.[39] Benchmarking can also increase sales, improve goal setting, and boost employee motivation.[40] The average cost of a benchmarking study is around $100,000 involving 30 weeks of effort.[41] Manco, Inc., a small Cleveland-area producer of duct tape regularly benchmarks itself against Wal-Mart, Rubbermaid, and PepsiCo to enable it to better compete with giant 3M. The American Productivity & Quality Center, a Houston research group, established the International Benchmarking Clearinghouse composed of 600 leading techniques from over 250 companies (see ⟨www.apqc.org⟩).

INTERNATIONAL MEASUREMENT ISSUES

The three most widely used techniques for international performance evaluation are return on investment, budget analysis, and historical comparisons. In one study, 95% of the corporate officers interviewed stated that they use the same evaluation techniques for foreign and domestic operations. Rate of return was mentioned as the single most important measure.[42] However, ROI can cause problems when it is applied to international operations: Because of foreign currencies, different rates of inflation, different tax laws, and the use of transfer pricing, both the net income figure and the investment base may be seriously distorted.[43]

A study of 79 MNCs revealed that **international transfer pricing** from one country unit to another is primarily used not to evaluate performance but to minimize taxes.[44] Taxes are an important issue for MNCs given that corporate tax rates vary from over 40% in Canada, Japan, Italy, and the United States to 25% in Bolivia, 15% in Chile, and 10% to 15% in Zambia.[45] For example, the U.S. Internal Revenue Service contends that many Japanese firms doing business in the United States have artificially inflated the value of U.S. deliveries in order to reduce the profits and thus the taxes of their American subsidiaries.[46] Parts made in a subsidiary of a Japanese MNC in a low-tax country like Singapore can be shipped to its subsidiary in a high-tax country like the United States at such a high price that the U.S. subsidiary reports very little profit (and thus pays few taxes), while the Singapore subsidiary reports a very high profit (but also pays few taxes because of the lower tax rate). A Japanese MNC can, therefore, earn more profit worldwide by reporting less profit in high-tax countries and more profit in low-tax countries. Transfer pricing is an important factor, given that 56% of all trade in the triad and one-third of all international trade is composed of intercompany transactions.[47] Transfer pricing can thus be one way the parent company can reduce taxes and "capture profits" from a subsidiary. Other common ways of transferring profits to the parent company (often referred to as the **repatriation of profits**) are through dividends, royalties, and management fees.[48]

An important issue in international trade is **piracy**. Firms in developing nations around the world make money by making counterfeit copies of well-known name brand products and selling them globally. See the **Global Issue** feature to learn how this is being done.

Global Issue

The Impact of Piracy on International Trade

Many foreign manufacturers in China conservatively estimate that 30% of their products in the mainland are counterfeits. This includes products from Tide detergent and Budweiser beer to Marlboro cigarettes. Yamaha estimates that five out of every six bikes bearing its brand name are fake. Procter & Gamble estimates that 15% of the soaps and detergents under its Head & Shoulders, Vidal Sassoon, Safeguard, and Tide brands in China are counterfeit, costing the company $150 million in lost sales. According to Joseph M. Johnson, President of the China division of Bestfoods Asia Ltd, "We are spending millions of dollars to combat counterfeiting." The trend in counterfeiting seems to be increasing. In the first four months of 2000, for example, Gillette seized more fake products than it did in the past two years combined.

Tens of thousands of counterfeiters are currently active in China. They range from factories mixing shampoo and soap in back rooms to large state-owned enterprises making copies of soft drinks and beer. Other factories make everything from car batteries to automobiles. Mobile CD factories with optical disk-mastering machines counterfeit music and software. These factories in southern Guangdong or Fujian provinces truck their products to a central distribution center, such as the one in Yiwu (five hours by train from Shanghai). They may also be shipped across the border into Russia, Pakistan, Vietnam, or Burma. Chinese counterfeiters have developed a global reach through their connections with organized crime.

According to the market research firm, Automotive Resources, the profit margins on counterfeit shock absorbers can reach 80% versus only 15% for the real ones. Counterfeiters charge up to 80% less for an oil filter for a Mercedes than the $24 for an authentic filter.

Counterfeit products can be found around the world—not just in China. The worldwide cost of software piracy is around $12 million annually. For example, 27% of the software sold in the United States is pirated. That figure increases to around 50% in Brazil, Singapore, and Poland, and to over 90% in Russia, Indonesia, China, and Vietnam. Thanks to Napster and others, the music and book industries are in serious danger from piracy sites, according to Forrester Research, Inc. "As piracy increases and artists and authors break away from the publishers to go independent, record labels and book publishers will lose $3.1 billion and $1.5 billion, respectively, by 2005," warns the report by Forrester Research.

Sources: D. Roberts, F. Balfour, P. Magnusson, P. Engardio, and J. Lee, "China's Piracy Plague," *Business Week* (June 5, 2000), pp. 44–48; "Emerging Market Indicators: Software Piracy," *The Economist* (June 27, 1998), p. 108; "Piracy's Big-Business Victims," *Futurist Update* (December 2000).

Authorities in international business recommend that the control and reward systems used by a global MNC be different from those used by a multidomestic MNC.[49] The *multidomestic MNC* should use loose controls on its foreign units. The management of each geographic unit should be given considerable operational latitude, but it should be expected to meet some performance targets. Because profit and ROI measures are often unreliable in international operations, it is recommended that the MNC's top management, in this instance, emphasize budgets and nonfinancial measures of performance such as market share, productivity, public image, employee morale, and relations with the host country government.[50] Multiple measures should be used to differentiate between the worth of the subsidiary and the performance of its management.

The *global MNC*, however, needs tight controls over its many units. To reduce costs and gain competitive advantage, it is trying to spread the manufacturing and marketing operations of a few fairly uniform products around the world. Therefore, its key operational decisions must be centralized. Its environmental scanning must include research not only into each of the national markets in which the MNC competes, but also into the "global arena" of the interaction between markets. Foreign units are thus evaluated more as cost centers, revenue centers, or expense centers than as investment or profit centers because MNCs operating in a global industry do not often make the entire product in the country in which it is sold.

10.3 Strategic Information Systems

Before performance measures can have any impact on strategic management, they must first be communicated to those people responsible for formulating and implementing strategic plans. Strategic information systems can perform this function. They can be computer-based or manual, formal or informal. One of the key reasons given for the bankruptcy of International Harvester was the inability of the corporation's top management to precisely determine its income by major class of similar products. Because of this inability, management kept trying to fix ailing businesses and was unable to respond flexibly to major changes and unexpected events. In contrast, one of the key reasons for the success of Toys "R" Us and Wal-Mart has been management's use of the company's sophisticated information system to control purchasing decisions. Cash registers in the many U.S. Toys "R" Us and Wal-Mart retail stores transmit information daily to computers at each company's headquarters. Consequently managers know every morning exactly how many of each item have been sold the day before, how many have been sold so far in the year, and how this year's sales compare to last year's. The information system allows all reordering to be done automatically by computers without any managerial input. It also allows the company to experiment with new products without committing to big orders in advance. In effect, the system allows the customers to decide through their purchases what gets reordered.

ENTERPRISE RESOURCE PLANNING (ERP)

Many corporations around the world have adopted or are adopting **enterprise resource planning (ERP)** software. ERP unites all of a company's major business activities from order processing to production within a single family of software modules. The system provides instant access to critical information to everyone in the organization from the CEO to the factory floor worker. Because of the ability of ERP software to use a common information system throughout a company's many operations around the world, it is becoming the business information systems' global standard. The major providers of this software are SAP AG, Oracle, J. D. Edwards, Peoplesoft, Baan, and SSA.

The German company SAP AG originated the concept with its R/3 software system. Microsoft, for example, used R/3 to replace a tangle of 33 financial tracking systems in 26 subsidiaries. Even though it cost the company $25 million and took 10 months to install, R/3 annually saves Microsoft $18 million. Coca-Cola uses the R/3 system to enable a manager in Atlanta to use her personal computer to check the latest sales of 20-ounce bottles of Coke Classic in India. Owens-Corning envisions that its R/3 system will allow sales people to learn what is available at any plant or warehouse and to quickly assemble orders for customers.

ERP is, nevertheless, not for every company. The system is extremely complicated and demands a high level of standardization throughout a corporation. Its demanding nature often forces companies to change the way they do business. There are three reasons why ERP could fail: (1) insufficient tailoring of the software to fit the company, (2) inadequate training, and (3) insufficient implementation support.[51] Over the two-year period of installing R/3, Owens-Corning had to completely overhaul its operations. Because R/3 was incompatible with Apple Computer's very organic corporate culture, the company was only able to apply it to its order management and financial operations, but not to manufacturing. Other companies having difficulty installing and using ERP are Whirlpool, Hershey Foods, and Stanley Works. At Whirlpool, SAP's software led to missed and delayed shipments, causing Home Depot to cancel its agreement for selling Whirlpool products.[52]

DIVISIONAL AND FUNCTIONAL IS SUPPORT

At the divisional or SBU level of a corporation, the information system should be used to support, reinforce, or enlarge its business-level strategy through its decision support system. An SBU pursuing a strategy of overall cost leadership could use its information system to reduce costs either by improving labor productivity or improving the use of other resources such as inventory or machinery. Merrill Lynch took this approach when it developed PRISM software to provide its 500 U.S. retail offices with quick access to financial information in order to boost brokers' efficiency. Another SBU, in contrast, might want to pursue a differentiation strategy. It could use its information system to add uniqueness to the product or service and contribute to quality, service, or image through the functional areas. FedEx wanted to use superior service to gain a competitive advantage. It invested significantly in several types of information systems to measure and track the performance of its delivery service. Together, these information systems gave FedEx the fastest error-response time in the overnight delivery business.

Increasingly, corporations are connecting their intranets to other firms via extranets to implement strategic decisions and monitor their results. For example, Chicago-based Navistar no longer maintains a tire-and-rim inventory at its Springfield, Ohio, truck assembly plant. That responsibility is now being handled electronically by Goodyear Tire & Rubber, one of Navistar's suppliers. A Goodyear office in New York receives Navistar's manufacturing schedule and tire-and-rim requirements by electronic data interchange. The information is then sent to a Goodyear plant in Ohio where tires are mounted on rims. The completed assemblies are shipped to Navistar's Springfield plant—arriving just eight hours ahead of when they are needed. [53]

10.4 Problems in Measuring Performance

The measurement of performance is a crucial part of evaluation and control. The lack of quantifiable objectives or performance standards and the inability of the information system to provide timely and valid information are two obvious control problems. Without objective and timely measurements, it would be extremely difficult to make operational, let alone strategic, decisions. Nevertheless, the use of timely, quantifiable standards does not guarantee good performance. The very act of monitoring and measuring performance can cause side effects that interfere with overall corporate performance. Among the most frequent negative side effects are a short-term orientation and goal displacement.

SHORT-TERM ORIENTATION

Top executives report that in many situations they analyze neither the long-term implications of present operations on the strategy they have adopted nor the operational impact of a strategy on the corporate mission. Long-run evaluations are often not conducted because executives (1) don't realize their importance, (2) believe that short-run considerations are more important than long-run considerations, (3) aren't personally evaluated on a long-term basis, or (4) don't have the time to make a long-run analysis.[54] There is no real justification for the first and last "reasons." If executives realize the importance of long-run evaluations, they make the time needed to conduct them. Even though many chief executives point to immediate pressures from the investment community and to short-term incentive and promotion plans to support the second and third reasons, evidence does not always support their claims.[55]

Many accounting-based measures do, however, encourage a **short-term orientation**. **Table 10–1** indicates that one of the limitations of ROI as a performance measure is its short-term nature. In theory, ROI is not limited to the short run, but in practice it is often difficult to use this measure to realize long-term benefits for the company. Because managers can often manipulate both the numerator (earnings) and the denominator (investment), the resulting ROI figure can be meaningless. Advertising, maintenance, and research efforts can be reduced. Mergers can be undertaken that will do more for this year's earnings (and next year's paycheck) than for the division's or corporation's future profits. Research of 55 firms that engaged in major acquisitions revealed that even though the firms performed poorly after the acquisition, the acquiring firms' top management still received significant increases in compensation![56] Expensive retooling and plant modernization can be delayed as long as a manager can manipulate figures on production defects and absenteeism.

Research supports the conclusion that many CEOs and their friends on the board of directors compensation committee manipulate information to provide themselves a pay raise. For example, CEOs tend to announce bad news—thus reducing the company's stock price—just before the issuance of stock options. Once the options are issued, the CEOs tend to announce good news—thus raising the stock price and making their options more valuable.[57] Board compensation committees tend to expand the peer group comparison outside of their industry to include lower performing firms to justify a high raise to the CEO. They tend to do this when the company performs poorly, the industry performs well, the CEO is already highly paid, and when shareholders are powerful and active.[58]

GOAL DISPLACEMENT

Monitoring and measuring performance (if not carefully done) can actually result in a decline in overall corporate performance. **Goal displacement** is the *confusion of means with ends* and occurs when activities originally intended to help managers attain corporate objectives become ends in themselves—or are adapted to meet ends other than those for which they were intended. Two types of goal displacement are behavior substitution and suboptimization.

Behavior Substitution

Behavior substitution refers to a phenomenon when people substitute activities that do not lead to goal accomplishment for activities that do lead to goal accomplishment because the wrong activities are being rewarded. Managers, like most people, tend to focus more of their attention on those behaviors that are clearly measurable than on those that are not. Employees often receive little to no reward for engaging in hard-to-measure activities such as cooperation and initiative. However, easy-to-measure activities might have little to no relationship to the desired good performance. Rational people, nevertheless, tend to work for the rewards that the system has to offer. Therefore, people tend to substitute behaviors that are recognized and rewarded for those behaviors that are ignored, without regard to their contribution to goal accomplishment. A U.S. Navy quip sums up this situation: "What you inspect (or reward) is what you get." Sears, Roebuck & Co. thought that it would improve employee productivity by tying performance to rewards. It, therefore, paid commissions to its auto shop employees as a percentage of each repair bill. Behavior substitution resulted as employees altered their behavior to fit the reward system. The result was over-billed customers, charges for work never done, and a scandal that tarnished Sears' reputation for many years.[59]

The law governing the effect of measurement on behavior seems to be that *quantifiable measures drive out nonquantifiable measures.*

Suboptimization

Suboptimization refers to the phenomenon when a unit optimizes its goal accomplishment to the detriment of the organization as a whole. The emphasis in large corporations on developing separate responsibility centers can create some problems for the corporation as a whole. To the extent that a division or functional unit views itself as a separate entity, it might refuse to cooperate with other units or divisions in the same corporation if cooperation could in some way negatively affect its performance evaluation. The competition between divisions to achieve a high ROI can result in one division's refusal to share its new technology or work process improvements. One division's attempt to optimize the accomplishment of its goals can cause other divisions to fall behind and thus negatively affect overall corporate performance. One common example of suboptimization occurs when a marketing department approves an early shipment date to a customer as a means of getting an order and forces the manufacturing department into overtime production for this one order. Production costs are raised, which reduces the manufacturing department's overall efficiency. The end result might be that, although marketing achieves its sales goal, the corporation as a whole fails to achieve its expected profitability.

10.5 Guidelines for Proper Control

In designing a control system, top management should remember that *controls should follow strategy.* Unless controls ensure the use of the proper strategy to achieve objectives, there is a strong likelihood that dysfunctional side effects will completely undermine the implementation of the objectives. The following guidelines are recommended:

1. **Control should involve only the minimum amount of information** needed to give a reliable picture of events. Too many controls create confusion. *Focus on the strategic factors by following the 80/20 rule: monitor those 20% of the factors that determine 80% of the results.*

2. **Controls should monitor only meaningful activities and results**, regardless of measurement difficulty. If cooperation between divisions is important to corporate performance, some form of qualitative or quantitative measure should be established to monitor cooperation.

3. **Controls should be timely** so that corrective action can be taken before it is too late. Steering controls, controls that monitor or measure the factors influencing performance, should be stressed so that advance notice of problems is given.

4. **Long-term and short-term controls should be used**. If only short-term measures are emphasized, a short-term managerial orientation is likely.

5. **Controls should aim at pinpointing exceptions**. Only those activities or results that fall outside a predetermined tolerance range should call for action.

6. **Emphasize the reward of meeting or exceeding standards** rather than punishment for failing to meet standards. Heavy punishment of failure typically results in goal displacement. Managers will "fudge" reports and lobby for lower standards.

To the extent that the culture complements and reinforces the strategic orientation of the firm, there is less need for an extensive formal control system. In their book *In Search of Excellence*, Peters and Waterman state that "the stronger the culture and the more it was directed toward the marketplace, the less need was there for policy manuals, organization charts, or detailed procedures and rules. In these companies, people way down the line know what they are supposed to do in most situations because the handful of guiding values is crystal clear."[60] For example, at Eaton Corporation, the employees are expected to enforce the rules themselves. If someone misses too much work or picks fights with coworkers, other members of the production team point out the problem. According to Randy Savage, a long-time Eaton employee, "They say there are no bosses here, but if you screw up, you find one pretty fast."[61]

10.6 Strategic Incentive Management

To ensure congruence between the needs of the corporation as a whole and the needs of the employees as individuals, management and the board of directors should develop an incentive program that rewards desired performance. This reduces the likelihood of agency problems (when employees act to feather their own nest instead of building shareholder value) mentioned earlier in **Chapter 2**. Incentive plans should be linked in some way to corporate and divisional strategy. For example, a survey of 600 business units indicates that the pay mix associated with a growth strategy emphasizes bonuses and other incentives over salary and benefits, whereas the pay mix associated with a stability strategy has the reverse emphasis.[62] Research does indicate that SBU managers having long-term performance elements in their compensation program favor a long-term perspective and thus greater investments in R&D, capital equipment, and employee training.[63] The typical CEO pay package is composed of 21% salary, 27% short-term annual incentives, 16% long-term incentives, and 36% stock options.[64]

The following three approaches are tailored to help match measurements and rewards with explicit strategic objectives and timeframes.[65]

1. **Weighted-Factor Method:** This method is particularly appropriate for measuring and rewarding the performance of top SBU managers and group level executives when performance factors and their importance vary from one SBU to another. One corporation's measurements might contain the following variations: the performance of high-growth SBUs is measured in terms of market share, sales growth, designated future payoff, and progress on several future-oriented strategic projects; the performance of low-growth SBUs, in contrast, is measured in terms of ROI and cash generation; and the performance of medium-growth SBUs is measured for a combination of these factors. (Refer to **Table 10–3**.)

2. **Long-Term Evaluation Method:** This method compensates managers for achieving objectives set over a multiyear period. An executive is promised some company stock or "performance units" (convertible into money) in amounts to be based on long-term performance. An executive committee, for example, might set a particular objective in terms of growth in earnings per share during a five-year period. The giving of awards would be contingent on the corporation's meeting that objective within the designated time. Any executive who leaves the corporation before the objective is met receives nothing. The typical emphasis on stock price makes this approach more applicable to top management than to business unit managers. Because rising stock markets tend to raise the stock price of mediocre companies, there is a developing trend to index stock options to competitors or to the Standard & Poor's 500.[66]

3. **Strategic-Funds Method:** This method encourages executives to look at developmental expenses as being different from expenses required for current operations. The accounting statement for a corporate unit enters strategic funds as a separate entry below the current ROI. It is, therefore, possible to distinguish between those expense dollars consumed

Table 10–3 Weighted-Factor Approach to Strategic Incentive Management

Strategic Business Unit Category	Factor	Weight
High Growth	Return on assets	10%
	Cash flow	0%
	Strategic-funds programs (developmental expenses)	45%
	Market-share increase	45%
	Total	100%
Medium Growth	Return on assets	25%
	Cash flow	25%
	Strategic-funds programs (developmental expenses)	25%
	Market-share increase	25%
	Total	100%
Low Growth	Return on assets	50%
	Cash flow	50%
	Strategic-funds programs (developmental expenses)	0%
	Market-share increase	0%
	Total	100%

Source: Reprinted by permission of the publisher from "The Performance Measurement and Reward System: Critical to Strategic Management," by Paul J. Stonich, from *Organizational Dynamics* (Winter 1984), p. 51. Copyright © 1984 with permission from Elsevier Science.

in the generation of current revenues and those invested in the future of the business. Therefore, the manager can be evaluated on both a short- and a long-term basis and has an incentive to invest strategic funds in the future. (See **Table 10–4**.)

An effective way to achieve the desired strategic results through a reward system is to combine the three approaches:

1. Segregate strategic funds from short-term funds as is done in the strategic-funds method.

2. Develop a weighted-factor chart for each SBU.

3. Measure performance on three bases: The pretax profit indicated by the strategic-funds approach, the weighted factors, and the long-term evaluation of the SBUs' and the corporation's performance.

Genentech, General Electric, and Textron are some of the firms in which CEO compensation is contingent upon the company's achieving strategic objectives.[67]

Table 10–4 Strategic Funds Approach to an SBU's Profit-and-Loss Statement

Sales	$12,300,000
Cost of sales	−6,900,000
Gross margin	$ 5,400,000
General and administrative expenses	−3,700,000
Operating profit (return on sales)	$ 1,700,000
Strategic funds (development expenses)	−1,000,000
Pretax profit	$ 700,000

Source: Reprinted by permission of the publisher from "The Performance Measurement and Reward System: Critical to Strategic Management," by Paul J. Stonich, from *Organizational Dynamics* (Winter 1984), p. 52. Copyright © 1984 with permission from Elsevier Science.

10.7 Using the Strategic Audit to Evaluate Corporate Performance

The **strategic audit** provides a checklist of questions, by area or issue, that enables a systematic analysis of various corporate functions and activities to be made. (See **Appendix 10.A** at the end of this chapter.) It is a type of management audit and is extremely useful as a diagnostic tool to pinpoint corporatewide problem areas and to highlight organizational strengths and weaknesses.[68] The strategic audit can help determine why a certain area is creating problems for a corporation and help generate solutions to the problem.

The strategic audit is not an all-inclusive list, but it presents many of the critical questions needed for a detailed strategic analysis of any business corporation. Some questions or even some areas might be inappropriate for a particular company; in other cases, the questions may be insufficient for a complete analysis. However, each question in a particular area of the strategic audit can be broken down into an additional series of sub-questions. Develop these sub-questions when they are needed.

The strategic audit summarizes the key topics in the Strategic Management Model discussed in **Chapters 1** through **10**. As you look through the major headings of the audit in **Appendix 10.A**, note that it identifies by chapter, section, and page numbers where information about each topic can be found. The strategic audit puts into action the strategic decision-making process illustrated in **Figure 1–5**. The headings in the audit are the same as those shown in **Figure 1–5**:

1. Evaluate Current Performance Results
2. Review Corporate Governance
3. Scan and Assess the External Environment
4. Scan and Assess the Internal Environment
5. Analyze Strategic Factors Using SWOT
6. Generate and Evaluate Strategic Alternatives
7. Implement Strategies
8. Evaluate and Control

10.8 Impact of the Internet on Evaluation and Control

Privacy is becoming a major issue with the use of the Internet. According to the American Management Association, nearly 75% of U. S. companies actively monitored their workers' communications and on-the-job activities in 2000—more than double the number four years earlier. Around 54% tracked individual employees' Internet connections and 38% admitted storing and reviewing their employees' e-mail. About 45% of the companies surveyed had disciplined workers (16% fired them). For example, Xerox fired 40 employees for visiting pornographic Web sites.[69] New desktop software products now allow anyone—boss, business partner, or spouse—to track a person's Internet activities. One software firm advertises: "Secretly record everything your spouse, children, and employees do online." The U.S. Congress was considering in late 2000 several bills regarding computer surveillance, but none would make monitoring illegal.[70] According to Paul Saffo, Director, Institute of the Future,

What will end up happening—and it already is happening—is that privacy becomes an increasingly scarce good that you will pay increasingly more for. That is, if you want an unlisted phone number, you pay for that privilege. If you don't want your transactions tracked. . . . (you know, theoretically an electronic transaction could be tracked. In fact, the system's so screwed up I don't think anyone can find anything.) But, in theory, if you didn't want your transactions tracked, you would get cash and put up with the inconvenience of doing that. . . .

Well, I think the fact is there's a multiplicity of players in this. And everybody's trying to have their role. The problem is that the boundaries between the roles are not clear. The legislative process is a very heavy club and not a precise tool. On the other hand, high-tech in particular has a dreadful history about protecting privacy. Companies just can't help but put unique serial numbers in chips or unique serial numbers in software. This is an industry that still calls its customers "users." As far as I know, there are only two high-growth industries on this planet that reserve such a scornful term for their customers. The other one's in Columbia.[71]

Privacy is also an issue for companies wanting to safeguard confidential information from unwanted visitors. Computer hackers are seemingly able to get into almost any company through their Internet Web sites. In October 2000, hackers were able to view Microsoft's source code. They entered the giant software company by infecting the company's network with a Trojan horse program. This was probably done by sliding past disabled antivirus programs, static IP addresses at Microsoft (a problem with any site constantly connected to the Internet via a T-1, cable, or DSL line), and employee laptops used while telecommuting. With this program, hackers obtained Microsoft IP addresses, user names, and passwords in order to access the corporate network from somewhere in Russia.[72]

Intelligence agencies from America, Britain, Canada, Australia and New Zealand jointly monitor all international satellite communications traffic via a system called "Echelon" that can identify specific words or phrases from hundreds of thousand of messages. The National Security Agency (NSA) of the United States and its partners have been accused in the European Parliament of tapping into billions of messages per minutes ranging from telephone calls to e-mail. The NSA was said to have used the Echelon system to assist U.S. corporations to win two large business contracts in the mid-1990s.[73]

Even though the U.S. Congress passed a law allowing digital signature in July 2000, many people are still concerned that the Internet is not a secure means of communicating important or confidential information. Don't expect the Internet to replace FedEx or UPS anytime soon.

Projections for the 21st Century

- From 1994 to 2010, the number of miles traveled by air will double from 1.5 trillion to 3 trillion.
- From 1994 to 2010, the number of credit card transactions will increase from 1.5 trillion to 2 trillion.[74]

Discussion Questions

1. Is **Figure 10–1** a realistic model of the evaluation and control process?

2. What are some examples of behavior controls? Output controls? Input controls?

3. Is EVA an improvement over ROI, ROE, or EPS?

4. How much faith can a manager place in a transfer price as a substitute for a market price in measuring a profit center's performance?

5. Is the evaluation and control process appropriate for a corporation that emphasizes creativity? Are control and creativity compatible?

Strategic Practice Exercise

Each year, *Fortune* magazine publishes an article entitled, "America's Most Admired Companies." It lists the 10 most admired and the 10 least admired. *Fortune*'s rankings are based on scoring publicly held U.S. companies on what it calls "eight key attributes of reputation": innovativeness, quality of management, employee talent, quality of products/services, long-term investment value, financial soundness, social responsibility, and use of corporate assets. *Fortune* asks Clark, Martire & Bartolomeo to survey more than 10,000 executives, directors, and securities analysts. Respondents are asked to choose the companies they admire most, regardless of industry. *Fortune* has been publishing this list since 1982. The 2000 *Fortune* listing of the top 10 most admired were (starting with #1): GE, Microsoft, Dell Computer, Cisco Systems, Wal-Mart Stores, Southwest Airlines, Berkshire Hathaway, Intel, Home Depot, and Lucent Technologies. The bottom 10 were: Humana, Revlon, Trans World Airlines, CKE Restaurants, CHS Electronics, Rite Aid, Trump Resorts, Fruit of the Loom, Amerco, and Caremark Rx (least admired).

TRY ONE OF THESE EXERCISES:

1. Go to the library and find a "Most Admired Companies" article from the 1980s or early 1990s and compare that list to the latest one. (See ⟨www.fortune.com⟩ for latest list.) Which companies have fallen out of the top 10? Pick one of the companies to investigate why it is no longer "admired."

2. How much of the evaluation is dominated by the profitability of the company? See how many of the top 10 are very profitable and how many of the bottom 10 are losing money. How many of these companies also appear in *Fortune*'s "The 100 Best Companies to Work For"?

3. Pick one of the least admired companies in any year of the survey (such as Trump Resorts) and find out why that company has such a poor reputation. How many of the least admired had received bad publicity the previous year? How many of the least admired companies were listed in multiple years compared to the most admired companies?

Key Terms

80/20 rule (p. 259)
activity-based costing (ABC) (p. 245)
balanced scorecard (p. 250)
behavior controls (p. 243)
behavior substitution (p. 258)
benchmarking (p. 254)
earnings per share (EPS) (p. 246)
economic value added (EVA) (p. 249)
enterprise resource planning (ERP) (p. 256)
evaluation and control information (p. 243)
evaluation and control process (p. 242)
expense center (p. 253)

goal displacement (p. 258)
input controls (p. 243)
international transfer pricing (p. 255)
investment center (p. 253)
ISO 9000 Standards Series (p. 245)
key performance measures (p. 251)
long-term evaluation method (p. 260)
management audits (p. 252)
market value added (MVA) (p. 250)
operating budgets (p. 252)
output controls (p. 243)
performance (p. 243)
periodic statistical reports (p. 252)
piracy (p. 255)

profit center (p. 253)
repatriation of profits (p. 255)
responsibility centers (p. 252)
return on equity (ROE) (p. 247)
return on investment (ROI) (p. 246)
revenue center (p. 252)
shareholder value (p. 248)
short-term orientation (p. 258)
stakeholder measures (p. 247)
standard cost center (p. 252)
steering controls (p. 243)
strategic audit (pp. 252, 262)
strategic-funds method (p. 260)
suboptimization (p. 259)
transfer pricing (p. 253)
weighted-factor method (p. 260)

Strategic Audit of a Corporation

I. Current Situation

A. Current Performance
See Section 10.2 on pages 243–256.

How did the corporation perform the past year overall in terms of return on investment, market share, and profitability?

B. Strategic Posture
See Section 1.3 on pages 7–8.

1. What are the corporation's current mission, objectives, strategies, and policies? Are they clearly stated or are they merely implied from performance?
2. **Mission:** What business(es) is the corporation in? Is the mission statement appropriate?
3. **Objectives:** What are the corporate, business, and functional objectives? Are they consistent with each other, with the mission, and with the internal and external environments?
4. **Strategies:** What are the current corporate, business, and functional strategies? Are they consistent with each other, with the mission and objectives, and with the internal and external environments?
5. **Policies:** What are they? Are they consistent with each other, with the mission, objectives, and strategies, and with the internal and external environments?
6. Do the current mission, objectives, strategies, and policies reflect the corporation's international operations—whether global or multidomestic?

II. Corporate Governance

A. Board of Directors
See Section 2.1 on pages 26–36.

1. Who are the directors? Are they internal or external?
2. Do they own significant shares of stock?
3. Is the stock privately held or publicly traded? Are there different classes of stock with different voting rights?
4. What do they contribute to the corporation in terms of knowledge, skills, background, and connections? If the corporation has international operations, do board members have international experience?
5. How long have they served on the board?
6. What is their level of involvement in strategic management? Do they merely rubber-stamp top management's proposals or do they actively participate and suggest future directions?

B. Top Management · · · · · · · · · See Sections 2.2 to 2.4 on pages 35–43.

1. What person or group constitutes top management?

2. What are top management's chief characteristics in terms of knowledge, skills, background, and style? If the corporation has international operations, does top management have international experience? Are executives from acquired companies considered part of the top management team?

3. Has top management been responsible for the corporation's performance over the past few years? How many managers have been in their current position for less than three years? Were they internal promotions or external hires?

4. Has it established a systematic approach to strategic management?

5. What is its level of involvement in the strategic management process?

6. How well does top management interact with lower level managers and with the board of directors?

7. Are strategic decisions made ethically in a socially responsible manner?

8. What role do stock options play in executive compensation?

9. Is top management sufficiently skilled to cope with likely future challenges?

III. External Environment: Opportunities and Threats (SW<u>OT</u>)

A. Societal Environment · · · · · · · · · See Section 3.1 on pages 52–60.

1. What general environmental forces are currently affecting both the corporation and the industries in which it competes? Which present current or future threats? Opportunities? See **Table 3–1** on page 53.
   a) Economic
   b) Technological
   c) Political-legal
   d) Sociocultural

2. Are these forces different in other regions of the world?

B. Task Environment (Industry) · · · · · · · · · See Section 3.2 on pages 60–70.

1. What forces drive industry competition? Are these forces the same globally or do they vary from country to country?
   a) Threat of new entrants
   b) Bargaining power of buyers
   c) Threat of substitute products or services
   d) Bargaining power of suppliers
   e) Rivalry among competing firms
   f) Relative power of unions, governments, special interest groups, etc.

2. What key factors in the immediate environment (that is, customers, competitors, suppliers, creditors, labor unions, governments, trade associations, interest groups, local communities, and shareholders) are currently affecting the corporation? Which are current or future threats? Opportunities?

C. Summary of External Factors · · · · · · · · · See EFAS Table on pages 73–74.

Which of these forces and factors are the most important to the corporation and to the industries in which it competes at the present time? Which will be important in the future?

IV. Internal Environment: Strengths and Weaknesses (S<u>W</u>OT)

A. Corporate Structure

See Sections 4.3 and 8.4 on pages 87–100 and 197–209.

1. How is the corporation structured at present?
    a) Is the decision-making authority centralized around one group or decentralized to many units?
    b) Is it organized on the basis of functions, projects, geography, or some combination of these?
2. Is the structure clearly understood by everyone in the corporation?
3. Is the present structure consistent with current corporate objectives, strategies, policies, and programs as well as with the firm's international operations?
4. In what ways does this structure compare with those of similar corporations?

B. Corporate Culture

See Section 4.3 on pages 87–100.

1. Is there a well-defined or emerging culture composed of shared beliefs, expectations, and values?
2. Is the culture consistent with the current objectives, strategies, policies, and programs?
3. What is the culture's position on important issues facing the corporation (that is, on productivity, quality of performance, adaptability to changing conditions, and internationalization)?
4. Is the culture compatible with the employees' diversity of backgrounds?
5. Does the company take into consideration the values of each nation's culture in which the firm operates?

C. Corporate Resources

1. Marketing

See Section 4.3 on pages 87–100.

   a) What are the corporation's current marketing objectives, strategies, policies, and programs?
      i. Are they clearly stated, or merely implied from performance and/or budgets?
      ii. Are they consistent with the corporation's mission, objectives, strategies, policies, and with internal and external environments?
   b) How well is the corporation performing in terms of analysis of market position and marketing mix (that is, product, price, place, and promotion) in both domestic and international markets? What percentage of sales comes from foreign operations? Where are current products in product life cycle?
      i. What trends emerge from this analysis?
      ii. What impact have these trends had on past performance and how will they probably affect future performance?
      iii. Does this analysis support the corporation's past and pending strategic decisions?
      iv. Does marketing provide the company with a **competitive advantage**?
   c) How well does this corporation's marketing performance compare with that of similar corporations?
   d) Are marketing managers using accepted marketing concepts and techniques to evaluate and improve product performance? (Consider product life cycle, market segmentation, market research, and product portfolios.)
   e) Does marketing adjust to the conditions in each country in which it operates?
   f) What is the role of the marketing manager in the strategic management process?

2. **Finance** See Sections 4.3 and 14.3 on pages 91–92 and 342–348.

a) What are the corporation's current financial objectives, strategies, policies, and programs?

    i. Are they clearly stated or merely implied from performance and/or budgets?

    ii. Are they consistent with the corporation's mission, objectives, strategies, policies, and with internal and external environments?

b) How well is the corporation performing in terms of financial analysis? (Consider ratios, common size statements, and capitalization structure.) How balanced, in terms of cash flow, is the company's portfolio of products and businesses?

    i. What trends emerge from this analysis?

    ii. Are there any significant differences when statements are calculated in constant versus reported dollars?

    iii. What impact have these trends had on past performance and how will they probably affect future performance?

    iv. Does this analysis support the corporation's past and pending strategic decisions?

    v. Does finance provide the company with a **competitive advantage**?

c) How well does this corporation's financial performance compare with that of similar corporations?

d) Are financial managers using accepted financial concepts and techniques to evaluate and improve current corporate and divisional performance? (Consider financial leverage, capital budgeting, ratio analysis, and managing foreign currencies.)

e) Does finance adjust to the conditions in each country in which the company operates?

f) What is the role of the financial manager in the strategic management process?

3. **Research and Development (R&D)** See Section 4.3 on pages 92–95.

a) What are the corporation's current R&D objectives, strategies, policies, and programs?

    i. Are they clearly stated, or merely implied from performance and/or budgets?

    ii. Are they consistent with the corporation's mission, objectives, strategies, policies, and with internal and external environments?

    iii. What is the role of technology in corporate performance?

    iv. Is the mix of basic, applied, and engineering research appropriate given the corporate mission and strategies?

    v. Does R&D provide the company with a **competitive advantage**?

b) What return is the corporation receiving from its investment in R&D?

c) Is the corporation competent in technology transfer? Does it use concurrent engineering and cross-functional work teams in product and process design?

d) What role does technological discontinuity play in the company's products?

e) How well does the corporation's investment in R&D compare with the investments of similar corporations?

f) Does R&D adjust to the conditions in each country in which the company operates?

g) What is the role of the R&D manager in the strategic management process?

4. **Operations and Logistics** See Section 4.3 on pages 95–97.

a) What are the corporation's current manufacturing/service objectives, strategies, policies, and programs?

    i. Are they clearly stated, or merely implied from performance and/or budgets?

    ii. Are they consistent with the corporation's mission, objectives, strategies, policies, and with internal and external environments?

b) What is the type and extent of operations capabilities of the corporation? How much is done domestically versus internationally? Is the amount of outsourcing appropriate to be competitive? Is purchasing being handled appropriately?

   i. If product-oriented, consider plant facilities, type of manufacturing system (continuous mass production, intermittent job shop, or flexible manufacturing), age and type of equipment, degree and role of automation and/or robots, plant capacities and utilization, productivity ratings, availability and type of transportation.

   ii. If service-oriented, consider service facilities (hospital, theater, or school buildings), type of operations systems (continuous service over time to same clientele or intermittent service over time to varied clientele), age and type of supporting equipment, degree and role of automation and/or use of mass communication devices (diagnostic machinery, videotape machines), facility capacities and utilization rates, efficiency ratings of professional/service personnel, availability and type of transportation to bring service staff and clientele together.

c) Are manufacturing or service facilities vulnerable to natural disasters, local or national strikes, reduction or limitation of resources from suppliers, substantial cost increases of materials, or nationalization by governments?

d) Is there an appropriate mix of people and machines in manufacturing firms, or of support staff to professionals in service firms?

e) How well does the corporation perform relative to the competition? Is it balancing inventory costs (warehousing) with logistical costs (just-in-time)? Consider costs per unit of labor, material, and overhead; downtime; inventory control management and/or scheduling of service staff; production ratings; facility utilization percentages; and number of clients successfully treated by category (if service firm) or percentage of orders shipped on time (if product firm).

   i. What trends emerge from this analysis?

   ii. What impact have these trends had on past performance and how will they probably affect future performance?

   iii. Does this analysis support the corporation's past and pending strategic decisions?

   iv. Does operations provide the company with a **competitive advantage**?

f) Are operations managers using appropriate concepts and techniques to evaluate and improve current performance? Consider cost systems, quality control and reliability systems, inventory control management, personnel scheduling, TQM, learning curves, safety programs, and engineering programs that can improve efficiency of manufacturing or of service.

g) Do operations and logistics adjust to the conditions in each country in which it has facilities?

h) What is the role of the operations manager in the strategic management process?

5. **Human Resources Management (HRM)** See Section 4.3 on pages 97–99.

a) What are the corporation's current HRM objectives, strategies, policies, and programs?

   i. Are they clearly stated, or merely implied from performance and/or budgets?

   ii. Are they consistent with the corporation's mission, objectives, strategies, policies, and with internal and external environments?

b) How well is the corporation's HRM performing in terms of improving the fit between the individual employee and the job? Consider turnover, grievances, strikes, layoffs, employee training, and quality of work life.

   i. What trends emerge from this analysis?

   ii. What impact have these trends had on past performance and how will they probably affect future performance?

    iii. Does this analysis support the corporation's past and pending strategic decisions?

    iv. Does HRM provide the company with a **competitive advantage**?

    v. Do the company's employees (skills, education, knowledge) provide the company with a **competitive advantage**?

c) How does this corporation's HRM performance compare with that of similar corporations?

d) Are HRM managers using appropriate concepts and techniques to evaluate and improve corporate performance? Consider the job analysis program, performance appraisal system, up-to-date job descriptions, training and development programs, attitude surveys, job design programs, quality of relationship with unions, and use of autonomous work teams.

e) How well is the company managing the diversity of its workforce? What is the company's position and record on human rights?

f) Does HRM adjust to the conditions in each country in which the company operates? Does the company have a code of conduct for HRM in developing nations? Are employees receiving international assignments to prepare them for managerial positions?

g) What is the role of the HRM manager in the strategic management process?

6. **Information Systems (IS)**   **See Section 4.3 on pages 99–100.**

a) What are the corporation's current IS objectives, strategies, policies, and programs?

    i. Are they clearly stated, or merely implied from performance and/or budgets?

    ii. Are they consistent with the corporation's mission, objectives, strategies, policies, and with internal and external environments?

b) How well is the corporation's IS performing in terms of providing a useful database, offering Internet access and Web sites, automating routine clerical operations, assisting managers in making routine decisions, and providing information necessary for strategic decisions?

    i. What trends emerge from this analysis?

    ii. What impact have these trends had on past performance and how will they probably affect future performance?

    iii. Does this analysis support the corporation's past and pending strategic decisions?

    iv. Does IS provide the company with a **competitive advantage**?

c) How does this corporation's IS performance and stage of development compare with that of similar corporations? Is it appropriately using the Internet?

d) Are IS managers using appropriate concepts and techniques to evaluate and improve corporate performance? Do they know how to build and manage a complex database, establish Web sites with firewalls, conduct system analyses, and implement interactive decision-support systems?

e) Does the company have a global IS and Internet presence? Does it have difficulty with getting data across national boundaries?

f) What is the role of the IS manager in the strategic management process?

D. Summary of Internal Factors   **See IFAS Table on pages 101–102.**

Which of these factors are *core competencies*? Which are *distinctive competencies*? Which of these factors are the most important to the corporation and to the industries in which it competes at the present time? Which of these factors will be important in the future?

V. Analysis of Strategic Factors (SWOT)
See Sections 5.1 and 5.2 on pages 109–114.

A. Situational Analysis   See SFAS Table on pages 110–112.

What are the most important internal and external factors (*Strengths, Weaknesses, Opportunities, Threats*) that strongly affect the corporation's present and future performance? List 8 to 10 strategic factors.

B. Review of Mission and Objectives   See Section 5.2 on page 114.

1. Are the current mission and objectives appropriate in light of the key strategic factors and problems?
2. Should the mission and objectives be changed? If so, how?
3. If changed, what will be the effects on the firm?

VI. Strategic Alternatives and Recommended Strategy

A. Strategic Alternatives   See Sections 5.3, 5.4, 6.2, and 7.1 on pages 114–115, 115–130, 138–150, and 165–177.

1. Can the current or revised **objectives** be met by the simple, more careful implementing of those strategies presently in use (for example, fine-tuning the strategies)?
2. What are the major feasible alternative **strategies** available to this corporation? What are the pros and cons of each? Can corporate scenarios be developed and agreed upon? **(Alternatives must fit societal environment, industry, and company for next 3–5 years.)**
   a) Consider *cost leadership* and *differentiation* as business strategies.
   b) Consider *stability*, *growth*, and *retrenchment* as corporate strategies.
   c) Consider any functional strategic alternatives that might be needed for reinforcement of an important corporate or business strategic alternative.

B. Recommended Strategy   See Sections 7.3 and 7.4 on pages 177–184.

1. Specify which of the strategic alternatives you are recommending for the corporate, business, and functional levels of the corporation. Do you recommend different business or functional strategies for different units of the corporation?
2. Justify your recommendation in terms of its ability to resolve both long- and short-term problems and effectively deal with the strategic factors.
3. What **policies** should be developed or revised to guide effective implementation?
4. What is the impact of recommended strategy on the company's core and distinctive competencies?

VII. Implementation   See Chapters 8 and 9.

A. What kinds of programs (for example, restructuring the corporation or instituting TQM) should be developed to implement the recommended strategy?

1. Who should develop these programs?
2. Who should be in charge of these programs?

B. Are the programs financially feasible? Can pro forma budgets be developed and agreed upon? Are priorities and timetables appropriate to individual programs?

C. Will new standard operating procedures need to be developed?

VIII. Evaluation and Control   See Chapter 10.

A. Is the current information system capable of providing sufficient feedback on implementation activities and performance? Can it measure strategic factors?

1. Can performance results be pinpointed by area, unit, project, or function?
2. Is the information timely?

B. Are adequate control measures in place to ensure conformance with the recommended strategic plan?

1. Are appropriate standards and measures being used?
2. Are reward systems capable of recognizing and rewarding good performance?
3. Who takes corrective action?

Notes

1. K. F. Iverson with T. Varian, "Plain Talk," *INC.* (October 1997), p. 81. Excerpted from Iverson's book, *Plain Talk: Lessons from a Business Maverick*, published by John Wiley, 1997.
2. D. Pickton, M. Starkey, and M. Bradford, "Understand Business Variation for Improved Business Performance," *Long Range Planning* (June 1996), pp. 412–415.
3. R. Muralidharan and R. D. Hamilton III, "Aligning Multinational Control Systems," *Long Range Planning* (June 1999), pp. 352–361. These types are based on W. G. Ouchi, "The Relationship Between Organizational Structure and Organizational Control," *Administrative Science Quarterly*, Vol. 20 (1977), pp. 95–113, and W. G. Ouchi, "A Conceptual Framework for the Design of Organizational Control Mechanisms," *Management Science*, Vol. 25 (1979), pp. 833–848. Muralidhara and Hamilton refer to Ouchi's clan control as input control.
4. W. G. Rowe and P. M. Wright, "Related and Unrelated Diversification and Their Effect on Human Resource Management Controls," *Strategic Management Journal* (April 1997), pp. 329–338.
5. Muralidharan and Hamilton, pp. 356–359.
6. F. C. Barnes, "ISO 9000 Myth and Reality: A Reasonable Approach to ISO 9000," *SAM Advanced Management Journal* (Spring 1998), pp. 23–30.
7. M. V. Uzumeri, "ISO 9000 and Other Metastandards: Principles for Management Practice?" *Academy of Management Executive* (February 1997), pp. 21–36.
8. A. M. Hormozi, "Understanding and Implementing ISO 9000: A Manager's Guide," *SAM Advanced Management Journal* (Autumn 1995), pp. 4–11.
9. J. K. Shank and V. Govindarajan, *Strategic Cost Management* (New York: The Free Press, 1993).
10. S. S. Rao, "ABCs of Cost Control," *Inc. Technology*, No. 2 (1997), pp. 79–81.
11. R. Gruber, "Why You Should Consider Activity-Based Costing," *Small Business Forum* (Spring 1994), pp. 20–36.
12. T. P. Pare, "A New Tool For Managing Costs," *Fortune* (June 14, 1993), pp. 124–129.
13. C. K. Brancato, *New Corporate Performance Measures* (New York: The Conference Board, 1995).
14. C. D. Ittner, D. F. Larcker, and M. V. Rajan, "The Choice of Performance Measures in Annual Bonus Contracts," Working paper reported by K. Z. Andrews in "Executive Bonuses," *Harvard Business Review* (January–February 1996), pp. 8–9; J. Low and T. Siesfeld, "Measures that Matter: Wall Street Considers Non-Financial Performance More than You Think," *Strategy & Leadership* (March/April 1998), pp. 24–30.
15. S. Tully, "America's Best Wealth Creators," *Fortune* (November 28, 1994), p. 143.
16. P. C. Brewer, G. Chandra, and C. A. Hock, "Economic Value Added (EVA): Its Uses and Limitations," *SAM Advanced Management Journal* (Spring 1999), pp. 4–11.
17. D. J. Skyrme and D. M. Amidon, "New Measures of Success," *Journal of Business Strategy* (January/February 1998), p. 23.
18. G. B. Stewart III, "EVA Works—But Not If You Make These Common Mistakes," *Fortune* (May 1, 1995), pp. 117–118.
19. S. Tully, "The Real Key to Creating Wealth," *Fortune* (September 20, 1993), p. 38.
20. A. Ehrbar, "Using EVA to Measure Performance and Assess Strategy," *Strategy & Leadership* (May/June 1999), pp. 20–24.
21. Brewer, Chandra, and Hock, pp. 7–9.
22. PRO: K. Lehn and A. K. Makhija, "EVA & MVA as Performance Measures and Signals for Strategic Change," *Strategy & Leadership* (May/June 1996), pp. 34–38. CON: D. I. Goldenberg, "Shareholder Value Debunked," *Strategy & Leadership* (January/February 2000), pp. 30–36.
23. Ehrbar, p. 21.

24. S. Tully, "America's Wealth Creators," *Fortune* (November 22, 1999), pp. 275–284, and A. B. Fisher, "Creating Stockholder Wealth: Market Value Added," *Fortune* (December 11, 1995), pp. 105–116.

25. A. B. Fisher, "Creating Stockholder Wealth: Market Value Added," *Fortune* (December 11, 1995), pp. 105–116.

26. Lehn and Makhija, p. 37.

27. R. S. Kaplan and D. P. Norton, "Using the Balanced Scorecard as a Strategic Management System," *Harvard Business Review* (January–February 1996), pp. 75–85; R. S. Kaplan and D. P. Norton, "The Balanced Scorecard—Measures that Drive Performance," *Harvard Business Review* (January–February, 1992), pp. 71–79.

28. D. I. Goldenberg, p. 34.

29. C. K. Brancato, *New Performance Measures* (New York: The Conference Board, 1995).

30. B. P. Stivers and T. Joyce, "Building a Balanced Performance Management System," *SAM Advanced Management Journal* (Spring 2000), pp. 22–29.

31. D. J. Skyrme and D. M. Amidon, p. 22.

32. R. Charan, *Boards At Work* (San Francisco, CA: Jossey-Bass, 1998), pp. 176–177.

33. T. D. Schellhardt, "Directors Get Tough: Inside a CEO Performance Review," *Wall Street Journal Interactive Edition* (April 27, 1998).

34. H. Threat, "Measurement Is Free," *Strategy & Leadership* (May/June 1999), pp. 16–19.

35. Z. U. Khan, S. K. Chawla, M. F. Smith, and M. F. Sharif, "Transfer Pricing Policy Issues in Europe 1992," *International Journal of Management* (September 1992), pp. 230–241.

36. H. Rothman, "You Need Not Be Big to Benchmark," *Nation's Business* (December 1992), p. 64.

37. C. W. Von Bergen and B. Soper, "A Problem with Benchmarking: Using Shaping as a Solution," *SAM Advanced Management Journal* (Autumn 1995), pp. 16–19.

38. "Tool Usage Rates," *Journal of Business Strategy* (March/April 1995), p. 12.

39. R. J. Kennedy, "Benchmarking and Its Myths," *Competitive Intelligence Magazine* (April–June 2000), pp. 28–33.

40. L. Mann, D. Samson, and D. Dow, "A Field Experiment on the Effects of Benchmarking & Goal Setting on Company Sales Performance," *Journal of Management*, Vol. 24, No. 1 (1998), pp. 73–96.

41. S. A. W. Drew, "From Knowledge to Action: The Impact of Benchmarking on Organizational Performance," *Long Range Planning* (June 1997), pp. 427–441.

42. S. M. Robbins and R. B. Stobaugh, "The Bent Measuring Stick for Foreign Subsidiaries," *Harvard Business Review* (September–October 1973), p. 82.

43. J. D. Daniels and L. H. Radebaugh, *International Business*, 5th ed. (Reading, Mass.: Addison-Wesley, 1989), pp. 673–674.

44. W. A. Johnson and R. J. Kirsch, "International Transfer Pricing and Decision Making in United States Multinationals," *International Journal of Management* (June 1991), pp. 554–561.

45. "Global Economy Makes Taxing Harder," *The Futurist* (March–April 2000), p. 11; "Financial Indicators," *The Economist* (August 26, 2000), p. 89.

46. "Fixing the Bottom Line," *Time* (November 23, 1992), p. 20.

47. T. A. Stewart, "The New Face of American Power," *Fortune* (July 26, 1993), p. 72; G. P. Zachary, "Behind Stocks' Surge Is an Economy in Which Big U.S. Firms Thrive," *Wall Street Journal* (November 22, 1995), pp. A1, A5.

48. J. M. L. Poon, R. Ainuddin, and H. Affrim, "Management Policies and Practices of American, British, European, and Japanese Subsidiaries in Malaysia: A Comparative Study," *International Journal of Management* (December 1990), pp. 467–474.

49. C. W. L. Hill, P. Hwang, and W. C. Kim, "An Eclectic Theory of the Choice of International Entry Mode," *Strategic Management Journal* (February 1990), pp. 117–128; D. Lei, J. W. Slocum, Jr., and R. W. Slater, "Global Strategy and Reward Systems: The Key Roles of Management Development and Corporate Culture," *Organizational Dynamics* (Autumn 1990), pp. 27–41; W. R. Fannin and A. F. Rodriques, "National or Global?—Control vs. Flexibility," *Long Range Planning* (October 1986), pp. 84–88.

50. A. V. Phatak, *International Dimensions of Management*, 2nd ed. (Boston: Kent, 1989), pp. 155–157.

51. S. McAlary, "Three Pitfalls in ERP Implementation," *Strategy & Leadership* (October/November/December 1999), pp. 49–50.

52. J. B. White, D. Clark, and S. Ascarelli, "This German Software Is Complex, Expensive—and Wildly Popular," *Wall Street Journal* (March 14, 1997), pp. A1, A8; D. Ward, "Whirlpool Takes a Dive with Software Snarl," *Des Moines Register* (April 29, 2000), p. 8D.

53. B. Richards, "The Business Plan," *Wall Street Journal* (November 11, 1996), p. R10.

54. R. M. Hodgetts and M. S. Wortman, *Administrative Policy*, 2nd ed. (New York: John Wiley & Sons, 1980), p. 128.

55. J. R. Wooldridge and C. C. Snow, "Stock Market Reaction to Strategic Investment Decisions," *Strategic Management Journal* (September 1990), pp. 353–363.

56. D. R. Schmidt and K. L. Fowler, "Post-Acquisition Financial Performance and Executive Compensation," *Strategic Management Journal* (November–December 1990), pp. 559–569.

57. D. Jones, "Bad News Can Enrich Executives," *Des Moines Register* (November 26, 1999), p. 8S.

58. J. F. Porac, J. B. Wade, and T. G. Pollock, "Industry Categories and the Politics of the Comparable Firm in CEO Compensation," *Administrative Science Quarterly* (March 1999), pp. 112–144.

59. W. Zellner, E. Schine, and G. Smith, "Trickle-Down Is Trickling Down at Work," *Business Week* (March 18, 1996), p. 34.

60. T. J. Peters and R. H. Waterman, *In Search of Excellence* (New York: HarperCollins, 1982), pp. 75–76.

61. T. Aeppel, "Not All Workers Find Idea of Empowerment as Neat as It Sounds," *Wall Street Journal* (September 8, 1997), pp. A1, A13.

62. D. B. Balkin and L. R. Gomez-Mejia, "Matching Compensation and Organizational Strategies," *Strategic Management Journal* (February 1990), pp. 153–169.

63. C. S. Galbraith, "The Effect of Compensation Programs and Structure on SBU Competitive Strategy: A Study of Technology-Intensive Firms," *Strategic Management Journal* (July 1991), pp. 353–370.

64. T. A. Stewart, "CEO Pay: Mom Wouldn't Approve," *Fortune* (March 31, 1997), pp. 119–120.

65. P. J. Stonich, "The Performance Measurement and Reward System: Critical to Strategic Management," *Organizational Dynamics* (Winter 1984), pp. 45–57.

66. A. Rappaport, "New Thinking on How to Link Executive Pay with Performance," *Harvard Business Review* (March–April 1999), pp. 91–101.

67. W. Grossman and R. E. Hoskisson, "CEO Pay at the Crossroads of Wall Street and Main: Toward the Strategic Design of Executive Compensation," *Academy of Management Executive* (February 1998), pp. 43–57.

68. T. L. Wheelen and J. D. Hunger, "Using the Strategic Audit," *SAM Advanced Management Journal* (Winter 1987), pp. 4–12; G. Donaldson, "A New Tool for Boards: The Strategic Audit," *Harvard Business Review* (July–August 1995), pp. 99–107.

69. L. Armstrong, "Someone to Watch Over You," *Business Week* (July 10, 2000), pp. 189–190.

70. B. Wallace and J. Fenton, "Is Your PC Watching You?" *PC World* (December 2000), pp. 59–63.

71. *The Charlie Rose Show* on PBS, transcript of May 24, 1999.

72. C. Machrone, "Security," *PC Magazine* (February 6, 2001), p. 159.

73. "The Surveillance Society," *The Economist*, May 1, 1999, p. 22.

74. J. Warner, "21st Century Capitalism: Snapshot of the Next Century," *Business Week* (November 18, 1994), p. 194.

Newbury Comics, Inc

IMPLEMENTATION AND CONTROL

ewbury Comics Cofounders Mike Dreese and John Brusger parlayed $2,000 and a comic book collection into a thriving chain of 22 stores spanning the New England region, known to be *the* place to shop for everything from the best of the underground/independent scene to major label superstars. The chain also stocks a wide variety of non-music related items such as T-shirts, Dr. (doc) Martens shoes, posters, jewelry, cosmetics, books, magazines, and other trendy items.

In Part Four, "**Strategy Implementation and Control**," the video focuses on Newbury Comics' used CD business. Mike, John, and Jan discuss the development of procedures and control processes for introducing the used CD program. Budgeting is indirectly mentioned in terms of huge expenditures made at the six-month point to greatly expand the program. The video also highlights the importance of having the right staff to implement a strategy.

As pointed out in Part 3 of the Video Case, the project of developing an implementation plan was assigned to Duncan Brown, Senior Vice President. Part of this plan was to begin the used CD program in a few stores and then evaluate how well the program was working. This was a very ad hoc approach to implementation, but it fit the very loose entrepreneurial approach Newbury Comics takes toward strategy formulation. Mike tells us that he is more interested in "continuous improvement" than in setting specific sales or profit objectives. He admits that one reason he wanted to enter the used CD business was because he likes being a "pioneer" (i.e., first mover). But being a pioneer has its problems.

Jan points out that when the used CD program was started, a store would just put up signs saying that it now bought and sold used CDs. It was then up to the manager to set both the buying and selling price for each CD (with no help from any computer). The headquarters office would then print tags for that store. As a result, stores (even the same store) would offer the same CD for a different price. Following Mike's belief in encouraging creativity and individual initiative, there were no attempts to place blame during this implementation period.

Mike points out that the used CD business is much more complicated than dealing with new CDs. Although management saw it as a risky business, they also believed that its potential for the company outweighed the risk. Because of the many complications of the used CD business, it resulted in a series of new activities in implementation, evaluation, and control, such as choosing what CDs to buy at what price, cleaning, and packaging them. These new activities resulted in adding new job duties at the store level, warehouse, and main office—thus changing the structure of the organization from one of being fairly decentralized at the store level to one with much more centralization of decision making at headquarters. The main office took control of pricing. The IBM AS-400 computer was part of the information system developed for the used CD bar code program to integrate information from all the stores. Duties were expanded and positions were added at the headquarters office and warehouse to deal with finding sources of bulk shipments, setting prices, and sorting, cleaning, and packaging used CDs. Special relationships were developed with some bulk suppliers of used CDs to make sure that Newbury Comics would get the first look at a new batch in return for paying more than other purchasers. A system of procedures was developed to sell non-selling used CDs to other retailers.

Concepts Illustrated in the Video

- Strategy Implementation: Programs, Budgets, and Procedures
- Achieving Synergy
- Job Design
- Staffing Follows Strategy
- Evaluation and Control: Measuring Performance
- Strategic Information Systems

Study Questions

1. Why was the used CD program at Newbury Comics a success?
2. What programs and procedures did management use to implement the growth strategy?
3. How important is staffing to this company's success?
4. How does the structure of Newbury Comics help or hinder the company's growth?
5. How is synergy achieved throughout the company?

chapter 11

Strategic Issues in Managing Technology and Innovation

Trilogy Software, Inc., is in the business of creating new businesses by properly managing new technology and innovative concepts. A private company with more than $200 million in revenues, Trilogy recruits the best engineers directly from campus by offering them a direct chance to build the company. The new employees attend a three-month intensive training program, called Trilogy University, taught by senior managers. Joe Liemandt, Cofounder and President of Trilogy, challenges every class to create at least 20% of new revenues within two years. Since the company is private, it doesn't motivate by offering stock options. Instead, it offers employees the chance to create and run new businesses. Thus far, Trilogy has spun off six new companies.

Liemandt uses the Internet to establish conversations with Trilogy's 1,500 employees. He asks them not only to respond to mission statements drafted by top management, but also to periodically assess managers online. According to President Liemandt, "Energy and excitement is why people do start-ups. But as the company gets larger, people don't feel as engaged. They feel as if they are spoken to instead of being engaged in a collaboration. The net provides a 10-to-20-fold increase in the level of interaction you can have."[1]

Trilogy is a good example of a company successfully energizing its people to create new products and services. Properly managing technology and innovation is crucial in a fast-moving interconnected world. Over the past 15 years, the top 20% of firms in an annual innovation poll conducted by *Fortune* magazine achieved double the shareholder returns of their peers.[2] Nevertheless, many large firms find it difficult to be continually innovative. A recent

277

Table 11–1 Executives Fear Their Companies Are Becoming Less Innovative

A survey of business executives conducted by *Fortune* with the consulting firm, Integral, Inc., revealed the percentages of those responding either **agree** or **strongly agree** to the following five statements:

■ Your company has recently lost relatively low-value customers in small market niches or low-end market segments.	55%
■ Your organization passes up growth opportunities it would have pursued when the company was smaller because the opportunities are now "too small to be interesting."	60%
■ There is a disconnect between the kind of innovations your frontline troops suggest and the types of innovations upper management invests in.	64%
■ When your organization sees a potentially disruptive technology, it defines it as a technical problem ("Will our customers accept the product?") instead of a market problem.	58%
■ New entrants have exploited opportunities where uncertainty over market size and customer needs resulted in inaction by your company.	68%

Source: "Don't Leave Us Behind," *Fortune* (April 3, 2000), p. 250. Copyright © 2000 Time, Inc. All rights reserved.

survey of business executives reveals that a significant majority are concerned that their companies are losing growth opportunities because they are not able to properly manage new technology (see **Table 11–1**).[3] Even innovative established companies, such as 3M, Procter & Gamble, and Rubbermaid, have had a recent slowing in their rate of successful new product introductions.[4]

In this chapter, we examine strategic issues in technology and innovation as they impact environmental scanning, strategy formulation, strategy implementation, and evaluation and control.

11.1 Role of Management

Due to increased competition and accelerated product development cycles, innovation and the management of technology is becoming crucial to corporate success. Research conducted by *Forbes*, Ernst & Young, and the Wharton School of Business found the most important driver of corporate value for both durable and nondurable companies to be innovation.[5] Approximately half the profits of all U.S. companies come from products launched in the previous 10 years.[6] What is less obvious is how a company can generate a significant return from investment in R&D as well as an overall sense of enthusiasm for innovative behavior and risk taking. One way is to include innovation in the corporation's mission statement. See the **boxed example** for mission statements from well-known companies. Another way is by establishing policies that support the innovative process. For

Examples of Innovation Emphasis in Mission Statements

To emphasize the importance of technology, creativity, and innovation to overall future corporate success, some well-known firms have added sections to this effect in their published mission statements. Some of these are listed here.

AT&T: "We believe innovation is the engine that will keep us vital and growing. Our culture embraces creativity, seeks different perspectives and risks pursuing new opportunities. We create and rapidly convert technology into products and services, constantly searching for new ways to make technology more useful to customers."

General Mills: "Innovation is the principal driver of growth. . . . To be first among our competitors, we must constantly challenge the status quo and be willing to experiment. . . . Our motivation system will strongly reward successful risk taking, while not penalizing an innovative idea that did not work."

Gerber: "[The mission will be achieved by] investing in continued product and body-of-knowledge, innovation, and research in the areas of infant nutrition, care, and development."

Gillette: "We will invest in and master the key technologies vital to category success."

Hallmark: "[We believe] that creativity and quality—in our concept, products and services—are essential to our success."

Intel: "To succeed we must maintain our innovative environment. We strive to embrace change, challenge the status quo, listen to all ideas and viewpoints, encourage and reward informed risk taking, and learn from our successes and mistakes."

Merck & Co.: "We are dedicated to achieving the highest level of scientific excellence and commit our research to maintaining human health and improving the quality of life."

Source: P. Jones and L. Kahaner, *Say It and Live It: The 50 Corporate Mission Statements That Hit the Mark* (New York: Currency Doubleday, 1995).

example, 3M has set a policy of generating at least 25% of its revenue from products introduced in the preceding three years. To support this policy, this $13 billion corporation annually spends nearly $1 billion in R&D.[7]

The importance of technology and innovation must be emphasized by people at the very top and reinforced by people throughout the corporation. If top management and the board are not interested in these topics, managers below them tend to echo their lack of interest. When Akio Morita, Chairman of Sony Corporation, visited the United Kingdom a number of years ago, he expressed disbelief at the number of accountants leading that country's companies. Uncomfortable because they lacked familiarity with science or technology, these top managers too often limited their role to approving next year's budget. Constrained by what the company could afford and guided by how much the competition was spending, they perceived R&D as a line expense item instead of as an investment in the future.[8]

Management has an obligation to not only encourage new product development, but also to develop a system to ensure that technology is being used most effectively with the consumer in mind. Between 33% and 60% of all new products that reach the market fail to make a profit.[9] A study by Chicago consultants Kuczmarski & Associates of 11,000 new products marketed by 77 manufacturing, service, and consumer-product firms revealed that only 56% of all newly introduced products were still being sold five years later. Only 1 in 13 new product ideas ever made it into test markets. Although some authorities argue that this percentage of successful new products needs to be improved, others contend that too high a percentage means that a company isn't taking the risks necessary to develop a really new product.[10]

The importance of top management's providing appropriate direction is exemplified by Chairman Morita's statement of his philosophy for Sony Corporation:

> The key to success for Sony, and to everything in business, science, and technology for that matter, is never to follow the others . . . . Our basic concept has always been this—to give new convenience, or new methods, or new benefits, to the general public with our technology.

Morita and his Cofounder, Masuru Ibuka, always looked for ways to turn ideas into clear targets. Says Morita, "When Ibuka was first describing his idea for the Betamax videocassette, he gave the engineers a paperback book and said, 'Make it this size.' Those were his only instructions."[11]

11.2 Environmental Scanning

EXTERNAL SCANNING

Corporations need to continually scan their external societal and task environments for new developments in technology that may have some application to their current or potential products. Stakeholders, especially customers, can be important participants in the new product development process.

Technological Developments

Motorola, a company well known for its ability to invest in profitable new technologies and manufacturing improvements, has a sophisticated scanning system. Its intelligence department monitors the latest technology developments introduced at scientific conferences, in journals, and in trade gossip. This information helps it build "technology roadmaps" that assess where breakthroughs are likely to occur, when they can be incorporated into new products, how much money their development will cost, and which of the developments is being worked on by the competition.[12]

Focusing one's scanning efforts too closely on one's own industry is dangerous. Most new developments that threaten existing business practices and technologies do not come from existing competitors or even from within traditional industries.[13] A new technology that can substitute for an existing technology at a lower cost and provide higher quality can change the very basis for competition in an industry. Consider, for example, the impact of Internet technology on the personal computer software industry. Microsoft Corporation had ignored the developing Internet technology while the company battled successfully with IBM, Lotus, and WordPerfect to dominate operating system software via Windows 95 as well as word processing and spreadsheet programs via Microsoft Office. Ironically, just as Microsoft introduced its new Windows 95 operating system, newcomer Netscape used Java applets in its user-friendly, graphically oriented browser program with the potential to make operating systems unnecessary. By the time Microsoft realized this threat to its business, Netscape had already established itself as the industry standard for browsers. Microsoft was forced to spend huge amounts of time and resources trying to catch up to Netscape's dominant market share with its own Internet Explorer browser.

One way to learn about new technological developments in an industry is to locate part of a company's R&D or manufacturing in those locations making a strong impact on product development. Large multinational corporations undertake between 5% and 25% of their R&D outside their home country.[14] For example, automobile companies like to have design centers in Southern California and in Italy, key areas for automotive styling. Software companies throughout the world know that they must have a programming presence in Silicon Valley if they are to compete on the leading edge of technology. The same is true of the semiconductor industry in terms of manufacturing.[15]

Impact of Stakeholders on Innovation

A company should look to its stakeholders, especially its customers, suppliers, and distributors, for sources of product and service improvements. These groups of people have the most to gain from innovative new products or services. Under certain circumstances, they may propose new directions for product development. Some of the methods of gathering information from key stakeholders are using lead users, market research, and new product experimentation.

Lead Users

Research by Von Hippel indicates customers are a key source of innovation in many industries. For example, 77% of the innovations developed in the scientific instruments industry came from the users of the products. Suppliers are often important sources as well. Suppliers accounted for 36% of innovations in the thermoplastics industry, according to Von Hippel.[16] One way to commercialize a new technology is through early and in-depth involvement with a firm's customer in a process called co-development.[17] This type of customer can be called a "lead user."

Von Hippel proposes that companies should look to lead users for help in product development, especially in high technology industries where things move so quickly that a product is becoming obsolete by the time it arrives on the market. These **lead users** are "companies, organizations, or individuals that are well ahead of market trends and have needs that go far beyond those of the average user."[18] They are the first to adopt a product because they benefit significantly from its use—even if it is not fully developed.

At 3M, for example, a product development team in 3M's Medical Surgical Markets Division was charged with creating a breakthrough in the area of surgical drapes—the material that prevents infections from spreading during surgery. At the time, 3M dominated the market but had not developed a new product improvement in almost a decade. After spending six weeks learning about the cause and prevention of infections, the project team spent six more weeks investigating trends in infection control. The team then worked to identify lead users—doctors in developing nations and veterinarians who couldn't afford the current expensive drapes. The team invited several lead users to a 2½-day workshop focused on "Can we find a revolutionary, low-cost approach to infection control?" The workshop generated concepts for six new product lines and a radical new approach to infection control. The team chose the three strongest concepts for presentation to senior management. 3M has successfully applied the lead user method in 8 of its 55 divisions.

Lead user teams are typically composed of four to six people from marketing and technical departments with one person serving as project leader. Team members usually spend 12 to 15 hours per week on the project for its duration. For planning purposes, a team should allow 4 to 6 weeks for each phase and four to six months for the entire project. The *four phases of the lead user process* are:

1. **Laying the Foundation:** Identify target markets and the type and level of innovations desired.
2. **Determining the Trends:** Research the field and talk with experts with a broad view of emerging technologies and leading-edge applications.

3. **Identify Lead Users:** Talk with users at the leading edge of the target and related markets to understand their needs.

4. **Develop the Breakthrough:** Host a two- to three-day workshop with several lead users and a half dozen marketing and technical people. Participants first work in small groups and then as a whole to design the final concepts that fit the company's and the users' needs.[19]

Market Research

A more traditional method of obtaining new product ideas is to use **market research** to survey current users regarding what they would like in a new product. This method has been successfully used by companies such as Procter & Gamble to identify consumer preferences. It is especially useful in directing incremental improvements to existing products. For example, the auto maker BMW solicits suggestions from BMW owners to improve its current offerings and to obtain ideas for new products.

Market research may not, however, necessarily provide the information needed for truly innovative products or services (radical innovation). According to Sony executive Kozo Ohsone, "When you introduce products that have never been invented before, what good is market research?" For example, Hal Sperlich took the concept of the minivan from Ford to Chrysler when Ford refused to develop the concept. According to Sperlich,

> [Ford] lacked confidence that a market existed because the product didn't exist. The auto industry places great value on historical studies of market segments. Well, we couldn't prove there was a market for the minivan because there was no historical segment to cite. In Detroit most product-development dollars are spent on modest improvements to existing products, and most market research money is spent on studying what customers like among available products. In 10 years of developing the minivan we never once got a letter from a housewife asking us to invent one. To the skeptics, that proved there wasn't a market out there.[20]

A heavy emphasis on being customer-driven could actually prevent companies from developing innovative new products. A study of the impact of **technological discontinuity** (explained earlier in **Chapter 4**) in various industries revealed that the leading firms failed to switch to the new technology not because management was ignorant of the new development, but rather because they listened too closely to their current customers. In all of these firms, a key task of management was to decide which of the many product and development programs continually being proposed to them should receive financial resources. The criterion used for the decision was the total return perceived in each project, adjusted by the perceived riskiness of the project. Projects targeted at the known needs of key customers in established markets consistently won the most resources. Sophisticated systems for planning and compensation favored this type of project every time. As a result, the leading companies continued to use the established technology to make the products its current customers demanded, allowing smaller entrepreneurial competitors to develop the new, more risky technology.[21]

Because the market for the innovative products based on the new technology was fairly small at first, new ventures had time to fine-tune product design, build sufficient manufacturing capacity, and establish the product as the industry standard (as Netscape did with its Internet browser). As the marketplace began to embrace the new standard, the customers of the leading companies began to ask for products based on the new technology. Although some established manufacturers were able to defend their market share positions through aggressive product development and marketing activity (as Microsoft did against Netscape), many firms, finding that the new entrants had developed insurmountable advantages in manufacturing cost and design experience, were forced out of the market. Even the established manufacturers that converted to the new technology were unable to win a significant share of the new market.[22]

New Product Experimentation   Instead of using lead users or market research to test the potential of innovative products, some successful companies are using speed and flexibility to gain market information. These companies developed their products by "probing" potential markets with early versions of the products, learning from the probes, and probing again.[23] For example, Seiko's only market research is surprisingly simple. The company introduces hundreds of new models of watches into the marketplace. It makes more of the models that sell; it drops those that don't.

The consulting firm Arthur D. Little found that the use of standard market research techniques has only resulted in a success rate of 8% for new cereals—92% of all new cereals fail. As a result, innovative firms, such as Keebler and the leading cereal makers, are reducing their expenditures for market research and working to reduce the cost of launching new products by making their manufacturing processes more flexible.[24]

From its beginning as a software company, Microsoft has successfully followed a strategy of monitoring the competition for new developments. It follows an *embrace and extend* strategy of imitating new products developed by pioneers, refining them, and outmarketing the competition. (This approach is nothing new. Procter & Gamble did this to *Lestoil* when P&G introduced *Mr. Clean*.) Microsoft's distinctive competency is its ability to change directions and adjust priorities when the market changes.[25] The company purchased the rights to a program that formed the basis for PC DOS, which it sold to IBM for its personal computers. It then imitated the "look and feel" of Apple's graphical user interface (which Steve Jobs had first seen at Xerox's Palo Alto Research Center) with its Windows operating system. Once the company realized the importance of the Internet browser, it developed its own Internet Explorer and has successfully battled Netscape for market share.

INTERNAL SCANNING

In addition to scanning the external environment, strategists should also assess their company's ability to innovate effectively by asking the following questions:

1. Has the company developed the resources needed to try new ideas?
2. Do the managers allow experimentation with new products or services?
3. Does the corporation encourage risk taking and tolerate mistakes?
4. Are people more concerned with new ideas or with defending their turf?
5. Is it easy to form autonomous project teams?[26]

In addition to answering these questions, strategists should assess how well company resources are internally allocated and evaluate the organization's ability to develop and transfer new technology in a timely manner into the generation of innovative products and services. These issues are important given that it takes on average seven ideas to generate a new commercial product, according to the Product and Development and Management Association.[27]

RESOURCE ALLOCATION ISSUES

The company must make available the resources necessary for effective research and development. Research indicates that a company's **R&D intensity** (its spending on R&D as a percentage of sales revenue) is a principal means of gaining market share in global competition.[28] The amount of money spent on R&D often varies by industry. For example, the computer software and drug industries spend an average of 11% to 13% of their sales dollar for R&D. Others, such as the food and the containers and packaging industries, spend less than 1%. A good rule of thumb for R&D spending is that a corporation should spend at a "normal" rate for that particular industry, unless its competitive strategy dictates otherwise.[29] Research indicates that consistency in R&D strategy and resource allocation across lines of business improves corporate performance by enabling the firm to better develop synergies among product lines and business units.[30]

Simply spending money on R&D or new projects does not, however, guarantee useful results. One study found that although large firms spent almost twice as much per R&D patent than did smaller firms, the smaller firms used more of their patents. The innovation rate of small businesses was 322 innovations per million employees versus 225 per million for large companies.[31] One explanation for this phenomenon is that large (especially older) firms tend to spend development money on extensions of their current products (incremental innovation) or to increase the efficiency of existing performance.[32] In contrast, small firms tend to apply technology to improving effectiveness through developing completely new products (radical innovation).[33] Other studies reveal that the maximum innovator in various industries often was the middle-sized firm. These firms were generally more effective and efficient in technology transfer. Very small firms often do not have sufficient resources to exploit new concepts (unless supported by venture capitalists with deep pockets), whereas the bureaucracy present in large firms rewards consistency over creativity.[34] From these studies, Hitt, Hoskisson, and Harrison propose the existence of an inverted U-shaped relationship between size and innovation. According to Hitt et al., "This suggests that organizations are flexible and responsive up to some threshold size but encounter inertia after that point."[35]

Sometimes most of the firms in an industry can waste their R&D spending. For example, between 1950 and 1979, the U.S. steel industry spent 20% more on plant maintenance and upgrading for each ton of production capacity added or replaced than did the Japanese steel industry. Nevertheless the top management of U.S. steel firms failed to recognize and adopt two breakthroughs in steelmaking—the basic oxygen furnace and continuous casting. Their hesitancy to adopt new technology caused them to lose the world steel market.[36]

Time to Market Issues

In addition to money, another important consideration in the effective management of research and development is **time to market**. A decade ago, the time from inception to profitability of a specific R&D program was generally accepted to be 7 to 11 years. According to Karlheinz Kaske, CEO of Siemens AG, however, the time available to complete the cycle is getting shorter. Companies no longer can assume that competitors will allow them the number of years needed to recoup their investment. In the past, Kaske says, "10 to 15 years went by before old products were replaced by new ones . . . now, it takes only 4 or 5 years."[37] Time to market is an important issue because *60% of patented innovations are generally imitated within 4 years at 65% of the cost of innovation.*[38] In the 1980s, Japanese auto manufacturers gained incredible competitive advantage over U.S. manufacturers by reducing new products' time to market to only 3 years (U.S. auto companies needed 5 years).[39]

11.3 Strategy Formulation

Research and development strategy deals not only with the decision to be a leader or a follower in terms of technology and market entry (discussed earlier in **Chapter 7** under R&D strategy), but also with the source of the technology. Should a company develop its own technology or purchase it from others? The strategy also takes into account a company's particular mix of basic versus applied and product versus process R&D (discussed earlier in **Chapter 4**). The particular mix should suit the level of industry development and the firm's particular corporate and business strategies. The 🌐 **Global Issue** feature illustrates how a company's com-

Global Issue

Impact of R&D on Competitive Advantage in China

China is one of the 10 largest economies in the world. Average income has tripled since 1978 for most rural people. Urban incomes have risen even faster as the country's economy has grown at an annual rate of 9% in real terms for the past 15 years. As income increases, people are using it to improve their standard of living.

China is the world's fastest growing and potentially most profitable market for bathroom fixture manufacturers. Western-style toilets, which are easier to keep clean and use less water than the traditional Chinese fixtures, have become the standard in thousands of new apartment and office buildings. Two globally oriented companies attempting to dominate this lucrative market are American Standard of the United States and Toto Ltd. of Japan. Both design their products in their home country, manufacture them in Thailand using low-cost labor, and then ship the products to China for sale.

Product design has a significant impact on each company's competitive strategy in China. Toto has an advantage in one part of the design process because its designers in Japan use computers to generate models from blocks of foam. Engineering design is its distinctive competency. Blueprints can be in the hands of factory engineers in four weeks. In contrast, American

Standard's process takes two months, on average. Models are crafted by hand by Jack Kaiser, an acknowledged design expert, and six associates. The personal touch is part of Standard's distinctive competency. Although the designers dominate the process, they work closely with marketing and production to develop a product to suit consumers' needs. In contrast, Toto's engineers dominate the process—building for production, but limiting creativity and neglecting markets in other countries. This limits Toto's ability to successfully enter a new market with unusual needs.

Toto dominates the luxury bathroom market in China, but it has been slow to adapt to the fast-growing low end of the market. "To ask a Japanese engineer to make something cheaper is harder than to ask him to make something better," explained Thibault Danjou, a Toto Marketing Manager. American Standard has another advantage in its flexible manufacturing facility in Thailand. It stocks only 14 days' worth of inventory. Its production process is flexible enough to produce to order. Toto, in contrast, has a much more rigid production process and must keep two months' inventory on hand. American Standard can also fill odd size orders that Toto finds too difficult to fill. In selling new-style toilets to China, manufacturers must customize toilets to line up with existing sewage pipes. Selling close to half of the bathroom fixtures imported into China, American Standard is certainly cleaning up!

Source: S. Glain, "Top Toilet Makers from U.S. and Japan Vie for Chinese Market," *Wall Street Journal* (December 19, 1996), pp. A1, A11; "Deng's China: The Last Emperor," *The Economist* (February 22, 1997), pp. 21–25.

petence in different aspects of R&D can affect its competitive strategy and its ability to successfully enter new markets. It shows not only how distinctive competencies in R&D can affect a company's competitive strategy, but also how emerging markets, such as China, are crucial to corporate growth strategies. Toto Ltd. is able to get from design to market quickly, but American Standard is able to design a product to better suit the needs of a new market.

In addition, R&D strategy in a large corporation deals with the proper balance of its product portfolio based on the life cycle of the products.

PRODUCT VERSUS PROCESS R&D

As illustrated in **Figure 11–1**, the proportion of product and process R&D tends to vary as a product moves along its life cycle. In the early stages, **product innovations** are most important because the product's physical attributes and capabilities most affect financial performance. Later, **process innovations** such as improved manufacturing facilities, increasing product quality, and faster distribution become important to maintaining the product's economic returns. Generally product R&D has been key to achieving differentiation strategies, whereas process R&D has been at the core of successful cost leadership strategies.

Figure 11–1

Product and Process R&D in the Innovation Life Cycle

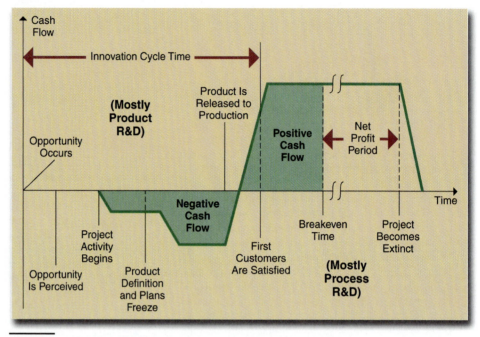

Source: Adapted from M. L. Patterson, "Lessons from the Assembly Line," *Journal of Business Strategy* (May/June 1993), p. 43. Permission granted by Faulkner & Gray, Eleven Penn Plaza, NY, NY 10001.

Historically, U.S. corporations have not been as skillful at process innovations as have German and Japanese companies. The primary reason has been a function of the amount of money invested in each form of R&D. U.S. firms spend, on the average, 70% of their R&D budgets on product R&D and only 30% on process R&D; German firms spend 50% on each form; and Japanese firms spend 30% on product and 70% on process R&D.[40] The traditionally heavy emphasis by U.S. major home appliance manufacturers on process R&D is one reason why they continue to have a strong position in the North American market. (See the **boxed example** on the U.S. major home appliance industry.)

To be competitive, companies must find the proper mix of product and process R&D. Even though the key to the success of the U.S. major home appliance industry has been its emphasis on process innovation, significant product innovation is more likely to result in a first mover advantage. For example, the first company to successfully use sound waves to clean clothes (instead of water and detergent) may very likely change the entire dynamics of the industry.

TECHNOLOGY SOURCING

Technology sourcing, typically a make-or-buy decision, can be important in a firm's R&D strategy. Although in-house R&D has traditionally been an important source of technical knowledge for companies, firms can also tap the R&D capabilities of competitors, suppliers, and other organizations through contractual agreements (such as licensing, R&D agreements, and joint ventures). One example is Matsushita's licensing of Iomega's Zip drive technology in 1996 so that Matsushita could also manufacture and sell removable cartridges for personal computers. When technological cycles were longer, a company was more likely to choose an independent R&D strategy not only because it gave the firm a longer lead time before com-

Product and Process Innovation in the Major Home Appliance Industry

Product innovation is being used in the major home appliance industry to provide consumers with new products as well as to add newer functions and features to existing products. The microwave oven was the last completely new product in this industry. Fuzzy logic technology is now being used to provide more effective, consumer-friendly appliances. Japanese appliance makers were the first to use this new technology to replace the many selector switches on an appliance with one start button. With fuzzy logic, a sophisticated set of electronic sensors and self-diagnostic software can measure the amount of detergent placed in a washing machine, check water temperature, gauge the amount of dirt on clothes, and decide not only how long the wash and rinse cycles should run, but also how vigorously the agitator should swish the water to get the clothes clean. Most major home appliance manufacturers have added fuzzy logic technology to top-end appliances in at least one of their product categories. Whirlpool added fuzzy logic to its VIP series of microwave ovens. Maytag did the same to its Intellisense™ line of dishwashers.

Process innovation for more efficient manufacturing of current products (as compared to new product development) has dominated research and development efforts in the U.S. major home appliance industry since the 1950s. Even though a refrigerator or a washing machine still looks and acts very much the same today as it did in the 1950s, it is built in a far different and more efficient manner. The components inside the appliances are being produced in highly automated plants using computer-integrated manufacturing processes. An example of this emphasis on product simplification was Maytag's "Dependable Drive" washer transmission, which was designed to have 40.6% fewer parts than the transmission it replaced. Fewer parts meant simplified manufacturing and less chance of a breakdown. The result was lower manufacturing costs and higher product quality.

Most industry analysts agreed that continual process improvements have kept U.S. major home appliance manufacturers dominant in the North American market. The emphasis on quality and durability, coupled with a reluctance to make major design changes simply for the sake of change, resulted in products with an average life expectancy of 20 years for refrigerators and 15 years for washers and dryers. Even though quality has improved significantly over the past 20 years, the average washer, dryer, and refrigerator cost no more than they did 20 years ago and yet last almost twice as long. If only the same could be said of the U.S. automobile industry!

petitors copied it, but also because it was more profitable in the long run. In today's world of shorter innovation life cycles and global competition, a company may no longer have the luxury of waiting to reap a long-term profit.

During a time of technological discontinuity in an industry, a company may have no choice but to purchase the new technology from others if it wants to remain competitive. For example, Ford Motor Company paid $100 million for 10.8% of the common stock of Cummins Engine Co., an expert in diesel engine technology. In return for its money, Ford got exclusive access to Cummins's truck engine technology. This allowed Ford to forgo the $300 million expense of designing a new engine on its own to meet U.S. emission standards.[41]

Firms that are unable to finance alone the huge costs of developing a new technology may coordinate their R&D with other firms through a **strategic R&D alliance**. By the 1990s, more than 150 cooperative alliances involving 1,000 companies were operating in the United States and many more were operating throughout Europe and Asia.[42] These alliances can be (a) joint programs or contracts to develop a new technology, (b) joint ventures establishing a separate company to take a new product to market, or (c) minority investments in innovative firms wherein the innovator obtains needed capital and the investor obtains access to valuable research. For example, Intel formed an alliance with Hewlett-Packard (HP) in 1994 to develop the Merced, a microprocessor combining elements of CISC (Complex Instruction Set Computing) and RISC (Reduced Instruction Set Computing) architecture. Up to this time Intel had little experience with designing general-purpose RISC chips. Since HP was already producing its own highly regarded RISC processor, Intel proposed the technology alliance. This alliance combined HP's knowledge of RISC with Intel's knowledge of CISC and Intel's manufacturing capabilities.[43]

When should a company buy or license technology from others instead of developing it internally? Following the resource-based view of the firm discussed previously in **Chapter 4**, a company should buy technologies that are commonly available but should make (and protect) those that are rare, valuable, hard to imitate, and have no close substitutes. In addition, *outsourcing technology may be appropriate when*:

- The technology is of low significance to competitive advantage.
- The supplier has proprietary technology.
- The supplier's technology is better and/or cheaper and reasonably easy to integrate into the current system.
- The company's strategy is based on system design, marketing, distribution, and service—not on development and manufacturing.
- The technology development process requires special expertise.
- The technology development process requires new people and new resources.[44]

Licensing technology to other companies may be an excellent R&D strategy—especially in a turbulent high tech environment where being the first firm to establish the standard dominant design may bring competitive advantage.[45] Matsushita successfully used this strategy to overcome the technologically superior Sony beta format with its VHS format for VCRs. By freely licensing the VHS format to all other VCR makers, Matsushita (through its Panasonic brand) became one of the dominant VCR manufacturers and Sony was relegated to a minority position in the market.[46]

IMPORTANCE OF TECHNOLOGICAL COMPETENCE

Firms that emphasize growth through acquisitions over internal development tend to be less innovative in the long run.[47] Research suggests that companies must have at least a minimal R&D capability if they are to correctly assess the value of technology developed by others. R&D creates a capacity in a firm to assimilate and exploit new knowledge. This is called a company's "absorptive capacity" and is a valuable by-product of routine in-house R&D activity.[48] **Absorptive capacity** is a firm's ability to value, assimilate, and utilize new external knowledge.[49] Firms having absorptive capacity are able to use knowledge obtained externally to increase the productivity of their research expenditures.[50] Further, without this capacity, firms could become locked out in their ability to assimilate the technology at a later time.

Those corporations that do purchase an innovative technology must have the **technological competence** to make good use of it. Some companies that introduce the latest technology into their processes do not adequately assess the competence of their people to handle it. For example, a survey conducted in the United Kingdom found that 44% of all companies that started to use robots met with initial failure and that 22% of these firms abandoned the use of robots altogether, mainly because of inadequate technological knowledge and skills.[51] One U.S. company built a new plant equipped with computer-integrated manufacturing and statistical process controls, but the employees could not operate the equipment because 25% of them were illiterate.[52]

A corporation may acquire a smaller high technology company in order to learn not only the new technology, but also a new way of managing its business. For example, Northern

Telecom, the Canadian telecommunications equipment manufacturer, was looking for renewal in 1998. CEO John Roth had identified the need for a cultural "right-angle turn." To become involved in the Internet, the company purchased Bay Networks. Roth made it clear from the beginning that the renamed company, Nortel Networks, would be culturally closer to Bay Networks than to the former Northern Telecom. Roth made Bay's CEO, Dave House, President of the entire company and installed House's people in key positions in development, operations, and customer service. Bay's Chief Technology Officer was promoted to the same position over all of Nortel. Together, Roth and House remade Nortel's planning and product development around the idea of shortened product life cycles and innovative new products.[53]

PRODUCT PORTFOLIO

Developed by Hofer and based on the product life cycle, the 15-cell **product/market evolution matrix** (shown in **Figure 11–2**) depicts the types of developing products that cannot be easily shown on other portfolio matrixes. Products are plotted in terms of their competitive

Figure 11–2
Product/Market Evolution Portfolio Matrix

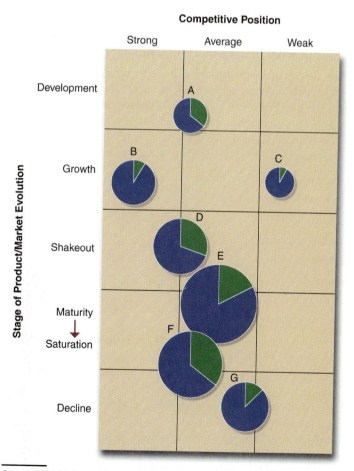

Source: C. W. Hofer and D. Schendel, *Strategy Formulation: Analytical Concepts* (St. Paul, MN: West Publishing Co., 1978), p. 34. From C. W. Hofer, "Conceptual Constructs for Formulating Corporate and Business Strategies" (Dover, MA: Case Publishing), no. BP-0041, p. 3. Copyright © 1977 by Charles W. Hofer. Reprinted by permission.

positions and their stages of product/market evolution. As on the GE Business Screen (depicted in **Figure 6.4** in **Chapter 6**), the circles represent the sizes of the industries involved, and the pie wedges represent the market shares of the firm's business product lines. Present and future matrixes can be developed to identify strategic issues. In response to **Figure 11–2**, for example, we could ask why product B does not have a greater share of the market, given its strong competitive position. We could also ask why the company has only one product in the developmental stage. A limitation of this matrix is that the product life cycle does not always hold for every product. Many products, for example, do not inevitably fall into decline but (like Tide detergent and Colgate toothpaste) are revitalized and put back on a growth track.

11.4 Strategy Implementation

If a corporation decides to develop innovations internally, it must make sure that its corporate system and culture are suitable for such a strategy. It must make sufficient resources available for new products, provide collaborative structures and processes, and incorporate innovation into its overall corporate strategy.[54] It must ensure that its R&D operations are managed appropriately. It must establish procedures to support all six **stages of new product development**. (See **Table 11–2**.) If, like most large corporations, the culture is too bureaucratic and rigid to support entrepreneurial projects, top management must reorganize so that innovative projects can be free to develop.

DEVELOPING AN INNOVATIVE ENTREPRENEURIAL CULTURE

To create a more innovative corporation, top management must develop an entrepreneurial culture—one that is open to the transfer of new technology into company activities and products and services. The company must be flexible and accepting of change. It should include a willingness to withstand a certain percentage of product failures on the way to success. Largeness is not a disadvantage. In his classic book, *Diffusion of Innovations*, Rogers reveals that innovative organizations tend to have the following characteristics:

- Positive attitude toward change
- Decentralized decision making
- Complexity
- Informal structure
- Interconnectedness
- Organizational slack (unused resources)
- Large size
- System openness[55]

Such a culture has been noted in 3M Corporation and Texas Instruments, among others. Research and development in these companies is managed quite differently from traditional methods. *First*, employees are dedicated to a particular project outcome rather than to innovation in general. *Second*, employees are often responsible for all functional activities and for all phases of the innovation process. Time is allowed to be sacrificed from regular duties to spend on innovative ideas. If the ideas are feasible, employees are temporarily reassigned to help develop them. They may become project champions who fight for resources to make the project a success. *Third*, these internal ventures are often separated from the rest of the company to provide them with greater independence, freedom from short-term pressures, different rewards, improved visibility, and access to key decision makers.[56]

The innovative process often involves individuals at different organizational levels who fulfill three different types of entrepreneurial roles: product champion, sponsor, and orchestrator.

Table 11–2 Six Stages of New Product Development

1. **Idea Generation:** New product concepts are identified and refined.
2. **Concept Evaluation:** Screening techniques are used to determine the concept's validity and market opportunity. Preliminary market research is conducted and a strategy is developed. A business plan is developed to present to management.
3. **Preliminary Design:** A new venture team is formed to prepare desired product specifications.
4. **Prototype Build and Test:** A functioning model of the product is built and subjected to numerous tests.
5. **Final Design and Pilot Production:** Final product and process designs are developed to produce small numbers of the product for use in test marketing. Suggestions from the users are fed back to the design team for possible inclusion in the final product.
6. **New Business Development:** The entire company is energized to launch the product.

Source: H.W. Oden, *Managing Corporate Culture, Innovation, and Intrapreneurship* (Westport, CT: Quorum Books, 1997).

A **product champion** is a person who generates a new idea and supports it through many organizational obstacles. A **sponsor** is usually a department manager who recognizes the value of the idea, helps obtain funding to develop the innovation, and facilitates its implementation. An **orchestrator** is someone in top management who articulates the need for innovation, provides funding for innovating activities, creates incentives for middle managers to sponsor new ideas, and protects idea/product champions from suspicious or jealous executives. Unless all of these roles are present in a company, major innovations are less likely to occur.[57]

Companies are finding that one way to overcome the barriers to successful product innovation is by using multifunctional teams with significant autonomy dedicated to a project. In a survey of 701 companies from Europe, the United States, and Japan, 85% of the respondents have used this approach with 62% rating it as successful.[58] Research reveals that cross-functional teams are best for designing and developing innovative new products, whereas the more traditional bureaucratic structures seem to be best for developing modifications to existing products, line extensions, and me-too products.[59] Chrysler Corporation was able to reduce the development time for new vehicles by 40% by using cross-functional teams and by developing a partnership approach to new projects.[60] International Specialty Products, a maker of polymers, used "product express" teams composed of chemists and representatives from manufacturing and engineering to cut development time in half. "Instead of passing a baton, we bring everyone into the commercialization process at the same time," explained John Tancredi, Vice-President for R&D. "We are moving laterally, like rugby players, instead of like runners in a relay race."[61] Companies throughout the world are beginning to realize the benefits from cross-functional teams in product development activities.

ORGANIZING FOR INNOVATION: CORPORATE ENTREPRENEURSHIP

Corporate entrepreneurship (also called intrapreneurship) is defined by Guth and Ginsburg as "the birth of new businesses within existing organizations, that is, internal innovation or venturing; and the transformation of organizations through renewal of the key ideas on which they are built, that is, strategic renewal."[62] A large corporation that wants to encourage innovation and creativity within its firm must choose a structure that will give the new business unit an appropriate amount of freedom while maintaining some degree of control at headquarters. Research reveals that corporate entrepreneurship has a positive impact on a company's financial performance.[63] Burgelman proposes (see **Figure 11–3**) that the use of a particular organizational design should be determined by (1) *the strategic importance of the new business to the corporation* and (2) *the relatedness of the unit's operations to those of the corpora-*

Figure 11–3
Organizational Designs for Corporate Entrepreneurship

Strategic Importance

		Very Important	Uncertain	Not Important
Operational Relatedness	**Unrelated**	**3** Special Business Units	**6** Independent Business Units	**9** Complete Spin-Off
	Partly Related	**2** New Product Business Department	**5** New Venture Division	**8** Contracting
	Strongly Related	**1** Direct Integration	**4** Micro New Ventures Department	**7** Nurturing and Contracting

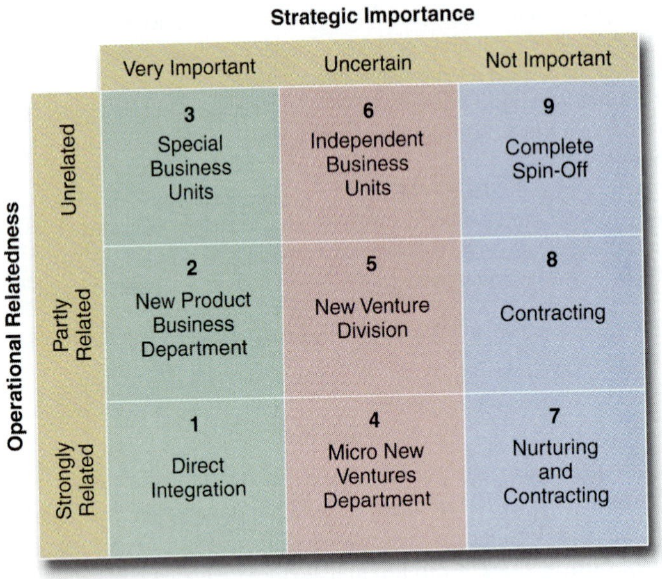

Source: Reprinted from R. A. Burgelman, "Designs for Corporate Entrepreneurship in Established Firms." Copyright © 1984 by the Regents of the University of California. Reprinted/condensed from *California Management Review*, Vol. 26, No. 3, p. 161. By permission of The Regents.

tion.[64] The combination of these two factors results in nine organizational designs for corporate entrepreneurship.

1. **Direct Integration:** A new business with a great deal of strategic importance and operational relatedness must be a part of the corporation's mainstream. Product champions—people who are respected by others in the corporation and who know how to work the system—are needed to manage these projects. Janiece Webb championed the incorporation of Internet Web browsers in Motorola's mobile phones and is now in charge of Motorola's Personal Networks Group. Since Webb's unit makes only software, she works with other divisions to shape their "product maps" that show what they hope to bring to market and when.[65]

2. **New Product Business Department:** A new business with a great deal of strategic importance and partial operational relatedness should be a separate department organized around an entrepreneurial project in the division where skills and capabilities can be shared. Maytag Corporation did this when it built a new plant near its current Newton, Iowa, washer plant to manufacture a wholly new *Neptune* line of energy and water efficient front-loading dishwashers.

3. **Special Business Units:** A new business with a great deal of strategic importance and low operational relatedness should be a special new business unit with specific objectives and time horizons. Teradyne tried this with a new product called Integra. The new product was based on a new, low-cost technology—something that might be good enough in a few years to replace Teradyne's current technology. Since the technology wasn't good enough for Teradyne's high-end applications, Teradyne's management treated Integra like an entrepreneurial venture. Integra's General Manager, Marc Levine, reported to a board of directors composed of Teradyne's top executives. Instead of a budget, Levine had a busi-

ness plan and venture capital (from Teradyne). This governance structure allowed Integra to operate autonomously by recruiting and purchasing from outside the company. According to Levine, "The idea was to think of this as a business from the start, not an R&D project. The board setup allows more of a coaching attitude." Says Teradyne's Rogas, "A division is always pressed to do the next logical thing—and make it compatible with the existing line. We told Marc: Be aggressive on the technology; do something no one else has done."[66]

4. **Micro New Ventures Department:** A new business with uncertain strategic importance and high operational relatedness should be a peripheral project, which is likely to emerge in the operating divisions on a continuous basis. Each division thus has its own new ventures department. Xerox Corporation, for example, uses its SBUs to generate and nurture new ideas. Small product-synthesis teams within each SBU test the feasibility of new ideas. Those concepts receiving a "go" are managed by an SBU product-delivery team, headed by a chief engineer, that takes the prototype from development through manufacturing.

5. **New Venture Division:** A new business with uncertain strategic importance that is only partly related to present corporate operations belongs in a new venture division. It brings together projects that either exist in various parts of the corporation or can be acquired externally; sizable new businesses are built. Lucent established an internal venture capital operation to fund the ideas of researchers from its Bell Labs R&D unit that didn't fit into existing business units. One new venture, Visual Insights, sells software that can detect billing fraud by analyzing patterns in large amounts of data. Another, Veridicom, does fingerprint authentication.[67]

6. **Independent Business Units:** Uncertain strategic importance coupled with no relationship to present corporate activities can make external arrangements attractive. Hewlett-Packard established printers as an independent business unit in Boise, Idaho (far from its Palo Alto, California, headquarters) because management was unsure of the desktop printer's future. According to Richard Belluzzo, head of HP's printer business, "We had the resources of a big company, but we were off on our own. There wasn't central planning . . . , so we could make decisions really fast."[68]

7. **Nurturing and Contracting:** When an entrepreneurial proposal might not be important strategically to the corporation but is strongly related to present operations, top management might help the entrepreneurial unit to spin off from the corporation. This allows a friendly competitor, instead of one of the corporation's major rivals, to capture a small niche. Techtronix has extensively used this approach. Because of research revealing that related spin-offs tend to be poorer performers than nonrelated spin-offs (presumably owing to the loss of benefits enjoyed with a larger company), it is especially important that the parent company continue to support the development of the spun-off unit in this cell.[69]

8. **Contracting:** As the required capabilities and skills of the new business are less related to those of the corporation, the parent corporation may spin off the strategically unimportant unit yet keep some relationship through a contractual arrangement with the new firm. The connection is useful in case the new firm eventually develops something of value to the corporation. For example, B.F. Goodrich offered manufacturing rights plus a long-term purchasing agreement to a couple of its managers for a specific raw material Goodrich still used (in declining quantities) in its production process but no longer wanted to manufacture internally.

9. **Complete Spin-Off:** If both the strategic importance and the operational relatedness of the new business are negligible, the corporation is likely to completely sell off the business to another firm or to the present employees in some form of ESOP (Employee Stock

Ownership Plan). The corporation also could sell off the unit through a leveraged buy-out (executives of the unit buy the unit from the parent company with money from a third source, to be repaid out of the unit's anticipated earnings). Because 3M wanted to focus its development money on areas with more profit potential, it decided to spin off its money-losing data storage and medical imaging divisions as a new company called Imation.

Organizing for innovation has become especially important for those corporations that want to become more innovative, but their age and size have made them highly bureaucratic with a culture that discourages creative thinking. These new structural designs for corporate entrepreneurship cannot work by themselves, however; they must have the support of management and sufficient resources. They must also have employees who are risk takers, willing to purchase an ownership interest in the new venture, and a corporate culture that supports new ventures.

11.5 Evaluation and Control

Companies want to gain more productivity at a faster pace from their research and development activities. But how do we measure the effectiveness or efficiency of a company's R&D? This is a problem given that a company shouldn't expect more than one in seven product ideas from basic research to make it to the marketplace. Some companies measure the proportion of their sales attributable to new products. For example, Hewlett-Packard measures how much of its revenues come from products introduced in the past three years.[70] At BellCore, the research part of seven regional Bell telephone companies, the effectiveness of basic research is measured by how often the lab's research is cited in other scientists' work. This measure is compiled and published by the Institute for Scientific Information. Other companies judge the quality of research by counting how many patents are filed annually.

A novel way of both evaluating and marketing new software products is to use potential consumers to sample the product. Microsoft routinely offers information systems people and other software users the opportunity to try beta (not quite ready for prime time) versions of its software. A cheap way to do quality control, users e-mail Microsoft about any problems they had with a program. At one time, beta testing was so popular that Microsoft actually charged people for the use of its betas! An even more novel approach to evaluation and control is that being used by Argus Systems Group, maker of PitBull computer security software. See the 🛡 **Internet Issue** feature to see how the company actually challenged hackers to attack its product.

Pittiglio Rabin Todd McGrath (PRTM), a high-tech consulting firm, proposes an **index of R&D effectiveness**. The index is calculated by dividing the percentage of total revenue spent on R&D into new product profitability, which is expressed as a percentage. When applying this measure to 45 large electronics manufacturers, only 9 companies scored 1.0 or higher, indicating that only 20% received a positive payback from their R&D spending. The top companies kept spending on marginal products to a minimum by running frequent checks on product versus market opportunities and canceling questionable products quickly. They also moved new products to market in half the time of the others. As a result, revenue growth among the top 20% of the companies was double the average of all 45 companies.[71]

A study of 15 multinational companies with successful R&D operations focused on three measures of R&D success: (1) improving technology transfer from R&D to business units, (2) accelerating time to market for new products and processes, and (3) institutionalizing cross-functional participation in R&D. The companies participated in basic, applied, and developmental research activities. The study revealed 13 **best practices** that all of the companies followed.[72] Listed in **Table 11–3**, they provide a benchmark for a company's R&D activities.

Internet Issue

Software Company Challenges Hackers to Attack Its Product

Akey problem with the Internet is computer security. The Web sites of companies like Yahoo!, eBay, and even Microsoft have been successfully attacked by hackers. Given time and patience, a software expert could get past most corporations' computer security systems. As a way of testing and marketing its PitBull software, Argus Systems Groups joined with *eWeek* magazine in 2001 to challenge computer hackers to penetrate its computer security product. Although hacking contests have been taking place since the mid-1980s, Argus raised the stakes to validate a product it contends is the Fort Knox of computer security. Hackers were given two weeks to complete four tasks relating to corrupting a Web site protected by PitBull. There were prizes for being the first to complete each task with a grand prize of $50,000 for being the first to complete all four. (Argus had originally thought to give away a car, but then realized that a significant number of the participants were not old enough to drive.)

In previous contests in Las Vegas and Munich, hackers had failed to break into Argus-protected systems. Argus joined the contest as a way of proving the worth of its product. Many in the computer industry argue that hacking contests such as this one prove little. "If you have the skills to break into a product that's secure, are you going to announce it to the world, or are you going to keep those skills to yourself?" asks Jeff Moss, a hacker and security expert at Blackhat, a computer company firm. For example, Riley Eller, known as "caezar" to fellow computer hackers known as the Ghetto Hackers, stated that he would not take part in the OpenHackIII competition. Randy Sandone, CEO of Argus, acknowledged that the test was imperfect. "Even if we survive the two weeks without breaches, we're not going to claim that our system is fundamentally impenetrable." Nevertheless, the contest provided some incentive to "some pretty serious people to give (the system) a good thrashing."

Source: J. Pope, "Computer Hacking Competition Begins," *The (Ames) Tribune* (January 16, 2001), p. A2.

Table 11–3 Thirteen "Best Practices" for Improving R&D

1. Corporate and business unit strategies are well defined and clearly communicated.
2. Core technologies are defined and communicated to R&D.
3. Investments are made in developing multinational R&D capabilities to tap ideas throughout the world.
4. Funding for basic research comes from corporate sources to ensure a long-term focus; funding for development comes from business units to ensure accountability.
5. Basic and applied research are performed either at a central facility or at a small number of labs, each focused on a particular discipline of science or technology. Development work is usually performed at business unit sites.
6. Formal, cross-functional teams are created for basic, applied, and developmental projects.
7. Formal mechanisms exist for regular interaction among scientists, and between R&D and other functions.
8. Analytical tools are used for selecting projects as well as for on-going project evaluation.
9. The transfer of technology to business units is the most important measure of R&D performance.
10. Effective measures of career development are in place at all levels of R&D.
11. Recruiting of new people is from diverse universities and from other companies when specific experience or skills are required that would take long to develop internally.
12. Some basic research is performed internally, but there are also many university and third-party relationships.
13. Formal mechanisms are used for monitoring external technological developments.

Source: I. Krause and J. Liu, "Benchmarking R&D Productivity," *Planning Review* (January/February 1993), pp. 16–21, 52–53. Copyright © MCB University Press Ltd. Reprinted with permission.

11.6 Impact of the Internet on Managing Technology and Innovation

The Internet is becoming essential for research and development in today's world. Cross-functional collaboration with colleagues around the world is possible only with modern communication. At the Royal Dutch/Shell Group, six teams of six people each meet every week at the Exploration and Production Divisions in Houston, Texas, and in Rijswijk, Netherlands, to consider ideas that have been sent to them by e-mail. Out of these "GameChanger" teams came four of the five top business initiatives for the corporation in 1999. One of them was Shell's new "Light Touch" oil-discovery method—a way of using lasers to sense hydrocarbon emissions released naturally into the air from underground reserves. Increasing numbers of companies are using the Internet to stimulate and manage innovation. The concept is for small entrepreneurial teams to drive innovation at a rate never before experienced in large corporations. According to Christensen, author of *The Innovator's Dilemma*, "The trend now is to decentralize operations, to build idea factories, or idea markets. This is a way to bring the startup mentality inside."[73]

Companies like Nortel Networks and Procter & Gamble are adopting this "knowledge market" approach to innovation. Nortel allocates *phantom stock* to those who volunteer for special high-risk innovative projects. Nortel buys the stock as if the project was an IPO. Employees are paid in chits redeemable for cash once when the project is finished and again after it has been on the market about a year. P&G has created a Corporate New Ventures (CNV) unit as an autonomous idea lab with a mission of encouraging new ideas for products and putting them into speedy production. Ideas bubbling up from P&G's worldwide workforce of 110,000 people are routed to the CNV innovation panel via *My Idea*, a corporate collaboration network. Employees submitting winning ideas are rewarded with stock options. CNV teams then analyze the ideas using the Internet to analyze markets, demographics, and cost information to learn if the idea is a feasible opportunity. Once the team agrees on an idea, a project is launched within days. The CNV has the authority to tap any resources in the company to bring a product to market. So far, CNV has generated 58 marketable products. One of these, a cleaning product called *Swiffer*, was commercialized in just 10 months, less than half the usual time. Swiffer is a disposable cloth that generates static electricity to attract dust and dirt. The idea for it was generated by P&G's paper and cleaning-agent experts during a discussion on the Internet. According to Craig Wynett, CNV President, "It was an exercise in speed, in breaking down the company's traditional division-by-division territories to come up with new ideas."[74]

Projections for the 21st Century

- From 1994 to 2010, the number of communications satellites worldwide will grow from 1,100 to 2,260.
- From 1994 to 2010, the number of McDonald's fast food restaurants will increase from 14,000 to 31,000—many of them outside the United States.[75]

Discussion Questions

1. How should a corporation scan the external environment for new technological developments? Who should be responsible?

2. What is technology research and how does it differ from market research?

3. What is the importance of product and process R&D to competitive strategy?

4. What factors help determine whether a company should outsource a technology?

5. How can a company develop an entrepreneurial culture?

Strategic Practice Exercise

HOW CREATIVE IS YOUR ORGANIZATION?

One of the keys to managing technology and innovation is to have a creative organization in which people are free to propose and try new ideas. The following questionnaire is taken from "Building a Creative Hothouse" by Barton Kunstler in the January–February, 2001, issue of *The Futurist*. It is a simplified version of the Hothouse Assessment Instrument presented in greater detail in the Spring 2000 issue of *Futures Research Quarterly*. This version describes many of the elements of a highly creative organization.

If you work or have worked full time in an organization, answer this questionnaire in light of your experience with that organization. If you have not worked full time anywhere, find someone who is working full time and ask them to complete this questionnaire. Then discuss their answers with them.

To assess the level of creativity in your organization's culture, score your level of agreement or disagreement with the statements below as follows: **Strongly Agree** (5 points), **Mildly Agree** (4 points), **Neutral** (3 points), **Mildly Disagree** (2 points), **Strongly Disagree** (1 point).

Values

_____ 1. We believe that our work can change the world.

_____ 2. The organization actively promotes a positive quality of life in our surrounding communities.

_____ 3. People here really believe our products and services are vital to others' well-being.

_____ 4. Virtually all who work here continually study and question the basic nature of their job and the technologies—human, organizational, technical—they work with.

_____ 5. Working here fills me with a sense of personal well-being and commitment to my higher values.

Mission and Vision

_____ 6. Principles of justice and compassion directly and significantly influence strategy, design, and development.

_____ 7. We explore the fundamental practices and principles of our industry and its disciplines as a source of creativity, values, and purpose.

_____ 8. We can fail without fear for our jobs.

_____ 9. My organization takes the long view.

_____ 10. Employees are free to develop their own vision of what their jobs entail.

Ideas

_____ 11. This organization cultivates the growth of knowledge into wisdom and views wisdom as a guide to action.

_____ 12. Organizational structure is shaped by innovative, idea-driven approaches to our challenges and tasks.

_____ 13. Organizational responses to crises are thoughtful and imaginative, not reactive and typical.

_____ 14. The organization respects thinkers.

_____ 15. I am respected for all my talents, whether or not they contribute to the bottom line.

Exchange

_____ 16. My organization rewards those who display mastery at their jobs and seeks their advice, whatever their title or position.

_____ 17. Institutionalized procedures enable anyone to make suggestions or raise objections.

_____ 18. Intellectually exciting and stimulating conversation directly influences product development and delivery.

_____ 19. "Idea people" share their vision with other employees and invite feedback.

_____ 20. The group uses conflict as an opportunity for personal and organizational growth.

Perception

_____ 21. How we perceive our tasks, our expertise, and the group itself is a legitimate object of inquiry.

_____ 22. Whole-minded thinking, including activities based on movement and heightening awareness of the five senses, is encouraged.

_____ 23. Employees are taught and encouraged to think creatively.

_____ 24. We continually re-vision our group's place within its industry and society as a whole.

_____ 25. Clear problem-solving algorithms are taught, practiced, developed, and applied wherever a need is perceived, without regard to concerns of status, tradition, or company politics.

Learning

_____ 26. To be viewed as a "continuous learner" at work benefits one's career.

_____ 27. We regularly challenge group norms, and anyone can initiate this process.

_____ 28. My organization is constantly engaged in learning about itself and the environments in which it operates.

_____ 29. The organization allocates resources toward employee involvement in cultural events as attendees, participants, or learners.

_____ 30. Projects are undertaken by integrated teams whose members bring multiple disciplines and diverse perspectives to the task.

Social

_____ 31. Our relationships at work are relaxed, irreverent, warm, and crackling with ideas.

_____ 32. People from different departments and organizational levels socialize together, either during or after work.

_____ 33. Committee meetings are reasonably productive and amicable.

_____ 34. When we form teams to work on special projects, the work is integrated into our day-to-day schedules.

_____ 35. We always produce effective leadership when and where we need it.

Festiva

_____ 36. Social occasions are planned and designed in highly creative ways.

_____ 37. The line between work and play is virtually nonexistent.

_____ 38. Developments in art, politics, science, and other fields not directly related to our work are discussed in relation to their impact upon our organization and industry.

_____ 39. We have a strong group vocabulary of terms and symbols that promotes communication, community, and creativity.

_____ 40. We are encouraged to play whimsically with ideas, materials, and objects as well as with new ways of doing things.

_____   **TOTAL POINTS**

SCORING YOUR ORGANIZATION'S CREATIVITY

If you Scored:	Organization Is in the Creative. . .
40–79	**Dead Zone**—a place where it is virtually impossible for creativity to flourish
80–159	**I-Zone**—where management thinks in terms of the next quarter and creativity is seldom transmitted from one person or department to another* OR. . . **O-Zone**—where creativity is valued but not consistently incorporated into the organization's strategy*
160–200	**Hot Zone**—where creativity is intense and productive

*Note: I-Zone organizations score higher on Values, Ideas, Perception, and Social questions. O-Zone organizations score higher on Mission and Vision, Learning, Exchange, and Festiva questions.

Source: B. Kunstler, "Building a Creative Hothouse," *The Futurist* (January–February 2001), pp. 22–29. Reprinted by permission.

Key Terms

Notes

1. J. A. Byrne, "Management by Web," *Business Week* (August 28, 2000), p. 96.
2. R. Jonash and T. Sommerlatte, *The Innovation Premium* (Perseus Books, 1999).
3. G. Getz and C. Christensen, "Should You Fear Disruptive Technology?" *Fortune* (April 3, 2000), pp. 249–250.
4. "Fear of the Unknown," *The Economist* (December 4, 1999), pp. 61–62.
5. M. S. Malone, "Which Are the Most Valuable Companies in the New Economy?" *Forbes ASAP* (May 29, 2000), pp. 212–214.
6. S. J. Towner, "Four Ways to Accelerate New Product Development," *Long Range Planning* (April 1994), p. 57.
7. R. Garud and P. R. Nayyar, "Transformative Capacity: Continual Structuring by Intertemporal Technology Transfer," *Strategic Management Journal* (June 1994), p. 379.
8. C. A. Ferland, book review of *Third Generation R&D—Managing the Link to Corporate Strategy* by P. A. Roussel, K. N. Saad, and T. J. Erickson, in *Long Range Planning* (April 1993), p. 128.
9. M. A. Schilling and C. W. L. Hill, "Managing the New Product Development Process: Strategic Imperatives," *Academy of Management Executive* (August 1998), pp. 67–81.
10. C. Power, K. Kerwin, R. Grover, K. Alexander, and R. D. Hof, "Flops," *Business Week* (August 16, 1993), pp. 76–82.
11. B. R. Schlender, "How Sony Keeps the Magic Going," *Fortune* (February 24, 1992), p. 77.
12. G. C. Hill and K. Yamada, "Motorola Illustrates How an Aged Giant Can Remain Vibrant," *Wall Street Journal* (December 9, 1992), pp. A1, A14.
13. N. Snyder, "Environmental Volatility, Scanning Intensity and Organizational Performance," *Journal of Contemporary Business* (September 1981), p. 16.
14. R. Nobel and J. Birkinshaw, "Innovations in MNCs: Control and Communication Patterns in International R&D Operations," *Strategic Management Journal* (May 1998), pp. 479–496.
15. P. Almeida, "Knowledge Sourcing by Foreign Multinationals: Patent Citation Analysis in the U.S. Semiconductor Industry," *Strategic Management Journal* (December 1996), pp. 155–165.
16. E. Von Hippel, *The Sources of Innovation* (Oxford: Oxford University Press, 1988), p. 4.
17. M. R. Neale and D. R. Corkindale, "Co-Developing Products: Involving Customer Earlier and More Deeply," *Long Range Planning* (June 1998), pp. 418–425.
18. E. Von Hippel, *The Sources of Innovation*, p. 107; E. Von Hippel, S. Thomke, and M. Sonnack, "Creating Breakthroughs at 3M," *Harvard Business Review* (September–October 1999), p. 48.
19. Von Hippel, Thomke, and Sonnack, p. 52.
20. G. Hamel and C. K. Prahalad, "Seeing the Future First," *Fortune* (September 5, 1995), p. 70.
21. C. M. Christensen, *The Innovator's Dilemma* (Boston: HBS Press, 1997); J. Wade, "A Community-Level Analysis of Sources and Rates of Technological Variation in the Microprocessor Market," *Academy of Management Journal* (October 1996), pp. 1218–1244.
22. C. M. Christensen and J. L. Bower, "Customer Power, Strategic Investment, and the Failure of Leading Firms," *Strategic Management Journal* (March 1996), pp. 197–218.
23. G. S. Lynn, J. G. Morone, and A. S. Paulson, "Marketing and Discontinuous Innovation: The Probe and Learn Process," *California Management Review* (Spring 1996), pp. 8–37.
24. W. I. Zangwill, "When Customer Research Is a Lousy Idea," *Wall Street Journal* (March 8, 1993), p. A10.
25. S. Baker, "What Every Business Should Learn from Microsoft," *Journal of Business Strategy* (September/October 1998), pp. 36–41.
26. D. F. Kuratko, J. S. Hornsby, D. W. Naffziger, and R. V. Montagno, "Implement Entrepreneurial Thinking in Established Organizations," *SAM Advanced Management Journal* (Winter 1993), p. 29.
27. "Business Bulletin," *Wall Street Journal* (May 1, 1997), p. A1. The number has improved from 58 ideas in 1967 to 11 in 1990, to 7 in 1995.
28. L. G. Franko, "Global Corporate Competition: Who's Winning, Who's Losing, and the R&D Factor as One Reason Why," *Strategic Management Journal* (September–October 1989), pp. 449–474. See also P. S. Chan, E. J. Flynn, and R. Chinta, "The Strategies of Growing and Turnaround Firms: A Multiple Discriminant Analysis," *International Journal of Management* (September 1991), pp. 669–675.
29. M. J. Chussil, "How Much to Spend on R&D?" *The PIMS-letter of Business Strategy*, No. 13 (Cambridge, Mass.: The Strategic Planning Institute, 1978), p. 5.
30. J. S. Harrison, E. H. Hall, Jr., and R. Nargundkar, "Resource Allocation as an Outcropping of Strategic Consistency: Performance Implications," *Academy of Management Journal* (October 1993), pp. 1026–1051.
31. S. B. Graves and N. S. Langowitz, "Innovative Productivity and Returns to Scale in the Pharmaceutical Industry," *Strategic Management Journal* (November 1993), pp. 593–605; A. Brady, "Small Is as Small Does," *Journal of Business Strategy* (March/April 1995), pp. 44–52.
32. J. B. Sorensen and T. E. Stuart, "Aging, Obsolescence, and Organizational Innovation," *Administrative Science Quarterly* (March 2000), pp. 81–112.
33. D. H. Freedman, "Through the Looking Glass," in "The State of Small Business," *INC.* (May 21, 1996), pp. 48–54.
34. N. Nohria and R. Gulati, "Is Slack Good or Bad for Innovation?" *Academy of Management Journal* (October 1996), pp. 1245–1264.
35. M. A. Hitt, R. E. Hoskisson, and J. S. Harrison, "Strategic Competitiveness in the 1990s: Challenges and Opportunities for U.S. Executives," *Academy of Management Executive* (May 1991), p. 13.
36. T. F. O'Boyle, "Steel's Management Has Itself to Blame," *Wall Street Journal* (May 17, 1983), p. 32.
37. M. Silva and B. Sjögren, *Europe 1992 and the New World Power Game* (New York: John Wiley & Sons, 1990), p. 231.
38. E. Mansfield, M. Schwartz, and S. Wagner, "Imitation Costs and Patents: An Empirical Study," *Economic Journal* (December 1981), pp. 907–918.
39. G. Stalk, Jr., and A. M. Webber, "Japan's Dark Side of Time," *Harvard Business Review* (July–August 1993), p. 99.
40. M. Robert, "Market Fragmentation Versus Market Segmentation," *Journal of Business Strategy* (September/October 1992), p. 52.
41. K. Kelly and M. Ivey, "Turning Cummins into the Engine Maker That Could," *Business Week* (July 30, 1990), pp. 20–21.
42. Silva and Sjögren, *Europe 1992 and the New World Power Game*, pp. 239–241. See also P. Nueno and J. Oosterveld, "Managing Technology Alliances," *Long Range Planning* (June 1988), pp. 11–17.
43. B. Schlender, "Killer Chip," *Fortune* (November 10, 1997), pp. 70–80.
44. P. R. Nayak, "Should You Outsource Product Development?" *Journal of Business Strategy* (May/June 1993), pp. 44–45.
45. C. W. L. Hill, "Establishing a Standard: Competitive Strategy and Technological Standards in Winner-Take-All Industries," *Academy of Management Executive* (May 1997), pp. 7–25.
46. M. H. Roy and S. S. Dugal, "The Effect of Technological Environment and Competitive Strategy on Licensing Decisions," *American Business Review* (June 1999), pp. 112–118.

47. M. A. Hitt, R. E. Hoskisson, R. A. Johnson, and D. D. Moesel, "The Market for Corporate Control and Firm Innovation," *Academy of Management Journal* (October 1996), pp. 1084–1119.

48. W. M. Cohen and D. A. Levinthal, "Absorptive Capacity: A New Perspective on Learning and Innovation," *Administrative Science Quarterly* (March 1990), pp. 128–152.

49. P. J. Lane and M. Lubatkin, "Absorptive Capacity and Inter-organizational Learning," *Strategic Management Journal* (May 1998), pp. 461–477.

50. M. B. Heeley, "Appropriating Rents from External Knowledge: The Impact of Absorptive Capacity on Firm Sales Growth and Research Productivity," paper presented to *Babson Entre-preneurship Research Conference* (Wellesley, MA), 1997.

51. "The Impact of Industrial Robotics on the World of Work," *International Labour Review*, Vol. 125, No. 1 (1986). Summarized in "The Risks of Robotization," *The Futurist* (May–June 1987), p. 56.

52. Hitt, Hoskisson, and Harrison, "Strategic Competitiveness in the 1990s: Challenges and Opportunities for U.S. Executives," p. 9.

53. S. Chaudhuri and B. Tabrizi, "Capturing the Real Value in High-Tech Acquisitions," *Harvard Business Review* (September/October 1999), pp. 123–130.

54. D. Dougherty and C. Hardy, "Sustained Product Innovation in Large, Mature Organizations: Overcoming Innovation-to-Organization Problems," *Academy of Management* (October 1996), pp. 1120–1153.

55. E. M. Rogers, *Diffusion of Innovations*, 4th edition (New York: Free Press, 1995).

56. C. A. Lengnick-Hall, "Innovation and Competitive Advantage: What We Know and What We Need to Know," *Journal of Management* (June 1992), pp. 399–429.

57. J. R. Galbraith, "Designing the Innovative Organization," *Organizational Dynamics* (Winter 1982), pp. 5–25.

58. P. R. Nayak, "Product Innovation Practices in Europe, Japan, and the U.S.," *Journal of Business Strategy* (May/June 1992), pp. 62–63.

59. E. M. Olson, "Organizing for Effective New Product Devel-opment: The Moderating Role of Product Innovativeness," *Journal of Marketing* (January 1995) as reported by K. Z. Andrews in *Harvard Business Review* (November–December 1995), pp. 12–13.

60. D. Rowe, "Up and Running," *Journal of Business Strategy* (May/June 1993), pp. 48–50.

61. N. Freundlich and M. Schroeder, "Getting Everybody Into the Act," *Business Week* (Quality 1991 edition), p. 152.

62. W. D. Guth and A. Ginsberg, "Corporate Entrepreneurship," *Strategic Management Journal* (Summer 1990), p. 5.

63. S. A. Zahra and J. G. Covin, "Contextual Measures on the Corporate Entrepreneurship–Performance Relationship: A Longitudinal Analysis," *Journal of Business Venturing*, Vol. 10 (1995), pp. 43–58.

64. R. A. Burgelman, "Designs for Corporate Entrepreneurship," *California Management Review* (Spring 1984), pp. 154–166; R. A. Burgelman and L. R. Sayles, *Inside Corporate Innovation* (New York: The Free Press, 1986).

65. W. J. Holstein, "Remaking Motorola Isn't Easy," *U.S. News & World Report* (October 23, 2000), p. 52; R. O. Crockett, "A New Company Called Motorola," *Business Week* (April 17, 2000), pp. 86–92.

66. T. A. Stewart, "How Teradyne Solved the Innovator's Dilemma," *Fortune* (June 10, 2000), pp. 188–190.

67. J. Carey, "An Ivory Tower That Spins Pure Gold," *Business Week* (April 19, 1999), pp. 167–170.

68. S. K. Yoder, "How H-P Used Tactics of the Japanese to Beat Them at Their Game," *Wall Street Journal* (September 8, 1994), pp. A1, A6.

69. C. Y. Woo, G. E. Willard, and S. M. Beckstead, "Spin-Offs: What Are the Gains?" *Journal of Business Strategy* (March–April 1989), pp. 29–32.

70. J. B. Levin and R. D. Hof, "Has Philips Found Its Wizard?" *Business Week* (September 6, 1993), pp. 82–84.

71. O. Port, "Rating R&D: How Companies Get the Biggest Bang for the Buck," *Business Week* (July 5, 1993), p. 98.

72. I. Krause and J. Liu, "Benchmarking R&D Productivity," *Planning Review* (January/February 1993), pp. 16–21, 52–53.

73. M. Stepanek, "Using the Net for Brainstorming," *Business Week E.Biz* (December 13, 1999), p. EB55.

74. Stepanek, pp. EB55–EB59.

75. J. Warner, "21st Century Capitalism: Snapshots of the Next Century," *Business Week* (November 18, 1994), p. 194.

chapter 12

Strategic Issues in Entrepreneurial Ventures and Small Businesses

Debbie Giampapa was at a party juggling her food plate and drink. "This is ridiculous," she thought. "Why doesn't somebody make something to hold this?" When she got home she pulled a piece of cardboard out of the trash and cut a hole large enough to hold a standard 10-ounce plastic cup. Then she added a smaller hole for a wine glass. After much trial and error and a lot of perseverance in obtaining funding, plus deciding how to make and market her product, she established her own company, FunZone. She went to die cutters and machinists to learn how machines could make her product. She told them she was doing door hangers because she didn't want them to steal her idea. Said Giampapa, "The more I understand what the machine can do, the better I can design the product." Giampapa is now selling thousands of "Party HOLDems" to customers like American Express, Walt Disney Company, and Coopers and Lybrand. When asked the secret of her success, she responded:

It's not having the idea. It's believing in yourself and your product enough to put up the money and time for that. I've put in 16-hour days, seven-day weeks for two years.[1]

12.1 Importance of Small Business and Entrepreneurial Ventures

Strategic management as a field of study typically deals with large, established business corporations. However, small business cannot be ignored. There are 22 million small businesses—over 95% of all businesses in the United States. During the 1990s, 85% of all new jobs in the United States were created by small firms and 70% of these by the fastest growing entrepreneurial firms.[2] Research reveals that not only do small firms spend almost twice as much of their R&D dollars on fundamental research as do large firms, but also that small companies are responsible for a high proportion of innovations in products and services.[3] For example, new small firms produce 24 times more innovation per research dollar than do the much larger *Fortune* 500 firms.[4] The National Science Foundation estimates that 98% of "radical" product developments result from the research done in the labs of small companies.[5] Nevertheless, not every country is as supportive of new ventures as is the United States. See the Global Issue feature to learn how different countries support entrepreneurship.

Despite the overall success of small businesses, however, every year tens of thousands of small companies fail. Figures from the U.S. Small Business Administration generally support the rule of thumb that 50% of businesses founded in any one year are not in business

Global Issue

Entrepreneurship: Some Countries Are More Supportive Than Others

Entrepreneurship is becoming increasingly important throughout the world. True to economist Joseph Schumpeter's view of entrepreneurship as "creative destruction," much of the world from Eastern Europe to South America to Asia envisions entrepreneurial ventures as the means to build successful free market economies. New entrepreneurial ventures are emerging daily in these countries. Unfortunately, not every country makes it easy to start a new business.

According to the World Economic Forum's *Global Competitiveness Report,* countries range from easy (7) to difficult (1) in terms of the ease of starting an entrepreneurial venture. The easiest is the United States with a rating of 6.06, followed by New Zealand, Iceland, Canada, Finland, Britain, and The Netherlands at 5.5. The most difficult countries listed are Austria at 3.96, followed by Japan, Italy, Spain, Belgium, France, and Germany at 4.5. A separate *Economic Creativity Index* developed by the World Economic Forum gauges countries' involvement in innovation. Based on observed data and survey results, the index measures the level of technology and the conditions favoring new business start-ups. Highest marks go to the United States (+2.1) followed by Finland, Singapore, Israel, Britain, Hong Kong, Germany, and Taiwan (+1.0). The lowest marks go to Columbia (−1.3) followed by Venezuela, Russia, Peru, China, Argentina, and Indonesia (−0.4).

Even though entrepreneurship is more difficult in many other parts of the world than in the United States, the situation is changing. For example, investors are flocking to young, fast-growing companies in Europe. The number of European entrepreneurs has been gradually increasing through the 1990s. Politicians are beginning to see entrepreneurs as part of a solution to unemployment rather than as grasping exploiters. In 1997, European venture capital firms accounted for $23 billion in new venture capital. The total amount spent by private equity firms increased by 42% to $11.3 billion. The EASDAQ, founded in 1996, is Europe's version of the NASDAQ. Companies can be listed on the EASDAQ regardless of size or history so long as they agree to international accounting standards and U.S. style financial reporting.

There is still an ingrained cultural aversion to the risk taking so necessary to entrepreneurship. The contradiction between the Marxist ideology and private ownership in China means that business entrepreneurs are not perceived as legitimate. The social stigma attached to business failure is deeply entrenched in many countries. According to Christophe Sapet, the French founder of a computer game company called Infogrames, "When you earn money, (French) people are jealous. They think you have done something wrong." From 1984 to 1991, the OECD estimates that the United States established new businesses at four times the rate of France.

Sources: J. Kahn, "Suddenly, Startups Are Chic," *Fortune* (February 15, 1999), p. 110; "Financial Indicators," *The Economist* (October 16, 1999), p. 109; "Emerging-Market Indicators," *The Economist* (September 23, 2000), p. 128; E. W. K. Tsang, "In Search of Legitimacy: The Private Entrepreneur in China," *Entrepreneurship Theory and Practice* (Fall 1996), pp. 21–30.

five years later.[6] Similar rates occur in the United Kingdom, The Netherlands, Japan, Taiwan, and Hong Kong.[7] Although an increasing number of studies are more positive regarding the survival rate of new entrepreneurial ventures, new businesses are definitely considered risky.[8] The causes of small-business failure (depending on the study cited) range from inadequate accounting systems to inability to cope with growth. The underlying problem appears to be an overall lack of strategic management—beginning with an inability to plan a strategy to reach the customer and ending with a failure to develop a system of controls to keep track of performance.[9]

DEFINITION OF SMALL-BUSINESS FIRMS AND ENTREPRENEURIAL VENTURES

The most commonly accepted definition of a small-business firm in the United States is one that employs fewer than 500 people and that generates sales of less than $20 million annually.

Although the meanings of the terms "small business" and "entrepreneurship" overlap considerably, the concepts are different. The **small-business firm** is independently owned and operated, not dominant in its field, and does not engage in innovative practices. The **entrepreneurial venture**, in contrast, is any business whose primary goals are profitability and growth and that can be characterized by innovative strategic practices.[10] The basic difference between the small-business firm and the entrepreneurial venture, therefore, lies not in the type of goods or services provided but in their fundamental views on growth and innovation. According to Donald Sexton, an authority on entrepreneurship, this explains why strategic planning is more likely to be present in an entrepreneurial venture than in the typical small-business firm:

> *Most firms start with just a single product. Those oriented toward growth immediately start looking for another one. It's that planning approach that separates the entrepreneur from the small-business owner.[11]*

THE ENTREPRENEUR AS STRATEGIST

Often defined as a person who organizes and manages a business undertaking and who assumes risk for the sake of a profit, the **entrepreneur** is the ultimate strategist. He or she makes all the strategic as well as operational decisions. All three levels of strategy—corporate, business, and functional—are the concerns of this founder and owner/manager of a company. As one entrepreneur puts it: "Entrepreneurs are strategic planners without realizing it."

The founding of FunZone described earlier captures the key elements of the entrepreneurial venture: a basic business idea that has not yet been successfully tried and a gutsy entrepreneur who, while working on borrowed capital and a shoestring budget, creates a new business through a lot of trial and error and persistent hard work. Similar stories can be told of other people, such as Debbie Fields, who created Mrs. Fields Cookies, and Will Parish, who founded National Energy Associates. Both were ridiculed at one time or another for their desire to start a business. Friends and family told Debbie Fields that starting a business to sell chocolate chip cookies "was a stupid idea." Will Parish, who built a power plant in California's Imperial Valley that burns "pasture patties," was called an "entre-manure." Every day the plant burned 900 tons of manure collected from nearby feedlots to generate 15 megawatts of electricity—enough to light 20,000 homes. The power was sold to Southern California Edison. Parish got the idea from a trip to India where the fuel used to heat a meal was cow dung. Once the plant was earning a profit, Parish planned to build a larger plant nearby that would burn wheat straw and other crop wastes. The plants provide an environmentally sound as well as profitable way to dispose of waste. Very interested in conservation, Parish says, "I wanted to combine doing well with doing good."[12]

Successful new ventures often propose an entirely new approach to doing business, called a "new business model." A **business model** describes the mix of activities a company performs to deliver goods and services to customers. Coined in the 1990s, the term is used to show how the Internet and global trade are changing how companies must do business today.

12.2 Use of Strategic Planning and Strategic Management

Research shows that strategic planning is strongly related to small-business financial performance.[13] A survey of the high growth *Inc.* 500 firms revealed that 86% performed strategic planning. Of those performing strategic planning, 94% reported improved profits.[14] Nevertheless, many small companies still do not use the process. The reasons often cited for the apparent lack of strategic planning practices in many small-business firms are fourfold:

- **Not enough time:** Day-to-day operating problems take up the time necessary for long-term planning. It's relatively easy to justify avoiding strategic planning on the basis of day-to-day crisis management. Some will ask: "How can I be expected to do strategic planning when I don't know if I'm going to be in business next week?"

- **Unfamiliar with strategic planning:** The small-business CEO may be unaware of strategic planning or may view it as irrelevant to the small-business situation. Planning may be viewed as a straitjacket that limits flexibility.

- **Lack of skills:** Small-business managers often lack the skills necessary to begin strategic planning and do not have or want to spend the money necessary to import trained consultants. Future uncertainty may be used to justify a lack of planning. One entrepreneur admits, "Deep down, I know I should plan. But I don't know what to do. I'm the leader but I don't know how to lead the planning process."

- **Lack of trust and openness:** Many small-business owner/managers are very sensitive regarding key information about the business and are thus unwilling to share strategic planning with employees or outsiders. For this reason, boards of directors are often composed only of close friends and relatives of the owner/manager—people unlikely to provide an objective viewpoint or professional advice.

DEGREE OF FORMALITY

Research generally concludes that the strategic planning process can be far more informal in small companies than it is in large corporations.[15] Some studies have even found that too much formalization of the strategic planning process may actually result in reduced performance.[16] It is possible that a heavy emphasis on structured, written plans can be dysfunctional to the small entrepreneurial firm because it detracts from the very flexibility that is a benefit of small size. *The process of strategic planning, not the plan itself, is probably the key to improving business performance.* Research does show, however, that as an entrepreneurial firm matures, its strategic planning process tends to become more formal.[17]

These observations suggest that new entrepreneurial ventures begin life in Mintzberg's *entrepreneurial mode* of strategic planning (explained in **Chapter 1**) and move toward the *planning mode* as the company becomes established and wants to continue its strong growth. If, after becoming successfully established, the entrepreneur instead chooses stability over growth, the venture moves more toward the *adaptive mode* so common to many small businesses.

USEFULNESS OF STRATEGIC MANAGEMENT MODEL

The model of strategic management (presented in **Figure 1–2** of **Chapter 1**) is also relevant to entrepreneurial ventures and small businesses. This basic model holds for both an established small company and a new entrepreneurial venture. As the research mentioned earlier concluded, small and developing companies increase their chances of success if they make a serious attempt to work through the strategic issues embedded in the strategic management model. The key is to focus on what's important—the set of managerial decisions and actions that determines the long-run performance of the company. The list of informal questions presented in **Table 12–1** may be more useful to a small entrepreneurial company than their more formal counterparts used by large established corporations.

USEFULNESS OF STRATEGIC DECISION-MAKING PROCESS

As mentioned in **Chapter 1**, one way in which the strategic management model can be made action oriented is to follow the strategic decision-making model presented in **Figure 1–5**. The eight steps presented in that model are just as appropriate for small companies as they are for large corporations. Unfortunately the process does not fit new entrepreneurial ventures. These companies must develop new missions, objectives, strategies, and policies out of a comparison of their external opportunities and threats to their potential strengths and weaknesses. Consequently we propose in **Figure 12–1** a modified version of the strategic decision-making process; this version more closely suits the new entrepreneurial business.

The proposed **strategic decision-making process for entrepreneurial ventures** is composed of the following eight interrelated steps:

1. **Develop the basic business idea**—a product and/or service having target customers and/or markets. The idea can be developed from a person's experience or generated in a moment of creative insight. For example, Debbie Giampapa conceived of the beverage-holding party tray long before such a product was feasible.

Table 12–1 Informal Questions to Begin the Strategic Management Process in a Small Company or Entrepreneurial Venture

Formal	Informal
Define mission	What do we stand for?
Set objectives	What are we trying to achieve?
Formulate strategy	How are we going to get there? How can we beat the competition?
Determine policies	What sort of ground rules should we all be following to get the job done right?
Establish programs	How should we organize this operation to get what we want done as cheaply as possible with the highest quality possible?
Prepare *pro forma* budgets	How much is it going to cost us and where can we get the cash?
Specify procedures	In how much detail do we have to lay things out, so that everybody knows what to do?
Determine performance measures	What are those few key things that will determine whether we can make it? How can we keep track of them?

Figure 12–1
Strategic Decision-Making Process for New Ventures

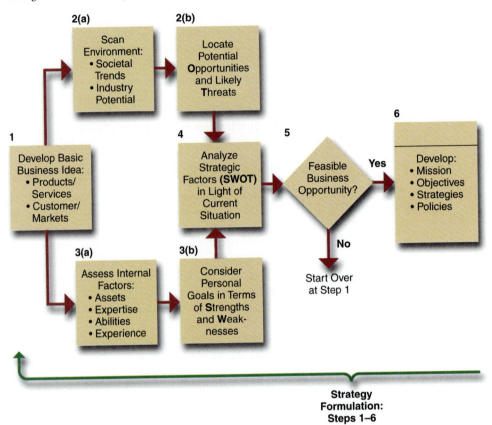

Strategy
Formulation:
Steps 1–6

2. **Scan and assess the external environment** to locate factors in the societal and task environments that pose opportunities and threats. The scanning should focus particularly on market potential and resource accessibility.

3. **Scan and assess the internal factors** relevant to the new business. The entrepreneur should objectively consider personal assets, areas of expertise, abilities, and experience, all in terms of the organizational needs of the new venture.

4. **Analyze the strategic factors** in light of the current situation using SWOT. The venture's potential strengths and weaknesses must be evaluated in light of opportunities and threats. Develop a SFAS Table (**Figure 5–1**) of the strategic factors.

5. **Decide go or no go.** If the basic business idea appears to be a feasible business opportunity, the process should be continued. Otherwise, further development of the idea should be canceled unless the strategic factors change.

6. **Generate a business plan** specifying how the idea will be transformed into reality. See **Table 12–2** for the suggested contents of a strategic **business plan**. The proposed venture's mission, objectives, strategies, and policies, as well as its likely board of directors (if a corporation) and key managers should be developed. Key internal factors should be specified and performance projections generated. The business plan serves as a vehicle through which financial support is obtained from potential investors and creditors. Research indicates that new ventures with business plans tend to have higher revenue and sales growth than do those without a business plan.[18] Starting a business without a busi-

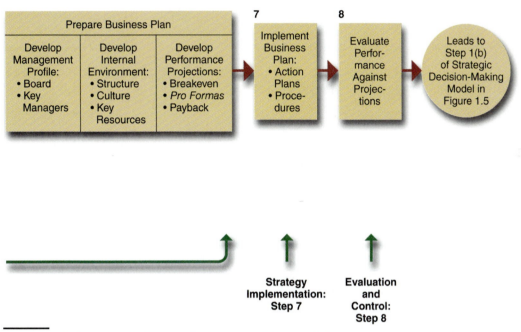

Source: T. L. Wheelen and C. E. Michaels, Jr., "Model for Strategic Decision-Making Process for New Ventures." Copyright © 1987 by T. L. Wheelen. Reprinted by permission.

ness plan is the quickest way to kill a new venture. For example, one study of 270 clothing retailers found that 80% of the successful stores had written a business plan, whereas 65% of the failed businesses had not.[19]

The strategic audit (see **Appendix 10.A at the end of Chapter 10**) can be used to develop a formal business plan. The audit's sections and subsections, along with the questions within them, provide a useful framework. Instead of analyzing the historical events of an existing company, use the questions to project the proposed company's future. The questions can be reoriented to follow the outline in **Appendix 10.A**. A crucial building block of a sound business plan is the construction of realistic scenarios for the pro forma financials. The pro formas must reflect the impact of seasonality on the cash flows of the proposed new venture.

7. **Implement the business plan** through the use of action plans and procedures.

8. **Evaluate the implemented business plan** through comparison of actual performance against projected performance results. This step leads to Step 1(b) of the strategic decision-making process shown in **Figure 1–5**. To the extent that actual results are less than or much greater than the anticipated results, the entrepreneur needs to reconsider the company's current mission, objectives, strategies, policies, and programs, and possibly make changes to the original business plan.

Table 12–2 Contents of a Strategic Business Plan for an Entrepreneurial Venture

I. Table of Contents	X. Human Resources Plan
II. Executive Summary	XI. Ownership
III. Nature of the Business	XII. Risk Analysis
IV. Strategy Formulation	XIII. Timetables and Milestones
V. Market Analysis	XIV. Strategy Implementation—Action Plans
VI. Marketing Plan	XV. Evaluation and Control
VII. Operational Plans—Service/Product	XVI. Summary
VIII. Financial Plans	XVII. Appendixes
IX. Organization and Management	

Note: **The Strategic Audit in Appendix 10A can be used to develop a business plan. It provides detailed questions to serve as a checklist.**

Source: Thomas L. Wheelen, "Contents of a Strategic Business Plan for an Entrepreneurial Venture." Copyright © 1988 by Thomas L. Wheelen. Reprinted by permission.

12.3 Issues in Corporate Governance

Corporate governance is much simpler in small entrepreneurial ventures than in large, established corporations. For one thing, the owners and the managers are usually the same people—the company founders (or their close relatives). If a venture is not incorporated, there is no need for a board of directors. It may be a sole proprietorship or a simple partnership. Those entrepreneurial ventures wishing to grow quickly or wishing to limit the liability of the owners often incorporate the business. Once incorporated, the company can sell shares of stock to others (such as venture capitalists) to finance its growth. Once the company is owned by shareholders (even if the shareholders are composed of only the founding owners who also manage the firm), the company must have a board of directors.

The boards of directors of entrepreneurial firms are likely to be either very passive or very active. Passive boards exist when the stock is closely held by the founding owners (and their immediate families) who manage the company on a day-to-day basis. As the only stockholders, they elect themselves to board offices and call meetings only when the law requires it—usually as a social occasion. There is no need for an active board, since there are no other stockholders and thus no agency problems. The board typically has no external directors. In most instances, the primary role of the board is simply to be a figurehead to satisfy the law.

Those entrepreneurial ventures financed by venture capitalists (VCs) will typically have very active boards of directors. The venture capitalists expect to obtain seats on the board in exchange for their investment.[20] Once on the board, VCs tend to be very powerful members of the board and are highly involved in strategic management.[21] The boards of directors of fast-growth entrepreneurial firms have around five directors, of whom about three are external. Almost 80% of them have written strategic plans with a time horizon of 12 to 24 months.[22]

Since closely held entrepreneurial ventures and small businesses tend to have relatively passive boards composed primarily of insiders, these types of businesses should use an advisory board to provide advice to the owner/managers. An **advisory board** is a group of external business people who voluntarily meet periodically with the owner/managers of the firm to discuss strategic and other issues. The members are usually invited to join the board by the president of the company. The advisory board has no official capacity but is expected to provide management with useful suggestions and act as a sounding board.

Since the members typically receive no compensation for serving, quarterly business meetings are often followed by cocktails and dinner at a nearby country club, hotel, or prestigious restaurant. It is important to staff the advisory board with knowledgeable people with significant business experience or skills who can complement the background and skills of the company's owner/managers. Advisory boards are an easy way to obtain free professional consulting advice. Research does indicate that advisory boards improve the performance of small businesses.[23]

12.4 Issues in Environmental Scanning and Strategy Formulation

Environmental scanning in small businesses is much less sophisticated than it is in large corporations. The business is usually too small to justify hiring someone to do only environmental scanning or strategic planning. Top managers, especially if they are the founders, tend to believe that they know the business and can follow it better than anyone else. A study of 220 small rapid-growth companies revealed that the majority of CEOs were actively and personally involved in all phases of the planning process but especially in the setting of objectives. Only 15% of the companies used a planning officer or formed a planning group to assist in the planning process. In the rest of the firms, operating managers who participated in strategic planning provided input only to the CEO, who then formulated the plan.[24] Unfortunately, the literature suggests that most small business owner/managers rely more on internal as opposed to external sources of information.[25] Few small businesses do much competitor analysis.

A fundamental reason for differences in strategy formulation between large and small entrepreneurial companies lies in the relationship between owners and managers. The CEO of a large corporation has to consider and balance the varied needs of the corporation's many stakeholders. The CEO of a small business, however, is very likely also to be the owner—the company's primary stakeholder. Personal and family needs can thus strongly affect the company's mission and objectives and can overrule other considerations.[26]

Size can affect the selection of an appropriate corporate strategy. Large corporations often choose growth strategies for their many side benefits for management as well for shareholders. A small company may, however, choose a stability strategy because the entrepreneur is interested mostly in (1) generating employment for family members, (2) providing the family a "decent living," and (3) being the "boss" of a firm small enough that he or she can manage it comfortably. Thus the goals of a small business are likely to be the same as the goals of the owner/manager.

Basic SWOT analysis is just as relevant to small entrepreneurial businesses as it is to established large ones. Both the greatest strength and the greatest weakness of the small firm, at least in the beginning, rest with the entrepreneur—the owner/manager of the business. The entrepreneur is *the manager*, the source of product/market strategy, and the dynamo who energizes the company. That is why the internal assessment of a new venture's strengths and weaknesses focuses in **Figure 12–1** on the founder's personal characteristics—his or her assets, expertise, abilities, and experience. Just as an entrepreneur's strengths can be the key to company success, personal weaknesses can be a primary cause of failure. For example, the study of clothing retailers mentioned earlier showed that the owner/managers of 85% of the failed stores had no prior retailing experience.

SOURCES OF INNOVATION

Peter Drucker, in his book *Innovation and Entrepreneurship*, proposes seven sources for innovative opportunity that should be monitored by those interested in starting an entrepreneurial venture, either within an established company or as an independent small business.[27] The first four **sources of innovation** lie within the industry itself; the last three arise in the societal environment. These seven sources are:

1. **The Unexpected:** An unexpected success, an unexpected failure, or an unexpected outside event can be a symptom of a unique opportunity. When Don Cullen of Transmet Corporation spilled a box of very fine aluminum flakes onto his company's parking lot, he discovered that their presence in the asphalt prevented it from turning sticky in high temperatures. His company now produces aluminum chips for use in roofing. Sales have doubled every year since the product's introduction and his company will soon dominate the business.

2. **The Incongruity:** A discrepancy between reality and what everyone assumes it to be, or between what is and what ought to be, can create an opportunity for innovation. For example, a side effect of retailing via the Internet is the increasing number of packages being delivered to the home. Since neither FedEx nor UPS can leave a package unless someone is home to sign for it, many deliveries are delayed. Tony Paikeday founded zBox Company to make and sell a hard-plastic container that would receive deliveries from any delivery service and would be accessible only by the owner and the delivery services. "We're amazed that it doesn't exist yet," says Paikeday. "We think it will be the next great appliance of the century."[28]

3. **Innovation Based on Process Need:** When a weak link is evident in a particular process, but people work around it instead of doing something about it, an opportunity is present for the person or company willing to forge a stronger one. Tired of having to strain to use a too-small keyboard on his personal computer, David Levy invented a keyboard with 64 normal-sized keys cleverly put into an area the size of a credit card.[29]

4. **Changes in Industry or Market Structure:** A business is ready for an innovative product, service, or approach to the business when the underlying foundation of the industry or market shifts. Black Entertainment Television, Inc. (BET) was born when Robert Johnson noticed that no television programmer was targeting the increasing number of black viewers. The BET brand has expanded into magazines and is now known by over 90% of African Americans.[30]

5. **Demographics:** Changes in the population's size, age structure, composition, employment, level of education, and income can create opportunities for innovation. For example, Pam Henderson started a company called Kids Kab to shuttle children and teenagers to private schools, doctor and dental appointments, lessons, and extracurricular activities. With the trend to dual careers, parents were no longer always available to provide personal transportation for their own children and needed such a service.

6. **Changes in Perception, Mood, and Meaning:** Opportunities for innovation can develop when a society's general assumptions, attitudes, and beliefs change. For example, the increasing dominance of a few national brewers have caused beer drinkers to look for alternatives to the same old national brands. By positioning Yuengling, a local Pennsylvania beer, as a full-flavored beer and providing it with an artsy, nostalgic-looking label, the small company was able to catch the fancy of young, trendy consumers who viewed it as Pennsylvania's version of Anchor Steam, the successful San Francisco beer.

7. **New Knowledge:** Advances in scientific and nonscientific knowledge can create new products and new markets. Advances in two different areas can sometimes be integrated to form the basis of a new product. For example, Medical Foods was formed to make foods that act like medicine to treat conditions from diabetes to arthritis. Its first product,

NiteBite is a chocolate-flavored snack bar designed to help diabetics manage nocturnal hypoglycemia, caused by low blood sugar. NiteBite gradually releases glucose into the bloodstream, where it lasts for six hours or more.[31]

FACTORS AFFECTING A NEW VENTURE'S SUCCESS

According to Hofer and Sandberg, three factors have a substantial impact on a new venture's performance. In order of importance, these **factors affecting new venture success** are (1) the structure of the industry entered, (2) the new venture's business strategy, and (3) behavioral characteristics of the entrepreneur.[32]

Industry Structure

Research shows that the chances for success are greater for entrepreneurial ventures that enter rapidly changing industries than for those that enter stable industries. In addition, prospects are better in industries that are in the early, high-growth stages of development.[33] Competition is often less intense. Fast market growth also allows new ventures to make some mistakes without serious penalty. New ventures also increase their chances of success when they enter markets in which they can erect entry barriers to keep out competitors.

Contrary to popular wisdom, patents may not always provide competitive advantage, especially for new ventures in a high-tech or hypercompetitive industry. A well-financed competitor could examine a newly filed application for a patent, work around the patent, and beat the pioneering firm to market with a similar product. In addition, the time and cost of filing and defending a patent may not be worth the effort. According to Connie Bagley, author of *The Entrepreneur's Guide to Business Law:*

> *It might take 18 months to get a patent on a product that has a 12-month life cycle. By the time you finally get the damn thing litigated, it's meaningless. So people are focusing less on proprietary assurance and more on first-mover advantage. . . . The law is just too slow for this high-speed economy.[34]*

Most new ventures enter industries having a low degree of industry concentration (that is, no dominant competitors).[35] Industry concentration is not necessarily bad. It may create market niches being ignored by large firms.[36] Hofer and Sandberg found that a new venture is more likely to be successful entering an industry in which one dominant competitor has a 50% or more market share than entering an industry in which the largest competitor has less than a 25% market share. To explain this phenomenon, Hofer and Sandberg point out that when an industry has one dominant firm, the remaining competitors are relatively weak and are easy prey for an aggressive entrepreneur. To avoid direct competition with a major rival, the new venture can focus on a market segment that is being ignored.

Industry product characteristics also have a significant impact on a new venture's success. First, a new venture is more likely to be successful when it enters an industry with heterogeneous (different) products than when it enters one with homogeneous (similar) products. In a heterogeneous industry, a new venture can differentiate itself from competitors with a unique product; or, by focusing on the unique needs of a market segment, it can find a market niche. Second, a new venture is, according to research data, more likely to be successful if the product is relatively unimportant to the customer's total purchasing needs than if it is important. Customers are more likely to experiment with a new product if its cost is low and product failure will not create a problem.

Business Strategy

According to Hofer and Sandberg, the key to success for most new ventures is (1) to differentiate the product from those of other competitors in the areas of quality and service and (2) to focus the product on customer needs in a segment of the market in order to achieve a domi-

Internet Issue

Web Site Provides Local Business a Global Presence

A few years ago, The Doll Collection was a barely profitable neighborhood retail shop in Louisville, Kentucky, with a staff of three people. Looking for an inexpensive way to boost its sales, one of the employees,

Jason Walters, suggested putting a Web page on the Internet. After spending two weeks learning the Internet computer language, html, Walters designed a simple site showcasing well-known dolls like Barbie and Madam Alexander to attract buyers. Employees of The Doll Collection were amazed by the response—much of which came from outside North America. Sales jumped 375%. By 1997, the shop had become a global retailer, marketing Barbie and Madam Alexander dolls to people in almost every country, including Japan, China, and Australia. Try its Web site at ⟨www.dollpage.com⟩.

Source: L. Beresford, "Global Smarts: Toy Story," *Entrepreneur* (February 1997), p. 38.

---

nant share of that part of the market (Porter's focused differentiation competitive strategy). Adopting guerrilla-warfare tactics, these companies go after opportunities in market niches too small or too localized to justify retaliation from the market leaders.[37]

To continue its growth once it has found a niche, the entrepreneurial firm can emphasize continued innovation and pursue natural growth in its current markets. It can expand into related markets in which the company's core skills, resources, and facilities offer the keys to further success.

Some studies do indicate, however, that new ventures can also be successful following strategies other than going after an undefended niche with a focus strategy. A narrow market approach may leave the new firm vulnerable and preordained to only limited sales. One possible approach would be to offer products that are substitutable to, but differentiated from, those offered by bigger firms.[38] As noted in the ⧅ **Internet Issue** feature, small businesses are finding it easy to enter global markets simply by developing a Web site on the Internet.

Entrepreneurial Characteristics

Four **entrepreneurial characteristics** are key to a new venture's success. Successful entrepreneurs have:

1. The *ability to identify potential venture opportunities* better than most people. They focus on opportunities—not on problems—and try to learn from failure. Entrepreneurs are goal oriented and have a strong impact on the emerging culture of an organization. They are able to envision where the company is going and are thus able to provide a strong overall sense of strategic direction.

2. A *sense of urgency* that makes them action oriented. They have a high need for achievement, which motivates them to put their ideas into action. They tend to have an internal locus of control that leads them to believe that they can determine their own fate through their own behavior. They also have a significantly greater capacity to tolerate ambiguity and stress than do many in established organizations.[39] They also have a strong need for control and may even be viewed as "misfits who need to create their own environment." They tend to distrust others and often have a need "to show others that they amount to something, that they cannot be ignored."[40]

3. A *detailed knowledge of the keys to success in the industry and the physical stamina* to make their work their lives. They have better than average education and significant work experience in the industry in which they start their business. They often work with partners to

Table 12–3 Some Guidelines for New Venture Success

- Focus on industries facing substantial technological or regulatory changes, especially those with recent exits by established competitors.
- Seek industries whose smaller firms have relatively weak competitive positions.
- Seek industries that are in early, high-growth stages of evolution.
- Seek industries in which it is possible to create high barriers to subsequent entry.
- Seek industries with heterogeneous products that are relatively unimportant to the customer's overall success.
- Seek to differentiate your products from those of your competitors in ways that are meaningful to your customers.
- Focus such differentiation efforts on product quality, marketing approaches, and customer service—and charge enough to cover the costs of doing so.
- Seek to dominate the market segments in which you compete. If necessary, either segment the market differently or change the nature and focus of your differentiation efforts to increase your domination of the segments you serve.
- Stress innovation, especially new product innovation, that is built on existing organizational capabilities.
- Seek natural, organic growth through flexibility and opportunism that builds on existing organizational strengths.

Source: C. W. Hofer and W. R. Sandberg, "Improving New Venture Performance: Some Guidelines for Success," *American Journal of Small Business* (Summer 1987), pp. 17, 19. Copyright © 1987 by C. W. Hofer and W. R. Sandberg. Reprinted by permission.

form a new venture (70% of new high-tech ventures are started by more than one founder).[41] More than half of all entrepreneurs work at least 60 hours a week in the start-up year, according to a National Federation of Independent Business study.[42]

4. *Access to outside help* to supplement their skills, knowledge, and abilities. Over time, they develop a network of people having key skills and knowledge whom the entrepreneurs can call upon for support. Through their enthusiasm, these entrepreneurs are able to attract key investors, partners, creditors, and employees. For example, the founders of eBay did not hesitate to bring in Meg Whitman as CEO because Whitman had the managerial skills that eBay needed to expand.

In summarizing their conclusions regarding factors affecting the success of entrepreneurial ventures, Hofer and Sandberg propose the guidelines presented in **Table 12–3**.

12.5 Issues in Strategy Implementation

Two key implementation issues in small companies are organizing and staffing the growing company and transferring ownership of the company to the next generation.

SUBSTAGES OF SMALL BUSINESS DEVELOPMENT

The implementation problems of a small business change as the company grows and develops over time. Just as the decision-making process for entrepreneurial ventures is different from that of established businesses, the managerial systems in small companies often vary from those of large corporations. Those variations are based on their stage of development. The stages of corporate growth and development discussed in **Chapter 8** suggest that all small businesses are either in Stage I or trying to move into Stage II. These models imply that all successful new ventures eventually become Stage II, functionally organized companies. This is not always true, however. In attempting to show clearly how small businesses develop, Churchill and Lewis propose five **substages of small business development**: (a) existence, (b) survival, (c) success, (d) take-off, and (e) resource maturity.[43] A review of these small business substages shows in more detail how a company can move through the entrepreneurial Stage I into a functionally oriented, professionally managed Stage II.

Stage A: Existence

At this point, the entrepreneurial venture faces the problems of obtaining customers and delivering the promised product or service. The organizational structure is simple. The entrepreneur does everything and directly supervises subordinates. Systems are minimal. The owner is the business.

Stage B: Survival

Those ventures able to satisfy a sufficient number of customers enter this stage; the rest close when their owners run out of start-up capital. Those reaching the survival stage are concerned about generating the cash flow needed to repair and replace capital assets as they wear out and to finance the growth to continue satisfying the market segment they have found.

At this stage, the organizational structure is still simple, but it probably has a sales manager or general supervisor to carry out the owner's well-defined orders. A major problem of many small businesses at this stage is finding a person who is qualified to supervise the business when the owner can't be present but who is still willing to work for a very modest salary. Entrepreneurs usually try to use family members rather than hiring an outsider who lacks the entrepreneur's dedication to the business and (in the words of one owner/manager) "steals them blind." A company that remains in this stage for a long time is often called a "mom and pop" firm. It earns marginal returns on invested time and capital (with lots of psychic income!) and eventually goes out of business when "mom and pop" give up or retire. This type of small business is viewed more as a **lifestyle company** in which the firm is purely an extension of the owner's lifestyle. Over 94% of small private companies are in this category.[44]

Stage C: Success

By this point, the company's sales have reached a level where the firm is not only profitable, but also has sufficient cash flow to reinvest in itself. The key issue at this stage is whether the company should be used as a platform for growth or as a means of support for the owners as they completely or partially disengage from the company. The company is transforming into a functionally structured organization, but it still relies on the entrepreneur for all key decisions. The two options are disengagement and growth.

C(1) Disengagement   The company can now successfully follow a stability strategy and remain at this stage almost indefinitely—provided that environmental change does not destroy its niche or poor management reduce its competitive abilities. By now functional managers have taken over some of the entrepreneur's duties. The company at this stage may be incorporated, but it is still primarily owned by the founder or founder's family. Consequently the board of directors is either a rubber stamp for the entrepreneur or a forum for family squabbles. Growth strategies are not pursued because either the market niche will not allow growth or the owner is content with the company at a size he or she can still manage comfortably. Strategic decisions make limited use of objective information and tend to be intuitive—based on personal desires and the founder's background.[45]

C(2) Growth   The entrepreneur risks all available cash and the established borrowing power of the company in financing further growth. Strategic as well as operational planning is extensive and deeply involves the owner. Managers with an eye to the company's future rather than for its current situation are hired. This is an entrepreneurial high-growth firm aiming to be included in the *Inc.* 500. The emphasis now is on teamwork rather than on the entrepreneur's personal actions and energy. The personal values and philosophy of the founder are slowly transferred into a developing corporate culture.

Stage D: Take-Off

The key problems in this stage are how to grow rapidly and how to finance that growth. By now the firm is incorporated and has sold or is planning to sell stock in its company via an initial public offering (IPO) or via a direct public offering (DPO).[46] The entrepreneur must learn to delegate to specialized professional managers or to a team of managers who now form the top management of the company.[47] A functional structure of the organization should now be solidly in place. Operational and strategic planning greatly involve the hired managers, but the company is still dominated by the entrepreneur's presence and stock control. Vertical and horizontal growth strategies are being seriously considered as the firm's management debates when and how to grow. The company is now included in the *Inc. 500* select group of firms.

At this point, the entrepreneur either is able to manage the transition from a small to a large company or recognizes personal limitations, sells his or her stock for a profit, and leaves the firm. The composition of the board of directors changes from dominance by friends and relatives of the owner to a large percentage of outsiders with managerial experience who can help the owner during the transition to a professionally managed company. The biggest danger facing the firm in this stage is the owner's desire to remain in total control (not willing to delegate) as if it were still a small entrepreneurial venture, even though he or she lacks the managerial skills necessary to run an established corporation.

Stage E: Resource Maturity

It is at this point that the small company has adopted most of the characteristics of an established, large company. It may still be a small-to-medium-sized company, but it is recognized as an important force in the industry and a possible candidate for the *Fortune 500* someday. The greatest concerns of a company at this stage are controlling the financial gains brought on by rapid growth and retaining its flexibility and entrepreneurial spirit. In terms of the stages of organizational growth and development discussed in **Chapter 8**, the company has become a full-fledged Stage II functional corporation.

TRANSFER OF POWER AND WEALTH IN FAMILY BUSINESSES

Small businesses are often **family businesses**. It is estimated that over a third of the U.S. *Fortune 500* companies are either family owned or dominated. For the world, the percentage is over half.[48] Even though the founders of the companies are the primary forces in starting the entrepreneurial ventures, their needs for business support and financial assistance will cause them to turn to family members, who can be trusted, over unknown outsiders of questionable integrity, who may demand more salary than the enterprise can afford. Sooner or later, the founder's spouse and children are drafted into business operations either because the family standard of living is directly tied to the business or the entrepreneur desperately needs help just to staff the operation. The children are guaranteed summer jobs, and the business changes from dad's or mom's company to "our" company. The family members are extremely valuable assets to the entrepreneur because they are often also willing to put in long hours at low pay to help the business succeed. Even though the spouse and children might have no official stock in the company, they know that they will somehow share in its future and perhaps even inherit the business. The problem is that only 30% of family firms in the United States make it to the second generation, and just 13% survive to the third generation.[49] A common saying among European family businesses is: "The first generation creates, the second inherits, and the third destroys."[50]

Table 12-4 Transfer of Power in a Family Business

Phase 1 **Owner-Managed Business:** Phase 1 begins at start-up and continues until the entrance of another family member into the business on a full-time basis. Family considerations influence but are not yet a directing part of the firm. At this point, the founder (entrepreneur) and the business are one.

Phase 2 **Training and Development of New Generation:** The children begin to learn the business at the dining room table during early childhood and then through part-time and vacation employment. The family and the business become one. Just as the entrepreneur identified with the business earlier, the family now begins to identify itself with the business.

Phase 3 **Partnership Between Generations:** At this point, a son or daughter of the founder has acquired sufficient business and managerial competence so that he or she can be involved in key decisions for at least a part of the company. The entrepreneur's offspring, however, has to first gain respect from the firm's employees and other managers and show that he or she can do the job right. Another issue is the lack of willingness of the founder to share authority with the son or daughter. Consequently a common tactic taken by sons and daughters in family businesses is to take a job in a large, established corporation where they can gain valuable experience and respect for their skills.

Phase 4 **Transfer of Power:** Instead of being forced to sell the company when he or she can no longer manage the business, the founder has the option in a family business of turning it over to the next generation as part of their inheritance. Often the founder moves to the position of Chairman of the Board and promotes one of the children to the position of CEO. Unfortunately some founders cannot resist meddling in operating affairs and unintentionally undermine the leadership position of the son or daughter. To avoid this problem, the founder should sell his or her stock (probably through a leveraged buy-out to the children) and physically leave the company and allow the next generation the freedom it needs to adapt to changing conditions.

Source: N. C. Churchill and K. J. Hatten, "Non-Market-Based Transfer of Wealth and Power: A Research Framework for Family Businesses," *American Journal of Small Business* (Winter 1987), pp. 51–64. Reprinted with the permission of Baylor University. All rights reserved.

Churchill and Hatten propose that family businesses go through four sequential phases from the time in which the venture is strictly managed by the founder to the time in which the next generation takes charge.[51] These phases are detailed in **Table 12–4**. Each of these phases must be well managed if the company is to survive past the third generation. Some of the reasons why family businesses may fail to successfully transfer ownership to the next generation are (1) inherited wealth destroys entrepreneurial drive, (2) the entrepreneur doesn't allow for a changing firm, (3) emphasis on business means the family is neglected, (4) the business's financial growth can't keep up with rising family lifestyles, (5) family members are not prepared to run a business, and (6) the business becomes an arena for family conflicts.[52] In addition, succession planning may be ignored because of the founder's or family's refusal to think about the founder's death, the founder's unwillingness to let go of the firm, the fear of sibling rivalry, or intergenerational envy.

12.6 Issues in Evaluation and Control

As a means by which the corporation's implementation of strategy can be evaluated, the control systems of large corporations have evolved over a long period of time in response to pressures from the environment (particularly the government). Conversely the entrepreneur creates what is needed as the business grows. Because of a personal involvement in decision making, the entrepreneur managing a small business has little need for a formal, detailed reporting system. Thus the founder who has little understanding of accounting and a shortage of cash might employ a bookkeeper instead of an accountant. A formal personnel function might never appear because the entrepreneur lumps it in with simple bookkeeping and uses a secretary to handle personnel files. As an entrepreneurial venture becomes more established, it will develop more complex evaluation and control systems, but they are often not the kind used in large corporations and are probably used for different purposes.

Financial statements, in particular, tell only half the story in small, privately owned companies. The formality of the financial reporting system in such a company is usually a result of pressures from government tax agencies, not from management's desire for an objective evaluation and control system. For example, the absence of taxes in Bermuda has been given as the reason why business owners keep little documentation—thus finding it nearly impossible to keep track of inventory, monitor sales, or calculate how much they are owed.[53]

Because balance sheets and income statements do not always give an accurate picture, standard ratios such as return on assets and debt-equity are unreliable. Research reveals systematic differences among liquidity and solvency measures for small compared to large companies. The mean averages of both the current ratio and the debt ratio are systematically larger for the small companies.[54] Cash flow is widely regarded as more important for an entrepreneurial business than is the traditional balance sheet or income statement. Even though a small business may be profitable in the accounting sense, a negative cash flow could bankrupt the company. Levin and Travis provide five reasons why owners, operators, and outside observers should be wary of using standard financial methods to indicate the health of a small, privately owned company.[55]

- **The line between debt and equity is blurred.** In some instances, what appears as a loan is really an easy-to-retrieve equity investment. The entrepreneur in this instance doesn't want to lose his or her investment if the company fails. Another condition is that retained earnings seldom reflect the amount of internal financing needed for the company's growth. This account may merely be a place in which cash is left so that the owner can avoid double taxation. To avoid other taxes, owner/managers may own fixed assets that they lease to the corporation. The equity that was used to buy those assets is really the company's equity, but it doesn't appear on the books.

- **Lifestyle is a part of financial statements.** The lifestyle of the owner and the owner's family is often reflected in the balance sheet. The assets of some firms include beach cottages, mountain chalets, and automobiles. In others, plants and warehouses that are used for company operations are not shown because they are held separately by the family. Income statements may not reflect how well the company is operating. Profitability is not so important in decision making in small, private companies as it is in large, publicly held corporations. For example, spending for recreation or transportation and paying rents or salaries above market rates to relatives put artificially high costs on the books of small firms. The business might appear to be poorly managed to an outsider, but the owner is acting rationally. The owner/manager wants dependable income or its equivalent with the least painful tax consequences. Because the standard profitability measures such as ROI are not useful in the evaluation of such a firm, Levin and Travis recommend return on current assets as a better measure of corporate productivity.

- **Standard financial formulas don't always apply.** Following practices that are in contrast to standard financial recommendations, small companies often use short-term debt to finance fixed assets. The absence of well-organized capital markets for small businesses, along with the typical banker's resistance to making loans without personal guarantees, leaves the private owner little choice. Even though a large amount of long-term debt is considered to be a good use of financial leverage by a large publicly held firm, it can drive a smaller firm into bankruptcy by raising its break-even point.

- **Personal preference determines financial policies.** Because the owner is often the manager of the small firm, dividend policy is largely irrelevant. Dividend decisions are based not on stock price (which is usually unknown because the stock is not traded), but on the owner's lifestyle and the tradeoff between taking wealth from the corporation and double taxation.

- **Banks combine personal and business wealth.** Because of the large percentage of small businesses that go bankrupt every year, bank loan officers are reluctant to lend money to a small business unless the owner also provides some personal guarantees for the loan. In some instances, part of the loan may be composed of a second mortgage on the owner's house. If the owner does not want to succumb to this pressure by lenders to include the owner's personal assets as part of the collateral, the owner/manager must be willing to pay high interest rates for a loan that does not put the family's assets at risk.

12.7 Impact of the Internet on Entrepreneurial Ventures and Small Business

The years from 1998 to 2000 were glory years for Internet-based entrepreneurial ventures. Most subsequently failed during 2000 and 2001 when venture capitalists and others began to doubt that many of these ventures would ever achieve profitability. Recent graduates had been founding Internet start-ups by the thousands. Some college students were even wooed by these Internet entrepreneurial ventures to leave school (at least temporarily) and join the dot-com boom. In his own words, this is one college student's story of his experience being a part of an Internet-based entrepreneurial venture:

> There I was, walking into some unknown building, about to meet some unknown people, and working for a company I barely knew. I wondered how I had gotten myself into this mess in the first place. I say "mess" jokingly because I did enjoy the experience and wouldn't trade it for the world. Life just never goes quite according to plan.
>
> I had been working for this small operation since last October (1999). It started off as just a little side job to make ends meet. In February (2000), I received a phone call from the founder of the company. He told me that the company was currently working with a venture capital firm to secure a few million dollars in funding. The founder wanted me to come to Chicago to work full time in March. Even though I saw huge potential for the company's future, I was still extremely hesitant to drop out of school and go chase after this opportunity. He then laid out his plan for the company: Get the funding, build up the company over the following months, and then sell it off for a large amount by the end of the year. It sounded fairly reasonable to me at the time. I started to sway, but I still wasn't convinced. We then looked at the track record of many other Internet start-ups over the past few years. All of our competitors had been bought out for substantial amounts with a year of VC funding. Almost all of them were acquired just after Christmas (1999). The potential numbers plus the amazing opportunity to work for a start-up as an undergraduate far outweighed the risks.
>
> At this time in my life, I had nothing to lose. Worst-case scenario: the company flops. In this worst case, I would still have a few months salary in the bank and I'd be back in school the next semester with a shiny new addition to my resume. Best-case scenario: I would own 1% of a company that was worth a few hundred million dollars. After much thought, advice from others, and a few loose ends to tie up, I decided to go for it.
>
> Things had been falling into place perfectly except the company was a little behind schedule. In the first week of March, the VC offered to fund us. It was the beginning of what they call "due diligence." A deal falling through at this point is so rare that due diligence is often accompanied with a term sheet (letter of intent) and a bridge note (3–5% of the capital). The second week of

March (2000) was my deadline to withdraw from school, so I did. The third week of March, the improbable happened; our deal with the VC fell apart.

The month that followed turned this once-in-a-lifetime opportunity into a giant mess. We ended up firing our financial advisor, who was ultimately to blame for the VC funding falling through. Shortly after that, the CTO/Cofounder decided to leave the company. To make things worse, the stock market fell. The technology sector, most notably, Internet companies, was to blame for the crash. We were down to three people on this project, the founder, the acting CEO, and me. That brings me to where I began this story—walking into a meeting to meet these two for the first time.

We were in Chicago trying to figure out what to do. Actually, I didn't have the slightest clue what to do, so I just sat, listened, and nodded my head. It was decided that we would bring in a "turnaround" guy. I nicknamed him "The Cleaner," pun and allusion intended. Once he stepped in, he devised a plan and re-established a connection with the Cofounder and some other people that were involved. He also brought in a new CEO and a new Chairman of the Board. His plan was to change the direction of the company in a way that was more appealing to investors. We could then obtain VC and angel funding. There were still thoughts of selling the company off sometime in the future, but it was no longer a goal. The biggest change was to our business model. We took our business plan, placed it in the paper shredder, and hit "mutilate."

Our original business model was a typical business to consumer model. We provided a service—price comparison-based Internet shopping. We had a few edges that let us stay competitive, such as superior technology, additional services, and a media partner program. The media partner program is worth explaining. We partner with content-driven Web sites and embed our technology into their sites. The Web sites can then participate in our revenue stream. Our original goal was to build a brand name doing this. For example, we could partner with MTV.com. Every time their site would bring up a music CD, there would be a button that would allow the customer to buy it online for the lowest price. The turnaround guy saw this as our primary asset and our best idea. So overnight, we changed from an Internet e-commerce company to an infrastructure technology company. Our financial model also dramatically changed.

Instead of spending millions of dollars on direct advertising to build a brand name (the number one reason why dot-coms are failing now), we would utilize our partner's existing traffic. A big Web site like MTV.com gets millions of hits a day. Of those, a certain percentage will click on our button to compare prices. A certain percentage of those will buy the item. We get a commission from every sale the retailer makes. As an incentive, we give a percentage of what we make back to the partner site. We end up with a small piece of the pie, but the pie is huge and growing every day. We packaged these ideas with a lot of other ones into a 50-page business plan. With our new business plan and a very impressive management team, we were now ready to go back to a VC.

It was at this time I decided to go back to school. Despite how bright things were looking now, we still had no money. The paychecks were smaller and the fall semester was about to start. Everyone on the team agreed that for the time being, it was a smart move for me. There was no telling if and when the funding would come through. Today, as far as things stand, we are scheduled to close with a VC from Florida sometime in November (2000). Our new Chairman has been aggressively pursuing angel funding and should have some capital within the next week or two. If the VC funding works out, I will have a plethora of options of how I want to be involved in the company. Likely, I will stay in school and become an independent consultant to the company part-time. That is generally what my role is now.

For a while the company was only a handful of people. Being one of those people, I had to, rather was able to work in many different areas outside my original position. I helped lay the original groundwork for the company, which was very exciting. My official title was Director of Content Development. My primary role was to lead the content team, which consisted of one other individual and me. My team was responsible for maintaining the external Web pages, running promotions, and keeping positive relations with our customers and retailers. One thing I really learned was that when you are working in a small company, everyone does everything. If there is something that needs to get done, everyone helps out. I've had the President of the company help me update Web pages. I've helped out the CEO with a PowerPoint presentation for potential investors. I've also helped the CFO with the financial planning; the CTO with java scripts, and explained the technology to potential partners. All of us worked on and wrote the business plan.

Looking back at the roller coaster ride this company has taken me on, I'm glad to have been and still be a part of it. This experience has raised my understanding to a whole new level of how the world works. I can't, nor would I want to, imagine how my life would be if I hadn't decided to take a risk and jump on this opportunity.[56]

Projections for the 21st Century

- From 1994 to 2010, the number of golf courses in the United States will increase from 14,648 to 16,800.
- From 1994 to 2010, gambling revenues will grow in the United States from $39.5 billion to $125.6 billion.[57]

Discussion Questions

1. In terms of strategic management, how does a new venture's situation differ from that of an ongoing small company?

2. How should a small entrepreneurial company engage in environmental scanning? To what aspects of the environment should management pay most attention?

3. What are the characteristics of an attractive industry from an entrepreneur's point of view? What role does innovation play?

4. What considerations should small-business entrepreneurs keep in mind when they are deciding if a company should follow a growth or a stability strategy?

5. How does being family owned (as compared to being publicly owned) affect a firm's strategic management?

Strategic Practice Exercise

Amazon.com began a new era in July 1995 when it offered a new proposition to the consumer: easy access to convenient ordering with seemingly endless selection. No longer did people need to drive to a local book store to search for and buy a book or CD. Amazon simplified the selection process through its search engines and huge databases. This Internet advantage was undermined, however, by an advantage only a bricks and mortar retailer like Barnes & Noble could offer: the ability for the customer to take home the book as soon as it is paid for.

In the United States, 55% of Internet deliveries are currently made by UPS, 32% by the Postal Service, and 10% by FedEx. The remaining 3% is composed of a new type of Internet service company—the Internet delivery firm. Entrepreneurial ventures like Webvan, Kozmo.com, Urbanfetch, and Pink Dot offer same-day delivery in certain locations. By combining the convenience of online ordering with nearly instant gratification, they offer a superior value proposition to those firms shipping by conventional means. Most of the Internet retailers offering same-day delivery typically focus on a mix of two broad product categories, impulse items such as videos, books, snacks, and routine necessities like grocery and household items. All offer delivery 24 hours a day, 7 days a week. Although most offer free delivery, some price their offerings to discourage small orders. The trade off with this type of business is speed of delivery versus variety of offerings. To achieve fast response, the local deliverer must hold product locally, rather than in large national distribution centers, like mass merchandisers and large catalogue companies. The speed advantage from being local means a decrease in variety. For example, Kozmo offered about

15,000 items in total versus more than 10 million total items at Amazon.[58]

1. Are there any Internet same-day local delivery firms in your city or town? How successful are they?

2. Evaluate the growth potential of the Internet same-day delivery company. It this the type of business you would like to start? If you were a venture capitalist, would you invest in this type of firm?

3. Who is the competition of the Internet same-day delivery firm? Large Internet firms such as Amazon? Local bricks and mortar retailers? National delivery operations such as UPS and the Postal Service?

4. How might new developments in technology effect this type of business?

Key Terms

advisory board (p. 308)

business model (p. 304)

business plan (p. 306)

entrepreneur (p. 303)

entrepreneurial characteristics (p. 312)

entrepreneurial venture (p. 303)

factors affecting new venture success (p. 311)

family businesses (p. 315)

lifestyle company (p. 314)

small-business firm (p. 303)

sources of innovation (p. 310)

strategic decision-making process for entrepreneurial ventures (p. 305)

substages of small business development (p. 314)

Notes

1. J. Norman, "Great Idea? That's the Easy Part," *Des Moines Register* (November 12, 1995), p. 3G.

2. J. Kahn, "Suddenly, Startups Are Chic," *Fortune* (February 15, 1999), p. 110.

3. *The State of Small Business: A Report to the President* (Washington, DC: U.S. Government Printing Office, 1987), p. 117.

4. B. Keats and J. Bracker, "Toward a Theory of Small Firm Performance: A Conceptual Model," *American Journal of Small Business* (Spring 1988), pp. 41–58; D. Dougherty, "A Practice-Centered Model of Organizational Renewal Through Product Innovation," *Strategic Management Journal* (Summer 1992), pp. 77–92.

5. J. Castro, J. McDowell, and W. McWhirter, "Big vs. Small," *Time* (September 5, 1988), p. 49.

6. B. Bowers, "This Store Is a Hit But Somehow Cash Flow Is Missing," *Wall Street Journal* (April 13, 1993), p. B2.

7. M. J. Foster, "Scenario Planning for Small Businesses," *Long Range Planning* (February 1993), p. 123; M. S. S. El-Namacki, "Small Business—The Myth and the Reality," *Long Range Planning* (August 1990), p. 79.

8. According to a study by Dun & Bradstreet of 800,000 small U.S. businesses started in 1985, 70% were still in business in March 1994. Contrary to other studies, this study only counted firms as failures if they owed money at the time of their demise. Also see J. Aley, "Debunking the Failure Fallacy," *Fortune* (September 6, 1993), p. 21.

9. R. N. Lussier, "Startup Business Advice from Business Owners to Would-Be Entrepreneurs," *SAM Advanced Management Journal* (Winter 1995), pp. 10–13.

10. J. W. Carland, F. Hoy, W. R. Boulton, and J. A. C. Carland, "Differentiating Entrepreneurs from Small Business Owners: A Conceptualization," *Academy of Management Review* (April 1984), p. 358; J. W. Carland, J. C. Carland, F. Hoy, and W. R. Boulton, "Distinctions Between Entrepreneurial and Small Business Ventures," *International Journal of Management* (March 1988), pp. 98–103.

11. S. P. Galante, "Counting on a Narrow Market Can Cloud Company's Future," *Wall Street Journal* (January 20, 1986), p. 17. Sexton's statement that entrepreneurial firms engage in more sophisticated strategic planning than do small businesses is supported by C. H. Matthews and S. G. Scott, "Uncertainty and Planning in Small Entrepreneurial Firms: An Empirical Assessment," *Journal of Small Business Management* (October 1995), pp. 34–52. See also W. H. Stewart, Jr., W. E. Watson, J. C. Carland, and J. W. Carland, "A Proclivity for Entrepreneurship: A Comparison of Entrepreneurs, Small Business Owners, and Corporate Managers," *Journal of Business Venturing* (March 1999), pp. 189–214.

12. D. Fields, "Mrs. Fields' Weekends," *USA Weekend* (February 3–5, 1989), p. 16; M. Alpert, "In the Chips," *Fortune* (July 17, 1989), pp. 115–116.

13. J. S. Bracker, B. W. Keats, and J. N. Pearson, "Planning and Financial Performance Among Small Firms in a Growth Industry," *Strategic Management Journal* (November–December 1988), pp. 591–603; J. Kargar and J. A. Parnell, "Strategic Planning Emphasis and Planning Satisfaction in Small Firms: An Empirical Investigation," *Journal of Business Strategies* (Spring 1996), pp. 120; C. R. Schwenk and C. B. Shrader, "Effects of Formal Strategic Planning on Financial Performance in Small Firms: A Meta-Analysis," *Entrepreneurship Theory & Performance* (Spring 1993), pp. 53–64; L. W. Rue and N. A. Ibrahim, "The Relationship Between Planning Sophistication and Performance in Small Businesses," *Journal of Small Business Management* (October 1998), pp. 24–32.

14. W. H. Baker, H. Lon, and B. Davis, "Business Planning in Successful Small Firms," *Long Range Planning* (December 1993), pp. 82–88.

15. A. Thomas, "Less Is More: How Less Formal Planning Can Be Best," in *The Strategic Planning Management Reader*, edited by L. Fahey (Upper Saddle River, NJ: Prentice Hall, 1989), pp. 331–336; C. B. Shrader, C. L. Mulford, and V. L. Blackburn, "Strategic and Operational Planning, Uncertainty, and Performance in Small Firms," *Journal of Small Business Management* (October 1989), pp. 45–60.

16. R. B. Robinson, Jr., and J. A. Pearce II, "The Impact of Formalized Strategic Planning on Financial Performance in Small Organizations," *Strategic Management Journal* (July–September 1983), pp. 197–207; R. Ackelsberg and P. Arlow, "Small Businesses Do Plan and It Pays Off," *Long Range Planning* (October 1985), pp. 61–67.

17. M. Berry, "Strategic Planning in Small High-Tech Companies," *Long Range Planning* (June 1998), pp. 455–466.

18. T. Mazzarol, "Do Formal Business Plans Really Matter? A Survey of Small Business Owners in Australia," Paper presented to the *45th International Conference on Small Business (ICSB) World Conference 2000*, Brisbane, Australia (June 7–10, 2000).

19. V. Fowler, "Business Study Focuses on Failures," *Des Moines Register* (August 9, 1992), p. G1. For information on preparing a business plan, see R. Hisrich and M. Peters, *Entrepreneurship*, 4th edition (New York: Irwin/McGraw-Hill, 1998).

20. L. W. Busenitz, D.D. Moesel, J. O. Fiet, and J. B. Barney, "The Framing of Perceptions of Fairness in the Relationship Between Venture Capitalists and New Venture Teams," *Entrepreneurship Theory & Practice* (Spring 1997), pp. 5–21.

21. V. H. Fried, G. D. Bruton, and R. D. Hisrich, "Strategy and the Board of Directors in Venture Capital-Backed Firms," *Journal of Business Venturing* (November 1999), pp. 493–503.

22. D. L. Sexton and F. I. Steele, *Leading Practices of Fast Growth Entrepreneurs* (Kansas City, Mo.: National Center for Entrepreneurship Research, 1997).

23. D. J. Garsombke and T. W. Garsombke, "An Empirical Investigation of the Utilization of External and Internal Boards of Directors and Management Advisory Assistance on the Performance of Small Businesses," *Journal of Business Strategies* (Fall 1996), pp. 167–184.

24. J. C. Shuman and J. A. Seeger, "The Theory and Practice of Strategic Management in Smaller Rapid Growth Firms," *American Journal of Small Business* (Summer 1986), p. 14.

25. R. C. Pineda, L. D. Lerner, M. C. Miller, and S. J. Phillips, "An Investigation of Factors Affecting the Information-Search Activities of Small Business Managers," *Journal of Small Business Management* (January 1998), pp. 60–71.

26. S. Birley and P. Westhead, "Growth and Performance Contrasts Between 'Types' of Small Firms," *Strategic Management Journal* (November–December 1990), pp. 535–557; J. L. Ward and C. E. Aronloff, "How Family Affects Strategy," *Small Business Forum* (Fall 1994), pp. 85–90.

27. P. F. Drucker, *Innovation and Entrepreneurship* (New York: HarperCollins, 1985), pp. 30–129.

28. F. Donnely, "Let zBox Accept Deliveries," *Des Moines Register* (October 31, 2000), p. TW1.

29. D. Stipp, "Inventor on the Verge of a Nervous Breakthrough," *Fortune* (March 29, 1999), pp. 104–117.

30. D. Whitford, "Taking BET Back From the Street," *Fortune* (November 9, 1998), pp. 167–170.

31. A. Bianchi, "Medical-Food Start-Up Offers Tasty Treatments," *Inc.* (January 1997), p. 15.

32. C. W. Hofer and W. R. Sandberg, "Improving New Venture Performance: Some Guidelines for Success," *American Journal of Small Business* (Summer 1987), pp. 12–23. See also J. J. Chrisman and A. Bauerschmidt, "New Venture Performance: Some Critical Extensions to the Model," Paper presented to *State-of-the-Art Symposium on Entrepreneurship*, Iowa State University (April 12–14, 1992).

33. K. C. Robinson, "An Examination of the Influence of Industry Structure on Eight Alternative Measures of New Venture Performance for High Potential Independent New Ventures," *Journal of Business Venturing* (March 1999), pp. 165–187.

34. Interview with C. Bagley by J. Useem, "Forget Patents, Says Stanford Prof," *Inc.* (October 1996), p. 23.

35. K. C. Robinson.

36. J. Wade, "A Community-Level Analysis of Sources and Rates of Technological Variation in the Microprocessor Market," *Academy of Management Journal* (October 1996), pp. 1218–1244.

37. Supported by R. C. Shrader and M. Simon, "Corporate Versus Independent New Ventures: Resources, Strategy, and Performance Differences," *Journal of Business Venturing* (January 1997), pp. 47–66, and R. Tonge, P. C. Larsen, and M. Sto, "Strategic Leadership in Super-Growth Companies—A Reappraisal," *Long Range Planning* (December 1998), pp. 838–847.

38. A. C. Cooper, G. E. Willard, and C. Y. Woo, "A Reexamination of the Niche Concept," in *The Strategy Process: Concepts, Contexts, and Cases*, 2nd edition, edited by H. Mintzberg and J. B. Quinn (Upper Saddle River, N.J.: Prentice Hall, 1991), pp. 619–628; P. P. McDougal, J. G. Covin, R. B. Robinson, Jr., and L. Herron, "The Effects of Industry Growth and Strategic Breadth on New Venture Performance and Strategy Content," *Strategic Management Journal* (September 1994), pp. 537–554; C. E. Bamford, T. J. Dean, and P. P. McDougall, "Initial Strategies and New Venture Growth: An Examination of the Effectiveness of Broad vs. Narrow Breadth Strategies," in *Frontiers of Entrepreneurial Research*, edited by P. D. Reynolds, et al. (Babson Park, MA: Babson College, 1997), pp. 375–389; G. H. Lim, K. S. Lee, and S. J. Tan, "SMEs' Market Entry Strategy: Substitution Instead of Niching," paper presented to the *International Council for Small Business Conference*, 1999.

39. H. P. Welsch, "Entrepreneurs' Personal Characteristics: Causal Models," Paper presented to *State-of-the-Art Symposium on Entrepreneurship*, Iowa State University (April 12–14, 1992); A. Rahim, "Stress, Strain, and Their Moderators: An Empirical Comparison of Entrepreneurs and Managers," *Journal of Small Business Management* (January 1996), pp. 46–58.

40. M. Kets de Vries, "The Dark Side of Entrepreneurship," *Harvard Business Review* (November–December 1985), pp. 160–167.

41. A. C. Cooper, F. J. Gimeno-Gascon, and C. Y. Woo, "Initial Human and Financial Capital as Predictors of New Venture Performance," *Journal of Business Venturing* (Vol. 9, 1994), pp. 371–395; H. R. Feeser and G. E. Willard, "Founding Strategies and Performance in High-Tech Firms," in *Handbook of Business Strategy, 1991/92 Yearbook*, edited by H. E. Glass and M. A. Hovde (Boston: Warren, Gorham & Lamont, 1991), pp. 2.1–2.18.

42. R. Ricklefs and U. Gupta, "Traumas of a New Entrepreneur," *Wall Street Journal* (May 10, 1989), p. B1.

43. N. C. Churchill and V. L. Lewis, "The Five Stages of Small Business Growth," *Harvard Business Review* (May–June 1983), pp. 30–50. The life cycle concept is supported by research by M. Beverland, "Organizational Life Cycles in Small Enterprises," paper presented to the *45th International Conference on Small Business (ICSB) World Conference*, Brisbane, Australia (June 7–10, 2000).

44. J. W. Petty and W. D. Bygrave, "What Does Finance Have to Say to the Entrepreneur?" *Journal of Small Business Finance* (Spring 1993), pp. 125–137.

45. K. D. Brouthers, F. Andriessen, and J. Nicolaes, "Driving Blind: Strategic Decision-Making in Small Companies," *Long Range Planning* (February 1998), pp. 130–138.

46. See C. Farrell, K. Rebello, R. D. Hof, and M. Maremont, "The Boom in IPOs," *Business Week* (December 18, 1995), pp. 64–72; S. Gruner, "When Mom & Pop Go Public," *Inc.* (December 1996), pp. 66–73.

47. A. Caruana, M. H. Morris, and A. J. Vella, "The Effect of Centralization and Formalization on Entrepreneurship in Export Firms," *Journal of Small Business Management* (January 1998), pp. 16–29.

48. J. Magretta, "Governing the Family-Owned Enterprise: An Interview with Finland's Krister Ahlstrom," *Harvard Business Review* (January–February 1998), pp. 113–123.

49. J. Ward, *Keeping the Family Business Healthy* (San Francisco: Jossey-Bass, 1987), as reported by U. Gupta and M. Robichaux, "Reins Tangle Easily at Family Firms," *Wall Street Journal* (August 9, 1989), p. B1.

50. J. Magretta, p. 119.

51. N. C. Churchill and K. J. Hatten, "Non-Market-Based Transfers of Wealth and Power: A Research Framework for Family Businesses," *American Journal of Small Business* (Winter 1987), pp. 51–64.

52. J. L. Ward and C. E. Aronoff, "Shirt Sleeves to Shirt Sleeves," *Nation's Business* (September 1992), pp. 62–63.

53. J. Applegate, "Business People in Bermuda Get Sloppy Without Taxes," *Des Moines Register* (July 6, 1992), p. 8B.

54. P. L. Huff, R. M. Harper, Jr., and A. E. Eikner, "Are There Differences in Liquidity and Solvency Measures Based on Company Size?" *American Business Review* (June 1999), pp. 96–106.

55. R. I. Levin and V. R. Travis, "Small Company Finance: What the Books Don't Say," *Harvard Business Review* (November–December 1987), pp. 30–32.

56. T. Atkins, "My Entrepreneurial Experience," paper submitted to Management 310, *Entrepreneurship & Innovation*, taught by J. David Hunger at Iowa State University (October 2000). Reprinted by permission of Todd Atkins.

57. J. Warner, "21st Century Capitalism: Snapshot of the Next Century," *Business Week* (November 18, 1994), p. 194.

58. T. Laseter, P. Houston, A. Chung, S. Byrne, M. Turner, and A. Devendran, "The Last Mile to Nowhere," *Strategy + Business*, Issue 20 (3rd Quarter, 2000), pp. 41–48.

chapter 13

Strategic Issues in Not-For-Profit Organizations

The New York City chapter of the American Heart Association (AHA) was in a difficult situation. Although it was one of 56 affiliates of the AHA, it had to generate revenue to put into its own projects. In recent years, the number of charitable organizations asking for corporate and foundation funds had proliferated at the same time that government dollars for human services and the arts were being drastically cut. Increasing costs had meant that the chapter would have to either increase its funding through more donations or drop some of its programs. The chapter's Board of Directors and management was unwilling to cut the chapter's programs on reducing death and disability from heart attacks and strokes. Unfortunately they would then have to raise an additional $1 million on top of the current budget—an impossible goal.[1] What should the organization do?

The American Heart Association was not alone in this situation. By the mid-1990s, most not-for-profit organizations were turning to strategic management and other concepts from business to ensure their survival. This was a significant change because most not-for-profit managers had traditionally felt that business concepts were not relevant to their situation. According to Peter Drucker:

> Twenty years ago, management was a dirty word for those involved in nonprofit organizations. It meant business, and nonprofits prided themselves on being free of the taint of commercialism and above such sordid considerations as the bottom line. Now most of them have learned that nonprofits need management even more than business does, precisely because they lack the discipline of the bottom line.[2]

A knowledge of not-for-profit organizations is important if only for the sole reason that they account for an average of 1 in every 20 jobs in nations throughout the world. A study by the Johns Hopkins University Institute for Policy Studies found that in 9 countries between 1990 and 1995, nonprofit jobs grew by 23% compared to 6.2% for the whole economy.[3] Not-for-profits employ over 25% of the U.S. workforce and own approximately 15% of the nation's private wealth.[4] In the United States alone, in addition to various federal, state, and local government agencies, there are about 10,000 not-for-profit hospitals and nursing homes (85% of all hospitals), 4,600 colleges and universities, over 100,000 private and public elementary and secondary schools, and almost 350,000 churches and synagogues, plus many thousands of charities and service organizations.[5]

Typically **not-for-profit organizations** include **private nonprofit corporations** (such as hospitals, institutes, private colleges, and organized charities) as well as **public governmental units or agencies** (such as welfare departments, prisons, and state universities). Traditionally studies in strategic management have dealt with profit-making firms to the exclusion of non-profit or governmental organizations. This, however, is changing. Not-for-profit organizations are adopting strategic management in increasing numbers.

Scholars and practitioners are concluding that many strategic management concepts and techniques can be successfully adapted for not-for-profit organizations.[6] Although the evidence is not yet conclusive, there appears to be an association between strategic planning efforts and performance measures such as growth.[7] The purpose of this chapter is, therefore, to highlight briefly the major differences between the profit-making and the not-for-profit organization, so that the effects of their differences on the strategic management process can be understood.

13.1 Why Not-For-Profit?

The not-for-profit sector of an economy is important for several reasons. First, society desires certain goods and services that profit-making firms cannot or will not provide. These are referred to as **public or collective goods** because people who might not have paid for the goods receive benefits from them. Paved roads, police protection, museums, and schools are examples of public goods. A person cannot use a private good unless she or he pays for it. Generally once a public good is provided, however, anyone can use or enjoy it.

Certain aspects of life do not appear to be served appropriately by profit-making business firms yet are often crucial to the well-being of society. These aspects include areas in which society as a whole benefits from a particular service, but in which a particular individual benefits only indirectly. It is in these areas that not-for-profit organizations have traditionally been most effective. Libraries and museums are examples. Although most people do not visit libraries or museums very often, they are usually willing to pay taxes and/or donate funds to support their existence. They do so because these people believe that these organizations act to uplift the culture and quality of life of the region. To fulfill their mission, entrance fees (if any) must be set low enough to allow everyone admission. These fees, however, are not profitable—they rarely even cover the costs of the service. The same is true of animal shelters managed by the Humane Society. Although few people want abandoned pets running wild through city streets, fees charged from the sale of these animals cannot alone pay the costs of finding and caring for them. Additional revenue is needed—either in the form of donations or public taxation. Such public or collective services cannot generate a profit, yet they are necessary for any successful civilization. Which aspects of society are most suited for being served by not-for-profit organizations rather than by profit-making business organizations? This is the issue being faced by govern-

Global Issue

Which Is Best for Society: Business or Not-For-Profit?

Many nations throughout the world are attempting to privatize state-owned enterprises to balance their budgets. **Privatization** is (1) the selling of state-owned enterprises to private individuals or corporations or (2) the hiring of a private business to provide services previously offered by a state agency. The British government, for example, sold British Airways, its state-owned airline to private investors. In the United States, many city governments now allow private companies to collect and dispose of trash—something that had previously been done by the city.

Problems can result, however, if privatization goes too far. For example, in converting from a communist-oriented, centrally managed economy to a more democratic, free-market economy, Eastern European countries are finding that profit-making business firms are unable to satisfy all of society's needs. What used to be provided by the state free of charge (tax-supported) in Russia and other countries may now be provided only for the rich or not at all. The same problem is evident in

the United States in the controversies over the provision of health care, retirement benefits, and private versus public education.

Some of the aspects of life that cannot easily be privatized and are often better managed by not-for-profit organizations are as follows:

- Religion
- Education
- Charities
- Clubs, interest groups, unions
- Health care
- Government

The privatization of state-owned business enterprises is likely to continue globally because most of these enterprises must expand internationally in order to survive in the increasing global environment. They cannot compete successfully if they are forced to follow inefficient, socially oriented policies and regulations (emphasizing employment over efficiency) rather than economically oriented, international practices (emphasizing efficiency over employment). The global trend toward privatization will probably continue until each country reaches the point where the efficiency of business is counterbalanced by the effectiveness of the not-for-profit sector of the economy. As political motives overcome economic ones, government will likely intervene in that decision.

ments when they privatize what was previously provided by the state. See the **Global Issue** feature to learn more about this development.

A second reason why the not-for-profit sector is important is that a private nonprofit organization tends to receive benefits from society that a private profit-making firm cannot obtain. Preferred tax status to nonstock corporations is given in section 501(c)(3) of the U.S. Internal Revenue code in the form of exemptions from corporate income taxes. Private nonprofit firms also enjoy exemptions from various other state, local, and federal taxes. Under certain conditions, these firms also benefit from the tax deductibility of donors' contributions and membership dues. In addition, they qualify for special third-class mailing privileges.[8] These benefits are allowed because private nonprofit organizations are typically service organizations, which are expected to use any excess of revenue over costs and expenses (a surplus rather than a profit) either to improve service or to reduce the price of their service. This service orientation is reflected in the fact that not-for-profit organizations do not use the term "customer" to refer to the recipient of the service. The recipient is typically referred to as a patient, student, client, case, or simply "the public."

13.2 Importance of Revenue Source

The feature that best differentiates not-for-profit (NFP) organizations from each other as well as from profit-making corporations is their **source of revenue**.[9] The **profit-making firm** depends on revenues obtained from the sale of its goods and services to customers, who typically pay for the costs and expenses of providing the product or service plus a profit. The not-for-profit organization, in contrast, depends heavily on dues, assessments, or donations from its membership, or on funding from a sponsoring agency such as the United Way or the federal government to pay for much of its costs and expenses.

SOURCES OF NOT-FOR-PROFIT REVENUE

Revenue is generated from a variety of sources—not just from clients receiving the product or service from the NFP. It can come from people who do not even receive the services they are subsidizing. One study of Minnesota nonprofits found that donations accounted for almost 40%, government grants for around 25%, and program service fees for about 35% of total revenues.[10] In other types of not-for-profit organizations—such as unions and voluntary medical plans—revenue comes mostly from the members, the people who receive the service. Nevertheless, the members typically pay dues in advance and must accept later whatever service is provided whether they choose it or not, whether it is what they expected or not. The service is often received long after the dues are paid.

In profit-making corporations, there is typically a simple and direct connection between the customer or client and the organization. The organization tends to be totally dependent on sales of its products or services to the customer for revenue and is therefore extremely interested in pleasing the customer. As shown in **Figure 13–1**, the profit-making organization (*organization A*) tries to influence the customer (through advertising and promotion) to continue to buy and use its services. Either by buying or not buying the item offered, the customer, in turn, directly influences the organization's decision-making process. The business is thus market oriented.

In the case of the typical not-for-profit organization, however, there is likely to be a very different sort of relationship between the organization providing and the person receiving the service. Because the recipient of the service typically does not pay the entire cost of the service, outside sponsors are required. In most instances, the sponsors receive none of the service but provide partial to total funding for the needed revenues. As indicated earlier, these sponsors can be the government (using taxpayers' money) or charitable organizations, such as the United Way (using voluntary donations). As shown in **Figure 13–1**, the not-for-profit organization can be partially dependent on sponsors for funding (*organizations B and C*) or totally dependent on the sponsors (*organization D*). The less money it receives from clients receiving the service or product, the less market oriented is the not-for-profit organization.

PATTERNS OF INFLUENCE ON STRATEGIC DECISION MAKING

The **pattern of influence** on the organization's strategic decision making derives from its sources of revenue.[11] As shown in **Figure 13–1**, a private university (*organization B*) is heavily dependent on student tuition and other client-generated funds for about 70% of its revenue. Therefore, the students' desires are likely to have a stronger influence (as shown by an unbroken line) on the university's decision making than are the desires of the various sponsors such as alumni and private foundations. The sponsors' relatively marginal influence on the organization is reflected by a broken line. In contrast, a public university (*organization C*) is more heavily dependent on outside sponsors such as a state legislature for revenue funding. Student tuition and other client-generated funds form a small percentage (typically less than 40%) of total revenue. Therefore, the university's decision making is heavily influenced by the sponsors (unbroken line) and only marginally influenced directly by the students (broken line).

In the case of *organization D*, however, the client has no direct influence on the organization because the client pays nothing for the services received. In this situation, the organiza-

Figure 13–1

The Effects of Sources of Revenue on Patterns of Client-Organization Influence

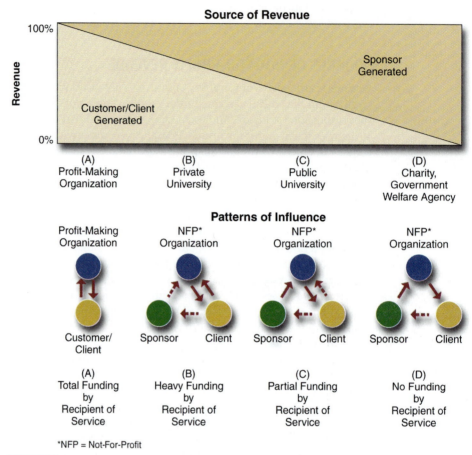

*NFP = Not-For-Profit

Source: Thomas L. Wheelen and J. David Hunger, "The Effect of Revenue Upon Patterns of Client-Organization Influence." Copyright ©1982 by Wheelen and Hunger Associates. Revised 1991. Reprinted by permission.

tion tends to measure its effectiveness in terms of sponsor satisfaction. It has no real measure of its efficiency other than its ability to carry out its mission and achieve its objectives within the dollar contributions it has received from its sponsors. In contrast to other organizations in which the client contributes a significant proportion of the needed revenue, *organization D* actually might be able to increase its revenue by heavily lobbying its sponsors while reducing the level of its service to its clients!

Regardless of the percentage of total funding that the client generates, the client may attempt to indirectly influence the not-for-profit organization through the sponsors. This is depicted by the broken lines connecting the client and the sponsor in *organizations B, C, and D* in **Figure 13–1**. Welfare clients or prison inmates, for example, may be able to indirectly improve the services they receive if they pressure government officials by writing to legislators or even by rioting. Students at public universities can lobby state officials for student representation on governing boards.

The key to understanding the management of a not-for-profit organization is thus learning who pays for the delivered services. If the recipients of the service pay only a small proportion of the total cost of the service, strategic managers are likely to be more concerned with satisfying the needs and desires of the funding sponsors or agency than those of the people receiving the service. The acquisition of resources can become an end in itself.

USEFULNESS OF STRATEGIC MANAGEMENT CONCEPTS AND TECHNIQUES

Some strategic management concepts can be equally applied to business and not-for-profit organizations, whereas others cannot. The marketplace orientation underlying portfolio analysis, for example, does not translate into situations in which client satisfaction and revenue are only indirectly linked. Industry analysis and competitive strategy are primarily relevant to not-for-profits that obtain most of their revenue from user fees rather than from donors or taxpayers. For example, as hospitals find themselves relying increasingly on patient fees for their revenue, they use competitive strategy to gain advantage versus other hospitals. Smaller NFP hospitals stress the "high touch" of their staff over the "high tech" of competitors having better diagnostic machinery. The concept of competitive advantage is less useful to the typical not-for-profit than the related concept of institutional advantage, which sets aside the profit-making objective of competitive advantage. A not-for-profit can be said to have **institutional advantage** when it performs its tasks more effectively than other comparable organizations.[12]

SWOT analysis, mission statements, stakeholder analysis, and corporate governance are, however, just as relevant to a not-for-profit as they are to a profit-making organization.[13] Portfolio analysis can be very helpful, but is used very differently from business firms. (See strategic piggybacking later in the chapter.) As with any corporation, nonprofits usually have boards of directors whose job is to ensure that the paid executive director and staff work to fulfill the organization's mission and objectives. Unlike the boards of most business firms, not-for-profit boards are often required, however, to take primary responsibility for strategic planning and fund-raising. Many not-for-profits are finding a well-crafted mission statement not only helps in finding donors, but also in attracting volunteers. Take the example of the mission statement of a local animal shelter:

> To shelter and care for stray, lost, or abandoned animals and to responsibly place animals in new homes and enforce animal laws. We are also here to better educate people in ways to be solutions to animal problems, not causes.[14]

Strategic management is difficult to apply when the organization's output is difficult to measure objectively, as is the case with most not-for-profit organizations. Thus it is very likely that many not-for-profit organizations have not used strategic management because its concepts, techniques, and prescriptions do not lend themselves to situations where sponsors, rather than the marketplace, determine revenue. The situation, however, is changing. The trend toward privatizing public organizations, such as converting subsidized community hospitals to independent (nonsubsidized) status, usually means that the clients/patients pay a larger percentage of the costs. As these not-for-profits become more market oriented (and thus client oriented), strategic management becomes more applicable and more increasingly used.[15] Nevertheless, various constraints on not-for-profits mean that strategic management concepts and techniques must be modified to be effective.

13.3 Impact of Constraints on Strategic Management

Several characteristics peculiar to the not-for-profit organization constrain its behavior and affect its strategic management. Newman and Wallender list the following five **constraints on strategic management:**

1. **Service is often intangible and hard to measure.** This difficulty is typically compounded by the existence of multiple service objectives developed to satisfy multiple sponsors.

2. **Client influence may be weak.** Often the organization has a local monopoly, and clients' payments may be a very small source of funds.

3. **Strong employee commitments to professions or to a cause may undermine allegiance** to the organization employing them.

4. **Resource contributors may intrude on the organization's internal management.** Such contributors include fund contributors and government.

5. **Restraints on the use of rewards and punishments** may result from constraints one, three, and four.[16]

It is true that several of these characteristics can be found in profit-making as well as in not-for-profit organizations. Nevertheless, as Newman and Wallender state, the ". . . frequency of strong impact is much higher in not-for-profit enterprises."[17]

IMPACT ON STRATEGY FORMULATION

The long-range planning and decision making affected by the listed constraints serve to add at least four **complications to strategy formulation.**

- **Goal conflicts interfere with rational planning.** Because the not-for-profit organization typically lacks a single clear-cut performance criterion (such as profits), divergent goals and objectives are likely, especially with multiple sponsors. Differences in the concerns of various important sponsors can prevent management from stating the organization's mission in anything but very broad terms, if they fear that a sponsor who disagrees with a particular, narrow definition of mission might cancel its funding. For example, a study of 227 public Canadian hospitals found that over half had very general, ambiguous, and unquantified objectives.[18] According to Heffron, an authority in public administration: "The greater openness within which they are compelled to operate—the fishbowl atmosphere—impedes thorough discussion of issues and discourages long-range plans that might alienate stakeholders."[19] In such organizations, it is the reduced influence of the clients that permits this diversity of values and goals to occur without a clear market check. For example, when a city council considers changing zoning to implement a strategic plan for the city, all sorts of people (including the press) will demand to be heard. A decision might be made based on pressure from a few stakeholders (who make significant contributions or who threaten to stir up trouble) to the detriment of the community as a whole.

- **An integrated planning focus tends to shift from results to resources.** Because not-for-profit organizations tend to provide services that are hard to measure, they rarely have a net bottom line. Planning, therefore, becomes more concerned with resource inputs, which can easily be measured, than with service, which cannot. Goal displacement (explained earlier in **Chapter 10**) becomes even more likely than it is in business organizations.[20]

- **Ambiguous operating objectives create opportunities for internal politics and goal displacement.** The combination of vague objectives and a heavy concern with resources allows managers considerable leeway in their activities. Such leeway makes possible political maneuvering for personal ends. In addition, because the effectiveness of the not-for-profit organization hinges on the satisfaction of the sponsoring group, management tends to ignore the needs of the client while focusing on the desires of a powerful sponsor. University administrators commonly say that people will donate money for a new building (which will carry the donor's name), but not for other more pressing needs, such as the maintenance of existing buildings. In this situation, powerful department heads might wine and dine the donor, hoping to get the money for their pet projects. This problem is compounded by the common practice of selecting people to boards of trustees/directors not on the basis of their managerial experience, but on the basis of their ability to contribute money, raise funds, and work with politicians. (A major role of the not-for-profit board is to ensure adequate resources—usually translated to mean fund-raising.)[21] Directors usually receive no compensation for serving on the board. Their lack of interest in overseeing management is reflected in an overall not-for-profit board-meeting attendance rate of only 50%, compared with 90% for boards of directors of business corporations. This is one reason why boards of not-for-profits tend to be larger than are boards of business corporations. Eckerd College, for example, has a 52-member, extremely passive board of directors.[22] Board members of not-for-profit organizations tend to ignore the task of determining strategies and policies—often leaving this to the paid (or sometimes unpaid) executive director. The larger the board, the less likely it is to exercise control over top management.[23]

- **Professionalization simplifies detailed planning but adds rigidity.** In not-for-profit organizations in which professionals play important roles (as in hospitals or colleges), professional values and traditions can prevent the organization from changing its conventional behavior patterns to fit new service missions tuned to changing social needs. This rigidity, of course, can occur in any organization that hires professionals. The strong service orientation of most not-for-profit organizations, however, tends to encourage the development of static professional norms and attitudes. As not-for-profits attempt to become more businesslike, this may be changing. One study of Minnesota nonprofits revealed that 29% of the program directors and 15% of the staff had degrees or experience in business administration.[24]

IMPACT ON STRATEGY IMPLEMENTATION

The five constraining characteristics also affect how a not-for-profit organization is organized in both its structure and job design. Three **complications to strategy implementation** in particular can be highlighted:

1. **Decentralization is complicated.** The difficulty of setting objectives for an intangible, hard-to-measure service mission complicates the delegation of decision-making authority. Because of the heavy dependence on sponsors for revenue support, the top management of a not-for-profit organization must be always alert to the sponsors' view of an organizational activity. This necessary caution leads to **defensive centralization**, in which top management retains all decision-making authority so that low-level managers cannot take any actions to which the sponsors may object.

2. **Linking pins for external-internal integration become important.** Because of the heavy dependence on outside sponsors, a special need arises for people in buffer roles to relate to both inside and outside groups. This role is especially necessary when the sponsors are diverse (revenue comes from donations, membership fees, and federal funds) and the service is intangible (for instance, a "good" education) with a broad mission and multiple shifting objectives. The job of a "Dean for External Affairs," for example, consists primarily of working with the school's alumnae and raising funds.

3. **Job enlargement and executive development can be restrained by professionalism.** In organizations that employ a large number of professionals, managers must design jobs that appeal to prevailing professional norms. Professionals have rather clear ideas about which activities are, and which are not, within their province. Enriching a nurse's job by expanding his or her decision-making authority for drug dosage, for example, can cause conflict with medical doctors who believe that such authority is theirs alone. Because a professional often views managerial jobs as nonprofessional and merely supportive, promotion into a management position is not always viewed positively.

IMPACT ON EVALUATION AND CONTROL

Special **complications to evaluation and control** arising from the constraining characteristics affect how behavior is motivated and performance is controlled. Two problems, in particular, are often noticed:

1. **Rewards and penalties have little or no relation to performance.** When desired results are vague and the judgment of success is subjective, predictable and impersonal feedback cannot be established. Performance is judged either intuitively ("You don't seem to be taking your job seriously") or on the basis of whatever small aspects of a job can be measured ("You were late to work twice last month").

2. **Inputs rather than outputs are heavily controlled.** Because its inputs can be measured much more easily than outputs, the not-for-profit organization tends to focus more on the resources going into performance than on the performance itself.[25] The emphasis is thus on setting maximum limits for costs and expenses. Because there is little to no reward for staying under these limits, people usually respond negatively to such controls.

Because of these and other complications, not-for-profits can waste money in many ways, especially on administrative costs and expenses. Because of this, it is becoming increasingly common to calculate ratios comparing total support and revenue with the amounts spent on specific service activities. For example, analysts become concerned when the total spent on the mission of the organization (e.g., community service or whatever) is less than 50% of total income received from sponsors and activities. Other rules of thumb are that a not-for-profit should not spend more than 35% on administrative expenses and that the costs of fund-raising should not account for more than 15% of total income.[26]

13.4 Popular Not-for-Profit Strategies

Because of various pressures on not-for-profit organizations to provide more services than the sponsors and clients can pay for, these organizations are developing strategies to help them meet their desired service objectives. In addition to a heavy use of volunteers to keep costs low, NFPs are choosing the strategies of strategic piggybacking, mergers, and strategic alliances.

STRATEGIC PIGGYBACKING

Coined by Nielsen, the term **strategic piggybacking** refers to the development of a new activity for the not-for-profit organization that would generate the funds needed to make up the difference between revenues and expenses.[27] The new activity is related typically in some manner to the not-for-profit's mission, but its purpose is to help subsidize the primary service programs. It appears to be a form of concentric diversification, but it is engaged in only for its money-generating value. In an inverted use of portfolio analysis, the organization invests in new, safe cash cows to fund its current cash-hungry stars, question marks, and dogs.

Although this strategy is not new, it has recently become very popular. As early as 1874, for example, the Metropolitan Museum of Art retained a professional to photograph its collections and to sell copies of the prints. Profits were used to defray the museum's operating costs. More recently, various income-generating ventures have appeared under various auspices, from the Girl Scouts to UNICEF, and in numerous forms, from cookies and small gift shops to vast real estate developments. A study by the U.S. General Accounting Office revealed that the amount of funds resulting from income-producing activities has significantly increased since the 1970s. Hospitals are offering wellness programs, ranging from meditation classes to aerobics. Some 70% of colleges and universities now offer "auxiliary" services, such as bookstores, conference rooms, and computer centers as sources of income.[28] The American Cancer Society earns millions annually from allowing its name to appear on products sold by private drug companies, such as Smith-Kline Beecham's Nicoderm chewing gum. The Metropolitan Museum of Art now has 16 stores outside the main museum and a fast-growing Web site—all of which generate money. The Baptist Hospital of Nashville, Tennessee, built and operates a $15 million, 18-acre office and training-field complex, which it rents to Nashville's professional football team.

The Small Business Administration, however, views this money-making activity as "unfair competition." The U.S. Internal Revenue Service (IRS) advises that a not-for-profit that engages in a business "not substantially related" to the organization's exempt purposes may jeopardize its tax-exempt status, particularly if the income from the business exceeds approximately 20% of total organizational revenues. The IRS requires not-for-profits to pay an unrelated business income tax on commercial activities that don't relate to the organization's central mission. So far, not-for-profits are still considered tax-exempt if their businesses are staffed by volunteers or if almost all their merchandise is donated. According to Marcus Owens, Director of tax-exempt organizations for the IRS, "The ultimate question is should these institutions continue as tax-exempt entities. And it's being raised more than ever before."[29]

Although strategic piggybacks can help not-for-profit organizations self-subsidize their primary missions and better use their resources, according to Nielsen, there are several potential drawbacks.[30] *First*, the revenue-generating venture could actually lose money, especially in the short run. *Second*, the venture could subvert, interfere with, or even take over the primary mission. *Third*, the public, as well as the sponsors, could reduce their contributions because of negative responses to such "money-grubbing activities" or because of a mistaken belief that the organization is becoming self-supporting. *Fourth*, the venture could interfere with the internal operations of the not-for-profit organization. To avoid these drawbacks, a not-for-profit should first carefully evaluate its resources before choosing this strategy. See the **boxed feature** to see the resources needed for a piggyback.

The U.S. National Association of College and University Business Officers predicts that within a few years over 90% of colleges and universities in the United States will be using strategic piggybacks.[31] Expect a similar trend for other not-for-profits that heavily rely on donations and taxpayer support for their revenue.

MERGERS

Dwindling resources are leading an increasing number of not-for-profits to consider mergers as a way of reducing costs. For example, the merger of Baptist Health Systems and Research Health Services created Health Midwest in Kansas City. The New York Hospital—Cornell Medical Center and Columbia-Presbyterian Medical Center combined to form the New York and Presbyterian Hospitals Health Care System. Between 1980 and 1991, more than 400 U.S. hospitals were involved in mergers and consolidations—more than half of them happening after 1987.[32]

STRATEGIC ALLIANCES

Strategic alliances involve developing cooperative ties with other organizations. Alliances are often used by not-for-profit organizations as a way to enhance their capacity to serve clients or to acquire resources while still enabling them to keep their identity.[33] Services can be pur-

Resources Needed for Successful Strategic Piggybacking

Based on his experience as a consultant to not-for-profit organizations, Edward Skloot suggests that a not-for-profit should have five resources before engaging in strategic piggybacking:

1. **Something to Sell:** The organization should assess its resources to see if people might be willing to pay for goods or services closely related to the organization's primary activity. Repackaging the Boston Symphony into the less formal Boston Pops Orchestra created a way to subsidize the deficit-creating symphony and provide year-round work for the musicians.

2. **Critical Mass of Management Talent:** Enough people must be available to nurture and sustain an income venture over the long haul. This can be very difficult, given that the most competent not-for-profit professionals often don't want to be managers.

3. **Trustee Support:** If the trustees have strong feelings against earned-income ventures, they could actively or passively resist commercial involvement. When the Children's Television Workshop began licensing its Sesame Street characters to toy companies and theme parks, many people criticized it for joining business in selling more things to children.

4. **Entrepreneurial Attitude:** Management must be able to combine an interest in innovative ideas with businesslike practicality.

5. **Venture Capital:** Because it often takes money to make money, engaging in a joint venture with a business corporation can provide the necessary start-up funds as well as the marketing and management support. For example, Massachusetts General Hospital receives $50 million from Hoechst, the German chemical company, for biological research in exchange for exclusive licenses to develop commercial products from particular research discoveries.

Source: E. Skloot, "Should Not-for-Profits Go into Business?" *Harvard Business Review* (January–February 1983), pp. 20–24. Copyright © 2001 by the President and Fellows of Harvard College, all rights reserved.

chased and provided more efficiently through cooperation with other organizations than if they were done alone. For example, four Ohio universities agreed to create and jointly operate a new school of international business. Alone, none of the business schools could afford the $30 million to build the school. The Collaborative Ventures Program of the Teagle Foundation has given more than $4 million in grants to help colleges set up money-saving collaborations. While only a handful of consortia existed in 1995, by 1998 there were at least 21 representing 125 colleges and universities.[34]

Strategic alliances and mergers are becoming commonplace among not-for-profit organizations. The next logical step is strategic alliances between business firms and not-for-profits. Already business corporations are forming alliances with universities to fund university research in exchange for options on the results of that research. Business firms find it cheaper to pay universities to do basic research than to do it themselves. Universities are in need of research funds to attract top professors and to maintain expensive labs. Such alliances of convenience are being criticized, but they are likely to continue.

13.5 Impact of the Internet on Not-for-Profit Organizations

The Internet is just beginning to have an impact on not-for-profit organizations. By far, the most impact has been upon government activities—especially in terms of taxation and the provision of services.

Taxation

The first impact of the Internet upon not-for-profit organizations (especially government) was the issue of taxation. Businesses in the United States must collect and pay sales taxes to the government of each state in which they operate. Mail order retailers—both catalogue and Internet—generally collect state sales tax from consumers only if the company operates a facility in the state where the merchandise is being sent. Since Internet companies usually don't have brick-and-mortar operations, they collect little sales tax. Many state and local government officials fear that as more of the economy shifts online, they will lose tax revenue needed for schools, police officers, and other basic services. These government officials have been supported by traditional retailers fearing that they will not be able to compete with Internet rivals who receive special tax advantages. Antitax activists and some business leaders have responded that the lack of tax has accelerated the growth of electronic commerce. According to them, a complex tax structure dealing with more than 6,000 different tax jurisdictions would stifle the growth of the Internet retail industry and hurt the overall economy. The U.S. Congress agreed in 1998 to a three-year moratorium on the taxation of sales by purely Internet-based businesses.[35]

The European Union (EU) is also concerned that the Internet will reduce its tax revenues. For example, if a German buys a CD from an American Internet retailer who delivers it by post, the German escapes paying the 16% value added tax (VAT) paid at the local shop. In addition, Internet businesses can avoid taxes by moving to low-tax countries or to tax havens, just as British gambling firms have done with online gambling. The European Commission has proposed that foreign companies with annual online sales of more than 100,000 Euros in the EU should register for VAT in at least one EU country and then collect the tax on all services downloaded from the Internet. According to *The Economist*, this tax would be almost impossible to enforce.[36]

Improvement of Government Services

After e-commerce (B2C) and business to business (B2B), the next Internet revolution will be in government services (G2C). The Internet can play an important role in helping government reduce its costs and improve its services. For example, a pioneering project called ServiceArizona allows the residents of Arizona to conduct transactions on the Web, from ordering personalized license plates for their cars to replacing lost identification cards. Instead of standing in line for hours, people can renew their registrations with the motor vehicle department in just a few minutes any hour or day of the week. The Web site was built, maintained, and hosted by IBM in return for 2% of the value of each transaction (about $4 for an auto registration). Because processing an auto registration costs only $1.60 compared to $6.60 in person, the state saves money. With 15% of renewals now being processed by ServiceArizona, the motor vehicles department saves around $17 million annually.

Governments around the world are realizing that they will need to construct Internet portals, similar to that of Yahoo! that can provide one location to satisfy all of its citizens' needs. A central government portal has been launched in Singapore; another is being developed in Austria. In Britain, BT won the contract to build UK Online, a portal to offer government services. Just as businesses are pushing their suppliers into doing business with them online, so can governments—thus streamlining the activities of government agencies. For example, EDS developed a Web-based intranet for the naval airbase at Corpus Christi, Texas, so that its mechanics could have access to spare parts anywhere in the world. IBM worked with Emekli Sandigi, a Turkish government social security organization to develop an intranet to link 17,000 pharmacies so that they can check the validity of a customer's health card and other factors. The new system reduces the amount of time pharmacists are paid from two months to less than a week. The Internet can also improve the quality of the relationship between a government and its citizens. For example, a Democratic primary in Arizona in which online voting was allowed boosted voter turnout to six times its usual level.[37]

Impact on Other Not-For-Profit Organizations

The Internet is also having an impact on not-for-profits other than government. Although the media tends to talk mostly of dot-coms (.com), three major Internet domains have

Internet Issue

The Not-For-Profit Organizations That Rule the Internet

There is a myth that the Internet has grown because of a complete absence of rules or regulations. In reality, the Internet is a highly organized place. What is unique about the Internet is that its regulation has developed from the bottom-up instead of from the top-down. The Internet Engineering Task Force (IETF) develops agreed technical standards, such as communication protocols. The Internet Corporation for Assigned Names and Numbers (ICANN) oversees the system of domain names, such as com (business), edu (education), gov (government), and org (nonprofit organizations). The World Wide Web Consortium (W3C) also oversees Internet standards. Without such global standards, there would be no way to connect modems to computers for Internet access or for viewers to read Web sites, let alone download files or host chat rooms. These not-for-profit bodies are largely self-created and self-governing. They are open in membership and willing to hear all arguments on an issue. According to David Clark of MIT, a member of IETF, "We reject kings, presidents, and voting. We believe in rough consensus and running code." Anyone can become a member of the IETF simply by signing up at the task force's Web site to a working group's mailing list. Anyone can come to the three meetings held annually by the task force.

These organizations seem to work so well because they are composed of like-minded individuals who have common interests even if located in various parts of the world. Very function-oriented, IETF decisions are based on effectiveness and efficiency. Since anyone can access all proposals, the process is very hard to manipulate. In 1999, the IETF argued about how far it should go to help law enforcement conduct wiretaps and eventually decided not to "consider requirements for wire-tapping." W3C is an organization founded by Tim Berners-Lee, the inventor of the World Wide Web, to develop standards for the Web. Most of the 400-plus members are companies paying $50,000 per year for membership. It also upholds the consensus principle in decision making. It has developed more than 20 technical specifications, including one on XML (Extensible Markup Language), which may replace HTML as the language used in Web sites. ICANN wrested monopoly control of Internet domain names from Network Solutions and has accredited over 120 registers who can sell domain names. It recently added a number of new top-level domains to the usual com, edu, gov, org, and net. ICANN also helps resolve conflicts over who has the right to a domain name. The World Intellectual Property Organization, one of four dispute-resolution bodies accredited by ICANN, recently ruled that Internet addresses bearing the names of British author, Jeanette Winterson, and the American actress, Julia Roberts, should be returned to their rightful owners. Both addresses had been registered by Internet "squatters" who had argued that the names of living people are not trademarks.

been edu, gov, and org. Along with net, these have been the primary Internet domains until the number of domains were increased in 2000 by ICANN. (See the ⧉ **Internet Issue** feature for who regulates the Internet.) Most every nonprofit organization now has its own Web site to provide services to its members and to interested outsiders.

According to Peter Drucker, the greatest impact of the Internet may be upon higher education and health care (85% of U.S. hospitals are nonprofit).[38] Internet access can enable medical practitioners to access the knowledge of specialists in distant locations. Patients can learn more about their illness by talking in Internet *chat rooms* with other people having the same illness. Around 75% of U.S. colleges and universities have Web sites enabling students to access course information (including the syllabus) and download assignments. Such Web sites are replacing library reserve rooms. Although 1.4 million people were enrolled in distance education courses during the 1997–1998 academic year, that number has risen considerably during the following years.[39] Some universities, like the University of Phoenix, are offering complete courses and degree programs over the Internet.

Projections for the 21st Century

- From 1994 to 2010, the number of AIDS cases worldwide will grow from 20 million to 38 million.
- From 1994 to 2010, the cost of a Wharton MBA will increase from $84,200 to $257,200.[40]

Discussion Questions

1. Are not-for-profit organizations less efficient than profit-making organizations? Why or why not?

2. How does the lack of a clear-cut performance measure, such as profits, affect the strategic management of a not-for-profit organization?

3. What are the pros and cons of strategic piggybacking? In what way is it "unfair competition" for NFPs to engage in revenue generating activity?

4. What are the pros and cons of mergers and strategic alliances? Should not-for-profits engage in alliances with business firms?

5. Recently, many not-for-profit organizations in the United States have been converting to profit making. Why would a not-for-profit organization want to change its status to profit making? What are the pros and cons of doing so?

Strategic Practice Exercise

1. Read the **Global Issue** feature in this chapter on page 326. It lists six aspects of society that it proposes are better managed by not-for-profit organizations than by profit-making organizations. Do you agree with this list? Should some aspects be deleted from the list? Should other aspects be added?

2. Examine a local college or university—perhaps the one you may be currently attending. What strategic issues is it facing? Develop a SFAS Table (**Figure**

5–1) of strategic factors. Is it attempting to use any strategic management concepts? If so, which ones? What sorts of strategies should it be considering for continued survival and future growth? Is it currently using strategic piggybacks to obtain additional funding? What sorts of additional piggybacks should it consider? Are strategic alliances with another college or university or business firm a possibility?

Key Terms

complications to evaluation and control (p. 332)

complications to strategy formulation (p. 330)

complications to strategy implementation (p. 331)

constraints on strategic management (p. 329)

defensive centralization (p. 331)

institutional advantage (p. 329)

not-for-profit organization (p. 325)

patterns of influence (p. 327)

private nonprofit corporations (p. 325)

privatization (p. 326)

profit-making firm (p. 326)

public governmental units or agencies (p. 325)

public or collective goods (p. 325)

source of revenue (p. 326)

strategic alliances (p. 333)

strategic piggybacking (p. 332)

Notes

1. B. Wiesendanger, "Profitable Pointers from Non-Profits," *Journal of Business Strategy* (July/August 1994), pp. 33–39.

2. P. F. Drucker, "What Business Can Learn from Nonprofits," *Harvard Business Review* (July–August 1989), p. 89.

3. "The Non-Profit Sector: Love or Money," *The Economist* (November 14, 1998), pp. 68–73.

4. G. Rudney, "The Scope and Dimensions of Nonprofit Activity," in *The Nonprofit Sector: A Research Handbook*, edited by W. W. Powell (New Haven: Yale University Press, 1987), p. 56; C. P. McLaughlin, *The Management of Nonprofit Organizations* (New York: John Wiley & Sons, 1986), p. 4.

5. M. O'Neill, *The Third America* (San Francisco: Jossey–Bass, 1989).

6. K. Ascher and B. Nare, "Strategic Planning in the Public Sector," *International Review of Strategic Management*, Vol. 1, edited by D. E. Hussey (New York: John Wiley & Sons, 1990), pp. 297–315; I. Unterman and R. H. Davis, *Strategic Management of Not-for-Profit Organizations* (New York: Praeger Press, 1984), p. 2.

7. P. V. Jenster and G. A. Overstreet, "Planning for a Non-Profit Service: A Study of U.S. Credit Unions," *Long Range Planning* (April 1990), pp. 103–111; G. J. Medley, "Strategic Planning for the World Wildlife Fund," *Long Range Planning* (February 1988), pp. 46–54.

8. J. G. Simon, "The Tax Treatment of Nonprofit Organizations: A Review of Federal and State Policies," in *The Nonprofit Sector: A Research Handbook*, edited by W. W. Powell (New Haven: Yale University Press, 1987), pp. 67–98.

9. B. P. Keating and M. O. Keating, *Not-for-Profit* (Glen Ridge, NJ: Thomas Horton & Daughters, 1980), p. 21.

10. K. A. Froelich, "Business Management in Nonprofit Organizations," paper presented to the *Midwest Management Society* (Chicago, 1995).

11. J. D. Hunger and T. L. Wheelen, "Is Strategic Management Appropriate for Not-for-Profit Organizations?" in *Handbook of Business Strategy, 1989/90 Yearbook*, edited by H. E. Glass (Boston: Warren, Gorham and Lamont, 1989), pp. 3.1–3.8. The contention that the pattern of environmental influence on the organization's strategic decision making derives from the organization's source(s) of income agrees with the authorities in the field. See R. E. Emerson, "Power-Dependence Relations," *American Sociological Review* (February 1962), pp. 31–41; J. D. Thompson, Organizations in Action (New York: McGraw-Hill, 1967), pp. 30–31; and J. Pfeffer and G. R. Salancik, *The External Control of Organizations: A Resource Dependence Perspective* (New York: HarperCollins, 1978), p. 44.

12. M. Goold, "Institutional Advantage: A Way into Strategic Management in Not-for-Profit Organizations," *Long Range Planning* (April 1997), pp. 291–293.

13. Ascher and Nare, "Strategic Planning in the Public Sector," pp. 297–315; R. McGill, "Planning for Strategic Performance in Local Government," *Long Range Planning* (October 1988), pp. 77–84.

14. Lorna Lavender, Supervisor of Ames (Iowa) Animal Shelter, quoted by K. Petty, "Animal Shelter Cares for Homeless," *ISU Daily* (July 25, 1996), p. 3.

15. E. Ferlie, "The Creation and Evolution of Quasi Markets in the Public Sector: A Problem for Strategic Management," *Strategic Management Journal* (Winter 1992), pp. 79–97. Research has found that for-profit hospitals have more mission statement components dealing with principal services, target customers, and geographic domain than do not-for-profit hospitals. See R. Subramanian, K. Kumar, and C. C. Yauger, "Mission Statements of Hospitals: An Empirical Analysis of Their Contents and Their Relationship to Organizational Factors," *Journal of Business Strategies* (Spring 1993), pp. 63–78.

16. W. H. Newman and H. W. Wallender III, "Managing Not-for-Profit Enterprises," *Academy of Management Review* (January 1978), p. 26.

17. Ibid., p. 27. The following discussion of the effects of these constraining characteristics is taken from pp. 27–31.

18. J. Denis, A. Langley, and D. Lozeau, "Formal Strategy in Public Hospitals," *Long Range Planning* (February 1991), pp. 71–82.

19. F. Heffron, *Organization Theory and Public Administration* (Upper Saddle River, NJ: Prentice Hall, 1989), p. 132.

20. Heffron, pp. 103–115.

21. R. T. Ingram, *Ten Basic Responsibilities of Nonprofit Boards*, 2nd edition (Washington, DC: National Center for Nonprofit Boards, 1997), pp. 9–10.

22. A. C. Smith, "Endowment Use Overlooked," *St. Petersburg Times* (June 23, 2000), p. 3B. Eckerd's board was strongly criticized because it had tolerated improper financial practices on the part of the President and had allowed the college's endowment to dissipate.

23. I. Unterman and R. H. Davis, *Strategic Management of Not-for-Profit Organizations* (New York: Praeger Press, 1984), p. 174; J. A. Alexander, M. L. Fennell, and M. T. Halpern, "Leadership Instability in Hospitals: The Influence of Board–CEO Relations and Organizational Growth and Decline," *Administrative Science Quarterly* (March 1993), pp. 74–99.

24. Froelich, "Business Management in Nonprofit Organizations," p. 9.

25. R. M. Kanter and D. V. Summers, "Doing Well While Doing Good: Dilemmas of Performance Measurement in Nonprofit Organizations and the Need for a Multiple-Constituency Approach," in *The Nonprofit Sector: A Research Handbook*, edited by W. W. Powell (New Haven: Yale University Press, 1987), p. 163.

26. J. P. Dalsimer, *Understanding Nonprofit Financial Statement: A Primer for Board Members*, 2nd edition (Washington, DC: National Center for Nonprofit Boards, 1997), p. 17.

27. R. P. Nielsen, "SMR Forum: Strategic Piggybacking—A Self-Subsidizing Strategy for Nonprofit Institutions," *Sloan Management Review* (Summer 1982), pp. 65–69; R. P. Nielsen, "Piggybacking for Business and Nonprofits: A Strategy for Hard Times," *Long Range Planning* (April 1984), pp. 96–102.

28. D. C. Bacon, "Nonprofit Groups: An Unfair Edge?" *Nation's Business* (April 1989), pp. 33–34; "Universities Push Auxiliary Services to Generate More Revenue," *Wall Street Journal* (April 27, 1995), p. A1.

29. M. Langley, "Nonprofit Hospitals Sometimes Are That in Little but Name," *Wall Street Journal* (July 14, 1997), p. A1, A6; D. Brady, "When Nonprofits Go After Profits," *Business Week* (June 26, 2000), pp. 173–178.; E. Skloot, "Should Not-for-Profits Go into Business?" *Harvard Business Review* (January–February 1983), p. 21; E. Felsenthal, "As Nonprofits Add Sidelines, IRS Takes Aim," *Wall Street Journal* (May 3, 1996), p. B1.

30. R. P. Nielsen, "Piggybacking Strategies for Nonprofits: A Shared Costs Approach," *Strategic Management Journal* (May–June 1986), pp. 209–211.

31. "Universities Push Auxiliary Services to Generate More Revenue," (Business Bulletin) *Wall Street Journal* (April 27, 1995), p. A1.

32. S. Collins, "A Bitter Financial Pill," *U.S. News & World Report* (November 29, 1993), pp. 83–86.

33. K. G. Provan, "Interorganizational Cooperation and Decision Making Autonomy in a Consortium Multihospital System," *Academy of Management Review* (July 1984), pp. 494–504; R. D. Luke, J. W. Begun, and D. D. Pointer, "Quasi-Firms: Strategic Interorganizational Forms in the Health Care Industry," *Academy of Management Review* (January 1989), pp. 9–19.

34. "More Colleges Are Opting for Mergers," *The (Ames, IA) Daily Tribune* (August 12, 1998), p. B3.

35. H. Fineman, "The Tax War Goes Online," *Newsweek* (December 20, 1999), p. 31; R. Chandrasekaran, "Tax Debate Heats Up Over On-line Sales," *International Herald Tribune* (December 14, 1999), p. B2; G. R. Simpson, "Internet Panel Pushes Reform of Sales Taxes," *Wall Street Journal* (December 16, 1999), p. A3.

36. "The End of Taxes?" *The Economist: A Survey of the New Economy* (Special insert: September 23, 2000), p. 30.

37. "The Next Revolution" and "Quick Fixes," *The Economist: A Survey of Government and the Internet* (Special insert: June 24, 2000), pp. 3–9, 13.

38. M. Williams, "Prophet Sharing," *Red Herring* (January 30, 2001), pp. 100–107.

39. A. Levinson, "Students Attend College Online," *The (Ames, IA) Tribune* (January 29, 2001), p. A2.

40. J. Warner, "21st Century Capitalism: Snapshot of the Next Century," *Business Week* (November 18, 1994), p. 194.

chapter 14

Suggestions for Case Analysis

A few years ago, AlliedSignal's free cash flow measure turned negative. Although the company reported a 16% gain in net income for the second quarter, the free cash flow was a negative $90 million. Top management dismissed the cash flow situation as only temporary, arguing that capital spending and increasing inventory during the first part of the year was needed to fuel the company's sales growth expected later in the year. A company spokesman predicted that the free cash flow for the year should hit $300 million and concluded, "There's no problem with cash flow here."

"Not so!" responded Jeffrey Fotta, President of Boston's Ernst Institutional Research. Fotta contended that Allied's growing sales and earnings masked a serious problem in the company. Over the past year, Allied's push to boost sales had caused it difficulty in meeting its cash needs from operations. "They're growing too fast and not getting the returns from capital investments they used to get. Allied peaked in mid 1995, and returns have been deteriorating since." Fotta predicted that without major changes, AlliedSignal would have increasing difficulty continuing its double-digit sales growth.[1]

This is an example of how one analyst used a performance measure to assess the overall health of a company. You can do the same type of in-depth analysis on a comprehensive strategic management case. This chapter provides you with various analytical techniques and suggestions for conducting this kind of case analysis.

341

14.1 The Case Method

The analysis and discussion of case problems has been the most popular method of teaching strategy and policy for many years. The case method provides the opportunity to move from a narrow, specialized view that emphasizes functional techniques to a broader, less precise analysis of the overall corporation. Cases present actual business situations and enable you to examine both successful and unsuccessful corporations. In case analysis, you might be asked to critically analyze a situation in which a manager had to make a decision of long-term corporate importance. This approach gives you a feel for what it is like to be faced with making and implementing strategic decisions.

14.2 Researching the Case Situation

Don't restrict yourself only to the information written in the case. You should undertake outside research into the environmental setting. Check the decision date of each case (typically the latest date mentioned in the case) to find out when the situation occurred and then screen the business periodicals for that time period. Use computerized company and industry information services such as COMPUSTAT, Compact Disclosure, and CD/International, available on CD-ROM or online at the library. On the Internet, Hoover's On Line Corporate Directory ⟨www.hoovers.com⟩ and the Security Exchange Commission's Edgar database ⟨www.sec.gov⟩ provide access to corporate annual reports and 10-K forms. This background will give you an appreciation for the situation as it was experienced by the participants in the case.

A company's annual report and 10-K form from the year of the case can be very helpful. According to the Yankelovich Partners survey firm, 8 out of 10 portfolio managers and 75% of security analysts use annual reports when making decisions.[2] They contain not only the usual *income statements* and *balance sheets*, but also *cash flow statements* and notes to the financial statements indicating why certain actions were taken. 10-K forms include detailed information not usually available in an annual report. An understanding of the economy during that period will help you avoid making a serious error in your analysis, for example, suggesting a sale of stock when the stock market is at an all-time low or taking on more debt when the prime interest rate is over 15%. Information on the industry will provide insights on its competitive activities. Some resources available for research into the economy and a corporation's industry are suggested in **Appendix 14.A**.

14.3 Financial Analysis: A Place to Begin

Once you have read a case, a good place to begin your analysis is with the financial statements. **Ratio analysis** is the calculation of ratios from data in these statements. It is done to identify possible financial strengths or weaknesses. Thus it is a valuable part of SWOT analysis. A review of key financial ratios can help you assess the company's overall situation and pinpoint some problem areas. Ratios are useful regardless of firm size and enable you to compare a company's ratios with industry averages. **Table 14–1** lists some of the most important financial ratios, which are (1) **liquidity ratios**, (2) **profitability ratios**, (3) **activity ratios**, and (4) **leverage ratios**.

ANALYZING FINANCIAL STATEMENTS

In your analysis, do not simply make an exhibit including all the ratios, but select and discuss only those ratios that have an impact on the company's problems. For instance, accounts receivable and inventory may provide a source of funds. If receivables and inventories are double the industry average, reducing them may provide needed cash. In this situation, the case report should include not only sources of funds, but also the number of dollars freed for use. Compare these ratios with industry averages to discover if the company is out of line with others in the industry. A typical financial analysis of a firm would include a study of the operating statements for five or so years, including a trend analysis of sales, profits, earnings per share, debt-to-equity ratio, return on investment, and so on, plus a ratio study comparing the firm under study with industry standards.

- **Scrutinize historical income statements and balance sheets**. These two basic statements provide most of the data needed for analysis. Statements of cash flow may also be useful.

- **Compare historical statements over time** if a series of statements is available.

- **Calculate changes that occur in individual categories from year to year**, as well as the cumulative total change.

- **Determine the change as a percentage** as well as an absolute amount.

- **Adjust for inflation** if that was a significant factor.

Examination of this information may reveal developing trends. Compare trends in one category with trends in related categories. For example, an increase in sales of 15% over three years may appear to be satisfactory until you note an increase of 20% in the cost of goods sold during the same period. The outcome of this comparison might suggest that further investigation into the manufacturing process is necessary. If a company is reporting strong net income growth but negative cash flow, this would suggest that the company is relying on something other than operations for earnings growth. Is it selling off assets or cutting R&D? If accounts receivable are growing faster than are sales revenues, the company is not getting paid for the products or services it is counting as sold. Is the company dumping product on its distributors at the end of the year to boost its reported annual sales? If so, expect the distributors to return the unordered product the next month—thus drastically cutting the next year's reported sales. The Securities and Exchange Commission brought 90 accounting fraud cases against U.S. companies during 1999, more than half involving falsifying revenue.[3]

Other "tricks of the trade" need to be examined. Until June, 2000, firms growing through acquisition were allowed to account for the cost of the purchased company through the pooling of both companies' stocks. This approach was used in 40% of the value of mergers between 1997 and 1999. The pooling method enabled the acquiring company to disregard the premium it paid for the other firm (the amount above the fair market value of the purchased company often called "good will"). Thus, when PepsiCo agreed to purchase Quaker Oats for $13.4 billion in PepsiCo stock, the $13.4 billion was not found on PepsiCo's balance sheet. As of June, 2000, merging firms must use the "purchase" accounting rules in which the true purchase price is reflected in the financial statements.[4]

Note that multinational corporations follow the accounting rules for their home country. As a result, their financial statements may be somewhat difficult to understand or to use for comparisons with competitors from other countries. For example, British firms such as British Petroleum and The Body Shop use the term "turnover" rather than sales revenue. In the case of AB Electrolux of Sweden, a footnote to the annual report indicates that the consolidated accounts have been prepared in accordance with Swedish accounting standards, which

Table 14–1 Financial Ratio Analysis

	Formula	How Expressed	Meaning
1. Liquidity Ratios			
Current ratio	$\dfrac{\text{Current assets}}{\text{Current liabilities}}$	Decimal	A short-term indicator of the company's ability to pay its short-term liabilities from short-term assets; how much of current assets are available to cover each dollar of current liabilities.
Quick (acid test) ratio	$\dfrac{\text{Current assets} - \text{Inventory}}{\text{Current liabilities}}$	Decimal	Measures the company's ability to pay off its short-term obligations from current assets, excluding inventories.
Inventory to net working capital	$\dfrac{\text{Inventory}}{\text{Current assets} - \text{Current liabilities}}$	Decimal	A measure of inventory balance; measures the extent to which the cushion of excess current assets over current liabilities may be threatened by unfavorable changes in inventory.
Cash ratio	$\dfrac{\text{Cash} + \text{Cash equivalents}}{\text{Current liabilities}}$	Decimal	Measures the extent to which the company's capital is in cash or cash equivalents; shows how much of the current obligations can be paid from cash or near-cash assets.
2. Profitability Ratios			
Net profit margin	$\dfrac{\text{Net profit after taxes}}{\text{Net sales}}$	Percentage	Shows how much after-tax profits are generated by each dollar of sales.
Gross profit margin	$\dfrac{\text{Sales} - \text{Cost of goods sold}}{\text{Net sales}}$	Percentage	Indicates the total margin available to cover other expenses beyond cost of goods sold, and still yield a profit.
Return on investment (ROI)	$\dfrac{\text{Net profit after taxes}}{\text{Total assets}}$	Percentage	Measures the rate of return on the total assets utilized in the company; a measure of management's efficiency, it shows the return on all the assets under its control regardless of source of financing.
Return on equity (ROE)	$\dfrac{\text{Net profit after taxes}}{\text{Shareholders' equity}}$	Percentage	Measures the rate of return on the book value of shareholders' total investment in the company.
Earnings per share (EPS)	$\dfrac{\text{Net profit after taxes} - \text{Preferred stock dividends}}{\text{Average number of common shares}}$	Dollars per share	Shows the after-tax earnings generated for each share of common stock.
3. Activity Ratios			
Inventory turnover	$\dfrac{\text{Net sales}}{\text{Inventory}}$	Decimal	Measures the number of times that average inventory of finished goods was turned over or sold during a period of time, usually a year.
Days of inventory	$\dfrac{\text{Inventory}}{\text{Cost of goods sold} \div 365}$	Days	Measures the number of one day's worth of inventory that a company has on hand at any given time.
Net working capital turnover	$\dfrac{\text{Net sales}}{\text{Net working capital}}$	Decimal	Measures how effectively the net working capital is used to generate sales.
Asset turnover	$\dfrac{\text{Sales}}{\text{Total assets}}$	Decimal	Measures the utilization of all the company's assets; measures how many sales are generated by each dollar of assets.

Table 14–1 (continued)

	Formula	How Expressed	Meaning
Fixed asset turnover	$\dfrac{\text{Sales}}{\text{Fixed assets}}$	Decimal	Measures the utilization of the company's fixed assets (i.e., plant and equipment); measures how many sales are generated by each dollar of fixed assets.
Average collection period	$\dfrac{\text{Accounts receivable}}{\text{Sales for year} \div 365}$	Days	Indicates the average length of time in days that a company must wait to collect a sale after making it; may be compared to the credit terms offered by the company to its customers.
Accounts receivable turnover	$\dfrac{\text{Annual credit sales}}{\text{Accounts receivable}}$	Decimal	Indicates the number of times that accounts receivable are cycled during the period (usually a year).
Accounts payable period	$\dfrac{\text{Accounts payable}}{\text{Purchases for year} \div 365}$	Days	Indicates the average length of time in days that the company takes to pay its credit purchases.
Days of cash	$\dfrac{\text{Cash}}{\text{Net sales for year} \div 365}$	Days	Indicates the number of days of cash on hand, at present sales levels.
4. Leverage Ratios			
Debt to asset ratio	$\dfrac{\text{Total debt}}{\text{Total assets}}$	Percentage	Measures the extent to which borrowed funds have been used to finance the company's assets.
Debt to equity ratio	$\dfrac{\text{Total debt}}{\text{Shareholders' equity}}$	Percentage	Measures the funds provided by creditors versus the funds provided by owners.
Long-term debt to capital structure	$\dfrac{\text{Long-term debt}}{\text{Shareholders' equity}}$	Percentage	Measures the long-term component of capital structure.
Times interest earned	$\dfrac{\text{Profit before taxes} + \text{Interest charges}}{\text{Interest charges}}$	Decimal	Indicates the ability of the company to meet its annual interest costs.
Coverage of fixed charges	$\dfrac{\text{Profit before taxes} + \text{Interest charges} + \text{Lease charges}}{\text{Interest charges} + \text{Lease obligations}}$	Decimal	A measure of the company's ability to meet all of its fixed-charge obligations.
Current liabilities to equity	$\dfrac{\text{Current liabilities}}{\text{Shareholders' equity}}$	Percentage	Measures the short-term financing portion versus that provided by owners.
5. Other Ratios			
Price/earnings ratio	$\dfrac{\text{Market price per share}}{\text{Earnings per share}}$	Decimal	Shows the current market's evaluation of a stock, based on its earnings; shows how much the investor is willing to pay for each dollar of earnings.
Divided payout ratio	$\dfrac{\text{Annual dividends per share}}{\text{Annual earnings per share}}$	Percentage	Indicates the percentage of profit that is paid out as dividends.
Dividend yield on common stock	$\dfrac{\text{Annual dividends per share}}{\text{Current market price per share}}$	Percentage	Indicates the dividend rate of return to common shareholders at the current market price.

Note: In using ratios for analysis, calculate ratios for the corporation and compare them to the average and quartile ratios for the particular industry. Refer to Standard and Poor's and Robert Morris Associates for average industry data. Special thanks to Dr. Moustafa H. Abdelsamad, Dean, Business School, Texas A&M University–Corpus Christi, Corpus Christi, Texas, for his definitions of these ratios.

differ in certain significant respects from United States generally accepted accounting principles (U.S. GAAP). For one year, net income of 4,830m SEK (Swedish kronor) approximated 5,655 SEK according to U.S. GAAP. Total assets for the same period were 84,183m SEK according to Swedish principle, but 86,658 according to U.S. GAAP.

For further information, see ⟨www.prenhall.com/wheelen⟩ to download "Understanding Financial Statements" by M. M. Rouse.

COMMON-SIZE STATEMENTS

Common-size statements are income statements and balance sheets in which the dollar figures have been converted into percentages. For the income statement, net sales represent 100%: calculate the percentage of each category so that the categories sum to the net sales percentage (100%). For the balance sheet, give the total assets a value of 100%, and calculate other asset and liability categories as percentages of the total assets. (Individual asset and liability items, such as accounts receivable and accounts payable, can also be calculated as a percentage of net sales.)

When you convert statements to this form, it is relatively easy to note the percentage that each category represents of the total. Look for trends in specific items, such as cost of goods sold, when compared to the company's historical figures. To get a proper picture, however, make comparisons with industry data, if available, to see if fluctuations are merely reflecting industrywide trends. If a firm's trends are generally in line with those of the rest of the industry, problems are less likely than if the firm's trends are worse than industry averages. (Raymond Morris Associates provides common-size statements for various industries.) Common-size statements are especially helpful in developing scenarios and pro forma statements because they provide a series of historical relationships (for example, cost of goods sold to sales, interest to sales, and inventories as a percentage of assets) from which you can estimate the future with your scenario assumptions for each year.

Z-VALUE, INDEX OF SUSTAINABLE GROWTH, AND FREE CASH FLOW

If the corporation being studied appears to be in poor financial condition, use **Altman's Bankruptcy Formula** to calculate its **Z-value**. The Z-value formula combines five ratios by weighting them according to their importance to a corporation's financial strength. The formula is:

$$Z = 1.2x_1 + 1.4x_2 + 3.3x_3 + 0.6x_4 + 1.0x_5$$

where:

x_1 = Working capital/Total assets (%)
x_2 = Retained earnings/Total assets (%)
x_3 = Earnings before interest & taxes/Total assets (%)
x_4 = Market value of equity/Total liabilities (%)
x_5 = Sales/Total assets (number of times)

Scores below 1.81 indicate significant credit problems, whereas a score above 3.0 indicates a healthy firm. Scores between 1.81 and 3.0 indicate question marks.[5]

The **index of sustainable growth** is useful to learn if a company embarking on a growth strategy will need to take on debt to fund this growth. The index indicates how much of the growth rate of sales can be sustained by internally generated funds. The formula is:

$$g^* = \frac{[P(1 - D)(1 + L)]}{[T - P(1 - D)(1 + L)]}$$

where:

P = (Net profit before tax/Net sales) $\times$ 100
D = Target dividends/Profit after tax
L = Total liabilities/Net worth
T = (Total assets/Net sales) $\times$ 100

If the planned growth rate calls for a growth rate higher than its g^*, external capital will be needed to fund the growth unless management is able to find efficiencies, decrease dividends, increase the debt/equity ratio, or reduce assets by renting or leasing arrangements.[6]

Takeover artists and LBO (leveraged buy-out) specialists look at a corporation's financial statements for **operating cash flow**: the amount of money generated by a company before the cost of financing and taxes. This is the company's net income plus depreciation plus depletion, amortization, interest expense, and income tax expense. LBO specialists will take on as much debt as the company's operating cash flow can support. A similar measure, **EBITDA** (**E**arnings **B**efore **I**nterest, **T**axes, **D**epreciation, and **A**mortization), is sometimes used, but is *not* determined in accordance with generally accepted accounting principles and is thus subject to varying calculations. Although operating cash flow is a broad measure of a company's funds, some takeover artists look at a much narrower **free cash flow**: the amount of money a new owner can take out of the firm without harming the business. This is net income plus depreciation, depletion, and amortization less capital expenditures and dividends. The free cash flow ratio is very useful in evaluating the stability of an entrepreneurial venture.[7] The danger in using these instruments is that they appear to be the same as cash flow—which they are not. According to Martin Fridson, chief of high-yield research with Merrill Lynch, "A capital intensive company isn't earning a profit if its assets are wearing down from wear and tear."[8]

USEFUL ECONOMIC MEASURES

If you are analyzing a company over many years, you may want to adjust sales and net income for inflation to arrive at "true" financial performance in constant dollars. **Constant dollars** are dollars adjusted for inflation to make them comparable over various years. See the 🌐 **Global Issue** feature to learn why inflation can be an important issue for multinational corporations. One way to adjust for inflation in the United States is to use the Consumer Price Index (CPI), as given in **Table 14–2**. Dividing sales and net income by the CPI factor for that year will change the figures to 1982–1984 constant dollars (when the CPI was 1.0).

Another helpful analytical aid provided in **Table 14–2** is the **prime interest rate**, the rate of interest banks charge on their lowest risk loans. For better assessments of strategic decisions, it can be useful to note the level of the prime interest rate at the time of the case. A decision to borrow money to build a new plant would have been a good one in 1993 at 6%, but less practical in 2000 when the rate reached 9.5%.

In preparing a scenario for your pro forma financial statements, you may want to use the **gross domestic product (GDP)** from **Table 14–2**. GDP is used worldwide and measures the total output of goods and services within a country's borders. The amount of change from one year to the next indicates how much that country's economy is growing. Remember that scenarios have to be adjusted for a country's specific conditions.

Global Issue

Why Consider Inflation in Case Analysis?

Inflation is a recent problem in the United States. Between 1800 and 1940, there was no clear trend up or down in the overall cost of living. A moviegoer in the late 1930s watching a drama set in the early 1800s would not notice prices to be unusual. For example, the cost of a loaf of bread in the late 1930s was roughly the same as in 1800. With the minor exceptions of 1949 and 1955, prices have risen every year since 1945. The Consumer Price Index (a generally used measure of the overall cost of living in the United States) increased nine times from 1945 to 1996. (Watch the movie *It's a Wonderful Life* to see how much prices have changed since 1948.) From 1970 to 1980, the CPI more than doubled. After an average rate of 7.1% during the 1970s, inflation slowed to 5.5% in the 1980s, and 3.4% during the 1990s. Inflation seemed to be under control in the United States. Although people complained about the rising price of retail gasoline, the average price in constant dollars in 2000 was the same as in 1970—before the OPEC oil embargo. Nevertheless, economist Milton Friedman warns of an increase in inflation. "We're in a period like the 1960s, when no one paid any attention to the money supply. Then we got inflation," says Friedman.

The rate of inflation in other countries varies and has a significant impact on a multinational corporation's profits. Although most countries in the developed parts of the world kept inflation under control during the five-year period from 1994 to 1999, the developing nations did not fare as well. For example, the average annual inflation rate in Turkey during 1994–1999 was 81%. Supermarkets were forced to list prices on electronic displays rather than on printed labels. Turkey's rate of inflation was high, but was a far cry from Bolivia's astounding annual rate during 1985 of 25,000%! During 1994–1999, the countries of the European Union had an inflation rate of around 2–3%, while Eastern European countries were dealing with higher rates, such as 64% in Russia and 19% in Hungary. During 1997 alone, Romania's annual inflation rate was 170%, while Bulgaria's was 1,268%. During the 1994–1999 time period in Latin America, Mexico's annual rate was 24%, Columbia's was 18%, and Brazil's was 17%. Although most Asian countries had a low rate of inflation (Singapore, Taiwan, and Malaysia increased less than 5%), Indonesia's increased 20% and India's increased 8%.

Before inflation is declared dead by politicians anxious to reduce cost-of-living increases to Social Security payments (to reduce government expenditures and thus government debt), note what happens with a relatively constant 3.4% rate of inflation. Through the working of compound interest, the price level rose about 40% during the 1990s. This means that companies have to be constantly monitoring not only their costs, but also the prices of the products they offer. Unless a company's dollar sales are increasing over 3.5% annually, its sales are actually falling (in constant dollars)! The same is true for net income. This point is often overlooked by the chief executive officers of troubled companies who are anxious to keep their jobs by fooling both the board and the shareholders.

Sources: P. W. Boltz, "Is Inflation Dead?" *T. Rowe Price Report* (Winter 1997), pp. 10–11; P. Brimelow with M. Friedman, "Beware the Funny Money," *Forbes* (May 3, 1999), pp. 138–141; "Managing Inflation: Talking Turkey," *The Economist* (October 11, 1997), p. 95; "Emerging Market Indicators," *The Economist* (December 9, 2000), p. 116; J. T. Allen and D. McGraw, "The Gas Crisis that Isn't—Yet," *U.S. News & World Report* (April 3, 1990), p. 22.

14.4 Format for Case Analysis: The Strategic Audit

There is no one best way to analyze or present a case report. Each instructor has personal preferences for format and approach. Nevertheless, we suggest an approach for both written and oral reports in **Appendix 14.B**, which provides a systematic method for successfully attacking a case. This approach is based on the **strategic audit**, which was presented at the end of **Chapter 10** in **Appendix 10.A**. We find that this approach provides structure and is very helpful for the typical student who may be a relative novice in case analysis. Regardless of the

Table 14–2 U.S. Economic Indicators: Gross Domestic Product (GDP) in Billions of Dollars; Consumer Price Index for All Items (CPI) (1982–1984 = 1.0); Prime Interest Rate (PIR)

Year	GDP	CPI	PIR
1983	3,514.5	.996	10.79
1984	3,902.4	1.039	12.04
1985	4,180.7	1.076	9.93
1986	4,422.2	1.096	8.33
1987	4,693.3	1.136	8.21
1988	5,049.6	1.183	9.32
1989	5,483.7	1.240	10.87
1990	5,743.8	1.307	10.01
1991	5,916.7	1.362	8.46
1992	6,244.4	1.403	6.25
1993	6,553.0	1.445	6.00
1994	6,935.7	1.482	7.15
1995	7,253.8	1.524	8.83
1996	7,661.6	1.569	8.27
1997	8,318.4	1.605	8.44
1998	8,790.2	1.630	8.35
1999	9,299.2	1.666	8.00
2000	9,965.7	1.720	9.23

Sources: Gross Domestic Product from *Survey of Current Business* (February 2001), Vol. 81, No. 2, Table 1.1, p. D-3. Consumer Price Index from U.S. Department of Commerce, *1997 Statistical Abstract of the United States,* 117th edition, Chart no. 752, p. 487; U.S. Bureau of Labor Statistics, *Monthly Labor Review* (October 1998), Chart no. 28, p. 74; *Survey of Current Business* (September 2000), Vol. 80, No. 9, Table D.1, p. D-41. Prime Interest Rates from D.S. Benton, "Banking and Financial Information," Table 1–2, p. 3 in *Thorndike Encyclopedia of Banking and Financial Tables,* 3rd. ed., 1998 Yearbook (Boston: Warren, Gorham and Lamont, 1998); *Survey of Current Business* (February 2001), Vol. 81, No. 2, Table D.1, p. D-41. Web sites of the Bureau of Economic Analysis, Economics & Statistics Administration, U.S. Department of Commerce ⟨www.stat-usa.gov⟩ and ⟨www.bea.doc.gov⟩.

format chosen, be careful to include a complete analysis of key environmental variables— especially of trends in the industry and of the competition. Look at international developments as well.

If you choose to use the strategic audit as a guide to the analysis of complex strategy cases, you may want to use the strategic audit worksheet in **Figure 14–1. You can download the Strategic Audit Worksheet from this book's Web site at ⟨www.prenhall. com/wheelen⟩.** Print a copy of the worksheet to use to take notes as you analyze a case. See **Appendix 14.C** for an example of a completed student-written analysis of a 1993 Maytag Corporation case (not the later 1996 version in the case portion of this book) done in an outline form using the strategic audit format. This is one example of what a case analysis in outline form may look like.

Case discussion focuses on critical analysis and logical development of thought. A solution is satisfactory if it resolves important problems and is likely to be implemented successfully. How the corporation actually dealt with the case problems has no real bearing on the analysis because management might have analyzed its problems incorrectly or implemented a series of flawed solutions.

Figure 14–1
Strategic Audit
Worksheet

Strategic Audit Heading	Analysis		Comments
	(+) Factors	(−) Factors	
I. Current Situation			
A. Past Corporate Performance Indexes			

B. Strategic Posture:
      Current Mission
      Current Objectives
      Current Strategies
      Current Policies			

SWOT Analysis Begins:			
II. Corporate Governance			
A. Board of Directors			
B. Top Management			
III. External Environment (EFAS): Opportunities and Threats (SW<u>OT</u>)			
A. Societal Environment			
B. Task Environment (Industry Analysis)			
IV. Internal Environment (IFAS): Strengths and Weaknesses (<u>SW</u>OT)			
A. Corporate Structure			
B. Corporate Culture			
C. Corporate Resources			
1. Marketing			
2. Finance			
3. Research and Development			
4. Operations and Logistics			
5. Human Resources			
6. Information Systems			
V. Analysis of Strategic Factors (SFAS)			
A. Key Internal and External Strategic Factors (SWOT)			
B. Review of Mission and Objectives			

Figure 14–1
Strategic Audit
Worksheet
(*continued*)

SWOT Analysis Ends. Recommendation Begins:			
VI. **Alternatives and Recommendations**			
A. Strategic Alternatives—pros and cons			
B. Recommended Strategy			
VII. **Implementation**			
VIII. **Evaluation and Control**			

Note: See the complete Strategic Audit on page 265–272. It lists the pages in the book that discuss each of the eight headings.

Source: T. L. Wheelen and J. D. Hunger, "Strategic Audit Worksheet." Copyright © 1989 by Wheelen and Hunger Associates. Revised 1991, 1994, and 1997. Reprinted by permission. Additional copies available for classroom use in Part D of *Case Instructors Manual* and on the Prentice Hall Web site ⟨www.prenhall.com/wheelen⟩.

14.5 Impact of the Internet on Case Analysis

The Internet is an excellent source of information about industries as well as individual companies. It can be especially useful if your instructor gives you the assignment to either update a case or to research an industry. To begin, you only need access to the Internet and a browser like Netscape Navigator or Microsoft's Internet Explorer. When "surfing" the net, you will be amazed by the amount of information (much of it worthless) you can find. A word of caution: Beware of getting caught by an online confidence game. (See the Internet Issue feature for the top 10 Internet scams.)

Finding a Company's Web Site

If you are looking for information about a particular company, you can first try using a simplified version of the firm's name to directly get to the firm's home (primary) Web page. For example, first type in the protocol—the standard first part of the **url** (uniform resource locator)—http://www. Don't capitalize any letters in the url. Then type in a likely name for the firm, such as maytag, ibm, toyota, hp (Hewlett-Packard), ti (Texas Instruments), or prenhall (Prentice Hall). This is referred to as the company's server name. Follow this name with the suffix .com. This is called a **domain**. In the United States, most business urls still end with the domain name .com. The same is true for other urls, such as edu for schools and colleges, gov for government agencies, org for not-for-profit organizations, and mil for the military. Outside of the United States each country has its own suffix, such as .uk for Great Britain, .au for Australia, .ca for Canada, .de for Germany, and .pe for Peru. This string of words and letters usually completes the url. For example, try typing ⟨http://www.maytag.com⟩ in the location line of your Internet browser and tap the Enter key. This takes you directly to Maytag's home Web page. In some instances, the url may also contain a more specific Web page beyond the company's home page. In this case, the .com is followed by /xxxx.html (xxxx can be anything). This indicates that this is another Web page that uses the html (hypertext markup language) of the World Wide Web.

Internet Issue

Top 10 Internet Scams

T he U.S. Federal Trade Commission reports the following list of most popular Internet-related complaints regarding confidence games being played on unsuspecting visitors to the information highway.

- **Auctions** (45%): Buyer pays but gets wrong item or none at all.
- **Internet Access** (21%): Supposedly "free" Internet access has hidden charges and high cancellation fees.
- **Credit Card Fraud** (9%): Adult-only sites ask for credit card data to verify age—resulting in unauthorized charges.
- **Personal Web Site** (5%): Offers free Web site for 30 days but charges via the phone bill.
- **Modem Scam** (5%): Download a "free" dialer to access adult sites but high charges soon follow.

- **Home Business** (3%): Pay a fee but earn nothing.
- **Travel Bargains** (2%): Inexpensive trip is either not what was promised or is nonexistent.
- **Sell Special Products** (2%): Sells product at low price, but there are no buyers.
- **Invest Now** (1%): Promises stock appreciation, but little actually happens after stock purchase.
- **Health Products** (1%): Miracle medicines sold as Internet "snake oil" to solve all problems.

The modem scam is especially ingenious. A pornographic Web site offers to download a special "viewer" or "dialer" program to see nude photos. When the file is downloaded, the Internet connection is disconnected and the program makes the computer dial a phone number to a small island in the southwest Pacific called Vanuatu (formerly New Hebrides) at a rate of $2 to $7 per minute. Few people report this scam because they don't want others to know they were visiting pornographic Web sites!

Sources: "Top Ten Scams on the Information Highway," *U.S. News & World Report* (November 13, 2000), p. 16; S. S. Woo, "Scam Prompts Surf Warning," *Des Moines Register* (February 17, 2001), pp. D1, D6.

Using a Search Engine

If typing in an obvious company name doesn't work, use a search engine. This is especially the case if you are investigating a non-U.S. corporation like AB Electrolux of Sweden. **Search engines** are services that act like a library's card file to help you find information on a topic. Type in http://www. followed by the search engine's url. Some of the common search engines are Yahoo! ⟨yahoo.com⟩, Alta Vista ⟨altavista.com⟩, Lycos ⟨lycos.com⟩, Google ⟨google. com⟩, Northern Light ⟨northernlight.com⟩, and Excite ⟨excite.com⟩. This url will take you to the search engine's Web page where you can type in the name of a company. The search engine finds any references to that firm. One of these references should include the company's url. Use it to get to the company's home Web page.

Finding More Information

Getting to the company's home Web page does not necessarily mean that you now have access to the firm's financials. If the Web site does include a link to a Web page containing the company's financials, that page will probably have only financials for the most recent year or two. In that case, try related business directories such as Hoover's On-Line ⟨hoovers.com⟩ or the U.S. Securities and Exchange Commission Edgar database ⟨sec.gov⟩. If the company's stock is publicly traded and listed on one of the major stock exchanges, these business directories should get you to the database containing the latest annual reports and 10-K reports, as well as quarterly reports. Other sites offering valuable information relating to business firms are:

- Annual Report Gallery ⟨www.reportgallery.com⟩
- Web 100 ⟨www.w100.com⟩
- CEO Express ⟨www.ceoexpress.com⟩
- Wall Street Research Net ⟨www.wsrn.com⟩
- Companies Online ⟨www.companiesonline.com⟩
- Corporate Financials Online ⟨www.cfonews.com⟩
- Corporate Information ⟨www.corporateinformation.com⟩
- Kompass International ⟨www.kompass.com⟩
- CorpTech Database of Technology Companies ⟨www.corptech.com⟩
- ZDNet Company Finder ⟨www.companyfinder.com⟩

Additional Web sites are listed in **Appendix 14.A** and at the Web site ⟨www.prenhall.com/wheelen⟩. Note that Web sites constantly change. Just because a particular url works one time does not mean that it will work a year or two later. If the company is doing a good job of managing its Web sites, it will leave a message on its abandoned Web page sending you to a new page. If nothing works, simply go to one of the search engines and begin again. Good luck!

Projections for the 21st Century

- From 1994 to 2010, expect consumer inflation to decline from 4.3% to 2.5%.
- From 1994 to 2010, expect the international value of the U.S. dollar to increase from 1.0 to 9.33.[9]

Discussion Questions

1. Why should you begin a case analysis with a financial analysis? When are other approaches appropriate?

2. What are common-size financial statements? What is their value to case analysis? How are they calculated?

3. When should you gather information outside the case by going to the library or using the Internet? What should you be looking for?

4. When is inflation an important issue in conducting case analysis? Why bother?

5. How can you learn the date a case took place?

Strategic Practice Exercise

Convert the following two years of income statements from the Maytag Corporation into common-size statements. The dollar figures are in thousands. What does converting to a common size reveal?

	1992	%	1991	%
Net sales	$3,041,223		$2,970,626	
Cost of sales	2,339,406		2,254,221	
Gross profits	701,817		716,405	
Selling, general, and admin. expenses	528,250		524,898	
Reorganization expenses	95,000		—	
Operating income	78,567		191,507	
Interest expense	(75,004)		(75,159)	
Other—net	3,983		7,069	
Income before taxes and accounting changes	7,546		123,417	
Income taxes	(15,900)		(44,400)	
Income before accounting changes	(8,354)		79,017	
Effects of accounting changes for post-retirement benefits	(307,000)		—	
Net income (loss)	$(315,354)		$79,017	

Key Terms

activity ratios (pp. 342, 344–345)
Altman's Bankruptcy Formula (p. 346)
common-size statements (p. 346)
constant dollars (p. 347)
domain (p. 351)
EBITDA (p. 347)
free cash flow (p. 347)

gross domestic product (GDP) (p. 347)
index of sustainable growth (p. 346)
leverage ratios (pp. 342, 345)
liquidity ratios (pp. 342, 344)
operating cash flow (p. 347)
prime interest rate (p. 347)

profitability ratios (pp. 342, 344)
ratio analysis (p. 342)
search engines (p. 352)
strategic audit worksheet (pp. 349–351)
url (p. 351)
Z-value (p. 346)

Resources for Case Research

Company Information

1. Annual reports
2. *Moody's Manuals on Investment* (a listing of companies within certain industries that contains a brief history and a five-year financial statement of each company)
3. Securities and Exchange Commission Annual Report Form 10-K (annually) and 10-Q (quarterly)
4. Standard and Poor's *Register of Corporations, Directors, and Executives*
5. Value Line's *Investment Survey*
6. *COMPUSTAT, Compact Disclosure, CD/International*, and *Hoover's Online Corporate Directory* (computerized operating and financial information on thousands of publicly held corporations)
7. Shareholders meeting notices

Economic Information

1. Regional statistics and local forecasts from large banks
2. *Business Cycle Development* (Department of Commerce)
3. Chase Econometric Associates' publications
4. U.S. Census Bureau publications on population, transportation, and housing
5. *Current Business Reports* (U.S. Department of Commerce)
6. *Economic Indicators* (U.S. Joint Economic Committee)
7. *Economic Report of the President to Congress*
8. *Long-Term Economic Growth* (U.S. Department of Commerce)
9. *Monthly Labor Review* (U.S. Department of Labor)
10. *Monthly Bulletin of Statistics* (United Nations)
11. *Statistical Abstract of the United States* (U.S. Department of Commerce)
12. *Statistical Yearbook* (United Nations)
13. *Survey of Current Business* (U.S. Department of Commerce)
14. *U.S. Industrial Outlook* (U.S. Department of Defense)
15. *World Trade Annual* (United Nations)
16. *Overseas Business Reports* (by country, published by U.S. Department of Commerce)
17. *The World Factbook* (U.S. CIA)

Industry Information

1. Analyses of companies and industries by investment brokerage firms
2. *Business Week* (provides weekly economic and business information, and quarterly profit and sales rankings of corporations)
3. *Fortune* (each April publishes listings of financial information on corporations within certain industries)

4. *Industry Survey* (published quarterly by Standard and Poor's Corporation)
5. *Industry Week* (late March/early April issue provides information on 14 industry groups)
6. *Forbes* (mid-January issue provides performance data on firms in various industries)
7. *Inc.* (May and December issues give information on fast-growing entrepreneurial companies)
8. *The Information Catalogue* (a listing by MarketResearch.com of over 11,000 studies conducted by leading research firms)

Directory and Index Information on Companies and Industries

1. *Business Periodical Index* (on computer in many libraries)
2. *Directory of National Trade Associations*
3. *Encyclopedia of Associations*
4. Funk and Scott's *Index of Corporations and Industries*
5. Thomas's *Register of American Manufacturers*
6. *Wall Street Journal Index*

Ratio Analysis Information

1. *Almanac of Business and Industrial Financial Ratios* (Prentice Hall)
2. *Annual Statement Studies* (Robert Morris Associates)
3. *Dun's Review* (Dun and Bradstreet; published annually in September–December issues)
4. *Industry Norms and Key Business Ratios* (Dun and Bradstreet)

Online Information

1. *Hoovers Online*—Financial statements and profiles of public companies ⟨www.hoovers.com⟩
2. *U.S. Securities & Exchange Commission*—Official filings of public companies in Edgar database ⟨www.sec.gov⟩
3. *Fortune 500*—Statistics for largest U.S. corporations ⟨www.pathfinder.com⟩
4. *Dun & Bradstreet's Online*—Short reports on 10 million public and private U.S. companies ⟨www.dbisna.com/dnb/dnbhome.htm⟩
5. *Ecola's 24-Hour Newsstand*—Links to Web sites of 2,000 newspapers, journals, and magazines ⟨www.ecola.com/news⟩
6. *Competitive Intelligence Guide*—Information on company resources ⟨www.fuld.com⟩
7. *The Economist*—Provides international information and surveys ⟨www.economist.com⟩
8. *Web 100*—Information on 100 largest U.S. and international companies ⟨www.w100.com⟩
9. *Bloomberg*—Information on interest rates, stock prices, currency conversion rates, and other general financial information ⟨www.bloomberg.com⟩
10. *The World Factbook*—Profiles of many countries ⟨www.odci.gov/cia/publications/factbook/index.html⟩

appendix 14.B

Suggested Case Analysis Methodology Using the Strategic Audit

1. READ CASE

First Reading of the Case

- Develop a general overview of the company and its external environment.
- Begin a list of the possible strategic factors facing the company at this time.
- List the research information you may need on the economy, industry, and competitors.

2. READ THE CASE WITH THE STRATEGIC AUDIT

Second Reading of the Case

- Read the case a second time using the strategic audit as a framework for in-depth analysis. (See **Appendix 10.A** on pages 265–272.) You may want to make a copy of the strategic audit worksheet (**Figure 14–1**) to use to keep track of your comments as you read the case.
- The questions in the strategic audit parallel the strategic decision making process shown in **Figure 1–5** (pages 20–21).
- The audit provides you with a conceptual framework to examine the company's mission, objectives, strategies, and policies as well as problems, symptoms, facts, opinions, and issues.
- Perform a financial analysis of the company using ratio analysis (see **Table 14–1**) and do the calculations necessary to convert key parts of the financial statements to a common-size basis.

3. DO OUTSIDE RESEARCH

Library and Online Computer Services

- Each case has a decision date indicating when the case actually took place. Your research should be based on the time period for the case.
- See **Appendix 14.A** for resources for case research. Your research should include information about the environment at the time of the case. Find average industry ratios. You may also want to obtain further information regarding competitors and the company itself (10-K forms and annual reports). This information should help you conduct an industry analysis. Check with your instructor to see what kind of outside research is appropriate for your assignment.
- Don't try to learn what actually happened to the company discussed in the case. What management actually decided may not be the best solution. It will certainly bias your analysis and will probably cause your recommendation to lack proper justification.

4. BEGIN SWOT ANALYSIS

External Environmental Analysis: EFAS

- Analyze the four societal forces to see what trends are likely to affect the industry(s) in which the company is operating.

- Conduct an industry analysis using Porter's competitive forces from **Chapter 3**. Develop an Industry Matrix (**Table 3–3** on page 69).

- Generate 8 to 10 external factors. These should be the *most important* opportunities and threats facing the company at the time of the case.

- Develop an EFAS Table, as shown in **Table 3–4**, for your list of external strategic factors.

- **Suggestion:** Rank the 8 to 10 factors from most to least important. Start by grouping the 3 top factors and then the 3 bottom factors.

Internal Organizational Analysis: IFAS

- Generate 8 to 10 internal factors. These should be the *most important* strengths and weaknesses of the company at the time of the case.

- Develop an IFAS Table, as shown in **Table 4–2** (page 102), for your list of internal strategic factors.

- **Suggestion:** Rank the 8 to 10 factors from most to least important. Start by grouping the 3 top factors and then the 3 bottom factors.

5. WRITE YOUR STRATEGIC AUDIT: PARTS I TO IV

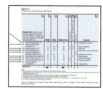

First Draft of Your Strategic Audit

- Review the student-written audit of an old Maytag case in **Appendix 14.C** for an example.

- Write Parts I to IV of the strategic audit. Remember to include the factors from your IFAS and IFAS Tables in your audit.

6. WRITE YOUR STRATEGIC AUDIT: PART V

Strategic Factor Analysis Summary: SFAS

- Condense the list of factors from the 16 to 20 identified in your EFAS and EFAS Tables to only the 8 to 10 most important factors.

- Select the most important EFAS and IFAS factors. Reconsider the weights of each. The weights still need to add to 1.0.

- Develop an SFAS Table, as shown in **Figure 5–1** (page 111), for your final list of strategic factors. Although the weights (indicating the importance of each factor) will probably change from the EFAS and IFAS Tables, the numerical rating (1 to 5) of each factor should remain the same. These ratings are your assessment of management's performance on each factor.

- This is a good time to reexamine what you wrote earlier in Parts I to IV. You may want to add to or delete some of what you wrote. Ensure that each one of the strategic factors you have included in your SFAS Table is discussed in the appropriate place in Parts I to IV. Part V of the audit is *not* the place to mention a strategic factor for the first time.

- Write Part V of your strategic audit. This completes your SWOT analysis.

- This is the place to suggest a revised mission statement and a better set of objectives for the company. The SWOT analysis coupled with revised mission and objectives for the company set the stage for the generation of strategic alternatives.

7. WRITE YOUR STRATEGIC AUDIT: PART VI

Strategic Alternatives and Recommendation

A. Alternatives

- Develop around three mutually exclusive strategic alternatives. If appropriate to the case you are analyzing, you might propose one alternative for growth, one for stability, and one for retrenchment. Within each corporate strategy, you should probably propose an appropriate business/competitive strategy. You may also want to include some functional strategies where appropriate.

- Construct a scenario for each alternative. Use the data from your outside research to project general societal trends (GDP, inflation, etc.) and industry trends. Use these as the basis of your assumptions to write pro forma financial statements (particularly income statements) for each strategic alternative for the next five years.

- List pros and cons for each alternative based on your scenarios.

B. Recommendation

- Specify which one of your alternative strategies you recommend. Justify your choice in terms of dealing with the strategic factors you listed in Part V of the audit.

- Develop policies to help implement your strategies.

8. WRITE YOUR STRATEGIC AUDIT: PART VII

Implementation

- Develop programs to implement your recommended strategy.

- Specify who is to be responsible for implementing each program and how long each program will take to complete.

- Refer to the pro forma financial statement you developed earlier for your recommended strategy. Do the numbers still make sense? If not, this may be a good time to rethink the budget numbers to reflect your recommended programs.

9. WRITE YOUR STRATEGIC AUDIT: PART VIII

Evaluation and Control

- Specify the type of evaluation and controls that you need to ensure that your recommendation is carried out successfully. Specify who is responsible for monitoring these controls.

- Indicate if sufficient information is available to monitor how the strategy is being implemented. If not, suggest a change to the information system.

10. PROOF AND FINE-TUNE YOUR AUDIT

Final Draft of Your Strategic Audit

- Check to ensure that your audit is within the page limits of your professor. You may need to cut some parts and expand others.

- Make sure that your recommendation clearly deals with the strategic factors.

- Attach your EFAS, IFAS, and SFAS Tables plus your ratio analysis and pro forma statements. Label them as numbered exhibits and refer to each of them within the body of the audit.

- Proof your work for errors. If on a computer, use a spell checker.

Special Note: Depending on your assignment, it is relatively easy to use the strategic audit you have just developed to write a written case analysis in essay form or to make an oral presentation. The strategic audit is just a detailed case analysis in an outline form and can be used as the basic framework for any sort of case analysis and presentation.

Example of Student-Written Strategic Audit

(For the 1993 Maytag Corporation Case—Not in This Book)

I. CURRENT SITUATION

A. Current Performance

Poor financials, high debt load, first losses since 1920s, price/earnings ratio negative.

B. Strategic Posture

1. **Mission**
   - Developed in 1989 for the Maytag Company: "To provide our customers with products of unsurpassed performance that last longer, need fewer repairs, and are produced at the lowest possible cost."
   - Updated in 1991: "Our collective mission is world class quality." Expands Maytag's belief in product quality to all aspects of operations.

2. **Objectives**
   - "To be profitability leader in industry for every product line Maytag manufactures." Selected profitability rather than market share.
   - "To be number one in total customer satisfaction."
   - "To grow the North American appliance business and become the third largest appliance manufacturer (in unit sales) in North America."
   - To increase profitable market share growth in North American appliance and floor care business, 6.5% return on sales, 10% return on assets, 20% return on equity, beat competition in satisfying customers, dealer, builder and endorser, move into third place in total units shipped per year.

3. **Strategies**
   - Global growth through acquisition and alliance with Bosch Siemens.
   - Differentiate brand names for competitive advantage.
   - Create synergy between companies, product improvement, investment in plant and equipment.

4. **Policies**
   - Cost reduction is secondary to high quality.
   - Promotion from within.
   - Slow, but sure R&D: Maytag slow to respond to changes in market.

II. STRATEGIC MANAGERS

A. Board of Directors

1. Fourteen members—eleven are outsiders.
2. Well-respected Americans, most on board since 1986 or earlier.
3. No international or marketing backgrounds.
4. Time for a change?

B. Top Management

1. Top management promoted from within Maytag Company.
2. Very experienced in the industry.
3. Responsible for current situation.
4. May be too parochial for global industry—may need new blood.

III. EXTERNAL ENVIRONMENT (EFAS see Exhibit 1)

A. Societal Environment

1. **Economic**
   a. Unstable economy but recession ending, consumer confidence growing—could increase spending for big ticket items like houses, cars, and appliances.
   b. Individual economies becoming interconnected into a world economy.
2. **Technological**
   a. Fuzzy logic technology being applied to sense and measure activities.
   b. Computers and information technology increasingly important.
3. **Political-Legal**
   a. NAFTA, European Union, other regional trade pacts opening doors to markets in Europe, Asia, Latin America that offer enormous potential.
   b. Breakdown of communism means less chance of world war.
   c. Environmentalism being reflected in laws on pollution and energy usage.
4. **Sociocultural**
   a. Developing nations desire goods seen on TV.
   b. Middle-aged baby boomers want attractive, high quality products, like BMWs and Maytag.
   c. Dual career couples increases need for labor-saving appliances, second cars, and day care.
   d. Divorce and career mobility means need for more houses and goods to fill them.

B. Task Environment

1. North American market is mature and extremely competitive—vigilant consumers demand high quality with low price in safe, environmentally sound products.
2. Industry going global as North American and European firms expand internationally.
3. *Rivalry High*: Whirlpool, AB Electrolux, GE have enormous resources and developing global presence.
4. *Buyers' Power Low*: Technology and materials used in manufacture can be sourced worldwide.
5. European design popular and consumer desire for technologically advanced appliances.
6. *Power of Other Stakeholders Medium*: Quality, safety, environmental regulations increasing.

7. *Distributors' Power High*: Super retailers more important, mom and pop dealers less.

8. *Substitutes unlikely.*

9. *Entry Barriers High*: New entrants unlikely; only large appliance firms can enter other markets.

IV. INTERNAL ENVIRONMENT (IFAS see Exhibit 2)

A. Corporate Structure

1. Divisional structure: appliance manufacturing and vending machines. Floor care managed separately.

2. Centralized major decisions by Newton corporate staff with a timeline of about three years.

B. Corporate Culture

1. Quality key ingredient—commitment to quality shared by executives and workers.

2. Much of corporate culture is based on founder F. L. Maytag's personal philosophy, including concern for quality, employees, local community, innovation, and performance.

3. Acquired companies, except for European, seem to accept dominance of Maytag culture.

C. Corporate Resources

1. **Marketing**

   a. Maytag brand lonely repairman advertising successful.

   b. Efforts focus on distribution—combining three sales forces into two, concentrating on major retailers. (Cost $95 million for this reconstructing.)

   c. Hoover's well-publicized marketing fiasco involving airline tickets.

2. **Finance** (see **Exhibits 4 and 5**)

   a. Revenues are up slightly, operating income is down significantly.

   b. Some key ratios are troubling, such as a 57% debt/asset ratio, 132% long-term debt/equity ratio. No room for more debt to grow company.

   c. Net income is 400% less than 1988, based on common-size income statements.

3. **R&D**

   a. Process-oriented with focus on manufacturing process and durability.

   b. Maytag is becoming a technology follower, taking too long to get product innovations to market (competitors put out more in last six months than prior two years combined), lagging in fuzzy logic and other technological areas.

4. **Operations**

   a. Maytag's core competence—continual improvement process kept it dominant in the U.S. market for many years.

   b. Plants are aging and may be losing competitiveness as rivals upgrade facilities.

5. **Human Resources**

   a. Traditionally very good relations with unions and employees.

   b. Labor relations increasingly strained, with two salary raise delays, and layoffs of 4,500 employees at Magic Chef.

   c. Unions express concern at new, more distant tone from Maytag Corporation.

6. **Information Systems**

   a. Not mentioned in case; Hoover fiasco in Europe suggests information systems need significant upgrading.

   b. Critical area where Maytag may be unwilling or unable to commit resources needed to stay competitive.

V. ANALYSIS OF STRATEGIC FACTORS

A. Situational Analysis (SWOT) (SFAS see **Exhibit 3**)

1. **Strengths**
   a. Quality Maytag culture.
   b. Maytag well-known and respected brand.
   c. Hoover's international orientation.
   d. Core competencies in process R&D and manufacturing.

2. **Weaknesses**
   a. Lacks financial resources of competitors.
   b. Poor global positioning; Hoover weak on continent.
   c. Product R&D and customer service innovation areas of serious weakness.
   d. Dependent on small dealers.

3. **Opportunities**
   a. Economic integration of European Community.
   b. Demographics favor quality.
   c. Trend to superstores.

4. **Threats**
   a. Trend to superstores.
   b. Aggressive rivals—Whirlpool and Electrolux.
   c. Japanese appliance companies—new entrants?

B. Review of Current Mission and Objectives

1. Current mission appears appropriate.
2. Some of the objectives are really goals and need to be quantified and given time horizons.

VI. STRATEGIC ALTERNATIVES AND RECOMMENDED STRATEGY

A. Strategic Alternatives

1. *Growth Through Concentric Diversification:* Acquire a company in a related industry like commercial appliances.
   a. *Pros:* Product/market synergy created by acquisition of related company.
   b. *Cons:* Maytag does not have the financial resources to play this game.

2. *Pause Strategy:* Consolidate various acquisitions to find economies and to encourage innovation among the business units.
   a. *Pros:* Maytag needs to get its financial house in order and get administrative control over its recent acquisitions.
   b. *Cons:* Unless it can grow through a stronger alliance with Bosch Siemens or some other backer, Maytag is a prime candidate for takeover because of its poor financial performance in recent years, and it is suffering from the initial reduction in efficiency inherent in acquisition strategy.

3. *Retrenchment:* Sell Hoover's foreign major home appliance businesses (Australia and the United Kingdom) to emphasize increasing market share in North America.
   a. *Pros:* Divesting Hoover improves bottom line and enables Maytag Corp. to focus on North America while Whirlpool, Electrolux, and GE are battling elsewhere.
   b. *Cons:* Maytag may be giving up its only opportunity to become a player in the coming global appliance industry.

B. Recommended Strategy

1. Recommend pause strategy, at least for a year, so Maytag can get a grip on its European operation and consolidate its companies in a more synergistic way.

2. Maytag quality must be maintained and continued shortage of operating capital will take its toll, so investment must be made in R&D.

3. Maytag may be able to make the Hoover U.K. investment work better since the recession is ending and the EU countries are closer to integrating than ever before.

4. Because it is only an average competitor, Maytag needs the Hoover link to Europe to provide a jumping off place for negotiations with Bosch-Siemens that could strengthen their alliance.

VII. IMPLEMENTATION

A. The only way to increase profitability in North America is to further involve Maytag with the superstore retailers, sure to anger the independent dealers, but necessary for Maytag to compete.

B. Board members with more global business experience should be recruited with an eye toward the future, especially with expertise in Asia and Latin America.

C. Product R&D needs to be improved, as does marketing, to get new products on line quickly.

VIII. EVALUATION AND CONTROL

A. MIS needs to be developed for speedier evaluation and control. While the question of control vs. autonomy is "under review," another Hoover fiasco may be brewing.

B. The acquired companies do not all share the Midwestern work ethic or the Maytag Corporation culture and Maytag's managers must inculcate these values into the employees of all acquired companies.

C. Systems should be developed to decide if the size and location of Maytag manufacturing plants is still correct and to plan for the future; industry analysis indicates that smaller automated plants may be more efficient now than in the past.

© Thomas L. Wheelen and J. David Hunger. Reprinted by permission of the authors.

Note: The following exhibits were originally attached in their entirety to this strategic audit, but for reasons of space only their titles are listed here:

Exhibit 1: EFAS Table

Exhibit 2: IFAS Table

Exhibit 3: SFAS Table

Exhibit 4: Ratio Analysis for five Years

Exhibit 5: Common-Size Income Statements

Notes

1. J. A. Sasseen, "Are Profits Shakier Than They Look?" *Business Week* (August 5, 1996), pp. 54–55.

2. M. Vanac, "What's a Novice Investor to Do?" *Des Moines Register* (November 30, 1997), p. 3G.

3. E. Iwata, "More Firms Falsify Revenue to Boost Stocks," *USA Today* (March 29, 2000), p. B1.

4. A. R. Sorking, "New Path on Mergers Could Contain Loopholes," *The (Ames, IA) Daily Tribune* (January 9, 2001), p. B7; "Firms Resist Effort to Unveil True Costs of Doing Business," *USA Today* (July 3, 2000), p. 10A.

5. M. S. Fridson, *Financial Statement Analysis* (New York: John Wiley & Sons, 1991), pp. 192–194.

6. D. H. Bangs, *Managing by the Numbers* (Dover, NH: Upstart Publications, 1992), pp. 106–107.

7. J. M. Laderman, "Earnings, Schmernings Look at the Cash," *Business Week* (July 24, 1989), pp. 56–57.

8. H. Greenberg, "EBITDA: Never Trust Anything That You Can't Pronounce," *Fortune* (June 22, 1998), pp. 192–194.

9. J. Warner, "21st Century Capitalism: Snapshot of the Next Century," *Business Week* (November 18, 1994), p. 194.

cases in strategic management

CONTENTS

The Recalcitrant Director at Byte Products, Inc.: Corporate Legality Versus Corporate Responsibility

Dan R. Dalton, Richard A. Cosier, and Cathy A. Enz

Byte Products, Inc., is primarily involved in the production of electronic components that are used in personal computers. Although such components might be found in a few computers in home use, Byte products are found most frequently in computers used for sophisticated business and engineering applications. Annual sales of these products have been steadily increasing over the past several years; Byte Products, Inc., currently has total sales of approximately $265 million.

Over the past six years increases in yearly revenues have consistently reached 12%. Byte Products, Inc., headquartered in the midwestern United States, is regarded as one of the largest volume suppliers of specialized components and is easily the industry leader with some 32% market share. Unfortunately for Byte, many new firms—domestic and foreign—have entered the industry. A dramatic surge in demand, high profitability, and the relative ease of a new firm's entry into the industry explain in part the increased number of competing firms.

Although Byte management—and presumably shareholders as well—is very pleased about the growth of its markets, it faces a major problem: Byte simply cannot meet the demand for these components. The company currently operates three manufacturing facilities in various locations throughout the United States. Each of these plants operates three production shifts (24 hours per day), 7 days a week. This activity constitutes virtually all of the company's production capacity. Without an additional manufacturing plant, Byte simply cannot increase its output of components.

James M. Elliott, Chief Executive Officer and Chairman of the Board, recognizes the gravity of the problem. If Byte Products cannot continue to manufacture components in sufficient numbers to meet the demand, buyers will go elsewhere. Worse yet is the possibility that any continued lack of supply will encourage others to enter the market. As a long-term solution to this problem, the Board of Directors unanimously authorized the construction of a new, state-of-the-art manufacturing facility in the southwestern United States. When the planned capacity of this plant is added to that of the three current plants, Byte should be able to meet demand for many years to come. Unfortunately, an estimated three years will be required to complete the plant and bring it on line.

This case was prepared by Professors Dan R. Dalton and Richard A. Cosier of the Graduate School of Business at Indiana University and Professor Cathy A. Enz of Cornell University. The names of the organization, individual, location, and/or financial information have been disguised to preserve the organization's desire for anonymity. This case was edited for SMBP-9th Edition. Reprinted by permission.

Jim Elliott believes very strongly that this three-year period is far too long and has insisted that there also be a shorter range, stopgap solution while the plant is under construction. The instability of the market and the pressure to maintain leader status are two factors contributing to Elliott's insistence on a more immediate solution. Without such a move, Byte management believes that it will lose market share and, again, attract competitors into the market.

Several Solutions

A number of suggestions for such a temporary measure were offered by various staff specialists, but rejected by Elliott. For example, licensing Byte's product and process technology to other manufacturers in the short run to meet immediate demand was possible. This licensing authorization would be short-term, or just until the new plant could come on line. Top management, as well as the board, was uncomfortable with this solution for several reasons. They thought it unlikely that any manufacturer would shoulder the fixed costs of producing appropriate components for such a short term. Any manufacturer that would do so would charge a premium to recover its costs. This suggestion, obviously, would make Byte's own products available to its customers at an unacceptable price. Nor did passing any price increase to its customers seem sensible, for this too would almost certainly reduce Byte's market share as well as encourage further competition.

Overseas facilities and licensing also were considered but rejected. Before it became a publicly traded company, Byte's founders decided that its manufacturing facilities would be domestic. Top management strongly felt that this strategy had served Byte well; moreover, Byte's majority stockholders (initial owners of the then privately held Byte) were not likely to endorse such a move. Beyond that, however, top management was reluctant to foreign license—or make available by any means the technologies for others to produce Byte products—as they could not then properly control patents. Top management feared that foreign licensing would essentially give away costly proprietary information regarding the company's highly efficient means of product development. There also was the potential for initial low product quality—whether produced domestically or otherwise—especially for such a short-run operation. Any reduction in quality, however brief, would threaten Byte's share of this sensitive market.

The Solution!

One recommendation that has come to the attention of the Chief Executive Officer could help solve Byte's problem in the short run. Certain members of his staff have notified him that an abandoned plant currently is available in Plainville, a small town in the northeastern United States. Before its closing eight years before, this plant was used primarily for the manufacture of electronic components. As is, it could not possibly be used to produce Byte products, but it could be inexpensively refitted to do so in as few as three months. Moreover, this plant is available at a very attractive price. In fact, discreet inquiries by Elliott's staff indicate that this plant could probably be leased immediately from its present owners because the building has been vacant for some eight years.

All the news about this temporary plant proposal, however, is not nearly so positive. Elliott's staff concedes that this plant will never be efficient and its profitability will be low. In addition, the Plainville location is a poor one in terms of high labor costs (the area is highly unionized), warehousing expenses, and inadequate transportation links to Byte's major markets and suppliers. Plainville is simply not a candidate for a long-term solution. Still, in the short run a temporary plant could help meet the demand and might forestall additional competition.

The staff is persuasive and notes that this option has several advantages: (1) there is no need for any licensing, foreign or domestic, (2) quality control remains firmly in the company's hands, and (3) an increase in the product price will be unnecessary. The temporary plant, then, would be used for three years or so until the new plant could be built. Then the temporary plant would be immediately closed.

CEO Elliott is convinced.

Taking the Plan to the Board

The quarterly meeting of the Board of Directors is set to commence at 2:00 P.M. Jim Elliott has been reviewing his notes and agenda for the meeting most of the morning. The issue of the temporary plant is clearly the most important agenda item. Reviewing his detailed presentation of this matter, including the associated financial analyses, has occupied much of his time for several days. All the available information underscores his contention that the temporary plant in Plainville is the only responsible solution to the demand problems. No other option offers the same low level of risk and ensures Byte's status as industry leader.

At the meeting, after the board has dispensed with a number of routine matters, Jim Elliott turns his attention to the temporary plant. In short order, he advises the 11-member board (himself, 3 additional inside members, and 7 outside members) of his proposal to obtain and refit the existing plant to ameliorate demand problems in the short run, authorized the construction of the new plant (the completion of which is estimated to take some three years), and plan to switch capacity from the temporary plant to the new one when it is operational. He also briefly reviews additional details concerning the costs involved, advantages of this proposal versus domestic or foreign licensing, and so on.

All the board members except one are in favor of the proposal. In fact, they are most enthusiastic; the overwhelming majority agree that the temporary plant is an excellent—even inspired—stopgap measure. Ten of the eleven board members seem relieved because the board was most reluctant to endorse any of the other alternatives that had been mentioned.

The single dissenter—T. Kevin Williams, an outside director—is, however, steadfast in his objections. He will not, under any circumstances, endorse the notion of the temporary plant and states rather strongly that "I will not be party to this nonsense, not now, not ever."

T. Kevin Williams, the senior executive of a major nonprofit organization, is normally a reserved and really quite agreeable person. This sudden, uncharacteristic burst of emotion clearly startles the remaining board members into silence. The following excerpt captures the ensuing, essentially one-on-one conversation between Williams and Elliott.

Williams: How many workers do your people estimate will be employed in the temporary plant?

Elliott: Roughly 1,200, possibly a few more.

Williams: I presume it would be fair, then, to say that, including spouses and children, something on the order of 4,000 people will be attracted to the community.

Elliott: I certainly would not be surprised.

Williams: If I understand the situation correctly, this plant closed just over eight years ago and that closing had a catastrophic effect on Plainville. Isn't it true that a large portion of the community was employed by this plant?

Elliott: Yes, it was far and away the majority employer.

Williams: And most of these people have left the community presumably to find employment elsewhere.

Elliott: Definitely, there was a drastic decrease in the area's population.

Williams: Are you concerned, then, that our company can attract the 1,200 employees to Plainville from other parts of New England?

Elliott: Not in the least. We are absolutely confident that we will attract 1,200—even more, for that matter virtually any number we need. That, in fact, is one of the chief advantages of this proposal. I would think that the community would be very pleased to have us there.

Williams: On the contrary, I would suspect that the community will rue the day we arrived. Beyond that, though, this plan is totally unworkable if we are candid. On the other hand, if we are less than candid, the proposal will work for us, but only at great cost to Plainville. In fact, quite frankly the implications are appalling. Once again, I must enter my serious objections.

Elliott: I don't follow you.

Williams: The temporary plant would employ some 1,200 people. Again, this means the infusion of over 4,000 to the community and surrounding areas. Byte Products, however, intends to close this plant in three years or less. If Byte informs the community or the employees that the jobs are temporary, the proposal simply won't work. When the new people arrive in the community, there will be a need for more schools, instructors, utilities, housing, restaurants, and so forth. Obviously, if the banks and local government know that the plant is temporary, no funding will be made available for these projects and certainly no credit for the new employees to buy homes, appliances, automobiles, and so forth.

   If, on the other hand, Byte Products does not tell the community of its "temporary" plans, the project can go on. But, in several years when the plant closes (and we here have agreed today that it will close), we will have created a ghost town. The tax base of the community will have been destroyed; property values will decrease precipitously; practically the whole town will be unemployed. This proposal will place Byte Products in an untenable position and in extreme jeopardy.

Elliott: Are you suggesting that this proposal jeopardizes us legally? If so, it should be noted that the legal department has reviewed this proposal in its entirety and has indicated no problem.

Williams: No! I don't think we are dealing with an issue of legality here. In fact, I don't doubt for a minute that this proposal is altogether legal. I do, however, resolutely believe that this proposal constitutes gross irresponsibility.

   I think this decision has captured most of my major concerns. These along with a host of collateral problems associated with this project lead me to strongly suggest that you and the balance of the board reconsider and not endorse this proposal. Byte Products must find another way.

The Dilemma

After a short recess, the board meeting reconvened. Presumably because of some discussion during the recess, several other board members indicated that they were no longer inclined to support the proposal. After a short period of rather heated discussion, the following exchange took place.

Elliott: It appears to me that any vote on this matter is likely to be very close. Given the gravity of our demand capacity problem, I must insist that the stockholders' equity be protected. We cannot wait three years; that is clearly out of the question. I still feel that licensing—domestic or foreign—is not in our long-term interests for any number of reasons, some of which have been discussed here. On the other hand, I do not want to take this project forward on the strength of a mixed vote. A vote of 6–5 or 7–4, for example, does not indicate that the board is remotely close to being of one mind. Mr. Williams, is there a compromise to be reached?

Williams: Respectfully, I have to say no. If we tell the truth, namely, the temporary nature of our operations, the proposal is simply not viable. If we are less than candid in this respect, we do grave damage to the community as well as to our image. It seems to me that we can only go one way or the other. I don't see a middle ground.

case 2

The Wallace Group

Laurence J. Stybel

Frances Rampar, President of Rampar Associates, drummed her fingers on the desk. Scattered before her were her notes. She had to put the pieces together in order to make an effective sales presentation to Harold Wallace.

Hal Wallace was the President of The Wallace Group. He had asked Rampar to conduct a series of interviews with some key Wallace Group employees, in preparation for a possible consulting assignment for Rampar Associates.

During the past three days, Rampar had been talking with some of these key people and had received background material about the company. The problem was not in finding the problem. The problem was that there were too many problems!

Background of The Wallace Group

The Wallace Group, Inc., is a diversified company dealing in the manufacture and development of technical products and systems (see **Exhibit 1**). The company currently consists of three operational groups and a corporate staff. The three groups include Electronics, Plastics, and Chemicals, each operating under the direction of a Group Vice President (see **Exhibits 2, 3,** and **4**). The company generates $70 million in sales as a manufacturer of plastics, chemical products, and electronic components and systems. Principal sales are to large contractors in governmental and automotive markets. With respect to sales volume, Plastics and Chemicals are approximately equal in size, and both of them together equal the size of the Electronics Group.

Electronics offers competence in the areas of microelectronics, electromagnetic sensors, antennas, microwave, and minicomputers. Presently, these skills are devoted primarily to the engineering and manufacture of countermeasure equipment for aircraft. This includes radar detection systems that allow an aircraft crew to know that they are being tracked by radar units on the ground, on ships, or on other aircraft. Further, the company manufactures displays that provide the crew with a visual "fix" on where they are relative to the radar units that are tracking them.

In addition to manufacturing tested and proven systems developed in the past, The Wallace Group is currently involved in two major and two minor programs, all involving display systems. The Navy-A Program calls for the development of a display system for a tactical fighter plane; Air Force-B is another such system for an observation plane.

This case was prepared by Dr. Laurence J. Stybel. It was prepared for class discussion rather than to illustrate either effective or ineffective handling of an administrative situation. Unauthorized duplication of copyright materials is a violation of federal law. This case was edited for SMBP-9th Edition. Reprinted by permission.

Exhibit 1

An Excerpt from the Annual Report

To the Shareholders:

This past year was one of definite accomplishment for The Wallace Group, although with some admitted soft spots. This is a period of consolidation, of strengthening our internal capacity for future growth and development. Presently, we are in the process of creating a strong management team to meet the challenges we will set for the future.

Despite our failure to achieve some objectives, we turned a profit of $3,521,000 before taxes, which was a growth over the previous year's earnings. And we have declared a dividend for the fifth consecutive year, albeit one that is less than the year before. However, the retention of earnings is imperative if we are to lay a firm foundation for future accomplishment.

Currently, The Wallace Group has achieved a level of stability. We have a firm foothold in our current markets, and we could elect to simply enact strong internal controls and maximize our profits. However, this would not be a growth strategy. Instead, we have chosen to adopt a more aggressive posture for the future, to reach out into new markets wherever possible and to institute the controls necessary to move forward in a planned and orderly fashion.

The Electronics Group performed well this past year and is engaged in two major programs under Defense Department contracts. These are developmental programs that provide us with the opportunity for ongoing sales upon testing of the final product. Both involve the creation of tactical display systems for aircraft being built by Lombard Aircraft for the Navy and the Air Force. Future potential sales from these efforts could amount to approximately $56 million over the next five years. Additionally, we are developing technical refinements to older, already installed systems under Army Department contracts.

In the future, we will continue to offer our technological competence in such tactical display systems and anticipate additional breakthroughs and success in meeting the demands of this market. However, we also believe that we have unique contributions to make to other markets, and to that end we are making the investments necessary to expand our opportunities.

Plastics also turned in a solid performance this past year and has continued to be a major supplier to Chrysler, Martin Tool, Foster Electric, and, of course, to our Electronics Group. The market for this group continues to expand, and we believe that additional investments in this group will allow us to seize a larger share of the future.

Chemicals' performance, admittedly, has not been as satisfactory as anticipated during the past year. However, we have been able to realize a small amount of profit from this operation and to halt what was a potentially dangerous decline in profits. We believe that this situation is only temporary and that infusions of capital for developing new technology, plus the streamlining of operations, has stabilized the situation. The next step will be to begin more aggressive marketing to capitalize on the group's basic strengths.

Overall, the outlook seems to be one of modest but profitable growth. The near term will be one of creating the technology and controls necessary for developing our market offerings and growing in a planned and purposeful manner. Our improvement efforts in the various company groups can be expected to take hold over the years with positive effect on results.

We wish to express our appreciation to all those who participated in our efforts this past year.

Harold Wallace
Chairman and President

Ongoing production orders are anticipated following flight testing. The other two minor programs, Army-LG and OBT-37, involve the incorporation of new technology into existing aircraft systems.

The Plastics Group manufactures plastic components utilized by the electronics, automotive, and other industries requiring plastic products. These include switches, knobs, keys, insulation materials, and so on, used in the manufacture of electronic equipment and other small made-to-order components installed in automobiles, planes, and other products.

The Chemicals Group produces chemicals used in the development of plastics. It supplies bulk chemicals to the Plastics Group and other companies. These chemicals are then injected into molds or extruded to form a variety of finished products.

Exhibit 2

Organizational Chart: The Wallace Group (Electronics)

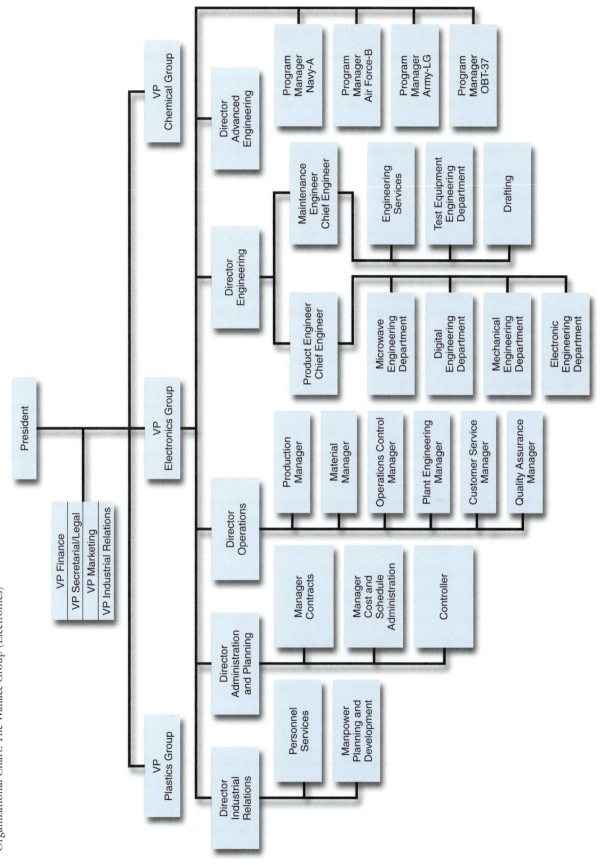

2-3

Exhibit 3

The Wallace Group (Chemicals)

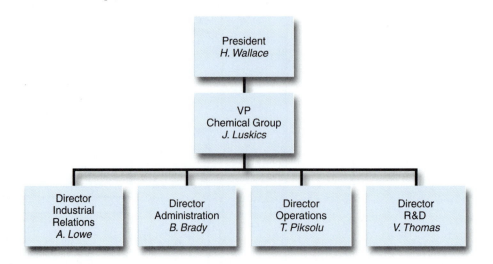

History of The Wallace Group

Each of the three groups began as a sole proprietorship under the direct operating control of an owner/manager. Several years ago, Harold Wallace, owner of the original electronics company, determined to undertake a program of diversification. Initially, he attempted to expand his market by product development and line extensions entirely within the electronics industry. However, because of initial problems, he drew back and sought other opportunities. Wallace's primary concern was his almost total dependence on defense-related contracts. He had felt for some time that he should take some strong action to gain a foothold in the private markets. The first major opportunity that seemed to satisfy his various requirements was the

Exhibit 4

The Wallace Group (Plastics)

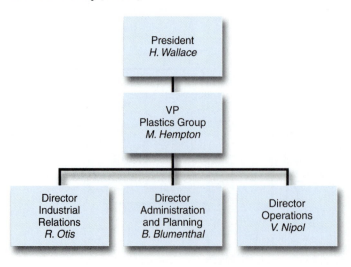

acquisition of a former supplier, a plastics company whose primary market was not defense-related. The company's owner desired to sell his operation and retire. At the time, Wallace's debt structure was such that he could not manage the acquisition and so he had to attract equity capital. He was able to gather a relatively small group of investors and form a closed corporation. The group established a Board of Directors with Wallace as Chairman and President of the new corporate entity.

With respect to operations, little changed. Wallace continued direct operational control over the Electronics Group. As holder of 60% of the stock, he maintained effective control over policy and operations. However, because of his personal interests, the Plastics Group, now under the direction of a newly hired Vice President, Martin Hempton, was left mainly to its own devices except for yearly progress reviews by the President. All Wallace asked at the time was that the Plastics Group continue its profitable operation, which it did.

Several years ago, Wallace and the Board decided to diversify further because two-thirds of their business was still defense-dependent. They learned that one of the major suppliers of the Plastics Group, a chemical company, was on the verge of bankruptcy. The company's owner, Jerome Luskics, agreed to sell. However, this acquisition required a public stock offering, with most of the funds going to pay off debts incurred by the three groups, especially the Chemicals Group. The net result was that Wallace now holds 45% of The Wallace Group and Jerome Luskics 5%, with the remainder distributed among the public.

Organization and Personnel

Presently, Harold Wallace serves as Chairman and President of The Wallace Group. The Electronics Group had been run by LeRoy Tuscher, who just resigned as Vice President. Hempton continued as Vice President of Plastics and Luskics served as Vice President of the Chemicals Group.

Reflecting the requirements of a corporate perspective and approach, a corporate staff has grown up, consisting of Vice Presidents for Finance, Secretarial/Legal, Marketing, and Industrial Relations. This staff has assumed many functions formerly associated with the group offices.

Because these positions are recent additions, many of the job accountabilities are still being defined. Problems have arisen over the responsibilities and relationships between corporate and group positions. President Wallace has settled most of the disputes himself because of the inability of the various parties to resolve differences among themselves.

Current Trends

Presently, there is a mood of lethargy and drift within The Wallace Group (see **Exhibits 1–11**). Most managers feel that each of the three groups functions as an independent company. And, with respect to group performance, not much change or progress has been made in recent years. Electronics and Plastics are still stable and profitable, but both lack growth in markets and profits. The infusion of capital breathed new life and hope into the Chemicals operation but did not solve most of the old problems and failings that had caused its initial decline. For all these reasons Wallace decided that strong action was necessary. His greatest disappointment was with the Electronics Group, in which he had placed high hopes for future development. Thus he acted by requesting and getting the Electronics Group Vice President's resignation. Hired from a computer company to replace LeRoy Tuscher, Jason Matthews joined The Wallace Group a week ago.

Last week, Wallace's annual net sales were $70 million. By group they were:

Electronics	$35,000,000
Plastics	$20,000,000
Chemicals	$15,000,000

On a consolidated basis, the financial highlights of the last 2 years are as follows:

	Last Year	Two Years Ago
Net sales	$70,434,000	$69,950,000
Income (pre-tax)	3,521,000	3,497,500
Income (after-tax)	2,760,500	1,748,750
Working capital	16,200,000	16,088,500
Shareholders' equity	39,000,000	38,647,000
Total assets	59,869,000	59,457,000
Long-term debt	4,350,000	3,500,000
Per Share of Common Stock		
Net income	$.37	$.36
Cash dividends paid	.15	.25

Of the net income, approximately 70% came from Electronics, 25% from Plastics, and 5% from Chemicals.

Exhibit 5

Selected Portions of a Transcribed Interview with H. Wallace

Rampar: What is your greatest problem right now?

Wallace: That's why I called you in! Engineers are a high-strung, temperamental lot. Always complaining. It's hard to take them seriously.

Last month we had an annual stockholder's meeting. We have an Employee Stock Option Plan, and many of our long-term employees attended the meeting. One of my managers—and I won't mention any names—introduced a resolution calling for the resignation of the President—me!

The vote was defeated. But, of course, I own 45% of the stock!

Now I realize that there could be no serious attempt to get rid of me. Those who voted for the resolution were making a dramatic effort to show me how upset they are with the way things are going.

I could fire those employees who voted against me. I was surprised by how many did. Some of my key people were in that group. Perhaps I ought to stop and listen to what they are saying.

Businesswise, I think we're O.K. Not great, but O.K. Last year we turned in a profit of $3.5 million before taxes, which was a growth over previous years' earnings. We declared a dividend for the fifth consecutive year.

We're currently working on the creation of a tactical display system for aircraft being built by Lombard Aircraft for the Navy and the Air Force. If Lombard gets the contract to produce the prototype, future sales could amount to $56 million over the next five years.

Why are they complaining?

Rampar: You must have thoughts on the matter.

Wallace: I think the issue revolves around how we manage people. It's a personnel problem. You were highly recommended as someone with expertise in high-technology human resource management.

I have some ideas on what is the problem. But I'd like you to do an independent investigation and give me your findings. Give me a plan of action.

Don't give me a laundry list of problems, Fran. Anyone can do that. I want a set of priorities I should focus on during the next year. I want a clear action plan from you. And I want to know how much this plan is going to cost me!

Other than that, I'll leave you alone and let you talk to anyone in the company you want.

Exhibit 6

Selected Portions of a Transcribed Interview with Frank Campbell,
Vice President of Industrial Relations

Rampar: What is your greatest problem right now?

Campbell: Trying to contain my enthusiasm over the fact that Wallace brought you in!
   Morale is really poor here. Hal runs this place like a one man operation, when it's grown too big for that. It took a palace revolt to finally get him to see the depths of the resentment. Whether he'll do anything about it, that's another matter.

Rampar: What would you like to see changed?

Campbell: Other than a new President?

Rampar: Uh-huh.

Campbell: We badly need a management development program for our group. Because of our growth, we have been forced to promote technical people to management positions who have had no prior managerial experience. Mr. Tuscher agreed on the need for a program, but Hal Wallace vetoed the idea because developing such a program would be too expensive. I think it is too expensive *not* to move ahead on this.

Rampar: Anything else?

Campbell: The IEWU negotiations have been extremely tough this time around, due to excessive demands they have been making. Union pay scales are already pushing up against our foreman salary levels, and foremen are being paid high in their salary ranges. This problem, coupled with union insistence on a no-layoff clause, is causing us fits. How can we keep all our workers when we have production equipment on order that will eliminate 20% of our assembly positions?

Rampar: Wow.

Campbell: We have been sued by a rejected candidate for a position on the basis of discrimination. She claimed our entrance qualifications are excessive because we require shorthand. There is some basis for this statement since most reports are given to secretaries in handwritten form or on audio cassettes. In fact, we have always required it and our executives want their secretaries to have skill in taking dictation. Not only is this case taking time, but I need to reconsider if any of our position entrance requirements, in fact, are excessive. I am sure we do not want another case like this one.

Rampar: That puts The Wallace Group in a vulnerable position, considering the amount of government work you do.

Campbell: We have a tremendous recruiting backlog, especially for engineering positions. Either our pay scales are too low, our job specs are too high, or we are using the wrong recruiting channels. Kane and Smith [Director of Engineering and Director of Advanced Systems] keep rejecting everyone we send down there as being unqualified.

Rampar: Gee.

Campbell: Being head of human resources around here is a tough job. We don't act. We react.

Exhibit 7

Selected Portions of a Transcribed Interview with Matthew Smith, Director of Advanced Systems

Rampar: What is your greatest problem right now?

Smith: Corporate brass keeps making demands on me and others that don't relate to the job we are trying to get done. They say that the information they need is to satisfy corporate planning and operations review requirements, but they don't seem to recognize how much time and effort is required to provide this information. Sometimes it seems like they are generating analyses, reports, and requests for data just to keep themselves busy. Someone should be evaluating how critical these corporate staff activities really are. To me and the Electronics Group, these activities are unnecessary.

An example is the Vice President, Marketing (L. Holt), who keeps asking us for supporting data so he can prepare a corporate marketing strategy. As you know, we prepare our own group marketing strategic plans annually, but using data and formats that are oriented to our needs, rather than Corporate's. This planning activity, which occurs at the same time as Corporate's, coupled with heavy work loads on current projects, makes us appear to Holt as though we are being unresponsive.

Somehow we need to integrate our marketing planning efforts between our group and Corporate. This is especially true if our group is to successfully grow in nondefense-oriented markets and products. We do need corporate help, but not arbitrary demands for information that divert us from putting together effective marketing strategies for our group.

I am getting too old to keep fighting these battles.

Rampar: This is a long-standing problem?

Smith: You bet! Our problems are fairly classic in the high-tech field. I've been at other companies and they're not much better. We spend so much time firefighting, we never really get organized. Everything is done on an ad hoc basis.

I'm still waiting for tomorrow.

Exhibit 8

Selected Portions of a Transcribed Interview with Ralph Kane, Director of Engineering

Rampar: What is your greatest problem right now?

Kane: Knowing you were coming, I wrote them down. They fall into four areas:

1. Our salary schedules are too low to attract good, experienced EEs. We have been told by our Vice President (Frank Campbell) that corporate policy is to hire new people below the salary grade midpoint. All qualified candidates are making more than that now and in some case are making more than our grade maximums. I think our Project Engineer job is rated too low.
2. Chemicals Group asked for and the former Electronics Vice President (Tuscher) agreed to "lend" six of our best EEs to help solve problems it is having developing a new battery. That is great for the Chemicals Group, but meanwhile how do we solve the engineering problems that have cropped up in our Navy-A and OBT-37 programs?
3. As you know, Matt Smith (Director of Advanced Systems) is retiring in six months. I depend heavily on his group for technical expertise, and in some areas he depends heavily on some of my key engineers. I have lost some people to the Chemicals Group, and Matt has been trying to lend me some of his people to fill in. But he and his staff have been heavily involved in marketing planning and trying to identify or recruit a qualified successor long enough before his retirement to be able to train him or her. The result is that his people are up to their eyeballs in doing their own stuff and cannot continue to help me meet my needs.
4. IR has been preoccupied with union negotiations in the plant and has not had time to help me deal with this issue of management planning. Campbell is working on some kind of system that will help deal with this kind of problem and prevent them in the future. That is great, but I need help now—not when his "system" is ready.

Exhibit 9

Selected Portions of a Transcribed Interview with Brad Lowell, Program Manager, Navy-A

Rampar: What is your . . .?

Lowell: . . . great problem? I'll tell you what it is. I still cannot get the support I need from Kane in Engineering. He commits and then doesn't deliver, and it has me quite concerned. The excuse now is that in "his judgment," Sid Wright needs the help for the Air Force program more than I do. Wright's program is one week ahead of schedule, so I disagree with "his judgment." Kane keeps complaining about not having enough people.

Rampar: Why do you think Kane says he doesn't have enough people?

Lowell: Because Hal Wallace is a tight-fisted S.O.B. who won't let us hire the people we need!

Exhibit 10

Selected Portions of a Transcribed Interview with Phil Jones, Director, Administration and Planning

Jones: Wheel spinning—that's our problem! We talk about expansion, but we don't do anything about it. Are we serious or not?

For example, a bid request came in from a prime contractor seeking help in developing a countermeasure system for a medium-range aircraft. They needed an immediate response and concept proposal in one week. Tuscher just sat on my urgent memo to him asking for a go/no go decision on bidding. I could not give the contractor an answer (because no decision came from Tuscher), so they gave up on us.

I am frustrated because (1) we lost an opportunity we were "naturals" to win, and (2) my personal reputation was damaged because I was unable to answer the bid request. Okay, Tuscher's gone now, but we need to develop some mechanism so an answer to such a request can be made quickly.

Another thing, our MIS is being developed by the Corporate Finance Group. More wheel spinning! They are telling us what information we need rather than asking us what we want! E. Kay (our Group Controller) is going crazy trying to sort out the input requirements they need for the system and understanding the complicated reports that came out. Maybe this new system is great as a technical achievement, but what good is it to us if we can't use it?

Exhibit 11

Selected Portions of a Transcribed Interview with Burt Williams, Director of Operations

Rampar: What is your biggest problem right now?

Williams: One of the biggest problems we face right now stems from corporate policy regarding transfer pricing. I realize we are "encouraged" to purchase our plastics and chemicals from our sister Wallace groups, but we are also committed to making a profit! Because manufacturing problems in those groups have forced them to raise their prices, should *we* suffer the consequences? We can get some materials cheaper from other suppliers. How can we meet our volume and profit targets when we are saddled with noncompetitive material costs?

Rampar: And if that issue was settled to your satisfaction, then would things be O.K.?

Williams: Although out of my direct function, it occurs to me that we are not planning effectively our efforts to expand into nondefense areas. With minimal alteration to existing production methods, we can develop both end-use products (e.g., small motors, traffic control devices, and microwave transceivers for highway emergency communications) and components (e.g., LED and LCD displays, police radar tracking devices, and word processing system memory and control devices) with large potential markets.

 The problems in this regard are:

1. Matt Smith (Director, Advanced Systems) is retiring and has had only defense-related experience. Therefore, he is not leading any product development efforts along these lines.
2. We have no marketing function at the group level to develop a strategy, define markets, and research and develop product opportunities.
3. Even if we had a marketing plan and products for industrial/commercial application, we have no sales force or rep network to sell the stuff.

 Maybe I am way off base, but it seems to me we need a Groups/Marketing/Sales function to lead us in this business expansion effort. It should be headed by an experienced technical marketing manager with a proven track record in developing such products and markets.

Rampar: Have you discussed your concerns with others?

Williams: I have brought these ideas up with Mr. Matthews and others at the Group Management Committee. No one else seems interested in pursuing this concept, but they won't say this outright and don't say why it should not be addressed. I guess that in raising the idea with you I am trying to relieve some of my frustrations.

The Problem Confronting Frances Rampar

As Rampar finished reviewing her notes (see **Exhibits 5–11**), she kept reflecting on what Hal Wallace had told her:

> Don't give me a laundry list of problems, Fran. Anyone can do that. I want a set of priorities I should focus on during the next year. I want a clear action plan from you. And I want to know how much this plan is going to cost me!

Fran Rampar again drummed her fingers on the desk.

case 3

The Audit

*John A. Kilpatrick, Gamewell D. Gantt,
and George A. Johnson*

Sue was puzzled as to what course of action to take. She had recently started her job with a national CPA firm, and she was already confronted with a problem that could affect her future with the firm. On an audit, she encountered a client who had been treating payments to a large number, but by no means a majority, of its workers as payments to independent contractors. This practice saves the client the payroll taxes that would otherwise be due on the payments if the workers were classified as employees. In Sue's judgment this was improper as well as illegal and should have been noted in the audit. She raised the issue with John, the senior accountant to whom she reported. He thought it was a possible problem but did not seem willing to do anything about it. He encouraged her to talk to the partner in charge if she didn't feel satisfied.

She thought about the problem for a considerable time before approaching the partner in charge. The ongoing professional education classes she had received from her employer emphasized the ethical responsibilities that she had as a CPA and the fact that her firm endorsed adherence to high ethical standards. This finally swayed her to pursue the issue with the partner in charge of the audit. The visit was most unsatisfactory. Paul, the partner, virtually confirmed her initial reaction that the practice was wrong, but he said that many other companies in the industry follow such a practice. He went on to say that if an issue was made of it, Sue would lose the account, and he was not about to take such action. She came away from the meeting with the distinct feeling that had she chosen to pursue the issue she would have created an enemy.

Sue still felt disturbed and decided to discuss the problem with some of her coworkers. She approached Bill and Mike, both of whom had been working for the firm for a couple of years. They were familiar with the problem because they had encountered the same issue when doing the audit the previous year. They expressed considerable concern that if she went over the head of the partner in charge of the audit, they could be in big trouble since they had failed to question the practice during the previous audit. They said that they realized it was probably wrong, but they went ahead because it had been ignored in previous years and they knew their supervisor wanted them to ignore it again this year. They didn't want to cause problems. They encouraged Sue to be a "team player" and drop the issue.

This case was prepared by Professors John A. Kilpatrick, Gamewell D. Gantt, and George A. Johnson of the College of Business, Idaho State University. The names of the organization, individual, location, and/or financial information have been disguised to preserve the organization's desire for anonymity. This case was edited for SMBP-9th Edition. Presented to and accepted by the refereed Society for Case Research. All rights reserved to the authors and the SCR. Copyright © 1995 by John A. Kilpatrick, Gamewell D. Gantt, and George A. Johnson. Reprinted by permission.

case 4

McKesson Makes a Deal

Phyllis G. Holland, John E. Oliver, Peter M. Bergevin, and Kenneth L. Stanley

Edward Lyle, a member of the Board of Directors of McKesson Corporation, was intrigued by the merger proposal that had just been described to him by Mark Pulido, McKesson's Chief Executive Officer (CEO). Lyle had been a McKesson director for a number of years and had seen McKesson acquire several other companies, with varying degrees of success. He knew that anticipated synergies were not always realized and was concerned about a tendency to pay premium prices when making acquisitions. He was also aware of a trend toward naming directors in stockholder suits about failed acquisitions. Most importantly, he knew that his responsibilities as a Director required that he give this proposal careful scrutiny (see **Exhibit 1**).

McKesson Corporation

McKesson Corporation was founded in 1833 and was a leading provider of health care products and services to independent and chain pharmacies, hospitals, and other health care organizations throughout the United States and Canada. Once the largest liquor distributor in the United States, McKesson had been through many cycles of acquisition and divestiture as it had sought to dominate various markets. Headquartered in San Francisco, the company distributed health and beauty products, bottled drinking water, specialty foods, and general merchandise. Current management believed that the health care industry offered the best opportunities for McKesson. The company was listed on the New York and Pacific Stock Exchanges.

McKesson was the major wholesale distributor in the pharmaceutical industry, an industry where net profits averaged around 2% and mergers were common. To compete, a company must be innovative and cost conscious. McKesson had managed this by offering high-margin generic drugs and investing in technologies that lowered both McKesson's and its customers' costs of distribution. Investments in information technology, including Web-based systems, enhanced McKesson's speed and accuracy in filling orders and managing its inventories. McKesson shared its technological advantages with its customers, and that made McKesson the supplier of choice for many pharmacies. McKesson systems supported every aspect of pharmacy operations (see **Exhibit 2**). The company was positioned to do well in the managed care environment, in which generic drugs are substituted for patent drugs and in which excellent information systems enable pharmacies to maximize profits.

This case was prepared by Professors Phyllis G. Holland, John E. Oliver, Peter M. Bergevin, and Kenneth L. Stanley of Valdosta State University. Copyright © 2002 by Phyllis G. Holland, John E. Oliver, Peter M. Bergevin, and Kenneth L. Stanley. This case was edited for SMBP-9th Edition. Reprinted by permission.

Exhibit 1

Board of Directors' Liability

The Delaware General Corporation Law (DGCL) permits a corporation to include a provision in its certificate of incorporation limiting the personal liability of a director or an officer to the corporation or its stockholders for damages for a breach of the director's fiduciary duty, subject to certain limitations. The McKesson Certificate includes such a provision, to the maximum extent permitted by law.

The DGCL also permits a corporation to indemnify officers, directors, employees, and agents for actions taken in good faith and in a manner they reasonably believed to be in, or not opposed to, the best interests of the corporation, and with respect to any criminal action, which they had no reasonable cause to believe was unlawful. The DGCL further provides that a corporation may advance expenses of defense (upon receipt of a written undertaking to reimburse the corporation if indemnification is not appropriate) and must reimburse a successful defendant for expenses, including attorneys' fees, actually and reasonably incurred, and permits a corporation to purchase and maintain liability insurance for its directors and officers. The DGCL provides that no indemnification may be made for any claim, issue, or matter as to which a person has been adjudged by a court of competent jurisdiction, after exhaustion of all appeals therefrom, to be liable to the corporation, unless and only to the extent a court determines that a person is entitled to indemnity for such expenses as the court deems proper. McKesson indemnifies its agents to the extent that they are found to be acting in good faith.

Source: Proxy Statement/Prospectus, McKesson Corporation, November 27, 1998.

Since the early 1990s, McKesson had acquired several companies in an effort to pursue its mission of becoming the world leader in health care supply management by assisting its customers in improving patient care while lowering or controlling costs. McKesson acquired General Medical, Inc. (the largest U.S. distributor of medical-surgical supplies), FoxMeyer Corporation (a bankrupt drug distributor), and Automated Healthcare, Inc., to improve supply management, information technologies, automated logistics, managed care, electronic connectivity, and customer service programs. Although the acquisitions were not

Exhibit 2

McKesson Programs and Systems for Pharmacy Operation

Front office (in-store) activities: Physically dispensing products (RXOBOT), promotions (Healthy Value$), point-of-sale applications (McKesson POS), catalogs of products (Home Health Catalogs)

Advice and support for business activities: Support for filling prescriptions (Pharmaserv), tracking dispensing records (Pharmaserv), providing advice on drug interaction (Omnilink), managing generics (McKesson Select Generics), monitoring benefits and health plan coverage (Omnilink, Caremax, Integrated Medical Systems)

Back office administration: Managing inventory (Econolink), managing store control and pharmacy (Pharmaserv)

Financial services: Providing automated reconciliation and reporting services, advanced payments, and offsets on receivables (Omnilink financial services)

Warehouse administration: Supplying products to major retailers from 41 warehouses nationwide, providing warehouse management tools (Acumax Plus)

Exhibit 3

Partial History of Acquisitions and Divestitures: McKesson Corporation

```
1833—McKesson founded
1855—Became McKesson and Robbins
1967—Became Foremost McKesson after merger with Foremost Dairies
1970s—Acquired 21 Brands, a portfolio of liquor brands including Mohawk, Ezra
        Brooks, and Ballantine's
      —Sold commercial sector of land development business
      —Acquired Armor All and C.F. Mueller (pasta)
1980s—Changed name to McKesson Corporation
      —Sold assets in hospital supply business
      —Divested homebuilding operations
      —Divested Foremost Dairies
      —Acquired Inland Chemical
      —Acquired California Culinary Academy
      —Sold C.F. Mueller and discontinued or sold other food operations
      —Sold chemical business
      —Acquired various medical or pharmaceutical companies
            Zee Medical Products
            Garrett-Hewitt International
            RDR Drug and Sundry
            3 PM, Inc.
            Lone Star Veterinary Supply
            AMBI Medical Management
            Mutual Supply Co.
            Johnson Drug Co.
            Spectro Industries
            S-P Drugs
      —Acquired American Legal Systems
      —Acquired Office Product Division of Champion International
      —Sold wine and spirits distribution business
1990s—Sold bottled water business
      —Acquired General Medical
      —Acquired FoxMeyer
      —Acquired Automated Healthcare
      —Sold Armor All
      —Sold Millbrook Distribution Services
```

without problems, it was generally acknowledged that the acquisitions had helped McKesson achieve the leadership position and competitive advantage it currently possessed. Two subsidiaries, Armor All Products Corporation and Millbrook Distribution Services, Inc., were sold off during the 1990s because they were not related to the health care mission (see **Exhibit 3**).

Financial statements for McKesson are shown in **Exhibit 4**.

HBOC

The merger proposal before the board involved HBO and Co. (HBOC). HBOC was the leading competitor in health care information, which was a high-growth segment of the information systems industry.

HBOC provided software solutions and other technological innovations to the health care industry (hospitals, physicians, HMOs). The company offered an array of integrated information programs to meet its clients' demands for financial, clinical, home, and managed

Exhibit 4

Selected Financial Data: McKesson Corporation

A. Income Statement (Dollars in millions, except per share data)

	Year Ended March 31,			Six Months Ended September 30,	
	1998	**1997**	**1996**	**1998**	**1997**
Revenues	$20,857.3	$15,710.8	$12,964.8	$12,812.4	$10,122.6
Costs and expenses					
Cost of sales	19,336.0	14,673.5	12,049.3	11,981.4	9,390.1
Selling, distribution and administration	1,159.1	944.5	674.2	684.1	554.9
Interest	102.5	55.7	44.4	57.4	48.1
Total line expenses	20,597.6	15,673.7	12,767.9	12,722.9	9,993.1
Income (loss) before income taxes and dividends on convertible preferred securities of subsidiary trust	259.7	37.1	196.9	89.5	129.5
Income taxes	98.6	31.3	76.2	34.9	49.2
Dividends on convertible preferred securities of subsidiary trust, net of tax benefit	(6.2)	(0.7)	—	(3.1)	(3.1)
Income (loss) after taxes					
Continuing operations	154.9	5.1	120.7	51.5	77.2
Discontinued operations (8)	—	128.8	14.7	—	—
Extraordinary item	—	—	—	—	—
Cumulative effect of accounting changes	—	—	—	—	—
Net income	$ 154.9	$ 133.9	$ 135.4	$ 51.5	$ 77.2
Diluted earnings (loss) per common share					
Continuing operations	$ 1.59	$ 0.06	$ 1.29	$ 0.51	$ 0.80
Discontinued operations	—	1.45	0.16	—	—
Extraordinary item	—	—	—	—	—
Cumulative effect of accounting changes	—	—	—	—	—
Total	$ 1.59	$ 1.51	$ 1.45	$ 0.51	$ 0.80
Diluted shares	101.2	89.4	93.2	106.2	100.7
Basic earnings (loss) per common share					
Continuing operations	$ 1.69	$ 0.06	$ 1.36	$ 0.54	$ 0.85
Discontinued operations	—	1.51	0.17	—	—
Extraordinary item	—	—	—	—	—
Cumulative effect of accounting changes	—	—	—	—	—
Total	$ 1.69	$ 1.57	$ 1.53	$ 0.54	$ 0.85

	Year Ended March 31,			Six Months Ended September 30,	
	1998	**1997**	**1996**	**1998**	**1997**
Basic shares	91.5	85.5	88.8	95.6	91.2
Cash dividends declared per common share	$ 0.50	$ 0.50	$ 0.50	$ 0.25	$ 0.25

B. Selected Balance Sheet Data (Dollar amounts in millions)

	Year Ended March 31			September 30,
	1998	**1997**	**1996**	**1998**
Cash, cash equivalents and marketable securities	$ 113.6	$ 229.8	$ 456.2	$ 131.6
Working capital	1,527.8	1,123.9	820.5	1,521.0
Total assets	5,607.5	5,172.8	3,360.2	7,016.9
Total debt	1,204.2	985.2	398.3	1,626.4
Convertible preferred securities of subsidiary trust	195.4	194.8	—	195.5
Stockholders' equity	1,406.8	1,260.8	1,064.6	1,630.8

Notes: The notes were deleted.

Source: McKesson Corporation, SEC Form S-4/A, November 27, 1998 and www.sec.gov/Archives/edgar/data.

care data. HBOC's software applications were based on an open-architecture system; this approach enabled customers to enhance their systems with HBOC software, regardless of the origins of their information systems. In addition to software applications, HBOC managed business offices, maintained information systems, and provided networking technologies and e-mail for many of its clients. The company numbered hospitals, pharmacies, laboratories, physicians' offices, home care providers, and managed care providers among its 9,000 global customers. HBOC's software products were complex and required up to 18 months to install. The company booked sales early in the installation process. Financial statements for HBOC are shown in **Exhibit 5**.

The Health Care Industry

The health care industry was very competitive and was changing rapidly. Competition in the industry, as in many others, compelled companies to deliver constantly increasing value to customers. Competitors believed the key to success was innovation to reduce costs, waste, and inefficiency. Technological change, they believed, could lead to dramatic and sustained improvements in price and service.

The wholesale drug industry played a central role in the U.S. health care delivery system. Drug wholesaling was a growth industry, expanding as an aging population increased its consumption of pharmaceuticals. The industry was characterized by declining profit margins and the need for national distribution systems to supply an expanding base of drug retailers. Economies of scale were a prerequisite for survival.

Exhibit 5

Selected Financial Data: HBO & Company (Dollar amounts in thousands, except per data)

	At and for the Year Ended December 31,			At and for the Nine Months Ended September 30,	
	1997	**1996**	**1995**	**1998**	**1997**
A. Income Statement Data:					
Revenue	$1,203,204	$950,911	$715,902	$1,119,170	$861,962
Net income (loss)	$ 143,537	$ 82,333	$ (7,895)	$ 224,161	$117,696
Diluted earnings (loss) per share	$ .33	$ .20	$ (.02)	$ .51	$ .28
Weighted average shares outstanding (diluted)	428,295	421,768	370,060	439,379	427,405
Cash dividends per share	$ .03	$ .02	$ .02	$ .05	$ .02
	1997	**1996**	**1995**	**1998**	**1997**
B. Balance Sheet					
Working capital	$ 519,140	$ 295,240	$156,488	$ 789,000	$ 489,792
Total assets	$1,312,586	$1,012,749	$771,550	$1,534,000	$1,177,016
Long-term debt	$ 1,022	$ 769	$ 4,054	$ 696	$ 368
Stockholders' equity	$ 900,582	$ 650,646	$500,787	$1,185,139	$ 857,039

Note: Notes were deleted.

Source: McKesson Corporation, SEC Form S-4/A, November 27, 1998 and www.hoovers.com.

The Proposed Merger

In the proposed merger, HBOC would become a wholly owned subsidiary of McKesson, and each share of HBOC's common stock would be traded for a partial share (.37) of McKesson's common stock. The exchange of stock would be tax free to stockholders for federal income tax purposes.

If the merger was completed, Charles W. McCall, President and CEO of HBOC, would become the Chairman of the board of directors of McKesson HBOC, Inc., and Mark A. Pulido, President and CEO of McKesson, would serve as the board's President and CEO. Following the merger, the board of directors would consist of 10 people, evenly split between former McKesson and HBOC directors. McKesson HBOC, Inc.'s bylaws would be written so that a three-fourths vote of the board would be required to replace either the Chairman or the CEO within the combined entity's first year of operations.

The Director's Concerns

Like most board members in large corporations, Lyle was a busy executive. A typical board member of a Fortune 500 firm has more than one directorate in addition to his or her own high-level, demanding executive position. Lyle was provided compensation and expenses for his work with the McKesson board of directors but primarily expected to see the value of his stock appreciate as McKesson expanded its presence in health care.

Exhibit 6
Interests of Executive Officers in the Merger

The executive officers of McKesson had financial interests in the merger that were beyond and, in some cases, different from those of stockholders. In the event of a merger,

1. Stock options would become exercisable. McKesson's officers held options totaling 3,900,257 shares, which could be exercised for prices ranging from $22.75 to $136.74. Ordinarily, a waiting period was required before options could be exercised, but a merger accelerated vesting of these options so that they might be exercised upon approval of the merger.

2. Stock restrictions would be lifted. McKesson's officers purchased stock on an interest-bearing full-recourse note. This stock cannot be sold for 5 years after the purchase. If the merger is approved, the restriction on sale will be lifted and the remaining balance of the note will be due.

3. Termination agreements would go into effect. If any of 14 executive officers were terminated by McKesson without "cause," or if they left McKesson for "good reason" within 2 years of approval of the merger, they would be entitled to a lump-sum cash payment of the maximum allowable under law. They could also continue to participate in McKesson's health and welfare plans and to accrue certain retirement benefits for an additional 12 to 24 months. Such arrangements were often called "golden parachutes."

Mark Pulido (McKesson's CEO), for example, purchased 80,000 shares at $27.88. In the event of a merger, this note would become due, and Pulido would be able to sell the shares. McKesson's stock price for the month following the merger announcement ranged from $74.0625 to $88.6875, so Pulido would benefit significantly from selling his stock. He could also benefit from the effects of vesting (Number 1) and the golden parachute (Number 3).

Lyle took seriously the oversight function of the board in corporate governance. Although he was protecting his own financial interests, he was also aware that he represented the interests of many other stockholders, some of whom might be much more dependent on McKesson's performance that he was. He knew that the protection that he had from personal liability for his decisions did not absolve him of responsibility for careful consideration of issues brought before the board. There was also the question of the financial interests of the executives involved (see **Exhibit 6**).

Determined to fulfill his responsibilities, Lyle pondered the questions he should ask and how aggressive he should be in studying this proposal. McKesson's mission of becoming "the world leader in health care supply management by assisting its customers in improving patient care while lowering or controlling costs" would be furthered by HBOC's products and services. Health care information services was the missing link in McKesson's overall strategy for dominating health care supply management. Lyle was also impressed by the possible synergies from the proposed merger. The ability to market HBOC's physician information products to McKesson's physician customer base was only one example of the two companies' potential to share resources and activities. Both Bear Stearns and Co. (financial advisors) and Skadden, Arps, Slate, Meagher, and Flom LLC (legal advisors) had completed due diligence investigations and submitted reports favoring the merger. Could one director have insight beyond that of a staff of attorneys?

Pulido, McKesson's CEO, had told Lyle that Pulido thought the merger would result in a unified organization with several advantages: a deep and talented pool of managers, the capability of becoming a world leader in the supply of health care products and services, the ability to increase revenues by cross-marketing each other's products, and the capacity to reduce expenses by eliminating redundant personnel and facilities.

Lyle, however, was concerned. Synergies anticipated from past mergers had not always materialized. He sometimes worried about whether the directors and managers of acquired companies had the same loyalty, ethics, and concern for stockholders that he did. He was also concerned about his fiduciary responsibility to other shareholders under agency law. He was not sure that mergers were always equally advantageous for each firm's stockholders.

case 5

Singapore Telecom: Strategic Challenges in a Turbulent Environment

Loizos Heracleous and Kulwant Singh

The financial year 1998/1999 has been a difficult and challenging year for the Singapore Telecom Group. We operated in a difficult business environment as a result of the regional economic crisis. We also faced increasing competition both locally and abroad (Koh Boon Hwee, Singapore Telecom Chairman).[1]

Singapore Telecom is preparing for battle. Having successfully met the challenge of changing from a government department to becoming the largest listed firm in Singapore, it is now facing its next major challenge—competition in its primary market. Its stated goal is to maintain its exceptional record of profitability and as much market share as possible, after StarHub, a full-service telecom provider starts operating in Singapore on April 1, 2000. StarHub will be the first competitor that Singapore Telecom will have in the fixed-line telecommunications (telecom) sector, having faced initial competition in the mobile sector with the entry of MobileOne in April 1997. The effects of StarHub's entry on the competitive landscape will be dramatic. StarHub is backed by some of the largest global telecom providers such as British Telecom and Nippon Telecom and Telegraph. Technologies Telemedia and Singapore Power will try to capture a significant part of the lucrative International Direct Dialing (IDD) market as well as of the large corporate business segment.

In addition to the intensifying competitive arena, the Asian crisis is taking its toll on Singapore Telecom's performance, and technological advancements such as Internet telephony mean that it is increasingly possible to bypass the networks of local telecom providers to make overseas calls, depriving telecom firms of an important source of income. The barriers that protected Singapore Telecom's market appear to be in danger of collapse.

It is no surprise that Singapore Telecom's chairman warned that earnings growth for the year ending March 2000 would be "negative and if I'm lucky, flat," unless there is a "significant recovery in the region's real economy."[2] For some observers, this warning foretold of more difficult times to come for Singapore Telecom.

The National Context: Singapore's National Development and Infrastructure Policy

> To promote a vibrant environment for the development of a worldclass infocommunication industry to enhance Singapore's economic competitiveness and quality of life … Singapore is a fully networked knowledge based society, connected to the world, connecting to the future.[3]

Singapore's strategic goals have largely focused on achieving rapid economic development through closely integrating its economy with global trade and development, accepting heavy foreign investments and attracting multinational corporations. These goals evolved from a mindset of survival in the 1960s, to the drive for efficiency in the 1970s, to the focus on people development, productivity, and value-added investments in the 1980s, to anticipating and embracing continuous change in the 1990s,[4] and lastly to the need to develop a "learning nation" in the late 1990s and beyond.

Singapore's broad strategic actions have focused on leveraging its natural advantage of having a strategic location by establishing worldclass transportation and materials handling facilities; extending this concept to the manufacturing, financial, and service domains by developing a sophisticated telecommunications and IT infrastructure; continuously improving workforce skills; and lastly, monitoring and absorbing global technological developments[5] through acting as a rapid adopter of tried and tested technologies to minimize the risk of adoption.[6] These strategies were guided by a sophisticated industrial policy that was developed and closely monitored by the government.

Singapore's economy has performed exceptionally well. Between 1960 and 1997, Singapore achieved real annual growth in GDP exceeding 8%, which in 1998 amounted to S$133 billion. Per capita GDP of S$27,480 is among the highest in Asia and matches or exceeds most developed countries. However, economic growth slowed drastically to 1.5% in 1998 from 8% in 1997 as the effects of the Asian economic crisis took their toll.[7] At the end of 1998, Singapore was in recession for only the second time since the early 1960s.

National infrastructure has played a key part in Singapore's development. Recognizing that infrastructure quality has a major positive impact on national economic development,[8] major resources were committed to developing the country's physical infrastructure. Singapore has placed particular importance on developing its information infrastructure, which it views as a national asset, and has implemented a number of forward-looking national plans. The "IT2000 Report: A Vision of an Intelligent Island," for example, was published in 1992, advocating the creation of a National Information Infrastructure aimed at making Singapore a more efficient switching center for goods, capital, information, and people, and at achieving further improvements in productivity.[9] In some respects, Singapore has about the most advanced information technology hardware infrastructure in the world. The Singapore government has invested in its rapid development by providing financial support, protection from market forces, and managerial talent, while urging the adoption of competitive rates and standards. In recent years, it has taken a more free market approach to the telecommunications industry, introducing a program to gradually privatize Singapore Telecom and to introduce competition into the industry.

The Industry Context: Trends in the Telecommunications Industry

For most of the 100 or so years the industry has been in existence, the big operators have provided mostly basic services on a take-it-or-leave-it basis, protected by the barriers of their monopoly status. Now, stripped of this protection and facing competition at home and abroad, the telecommunications industry is rapidly becoming one of the most competitive and turbulent industries. Operators are seeking ways to secure new customers and to hold on to as many existing customers as possible. It is clear that only a few years after the opening of telecom markets to full competition, the gloves are off and no holds are barred.[10]

THE GLOBAL COMPETITIVE ENVIRONMENT

Trends of deregulation, technological advancement and privatization, and more sophisticated and demanding consumers are causing turmoil in a once stable and highly profitable industry. The advent of competition is exerting continuous downward pressure on prices with margins falling as a result, and necessitating the introduction of value-added services by telecom providers in an effort to sustain volume and profitability. Asia has not been spared these trends, which are global and sweeping in scope.

The rulings of global organizations such as the World Trade Organization and the European Union, and a general movement toward more open and competitive markets, are having an unprecedented effect on the global telecom environment. In Asia, Japan and Hong Kong were among the first countries to liberalize their telecom markets. Though in 1990 only 35% of outgoing international telecom traffic was open to competition, by 1998 this amount had risen to 74%.[11] In 1990, only three countries (Japan, the United Kingdom, and the United States) permitted competition in basic telecom services; by 1998 over 30 countries did so, a number that continues to grow (see **Exhibit 1**).[12]

RAPID TECHNOLOGICAL CHANGE

The convergence of the technologies underlying telecommunications, computers, television, movies, and publishing is increasingly leading to overlapping products, markets, and competition and to firms moving among these industries. During the 1990s, there has also been a pronounced movement toward wireless communications, with mobile phones representing the fastest growth segment in almost all national markets and one of the fastest growing markets in the world. Such technological advancements are a huge threat for telecom companies, but they are also an opportunity for entrepreneurial, innovative firms to invest in and develop new technologies, products, and services. The telecommunications industry is shifting from proprietary to open standards, much as the computer industry did in the 1980s. Telecom technology is progressing so fast that forecasts of more than a few years are seldom attempted. In this industry, the long term is often viewed as the period beyond three years. Arguably, only the computer industry is experiencing the same rate of technological change as the telecommunications industry.

To become effective competitors in such conditions would require a cultural change for most telecommunication companies, which have historically operated in a slow-moving, monopolistic, and protectionist world. "The idea is to create a company run by people who think in terms of a world where the ratio of performance to price doubles every 18 months, and where deals have to be snapped up at once."[13]

New services such as Internet telephony or Virtual Private Networks, which are forecasted to be widely adopted in Singapore,[14] are threatening to gain substantial market share in

Exhibit 1
Countries Allowing Competition in Basic Telecom Services in 1998

Australia	Germany	Netherlands
Austria	Ghana	Norway
Belgium	Hong Kong	Philippines
Canada	Israel	Russia
Chile	Italy	Spain
China	Ireland	Sweden
Denmark	Japan	Switzerland
El Salvador	Korea	Uganda
Finland	Mexico	United Kingdom
France	New Zealand	United States

domestic and international voice traffic at the expense of established telecommunication companies. A major feature of these new services is that they often bypass the existing infra-structure, allowing providers to deal directly with customers. In time, these services will challenge the importance of national boundaries, regulatory constraints, licensing approval, and domestic telecommunications providers.

The pressure of Internet telephony will be felt most in international traffic, which produces an estimated 12 to 15% of the revenues of large international operators but 30 to 40% of profits.[15] In Singapore Telecom's case, international calls account for around 38% of total revenues. Internet telephony is forecasted to account for as much as 15 to 30% of the global market for voice and fax calls within five years. Internet telephony is inexpensive for users and allows closer customization of services, where consumers can choose the level of service they require and be charged accordingly. It also enables the provision of several value-added services to consumers, for example real-time billing, cheaper videoconferencing and unified messaging. In Asia, Internet telephony is said to be a "regulatory minefield," with some countries banning it, others embracing it, and some unsure as to how to handle it.[16]

In addition to deregulation and the effects of technology, another major force for change are consumers themselves, who expect consistently high quality of services and support the liberalization of telecom markets and the global harmonization of technological and regulatory standards.[17]

MERGERS AND ACQUISITIONS

The greater financial and competency resources required to deal with rapidly changing technology, the growing pressures of globalization and increased competition, and the convergence between industries led to a wave of mergers, acquisitions, and alliances in the industry from the mid-1990s. The resulting large firms are believed to be more likely to have the resources and strength to survive in the new environment. Consequently, there was a clear move toward larger, more global, and better endowed firms in the industry. Many of these industry-leading organizations emerged from mergers that combined firms that were unknown even months before. Many incumbents merged with firms not traditionally viewed to be part of the industry, to integrate new skills, or to pool their resources. The growing belief is that only a relatively few large global firms will prosper in the future, with the bulk of the industry serving as their local partners or suppliers. Mergers and acquisitions are greatly accelerating the pace of change and consolidation in the industry, with each megamerger being exceeded by a bigger one. According to the CEO of Cable and Wireless,

> We had 10 years in which every operator was suppressed because they were regulated and government-owned. While industries like the oil business were consolidating, telecom was not. Suddenly, 10 years' activity is being squeezed into 24 months. Sometimes it feels like 24 weeks.[18]

THE ASIAN COMPETITIVE ENVIRONMENT

The huge telecom overcapacity in certain Asian markets, such as mobile telecommunications in Malaysia and fixed-line services in Hong Kong, intensifying competition in general, and the Asian economic crisis of the late 1990s, are increasing competition and pressures for industry consolidation. Downward pricing pressures in Asia have been intense. The average reduction in the cost of a basket of business telecom services in Asia for the year ending April 30, 1998, was 16%. Some countries experienced high reductions, such as Indonesia with a decrease of 65% and South Korea with a decrease of 57%. Singapore was relatively buffered, with a reduction of only 6% for the same period (Singapore's cost for this basket of telecom services was US$2,657, lower than the Asian average of US$3,685).[19]

Analysts believe, moreover, that mergers and acquisitions will radically restructure the industry in the near future, especially in countries that have awarded too many telecom licenses and whose telecom companies have massive overcapacity. Telecom companies that are cash rich and have limited growth opportunities domestically, such as Hong Kong Telecom and Singapore Telecom, are believed to be scouting for good investment opportunities. One interesting outcome of the economic crisis is that it gives some "breathing space" to the established players since newer and smaller challengers are finding it much harder to realize their expansion plans.[20]

Large telecom companies such as British Telecom (BT) are investing heavily in the Asian region. In the six months leading up to April 1999, BT has invested a total of around S$1.8 billion to acquire various stakes in the region.[21] These ventures have immediately made it one of the major players on the continent, one of very few firms with multicountry operations. BT's longer term goal is to invest as much in Asia as it has in Europe; current investments in Europe are five times as large as those in Asia. According to the CEO of BT Worldwide,

> There's no question that over the long term, Asia has to be the engine for growth in telecoms worldwide. At the moment, Asia probably accounts for 22% of the total market . . . Within 10 years, most of the projections say Asia will be 60% of the market.[22]

The Asian competitive climate in telecommunications differs from the global climate in some respects. For example, major investments are needed in many Asian countries such as China and India, as their telecommunications infrastructure is relatively undeveloped, in contrast with Western Europe, which has a mature infrastructure. For example, China has in recent years been adding as many new telephone lines *each year* as are available in the whole of Switzerland. However, service availability and quality in many parts of Asia lag significantly behind those of developed countries. Key characteristics of and trends in Asian telecommunications are shown in **Exhibit 2**.[23]

While the characteristics and trends described in **Exhibit 2** apply to many Asian countries, companies such as Singapore Telecom and Hong Kong Telecom operate under very different conditions, illustrating the contrast between national competitive environments within Asia. With regard to industry characteristics for example, Singapore has high teledensity, high quality fixed-line services, higher demand for specialized features, lower vulnerability to credit risks, and falling tariffs. Hong Kong, while similar to Singapore in many of these characteris-

Exhibit 2
Characteristics and Trends in Asian Telecommunications

Characteristics
- Extremely low teledensity
- Lower quality and availability of fixed-line services
- Higher concentration of residential users
- Less demand for specialized features
- Higher vulnerability to credit risks
- Highly regulated tariffs
- Relatively limited competition among service providers

Trends
- Strong emphasis on telecommunications infrastructure development by most governments
- Strong growth of fixed line and mobile telecommunications networks
- Acceleration of deregulation and privatization
- Increased competition from entry of Western telecommunications firms
- Concession/licensing periods of 15–25 years utilizing the Build-Transfer-Operate model or a variation thereof
- Strong demand for debt and equity capital to finance expansion
- Industry rationalization through mergers and acquisitions
- Upgrading of telecommunications technology, with significant pricing impact

Exhibit 3

Penetration Rates in Singapore and Developed Countries (%)

	Singapore (Sept. 1999)	Developed Countries Average
Fixed lines	57.6	50.0
Mobile phones	41.4	9.7
Paging lines	39.1	15.3

tics, is a highly competitive market with many firms competing in every segment of the industry. **Exhibit 3** shows the penetration rate per 100 people of fixed phone lines, mobile phones, and pagers in Singapore, as well as the average figures for developed countries.[24] A more detailed look at the size and growth of telecommunications in various countries is provided in **Exhibit 4** (figures denote lines per 100 inhabitants).

Exhibit 4

Telecommunications Growth in Selected Countries

	Number of Fixed Lines (2000)			Lines Per 100 People		
	2000F	1995	1990	2000F	1995	1990
Australia	10,870	9,200	7,787	57.2	50.7	45.7
Belgium	11,044	8,850		58.1	49.6	
China	241,884	40,706	6,850	19.3	3.4	0.6
Denmark	3,494	3,123		69.9	60.4	
Hong Kong	4,342	3,278	2,475	72.2	53.0	43.4
India	28,272	11,978	5,074	2.8	1.3	0.6
Indonesia	10,157	3,291	1,066	4.9	1.7	0.6
Japan	68,477	61,106	54,528	53.9	48.8	44.1
South Korea	26,059	18,600	13,276	55.4	41.5	31.0
Malaysia	7,003	3,332	1,588	31.8	16.6	9.0
Norway	2,838	2,392		71.0	55.4	
Philippines	3,257	1,410	610	4.2	2.1	1.0
Singapore	1,938	1,429	1,053	64.6	47.9	39.0
Sweden	6,357	5,967		70.7	68.3	
Thailand	9,154	3,482	1,325	14.1	5.9	2.4
Vietnam	6,095	775	96	7.5	1.1	0.2
United Kingdom	33,770	28,389		57.2	48.9	
United States	198,781	164,624	136,337	72.0	62.6	54.6
Asia	459,954	182,454	109,759	12.7	5.4	3.5
World	1,107,094	692,101	519,203	18.1	12.1	9.9

Note: F means forecasted information.
Source: K. Singh, 1999. Singapore Telecom in Europe. *ASEAN-EU Management Centre* cases series.

Exhibit 5

Penetration Figures in Various Regions in 1998 (%)

	Africa	**Americas**	**Asia**	**Europe**	**Oceania**	**World**
Fixed lines	2.24	32.33	7.34	37.25	40.29	14.26
Mobile phones	0.45	12.09	3.05	13.15	24.87	5.39

The penetration rates of fixed and cellular lines in Asia as a whole, however, are considerably lower than for other continents (other than Africa) and for the world as a whole (see **Exhibit 5**; figures denote lines per 100 inhabitants).[25] The lower penetration rates suggest high potential for growth, particularly when economic growth resumes after the economic crisis of the late 1990s.

Some industry observers believe that mobile phone penetration rates in developed markets and in some high growth developing countries could reach as high as 70% in the near term. This growth will be fueled, it is thought, by new third generation phones and technologies that will be capable of linking to the Internet, thus providing a whole range of additional information and video services.[26] Even more conservative observers estimate that cellular penetration in Singapore could reach 50% by 2001.[27]

Singapore's domestic telecom environment is more similar to those of developed countries than to most of Asia in areas such as service quality and penetration levels. Singapore has therefore experienced a higher intensity of global trends such as deregulation and privatization, technological advancement, and increased sophistication of consumers who increasingly demand higher standards of quality and service, as well as a greater choice of telecom providers.

Singapore Telecom's Strategy, Performance, and Local Competitive Context

EARLY DAYS AND PRIVATIZATION

Singapore Telecom traces its roots to the introduction of telephone services in Singapore in 1879, just three years after Alexander Graham Bell's invention. The amalgamation of many private and government service providers over the following decades ultimately resulted in a single organization providing telephone and postal services in Singapore. After many permutations in its administrative structure and product portfolio, Singapore Telecom in 1972 became the monopoly government-owned postal and telecommunications services provider. Following a global trend, the government announced plans in 1986 to privatize Singapore Telecom.

Privatization is often carried out to raise private capital for infrastructural development, to ease the fiscal burden of the state, to improve the quality of service, and to reduce prices for consumers.[28] In Singapore's case, however, these traditional objectives of privatization were not the primary motivating factors, as Singapore Telecom has been performing to world standards even without privatization. Instead, the privatization of Singapore Telecom was part of a wider effort aimed at reducing the state's involvement in business.[29] The main aims were to increase Singapore Telecom's flexibility, to prepare it for the challenges of global competition and technological advancements,[30] and to stimulate the development of the Singapore stock market, which lacked depth and scope.[31]

However, as a small country that lacks natural resources and that has a strategic interest in ensuring the development and control of its telecommunications sector, the government endorsed only limited privatization. This would allow it to retain control of the telecommunications infrastructure[32] while achieving the broader objectives. An additional advantage would be control over the potentially negative social implications from the uncontrolled flow of information into Singapore. Consequently, despite privatization, the government continues to own about 80% of Singapore Telecom.[33]

SINGAPORE TELECOM'S STRATEGY

The main elements of Singapore Telecom's strategy have been a focus on the achievement of short- and medium-term profitability, pursuit of globally competitive service and efficiency standards, high investments in proven technologies, and the establishment of a worldclass telecom infrastructure. More recently, Singapore Telecom has initiated foreign investments in several countries, has engaged in strategic alliances in order to gain market entry and acquire technological skills, and has undertaken diversification into IT and value-added services in order to sustain its growth and profitability levels.[34]

According to Singapore Telecom's Chairman, in the area of e-commerce Singapore Telecom "intends to exploit synergies and capabilities to offer total solutions."[35] Singapore Telecom Mobile, SingNet, and Singapore Post are major partners in the recently formed Asia Mobile Electronic Services alliance aiming to provide various cross-border mobile electronic services through mobile phones. These services include mobile banking, electronic bill payment, electronic ticketing, secure postal services, e-mail, and information access. According to Singapore Telecom's CEO, "This is truly a convergence between e-commerce, Internet, and mobile services."[36] New services initiated over the last five years, such as maintenance of cable chips and ownership of Singapore Telecom's own satellite, contribute to about 12–15% of revenues (around $700 million).[37]

Some investors believe that the addition of Internet services will be an important growth platform for Singapore Telecom. According to the managing director of Bear Sterns Singapore, "You've got the prospect that Singapore Telecom will start to be looked at by investors not as a rusty telecom company but an Internet stock."[38]

Singapore Telecom's internationalization strategy began in the late 1980s. This effort was driven by several trends, including the increasing maturity of the small Singapore market, the prospective entry of competitors into Singapore Telecom's previously closed domestic market, the globalization of business and telecommunications, the emergence of major opportunities globally, and the need to find productive uses for Singapore Telecom's large cash reserves. By June 1999, Singapore Telecom had invested $2.3 billion in 55 overseas ventures and operations in 19 countries.[39] Though initial efforts were in Asian countries such as Thailand, Vietnam, and Sri Lanka, the focus of international efforts quickly switched to Europe. Most investments were made in cable television and mobile communications services in England and Western Europe. With few exceptions these were not profitable and Singapore Telecom has so far been unable to achieve its target of drawing 15 to 20% of total sales from its foreign ventures.[40] As a consequence, Singapore Telecom disposed of all of its significant investments in Europe, most of these less than five years after the initial investments, unusual in an industry with fairly long gestation periods. Many observers viewed these ventures as expensive lessons for Singapore Telecom, which taught it that success in the protected domestic market did not necessarily prepare it for success in distant and competitive markets against large and technologically sophisticated firms. Results have been improving, however, and in financial year 1999, overseas investments contributed 11% of pre-tax profits at S$292 million. Singapore Telecom is on track to achieve its target of 20% foreign sales by 2005.

More recently, Singapore Telecom has refocused its overseas investments on Asia. Significant investments include S$55.6 million in AAPT of Australia, which provides switched and leased-line communications services; S$47.1 million in PT Bukaka Singapore Telecom International in Indonesia, which operates fixed public switch telephone services; S$155.7 million in Globe Telecom in the Philippines, which provides mobile phone, international, and fixed-line services; S\$36.9 million in Shinawatra Datacom and Shinawatra Paging, which provide data communication and paging services; and S\$551 million in Advanced Info Services of Thailand, a cellular phone operator.[41] In November 1999, Singapore Telecom and KDD, Japan's largest international telecommunications operator established an equity joint venture to integrate their services. However, it also pulled back from some regional ventures, as it became clear that these were too minor to significantly impact Singapore Telecom's profitability.

Faced with competition from foreign callback services, Singapore Telecom has continually reviewed and reduced its international direct dialing rates in order to retain globally competitive standards and continuously introduced newer and cheaper pricing packages. The average international call charge declined by 42% between 1993 and 1998.[42] Several new value-added services for private and business users were also introduced to improve the quality of services, to provide new streams of revenue, and to meet customer demands. Yet the challenges ahead probably dwarf those that Singapore Telecom has faced to date:

> With the rapid advancement in communications technology, Singapore Telecommunications may have no option but to offer a fixed monthly charge to those who use its service for international calls in two years' time. In five years, it might even have to offer long-distance calls for free . . . bandwidth is growing by leaps and bounds, tripling annually by some estimates. In five years, the amount of information that can be carried through a network could be some 250 times that of the current level. In 2004, a "phone" call could include real-time video of the two (or more) parties conversing. It could also feature pictures and graphics, and at the same time link the many users to the Internet. Faced with a huge bandwidth, it makes no sense for a telco to charge for a specific service.[43]

Perhaps in anticipation of the prospective entry of more competition, Singapore Telecom launched a new effort in 1999 to establish long-term service agreements with its major commercial customers. These efforts locked major customers into multiyear service agreements in Singapore and in the region in return for preferential rates. By this means, Singapore Telecom appears to be preventing defection among its existing customers to new service providers.

The turnover composition of Singapore Telecommunications' various services is shown below in **Exhibit 6**.[44]

Exhibit 7 contains Singapore Telecom Chairman's 1999 statement to shareholders, giving more information on the various aspects of Singapore Telecom's strategy.

Exhibit 6

Group Turnover Composition

	FY 98/99		FY 97/98	
	S\$ million	%	S\$ million	%
International telephone	1,843.7	37.8	2,057.9	41.6
Mobile communications	880.0	18.0	805.9	16.3
Public data and private network	620.6	12.7	561.6	11.4
National telephone	546.6	11.2	539.2	10.9
Postal services	307.9	6.3	311.8	6.3
IT and engineering services	262.3	5.4	157.5	3.2
Sale of equipment	216.8	4.4	275.0	5.6
Directory advertising	125.8	2.6	130.2	2.6
Public messages	37.3	0.8	54.4	1.1
Others	42.5	0.8	48.7	1.0
Total	4,883.5	100.0	4,942.2	100.0

Exhibit 7

Singapore Telecom Chairman's Statement to Shareholders, 1998/1999

Dear Shareholder,

Financial year 1998/1999 has been a difficult and challenging year for the Singapore Telecom Group. We operated in a difficult business environment as a result of the regional economic crisis. We also faced increasing competition both locally and abroad.

Corporate Reorganisation

As the business landscape and market environment change, Singapore Telecom must also evolve to meet the company's and customers' changing needs. To this end, Singapore Telecom reorganized in April 1999 to increase our focus on the people that matter most to us—our customers. Specific customer units have been set up to manage the diverse telecommunications needs of our different customer segments including corporate clients, small and medium sized enterprises, and residential consumers. In addition, the new organisational structure also emphasises new growth areas such as our overseas ventures and new businesses like e-commerce, systems integration, multimedia, and Internet-based services.

Growth

Singapore Telecom has identified e-commerce and Internet-based activities as areas where there are significant growth opportunities. The Singapore Telecom Group of companies is uniquely positioned to offer services throughout the e-commerce value chain, from providing terminals to end users to fulfilling the orders of consumers. For example, Singapore Telecom, Singapore Telecom Mobile, and SingNet provide the infrastructure for e-commerce, NCS can provide the systems integration capabilities, and SingPost can support the physical fulfilment of orders. Singapore Telecom will also take advantage of the growing trend towards the convergence of telecommunications, IT, and media to introduce new services. Our broadband multimedia service, Singapore Telecom Magix, is a good example.

Infrastructure Development

Despite an already extensive domestic and international infrastructure, we continue to invest heavily in infrastructure to ensure that we have sufficient capacity to meet the growing demands of our customers. At the same time, we actively implement the latest technologies to offer innovative services.

For the financial year 1998/1999, our capital expenditure amounted to approximately S$1 billion. In the current year, we expect to spend another S$900 million to build and improve our networks, particularly to support mobile and e-commerce services. For example, Singapore Telecom Mobile is currently conducting a wideband CDMA trial. It will also be introducing various high speed data services (e-ideas) to give our customers the convenience of e-commerce applications such as mobile stock trading, banking, and ticketing services.

To provide our corporate customers with the global connectivity that is essential in today's competitive business environment, we will continue to invest in international network and cable systems. This also ensures that there will always be sufficient capacity to support increasing demand for bandwidth. Singapore Telecom has invested a total of more than US$500 million in digital submarine cable networks. An extensive international infrastructure provides our multinational customers with the redundancy and diversity they require. This is a strategic advantage that new entrants to the market cannot offer.

Overseas Investments

Our overseas investments have done well, contributing 11.2% to our pre-tax profit this year. In fact, the success of our internationalisation efforts has contributed significantly to

Exhibit 7
(*continued*)

our earnings growth this year. Belgacom in Belgium and Globe Telecom in the Philippines are the Group's two most successful overseas investments. We target contributions from our overseas investments to increase to 20% of pre-tax profit by 2005.

It is our strategy to participate actively in the companies in which we invest and to add value through our expertise. Of the S$2.5 billion that we have invested in 19 countries, S$1.3 billion are now in listed companies. Today, the value of these companies is more than double the invested amount.

Besides the financial returns we receive from our overseas projects and ventures, Singapore Telecom also seeks to maximise synergies from its investments. For example, Singapore Telecom Mobile is exploring the feasibility of launching regional mobile products and services jointly with our partners, Advanced Info Service of Thailand and Globe Telecom. Such products and services, which include local SIM cards and preferred roaming, offer significant value to frequent travellers in the region. The three cellular companies are also looking at bulk purchasing of handsets and network equipment to achieve greater savings through economies of scale. Singapore Telecom will continue to look for investment opportunities overseas that will make meaningful contributions to our bottom line.

Looking Forward
Singapore Telecom's businesses are closely linked to economic activities in Singapore and the region. Although the worst seems to be over for the regional economies, the outlook nonetheless remains uncertain. The impact of significant rate cuts implemented in the first quarter of this year will be fully realised in the financial year 1999/2000. However, we expect contributions from our associated companies overseas to continue to improve, which will mitigate the expected weaker operating results.

Singapore Telecom commemorates 120 years of telecommunications services in Singapore this year. We are proud to have contributed to Singapore's success as a telecommunications hub for the region. Our many years of experience and expertise in providing telecommunications services to Singapore homes and businesses will put us in good stead notwithstanding the introduction of competition next year.

We will strive, through innovation and continued customer service improvements, to build on the relationships we have established with our customers so that we can continue to serve them in the years ahead.

Enhancing shareholder value is one of Singapore Telecom's key objectives. To achieve this, we intend to create a more efficient capital structure through various measures, including a share buyback programme, if and when appropriate, and the payment of special dividends. Our aim is to work towards a debt to equity ratio of 20 to 30%. This will, however, not inhibit the Group's ability to continue with its expansion plans and overseas investments.

I would like to thank my fellow Directors of the Singapore Telecom Board for their contributions to the success and development of the Group. I also thank the Management, Union, and Staff of the Group. Through their unstinting efforts, Singapore Telecom has been able to perform well given the difficult circumstances. With their continued support and dedication, Singapore Telecom will be more than able to meet the demands of the coming year.

KOH BOON HWEE
Chairman

SINGAPORE TELECOM'S STRUCTURE

Singapore Telecom's subsidiaries include National Computer Systems, Singapore Aeradio, Singapore Post, Singapore Telecom International, Singapore Telecom Investments, Singapore Telecom Mobile, Singapore Telecom Paging, Singapore Telecom Yellow Pages Pte Ltd, and Telecom Equipment. Singapore Telecom provides fixed-line, mobile, Internet and satellite services, as well as systems integration through its wholly owned subsidiary National Computer Systems, and aspires to be "a total service provider with a range that covers the entire spectrum of the telecom business."[45]

Singapore Telecom's organizational structure up to early 1999 involved the grouping of businesses into international, domestic mobile, and domestic fixed-line businesses. In March 1999, Singapore Telecom announced a major restructuring, whose primary aim was to focus on growth areas such as overseas ventures and new business areas such as e-commerce, systems integration, multimedia, and Internet-based services.[46]

The restructuring involves the creation of three new units: the consumer business unit, covering residential customers and small and medium-sized enterprises; the corporate business unit dealing with corporate accounts; and the global business unit concerned with Singapore Telecom's overseas investments. A new Chief Operating Officer (COO) position and three customer units under the COO were also created. This new post is intended to relieve the Chief Executive Officer from running day-to-day operations and allow him to focus on growth areas such as overseas ventures and new business areas such as e-commerce, systems integration, multimedia, and Internet-based services.

THE ADVENT OF COMPETITION

Despite Singapore Telecom's success in building Singapore's telecommunications infrastructure, the government embarked on a program of gradually introducing competition. This decision reflected global trends of deregulation and increased competition and the government's belief that competitive pressures would prepare Singapore Telecom for increased international competition and expansion, thus ensuring the competitiveness of Singapore's telecommunications infrastructure and services.[47] Competition was introduced in phases to allow Singapore Telecom to prepare.

The first direct competitor to Singapore Telecom, MobileOne, commenced mobile phone services in April 1997. MobileOne (M1) is a consortium of two foreign firms (Cable & Wireless of UK and its partially owned subsidiary HongKong Telecoms) and two local firms (Singapore's sole newspaper publisher SPH and the diversified, government-linked Keppel Corporation). MobileOne's entry had the usual dramatic results associated with the introduction of competition in a previously protected market: MobileOne captured significant market share, prices declined by between 50 and 70% within a year, the range and quality of services improved significantly, and the market expanded rapidly. In the process, the mobile phone penetration rate rose from 14% at the start of 1997 to 33% by the end of 1998. According to analysts,

> M1's success—it grabbed 32% of the market share within two years, a phenomenal achievement by world standards—was largely due to its marketing savvy, attention to customer service, and network quality.[48]

As an example of the price wars that erupted with the entry of MobileOne, in January 1999, Singapore Telecom was forced to cut its rates twice in one day, by a total of 18%, when MobileOne responded to its first rate cut. In the next few days Singapore Telecom also reduced some monthly subscriptions by 35 to 40%.[49] According to the *Business Times*, it is a "monumental task" to compare which package would offer the best value, given that Singapore Telecom and MobileOne have different peak hours and denominate free talk time differently, in dollars or in minutes. After a comparison of the competitive packages, it concluded that:[50]

> Singapore Telecom is the bigger culprit in trying to 'confuse' consumers. Besides different charges for the different times of the day, it also has separate rates for incoming and outgoing calls.

The two competitors in the mobile market constantly monitor each others' performance and make countermoves. In January 1999, for example, about 90% of the 15,000 new mobile phone subscribers signed on with M1.[51] Singapore Telecom immediately carried out a promotion and announced that it had attracted more than 50% of new mobile subscribers for February as a result of this promotion. Advertising in the telecom industry is intense and growing in value. In financial year 1996 it was S$27.4 million, which rose sharply in 1997 to S$70 million with the entry of MobileOne. In 1998 advertising spending rose to S$76.4 million, and it is expected to surpass S$100 million in financial year 1999, with the entry of StarHub, which announced:

> StarHub's advertising and promotion budget will be significant—in the double-digit, multi-million-dollar region—to enable us to create a strong presence in the marketplace.[52]

Although Singapore's mobile market may appear saturated, given global levels of mobile phone penetration, industry analysts forecast that the penetration may rise to about 50 to 60% in the short run. It is also forecasted that the Asia-Pacific region's number of mobile subscribers would nearly treble by 2003, from 109 million to 296 million, while the average monthly revenue per subscriber would decline from US$41 to US$29. This will lead to an increase in annual mobile subscriber revenue from US$69.4 billion to US$104 billion.[53] In the medium term, mobile phone penetration rates are forecasted to exceed fixed-line rates. In the longer term, mobile communications will become a part of many types of home and office devices, and the industry will lose its identity as a distinct industry primarily offering voice telecommunications services.

Continuing with its plan for introducing competition, the government in 1998 issued two more licenses for mobile phone services and one for fixed telephone services to start operations in April 2000. All license winners were consortia that comprised at least one government-linked corporation. The primary factor driving this liberalization was the recognition that competition would bring the same positive benefits to the fixed-line market as it did in the mobile phone market. The failure to do this would, on the other hand, handicap the country with higher telecommunications costs and older technology than in competitor economies with more effective telecommunications industries.

SINGAPORE TELECOM'S PERFORMANCE

Singapore Telecom's performance in the 1990s has been spectacular, with profitability being unmatched in Singapore, and arguably, in much of the global telecom industry. Operating returns are high enough to replace net fixed assets in less than two years, while shareholders' funds can be repaid with about three years' profits. **Exhibit 8** shows Singapore Telecom's financial summary for the period 1990–1999. Despite intensifying competition and falling international call rates, Singapore Telecom has continued to deliver in terms of service quality and financial returns.

The quality of Singapore's telecommunications infrastructure ranked first in a survey of 10 Southeast Asian countries in 1997.[54] Its telecom infrastructure in particular has also ranked first in the Asia-Pacific Telecommunications Index 1999, compiled by the National University of Singapore's Centre for Telemedia Studies. However, Singapore's telecom infrastructure scored poorly in the "choice" and "regulation" subindex of this survey, where it was perceived as offering limited choice of service providers and having a regulator that was not responsive

Exhibit 8

Singapore Telecom's Financial Performance

	1999	1998	1997	1996	1995	1994	1993	1992	1991	1990
Turnover	4,883.5	4,942.2	4,240.9	3,999.0	3,516.0	3,190.8	2,759.3	2,479.7	2,221.7	1,998.6
Operating expenses	2,910.4	2,738.1	2,337.9	2,029.6	1,791.2	1,677.1	1,526.6	1,390.8	1,351.2	1,266.5
Operating profit	1,973.1	2,204.1	2,083.0	1,969.4	1,724.8	1,513.7	1,232.7	1,088.9	870.5	732.1
Profits and losses of associated firms	291.7	(154.0)	47.6	(87.8)	(38.7)	(15.6)	(0.9)	3.3	(1.8)	(0.7)
Restructuring costs	–									
Net profit	1,955.4	1,886.1	1,687.5	1,501.4	1,333.0	1,205.8	1,005.3	‡	‡	‡
Fixed assets	4,549.1	4,005.3	3,535.0	3,341.1	3,100.3	2,908	2,559.3	2,449.5	1,684.5	1,498.4
Cash and bank deposits	‡	4,112.0	3,987.5†	1,481.4	2,153.2	1,106.1	1,621.3	‡	‡	‡
Net current assets	4,438.7	3,998.6	2,970.9	441.4	602.5	192.0	(410.7)*	3,351.7	3,161.1	2,634.9
Noncurrent liabilities	503.6	418	255.7	468.4	396.0	522.4	190.9	31.2	32.2	30.8
Shareholders' funds	7,967.9	6,873.2	5,558.1	4,188.5	4,123.1	3,297.1	2,450.0	6,273.3	5,266.1	4,374.0
Turnover growth (%)	-1.2	16.5	6.0	13.7	10.2	15.6	11.2	11.6	11.1	–
Net profit growth (%)	3.7	11.8	12.4	12.6	10.5	19.9	–	‡	‡	‡
Earnings per share (¢)	12.82	12.37	11.07	9.85	8.74	7.91	6.59	‡	‡	‡
Net tangible asset per share (¢)	52.25	45.07	36.45	27.47	27.04	21.62	16.02	‡	‡	‡
Dividends (¢)	5.5	5.0	4.5	4.0	3.5	3.0	5.2	‡	‡	‡
Return on shareholders funds (%)	26.4	30.3	34.6	36.1	35.9	32.8	27.4	‡	‡	‡
Return on total assets (%)	15.1	17.5	20.3	22.3	22.5	23.2	22.2	‡	‡	‡
Operating return on turnover (%)	40.4	44.6	47.1	49.2	49.1	47.4	44.7	43.9	39.2	36.6
Operating return on net fixed assets (%)	‡	58.5	60.6	61.1	57.4	55.4	50.2	52.7	54.7	48.6
Turnover per employee ($,000)	‡	434.6	414.1	359.5	316.5	292.1	255.3	230.9	207.0	177.9

*Singapore Telecom transferred large funds back to the government prior to its public listing.
†Includes a $1.5 billion cash compensation from the government for bringing forward the end of Singapore Telecom's exclusive license by seven years.
‡Figures are not available or not comparable due to its then status as a government department.

Source: Singapore Telecom annual reports 1990–1998.

or transparent.[55] Singapore Telecom was also ranked 7th out of 26 international carriers in a 1999 Data Communications survey that rated telecom providers on value, quality reliability, speed of repairs, billing, and general responsiveness for frame relay and leased-line services.[56]

In terms of absolute profit figures, Singapore Telecom remains the most profitable Singapore firm, with a profit of S$1.88 billion for financial year 1998 and S$1.95 billion for 1999.[57] Although the company managed to go through the worst of the Asian crisis relatively unscathed in 1988, the outlook appears gloomy. According to Singapore Telecom's Chairman, growth earnings were flat.[58] Group revenue in 1999 fell by 1.2%, operating profits fell by 10.5%, and operating expenses increased by 6% from 1998. Singapore Telecom's IDD (international direct dialing) revenue, its largest revenue contributor, fell by 10.4% in 1999, largely due to lower call rates, which fell by 13%. Singapore Telecom's growth rate in recent years has become relatively unstable (see **Exhibit 8**).

What Does the Future Hold?

The competitive environment will become more intense with the entry of StarHub in April 2000. StarHub aims to be "the first infocommunications company in Asia-Pacific to offer total convergence of fixed and mobile communications on a single, integrated platform. This means your home, office, and mobile phones can all be linked, so you can be reached anywhere with just one number."[59]

The relative contribution of IDD revenues has been declining over the years, from 50% at the time of Singapore Telecom's listing in 1993, to 38% in financial year 1999.[60] StarHub's entry is expected to spell even steeper decline as market share is inevitably lost to the new competitor. Singapore Telecom expects to lose between 20 and 40% of the fixed-line and IDD markets to StarHub within the next two to three years.[61] According to Singapore Telecom's Vice-President for Corporate Products, the decrease in IDD's revenue contribution will depend on StarHub's price aggressiveness, the growth of new revenue streams, and new technological advancements and industry trends.[62] Corporate customers account for about 80% of Singapore Telecom's S$5 billion revenue; StarHub's CEO believes that once StarHub enters the market in April 2000, it can attract a significant amount of business from these customers:

> Corporate customers were quite keen to talk to us . . . and we haven't come across a locked door yet . . . You hear things like why can't I get this particular kind of service in Singapore. I can get that in the U.S., why does it cost me so much, why does it take two months to get this installed.[63] . . . our strength is that Singapore Telecom can't imagine where we're coming from.[64]

Singapore Telecom stresses that it will match or surpass all offers StarHub makes when it begins operations:

> We will never let our competitor get the better of us.[65]
> . . . firstly, we want to ensure that we are price-competitive, that we offer value-for-money. We also need to deliver appropriate levels of customer service. There we have been continuously trying to improve the service delivery . . . The other area is, we will continuously look for new products and services . . . I think there is always a problem that you are an incumbent, you are large and people feel that therefore they favor the underdog.[66]

According to the Minister for Communications, Mah Bow Tan, the Telecommunications Authority of Singapore will continue to ensure high service standards and a sustainable competitive environment; but when the playing field is more even, it will adopt a more relaxed regulatory attitude. They will also ensure that customers are free to switch between providers and that there will be no penalty involved in the switch.[67] In the past, charges for switching have been finely balanced to avoid penalizing or encouraging switching between providers.[68]

The newly appointed head of Singapore Telecom Mobile, however, fears that public sympathy is not with Singapore Telecom, as it was a former monopoly in the mobile market and has a current monopoly in the fixed-line market until April 2000. Consumer response to new offerings by MobileOne since April 1997 demonstrated that consumers were glad to have a choice of mobile providers and may have felt that prices were maintained at an artificially high level before the opening of the market to competition:[69]

> When I took the job, I really felt the public sympathy was not with us, it was with the newcomer. People will not be very forgiving if Singapore Telecom makes a mistake . . . We need to go back to tell the customers that first of all, we are sorry for all the things that we've done to you in the past . . . .

A recent event in which SingNet (a Singapore Telecom subsidiary) subscribers' computers were secretly scanned suggests that improvements are needed. According to the Asian *Wall Street Journal*:

> At the request of an Internet service provider, Singapore's internal-security agency secretly scanned 200,000 computers last month to trace a virus that allows hackers to steal computer passwords and credit-card numbers. The action came to light last week only after a law student who had installed antihacking software filed a police report, alleging that her computer had been entered into by the Ministry of Home Affairs on 10 different occasions in mid-April. The revelation has caused such a controversy in the island-state that this week the Internet service provider involved, SingNet, issued a public apology headed, "We should have informed you first." SingNet insisted that the scanning was only for the purpose of identifying computers susceptible to hackers, and that no computers were actually entered to access confidential information . . . But SingNet's reassurance did little to calm computer users in Singapore . . . Online discussion groups have been filled with protests charging invasion of privacy and expressing suspicions of hidden motives for the intrusion.[70]

In March Singapore Telecom said that it was searching for the identity of an Internet user who claimed in a newsgroup posting that Singapore Telecom Mobile's users had not benefited from the company's recent price cuts, and threatened to sue him.[71] Singapore Telecom's stern reaction to this Internet user's allegedly libelous comments about its packages is a telling indication of the intense rivalry in this industry sector.

The outlook for the near term is seen to be negative by Singapore Telecom. Downward trends are expected to continue in its "key business drivers," international telephone traffic, mobile subscribers, and business lines. Singapore Telecom intends to implement stricter cost control measures to protect its bottom line.[72] Cost cutting measures included reducing the salaries of senior managers by 10% and management flying economy instead of business class. According to the Singapore Telecom Group Director of Human Resources:

> The wage cuts will help SingTel to better manage its costs in the current economic slowdown . . . Being leaders in the company, we must show our staff that we are willing to live through good and bad times with them together . . . .[73]

In the most recent announcement of Singapore Telecom's planned competitive strategy, Singapore Telecom's Chairman explained how the company would focus on the competition and on growth:

> SingTel has consistently regarded competition as a regional challenge . . . . In the Asia Pacific, we continue to outperform our competitors . . . . Besides getting ready for the competition, our other focus is to develop our growth strategy. We have a four-pronged approach. Firstly, we will take advantage of the business opportunities that come with the convergence of telecommunications, IT, and media. Our broadband multimedia service, Singapore Telecom Magix, is a good example of a "convergent service." Secondly, we will seek new business opportunities as they emerge and synergize them with our existing services and operations. Examples of these include

e-commerce and Internet hubbing. Thirdly, we will pursue global and regional expansion through investments overseas. Finally, we will also take advantage of our existing assets, such as our billing systems, telecom networks, and real estate, to generate new revenues through services such as facility management and billing services.[74]

Notes

1. *Annual Report 1998/99,* Chairman's statement.
2. H. L. Teh, "Singapore Telecom Warning Even as Its Profits Rise 3.7%," *Business Times* (June 5, 1999).
3. Telecommunications Authority of Singapore, *1998/1999 Annual Report* (1999).
4. S. G. Lim, "Sustaining Excellence in Government: The Singapore Experience," *Public Administration and Development* 17 (1997), pp. 167–174.
5. R. S. Sisodia, "Singapore Invests in the Nation-Corporation," *Harvard Business Review* (May–June, 1992), pp. 5–11.
6. K. Singh, 1995.
7. Ministry of Trade and Industry, *Economic Survey of Singapore, 1998* (Singapore: SNP Publishers, 1999).
8. S. Durchslag, T. Puri, and A. Rao, "The Promise of Infrastructure Privatisation," *McKinsey Quarterly* 1 (1994), pp. 3–19.
9. C. I. Knoop, L. M. Applegate, B. S. Neo, and J. L. King, "Singapore Unlimited: Building the National Information Infrastructure," *Harvard Business School Case 9-196-012* (1996).
10. *Financial Times* (September 30, 1999).
11. International Telecommunications Union <www.itu.int>.
12. International Telecommunications Union <www.itu.int>.
13. "Managing Telecoms: Old Champions, New Contenders," *The Economist* (October 11, 1997).
14. "Virtual Private Network Posed for Big Take-off Here," *The Business Times* (April 12, 1999).
15. "Telecommunications: The Death of Distance," *The Economist* (September 30, 1995).
16. "Asian Telecommunications," *Asian Wall Street Journal* (June 2, 1998).
17. *BT World Communications Report 1998/9.*
18. *Financial Times* (September 30, 1999).
19. *Asian Wall Street Journal* (1998).
20. *Asian Wall Street Journal* (1998).
21. C. Ong, "Another British Invasion of Asia," *Business Times* (April 7, 1999).
22. "British Tel Still Hungry for More Asian Acquisitions," *Business Times* (March 11, 1999).
23. Bank of America, *Guide to Telecommunications in Asia* (Hong Kong: Euromoney Publications, 1996) pp. 1–6.
24. Telecommunications Authority of Singapore <www.tas.gov.sg>.
25. International Telecommunications Union <www.itu.int> (data dated October 4, 1999).
26. "Mobile Phone Penetration Seen Hitting 70%," *Business Times* (February 13–14, 1999).
27. C. Ong, "Corporate Customers Willing to Give Business to Us: StarHub Chief," *Business Times* (April 9, 1999).
28. L. Heracleous, "Privatisation: Global Trends and Implications of the Singapore Experience," *Research Paper Series,* Faculty of Business Administration, National University of Singapore, RPS #98–45 (1998).
29. L. Low, "Privatisation in Singapore: The Big Push," paper for Symposium on Privatisation organised by the Asian Productivity Organisation, Bangkok, July 4–6; C. H. Tan, "Singapore Telecom: From Public to Private Sector," *International Journal of Public Sector Management* 5, 4 (1995), pp. 4–14.
30. K. Singh, 1995.
31. Kuo, Low, and Toh, 1989; L. Low, 1995; M. H. Toh and L. Low, "Towards Greater Competition in Singapore's Telecommunications," *Telecommunications Policy* (August, 1990), pp. 303–314; M. H. Toh and L. Low, "Privatisation of Telecommunications Services in Singapore," in J. Pelkmans and N. Wagner (eds.), *Privatisation and Deregulation in ASEAN and EC: Making Markets More Effective* (1990), pp. 82–93.
32. E. C. Y. Kuo, L. Low, and M. H. Toh, "The Singapore Telecommunications Sector and Issues Affecting Its Competitive Position in the Pacific Region," *Colombia Journal of World Business* (Spring, 1989), pp. 59–71.
33. K. Singh, "Guided Competition in Singapore's Telecommunications Industry," presented at 4th Annual Conference of the Consortium for Research on Telecommunications Policy and Strategy, University of Michigan, Ann Arbor (June 1998).
34. K. Singh, 1995.
35. "Group Wants Bigger Role in E-Commerce," *Business Times* (June 5, 1999).
36. "E-Commerce, Internet and Mobile Services Coverage," *Keylines* (June 7, 1999).
37. T. Tan, "Singapore Telecom Reaps $700m from New Services," *Straits Times* (April 12, 1999).
38. "Singapore Telecom Seen Growing on Internet, Asian Expansion," *Business Times* (April 28, 1999).
39. "Singapore Telecom's Overseas Earnings on the Rise," *Business Times* (June 5, 1999) <www.Singtel.com>.
40. K. Singh, 1998; K. Singh, "Singapore Telecom in Europe," *ASEAN-EU Management Centre Cases Series,* 1999.
41. T. Tan, "Singapore Telecom to Pay $551m for Thai Stake," *Business Times* (January 7, 1999).
42. K. Singh, 1998.
43. H. S. Lee, "Singapore Telecom's Cash Cow Could Turn into a Free Service," *Business Times* (September 30, 1999).
44. Singapore Telecom Annual Report, 1998/99.
45. "Singapore Telecom's Competitive Strategy," *Keylines* (May 8–9, 1999).
46. H. L. Teh, "Singapore Telecom Unveils Major Restructuring," *Business Times* (March 12, 1999); T. Tan, "Major Shake-Up at Singapore Telecom," *Straits Times* (March 12, 1999).
47. K. T. Leong, "Lessons of Regulatory Changes for Asian Needs," in Proceedings of Special Session on Effective Transition Through Regulation, World Telecommunications Forum, Singapore (May 1993), pp. 113–116.
48. C. Ong, "Pro-Choice, Pro-Competition," *Business Times* (May 6, 1999).
49. H. L. Teh, "Singapore Telecom Mobile Cuts Rates Twice in a Day to Fend Off M1 Challenge," *Business Times* (January 30–31, 1999); T. Tan, "Singapore Telecom, M1 Slug It Out in Price War," *Straits Times* (January 30, 1999).
50. H. L. Teh, "Packing a Punch: Hi and Low of Handphone Packages," *Business Times* (February 19, 1999).
51. T. Tan, "M1 Gains on Singapore Telecom Mobile," *Business Times* (March 10, 1999).
52. H. L. Teh, "Telcos' Advertising Tab Seen Topping $100m in '99," *Business Times* (April 28, 1999).
53. H. L. Teh, "US$450b to Be Made in Region's Mobile Market," *Business Times* (June 5, 1999).

54. "Singapore Is Tops for Business," *Straits Times* (August 22, 1997).

55. "S'pore Is Tops Again in Telecoms Ranking," *Straits Times* (January 19, 1999).

56. "Singapore Telecom Shines in Telecom Survey," *Straits Times* (May 14, 1999).

57. J. Chia, "Singapore Telecom Takes the Lead with $1.88b Net Profit," *Straits Times* (March 2, 1999).

58. H. L. Teh, "Singapore Telecom Warning Even as Its Profits Rise 3.7%," *Business Times* (June 5, 1999).

59. <www.StarHub.com.sg>

60. W. Choong and T. Tan, "IDD Revenue Drops for the First Time," *Straits Times* (June 5, 1999).

61. "20%–40% Loss in Market Share Expected," *Business Times* (June 5, 1999).

62. T. Tan, "Singapore Telecom to Reap Less from IDD Calls," *Straits Times* (June 14, 1999).

63. C. Ong, "Corporate Customers Willing to Give Business to Us: StarHub Chief," *Business Times* (April 9, 1999).

64. T. Tan, "StarHub Eyes 25% of IDD Market," *Straits Times* (April 9, 1999).

65. T. Tan, "Singapore Telecom to Match Prices," *Straits Times* (April 12, 1999).

66. C. Ong and H. L. Teh, "Standing Above the Fray," *Business Times* (May 6, 1999).

67. "TAS Will 'Step Back' Once Market Opens Up," *Business Times* (February 12, 1999); C. Ong, "New TAS Rule May Spell End of Handphone Subscription Perks," *Business Times* (November 27, 1998).

68. K. Singh, 1998.

69. C. Ong, "Singapore Telecom Mobile Takes Battle to the Competition," *Business Times* (January 11, 1999).

70. S. Sesser, "SingNet Apologizes for Virus Scanning," *Asian Wall Street Journal* (May 7, 1999).

71. T. Tan, "Singapore Telecom Mobile May Sue Net User," *Business Times* (March 22, 1999).

72. <www.SingaporeTelecom.com>

73. T. Tan, "Singapore Telecom's Top Earners Take Extra Pay Cut," *Straits Times* (January 19, 1999).

74. Transcript of comments by Mr. Koh Boon Hwee, Singapore Telecom Chairman, at news conference of June 4, 1999.

case 6

Hewlett-Packard Company in Vietnam

Dr. Geok Theng Lau

In September 1995, John Peter, a Marketing Manager of Hewlett-Packard Asia Pacific (HPAP) was evaluating HPAP's long-term strategic investment options for doing business in Vietnam. HPAP was a subsidiary of the Hewlett-Packard (HP) Company and its headquarters was located in Singapore. Vietnam had recently adopted an open door policy after the United States lifted its embargo on the country in February 1994. The country had a population of over 70 million with a literacy rate of over 90%. Foreign investment in the country had climbed steadily and had reached almost US$12 billion by the end of 1994.

An environmental and market analysis revealed that the information technology (IT) market in Vietnam had potential. However, the market was currently small and market growth was uncertain. Several business units within HP had begun to distribute some HP products in Vietnam. John needed to make a recommendation on whether the HPAP should enter the Vietnam market in a more strategic fashion, that is, to give serious consideration to Vietnam as a major market for HP. If so, what form should the market entry take and how should it be done?

The Country of Vietnam and Its Business Environment

Vietnam is situated in the east of the Indochina Peninsula with a total land area of 330,363 square kilometers (see **Exhibit 1**). It shares borders with China in the north, Laos in the west, and Cambodia in the southwest. The coastline in the east stretches 3,400 km. The country has 56 provinces. Its major cities included the capital city of Hanoi, Ho Chi Minh City (formerly Saigon), and the port cities of Haiphong and Danang. The official language is Vietnamese.

This case was prepared by Dr. Geok Theng Lau. This case was written as a basis for class discussion rather than to illustrate effective or ineffective handling of an administrative situation. Names of individuals were disguised. The author wishes to acknowledge the cooperation of Hewlett-Packard Asia Pacific Limited in the writing of this case and especially to thank Mr. Dennis Khoo, who provided the main structure and the information for this case. The involvement and advice of Dr. A. N. Hakam in this case development project is also recognized. This case was edited for SMB-9th Edition. All other rights reserved jointly to the author and the North American Case Research Association (NACRA). This case appeared in *Case Research Journal*, Summer, 2000, pp. 115–138. Copyright © 2000 by *Case Research Journal* and Geok Theng Lau. Reprinted by permission of author.

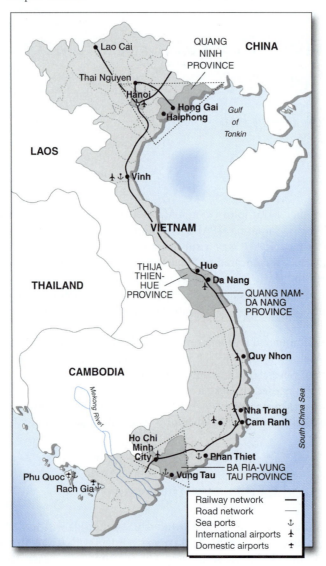

HISTORY

For over a thousand years, from 111 B.C. to 939 A.D., Vietnam was governed as a Chinese province, Giao Chia. After it liberated itself, Vietnam frequently had to resist Chinese invasions. The country remained free from foreign control until 1885 when France brought all of Vietnam under its rule. After the Japanese surrender in August 1945, Ho Chi Minh, founder of the Vietminh, proclaimed the independence of the Provisional Democratic Republic of Vietnam.

France's refusal to give up its colony led to a protracted war. China and the Soviet Union backed the Vietminh, while the United States backed the French. In subsequent years, the United States-backed Ngo Dinh Diem took power in the South. A united front organization called the National Front for the Liberation of South Vietnam was formed to oppose Diem.

The conflict escalated and turned into an American war, with the United States deploying 500,000 troops in Vietnam by 1968. The Southern forces collapsed after the U.S. withdrawal and on April 30, 1975, the communists entered Saigon and Vietnam's 30-year war of independence was over.

After the fall of Saigon, the North proceeded to reunify the country. Vietnam subsequently found itself treated with suspicion and, after its invasion of Cambodia in late 1978, was isolated by the international community. After the final withdrawal of Vietnamese troops from Cambodia in late 1989, the process of normalization of economic ties with ASEAN (Association of South East Asian Nations), Western Europe, Northeast Asia, Australia, and New Zealand began to gather pace. In late 1991, after the Paris agreement on Cambodia, diplomatic and economic relations with many countries, including China, were fully normalized.

POLITICAL ENVIRONMENT

The supreme organ of state power in Vietnam was the National Assembly, which performed functions such as promulgation of laws; ratification of the annual and long-term plans for economic and social development; budget planning; election of top officials; and selection of the cabinet members. The Government was the executive body responsible for the enforcement of the laws of the country issued by the National Assembly.

Until the mid-to-late 1980s, the leadership of the Vietnamese Communist Party (VCP) held orthodox Marxist-Leninist beliefs, which viewed the world as a mortal struggle between imperialist and revolutionary camps. In the late 1980s to early 1990s, due partly to the end of the Cold War, the Vietnamese Political Bureau acknowledged the need for Vietnam to participate actively in the global capitalist economy, since the socialist organization for economic cooperation (COMECON) was becoming less relevant. The leadership sought to achieve a breakthrough in trade with the capitalist countries and an expansion of external cooperation, including taking out loans for capital investment and promoting joint venture projects.

Elements of the old world view, however, continued to coexist with the new one. The aging leadership continued to adopt an autocratic political system, and there was conflict between a closed political system and the economy opening up. This resulted in continuing debates and shifts in emphasis from struggle against imperialism to economic interdependence.

THE PEOPLE AND WORKFORCE

The population of Vietnam was approximately 71 million people, 70% of them under 35 years old. The annual population growth was 2.2%. The population was basically rural and was concentrated in the two main rice-growing deltas: the Red River in the north and the Mekong in the south. The river delta population was almost entirely ethnic Vietnamese (Kinh), who made up 87% of the total population. The minority groups (including Khmer, Cham, Muong, and Thai peoples), whose cultures and languages were quite distinct from those of the Kinh Vietnamese, were found in the upland areas. The overseas Chinese community, which was largely concentrated in the south, was depleted by the decision of many to leave the country, often as "boat people." This community had partly recouped its position in the economy since the late 1980s, largely on the strength of its links with Hong Kong and Taiwan.

Vietnam was underurbanized in comparison with many other developing countries in Southeast Asia. The largest city was Ho Chi Minh (Saigon) with a population of well over four million. The capital, Hanoi, had a registered population of 3.1 million. The level of primary education was comparatively high. The population, especially in the north, was basically literate, with a literacy rate of over 90%. The average wages in Vietnam and some neighboring countries are shown in **Exhibit 2**.

Exhibit 2

Monthly Minimum Wage Rates of Selected Countries in Asia

Country	Monthly Wage Rates (US$)
China	50
Hong Kong	525
Indonesia	80
Malaysia	290
Philippines	95
Singapore	600
Taiwan	650
Thailand	165
Vietnam	35

Source: World Bank, Trends in Developing Countries.

ECONOMIC ENVIRONMENT

Vietnam was the largest of the three Indo-Chinese nations, accounting for about 44% of total land area and 75% of the combined population of the region. The country was endowed with oil reserves and extensive mineral resources. It was an agro-based economy with the agricultural sector absorbing 70% of the workforce (numbering about 32 million people) and contributing some 40% to the GNP and nearly 40% to total exports. Since 1989, Vietnam had become an important rice exporter and was the world's third largest rice exporter, after Thailand and the United States.

Light industries, including textiles, garments, footwear, paper, food processing, electrical, and electronics, though scattered throughout the country, were more concentrated in the south. Heavy industries, including iron and steel, power generation, cement, mining, chemicals, fertilizers, and machine tools were mainly concentrated in the north. The number of industrial establishments in Vietnam is shown in **Exhibit 3**.

In the past, Vietnam relied mainly on the former Soviet Union and Eastern European countries for trade and economic cooperation and assistance. All of its foreign aid and one-half of its export markets vanished with the collapse of the Eastern bloc in 1991. The country, however, survived this crisis and economic growth rebounded to an official 8.3% in 1992 after a mild slowdown to around 5% in 1990. Inflation eased from about 700% in 1986 to 17.5% in 1992. Foreign investment approvals rose by 73% in 1992 and accounted for 26.2% of total investments. Exports rose by 19% to US$2.5 billion, while imports climbed by 9% during the same year. For the first time in several decades, Vietnam was estimated to have registered a trade and current account surplus in 1992. **Exhibit 4** shows some key economic indicators for Vietnam from 1991 to 1994.

The government encouraged greater exports and imports. Exports were encouraged and only a few items were subject to export duty, which had been kept low. The import of capital goods and materials for domestic production was encouraged, while the import of consumer goods, which could be produced at home or were considered luxurious, were discouraged. The list of items subjected to export and import prohibition or quota had been substantially cut down. Greater autonomy had been given to companies and enterprises in their export and

Exhibit 3

Number of Industrial Establishments in Vietnam

Year	State			Nonstate		
	Central	**Local**	**Total**	**Cooperatives**	**Private Enterprises**	**Private Household**
1985	711	2,339	3,050	35,629	902	-
1986	687	2,454	3,141	37,649	567	-
1987	682	2,457	3,139	33,962	490	-
1988	681	2,430	3,111	32,034	318	318,557
1989	666	2,354	3,020	21,901	1,248	333,337
1990	589	2,173	2,762	13,086	770	376,900
1991	546	2,053	2,599	8,829	959	446,771
1992	537	1,731	2,268	5,723	1,114	368,000

Source: General Statistical Office (Vietnam).

import business. State subsidies and price controls on export and import had ended except for some major items. The country established its first Export Processing Zone named Tan Thuan in Ho Chi Minh City in 1991.

Vietnam had diversified its export and import markets to other parts of the world. As a result, about 80% of total trade were now with Asia-Pacific countries, with Singapore, Japan, Hong Kong, South Korea, Taiwan, Australia, and Thailand as the main trade partners. Meanwhile, widespread tax reforms and improved collection had raised government revenue by 82%. Reflecting these strengths, the Vietnamese currency, the Dong, appreciated almost 5% against the U.S. dollar in 1993, in contrast to 1991, when its value was almost halved (see exchange rates of the Dong in **Exhibit 5**). Vietnam had normalized relations with the World Bank, the International Monetary Fund (IMF), and the Asian Development Bank (ADB) and had attracted many sources of bilateral and multilateral financial support. Vietnam joined ASEAN in July 1995.

Exhibit 4

Some Key Economic Indicators for Vietnam (1991–1994)

Year	GDP Growth	Industrial Growth	Services Growth	Agricultural Growth
1991	6.0%	10.0%	2.2%	8.2%
1992	8.6%	15.0%	7.2%	8.3%
1993	8.1%	12.0%	4.4%	13.0%
1994	8.5%	13.5%	4.5%	12.5%

Source: General Statistical Office (Vietnam).

Exhibit 5

Exchange Rates of the Dong

Year	Exchange Rates (Dong per US$)
1989	4,000
1990	5,200
1991	9,390
1992	11,181
1993	10,641
1994	11,080

Source: Economic Intelligence Unit, Business in Vietnam.

Exhibit 6 shows the distribution of foreign investments by sectors. **Exhibit 7** shows the foreign investments from the top 10 countries. Joint ventures accounted for about 74% of the foreign investments, totally foreign-owned companies accounted for 11%, and business cooperation contracts accounted for 15%.

The lifting of the U.S. trade embargo on Vietnam in February 1994 brought benefits such as direct access to U.S. technology and investment and smoother access to soft loans and aids from multilateral institutions. A survey of 100 American companies by the US-ASEAN council (reported in the *Business Times* of Singapore on February 5, 1994) indicated that trade and investment opportunities in Vietnam were worth US$ 2.6 billion in the first two years following the lifting of the embargo. Foreign investment had climbed steadily and reached US$11.05 billion (from 1,201 projects) as of the beginning of January 1995.

The government had set the target growth rates of 3.5 to 4% for the agriculture, aqua-culture, and livestock husbandry sectors and 7 to 8% for the industrial sector. The food processing indus-

Exhibit 6

Foreign Direct Investments by Economic Activities

Activity	(as of January 4, 1995) Number of Projects	Investment Capital (US$ million)
Industry (manufacturing)	548	4,334
Oil and gas	26	1,303
Agriculture and forestry	74	369
Aqua- and mariculture	21	62
Transportation and communication	128	951
Tourism and hotels	113	2,235
Services	134	1,254
Finance and banking	15	177
Housing	14	71
Others	8	14
Export processing zone	29	109
Industrial zone	2	167
Total	1,201	11,046

Source: State Committee for Cooperation and Investment in Vietnam.

Exhibit 7

Foreign Direct Investments In Vietnam—Top Ten Countries

Country	Number of Projects	Investment Capital (US$ million)
	(as of January 4, 1995)	
Taiwan	179	1,968
Hong Kong	171	1,796
Singapore	76	1,028
Korea, Republic of	98	889
Japan	73	789
Australia	42	861
Malaysia	32	585
France	58	510
Switzerland	14	463
United Kingdom	15	376

Source: State Committee for Cooperation and Investment in Vietnam.

try would give priority to the development of the Mekong and Red River Delta regions in order to upgrade the quality of processed agro-products and aquatic products to export standards. In the production of consumer goods, attention would be paid to the rehabilitation of current equipment and installation of new ones to improve the quality of manufactured products. Electronics assembling and manufacturing facilities would be established. Oil and gas exploitation on the continental shelf would be carried out and an oil refinery would be constructed. The mining, cement production, steel and mechanical industries were also targeted for development.

Despite the preceding positive economic outlook, some economic observers had pointed out several problems. The low savings rate and lack of hard currency constrained investment growth. Vietnam had an estimated US$15 billion of foreign debt, and the foreign exchange reserve constituted only about one month of imports. Three-quarters of export revenues were generated from only two sources—unprocessed farm products and crude oil. The annual inflation rate in Vietnam had ranged from a high of 400% in 1988 to a low of 15% in 1992. The annual inflation forecast for 1994 to 1998 was 40%. The Vietnam currency, the Dong, was not a fully convertible currency. The official exchange rate had depreciated from 5,200 dong per U.S. dollar to 9,390 dong per U.S. dollar in 1991 (see **Exhibit 5**). The state-owned enterprises appeared inefficient. They used 85% of the total fixed capital, 80% of total credit volume, 100% of savings, 60% of forestry output, and 90% of trained and high-school educated people, but they contributed less than 15% of total GDP in 1992.

FOREIGN EXCHANGE AND INVESTMENT REGULATIONS

Prior to 1980, in Vietnam, all transactions had to pass through the state export and import corporations. Beginning in 1980, however, provinces, cities, and individual enterprises were given some freedom to sign contracts with foreign traders. Exchange control was administered by the State Bank, which had branches in Hanoi and Ho Chi Minh City.

On January 1, 1988, a new Foreign Investment Law was promulgated to supersede the one dating from 1977. The new code allowed foreigners to own up to 100% of a venture, against a previous maximum of 49%. The old requirement that foreign investors should take a minimum 30% stake in joint ventures was retained. Priority areas for investment specified in the code were production for export and import substitution. Investors were expected to meet their own foreign exchange needs. The duration of a venture with foreign capital generally might not exceed 20 years, but it could be extended in special cases.

The corporate income tax rate had been reduced from between 30% and 50% in the old code to between 15% and 25% in the new one. There was provision for tax holidays of up to two years after the company made a profit. A statute governing labor relations and remuneration in foreign-invested companies was issued in 1990. Some main provisions in the statute specified the minimum wages, working hours, day of rest and holidays, minimum working age, rights to join a union, and labor arbitration process. The State Committee for Cooperation and Investment was created to manage and administer all foreign direct investment in 1988.

Land in Vietnam could not be purchased, only leased for a period, which depended on the duration of investment. The cost of land lease ranged from US$0.50 to US$18.00 per square meter per year in 1995.

INFRASTRUCTURE AND BANKING SYSTEM

The existing telecommunications system in Vietnam was found by many to be expensive and inefficient. The country relied mainly on waterways for transportation. The port facilities were felt to be backward, and it was thought that they might hinder the distribution system, especially when volume increased with the expected surge in economic activities. Many observers from the financial sector felt that the banking system, though reformed, was still far from those in capitalist countries, and might cause delays and confusion, especially in the handling of foreign exchange remittances.

The Vietnamese government had directed the state to invest in the construction of infrastructures, such as water supply and drainage systems in big cities, in-town traffic projects, highway network connecting the big cities, North-South railway network, restoration and improvement of sea ports, and upgrading of airports in major cities. There were plans to construct new hydropower plants and thermopower plants with a target production of 16 to 17 billion KWH (kilowatt hours) for 1995.

Information Technology Market in Vietnam

MARKET CHARACTERISTICS

The computer industry in Vietnam was in its infancy. The 18-year-old trade embargo imposed by the United States had effectively prevented computer technology from being transferred into the country by any of the major computer manufacturers and restricted heavily any capital inflow. Since the number of computer installations currently was small and located mostly in Ho Chi Minh City, many businessmen viewed the computer industry as an emerging industry with good market potential. There were not many competitors in the market, and there were no clear leaders in the market yet. Distribution channels for the industry were also not fully developed.

An analysis of Vietnam's IT end-user market showed that the government, together with its related agencies and institutions, made up 35% of the market, followed by multinationals (35%), small and medium enterprises (25%), and small home or office users making up the remaining market. The buyers in the foreseeable future would be the public sector and major foreign companies. The deal sizes were forecast to be large as the government departments and foreign companies made initial investments in information technology infrastructure.

Different types of computers, such as personal computers, minicomputers, RISC based workstations, and mainframes, could be used by businesses in their operation in Vietnam. The price differences among them would be an important consideration for these different business customers in their buying decision. Skilled local expertise in IT in Vietnam was somewhat limited. The Vietnamese workforce, however, was hardworking and well-educated and could possibly be trained quickly.

Computer products had limited intrinsic proprietary attributes and most innovations were easily imitated. Computer products, thus, were increasingly becoming less differentiated. The market, especially the low-end segment, tended to have fierce price competition and switching costs from one manufacturer to another was low. The Vietnamese users tended to favor U.S. brands of computers, even though brand loyalty for the product area was currently not strong.

There were problems associated with the lack of normalized ties between the United States and Vietnam, although the trade embargo had been lifted. As a result, American banks were not able to provide credit, although financing for their operation was a necessity in doing business in Vietnam. This was because hard currency was still hard to come by. American IT companies such as UNISYS had invested heavily in at least two large IT bids, only to find that their European and Japanese competitors had the edge against them when it came to extending credit. This problem might be resolved in the near future, as U.S. Secretary of State Warren Christopher had recommended that ties with Vietnam be normalized.

As in other Asian countries, "guanxi" was an important factor in doing business in Vietnam. "Guanxi" is a Chinese term denoting the use of personal connections, relationships, or networks to win business deals, forge business ventures, or to get business approvals for government authorities. Local and regional competitors could have a better understanding of such culture and practices, and they could have built up their own networks since they entered the market before the trade embargo was lifted.

VIETNAM'S IT-2000 PROGRAM

Vietnam planned to propel itself into the twenty-first century through a billion-dollar program called IT-2000. It was based on a similar development model created in Singapore. The IT-2000 called for expenditures of up to U.S. $2 billion over the next five years to set up the hardware necessary to create a national data communications network, establish a domestic industry in component manufacturing, and educate over 5,000 Vietnamese in the use of computer technology. The government adopted the IT-2000 on August 4, 1993, designating it a national initiative. The Ministry of Science Technology and Environment had been given the formidable task to oversee the plan.

Part of this plan was to create online computer networks for almost all government agencies and the financial sector, build the Vietnam Education Research and Development Network (VERDNet), and provide each secondary school and university student in Vietnam with access to an integrated computer complete with Vietnamese educational software. The IT-2000 also addressed government policies for financial management and support. The State Bank of Vietnam and the Ministry of Finance were desperately in need of an integrated nationwide data processing network to manage the chaos of transactions in banking, financial markets, and tax collection.

The Minister of Science, Technology and the Environment, and Chairman of IT-2000, Dr. Dang Hua, was quoted as saying:

> The purpose of IT-2000 is to build a foundation for basic information demands in the management of government and socioeconomic activities, and to develop the IT industry to a level where it can help in national development. We have stated very clearly in the masterplan for IT-2000 that an integrated system of different computing networks must be built, with strong enough software and database systems which are able to service the Government and other key essential activities. Some domestic services will be integrated with international systems.

Customer Groups in the IT Market

Two segmentation approaches, by industry and by benefits, were adopted to examine customer groups in the IT market. The industry segmentation identified the high growth business segments of the Vietnamese economy which, from HP's experience in other countries, might be heavy and early adopters of IT. The benefit segmentation further defined the characteristics and needs of these segments.

INDUSTRY SEGMENTATION

Financial Services

The Vietnam government had increasingly liberalized foreign bank participation. As of the beginning of 1995, investments totaling US$1.77 billion had been made in financial and commercial services. Apart from the lucrative trade finance business, which was forecast to expand rapidly, other financial services, especially venture capital, leasing, and project financing, had potential, too. In the short- to medium-term, this was generally the segment most Vietnam watchers and experts deemed likely to experience explosive growth. Funds from lenders were desperately needed to fuel the growth of the economy. In addition, the government was trying to encourage savings to create a pool of investment money. The financial industry had long viewed IT as a competitive advantage and, thus, IT investment in this segment was expected to pick up strongly. Due to the mission critical nature of financial applications, financial customers demanded a high level of support services.

Telecommunications

Vietnam's telecommunications infrastructure was still in its infancy. Explosive growth was expected here as well, especially in mobile communications and high-speed data communications links for businesses. The postal and telecommunications sectors were still very much a monopoly in Vietnam in 1995, so any investor wanting to offer a public telecommunications service would have to work with VNPT, the Vietnam Post and Telecommunications Department. Some announcements of foreign joint ventures in the telecommunications sector are shown in **Exhibit 8**.

Exhibit 8
Foreign Joint Ventures in the Telecommunications Sector

France: Alcatel Alsthom said it had been selected by the Ministry of the Interior to supply the first private national communications network in Vietnam. The contract covered the supply, installation, implementation, and maintenance of a service integration network, which would eventually cover the entire country and represent 50,000 lines. The first part of the network was to be operational in March 1995.

Sweden: Three Swedish companies and Vietnam's Posts and Telecommunications Department had applied for a license to set up a US$340 million mobile phone network covering the whole of Vietnam. They hoped to install and operate a cellular telephone and paging system connected by hubs in Hanoi in the north, Danang in the center, and Saigon in the south by the end of 1995. The Swedish companies were reported to be Industriforvaltings, Kirnevik, and Comvik International, and they said their combined investment would be US$159 million.

Canada: Montreal-based Teleglobe, Inc., said its cable systems arm and Telesystem International Wireless Services, Inc., had signed a deal to study the feasibility of a multiregional wireless and communication service and coastal submarine fiberoptic cable system in Vietnam. The study would cost US$720,000 and the project itself would cost US$100 million.

Source: Internal company file—extracted from various sources.

Hotels and Tourism

Vietnam had increasingly become a new tourist destination and business travels continued to surge. This would create demand for hotel facilities, as well as spark the growth of a retail sector. Some international hotel groups, such as the Accor Group and Pullman International Hotels, and some Singapore companies, had begun a number of hotel projects in Vietnam. As of the beginning of 1995, foreign investment projects totaling US$2.235 billion had been made in this sector.

Manufacturing

Vietnam was an attractive location for labor-intensive industries due to low wages and a relatively skilled and productive workforce. The government encouraged export-oriented and resource- or agricultural-based manufacturing, such as assembly operations for electronic goods, garment, and food-processing industries.

Utilities

There would be explosive growth in this area as Vietnam sought to build its power infrastructure to cope with the demands of a modern economy. The Phu My thermal power plant project, worth US$900 million, was expected to provide 600 megawatts of power.

Oil and Gas

There were extensive offshore crude extraction activities going on. The Vietnamese government wished to promote local refining of crude oil. Many joint ventures with the various international and regional oil extraction and refining companies like BHP, Mobil, Shell, and Petronas were already in place. Total foreign investments as of the beginning of 1995 in this sector totaled US$1.3 billion.

Government

The government was expected to play a major role in influencing the use and penetration of IT in the Vietnamese economy. With its IT-2000 plan, the Vietnamese government hoped to follow in Singapore's footsteps and accelerate the country's entry into high technology.

BENEFIT SEGMENTATION

The benefit segmentation of IT customers is shown in **Exhibit 9**. Benefit segmentation distinguishes customers by choice criteria, technology requirements, and primary needs. Four benefit segments were identified.

The Economy Segment

This segment used IT mainly for productivity gains. PCs, simple networks, and off-the-shelf software were generally preferred because of cost reasons. Price-to-performance ratio was an important buying criterion, and these customers were extremely cost sensitive and also did not require high-quality, round-the-clock support.

The Technology Segment

This segment planned IT implementation so that they could be seen as technology leaders. Customers here generally had deep pockets and were willing to pay for the latest and the best technology.

The Mission Critical–Mission Sensitive Segment

This segment used IT for competitive advantage. The failure of its information systems would interrupt business operations, sometimes bringing it to a standstill, thus affecting revenue and profit. Hence, these customers looked for high availability, near-zero downtime, round-the-

Exhibit 9

Benefit Segments

Segments	Some Customers	Choice Criteria	Technology Requirements	Primary Needs
Economy (low price)	Consumer products; retail sector	Low price; low design content	Simple	Low costs; productivity gains
Technology	Oil and gas utilities	Leading edge solution	Complex	Technology leadership
Mission critical, mission sensitive	Banking and finance; couriers	High reliability; good and fast service	Proven and tested	Maximum uptime; performance
Geographical coverage	MNCs	Regional or worldwide presence	Wide area requirement	Branch connectivity; consistent support

clock support, and reliable solutions. They might also be uncomfortable with new technologies and view them as risky unless they saw a distinct competitive advantage in implementing them.

The Geographical Coverage Segment

This segment consisted of multinational corporations who operated worldwide or regionally and had a need to connect their dispersed operations together to ensure that information was disseminated quickly and reliably. Consistent, global support was critical when serving this segment.

Some Players in the IT Market in Vietnam

Exhibit 10 shows selected information on some major players in the IT market.

Exhibit 10

Some Players in the IT Market

Company	(Dollar amounts in millions, except employee revenues per employees)				
	1994 Annual Revenue	1994 Net Income	1993 Net Income	Number of Employees	Revenue per Employee
IBM	$62,716.0	$(8,101.0)	$(4,965.0)	267,196	$234,719
Hewlett-Packard	24,991.0	1,599.0	1,177.0	98,400	253,974
DEC	13,450.8	(2,156.1)	(251.0)	78,000	172,466
Unisys	7,742.5	565.4	361.2	49,000	158,010
Compaq	7,191.0	462.0	213.0	10,043	716,021

Source: Software Asia Magazine (June/July, 1995).

DIGITAL EQUIPMENT CORPORATION (DEC)

Digital Equipment Corporation or DEC was a leading supplier of networked computer systems, software, and services. Its areas of differentiation were open systems, client-server knowledge and experiences, and multivendor experiences. Its strategy was to invest in technical research, build up technical capabilities, and to focus on training.

Over the past few years, DEC's financial results had been poor and DEC had a net loss of US$2 billion in 1994. DEC's poor performance caused the ouster of DEC's founder and CEO, Ken Olsen. His replacement from within was Robert Palmer, who had since sold off a number of DEC's noncore divisions, such as the disk drive operation, database software, and the consulting unit. He sought to focus on DEC's core hardware business and increase margin by adding value in networking. Palmer had positioned DEC to take advantage of key trends, such as mobile computing and video on demand. Palmer had also shifted most sales to indirect distribution channels and sought to slash costs by signing on computer resellers as key partners. Salomon Brothers, Inc., expected DEC's new Alpha system sales to soar in 1995 by 84% to US$1.7 billion and by another 55% in 1996.

In 1992, DEC had 45% of its turnover in the United States, 40% in Europe, 10% in Asia-Pacific (including Japan), and 5% in Canada. Alpha still faced a long-term problem: The chip had not won a single influential convert among computer makers. That could ultimately prove fatal when it came time to fund the mind-boggling cost of succeeding generations of chips. Most industry analysts believed that Palmer's accomplishments of the past year had merely brought DEC to the point where it was ready to compete again. If Palmer could not make DEC stand out with his networking strategy, the company risked following the path of another former industry, number two, Unisys Corp., which now served mostly its old customers, and its revenue was shrinking slowly. Digital had a strong client base in government, banking and finance, insurance, and telecommunications. DEC had also done projects in health care, transportation, utilities, and retail. DEC currently had a representative office in Hanoi. So far, their main area of activity seemed to be on large internationally funded tenders. They had appointed three distributors in Vietnam as sales outlets and as service providers.

INTERNATIONAL BUSINESS MACHINES (IBM)

Despite losses amounting to over US$8 billion in 1994, IBM was still the world's largest information systems and services company. In 1995, IBM CEO Lou Gertsner had engineered a turnaround. Recently, IBM purchased Lotus Corporation for US$3.5 billion. IBM's worldwide revenues had declined since 1990, slipping to US$62.7 billion in 1994. In 1992, IBM had 1,500 consultants worldwide. While these consultants provided support to all industries, their key focus was on finance, retail, and manufacturing.

IBM's key area of differentiation was its ability not only to provide insights, experience, and specialized skills to its customers, but also to deliver results and increase the value of IBM products and services to customers. Its strategy was to focus on customer relationship and develop account presence. Its global organization allowed IBM to bring its best intellectual capabilities to bear on any project. IBM, however, was still encumbered by a mainframe image it might never completely shake. Still in recovery mode and uncertain about its strategic directions, IBM supported more than a half dozen operating systems as well as dual desktop hardware platforms with PowerPC and X86.

IBM had set up IBM Vietnam in Hanoi in 1995. The operation provided sales and marketing support to distributors and dealers as well as customers. They had also appointed their dealers as service providers for hardware repair and support.

UNISYS

In 1994, Unisys was the ninth largest systems and PC vendor in the world. Unisys manufactured and marketed computer-based networked information systems and software. The company also offered related services, such as systems integration and IT outsourcing. As such, its strategy was to provide a full spectrum of services and solutions. It sought to develop leading edge hardware and technology in open systems.

Unisys specialized in providing business-critical solutions based on open information networks for organizations that operated in transaction-intensive environments. In 1992, Unisys generated 49% of its revenue from the United States, 30% from Europe, 9% from Canada, 5% from Asia-Pacific, and 7% from Japan. For international projects, local resources were normally relied upon. Vertically, Unisys focused on airlines, public sectors, financial services, and telecommunications. Horizontally, they focused on networking and online transaction processing. Unisys had also established a representative office in Vietnam. With 15 marketing staff based in the country, it appeared that they had adopted an aggressive strategy in Vietnam. In 1995, they installed their equipment for the banking sector in the country for SWIFT (Society for Worldwide Interbank Financial Telecommunications) transactions. Unisys was targeting to set up an operation (subsidiary) in Vietnam in 1996.

COMPAQ

In 1995, Compaq completed yet another record year with sales of US$10.9 billion, up 51% from the previous year. Net income grew by a healthy 88% to reach US$867 million. As the leading manufacturer of PC systems (desktops, portables, and servers), Compaq was currently positioned to tackle both the consumer and corporate computing markets and was now a major player in the commercial server market.

The reasons for Compaq's success to date included aggressive expansion of distribution channels, efficient manufacturing, ability to bring new products and technologies into the market early, ability to deliver top-quality products, and ability to include added-value features in its products.

Hewlett-Packard Businesses in Southeast Asia

THE HEWLETT-PACKARD COMPANY

In January 1939, in a garage in Palo Alto, California, two graduates from nearby Stanford University, William Hewlett and David Packard, set up a company called the Hewlett-Packard (HP) Company with an initial capital of US$538. They marketed their first product (invented by Bill), a resistance-capacity audio oscillator. HP's initial emphasis was on instrumentation. It was not until 1972 that the company finally acknowledged that it was in the computer field, with the introduction of its first business computer, the HP3000.

In 1995, HP was a sprawling corporate giant with annual sales in excess of US$25 billion and about 90,000 employees worldwide. It was involved principally in the manufacture, supply, marketing, and distribution of computer-based products, test and measurement products, medical and analytical products, electronic components and Information Technology related service and support. In 1985, HP was ranked by a *Fortune* magazine survey as one of the two most admired companies in America. In 1995, the bulk of the company's business, a good 76.6% of the net revenue, came from computational products and services.

Years ago, Bill Hewlett and Dave Packard developed a set of management objectives for the company. With only slight modification, these became the corporate objectives of HP and were first published in 1957. These objectives gave a clear idea as to how the company viewed itself and its position in society. The HP Statement of Corporate Objectives (October 1986) is shown in **Exhibit 11**.

Exhibit 11

Objectives: Hewlett-Packard

a. **Profit.** To achieve sufficient profit to finance our growth and to achieve corporate objectives through self-generated resources.

b. **Customers.** To provide products and services of the highest quality and the greatest possible value to customers, thereby gaining and holding their respect and loyalty.

c. **Fields of Interest.** To participate in those fields of interest that build upon our technology and customer base, that offer opportunities for continuing growth, and that enable us to make a needed and profitable contribution.

d. **Growth.** To let growth be limited only by our profits and ability to develop and produce innovative products that satisfy real customer needs.

e. **People.** To help HP people share in the company's success which they make possible; to provide employment security based on their performance; to ensure them a safe and pleasant work environment; to recognize their individual achievements; and to help them gain a sense of satisfaction and accomplishment from their work.

f. **Management.** To foster initiative and creativity by allowing the individual great freedom of action in attaining well-defined objectives.

g. **Citizenship.** To honor our obligations to society by being an economic, intellectual, and social asset to each nation and each community in which we operate.

These corporate objectives formed the basis of what was known as "The HP Way," which sought to create a work environment geared to produce capable, innovative, well-trained, and enthusiastic people who could give their best to the company. HP's guiding strategic principle had been to provide customers with devices superior to any competitive offering in performance, quality, and overall value. To this day, HP corporate strategy was pursued with three measures in mind:

1. Getting the highest return out of the company's most important asset, its people.
2. Getting the best output from a given technology.
3. Giving the customer the best performance for price paid.

Around the world, Hewlett-Packard was organized broadly into several strategic business units as shown in **Exhibit 12**. Each business unit was represented at HP's top management and was more or less run as an independent entity within HP.

Exhibit 12

Strategic Business Units: Hewlett-Packard

a. **Computer Systems Organization (CSO)** which manufactured and marketed HP minicomputers and workstations.

b. **Computer Products Organization (CPO)** which manufactured and marketed PCs, PC peripherals, and networking products.

c. **Tests and Measurements Organization (TMO)** which manufactured, marketed, and serviced test and measurement products.

d. **Analytical Products Group (APG)** which manufactured, marketed, and serviced analytical chemical compound products.

e. **Medical Products Group (MPG)** which manufactured, marketed, and serviced products, such as defibrillators, ECG, and monitoring equipment, that were used in the medical industry.

f. **Components Group** which manufactured and marketed opto-electronic components.

g. **Worldwide Customer Support Organization (WCSO)** which provided services for HP's computer-related business (i.e., the CSO and CPO).

HP'S MARKET POSITION AND CAPABILITIES

HP had established its presence in countries like Hong Kong, Singapore, Japan, Taiwan, and Korea for more than 25 years. It had extensive experience in entering into emerging Asian markets such as China, Indonesia, and the Philippines. Though a subsidiary of an American company, HP Southeast Asia had a largely Asian management team. They shared similar norms, practices, beliefs, customs, and languages with many local markets. Nevertheless, HP was still an American company with its own stringent code of business and the requirement to comply with American laws.

HP had, over the years, built up many major customer accounts, some of which were multinational corporations with offices worldwide. It had developed a strong reputation and brand identity. The HP name was often synonymous with quality products and high technology, albeit at a premium price. HP could not be as aggressive in product pricing due to its higher cost structure and overhead. HP had, for many years, come up tops in many independent customer satisfaction surveys conducted by organizations such as Datapro and IDC.

HP had a large network of subsidiaries and associated companies in different countries in the Asia Pacific. It was, thus, able to source for raw materials and parts in these countries at the cheapest prices, manufacture at locations with the lowest costs, and establish an efficient distribution and warehousing network to transport products from manufacturing sites to markets.

Exhibit 13 shows some information related to the turnover and earnings of HP from 1989 to 1994. In the brutal, fast-paced world of IT, customers looked for financial stability to ensure that vendors would still be around when their projects were completed, especially for large multiyear, infrastructural projects.

HP was a diversified company and had products and services in computation, measurement, and communications. This gave it a breadth that few computer vendors could match. The autonomous units dealing with measurement, communications, and computers in the HP setup, however, often acted as separate companies and, thus, created functional silos that might not effectively leverage HP's knowledge and diversity.

Exhibit 13
Income and Earnings (1994–1989): Hewlett-Packard

	(U.S. Dollar amounts in millions)					
	1994	**1993**	**1992**	**1991**	**1990**	**1989**
Revenue	$24,991	$20,317	$16,410	$14,494	$13,233	$11,889
Cost of revenue	15,490	12,123	9,152	7,858	6,993	6,091
Gross profit	9,501	8,194	7,258	6,636	6,240	5,808
R&D	2,027	1,761	1,619	1,463	1,367	1,269
Mktg, gen, & admin	4,925	4,554	4,224	3,963	3,711	3,327
Operating income	2,549	1,879	1,415	1,210	1,162	1,212
Other income/exp	(126)	(96)	(79)	(83)	(106)	(61)
Pre-tax income	2,423	1,783	1,336	1,127	1,056	1,151
Income tax	824	606	449	372	317	322
Net income	1,599	1,177	887	755	739	829

Source: Salomon Brothers.

HP was the industry leader in open systems technology and solutions and it had a specialized knowledge and extensive experience in this area. HP moved into RISC Technology long before DEC, IBM, and other rivals and was now collecting the dividends. HP was strong in client/server computing involving PCs, workstations, and large systems and servers. HP opened up its proprietary HP3000 systems and it had become a whirlwind of success.

While HP served a cross-section of the IT industry, it had in particular established significant presence in three industry groups: manufacturing, telecommunications, and financial services. In addition, HP also had large installed bases in industries such as retail, hospitality, government, and health services. In manufacturing, HP was the dominant worldwide supplier of UNIX systems accounting for 45% of this market. HP had a wide range of customers in the manufacturing sector, which remained HP's largest vertical market.

HP sought to use the distribution channel as a means to support its customers. In 1988, HP sold its products primarily through a direct sales force. HP foresaw the rapid fall in gross margins as standardization, volumes, and competitiveness increased, and so developed two distinct sales strategies, one for volume sales where sales was indirect and took place through sales channels, and the other direct, providing value sales to large HP target accounts around the world. While many high-tech companies viewed distribution channels as their customers, HP had identified end users as its customers. HP recognized that the computer industry had become a demand-driven (pull) environment, and HP had sought to create demand for its products among end users. HP tracked very closely consumer buying preferences and responded quickly to changes in the market.

HP'S BUSINESSES IN SOUTHEAST ASIA

Hewlett-Packard Southeast Asia had its headquarters in Singapore with fully owned subsidiaries in Singapore, Malaysia, and Thailand. In Indonesia, the Philippines, and Brunei, HP appointed distributors. In addition, HP had a joint venture in Indonesia with its distributor, Berca, called HPSI which was primarily an IT services company.

In Southeast Asia, HP's Worldwide Customer Support Organization (WCSO) was represented by the Southeast Asia (SEA) Customer Support Organization, whose role was to provide services and support in satisfying customers' needs in financing, implementing and operating their IT operations. The SEA Customer Support Organization managed the following product lines:

PL72	Hardware Support for Computer Systems and Networks
PL3D	Software Support for Computer Systems
PL71	Support for Personal Computers and Peripherals
PL6N	Outsourcing Services
PL6L	Network Integration Services

Product Lines 72, 3D, and 71 were the traditional maintenance services that HP had provided for buyers and users of its computer systems and was primarily focused on post-sales maintenance. In recent years, these businesses had experienced declining growth rate. Prices of computer products continued to drop, even as their performance improved. This trend was especially prevalent in the hardware maintenance business. Support expenditure, typically capped at a percentage of total IT expenditure, was thus greatly affected by this trend.

Product Lines 6N and 6L were the newer businesses WCSO had set up to counter the slower growth of the traditional maintenance businesses. They required higher investment and typically had lower profitability. The selling model for these product lines was also different, requiring more direct selling as it was not always possible to leverage support revenues off computational product sales as was more often the case in the traditional maintenance businesses.

CURRENT STATUS OF HP'S BUSINESS IN VIETNAM

Since the lifting of the U.S. embargo on February 3, 1994, different business units in HP had taken initial and ad hoc steps to develop their businesses in Vietnam in response to the current changes taking place in the country. The HP business units Customer Systems Organization (CSO), Computer Products Organization (CPO), and Test and Measurements Organization (TMO) had signed up distributors in Vietnam to distribute their products. The CSO currently had one main distributor, the High Performance Technology Corporation (HiPT). HiPT was 100% privately owned. One of the owners, Dr. Binh, had good contacts with the Vietnamese government. CSO was ready to appoint a second distributor (the Peregrine Group) for the south of Vietnam. TMO had also appointed a distributor, Systems Interlace, while CPO had appointed several wholesalers and resellers in Vietnam. Projected orders from these product organizations were expected to hit US$10 million at the end of October 1995. HP's computer support business, WCSO, was not represented in Vietnam in 1994.

Hewlett-Packard and its CSO distributor in Vietnam, the HiPT, officially opened a Center for Open Systems Computing Expertise in Hanoi on July 1, 1995. Its establishment was part of a formal memorandum of understanding that HP and the Ministry of Science, Technology and the Environment (MOSTE) had signed in March 1995. MOSTE was the body responsible for the promotion and development of information technology in Vietnam. The center would assist MOSTE's goal of developing a pool of qualified IT professionals to implement the Vietnam IT-2000 plan, based on the open systems concept.

Field Trip To Vietnam

In January 1995, John made a business visit to Vietnam to assess first hand the business climate and investment opportunities and to provide ideas on how WCSO in Southeast Asia should plan its overall investment strategy in Vietnam, rather than the current ad-hoc involvement of its CSO, CPO, and TMO in the Vietnamese market. The first stop was Ho Chi Minh City, a bustling city of 5 million people, 1 hour and 25 minutes from Singapore by air.

MEETING WITH DR. VO VAN MAI (MANAGING DIRECTOR OF HiPT)

Dr. Vo Van Mai was the Managing Director of High-Performance Technology (HiPT), HP's distributor in Vietnam. He was educated in Hungary. Dr. Mai expected the IT market in Vietnam to hit US$300 million by the year 2000. The market size had doubled each year for the past few years and Dr. Mai expected the IT market to grow even more rapidly in the next two years. Currently, IT took the form of mainly personal computers (PCs) with some limited local area networks. Vietnam, being an IT greenfield, looked likely to adopt client-server technology in a big way, bypassing legacy and proprietary systems common in most developing and developed countries. The PC brands available in Vietnam included Compaq, HP, ACER, Wearnes, AST, Digital, Unisys, and IBM.

Dr. Mai felt that the most attractive segments of the IT market would be finance, utilities, telecommunications, petrochemicals, and airlines. Currently, within Vietnam, the primary means of data transmission was using phone lines and modems. Between Hanoi and Ho Chi Minh City, more sophisticated and higher bandwidth transmission methods were available through fiber optic links and X.25.

IBM had representative offices in Hanoi and Ho Chi Minh City, with staff strength of 10. They had six to seven distributors in Vietnam, and it was known that they had applied for a license to operate a service operation in Vietnam.

Dr. Mai's conclusions were that it would be three to four years before the Vietnamese market became really significant in IT revenues. He felt that the next two years would be critical in establishing a presence and building relationships and awareness of products and services. Obtaining budgets for IT expenditure was still a problem. The government's IT-2000 plan, however, was a clear indication of the government's commitment to IT.

MEETING WITH ROSS NICHOLSON (GENERAL MANAGER OF DHL WORLDWIDE EXPRESS)

Nicholson felt that he had access to good market information as DHL had been operating in Vietnam since 1988. DHL worked through the Vietnam Post Office as the Vietnamese government still controlled the provision of mail and postal services tightly. Nicholson was assigned to Vietnam as a Technical Advisor in April 1994. He told John that things had not boomed as expected since the American embargo was lifted. Some obstacles like chaotic taxation laws and investment risks still plagued potential investors. In the short term, the fluctuating Mexican peso incident was likely to affect investor outlook, especially in emerging economies like Vietnam. In his opinion, the Asians, especially Japanese, were moving in very quickly. Hotels in Hanoi were usually full of Japanese.

In Nicholson's opinion, the finance industry had the highest prospects for growth in the immediate future. Presently, agriculture was DHL's biggest customer for the provision of shipping facilities. In time, more technologically advanced production activity would take place. DHL would then have the opportunity to sell logistics services to these new entrants, leveraging on their long experience in the Vietnamese market. DHL would like to get itself integrated into these companies, which would be very happy to listen because they were in startup mode.

Nicholson believed that there would not be anything spectacular until two to three years later. He cited the lack of skilled IT personnel as one of the obstacles to IT growth. Still, he felt that it was well worth the investment of establishing a presence in Vietnam now, so that when the boom came, companies like DHL would be well positioned to capitalize on the ensuing growth. DHL currently used a stand-alone PC for its IT needs. This was certainly not suitable for the anticipated growth. Nicholson intended to upgrade to a nationwide system comprising two HP9000 E45s.

MEETING WITH DR. TRUENE GIA BINH (MANAGING DIRECTOR OF FPT)

The Corporation for Financing and Promoting Technology (FPT) was a wholly government-owned company incorporated under the auspices of the Ministry of Science, Technology and the Environment (MOSTE). Dr. Binh, the Managing Director of FPT and son-in-law of a prominent general in Vietnam, elaborated on the difference in status between a representative office and an operating office. Basically, a representative office could only acquire goods required for the operation of the office. It was not allowed to receive payment for any products or services rendered but could provide marketing and support services as part of its distributor support service. Commenting on the attractiveness of the IT market, Dr. Binh felt that the financial sector would be very attractive due to the high growth prospects and the prominence placed on it by the Vietnamese economy in the next three to four years.

MEETING WITH HAI CHAO DUY (DIRECTOR OF TECHNICAL SERVICES AND OPERATIONS, VIETNAM MOBILE TELECOMMUNICATION SERVICES)

Hai Chao Duy expressed that he looked forward to a long-term relationship with HP. He mentioned the tremendous opportunities in Vietnam Mobile Telecom Services (VMS) to build networks. Today, VMS supplied cellular services to 9,000 subscribers in Ho Chi Minh City and Hanoi. The IT projects needed to facilitate the provision of cellular services were in operation, transmission, business support, finance, end-user computing, and e-mailing. He also mentioned that the next project would involve some management system software for the telecommunication network.

MEETING WITH NGUYEN TRANG (CHAIRMAN OF HCMC COMPUTER ASSOCIATION)

Nguyen Trang was a very influential personality in IT and was the Chairman of the Ho Chi Minh City Computer Association. The Vietnam IT-2000 plan would be driven centrally from Hanoi. The city also had a board that would oversee the implementation of the IT-2000 plan. That plan had been approved, and Nguyen revealed details regarding two other projects.

One project was IT applications for municipal and government administration in the areas of transportation and traffic control, financial control, industrial administration, land property, city planning, trade services, and manpower development.

The other project was governmental IT infrastructural development. This included the setup of units such as the Center for System Analysis and Design and the Center for Manpower Development, and projects such as the feasibility study for Ho Chi Minh EDI, a museum for IT development, and an Internet gateway for Vietnam. In his estimate, the market size of the Vietnamese IT industry would be US$500 million by the year 2000.

Market Entry Decisions

Vietnam represented a promising market with untapped potential. There were, however, risks. Despite all the recent rapid progress toward a free economy, the basic political structure in Vietnam had not changed. Although Vietnam had recently adopted an open-door policy, economic development in the country was only beginning to take off and the pace and direction of reform was still uncertain. Although economic growth was robust, the economy recently suffered from high inflation, and the dong was expected to depreciate against the U.S. dollar. There were gaps in Vietnam's legal framework with two instances where business firms were subjected to different interpretations of the law by authorities at different levels in the government, which resulted in different applications of the same law. This had caused uncertainties and delay in the business setup.

Although the information technology (IT) market in Vietnam had potential, the market was currently small and market growth was uncertain. HPAP management needed to weigh the positive and negative factors before deciding if the company should enter the Vietnam market in a more strategic manner.

POSSIBLE MODES OF ENTRY

The following are some possible entry strategies available to HP to set up its presence in Vietnam if it decides to enter the market.

Majority Joint Venture with Local Partner

HP could use the joint venture strategy to enter the Vietnam market. In Southeast Asia, a HP joint venture existed in Indonesia where an agreement was entered into with Berca, a distributor, to set up a service company, HPSI. Berca retained the primary responsibility for the sale of HP products, while HPSI was charged with providing HP services to the marketplace. This option required less initial investment, compared to the direct presence strategy, thus reducing the risk involved. A local joint-venture partner could be a valuable resource where "guanxi" was vital for doing business.

Distribution (Independent Partner)

HP could appoint one or more independent organizations as distributors, as well as service and support providers. In the initial years, it was likely that products from each business unit would be sold only through one distributor, although the same distributor might be chosen for the products of more than one business unit.

This strategy offered a quick start-up for HP and was especially suited for the off-the-shelf, mass-market, plug-and-play type of products offered by CPO. To be successful, HP needed to commit resources to train and develop the distributor to build up their service capability. The disadvantage of this strategy was that it would result in the cultivation of future competitors for support services. Where services in many other markets were concerned, HP had not found a way to provide support to its mission-sensitive and mission-critical end users through channel members and still maintain the high quality and responsiveness that customers required. In addition, the margins on services were high and services contributed significantly to HP's profit. The profit was likely to drop if HP allowed its channels to sign support contracts directly with the end users.

Distribution (Ex-HP Employee Start-Up)

A modified form of the entry strategy was to appoint a start-up company founded by ex-HP employees as its distributor. These ex-HP employees could be trusted to deliver quality service. In the future, this company would probably be more obliged to pay off the goodwill shown by HP in giving it the opportunity to be HP's service provider in Vietnam. When HP decided to establish a direct presence in Vietnam, the former employees could also be rehired as key managers in the new subsidiary.

Cooperative Venture/ Franchising

Investment in the form of a cooperative venture was also viable. HP could initially franchise the support services and provide advisory services to a partner on how to establish and manage a support business. HP could act as a supplier of spares to its Vietnamese partner. HP would not have to take the risks incurred in direct investment, and trade ties could still be forged because of the special relationship with a local firm. At present, Singapore firms like Rothmans of Pall Mall (cigarettes) and Cold Storage (retail supermarkets) had established such ventures with Vietnam firms Agrex Saigon and Saigon-Intershop, respectively.

Direct Presence

HP could have a direct presence in Vietnam by setting up a subsidiary or representative office to provide marketing, sales support, and management services. This strategy required the largest investment and commitment of resources. It also offered maximum control and flexibility and the best payoff. HP's direct presence in the market would allow it to keep in touch with customers. HP would gain invaluable access to markets and customers. To reduce the risk, uncertainty, and investment requirement, it was possible to start off with limited staff on a smaller scale and increase staffing as required.

case 7

The Body Shop International PLC: Anita Roddick, OBE

Ellie A. Fogarty, Joyce P. Vincelette, and Thomas L. Wheelen

I am not taking a back seat. I have no intention of marginalizing myself from this business as a nonworking director. I just can't see myself retiring. I will still do what I do best—that's marketing, styling, image, store design and so on.

> —Comment from Anita Roddick on the prospect of handing over the reins at the company she founded.[1]

Asked what her new role as Co-Chairman would actually mean, she said: "I have no bloody idea."[2]

On May 12, 1998, Anita Roddick announced that she would cede her post of Chief Executive Officer of The Body Shop International PLC to Patrick Gournay. She admitted she was bored with basic retail disciplines such as distribution. Anita would rather spend time with the Dalai Lama, whom she met the day before stepping down. Anita moved alongside her husband Gordon as Executive Cochairman. She said titles are meaningless and "tomorrow's job is exactly the same as yesterday's."[3]

Patrick Gournay, an experienced international business manager, had worked 26 years with Groupe Danone, the multiproduct food group headquartered in Paris with sales of £8 billion. He was the Executive Vice President of Danone's North and South American division, with strategic responsibilities for eight companies in five countries.[4] Gournay had never heard of The Body Shop until he was approached by headhunters (executive recruiters). He met Anita and Gordon to ask them if they really wanted to change." It was important to me to establish that Anita in particular was ready for a change, for someone to come in and take responsibility for the business. We spent a lot of time talking about that and the conclusion is clear."[5] Although he admitted he was not an activist, he realized that The Body Shop "is not just an average cosmetics company, it is something unique."[6]

Gournay was granted options of over 2.5 million shares that may be exercised at £123 British. Half the performance-related options were exercisable between May 2001 and May 2008. The other half were exercisable between May 2003 and May 2008. These options may be exercised only if normalized earnings per share over any three consecutive years exceed growth in the retail prices index for the same period by at least 4%.[7]

On July 14, 1998 (Bastille Day), Gournay began his work at The Body Shop. He planned to focus on defining the roles and processes within the company. He felt the operations needed to be made more flexible and more innovative. Gournay thought the expansion program

---

should continue with South America as an obvious starting point, based on his previous experience. His long-term targets included India and China. He and Anita agreed that due to high store rents, more emphasis should be placed on direct selling operations, perhaps even replacing some stores with this effective new method. Gournay's future plans included tackling the issue of extending the Body Shop brand. Anita was interested in directing that expansion to include leisure services such as weekend retreats.

Also in 1998, The Body Shop shareholders approved a joint venture with Bellamy Retail Group LLC to manage the operations of The Body Shop, Inc., in the United States, giving the owner up to 51% of the company at a future date.

Anita admitted that several previous senior appointments from outside failed to work. But she promised this time would be different. "It will have to work. There is no option."[8]

Anita Roddick: The Entrepreneur

> I certainly had no ambition to start a big international company. I did not want to change the world; I just wanted to survive and be able to feed my children.
>
> —Anita Roddick, OBE

In 1942, Anita Perellas was born to Italian immigrant parents and grew up working in the family-owned cafe, the Clifton Cafe, in Littlehampton, West Sussex, England. She wanted to be an actress, but her mother, Gilda, wanted her to be a teacher. Her mother told her to "be special" [and] "be anything but mediocre."[9] She received a degree in education from Newton Park College of Education at Bath. In 1963, her senior year, she received a three-month scholarship to Israel, which enabled her to do research for her thesis, "The British Mandate in Palestine."

After graduation, she taught for a brief time at a local junior school. She then accepted a position in Paris with the *International Herald Tribune* in its library. Her next position was with the United Nations International Labour Organization in Geneva. She worked on women's rights in Third World countries. She said of her United Nations experience that she learned "the extraordinary power of networking, but I was appalled by the money that was squandered on red tape and all the wining and dining that was going on with no apparent check on expenses. I found it offensive to see all of those fat cats discussing problems in the Third World over four-course lunches at the United Nations Club."[10]

With the money saved from her United Nations position, she decided to satisfy her quest to travel. She boarded a boat bound for Tahiti via the Panama Canal. She went on to visit Africa. During her travels, she developed a deep interest in and curiosity about the beauty practices of women that she encountered. She focused on the effectiveness and simplicity of these beauty practices.

After returning to England, she met Gordon Roddick at El Cubana, her family-owned club. He was an adventurer who loved to travel and write poetry. They got married in Reno, Nevada, on a trip to San Francisco to visit friends in 1970. After the birth of their two daughters, Justine in 1969 and Samantha in 1971, they decided to settle down. They purchased a Victorian hotel, St. Winifred Hotel, in Littlehampton, which required substantial renovations. They resided in part of the hotel while renovating the guest quarters. The next Roddick enterprise was the Paddington's restaurant in the center of Littlehampton. They borrowed £10,000 from the bank to lease and renovate the restaurant.[11] This was a time-consuming enterprise for the couple. They had no social or family life while running the Paddington and residing in and staffing the hotel, St. Winifred. Anita said, "We did not have time for each other and our marriage was beginning to suffer as a result, exacerbated by the fact we had no privacy; being at St. Winifred's was like living in a commune with a lot of elderly people. And despite all the leisure time we had sacrificed, we were not making much money. All we were doing was surviving."[12] Paddington became the most popular place in the town, especially on a Saturday night. Gordon crawling into bed one night said, "This is killing us," . . . [and] "I can't cope with it any more. Let's pack it in."[13]

In 1976, Gordon and Anita agreed that Gordon should fulfill his dream of riding horseback across the Americas from Buenos Aires to New York City. The 5,300-mile horseback trek would take about two years to complete. Anita said, "I have admired people who want to be remarkable, who follow their beliefs and passions, who make grand gestures."[14] Anita wanted a real home life, which as entrepreneurs they had never had, and she wanted to spend some time with her children, who were four and six. She needed a business to survive and feed the children, so they decided she needed to open a shop.

The Body Shop

Anita decided to sell naturally based cosmetics in five sizes so that her customers had a choice. She felt that "people tend not to trust their gut instincts enough, especially about those things that irritate them, but the fact is that if something irritates you it is a pretty good indication that there are other people who feel the same. Irritation was a great source of energy and creativity."[15] She had been dissatisfied with the purchase of body lotion because most stores sold only one size.[16] Her dissatisfaction led her to question why she could not buy cosmetics by weight or bulk, like groceries or vegetables, and why a customer could not buy a small size of a cream or lotion to try it out before buying a big bottle. These were simple enough questions, but at the time there were no sensible answers.[17] She and Gordon discussed her concept for a shop where she could sell cosmetic products in a cheap container and in different sizes. He liked the concept. Anita decided to sell products made from "natural ingredients." The environmental green movement had not yet started.

She obtained a £4,000 bank loan (approximately $6,000) to open the first Body Shop at 22 Kensington Gardens, Brighton. The shop opened Saturday, March 26, 1976, at 9:00 A.M. By noon, Anita had to call Gordon and ask him to come to the shop and work. At 6:00 P.M., they closed the shop and counted the daily receipts of exactly £130. She had a goal of £300 of weekly receipts to cover her living costs.[18]

Just before she opened the shop, she had encountered opposition over the shop name, The Body Shop. The name came from the generic name for auto repair shops in the United States. Two nearby funeral homes threatened to sue her over the shop's name. She contacted the local newspaper about the pending lawsuits. The article on her plight helped draw attention to her new shop. Based on this experience, she developed a company policy of never spending a cent on advertising.[19] It has been estimated that The Body Shop receives £2,000,000 of free publicity each year based on the company's and Anita's position on key social problems. The shop's logo was designed by a local art student at a cost of £25.

In developing the design of The Body Shop, Anita based it on "a Second World War mentality (shortages, utility goods, and rationing) imposed by sheer necessity and the fact that I had no money. But I had a very clear image in my mind of the kind of style I wanted to create: I wanted it to look a bit like a country store in a spaghetti western."[20]

The first products—all 25 of them—were composed of natural ingredients that Anita could gather and mix together herself rather inexpensively. The cheapest bottles she could find were those used by hospitals to collect urine samples and she offered to fill any bottle the customer would bring in. The labels were plain and simple, as they still are today, and handwritten. The store also carried knickknacks to fill space, including cards, books, and jewelry; sometimes this merchandise accounted for 60% of the turnover. She developed loyal clients.

Perhaps because Anita sprayed Strawberry Essence on the sidewalks in the hopes that potential customers would follow it, the first store did well. After a successful summer, Anita

Exhibit 1

A Timeline: The Body Shop

1976	Anita Roddick opens the first branch of The Body Shop in Brighton on England's south coast.
1977	The first franchise of The Body Shop opens in Bognor Regis, England.
1978	The first branch opens outside the United Kingdom in Brussels, Belgium.
1984	The Body Shop goes public. With a placing of 95p ($1.38), shares close at £1.65 ($2.39) on the first day of dealing.
1985	The Body Shop runs its first in-shop campaign, "Save the Whale" with Greenpeace.
1986	The Body Shop launches its cosmetic range, called Colourings, and Mostly Men, a skin care line for men.
1987	The Body Shop establishes its first Trade Not Aid initiative in Nepal.
1988	The first U.S. branch of The Body Shop opens in New York.
	Soapworks, a soap-making plant for The Body Shop, opens in Easterhouse, Scotland.
	Queen awards Anita Roddick the Order of the British Empire (OBE).
1989	One million people sign The Body Shop's petition to "Stop the Burning" in the Amazon Rainforest.
	Anita receives the United Nations' Global 500 Environment Award.
1990	2.6 million people sign The Body Shop's "Against Animal Testing" petition.
	The Body Shop launches its Eastern European Drive of volunteers to renovate three orphanages in Halaucesti, Romania.
	The Body Shop opens in Tokyo, Japan.
1991	*The Big Issue*, a paper sold by and for the homeless, is launched by The Body Shop in London.
	Anita is awarded the World Vision Award by the Centre for World Development Education in recognition of Trade Not Aid initiative.
	The Body Shop marks Amnesty International's 30th anniversary with a campaign to increase membership.
1992	The Body Shop's voter registration drive in the United States signs up more than 33,000 voters.
	The Company publishes the results of the first environmental audit, *The Green Book*, in the United Kingdom.
	The Body Shop opens its first American community-based shop on 125th Street, Harlem, New York.
1993	The Body Shop opens its 1,000th shop.
	The American "Reuse/Refill/Recycle" campaign increases awareness of the refill and recycling services available at The Body Shop.
	The Body Shop USA joins with other corporations in signing the CERES Principles, an environmental code of conduct.
	The Body Shop USA joins forces with the Ms. Foundation to support the first annual Take Our Daughters to Work Day.
	The Body Shop USA is honored by the NAACP for excellence in minority economic development.
	"Protect & Respect" project, on AIDS education and awareness, is launched.
1994	The Body Shop launches its biggest ever international campaign in 30 markets and more than 900 shops to gain public support influencing the U.N. Convention on International Trade in Endangered Species to enforce regulations governing trade in endangered species.
1995	The Body Shop introduces The Body Shop Direct home selling operation.
1996	The first shop in the Philippines opens.
	First social audit published.
	The Body Shop is recognized in the 1996 PR Week award categories for Best International Campaign and Best Overall PR Campaign in the United Kingdom for the Ogoni people of Nigeria campaign.
	Largest ever petition on animal testing—over 4 million signatures from 16 countries—was presented to the European Parliament and Commission in Brussels in November.
1997	Created an international Franchisee Advisory Board.
	Won the Retail Week Store Design of the Year Award for its new format stores.
1998	With Amnesty International, launched Make Your Mark on May 11 in Atlanta, Georgia, with the Dalai Lama.
	Published *Naked Body*, a 50-page magazine featuring articles on hemp, beauty tips, a photo of a woman's naked lower body, and an interview with a London prostitute.

Source: The Body Shop, "This Is the Body Shop" (November 1994), pp. 3–4, and author's additions.

decided to open a second store in Chichester and approached the bank for a £4,000 loan. She was turned down because she had no track record. So, she turned to a friend, Ian McGlinn, who owned a local garage. Ian received a 50% interest in the company for his investment.[21] In 1998, he owned 45,666,768 (23.5%) of the ordinary shares. The Roddicks owed 48,237,136 shares. Ian played no role in the management of the company. Anita felt, "To succeed you have to believe in something with such a passion that it becomes a reality."[22] This was one of the two principal reasons for the company's initial success. The other was that Anita had to survive while Gordon was away. **Exhibit 1** shows a timeline of the key highlights of the company.

Franchising as a Growth Strategy

A friend's daughter, Chris Green, wanted to open her own shop in Hove. The Roddicks agreed and thought it was a great idea. Their only interest was in her selling their products. There were no fees or contracts. Another friend, Aidre, wanted to open a shop with her parents in Bognor Regis. They gave her the same deal.

Gordon had returned home before the two shops were opened. He could see the potential of the business to grow, but no bank wanted to lend them money.

Gordon hired a lawyer to develop a franchising contract. The formula was based on a license to use The Body Shop name and to sell its products, and the franchisee would put up the money. In 1978, the first franchise outside the United Kingdom was opened in Brussels. The franchise fee was £300.[23] Women owned all the initial franchises. Anita felt that "men were good at the science and vocabulary of business, at talking about economic theory and profits and loss figures (some women are, too, of course). But I could also see that women were better at dealing with people, caring, and being passionate about what they are doing."[24]

During this time, the company was developing its own style of "respond[ing] to needs rather than creating them."[25] The company was run in an informal way as an extended big family. Anita understood the concept of developing a niche around a competitive advantage. She said, "A true key to success is knowing what features set you apart from the competitor."[26] And also, "We had stuck closely to a policy of being open and honest about our products, and it was paying dividends among our customers who were increasingly irritated by the patently dishonest advertising of the cosmetics industry. Women in the 1980s were less and less inclined to fall for the 'buy this mixture of oil and water and you will be a movie star' pitch dreamed up in the expensive offices of advertising agencies."[27]

By 1982, the Roddicks were exercising much stricter control over what could and could not be done in the shop. They had learned, from experience, that it was absolutely essential to maintain a strong identity.[28] The company opened shops at the rate of two a month. They had shops in Iceland, Denmark, Finland, Holland, and Ireland.

During these early franchising years, the biggest mistake management made was offering three choices of shop styles to franchisees—dark green, dark mahogany stain, or stripped pine. Anita quickly recognized that the shops looked different, and as such the shops lost their distinctiveness. So she persuaded all the shops to return to the dark green.[29]

Anita kept strict control over the franchising process. At times, 5,000 franchise applications were in process. The franchise process included a home visit, a personality test, and an assessment of the applicant's attitude toward people and the environment. The process could take three years to complete. In the final interview with Anita, she was known to ask unexpected questions ("How would you like to die?" "Who is your favorite heroine in literature?") This type of applicant process could ensure that the franchisee would adhere to the principles and image of The Body Shop. After being selected to own a franchise, owners underwent extensive training on products, store operations, and merchandising techniques.

In 1985, The Body Shop Training School opened. The curriculum focused on human development and consciousness-raising. Anita said, "Conventional retailers trained for a sale; we

Exhibit 2
Shop Locations by Regions: The Body Shop[1]

	Number of Shops			First Shop
	February 1998	February 1997	February 1996	Opening
Europe				
Austria	17	17	15	1979
Belgium	18	18	18	1978
Cyprus	3	3	3	1983
Denmark	19	20	19	1981
Eire	11	11	10	1981
Finland	24	23	21	1981
France	23	32	34	1982
Germany	72	67	60	1983
Gibraltar	1	1	1	1988
Greece	51	46	44	1979
Holland	50	51	50	1982
Iceland	3	2	2	1980
Italy	53	50	46	1984
Luxembourg	2	2	2	1991
Malta	3	1	1	1987
Norway	24	24	21	1985
Portugal	12	11	9	1986
Spain	65	63	59	1986
Sweden	48	44	42	1979
Switzerland	28	28	27	1983
Total Shops	**527**	**514**	**484**	
United Kingdom				
Total Shops	**263**	**256**	**252**	1976
Asia				
Bahrain	2	2	2	1985
Brunei	3	3	3	1993
Hong Kong	16	13	11	1984
Indonesia	17	13	8	1990
Japan	116	87	58	1990
Korea	5	0	0	1997
Kuwait	9	8	3	1986
Macau	3	2	2	1993
Malaysia	25	22	21	1984
Oman	4	4	2	1986
Philippines	7	3	0	1996
Qatar	1	1	1	1987
Saudi Arabia	33	25	21	1987
Singapore	16	15	12	1983
Taiwan	34	21	14	1988
Thailand	12	9	8	1993
UAE	5	5	4	1983
Total Shops	**308**	**233**	**170**	

(*Continued*)

Exhibit 2

Shop Locations by Regions: The Body Shop *(continued)*

	Number of Shops			First Shop Opening
	February 1998	**February 1997**	**February 1996**	
Australia and New Zealand				
Australia	62	59	57	1983
New Zealand	14	12	11	1989
Total Shops	**76**	**71**	**68**	
America Excluding USA				
Antigua	1	1	1	1987
Bahamas	3	3	3	1985
Bermuda	1	2	2	1987
Canada	119	119	115	1980
Cayman Islands	1	1	1	1989
Mexico	5	4	4	1993
Total Shops	**130**	**130**	**126**	
USA				
Total Shops	**290**	**287**	**273**	1988
Grand Total Shops	**1,594**	**1,491**	**1,373**	

Note:
1. The Company shops (1998) are located as follows:
   - USA 210, UK 67, Singapore 16, France 15
   - Number of countries: 47
   - Number of languages company traded in: 24

Source: The Body Shop, *1998* and *1997 Annual Reports*, pp. 68 and 48.

trained for knowledge. They trained with an eye on the balance sheet; we trained with an eye on the soul."[30] The courses centered on "educating" the participant, not training. In the customer care course, the teacher "encouraged the staff to treat customers as potential friends, to say hello, smile, make eye contact and to offer advice if it was wanted, to thank them and always to invite them back."[31] She viewed money spent on staff training as an investment and not as an expense.

Franchisees had mixed feelings over developments at The Body Shop to pursue direct selling at home parties through Body Shop Direct and sales of products over the Internet. Some felt threatened and wanted to sell back their stores. They felt customers would bypass their shops and order on the Web. Others felt these new distribution channels would help them rather than take sales away.

In 1998, The Body Shop had over 1,594 shops in 47 countries (see **Exhibit 2**) and traded in 24 languages worldwide. The Body Shop expected to open 70 new stores in 1999, almost all of which would be franchised.[32]

Anita Roddick's Philosophy and Personal Values Translate into Corporate Culture and Citizenship

Below are some of Anita's most salient quotes on the issues of our time:

It is immoral to trade on fear. It is immoral to make women feel dissatisfied with their bodies. It is immoral to deceive a customer by making miracle claims for a product. It is immoral to use a photograph of a glowing 16-year-old to sell a (beauty) cream aimed at preventing wrinkles in a 40-year-old.[33]

I think all business practices would improve immeasurably if they were guided by "feminine" principles—qualities like love and care and intuition.[34]

I honestly believe I would not have succeeded if I had been taught about business.[35]

We communicate with passion, and passion persuades.[36]

I learned there was nothing more important to life than love and work.[37]

Passion persuades, and by God I was passionate about what I was selling.[38]

In a society in which politicians no longer lead by example, ethical conduct is unfashionable, and the media does not give people real information on what is happening in the world, what fascinates me is the concept of turning our shops into centers of education.[39]

You can be proud to work for The Body Shop and boy, does that have an effect on morale and motivation.[40]

I have never been able to separate Body Shop values from my personal values.[41]

I think the leadership of a company should encourage the next generation not just to follow, but to overtake.[42]

When you take the high moral road, it is difficult for anyone to object without sounding like a fool.[43]

Whenever we wanted to persuade our staff to support a particular project we always tried to break their hearts.[44]

You have to look at leadership through the eyes of the followers and you have to live the message. What I have learned is that people become motivated when you guide them to the source of their own power and when you make heroes out of employees who personify what you want to see in the organization.[45]

I do not believe women have a chance in hell of achieving their desired status and power in business within the foreseeable future. My daughters might see it, but I won't.[46]

If you have a company with itsy-bitsy vision, you have an itsy-bitsy company.[47]

The thought that every day might be my last, and the desire to make the most of every moment, drives me on.[48]

These were the statements of a unique woman who had a strong personal value system that she clearly articulated. She saw herself as a concerned citizen of the world, who continuously searched and developed solutions for its problems; a leader in the green political movement; a very successful business leader; a spokesperson for those without a voice in the world arena; a wife; a mother; and a daughter. She served the needs of the underprivileged and the environment. Anita was a trader. She said, "I am not rushing around the world as some kind of loony do-gooder; first and foremost I am a trader looking for a trade."[49]

In 1988, Anita was knighted by Queen Elizabeth into the Order of the British Empire (OBE).

United States Market

HISTORY

By 1987, the company received about 10,000 letters from the United States inquiring about franchising opportunities and asking when stores would be opened so they could purchase products.

Before opening the first U.S. store, the Roddicks negotiated for the trademark to The Body Shop. Two companies, owned by the Saunders and Short families, held the rights between them to "The Body Shop" name. Their trademark covered the United States and

Japan, which represented 40% of the world's consumers. Gordon negotiated to buy the rights in both countries for $3,500,000.

The first shop was opened in New York on Broadway and 8th Street on July 1, 1988. A few weeks before opening, there was much questioning whether The Body Shop could succeed in the United States without advertising. A Harvard Business School professor was quoted in the *Wall Street Journal* saying that the company needed, "at minimum," a major launch advertising campaign. Anita had the quote reprinted on a postcard with her response: "I'll never hire anyone from the Harvard Business School."[50]

The first shop was an instant success, and over the next two years, 13 more company-owned shops were opened. Initially the company had a hard time trying to locate in malls because it was an unknown. Management asked their mail-order customers, who lived within a 110-mile radius of a proposed shop, for a letter-writing campaign. It was very successful. The first franchised store in the United States was opened in Washington, DC, in 1990.

After this successful start in the United States, The Body Shop began to run into trouble. Unsuccessful managers, too many product lines, copycat rivals who discounted, and too few products created specifically for the U.S. consumer were some of the biggest problems. Many U.S. stores were located in expensive major cities that led to high real estate costs. By 1995, critics were saying that U.S. consumers no longer bought into the company's political message. Price-driven consumers did not rate The Body Shop as a premium brand. Instead, they enjoyed the aggressive discounting by Body Shop rivals Garden Botanica and Bath & Body Works. Turnover in Body Shop U.S. leadership and low brand recognition due to lack of advertising contributed to the problem.

JOINT VENTURE

In January 1997, Adrian Bellamy became a Non-Executive (outside member of The Body Shop's Board of Directors). From 1983 until he retired in 1995, Bellamy had served as Chairman and CEO of DFS Group Limited—the U.S.-based global duty-free and luxury goods retailer. He also served as a Non-executive Director of GAP Inc., Gucci Group NV, and Williams-Sonoma. He approached The Body Shop board with the idea for a joint venture. The terms of the deal were as follows:

- Bellamy Retail Group (BRG) LLC would pay The Body Shop a nonrefundable $1 million to acquire options over the U.S. business.
- BRG would immediately take over management responsibility of The Body Shop in the United States with options to buy 49% of the company at its net asset value between 2000 and 2002, provided it met performance targets.

Bellamy had a further option to acquire another 2% of the company at a later date. The targets were to reach breakeven by 2000, a profit of $1 million in 2001, and $4 million in 2002. The option lapsed if aggregate losses of $4 million or more occurred in the United States in 2000 and 2001.[51]

At the June 19, 1998, shareholders' meeting, only a handful of shareholders voted against the management.[52] Bellamy planned to focus the new U.S. regime on boosting sales per square foot by improving retail operations and marketing and also by cutting operating costs. He planned to focus on better customer service, improved promotions, and a balanced product range.[53]

As of February 1998, there were 290 shops in the U.S. Retail sales were £98.5 million ($161.6 million) and £100.6 million ($165.0 million) for 1998 and 1997, respectively. As of June 1998, The Body Shop U.S. was not taking applications for new franchises.

Mission Statement

The company's mission statement dedicated its business to the pursuit of social and environmental change:

> To creatively balance the financial and human needs of our stakeholders: employees, customers, franchisees, suppliers, and shareholders.
>
> To courageously ensure that our business is ecologically sustainable, meeting the needs of the present without compromising the future.
>
> To meaningfully contribute to local, national, and international communities in which we trade, by adopting a code of conduct which ensures care, honesty, fairness, and respect.
>
> To passionately campaign for the protection of the environment and human and civil rights, and against animal testing within the cosmetics and toiletries industry.
>
> To tirelessly work to narrow the gap between principle and practice, while making fun, passion, and care part of our daily lives.[54]

Corporate Governance

BOARD OF DIRECTORS

The *Annual Report* stated the Directors' responsibilities. The Directors were required by company law to prepare financial statements for each financial year that give a true and fair view of the state of affairs of the company and the group and of the profit or loss of the group for that period.

In preparing those financial statements, the Directors were required to:

- Select suitable accounting policies and then apply them consistently.
- Make judgments and estimates that are reasonable and prudent.
- State whether applicable accounting standards have been followed, subject to any material departures disclosed and explained in the financial statements.
- Prepare the financial statements on the going concern basis unless it is inappropriate to presume that the company will continue in business.

The Directors were responsible for maintaining proper accounting records that disclosed with reasonable accuracy at any time the financial position of the company and to enable them to ensure that the financial statements comply with the Companies Act. They were also responsible for safeguarding the assets of the company and hence for taking reasonable steps for the prevention and detection of fraud and other irregularities.[55]

There were 11 board members, of which 8 were Executive and 3 Non-Executive Directors. The first Non-Executive Directors had been appointed in 1995.

The board members were as follows:[56]

Anita L. Roddick, OBE	Chief Executive
T. Gordon Roddick	Chairman
Stuart A. Rose	Managing Director
Eric G. Helyer	Executive
Ivan C. Levy	Executive
Jane Reid	Executive
Jeremy A. Kett	Executive
Terry G. Hartin	Executive
Penny Hughes	Non-Executive
Aldo Papone	Non-Executive
Adrian D. Bellamy	Non-Executive

Remuneration for the Executive Directors in 1998 was as follows:[57]

(British pound amounts in thousands)

Name	Salary	Benefits	Total
A. L. Roddick	140	22	162
T. G. Roddick	140	22	162
S. A. Rose	250		250
E. G. Helyer	161		161
J. Reid	220		220
J. A. Kett	155		155
T. G. Hartin	286	7	293
I. C. Levy	198	56	254

The Remuneration Committee recommended that the total salaries of both Anita and Gordon Roddick be at a rate of £300,000 per annum, but the Roddicks have chosen to be remunerated at the level set out in the preceding table (an increase of £5,000 each).

Directors' share holdings in 1998 were as follows:[58]

A. L. Roddick	24,010,456
T. G. Roddick	24,226,680
E. G. Helyer	10,000
I. C. Levy	300
T. G. Hartin	15,785
A. Papone	3,000

Ian McGlinn, who had loaned £6,000 to Anita to open her second shop, owned 45,666,768 (23.5%) ordinary shares. The Prudential Corporation owned 6,911,146 (3.6%) ordinary shares, and the Aeon Group had an interest in 6,700,000 (3.5%).

TOP MANAGEMENT

Anita said about Gordon and her roles that "Gordon rarely accompanies me on shop visits because we are each more comfortable in our chosen roles of high profile and low profile. Outsiders often think of Gordon as a shadowy figure, but that is certainly not how he is viewed within The Body Shop. He is well known to everyone, much loved, and deeply respected as the real strength of the company. Our relationship bequeathed a very distinct management style to the company—loosely structured, collaborative, imaginative, and improvisatory, rather than by the book—which matured as the company expanded. I think Gordon provides a sense of constancy and continuity, while I bounce around breaking the rules, pushing back the boundaries of possibility, and shooting off my mouth. We rarely argue . . . it is never about values. His calm presence and enormous influence are rarely taken into account by critics who see The Body Shop as a flaky organization led by a madwoman with fuzzy hair."[59]

Group Structure and Organization

The Body Shop International PLC had stakes in six principal subsidiaries as of February 28, 1998 (see **Exhibit 3**). The operating structure is shown in **Exhibit 4.**

Marketing and Advertising

The company had no marketing or advertising department. In 1979, Janis Raven was hired to handle public relations. She helped to publicize the company for its image and stances on public social issues. An analyst felt that the lack of an advertising and marketing budget con-

Exhibit 3
Principal Subsidiaries: The Body Shop International PLC

The Body Shop Inc. (90% owned, USA)[1]
Responsible for U.S. retail activities.
The Body Shop (Singapore) Pte Limited (100% owned, Singapore)[1]
Responsible for The Body Shop retail outlets in Singapore.
Soapworks Limited (100% owned, Great Britain)[1]
Manufactures soap and related products.
Skin & Hair Care Preparations Inc. (100% owned, USA)[1]
U.S. holding company. Does not trade.
The Body Shop Direct Limited (100% owned, Great Britain)[1]
Makes direct sales through a home-selling program.
The Body Shop (France) SARL (100% owned, France)[1]
Operates The Body Shop retail outlets in France.

Note:
1. Shows % holding ordinary shares and country of incorporation and operation.

Source: The Body Shop, *1998 Annual Report*, p. 52.

tributed to low repeat customer sales. Customers came in looking for a gift for a friend or out of curiosity. Once the customer satisfied his or her need, there seemed to be little incentive for the customer to come back. Product Information Manuals (PIMs) were available to all customers and staff to increase their knowledge or answer questions about every Body Shop product. These manuals contained information about how the products were made, a listing of product ingredients, and the uses for each product. Many potential customers were not sure what products the company offered.

Anita Roddick used regular visits by regional managers to keep tight control over shop layout, window displays, PIM handouts, and operating style. Anita viewed marketing as hype;

Exhibit 4
Operating Structure

*Group-owned.

Source: The Body Shop, *1996 Annual Report*.

instead she wanted to establish credibility by educating the customer. She viewed the shop as the company's primary marketing tool. In 1990, The Body Shop was nominated to the United Kingdom Marketing Hall of Fame.

By 1997, Body Shop products were regularly accused of being "tired" and "lacking innovation."[60] One critic went so far as to say that the product mix would not be out of place in Woolworth's.[61] Recognizing this, The Body Shop placed a high priority on reorganizing the product range. The goal was to refocus on core lines and values, communicate effectively with consumers, and create new products that were young, funky, energizing, and marketed efficiently.[62]

Packaging also received a new look in 1997. Instead of continuing with dark green labels, clear labels were phased in to create a more sophisticated look. Colorings of makeup cases went from gun metal gray to metallic green.[63]

Complaints of cluttered, dark, uninviting shops led The Body Shop to design a new store format. The new store format performed well in the United Kingdom during the first year, 1997. The Body Shop planned to open up to 150 new format stores within 2 years.[64] Five U.S. stores scheduled to undergo face lifts in 1998 were straying from the signature green look of old stores. Brighter lighting, hardwood floors, a bolder storefront logo, and light green, bright orange, and yellow colors were intended to help consumers locate products more easily.[65]

In 1997, The Body Shop launched a self-esteem campaign featuring Ruby Rubenesque, a plus-sized doll, as the spokeswoman. A strategic alliance formed with British Airways provided amenity kits from The Body Shop to over two million passengers who flew Club World each year.

Product Development and Production

In 1998, the company introduced three major new lines of products: Hemp, Aromatherapy, and Bergamot. In May 1998, The Body Shop unveiled a five-product body care line for dry skin formulated with hemp. It featured hand protector, lip conditioner, soap, elbow grease, and 3-in-1 oil for dry skin sold in metal tins with hemp leaf designs on the packaging. The Body Shop developed educational pamphlets to distribute in stores describing the essential fatty acids and amino acids found in the herb. Support of hemp farmers at the local level was begun immediately. In the United States, the 1970 Controlled Substance Act made it illegal to grow marijuana. The difference between drug-grade marijuana and industrial hemp is the level of tetrahydrocannabinol (THC). Marijuana contains high levels of THC, which is psychoactive, whereas hemp has so little THC that it's virtually drug-free.[66]

Anita handed out packets of hemp seeds that carried the message: "Do not attempt to use this plant as a narcotic. You would need to smoke a joint the size of a telegraph pole to get high." Within a week of going on sale, the Hemp range accounted for 5% of total sales.[67]

Aromatherapy—the use of essential oils to enhance physical and mental well-being—fit in well with the value of The Body Shop. Products in this range included shower gel, massage oils, foaming milk bath, and bath oils organized into four collections: Energizing, Balancing, Relaxing, and Sensual.

Products made with Bergamot oil were a key component of the Aromatherapy range. A bergamot is a small bitter, yellow-green citrus fruit grown in Calabria, Italy. Bergamot oil was reputed to have a stimulating effect that reinvigorated the mind and imparted a feeling of well-being. Because its oil could be produced synthetically at very low cost, the bergamot orchards in Italy had been cleared, destroying the local economy. Anita was trying to reverse the decline in the region by increasing the demand for the fruit and thereby bringing jobs and income to the area. This Community Trade relationship had been developed from the collaboration between Simone Mizzi, the Italian Head Franchisee of The Body Shop, The Body Shop International, and the Calabrian authorities. The Body Shop's Trading Charter and Mission are included in **Exhibit 5**.

Exhibit 5
Trading Charter and Mission: The Body Shop

A. OUR TRADING CHARTER

The way we trade creates profits with principles.

We aim to achieve commercial success by meeting our customers' needs through the provision of high quality, good value products with exceptional service and relevant information which enables customers to make informed and responsible choices.

Our trading relationships of every kind—with customers, franchisees, and suppliers—will be commercially viable, mutually beneficial, and based on trust and respect.

Our trading principles reflect our core values.

We aim to ensure that human and civil rights, as set out in the Universal Declaration of Human Rights, are respected throughout our business activities.

We will establish a framework based on this declaration to include criteria for workers' rights embracing a safe, healthy working environment, fair wages, no discrimination on the basis of race, creed, sex or sexual orientation, or physical coercion of any kind.

We will support long-term, sustainable relationships with communities in need.

We will pay special attention to those minority groups, women, and disadvantaged peoples who are socially and economically marginalized.

We will use environmentally sustainable resources wherever technically and economically viable. Our purchasing will be based on a system of screening and investigation of the ecological credentials of our finished products, ingredients, packaging, and suppliers.

We will promote animal protection throughout our business activities. We are against animal testing in the cosmetics and toiletries industry. We will not test ingredients or products on animals, nor will we commission others to do so on our behalf. We will use our purchasing power to stop suppliers' animal testing.

We will institute appropriate monitoring, auditing, and disclosure mechanisms to ensure our accountability and demonstrate our compliance with these principles.

B. DIRECT TRADING: OUR MISSION

The Body Shop believes that all trading should be viewed as an exercise in ethics. This is the attitude we seek to apply to all goods and services within the company and its retail shops.

Our ethical trading program helps create livelihoods for economically stressed communities, mostly in the majority world. Although trading with such communities is currently just a small percentage of all our trade, we intend to increase this practice wherever possible.

Fair Prices. The Body Shop will pay for the products it purchases. While our program aims to benefit the primary producers directly, we also recognize the value of commercial intermediaries. Where world market prices are applicable, we commit ourselves to pay these prices or more.

Partnership. Both sides must benefit commercially. We aim to develop long-term relationships if possible, and plan to work in partnership to solve potential problems. We aim to help our trade partners achieve self-reliance.

Community Benefits. The company will work with a variety of trading partners—cooperatives, family businesses, tribal councils—with the intention of benefiting the individual worker as much as possible. We can't control the dispersal of community benefits that we provide. That process is determined by local needs, which may mean anything from funds managed by consensus to direct payments to individual producers.

(Continued)

Exhibit 5
Trading Charter and Mission: The Body Shop *(continued)*

Respect. Our trading relationships are based on respect. The guidelines we are developing for sustainable development ensure that we respect all environments and cultures that may be affected by our trade. Wherever possible, we use renewable natural materials and skills that are appropriate to local cultures.

Cooperation. The Body Shop is committed to an open relationship with other fair trade organizations and places great emphasis on maintaining dialogue with organizations that are helping to define the path to sustainable development.

Accountability. We believe it is essential that our trading policy be measurable, audited, and open to scrutiny, and we are energetically seeking the mechanisms to achieve that goal. We already use an open approach to assess our impact on the environment and to promote our opposition to animal testing in the cosmetics industry by monitoring our suppliers.

Our trading practices are not the solution to everyone's needs. We simply see them as one component of the help we feel qualified to give. We will also help trading partners to broadly assess the likely social and environmental impact of developing trade.

In committing itself to the above aims, The Body Shop believes it is creating a trading policy that will satisfy the needs of our business, our trading partners, and our customers. Letting consumers know that neither places nor peoples have been exploited in getting our products to market helps The Body Shop customer make informed, responsible choices.

Source: The Body Shop, handouts.

In-house manufacturing facilities at Littlehampton, Glasgow, and Wake Forest in the United States produced approximately 60% of The Body Shop products, excluding accessories. Bulk production of toiletries rose 13% to 9,427 tons from 1997 at the Watersmead plant. The U.S. facility filled 11.8 million units, up 4% from 1997.

Soapworks, a wholly owned subsidiary of The Body Shop, manufactured soap and essential oil filling for the Aromatherapy range. Anita opened the facility in Easterhouse, Scotland, an area with historically high unemployment. When Soapworks was founded, the company made a commitment to donate 25% of its cumulative after-tax profits to local community projects. Between 1989 and 1998, the group had made or provided for donations of £274,810. Soapworks manufactured 30 million units in 1998, which was an increase of 4% over 1997.

Anita spent up to five months a year traveling the world looking for new product ideas and ingredients. Her samples were brought back to Watersmead where they were analyzed for their potential and durability. The department was backed up by anthropological and ethnobotanical research in traditional uses of plants, herbs, fruits, flowers, seeds, and nuts.

Human Resources Management

Most of the employees in the company were women under 30. Anita constantly worked at communications within the company. Each shop had a bulletin board, a fax machine, and a video player with which she provided the staff a continuous stream of information concerning new products, causes that she supported, or status reports on her latest trip. The in-house video production company produced "Talking Shop," which was a monthly multilingual video magazine. It also produced training tapes and documentaries on social campaigns.

Anita encouraged upward communication through a suggestion system, DODGI (The Department of Damned Good Ideas), and through regularly scheduled meetings of a cross-section of staff, often at her home. She set up the "Red Letter" system so an employee could directly communicate with a director and bypass the normal chain of communications.

She believed in educating her employees and customers. In 1985, The Body Shop Training Center was opened in London and began offering courses on the company's products and philosophy, customer services, and hair and skin care problems. Sessions were held on key social issues such as AIDS, aging, management by humor, drug and alcohol abuse, and urban survival. She discussed the idea of opening a business college. She said, "You can train dogs and you can train horses, but we wanted to educate and help the people realize their potential."[68]

The Body Shop empowered its staff. It encouraged debate, encouraged employees to speak out and state their views. Anita wanted her staff to be personally involved in social campaigns. She said, "One of the risks of corporate campaigning is that the staff start to fall in love with doing good and forget about trading."[69]

Anita had problems recruiting staff for the U.S. headquarters, located in New Jersey, because employees were not willing or able to embrace the company's culture. She went on to say, "Most of them came from conventional, moribund jobs and seemed confused by the idea of a company being quirky or zany or contemptuous of mediocrity. I could never seem to get their adrenaline surging. We are a company in which image, design, style, and creativity are of paramount importance, but we were unable to find employees who appreciate these qualities."[70] Headquarters for the United States were moved to Wake Forest (Winston-Salem), North Carolina, in 1993. Although in 1998, in the face of the troubled U.S. market, Anita admitted that it had been a mistake to move the U.S. headquarters to North Carolina instead of a big city like New York or San Francisco.

The company created "the Company Care Team, a five-person group that is taking responsibility for The Body Shop's performance as a caring employer. The team coordinated child care through the company's Family Centre and through the launch in April 1994 of programs offering financial help with child care for all company staff. A counselor service provided 24-hour confidential counseling services for employees and their families."[71]

Global Corporate Citizenship

The company clearly stated its position on the key global issue of corporate citizenship in its publication, *This Is the Body Shop*:[72]

Human and Civil Rights

The Body Shop is committed to supporting and promoting social and environmental change for the better. We recognize that human and civil rights are at the very heart of such change.

We're All in This Together

Working with organizations like Amnesty International, Human Rights Watch, the Unrepresented Nations and Peoples Organization, and the Foundation for Ethnobiology, The Body Shop has tried to promote awareness of our responsibility as human beings. What happens to one of us affects us all. We can no longer pretend it is none of our business if people suffer, whether they're on the other side of the world or in our own backyards. Here are a few successful examples of work by The Body Shop in both those areas:

- In 1990, The Body Shop started a relief drive to fund volunteers to renovate orphanages in Romania, where thousands of children had been abandoned under the regime of dictator Nicolae Ceacescu. The Project has been so successful that we've now extended it to Albania.

- In 1993, the Body Shop Foundation donated £162,000 ($234,900) to "Rights and Wrongs," a weekly human rights television series created by Globalvision Inc. on a nonprofit basis. By focusing on the human rights revolution around the world, the series explained how interrelated many of our problems are.

- In 1993, our biggest campaign in the U.S. focused attention on people living with HIV and AIDS. Working with groups like the American Red Cross, the San Francisco AIDS Foundation, the Gay Men's Health Crisis, and the National Leadership Coalition on AIDS, we developed a multifaceted campaign, focusing particularly on women and teenagers who are the fastest growing risk groups for HIV infection. Using the theme "Protect & Respect," our campaign included a new corporate policy on life threatening illness; training for all our employees; educational materials on safer sex and living with HIV and AIDS for distribution in our shops; outreach to local community groups; and funding support for organizations which assist people with HIV and AIDS.

- The Body Shop Foundation was founded in1989. The company donated £0.9 million to the foundation in 1997/98, up from £0.75 million in 1996/97.[73]

Against Animal Testing

The Body Shop is against animal testing of ingredients and products in the cosmetics industry. We do not test our products or ingredients on animals. Nor do we commission others to test on our behalf. We never have and we never will.

We will never endorse the use of animal tests in the cosmetics or toiletries industry. However, no cosmetics company can claim that its manufactured ingredients have never been tested on animals by somebody at some stage for someone. We support a complete ban on the testing of both finished cosmetic products and individual ingredients used in cosmetic products.

We work with leading animal welfare organizations to lobby for a complete ban on animal testing of cosmetic ingredients and products. We also encourage our ingredient suppliers and those who want to become our suppliers to stop animal testing by making our position on animal testing clear to them. We require our suppliers of raw materials to provide written confirmation every six months that any material they supply to us has not been tested by them for the cosmetics industry for the last five years.

The "five-year rolling rule" is the most effective mechanism for change. Every six months, our technical information specialists send out hundreds of declarations requiring all our suppliers to certify the last date of any animal testing they have conducted on behalf of the cosmetics industry on any ingredient which they supply to us.

If a supplier fails to complete the form, the company is pursued until we get the information we need. If no declaration is forthcoming, or if the company reports conducting an animal test for any part of the cosmetics industry within the last five years, we immediately stop buying the ingredient from that supplier and look for alternative suppliers who have not tested on animals within the previous five years. If no supplier can be found who meets the five-year rule, we will try to reformulate the product without that ingredient. If we cannot reformulate, we will stop making the product.

Some companies who adopt an against-animal-testing policy take a "fixed cut off date" stance, declaring they will not use an ingredient which comes into existence after a specific date. This position does little to persuade ingredient suppliers, who continue to develop new ingredients, to stop animal testing. A "fixed cut off date" company provides no market for new ingredients, forcing suppliers to continue dealing with those cosmetic companies which require tests. In addition, the extent to which a company's suppliers adhere to its rule may be questionable since most "cut-off" date companies never recheck with their suppliers to see if previously untested ingredients have been retested.

The Body Shop polices the five-year rule. It's not just the rule itself that provokes the changes we want. It's the policing with regard to each ingredient. As our ingredient suppliers trade with new customers and in new markets, they are confronted by additional demands for animal testing. Our twice yearly declarations ensure they continue to meet our requirements.

We rely upon a number of alternative techniques to help assess a product's safety. At The Body Shop, customer safety is paramount. We believe (as do many experts) that the reliability of animal testing is questionable. In developing products we use natural ingredients, like bananas and Brazil nut oil, as well as others with a long history of human usage. Our ingredients and/or finished products are subject to in-vitro testing methods such as Eytex, human patch testing, SPF testing, and analytical procedures.

Working for the World's Wildlife

All around the world animals are in danger of extinction as their food sources are threatened, their natural habitats diminish, and environmental degradation takes its toll. The Body Shop takes action on several fronts to keep this critical issue in the public eye.

The Body Shop has a long established commitment to helping endangered species. Over the years, The Body Shop and its franchisees have raised hundreds of thousands of dollars, locally, nationally, and internationally, to support a host of campaigns and projects. We also work hard to inform the public and influence governments the world over to protect the environment and stop the illegal trade in endangered species.

Care for the Environment

The Body Shop believes it just isn't possible for any business to claim to be environmentally friendly because all commerce involves some environmental impact. But at The Body Shop, we take responsibility for the waste we create. We aim to avoid excessive packaging, to refill our bottles, and to recycle our packaging and use raw ingredients from renewable sources whenever technically and economically feasible.

The most accessible aspect of our environmental practice for customers is our refill service. Customers bring back their empty, clean containers and we refill them with the same product at a discount. This conserves resources, reduces waste, and saves money. We also accept our packaging back for recycling. At the same time, we're always searching for new ways to reduce our impact on the environment. In the United Kingdom, we are investing in wind energy with the ultimate aim of putting back into the national grid as much electricity as we take out.

In the United States, we've yet to achieve the level of environmental management reached in the United Kingdom and, unsurprisingly, we've had some growing pains which we've done our best to minimize. For instance, we discovered that because of regulations in some states, our larger bottles required special labels to comply with the state's recycling program. So we used a special stick-on label while we phased out stock of that particular bottle.

A New Kind of Audit

To create a framework for our environmental commitment, we have introduced an annual environmental audit pursuant to European Community Eco-management and Audit Regulation at our U.K. headquarters. The results of the audit are publicly available. [See **Exhibit 6** for results of first social audit.] By setting targets to meet on a yearly basis, the audit process is a constant challenge to our commitment, as well as a campaigning platform for us and a role model for other companies. And it's a constant reminder to staff that good environment housekeeping is everyone's business.

Having relocated our headquarters to Wake Forest, NC, from Cedar Knolls, NJ, we are now committed to publishing a comprehensive and externally verified environmental audit statement like "The Green Book," which is published annually in the United Kingdom. Our internal reviews have helped us identify problems to work on and get our staff more involved in environmental management as well.

We are beginning to execute environmental reviews at our principal subsidiaries, retail outlets, and overseas franchises. All will be subject to independent examinations which will eventually result in separately accountable environmental management procedures.[74]

In 1995, the company commissioned Professor Kirk Hanson, a leading American professor in business ethics and social responsibility at the Graduate School of Business of Stanford University, to conduct an independent evaluation of the company's social performance and make recommendations for improvements.[75]

A Brief Summary of Our Environmental Policy

1. Think Globally as a constant reminder of our responsibility to protect the environment.
2. Achieve Excellence by setting clear targets and time scales within which to meet them.
3. Search for Sustainability by using renewable resources wherever feasible and conserving natural resources where renewable options aren't available.

Exhibit 6
Results of Social Audit—The Good News and *The Bad News*: The Body Shop

Employees	Franchisees	Customers
93% agreed or strongly agreed that The Body Shop lives up to its mission on the issues of environmental responsibility and animal testing.	94% of U.K. and 73% of U.S. franchisees agreed or strongly agreed that The Body Shop campaigns effectively on human rights, environmental protection, and animal testing.	The Body Shop scored an average of 7.5 out of 10 for campaigning effectively on human rights, environmental protection, and animal protection.
79% agreed or strongly agreed that working for The Body Shop has raised their awareness of pressing global issues.	90% of U.K. and 80% of U.S. franchisees felt that the company provides reliable and honest information to them on social issues.	The Body Shop scored an average of 9 out of 10 for its stance against animal testing among British customers.
23% felt the best way for them to develop their career was to change companies.	*More than one-fifth of U.K. and U.S. franchisees expressed no opinion on the majority of issues related to doing business with The Body Shop.*	*Many customers in the U.K. and U.S. are still confused by what is natural.*
53% disagreed or strongly disagreed that the behavior and decision making of managers was consistent throughout the company.	*43% of U.K. and 64% of U.S. franchisees disagreed that The Body Shop's sales divisions communicated their long-term strategy clearly to the franchisees.*	*U.K. customer complaints rose from 18.3 per 100,000 transactions in 1992/93 to 20.9 per 100,000 transactions in 1994/95.*

Suppliers	Shareholders	Community Involvement
95% agree or strongly agree that The Body Shop takes active steps to make its business more environmentally responsible.	90% agreed or strongly agreed that The Body Shop takes active steps to make its business more environmentally responsible.	In 1994/95 The Body Shop's directly employed staff gave an estimated 19,500 hours to projects in the community.
Prompt payment, clarity of delivery and purchase order requirements, and fairness of quality assurance arrangements were all recognized by 80% or more.	78% were satisfied with the information they receive on The Body Shop's financial performance.	87% of recipients of funding from The Body Shop Foundation agreed or strongly agreed that The Body Shop takes active steps to make its business more environmentally responsible.
One-fifth disagreed or strongly disagreed that The Body Shop's purchasing and logistics functions are well structured and efficient.	*29% disagreed or strongly disagreed that the company enjoys the trust of the financial community.*	*75% of The Body Shop employees do not participate actively in the community volunteering program.*
8% claimed to have experienced ethically corrupt behavior in their dealings with individual members of The Body Shop staff.	*33% had no opinion or disagreed that The Body Shop has a clear long-term business strategy.*	*Nearly half the recipients of funding disagreed or strongly disagreed that it was easy to identify the right decision makers in The Body Shop Foundation.*

Source: The Body Shop.

4. Manage Growth by letting our business decisions be guided as much by their environmental implications as by economics.

5. Manage Energy by working towards replacing what we must use with renewable resources.

6. Manage Waste by adopting a four-tier approach: reduce, reuse, recycle, and as last resort, dispose by the safest and most responsible means possible.

7. Control Pollution by protecting the quality of land, air, and water on which we depend.

8. Operate Safely by minimizing risk at every level of our operations: for staff, for customers, and for the community in which the business operates.

9. Obey the Law by complying with environmental laws at all times.

10. Raise Awareness by continuously educating our staff and our customers.

Community Outreach

The Body Shop believes that businesses should give something back to the communities in which they trade. We try to do that in a number of different ways.

Harlem

We opened our 120th American shop on 125th Street in Harlem in 1992. Staffed in part by residents of the community, this shop is helping to contribute to the economic revitalization of the Harlem community. Fifty percent of the post-interest, pre-tax profits from the shop are placed in a fund which will be used to open other community-based shops around the country, while the other 50% is given to a fund (monitored by an advisory group of local community leaders) for Harlem community projects.

Community Projects

We encourage all of our employees to do volunteer work and allow them four hours each month of paid time to do it! Community projects are as diverse as our staff and the communities in which we trade. They range from Adopt-a-Highway clean-ups, to delivering meals to homebound people with AIDS, to working with children who have been physically abused, to serving meals to the homeless.

Local Events

In addition to regular community projects work, our employees frequently help out with local events. Recent projects have included a Harlem street fair, participation in AIDS walkathons, and benefit dances to raise money for the Kayapo Indians in Brazil. Many shops do makeovers, foot and hand massages, and aromatherapy massages and donate the proceeds to local organizations. And staff also frequently give talks to various community groups on a wide range of topics—from endangered species to how The Body Shop does business to the rights of indigenous people.[76]

Global Operations and Financial Results

RETAIL SALES

Worldwide retail sales grew by 5% to £604.4 million in 1998. This reflected growth of 14% in Asia, 9% in the Americas (excluding the United States), 6% in Europe, 4% in Australasia, 3% in the United Kingdom, and a decline of 2% in the United States. The retail sales by region are shown below, with prior year figures restated at comparable exchange rates:[77]

Retail Sales by Region
(British pound amounts in millions)

Region	1998	1997	% Change	% of Operating Profit
United Kingdom	£165.0	£161.0	3	27
Europe	148.0	139.5	6	25
United States	98.5	100.6	(2)	16
Americas (excluding USA)	50.0	45.9	9	8
Asia	108.3	95.2	14	18
Australia and New Zealand	33.8	32.6	4	6
Total	£603.6	£574.8		

Worldwide, comparable shop sales growth was unchanged year to year, reflecting a combination of 7% growth in the Americas (excluding the United States), 2% growth in the United Kingdom, 1% growth in Europe, an unchanged position in Australia, a 5% decline in the United States, and a 6% decline in Asia. Japan was the major influence on the performance in Asia where comparable store sales declined by 19%.

Customer transactions showed a 1% decrease during 1998 to 86.5 million. The average transaction per customer increased by 5% to £6.84. Customer transactions in 1998 by geographic region were: United Kingdom—37%; Europe—24%; United States—12%; Americas (excluding the United States)—9%; Asia—13%; and Australia and New Zealand—5%.

TURNOVER

Turnover (a term used in the United Kingdom) was a combination of retail sales (excluding sales taxes) through company-owned shops and wholesale revenue for goods sold to franchisees.[78]

The *1998 Annual Report* stated "Group turnover for the year increased by 8% to £293.1 million, of which 60% relates to international markets. Of the total turnover, 60% represented wholesale sales to franchisees and 40% was achieved in retail sales through company-owned stores, mail order, and The Body Shop Direct. The change reflects the higher proportion of company-owned stores, with retail sales of £117.7 million being 24% higher than in the previous year. The growth in 1998 turnover also reflects higher exports, which, including sales to overseas subsidiaries, increased by 7% to £107.8 million."[79]

OPERATING PROFITS

The operating profits of the company's six geographic regions were as follows:[80]

Operating Profit (Loss) by Region
(British pound amounts in millions)

Region	1998	1997	% Change	% of Operating Profit
United Kingdom	£11.2	£13.6	−18	37
Europe	8.0	8.1	−1	20
United States	(1.7)	(3.0)	—	—
Americas (excluding USA)	3.4	3.0	13	16
Asia	15.4	14.7	5	8
Australia and New Zealand	1.8	2.0	−10	5
Total	£38.1	£38.4		

MANAGEMENT ANALYSIS BY REGIONS

This section is management analyses of operations by geographic regions as reported in the Company's *1998 Annual Report*.[81]

United Kingdom

The company acted as the head franchisee in the United Kingdom, managing wholesale and retail activities. Seven new shops were opened during the 1998 financial year, giving a total of 263 stores at year's end of which 67 were company-owned. In line with the company's strategy to operate stores located in large cities, 10 shops were purchased from franchisees during the year.

Region: United Kingdom	1998	1997	
Shops at year end	263	256	
Shop openings	7	4	
Category	**£m**	**£m**	**Change**
Retail sales	£165.8	£161.2	+3%
Turnover	116.2	103.1	10%
Operating profit	11.2	13.6	−18%

Total retail sales grew by 3% in the year to February 1998, with comparable store sales up by 2% from the previous year. The comparable store sales excluded sales realized though The Body Shop Direct, the home selling program, which were included in the total retail sales figure. The Body Shop Direct continued to move forward, with over 1,100 registered consultants at the year's end. More than 60,000 parties were held during the year, reaching some 625,000 customers.

The testing of the new store design progressed, with seven of these stores operating by the year's end. The Body Shop anticipated that up to 15 of these new designs would be fitted in existing and new stores during 1998.

Turnover in the United Kingdom grew by 10%, ahead of the growth in retail sales due to the larger number of company-owned stores. Operating profit was 18% lower, with the profit from the additional company-owned stores being offset by an increase in marketing expenses and higher costs associated with The Body Shop Direct.

United States

The company's subsidiary, The Body Shop Inc., functioned as the head franchisee for the United States. The head office, filling facilities, and main distribution center were based in Wake Forest, North Carolina.

Store openings were minimal, with a net increase of 3 stores during the year. Of the 290 stores at the period's end, 210 were company-owned with 68 stores that were purchased from franchisees during the year. This number included 16 shops that were acquired with the southeastern distributorship. Once most of the lowest performing franchised stores had been bought, The Body Shop anticipated few store buy-backs in 1998.

Region: USA	1998	1997	
Shops at year end	290	287	
Shop openings	3	14	
Category	**$m**	**$m**	**Change**
Retail sales	161.6	165.0	−2%
Turnover	128.1	119.6	+7%
Category	**£m**	**£m**	**Change**
Retail sales	98.5	100.6	−2%
Turnover	78.0	73.1	+7%
Operating profit	(1.7)	(3.0)	

Total retail sales in the United States were 2% lower than in the previous year, reflecting the low number of new store openings together with a comparable store sales decline of 5%. Other than Manhattan, which performed slightly better than the average, sales performances were similar across the regions.

Fewer new product introductions, poor retailing, and competitive pressures continued to affect sales performance.

Turnover in the United States was 7% higher given the larger number of company-owned stores. The U.S. operating results were a combination of the margin realized in the United Kingdom on supplying goods to the United States, together with the margin arising from wholesale and retail activities within the United States. The operating loss of £1.7 million showed an improvement on the 1997 result although the result was similar year to year if the effect of currency changes were excluded.

Europe

The 13 net store openings in Europe reflected 41 openings and 28 closures, with 9 closures in France. The 6% total retail sales growth achieved in Europe reflected the store openings and a 1% increase in comparable store sales.

Region: Europe United	1998	1997	
Shops at year end	527	514	
Shop openings	13	30	
Category	**£m**	**£m**	**Change**
Retail sales	148.0	139.5	+6%
Turnover	42.0	39.3	+7%
Operating profit	8.0	8.1[1]	−1%

Note: 1. Excluding the exceptional item relating to France. The exceptional item related to a provision of £6.5 million (£4.3 million after tax) in respect of facilities extended to the former head franchisee in France prior to the acquisition of the French business in November 1997.

Comparable store sales performance varied across the region with markets such as Holland, Sweden, Finland, and Ireland showing the strongest underlying growth. Other markets, such as France, Germany, and Spain, showed improving trends with negative comparable store sales reversing in the second six months. The improvements being achieved in France reflected a rationalization of the store base there and the successful introduction of a stronger retail agenda following the acquisition of the business during the year.

Turnover in Europe grew by 7%, with operating profit similar to the previous year.

Asia

Of the 75 new store openings in Asia, 29 were in Japan. The Body Shop anticipated fewer store openings in Asia during the current year given the economic difficulties in a number of Southeast Asian Countries.

Region: Asia	1998	1997	
Shops at year end	308	233	
Shop openings	75	63	
Category	**£m**	**£m**	**Change**
Retail sales	108.3	95.2	+14%
Turnover	37.5	35.7	+5%
Operating profit	15.4	14.7	+5%

Retail stores in the Asian region showed growth of 14%, with comparable store sales declining by 6%. Excluding the impact of Japan, where comparable store sales declined by 19%, comparable store sales in the region grew by 4%. Although Taiwan, Malaysia, Indonesia, and Saudi Arabia all showed strong positive underlying growth, other markets such as Singapore and Thailand saw comparable store sales declines. The first shop opened in Korea at the end of March 1997, with five stores opening by the year's end.

Americas (excluding the United States)

Total retail sales grew by 9%, with comparable store sales growth of 7%. These results were mainly influenced by the sales performance in Canada, which continued to benefit from a focused marketing and retail program.

Region: Americas (excluding the United States)	1998	1997	
Shops at year end	130	130	
Shop openings	—	4	
Category	**£m**	**£m**	**Change**
Retail sales	50.0	45.9	+9%
Turnover	12.8	9.9	+29%
Operating profit	3.4	3.0	+13%

Turnover was 29% higher, with operating profit 13% up from the previous year.

Exhibit 7

Balance Sheets: The Body Shop[1,2]
(British pounds in millions)

Year Ending February 28	Group		Company	
	1998	1997	1998	1997
Fixed Assets				
Tangible assets	78.4	74.9	50.7	52.7
Investments	2.0	0.5	50.5	15.8
	80.4	75.4	101.2	68.5
Current Assets				
Stocks	47.7	34.8	28.5	21.2
Debtors	47.0	45.0	59.5	65.6
Cash at bank and in hand	29.6	47.1	21.3	39.0
	124.3	126.9	109.3	125.8
Creditors: amounts falling due within one year	70.4	59.0	59.3	44.9
Net current assets	53.9	67.9	50.0	80.9
Total assets less current liabilities	134.3	143.3	151.2	149.4
Creditors: amounts falling due after more than one year	2.9	13.0	0.0	0.1
Provisions for liabilities and charges				
Deferred tax	1.1	0.2	1.9	0.6
Total assets	£130.3	£130.1	£149.3	£148.7
Capital and Reserves				
Called up share amount	9.7	9.7	9.7	9.7
Share premium account	42.8	42.1	42.8	42.1
Profit and loss account	77.8	78.3	96.8	96.9
Shareholders' funds	£130.3	£130.1	£149.3	£148.7

Notes:
1. These financial statements were approved by the Board on May 13, 1998.
2. Notes were deleted.

Source: The Body Shop, *1998 Annual Report*, p. 39.

Australia and New Zealand

Total retail sales in Australia and New Zealand increased by 4%, with comparable store sales unchanged from the previous year.

Region: Australia and New Zealand	1998	1997	
Shops at year end	76	71	
Shop openings	5	3	
Category	**£m**	**£m**	**Change**
Retail sales	33.8	32.6	+4%
Turnover	6.6	6.7	−1%
Operating profit	1.8	2.0	−10%

Turnover was down 1% and operating profit was down 10% from the previous year mainly due to the timing of product shipments.

Exhibits 7 and **8** show the company's balance sheets and consolidated profit and loss accounts.

Exhibit 8

Consolidated Profit and Loss Accounts: The Body Shop[2]
(British pounds in millions, except per ordinary share data)

Year Ending February 28	1998	1997
Turnover[1]	£293.10	£270.80
Cost of sales	115.90	111.90
Gross Profit	177.20	158.90
Operating expenses—excluding exceptional item	139.10	120.50
Operating expenses—exceptional item	0	6.50
Operating Profit	38.10	31.90
Interest payable (net)	0.10	0.20
Profit on Ordinary Activities Before Tax	38.00	31.70
Tax on profit on ordinary activities	15.20	14.10
Profit for the Financial Year	22.80	17.60
Dividends paid and proposed	10.80	9.10
Retained profit	£ 12.00	£ 8.50
Earnings per ordinary share including exceptional item	11.8p	9.2p
Earnings per ordinary share excluding exceptional item	11.8p	11.4p

Notes:
1. Turnover represents the total accounts receivable in the ordinary course of business for goods sold and services provided and excludes sales between companies in the Group, discount given, Value Added Tax (VAT), and other sales taxes.
2. Other notes were deleted.

Source: The Body Shop, *1998 Annual Report*, p. 38.

Notes

1. Nigel Cope, "Roddick Quits Helm at Body Shop," *Independent* (May 21, 1998), p. 21.
2. *Ibid.*
3. "They Said It," *Daily Telegraph* (May 16, 1998), p. 33.
4. "Body Shop, Capitalism and Cocoa Butter," *The Economist* (May 16, 1998), p. 66.
5. Rufus Olins, "Body Shop Calls in Corporate Man," *The Sunday Times* (May 17,1998).
6. *Ibid.*
7. Sarah Cunningham, "Body Shop Offers Golden Handcuffs," *Times* (May 15, 1998).
8. Rufus Olins, "Body Shop."
9. Anita Roddick, *The Body Shop* (NY: Crown Publishers, Inc.), 1991, p. 43.
10. *Ibid.*, p. 52.
11. *Ibid.*, pp. 55–62.
12. *Ibid.*, p. 66.
13. *Ibid.*
14. *Ibid.*, p. 67.
15. *Ibid.*, p. 68.
16. *Ibid.*
17. *Ibid.*
18. *Ibid.*, p. 77.
19. *Ibid.*, p. 68.
20. *Ibid.*, p. 74.
21. *Ibid.*, pp. 85–86.
22. *Ibid.*, p. 86.
23. *Ibid.*, p. 92.
24. *Ibid.*, pp. 94–95.
25. *Ibid.*, pp. 96–97.
26. *Ibid.*, p. 101.
27. *Ibid.*
28. *Ibid.*, p. 100.
29. *Ibid.*
30. *Ibid.*, p. 143.
31. *Ibid.*, p. 144.
32. The Body Shop, *1998 Annual Report*, p. 25.
33. The Body Shop, *1995 Annual Report*, p. 15.
34. *Ibid.*, p. 17.
35. *Ibid.*, p. 20.
36. *Ibid.*, p. 25.
37. *Ibid.*, p. 49.
38. *Ibid.*, p. 81.
39. *Ibid.*, p. 108.
40. *Ibid.*, p. 115.
41. *Ibid.*, p. 123.
42. *Ibid.*, p. 226.
43. *Ibid.*, p. 158.
44. *Ibid.*, p. 178.
45. *Ibid.*, p. 214.
46. *Ibid.*, p. 217.
47. *Ibid.*, p. 223.
48. *Ibid.*, p. 231.
49. *Ibid.*, p. 181.
50. *Ibid.*, p. 137.
51. James Fallon, "Body Shop Shakeup Brings New CEO," *WWD* (May 13, 1998), p. 3.
52. Robert Wright, "Body Shop U.S. Venture Approved," *Financial Times* (June 23, 1998), p. 28
53. Ernest Beck, "Body Shop Founder Roddick Steps Aside as CEO," *Wall Street Journal* (May 13, 1998), p. B14.
54. The Body Shop. *Our Reason for Being* (handout).
55. The Body Shop. *1998 Annual Report*, p. 25.
56. *Ibid.*, p. 32.
57. *Ibid.*, p. 36.
58. *Ibid.*
59. Anita Roddick, pp. 235–236.
60. "Loosening One's Grip," *Cosmetic Insiders' Report*, no. 11, vol. 17.
61. Ruth Nicholas, "New Age Finds a New Face," *Marketing* (May 21, 1998), p. 15.
62. *Ibid.*
63. Diane Seo, "Body Shop Hopes Hemp Will Plant Seeds of Recovery," *LA Times* (February 26, 1998), p. D1.
64. Fallon, p. 3.
65. Seo, p. D1.
66. Alev Aktar, "Hemp: A Growing Controversy," *WWD* (February 13, 1998), p. 8.
67. Nicholas, p. 15
68. *Ibid.*, p. 143.
69. *Ibid.*, p. 125.
70. *Ibid.*, p. 135.
71. The Body Shop. *1994 Annual Report*, p. 22.
72. The Body Shop. *This Is The Body Shop*, (November 1994), p. 57. All 5 paragraphs below are directly taken from this source.
73. The Body Shop. *1998 Annual Report*, p. 67.
74. The Body Shop. *This Is The Body Shop* (November 1994), pp. 6–8. All 15 paragraphs below are directly taken from this source.
75. The Body Shop. *1995 Annual Report*, p. 3.
76. The Body Shop. *This Is The Body Shop* (November 1994), pp. 8–9.
77. The Body Shop. *1998 Annual Report*, pp. 25–29.
78. *Ibid.*
79. *Ibid.*
80. *Ibid.*, pp. 18–20.
81. *Ibid.*

case 8

Waterford Wedgwood PLC. (2000): The Millennium (Revised)

Kathryn E. Wheelen

On March 14, 2000, P. Redmond O'Donoghue, Chief Executive Officer (CEO), of Waterford Crystal Limited was chairing a meeting. The focus of the meeting was on the sale of Millennium products. A Millennium Waterford Crystal ball, the "Star of Hope," was used in Times Square to ring in the New Year and the Millennium. The 500 pound Waterford Crystal ball was lowered down a 77 foot flag pole, that was 22 stories above the ground. It took a team of 40 designers and 10 months to assemble the six-foot diameter geodesic sphere. O'Donoghue was curious about the impact the Millennium Crystal Ball had on the sale of the company's products.

Overview of the Crystal Business and History of Waterford Crystal[1]

MANUFACTURING OF CRYSTAL

The crystal manufacturing business was by nature very labor intensive. Each piece of crystal had gone through the processes of mixing, blowing, cutting, and polishing. Mixing involved the heating of raw materials in a furnace to temperatures in excess of 1400 degrees centigrade to create molten crystal. Blowing forms the molten crystal into a basic item such as a wine goblet or vase. The cutting process etched a design pattern into the blank piece. Finally, the piece was polished to smoothen the edges of the cuts and give the piece the luster and sparkle for which crystal is known. Labor costs typically represented 50–55% of the cost of manufacturing crystal.

Blowing was done either by machine or is mouth-blown by a skilled craftsman. Similarly, crystal pieces can be cut by machine or hand-cut. Three different technologies were used in the crystal cutting process. They were (1) fully hand-cut, (2) semi-automated and slow speed-automated, and (3) high speed-automated. Crystal pieces which were both mouth-blown and hand-cut had the highest image of quality of all crystal products.

Developing craft skills was a key element in a manufacturer's ability to increase its production output. This was particularly critical in the case of mouth-blown and hand-cut products. In addition to the wages paid to craftsmen (i.e., blowers and cutters). An intensive

---

apprenticeship program must be maintained. Apprenticeships typically lasted for four or more years. Each craftsman usually oversaw several apprentices. The availability of craft and design skills was a major factor in establishing and maintaining competitive advantage. Relative to the labor component involved in manufacturing crystal, raw materials were inexpensive and readily available.

Labor cost efficiency was not a significant issue until the late 1970s. At that time, pressure on prices forced manufacturers to focus on costs in order to maintain gross profit margins. The pressure on prices came from multiple sources. Primary among these were general economic conditions, an increasing number of competitors (most of them European), and new technology. The technology of glass blowing had changed little since crystal making began. The traditional tools, hollow irons and wooden templates, were still used by glass blowers to create the crystal pieces that were then passed on to cutters and hand-cut the design patterns. Recently, improved processing of machine-cut crystal had been introduced into the industry.

While the quality of machine-cut crystal had improved, its level varied and was not equal to hand-cut crystal. Machine-cut crystal was lower in price relative to hand-cut crystal.

Lead crystal manufacturing was not a fixed capital intensive business. However, it did require a significant level of investment and its working capital needs are high. High-valued finished inventories had to be maintained throughout the distribution channels. In addition, work-in-progress inventories contained a high value-added component which must be financed, reflecting significant cash requirements.

The technology differences used in the manufacture of crystal products translate into three market segments; *high-end*, *medium*, and *low-end*. These three segments were based on price and brand name recognition

HISTORY OF WATERFORD

In 1783, businessmen George and William Penrose founded the Waterford Glass House in the busy port of Waterford, Ireland, and began to make crystal "as fine a quality as any in Europe. . . in the most elegant style." The Penroses knew the secret of mingling minerals and glass to create crystal with beauty and mystery. When tapped, it sang sweetly. When touched, it felt warm and soft. Yet it possessed strength and durability and, most wonderful of all, the crystal shone with a romantic, silvery brilliance. Patience, skill, and artistry had forged a triumph.

In 1851, Waterford Crystal won several gold medals and universal acclaim at the Great Exhibition in London, but just as Waterford's art was reaching its full bloom, the financial climate turned grim. In the same year, the Waterford factory was forced to close, largely due to heavy excise duties.

Waterford Crystal's great tradition lay dormant for a hundred years. But when Irish independence rekindled a passion for the Irish arts in the 1940s and 1950s, a group of businessmen resolved to bring back to life the legacy that had made Waterford synonymous with the finest crystal in the world.

In 1947, they recruited a small group of artisans and, under the guidance of these masters, young apprentices learned the art of Waterford Crystal made famous by their skilled countrymen decades before. By 1951, Waterford Crystal was again launched on the world market. When, in the early 1960s, demand began to exceed supply, a larger glass works was built. This was later expanded until, by the 1980s, Waterford Crystal was the largest producer of hand-crafted crystal in the world.

In 1991, Waterford launched Marquis by Waterford Crystal, the first new brand in the company's 200-year history fine enough to carry the name Waterford Crystal. Today, Marquis by Waterford Crystal is the most successful new entry in the tabletop industry . . . and the number four brand. Marquis offers innovative crystal patterns ranging from contemporary to traditional design, designed by Waterford and brought to life by the great crystal makers in Europe.

In 1992, after extensive consumer research, Waterford learned that many consumers desired Waterford Crystal in less formal designs. In a move to broaden Waterford's design and consumer appeal, some new products were successfully introduced from the finest crystal facilities in Europe—all manufactured to the same exacting standards of Waterford, Ireland.

Each piece of Waterford Crystal stands today as a testament to the traditions and standards of excellence that have survived with the Waterford name for more than 200 years ". . . . to be enjoyed and displayed now . . . to be cherished as an heirloom for generations to come."

Corporate Governance Board of Directors

The *Annual Report* stated the Directors' responsibilities.

> "The Directors are required by Irish company law to prepare financial statements for each financial year which give a true and fair view of the state of affairs of the Company and the Group and of the profit or loss of the Group for that financial year.
>
> In preparing those financial statements, Directors are required to: select appropriate accounting policies and apply them consistently; make reasonable and prudent judgments and estimates; and state that all accounting standards which they consider to be applicable have been followed.
>
> The Directors have responsibility for ensuring that the Group keeps accounting records which disclose with reasonable accuracy at any time the financial position of the Group and which enable them to ensure that the financial statements are prepared in accordance with accounting standards generally accepted in Ireland and comply with Irish statute, comprising the Companies Acts 1963 to 1999 and the European Communities (Companies: Group Accounts) Regulations, 1992. The Directors confirm that the financial statements comply with the above requirements. The Directors also have responsibility for taking such steps as are reasonably open to them to safeguard the assets of the Group and to prevent and detect fraud and other irregularities."[2]

Exhibit 1 provides the names of the 17 board members. Eight are internal members. Eight are classified as Non-executive Independent Directors. Dr. O'Reilly announced that Lord Wedgwood would join the Board as an Executive Director at the next board meeting. Lord Wedgwood was a direct descendant of Josiah Wedgwood, founder of Wedgwood, and has served for years as Wedgwood's International Ambassador.

In February, 2000, Dr. O'Reilly announced the appointment of Peter John Goulandris as Executive Chairman of Ceramics. Goulandris was a major shareholder (see **Exhibit 2**) and Deputy Chairman of Waterford Wedgwood since 1999. He was the Chairman's brother-in-law.

R. A. Barnes, O. C. Küsel, C. J. McGillivary, K. C. McGoran, and F. A. Wedgwood were reelected at the 2000 Annual Meeting.

Exhibit 2 shows the stock ownership of Dr. A. J. F. O'Reilly, Mrs. C. J. O'Reilly and P. J. Goulandris, Mrs. O'Reilly's brother, and other substantial ordinary shareholders.

TOP MANAGEMENT

The Executive Directors are P. J. Goulandris, Richard A. Barnes, P. R. O'Donoghue, B. D. Patterson, O. C. Küsel, C. J. McGillivary, S. Michaels, and C. J. S. Johnson (see **Exhibit 1**).

Exhibit 1

Board of Directors: Waterford Wedgwood plc

Dr. Anthony J. F. O'Reilly[1]

Chairman, had been a Director of the Group since 1990 and was appointed Chairman on 1 January 1994. He was Chairman of H.J. Heinz Company and Executive Chairman of Independent News & Media plc.

Peter John Goulandris

Joined the Group as a Director in 1996. He was Deputy Chairman of the Group and Executive Chairman, Ceramics. His other directorships included Fitzwilton Limited.

Chryssanthie J. O'Reilly[1]

Joined the Group as a Director in 1995. She was also Chairperson of the Irish National Stud Company Limited.

Richard A. Barnes

Joined the Group in 1988. He was appointed a Director in 1993. He was Waterford Wedgwood Group Finance Director and a Director of West Midlands Regional Development Agency, a U.K. Government appointment.

P. Redmond O'Donoghue

Joined the Group as a Director in 1985. He was Chief Executive Officer of Waterford Crystal Limited. Additionally he was Nonexecutive Chairman of Bord Failte (Irish Tourist Board) and Nonexecutive Director of Greencore plc.

Brian D. Patterson

Joined the Group in 1987. He was appointed a Director in 1992. He is Chief Executive Officer of Wedgwood and Chairman of Competitiveness Council of Ireland, a Government appointment.

Ottmar C. Küsel

Is Chief Executive Officer of Rosenthal AG. He was appointed a Director of the Group in 1997. He was Chairman of the Ceramics Industry Association in Germany and of the Ambiente/Tendence Trade Show Committee in Frankfurt.

Christopher J. McGillivary

Joined the Group in 1990. He was appointed a Director in 1996. He was Chief Executive Officer of Waterford Wedgwood U.S.A., Inc. He was also Co-Chairman of All-Clad Holdings, Inc.

Sam Michaels

Joined the Group as a Director on 2 July 1999. He was Co-Chairman and Chief Executive Officer of All-Clad Holdings, Inc., and Chairman of Pittsburgh Annealing Box Company.

Robert H. Niehaus[1]

Joined the Group as a Director in 1990. He was Chairman of Waterford Wedgwood U.K. plc. He was also Chairman and Managing Partner of Greenhill Capital Partners, a private equity investment fund in New York. His other directorships included the American Italian Pasta Company.

David W. Sculley[1]

Is a partner in the New York based investment firm, Sculley Brothers. He joined the Group as a Director in 1997. He serves on the board of a number of private companies.

Tony O'Reilly, Jr.[1]

Joined the Group as a Director in 1998. He was a Director and Chief Executive Officer of Arcon International Resources plc. His other directorships included Tedcastle Holdings Limited, Lockwood Financial Group, Inc. (U.S.A.), Providence Resources plc, and Independent News & Media plc.

Dr. F. Alan Wedgwood[1]

Joined the Group as a Director in 1986 and before that was a Director of Josiah Wedgwood & Sons Limited since 1966. He was also a Director of Waterford Wedgwood U.K. plc.

Kevin C. McGoran[1]

Joined the Group as a Director in 1990. He was Deputy Chairman of Fitzwilton Limited, and Chairman of Waterford Crystal Limited.

Gerald P. Dempsey[1]

Joined the Group as a Director in 1986. His other directorships included UNM Financial Services Ireland and Design and Project Management Limited.

Christopher J. S. Johnson

Joined Wedgwood in 1968. He was appointed a Group Director in 1988. He was Manufacturing and Technical Director of Wedgwood.

Lewis L. Glucksman[1]

Joined the Group as a Director in 1998. He acted as a senior adviser at Salomon Smith Barney, New York, and was a member of the Advisory Committee of the National Treasury Management Agency in Ireland—a Government appointment. His directorships included Risk Capital Holdings (U.S.A.).

Notes:

1. Non-executive Independent Director

Source: Waterford Wedgwood plc, *1999 Annual Report*, p. 11.

Exhibit 2

Substantial Ordinary Shareholders: Waterford Wedgwood plc
March 7, 2000

A. General Ownership

Name	Holding	Percentage
Greater than 10%		
Stoneworth Investment Ltd.	119,666,795	16.20%
Bank of Ireland Nominees Ltd.	112,016,276	15.17%
Between 5% and 10%		
Allied Irish Banks plc & its subsidiaries	42,136,373	5.71%
Ulster Bank Markets (Nominees) Ltd.	37,293,695	5.05%
Between 3% and 5%		
Irish Life Assurance plc	29,541,431	4.00%
Araquipa International Ltd.	27,111,201	3.67%
Albany Hill Ltd.	26,778,362	3.63%

B. A. J. F. O'Reilly, Mrs. C. J. O'Reilly, and P. J. Goulandris (Mrs. O'Reilly's brother) Stock Ownership

Name	Stock Owner	Percentage	Shares
Indexia Holdings Ltd.	A. J. F. O'Reilly	100%	250,000
Mystic Investments (Cayman) Ltd.			420,097
Albany Hill Limited	A. J. F. O'Reilly	100%	26,778,362
	Mrs. C. J. O'Reilly		
	combined		
	P. J. Goulandris		
Stoneworth Investments Ltd.	A. J. F. O'Reilly	49%	119,666,795
	P. J. Goulandris	49%	
	L. L. Glucksman	2%	

Source: Waterford Wedgwood plc, *1994 Annual Report*, pp. 7 and 10.

GROUP STRUCTURE AND ORGANIZATION

Exhibit 3 shows the four product lines for the company. The principal executives of these units are:

Name	Title	Unit
P. R. O'Donoghue	CEO	Waterford Crystal Ltd.
B. D. Patterson	CEO	Wedgwood
O. C. Küsel	CEO	Rosenthal
C. J. McGillivary	CEO	Waterford Wedgwood, U.S.A., Inc.
S. Michael	CEO Co-Chairman	All-Clad Holdings
C. J. S. Johnson	Manufacturing and Technical Director	Wedgwood
P. J. Goulandris	Deputy Chairman Executive Chairman	Ceramics

Exhibit 4 shows principal subsidaries of the company.

Exhibit 3

Product Lines: Waterford Wedgwood plc

Source: Waterford Wedgwood plc, *1999 Annual Report*, backside of cover page.

Strategic Group Units

WATERFORD CRYSTAL CEO'S STRATEGIC REPORT

"Group Crystal sales increased by 31.5% in 1999, an all time record year for the peerless Waterford and our other luxury crystal brands."[3]

P. R. O'Donoghue, CEO

I am delighted to report that Group Crystal operating profit in 1999 was €57.0 million, an increase of no less than 39% (see **Exhibit 5**). Sales were €395.2 million, up 31.5% (€395.2 million [IR £501.8 million]). Our record 1999 performance was based on many things, but most particularly on our successful design and marketing of exciting new products, on reaping the benefits of investments, over the past several years, in reducing unit costs and on manufacturing and logistics skills.

Waterford Crystal is the only truly global luxury crystal brand. Last year's success was repeated in all of our major international markets, with the sole exception of Japan where consumer demand remained depressed. In the world's largest market, the United States, our outstandingly professional team, under the inspired leadership of Chris McGillivary, increased sales by 37%. Working closely with Ireland, the products development effort in America has gone from strength to strength. At home in Ireland sales increased by 28%, while the United Kingdom showed 17% growth and Europe grew 8%. Furthermore, we achieved strong growth in Australia and Canada with sales up by 42% and 39% respectively.

Exhibit 4

Principal Subsidiaries, 2000: Waterford Wedgwood plc

Company	Registered office and country of incorporation	Nature of business
A. Manufacturing		
Waterford Crystal (Manufacturing) Ltd.	Kilbarry, Waterford, Ireland	Crystal glass manufacturer
Josiah Wedgwood & Sons Ltd.	Barlaston, Stoke-on-Trent, England	Ceramic tableware/giftware manufacturer
Rosenthal AG	Selb, Germany	Ceramic tableware/giftware manufacturer
All-Clad Metalcrafters LLC	Delaware, U.S.A.	Kitchenware manufacturer
Stuart & Sons Ltd.	Stourbridge, West Midlands, England	Kitchenware manufacturer
B. Distribution		
Waterford Crystal Ltd.	Kilbarry, Waterford, Ireland	Distributor
Waterford Crystal Gallery Ltd.	Kilbarry, Waterford, Ireland	Product display and sales center
Waterford Wedgwood Australia Ltd.	Barlaston, Stoke-on-Trent, England	Distributor
Waterford Wedgwood Canada, Inc.	Toronto, Canada	Distributor
Waterford Wedgwood U.S.A., Inc.	New York, U.S.A.	Distributor
Waterford Wedgwood Japan Ltd.	Tokyo, Japan	Distributor
Waterford Wedgwood Retail Ltd.	Barlaston, Stoke-on-Trent, England	Retailer
Josiah Wedgwood & Sons (Exports) Ltd.	Barlaston, Stoke-on-Trent, England	Exporter
Josiah Wedgwood (Malaysia) Sdn Bhd.	Kuala Lumpur, Malaysia	Retailer
Waterford Wedgwood Trading Singapore Pte. Ltd.	Singapore	Distributor
Waterford Wedgwood (Taiwan) Ltd.	Taipei, Taiwan	Distributor
Wedgwood GmbH	Selb, Germany	Sales office
C. Finance		
Statum Limited	Barlaston, Stoke-on-Trent, England	Finance
Waterford Wedgwood International Financial Services	Dublin, Ireland	Finance
D. Other		
Waterford Wedgwood U.K. plc	Barlaston, Stoke-on-Trent, England	Subsidiary holding company
Wedgwood Ltd.	Barlaston, Stoke-on-Trent, England	Subsidiary holding company
Waterford Wedgwood, Inc.	Delaware, U.S.A.	Subsidiary holding company
Waterford Glass Research and Development Ltd.	Kilbarry, Waterford, Ireland	Research and development
Dungarvan Crystal Ltd.	Kilbarry, Waterford, Ireland	Dormant
Waterford Wedgwood Employee Share Ownership Plan (Jersey) Ltd.	St. Helier, Jersey	Trustee company
Waterford Wedgwood GmbH	Dusseldorf, Germany	Subsidiary holding company
All-Clad Holdings, Inc.	Canonsburg, Pennsylvania, U.S.A.	Subsidiary holding company

One of the key factors in our success in recent years has been the continuous introduction of innovative, market-led new products, which have attracted new consumers to our brands at the same as keeping existing consumers loyal. On top of the success of new products we have been able to maintain and increase sales of existing products. This unique combination of new contemporary products and traditional products has been the driving force behind our sales growth rate which has been so dramatic year after year since the early 1990's. In 1999, however, we elevated our performance onto an entirely new plane with a range of Waterford Crystal Millennium products. These were a particular success for two main reasons. Firstly, they

Exhibit 5

Segment Information: Waterford Wedgwood plc
(Stated in pounds)

Year Ending December 31	1999			1998				
	Turnover	Operation Profit	1999 Net Assets	Turnover	Operating Profit Before Exceptional Cost	Exceptional Costs	Operating Profit/(Loss)	1998 Net Assets Restated
Crystal	£ 395.2	£ 57.0	£ 213.5	£ 300.5	£ 41.0	(£ 4.5)	£ 36.5	£ 182.8
Ceramics	396.8	14.0	227.2	382.1	13.9	(26.7)	(12.8)	186.9
Other	87.6	11.9	110.2	47.9	8.8	—	8.8	4.9
Group Net Borrowings	—	—	(311.8)	—	—	—	—	(190.8)
Minority Interests	879.6	82.9	239.1	730.5	63.7	(31.2)	32.5	183.8
Total Group	579.6	82.9	236.0	730.5	63.7	(31.2)	32.5	180.0

Note:

1. The segmental analysis provided has been changed from business segment to product category analysis reflecting the greater integration of the Group's ceramic businesses and the acquisition of All-Clad. Crystal includes the manufacture and distribution of the Group's crystal products. Ceramics includes the manufacture and distribution of the group's ceramic products. "Other" includes products manufactured and distributed by All-Clad together with the Group's other non-crystal and ceramic products.

Source: Waterford Wedgwood plc, *1999 Annual Report*, p. 19.

appealed to gift buyers by providing attractively packaged, well priced gift solutions. Secondly, they were linked by a series of related themes and collectors were delighted to own several pieces or, indeed, the whole collection.

In addition to the growth in our core crystal business, line and brand extensions have continued to expand and are now making a valuable contribution to our overall performance. Thus a combination including John Rocha at Waterford, Waterford China, Waterford Holiday Heirlooms, the newly launched Waterford Jewelry and our licensed products (table linen, cutlery and writing instruments) accounted for retail sales in 1999 of €70 million. And none of these products existed before mid 1997! The John Rocha line was particularly strong showing 1999 growth of 75%.

Marquis and Stuart Crystal brands also had a successful year. Stuart launched the Jasper Conran at Stuart range designed to appeal to more contemporary taste and attract younger consumers. It was greeted with acclaim and immediate sales success. The 'livery' and identity of the core Stuart brand was tastefully rejuvenated and has already won a national U.K. design award. At home in Waterford the Visitor Center remained one of Ireland's most popular tourist attractions with 315,000 visitors and sales up 24%.

Waterford has continued its strategy of investing in appropriate manufacturing technology, together with maintaining the largest team of traditional craftspeople in our industry. Our three Waterford plants have now been smoothly consolidated into two, the Kilbarry tank furnace rebuilt, while the Stuart plant in Stourbridge has been fully integrated into Waterford's manufacturing organization. As a result of this streamlining, we were able to meet last year's record consumer demand and so achieve our remarkable sales and profit results.

Waterford's greatest public highlight of last year—indeed of the last century—was, of course, the Times Square Millennium crystal ball, which received front page coverage in hundreds of newspapers and was watched by around 1.4 billion television viewers around the world. The visual excitement of this spectacular event was literally overwhelming for every member of the Waterford family and a source of pride for Irish people everywhere. It was the emotional zenith of a stunningly successful year and I want to thank everyone, both in Ireland

and in America, who worked on the ball and, in doing so, met a near impossible challenge—in terms of crystal making, engineering and logistics—in record time and to glorious effect. At the same time, my sincere thanks go to all of Waterford's employees everywhere whose talent, determination and skill produced the finest year in our company's history.

The next challenge is to use the platform of our 1999 achievements as a base for further innovation, more growth and ever wider Waterford brand awareness. Even though our Millennium products remain on sale in 2000 (and are selling well) we already have in the pipeline a broad range of exciting new products to maintain and extend sales momentum. These will replicate the key attributes of the Millennium Collection and will appeal to consumers looking for the ideal gift and to collectors who enjoy owning a series of beautiful pieces of crystal linked by a theme or story. Additionally there is significant potential for further expansion of line and brand extensions which are still at an early stage of their lives. Our recently launched Waterford Jewelery is a particularly exciting prospect. Given the proven creativity of our people and the responsiveness of our organization to market trends we are sure of continued success.

Waterford Crystal has been a great brand for a long time. In the past decade, we have nurtured and promoted our brand with the utmost care and thoughtfulness. We have made it more accessible to many more consumers. We continue to refuse to sell seconds and we discourage discounting, while insisting that we distribute only in the finest stores. We have extended the brand carefully, protectively, intelligently. We have invested in effective advertising and wonderful, indeed spectacular, public relations. We have maintained the highest standards of craftsmanship which, allied to the most suitable technology available, assures the breathtaking beauty and quality of our products. We have transformed a brand that was once heavily identified with stemware, (i.e. drinking glasses) into a multi faceted brand that today provides our consumers all over the world with perfect solutions to gift giving challenges. We have made a great international luxury brand even greater which allows us to look forward with confidence to the continuing profitable growth of Waterford in the years ahead.[4]

We have extended the brand carefully, protectively, intelligently.

Waterford Crystal Products *Waterford Crystal product offerings are crystal and table lamps; ceiling and wall fixtures; crystal chandeliers; table items; candle sticks; cutlery; hurricane lamps; collectibles (baby, sport, religious); vanity (picture frames, vanity items, bridal items); executive desk items; crystal animals; clocks and time pieces; vases and bowls.*[5]

Waterford Linens *In spring, 1996, Waterford Linens were introduced. W-C Design of New York manufactured these linens. The label bore Waterford name and W-C Design name in smaller letters. The initial linens were tested in the Irish market before being sold in the U.S. The prices varied from $450 for a tablecloth and $8 for napkins. These linens were sold through selected department stores with limited advertising.*

Waterford Writing Instruments *In April 1996, Lodis Corporation of Los Angeles was granted exclusive rights to manufacture and distribute writing instruments with the Waterford name.*

Waterford Holiday Heirlooms *In December 1996, the company introduced a line of crystal and glass holiday ornaments and tree toppers. Each Christmas (dated-year) new items offered.*[6]

WEDGWOOD—CEO'S STRATEGIC REPORT

"Happily, Wedgwood today stands more firmly than ever at the top of its league, leaner, hungrier, stronger, the world's pre-eminent luxury ceramic brand."[7]

B. Patterson, CEO

In a tough global ceramics industry, Wedgwood is doing well. Several years ago, we determined that our prime strategic goal was to increase and maintain our international competitiveness in the face of an industry increasingly under pressure from over capacity, widespread discounting and cheap, imported products. We recognized that the Wedgwood brand was unique in its international appeal, its centuries-old reputation for quality and craftsmanship and because of its symbolic stature as one of the greatest of all English brands.

In order to generate the oxygen to power the Wedgwood brand, we initiated early action—starting in 1997—to take substantial costs out of our business. This included further investment in—and radical restructuring of—our manufacturing and supply chain operations. We are now the leader in applying appropriate technology in manufacturing, while preserving the traditional hand-crafted element that makes Wedgwood so desirable to discerning consumers. Our restructuring program included over 100 different projects.

I am pleased to report this is now virtually complete. It has not been easy. We now manufacture in five rather than eight factories and we employ 1,800 fewer people, as a result of restructuring, than we did at the end of 1996. Our costs of manufacturing have decreased greatly, while our customer service is more efficient and cost-controlled than ever before in the company's history. We know that had we not acted decisively and in time, Wedgwood might be in a similar unfortunate position to some of our competitors. Happily, Wedgwood today stands more firmly than ever at the top of its league, leaner, hungrier, stronger, the world's pre-eminent luxury ceramic brand.

Total sales in 1999 increased by 5.4%. Our sales in the U.K. increased by an encouraging 6.2%. In the widest context, Wedgwood remains the number one premium ceramic brand in the nation. We continue to have wonderful relationships with the best British and Irish retailers and we are confident the success of recently launched product lines like Sarah's Garden and Contrasts will be repeated with new lines such as Time for Wedgwood, Fruit Symphony and the exclusive ceramic creations of leading designers Nick Munro and Paul Costelloe.

Japan's prolonged recession did not abate during 1999, although there were several encouraging signs. In common with overall retail sales, Wedgwood sales in Japan were down 4% year on year. The effect of the recession is felt far beyond the national boundaries of Japan itself, for Japanese tourists have in the past spent considerable sums on Wedgwood products in foreign markets from Hong Kong to London, from Singapore to Hawaii. However, research shows that these same consumers continue to hold the Wedgwood brand in the highest esteem, which has allowed us over the past decade to extend our brand into food, crystal, cutlery and linen. But the Japanese consumer is changing as well and, as a result, the traditional gifting market is evolving too. Hence we have taken a number of major steps to strengthen our brand—and our distribution efforts—in Japan, aimed at encouraging consumers to self-buy our products as well as purchase for gifts. To this end, we have an outstanding team in place, led by company President Hanspeter Kappeler. Our network of retail shops is being focused and strengthened and our advertising and promotion reinvigorated. The prestige accorded to Wedgwood in Japan continues to flourish, most recently evident in a series of exclusive high-end gift items—some costing £15,000 [IR £19,046]—currently being produced for Takashimaya, the leading department store chain. We are confident that the economy will continue to improve in Japan during the course of 2000 and, as a result of our wide-ranging efforts in 1999, we will be ideally placed to meet the rise in consumer demand.

We made excellent sales progress in the United States, up 14.5%. In this market, which still holds enormous potential for Wedgwood, our brand is perceived in more traditional terms than in either the U.K. or Europe, hence the continuing success of our formal bone china lines. During the year we introduced ranges of specially designed giftware along with new tableware lines at more affordable price points. Plans for 2000 include innovative marketing initiatives, improved merchandising and the penetration of new distribution channels. The dedicated efforts of our Wedgwood spokesperson, Sarah, Duchess of York, paid handsome dividends for us throughout America in both brand awareness and customer loyalty. I continue to receive a stream of letters from Americans who admire and respect the Duchess of York and who are impressed by Wedgwood's association with her.

Outside our three main markets, Wedgwood achieved some outstanding results. In Australia, sales increased by a record 13% in 1999. As one of the official licenses for the Sydney Olympic Games, opening in September 2000, we foresee even greater rewards ahead in Australia where our brand has been virtually adopted by a nation, which first started trading with Josiah Wedgwood back in the 18th century. In Canada, too, we enjoyed a second great year of sales in a market that ranks Wedgwood at the very highest level of premium desirability.

In Continental Europe, despite the difficult conditions in the German market, we achieved some important new sales breakthroughs. Italy, thanks to our integration with the highly successful existing Rosenthal marketing and distribution team, saw Wedgwood firmly establish itself as one of the best-selling brands of premium ceramics. In Holland, always a strong national market for Wedgwood, we saw sales grow significantly. We developed new distribution in the Scandinavian countries—which hold great promise—and we re-established our position in the promising Spanish market, through our relationship with leading retail chain El Corte Ingles.

During 1999, we made an important step into Taiwan—a sophisticated market of 22 million people with high disposable income. Setting up our own operation under Michael Boyle in Taipei, we already operate eight stores with more to come. The results so far are very encouraging.

The world of distribution and retailing is being shaken by rapid developments in e-commerce. We already use the Internet for business-to-business transactions with our key customers and in 1999, Wedgewood opened its own e-commerce site promoting initially a limited range of giftware items.

Wedgwood is now emerging from some years of rationalization and investing in manufacturing and supply chain operations—making us the least cost manufacturer with leading customer service. In the years ahead the focus of investment can now shift to the front end of the business—our retail partners and our consumers.

In the last year we have carried out some important work on the Wedgwood brand. Working with the London consultancy, The Partners, we sought to refresh our emotional conviction about its consumer appeal—and to renew ourselves with the qualities that make Wedgwood so special. Working through a 'right brain' process of visualization and emotional cues, we arrived at a three word summation that epitomizes for all of us the essence of our brand—"Authentic English Style."

- *Authentic* because in the age of 'hype,' consumers increasingly value things that are real. And with its roots going back nearly 250 years to the founder Josiah Wedgwood, our brand has a heritage and tradition which is truly genuine. For Wedgwood, authenticity is a given.

- *English* because, Englishness is aspirational in all of our markets—from the United States to Germany to Japan.

- *Style* has within it a dynamic which can embrace both the traditional and the modern—and English style has a unique capability of taking an old idea and re-expressing it in a modern way—often with a twist of humor or surprise. Style then, is dynamic—and positions us as highly desirable in today's fashion conscious world.

"Authentic English Style" is the message which Wedgwood will consistently communicate to our consumers as we advance as one of the world's leading luxury lifestyle brands in the century ahead.[8]

We plan to increase our brand advertising in lifestyle magazines and other media, in keeping with our long-term strategy of being a global luxury brand.

If we look at recent Wedgwood brand achievements, there are a number of outstanding success stories. At home, British Airways has chosen Wedgwood to provide the special gift which all Concorde passengers will receive as they fly through the Millennium date change and Wedgwood is the sole licensee for premium ceramics in the U.K.'s Millennium Experience. Also in the U.K., we have embarked on a major study of our national retailing perspectives.

In the United States, Sarah, Duchess of York has begun her active association with Wedgwood to very favorable press reaction. We are confident that she will bring to our brand the same kind of excellent U.S. consumer awareness that she achieved for Weight Watchers through her energetic, high profile endorsement.

In Australia, Wedgwood—like Waterford—has been selected as an official licensee for next year's Olympic Games in Sydney. While such licenses were open only to Australian companies, our innovative enterprise—and the strong historical links with Wedgwood, dating back to the 18th century (when Joseph Banks sent back to Josiah Wedgwood clay from Sydney Cove)—resulted in the manufacturing processes incorporating Australian materials in a line of luxury gifts, thus opening the door to a unique Australian-U.K.-Irish partnership, in keeping with the international Olympic spirit.

Wedgwood sells 35% of its products worldwide through its own 320 retail shops, outlets and shops-in-shops. We have embarked on a program of refurbishment to ensure that the Wedgwood shopping environment will appeal to the affluent, younger consumer targeted by our marketing strategy.

In Tokyo, our flagship store in the Ginza will be used to test future retail environments for the Japanese market, including "super boutiques" and other new concepts.

Our strategy calls for increased "relationship" marketing of our products, with direct marketing in appropriate areas, including the Internet, and through expanding our presence in lifestyle retail shops. We plan to increase our brand advertising in lifestyle magazines and other media, in keeping with our long-term strategy of being a global luxury brand.

It would be remiss not to mention the dedication and energy of Lord Wedgwood, our international ambassador, who has travelled the globe for week after week to promote the brand with his own unique combination of knowledge, eloquence and conviction. His appearances on television and radio and in the press around the world have won many new friends for Wedgwood. In addition to his efforts, our public relations achievements include numerous craft events, the Wedgwood Chef & Potter competition in Ireland and the United Kingdom and a host of other PR successes.

In July, Wedgwood Brand Director, Gavin Haig and I met in Barlaston, together with other Wedgwood marketing colleagues from around the world, for the Strategic Marketing and International Marketing meetings. Held over a three day period, this was a most constructive series of reporting and planning sessions. We were particularly encouraged by the support and direction provided over the entire three days by Deputy Chairman Peter John Goulandris.

All the above can be seen in the context of our three-part strategy to achieve our medium and long term goals for the Wedgwood brand. First, we have been working hard to develop new products, which will reach the right markets at the optimum price. Second, we have been concentrating on enhancing our existing retail distribution network and on expanding in a manner consistent with a successful modern premium lifestyle brand. Finally, we have taken a number of important steps to communicate directly with consumers the contemporary excitement and appeal of today's Wedgwood products—and the relevance to their lives of the great Wedgwood brand.[9]

Rosenthal—CEO's Strategic Report

"Last year was a very exciting one for us at Rosenthal."[10]

O. C. Küsel, CEO

Though conditions in our home consumer market of Germany were difficult, particularly in the first half of the year, there were definite signs of improvement in the second half. At the same time, we increased our leading market share in Germany, crossing the significant 25% hurdle for the first time in our history. Overall the German ceramics market was down about 13%, while Rosenthal managed to hold its sales decrease to just 2.5%.

The forecasts for the German economy in 2000 are good, predicting double the growth of last year, and we know from past history that, if correct, this should make a substantial impact on Rosenthal's sales, particularly in the second half of this year.

Looking at our other markets offers a more comprehensive and realistic view of where Rosenthal truly stands some two years after joining the Waterford Wedgwood group. Thanks to the successful integration which has been achieved, Rosenthal saw double digit sales growth in the United States and in Continental Europe (outside Germany). In Japan, where conditions remain difficult, sales growth was less dramatic but this should improve in 2000 as that market improves and as major steps are completed in our integration with the powerful Wedgwood marketing organization in that country.

Italy, in particular, is one market that stood out as a major success story for Rosenthal in 1999. Not only are we the market leader in Italy, but now that we have completed integration with Wedgwood, we find ourselves on-par in the Italian ceramics rankings and, collectively, miles ahead of any other challenger. This is a model that I am confident we will see repeated in many other European countries in the next few years.

Our single proudest achievement of last year, of course, came with the overwhelming success of the new Bulgari luxury tableware and gifts lines. Following much the same trajectory as our earlier phenomenally successful partnership with Versace, the elegant new Bulgari range sold a total of DM 10 million [German marks] by year end, which was 2.5 times more than we had forecast. Not only have discerning consumers in the major markets around the world taken our Bulgari products to their hearts, but they have also received fantastic coverage in the most important lifestyle publications.

We fully intend to develop the Bulgari range in future as we have done with the Versace range and look forward to many years of handsome returns from both partnerships. Naturally, we are also currently exploring other possible collaborative relationships with a handful of the world's leading luxury goods designers.

"Design Your Life" remains our corporate and consumer rallying cry and nowhere in our product range is this better expressed than in both our medium-market Thomas line of products and the distinguished new additions to our famous Rosenthal Studio Line. The latter is in brilliant accord with an international consumer trend today towards what is to be called "emotional purism": simple, elegant, functional and highly desirable. The reception to these products had been very favorable, most particularly in Germany, and as the consumer market recovers there, we are confident that we have the exciting new products to take full advantage of improved conditions.

I am pleased to report that our major restructuring efforts are now almost 100% completed. The strategy set out in 1997 called for a number of goals to be achieved: reduction in capacity, a re-focus on our key businesses and an improvement in the profitability of our retail business. To these ends, four factories have either been closed or sold; we have disposed of our other non-ceramics related businesses and completed the high-tech modernization of our Rothbuhl factory. The program at our factory at Thomas am Kulm, including new cup and plate lines, will be completed in a matter of weeks as I write this.

Our 1997 strategy called for an investment of DM 65.8 million in our manufacturing process to effect cost savings of DM 17.6 million per annum. By last summer, having invested slightly more—DM 66.9 million—we had achieved our goal and were saving at a rate of DM 17.6 million. Our strategy also called for us to outsource 20% of our production in order to increase our global competitiveness and maintain maximum production and price-structure flexibility. We have now achieved that goal as well.

By the end of 1999, I was very pleased by the progress Rosenthal had made in reaching the above and many other goals, first set two years earlier. The restructuring program has been successfully implemented with immediately conclusive results. Our concept of Rosenthal 'meets' some of the world's leading luxury designer brands—Bulgari and Versace—has been an absolute triumph, and will continue to be developed.

Finally, and above all, Rosenthal has traveled an immense distance in a very short time towards becoming one of the world's leading premium lifestyle brands in table and giftware. As our reputation begins to soar ever higher in markets like the United States and the Far East, and together with our Waterford Wedgwood partners, I look forward to the next century as one that offers almost unlimited opportunity to our company and our great brand.[11]

WATERFORD WEDGWOOD AND ROSENTHAL: CHAIRMAN O'REILLY'S FINANCIAL REPORT

Waterford Wedgwood's operating profit increased by 19.7% to a record-breaking €21.3 million [IR £27.0 million] up from €17.8 million [IR £22.6 million] in 1998. Total Group sales increased 5.5% to €342.6 million (from €324.7 million [IR £435.2 million] in 1998), with Waterford sales growing particularly strongly. Interest costs were up by 23.3% on 1998, reflecting the cash outflow of the Rosenthal acquisition, restructuring and capital expenditure. Our group pre-tax profits increased by 17.5% to €13.4 million [IR £17.0 million], from €11.4 million [IR £14.4 million] in 1998. The Group ROS of 6.2% showed a gain of 0.7% points on 1998.

Earnings per share before goodwill amortization increased by 13.8% to 1.73¢; this represents a compound growth of 18% in the past five years. The Directors are proposing an interim dividend of 0.5714¢ (IR 0.45p) up 12.5%, to be paid to shareholders on the register on 15 October 1999. A scrip dividend alternative will be available to shareholders.[12]

ACQUISITION OF ALL-CLAD

In June 1999, the management acquired All-Clad, which was a premier U.S. luxury cookware company. The acquisition price was $100 million, which was more than double last year's sales of $51.6 million, and 11.2 times operating profits. The goodwill cost was estimated to be $80 million. All-Clad sales had increased more than three fold from $51.5 million in 1993 to $51.5 million in 1998.[13]

Waterford Wedgwood provided figures to show All-Clad's premium sector growth rate of more expensive cookware and kitchen was about 18% from 1990 to 1998, while overall sector grew about 7% during the same period.[14]

Chairman O'Reilly said, "The single most important strategic decision by Waterford Wedgwood last year [1999] was the acquisition of All-Clad."[15] He further stated, "At the heart of any successful luxury brand, of course, are truly great products."[16]

At acquisition time, 97% of All-Clad sales were in the U.S. An executive said, "All-Clad is an important brand in the United States and we are going to make it important elsewhere be it U.K. or Japan, Australia or Italy."[17]

Chairman O'Reilly said, "Our strategy is based firmly on a long tradition of quality, style and confidence—embodied in our existing luxury brands in all the world's markets—and on a dynamic approach to promoting and strengthening them in the future."[18] Thus became a crucial criteria for the selection of companies to acquire or invest in.

ALL-CLAD: CO-CHAIRMAN'S STRATEGIC REPORT

"Record sales in 1999 continued the outstanding growth which has made All-Clad the envy of the rest of its industry."

C. McGillivary, Co-Chairman

On behalf of my Co-chairman, Sam Michaels, I [C. McGillivary] am delighted to report that All-Clad's total sales reached US $69.2 million in 1999, representing a rise in our cookware sales of 39%. With the overall U.S. cookware industry growing by between 4 and 6% per year, All-Clad has averaged 32% a year growth over the past five years. This truly outstanding achievement is a result of All-Clad's success in distinguishing and separating itself from the rest of its market. Indeed, the company has virtually created its own category at the very top end of the market.

Innovative new products, strong relationships with leading U.S. retailers and a distinct vision of its future: these are the three key elements which first attracted Waterford Wedgwood to All-Clad and, subsequently, have produced another record year in 1999. It is remarkable but true that, while averaging 32% sales growth, we see enormous promise for All-Clad to sustain and advance its growth in the U.S. market—at an even faster rate. Having already taken so much market share from our competitors, the All-Clad team is full of enthusiasm, ideas and determination.

I strongly dispute those who say that the gourmet cookware sector is a trend that will peak in a few years. In fact, it seems clear that if you take the sales trend of All-Clad over the past five years together with the huge popularity of celebrity chefs on television, the high sales of cookbooks, and the continuing expansion of fine restaurants around the world, you must conclude that this category is on the upside of the bell curve, far from having peaked.

Breaking down our sales in terms of product lines, Stainless increased by 34%, LTD by 24% and Master Chef was up 20%. In its first year, our All-Clad Kitchen Tools range sold $2.90 million worth of product. When Waterford Wedgwood acquired All-Clad in June 1999, the strategy was to enhance its growth capabilities and improve its ability to better service the U.S. market. Thereafter, in careful stages, we look to expand into selected foreign markets where Waterford Wedgwood already has a strong presence. One of our first decisions was to invest about $5 million in order to increase the manufacturing capacity of the Pittsburgh plant by 33%. Second, we decided to expand the shopping warehouse in order to increase its capacity by 50%. Both of these programs are on track, with the manufacturing increase due to be completed by the summer of 2000.

We fully expected to find a great deal of synergy between All-Clad and the Waterford Wedgwood group, and we have not been disappointed. Distribution and purchasing are two of the most important areas in which we have already begun to merge our efforts. However, the Waterford Wedgwood philosophy is firm in its determination to allow each brand considerable independence. We don't want to homogenize a new business. On the other hand, both Waterford Wedgewood and All-Clad have considerable influence on major U.S. retailers and, working together, expect this influence only to increase.

For instance, both Waterford and Wedgwood have outstanding relations with the leading U.S. department stores' bridal registry departments. Brides are, above all, seeking information. Surely there is no better company to advise a new bride on setting up her first home kitchen than All-Clad. We foresee marketing several starter kits of All-Clad cookware that will enable a bride to receive, along with her heirloom bone china and crystal tableware, the finest cookware available in the land. Our WW group clout with bridal registry departments will enable this marketing plan to become reality.

I believe that new ideas are what really drive successful businesses, and I have been very pleased by the quality of innovative thinking that I have found within All-Clad. I am particular optimistic about the launch of the new line of Emeril Ware in co-partnership with America's leading gourmet television chef, Emeril Lagasse. When the idea was first presented to us at Waterford Wedgwood, it met our own thinking exactly, based on our previous success in launching the Marquis sub-brand for Waterford Crystal. Just as Marquis has been an outstanding success and allowed Waterford to move into the middle market without in any way tarnishing its own prestige value, so I believe the Emeril Ware product line can rapidly and profitably expand All-Clad's market presence.

When it comes to the great opportunities for foreign expansion outside the United States, we are determined to make this move in a manner that will ensure a solid, long-term success for our brand. Rather than leak product into a market, we will have full business plans, full marketing strategies and, when we enter a market, it will be with a splash. All-Clad is an important brand in the United States and we are going to make it equally important elsewhere, be that the U.K. or Japan, Australia or Italy. No doubt we will look to All-Clad's previously successful strategy of seeding its products with top professionals who recognize that this is truly an outstanding, high-performance range of cookware. These professionals have gone on to be our most loyal and enthusiastic advocates.

Ideally, we want to make All-Clad a very strong supplier to a number of categories of housewares. The outstanding thing about the All-Clad brand is that it carries a real emotion with the consumer. Its strongest advocate is the user, whether a professional chef or an enthusiastic amateur, who actually owns All-Clad products, who endorse them to friends, who shows them off in the kitchen. This emotional strength residing in the All-Clad brand—the same kind of emotional strength possessed by Waterford Crystal and Wedgwood—should enable a carefully planned and innovative expansion into new categories and, as a result, even higher levels of growth in sales and profits in what is already a lucrative business.

Finally, I want to thank all of the people at both All-Clad and Waterford Wedgwood who have worked hard and intelligently to make this union between the two companies a success. I have discovered that the All-Clad team, led by my Co-chairman and CEO Sam Michaels, is very similar to the Waterford Wedgwood team: highly professional, thoughtful, not easily satisfied, aggressive and excellent at working together. I am confident that, thanks to our new products, the new resources brought by Waterford Wedgwood, and our new strategic thinking, all-Clad has only just begun its journey towards becoming one of the world's leading home lifestyle brands.[19]

At All-Clad, each and every item of cookware is individually built and finished. As part of the process, we have recently installed our Canonsburg, Pennsylvania facility state-of-the art buffing equipment. These buffers enhance our staff's productivity; at the same time this new technology helps our experienced team to hone and perfect All-Clad's finished quality, already renowned as the best in the world.[20]

ALL-CLAD: CHAIRMAN O'REILLY'S FINANCIAL REPORT

All-Clad Inc. is the leading premium cookware brand in the United States. Its acquisition was another major step towards achieving Waterford Wedgwood's strategic goals. Not only is All-Clad a company with a strong reputation and unique products, its financial performance over the past five years has been outstanding. Sales have gone up more than 300% in that period, to U.S. $51.5m in 1998. The company has 300 employees at its two plants outside Pittsburgh, Pennsylvania. All-Clad has superb relationships with the top premium lifestyle retail groups in the United States.

All-Clad's products are based on a special process of metal bonding. Its high-quality cookware has been widely hailed by the top U.S. professional chefs and food writers and is the fastest growing product range in a very fast-growing sector in the U.S. We see enormous opportunities to take it to new markets in the U.K. Continental Europe and the Far East markets where Waterford Wedgwood has great presence and expertise.

In specific terms, Waterford Wedgwood currently derives 46% of its sales in Europe, 12% in Australia and 40% in North America. All-Clad has no significant market presence outside the U.S. With Continental Europe the fastest growing market in the world for cookware, there is an enormous opportunity for our Group, particularly Rosenthal and Wedgwood, to bring All-Clad into this dynamic new European market. In Japan, Wedgwood's great brand strength will lend a very important helping hand to All-Clad. At the same time, All-Clad's market share in the United States will further strengthen all our Group's brands in that important retail arena. Adding All-Clad products to our Waterford, Wedgwood and Rosenthal contemporary ranges will extend our Group's presence across a fuller spectrum of the premium lifestyle marketplace.

The European launch of All-Clad is scheduled for the year 2000, which other markets to follow.

Sam Michaels will continue as Chairman and CEO of All-Clad—a role which he has held since 1988. I am very pleased that he has also joined the main Board of Waterford Wedgwood plc as an Executive Director. His past success and vast business experience will be extremely valuable in guiding the future development of All-Clad within our Group.

All-Clad sales and profits are not included in these interim results, as All-Clad was acquired on 30 June 1999.[21]

Other Irish Crystal Companies

Galway Crystal Ltd. was part of Fermanagh-based Belleek Pottery Group. Galway Crystal was established over 25 years ago. In June 1993, Belleek Galway Irish Crystal. At the time of purchase, Galway Crystal ". . . was struggling with 35 employees and heavy financial losses." The company went into receivership on April 17, 1993. George Moore, who owned Belleek, turned the company around. It now employed 80 and was profitable. Moore purchased Belleek Pottery in 1990, when it was losing money. Moore established ". . . strong links with U.S. distributors, aggressive marketing and improved brand image were the ingredients which led to a turnaround in that business."[22] These are basically the same strategies he employed in the mid-1990's.

Tipperary Crystal was purchased in 1992 by Ray Stafford and had a debt of one million Irish pounds in 1996. The company was sold. During October-December months of 1997, the business was at break-even. In 1998, Yeoman International Holdings reduced their 100 stake to 52%. Two minority partners, Irelandia Investments and Nial Wall acquired 30% and 18%, respectively. In September, 1999, Louise Kennedy, noted Irish designer, agreed to create a new range of products, Kennedy was compared with John Rocha, who designed a modern line of products for Waterford Crystal. Kennedy said, my work will be ". . . a different look and appeal to a different consumer."[23]

Some 60,000 visitors come yearly to the thatched cottage style showroom in the Tipperary Crystal plant. There are several small regional crystal companies.

Royal Doulton Investment

On November 19, 1999, Waterford Wedgwood management bought 12,380,000 shares of Royal Doulton at 90 p sterling. The shares opened on the previous day at 78 p. The shares were garnered from five institutions.

Royal Doulton expected losses for 1999 to be £16 million; the company had recorded a £14.4 million tax loss for the first-half of the year. A new software system delivery was delayed for 10 weeks. This cost Royal Doulton to lose about 5% of its annual turnover, the estimated loss was between £10 to £12 million.[24]

Royal Doulton has been undergoing ". . . a major rationalization program, announcing the laying off of 1,200 employees, a fifth of its workforce, last December [1998]."[25] Royal Doulton raised £31 million by issuing shares.

Royal Doulton generated £225 million in sales. The company's primer products are—Royal Crown Derby, Minton, Royal Doulton and Royal Albert. The company had three plants in Stoke-on-Trent and one in Indonesia.

Richard Barnes, Group Finance Director for Waterford Wedgwood, said, "the purchase represented 'good value,' provided closer cooperation between the two companies and gave it 'flexibility'. [Barnes was] ". . . adamant the group had 'no intention' of making a bid for the whole company." He further stated, "We are pursuing our strategy of becoming the world's largest luxury lifestyle group."[26]

Royal Doulton's management remained neutral on their reaction to the purchase of a 14.9 equity stake by Waterford Wedgwood.

Royal Doulton's management stressed that the company had "outstanding brand portfolio and strong positions in major markets worldwide and stressed its determination to realize the values of those brands and strategic market positions to the benefit of all its shareholders, employees and customers."[27]

Waterford Wedgwood management did not seek board representation and described the investment as a "strategic investment."

An analyst said Waterford Wedgwood and Royal Doulton brands each have suffered from 'grandmother's inheritance syndrome.' A young bride or couple will not purchase these brands, since the couple will inherit these family treasurers. This has been hurting these brands for a decade or more. This has acted as a stimulant for these companies to make new designs (Jasper Conran by Stuart, John Rocha by Waterford). This is their future—new brands and products for the modern couple who want luxury.

Technology/Research and Product Development

How had advanced technology been adapted to Waterford Crystal's requirements? For centuries glass was formed by pot-melting, then hand-gathered. This method resulted in wastage of up to 75%, and glass pulled from the surface was of necessity marred with impurities. At Waterford we have installed three of the most advanced continuous-melt, automatically gathered furnaces in the world, at a cost of tens of millions of Euros. Operating this state-of-the art technology we have more than doubled our previous yield. More importantly, special gathering equipment (inelegantly called 'gob-feeders') pulls glass from the purest part of the molten stream of liquid crystal—eliminating all inclusions, air or foreign matter—and delivers it to Waterford's master blowers and cutters. As a benefit of our investment in sophisticated technology, our craftspeople are therefore not only more productive, but they are today creating crystal pieces unprecedented in their quality and purity, each one a masterwork.

But our application of technology is much more than a mathematical exercise. At Waterford Wedgwood we also assure that the science to be applied is befitting of our product, consistent with our traditions, supportive of our craftspeople, and enhancing of quality. This is one of our Group's true marks of genius. Building upon a heritage of several centuries, our Irish, English, German and American engineers, a brilliant team, are without rival in adapting the latest technology to ensure that it is appropriate to the Group's special production needs.

Rosenthal's facility on the outskirts of Selb in southern Bavaria, designed by Walter Gropius, is architecture of great sensitivity—a work-environment of harmony and light. Here, Ralf Kuhn and his team have put in place state-of-the-art mechanical handling equipment. This equipment eliminates tedious and heavy manual work, avoids breakage and other handling damage, and frees up Rosenthal's superb manufacturing craftspeople to concentrate their full attention on the making of their product. The result is greater efficiency with improved production quality.[28]

The company spent £5.6 million on design and development in 1999.[29]

Internet Strategy

With the market for business to business e-commerce predicted to rise from US $145 billion in 1999 to $7.29 trillion in 2004, Waterford Wedgwood's excellent corporate web sites are a vital asset for safeguarding the future of the leading luxury home lifestyle brand company in the 21st century.

Since the launch of <www.wreview.com> last year, Waterford Wedgwood has expanded its corporate presence on the Internet to two more sites: <wwinterim.com> and <wwelegance.com>. All have proved extremely popular, with <wwreview.com> registering over half a million users in just four months.

As any visitor can quickly see, the Waterford Wedgwood group sites contain highly useful information in a very stylish format for both investors and consumers alike. As well as the most up-to-date Waterford Wedgwood financial news, including annual and interim reports, analyst presentations, statements from Chairman Dr. Tony O'Reilly, fascinating features about our products and our co-partners like Bulgari and Versace, users can access detailed information on each individual brand within the WW group.

Waterford Crystal, Wedgwood, Rosenthal and All-Clad: if you are searching for company history, product information and news on the latest happenings for each of these brands, check out the group site first. Visitor can also watch video footage of special statements and events, access the latest press releases and e-mail a request for corporate literature or any comments or inquiries. Soon other useful information including contact details for retail stockists in each market, details of regional or national Waterford Wedgwood headquarters and even advice on caring for your product will be available.

Click us up today and soon you will be a regular visitor to one of the Internet's most informative, exciting and easy-to-use corporate sites.

KEY FACTS ABOUT THE INTERNET AND TODAY'S BUSINESS

- Britain is the market leader for e-commerce in Europe, accounting for an amazing 95% of EU companies claiming a Web site, and more than half of business leaders using the Net for buying and selling.

- Total global sales transactions will reap $105 trillion in revenue by 2004, with e-commerce accounting for 7% of those.

- The Internet grows by 10,900 people a day in the UK. Currently, there are 10.6 million people with Internet access in the UK.

- By 2004, 58.5 million people in the United States will have access to the Internet. (That's 55% of all households and 89% of PC-owning households.)

- Three million people in the UK search for financial information on the net every year.

- Spending on Internet infrastructure is expected to quadruple to $41.5 trillion by 2003, surpassing the $1.3 trillion spent on e-commerce that year.[30]

The Internet site has proved extremely popular with <www.wwreview.com> registering over half a million users in just four months.[31]

Financial Report by Chairman O'Reilly

REGIONAL FINANCIAL INFORMATION

North America—40% of Group Sales

Waterford continues to make great gains in the United States with sales up 26% over the same period in 1998 (see **Exhibit 6**). As the American economy continues to thrive, Waterford Crystal has increased its U.S. market share to well over 50% of the premium crystal market.

The Times Square New Year's Eve Ball by Waterford Crystal that will be lowered to mark the Millennium celebrations has already captured the imagination of the American people and hundreds of millions of people around the world will observe, via television and other media, the start of the new Millennium in New York City, focusing on the magnificent Waterford Crystal ball.

Exhibit 6

Selected Financial Information: Waterford Wedgwood plc

(Geographical segment by country of operation. Amounts stated in millions of pounds)

Year Ending December 31	Turnover by Destination	Turnover by Country of Operation	Operating Profit/(Loss)	1999 Net Assets	Destination	Turnover by Country of Operation	Operating Profit Before Exceptional Costs	Exceptional Costs	Operating Profit/(Loss)	1998 Net Assets Restated
Europe	€356.8	€651.6	€68.1	€421.7	€354.9	€579.4	€55.5	(€28.4)	€27.1	€288.6
North America	406.9	399.8	14.3	96.8	283.4	276.2	7.1	(1.1)	6.0	58.8
Asia Pacific	79.8	63.2	(1.1)	24.4	58.7	54.8	–	(1.3)	(1.3)	21.4
Rest of World	36.1	25.2	1.6	8.0	33.5	20.7	1.1	(0.4)	0.7	5.8
	879.6	1,139.8	82.9	550.9	730.5	931.1	63.7	(31.2)	32.5	374.6
Inter Segment Sales[1]	—	(260.2)	—	—	—	(200.6)	—	—	—	—
Group Net Borrowings				(311.8)						(190.8)
	879.6	879.6	82.9	239.1	730.5	730.5	63.7	(31.2)	32.5	183.8
Minority Interest				(3.1)						(3.8)
Total Group	879.6	879.6	82.9	236.0	730.5	730.5	63.7	(31.2)	32.5	180.0

Exchange rates used between the euro and the principal foreign currencies in which the Group does business were as follows:

	Profit and Loss Transactions		Balance Sheet	
	1999	1998	1999	1998
U.S. Dollar	$1.06	$1.13	$1.00	$1.17
Sterling	£0.66	£0.68	£0.62	£0.71
Yen	¥121.33	¥146.91	¥102.93	¥132.80

Note:
1. All intersegment sales originate from Europe.

Source: Waterford Wedgwood plc, *1999 Accounts*, p. 19.

This momentous event, and the imaginative new crystal products created to celebrate it, are winning huge numbers of new customers for the Waterford brand—seed corn for new sales opportunities in the years ahead.

I am glad to report that Wedgwood's sales in the U.S. have reached double digit growth rates, up by 11%. In April we appointed Sarah, Duchess of York as our official Wedgwood ambassador in the United States. As her program of events begins in Fall 1999, we expect further growth arising from this exciting alliance. I am also pleased to report that Rosenthal's sales in the U.S. have increased by 5%.

I have already discussed the benefits that All-Clad's strong position in its sector of the premium homewares market will bring to our Group. I am sure these benefits will lead not only to increased sales for our Waterford, Wedgwood and Rosenthal brands, but also to a further increase in All-Clad's advancing market share in the U.S.

Were All-Clad sales consolidated into the first half, sales in the continuingly robust North American market would be close to 45% of the worldwide total.

U.K. and Ireland and 24% of Group Sales

Wedgwood's sales remained steady during the first six months and a growth trend is already apparent for the second half of 1999. Highly successful product lines like *Sarah's Garden*, *Variations* and our new *Weekday Weekend*, have enjoyed steady sales increases. The upcoming launch of a new Paul Costelloe range of ceramic tableware, new giftware and jewelry lines and Wedgwood's appointment as sole premium ceramics licensee for the U.K.'s Millennium Experience will underpin the growth trend. The completion and launch of our state-of-the-art Global Processing Center (distribution facility) in Staffordshire is already bringing significant benefits to our cost efficiency and customer service.

Waterford Crystal had an excellent year in the U.K. and Ireland, echoing its success in the U.S., with sales up 18%. With the John Rocha range continuing to grow strongly and the imminent launch of the superb new Jasper Conran-designed range of crystal from Stuart, Waterford's subsidiary in the U.K., we expect even greater returns by the end of 1999.

Continental Europe—22% of Group Sales

The Group's sales in Europe, particularly Rosenthal in Germany, reflected difficult market conditions there. Despite this, several of our new product launches were very successful. The Bulgari collection from Rosenthal has been a fantastic success and has already sold €2.6 million in three months, the figure originally estimated for its first year's sales, and Versace remains strong. The lower cost Benetton range, designed to introduce the Rosenthal brand to a new younger consumer group, has begun to take off—all indications show that sales will exceed our expectations.

Wedgwood sales in Europe were affected by restructuring of distribution in order to change from third party distribution to joint Rosenthal/Wedgwood distribution to our customers. In Holland, Scandinavia and Spain, Wedgwood continued to report strong growth.

Australia—12% of Group Sales

Overall Australian sales declined by 3.6%, continuing to recognize the slowdown in Japan but gaining in the rest of this region.

In Australia, our Waterford Wedgwood team achieved a considerable triumph with the appointment of both Waterford and Wedgwood brands as licensees for the creation of commemorative ranges for the next Olympic Games in Sydney. I am proud that Waterford and Wedgwood will both be linked to the Olympics in 2000.

In the difficult Japanese economy of recent years, Wedgwood has held market share and is continuing to invest in the brand, to develop new products—both ceramic and licensed non-ceramic ranges—and to position at price points to meet customer needs. The economy in Japan is now showing signs of picking up momentum and we are looking to an expanding market in 2000.

Wedgwood is planning two major exhibitions of prestige products in Japan in the year 2000: the first with leading store group Takashimaya and the second with one of Japan's top daily newspapers, *Sankei Shimbun*.[32]

Chairman O'Reilly believes people who come to the games will want true heirlooms to remember them by, not just tee-shirts or caps.[33]

Overall

During the first half the Group has invested €25 million [IR £31.7 million] in advertising and marketing its brands. This represents 7.3% of revenue, maintaining the 1998 standard. Gross capital investment at €16.7 million [IR £21.2 million] primarily reflects the completion of the Rosenthal capital expenditure programs. At both Wedgwood and Rosenthal the extensive restructuring is nearing completion. We have now, we believe, the three most modern and progressive ceramic manufacturing locations in the world. The Group has again shown its growth capability in both sales and profits, as well as through acquisition. Our Group today is twice the size it was in 1994 in sales and profitability, and our brand portfolio is more widely spread by category and these brands are more widely known for their "luxury living" qualities. We shall continue this strategy.

The sustained nature of the Group's growth encourages me for the future. The opportunity for top line improvements presented by All-Clad, the strong performance of our brands in the U.S., the global exposure of the Times Square New Year's Eve Ball by Waterford Crystal for the Millennium, the success of our wide ranging new product development and the easing of the Asian economies all point to the Group increasing its momentum.[34]

Other Selected Financial Information

Exhibits 7 and **8** are consolidated profit and loss accounts. **Exhibit 7** was stated in million of Euros (€) for 1999—1995, and **Exhibit 8** was stated in millions of Irish pounds (IRE) for 1998–1995. In 1999, the company started stating its financial statements in Euros (€),

Exhibit 7

Consolidated Profit and Loss Account (1999–1995): Waterford Wedgwood plc
(Amounts stated in millions of Euros, except per share data)

Year Ending December 31	1999	1998	1997	1996	1995
Turnover	€879.6	€730.5	€529.7	€477.8	€437.4
Operating profit before exceptional charge	82.9	63.7	57.4	49.8	42.3
Operating profit after exceptional charge	82.9	32.5	22.1	49.8	42.3
Share of profits of associated undertaking	—	—	0.6	—	—
Net interest cost	(17.4)	(13.6)	(7.2)	(5.5)	(6.6)
Profit on ordinary activities before taxation	65.5	18.9	15.5	44.3	35.7
Taxation on profit on ordinary activities	(9.4)	(2.5)	(7.4)	(7.5)	(5.1)
Profit on ordinary activities after taxation	56.1	16.4	8.1	36.8	30.6
Minority interests	0.9	(0.3)	—	—	—
Profit attributable to members of parent company	57.0	16.1	8.1	36.8	30.6
Dividends	(19.1)	(16.1)	(14.1)	(12.8)	(11.2)
Retained profit/(loss) for the year	37.9	—	(6.0)	24.0	19.4
Earnings per share (cents)	7.82¢	2.21¢	1.12¢	5.08¢	4.30¢
Diluted earnings per share (cents)	7.80¢	2.18¢	1.10¢	5.03¢	4.23¢
Earnings per share (before exceptional charge and goodwill amortization)—(cents)	8.26¢	6.59¢	5.97¢	5.08¢	4.30¢

Source: Waterford Wedgwood plc, *1999 Annual Report*, p. 34.

Exhibit 8

Consolidated Profit and Loss Account (1998–1995): Waterford Wedgwood plc
(Amounts stated in millions of Irish pounds (IR£), except per share data)

Year Ending December 31	1998	1997	1996	1995
Turnover	£575.3	£417.2	£376.3	£344.5
Operating profit before exceptional charge	50.2	45.2	39.2	33.3
Operating profit after exceptional charge	25.6	17.4	39.2	33.3
Share of profits of associated undertaking	—	0.5	—	—
Net interest cost	(10.7)	(5.7)	(4.3)	(5.2)
Profit on ordinary activities before taxation	14.9	12.2	34.9	28.1
Taxation on profit on ordinary activities	(2.0)	(5.8)	(5.9)	(4.0)
Profit on ordinary activities after taxation	12.9	6.4	29.0	24.1
Minority interests	(0.2)	—	—	—
Profit attributable to members of parent company	12.7	6.4	29.0	24.1
Dividends	(12.7)	(11.1)	(10.1)	(8.8)
Retained profit/(loss) for the year	0.0	(4.7)	18.9	15.3
Earnings per share	1.74p	0.88p	4.00p	3.39p
Diluted earnings per share	1.72p	0.87p	3.96p	3.33p
Earnings per share (before exceptional charge and goodwill amortization)	5.19p	4.70p	4.00p	3.39p

Source: Waterford Crystal plc, *1999 Accounts*, p. 32.

Exhibit 9 shows the company's consolidated profit and loss account in millions of Euros (€).
Exhibit 10 shows the company's consolidated balance sheet in millions of Euros (€), **Exhibit 11** provided selected financial information in three currencies—Euros (€), British pound sterling (STG) (£), U.S. dollars ($).

Exhibit 9

Consolidated Profit and Loss Account: Waterford Wedgwood plc
(Amounts stated in millions of Euros (€), except per share data)

Year Ending December 31	Continuing Operations 1999	Acquisitions All-Clad 1999	Total 1999	1998 Restated
Turnover	€842.9	€36.7	€879.6	€730.5
Cost of sales	(425.4)	(20.1)	(445.5)	(389.7)
Gross profit	417.5	16.6	434.1	340.8
Distribution costs	(250.6)	(7.5)	(258.1)	(233.5)
Administrative expenses	(89.7)	(4.7)	(94.4)	(74.9)
Other operating income	1.3	—	1.3	0.1
	(339.0)	(12.2)	(351.2)	(308.3)
Operating profit	78.5	4.4	82.9	32.5
Net interest payable			(17.4)	(13.6)
Profit on ordinary activities after taxation			65.5	18.9
Taxation on profit on ordinary activities			(9.4)	(2.5)
Profit on ordinary activities after taxation			56.1	16.4
Minority interests			0.9	(0.3)
Profit attributable to members of the parent company			57.0	16.1

(continued)

Exhibit 9
(*continued*)

Year Ending December 31	Continuing Operations 1999	Acquisitions All-Clad 1999	Total 1999	1998 Restated
Dividends			(19.1)	(16.1)
Retained profit for the year			37.9	0.0
Transfer to/(from) reserves and translation adjustments			16.9	(17.8)
Increase/(decrease) in balance during year			54.8	(17.8)
Balance at beginning of year			(62.9)	(45.1)
			(8.1)	(62.9)
Earnings per share			7.82¢	2.21¢
Diluted earnings per share			7.80¢	2.18¢
Earnings per share before exceptional charge and goodwill amortization			8.26¢	6.59¢

Note: Notes were deleted.

Source: Waterford Wedgwood plc, *1999 Annual Report*, p. 14.

Exhibit 10
Consolidated Balance Sheet: Waterford Wedgwood plc
(Amounts stated in millions of Euros [€])

Year Ending December 31	1999	1998 Restated
Fixed assets		
Intangible assets	104.8	16.8
Tangible assets	259.5	226.6
Financial assets	22.6	6.7
Total of fixed assets	386.9	250.1
Current assets		
Stocks	238.8	203.9
Debtors	167.0	132.9
Cash and deposits	87.4	68.2
Total of current assets	493.2	405.0
Creditors (amount falling due within 1 year)	(202.3)	(171.6)
Net current assets	290.9	233.4
Total assets less current liabilities	677.8	483.5
Creditors (amounts falling due after more than 1 year)	(430.1)	(291.5)
Provisions for liabilities and charges	(8.6)	(8.2)
Total assets	239.1	183.8
Capital and reserves		
Called up share capital	56.6	56.5
Share premium account	176.7	175.6
Revaluation reserve	10.8	10.8
Revenue reserves	(8.1)	(62.9)
Shareholders' funds—equity interests	236.0	180.0
Minority interests—equity interests	3.1	3.8
Shareholders' funds	239.1	183.8

Note: Notes were deleted.

Source: Waterford Wedgwood plc, *1999 Annual Report*, p. 15.

Exhibit 11

Summary Financial Statements: Waterford Wedgwood plc

To assist overseas investors, the consolidated financial statements of Waterford Wedgwood plc are presented in summary form below, prepared in accordance, with generally accepted accounting principles applicable in the Republic of Ireland ("Irish GAAP"), translated at the year-end exchange rates of €1 = STG£0.62 and US$1.00.

Statement stated in euros (€), Irish pounds (IR£), and U.S. dollars ($):
Waterford Wedgwood plc

A. Consolidated Income Statement	1999 €mils	1999 STG £mils	1999 US $mils
Net sales	879.6	545.4	879.6
Net income before taxes	65.5	40.6	65.5
Taxes on income	(9.4)	(5.8)	(9.4)
Minority interests	0.9	0.6	0.9
Net income	57.0	35.4	57.0
Income per ordinary share	7.82c	4.85p	7.82c
Diluted income per ordinary share	7.80c	4.84p	7.80c
Income per ordinary share before exceptional charge and goodwill amortization	8.26c	5.12p	8.26c

B. Consolidated Balance Sheet	1999 €mils	1999 STG £mils	1999 US $mils
Fixed assets	386.9	239.9	386.9
Current assets	493.2	305.8	493.2
Total assets	880.1	545.7	880.1
Current liabilities	202.3	125.4	202.3
Long-term liabilities	438.7	272.1	438.7
Shareholders' funds	236.0	146.3	236.0
Minority interests	3.1	1.9	3.1
Total liabilities, shareholders' funds, and minority interests	880.1	545.7	880.1

Note: 1998 conversion rates were based on IR£ (not € as in 1999). The exchange rates were IR£ 1 = US $1.43 and STG£0.86.

Source: Waterford Wedgwood plc, *Accounts 1999*, p. 36.

Notes

1. This case was written in the present tense to directly represent the quoted materials of Waterford Wedgwood executives. This section—An Overview of Crystal Business from Philip H. Anderson's case, "Waterford Crystal Ltd.". These sections were directly quoted with minor editing, and "History of Waterford Crystal" was from www.wwreview.com.
2. Waterford Wedgwood plc, *1999 Accounts*, p. 9. The above paragraphs were directly quoted with minor editing.
3. Waterford Wedgwood plc, *Interim Review 1999*, p. 22. Just this sentence.
4. Waterford Wedgwood plc, *Review of 1999*, pp. 72, 74 and 75. The above nine paragraphs were directly quoted with minor editing.
5. Waterford Crystal, 2000 *Give the Gift You Love To Receive*, p. back side of the cover.
6. *Ibid.*
7. Waterford Wedgwood, plc, *Review of 1999*, p. 81. Just this sentence.
8. Waterford Wedgwood plc, *Review of 1999*, pp. 81–83. The above 16 paragraphs were directly quoted with minor editing.
9. Waterford Wedgwood plc, *Interim Review 1999*, p. 19. The above nine paragraphs were directly quoted with minor editing.
10. *Ibid.*, *Review of 1999*, p. 89. Just this sentence.
11. *Ibid.*, pp. 89–90. The above 11 paragraphs are directly quoted with minor editing.
12. Waterford Wedgwood plc, *Interim Review 1999*, p. 1 of the Chairman's Statement. These two paragraphs were directly quoted with minor editing.
13. "All-Clad Has Right Ingredient for Waterford," *Irish Times*, May 31, 1999, p. 12.
14. "All-Clad Has Right Ingredient for Waterford," p. 10.
15. Waterford Wedgwood plc, *Review of 1999*, p. 9.
16. Waterford Wedgwood plc, *Review of 1999*, p. 10.
17. *Ibid.*, p. 95.

18. *Ibid.*, p. 12. Waterford Wedgwood plc, *Interim Review 1999*, p. 1 of the Chairman's Statement. The above six paragraphs were directly quoted with minor editing.

19. *Ibid.*, p. 93.

20. *Ibid.*, pp. 93–96. The above 11 paragraphs were directly quoted with minor editing.

21. Waterford Wedgwood plc, *Interim Review 1999*, p. 1 of the Chairman's Statement. The above six paragraphs were directly quoted with minor editing.

22. Alex Meehan, "Hordes Expected at Galaway Crystal Centre," *Sunday Business*, May 5, 1996 and Eddie Doyle, "Moore Plans £2.5m Galaway Centre," *Sunday Business*, May 8, 1994.

23. "Crystal Firm Hoping Things Will Take Shape with Louise Kennedy Designs," *Irish Times*, September 16, 1999.

24. Bill Murdock, "Waterford Wedgwood Takes 14.9% Equity Stake in Royal Doulton," *Irish Times*, November 20, 1999.

25. *Ibid.*

26. *Ibid.*

27. *Ibid.*

28. Waterford Wedgwood plc, *Review of 1999*, p. 65. The above four paragraphs were directly quoted with minor changes.

29. Waterford Wedgwood plc, *Accounts 1999*, p. 10.

30. Waterford Wedgwood plc, *Review of 1999*, pp. 34–35. The above six paragraphs were directly quoted with minor editing.

31. *Ibid.*, p. 35.

32. Waterford Crystal plc, *Interim Review 1999*, pp. 1–2 of the Chairman's Statement. The above 14 paragraphs were directly quoted with minor editing.

33. Waterford Wedgwood plc, *Review of 1999*, p. 25.

34. Waterford Crystal plc, *Interim Review 1999*, p. 2 of the Chairman's Statement. The above two paragraphs were quoted with minor editing.

case 9

Larry J. Ellison—Entrepreneurial Spirit at Oracle Corporation (2000)

Joyce P. Vincelette, Ellie A. Fogarty, and Thomas L. Wheelen

Larry J. Ellison has been Chief Executive Officer (CEO) since he cofounded Oracle in 1977, and he became Chairman in June 1995. His business philosophy is "to heck with cooperation, this means war." He is obsessed with toppling the number one software company (Microsoft and Bill Gates) from its perch, but occasionally trains his guns on other competitors as well."[1]

He was known as a loose cannon among industry leaders. His best friend, Steve Jobs, Chairman and CEO of Apple Computer, calls Ellison the "outrageous poster child."[2]

He has been accused of company bashing of competitors and their products. Some executives felt that some of Oracle's advertising sometimes goes overboard. Scott McNeally, Chairman of Sun Microsystems, said with some admiration, "There's a bit of P. T. Barnum in him."[3]

Jim Barksdale, CEO of Netscape, said, Ellison ". . . is talking down Netscape's stock because he wants to acquire the company."[4] AOL acquired Netscape.

Ellison was very competitive in all aspects of his life. He had a passion for ocean yachting and competed once in the Trans Pacific race and won it. His other passions were piloting jets, fitness, fine art, Asian culture, and women. He was frequently listed among the most eligible bachelors in Silicon Valley.

Ellison's management style was that he was a big-picture individual all the way. He delegated the day-to-day management to two of his trusted lieutenants. Others said that he had centralized decision making over the past few years.

Ellison's Internet strategy was "To be the company that makes the software that runs e-commerce. The largest retail sites are all powered by Oracle, most large Web sites use Oracle's database products, and the company was investing heavily in ventures for wireless data devices. Ellison was creating a network within Oracle as well, linking international offices and sharing sales, marketing, and other data. The effort has already saved the company about $1 billion."[5]

His personal strengths were "A rare blend of technology savvy and super salesmanship."[6] His personal weaknesses were "Not the most popular guy in the Valley. Loquacious, opinionated, abrasive, given to missing product-introduction. Until last year's [1999] decision to work 50-hour weeks, rarely had he showed at the office before 10 A.M."[7]

His stockholders had about 300% increase in their stock in 1999. The stock was scheduled to split 2 for 1 in October, 2000. Ellison was ranked the 15th Best CEO by *Worth* magazine.[8]

This case was prepared by Professor Joyce P. Vincelette; Ellie A. Fogarty, Business Librarian of the College of New Jersey; and Professor Thomas L. Wheelen of the University of South Florida. This case was edited for SMBP-9th edition. This case may not be reproduced in any form without written permission of the copyright holder, Thomas L. Wheelen. Copyright © 2000 by Thomas L. Wheelen. Reprinted by permission.

His passion for Asian culture and art led him to build a $40 million palace, which was modeled after a sixteenth century imperial Japanese residence, on his San Francisco property.

In 2000, he was ranked number two in the world with a net worth of $52 billion. Only Bill Gates', his arch rival, fortune exceeded Ellison's net worth. In late 2000, he passed Gates as the richest man in the world. This was during the slump in high-tech stocks.

Corporate Governance

TOP MANAGEMENT

On June 30, 2000, Raymond Lane, President and Chief Operating Officer (COO) resigned but remained on the Board of Directors until the Annual Meeting on October 16, 2000. No one was appointed to these positions. Raymond Lane joined Oracle in 1992, when Oracle ". . . was still struggling to rebound from a downturn caused by lax financial controls and hyperaggressive sales practices." In 1990, Oracle ". . . almost floundered . . . when auditors discovered that its sales force had been concocting sales in pursuit of commissions."[9] Oracle had to restate its earnings, which resulted in a loss from previously stated earnings with a profit. This re-statement resulted in the stock falling 80%.

This resulted in Ellison hiring Raymond Lane, in 1992, who became President and received many accolades for the company's recovery strategy. Lane had been a top executive at consulting firm Booz-Allen & Hamilton. Ellison said, "Ray's job had changed dramatically [and] he has gradually been decommissioning himself."[10] During Lane's tenure, Ellison focused mainly on product development, and Ellison reasserted his influence to overhaul many of the company's operations. He was able to harness the potentials of the Internet to cut costs by $1 billion and increased efficiencies. These changes according to Ellison, ". . . also reduced Mr. Lane's authority over sales and other operations."[11] Ellison further stated, "He [Lane] used to be more autonomous," and "The line had always been that Ray wanted to run his own show, and there is only one show at Oracle."[12] During this time, two executive Vice Presidents, Safra Catz and Gary Bloom, had been granted more responsibilities. David Roux, former Oracle executive, said, "Ray was the keel to Larry's sail, [and] the fact is the boat would have flipped over without him."[13]

Lane said he was concerned about "Larrygate." He further stated, "Larry intruded on my duties and made it difficult for me to fit into the system the past year; I had no choice but to leave."[14]

Charles Fitzgerald, Director of Business Development at Microsoft, said "without Ray, there is no adult supervision."[15]

The Lane announcement came two days (June 28, 2000) after Ellison admitted that Oracle had hired a Washington, DC detective agency, Investigative Group International, ". . . to help prove that archrival Microsoft Corp. had given financial support to groups expressing opposition to a federal antitrust against the dominant software maker."[16] The detectives offered money [up to $1,200] for the garbage of Microsoft allies."[17] A former Oracle executive said ". . . the two episodes reinforce a stereotype of Oracle as a brash company that hadn't been to college."[18]

Charles Fitzgerald said, "Make Oracle to be your trusted technology adviser? You can't even trust them to take out the trash."[19] Some observers called the incident "cash for trash," or "Larrygate."

The executive officers of Oracle were:[20]

Lawrence J. Ellison, 54, had been Chief Executive Officer since he cofounded the company in May 1977. Mr. Ellison had been Chairman of the Board since June 1995 and served as Chairman of the Board from April 1990 until September 1992. He also served as President of the company from May 1977 to June 1996. Mr. Ellison was Co-Chairman of California's Council on Information Technology. He was also a Director of Apple Computer, Inc.

Jeffrey O. Henley, 55, had been Executive Vice President and Chief Financial Officer of the company since March 1991 and had been a Director since June 1995. Prior to joining Oracle, he served as Executive Vice President and Chief Financial Officer of Pacific Holding Company, a privately held company with diversified interests in manufacturing and real estate, from August 1986 to February 1991.

Gary L. Bloom, 39, had been Executive Vice President (currently responsible for server development, platform technologies, marketing, education, customer support, and corporate development) of the company since May 1999 and the Executive Vice President of the System Products Division from March 1998 to May 1999. He had held various positions at Oracle, including Senior Vice President of the System Products Division from November 1997 to March 1998, Senior Vice President of the Worldwide Alliances and Technologies Division from May 1996 to May 1997, Vice President of the Mainframe and Integration Technology Division, and Vice President of the Massively Parallel Computing Division from May 1992 to May 1996. Prior to joining Oracle, Mr. Bloom worked at IBM and at Chevron Corporation where he held various technical positions in their mainframe system areas.

Safra Catz, 38, had been Executive Vice President (currently responsible for global business practices) of the company since November 1999 and was a Senior Vice President between April 1999 and October 1999. Prior to joining Oracle, Ms. Catz was at Donaldson, Lufkin & Jenrette, a global investment bank, where she was Managing Director from February 1997 to March 1999 and a Senior Vice President from January 1994 until February 1997 and had previously held various investment banking positions since 1986.

Sergo Giacoletto, 50, had been Executive Vice President for Europe, Middle East and Africa, since June 2000, and Senior Vice President, Business Solutions, since November 1998. He was Vice President of Alliances and Technology of the company from March 1997 to November 1998. Before joining Oracle, he was President, AT&T Solutions for Europe, since August 1994. Previously, he spent 20 years with Digital Equipment Corporation in various positions in marketing and services in the European unit.

Jay H. Nussbaum, 56, had been Executive Vice President, Oracle Service Industries, since October 1998, and Senior Vice President and General Manager of the company's Federal group since 1992. Prior to joining Oracle, Mr. Nussbaum worked at Xerox Corporation where he held various management roles during his 24-year tenure, including President of Integrated Systems Operations. Mr. Nussbaum had served on several key advisory boards for George Mason University, James Madison University, and the University of Maryland.

George J. Roberts, 43, had been Executive Vice President, North American Sales, since June 1999 and served as Senior Vice President, North American Sales from June 1998 to May 1999. Mr. Roberts served as Senior Vice President, Business Online, from March 1998 to June 1998. He took a leave of absence from July 1997 to March 1998. Mr. Roberts joined Oracle in March 1990 and from June 1990 to June 1997, he served as Group Vice President, Central Commercial Sales.

Charles A. Rozwat, 52, had been Executive Vice President, Database Server, since November 1999 and served as Senior Vice President, Database Server from December 1996 to October 1999. Mr. Rozwat served as Vice President of Development from May 1995 to November 1996.

Edward J. Sanderson, 51, had been Executive Vice President, Consulting and Latin American Division, since June 1999, and Senior Vice President of Consulting and the Latin American Division of the company from July 1998 to May 1999. He served as Senior Vice President of Americas Consulting for the company from July 1995 to July 1998. Before joining Oracle, Mr. Sanderson served as President of Worldwide Information Services for Unisys Corporation from February 1994 to June 1995. Prior to Unisys, he spent 18 years in the consulting industry at McKinsey & Company and Andersen Consulting.

Frank Varasano, 54, had been Executive Vice President, Oracle Product Industries since October 1999. Before joining Oracle, Mr. Varasano was a Senior Partner at Booz Allen & Hamilton from October 1998 to September 1999. Mr. Varasano held several positions at Booz Allen & Hamilton, including Managing Officer United States, Global Managing Officer Engineering and Manufacturing Industries, and Managing Officer, New York office. He also served on Booz Allen & Hamilton's Executive Committee and Board of Directors.

Ronald Wohl, 39, had been Executive Vice President, Applications Development, since November 1999 and served as Senior Vice President, Applications Development, from December 1992 to October 1999. From September 1989 until December 1992, Mr. Wohl was Vice President and Assistant General Manager of the Systems Product Division.

Daniel Cooperman, 49, had been Senior Vice President, General Counsel, and Secretary of the company since February 1997. Prior to joining Oracle, Mr. Cooperman had been associated with the law firm of McCutchen, Doyle, Brown & Enersen since October 1977, and had served there as a partner since June 1983. From September 1995 until February 1997, Mr. Cooperman was Chair of the law firm's Business & Transactions Group, and from April 1989 through September 1995, he served as the Managing Partner of the law firm's San Jose Office.

Jennifer L. Minton, 39, had been Senior Vice President and Corporate Controller of the company since April 2000, and Vice President and Corporate Controller since November 1998. From May 1989 to November 1998, Ms. Minton held various positions in Oracle's finance organization including Assistant Corporate Controller, and was a Vice President of the Company since August 1995. Prior to joining Oracle, Ms. Minton held various positions in the Audit Division of Arthur Andersen firm since December 1983.

Ellison had relinquished his $200,000 salary and bonuses through May 2003 for 20 million stock options, worth potentially $1.4 billion. **Exhibit 1** shows the salaries and stock own-

Exhibit 1

Executive Compensation: Oracle Corporation
Summary Compensation Table

Name and Principal Position	Fiscal Year	Annual Compensation		Long-Term Compensation Awards Securities Underlying Options/ SARs (#)
		Salary ($)	Bonus ($)	
Lawrence J. Ellison	2000	$ 208,000		20,000,000[1]
Chairman and	1999	1,000,000	$ 2,752,000	3,000,000
Chief Executive Officer	1998	999,987	$ 530,000	1,500,000
Raymond J. Lane[2]	2000	1,000,000	2,180,000	1,500,000
President and Chief	1999	1,000,000	2,250,000	2,250,000
Operating Officer	1998	974,991	$ 206,250	0
Gary L. Bloom	2000	1,000,000	1,915,000	2,400,000
Executive Vice President	1999	888,864	2,352,919	3,600,000
	1998	334,713	200,000	2,100,000
Jeffrey O. Henley	2000	806,250	1,361,250	1,000,000
Executive Vice President	1999	727,500	1,334,609	1,200,000
and Chief Financial Officer	1998	645,000	113,437	0
Jay Nussbaum	2000	742,897	1,772,069	800,000
Executive Vice President	1999	525,000	1,151,730	1,500,000
Oracle Service Industries	1998	345,600	386,996	360,000
George Roberts	2000	643,182	4,020,158	800,000
Executive Vice President	1999	406,458	357,967	875,000
	1998	106,831	115,844	180,000

Notes:
1. All figures in this column reflect options to purchase common stock and adjustments, to the extent applicable, for two 3-for-2 stock splits and one 2-for-1 stock split effective August 15, 1997, February 26, 1999, and January 18, 2000, respectively. Mr. Ellison's option grant is intended to be the only option grant that he receives in the four-year period from fiscal year 2000 to fiscal year 2003.
2. Mr. Lane is no longer an employee of the company.

Source: Oracle Corporation *Annual Stockholders Meeting,* September 11, 2000, p. 7.

Exhibit 2

Executives' Stock Ownership: Oracle Corporation

Name and Address of Beneficial Owner	Amount and Nature of Beneficial Ownership	Percent of Class
Lawrence J. Ellison 500 Oracle Parkway, Redwood City, CA 94065	696,356,050	24.16%
Raymond J. Lane	10,104,298	1*
Gary L. Bloom	3,007,982	1*
Jeffrey O. Henley	7,534,010	1*
Jay Nussbaum	618,954	1*
George Roberts	695,178	1*
Donald L. Lucas	439,815	1*
Michael J. Boskin	477,060	1*
Jack Kemp	18,351	1*
Jeffrey Berg	179,250	1*
Richard A. McGinn	13,500	1*
Kay Koplovitz	79,300	1*
All current executive officers and directors as a group (19 persons)	725,171,403	25.16%

* Means less than 1%.
Note: Original notes were deleted.

Source: Oracle Corporation *Annual Stockholders Meeting*, September 11, 2000, p. 5.

erships of 25.16% by Oracle's executives. **Exhibit 2** shows stock options. Ellison owned 696,356,050 shares (24.16%), so the other 18 executives owned 1.0% of the stock. Institutions owned 44.5%, and insiders owned 46.7%.

BOARD OF DIRECTORS

The eight directors were:[21]

Mr. Ellison, 56, had been Chief Executive Officer and a Director of the company since he cofounded it in May 1977. Mr. Ellison had been Chairman of the Board since June 1995 and served as Chairman of the Board from April 1990 until September 1992. He also served as President of the company from May 1977 to June 1996. Mr. Ellison was Co-Chairman of California's Council on Information Technology. He was also a Director of Apple Computer, Inc.

Mr. Lucas, 70, had been a Director of the company since March 1980. He had been Chairman of the Executive Committee since 1986 and Chairman of the Finance and Audit Committee since 1987. Mr. Lucas had been a member of the Committee on Compensation and Management Development (the "Compensation Committee") since 1989 and a member of the Nominating Committee since December 1996. He was Chairman of the Board from October 1980 through March 1990. He had been a venture capitalist since 1960. He also served as a Director of Cadence Design Systems, Inc., Coulter Pharmaceutical, Inc., Macromedia, Inc., Transcend Services, Inc., Preview Systems, Inc., and Tricord Systems, Inc.

Dr. Boskin, 54, had been a Director of the company since May 1994. He had been a member of the Finance and Audit Committee and the Nominating Committee since July 1994 and a member of the Compensation Committee since July 1995. He was appointed Chairman of the Compensation Committee by the Board in July 1997. Dr. Boskin had been a Professor of Economics at Stanford University since 1971 and was Chief Executive Officer and President of

Boskin & Co., Inc., a consulting firm. He was Chairman of the President's Council of Economic Advisers from February 1989 until January 1993. Dr. Boskin also served as a Director of Exxon Mobil Corporation, First Health Group Corp., and Vodafone AirTouch Public Limited Company.

Mr. Henley, 55, had been Executive Vice President and Chief Financial Officer for the company since March 1991 and had been a Director since June 1995. Prior to joining Oracle, he served as Executive Vice President and Chief Financial Officer of Pacific Holding Company, a privately held company with diversified interests in manufacturing and real estate, from August 1986 to February 1991.

Mr. Kemp, 65, had served as a Director of the company since February 1997 and previously served as a Director for the company from February 1995 until September 1996. Mr. Kemp had been Co-director of Empower America from 1993 to the present. Mr. Kemp served as a member of Congress for 18 years and as Secretary of Housing and Urban Development from February 1989 until January 1992. In 1996, Mr. Kemp was the Republican candidate for Vice President of the United States. Mr. Kemp also served as a Director of Hawk Corporation, JumpMusic.com, Inc., Proxicom, Inc., Speedway Motorsports, Inc., and ZapMe! Corporation. He was a former quarterback for the Buffalo Bills football team.

Mr. Berg, 53, had been a Director of the company since March 1997. He had been a member of the Finance and Audit Committee since April 1997. Mr. Berg had been an agent in the entertainment industry for over 25 years and the Chairman and Chief Executive Officer of International Creative Management, Inc., a talent agency for the entertainment industry, since 1985. He served as Co-Chair of California's Council on Information Technology and was President of the Executive Board of the College of Letters and Sciences at the University of California at Berkeley.

Mr. McGinn, 53, had been a Director of the company since March 1997. Mr. McGinn had served as the Chairman of the Board of Lucent Technologies, Inc., since February 1998 and had been its Chief Executive Officer since October 1997. He had been President since February 1996, and was Chief Operating Officer from February 1996 to October 1997. Lucent Technologies was the communications and technology subsidiary of AT&T and was spun off in April 1996. Mr. McGinn served as Executive Vice President of AT&T and Chief Executive Officer of AT&T Network Systems from October 1994 to April 1996. He served as President and Chief Operating Officer of AT&T Network Systems from August 1993 to October 1994 and as a Senior Vice President from August 1992 to August 1993. Mr. McGinn also served as a Director of the American Express Company.

Ms. Koplovitz, 55, had been a Director of the company since October 1998. She had been a member of the Nominating Committee since July 1999. Since January 2000, she had been CEO of Working Woman Network, Inc., which operated a Web site aimed at women and provides business tools. From June 1998 to January 2000, she served as Chief Executive Officer of Koplovitz & Co., a company specializing in media start-up ventures. She was the Founder of USA Networks, and served as its Chairman and Chief Executive Officer from its premiere in 1977 as television's first advertiser-supported basic cable network until June 1998. In 1992, Ms. Koplovitz launched the Sci-Fi Channel, which had become one of the industry's fastest growing networks. Ms. Koplovitz was also a director of Liz Claiborne, Inc. In June 1998, Ms. Koplovitz was appointed by President Clinton to Chair the National Women's Business Council.

The outside directors, Kemp, Berg, McGinn, Lane, and Koplovitz, were paid an annual retainer of $40,000 each. Dr. Boskin was paid $100,000 and Mr. Lucas was paid $160,000 in connection with their additional board committee duties. Nonemployee members of the Board also receive directors fees of (1) $1,500 for each Board meeting attended; (2) $3,000 for each meeting of the Finance and Audit Committee attended, and (3) $2,000 per day for each special meeting or committee attended. Nonemployee members are granted stock option (30,000 to 90,000) depending on specific time constraints.

The Organization

Oracle Corporation was the world's leading supplier of software for information management. The company developed, manufactured, marketed, and distributed computer software that helped corporations manage and grow their businesses. The company's software products were categorized into two broad areas: *Systems software* and *Internet business applications software.* Systems software was a complete Internet platform to develop and deploy applications on the Internet and corporate intranets, and included database management software and development tools that allowed users to create, retrieve, and modify the various types of data stored in a computer system. Internet business applications software allowed users to access information or use the applications through a simple Internet browser on any client computer, and automates the performance of specific business data processing functions for financial management, procurement, project management, human resources management, supply chain management, and customer relationship management. The company's software ran on a broad range of computers, including mainframes, minicomputers, workstations, personal computers, laptop computers, and information appliances (such as hand-held devices and mobile phones) and was supported on more than 85 different operating systems, including UNIX, Windows, Windows NT, OS/390, and Linux. In addition to computer software products, the company offered a range of consulting, education, and support services for its customers. Also, for customers who choose not to install their own applications, Oracle's Business On-Line offered an online service that hosted and delivered Internet business applications across a network that could be accessed via any standard Web browser.[22]

Product Development Architecture

ORACLE INTERNET PLATFORM

Oracle's product development platform was based on an Internet computing architecture. The Internet computing architecture was comprised of data servers, application servers, and client computers or devices running a Web browser. Internet computing centralized business information and applications allowed them to be managed easily and efficiently from a central location. End users were provided with ready access to the most current business data and applications through a standard Internet browser. Database servers managed all business information, while application servers ran all business applications. These servers were managed by professional information technology managers. By contrast, the traditional, client-server computing architecture required that each client computer ran and managed its own applications, and also be updated every time an application changed. The company believed that the design of its software for Internet computing improved network performance and data quality and helped organizations decrease installation, maintenance, and training costs associated with information technology.

ELECTRONIC BUSINESS

Oracle believed that electronic commerce (the exchange of goods and/or services electronically over the Internet) was revolutionizing business by providing a relatively low cost means of distributing products and expanding markets globally, increased efficiencies, and provided better, more personalized customer services. Because organizations were changing the way employees work, communicate, share knowledge, and deliver value, the company believed that to remain competitive, they needed to develop and deploy Web-based business and commerce applications on the Internet.[23]

Major Product Groups

Oracle had three major product groups.[24]

1. SYSTEMS SOFTWARE

The Oracle relational database management system (DBMS)—the key component of Oracle's Internet platform—enabled storing, manipulating, and retrieving relational, object-relational, multidimensional, and other types of data.

- Oracle Version 8*i* was a database specifically designed as a foundation for Internet development and deployment, extending Oracle's technology in the areas of data management, transaction processing, and data warehousing to the new medium of the Internet. Built directly inside the database, Internet features such as Java Server (Jserver), Internet File System (iFS), Internet Directory, Internet Security, and Intermedia, allowed companies to build Internet applications that lower costs, enhance customer and supplier interaction, and provide global information access across different computer architectures and across the enterprise.

- *Oracle Lite Version 8i* was the company's mobile database for Internet computing. The Oracle Lite database management system could be used to run applications on portable devices and to temporarily store data on these devices, which could be replicated back to Oracle. Oracle Lite was a complete and comprehensive platform for building, deploying, and managing mobile applications that principally ran on laptops and information appliances such as hand-held devices, cell phones, smart phones, pagers, smart cards, and television set-top boxes.

- *Oracle Internet Application Server Version 8i* was introduced in June 2000, which was an open software platform for developing, deploying, and managing distributed Internet software application programs. Oracle Internet application *Server 8i* provided the infrastructure necessary to run Internet computing applications, and it enabled customers to build and deploy portals, transactional applications, and business intelligence facilities with a single product.

- *Internet Application Server (IAS) Wireless Edition* was formerly Portal-to-Go, which enabled information and services to be accessed through wireless and other devices. These devices included smart phones, wireless personal digital assistants, standard phones connected to Interactive Voice Recognition systems, modem-equipped personal organizers and television set-top boxes. Using *IAS Wireless Edition*, mobile operators, content providers, and wireless Internet service providers could quickly implement wireless portals (access hubs offering content formatted for small devices) for providing personalized services and content through wireless devices.

2. APPLICATION DEVELOPMENT TOOLS

The company's Oracle Internet Developer Suite contained application development tools, enterprise portal tools, and business intelligence tools.

The company's application development tools supported different approaches to software development. For a model-based approach to development, Oracle offered two products: *Oracle Designer* and *Oracle Developer*. *Oracle Designer* allowed business processes to be visually modeled and enterprise database applications to be generated. *Oracle Developer* was a development tool for building database applications that can be deployed, unchanged, in both Internet and client/server based environments. For Java programmers, Oracle offered *Oracle*

JDeveloper, a Java development tool suite for building enterprise applications for use on the Internet. The *Oracle JDeveloper* suite provided a complete Java development environment for developing and deploying applications from Java and HTML clients to server based business components across the enterprise.

Oracle offered *Oracle iPortal* to build portal sites that provided access to database applications. *Oracle iPortal* features a unique browser-based interface and allowed portal sites to be rapidly assembled from "portlets"—reusable information components that wrap commonly accessed pieces of information and application services. Portal sites built with *Oracle iPortal* may be personalized by role and customized by end users.

Oracle's Business Intelligence tools were designed for the Internet and provided a comprehensive and integrated suite of products that enabled companies to address the full range of user requirements for information publishing, data exploration, advanced analysis, and data mining. *Oracle Warehouse Builder* was an extensible data warehouse design and deployment environment that automated the process of creating a single database for business analysis. *Oracle Warehouse Builder* could quickly and easily integrate historical data with the massive, daily influxes of online data from Web sites. After collecting the data, *Oracle Warehouse Builder* cleaned, transformed, and loaded the data into an *Oracle8i*-based data warehouse.

3. INTERNET BUSINESS APPLICATIONS AND ONLINE BUSINESS EXCHANGES

- *E-Business Suite Version 11i* was a fully integrated and Internet-enabled set of Enterprise Resource Planning (ERP), Supply Chain and Customer Relationship Management (CRM) software applications for the enterprise. Oracle was the only company to offer a fully integrated suite of Internet business applications. This integrated suite, which also was available on a component basis, provided integrated enterprise information so that companies can manage their entire business cycle, from initial contact with customers through planning, production, and delivery, to postsale service and support (see **Exhibit 3**). This allowed companies to better align strategic and tactical goals across the entire organization. Available in approximately 30 languages, Oracle's Internet business applications allowed companies to operate in multiple currencies and languages, support local business practices and legal requirements, and handle business-critical operations across borders.

- *Oracle's ERP* applications consisted of integrated software modules to automate business functions such as financial management, supply chain management, procurement, manufacturing, project systems, and human resources for large and mid-sized commercial and public sector organizations throughout the world. These applications combined business functionality with innovative technologies, such as workflow and self-service applications, and enabled customers to lower the cost of their business operations by providing their customers, suppliers, and employees with self-service access to both transaction processing and selected business information using the Internet platform. Self-service applications automated a variety of business functions such as procuring and managing inventories of goods and services and employee expense reporting and reimbursement.

- *Oracle's CRM* applications helped automate and improve the business processes associated with managing customer relationships in the areas of sales, marketing, customer service and support, and call centers. Oracle's CRM applications allowed multichannel customer interactions over the Internet, such as through a call center. *I-store* (an Internet-based storefront used for selling products and services directly to customers over the Web), helped to maximize the use of technology to improve customer relationships. Integrated with Oracle's ERP applications, Oracle's CRM products also allowed enterprises to coordinate global sales forecasting and lead generation with order capture capabilities to help increase the overall efficiency of running a business.

- *OracleExchange.com* was an Internet marketplace that allowed contract and spot buying capabilities, online auctioning, and reverse auctioning. Branded exchanges were company specific versions of *OracleExchange.com,* allowing businesses to take control of their supply chain. Major corporations in the same industry were partnering to bring all their suppliers online with the goal of reducing supply chain costs through increased visibility into demand. Demand that could be fulfilled using their existing supply chain plans could be auctioned out to exchanges. In addition to the exchange platform, Oracle provided procurement software to allow businesses to collect demand from within their organization. Oracle also provided supply-chain planning software so businesses can check and reconfigure their supply chains based on demand.

Services

The company offered the following three services:

- **Consulting:** In most of Oracle's sales offices around the world, the company had trained consulting personnel who offer consulting services. Consultants supplemented the company's product offerings by providing services to assist customers in the implementation of applications based on the company's products. Consulting revenues represented approximately 22%, 27%, and 25% of total revenues in fiscal years 2000, 1999, and 1998, respectively.

- **Support:** The company offered a wide range of support services that included on-site, telephone, or Internet access to support personnel, as well as software updates. Telephone support was provided by local offices as well as Oracle's five global support centers located around the world. Support revenues represented approximately 29%, 27%, and 25% of total revenues in fiscal years 2000, 1999, and 1998, respectively.

- **Education:** The company offered both media-based and instructor-led training to customers on how to use the company's products. Education revenues represented approximately 5%, 5%, and 6% of total revenues in fiscal years 2000, 1999, and 1998, respectively.[25]

Marketing and Sales

KEY MARKET SEGMENTS

The Company had identified two key market segments where its products were sold; the *enterprise business market* and the *general business market.* The enterprise business market segment was defined by the company as those businesses with total revenues of $500 million and above. In the enterprise business market segment, the company believed that the most important considerations for customers were performance, functionality, product reliability, ease of use, quality of technical support, and total cost of ownership, including the initial price and deployment costs as well as ongoing maintenance costs. The general business market segment was defined by the company as those businesses with total revenues of less than $500 million. In the general business market segment, the company believed that the principal competitive factors are strength in distribution and marketing, brand name recognition, price/performance characteristics, ease of use, ability to link with enterprise systems, and product integration. The company believed that it competed effectively in each of these markets, although the competition was intense.

SALES DISTRIBUTION CHANNELS

In the United States, Oracle marketed its products and services primarily through its own direct sales and service organization. The sales and service group was based in the company's headquarters in Redwood City, California, and in field offices that, as of May 31, 2000, were located in approximately 90 metropolitan areas within the United States.

Outside the United States, the company marketed its products primarily through the sales and service organizations of approximately 60 subsidiaries. These subsidiaries licensed and supported the company's products both within their local countries and in certain other foreign countries where the company did not operate through a direct sales subsidiary.

The company also marketed its products through indirect channels, which were called Oracle Alliance partners. The partners included value-added relicensors, value-added distributors, hardware providers, systems integrators, and independent software vendors that combined the Oracle relational DBMS, application development tools, and business applications with computer hardware, software application packages, or services for redistribution.

The company also marketed its products through independent distributors in international territories not covered by its subsidiaries' direct sales organizations.

As of May 31, 2000, in the United States, the company employed 12,485 sales, service, and marketing employees, while the international sales, service, and marketing groups consisted of 18,224 employees.

Revenues from international customers (including end users and resellers) amounted to approximately 48%, 49%, and 50% of the company's total revenues in fiscal years 2000, 1999, and 1998, respectively.

ORACLE PARTNER PROGRAM

The Oracle Partner Program allowed Oracle to pursue new business opportunities with partners as well as direct customers. The types of partners in the Oracle Partner Program were consultants, education providers, Internet service providers, network integrators, resellers, independent software vendors, and system integrators. Partners could join the Oracle Technology Network (OTN), a program specifically designed for the Internet developer community. Oracle provided the technology, education, and technical support that enabled a partner to effectively integrate Oracle products into its business. The combination of Oracle technology and a partner's expertise broadened the company's exposure in new markets, such as the Internet.

HOSTED ONLINE SERVICES

Oracle offered Oracle Business OnLine, a service that delivered enterprise applications and technology across a network from a server that was hosted in a professionally managed environment at a remote data center. With a simple browser and network connections, companies could access Oracle's Internet business applications at costs significantly lower than a traditional deployment. While the customer owned the applications, Oracle owned the hardware, managed the application and server architecture, maintained and upgraded the software, and provided technical support for the customer's operations.[26]

Competition

The computer software industry was intensely competitive and rapidly evolving. Historically, the company had competed in various markets including the database, application development tools, business applications, and services sectors. The principal software competitors in the enterprise DBMS marketplace were International Business Machines Corporation, Sybase, Inc., and Informix Corporation. In the workgroup and personal DBMS marketplace, the company competed with several desktop software vendors, including Microsoft Corporation. In the data warehousing market, the company's OnLine Analytical Processing ("OLAP") products competed with those of Business Objects, S.A., Cognos, Inc., and Hyperion Solutions. In the application server market, competitors included IBM, and BEA Systems, Inc. In the business applications software market, competitors included J. D. Edwards, Peoplesoft Inc., and SAP Aktiengeschellschaft. The company continued to compete in these traditional markets as well as in some new, rapidly expanding marketed like the CRM, procurement and supply-chain marketplaces where the competition includes Siebel Systems, Ariba, Inc., Commerce One, and 12 Technologies.[27]

Product and Services Revenues

The Oracle's standard end-user license agreement for the company's products provided for an initial fee to use the product in perpetuity up to a maximum number of power units (processing power of the computers in the customer's network) or a maximum number of named users. The company also entered into other license agreement types, which allowed for the use of the company's products, usually restricted by the number of employees or the license term. Fees from licenses were recognized as revenue upon shipment, provided fees were fixed and determinable and collection were probable. Fees from licenses sold together with consulting services were generally recognized upon shipment, provided that the above criteria had been met, payment of the license fees was not dependent upon the performance of the consulting services, and the consulting services were not essential to the functionality of the licensed software. In instances where the aforementioned criteria had not been met, both the license and consulting fees were recognized under the percentage of completion method of contract accounting.

The company received sublicense fees from its Oracle Alliance Partners (value-added relicensors, value-added distributors, hardware providers, systems integrators, and independent software vendors) based on the sublicenses granted by the Oracle Alliance partner. Sublicense fees were typically based on a percentage of the company's list price and were generally recognized as they were reported by the reseller.

Support revenues consisted of two components: (1) updates for software products and end-user documentation; and (2) technical product support services that included on-site, telephone, or Internet access to support personnel. The company priced technical product support services as a percentage of the license price while on-site support services were based on the level of support services provided. Software subscription update rights were also priced as a percentage of the license price and can be purchased separately from technical product support. Most customers purchased support initially and renew their support agreements annually. The company generally billed support fees at the beginning of each support period. Support revenues were recognized ratably over the contract period.

Revenues related to consulting and education services to be performed by the company generally were recognized over the period during which the applicable service was to be performed or on a services-performed basis.

The company's quarterly revenues and expenses reflected distinct seasonality.[28]

Employees

As of May 31, 2000, the company employed 41,320 full-time persons, including 29,564 in sales and services, 1,145 in marketing, 6,650 in research and development, and 3,961 in general and administrative positions. Of these employees, 19,771 were located in the United States and 21,549 were employed in approximately 60 other countries.

None of the company's employees were represented by a labor union. The company had experienced no work stoppages and believes that its employee relations are good.[29]

E-Business Suite (Oracle 11i)

In May, 2000, Ellison introduced e-business suite, Oracle 11i, which was the most important new product introduced by the company in years. It ". . . was a suite of business applications that worked seamlessly with one another to handle everything from customer service on one end to relationships with suppliers on the other. And it's all rejiggered to run on the Web."[30]

Ellison's vision of the e-business suite was to make it as popular as Microsoft's Office Desktop Suite. Ellison figured this allowed every size business, from giant corporations to small dot-coms, to buy a single package from Oracle to run their e-business, instead of buying software from many competitors and then trying to merge and integrate these different softwares (see **Exhibit 3**).

David Yockelson, Director of E-business Strategies of Mesa Group, Inc., said that he believed there's no way Oracle can build all this technology itself and match the capabilities of its rivals."[31] He further stated that ". . . building it all themselves is going to be too slow."[32] Oracle's e-business suite was already a year behind in delivery. Yockelson warned his corporate customers that Oracle's e-business suite wouldn't be stable enough until the end of the year to

Exhibit 3
Seamless e-business Suite Software: Oracle Corporation

Seamless e-business
demands
seamless software.

E-business Kit		E-business Suite
Microsoft	Database	Oracle
Epiphany	Marketing	Oracle
Siebel	Sales	Oracle
Clarify	Support	Oracle
IBM	Webstore	Oracle
Commerce One	Procurement	Oracle
SAP	Manufacturing	Oracle
i2	Supply Chain Mgnt	Oracle
SAP	Financials	Oracle
PeopleSoft	Human Resources	Oracle

A complete e-business suite from Oracle. Or an e-business kit from lots of vendors. The choice is yours.

ORACLE
SOFTWARE POWERS THE INTERNET

Source: Oracle Corporation.

handle a company's most crucial jobs. Another analyst wondered how Yockelson felt with the e-commerce suite announcement.

Ellison conceded that the development of Oracle's e-business suite had been devilish. "It's a huge job," he said, "but it's the right strategy for Oracle."[33] Ellison insisted that Oracle Release 11i was on target for a May launch. Ellison vowed that "You ain't seen nothin' yet!" and further stated, "If this e-business suite plan works, we're going to be an extraordinary company."[34]

Exhibit 4 shows Oracle's e-business strengths in data storage, business applications, and e-market places, and prospects for each market.

An analyst remembered that Ellison had three years ago predicted that the personal computer (PC) was finished. He predicted it would be replaced by the network computer or NC, which Oracle had just built. The new machine would be like an ordinary appliance—cheap, reliable, and solid state. It would not be dependent on Intel chips or Microsoft software. Ellison made this announcement at a gala press conference at Radio City Music Hall in New York City. Pablo Galarza and Brian L. Clark said, "The NC . . . was a spectacular failure . . ."[35] They said, "We are undoubtedly entering a new age of computing dominated by the Internet, where having a PC is no longer a requirement. Welcome to the post-PC era."[36] These analysts wonder if Oracle's e-business suite would be a major success or be like the NC.

Projects for the Internet needed to be done at Internet speed. Wolfgang Kenna, CEO, SAP Americas, said "Our old projects took 18 months or two years. Internet speed means

Exhibit 4

Assembling an E-Business Powerhouse: Oracle Corporation

Oracle Corp.'s software is the foundation for Web sites, e-commerce, and corporate networks. Here are its most crucial markets:

Data Storehouses	Business Applications	E-Marketplaces
Database software for storing and analyzing corporate data, inventories, and customer info.	*For running everything from accounting to customer management to Web sales.*	*Web-site and internal software for transactions between companies, including auctions.*
Market Size: $10.5 billion in 1999 for software and maintenance; heading for $16.6 billion in 2003.	**Market Size:** $26 billion in 1999; heading for $33 billion this year.	**Market Size:** $3.9 billion in 1999; heading for $18.6 billion in 2003.
Oracle's Third-Quarter Sales: Software-license sales grew 32%, to $778 million.	**Oracle's Third-Quarter Sales:** Up 35%, to $199 million.	**Oracle's Third-Quarter Sales:** $26 million for supply-chain and procurement software.
Market Share: 40%, compared to 18% for IBM, 5.7% for Informix, and 5.1% for Microsoft.	**Market Position:** Oracle is a distant second behind SAP in the market for core corporate applications. Siebel Systems leads in customer-management software.	**Market Position:** The procurement market is expanding into e-exchanges, and Oracle is an early leader along with Commerce One, Ariba, and i2.
Prospects: Oracle dominates the database-software realm on both Unix and Windows NT operating systems. Analysts predict it will hold off the competition indefinitely, thanks to its strong technology and new cachet with dot-coms.	**Prospects:** In May, Oracle plans to release the most comprehensive package of business applications available. It has a good chance to gain market share because its applications are integrated, while others offer pieces that have to be stitched together.	**Prospects:** Oracle has deals to power exchanges for Ford, Sears, and Chevron and is expected to have staying power, thanks to its army of 7,000 software programmers.

Source: Steve Hamm, "Why It's Cool Again," *Business Week* (May 8, 2000), p. 120.

four weeks, six weeks."[37] Many executives referrred to Internet planning in terms of "dog years." Internet executives did six to seven years of strategic planning for every one year of planning done by old brick and mortar companies. This was due to the dynamic changing environment of the Internet.

Oracle's one-stop-shopping approach appeared to have strong appeal to start-up and mid-market companies because of the ". . . tantalizing prospects of more seamless automation."[38] Doug Allen, CIO of Hostcentric, which was a Web-hosting company in Houston, said, the suite's up-front cost wasn't any less than buying the pieces from different providers. "But it's the ongoing cost of ownership where you don't have to manage different releases from different vendors that is going to make us more successful."[39] Allen's company acquired Oracle's e-commerce suite in the spring and were working its way through the modules. They were installing one at a time. Allen thought Ellison's vision "of automating most of a company's customer interaction isn't a pipe dream."[40] He further stated, "If we can automate 85%, that would be pretty good."[41]

Ellison felt the balance of power in software and computing began to shift from desktop computers linked by small servers, which he viewed as Microsoft's market, to giant servers and databases that ran the Internet and electronic-commerce platforms, which was Oracle's market.[42] Ellison felt with this shift in the market, that "I actually believe now we will pass Microsoft." In a recent interview, he said, "I think they [Microsoft] are so late."[43]

Oracle Practices What It Practices

In 1997, Ellison decided to take a few months to find out why Oracle's application business—mainly accounting, ordering, and software sales that ran on Oracle's databases—was having problems. He didn't understand at the time, he admitted, because he had never used his own applications. Ellison said, "The earliest revelations were that I've never even see the applications, because the applications don't provide any information."[44] He was shocked to find the purchasing system could not ". . . identify who the best suppliers were by price, quality, and other metrics."[45] The information was scattered among 70 different computer systems and 70 databases in 70 different countries. He found the same type of problems existed for sales data and human-resources data.[46]

Ellison found the knowledge gaps from his investigation to be "galling." "I'm the CEO of the number one company in the world providing technology to manage information," he said. "Well, this is insane. We've got to build a global system, we've got to unfragment our data."[47] Ellison blamed Gates for the fragmentation and complexity issues that existed in the industry.

After Ellison's investigation, he ". . . discovered that there were huge holes in our applications."[48] So he said, "It was very clear to me that we had to build complete suite applications; we had to build a sales system, a marketing system; we had to build it so it is a global system, put it on the Internet; and then we had to roll it out inside of Oracle."[49]

Ellison quickly realized that the first step was to dismantle his country managers. Each manager had his/her own e-mail, human resource, and financial reporting systems, which were supported by 43 data centers around the world. Ellison said, "Not only did we have to separate accounting systems into different countries, but all of these countries hired IT departments to change them in different ways."[50] Ellison decreed that there be only two data centers—headquarters and a backup one in Colorado Springs—and only one global database for each major function, such as sales and accounting. Ellison realized that knowledge was power and he was asking his managers to give up their power. Many of the units used passive resistance to stop or slow down the changes. Ellison recalls, laughing, that "we had to make numerous management changes. I mean, we had to send a Navy Seal team to blow up the Canadian data center."[51]

Other findings before the complete changeover were:

1. Oracle prices varied from country to country. This made financial forecasts more difficult to develop.[52]

2. Oracle had 250 people whose sole job was to review requests for discounts. This group has been cut to four. There was one global Web store price for each product. The customer goes to Oracle's Web store and gets prices and specifications.[53]

3. Each sales person cut their own compensation plan. Ellison felt vast amounts of time were wasted by the salespeople on this issue. In 2000, headquarters decreed all compensation plans were to be distributed via the Internet. This change was not well received by the managers or the salespeople. Two thirds of the plans were held up by the managers. Ellison said, "I said, the managers don't need to approve them . . . we can bypass the managers."[54]

4. Ellison discovered that by centralizing information and automating relationships with employees and customers, he could cut out a huge amount of costs. He became so enthused about the rewards of "management-by-computer" that he was able to eliminate Lane's $100 million headquarters budget. Ellison was able to wipe out most of the headquarters functions and distribute some of it to division heads. This could be why Lane resigned.[55]

Some specific results of implementing the e-commerce suite were:

1. Oracle estimated that each customer call handled by an employee cost about $350 to process. The new customer service system required customers to enter their own complaints on products. Mike Javis, Oracle's Vice President, said, "We make our customers enter their own bug reports [on problems with software]. That saves us money because we don't have people sitting by telephones." Using the global-sales database, says Javis, "Customers buy Oracle products themselves by going online. That improves the accuracy of everything we do and lowers our costs." Handling a customer "call" on the new Web site was estimated to cost $20, "and twice as likely to be resolved without more follow-up."[56]

2. Gary Roberts, Senior Vice President, cited the tangible benefits as "250 IT staffers; 2,000 fewer servers (which will be auctioned off using Oracle's business-exchange software); 80% reduction in leased space for computer operations when the two data centers come online in December, 2000."[57] In 1999, Oracle saved $200 million in IT costs. By the end of 2000, he expected to cut the 450 staff to 50 who supported Oracle's desktop computers.

3. The company was able to expand its online store, which opened in the summer of 1999, to sell all Oracle products to thousands of businesses. The e-business suite allowed Oracle to build a Web-based store operation. Ellison predicted that 100% of revenue in 2000 would be from online sales. It was 10 to 15% in the fall of 1999.[58]

Craig Conway, CEO of PeopleSoft, said that Ellison ran ". . . a sociopathic company" addicted to "lying."[59] He doubted the cost-cutting claims as marketing hype. Conway was a former executive of Oracle.

Other benefits of the new system were:

1. Oracle's aggressive marketing campaigns, which cost $30 million. These campaigns focused on conferences and seminars on Internet computing that had drawn legions of developers. An analyst said, "Oracle will be a monster in this market." And, they are doing it "by winning the hearts and minds of the developers."[60]

2. Oracle forged partnerships with *Fortune 500* giants and small businesses that were moving into e-commerce. Ford and Oracle developed Auto X-Changed, an online exchange for Ford's 30,000 suppliers. Jim Pickert, an analyst at Hambrecht & Quist, said, "They make a great partner for companies trying to figure out their e-business strategies."[61]

Ellison said, "We couldn't beat Microsoft in PC or IBM in mainframes, but we can be number one software provider on the Internet. We're the odds-on favorite."[62]

Neil Herman of Lehman Bros. said "Oracle is one of the key Internet infrastructure companies, along with Sun, Cisco, and EMC." Another analyst said, "with all the emphasis on the e-business suite don't forget Oracle had 40% of the global market for database software. IBM was in second place with 18%; followed by Informix with 6%; in fourth place Microsoft with 5%; then Sybase with 4% and all others with 27%."[63]

Oracle Venture Fund

In 1999, Oracle management established an in-house venture-capital fund with a $100 million authorization from the company's Board of Directors. During 2000, the fund attained a rate of return of 504%, thanks in part to a stake in Red Hat Inc., which was a popular Linux operating system. Red Hat went public in August, 1999.[64]

In 2000, the Board of Directors approved quintupling the size of the fund. The company anticipated having stakes in about 70 companies by the end of 2000.

Only two of Oracle's companies have gone public. Broom, Executive Vice President, said ". . . he expected the number to grow to eight by the end of the year."[65]

General Electric Company was the number one investor in new companies. In 1999, General Electric invested in 100 companies, and Microsoft was second with 44 investments.[66]

Ellison had invested more than $500 million of his money in approximately 30 companies (biotech, e-commerce, and network appliance companies). A few of his investments were (1) Salesforce.com—$2 million investment—which will replace desktop software for salespeople; (2) Supergen Inc.—$23 million investment—which was working on treatment for the cancer that killed his mother; and (3) New Internet Computer Co.—$10 million investment—which produces a device to replace the PC for the Internet.[67]

In-house investment funds have become somewhat controversial, since some companies (Microsoft, Cisco, etc.) have used the capital gains from their investments to enhance their earnings. Broom said Oracle had not engaged in this practice. On cable finance channels (NBC, Bloomberg, Tech Channel, CNN), the analyst will usually note the earnings per share derived from this type of investment, and state what the company's actual earnings were less the income derived by these types of investments.

Management's Discussion and Analysis of Financial Condition and Results of Operations

RESULTS OF OPERATIONS

Total revenues grew 15%, 24%, and 26% in fiscal years 2000, 1999, and 1998, respectively (see **Exhibit 5**). The lower overall revenue growth rates in both fiscal 2000 and fiscal 1999 as compared to the prior corresponding periods were primarily due to lower consulting services revenue growth rates than those experienced in prior years, partially offset by higher license revenue growth. Sales and marketing expenses continued to represent a significant portion of operating expenses, constituting 26%, 30%, and 33% of revenues in fiscal 2000, 1999, and 1998, respectively, while cost of services as a percentage of total revenues decreased to 29% in fiscal year 2000 from 35% in fiscal year 1999 and 32% in fiscal year 1998 (see **Exhibit 6**). The decline in the sales and marketing and cost of services percentages in fiscal year 2000 was primarily the result of increased license revenues and productivity improvements that reduced headcount and related expenditures. The company's investment in research and development amounted to 10% of revenues in fiscal years 2000, 1999, and 1998. General and administrative expenses as a percentage

Exhibit 5

Revenues by Licensing and Services: Oracle Corporation

(Dollar amounts in thousands)					
	Fiscal Year 2000	Change	Fiscal Year 1999	Change	Fiscal Year 1998
Licenses and other	$4,446,795	21%	$3,688,366	15%	$3,193,490
Percentage of revenues	43.9%		41.8%		44.7%
Services	$5,683,333	11%	$5,138,886	30%	$3,950,376
Percentage of revenues	56.1%		58.2%		55.3%
Total revenues	**$10,130,128**	**15%**	**$8,827,252**	**24%**	**$7,143,866**

Source: Oracle Corporation, *Form 10-K* (May 31, 2000), p. 11.

of revenues were 5% in fiscal years 2000, 1999, and 1998. Overall, operating income as a percentage of revenues was 30%, 21%, and 17% (20% prior to the charges for acquired in-process research and developments), in fiscal years 2000, 1999, and 1998, respectively.

Domestic revenues increased 17% in fiscal year 2000 and 27% in fiscal year 1999, while international revenues increased 12% and 21% in fiscal years 2000 and 1999, respectively. International revenues were unfavorably affected in both fiscal years 2000 and 1999 when compared to the corresponding prior year periods as a result of the strengthening of the U.S. dollar against certain major international currencies. International revenues expressed in local currency increased by approximately 17% and 24% in fiscal years 2000 and 1999, respectively. Revenues from international customers were approximately 48%, 49%, and 50% of revenues in fiscal years 2000, 1999, and 1998, respectively. Management expected that the company's international operations would continue to provide a significant portion of total revenues. However, international revenues could be adversely affected if the U.S. dollar continued to strengthen against certain major international currencies.

Exhibit 6

Operating Expenses: Oracle Corporation

(Dollar amounts in thousands)					
Operating Expenses	Fiscal Year 2000	Change	Fiscal Year 1999	Change	Fiscal Year 1998
Sales and marketing	$2,616,749	0%	$2,622,379	11%	$2,371,306
Percentage of revenues	258%		29.7%		33.2%
Cost of services	$2,942,679	(4)%	$3,064,148	35%	$2,273,607
Percentage of revenues	29.0%		34.7%		31.8%
Research and development	$1,009,882	20%	$841,406	17%	$719,143
Percentage of revenues	10.0%		9.5%		10.1%
General and administrative	$480,658	13%	$426,438	16%	$368,556
Percentage of revenues	4.7%		4.8%		5.2%
Acquired in-process research and development	—		—		$167,054
Percentage of revenues	—		—		2.3%

Source: Oracle Corporation, *Form 10-K* (May 31, 2000), p. 121.

Licenses and Other Revenues

License revenues represented fees earned for granting customers licenses to use the company's software products. License and other revenues also included documentation revenues and other miscellaneous revenues, which constituted 3% of total license and other revenues in fiscal years 2000, 1999, and 1998. License revenues, excluding other revenues, grew 20% and 16% in fiscal year 2000 and fiscal year 1999. Systems software license revenues, which included server and development tools revenues, grew 15% and 16% in fiscal year 2000 and fiscal year 1999, respectively. Business applications license revenues grew 42% and 16% in fiscal year 2000 and fiscal year 1999, respectively. The higher license revenue growth rate experienced in fiscal year 2000 was primarily due to stronger demand for the company's business applications products, and the introduction and market positioning of new Internet business application products and versions, which had stimulated demand for the company's products.

SERVICES REVENUES

Services revenues consisted of support, consulting, and education services revenues, which comprised 52%, 40%, and 8% of total services revenues, respectively, during fiscal year 2000 (see **Exhibit 9-5**). Support revenues grew 27% and 31% in fiscal year 2000 and fiscal year 1999, respectively, reflecting an increase in the overall customer installed base. The support revenue growth rate will continue to be affected by the overall license revenue growth rates. Consulting revenues declined 4% in fiscal year 2000, as compared to a 34% growth rate in fiscal year 1999. The decline in the consulting services revenues experienced in fiscal year 2000 was primarily due to a decrease in the demand for these services as a result of the following: (1) a slowdown in the business applications market in fiscal year 1999; (2) the company's strategy to focus only on profitable business; (3) a push toward a partner model, leveraging third-party consulting firms who provided consulting services to the company's customers; and (4) shorter implementation engagements for Oracle's newer generation of products. Education revenues, which grew 4% and 12% in fiscal year 2000 and fiscal year 1999, respectively, were also affected by the lower business applications growth rate experienced in fiscal year 1999 and will continue to be affected by the overall mix in the systems and applications license revenue growth rates. Consulting and education revenue growth rates were expected to increase in fiscal year 2001 as compared to the prior year corresponding period due to the increased demand for the company's business applications products experienced in fiscal year 2000.

International expenses were favorably affected in both fiscal years 2000 and 1999 when compared to the corresponding prior year periods due to the strengthening of the U.S. dollar against certain major international currencies. The net impact on operating margins, however, was unfavorable, since the negative effect on revenues was greater than the positive effect on expenses.[68]

SALES AND MARKETING EXPENSES

Oracle continued to place significant emphasis, both domestically and internationally, on direct sales through its own sales force. However, the company also continued to market its products through indirect channels as well. Sales and marketing expenses as a percentage of both total revenues and license revenues decreased in both fiscal year 2000 and fiscal year 1999 as compared to the corresponding prior year periods. As a percentage of license and other revenues, sales and marketing expenses decreased to 59% in fiscal year 2000 from 71% in fiscal year 1999 and 74% in 1998. These decreases were primarily related to increased license revenues and productivity improvements that favorably affected headcount and related expenditures.[69]

Sales and marketing expenses were 25.8%, 29.7%, and 33.2% of total revenue in fiscal years 2000, 1999, and 1998 respectively (see **Exhibit 6**).

COST OF SERVICES

The cost of providing services consisted largely of consulting, support, and education personnel expenses. As a percentage of services revenues, cost of services decreased to 52% in fiscal year 2000 from 60% in fiscal year 1999. The decrease in cost of services as a percentage of services revenues in fiscal year 2000 was due primarily to support revenues, which have relatively higher margins; constituting of higher percentage of total services revenues; improved consulting utilization rates; increased productivity efficiencies; and controls over headcount and related expenditures as the company continued to focus on margin improvement. As a percentage of services revenues, cost of services increased to 60% in fiscal year 1999 from 58% in fiscal year 1998, primarily due to lower consulting and education utilization rates as a result of lower than anticipated revenue growth.[70] Cost of services expenses were 29.0%, 34.7%, and 31.8% of total revenue in fiscal years 2000, 1999, and 1998, respectively (see **Exhibit 6**).

RESEARCH AND DEVELOPMENT EXPENSES

Research and development expenses were 10.0%, 9.5%, and 10.1% for fiscal year 2000, 1999, and 1998 (see **Exhibit 6**). Research and development expenses increased 20% and 17% in fiscal years 2000 and 1999, respectively, when compared to corresponding prior year periods. The higher expense growth rate in fiscal year 2000 was due to planned increases in research and development headcount in fiscal year 2000. The company believed that research and development expenditures were essential to maintaining its competitive position and expected these costs to continue to constitute a significant percentage of revenues.[71]

GENERAL AND ADMINISTRATIVE EXPENSES

General and administrative expenses as a percentage of revenues were 4.7%, 4.8% and 5.2% in fiscal years 2000, 1999, and 1998, respectively (see **Exhibit 6**).

Financial Performance

Oracle's Board of Directors had approved the repurchase of up to 548,000,000 shares of common stock to reduce the dilutive effect of the company's stock plans. Pursuant to this repurchase program, the company had repurchased a total of 467,182,575 shares for approximately $7,725,489,000. In fiscal years 2000 and 1999, shares outstanding were 2,807,572,142 and 2,862,267,300 respectively.

The company's stock had two 3-for-2 stock splits and two 2-for-1 stock splits in August 15, 1997, February 26, 1999, January 18, 2000, and one scheduled for fall of 2000.

Exhibits 7 and **8** are the company's consolidated statement of operations and the consolidated balance sheets.

In early May, 2000, Lawrence J. Ellison, Chairman, CEO, and Founder of Oracle met with his executive officers to review and discuss the company's new ad to introduce its new e-business suite. The advertisement focused on Oracle's potential competitive advantage of one-stop shopping; buying e-business suite versus buying software from many sources. Multisourcing means the e-business must integrate these different software packages into one package and deal with each supplier when a problem arises. **Exhibit 3** shows the proposed advertisement.

Exhibit 7

Consolidated Statements of Operations: Oracle Corporation
(Dollar amount in thousands, except per share data)

Year Ending May 31	2000	1999	1998
Revenues			
Licenses and other	$ 4,446,795	$ 3,688,366	$ 3,193,490
Services	5,683,333	5,138,886	3,950,376
Total revenues	10,130,128	8,827,252	7,143,866
Operating expenses			
Sales and marketing	2,616,749	2,622,379	2,371,306
Cost of services	2,942,679	3,064,148	2,273,607
Research and development	1,009,882	841,406	719,143
General and administrative	480,658	426,438	368,556
Acquired in-process research and development	—	—	167,054
Total operating expense	7,049,968	6,954,371	5,899,666
Operating income	3,080,160	1,872,881	1,244,200
Other income (expenses)			
Net investment gains related to marketable securities	6,936,955	24,457	4,300
Interest income	141,904	118,486	85,986
Interest expense	(18,894)	(21,424)	(16,658)
Other	(16,691)	(12,322)	9,991
Total other income (expense)	7,043,274	109,197	83,619
Income before provision for income taxes	10,123,434	1,982,078	1,327,819
Provision for income taxes	3,826,631	692,320	514,124
Net income	**$ 6,296,803**	**$ 1,289,758**	**$ 813,695**
Earnings per share			
Basic	$2.22	$0.45	$0.28
Diluted	$2.10	$0.43	$0.27
Shares outstanding			
Basic	2,839,419	2,891,176	2,932,798
Diluted	2,997,921	2,968,450	2,999,176

Source: Oracle Corporation, *Form 10-K* (May 31, 2000), p. 31.

Exhibit 8

Consolidated Balance Sheets: Oracle Corporation
(Dollar amount in thousands, except per share data)

	2000	1999
Assets		
Current assets		
Cash and cash equivalents	$ 7,429,206	$1,785,715
Short-term cash investments	332,792	777,049
Trade receivables, net of allowance for doubtful accounts of $272,203 in 2000 and $217,096 in 1999	2,533,964	2,238,204
Other receivables	256,203	240,792
Prepaid and refundable income taxes	212,829	299,670
Prepaid expenses and other current assets	118,340	105,844
Total current assets	10,833,334	5,447,274
Long-term cash investments	110,000	249,547
Property, net	934,455	987,482
Intangible and other assets	1,148,990	575,351
Total assets	**$13,076,779**	**$7,259,654**

(continued)

Exhibit 8
(*continued*)

	2000	1999
Liabilities and stockholders' equity		
Current liabilities		
Notes payable and current maturities of long-term debt	$ 2,691	$ 3,638
Accounts payable	287,495	283,896
Income taxes payable	2,821,776	277,700
Accrued compensation and related benefits	725,860	693,525
Customer advances and unearned revenues	1,133,482	1,007,149
Value added tax and sales tax payable	165,304	128,774
Other accrued liabilities	725,630	651,741
Total current liabilities	5,862,238	3,046,423
Long-term debt	300,770	304,140
Other long-term liabilities	186,178	77,937
Deferred income taxes	266,130	135,887
Commitments (Note 5)		
Stockholders' equity	—	—
Preferred stock, $0.01 par value—authorized, 1,000,000 shares; outstanding: none	—	—
Common stock, $0.01 par value, and additional paid in capital—authorized, 11,000,000,000 shares; outstanding 2,807,572,142 shares in 2000 and 2,862,267,330 shares in 1999	3,112,126	1,475,763
Retained earnings	3,343,857	2,266,915
Accumulated other comprehensive income (loss)	5,480	(47,411)
Total stockholders' equity	6,461,463	3,695,267
Total liabilities and stockholders' equity	**$13,076,779**	**$7,259,654**

Source: Oracle Corporation, *Form 10-K* (May 31, 2000), p. 30.

Notes

1. Larry Olmsted, "The Best CEOs," *Worth* (May 2000). He was ranked 14th.
2. Janice Maloney, "Larry Ellison Is Captain Ahab and Bill Gates Is Moby Dick," *Fortune* (October 28, 1996), p. 120.
3. *Ibid.*
4. *Ibid.*, pp. 120–121.
5. Olmsted, "The Best CEOs."
6. *Ibid.*
7. *Ibid.*
8. *Ibid.*
9. G. Christian Hill, "Dog Eats Dog Food and Damn If It Ain't Tasty," *e-company* (November, 2000), p. 170.
10. Don Clark and Lee Gomes, "Oracle President, Operations Chief Quits," *Wall Street Journal* (September 30, 2000).
11. *Ibid.*
12. *Ibid.*
13. *Ibid.*
14. Jon Swartz, "Put Up Your Dukes, Microsoft," *USA Today* (September 28, 2000), p. 2B.
15. *Ibid.*
16. *Ibid.*
17. *Ibid.*
18. *Ibid.*
19. *Ibid.*
20. Oracle Corporation, *Form 10-K* (May 31, 2000), pp. 7–8. This section was directly quoted, except for minor editing.
21. Oracle Corporation, *Annual Stockholders Meeting Announcement* (September 11, 2000), pp. 2–3. This section was directly quoted, except for minor editing.
22. *Form 10-K* (May 31, 2000), pp. 2–3. This section was directly quoted, except for minor editing.
23. *Ibid.*, pp. 2–3. This section was directly quoted, except for minor editing.
24. *Ibid.*, pp. 2–4. This section was directly quoted, except for minor editing.
25. *Ibid.*, p. 4. This section was directly quoted, except for minor editing.
26. *Ibid.*, pp. 4–5. This section was directly quoted, except for minor editing.
27. *Ibid.*, pp. 5–6. This section was directly quoted, except for minor editing.
28. *Ibid.*, p. 6.

29. *Ibid.* This section was directly quoted, except for minor editing.
30. Steve Hamm, "Why It's Cool Again," *Business Week* (May 8, 2000), p. 115.
31. *Ibid.*, p. 188.
32. *Ibid.*
33. *Ibid.*
34. *Ibid.*
35. Pablo Galarza and Brian L. Clark, "Winners & Losers Investing in the Post PC Era," *Money* (May 2000), p. 76.
36. *Ibid.*
37. Stephen Baker and Spencer E. Ante, "Can SAP Swim with the Swiftest?" *Business Week* (June 26, 2000), p. 188.
38. Hill, "Dog Eats Dog Food and Damn If It Ain't Tasty," p. 178.
39. *Ibid.*
40. *Ibid.*
41. *Ibid.*
42. *Ibid.*, p. 171.
43. *Ibid.*
44. *Ibid.*
45. *Ibid.*, p. 172.
46. *Ibid.*
47. *Ibid.*
48. *Ibid.*, p. 172.
49. *Ibid.*, p. 174.
50. *Ibid.*
51. *Ibid.*
52. *Ibid.*, p. 178.
53. *Ibid.*
54. *Ibid.*
55. *Ibid.*
56. *Ibid.*, p. 174.
57. *Ibid.*
58. Edward Iwata, "Oracle Sees Future as No. 1 Software Source on Net," *USA Today* (December 27, 1999), p. 4B.
59. Hill, "Dog Eats Dog Food and Damn If It Ain't Tasty," p. 176.
60. Iwata, "Oracle Sees Future as No. 1 Software Source on Net," p. 4B.
61. *Ibid.*
62. *Ibid.*
63. Jon Swartz, "Put Up Your Dukes, Microsoft," p. 2B.
64. Lee Gomes, "Oracle, After a Good Year, Quintuples Size of In-House Venture-Capital Fund," *Wall Street Journal* (February 4, 2000), p. B4.
65. *Ibid.*
66. *Ibid.*
67. Jim Kerstetter, "Putting His Money Where His Passion Is," *Business Week* (May 8, 2000), p. 124.
68. *Form 10-K* (May 31, 2000), pp. 10–11. The above sections were directly quoted, with minor editing.
69. *Ibid.*, p. 12. This section was directly quoted, with minor editing.
70. *Ibid.* This section was directly quoted, with minor editing.
71. *Ibid.* This section was directly quoted, with minor editing.

case 10

Palm Computing, Inc., 2002: How to Survive in the Crowded PDA Market

Cynthia J. Tonucci and Alan N. Hoffman

On October 29, 2002, Palm, Inc., introduced two new handheld computer models, including its first with built-in Bluetooth wireless technology, as it battled to maintain its market dominance. The new Tungsten T (priced at $499) was the first Palm-branded handheld with the company's 5.0 operating system. This personal digital assistant (PDA) was also Palm's first to feature built-in technology for communicating wirelessly with Bluetooth-enabled devices, including printers and cell phones. Bluetooth allows users to dial a cell phone merely by calling up a number in the Tungsten T's address book and tapping it on the handheld's touchscreen.

closed · open

Compact "Slider" Design

These new product introductions came on the heels of Handspring's introduction of its Treo line of communicators during the summer of 2002 (Treo = phone+organizer+ e-mail+Web). The *Wall Street Journal* called Treo "the best combination of phone and personal digital assistant available." The Treo Model 180 sells for $399.

Treo 180g · Treo 180

This case was prepared by Cynthia J. Tonucci, MBA student, and Professor Alan N. Hoffman of Bentley College. The authors would like to thank Ann Lawrence, Robert Webb, Heather Winn, and Christopher Gallagher for their research and contributions to this case. This case was edited for SMBP-9th edition. Reprinted by permission of Dr. Alan N. Hoffman.

Palm, Inc., found itself in 2002 in the midst of a highly competitive and maturing market-place. Palm's CEO Eric Benhamou was faced with reevaluating Palm's objectives, "to build its leadership position in handheld computing by providing wireless functionality to all Palm hand-held devices and by establishing the Palm platform as the leading operation system for PDAs."

Benhamou had three options: (1) to continue to slug it out in the crowded PDA organizer market, (2) to move into the communicator marketplace, or (3) to exit the hardware business and focus 100% of the business on the industry-leading Palm OS operating system, which was at the time licensed by 75% of the PDA industry.

Corporate Goverance[1]

ERIC BENHAMOU, CHAIRMAN AND CEO

Eric Benhamou's professional and personal accomplishments centered on the creation and intelligent deployment of information technology, around the world, both in business and nonprofit environments.

Benhamou was the Chairman of the board of directors of 3Com Corporation, of Palm, Inc., and of PalmSource, Inc. He served as CEO of 3Com Corporation from September 1990 until December 31, 2000.

In 1981 Benhamou co-founded Bridge Communications, an early networking pioneer, and was Vice President of Engineering until its merger with 3Com in 1987. Before joining Bridge Communications, he worked for four years at Zilog, Inc., serving as Project Manager, Software Engineering Manager, and Design Engineer. In 1992, he received the President's Environment and Conservation Challenge Award, the highest environmental award in the United States. In 1997, then-President Bill Clinton appointed Benhamou to the President's Information Technology Advisory Committee, which advised the U.S. President on research and development focal points of federal programs to maintain U.S. leadership in advanced computing and communications technologies and their applications.

In 1998, Benhamou was recognized by former Israeli Prime Minister Benjamin Netanyahu with the Foreign Investor Jubilee Award for investments and contributions made by Palm, Inc., in furthering the ongoing development of Israel's economy. That same year, he received the Ellis Island Medal of Honor, which paid homage to the immigrant experience, and to individual achievement of U.S. citizens from various ethnic backgrounds. He was also a graduate of the American Leadership Forum, which sought to revitalize leadership within communities across the nation. In 1997, Benhamou received the Medaille Nessim Habif from Ecole Nationale Supérieure d'Arts et Métiers, Paris, and in 1998, he became a Fellow of the International Engineering Consortium.

Benhamou served on the Stanford University School of Engineering Board of Advisors. He served as Vice Chairman of the Board of Governors of Ben Gurion University and as Chairman of the Israel Venture Network.

Benhamou, 46, holds honorary doctoral degrees from Ben Gurion University of the Negev, Widener University, and the University of South Carolina. He has a master of science degree in electrical engineering from Stanford University and a Diplôme d'Ingénieur from Ecole Nationale Supérieure d'Arts et Métiers, Paris.

BOARD OF DIRECTORS AND TOP MANAGEMENT

Exhibit 1 shows the eight members of the Board of Directors of Palm, Inc. Five members are external directors. Outside directors were paid $25,000 if they were members of a standing committee and $20,000 if they were not members of a standing committee. Each outside board member is eligible to receive stock options under the 2001 Director Plan.

Exhibit 1

Board of Directors and Key Board Committees: Palm, Inc.

---

1. Board of Directors

Eric Benhamou[1]
Chairman of the Board and CEO (Interim)
Palm, Inc.

David Nagel
President and CEO
PalmSource, Inc.

Gordon A. Campbell[1,2]
President and Chairman of the Board
Techfarm, Inc.

Jean-Jacques Damlamian
Group Executive Vice President,
Development Division
France Telecom

Susan G. Swenson[1,2]
President and COO
Leap Wireless International, Inc.

Gareth C. C. Chang
Chairman and Managing Partner
GC3 & Associate International, LLC
Executive Chairman
click2Asia and Amedia

Michael Homer[2]
CEO and Chairman
Kontiki, Inc.

Todd Bradley
President and CEO,
Palm Solutions Group
Palm, Inc.

2. Key Board Committees

Audit Committee: Reviews Palm's auditing accounting, financial reporting, and internal control function and makes recommendations to the Board of Directors for the selection of independent accountants. In addition, the Audit Committee monitors the quality of Palm's accounting principles and financial reporting, as well as the independence of and nonaudit services provided by Palm's independent accountants.

Compensation Committee: Determines, approves, and reports to the Board of Directors on all elements of compensation for Palm's executive officers, including salaries, bonuses, stock options, benefits, and other compensation arrangements.

Nominating and Governance Committee: Provides assistance to the Board in the areas of membership selection, committee selection and rotation practices, evaluation of the overall effectiveness of the Board, and review and consideration of developments in corporate governance practices.

Source: Palm, Inc., www.Palm.com, company document.

Notes:
1. Member of Palm Compensation Committee.
2. Member of Palm Audit Committee.

Exhibit 2 shows the 15 members of Palm's management team.

COMPANY BACKGROUND

Palm Computing, Inc., was founded in 1992 and was acquired by U.S. Robotics in 1995. Palm successfully introduced its first Palm Pilot in 1996. The Palm Pilot became the industry standard, and sales soared. The very next year, Palm was acquired by 3Com, Inc.

In July 1998, founder Jeff Hawkins, CEO Donna Dubinsky, and Ed Colligan left Palm to start a new company called Handspring, Inc., which would eventually become one of Palm's main competitors.

Exhibit 2
Management Team: Palm, Inc.

Eric Benhamou Chairman of the Board and CEO (Interim) Palm, Inc.	**Michael Mace** Chief Competitive Officer PalmSource, Inc.	**Glenn Cross** Senior Vice President, American Sales, Services, and Palm Enterprise Business Development, Solutions Group Palm, Inc.
Judy Bruner Senior Vice President and Chief Financial Officer Palm, Inc.	**Steve Sakoman** Chief Products Officer and Executive Officer, Solutions Group Palm, Inc.	**Steve Manser** Senior Vice President, Worldwide Product Development, Solutions Group Palm, Inc.
David Nagel President and CEO PalmSource, Inc.	**Todd Brantly** President and CEO, Solutions Group Palm, Inc.	**Doug Solomon** Senior Vice President, Worldwide Product Development, Solutions Group Palm, Inc.
Doreen S. (Dory) Yochum Chief Administrative Officer PalmSource, Inc.	**Ken Wirt** Senior Vice President, Marketing and Product Management, Solutions Group Palm, Inc.	**Marianne Jackson** Senior Vice President and Chief Human Resource Officer Palm, Inc.
Gabi Schindler Senior Vice President, Marketing PalmSource, Inc.	**Angel Mendez** Senior Vice President, Global Operations and Accessories and Peripherals, Solutions Group Palm, Inc.	**Albert B. Chu** Vice President, Development PalmSource, Inc.

Source: Palm, Inc., www.Palm.com, company document.

In September 1999, 3Com announced its plan to take the company public. Palm completed its initial public offering (IPO) in March 2000, generating net proceeds of $947.5 million. Palm received additional proceeds of $225 million from the private placement sale of stock to AOL Time Warner, Motorola, and Nokia. In July 2000, 3Com, Inc., decided to spin off Palm and distributed all its shares of Palm, Inc., to 3Com stockholders.

Under the guidance of CEO Carl Yankowski, the company continued to experience rapid growth, generating revenue of $1,058 billion in fiscal year 2000, increasing 88% in one year and 289% over a two-year period. Profits grew as well, increasing $42 million, from $4 million to $46 million during the same two-year period.

Palm's stock performance was equally exceptional. Palm stock grew 357% during its first quarter and fiscal year ending June 2000, from its IPO price of $20.81 to a high of $95.06 per share.

The high was short-lived because new competitors, such as Hewlett-Packard, Compaq, Sony, and Handspring put downward pressure on PDA prices and profit margins. Furthermore, an inability to efficiently manage inventory levels resulted in lost revenue during the first nine months of fiscal year 2001 and was followed by a sudden and severe decline in consumer demand in the fourth quarter. This resulted in a significant oversupply of inventory, requiring a writedown of obsolete inventory in fourth-quarter 2001 and contributing to a fiscal net loss for 2001.

In July 2001, following six months of disappointing results, Palm announced its decision to create a separate software company. Recognizing that the Palm OS platform provided significant opportunities for Palm to further grow, top management made the strategic decision to reorganize the company into two separate divisions, creating Palm Solutions Inc. (hardware) and its subsidiary, PalmSource (software).

The decision to divide into two operations was not enthusiastically received by everyone. In November 2001, Carl Yankowski, CEO, announced his decision to resign from the company, explaining that Palm's decision to form two separate operations had changed his role in the company. The decision to form two businesses had created uncertainty among management and staff and conflict between coworkers; as opportunities and responsibilities for some Palm employees increased, they decreased for others.

Tod Bradley, formerly the Executive VP and Chief Operating Officer (COO), was appointed CEO of Palm Solutions, and Palm board member David Nagel, formerly the President and Chief Technology Officer at AT&T Labs, was appointed CEO of the newly created PalmSource.

The creation of PalmSource was seen as an opportunity to unlock future growth for Palm. Representing 4% of annual revenue in fiscal year 2001, the subsidiary was anticipated to return Palm to profitability and provide a strong stream of revenue and earnings.

Palm's Product Line

Palm was early to market in the handheld information system, introducing its first device in 1996. Its combination of simplicity and functionality created an early barrier for other competitors entering the market place (see **Exhibit 3**).

PalmSource, Inc.

In an effort to bring greater clarity to its mission "to be the global leader in mobile information management, better serve its licensees and ultimately increase shareholder value,"[2] Palm made the strategic decision to separate its platform business from its handheld solutions business in the middle of fiscal year 2001. "Throughout the industry the Palm platform was the standard of excellence for robust service, mobile access for personal and corporate data and enterprise systems. The Palm served enterprises well with its design, pen developer handheld platform that seamlessly integrated content and applications and empowered CIO's and CFO's alike."[3] The Palm platform integrated a number of components around the Palm OS and consisted primarily of the Palm OS operating system and the Palm user interface (now Palm Source). The Palm user interface enabled users to interact with a Palm-Powered device and allowed developers to write applications that run on devices based on the Palm platform.

The numerous benefits of the Palm platform resulted in its market leadership position, with more than 57% of the market using the Palm OS. Significant market acceptance of Palm OS devices attracted a number of licensees. By the end of fiscal year 2001, there were more than 160,000 third-party developers registered to create applications based on the Palm platform. It was Palm's belief that "strong developer support was due in part to the relative simplicity of developing applications for the Palm platform and represents a significant competitive advantage compared to alternative systems."[4] In addition, Palm licensed the platform to

Exhibit 3

The Palm Product Family, 2002

The Palm handheld computer family is known for its unique commitment to an elegant, simple interface that was easy to use. Today, the handheld family consists of the Palm m100 and m500 series handhelds and the Palm i705 wireless handheld. These Palm products are equipped with a comprehensive suite of personal information management (PIM) software, including Date Book, Address, To Do List, and Memo Pad; infrared beaming capabilities; expense-management software; a calculator; note-taking applications; games; and a backlit screen. They also come with the Palm Desktop software, a companion desktop PIM, and HotSync® technology, Palm's innovative local and remote synchronization software.

The Palm m100 Series

The stylish **Palm m100 handheld** series was the lowest-priced Palm handheld series ever introduced and offered users who are new to handhelds easy personalization and use of their handheld. These products—the Palm m105 and m125 monochrome handhelds and the Palm m130 color handheld—offered colorful, changeable faceplates to suit users' tastes and easy-to-use features, such as an introductory tutorial and a Notepad application that allowed users to create and store virtual sticky-notes in their own handwriting on the handheld.

The fun, functional **Palm m105 handheld** had 8MB of memory for appointments, addresses, and to-do items. Users could take advantage of thousands of third-party applications that could be downloaded from the Internet for offline browsing. And the included **Palm Mobile Internet Kit** could be used with a compatible data-enabled mobile phone or modem to wirelessly connect to the Internet via the user's ISP account.

The **Palm m125 handheld** featured Palm's elegant dual-expansion architecture—the Palm Expansion Card Slot for postage-stamp–sized content cards and the Palm Universal Connector for hardware accessories. Users could carry and share office-productivity and education software, eBooks, photos, short videos, extensive reference materials, and extra memory, and they could attach add-on modules, such as collapsible keyboards, digital cameras, and modems. The m125 also included bundled software solutions valued at more than $100.

The **Palm m130 color handheld** offered one of the most affordable Palm color handhelds available today. An easy-to-use, durable, and flexible product, the Palm m130 handheld was ideal for value-conscious consumers who valued a bright color display and a rechargeable battery, including young professionals, first-time buyers, students, and users who wanted to upgrade from the Palm m100 and m105 handhelds. Like the Palm m125 handheld, the m130 included bundled software solutions valued at more than $100 and featured Palm's dual-expansion technology to give users the ability to add on as their need for more powerful handheld applications grew.

The Palm m500 Series

The **Palm m500 handheld** offered Palm's dual-expansion technology—the Palm Expansion Card Slot and the Palm Universal Connector, which provided either serial or USB connectivity—in addition to the traditional functions and features of the Palm handheld series. The expansion slot offered an easy way for users to add storage, applications, content, and add-ons, such as a portable keyboard

Source: Company documents, www.palm.com.

Exhibit 3
The Palm Product Family, 2002 (*continued*)

and wireless modems. The Palm m500 shipped with bonus software—Palm's Mobile Connectivity software, Palm Reader, DataViz Documents To Go 3.0, MGI PhotoSuite Mobile Edition, Infinity Softworks powerOne Personal calculator, AvantGo, AOL, and Chapura Pocket Mirror 3.02.

A stylish marriage of form and function, the **Palm m515 color handheld** provided the tools mobile professionals needed in a sophisticated, elegant handheld. The new brighter color display and 16MB of memory let users work at their best, no matter where they were, making the Palm m515 handheld the premier choice for managing a busy executive's mobile lifestyle. Palm's dual-expansion technology enabled users to back up the handheld on-the-go; add new software, business applications, or memory; and attach peripherals, such as a keyboard, a GPS receiver, or a wireless modem—for a tool that grows with the user's needs. The Palm m515 handheld's powerful organizer software and support for familiar office software, such as Microsoft Word, Excel, and PowerPoint, made it the smart professional choice. In addition, the Palm m515 handheld shipped with a bonus CD-ROM with software applications that could be installed for added capabilities. If bought separately, these bundled products would cost more than $100.

The Palm i705 Wireless Handheld
The **Palm i705 wireless handheld*** and **Palm.Net**® wireless service[1] kept users on top of business, even when they were away from the office. It was the only wireless solution in the marketplace that delivered all the following benefits: always-on[1] push e-mail from up to eight e-mail accounts; secure, end-to-end, behind-the-firewall e-mail for corporate users; Web browsing via Google search or URL entry; plus classic Palm PIM features, such as Date Book and Address Book, combined in a sleek silver one-piece package.

The Palm i705 handheld also provided notification of new e-mail by LED, sound, or vibration; on-the-fly filtering of mail from different sources; multiple forms of data entry, including an optional Palm Mini Keyboard, which slipped over the bottom of the i705 and provided for "thumb typing"; and powerful complementary business software valued at more than $100. Included in-box was DataViz Documents To Go 4.0, Professional Edition, which provided an unparalleled ability to read and edit Word and Excel documents while preserving formatting. It also permitted viewing of PowerPoint presentations sized for the handheld's screen. The i705 also featured Palm's dual-expansion technology—the Palm Expansion Card Slot and the Palm Universal Connector.

The Palm i705 Wireless Messaging Solution
The **Palm i705 Wireless Messaging Solution**—an enterprise-class, end-to-end, behind-the-firewall, wireless messaging solution based on the Palm i705 wireless handheld—directly addressed the manageability, support, and security concerns of IT managers who were deploying handhelds to large numbers of mobile workers. The new enterprise solution comprised the Palm i705 handheld; the secure, behind-the-firewall Palm Wireless Messaging Server; the Enterprise Software Suite; Palm IT technical support; and the Palm.Net[2] enterprise wireless service.

HotSync® Technology
Palm's innovative HotSync technology was a robust, open architecture that allowed fast and easy synchronization of data, including all contact, scheduling, e-mail, and other personal information between Palm devices and a personal computer; networked computer; or Apple Macintosh, iBook, iMac, or PowerBook.

(continued)

Notes: [1] and [2] The Palm.Net® wireless service was a paid subscription service sold separately. The Palm i705 wireless handheld and the Palm.Net service were available in the United States only.

Exhibit 3

The Palm Product Family, 2002 (*continued*)

> To use HotSync technology, the user simply placed the Palm handheld into the small docking cradle and pressed the HotSync button. The HotSync technology, coupled with a Palm modem cable, also allowed a user to dial in to his or her company's server to synchronize with a PC.
>
> The HotSync architecture featured an extensive set of application programming interfaces (APIs) and conduit development tools that allowed third-party developers to create applications that easily take advantage of the HotSync capabilities in their own Palm OS solutions.
>
> **E-mail**
>
> With most Palm handheld computers, users could also take advantage of e-mail support for leading e-mail applications, including Eudora, Lotus cc: Mail, Microsoft Exchange, Microsoft Outlook 97 and 2000, Windows Messaging, and other POP3 Internet e-mail. The Palm family of products also supported Microsoft Mail, Windows for Workgroups Mail, and Microsoft Outlook Express. With Palm's MultiMail software, Palm offered the leading client software for e-mail and for viewing attachments. Palm offered a wide array of wireless and wireline e-mail solutions to meet a wide range of customer needs.

other manufacturers, including Sony, for multimedia and entertainment capabilities, and to Handspring, one of its PDA competitors.

To maintain this competitive position, Palm subsequently developed and distributed Palm OS5 in June 2002 to developers and licensees. The new system software included ARM-based computer chips and provided a broad range of expanded performance capabilities, including a longer battery life, enhanced security, and increased multimedia and wireless capacity. One of the key benefits to the Palm OS5 system was the Palm Powered Compatible Solutions logo, which developers could display with their software to indicate Palm OS compatibility. In promoting the program, Palm focused on keeping compatibility between its current programs and future programs and maintaining its "preferred system of choice" reputation. "Experts have suggested that Palm buyers are awaiting new devices with faster processors and more powerful software due later in 2002. The new processors and Palm operating software will bring most of the software applications to Palm based devices that are now only available on Microsoft based devices."[5]

Palm's Competition

Although Palm enjoyed strong brand name recognition, its market leadership position had weakened, as demonstrated by a one-year decline in its PDA market share from 75.9% in April 2000 to 63% in April 2001, with its OS market share slipping to 57% in 2001 from 75% in 2000 (per Gartner Dataquest). In addition to new competitors entering the PDA, OS, and wireless services markets, the power of existing competitors was high, with some competitors having significantly greater financial, technical, and marketing resources than Palm. Microsoft continued to be Palm's strongest competitor in the OS market. Whereas Palm originally focused on the consumer market to sell its product, Microsoft sold its Pocket PC primarily to businesses, with customers purchasing in volume. Like Palm, Microsoft was aggressive in building relationships with developers and licensees to create software applications that support Microsoft's handheld operating system. Microsoft's position was further strengthened by the merger of Compaq and Hewlett-Packard, manufacturers of the iPaq and Jordana PDAs, with HPCompaq becoming the number-two manufacturer of handheld PDAs. During the second quarter of fiscal year 2002, HPCompaq shipped 19% of total handhelds, and Palm's percentage slipped from 40.6% in first-quarter 2001 to 32% in first-quarter 2002. Sony, whose PDAs operated with Palm OS, has risen to the number-three position, controlling a 10% market share. Handspring, once Palm's closest competitor and the number-two manufacturer of handhelds, had slipped to fourth place, representing 6.5% of market share (this figure does not include communicators). With its position declining, Handspring decided that the handheld market could not sustain a company of its size and chose also to create communicators, such as the Treo. "Palm's software business has also come under increasing competition from Symbian, an operating system for wireless communication systems supported by major mobile-phone makers including Ericsson, Motorola, and Nokia. Symbian was moving from cell phones to PDA, while Palm was doing the reverse."[6]

Microsoft developed, manufactured, licensed, and supported a wide range of software products for a multitude of computing devices. Microsoft (MS) software included scalable operating systems for servers, PCs, and intelligent devices; server applications for client/server environments; knowledge worker productivity applications; and software development tools. The company's online efforts included the MSN network of internet products and services and alliances with companies involved with broadband access and various forms of digital interactivity. Microsoft also licensed consumer software programs, sold hardware devices, provided consulting services, trained and certified system integrators and developers, and researched and developed advanced technologies for future software products. Microsoft had four product segments: Desktop and Enterprise Software and Services; Consumer Software, Services and Devices; Consumer Commerce Investments; and Other. For the fiscal year ending June 30, 2002, MS revenues rose 12%, to $28.37 billion. Net income before accounting changes rose 1%, to $7.83 billion. Results reflected higher demand for client operating systems, which was partially offset by increased investment loss.

Hewlett-Packard Company was a global provider of products, technologies, solutions, and services. The company's offerings spanned information technology (IT) infrastructure, personal computing and access devices, global services, and imaging and printing. In May 2002, the company merged with Compaq. As a result of the merger with Compaq, the two companies' previous businesses and product lines were integrated and reorganized into four major groups. The Enterprise Systems Group provided key technology assets of enterprise IT infrastructure, including enterprise storage, servers, management software, and solutions. HP Services provided mission-critical infrastructure services, services for open IT environments, and enterprise-ready Microsoft integration and support services. The Imaging and Printing Group provided printing and imaging solutions for consumer and business markets. The Personal Systems Group was a provider of personal computing solutions. For the 6 months ending April 30, 2002, HP Compaq's net revenues fell 9%, to $22 billion. Net income before extraordinary items rose 68%, to $716 million. Results reflected a weak global economy, offset by the absence of a $400 million litigation settlement.

Sony Corporation and its consolidated subsidiaries developed, designed, manufactured, and sold electronic equipment, instruments, and devices for consumer and industrial markets. It also developed, produced, manufactured, and marketed home-use game consoles and software, and it developed, produced, manufactured, and distributed, recorded music in all commercial formats and musical genres. It was also engaged in the development, production, manufacture, marketing, distribution, and broadcasting of image-based software, including film, video, and television. It was also involved in various financial service businesses, including insurance operations through a Japanese life insurance subsidiary and non-life insurance subsidiaries, banking operations through a Japanese Internet-based banking subsidiary, and leasing and credit financing operations in Japan. Sony also had Internet-related businesses, an advertising agency business in Japan, and location-based entertainment businesses in Japan and the United States. For the three months ending June 30, 2002, Sony revenues rose 5%, to ¥1.722 trillion. Net income before accounting change totaled ¥57.18 million, versus a loss of

¥36.06 million. Results reflected higher demand for audiovisual products, DVD software, and the performance of *Spiderman, the Movie*.

Handspring, Inc., was engaged in personal communications and handheld computing. The company developed, manufactured, and marketed the Treo wireless communicators and Treo 90 organizer, the Visor expandable handheld computers, and client and server software for fast Web access from handheld devices and mobile phones. Founded in 1998, the company established itself with its Springboard platform, which provided a simple and easy method for hardware and software expansion. Handspring sold its Treo and Visor lines of wireless communicators, handheld computers, and Springboard expansion modules at www.handspring.com and through select Internet and retail partners in the United States, Europe, Asia, Australia, New Zealand, Canada, and the Middle East. For the nine months ending March 30, 2002, Handspring revenue fell 38%, to $191.6 million. Net losses rose 30%, to $76.2 million. Results reflected reduced demand for the company's products, which was partially offset by lower non-cash costs.

RIM/Blackberry, with more solid financial backing, should become a force in the market. The Blackberry 957 had PDA and phone capabilities, with a battery that lasted up to 80 hours. Blackberry was the first to develop the thumb keyboards and was widely preferred by its users. Compatible with applications such as Outlook and corporate networks, Blackberry had more than 13,000 companies using its product. Although the Blackberry 957 could not receive attachments via e-mail, the system was always ready to receive mail. Even with a price tag of $499, Blackberry was struggling to improve its financial performance.

Palm's Marketing Campaign

Although Palm held a leadership position in the consumer market, it did not enjoy the same strength in the corporate sector as did Blackberry and Microsoft. To raise awareness of its products and platform solutions, Palm, under Benhamou's guidance, launched a major advertising campaign in spring 2002, aimed at educating buyers about the benefits of Palm devices and solutions in the workplace. In addition to advertisements that appeared in the *Wall Street Journal, Business Week, Fortune, Information Week*, and *CIO Insight*, Palm created a special section on its Web site specifically to meet the needs of corporate buyers. The Web site informed and assisted corporate purchasers with the many products and business solutions Palm offered, with the capability to customize their products to specific industries, such as health care, retail, manufacturing, and financial services (see **Exhibit 4**).

The campaign stressed Palm's ease of use and lower total cost of ownership (TCO) for businesses and organizations as its main advantages over competitors and advertised its successful partnerships with companies including Siebel Systems, IBM, McKesson, and BEA Systems. In an independent study completed by the Gantry Group, leading operating systems Palm OS and the Pocket PC (from Microsoft) were compared. The study showed that the Palm OS platform delivered a 41% annual cost savings to enterprises compared with the Pocket PC platform. The study compared multiple cost factors associated with buying, deploying, managing, and supporting handheld devices. Of the six factors studied, the Palm OS–based devices were less expensive for every component and were at least 60% less expensive for software, IT services, and training. To reinforce its advertising campaign, Palm actively attended and participated in technology and business conferences to inform business leaders and business analysts about its new programs and strategy. In his presentations, Benhamou emphasized Palm's current rebuilding, which included Palm's decision to separate the two well-capitalized, profitable, high-growth companies, the recent rollout of the Palm OS5, and Palm's objective of gaining market share through new industry segments and expanded geographic presence.

Exhibit 4
Palm's Industry Solutions

- **Financial services:** Banks, brokerage firms, and insurance companies can keep their business and financial data flowing, no matter where they are. Palm-powered handhelds can provide constant access to real-time financial data and market activities.

- **Government:** Versatile handheld solutions help government agencies manage the collection, analysis, and distribution of data. For example, using Palm handhelds, fire safety inspectors with the National Naval Medical Center can document code violations and then upload the information to a master database for analysis and report generation.

- **Health care:** With Palm-powered handhelds, health care providers can deliver better patient care while controlling costs and streamlining processes. For example, physicians with BlueCross/BlueShield in Rochester, New York, use Palm handhelds for mobile access to medical information such as specialist listings and drug data; this improves the efficiency and quality of patient care.

- **Manufacturing:** With Palm handhelds, information management can be instant and wireless. Inspections can be automated, clipboards can be eliminated, and data entry can be fast and secure. For example, at auto races, BFGoodrich tire designers use Palm handhelds to quickly collect performance data during pit stops; the data are used to develop better, safer tires for both racers and consumers.

Source: Company document, www.Palm.com/solutions. This section was edited.

Palm's Licensing Strategy

Significant market acceptance of Palm platform devices had attracted a number of licensees. Palm licensed its platform for handheld devices to companies including Acer, HandEra, Handspring, Nokia, Sony, and Symbol. Other licensees included Kyocera, a maker of digital mobile phones, which had introduced its second-generation pdQ digital smart phone, combining the functionality of the Palm handheld device with that of a mobile phone. Handspring and Symbol recently extended their Palm OS licenses until 2009 and 2005, respectively. Palm marketed three primary Internet and wireless services and applications that addressed these opportunities: Palm.Net, My Palm portal, and Palm.com. Although these licensees competed with Palm for customers for handheld devices and reduced Palm's market share, the PDAs relied on the Palm platform for operations, further strengthening the consumer's reliance on Palm. "As of June 1, 2001 more than 160,000 developers had registered to use Palm developer tools to create software for the Palm platform."[7] Palm reached end users primarily through distributors, retailers, and resellers, with distributors representing the largest channel. Distributors generally sold to retailers (including Internet retailers) and resellers (enterprise and education resellers). The retail channel was the second largest U.S. distribution channel, and it included office supply stores, computer superstores, consumer electronics retailers, and catalog and mail-order companies.

Palm also sold products through third parties that had significant market presence or access to new products that could be more efficiently developed and managed than by Palm. For example, in the United States, Europe, Japan, Latin America, and Asia, IBM sold in the enterprise market Palm-based products branded as the IBM WorkPad PC Companion.

The Palm Model m500 Delay

As the originator and leader of the PDA market, Palm had experienced exceptional revenue growth since its inception. Palm had reported triple-digit revenue growth from 1997 to 2000. Fiscal years 1998 through 2000 were highly profitable, with earnings multiplying tenfold, growing from $4,171 million in 1999 to $45,910 million in 2000.

During the second half of fiscal year 2001, the company's performance was affected by a series of factors that led to a net loss, a decline in share price, and a change in management. Poor rollout of the company's Palm m500 model resulted in disastrous performance in the second half of fiscal year 2001, causing a $356,476 million loss for the year. In early fiscal year 2001, Palm introduced the Palm m500, which was expected to be available to customers in early spring 2001. Customers and potential customers put off purchasing PDAs in anticipation of buying the newest version, which was to be light, expandable, and Internet compatible. Supply shortages of several key components created difficulties at Flextronics International Ltd.,[8] one of two primary suppliers, resulting in a long delay in delivering the newest PDA model. The decision by many customers to delay purchasing PDAs until delivery of the newest model resulted in significant lost revenue during the period. Although outsourcing all of its production (to two primary manufacturers/suppliers) allowed the company to develop and market new products, as well as minimize working capital expenditure requirements, it left the company vulnerable to weaknesses on the part of the supplier. Compounding the problem was the fact that Palm had noncancelable contracts with Flextronics to manufacture the older (mature) Palm models, which were experiencing a softening of demand. The unexpected decline in demand resulted in inventory levels that exceeded forecasted requirements, requiring markdowns to move older inventory and drive revenue. In addition to lost revenue and lower gross profit margin, the company recorded a fourth-quarter restructuring charge of $60,900 million related to a series of cost-reduction initiatives implemented by Palm to minimize the impact of the ongoing economic slowdown.

Increased competition, coupled with prolonged recessionary conditions, continued to significantly affect demand, revenue, and profits during 2002. For the nine months ending March 1, 2002, Palm reported a net loss of $54.7 million (included additional restructuring charges of $25.9 million) compared to the previous year's $35.6 million profit. Total revenue for the same nine-month period decreased 43% over the previous year. At Solutions Group, revenue was $779 million, a 43% decline over the previous year, with Palm Source reporting revenue of $48.2 million, a 27% decrease due to lower Palm OS device shipments. Management attributed the decline in revenue at Palm Solutions to a decline in unit shipments and a lower average selling price of Palm PDAs due to recessionary economic conditions, a reduction in inventories held by channel partners, and increased competition. Low average selling price was due to a high percentage of entry-level and older products, which carried lower sales prices.

Despite the ongoing losses, the balance sheet was satisfactory, with working capital of $247 million and leverage of only 0.76/1 (tangible). More troubling was the rapidly eroding market capitalization. Time seemed to be running out for Palm. Although the company did not have debt service constraints, operating losses had resulted in negative cash flow, reducing Palm's cash position to only $285,645 million as of March 31, 2002.

2002, A Dreadful Year

In May 2002, Palm introduced the i705 model, with "always on e-mail." Benefits of the i705 were instant messaging as well as access to AOL, e-mail, and portal information. Criticisms included poor reliability and incomplete support for the Mac version. In presentations and discussions with investor and industry analysts, Benhamou acknowledged that "the $100 price point [had] proven significant for many products like the walkman and DVD player."[9] Although this was not the original price point of Palm's PDA, he believed the company could offer a product at that price and remain profitable by increasing the number of Palm customers fourfold. By gaining new customers at a low price point, Palm hoped customers would upgrade within 18 months. In addition to producing a lower-priced PDA, Palm's strategy included offering the new low-cost devices with wireless e-mail capabilities and development of a new PDA operating on Palm's new OS5 operating system that would be capable of making phone calls.

By June 2002, Palm's stock was trading at a low of $1.50. Benhamou was hopeful that the company's presentation to industry and business analysts in May 2002 would be the beginning of a strong turnaround for the company. Focused on building shareholder value through clear business objectives, Benhamou explained Palm's three key objectives: first, to "turn Palm into two, well capitalized, profitable, high growth companies; second, to execute enterprise strategy, on time and on budget; and finally, to introduce the industry's best ARM-based wireless solution."

In June 2002, the company began its rollout of the final Palm OS5 system to developers, which was anticipated to generate renewed demand for Palm-brand products and solutions. To raise additional awareness, Palm launched a major print advertising campaign. The one-year program aimed to educate corporate buyers and IT professionals about the advantages of using Palm products and solutions. Integrated in this campaign were the results from its white paper, prepared by Gantry Research, which compared the Palm OS and Microsoft Pocket PC platforms and found that the Palm OS devices were 41% less expensive on an annual basis than the Pocket PC.

For Palm, the leader in the PDA industry, competition was constant and intense, and Palm was tenacious in its effort to defend its position globally. In June 2002, Todd Bradley, President and CEO, Palm Solutions Group, traveled to China as the company prepared to enter the only market in Asia that Palm had not penetrated. Markets outside North America accounted for 40% of Palm's revenue.

Palm's Strategy Going Forward

Benhamou was dedicated to meeting the company's objectives and formulating its competitive strategy. Reflecting on the series of changes that had transpired during the past 24 months and looking ahead left him at a crossroads. With its market cap considerably reduced, could Palm continue to grow operations under two separate companies, Palm Solutions and PalmSource? Where should the company allocate resources for its future growth and development? Benhamou considered some of his options:

1. Focus on maintaining and building Palm's leadership position by developing new wireless functionality at different price points in all Palm PDA products.

2. Switch Palm's focus and invest in developing the next generation of PDA communicator technology. The Handspring communicator (Treo), which combines wireless messaging and Web access under Palm's operating system with a telephone, has been well received. Should Palm expand on the concept of a communicator and design an enhanced and improved product?

3. Exit the PDA hardware business and concentrate its resources on growing PalmSource, building and expanding its operating system capabilities. This would allow other competitors to struggle for market dominance in the PDA sector. Recently, Sony Corporation announced its $20 million investment in PalmSource in exchange for a 6% equity position in the company. The investment represented Sony's interest in expanding its business and technical collaboration with Palm.

Finanical Results

Exhibit 5 and Exhibit 6 are Palm's consolidated statement of operations and consolidated balance sheet.

Exhibit 5

Consolidated Statements of Operations: Palm, Inc.
(Dollars amount in thousands, except per share amounts)

	Year Ending		
	May 31, 2002	June 1, 2001	June 2, 2000
Revenues	$1,030,831	$1,559,312	$1,057,597
Costs and operating expenses:			
Cost of revenues	747,221	1,062,042	613,120
Cost of revenues—charge (reduction) for special excess inventory and related costs	(101,844)	268,930	—
Sales and marketing	236,214	337,029	236,275
Research and development	141,013	158,132	72,889
General and administrative	56,444	87,842	50,916
Amortization of goodwill and intangible assets (1)	12,531	37,321	3,378
Restructuring charges	46,553	60,888	—
Impairment charges	—	106,669	—
Legal settlements	—	5,450	—
Separation costs	1,542	5,468	19,570
Purchased in-process technology	—	1,063	—
Total costs and operating expenses	1,139,674	2,130,834	996,148
Operating income (loss)	(108,843)	(571,522)	61,449
Interest and other income (expense), net	938	47,331	16,364
Income (loss) before income taxes	(107,905)	(524,191)	77,813
Income tax provision (benefit)	(25,737)	(167,715)	31,903
Net income (loss)	$ (82,168)	$ (356,476)	$ 45,910
Net income (loss) per share:			
Basic	$ (0.14)	$ (0.63)	$ 0.09
Diluted	$ (0.14)	$ (0.63)	$ 0.09
Shares used in computing net income (loss) per share:			
Basic	572,796	566,132	539,739
Diluted	572,796	566,132	539,851

Note 1:
Amortization of goodwill and intangible assets:

Cost of revenues	$ 6,306	$ 4,135	$ 1,350
Sales and marketing	11	556	506
Research and development	6,137	32,610	1,494
General and administrative	77	20	28
Total amortization of goodwill and intangible assets	$ 12,531	$ 37,321	$ 3,378

Source: http://ir.palm.com/ireye/ir_site

Exhibit 6

Consolidated Balance Sheets: Palm, Inc.

(Dollar amounts in thousand except par value amounts)

	May 31, 2002	June 1, 2001
Assets		
Current assets:		
Cash and cash equivalents	$ 278,547	$ 513,769
Short-term investments	17,970	—
Accounts receivable, net of allowance for doubtful accounts		
of $8,485 and $14,899, respectively	63,551	115,342
Inventories	55,004	107,813
Deferred income taxes	48,985	154,362
Prepaids and other	14,122	12,867
Total current assets	478,179	904,153
Restricted investments	2,326	500
Land, property and equipment, net	211,556	223,422
Goodwill, net	68,785	43,169
Intangible assets, net	9,585	18,218
Deferred income taxes	205,440	90,656
Other assets	13,225	17,133
Total assets	$ 989,096	$1,297,251
Liabilities and Stockholders' Equity		
Current liabilities:		
Accounts payable	$ 88,909	$ 238,235
Accrued restructuring	35,512	32,399
Other accrued liabilities	108,577	282,851
Total current liabilities	232,998	553,485
Noncurrent liabilities:		
Long-term convertible debt	50,000	—
Deferred revenue and other	15,250	9,614
Stockholders' equity:		
Preferred stock, $.001 par value, 125,000 shares authorized;		
none outstanding	—	—
Common stock, $0.001 par value, 2,000,000 shares authorized;		
outstanding: May 31, 2002, 579,200 shares; June 1, 2001, 567,215 shares	579	567
Additional paid-in capital	1,122,124	1,092,329
Unamortized deferred stock-based compensation	(5,743)	(14,929)
Accumulated deficit	(426,207)	(344,039)
Accumulated other comprehensive income	95	224
Total stockholders' equity	690,848	734,152
Total liabilities and stockholders' equity	$ 989,096	$1,297,251

Source: http://ir.palm.com/ireye/ir_site

Notes

1. www.palm.com/about/corporate executive.html
2. Palm.com, Media Backgrounder. www.palm.com/solutions
3. Palm, Inc., *Form 10-K*, year ending June 2001.
4. *Ibid.*
5. P. Franklin, "Handheld Computer Shipments Dip, Palm's Grip Slips," *Renters Market News* (July 25, 2002).
6. Hellweg, "Danger Signs for Palm and Handspring" *Business 2.0 Tech Investor* (May 6, 2002).
7. Palm Computing, Inc., 2001 SEC 10-K.
8. Headquartered in Singapore, Flextronics provides electronics manufacturing services to OEMs in the networking, computer, medical, consumer, and telecommunications industries. The company currently had a market cap of $4,201.92 million based on 513.05 million shares outstanding. Comparable to other manufacturers in the technology sector, Flextronics had struggled with declining sales due to continued shortfall in IT spending. For the three months ending June 30, 2002, Flextronics's revenue increased 1%, to $3.13 billion due to acquisitions during fiscal 2002. Net loss ($131.2 million) versus net income of $88.3 million last year includes $207.8 million in unusual charges related to plant closures and workforce reductions. June 30, 2002, Financial Strength: Quick Ratio .78; Current Ratio 1.39; LT Debt/Equity 0.20; Total Debt/Equity 0.24. money.cnn.com/MGI/snap/A0AF2.htm.
9. Yahoo.

case 11

Handspring, Inc., 2002

Lisa-Marie Mulkern and Alan N. Hoffman

M*y focus today, 100 percent, is making Handspring successful, making handheld computing successful. I still view the handheld computing industry as very embryonic; it's very early on. It's like 1982 of the PC world. And the big things haven't happened yet. As much success as Palm has had, and as much success as Handspring is currently having, it's just the beginning, and it takes a lot of concentrated effort to build a big business. And we think Handspring's going to be a very big business.*[1]

Jeff Hawkins, Handspring's Chairman and Chief Product Officer

Jeffrey Hawkins: The Journey from GRiD Systems to Treo

Handspring was founded in 1998 by three key executives from Palm Computing, Jeff Hawkins, currently Handspring's Chairman and Chief Product Officer; Donna Dubinsky, President and CEO; and Ed Colligan, the Chief Operating Officer (CEO). At Palm Computing, Hawkins had been the chief inventor, Dubinsky the President and CEO, and Colligan the Vice President (VP) of Marketing. The three veterans of handheld computing were credited with reviving the industry through their successful launch of the Palm Pilot in 1996.

The widespread success and ongoing technological improvements found in today's handheld computing devices are a direct result of Hawkins's design work at GRiD Systems back in the early 1980s. After graduating from Cornell University in 1979 with a bachelor of science degree in electronic engineering and a short tenure at Intel, Hawkins left to begin working at GRiD Systems in 1982. While at GRiD Systems, he developed a high-level programming language called GRiDTask that would later fuel further technological advancements in handheld computing, particularly in the area of text entry. Hawkins's work on GRiDTask also increased his own personal interest in the area of brain research.

In response to his related interest, Hawkins left his position at GRiD in 1986 in order to pursue a Ph.D at Berkeley. As Hawkins explained, he was in search of answers to questions such as "What does it mean for a brain, or for a system like a brain, to understand its environ-

This case was prepared by Lisa-Marie Mulkern, MBA student, and Professor Alan N. Hoffman of Bentley College. This case was edited for SMBP-9th Edition. Reprinted by permission of Dr. Alan N. Hoffman. The authors would like to thank Scott Barry, Wendy Dalwin, Lindsey Fuller, Bob Mammarella, and Diane Shaffer for their research and contributions to this case.

ment? What is a reductionist approach to understanding language, vision, and hearing? and What are the concepts underlying that?"[2] Although his Ph.D. thesis proposal was rejected on the basis that no other professors at Berkeley were pursuing similar research, a pattern classifier program that Hawkins had written was patented and used as a hand-printed-character recognizer. With his thesis proposal rejected and experiencing difficulties with being a graduate student after having had a successful career, Hawkins decided that he would return to the computer industry in lieu of pursuing his academic interests. Hawkins returned to GRiD Systems as Vice President of Research and began working on the first handheld computing device, the GRiDPad, which was released in 1989. Hawkins's personal goal at the time he rejoined GRiD Systems was "to become famous enough to and wealthy enough to really promote and sponsor significant research in neurobiology and theoretical neurobiology."[3]

The GRiDPad measured 9×12×1.4 inches and ran on a 10MHz 80C86 processor with a DOS platform. The handheld used GRiD's own software solutions that were written in GRiDTask. With a color graphics adapter (640×400) display, the GRiDTask cost $2,370, exclusive of software, and used 256KB or 512KB battery-backed RAM cards. Using the character-recognition engine that Hawkins had developed, users were able to enter text by using either a pen or a keyboard. The GRiDPad was marketed primarily to data collection users in areas such as transportation and warehousing as well as to police, nurses, and census takers.

In Hawkins's mind, the GRiDPad was only a first step toward his revolutionary vision for handheld computing. Hawkins believed that the success of handheld computers depended on developing a product that was both small and lightweight enough for people to carry around with them all the time. Hawkins developed the specifications for a handheld computing device that was aptly named "Zoomer"—short for consumer, the device's intended market. However, the executives at GRiD were opposed to plans for entering the consumer market. Unable to find support from within, Hawkins left GRiD in 1992 with a software license for the GRiDPad and founded Palm Computing.

Corporate Governance

Exhibit 1-A shows the 7 members of the Board of Directors of Handspring, Inc., 5 of whom are external directors. **Exhibit 1-B** shows the 10 members of Handspring's executive team.

The Palm Pilot Era

On the heels of the GRiDPad's success, several high-tech companies, including IBM, NCR, NEC, and Samsung, joined in the rush to develop the next smaller computing device. Apple had been in the development phase of a handheld computing device since 1987. In 1992, John Sculley, then CEO of Apple, coined the termed "personal digital assistant" (PDA).[4]

Following an initial commercial failure with the launch of the Zoomer, Palm went back to the drawing board and re-emerged in 1996 with its second product, the Palm Pilot. U.S. Robotics funded the development of the Palm Pilot through its acquisition of Palm Computing in 1995 for $44 million in stock. It was at this time that Palm transformed itself from a strictly software company to one that would develop an entire product—both hardware and software. Hawkins created what he calls "a virtual company" by partnering with several hardware design and contract-manufacturing companies to bring the product to market. The Palm Pilot was a success, and as a result, Jeff Hawkins, along with his colleagues Donna Dubinsky and Ed Colligan, were credited with reviving the handheld computing industry. The Palm Pilot was the most successful product launch in computing history, selling faster than VCRs, color TVs, cell phones, and personal computers.

Exhibit 1
Board of Directors and Executive Team: Handspring, Inc.

A. Board of Directors

Donna L. Dubinsky
President, CEO and Acting
Chief Financial Officer
Handspring, Inc.

Kim B. Clark
Dean
Harvard Business School

Bruce W. Dunlevie
Managing Member
Benchmark Capital

Mitchell E. Kertzman
CEO and Chairman
Liberate Technologies

Jeffrey C. Hawkins
Chairman and Chief Product Officer
Handspring, Inc.

L. John Doerr
General Partner
Kleiner, Perkins, Caufield & Byers

William E. Kennard
Managing Director
The Carlyle Group

B. Executive Team

Jeffrey Hawkins
Founder, Chairman and Chief Product Officer

Jeff Hawkins co-founded Handspring with Donna Dubinsky in July of 1998 after 5 years together at Palm Computing. In 1994, Hawkins invented the original PalmPilot products and founded Palm Computing. He was often credited as the designer who reinvented the handheld market.

An industry veteran with nearly 20 years of technical expertise, Hawkins currently holds nine patents for various handheld devices and features. His vision for handheld computing dates back to the 1980s, when as Vice President of Research at GRiD Systems Corporation he served as principal architect and designer for the GRiDPad and GRiD Convertible. Prior to that, he held key technical positions with Intel Corporation. Hawkins earned a B.S. in electrical engineering from Cornell University.

He was also the Founder and Executive Director of the non-profit Redwood Neuroscience Institute, a scientific research institute working on theories and mathematical models of brain function (www.rni.org).

Donna Dubinsky
Founder and CEO

Donna Dubinsky co-founded Handspring with Jeff Hawkins in July 1998 to create a new breed of handheld computers for consumers. As President and CEO of Palm Computing, Dubinsky helped make the PalmPilot the best-selling handheld computer and the most rapidly adopted new computing product ever produced. When Dubinsky first joined Hawkins at Palm Computing in 1992, shortly after the company was founded, she brought with her more than 10 years of marketing and logistics experience from Apple and Claris. Dubinsky and Hawkins introduced the original PalmPilot in February 1996, a move that revitalized the handheld computing industry.

In addition to her position as CEO of Handspring, Dubinsky currently serves as a Director of Intuit Corporation and is a Trustee of the Computer History Museum. She earned a B.A. from Yale University and an M.B.A. from the Harvard Graduate School of Business Administration.

Exhibit 1

Board of Directors and Executive Team: Handspring, Inc. (*continued*)

Ed Colligan
Founder, President and COO

Ed Colligan joined Handspring to lead the development and marketing efforts for a new generation of handheld computers. As the Vice President of Marketing for Palm Computing, Ed Colligan worked with Jeff Hawkins and Donna Dubinsky to lead the product marketing and marketing communications efforts for Palm, including the successful positioning, launch, and marketing of the popular Palm product family.

Prior to Palm, Colligan was Vice President of Strategic and Product Marketing at Radius Corporation. During his eight years there, Colligan helped make Radius the brand leader in Macintosh graphics, graphic imaging, and hardware development.

Colligan's multiple successes had earned him several marketing industry accolades. Marketing Computers Magazine named him the 1997 Marketer of the Year, and *Advertising Age* named him one of the Top 100 Marketers of 1997, an award that spanned all product categories. He earned an B.A. from the University of Oregon.

Bill Slakey
Chief Financial Officer

Before joining Handspring in September, 2002 Bill Slakey was Chief Financial Officer at W J Communications, a leading RF semiconductor company. Prior to that, he was CFO at SnapTrack, a QUALCOMM company that pioneered the industry's most advanced GPS-based wireless tracking system for pinpointing wireless phones, PDAs, pagers and other wireless devices.

Slakey had over 16 years of experience in financial management, including a senior controller position at 3COM's Palm Computing Division and various financial roles spanning 10 years at Apple Computer.

Slakey earned a B.A. from the University of California and an M.B.A. from the Harvard Graduate School of Business Administration.

John Hartnett
Vice President, Worldwide Operations

John Hartnett joined Handspring from MetaCreations, where he served most recently as Senior Vice President of Marketing, Support & Operations for the United States. At MetaCreations, he was responsible for developing the marketing, branding and advertising strategies including online marketing and web site redesign.

Prior to MetaCreations, Hartnett served as Director of International Operations at Claris, where he developed and managed the operations business plan and was part of the lead team in the merger of the Applesoft and Claris business. Hartnett also spent time at AT&T GIS, Digital Equipment, and Wang.

Hartnett earned a Marketing Degree through the Marketing Institute of Ireland and a post grad diploma in Finance through the ACCA.

Exhibit 1

Board of Directors and Executive Team: Handspring, Inc. (*continued*)

Patricia Tomlinson
Vice President, Human Resources

With over 20 years of experience in the human resources field, Patricia Tomlinson came to Handspring from Edify Corporation where she was responsible for the worldwide human resources department. She also designed and implemented all HR-related programs and led the worldwide integration of all HR-functions for the merger of Edify with Security First Technologies.

Prior to Edify Corporation, Tomlinson's previous work experience was at Xerox Corporation, Synopsys, Inc., and Apple Computer, Inc. She earned a B.A. in Sociology from Pomona College in Claremont, California and completed the Program for Management Development from Harvard Business School.

Celeste Baranski
Vice President, Engineering

Celeste Baranski joined Handspring with over 18 years of engineering, design, and management experience in the mobile computing industry. Most recently, Baranski worked at Hewlett Packard Company as Research and Development Manager of its Mobile Computing Division, where she led R&D, manufacturing introduction, and quality assurance for the company's laptop computer product line.

Before Hewlett Packard, Baranski worked as a consultant and Director of R&D for Norand Corporation, where she was in charge of product design and engineering management for various companies including Plantronics, Kalidor, IDEO and Divicom. Prior to that she co-founded and served as Vice President of Hardware Engineering for EO Incorporated, and was also among the first employees at GO Corporation where she designed the first GO pen-based computer.

Baranski has also held technical staff positions at GRiD Systems and Rolm Corporation. She earned both a B.S. and a M.S. in Electrical Engineering from Stanford University.

David Pine
Vice President and General Counsel

David joined Handspring in May 2000 as Vice President and General Counsel. Prior to Handspring, he served as Senior Vice President and General Counsel for Excite@Home, a broadband online service provider. Before that he was Vice President, General Counsel of Radius Inc., a manufacturer of Macintosh computer peripherals. He started his career in private practice with Fenwick & West, LLP, a Silicon Valley law firm representing startup and high-growth technology companies. He also has been involved in government and politics and has served as a State Representative in the New Hampshire Legislature.

He earned a B.A. degree in government from Dartmouth College, where he was awarded a Harry S. Truman Scholarship, and a J.D. degree from the University of Michigan Law School.

Joe Sipher
Vice President, Worldwide Marketing

Joe Sipher joined Handspring in May 2000. Sipher was a long time veteran of the handheld industry, having joined Palm, Inc. in 1993. His most recent role there was serving as Palm's first and only "Palm Fellow."

Before his fellowship, Joe managed Palm's wireless business, including the definition, development, and introduction of the Palm VII wireless Internet handheld. Joe was responsible for the hardware and software development of the breakthrough Palm VII product, and spearheaded the creation of Palm's wireless Internet service, Palm.Net. Before the Palm VII, Joe managed the PalmPilot product line and was a product manager on the original Pilot project.

Prior to Palm, Inc., Joe's work experience included positions at Microsoft and Apple. He held five patents pertaining to handheld and wireless technology. He earned a B.A. and an M.B.A. with high distinction from the University of Michigan.

Gregory Woock
Vice President, Worldwide Sales

Gregory Woock joined Handspring in 1999 with over 10 years of experience in sales and marketing within the high-tech industry. Prior to Handspring, Woock served as VP of Sales, at Creative Labs, Inc. As one of the original members of the pre-IPO team, Mr Woock helped build Creative from a small start-up into a dominant brand. Mr Woock was responsible for Sales, Channel marketing, Sales training and Sales operations in the United States, Canada and Latin America.

Woock earned his B.A. from Columbia College in Chicago

Source: Company document www.handspring.com/company/execteam.html. This section was edited.

The Exodus at Palm

By 1998, Hawkins, Dubinsky, and Colligan were already setting the stage for their departure from Palm and the formation of their own handheld computing company. Collectively, the three executives did not believe that Palm was a strategic match for 3Com (previously U.S. Robotics) and requested that Palm be spun off as a separate company. Eric Benhamou, 3Com's CEO, insisted that Palm would never be spun off because it was simply too important to the business. In addition to wanting a Palm spinoff, the trio also felt pressured to deliver products too quickly. As an example, Hawkins pointed to the fact that he felt pressured to deliver a wireless handheld in the form of the Palm VII. As Hawkins describes, "We were still at U.S. Robotics at the time, and the CEO, Casey Coswell, kept saying, 'I want you to do a wireless Palm.'" Hawkins objected on the basis that he would not have a great solution to deliver, but he ultimately yielded to the pressure by doing the best that he could with the development and subsequent release of the Palm VII wireless handheld in 1999.[5]

In response to these frustrations and armed with a license for the Palm operating system as well as the confidence that they could develop improved handheld computing devices, the three executives left Palm in July 1998 to form Handspring. September 14, 1999, one day after

3Com announced its plans to spin off Palm, Handspring unveiled its first handheld computing device, the Visor.

The Handspring Visor

The Visor featured the Springboard expansion slot, consisting of a series of modules for adding the capabilities of a digital camera, a wireless Web device, a cellular phone, or an MP3 music player. Many Palm enthusiasts followed Hawkins and his colleagues over to Handspring. The new company was overwhelmed with orders, and it took nearly four months before the supply was satisfying consumer demand for the new product. By the summer of 2000, Handspring's market share for Palm-based PDAs had reached 40%. Handspring went public in June 2000, with an initial public offering (IPO) price of $20 per share. By October 2000, Handspring's stock price skyrocketed to $95 per share. These successes attracted the attention of Palm and, throughout most of 2001, Palm and Handspring engaged in a price war with their competing handheld computing devices. Meanwhile, Microsoft was pressing ahead with its own version of a handheld computer, the Pocket PC, which had been introduced in early 1998.

In response to the increasing competition and pricing pressure in the handheld computing market, Handspring refocused its strategy with the introduction of the Treo line of communicators in fall 2001. Handspring's executives had decided that the market for strictly PDAs had become too crowded. The resulting price wars had eroded Handspring's margins and prevented the start-up from achieving its much-anticipated profitability.

THE TREO COMMUNICATOR

Handspring had learned a lot of valuable lessons through the development of its Visor product line. In particular, the two-year development process of the VisorPhone module taught the company several valuable lessons about phone and radio technology. In turn, Handspring's designers were able to utilize this experience in the development of the Treo product line, which began in summer 2000 and was completed within 14 months.

Under the code name "Manhattan," the Treo product development team consisted of both hardware and software developers. Each of the communicator's component parts also had New York–inspired names, such as "Shea Stadium" for the Graffiti handwriting system, "Central Park" for the screen, and "Metro" for the circuit board. In stark contrast to their rival Palm Computing, which had recently split its hardware and software businesses into two separate companies, Handspring's hardware and software developers worked together to design a communicator that addressed how and where people actually used their wireless devices. In addition, rather than employ traditional focus groups, Handspring employed an ethnographer who observed how people used both their cell phones and PDAs in everyday situations such as while driving or riding the subway.[6] Such observations indicated that people preferred to use a cell phone with one hand to avoid the distractions of juggling. With Treo's thumb-touch QWERTY keyboard and the capability to look up addresses and telephone numbers by typing initials, Handspring's executives were confident that the Treo would set the company back on course toward near-term profitability.

In December 2001, Dubinsky announced that the Visor line would be phased out of production and that the company planned to achieve profitability by its fiscal year end on June 30, 2002. Handspring would eventually focus exclusively on the Treo platform of communicators, which in contrast to the hardware-based Visor products allowed users to increase functionality through additional software as opposed to bulky hardware expansions (see **Exhibit 2**).

Exhibit 2

Handspring's Family of Organizers, Communicators, and Related Products

Visor™ Expandable Handheld Computers

The Visor model line featured both B&W and color screens, used rechargeable or alkaline batteries, and ranged in list price from $169 to $229. This was Handspring's original product offering.

Springboard™ modules transformed the Visor into a digital camera, wireless Web device, MP3 player, and more.

Handspring offered more than 70 different modules. Some modules were included free with the purchase of a Visor handheld, whereas other modules had a list price in excess of $400.

Treo™ 90 Handheld Computer Organizer

The Treo 90 featured a color screen, rechargeable battery, QWERTY keyboard, and SD/MMC expansion capabilities. It listed for $299.

Treo™ communicators were combination phone, messaging, data organizer, and Web access devices

The original Treo 180 listed for $399, and the improved Treo 270 —offering global telephone coverage and released in 2002—listed for $499. The Sprint PCS Treo 300—the result of a highly collaborative partnership and scheduled for release in late 2002—was to run on Sprint PCS's nationwide 3G data network. The Treo 300 was listed at $449 after mail-in rebate.

Software and Accessories (Cases, Cables, Cradles, Keyboards, etc.) for Visor and Treo Products

A variety of accessories and additional software were available from Handspring and other third-party providers. Accessories for Handspring's family of products ranged in price from $10.00 to $50.00 and were model specific. The Treo e-mail annual subscription ranged in price from $49.99 to $99.99.

Source: Company document, www.handspring.com/products/treo/photos.html.

Handspring's Competitors

Because Handspring continued to serve the traditional PDA market while refocusing its strategy on becoming a leading provider of communicators, the company faced competition from a variety of providers. The competition between PDAs and smart phones continued to fuel the convergence of these two traditionally separate markets. Industry analysts expected PDA sales after 2004 to be strongly affected by smart phones.[7] A Strand Consulting report stated that Palm and Handspring would have difficulty surviving in the smart phone market because they lacked experience in the mobile phone market and were faced with strong competition. Some analysts believed that Microsoft's 2.5G Smart Phone platform would succeed because of the company's strong customer base.[8] Nokia, Sony, Ericsson, Siemens, and Motorola had more financial strength to compete in the market for smart phones and smart handheld devices.[9] Traditional PDA providers such as Palm, Sharp, and Sony competed most directly with Handspring's Visor product line, while software and cell phone giants such as Microsoft and Nokia were concentrating their resources on combining the capabilities of wireless and handheld computing into their own versions of communicators that would compete for market share alongside Handspring's Treo products.

PALM i705

Palm was still the undisputed market share leader in the PDA market. However, the company had been under fire by competitors for several years and was clearly in the crosshairs of Microsoft and its Pocket PC operating system. Palm's current competitive advantage was its operating system, which was licensed to many PDA makers. The Palm i705 was the upgrade from the Palm VIIx. The i705 provided wireless e-mail and Internet access but lacked a long battery life and a color screen, and it had only 8MB of memory. Although the Palm i705 did not have cellular capability, it had "always-on" access to e-mail. This feature notified the user by a blink, beep, or vibration when there was new e-mail and had a very comprehensive support system that was second to none.

SHARP ZAURUS SL-500

Sharp was not a major player in the PDA market, but it was making some changes to its product in order to gain recognition and market share. The Zaurus SL-500 offered a hidden thumb keyboard as well as built-in handwriting-recognition software. Perhaps most noteworthy, the Sharp PDA was operating on a Linux operating system, which was getting some attention from software developers. The Zaurus also had a wide range of accessories, 64MB of RAM, and an Intel processor. Although Sharp had taken a big step forward, there were still some bugs that needed to be worked out to simplify software installation and Outlook access before it became a force in the current market.

SONY CLIE PEG-N760C

Sony had one of the best products in the PDA market. Its long-term commitment to R&D and innovation made it a market leader in almost every industry in which it competed. Although it was more expensive than other Palm OS devices, the CLIE offered a 65,334-color display screen along with MP3 audio capability, easy-to-use controls, remote control headphones, and picture/video viewing software. With some changes in its price and improvements in memory, Sony had the potential to utilize its deep pockets and strong product development capabilities to either enter into the cellular PDA market or work with a phone producer to enter into the market.

COMPAQ iPAQ 3835

The iPaq was one of the newest products in the PDA market. With a color screen, 64MB of RAM, the Pocket PC 2002 operating system, and improvements to iPaq's memory card and speakers, Compaq was positioned to increase its market share. Compaq's only setback at this time was the price of its PDA. At $699, the iPaq was more expensive than its competitors' products. With the merger of HP and Compaq, the market for the iPaq had the potential to increase through the combined efforts of these two leaders in personal computing.

RIM/BLACKBERRY 957

With more solid financial backing, Blackberry should become a force in the market. The Blackberry 957 had PDA and phone capabilities, with a battery that lasted up to 80 hours. Blackberry was the first to develop the thumb keyboards and was widely preferred by its users. Compatible with applications such as Outlook and corporate networks, Blackberry had more than 13,000 companies using its product. Although the Blackberry 957 could not receive attachments via e-mail, the system was always ready to receive mail. Even with a price tag of $499, Blackberry was struggling to improve its financial performance.

SAMSUNG SPH-M330

The Samsung PDA was positioned to compete directly with the Handspring Treo, Blackberry, and Kyocera models. The SPH-M330 had a color screen, support for an external camera, and cellular capability, and it ran on the Palm OS. The device also used gpsOne, a service that could display a map of the user's location and immediate vicinity on the LCD screen. Samsung was to launch the product through Sprint PCS but still lacked the brand recognition of Handspring and the other market-share leaders.

KYOCERA SMARTPHONE QCP 6035

Kyocera was Japan's version of the smart phone. The PDA portion of the device ran on the Palm OS and was compatible with most third-party applications. Kyocera was new to the U.S. market but would likely thrive in the Japanese market, which was usually protected by strict tariffs and import regulations.

NOKIA 9290 COMMUNICATOR

The Nokia 9290 Communicator was released into the U.S. market in 2002. It ran on the Symbian operating system and offered a full-color screen. The 9290 was capable of sending and receiving images, sound, and video clips. The handheld combined phone, fax, e-mail, calendar, and Internet capabilities as well as support for PC applications such as Microsoft Word, Excel, and PowerPoint. It was marketed as "the one device that does it all" and listed for $599.

MICROSOFT POCKET PC PHONE EDITION

Microsoft was focused on the enterprise/corporate users who used products that were compatible with the operating systems and software controlled by Microsoft. It was more profitable to sell and support 5,000 Pocket PCs to one business than to 5,000 consumers. Microsoft's deep pockets and R&D capability posed the largest threat to reposition the PDA/phone market share. Although the product did not possess the capabilities of the Treo, Microsoft had just entered this market. The current device provided access to Outlook, e-mail

Exhibit 3

PDA Worldwide Market Share, 2001 and 2002

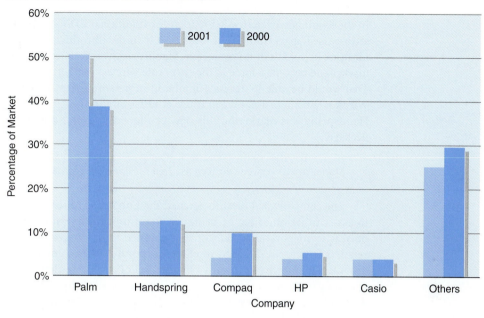

Exhibit 3 shows the market shares for key companies in the PDA market. Exhibit 4 shows growth in the number of units shipped.

functions, and browsing. It was to be eventually tied into Microsoft's new Mobile Information Server software, which acted as a liaison between phones and exchange. The Microsoft Pocket PC 2002 Phone Edition combined a phone and an organizer into a device that contained versions of Microsoft Word and Excel with an Internet browser. The device listed for $549.

Exhibit 3 shows the market shares for key companies in the PDA market. **Exhibit 4** shows growth in the number of units shipped.

Exhibit 4

Percentage Growth in Number of Devices Shipped

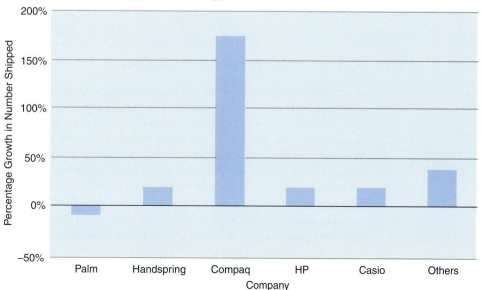

Handspring's Strategy for the Treo Communicators

In the seemingly overcrowded market for traditional PDAs, Handspring was committed to setting itself apart from the competition with the introduction of the Treo line of communicators. In pursuit of this objective, Handspring was seeking to reach beyond the consumer market and become a force in the corporate wireless market. Corporate customers using the Treo would be able to access e-mail and more sophisticated corporate data through the Wireless Business Engine, or they could opt for the try-then-buy desktop software. Handspring was marketing this new product as "several digital products all in one tiny package".

Management viewed the Treo as: *Treo = Phone + Organizer + E-mail + Web*

The company had recently formed the Enterprise Alliance Partnership (EAP) Program to assist in its objective of bringing communications solutions and wireless handheld devices to corporations. Handspring planned to maximize its existing relationships with retailers, enterprise-focused resellers, corporate systems integrators, and wireless service providers to branch out toward a broader set of corporate clients. A primary example of the company's commitment to the EAP Program was its highly collaborative experience in developing the Sprint PCS Treo 300. The Treo 300, scheduled for release in fall 2002, was designed exclusively for Sprint's nationwide 3G data network. According to Handspring COO Colligan, "By working with the best integrators and back-end software providers in the industry, we can leverage each other's experience to give corporate customers exactly what they want."[10]

Handspring was also committed to increasing its marketing and distribution channels through similar partnership arrangements. On December 17, 2001, Handspring announced a strategic marketing and sales partnership with Neomar, a leading developer of wireless enterprise software solutions. The companies intended to work together on product evaluation, testing, and training. They would also combine sales and marketing efforts for Handspring's Visor and Treo product lines with Neomar's mobile infrastructure software for corporate customers.[11] Other strategic partnerships included Wireless Knowledge, Inc. (a subsidiary of QUALCOMM, Inc.), Visto Corporation, Aether Systems, AvantGo, Extended Systems, and Synchrologic.

HOW IMPORTANT IS THE MICROSOFT OS?

According to Neil Ward-Dutton of Ovum, most consumers of PDAs were business users who were reimbursed by their companies. The general consumer market was not yet developed. This gave Microsoft and companies using the Microsoft operating system an advantage over Handspring's use of the Palm operating system. Company IT departments preferred products that used the same operating system as the company computer systems.[12] The Microsoft Pocket PC ran versions of Word and Excel. Other people contended that compatibility with the desktop was more important than compatibility with back-end applications.[13] In a 2001 interview with Business 2.0, Jeff Hawkins claimed that he did not believe the operating system was nearly as important to handhelds as it was to PCs. When asked if he had made a decision to use another operating system in lieu of continuing to license Palm's technology, Hawkins responded, "Long term, if Handspring grows as large as I think it will be . . . it is almost certain that we will have products that do not run on Palm. But that is not a product announcement."[14]

ENSURING PROFITABILITY PROJECTIONS ON THE BASIS OF TREO'S INITIAL SUCCESS

In the midst of Handspring's attempts to refocus its strategy on the communicator market, the young company was still struggling to achieve profitability. It had had a net loss every year since its inception.[15] While its sales were increasing, net profit was decreasing. Worldwide, the market for PDAs was increasing. According to Gartner Dataquest, the number of PDAs shipped increased 18% from 2001 to 2002.[16] Handspring's net profit, however, decreased as a result of downward pricing pressures from an increasing number of competitors. Gross margins fell from 31% to 9% during fiscal year 2001. Although Handspring received an additional $57 million in funding in January 2002, Dubinsky knew that the shareholders were expecting profitability in the near future.

Dubinsky was reviewing her comments from the company's quarterly and fiscal year end conference call for June 30, 2002. During the conference call, Handspring announced that Hawkins had recently formed the nonprofit Redwood Neuroscience Institute to pursue his lifelong passion for brain research. He would be splitting his time between the institute and serving as Handspring's Chief Product Officer and Chairman of the Board of Directors. Now that Hawkins was no longer 100% focused on Handspring, Dubinsky wanted to assure shareholders that the company would continue to successfully execute on its plans for the Treo communicators in both the near and long terms.

When Handspring unveiled its plans to transition to a communicator-based company, Dubinsky also predicted profitability by mid-2002. However, consumers were still taking a wait-and-see approach and looking for a compelling technological breakthrough to convince them that an upgrade to a communicator was warranted. Consumer reluctance combined with an economic slowdown prevented the company from achieving its fiscal year end profitability as predicted.

Although profitability objectives were still unmet, Dubinsky reported that the Treo was being well received in the marketplace, with more than 93,000 units shipped to date. The Treo product line had significantly improved margins from 9.2% to 24.5% over the prior fiscal year end. Unlike the Visor product line, the Treo products were not experiencing any pricing pressure from competing products. Telecommunications service providers were reportedly very happy with the Treo line, and studies indicated that Treo users represented a 20% to 90% increase in average revenue per user over traditional cell phone users.

Handspring remained confident that its new line of Treo communicators would succeed in the marketplace and revised its outlook by stating that the company intended to achieve profitability by the second quarter, ending December 30, 2002. Dubinsky needed to decide how Handspring could best realize this goal and considered the following approaches to ensure that the company's profitability objectives were met:

1. Accelerate the company's plan to phase out of the Visor product line and concentrate all of Handspring's resources on the development and marketing of the Treo communicators through increased alliances with telecommunications service providers.

2. Dedicate resources to a costly marketing and advertising campaign to increase awareness of communicators rather than rely on the early adopters of the new Treo products to educate other consumers.

3. Focus resources on developing an operating system to compete with products offered by Palm, Microsoft, and Symbian.

Financial Performance

Exhibit 5 shows Handspring's consolidated statement of operations, and Exhibit 6 shows its consolidated balance sheet.

Exhibit 5

Consolidated Statements of Operations: Handspring, Inc.
(Dollar amounts in thousands, except per share amounts)

Year Ending	June 29, 2002	June 30, 2001	July 1, 2000
Revenue	$240,651	$ 370,943	$101,937
Costs and operating expenses			
Cost of revenue	205,917	292,311	69,921
Research and development	24,739	23,603	10,281
Selling, general and administrative	85,612	145,132	42,424
In-process research and development	—	12,225	—
Amortization of deferred stock compensation and intangibles[1]	20,181	32,830	40,077
Total costs and operating expenses	336,449	506,101	162,703
Loss from operations	(95,798)	(135,158)	(60,766)
Interest and other income, net	5,259	12,195	675
Loss before taxes	(90,539)	(122,963)	(60,091)
Income tax provision	1,050	3,000	200
Net loss	$ (91,589)	$(125,963)	$ (60,291)
Basic and diluted net loss per share	$(0.71)	$(1.21)	$(1.77)
Shares used in calculating basic and diluted net loss per share	128,221	103,896	34,015

Note: 1. Amortization of deferred stock compensation and intangibles:

Cost of revenue	$ 2,586	$ 4,521	$ 5,904
Research and development	4,672	6,926	8,059
Selling, general and administrative	12,923	21,383	26,114
	$ 20,181	$ 32,830	$ 40,077

Source: Handspring, Inc., *SEC Form 10-K*, June 29, 2002, p. 37.

Exhibit 6

Consolidated Balance Sheets: Handspring, Inc.
(Dollar amounts in thousands, except share and per share amounts)

Year Ending	June 29, 2002	June 30, 2001
Assets		
Current assets		
Cash and cash equivalents	$ 85,554	$ 87,580
Short-term investments	15,235	33,943
Accounts receivable, net of allowance for doubtful accounts of $3,711 and $2,239, as of June 29, 2002, and June 30, 2001, respectively	20,491	12,850
Prepaid expenses and other current assets	3,667	19,473
Inventories	20,084	2,857
Total current assets	145,031	156,703
Long-term investments	50,644	80,237
Property and equipment, net	19,092	15,041
Other assets	1,408	1,254
Total assets	$216,175	$253,235
Liabilities and Stockholders' Equity		
Current liabilities		
Accounts payable	$ 44,490	$ 37,881
Accrued liabilities	48,779	70,152
Total current liabilities	93,269	108,033
Commitments and contingencies		
Stockholders' equity		
Preferred stock, $0.001 par value per share, 10,000,000 shares authorized; nil shares issued and outstanding at June 29, 2002, and June 30, 2001	—	—
Common stock, $0.001 par value per share, 1,000,000,000 shares authorized; 143,126,516 and 129,949,768 shares issued and outstanding at June 29, 2002, and June 30, 2001, respectively	143	130
Additional paid-in capital	419,256	368,166
Deferred stock compensation	(9,468)	(29,445)
Accumulated other comprehensive income (loss)	(793)	994
Accumulated deficit	(286,232)	(194,643)
Total stockholders' equity	122,906	145,202
Total liabilities and stockholders' equity	$216,175	$253,235

Note: The notes were deleted.
Source: Handspring, Inc., *SEC Form 10-K*, June 29, 2002, p. 36.

Notes

1. S. Barnett, "Jeff Hawkins," *Pen Computing* (April 2001), www.pencomputing.com/palm/Pen33/hawkins1.html.
2. *Ibid.*
3. *Ibid.*
4. P. Dillon, "The Next Small Thing," *Fast Company* (June 1998), www.fastcompany.com/online/15/smallthing.html.
5. J. Lardner, "Hawkins Talks," *Business 2.0* (March 2001).
6. V. Hua, "Three in One: Meet the Innovative Force Behind the New Treo, Which Combines PDA, Wireless Internet Access and a Mobile Phone," *San Francisco Chronicle* (January 6, 2002).
7. "Future Trends for Mobile Technologies Outlined by Gartner," *EDP Weekly's IT Monitor* (April 8, 2002) p. 5.
8. "Palm, Handspring Fighting a Losing Battle Against Microsoft?" *CommWeb* (April 2, 2002).
9. "Palm and Handspring May Be Victims of Mobile Convergence," *Europemedia* (March 25, 2002).
10. J. Wrolstad, "Handspring Vaults Toward Corporate Market," CRMDaily.com (November 13, 2001), www.crmdaily.com/perl/story/14751.html.
11. www.handspring.com/company/pr/pr_neomar_121701.html.
12. "PDA Market Stumbles As Yuppie Buyers Dry Up," *Ovum Comments* (April 4, 2002).
13. C. Zeite, "PDA Wars: Round Two," *InformationWeek.com* (April 1, 2002).
14. J. Lardner.
15. Handspring, *SEC Filing 10-Q* (February 12, 2002).
16. "Worldwide PDA Shipments Scoot Up," *PDA Cortex* (February 19, 2002, April 9, 2002).

case 12

Apple Computer, Inc. (2000): Here We Go Again

David B. Croll, Gordon P. Croll, and Andrew J. Croll

The Warm Glow of Success

It was 10 days before the July 19, 2000, Macworld trade show in New York, when Apple Computer, Inc., Chief Executive Steven P. Jobs once again wowed the masses with his P.T. Barnum-style product introductions. First came the small stuff: a see-through plastic keyboard and a sleek mouse. Then, off came the covers from new versions of Apple's popular iMac computer—now in four rich new colors, including ruby and indigo. Finally the climax—an eight-inch cube-shaped Mac that packed Apple's most powerful technology into a clear plastic case about the size of a toaster.

The reporter *Business Week* sent to the trade show gushed "Since returning three years ago to the company he founded, Jobs, 44, has worked the most unlikely comeback since the 1969 Amazin' Mets."[1] Close to death in 1997 with mounting losses and shriveling market share, Apple was back to making the most stylish products. Revenues were up 17% to $1.8 billion in the quarter reported on July 18. The stock was up eight-fold since Jobs returned. Stock analysts expected 25% plus revenue growth in the year that ended September 30, 2001 (see **Exhibits 1** and **2**).[2]

Thanks to the coolness factor of Apple's products, they had gotten away with charging up to 25% more than their competitors for a machine with similar capabilities. That helped Apple gain a gross profit margin of 29.8% in the quarter ending June 30. More amazing is that in a company known for its free-spirited, free-spending ways Apple had become a master of operating efficiencies. Jobs slashed expenses from $8.1 billion in 1997 to $5.7 billion in 1999. This was accomplished by outsourcing manufacturing, trimming inventories, shifting 25% of sales to an online store, and slicing the number of distributors from the double digits to two.[3]

Three Months Later

Under the headline "Apple Computer Plunges 52%, Drags Down Rest of Market"[4] the *Wall Street Journal* noted that on Friday, September 30, 2000, the value of a share of Apple Computer, Inc., dropped from $53.00 to $25.75 a share in heavy trading on the Nasdaq

This case was prepared by Professor David B. Croll of the McIntire School of Commerce at the University of Virginia; Gordon P. Croll, President and Founder of Cavalier Videography of Charlottesville; and Andrew J. Croll of The Discovery School of Virginia. This case was edited for SMBP-9th Edition. This case may not be reproduced in any form without written permission of the copyright holder, David B. Croll. Copyright © 2001 by David B. Croll.

Exhibit 1

Yes, Steve, You Fixed It. Congrats!

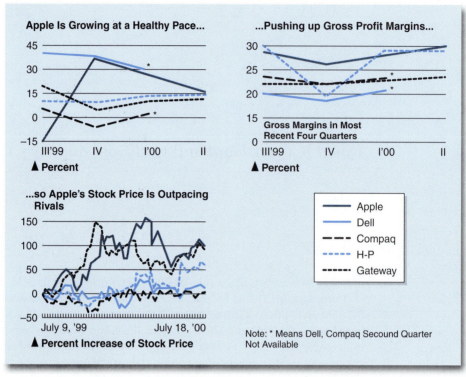

Apple Is Growing at a Healthy Pace...

▲ Percent

...Pushing up Gross Profit Margins...

Gross Margins in Most Recent Four Quarters

▲ Percent

...so Apple's Stock Price Is Outpacing Rivals

July 9, '99 — July 18, '00

▲ Percent Increase of Stock Price

Apple
Dell
Compaq
H-P
Gateway

Note: * Means Dell, Compaq Secound Quarter Not Available

Source: *Business Week* (July 31, 2000), pp. 104, 105.

Stock Market (see **Exhibit 3**).[5] The loss came after the Cupertino, California, personal-computer maker issued a warning late Thursday 9/29 that its fiscal fourth quarter profits were predicted to be far less than expected. Apple Computer's fiscal year 2000 ended on September 30. By contrast when an embattled Apple released a far more dire news release prompting one analyst at the time to question "the viability of the whole turnaround plan." Apple's shares fell just 18% that day.[6] What was it about Apple now that had the market spooked?

The Stock Market in Year 2000

In the year 2000 investors lived through one of the most extraordinary years in stock-market history. The rapid drop of technology and Internet stocks marked the end of what many consider the U.S.'s biggest financial mania of the last 100 years. Yet it was a drop that left much of the market relatively unscathed.

The Nasdaq Composite Index plunged 39.3%, the worst year since it was created in 1971, giving back almost all of 1999's record increase. Its peak-to-trough 54% plunge represented a loss of $3.3 trillion in paper wealth, equivalent, in dollars, to one third of the houses in America sliding into the ocean. But the Dow Jones Industrial Average fell only 6.2% for the year. Though that broke a nine-year winning streak and represented its worst calendar year since 1981, the Dow's peak-to-trough decline of just 16% was less than that of 1990. The

Exhibit 2

Steve Job's Unfinished Business

Apple has been winning back U.S. market share since 1997. Still, it's nowhere near its peak as a leader in home and education products.
(All based on U.S. unit sales)

Home Market

Maker	1994	Maker	1997	Maker	1999
Packard Bell	32.4%	Packard Bell NEC	23.3%	Compaq	19.0%
Apple	**14.7**	Compaq	18.8	H-P	16.1
Compaq	11.5	Gateway	11.1	Gateway	15.3
IBM	6.1	IBM	7.0	Emachine	11.0
Gateway	5.5	Acer	5.9	Packard Bell NEC	7.3
		Apple	**5.0**	**Apple**	**7.1**
Others	29.8	Others	28.9	Others	24.2

Business Market

Maker	1994	Maker	1997	Maker	1999
Compaq	14.2%	Compaq	15.7%	Dell	22.4%
IBM	10.1	Dell	12.8	Compaq	15.0
Apple	**6.4**	IBM	9.5	IBM	9.2
Dell	5.9	H-P	8.0	H-P	6.0
Gateway	5.3	Toshiba	5.6	Toshiba	4.7
		Apple	**1.4**	**Apple**	**1.3**
Others	58.1	Others	47.0	Others	41.4

Education Market

Maker	1994	Maker	1997	Maker	1999
Apple	**47.0%**	**Apple**	**27.2%**	Dell	21.4%
IBM	8.5	Compaq	13.2	**Apple**	**16.5**
Dell	4.3	Dell	10.7	Gateway	13.6
Gateway	3.3	Gateway	7.8	Compaq	9.2
Compaq	3.2	IBM	6.9	IBM	3.8
Others	33.7	Others	34.2	Others	35.5

Source: Business Week (July 31, 2000), p. 108.

Standard & Poor's 500-stock index lost 10.1% in 2000, its worst since 1977. But excluding its technology components, the index was down just 4% (see **Exhibit 4**).[7]

By contrast, the 1973–74 bear market affected all stocks. The Nasdaq's 60% slide then was the only time it had fallen further than the previous year. The Dow lost 45% and the S&P 500 ended 1974 at its lowest levels since 1963. Year 2001 began with investors wondering if Nasdaq's drop was the vanguard of a broad-based bear market. The answer depended mostly on whether the economy's downshift in the end of 2000 was a pause in the longest expansion in a century or the first stage of a recession. UBS Warburg strategist Edward Kerschner thought Apple was one of the five most attractive opportunities to own stocks in 20 years, and he predicted the S&P 500 would gain 30% in 2001. Strategists as a group were the most bullish they had been in the 16 years Merrill Lynch surveyed them. Merrill's head

Exhibit 3
Apple's Unseasonable Fall

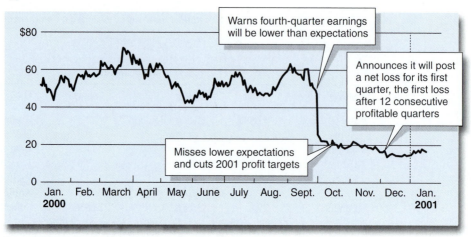

Source: *Wall Street Journal* (January 18, 2000), p. B8.

of quantitative research, Richard Bernstein, found this enthusiasm ironic, given that cash and bonds both performed better than stocks in 2000, and that markets usually bottom at the point of maximum pessimism, not optimism.[8]

Historical Background

Founded in a California garage in 1976, Apple created the personal computer revolution with powerful, yet easy-to-use, machines for the desktop. Steve Jobs sold his Volkswagen van and Steve Wozniak hocked his programmable calculator to raise seed money to begin the business.

Exhibit 4
Tale of the Tickers

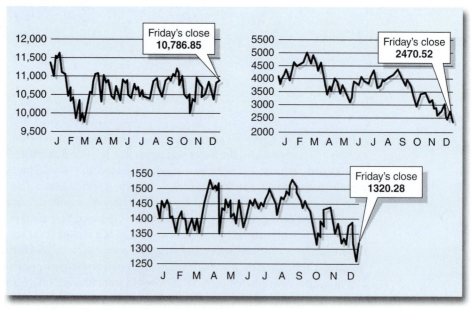

Source: *Washington Post* (Sunday, December 31, 2000).

Not long afterward, a mutual friend helped recruit A. C. "Mike" Markkula to help market the company and give it a million-dollar image. All three founders had left the company's management team in the 1980s but Mike Markkula remained as a member of the Board of Directors until August 1997.

The early success of Apple was attributed largely to marketing and technological innovation. In the high growth industry of personal computers in the early 1980s, Apple grew quickly. It stayed ahead of its competitors by contributing key products that stimulated the development of software specifically for their computers. Landmark programs such as Visicalc (forerunner of Lotus 1-2-3 and other spreadsheet programs) were developed first for the Apple II. Apple also secured early dominance in the education and consumer markets by awarding hundreds of thousands of dollars in grants to schools and individuals for the development of education software.

Even with enormous competition, Apple's revenues continued to grow at unprecedented rates, reaching $583.1 million by fiscal 1982. The introduction of the Macintosh graphical user interface in 1984, which included icons, pull-down menus, and windows, became the catalyst for desktop publishing and instigated the second technological revolution attributable to Apple. Apple kept the architecture of the Macintosh proprietary, i.e., it could not be cloned like the "open system" IBM PC. This allowed the company to charge a premium for its distinctive "user-friendly" features.

A shakeout in the personal computer industry began in 1983, when IBM entered the PC market, first affecting companies selling low-priced machines to consumers. Companies that made strategic blunders or that lacked sufficient distribution or brand awareness of their products disappeared. By 1985, only the largest computer and software companies survived.

In 1985, amid a slumping market, Apple saw the departure of its founders, Jobs and Wozniak, and instituted a massive reorganization to streamline operations and expenses. Under the leadership of John Sculley, Chief Executive Officer and Chairman of the Board, the company engineered a remarkable turnaround. Macintosh sales gained momentum throughout 1986 and 1987. Sales increased 40% from $1.9 billion to $2.7 billion in fiscal 1987, and earnings jumped 41% to $217 million.

In the early 1990s, Apple sold more personal computers than any other computer company. Net sales grew to over $7 billion, net income to over $540 million, and earnings per share to $4.33. The period from 1993 to 1995 was a time of considerable change in the management of Apple. In June 1993, John Sculley was forced to resign and Michael H. Spindler was appointed CEO of the company. Many of the company's executives advocated Apple's merging with another company, and when that didn't happen left Apple.

Spindler was forced out and Gilbert Amelio was hired from outside of Apple to serve as CEO. Amelio's regime presided over an accelerated loss of market share, deteriorating earnings, and stock that had lost half of its value. Apple had failed to license the Mac operating system to other manufacturers early enough that it might today be as ubiquitous as Windows. Both Amelio and his immediate predecessor, Michael Spindler, failed to accept any of the buyout offers proposed to Apple. By the end of Amelio's tenure, Apple seemed to be in utter disarray. In July of 1997 Gilbert Amelio resigned and was replaced by Steve Jobs, one of the two founders of the company. Jobs was back 14 years after being replaced as CEO by John Sculley.

Corporate Governance

Exhibit 5 lists the seven members of Apple's Board of Directors, a board that has not changed since the profound change that took place when Steve Jobs returned as CEO in 1997. Mr. Jobs was the only internal member of Apple's Board of Directors. Apple's top management as of October 1, 2000, is listed in **Exhibit 6**.[9]

Exhibit 5

Board of Directors: Apple Computer, Inc.

William V. Campbell has been Chairman of the Board of Directors of Intuit, Inc., since August of 1998. From September 1999 to January 2000, Mr. Campbell acted as Chief Executive Officer of Intuit.

Gareth C.C. Chang is the Chief Executive Officer and Chairman of the Board of PingPong Technology. He is also the Executive Chairman of click2Asia.com. Formally, Mr. Chang served as Chairman and Chief Executive Officer of STAR TV and Executive Director of News Corporation. He is currently a member of the Advisory Council of Nike, Inc., and serves on the board of SRS Labs Inc.

Millard S. Drexler has been Chief Executive Officer of Gap, Inc., since 1995, and President since 1987. Mr. Drexler has been a member of the Board of Directors of Gap, Inc., since November 1983. He also served as the President of the Gap Division from 1983 to 1987.

Lawrence J. Ellison has been Chief Executive Officer and a Director of Oracle Corporation since he cofounded Oracle in May 1977, and was President of Oracle until June 1996. Mr. Ellison has been Chairman of the Board of Oracle since June 1995.

Steven P. Jobs is one of the company's Cofounders and currently serves as its Chief Executive Officer. Mr. Jobs is also the Chairman and Chief Executive Officer of Pixar Animation Studios. In addition, Mr. Jobs cofounded NeXT Software, Inc. and served as the Chairman and Chief Executive Officer of NeXT from 1985 until 1997 when NeXT was aquired by the Company. Mr Jobs is currently a Director of Gap, Inc.

Arthur D. Levinson, Ph.D., has been President, Chief Executive Officer, and a Director of Genentech, Inc., since July 1995. He joined Genentech in 1980 and served in a number of executive positions, including Senior Vice President of R&D from 1993 to 1995.

Jerome B. York is Chairman and Chief Executive Officer of Micro Warehouse, Inc. Previously, he was Vice Chairman of Tracinda Corporation from September 1995 to October 1999. In May 1993 he joined International Business Machines Corporation as Senior Vice President and Chief Financial Officer, and served as a Director of IBM from January 1995 to August 1995. Prior to joining IBM, Mr. York served in a number of executive positions at Chrysler Corporation, including Executive Vice President–Finance and Chief Financial Officer from May 1990 to May 1993. Mr. York is also a Director of MGM Mirage, Inc., Metro-Goldwyn-Mayer, Inc., and National TechTeam, Inc.

Apple Computer, Inc.'s head of worldwide sales announced his retirement two weeks after the company warned of slowing product sales. Mitch Mandich, a longtime member of the management team of Apple's Chief Executive, Steve Jobs, announced he would retire at the end of December 2000.

Mr. Mandich temporarily was replaced by Tim Cook, Apple's Senior Vice President of Operations. The unexpected retirement of Mandich hints at trouble at the computer maker. "If Mitch is taking the fall for this, it's undeserved," said Steven Fortuna, a First Vice President at Merrill Lynch & Co.[10] Mitch Mandich was the first member of Apple's current executive team to leave since Mr. Jobs assembled the team in 1997.

Mr. Mandich, who previously worked with Mr. Jobs at NeXT Software, Inc., followed him to Apple in 1997. He was quickly promoted from Vice President of Apple's North America Business Division to Senior Vice President of North American Sales before taking responsibility for worldwide sales.

Current Situation in the Education Market

Many schools and universities, the mainstays of Apple's customer base for years, were phasing out their Macs in favor of personal computers based on the rival Windows operating system. The trend accelerated over the 12-month period ending September 30, 2000. In 1999, Dell moved ahead of Apple and became the largest supplier to education claiming 15.1% of the

Exhibit 6

Executive Officers: Apple Computer, Inc.

Fred D. Anderson, Executive Vice President and Chief Financial Officer (age 56), joined the Company in April 1996. Prior to joining the Company, Mr. Anderson was Corporate Vice President and Chief Financial Officer of Automatic Data Processing, Inc., a position he held from August 1992 to March 1996.

Timothy D. Cook, Senior Vice President, Worldwide Operations, and interim Senior Vice President, Worldwide Sales, Service & Support (age 40), joined the Company in February. Prior to joining the Company Mr. Cook held the position of Vice President, Corporate Materials, for Compaq Computer Corporation. Previous to his work at Compaq, Mr. Cook was the Chief Operating Officer of the Reseller Division at Intelligent Electronics. Mr. Cook also spent 12 years with IBM, most recently as Director of North American fulfillment.

Nancy R. Heinen, Senior Vice President, General Counsel, and Secretary (age 44), joined the Company in September. Prior to joining the Company, Ms. Heinen held the position of Vice President, General Counsel, and Secretary of the Board of Directors at NeXT from February 1994 until the acquisition of NeXT by the Company in February 1997.

Ronald B. Johnson, Senior Vice President, New Business Development (age 42), joined the Company in February 1997. Before joining the Company, Mr. Johnson was Executive Vice President and Chief Operating Officer of FirePower Systems Incorporated, from May 1993 to August 1996. Mr. Johnson also serves as member of the Board of Directors of Immersion Corporation.

Avadis Tevanian, Jr., Ph.D., Senior Vice President, Software Engineering (age 39), joined the Company in February 1997 upon the Company's acquisition of NeXT. With NeXT, Dr. Tevanian held several positions, including Vice President, Engineering, from April 1995 to February 1997. Prior to April 1995, Dr. Tevanian worked as an engineer with NeXT and held several management positions.

Sima Tamaddon, Senior Vice President, Applications (age 43), joined the Company in September 1997. Mr. Tamaddon has also served with the Company in the position of Senior Vice President Worldwide Service and Support, and Vice President and General Manager, Newton Group. Before joining the Company, Mr. Tamaddon held the position of Vice President, Europe with NeXT from September 1996 through March 1997. From August 1994 to August 1996, Mr. Tamaddon held the position of Vice President, Professional Services with NeXT.

Mitchell Mandich, Senior Vice President, Worldwide Sales (age 52) joined the Company in February 1997 upon the Company's acquisition of NeXT. Mr. Mandich has also served the Company in the position of Vice President, North American Business Division. Prior to joining the Company, Mr. Mandich held the position of Vice President, Worldwide Sales and Service, with NeXT from December 1995 through February 1997.

market (see **Exhibit 7**).[11] Apple dropped to a 12.5% market share, down from its 14.6% share in 1998 and its 16.5% share in 1999.

The shift hurt Apple's bottom line. Education had accounted for 40% of Apple's total U.S. sales over the past few quarters. Apple machines, however, were still used in 40% of the schools across the country, according to market tracker Quality Education Data, and the computer maker continued to make numerous education sales.

"Apple has done well in the past to show they're on the side of education," said Wayne Grant, Chief Executive of the educational software company ImagiWorks, Inc.[12] When the big push to wire classrooms more than a decade ago started, Apple jumped on the market and Macs became educators' top choice because of their ease of use and friendly graphical interface. The company deluged the market with special marketing programs, often at a discount, and created a widespread network of education sales agents. "But Apple has come under more pressure in pricing and ease of use recently as Windows 98 has come on board. It's more difficult for Apple to differentiate itself now," said Charles Smulders, an analyst at Gartner Group.[13]

Exhibit 7

Apple Crunch

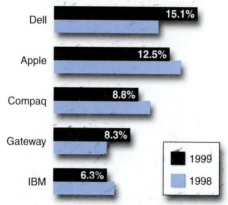

Top education PC vendors, by market share

Source: *Wall Street Journal* (October 17, 2000), pp. B1, B4.

In addition, many educational software developers have migrated away from the Mac platform over the past few years, analysts say. "Software developers now develop for Windows only because they don't think the Mac market is big enough anymore," said Roger Kay, research manager at International Data Corp. "That's a crushing economic reality."[14]

Apple was doing what it could to hold onto the education niche. It hoped to sell iMacs with preloaded software, such as its popular iMovie video-editing program. It planned to launch its next generation operating system OS X to attract new software developers to the Mac platform.

Since the start of fiscal year 2000, Apple's education sales team had also undergone confusing changes, many schools complained. Mike Lorion, an Apple executive overseeing education sales, left the company and joined hand-held device maker Palm, Inc. After his departure, Apple eliminated its contracted education sales force and brought the team in-house. This resulted in Apple having far less direct contact with schools than it had. Instead, the company trained schools to deal with Apple primarily through the Internet. That left many educational districts displeased.

Such stumbles have given rivals like Dell and Gateway, Inc., an opportunity. Bill Rodrigues, Dell's Vice President in charge of education and health care, said Dell's sales to schools had grown so much over the previous two years that it split its education operations into a higher education unit and a K–12 division. Dell also boosted its education field operatives to more than 100 people across the United States, and it was partnering with software developers such as Computer Curriculum Corp. and Compass Learning Corp. to provide educational software solutions to schools.

Competition[15]

The personal computer industry was highly competitive and was characterized by aggressive pricing practices, downward pressure on gross margins, frequent introduction of new products, short product life cycles, continual improvement in product price/performance characteristics, price sensitivity on the part of consumers, and a large number of competitors. Rapid technological advances in software performance features based on existing or emerging industry standards had also characterized the personal computer industry. As the personal computer industry and its customers placed more reliance on the Internet, an increasing number of Internet devices that were smaller and simpler than traditional personal computers competed for market share with Apple's existing products. Further, several competitors have either targeted or announced their intention to target certain of the company's key market segments, including consumer, education, and design and publishing. These competitors had greater financial, marketing, manufacturing, and technological resources, as well as broader product lines and larger installed customer bases than those of Apple.

Apple was the only maker of hardware using the Mac OS. The Mac OS had a minority market share in the personal computer market, which was dominated by makers of computers utilizing Microsoft Windows operating systems. Apple's future operating results and financial condition were substantially dependent on its ability to continue to develop improvements in the Macintosh platform in order to maintain perceived design and functional advantages over competing platforms.

Computer and Peripherals Industry

The computer and peripherals industry did not turn in quite as good a performance in year 2000 as had been expected. The sector's prospects for the next year, and at least through mid-decade, were good. It was widely expected by analysts that the industry would get off to a slow start in year 2000 because many businesses spent heavily in 1999 so they would correctly handle dates in the new century.

The second half of the year 2000 was expected to be better than the first half. However there were reports of slowing demand from some chipmakers, notably Intel, which raised fears that personal computer sales might be slowing. The strong dollar could trim overseas sales figures especially from Europe.

Over the next three to five years there should be continued growth in the industry. Businesses were going to continue to spend on computer gear to increase their efficiency and become more competitive. They were increasingly using the Internet to hook up with their customers and suppliers to cut costs and to speed up business processes. The increasing computerization of operations also meant more data were generated and stored electronically, which boosted demand for storage devices and printers to turn the digital data into hardcopy.[16]

COMPAQ COMPUTER

Compaq Computer Corp. was the second largest computer company in the world in 1999. It manufactured mainframes, servers, and workstations. Compaq also provided professional services that accounted for 52% of 1999 revenue, with commercial desktops and portables accounting for 32%, and personal computers for the consumer market 16%.

Compaq computer's effort to increase earnings growth was working. The commercial personal computer group returned to profitability after several periods of deficit results. New products with simpler designs and higher margins helped, as did lower costs aided by a shift to more direct sales. Whereas the commercial PC unit's focus in the past year has been on profitability rather than market share, management planned to also emphasize market share growth in the future. In Compaq's industry standard server business, sales benefited from shipments of a new ultra thin two-way server, as well as from companies building their Internet infrastructures.

However, Compaq still faced a number of challenges. The operating climate no doubt had become more difficult since mid-2000, especially in Europe, which together with the Middle East and Africa, accounted for about a third of their sales. It was also unclear whether the component shortages that held back shipments of Compaq's new AlphaServer in the June period will continue to restrain sales. At mid-year, there were over $200 million of orders for the AlphaServer in the backlog. Although Compaq now appeared on the recovery track, it still had a lot of work ahead of it.[17]

DELL COMPUTER

Dell Computer Corp. was the world's largest direct computer systems company in 1999. Dell made notebook and desktop computers, network servers, storage products, workstations, peripheral hardware, and computing software. They marketed their products via sales teams to corporate and institutional customers, as well as via the telephone and Internet. The majority of Dell's sales, 71%, were to the Americas; with 22% in Europe, Middle East, and Africa; and 7% in the Asia/Pacific market.

Dell Computer's top-line growth was slowing down. Management attributed the slowdown in sales to weak demand in Europe, lower sales to the U.S. government, and below-projected sales to small businesses worldwide. To recharge sales growth Dell announced price reductions across many product lines.

Dell's direct-to-consumer business model and efficient supplier alliances allowed it to keep its costs low. A continued shift in the sales mix from workstations to higher margined products was expected to enhance margins. The growth in Dell's cash flow seemed to be accelerating while its capital spending requirements were moderating, leaving it room to buy back stock, invest in promising technology ventures, and perhaps use some for acquisitions. The company expected to be successful in implementing its plans to expand overseas as well as in the storage systems market.[18]

GATEWAY, INC.

Gateway, Inc., manufactured, marketed, and supported a product line of Windows-compatible desktop, notebook, and subnotebook personal computers. The company marketed directly to businesses, individuals, government agencies, and educational institutions. Only 14.6% of their total sales were outside the United States.

While Dell computer saw its sales growth falter, Gateway's revenues rose by mid-year 2000. Strong consumer demand and "Gateway's limited exposure to the slowing corporate market" was given credit for this strong showing. Also, the move by management into products other than personal computers has been more profitable than even Gateway's management expected.

Gateway was no longer relying on processor chips from only one supplier. Using chips from both AMD and Intel broadened the company's product line and partially protected it from the processor shortages that occurred in the fall of 1999. Analysts predicted that dollar sales in the future would not rise as fast as earlier projected, due to falling prices not unit sales.[19]

INTERNATIONAL BUSINESS MACHINES CORPORATION

IBM Corporation was the world's largest supplier of advanced information processing technology and communication systems and services in 1999. The revenue breakdown was 43% hardware, 37% global services, 14% software, and 6% other. Business outside of the United States accounted for 58% of total revenue.

IBM had some positive and negative results in year 2000. On the minus side, unfavorable currency trends were having a negative impact on revenues. During the year, the hard disk drives—the company's new 10,000 RPM drives—were not ready when they were expected to be, causing personal computers to be a drag on total sales.

A new generation system, 309s, that was introduced in 2000 was expected to provide an increase in sales with a greater increase in year 2001. Also on the plus side, the amount of new service contract signings had picked up, thanks in part to strong demand for the company's e-business services. The demand for the company's servers, especially Web servers, and high-end hard disk drives improved.

IBM was positioning itself for further growth. For one thing, management expected the company's new G7 mainframes to sell extremely well, since they would be much more powerful than the older G6 generation. However, the major increase in growth was likely to be in the services area. IBM was also investing in Web products and services and such growth areas as customer relation and supply-chain management. What's more, IBM was providing services, such as storage, Web hosting, and facilities for application service providers, on a rental basis.[20]

HEWLETT-PACKARD COMPANY

Hewlett-Packard Company was a leading provider of computing and imaging solutions and services for business and home. Its 1999 revenue breakdown was 43.7% imaging and printing systems, 42.6% computing systems, and 13.7% IT services. Business outside of the United States accounted for 55% of total revenue.

Year 2000 got off to a slow start, as a number of factors, including a sales mix shift to low-end home personal computers and printers, a drop in the yen–dollar exchange rate, and costs associated with an early retirement program dragged net income down. Growth increased in July thanks to strong demand for home personal computers, laptops, printers, and supplies and services.

The company was positioning itself to post good gains over the next five years. A new family of high-end servers that would round out that product line and was expected to boost sales. A shift to color printing in offices lifted sales of the company's color laser printers and the move to digital photography fueled demand for HP's color inkjet printers. Analysts thought that the company's emphasis on the fast-growing Internet infrastructure market would lead to good demand for its servers, storage products, and consulting and services. Finally, Hewlett-Packard was in talks to acquire the consulting business of PricewaterhouseCoopers for roughly $18 billion of cash and stock.[21]

Semiconductor Industry

In year 2000 some factors changed in the semiconductor industry. A considerable number of companies in the chip industry, including industry leader Intel, announced they were about to encounter earnings or revenue shortfalls. It appeared that most of the disappointment was stemming from the personal computer area, but there was also some concern about the wireless handset market.

Intel's management blamed their lower gains almost entirely on its European exposure. Indeed the company sold its personal computer chips in Europe in U.S. dollars, which made its products much more expensive due to a weak euro.

Many stocks in the semiconductor universe had experienced significant price erosion over the past few months. It appeared that there might be some potential signs that the boom in the chip market could be coming to an end. However this drop seemed to be almost entirely on the personal computer side of the industry.[22]

INTEL CORPORATION

Intel Corporation was a leading manufacturer of integrated circuits. These they marketed primarily to makers of personal computers. Their main products were microprocessors and memory chips. They also sold computer modules and boards and network products. Foreign business represented 57% of total revenue.

Intel achieved only modest 3% to 5% growth during 2000. Lackluster European demand was the primary reason for the low growth rate. Intel has canceled plans for the Timna microprocessor, which was targeted toward computers in the sub-$600 price category. Intel's management cited design delays and lackluster demand by personal computer makers. Furthermore, the introduction of the company's high-end Pentium 4 chip was delayed until the fourth quarter of 2000.

Analysts warned that Intel was subject to a high degree of volatility. The current decrease in growth that had occurred in the industry was mostly personal computer related. Intel's efforts to increase its stake in the communications arena was expected to help it diversify beyond the traditional computer market and add some stability to their earnings.[23]

MOTOROLA, INC.

Motorola, Inc., was a leading manufacturer of electronic equipment and components. Their product mix in 1999 was 39% personal communications; 19% semiconductor products; 21% network systems; 13% commercial, government, and industrial systems; and 8% other. Foreign business represented 63% of total sales.

Motorola's handset business had some problems, causing orders to be down 23% compared to 1999. The company stated that concerns over the previous year's supply problems led customers to preorder at very high levels, but since component shortages were no longer an issue, orders had consequently fallen. Motorola was intent on revitalizing the phone unit sales. It rolled out low-tier products and began the transition to mid- and high-tier digital devices.

The broadband communications sector of Motorola was achieving record results. This segment continued to exceed expectations due to surging demand for digital set-top terminals and cable modems. Additionally, momentum was building outside of North America for large sales.[24]

Computer Software and Services

Year 2000 was not a good year for the computer software and services industry. Businesses had spent heavily on new computer gear and software in 1999 to be sure that their systems could handle dates after the turn of the century. This overhang of equipment purchase had to be worked off before new systems were needed. The fall of the dot-com boom also restricted growth in software sector. Many of these ventures have shut down as profits failed to materialize and funds ran out.

Some analysts thought that spending on computer services and equipment would rise at a faster rate than the economy as a whole. There were some signs that demand was accelerating in Europe. If that were true, that drag on sales would be eliminated.

The trend to move more activities to computers wasn't likely to end any time soon. Now that the most basic business functions, such as accounting and human resources, were computerized, companies were moving additional activities, such as ordering, billing, and customer relationship management on to computers. These trends should continue to drive strong demand for software and services.[25]

MICROSOFT CORPORATION

Microsoft Corporation was the largest independent maker of software. Its fiscal year 2000 revenue breakdown was 41% Windows platforms (operating systems and server applications and Internet products); 46% productivity applications and development (desktop applications, server applications, and developer tools); 13% consumer, commerce, and other (learning and entertainment software and PC input devices).

The company suffered a big loss in June when the presiding judge in the antitrust suit ruled that the company had violated antitrust laws. He proposed that as a remedy the company should be broken into two parts and that restrictions should be placed on its operations.

But then, in September of 2000, the Supreme Court decided against accepting the case directly without having it go through the appeals process. That was expected to be good for Microsoft, because the appeals court previously ruled in the company's favor on other matters.

Microsoft continued to broaden and upgrade its product line it rolled out. In early 2000 the Windows 2000 Datacenter Server, its high-end server software for businesses. Coupled with new versions of its database offering and its messaging server, that was expected to enable it to make inroads against UNIX-based products. The Windows 2000 operating system was gaining ground in the corporate world and that should also boost sales of its applications product suite, Office 2000.

Microsoft's efforts to move into new areas, such as television set-top boxes and Internet access appeared to be paying off. The company was working to expand its Web-based offerings such as providing access to applications on a subscription basis over the Internet.[26]

Foreign and Domestic Operations and Geographic Data[27]

The United States represented Apple's largest geographic marketplace. Approximately 54% of the company's net sales in fiscal 2000 came from operations inside the United States. Sales margins on Apple products in foreign countries, and on sales of products that include components obtained from foreign suppliers, could be adversely affected by foreign currency exchange rate fluctuations.

Apple managed its business primarily on a geographic basis. There were four geographic segments within the Company, the Americas, Europe, Japan, and Asia-Pacific. Each geographic operating segment provided similar hardware and software products and similar services. The European segment included European countries as well as the Middle East and Africa. The Japan segment included only Japan, while the Asia-Pacific segment included Australia and Asia except for Japan.

Net sales and unit sales in the Americas segment increased 22% and 24%, respectively, during fiscal 2000. The growth of the Americas' net sales in 2000 was indicative of strong growth in unit sales of iMac and iBook and relatively flat unit sales of professionally oriented Macintosh systems.

Net sales in the Europe segment increased 38% during 2000 driven by a 53% increase in Macintosh unit sales. Growth in unit sales resulted from a 96% increase in combined unit sales of iMac and iBook and an increase of 19% in combined unit sales of the company's professionally oriented Macintosh systems.

Net sales in the Japan segment increased 57% to $1.345 billion in fiscal 2000 with Japan's Macintosh unit sales increased 39%. The fact that Japan's net sales rose at a higher rate than its unit sales reflects several factors. First iMac unit sales in Japan were relatively flat. Second, unit sales of iBook, which generally carry a higher price than iMac units, accounted for approximately 17% of Japan's total Macintosh unit sales. Third, Japan saw a 43% increase in combined unit sales of the company's professionally oriented Macintosh systems.

The majority of the increase in both net sales and unit sales in the Asia Pacific segment can be attributed to sales of the G4 Cube and iBook, both of which were introduced in the region during fiscal 2000. Macintosh unit sales in the Asia Pacific segment increased 37% due in large part from the general economic recovery experienced in the region.

Product Introductions[28]

Due to the highly volatile nature of the personal computer industry, which was characterized by dynamic customer demand patterns and rapid technological advances, Apple needed to continually introduce new products and technologies and enhance existing products in order to remain competitive. The success of new product introductions was dependent on a number of factors, including market acceptance, Apple's ability to manage the risks associated with product transitions, the availability of products in appropriate quantities to meet anticipated demand, and the risk that new products might have quality or other defects in the early stages of introduction.

During fiscal 2001 Apple planned to introduce a new client operating system, Mac OS X, which would offer advance functionality based on Apple and NeXT software technologies. Inability to successfully introduce Mac OS X on a timely basis, gain customer acceptance, obtain the commitment of developers to transition existing applications to run on Mac OS X, or ensure adequate backward compatibility of Mac OS X with applications authored for previous versions of the Mac OS, might have an adverse impact on Apple's operating results.

Inventory and Supply[29]

Apple has recorded a write-down of inventories of components and products that have become obsolete or are in excess of anticipated demand. Apple ended fiscal year 2000 with substantially more inventory in its distribution channels than planned due to the lower than expected unit sales of products in September. Apple currently anticipated a significant sequential decline in quarterly net sales during the December quarter of year 2000, due in part to the company's plan to reduce substantially the level of inventory in its distribution channels.

Although certain components essential to Apple's business were generally available from multiple sources, other key components (including microprocessors and application specific integrated circuits) were currently obtained from single sources. In addition, new products introduced by Apple often utilized custom components obtained from only one source until Apple evaluated whether there was a need for additional suppliers. Apple's ability to produce and market competitive products was dependent on the ability and desire of IBM and Motorola, the sole suppliers of the PowerPC RISC based microprocessor for the Macintosh computers.

Support from Third-Party Software Developers[30]

Apple Corporation believed that decisions by customers to purchase its personal computers, as opposed to a Windows based system, were often based on the availability of particular applications. Management believed the availability of software for its hardware products depended in part on third-party developers' perception of the relative benefits of developing, maintaining, and upgrading such software versus software for the larger Windows market. To the extent that financial losses in prior years and the minority market share held by Apple in the personal computer market had caused software developers to question Apple's prospects in the personal computer market, developers might not develop new application software or upgrade existing software.

In August 1997, Apple and Microsoft Corporation entered into patent cross-licensing and technology agreements. For a period of five years from August 1997, Microsoft would make future versions of its Microsoft Office and Internet Explorer products for the Mac OS. Although Microsoft had announced its intention to do so, these agreements did not require Microsoft to produce future versions of its products that were optimized to run on Mac OS X. While Apple's management believed its relationship with Microsoft had been and would continue to be beneficial, the relationship was for a limited term and did not cover many of the areas in which they competed. Accordingly, Microsoft's interest in producing application software for the Mac OS, including Mac OS X, might be influenced by Microsoft's perception of its interests as the vendor of the Windows operating system.

Education Market[31]

Several competitors of Apple have announced their intention to target the education market for personal computers. As a result, Apple's overall share of this market has declined. Additionally, net sales in the company's education market fell short of expectations by approximately $60 million during the September quarter of year 2000, the quarter most school purchases are made. This may have been the result of Apple's transition to a more direct sales model from a model heavily dependent on third-party sales agents. Failure to increase or maintain market share in Apple's traditionally strong education market could have serious impact on operating results.

Markets and Distribution[32]

Apple's customers were primarily in the education, creative, consumer, and business markets. Certain customers were attracted to Macintosh computers for a variety of reasons, including the reduced amount of training resulting from the intuitive ease of use, advanced graphics capabilities, industrial design features of the hardware products, ability of the computers to network and communicate with other computer systems, and availability of application software. Apple was one of the major suppliers of personal computers for both elementary and secondary school customers.

Apple distributed its products through wholesalers, resellers, national and regional retailers, and cataloguers. During fiscal 2000, a single distributor, Ingram Micro, Inc., accounted for approximately 11.5% of Apple's net sales. Apple also sold many of its products to consumers, certain education customers, and certain resellers either directly or through 1 of its online stores around the world. During fiscal 2000, net sales attributable to the company's online stores totaled approximately $1.7 billion.

Two years after practically disappearing from many U.S. retail stores, Apple Computer, Inc., was back on the shelves. This store invasion signaled a marked turnaround in Apple's rocky relationships with retailers. In the early to mid-1990s, many stores complained about inventory problems and battled over Apple's rigid sales rules. The company, for example, once set a $500,000 annual sales cap for dealers, cutting many small distributors on strong growth tracks out of much needed business. Apple, in the past, would often change its mind about who could sell to the big education market, causing turmoil among dealers while keeping them in the dark on fast changing product strategies. "Apple used to be among the worst companies to deal with for a long time," said Larry Mondry, chief operating officer of CompUSA, Inc. "Apple is a different company today."[33]

For retail outlets such as the Wiz, a 41-store northeastern electronics chain, this translated into a revived give-and-take with Apple. Three years ago, the Wiz stopped selling Apple products after demand for the computers stalled at the same time that Apple began trimming its retail presence. Then in 1999, after Apple posted strong sales increases led by strong sales of its PowerBook laptops and its G4 high-end desktop model, Wiz executives called the computer company back. Unlike before when Apple didn't respond to many retailers' requests, the company was "very receptive" and "wanted us badly," says Tasso Koken, the Wiz's Executive Vice President of Merchandising.[34]

Behind this latest change was a renewed focus on giving customers a particular experience when they shop for Apple computers, an issue brought to the forefront by Steve Jobs. By improving the shopping environment for Apple buyers, marketing experts said, the company hoped to attract more of the first-time computer buyers. In a market inundated with lower-cost machines, Apple needed to capitalize on its successful iMac line, which had set milestones in computer design and offered candy-colored hardware that made for an attractive store display.

Besides renewing ties with the likes of the Wiz, Apple recruited department store chain Sears Roebuck & Co. in May 1999 to carry its computers. Apple then added new distributors, middlemen that sold to a variety of retailers, including mom-and-pop shops. The retail push was also going global to Europe and Japan, where Apple traditionally enjoyed strong sales. Stores such as Japan's DeoDeo Corp. and Comp Mart Company Ltd. boasted distinct Apple spaces.

Legal Proceedings[35]

Apple Corporation was subject to certain legal proceedings and claims, which have arisen in the ordinary course of business and had not been fully adjudicated. In the opinion of management, the company did not have a potential liability related to any existing legal proceedings and claims that will have a material adverse effect on its financial condition or operating results.

Financials[36]

During the fiscal year 2000, Apple experienced a 30% increase in net sales the result of a 32% increase in Macintosh unit sales. This increase in Macintosh unit sales was primarily attributable to increased sales of iMac, the company's moderately priced desktop Macintosh system designed for the education and consumer markets, and the introduction of iBook, the company's consumer and education oriented notebook computer introduced at the beginning of year 2000. Growth in net sales and unit sales was strong in fiscal 2000 in all of Apple's geographic operating segments with particular strength in Europe and Japan.

Apple experienced improved profitability in fiscal 2000 as well. Operating income before special charges rose 61% to $620 million. Improved profitability was driven by the 30% increase in net sales and stable overall gross margins. Special charges included both restructuring actions and executive bonuses. During the first quarter of fiscal 2000 Apple initiated restructuring actions resulting in recognition of an $8 million restructuring charge. This charge comprised $3 million for the write-off of various operating assets and $5 million for severance payments to approximately 95 employees associated with various domestic and international sales and marketing functions. Also during the first quarter of fiscal 2000, Apple's Board of Directors approved a special executive bonus for the company's Chief Executive Officer for past services in the form of an aircraft with the total cost to the Company of $90 million dollars (see **Exhibits 8, 9,** and **10**).[37]

Despite overall increases during fiscal 2000 in net sales, unit sales and profitability, Apple's performance in the fourth quarter ending in September of year 2000 was disappointing. Net sales during this quarter fell short of the company's expectations by approximately $180 million causing operating margin before special charges to fall to 4% for the quarter. The fourth-quarter revenue shortfall was primarily the result of three factors. First, fourth-quarter net sales of the G4 Cube, a new Macintosh system announced and introduced by the company during the fourth quarter, did not meet the company's expectations. G4 sales were approximately $90 million short of expectations. Second, net sales in the company's education market fell short of expectations by approximately $60 million. Third, although total fourth quarter Power Mac unit sales were close to expectations, the company experienced an unanticipated mix shift toward lower priced Power Mac configurations resulting in lower than anticipated net sales of approximately $30 million. Apple ended fiscal 2000 with substantially more inventory in its distribution channels than planned due to the lower than expected sell-through of the company's products during the fourth quarter.

Exhibit 8

Consolidated Balance Sheets: Apple Computer, Inc.
(Dollar amounts in millions, except share amounts)

	Sept 30, 2000	Sept 25, 1999
Assets		
Current assets:		
Cash and cash equivalents	$1,191	$1,326
Short-term investments	2,836	1,900
Accounts receivable, less allowances of $64 and $68, respectively	953	681
Inventories	33	20
Deferred tax assets	162	143
Other current assets	252	215
Total current assets	5,427	4,285
Property, plant, and equipment, net	313	318
Non-current debt and equity investments	786	339
Other assets	277	219
Total assets	6,803	5,161
Liabilities and shareholders' equity		
Current liabilities:		
Accounts payable	1,157	812
Accrued expenses	776	737
Total current liabilities	1,933	1,549
Long-term debt	300	300
Deferred tax liabilities	463	208
Total liabilities	2,696	2,057
Commitments and contingencies		
Shareholders' equity:		
Series A nonvoting convertible preferred stock, no par value; 150,000 shares authorized, 75,750 and 150,000 issued and outstanding, respectively	76	150
Common stock, no par value; 900,000,000 shares authorized; 335,676,889 and 321,598,122 shares issued and outstanding, respectively	1,502	1,349
Retained earnings	2,285	1,499
Accumulated other comprehensive income	244	106
Total shareholders' equity	4,107	3,104
Total liabilities and shareholders' equity	6,803	5,161

Future

Apple Computer anticipated a significant sequential decline in quarterly net sales during the first quarter of fiscal 2001(the quarter ending December 31, 2000) of approximately $1.0 billion. This decline was anticipated because of a perceived continued deterioration in demand, price cuts and a plan to reduce substantially the level of inventory in the Company's distribution channels.

For all of fiscal 2001, Apple anticipated net sales would decline as compared to fiscal 2000. Apple's future operating results and financial condition were dependent upon general economic conditions, market conditions within the PC industry, and the company's ability to successfully develop, manufacture, and market technologically innovative products within the highly competitive market for personal computers.[38]

Exhibit 9

Consolidated Statements of Operations: Apple Computer, Inc.
(Dollar amounts in millions, except share and per share amounts)

Fiscal Years Ending September 30	2000	1999	1998
Net sales	$7,983	6,134	5,941
Cost of sales	5,817	4,438	4,462
Gross margin	2,166	1,696	1,479
Operating expenses:			
Research and development	380	314	303
Selling, general, and administrative	1,166	996	908
Special charges:			
Executive bonus	90	—	—
Restructuring costs	8	27	—
In-process research and development	—	—	7
Total operating expenses	1,644	1,337	1,218
Operating income	552	359	261
Gains from sales of investment	367	230	40
Interest and other income, net	203	87	28
Total interest and other income, net	507	317	68
Income before provision for income taxes	1,092	676	329
Provision for income taxes	306	75	20
Net income	786	601	309
Earnings per common share:			
Basic	2.42	2.10	1.17
Diluted	2.18	1.81	1.05
Shares used in computing earnings per share (in thousands):			
Basic	324,568	286,314	263,948
Diluted	360,324	348,328	335,834

Apple was in the process of changing its message. The company decided to try to remake its image into a purveyor of "killer applications" or groundbreaking software programs that computer users can't live without. The Apple executives believed that new Apple applications would give Wintel users a reason to supplement their existing Windows-based systems with Apple hardware.

Apple's focus on applications was the latest effort by the computer company to reinvent itself. Following an unexpected profit warning in September of 2000, the company began offering rebates on several of its hardware lines to boost sales. The rebates had little effect, and Apple issued another profit warning in December.

The Company knew that lowering prices wasn't enough. The company hadn't managed to gather very much business from non-Mac users. For the first three fiscal quarters of 2000, Apple derived only 15% of its revenue from former Wintel customers. While an additional 28% of the company's sales came from first-time computer buyers, the majority of sales were generated by repeat Mac customers.

Hardware remained a core business for Apple. Steve Jobs has been highlighting Apple software applications for the past year, especially as the company readied its next generation operating system, Mac OS X, for release. Steven Jobs was a vocal champion of iMovie, Apple's home-movie editing software. He once said iMovie was at the heart of the company's philosophy of being at "the intersection of art and technology."

Exhibit 10

Consolidated Statements of Cash Flows: Apple Computer, Inc.
(Dollar amounts in millions)

Fiscal Years Ending September 30	2000	1999	1998
Cash and cash equivalents, beginning of the year	$1,326	$1,481	$1,230
Operating:			
Net income	786	601	309
Adjustments to reconcile net income to cash generated by operating activities:			
Depreciation and amortization	84	85	111
Provision for deferred income taxes	163	(35)	1
Loss on sale of property, plant, and equipment	3	—	—
Gains from sales of equity investment	(367)	(230)	(40)
In-process research and development	—	—	7
Changes in operating assets and liabilities:			
Accounts receivable	(272)	274	72
Inventories	(13)	58	359
Other current assets	(37)	(32)	31
Other assests	(15)	(3)	83
Accounts payable	345	93	34
Accrued restructuring costs	(27)	2	(107)
Other current liabilities	176	(15)	(85)
Cash generated by operating activities	826	798	775
Purchase of short-term investments	(4,267)	(4,236)	(2,313)
Proceeds from maturities of short-term investments	3,331	3,155	1,723
Purchases of long-term investments	(232)	(112)	—
Proceeds from sale of property, plant and equipment	11	23	89
Purchase of property, plant, and equipment	(107)	(47)	(46)
Proceeds from sales of equity investment	372	245	24
Other	(38)	8	(20)
Cash used for investing activities	(930)	(964)	(543)
Financing:			
Decrease in notes payable to banks	—	—	(22)
Proceeds from issuance of common stock	85	86	41
Cash used for repurchase of common stock	(116)	(75)	—
Cash generated by (used for) financing activities	(31)	11	19
Increase (decrease) in cash and cash equivalents	(135)	(155)	251
Cash and cash equivalents, end of the year	$1,191	$1,326	$1,481
Supplemental cash flow disclosures:			
Cash paid during the year for interest	$10	$58	$59
Cash paid (received) for income taxes, net	$47	$33	$(15)
Noncash transactions:			
Issuance of common stock for redemption of long-term debt	—	654	—
Issuance of common stock for acquisition of PCC assets	—		80
Issuance of common stock for conversion of Series A Preferred Stock	74	—	—

"Apple has needed to change its marketing for a long time," says Mark Macgillivray, a consultant at H&M Consulting, a market-research firm in Sunnyvale, California, that has worked with Apple in the past. "It's when Apple has focused on solutions that they've done reasonably well, because they've given customers a distinctive reason to buy a Mac."[39]

As Apple prepared in January of 2001 to hold the latest of the twice-annual expos in San Francisco, did Steven Jobs have enough flash left to rejuvenate Apple once again? Apple's stock was trading near its 52-week low. It wouldn't even come close to meeting its earnings projections for its most recent quarter. To top it all off, Apple was even losing some of its tiny share of the personal computing market.

All eyes were on the expo. Some who watched the company closely said they expected Apple to introduce new lines of laptops and desktops, perhaps a wireless gadget or two, and maybe expound more on its fledgling plans for a line of retail stores. Jobs, in his keynote address, also would likely disclose more details about the long awaited release of Mac OS X operating system, slated for February 2001, which would contain new Internet features. At some point, Jobs probably would feel compelled to address the company's financial condition.

Jobs and his associates are still running Apple, and they've never failed to rejuvenate the company. When Apple couldn't get a foothold in the consumer desktop market in the early 1980s, they came up with the revolutionary Macintosh that helped build the foundations of desktop publishing. When Apple found itself being devastated by Windows-based computers in the early 1990s, it came up with the Power PC, and later the iMac and the iBook. In 1996, when tired and flagging Apple and its partners were badly in need of some new flash and some profits, Steve Jobs was the one who arrived on the scene to provide it. "The Apple Corporation and Steve Jobs personally have been masters at repositioning that company," said John Kortier, Vice President of channel sales for Atlanta-based EarthLink Inc.[40]

Notes

1. Peter Burrows, "Yes, Steve, you fixed it. Congrats! Now What's Act Two? Apple," *Business Week* (July 31, 2000), p. 102.
2. Ibid., pp. 105, 108.
3. Ibid., p. 104.
4. Robert O'Brien, "Apple Computer Plunges 52%, Drags Down Rest of the Market," *Wall Street Journal* (October 2, 2000), p. C2.
5. Pui-Wing Tam, "Apple Reports First Loss in 3 Years; Stock Slips," *Wall Street Journal* (January 18, 2000), p. B6.
6. O'Brien, "Apple Computer Plunges 52%, Drags Down Rest of the Market," p. C2.
7. Terrence O'Hara, "It Was the Best of Times and the Worst of Times, and the Difference Was All in the Numbers," *The Washington Post* (December 31, 2000), p. H18.
8. Greg Ip, "A Year of Living Dangerously," *Wall Street Journal* (January 2, 2001), p. R1.
9. Apple Computer Inc., *Form 10-K* (2000), pp. 63, 64.
10. Staff reporter, "Apple Sales Executive Says He Is Leaving Post at End of Year," *Wall Street Journal* (October 11, 2000), p. B23.
11. Pui-Wing Tam, "Dwindling Education Sales Take a Bite Out of Apple's Bottom Line," *Wall Street Journal* (October 17, 2000), p. B1.
12. Ibid., p. B4.
13. Ibid., p. B4.
14. Ibid., p. B4.
15. Apple Computer Inc., *Form 10-K* (2000), p. 4.
16. "Computer and Peripherals Industry," *Value Line* (October 20, 2000), p. 1095.
17. "Compaq Computer," *Value Line* (October 20, 2000), p. 1101.
18. "Dell Computer," *Value Line* (October 20, 2000), p. 1102.

19. "Gateway, Inc.," *Value Line* (October 20, 2000), p. 1105.
20. "International Business Machines," *Value Line* (October 20, 2000), p. 1110.
21. "Hewlett-Packard," *Value Line* (October 20, 2000), p. 1109.
22. "Semiconductor Industry," *Value Line* (October 20, 2000), p. 1051.
23. "Intel," *Value Line* (October 20, 2000), p. 1067.
24. "Motorola," *Value Line* (October 20, 2000), p. 1075.
25. "Computer Software & Services," *Value Line* (December 1, 2000), p. 2171.
26. "Microsoft," *Value Line* (December 1, 2000), p. 2202.
27. Apple Computer, Inc., *Form 10-K* (2000), p. 6. The material in this section, Foreign and Domestic operations and Geographic Data, was directly abstracted. The verb tense was changed and some material altered.
28. Ibid., p. 21. The material in this section, Product Introductions, was directly abstracted. The verb tense was changed and some material altered.
29. Ibid., p. 21. The material in this section, Inventory and Supply, was directly abstracted. The verb tense was changed and some material altered.
30. Ibid., p. 24. The material in this section, Support from Third-Party Software Developers, was directly abstracted. The verb tense was changed and some material altered.
31. Ibid., p. 23. The material in this section, Education Market, was directly abstracted. The verb tense was changed and some material altered.
32. Ibid., p. 4. The material in this section, Markets and Distribution, was directly abstracted. The verb tense was changed and considerable additional material was added.

33. Pui-Wing Tam, "Apple Computer Tries Courting Retailers Again," *Wall Street Journal* (July 7, 2000), p. B1.

34. *Ibid.*

35. Apple Computer, Inc., *Form 10-K* (2000), p. 8. The material in this section, Legal Proceedings, was directly abstracted. The verb tense was changed.

36. *Ibid.*, p. 12. The material in this section, Financials, was directly abstracted. The verb tense was changed and some material altered.

37. *Ibid.*, pp. 33–36.

38. *Ibid.*, p. 13. The material in this section, Future, was directly abstracted. The verb tense was changed and considerable material was added.

39. Pui-Wing Tam, "Apple Seeks New Image as Producer of Killer Apps," *Wall Street Journal* (Jan 5, 2001), pp. B1, B4.

40. Bob Keefe, "Steve Jobs to Carry Extra Burden at Expo," *The Atlanta Constitution* (January 7, 2001), p. 5G.

case 13

WingspanBank.com

Laura Cooke, Liza Hovey, Hyung Kim, and Paul Rakouski

W*ingspanBank cannibalize[s] existing business to build new business.*[1]

—John B. McCoy, President and CEO
BANK ONE CORPORATION

It was Monday, November 15, 1999, and John B. McCoy already felt like it had been a long week. The *Wall Street Journal* had announced the impending departure of James Stewart,[2] Chief Executive of Wingspan, and investors and media hounds alike were clamoring for more details.

McCoy remembered the beginning, when he worried about the many Internet start-ups beginning to offer a wide array of financial services. Reasoning that bankone.com was insufficient to stem the tide, he launched WingspanBank.com as a freestanding Internet bank.[3] After all, he thought, if customers were going to abandon bricks and mortar banks in favor of Internet banks, BANK ONE should offer the best choice: WingspanBank.com.

Thus, WingspanBank.com was launched on June 24, 1999, under the auspices of the First USA division of BANK ONE. Unfortunately, the First USA division had performed poorly since then, and analysts had been questioning whether the excitement of launching WingspanBank.com had distracted management from its core business—credit cards.[4]

As McCoy considered the situation, several questions came to mind: Had he been right about permitting cannibalization? What is the role of Wingspan at BANK ONE? What is the future of BANK ONE in the era of e-commerce?

Background

There was a lot for McCoy to consider. The final decades of the twentieth century had brought changes to every possible dimension of banking. From changes in government regulations to the emergence of the Internet, the ever-changing landscape for financial service companies brought difficult challenges and uncertain opportunities.

MBA candidates Laura Cooke, Liza Hovey, Paul Rakouski, and Hyung Kim prepared this case under the supervision of Professor Allan Afuah as the basis for discussion in University of Michigan Business School class "Strategy, Technology and the Management of Innovation," not to demonstrate effective or ineffective handling of an administrative situation. Some data, names, and situations have been disguised to maintain confidentiality. Copyright ©1999 by Laura Cooke, Elizabeth Hovey, and Hyung Kim. This case was edited for SMBP-9th Edition. All rights reserved. Reprinted by permission.

HISTORY OF BANK ONE

Just as its all-caps name BANK ONE CORPORATION (hereinafter Bank One) proclaims, this financial institution thinks big, and its recent history (see **Exhibit 1**) shows that it embraces innovations. Among them are the first Visa (then called BankAmericard) credit card service outside California in 1966, and the first cash management account in 1977, which combined the higher interest rates of a brokerage account with the flexibility of checking services.

The bank—founded in 1868 and called City National Bank after the merger of two Columbus, Ohio, banks in 1929—also has a strong history of acquisitions. In 1967, its management created a holding company to enable expansion and named it First Banc Group of Ohio to skirt legal restrictions on the use of the word "bank." Its acquisition of a bank in neighboring Mansfield, Ohio, initiated a string of intrastate acquisitions. When restrictions on interstate banking were removed in 1984, BANC ONE (changed from First Banc in 1979) expanded into Arizona, Illinois, Indiana, Kentucky, Michigan, Texas, Utah, and Wisconsin—primarily through stock swaps.

Following its "merger of equals" (under BANC ONE leadership) with First Chicago NBD in 1998, Bank One (so renamed after the merger) was the fourth largest banking company in

Exhibit 1
Milestones: BANK ONE

1999	Becomes world's largest issuer of Visa credit cards
	Launches WingspanBank.com (as unit of First USA division), which offers wide array of financial services—including insurance, mortgage, mutual fund services
1998	Acquires First Chicago NBD in $30 billion stock swap
	Changes name to BANK ONE CORPORATION, based in Chicago, Illinois
	BANK ONE is number four banking company in United States
	Launches <bankone.com>, which offers traditional banking services to current customers (and general information about BANK ONE CORPORATION)
1997	Acquires number four credit card issuer First USA
	Buys Liberty Bancorp of Oklahoma
1996	Buys Premier Bancorp., Louisiana's #3 bank
1994	Begins major consolidation effort
1992	Enters Arizona and Utah
1991	Enters Illinois
1989	Enters Texas market with acquisition of 20 failed Mcorp and other banks
1984	John (B.) McCoy becomes third (and present) bank president
	Federal government relaxes restrictions on interstate banking
	BANC ONE expands into Indiana, Kentucky, Michigan, and Wisconsin
1979	Changes name to BANC ONE; all affiliated banks renamed Bank One
1977	Introduces first cash management account in partnership with Merrill Lynch
1967	First Banc Group of Ohio formed as holding company for City National
	Buys Farmers Savings and Trust of Mansfield, Ohio
1966	Introduces first Visa (then BankAmericard) credit card outside California
1958	John (G.) McCoy becomes second bank president
1935	John (H.) McCoy becomes first bank president
1929	Commercial National and National Bank of Commerce combine to form City National Bank and Trust
1868	F. C. Session founds Commercial National Bank in Columbus, Ohio

Sources: BANK ONE CORPORATION, 1998 Annual Report, Hoover's Company Capsules, WingspanBank Marketing.

Exhibit 2

Summary Balance Sheet: BANK ONE
(Dollar amounts in millions)

Year Ending December 31	1998	1997
Assets		
Cash and due from banks	$ 19,878	$ 15,380
Interest-bearing due from banks	4,642	6,910
Funds and securities under resale agreements	9,862	9,168
Trading and derivative products	12,299	9,869
Investment securities	44,852	26,039
Loans, net	153,127	156,762
Bank premises and equipment, net	3,340	3,426
Other assets	13,496	11,818
Total assets	$261,496	$239,372
Liabilities		
Deposits, total	$161,542	$153,726
Short-term borrowings, total	40,101	33,152
Long-term debt	21,295	20,543
Other liabilities	17,998	12,901
Total liabilities	$240,936	$220,322
Stockholders' equity		
Preferred stock	190	326
Common stock, $0.01 par value	12	12
Surplus	10,769	12,584
Retained earnings	9,528	8,063
Other	61	(1,935)
Total stockholders' equity	$ 20,560	$19,050
Total liabilities and stockholders' equity	$261,496	$239,372

Sources: BANK ONE CORPORATION, 1998 Annual Report.

the United States (see **Exhibits 2** and **3**). In addition, the recent acquisition of credit card issuer First USA made Bank One the largest issuer of Visa credit cards in the world.

First USA featured a more entrepreneurial culture and also brought significant e-commerce expertise in the form of its Internet Marketing Group. In its efforts to develop an e-commerce strategy for First USA and implement <firstusa.com>, this group had learned important lessons and forged useful relationships. The Internet Marketing Group made it possible for Bank One to take fuller advantage of the mounting Internet explosion than its current presence. BankOne.com (see **Exhibit 4**) was meant simply to offer online services to current customers of Bank One and to serve as the corporation's online information presence.

Explosion of the Internet

By the late 1990s, the Internet had already transformed itself from a convenience for academics and curiosity for intellectuals to a viable commercial force and powerful business tool. Three primary phenomena converged to spur this emergence:

1. **More people had access to the Internet**. Personal computers (PCs) and Internet access became increasingly affordable and reliable. Frenetic competition, learning effects, and scale economies in the PC and Internet industries even made it possible for some com-

Exhibit 3

Summary Income Statement: BANK ONE
(Dollar amounts in millions, except share data)

Year Ending December 31	1998	1997
Interest income		
Interest income, total	$17,524	$17,545
Interest expense, total	8,177	8,084
Less provision for credit losses	1,408	1,988
Net interest income after credit losses	$ 7,939	$ 7,473
Noninterest revenue		
Market-driven revenue	546	552
Fee-based revenue	6,728	5,645
Other	797	497
Total noninterest revenue	$ 8,071	$ 6,694
Noninterest expense		
Salaries and benefits	4,477	4,224
Net occupancy and equipment	845	739
Depreciation and amortization	680	693
Outside service fees and processing	1,349	1,145
Marketing and development	1,024	837
Communication and transportation	781	711
Merger-related and restructuring charges	1,062	337
Other	1,327	1,054
Total	$11,545	$ 9,740
Earnings before income taxes	**$ 4,465**	**$ 4,427**
Applicable income taxes	$ 1,357	$ 1,467
Net income	**$ 3,108**	**$ 2,960**
Earnings per share, basic	$ 2.65	$ 2.48
Earnings per share, diluted	$ 2.61	$ 2.43

Source: BANK ONE CORPORATION, 1998 Annual Report.

panies to offer free PCs to consumers willing to purchase Internet access (and vice versa). In addition, the network software offered security and ease of use. By 1998, over 50% of U.S. households had personal computers (PCs), and over 30% had Internet access (see **Exhibit 5**).

2. **The Internet offered something for everyone**. Internet companies were enjoying extraordinary market valuations, and no one wanted to be left out. For instance, the market value of online toy merchant eToys surpassed the market value of Toys 'R' Us within its first day of trading. As a result, seemingly every business looked for ways to offer its products and services on the Internet, and consumers invested what they could. With this infusion of capital and labor, the Internet grew, and the number of online destinations grew six-fold between 1996 and 1999.[5]

3. **People became comfortable with e-commerce**. Consumers were doing more and more business on the Internet. Advances in Internet security assuaged fears, and peoples' familiarity with and the affordability of the Internet meant people could and would spend more time "surfing" and buying. As a result, the $7.8 billion online retail market of 1998 is projected to reach $108 billion by 2003 (see **Exhibit 6**).

With the longest economic expansion in the history of the United States as a backdrop, the Internet was real, and e-commerce was an undeniable force.

Exhibit 4

BankOne.com Start Page, Wednesday, December 31, 1999

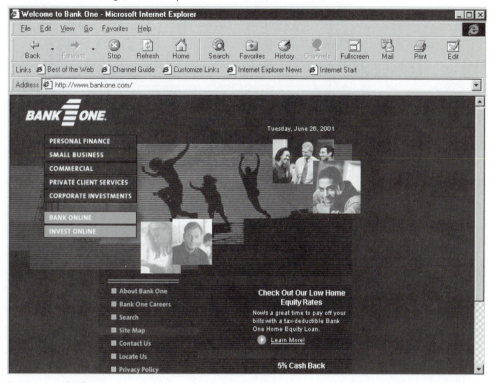

Source: <www.bankone.com>.

Exhibit 5

Number of U.S. Consumers with PCs and Internet Access

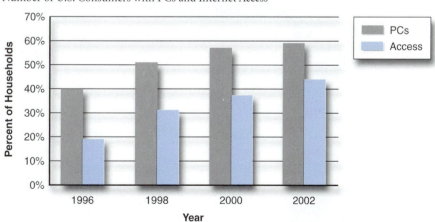

Source: Forrester Research.

Exhibit 6

U.S. Online Retail Spending

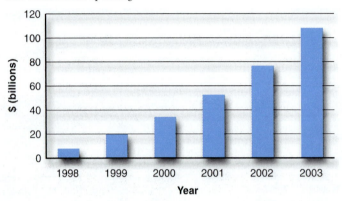

Source: Forrester Research.

Internet Banking

As the Internet achieved greater prominence, online banking emerged. Early Internet-only entrants included Telebank, Netb@nk (see **Exhibits 7** and **8**) and Security First Network Bank. Offering cost savings to suppliers and convenience to consumers, Internet banking appeared poised for tremendous growth. In addition to the lack of overhead expenses from bricks and mortar locations, an online transaction cost only $0.01, compared to $1.07 for a traditional

Exhibit 7

Start Page: NetB@nk.com

Source: <www.netbank.com>.

Exhibit 8

Summary Income Statement: NetB@nk
(Dollar amount in millions)

Six Months Ending June 30	1999	1998
Interest income		
Interest income, total	$17,979	$ 6,459
Interest expense, total	10,290	4,017
Net interest income	$ 7,689	$ 2,442
Noninterest income		
Noninterest income, total	477	226
Noninterest income, total	5,851	2,570
Net noninterest income	$(5,374)	$(2,344)
Provision for loan loss	$ 105	$ 10
Earnings before income taxes	$ 2,210	$ 88
Income tax (expense) benefit	$ (751)	$ (30)
Tax benefit of loss	$ —	$ 3,059
Net income	$ 1,459	$ 3,117

Source: NetB@nk Investor Relations.

face-to-face bank teller transaction (see **Exhibit 9**). Internet banks could pass these cost savings onto customers as higher interest rates and lower service fees (see **Exhibits 10** and **11**).

In the mid-1990s, the industry began its climb despite Federal banking regulations that limited its growth. For instance, unlike other Internet ventures, online banks had to generate sufficient revenue to cover such expenses as marketing and administration. Nevertheless, pure play Internet banks continued to appear, and in October 1998, CompuBank became the first national virtual bank to receive a charter from the Office of the Comptroller of the Currency and approval from the FDIC.

With interest rates rising and fees falling at online banks, Internet banking burgeoned in the late 1990s. In 1998 alone, the number of households using online banking nearly doubled to seven million, and estimates suggested that this number would reach 24 million by 2002.[6] Ominously, this growth, while rapid, paled in comparison to that of other financial services like online brokerage.

Witnessing this growth, traditional "bricks and mortar" banks began to acknowledge the importance of this new channel and worked to develop Internet strategies. Among the first were large national banks like Bank of America, Citibank, and Wells Fargo. Their initial

Exhibit 9

Estimated Banking Transaction Costs

Transaction Type	Per unit Cost
Face-to-face (with teller)	$1.07
Mail-in	$0.73
Telephone*	$0.54
Automatic teller machine	$0.27
Internet	$0.01

*Balance inquiry or money transfer.

Source: "Cyber-Banking Breaks New Ground Expands Towards Mainstream," *Bank Rate Monitor* (January 12, 1999).

Exhibit 10

Banks' Interest Rates

Bank	Checking[1]	Savings[1]
AmEx Membership Bank	2.00%	2.00%
Bank One	1.49%	1.49%
Bank of America	0%	1.00%
Chase.com	0.75%	2.13%
Citi f/I	0%	2.47%
CompuBank	3.00%	3.50%
NetB@nk	Up to 3.93%	N/A
Telebank	Up to 3.68%	Up to 4.88%
WingspanBank	Up to 4.5%	N/A
Mean	**0.84%**	**2.13%**

Note:
1. For balances of $0–$15,000.

Source: Company Web sites as of December 13, 1999.

Internet attempts meant limited services such as the ability to check balances and transfer funds. The primary purpose of their Internet sites was to retain existing customers and provide information about retail products at bricks and mortar locations. Soon, however, such other banking giants as Citibank, American Express, and Bank One would work to create separate entities under which to develop true online offerings (see **Exhibit 12**).

Traditional banks had many assets to leverage in developing Internet products. Customers could use pre-existing ATM networks without "per-use" transaction fees. In addition, individuals could make deposits at bank locations, electronically or by "snail mail." Finally, traditional banks' strong brand recognition meant virtually instant trust with potential online clientele.

Exhibit 11

Online Banks' Fees

	Savings Account	Bill Payment Services	Out-network ATM	Monthly Service Fee	Minimum Account Balance	Online Brokerage Link	Instant Credit Access
AmEx Membership B@nking	Free	Free	Free[1]	None	Yes	Yes	
Bankofamerica.com	Free				Yes		
Bankone.com	Free						Yes
Citi f/I	Free	Free	Free	None		Yes	
Chase.com	Free						Yes
CompuBank	Free	Free	Free[1]	None	Yes		
Net.B@nk		Free		None		Yes	
Telebank	Free	Free		None	Yes[2]	Yes	
Wellsfargo.com	Free	Free[3]			Yes	Yes	
WingspanBank.com		Free	Free[4]	None		Yes	Yes

Notes:
All offer free Interest Checking and In-network ATM use.
1. Maximum four surcharges per month reimbursed.
2. Interest not paid on balance below $1,000.
3. With minimum balance.
4. Up to $5 per month.

Source: Company Web sites as of December 6, 1999.

Exhibit 12

Internet Only Divisions of Established Banks

	Internet-only Division	**Launch Date**
BANK ONE	WingspanBank.com	June, 1999
Citibank	Citi f/I	August, 1999
American Express	Membership B@nking	July, 1999
Central Bank USA	USAccess Bank	Pending
Texas Capital Bank	BankDirect	Pending

Source: Team Research.

Established banks faced special challenges, too. General concerns about online privacy and security took on heightened importance when considering individuals' finances. In addition, the considerable investments were unlikely to bring short-term returns. Indeed, this new channel could cannibalize existing business. Furthermore, their conservative outlook coaxed most traditional banks to view the Internet as a revenue source—not as another "branch" location—and many actually charged customers for online transactions.

Quickly, however, online banks began to recognize that banking services—not venue— would continue to provide most of the revenue. Pete Kight, CEO of CheckFree Corporation, the premier bill payment and presentment service for online banks, sums it up:

> *You don't open a new branch and ask your customers to pay to bank there. You need to open a branch online because that's where your customers are.*

By November 1999, the landscape looked fragmented, and the competition fierce. Already there were more than 500 online banks,[7] and another 1000 were predicted to launch in the next year. The Federal government further spurred competition in November with the repeal of the Glass-Steagall Act, removing barriers among banks, brokerages, and insurance companies (see **Exhibit 13**). E*Trade quickly announced its intention to pur-

Exhibit 13

Glass-Steagall Act

On November 12, 1999, United States President Bill Clinton signed a new financial modernization bill into law, the Gramm-Leach Act, thus repealing the significant restrictions that had been placed on financial institutions in the United States by the Depression-era legislation, the Glass-Steagall Act. That bill had regulated the industry by preventing banks, insurance companies, and brokerage firms from entering into each other's lines of business.

The essence of the Glass-Steagall Act had been to separate commercial and investment banking. Its intention was to protect the commercial customers since it was born out of the concept that the investing activities of bankers in the 1920s had led to the stock market crash and resulting Great Depression of the 1930s. As financial markets have become more accessible to the consumer through such means as the Internet and the Securities and Exchange Commission has been diligent in keeping the markets transparent, such protection no longer was relevant.

While for the most part individual consumers were unaware of the restrictions caused by Glass-Steagall, much infighting had resulted over the years between various financial institutions desiring to offer a wider variety of services to their customers. It is anticipated that with the Act's repeal, many mergers will take place in the financial services industry and that competition will increase significantly. The lines between banks, brokerage firms, and insurance companies have certainly been blurred.

Source: Dee DePass, *Minneapolis Star Tribune* (November 13, 1999).

chase Telebank, an early Internet-only bank. Bill Wallace, CIO of Wingspan, describes an even more chaotic scenario:

> The other potential competitors that keep me up at night are the Yahoo's and AOL's of the world. They have the customer base, but currently face a barrier to entry in being unable to secure charters. If this [barrier] opens up, . . .

New entrants vying for space would simply overrun the online banking industry.

WingspanBank.com

Making 119 acquisitions in the past 15 years had helped make Bank One the fourth largest bank in the U.S. For the twenty-first century, however, CEO John McCoy looked to another avenue for growth—the Internet.[8]

THE DECISION TO LAUNCH

This fundamental shift in strategy came during a Fall 1998 trip which McCoy took with Dick Vague, then head of the First USA Division and a Bank One Executive Vice President. McCoy and Vague visited Internet companies like Yahoo!, Excite, and America Online. The ostensible purpose was for Vague to negotiate marketing deals for First USA's credit cards.[9] Importantly, however, McCoy began to see the power of the Internet in general and of online banking in particular.

This exposure served as the foundation for a new type of bank within Bank One and a new growth strategy. McCoy quipped that Bank One might never buy another bank because of the tremendous growth potential he saw in the Internet.

After the trip, McCoy gathered key Bank One executives in February 1999 to discuss what type of online bank to create. The result was WingspanBank.com—a broad-based, Internet-only bank that met all of a customer's financial service needs through one integrated user I.D.

THE VISION

> If your bank could start over, this is what it would be.
>
> —WingspanBank.com slogan

To herald this new Internet-only bank, senior management wanted to create a new brand. James Stewart, the original CEO of Wingspan, explains:

> We wanted something that was unique to online and financial services. We wanted a name that was not necessarily a literal name like Internet bank.com but something that could ultimately come to mean something. Like Amazon didn't mean "books online" and Excite didn't mean "search engine" —but now they do.[10]

The team looked to the market for this new name. After a series of focus groups, potential customers and senior management agreed upon Wingspan. Wingspan symbolized the breadth of new products and emphasized the fresh start. With their early entry into the market, the team hoped that WingspanBank would soon become synonymous with "Internet banking."

WingspanBank should be more than simply Bank One online—indeed, bankone.com already existed. WingspanBank should be a "one-stop shop" for financial services: checking, savings, direct deposit, credit cards, installment and other loans, investments, bill payment, financial planning, CDs, mortgages, insurance, and more. Multiple "best in class" vendors would provide these services, permitting WingspanBank customers to use a variety of financial institutions through one channel.

Michael Cleary, President of Wingspan comments:

Bank One has a multibrand strategy on the Internet. Our goal is to create different products for different customers with different needs. Bank One is for the bricks and mortar customer with a regional focus. Wingspan is for an Internet-customer with a national focus. To make a consumer products analogy, you may not know whether a customer wants Tide or Wisk, but either way, P&G will make sure to provide it.

The essence of WingspanBank, however, would be convenient, comprehensive, and objective solutions to customers' problems at competitive prices—not products. Wingspan committed to becoming a "trusted advisor" to its customers. Cleary notes:

Offline banks have promised for years to be the trusted advisor for customers. The Internet provides us with the tools to do that. [But] only time will tell whether people will provide the information we need to deliver that value.

The scope was national—extending beyond the 14 states where Bank One operated. The primary target market for WingspanBank.com was a segment that bankone.com could not reach—the growing core group of Internet users who disdain the bricks and mortar of traditional banks. Wingspan wanted both present and future users of Internet banks, especially those who currently bank with Bank One competitors. Even taking Bank One's own customers was deemed acceptable.

IMPLEMENTATION

Jim Stewart was selected to be CEO of Wingspan and an "iBoard of Directors" of technology leaders was created. Together, they set a timeframe of 90 days to launch, but where should WingspanBank be born in order to foster creativity, innovation and speed to market?

The answer was First USA. According to Cleary:

Bank One bought First USA for its speed and marketing savvy. First USA has the entrepreneurial spirit and acts quickly. I never thought it could move so fast, but indeed it is a fast company.

First USA understood direct marketing and lived to "test and learn." In addition, its Internet Marketing Group had recent experience in the Internet world, and its culture appeared to align well with the goals of Wingspan.

Over 30 external vendors were selected to speed launch and expand product offerings in keeping with the Wingspan vision. These partners comprised the best service providers for each product area. Though invisible in most cases to WingspanBank customers, they directly represented the brand and were thus crucial to the success of the venture. All partners began work based on verbal agreements—time constraints prevented legal negotiations. The work required to implement so much functionality in so little time meant 18-hour days for Wingspan employees and partner staff alike.

Meanwhile Carol Knight, a former First USA consultant, had been selected to head up the marketing and PR efforts. Within the first month, her group conducted over 60 focus groups! These groups clarified what consumers wanted from an Internet bank and helped refine the Wingspan goals.

For instance, consumers were most concerned about trustworthiness of the site (followed closely by price). Ease of use and customer service became paramount, increasing the importance of site design and seamless integration of the multiple vendors. Thorough testing before launch was essential—any technical difficulty with the site could sabotage the new brand. A customer's first impression of WingspanBank.com was critical.

Customers also believed putting all of their assets in one place was risky, but using multiple vendors made them feel more secure. This sentiment reassured Wingspan management that partnerships and offerings of non-Bank One products on the site were keys to success.

Customers also desired Personal Financial Management (PFM). Although these checking and bill payment services offered no profit margin, customized PFM could ultimately generate revenue by permitting targeted products such as loans to be "pushed" to consumers.

The marketing team of 30—including Wingspan's advertising and PR agencies, First USA staff and external consultants—was also developing a plan in keeping with the Wingspan vision. The perceived importance of marketing shows in the nearly $100 million allocated from a total annual operating budget for Wingspan of approximately $150 million.[11] The plan included network TV spots, radio ads, celebrity personalities, press releases, and news features. Each of these activities was critical to the establishment of a stand-alone brand.

Unlike traditional Bank One advertising, which was regional, this campaign demanded national exposure, especially in markets where Bank One did not have a presence (to minimize cannibalization). Cities such as Boston, Seattle, and Philadelphia were ideal. However, the campaign also had a presence in California and Texas, existing Bank One markets.

The timeliness was critical to the plan:

> *The ad agency had eight weeks to design a campaign and shoot a commercial. The actors practiced a script with no bank name because it was not yet determined. The day of the commercial shoot when the name was revealed, the biggest concern was whether the actors would be able to make this change.*[12]

WingspanBank.com was launched on June 24, 1999 (see **Exhibit 14**)—just 123 days from kick-off. McCoy was very visible during this time, including an interview for the *Wall Street Journal* where he announced the financial impact to Bank One. In the first year, WingspanBank was expected to dilute the value of Bank One's stock by 5¢ per share; in the second year, to add 5¢ per share; and in the third year, to add 20¢ per share.

Exhibit 14

Start Page: WingspanBank.com

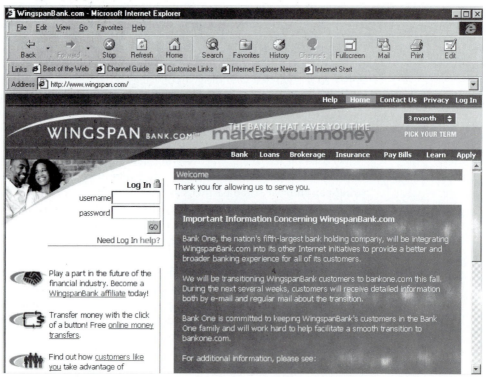

Source: <www.wingspanbank.com>.

CURRENT STATE (1999)

By most measures, Wingspan succeeded in meeting its goals.

Culture

Being an Internet start-up within a larger organization offered both opportunities and challenges. Kevin Watters, Wingspan's Marketing Senior Vice President, summarized the advantages:

> Compared to other Internet banks Wingspan has the cash resources of Bank One and First USA, which means enormous marketing dollars. In addition, we are able to mine data from First USA to provide better offers via direct mail and e-mail than competitors. That's a 70 million cardholder database to pull from. There is also shared learning across the three organizations (Bank One, First USA and Wingspan).

Cleary noted the challenges:

> It's sometimes hard to act like an Internet company. There is no currency like an E-Trade—currency for marketing deals, advertising, and talent. Businesses are about people and if we don't have what Internet savvy people want, we're handcuffed. We're also responsible for part of an earnings stream at Bank One, and we all know that at Internet start-ups, earnings don't drive success. We're forced to look at profitability [earlier].

Customer Base

Within its first 90 days of operations, Wingspan had signed up 50,000 customer accounts. By comparison, Net.B@nk, which has been operating for over three years, had only 35,000 customers. On the other hand, bankone.com had 350,000 customers, nearly 8 million people were online, and 200,000 of them used Internet-only banks.

Wingspan wanted to know whether their customers will switch among banks or remain loyal. Wingspan's "stickiest" products so far included online bill payment and direct deposit. With these products, customers spent a great deal of time and provided specific information to the bank, thus increasing their switching costs. In fact, Wells Fargo research indicated that online customers using bill payment services were 16 times more likely than bricks and mortar customers to stay with the bank and be profitable.[13]

In terms of "mindshare" and general awareness, Wingspan had hit its goals, but hoped to target better the core Internet banking consumer through both traditional and Internet advertising. In addition, a recent alliance with Lycos through which Lycos customers can bank through a co-branded Wingspan and Lycos site may represent future direction.

Services

Customers can use Bank One's ATM machines for free—but not the tellers and other face-to-face branch services. Customers can complete applications online, get approved, and start banking in the same online session, which is unusual—most online banks make customers wait for passwords received via e-mail. Customers can also receive virtually instant decisions on products ranging from credit cards to installment loans—the response to an online home equity loan application took only 50 seconds! Many WingspanBank services and rates were not available to Bank One customers. For example, they paid $4.95 per month for the same bill payment services Wingspan customers got for free.

Since the launch, Wingspan continued to demonstrate its commitment to its vision through continual spending and maintenance of product quality. For example, in its commitment to maintain the best portfolio of products and services, management added CheckFree Corporation, the leading supplier of bill payment services, to the list of vendors. According to CIO Wallace, "Wingspan will continue to look at all vendors in the marketplace and select the best ones."

The original plan added novel, meaningful functionality to the site every four to six weeks. Wingspan ran at a six- to eight-week time frame, but continued to innovate. According to Cleary, there was still much to do:

> *We launched quickly to beat Citibank and American Express, to test and to learn. There are many things not done at launch that we must complete in order to reach our goals. For example, we have not yet implemented many of our cross-selling techniques. Wingspan needs to recognize customers when they come to the site using CRM (Customer Relationship Management) tools to deepen the relationship.*

Wallace reflected on the future as well:

> *The model for Wingspan must change from product- to relationship-focused. In the past 25 years, banks created complicated views of banking and took away customers' control over their finances. Wingspan can erase the complexity and give customers back this control. For example, if there is $10,000 in a checking account, we can automatically issue a CD for the unused portion so that customer earns an extra $25. This adds value to the relationship.*

Wingspan planned to continue its furious growth and use its flexibility and size to its advantage. Relative to other Internet banks, Wingspan had higher brand awareness, better prices and leaner operations, meaning it could provide customer enhancements that other companies could not match.

The Dilemma

John McCoy liked what Wingspan had achieved, but was concerned. Shares of Bank One had fallen more than 40% since May. The First USA division suffered $70 billion in outstanding receivables, and expensive advertising campaigns had yet to deliver predicted returns.[14] Furthermore, the press unrelentingly included Wingspan in their criticism of Bank One even though Wingspan revenues meant little to a banking behemoth with $260 billion in assets. Was it because several executives at Wingspan—including Dick Vague and now James Stewart—had departed?

It's ironic, McCoy thought, that Wingspan had met virtually all of its goals and leads the industry, yet remains underappreciated outside—and maybe even inside—Bank One. Given all this, he had to ask himself: Now what?

Notes

1. "Internet Defense Strategy: Cannibalize Yourself," *Fortune* (September 6, 1999), p. 122.
2. "Bank One Says CEO of Internet Venture, Wingspan, Will Resign at Year's End," *Wall Street Journal* (Monday, November 15, 1999), p. B11.
3. "Internet Defense Strategy: Cannibalize Yourself," *Fortune* (September 6, 1999), pp. 121–134.
4. "WingspanBank: Losing Its Wings?" <www.thestandard.com/article/display/0,1151,7658,00.html?05>, *The Industry Standard*.
5. <Forrester.com> (October 15, 1999).
6. "Take Your Banking Online," <cnnfn.com/1999/05/21/banking/q_online_banks/> (May 21, 1999).
7. "True U.S. Internet Banks," *Online Banking Report* (November 29, 1999).
8. "Taking Flight with Wingspan," *Crain's Chicago Business* (August 2, 1999).
9. "Bank One: Nothing but Net," *Business Week* (August 2, 1999).
10. *Crain's Chicago Business* (August 2, 1999).
11. "Bank One Says CEO of Internet Venture, Wingspan, Will Resign at Year's End," *Wall Street Journal* (Monday, November 15, 1999), p. B11.
12. Telephone interview with Michael Cleary, President, Wingspan (December 6, 1999).
13. Telephone Interview with Peter Kight, Chief Executive Officer, CheckFree Corporation (December 1, 1999).
14. *Ibid.*

case 14

drkoop.com

Nicole Herskowitz, Fred Howard, Michael Iversen, Janet Mehlhop, and Pilar Speer

As Dennis Upah, Cofounder of drkoop.com, sat in his small, dimly lit office sipping a glass of water, he thought back to his conversation the previous day with his partner C. Everett Koop, former Surgeon General of the United States. He kept coming back to the comment that Everett had made.

> "I am excited about how the Web has greatly enhanced consumers' abilities to access healthcare information," Everett had said. "I firmly believe that empowered consumers make better, more informed decisions with their physicians. Our new Web site gives Americans one premier location on the Net to find trusted, quality healthcare information."[1]

Since the drkoop.com launch less than a year ago, the company had quickly grown to be the largest Web-based health information service, but it had yet to make a profit. Although Dennis and Everett's focus was on providing healthcare information, Dennis knew the site had to make a profit to keep its shareholders happy and to ensure that the business would survive. He thought to himself, "This tap water is terrible. I hope we soon turn a profit so we can afford a water cooler!" But more importantly, he wrestled with the question: What is the right strategy for drkoop.com to ensure that its early success will be sustainable in the long run?

The History of Medical Advice

People have always sought to obtain knowledge about their ailments. One can go back to ancient civilizations when medicine men performed spells and advised people on their spiritual and mental health. In the more modern world, people have relied on doctors for medical advice. For sicknesses like the flu or the common cold, this is still the case. There are also numerous books available for the "home doctor." In the case of more serious illnesses or prolonged illness such as cancer or diabetes, there is a wealth of support organizations available to the afflicted individual. These organizations not only offer support, but in many cases also give advice and support research.

The pharmaceutical industry plays an important role as a major contributor to these organizations. Bristol-Myers Squibb, for example, donated $23 million through the Bristol-Myers Squibb foundation in 1997. A large portion of this money went to organizations such as

This case was prepared by Nicole Herskowitz, Fred Howard, Michael Iversen, Janet Mehlhop, and Pilar Speer for class discussion in Professor Alan Afuah's Corporate Strategy Lecture on Strategy, Technology, and Innovations at the University of Michigan. This case was edited for SMBP-9th Edition. Reprinted by permission.

the National Cancer Foundation and the National Diabetes Foundation. The industry also does a great deal to inform patients of new treatment options through advertising, Web sites, and other forms of publications. Another important characteristic of the industry is that firms continue R&D efforts not only into broad areas of medicine that affect many consumers, but also into more obscure areas that affect only a small population.

In addition, all pharmaceutical companies today have extensive Web sites with numerous links and information options that address their primary treatment areas. Companies like Medtronic and Guidant have Web sites with specific areas dedicated to various types of cardiovascular problems. On Medtronic's site, for example, there are pages dedicated to ventricular fibrillation, which feature not only medical advice, but also contain many links to associated sites such as the American Heart Association. Beyond this, they work extensively with various patient support and prevention groups.

Medical Web Site History

The first Web sites to appear that pertained to the medical industry were those by pharmaceutical firms, which began to conduct business-to-business e-commerce with their customers. Most firms began their online presence by advertising their services in an effort to attract more business. However, those firms neglected to examine the aspect of the Internet that actually attracts most users: information. The sites that provided a free wealth of content were the ones that began seeing thousands and then millions of unique hits each quarter. This is where medical information sites got their start.

Medical information sites formed with the original purpose of providing the public with as much information as they could find in one place. Instead of having to try to call or get an appointment with a physician (or specialist, in many cases), patients could read everything on their own. Founders of these sites espoused a desire to foster a public environment for people to have access to trusted healthcare information. Through these sites, "the public has open access to tens of thousands of pages of reliable healthcare information." Site leaders embrace "the value of the Internet as a viable tool for educating the public . . ."[2] World-class sources of information include well-known physicians, information partners, a medical advisory board, and various authors and experts.

Medical information Web sites are popping up left and right. With competition on the rise, sites have been forced to add services to their sites in order to maintain growth in number of hits and unique viewers. Following the business models from other content provider Internet companies, the idea of "chat rooms" emerged into the healthcare scene. Due to the importance of accurate, timely information, which is often jeopardized by these "chat rooms," most medical sites added an "Ask the Expert" feature. Experts including physicians and specialists have joined the sites as partners who give feedback and advice to its questioners. Additionally, most sites ensure accuracy by setting up "stringent rules governing the ethics of the sites, including how advertising and editorial content should be addressed."[3]

Who Is Dr. Koop?

C. Everett Koop, M.D., is best known as the controversial Surgeon General who served under President Ronald Reagan. He built awareness of the destructive effects of tobacco and the AIDS virus. Today, Dr. C. Everett Koop continues his mission of encouraging good health. His latest effort is the launch of a health Web site, <www.drkoop.com>.

Dr. Koop was born in Brooklyn in 1916. After earning his M.D. from Cornell University in 1941, he worked at Children's Hospital at the University of Pennsylvania for 35 years. During his tenure, he built a reputation as one of the nation's best pediatric surgeons.

From 1981 to 1989, Dr. Koop served as Surgeon General of the United States Public Health Service and Director of International Health. Today, Dr. Koop continues to lead an active role in the health community and health education through writings, electronic media, public appearances, and personal contacts. He teaches medical students at Dartmouth College, where the Koop Institute is based. He is chairman of the National Safe Kids Campaign, Washington, D.C., and is producing 75 point-of-diagnosis videos over the next two years for Time-Life Medical, of which he is Chairman of the Board.

Why name a Web site after the 83-year-old Cofounder? The name provides credibility in a highly competitive and controversial environment. "It's an incredible asset," say Cofounder Dennis Upah. "He's the most trusted man in healthcare. He's an icon. With that comes a tremendous responsibility and scrutiny."[4] "In a recent survey by Bruskin-Goldring, almost 60% of consumers recognize Dr. Koop, and of those, nearly 50% percent believe him to be a top authority on healthcare issues," noted Donald Hackett, President and Chief Executive Officer of drkoop.com.[5]

drkoop.com Is Born

On July 20, 1998, Empower Health Corporation launched drkoop.com. Key to this new company was the name and guidance of C. Everett Koop, the former U.S. Surgeon General and the Chairman of Empower. "I am excited about how the Web has greatly enhanced consumers' abilities to access healthcare information," said Dr. Koop. "I firmly believe that empowered consumers make better, more informed decisions with their physicians. Our new Web site gives Americans one premier location on the Net to find trusted, quality healthcare information."[6]

To build drkoop.com brand awareness, they partnered with USWeb Corporation. Together they devised a strategy implementing innovative banner advertising and media placement, search engine optimization, and online public relations and promotions.[7] The strategies paid off with more than one million visitors in the first 90 days of operation. "The success of drkoop.com demonstrates the effectiveness of audience development techniques and reflects the strong demand for branded healthcare content on the Web," said Keith Schaefer, Managing Partner of the USWeb Audience Development Practice.[8]

The initial success that drkoop.com had during the first 90 days of existence continued over the next year. drkoop.com drew over 15 million page views for the month of October in 1999 according to Nielsen I/PRO.[9] In November 1999, both PC Data and Media Metrix ranked the site as the number 1 health Web site. According to PC Data's December 1999 records, drkoop.com held this position for the past eight months. Media Metrix also recognized drkoop.com as the number 25 site in its News/Information/ Entertainment category.

drkoop.com Web Site

The Web site is designed to better inform consumers about their health. The site has over 70,000 pages of health information and tools for users. The header of the site quotes Dr. Koop's philosophy, "The best prescription is knowledge." Currently, the site serves as a content and community portal that provides links to other information sources. The site includes the following categories:

- News
- Family
- Resources
- Wellness
- Community
- Conditions

Users can join as drkoop.com members, enabling them to access interactive tools, community bulletin boards, and chat rooms. The site allows members to customize their own drkoop.com homepage to cover topics, health issues, and diseases relevant to them.

NEWS

drkoop.com puts the latest and most critical information about health in the hands of consumers. Users can locate information about recalls, editorials, health events, polls, special reports, and sports medicine. The site includes reports and press releases from credible sources including the American Council on Science and Health (ACSH) and Occupational Safety and Health Administration (OSHA). Users also have searchable access to archived articles related to their health concerns. drkoop.com's HealthSearch™ provides access to a variety of resources for credible information. The search function not only scans the drkoop.com site, but also searches the MedLine database of medical journals and the National Cancer Institute's bibliographic database for relevant articles or abstracts.

Family

The Family section of the drkoop.com Web site is divided into categories including Children, Men, Women, and Elderly. The Web site has received accolades as a superior healthcare destination for women and children. On November 8, 1999, eHealthCare World awarded drkoop.com a gold medal for the "Best Site for Women" based on meeting women's needs for its health and medical news, information, education, advice, support, and community events.[10]

RESOURCES

drkoop.com includes a variety of content and tools that provide consumers with convenience and knowledge to make better-informed decisions.

drkoop.com's Personal Drugstore is a central location where consumers can refill their prescriptions, find drug information, and check drug interactions. The site provides links to pharmacy sites where consumers can order and reorder their prescriptions with doctor approval. Consumers can not receive prescriptions from the Web site. When asked if prescriptions will be given almost exclusively online, Donald Hackett, president and CEO of drkoop.com expresses his viewpoint as,

> Absolutely not. Although I'm a technologist at heart, there's a tremendous amount of human interaction that needs to take place. But even when the consumer needs to schedule the appointment, you can eliminate waste from the system with new technology. This technology is about streamlining the screening process.[11]

One of the most outstanding features on the site is the Drug Checker™, a proprietary drkoop.com technology that enables consumers to ensure that their medications do not interact with each other or with food to cause an adverse reaction in their bodies. Drug Checker™ provides users with critically vital information, considering the fact that the American Medical Association reported that adverse drug interactions are the fourth leading cause of death in the United States. Over 100,000 deaths in 1997 were attributed to these adverse affects.[12] The Drug Checker™ technology received a gold medal for the "Best Interactive Assessment Tool" in eHealthcare World awards.[13] drkoop.com allows its customers to download the tool and add it to their Web site, free of charge. Currently, over 9,500 Web sites provide this unique tool to their users.[14]

drkoop.com's Personal Insurance Center helps consumers evaluate insurance plans through access to an insurance library, glossary of terms and expert advice. Users can review frequently asked questions, search archived questions, and send their questions to insurance expert, Jim Perry, the Director of State Affairs for the Council for Affordable Health Insurance. The site includes direct links/advertisements to several health insurance sites, eHealthInsurance.com and Quotesmith.com, which provide online policy information and quotes. drkoop.com won a silver medal at the eHealthcare World Awards for the "Best Managed Care Site." The site was recognized for its extensive library of insurance articles, information on insurance programs by state, Medicare and Medicaid information, and an insurance policy chooser.[15]

Prior to the proliferation of the Internet, information about clinical trial results and registration was limited for patients. drkoop.com has taken initial steps to provide consumers with information about clinical studies such as patient information, trial procedures, how research is conducted, and how consumers can participate in a Quintiles clinical study. drkoop.com formed a partnership with Quintiles, the world's leading provider of healthcare services to the pharmaceutical industry and largest clinical trials management organization, in which drkoop.com is compensated for successfully recruiting qualified participants into clinical trials.

The strength of the Dr. Koop name in healthcare sets the stage for well-perceived recommendations. For example, the site provides drkoop.com's rankings of other health sites; however, it does not include major competitors such as WebMD and OnHealth.com. drkoop.com includes a list of books recommended by drkoop.com experts and community leaders. A partnership with Amazon.com provides online content and purchase capabilities. To buy a book, users are transferred to the Amazon.com site from drkoop.com.

drkoop.com provides consumers with information about health resources in their local communities. A regional directory helps consumers locate hospitals; however, it is limited to hospitals that participate in the drkoop.com Community Partner Program.[16] The site also includes a Physician Locator, provided by the American Board of Medical Specialties (ABMS). This service allows consumers to search and verify the location and specialty of any physician certified by the Member Boards of the ABMS. When accessing this portion of the site, users exit the drkoop.com and enter ABMS's site.

WELLNESS

The fourth section of drkoop.com focuses on personal wellness. The primary topics in this section are fitness and prevention. Consumers can access pages that help plan a workout routine to match a specified diet and time constraints. The section's theme is that by staying healthy and fit, one can prevent many illnesses.

To support this theme, there are pages that address one of C. Everett Koop's favorite subjects: smoking. Here one can find extensive information on the effects of smoking on the body, along with information on quitting programs and support groups. The Web site carries the banner for the most ardent issues during Dr. Koop's term in office as Surgeon General. Although most consumers may agree that smoking is bad for one's health, many of the drkoop.com claims could be considered biased, as this part of the Web site is clearly tainted by his personal views.

Finally, the *Wellness* section offers advice on weight loss. Through online chat rooms, users can design diet plans and obtain recipes for diet foods.

Community

drkoop.com's underlying philosophy of getting people together and giving them tools to help themselves is clear in this portion of the Web site, which is dedicated to health information and interactive chat boards. Here, one has the ability to select a specific affliction and log onto a message board or participate in online chat rooms. This portion of the Web site boasts more than 140 interactive information opportunities. In addition, there are daily topics of discussion where participants can "listen in" on discussions not only with other patients, but also with doctors. Visitors to the site can also find numerous stories of other patients who share the same affliction.

In this *Community* section, advertising is constant in the form of banners and large sidebars with ads from sites such as drugemporium.com. The ads often focus on the particular disease that one is currently examining.

Conditions

The last of the six main pages is designed to function as an online encyclopedia of medical advice. Visitors can come to this section and look up almost any disease or mental health issue they have questions about. It also offers shortcuts to advice pages for first aid and for common symptoms such as back pain or insomnia. The first aid section is particularly helpful in that it gives advice on anything from animal bites to sunburn. As in the *Community* section, the focus here is to provide people with information to help them help themselves.

Marketing

To build brand awareness and traffic, drkoop.com advertises on high frequency Web sites such as Yahoo!. Competitors also follow similar strategies. For example, WebMD.com advertises on NetZero, a free ISP for consumers, and OnHealth.com also advertises on Yahoo!.

drkoop.com has arrangements with local TV stations, which give the stations content for their Web sites in exchange for a drkoop.com "plug" at the end of a news story on a health issue.

In late 1999, drkoop.com is expected to launch a $10 million to $15 million advertising campaign supported by Lowe & Partners/SMS, New York.[17] The competitive market increasingly requires higher spending to build brand name recognition in the medical information industry. drkoop.com's planned marketing expenditures are shown in **Exhibit 1**.

Recently, drkoop.com established an exclusive relationship with Creative Artists Agency (CAA).[18] Dan Adler who is heading up the CAA's effort on drkoop.com stated, "We are excited by the opportunity to help broaden the reach of the most respected and recognized eHealth brand. We are confident that the strategic partnerships we help to build will secure drkoop.com's preeminent position in the eHealth category and will help it in its mission to revolutionize healthcare for consumers."[19]

drkoop.com Revenue Sources

drkoop.com is well positioned to take advantage of the mass amounts of money spent around the health care industry. This is further enhanced due to drkoop.com's broad positioning throughout the medical world. **Exhibits 2** and **3** show current financial information. **Exhibit 4** is an estimate of the market size to which drkoop.com has access.

ADVERTISING

drkoop.com generates most of its revenues through advertisements on its site. DrugEmporium is the only "sponsor" of the Web site. The site is covered with DrugEmporium advertisements and direct links to allow for over-the-counter medication purchases. drkoop.com also generates advertising revenues from Community Partners (i.e., hospitals) and health insurance companies. drkoop.com also receives advertising rates for Web banners by selling banner space to advertisers.

Exhibit 1

drkoop.com: Annual Statement of Earnings, 1997–2001
(Dollar amounts in millions, except for share data)

Year Ending December 31	Revenue Analysis					Revenue Analysis				
	2001E¹	2000E¹	1999¹	1998	1997	2001E	2000E	1999	1998	1997
Revenues										
Advertising	$ 42.3	$ 23.3	$ 7.0	$ —	$ —	63.4%	72.7%	77.2%	N/A	N/A
Content Licensing	$ 17.1	$ 6.7	$ 1.9	$ —	$ —	25.6%	20.8%	21.2%	N/A	N/A
Other	$ 7.4	$ 2.1	$ 0.1	$ —	$ —	11.0%	6.5%	1.6%	N/A	N/A
Total revenues	**$ 66.7**	**$ 32.1**	**$ 9.0**	**$ 0.04**	**$ —**	**100.0%**	**100.0%**	**100.0%**	**N/A**	**N/A**
Cost of operations										
Production, content and Product Development	$ 23.5	$ 20.8	$ 13.7	$ 4.4	$ 0.5	35.2%	64.9%	151.5%	N/A	N/A
Sales and Marketing	$ 35.8	$ 34.6	$ 29.5	$ 2.0	$ —	53.6%	107.7%	326.5%	N/A	N/A
Total cost of sales	**$ 59.3**	**$ 55.4**	**$ 43.2**	**$ 6.4**	**$ 0.5**	**88.8%**	**172.6%**	**478.0%**	**N/A**	**N/A**
Gross income	**$ 7.4**	**$ (23.3)**	**$ (34.1)**	**$ (6.4)**	**$ (0.5)**					
Gross Margin %	*(11.1%)*	*(72.6%)*	*NM*	*NM*	*NM*					
G & A Expense	$ 12.2	$ 10.6	$ 8.8	$ 2.6	$ 0.2	18.3%	33.0%	97.7%	N/A	N/A
Operating income	**$ (4.8)**	**$ (33.9)**	**$ (42.9)**	**$ (9.0)**	**$ (0.6)**					
Operating Margin	*(7.2%)*	*(105.6%)*	*NM*	*NM*	*NM*					
Nonoperating income and expenses										
Interest (Net)	$ 1.7	$ 1.7	$ 1.1	$ —	$ —	2.5%	5.3%	12.6%	N/A	N/A
Other	$ —	$ —	$ —	$ —	$ —	0.0%	0.0%	0.0%	N/A	N/A
Pretax income	**$ (3.1)**	**$ (32.2)**	**$ (41.8)**	**$ (9.0)**	**$ (0.6)**	**(4.6%)**	**(100.3%)**	**(463.1%)**	**N/A**	**N/A**
Pretax Margin	*(4.6%)*	*(100.3%)*	*NM*	*NM*	*NM*					
Provision for Income Taxes	$ 0.6	$ —	$ —	$ —	$ —					
Tax Rate	*(18.0%)*	*0%*	*0%*	*0%*	*0%*					
Income	**$ (3.6)**	**$ (32.2)**	**$ (41.8)**	**$ (9.0)**	**$ (0.6)**	**(5.4%)**	**(100.3%)**	**(463.1%)**	**N/A**	**N/A**
Nonrecurring items	$ —	$ —	$ (26.4)	$ —	$ —					
Net income	**$ (3.6)**	**$ (32.2)**	**$ (68.2)**	**$ (9.0)**	**$ (0.6)**	**(5.4%)**	**(100.3%)**	**(755.8%)**	**N/A**	**N/A**

Note:
1. Rounding error(s) in columns 1999, 2000E, and 2001E.

Source: Company reports; Bear, Stearns & Co. Inc. estimates.

14-7

Exhibit 2

Balance Sheet, 2001E–1998
(Dollar amounts in millions, except for share data)

Year Ending December 31	2001E[1]	2000E[1]	1999[1]	1998
Assets				
Current assets				
Cash and Equivalents	$ 11.1	$ 19.9	$ 56.6	$ —
Accounts Receivable	$ 14.5	$ 9.6	$ 4.7	$ —
Other	$ 5.9	$ 5.9	$ 5.9	$ —
Total current assets	**$ 31.5**	**$ 35.4**	**$ 67.1**	**$ 0.1**
Property, plant, and equipment	**$ 2.2**	**$ 1.0**	**$ 0.6**	**$ 0.3**
Investment	$ 5.0	$ 5.0	$ 5.0	$ —
Licenses	$ 1.2	$ 2.1	$ 3.0	$ —
Other	$ —	$ —	$ —	$ —
Total assets	**$ 39.9**	**$43.6**	**$ 75.8**	**$ 0.4**
Liabilities				
Current liabilities				
Accounts Payable	$ 5.0	$ 5.0	$ 5.0	$ 2.0
Accrued Liabilities	$ 2.7	$ 2.7	$ 2.7	$ 0.5
Deferred Revenue	$ 0.7	$ 0.7	$ 0.7	$ —
Notes Payable	$ 0.3	$ 0.3	$ 0.3	$ 0.5
Total current liabilities	**$ 8.7**	**$ 8.7**	**$ 8.7**	**$ 3.0**
Other	$ —	$ —	$ —	$ —
Redeemable Preferred Stock	$ —	$ —	$ —	$ 12.8
Stockholder's Equity				
Preferred Stock	$ —	$ —	$ —	$ —
Common Stock	$ —	$ —	$ —	$ —
Capital in Excess of par	$129.9	$133.5	$133.5	$ (0.3)
Retained Earnings (Deficit)	(94.9)	$ (94.8)	$(62.6)	$(15.2)
Other	$ (3.9)	$ (3.8)	$ (3.8)	$ –
Total stockholders' equity	**$ 31.2**	**$ 34.8**	**$ 67.0**	**$ (15.4)**
Total liabilities and stockholders' equity	**$ 39.9**	**$ 43.6**	**$ 75.8**	**$ 0.4**

	Dec–01E	Dec–00E	Dec–99	Dec–98
Current Ratio	3.6	4.1	7.7	0
Days Sales Outstanding	65.2	80.4	94	N/A
Book Value/Share	$ 0.99	$ 1.14	$ 2.23	N/A
Return on Equity	N/A	N/A	N/A	N/A
Cash Flow per Share	$(0.06)	$(1.00)	$(0.41)	$(0.32)
Free Cash Flow per Share	$(0.12)	$(1.04)	$(0.41)	$(0.33)
Long-Term Debt/Total Capital	0%	0%	0%	0%

Note:
1. Rounding error(s) in columns 1999, 2000E, and 2001E.

Source: Company reports; Bear, Stearns & Co. Inc. estimates.

PARTNERSHIPS

drkoop.com has revenues from numerous partnership agreements. These range from the arrangement with Quintiles, for which drkoop.com receives revenue for every referral generated, to the agreements that generate licensing fees for products and services that drkoop.com co-develops with partners.

Exhibit 3

Statement of Cash Flows, 2001E–1998
(Dollar amounts in millions, except for share data)

Year Ending December 31	2001E[1]	2000E[1]	1999[1]	1998[1]
Net income	$ (3.6)	$ (32.2)	$ (68.2)	$ (9.0)
Depreciation and amortization	$ 1.8	$ 1.8	$ 1.4	$ 0.1
Other	$ —	$ —	$ 26.5	$ 0.1
Change in current account				
Accounts receivable	$ (4.9)	$ (4.9)	$ (4.7)	$ —
Increase in other assets	$ —	$ —	$ —	$ —
Accounts payable	$ —	$ —	$ (0.1)	$ 2.1
Accrued liabilities and other assets	$ —	$ —	$ (0.2)	$ —
Deferred revenue	$ —	$ —	$ 0.5	$ —
Other	$ —	$ —	$ (6.0)	$ —
Cash provided by operating activities	$ (6.7)	$ (35.4)	$ (50.7)	$ (6.8)
Cash flows from investing activities				
Capital expenditures	$ (2.1)	$ (1.3)	$ (0.6)	$ (0.3)
Net cash used in investing activities	$ (2.1)	$ (1.3)	$ (0.6)	$ (0.3)
Cash flows from financing activities				
Net long-term financing	$ —	$ —	$ —	$ 0.5
Preferred stock issuances	$ —	$ —	$ 5.8	$ 6.6
Common stock issuances	$ —	$ —	$ 90.0	$ —
Other	$ —	$ —	$ 12.0	$ —
Net cash provided in financing activities	$ —	$ —	$ 107.8	$ 7.1
Net increase (decrease) in cash	$ (8.8)	$ (36.7)	$ 56.6	$ —
Cash beginning of year	$ 19.9	$ 56.6	$ —	$ —
End of year	$ 11.1	$ 19.9	$ 56.6	$ —
Cash flow/share	$ (0.06)	$ (1.00)	$ (2.25)	$ (0.3)
Free cash flow (FCF) per share	$ (0.12)	$ (1.04)	$ (2.27)	$ (0.3)
	2001 E	2000 E	1999	1998
CFFO-NI	$ (3.1)	$ (3.1)	$ 17.5	$ 2.2
EBITDA	$ (3.0)	$ (32.1)	$ (41.6)	$ (9.0)
Free cash flow (FCF)	$ (4.6)	$ (34.1)	$ (50.1)	$ (6.5)

Note:
1. Rounding error(s) in columns 1998, 1999, 2000E, and 2001E.

Source: Company reports; Bear, Stearns & Co. Inc. estimates.

CONTENT PROVIDER

drkoop.com has signed numerous deals with hospitals, for $50,000 to $100,000 a year, and the firm provides them with content to support their own hospital Web sites. drkoop.com also receives fees as a content provider for various other entities, such as the GO! Network and America Online.

Strategic Partnerships

One of the major strategies drkoop.com has employed since inception is that of partnerships. These partnerships have focused on numerous areas including those that broaden the firm's service offerings, expand its viewing base, and further expand its business model into traditional areas of the healthcare industry. drkoop.com currently has over one dozen portal agree-

Exhibit 4

1999 Potential Annual Market Size (in billions)

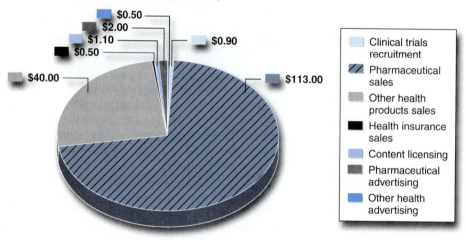

Legend:
- Clinical trials recruitment
- Pharmaceutical sales
- Other health products sales
- Health insurance sales
- Content licensing
- Pharmaceutical advertising
- Other health advertising

Pie chart values: $0.50, $2.00, $1.10, $0.50, $40.00, $113.00, $0.90

ments where drkoop.com is the exclusive or preferred provider of health care information. These partnerships range from The Dartmouth Medical School to the American Council on Science and Health.

Some of the most beneficial strategies are described below.

ADVENTIST HEALTH SYSTEMS

In January of 1999, drkoop.com exchanged 2,615,677 shares of preferred stock for $3.5 million in cash plus a 10% share of HealthMagic. HealthMagic is a subsidiary of Adventist Health Systems and a developer of a personal medical record application.[20] This was a key partnership for drkoop.com in that it allowed the firm access to and use of a personal medical record application and secured Adventist as a customer in its community partner program.

FHC INTERNET

FHC purchased $10 million of drkoop.com common stock at the offering price. FHC Internet is a subsidiary of Foundation Health Systems that specializes in the outsourcing of disease management programs for local health care organizations. FHC and drkoop.com have entered into an agreement whereby FHC is sponsoring drkoop.com's mental health center.[21]

QUINTILES TRANSNATIONAL

Quintiles purchased $5 million worth of shares of drkoop.com at the IPO price of $9. Quintiles is currently the world's largest provider of clinical research services to pharmaceutical companies. The firm has entered into an agreement with drkoop.com to jointly develop a clinical trials information center. This center allows drkoop.com visitors to view information about clinical trials that are currently going on across the country, to fill out an online prescreen form for various clinical trials, and then refers these prescreens to study sites. drkoop.com receives approximately $100 for each referral. Quintiles receives an expectation of realizing faster recruiting of patients, lower prescreening costs, and a larger pool of potential candidates for clinical trials.[22]

AMERICA ONLINE

drkoop.com entered into an agreement with America Online to offer services to its Internet Service Providers, America Online and CompuServe, as well as to its portals, AOL.com, Netscape.com, and DigitalCity.com. While all of the details of the deal have not been released, drkoop.com will pay AOL $89 million over the next four years and give the firm 1.6 million warrants with an exercise price of $15.94. In exchange, drkoop.com has access to over 70.3 million users from the five entities combined. In addition, drkoop.com receives an $8 million license fee for the use of a co-developed personal medical record as well as the use of AOL's salesforce.

PHAR-MOR

A cross partnership has been established between Phar-Mor, an online drugstore, and drkoop.com. Phar-Mor will sponsor a monthly drkoop.com pharmacy newsletter. Users of Phar-Mor's Web site will be directed to drkoop.com to gain further necessary information. In return, visitors to drkoop.com will be able to access Phar-Mor's Web site directly from drkoop.com's site. "Our relationship with drkoop.com allows us to provide our on line shoppers with the best health care content available so they can make sound purchasing decisions," said Phar-Mor president and CEO David Schwartz.[23]

DRUGEMPORIUM.COM

DrugEmporium.com and drkoop.com signed an agreement on October 4, 1999, to work together. Under the agreement drkoop.com visitors have access to over 20,000 discounted products sold by DrugEmporium.com. Shoppers at DrugEmporium.com can now go directly to drkoop.com for further information on products they are considering. Further, drkoop.com's Drug Checker™ has been integrated into the purchase of all prescription drugs, automatically checking for any potential problems.

Some of the additional drkoop.com selected affiliations include:

- ABC Television Affiliates (through the GO! Network)
- Dell Computer Corporation
- Element Media
- GO! Network (GO! Health Center, ESPN.com training room and Family.com Health Channel)
- Highmark
- iSyndicate
- MemorialCare
- Physicians' Online
- Salon Magazine
- Scott and White Hospital and Clinic
- Tallahassee Memorial HealthCare
- The Weather Channel

drkoop.com has numerous partnerships with various health care providers and HMOs including: Highmark (1 of the 10 largest insurers in the United States); MemorialCare (a large health care system serving more than 14 million residents in Los Angeles and Orange County); Scott and White Hospital and Clinic (one of the largest multispecialty hospitals in the U.S.); Promina Health Systems (a nonprofit health care organization serving 4.3 million residents in the Atlanta area); the Cleveland Clinic (with a staff of over 850 physicians); and the Baptist Health System (serves the 3.5 million residents in the Miami area).

Competition

Many would argue that drkoop.com is the leader in the online healthcare industry, yet the competition is intense. Hundreds of new medical sites have emerged over the past year and it is difficult to distinguish between the leaders in the market. All of the most popular sites provide extensive consumer health information, chat rooms, expert advice, links to products and comprehensive, fully tailored health care publications for professionals of all specialties.

In addition to the companies that specialize primarily in online health information, large medical companies are establishing an Internet presence by acquiring information and service firms such as insurance or drug products. Most pharmaceutical companies have portions of their corporate Web sites dedicated to consumer health information. One big player in this area is Merck, which publishes an online "medical bible." These pharmaceutical companies are not direct competitors of drkoop.com because their main focus is to sell products, but they are still "players" in the market.

In October 1999, PC Data ranked drkoop.com as the number one dedicated healthcare site for the seventh consecutive month.[24] According to PC Data, the site is the forty-third most popular site on the Internet overall. See **Exhibit 5** for the ranking for unique users for healthcare sites.

The following is a brief overview of some of the leading sites and how they position themselves in the competitive marketplace.

HEALTHEON/WEBMD.COM—REVENUES FOR QUARTER ENDING SEPTEMBER 1999: $28.7 M

drkoop.com's top competitor is Healtheon/WebMD, which claims to be the first comprehensive, online healthcare portal.[25]

Following the trend in consolidation, Healtheon and WebMD announced their merger in May 1999 to form Healtheon WebMD Corporation (HLTH). As a part of this merger, the companies combined their consumer Web sites, MyHealtheon.com and MyWebMD.com, into one site, www.webmd.com.

Exhibit 5
Traffic on competitive Web sites

Company	No. of Unique Hits 9/99
drkoop.com	5,539,000
onhealth.com	2,262,000
discoveryhealth.com	1,077,000
webmd.com	765,000
thriveonline.com	753,000
healthyideas.com	714,000
intelihealth.com	675,000
allhealth.com	596,000
AOLhealth.com	568,000
healthcentral.com	532,000
medscape.com	415,000
ama-assn.org	404,000
mediconsult.com	225,000

In early December 1999, Rupert Murdoch's News Corp. formed a $1 billion partnership with Healtheon/WebMD. According to CBS Market Watch's Barbara Kollmeyer, it's being "billed as the largest media and Internet deal to date."[26]

News Corp. is taking a 10.8% stake in Healtheon/WebMD, providing $700 million in "branding services" over 10 years, purchasing $100 million of Healtheon/WebMD, investing $100 million cash in the Internet company and signing a $62.5 million 5-year licensing deal to syndicate WebMD's daily broadcast content.

The licensing part of the deal is innovative because it changes the way media content is ordinarily used across media. Reuters quoted News Corp. President and Chief Operating Officer Peter Chernin, "Companies traditionally re-purpose print or broadcast content for the Web. With this deal, we're using the Web as a source for original, unique programming which will be leveraged across all media owned by News Corp."[27]

The goal of this partnership is to drive television viewers to medical Web sites and vice versa, creating single health care information brands across all media. The News Corp. partnership could give Healtheon/WebMD an advantage in internationalizing online health care.

The company is building a system of software and services to automate such tasks as HMO enrollment, referrals, data retrieval, and claims processing for use by insurers, doctors, pharmacies, and consumers. The site also offers physician communications services, physician references, medical information and news, and personalized content to its users.

The company has high aspirations for success, but whether it can surmount the daunting technological and economic challenges in rewiring the health-care industry remains to be seen.

MEDICONSULT.COM—REVENUES FOR QUARTER ENDING SEPTEMBER 1999: $3.1 M

The company's mission is to provide timely, comprehensive, and accessible information on chronic medical conditions, utilizing the latest available to deliver information efficiently. It features a fee-based service, *MediXpert*, which lets visitors present a case to a medical specialist who responds with a confidential report.

The company is completely independent of another company, HMO, hospital, or other healthcare organization in order to ensure unbiased, objective, credible information. All information that appears on the site "must pass a rigorous clinical review process before we deem it worthy" of the consumer.[28]

On September 7, Mediconsult.com acquired Physicians Online in a stock deal valued at $180 million. The acquisition could help Mediconsult.com take advantage of the recent introduction of online medical records and other services designed to connect doctors and patients and deliver health care.[29]

The site also has a powerful search engine, "Medisearch" which allows quick keyword inquiries.

AHN.COM (THE HEALTH NETWORK)—QUARTERLY REVENUES NOT AVAILABLE

Los Angeles based The Health Network, or ahn.com, is the one-stop television and Internet site where consumers can find information and motivation about leading a healthy life. Twenty-four hours a day, seven days a week, doctors and other medical experts provide credible, relevant information in a clear, interesting and easy-to-understand manner.

A 50/50 partnership between FOX Entertainment Group and AHN Partners, LP, The Health Network combines the leading health cable television network with one of the most visited health information sites on the Internet. The site is the premier source of live medical events, such as the first live Internet birth and the first live Internet triplet birth.

MEDSCAPE—REVENUES FOR QUARTER ENDING SEPTEMBER 1999: $3.1 M

The site's homepage is comprehensive, well organized, and more user-friendly than many competitors. It features the *Medscape Network* (for student, nurses, physicians), *Medscape Resources, My Medscape* (records personalized info from previous visits) and an *Editorial Board*.

In July 1999, CBS (CBS) took a 35% stake in Medscape, in exchange for $157 million in advertising and branding services. The company produces the consumer oriented CBS *HealthWatch* and provides information through AOL. In addition, Medscape publishes *Medscape General Medicine*, an online, peer-reviewed medical journal, and it offers a database of continuing medical education programs, an online bookstore, and physician Web sites for its members.

The company recently announced a content agreement with America Online. The three-year arrangement calls for Medscape to develop co-branded health sites for AOL's 18 million subscribers. In exchange, Medscape will pay AOL $33 million for two years.

WWW.AMA-ASSN.ORG—QUARTERLY REVENUES NOT AVAILABLE

The American Medical Association is primarily a membership organization. Its core objective is to be the world's leader in obtaining, synthesizing, integrating, and disseminating information on health and medical practice. It publishes numerous journals and its Web site provides valuable online information, which is accessible to "members only."

In addition to providing valuable information to its members, the AMA's corporate Web site contains a large variety of information available to the public. Consumers can use the site to look for medical groups and physician locators, to get medical advice about injuries, illnesses and specific conditions, and to read about general health information. Consumers can also learn about the Association's advocacy and legislative initiatives and read about topics on medical ethics and education.

Membership has been declining: the AMA represents about 35% of U.S. doctors (down from 50% in 1975). Most likely this decline will continue due to the emergence of medical information Web sites. Therefore, the AMA may devote time and funding to developing its consumer site and look for new revenue sources in addition to membership fees and publication sales.

ONHEALTH.COM—REVENUES FOR QUARTER ENDING SEPTEMBER 1999: $1 M

OnHealth Network Co. is a consumer health information company based in Seattle. Its site is not tied to a particular doctor, health system, or insurance company.

The site is supported by advertising, but the authors claim to keep the ads and the articles separate from each other—both behind the scenes and on the pages one sees. Information about a topic is not influenced by the advertisements displayed on that page. Authors write, "If it ever appears otherwise to you, please let us know."[30]

OnHealth Network offers both proprietary and syndicated content, and the company has negotiated many distribution deals with entities ranging from America Online to WebTV, as well as advertising deals with companies such as Johnson & Johnson and Pfizer.

In December 1999, OnHealth.com signed an agreement with Ask Jeeves, Inc., a leading provider of natural-language question answering services on the Web for consumers and businesses. This deal will provide OnHealth with prominent brand positioning.[31]

Most information comes from the publishers of the *New England Journal of Medicine*, from Cleveland Clinic, from Beth Israel Deaconess Medical Center, and from physicians who teach at Harvard, Columbia, and Stanford. A unique feature on the site's homepage is the Herbal Index, which contains 140 descriptions of alternative health remedies. About 80% of OnHealth's audience is female. Affiliates of Van Wagoner Capital Management own about 39% of the company.

iVILLAGE'S WWW.ALLHEALTH.COM—REVENUES FOR QUARTER ENDING SEPTEMBER 1999: $10.7 M

iVillage's Web site targets women aged 25 to 49 through more than 15 "channels" focusing on topics such as health, food, parenting, relationships, and shopping. The health sections of the site can be found at <betterhealth.com> or <allhealth.com>. The underlying themes of the site are "Take Charge of Your Health!" and "Information you need from a Community you can trust."[32] The site also features extensive chat rooms, weekly polls and shopping, and allows iVillage members to "ask the experts" for medical advice.

CEO Candice Carpenter recently commented on the merger between Healtheon and WebMD by saying, "I think it's pretty obvious there needs to be some (more) consolidation. We've got to clean this up a little. I don't know who's going to do it, but somebody should step up to the plate to do that job."[33]

iVillage generates more than 80% of its revenue from advertising, but the company is looking to enlarge its e-commerce presence with offerings such as its iBaby.com online baby products retailer. Perhaps the allhealth.com section will follow this trend.

Other Considerations

DISCLAIMERS/ LIABILITY

Similar to the competition, the drkoop.com site includes a disclaimer that states, "This information is not intended to be a substitute for professional medical advice. You should not use this information to diagnose or treat a health problem or disease without consulting with a qualified healthcare provider. Please consult your healthcare provider with any questions or concerns you may have regarding your condition."[34]

HIGH-ETHICS ALLIANCE/ LEGALITY

The growing concern of potential conflicts of interests related to inaccurate information, diagnosis, and prescribing drugs online resulted in the formation of a coalition of 16 companies including Healtheon/WebMD, Medscape Inc., America Online Inc., and drkoop.com. Dr. C. Everett Koop called this group together to develop an ethical code of conduct for consumers. Alliance members include 27% of total Internet audience traffic according to PC Data.[35] The committee will create policies for advertising, privacy and content and ensure the reliability of health information that consumers access through e-health providers. Donald Kemper, the chairperson of Hi-Ethics states that, "our ultimate goal is to guide a future of consumer confidence in healthcare information."[36]

On November 4, 1999, drkoop.com won the most awards of any e-healthcare Web site at eHealthcare World Awards in New York. The site received two Gold and two Silver awards, honoring the site for its trusted content and healthcare information for consumers. However, the drkoop.com Web site has been criticized by the American Medical Association for not providing sufficient information related to sponsorship and commerce relationships.

Conclusion

Dennis Upah knew the challenges were numerous, and the competitive field seemed to increase daily. He wondered which business model was the correct choice. Companies like Healtheon/WebMD, who were partnering with hospitals to provide other services, were definitely on the right track. In addition, WebMD and News Corp's recent announcement to put more than $1 billion into developing their site was also worrying. Although he felt drkoop.com had a significant advantage in its brand name, he knew this was not enough. How, then, could he continue to build on the important partnerships he had helped establish, such as the one with Quintiles? And how could he leverage the important innovations the firm had made, such as Drug Checker™? It was obvious to him that there were many opportunities out there, and his task was now to identify the best ones to pursue.

Notes

1. "Dr. Koop's Community" *1998 Business Wire, Inc.* (July 20, 1998).
2. <www.drkoop.com/aboutus/koop/>
3. *Ibid.*
4. "i:20 drkoop.com's Dennis Upah," *Crain Communications*, November 1999.
5. PR Newswire Association, Inc. March 29, 1999.
6. "Dr. Koop's Community" *1998 Business Wire, Inc.* (July 20, 1998).
7. "USWeb Audience Development Practice Helps Establish Success of Leading Consumer Healthcare Site," *1998 Business Wire, Inc.* (November 19, 1998).
8. "USWeb Audience Development Practice Helps Establish Success of Leading Consumer Healthcare Site," *1998 Business Wire, Inc.* (November 19, 1998).
9. "drkoop.com Breaks 15 million Page Views for October," *PR Newswire* (November 22, 1999).
10. "drkoop.com Web Site Dominates Awards at eHealthcareWorld," *PR Newswire* (November 8, 1999).
11. "Posts," *The Standard* (June 28, 1999).
12. "Dr. Koop's Community," *Business Wire, Inc.* (July 20, 1998).
13. "drkoop.com Web Site Dominates Awards at eHealthcareWorld," *PR Newswire* (November 8, 1999).
14. *Ibid.*
15. *Ibid.*
16. Hospitals that participate in the Community Partner pay $50,000 to $100,000 per year to license drkoop.com healthcare information to use on their Web sites. In addition, direct links are provided from the drkoop.com site to their individual Web sites.
17. "i:20 drkoop.com's Dennis Upah," *Crain Communications* (November 1999).
18. CAA provides strategic consulting services in marketing and technology areas and holds alliances with Internet incubator, idealab! And communications consulting and advertising company, Shepardson, Stern and Kaminsky.
19. "CAA to Provide Exclusive eHealth Representation to drkoop.com," *PR Newswire* (November 10, 1999).
20. Bear Stearns Equity Research, Health Care Industry, July 27, 1999.
21. *Ibid.*
22. Bear Stearns Equity Research, Health Care Industry, July 27, 1999.
23. "Phar-Mor, drkoop.com Enter Pact," FirstSearch database MMR, vol.16, no. 17, 990823, p. 19.
24. PR Newswire Association, Oct. 7, 1999, Financial News section.
25. <www.ixl.com/success/webmd/index.html>
26. <www.thestandard.com/article/display/0,1151,6224,00.html>
27. <thestandard.com>
28. <www.mediconsult.com>
29. <www.thestandard.com/article/display/0,1151,6224,00.html>
30. <nhealth.com/ch1/info/item.asp>
31. <www.askjeeves.com. Investor Relations>
32. <www.allhealth.com>
33. <www.thestandard.com/article/display/0,1151,4839,00.html>
34. Disclaimer present on every page of the drkoop.com Web site.
35. "Leading E-Healthware Companies Form Alliance to Benefit Internet Consumers," *Business Wire* (November 4, 1999).
36. *Ibid.*

Harley-Davidson, Inc. 2002: The 100th Anniversary

Patricia A. Ryan and Thomas L. Wheelen

T he year 2001 was our 16th consecutive year of records revenue and income, in spite of the weaker global economy," said Jeffrey L. Bleustein, Chairman and Chief Executive Officer of Harley-Davidson, Inc. "Worldwide retail sales of Harley-Davidson motorcycles in the fourth quarter were strong with 12.9 percent unit growth over last year.[1]

The theme filled the room as the Planning Committee for the 100th Anniversary Celebration met in preparation of the year-long event. It was a hot day in mid July and committee members were planning the final stages of the year long 100th anniversary celebration of Harley-Davidson. The culmination would entail an open tour starting in mid August in Portland, Las Vegas, Baton Rouge, and New York City and end in Milwaukee on August 29, 2003 in time for the three-day party and celebration. **Exhibit 1** shows the motorcycle routes for the participants. Company officials were expecting upward of 250,000 to participate in the final 100-year anniversary party celebration. At the end of the meeting, the committee discussed how to make the celebration one that Harley riders would never forget while at the same time encouraging a new, younger customer base to add to their aging baby boomer clientele.

History[2]

In 1903, William Harley (age 21), a draftsman, and his friend, Arthur R. Davidson, began experimenting with ideas to design and build their own motorcycles. They were joined by Arthur's brothers, William, a machinist, and Walter, a skilled mechanic. The Harley-Davidson Motor Company started in a 10×15 foot shed in the Davidson family's backyard in Milwaukee, Wisconsin.

In 1903, three motorcycles were built and sold. The production increased to eight in 1904. The company then moved to Juneau Avenue, which is the site of the company's present offices. In 1907, the company was incorporated.

In 1969, AMF, Inc., a leisure and industrial products conglomerate, acquired Harley-Davidson. The management team expanded production from 15,000 in 1969 to 40,000 motor-

Exhibit 1

Map of Harley-Davidson 100th Anniversary Celebration Roadtrip, 2003

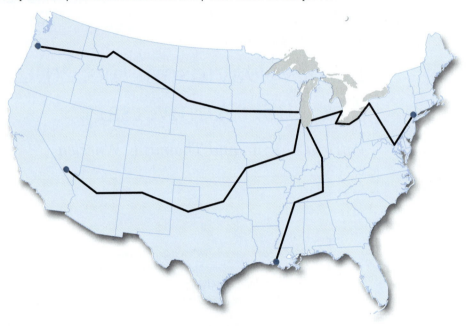

Source: www.harleydavidson.com, accessed December 3, 2002.

cycles in 1974. AMF favored short-term profits instead of investing in research and development and retooling. During this time, Japanese competitors continued to improve the quality of their motorcycles, while Harley-Davidson began to turn out noisy, oil-leaking, heavily vibrating, poorly finished, and hard-to-handle machines. AMF ignored the Japanese competition. In 1975, Honda Motor Company introduced its Gold Wing, which became the standard for large touring motorcycles. Harley-Davidson had controlled that segment of the market for years. There was a $2,000 price difference between Harley's top-of-the-line motorcycles and Honda's comparable Gold Wing. This caused American buyers of motorcycles to start switching to Japanese motorcycles. The Japanese companies (Suzuki and Yamaha) from this time until the mid-1980s continued to enter the heavyweight custom market with Harley lookalikes.

During AMF's ownership of the company, sales of motorcycles were strong, but profits were weak. The company had serious problems with poor-quality manufacturing and strong Japanese competition. In 1981, Vaughn Beals, then head of the Harley Division, and 13 other managers conducted a leveraged buyout of the company for $65 million.

New management installed a Materials as Needed (MAN) system to reduce inventories and stabilize the production schedule. Also, this system forced production to work with marketing to create more accurate forecasts. This led to precise production schedules for each month, allowing only a 10% variance. The company forced its suppliers to increase their quality in order to reduce customer complaints.

Citicorp, Harley's main lender, refused to lend the company more money in 1985. On New Year's Eve, four hours before a midnight that would have meant Harley's demise, the company inked a deal with Heller Financial that kept its doors open. Seven months later, amid a hot market for new stock, Harley-Davidson went public again. James L. Ziemer, the CFO, puts it more bluntly: "You throw cash at it, try to grow too fast, you'd destroy this thing."[3]

During the time Harley-Davidson was a privately held firm, management invested in research and development. Management purchased a Computer-Aided Design (CAD) system that allowed the company to make changes in the entire product line and still maintain its traditional styling. These investments by management had a quick payoff in that the break-even point went from 53,000 motorcycles in 1982 to 35,000 in 1986.

In June 1993, over 100,000 members of the worldwide Harley-Davidson family came home (Milwaukee) to celebrate the company's 90th anniversary. Willie G. Davidson, Vice President-Styling, grandson of the co-founder, said, "I was overwhelmed with emotion when our parade was rolling into downtown Milwaukee. I looked up to heaven and told the founding fathers, 'Thanks, guys.'"

During 1993, the company acquired a 49% interest in Buell Motorcycle Company, a manufacturer of sport/performance motorcycles. This investment in Buell offered the company the possibility of gradually gaining entry into select niches within the performance motorcycle market. In 1998, Harley-Davidson owned most of the stock in Buell. Buell began distribution of a limited number of Buell motorcycles during 1994 to select Harley-Davidson dealers. Buell sales were:

Year	Sales	Units (thousands)
1994	$ 6 million	576
1995	$14 million	1,407
1996	$23 million	2,762
1997	$40 million	4,415
1998	$53.5 million	6,334
1999	$63.5 million	7,767
2000	$58.1 million	10,189
2001	$61.9 million	9,925

Buell's mission "is to develop and employ innovative technology to enhance 'the ride' and give Buell owners a motorcycle experience that no other brand can provide." The European sport/performance market was four times larger than its U.S. counterpart. In 1997, there were 377 Buell dealers worldwide.

On November 14, 1995, the company acquired substantially all of the common stock and common stock equivalents of Eaglemark Financial Services, Inc., a company in which it held a 49% interest since 1993. Eaglemark provided credit to leisure product manufacturers, their dealers, and customers in the United States and Canada. The transaction was accounted for as a step acquisition under the purchase method. The purchase price for the shares and equivalents was approximately $45 million, which was paid from internally generated funds and short-term borrowings. The excess of the acquisition cost over the fair value of the net assets purchased resulted in approximately $43 million of goodwill, which was amortized on a straight-line basis over 20 years.

On January 22, 1996, the company announced its strategic decision to discontinue the operations of the Transportation Vehicles segment in order to concentrate its financial and human resources on its core motorcycle business. The Transportation Vehicles segment was comprised of Recreation Vehicles division (Holiday Rambler trailers), the Commercial Vehicles division (small delivery vehicles), and B & B Molders, a manufacturer of custom or standard tooling and injection-molded plastic pieces. During 1996, the company completed the sale of the Transportation Vehicles segment for an aggregate sales price of approximately $105 million—approximately $100 million in cash and $5 million in notes and preferred stock.

In the fall of 1997, GT Bicycles manufactured and distributed 1,000 Harley Limited Edition bicycles at a list retail price of $1,700. The pedal-powered bike had a real Harley paint job, signature fenders, a fake gas tank, and the chrome of a Harley Softail motorcycle. GT Bicycles manufactured the Velo Glide bikes and was licensed by Harley to produce the limited version. The four-speed bike weighed 40-plus pounds. Ken Alder, cycle shop owner, said, "It's a big clunker that no one would really want to ride." Nevertheless, the bicycles sold out in less than four months to buyers. The resale price for the Limited Edition jumped to $3,500, and one collector advertised his for $5,000. In contrast, a person could purchase an actual Harley XHL 883 Sportster motorcycle for $5,245.

Since 1997, Harley-Davidson had created an internal makeover. The unsung hero of Harley-Davidson's supply-chain makeover was an intense procurement expert named Garry Berryman, 48, Vice President of Materials management/Product Cost. He came to Harley by way of John Deere and Honda Motors. Berryman joined the company in 1995 to find that its supply-chain management has been neglected. There were nine different purchasing departments operating from different plant locations, 14 separate sets of representative terms and conditions, and nearly 4,000 suppliers. Engineers with little or no expertise in supply management were doing the bulk of the buying. To top it off, "the voice of supply management was buried three layers deep in the corporate hierarchy," said Berryman.

While at Honda, Berryman studied Japanese *keiretsu*—huge, vertically integrated companies that fostered deep, trusting relationships with suppliers. He wanted to form similar strategic alliances with Harley's top suppliers, bringing them into the design and planning process. Berryman felt that new technology and the Web would make it easier than ever to form these bonds and collaborate. He made it clear that relationship and strategy should drive applications, not vice versa. As Dave Cotteleer, the company's manager of planning and control, explained, "We're using technology to cut back on communication times and administrative trivia, like invoice tracking, so we can focus the relationships on more strategic issues. We're not saying, 'Here's a neat piece of technology. Let's jam it into our model.'"[4]

Also, in the 1990s, Harley-Davidson saw the need to build a motorcycle to try to appeal to the younger and international markets, which preferred sleeker, faster bikes. Harley-Davidson spent an undisclosed amount of research and development dollars over several years to develop the $17,000 V-Rod motorcycle. The V-Rod, introduced in 2001, had 110 horsepower, nearly double that of the standard Harley bike. The V-Rod was the quickest and fastest production model the company had ever built, capable of reaching 60 miles per hour in 3.5 seconds and 100 mph in a little over 8 seconds. Its top speed was about 140 mph. All in all, the V-Rod was faster and handled better than the traditional bulky Harley bikes.

All other Harley models were powered by 45-degree V-twin air-cooled engines with camshafts in the block; the new V-Rod had a 1,130cc 60-degree engine with double overhead cams and four values for each cylinder. The V-Rod had a very long 67.5-inch wheelbase, and it handled better than other Harleys because it is so much lighter. Furthermore, the V-Rod was only 26 inches off the ground, so it would accommodate a wide range of rides.[5] Harley-Davidson hoped to gain some of the younger markets with this new bike.

Corporate Governance

BOARD OF DIRECTORS

The Board of Directors consisted of nine members, of which only two were internal members—Richard E. Terlink, past Chairman, and Jeffrey L. Bleustein, Chairman and CEO. **Exhibit 2** highlights board members before the 2002 vote. In accordance with company bylaws, two of the directors, Richard J. Hermon-Taylor and Teerlink, whose term would expire at the 2002 meeting, were not eligible for re-election. The board recommended George H. Conrades, 63, to fill one of those seats. Conrades had been Chairman and CEO of Akamai Technologies since April 1999, and since August 1998, he has been associated with Polaris Venture Partners, an early-stage investment company. Previously, he had served as Executive Vice President of GTE. The other seat would remain empty, dropping the board size from nine to eight members.

Exhibit 2

Board of Directors: Harley-Davidson, Inc.

Barry K. Allen, *President, Allen Enterprises, LLC*
Barry has been a member of the Board since 1992. His distinguished business career has taken him from the telecommunications industry to leading a medical equipment and systems business and back again. Barry's diverse experience has been particularly valuable to the Board in the areas of marketing and organization transformation.

Richard I. Beattie, *Chairman of the Executive Committee, Simpson, Thacher & Bartlett*
Dick has been a valued advisor to Harley-Davidson for nearly 20 years. His contributions evolved and grew with the company over time. In the early 1980s, he provided legal and strategic counsel to the 13 leaders who purchased Harley-Davidson from AMF, taking it back to private ownership. He also advised the team when it was time to take the company public again in 1986. Dick was elected to the Board in 1996.

Jeffrey L. Bleustein, *Chairman and CEO, Harley-Davidson, Inc.*
Jeff began his association with Harley-Davidson in 1975, when he was asked to oversee the Engineering Group. During Jeff's tenure as Vice President–Engineering, Harley-Davidson developed the Evolution engine and established the foundations of its current line of cruiser and touring motorcycles. Jeff has demonstrated creativity and vision across a wide range of senior leadership roles. In 1996 he was elected to the Board, and in June 1997, he was appointed to his current position.

Richard J. Hermon-Taylor, *President, BioScience International, Inc. (term expires in 2002; not eligible for reelection)*
Richard joined the Board in 1986 and has been advising on marketing and manufacturing strategy for Harley-Davidson for nearly 20 years. His association with the company began when he was with the Boston Consulting Group in the mid-1970s and has been valued through the intervening years.

Donald A. James, *Vice Chairman and CEO, Fred Deeley Imports, Inc.*
Don's wisdom and knowledge of the motorcycle industry has guided the Board since 1991. As a 31-year veteran of Harley-Davidson's exclusive distributor in Canada, he has a strong sense for our core products. Don has a particularly keen understanding of the retrial issues involved with motorcycles and related products and the competitive advantage inherent in strong, long-lasting dealer relationships.

Richard G. LeFauve, *President, GM University; Senior Vice President, General Motors Corporation, retired*
Skip joined the Board in 1993. He has generously shared his vehicle industry experience with Harley-Davidson, including learning from his prior role as President of Saturn. Parallels in durable goods manufacturing, consumer trends, and lifelong customer marketing strategy has provided considerable creative stimuli for Board discussions.

Sara L. Levinson, *ChairMom and CEO, ClubMom, Inc.*
Sara joined the Board in 1996. She understands the value and power of strong brands, and her current senior leadership role in marketing and licensing, together with her previous experience at MTV, give her solid insights into the entertainment industries and younger customer segments.

James A. Norling, *Executive Vice President, Motorola, Inc.; President, Personal Communica-tions Sector, retired*
Jim has been a Board member since 1993. His career with Motorola has included extensive senior leadership assignments in Europe, the Middle East, and Africa, and he has generously shared his international experience and understanding of technological change to benefit Harley-Davidson.

Richard F. Teerlink, *Former Chairman and CEO, Harley-Davidson, Inc., retired (term expires in 2002; not eligible for reelection)*
Rich joined Harley-Davidson in 1981 and was elected to the Board in 1982. In 1988 he was appointed President of the company; in 1989, CEO. In 1996 he was named Chairman of the Board. Rich is credited with the financial restructuring of Harley-Davidson from private to public during the mid-1980s. His leadership was instrumental in creating at the company a values-based culture that revolves around developing mutually beneficial relationships with all stakeholders.

Source: Harley-Davidson, Inc., *2001 Annual Report*, p. 83.

The terms of the Board of Directors were a three-year stagger system: (a) the term expiring in 2002 was Sara L. Levinson (51); (b) terms expiring in 2003 were Bleustein (62), Donald James (58), and James A. Norling (60); and (c) terms expiring in 2004 were Barry K. Allen (53), Richard I. Beattie (62), and Richard G. LeFauve (67).

Directors who were employees of Harley-Davidson did not receive any special compensation for their services as directors. Directors who are not employees of Harley-Davidson receive an annual fee of $25,000 plus $1,500 for each regular meeting of the board, $750 for each special meeting of the board, $750 for each board committee meeting and a clothing allowance of $1,000 to purchase Harley-Davidson® MotorClothes™ apparel and accessories. Pursuant to the 1998 Director Stock Plan, an outside director could elect to receive 50% or 100% of the annual fee to be paid in each calendar year in the form of stock based on the fair market value at the time of the annual meeting. In 2001, each outside Director received an option to purchase 600 shares of common stock.[6]

All directors and executive officers as a group (19 individuals) owned 4,311,178 shares (1.4%). Jeffrey E. Bleustein owned the largest block with 1,785,993 shares, which was 0.5% of the outstanding stock. AXA Assurance I.A.R.D. Mutuelle owned 22,324,662 shares (7.4%) and was the largest shareholder.

The company's mission statement was as follows: "We fulfill dreams through the experience of motorcycling by providing to motorcyclists and to the general public an expanding line of motorcycles, branded products and services in selected market segments."[7]

TOP MANAGEMENT

Jeffrey E. Bleustein had been a director of the company since 1986. He was appointed Executive Vice President in 1991 and President and Chief Operating Officer of the Motor Company in 1993. In 1997, Bleustein succeeded Richard E. Teerlink as Chairman and CEO. Bleustein, a former Yale engineering professor, joined AMF in the early 1970s. In 1981, he joined Harley-Davidson. Thirteen Harley executives, including Bleustein, bought the company in a highly leveraged buyout—$80 of debt for every $1 of equity- in February 1981. "Before the ink had dried on our paper we were in violation of most of our loan covenants," he said. His current stake, at less than 1%, was worth $40 million.[8]

Exhibit 3 shows the corporate officers for Harley-Davidson and its business segments—motor company, Buell, and financial services.

The 100th Anniversary Celebration

Forbes named Harley-Davidson its "Company of the Year" for 2001 and was selected by *Business Week* as one of the nations' "Most Admired Companies." Additionally, in 2001, it was named to *Fortune*'s list of the "Top 100 Companies to Work for" for the fourth time in five years. The company unveiled its newest bike, the V-Rod, aimed at the younger, affluent riders with a list price of $16,995. The V-Rod was named *Motorcycle News* "Bike of the Year" the same year. Retail sales of Harley-Davison bikes were up 14.4% in 2001 in the United States. In Japan, Harley-Davidson celebrated its 17th consecutive year of growth with retail sales up 10.7% in 2001. In 2000 and 2001, Harley-Davidson was the best-selling heavyweight motorcycle in Japan.[9] With all this going for the company, they were moving to their year-long 100th Anniversary Celebration with excitement, hope for the future, and satisfaction for past accomplishments. The party was planned to be a year-long celebration, from summer 2002 culminating in a three-day party in Milwaukee in late August 2003.

All was not rosy for the century-old company. Harley-Davidson, which had fought back from near demise in the 1980s was to face new rivals in the competitive market, the aging customer base, and the lasting recession. The projected sales figures looked strong through 2003, but after the collectors' editions were sold, what would 2004 hold for Harley-Davidson? It's

Exhibit 3
Corporate Officers, Harley-Davidson, Inc.

Jeffrey L. Bleustein
Chairman and CEO

James M. Brostowitz
Vice President, Controller, and Treasurer

Gail A. Lione
Vice President, General Counsel, and Secretary

James L. Ziemer
Vice President and Chief Financial Officer

Motor Company Leadership

Jeffrey L. Bleustein
CEO

Garry S. Berryman
Vice President, Materials Management/Product Cost

Joanne M. Bischmann
Vice President, Marketing

James M. Brostowitz
Vice President and Controller

Roy Coleman
General Manager, Tomahawk Operations

Ruth M. Crowley
Vice President, General Merchandise

William B. Dannehl
Vice President and General Manager, York Operations

William G. Davidson
Vice President, Styling

Karl M. Eberle
Vice President and General Manager, Kansas City Operations

Jon R. Flickinger
Vice President, North American Sales and Dealer Services

John A. Hevey
Vice President

Jorge F. Hidalgo
General Manager, Pilgrim Road Operations

Timothy K. Hoelter
Vice President, Government Affairs

Ronald M. Hutchinson
Vice President, Parts and Accessories

Michael D. Keefe
Vice President and Director, Harley Owners Group®

Donald C. Kieffer
General Manager, Capitol Drive Operations

Kathleen A. Lawler
Vice President, Communications

Gail A. Lione
Vice President and General Counsel

James A. McCaslin
President and Chief Operating Officer

Steven R. Phillips
Vice President, Quality, Reliability, and Technical Services

John Russell
Vice President and Managing Director, Europe

Harold A. Scott
Vice President, Human Resources

W. Kenneth Sutton, Jr.
Vice President, Continuous Improvement

Earl K. Werner
Vice President, Engineering

Jerry G. Wilke
Vice President and General Manager, Asia/Pacific and Latin America Regions

Harley-Davidson Financial Services Leadership

Lawrence G. Hund
Vice President and Chief Financial Officer

Donna F. Zarcone
President and Chief Operating Officer

Buell Motorcycle Company Leadership

Erik F. Buell
Chairman and Chief Technical Officer

John A. Hevey
President and Chief Operating Officer

Source: Harley-Davidson, Inc., *2001 Annual Report*, p. 84.

losing market share to Japanese rivals such as Honda Motors Co., seeing lower prices for some older bikes that used to trade at a premium, and facing a peculiar marketing headache stemming from its upcoming 100th anniversary. Buyers seem to be hanging back, awaiting 2003's collector-edition models.[10] The coming year was less certain. These were issues management wrestled with during the celebration gala. One theme during the attention-getting celebration was to gain new, younger customers to move Harley-Davidson into its second century.

Harley-Davidson, the marvel of Milwaukee, which roared back from near-ruin in 1986 to dazzle investors and bikers alike with its marketing artistry, financial savvy, and sheer mystique may be facing a patch of rough road.

Harley Owners Group (H.O.G.)

A special kind of camaraderie marked the Harley Owners Group (H.O.G.) rallies and other motorcycle events. At events and rallies around the world, members of the H.O.G. came together for fun, adventure, and a love of their machines and the open road. As the largest

Exhibit 4

2002 Profile of the H.O.G. and BRAG: Harley-Davidson, Inc.

H.O.G.-Sponsored Events: In 2001 H.O.G. continued to sponsor motorcycling events on local, regional, national, and international levels, including U.S. national rallies in Worcester, Maine, and Milwaukee, Wisconsin, as well as a special touring journey rally that took participants through Americana on legendary Route 66 from Chicago, Illinois, to Santa Monica, California. The 11th annual international H.O.G. Rally, held in Saint-Tropez, France, drew tens of thousands of members.

H.O.G. Membership: Any Harley-Davidson motorcyclist could become a member of H.O.G.. In fact, the first year of membership was included with the purchase of a new Harley-Davidson motorcycle. The number of H.O.G. members had grown rapidly since the motorcycle organization began in 1983 with 33,000 members. There were 660,000 H.O.G. members in 115 countries worldwide. Sponsorship of H.O.G. chapters by Harley-Davidson dealers grew from 49 chapters in 1985 to 1,200 chapters at the close of 2001.

A Snapshot of H.O.G.

Worldwide members	660,000
Worldwide dealer-sponsored chapters	1,200
Countries with members	115

A Snapshot of BRAG (Buell Riders Adventure Group)

Created in	1995
Worldwide members	10,000
Number of clubs	55

Source: Harley-Davidson, Inc., *2001 Annual Report*, pp. 28–29.

motorcycle club in the world, H.O.G. offered customers organized opportunities to ride their famed bikes. H.O.G. rallies visibly promoted the Harley-Davidson experience to potential new customers and strengthened the relationships among members, dealers, and Harley-Davidson employees.

William G. Davidson, grandson of the co-founder, biker to the core, and known to all as Willie G. dismissed the charge without quite denying it. "There's a lot of beaners, but they're out on the motorcycles, which is a beautiful thing," he says, noting that he recently co-led a national rally of Canadian H.O.G. groups with Harley's top executive, CEO Jeff Bleustein.[11]

In 1995, the Buell Riders Adventure Group (BRAG) was created to bring Buell motorcycle enthusiasts together and to share their on-road experiences. In 2001, BRAG held a homecoming event in East Troy, Wisconsin. Harley-Davidson plans to grow both organizations with new members and chapters in the years to come.

Exhibit 4 provides a profile of H.O.G and BRAG clubs. As of 2001, there were about 660,000 H.O.G. members in about 1,200 clubs. The newer BRAG club for Buell riders numbered 10,000 members over 55 clubs.

Foreign Operations[12]

EUROPE/MIDDLE EAST/AFRICA

In the European Region there were currently 381 independent Harley-Davidson dealerships serving 32 country markets. This included 280 combined Harley-Davidson and Buell dealerships. Buell was further represented by 10 dealerships that did not sell Harley-Davidson motorcycles. They had an established infrastructure in Europe, based out of its headquarters in the United Kingdom, and it operated through a network of independent dealers served by eight independent distributors and by five wholly owned sales and marketing subsidiaries in France, Germany, Italy, The Netherlands, and the United Kingdom. The European management team is continuing to focus on the expansion and improvement of distributor and dealer relationships through the dealer development team, specialized training programs, retail financing initiatives, ongoing product development, and coordinated Europe-wide and local marketing programs aimed at attracting new customers. Other initiatives included the development of information systems linking European subsidiaries directly with each of the major independent distributors and most of the dealers located in the subsidiary markets.

ASIA-PACIFIC

There were currently 240 Harley-Davidson outlets serving eight country markets of which 82 are combined Harley-Davidson/Buell dealerships, and 27 were service-only outlets. In addition, there were currently only two Buell dealerships. Management expected the majority of its growth opportunities in the Asia-Pacific region to come from its existing markets in Japan and Australia. Harley-Davidson would continue to support its objectives of maintaining and growing its business in southeast Asia, where markets had continued to stabilize over recent years.

LATIN AMERICA

This market consisted of 15 country markets managed from Milwaukee, Wisconsin. The Latin American market had a diverse dealer network including 28 Harley-Davidson dealerships. Management planned to continue developing its distribution in Brazil and Mexico, its two biggest Latin American markets, as well as broaden brand management and marketing activities across the entire region.

CANADA

In Canada, there were currently 75 independent Harley-Davidson dealerships and one independent standalone Buell dealership served by a single independent distributor. This network included 25 combined Harley-Davidson and Buell dealerships, resulting in a total of 26 Buell dealerships in Canada.

Business Segments

Running a company is like riding a motorcycle. Go too slow, and you tip over. Go too fast, and you crash. At the moment, Harley has a perfect balance.[13]

Harley-Davidson operates in two principal business segments: Motorcycles and Related Products (Motorcycles) and Financial Services. The segments will be discussed in that order. **Exhibit 5** provides financial information on the company's two business segments.

Motorcycles and Related Products Segment

The longer the waits, the more Wall Street loved Harley.[14]

The primary business of the motorcycles segment was to design, manufacture and sell premium motorcycles, for the heavyweight market. It was best known for its Harley-Davidson® motorcycle products, but also offered a line of motorcycles and related products under the Buell® brand name. Its worldwide motorcycle sales generated 80.0%, 79.4% and 79.7% of the total net sales in the motorcycles segment during 2001, 2000, and 1999, respectively.

Exhibit 5

Information by Industry Segment: Harley-Davidson, Inc.
(Dollar amounts in thousands)

A. Revenues and Income from Operations

Year Ending December 31	2001	2000	1999
Net sales and financial services income			
Motorcycles and related products net sales	$3,363,414	$2,906,365	$2,452,939
Financial services income	181,545	140,135	132,741
	$3,544,959	$3,046,500	$2,585,680
Income from operations			
Motorcycles and related products	$613,311	$487,485	$397,601
Financial services	61,273	37,178	27,685
General corporate expenses	(12,083)	(9,691)	(9,427)
Operating income	$662,561	$514,972	$415,859

B. Assets, Depreciation, and Capital Expenditures

	Motorcycles and Related Products	Financial Services	Corporate	Consolidated
1999				
Identifiable assets	$1,058,934	$868,711	$184,432	$2,112,077
Depreciation and amortization	107,737	5,813	272	113,822
Net capital expenditures	162,071	3,565	150	165,786
2000				
Identifiable assets	$1,158,813	$856,961	$420,630	$2,436,404
Depreciation and amortization	127,085	6,012	251	133,348
Net capital expenditures	199,306	4,177	128	203,611
2001				
Identifiable assets	$1,385,932	$1,096,239	$636,324	$3,118,495
Depreciation and amortization	146,260	6,618	183	153,061
Net capital expenditures	285,023	5,193	165	290,381

Source: Harley-Davidson, Inc., *2001 Annual Report*, pp. 80–81.

The majority of the Harley-Davidson branded motorcycle products emphasized traditional styling, design simplicity, durability, ease of service, and evolutionary change. Harley's appeal straddled class boundaries, stirring the hearts of grease monkeys and corporate titans alike. Malcolm Forbes, the late owner of *Forbes* magazine, was pivotal in introducing Harleys to the business elite in the early 1980s.[15]

The typical rider was a 38-year-old male who was married, had attended college, and earned $44,250 a year. Based on data from the 1998 Motorcycle Industry Council owner survey, nearly one out of every 12 motorcycle owners in the United States was a woman.[16] The average U.S. Harley-Davidson motorcycle purchaser was a married male in his mid-40s with a household income of approximately $78,300, who purchased a motorcycle for recreational purposes rather than to provide transportation and was an experienced motorcycle rider. Over two-thirds of the firm's U.S. sales of Harley-Davidson motorcycles were to buyers with at least one year of education beyond high school, and 31% of the buyers had college degrees (see **Exhibit 6**).

Buell motorcycle products emphasize innovative design, responsive handling, and overall performance. The Buell motorcycle product line has traditionally consisted of heavyweight performance models, powered by the 1200cc V-Twin engine. However, in 2000, they intro-

Exhibit 6

Purchaser Demographic Profile: Harley-Davidson, Inc.

	2001	**2000**	**1999**	**1998**	**1997**	**1990**	**1983**
Gender							
Male	91%	91%	91%	93%	93%	96%	98%
Female	9%	9%	9%	7%	7%	4%	2%
Median Age (years)	45.6	45.6	44.6	44.4	44.6	36.7	34.1
Median household income							
($000)	$78.3	$77.7	$73.8	$73.6	$74.1	$47.3	$38.3

2001 Purchasers

41%	Owned Harley-Davidson motorcycle previously
31%	Coming off competitive motorcycle
28%	New to motorcycling or haven't owned a motorcycle for at least 5 years

Source: Harley-Davidson Inc., Demographics.com accessed August 4, 2002.

duced the Buell Blast®, a new vehicle designed specifically to attract new customers into the sport of motorcycling. This vehicle is considerably smaller, lighter, and less expensive than the traditional Buell heavyweight models and is powered by a 492cc single-cylinder engine.

The average U.S. purchaser of Buell heavyweight motorcycles is a male with a median age of 39, with a median household income of approximately $61,600. Approximately 3% of all Buell heavyweight U.S. retail motorcycle sales are to females. Internal documents indicate that half of Buell Blast purchasers have never owned motorcycles before, and in excess of 95% of them had never owned Buell motorcycles before. The median age of Blast purchasers is 38, with over one-half of them being female.

The motorcycle market was composed of four segments: standard, which emphasized simplicity and cost; performance, which emphasized handling and acceleration; touring, which emphasized comfort and amenities for long-distance travel; and custom, which emphasized styling and individual owner customization.

Harley-Davidson presently manufactured and sold 28 models of Harley-Davidson *touring and custom heavyweight* motorcycles, with domestic manufacturer's suggested retail prices ranging from approximately $5,695 to $24,995 (see **Exhibit 7.**) The touring segment of the heavyweight market was pioneered by Harley-Davidson and included motorcycles equipped for long-distance touring with fairings, windshields, saddlebags, and Tour Pak® luggage carriers. The custom segment of the market included motorcycles featuring the distinctive styling associated with classic Harley-Davidson motorcycles. These motorcycles were highly customized through the use of trim and accessories.

Harley-Davidson's traditional heavyweight motorcycles were based on variations of five basic chassis designs and were powered by one of four air-cooled, twin-cylinder engines with a 45-degree "V" configuration, which had displacements of 883cc, 1200cc, 1450cc, and 1550cc. The recently introduced V-Rod™ had its own unique chassis design and is equipped with the new Revolution™ powertrain, a new liquid-cooled, twin-cylinder, 1130cc engine, with a 60-degree "V" configuration.

Although there were some accessory differences between the top-of-the line touring motorcycles and those of its competitors, suggested retail prices were generally comparable. The prices for the high end of the Harley-Davidson custom product line ranged from being competitive to 50% more than its competitors' custom motorcycles. The custom portion of the Harley-Davidson product line represents its highest unit volumes and continued to command a premium price because of the features, styling, and high resale value associated with

Exhibit 7

2002 Motorcycles Product Line: Harley-Davidson, Inc.

Motorcycle	Suggested Selling Price ($)
Buell Blast![1]	4,595
XLH Sportster 883	6,145
XLH Sportster 883 Hugger®	6,545
XL Sportster 883R	6,795
XL883C Sportster 883 Custom	7,690
XLM Sportster1200	8,425
XL 1200S Sportster 1200 Sport	9,130
XB9S Buell Lightning[1]	9,995
XB9R Buell Firebolt[1]	9,995
XL 1200C Sportster 1200 Custom	10,040
FXD Dyna Glide Super Glider®	12.490
FXST Softail® Standard	13,870
FXDX Dyna Glide Super Glide® Sport	14,510
FLHT/FLHTI Electra Glide® Standard	14,710
FXDXT Dyna Glide Super Glide® T-Sport	15,520
FXSTB Softail® Night Train®	15,575
FXDL Dyna Glide Low Rider®	16,090
FLSTS/FLSTSI Springer®	16,630
FLHR/FLHRI Road King®	16,650
VRSCA V-Rod	16,995
FLSTF/FLSTFI Fat Boy®	17,100
FXDWG Dyna Glide Wide Glider®	17,215
FXSTD Softail® Deuce	17,870
FLTSC/FLSTCI Heritage Softail® Classic	17,870
FLHTC/FLHTCI Electra Glide® Classic	18,070
FLHRCI Road King® Classic	18,310
FLTR/FLTRI Road Glide	18,520
FLSTS/FLSTSI Heritage Springer®	18,615
VRSC V-Rod® VRSCA	18,695
FLHTCUI Ultra Classic®	21,065

Note:

1. The Buell Blast!, Buell Lightning, and Buell Firebolt are manufactured by Buell Motorcycle Company, which partnered with Harley-Davidson in 1993 and was purchased by Harley-Davidson in 1998.

Source: www.harley-davidson.com payment calculator schedule, accessed December 12, 2002.

Harley-Davidson custom products. The smallest displacement custom motorcycle (the 883cc Sportster®) was directly price competitive with comparable motorcycles available in the market. The surveys of retail purchasers indicated that, historically, over three-quarters of the purchasers of its Sportster model either had previously owned competitive-brand motorcycles or were completely new to the sport of motorcycling or had not participated in the sport for at least five years. Since 1988, research had consistently shown that purchasers of Harley-Davidson motorcycles had a repurchase intent in excess of 90%, and management expected to see sales of its 883cc Sportster model partially translated into sales of its higher-priced products in the normal two- to three-year ownership cycle.

The major Parts and Accessories (P&A) products were replacement parts (Genuine Motor Parts) and mechanical and cosmetic accessories (Genuine Motor Accessories). Worldwide P&A net sales comprised 15.1%, 15.4%, and 14.8% of net sales in the Motorcycles segment in 2001, 2000, and 1999, respectively.

Worldwide net sales of General Merchandise, which included MotorClothes™ apparel and collectibles, comprised 4.9%, 5.2%, and 5.4% of net sales in the Motorcycles segment in 2001, 2000, and 1999, respectively.

Management also provided a variety of services to its dealers and retail customers, including service training schools, customized dealer software packages, delivery of its motorcycles, an owners' club membership, a motorcycle rental program, and a rider training program that was available in the United States through a limited number of authorized dealers.

PRESIDENT AND CEO'S COMMENTS[17]

President Jeffrey L. Bluestein said in the 2001 *Annual Report*,

> *It is a legacy forged by generations of people with a passion for motorcycling, a commitment to honor and build on the past, and the determinations to seek out new opportunities for the future. In 2001, despite the global economic downturn, Harley-Davidson achieved its 16th consecutive year of record revenue and earnings. Consolidated revenue for Harley-Davidson, Inc. was $3.36 billion, a 15.7% increase over 2000, while net income was $437.7 million, a 25.9% increase over the previous year, As a result, diluted earnings per share climbed from $1.13 to $1.43—a 26.4% increase. [see **Exhibits 8** and **9**]*

OVERVIEW

The venerable motorcycle company was anything but set in its ways.[18] Consider Harley customer Bob Johnson, 52, vice-president of an Oren, Utah maker of oil-industry tools. Back in 2000, when Johnson bought his Softail Fat Boy, he had to wait five months and pay $1,000 over suggested retail. Even then, he considered himself lucky: In Texas, Harleys were fetching $4,000 to $5,000 over list. But last December, he snared an Electra Glide Classic for $1,200 below retail and rode away on his tricked-out $16,770 touring machine. "They had inventory, and they were actually discounting," he crowed.[19]

The customer waiting list for new motorcycles had shrunk from as much as two years to a matter of months. Dealer premiums that used to range between $2,000 and $4,000 have disappeared for most models. Dealers were grateful the company was playing the centennial to the hilt. But the question, says a dealer, was "What's going to happen in 2004?" The answer: Harley must get ahead of the demographics curve with new customers while somehow keeping faith with its fanatical old ones. If it doesn't, the born-to-be-wild company will begin its second century with profit growth that is doomed to be mild.[20]

NEW BIKES: THE BUELL AND THE V-ROD

Harley's new V-Rod was introduced in the Los Angeles Convention Center on July 12, 2001. More than 4,000 packed into the center for the company's long-awaited announcement. The cavernous room went black. The engines roared in the darkness. Spotlights clicked on and followed two glinting new hot rods as they roared onto center stage.[21]

Harley-Davidson deviated from its traditional approach to styling, with the introduction of the V-Rod™ motorcycle. The new, liquid-cooled V-Rod, inspired by Harley-Davidson's drag racing heritage, combines the characteristics of a performance motorcycle with the styling of a custom.[22] Liquid cooling allowed riders to rev a little higher and hotter in each gear, boosting acceleration. This was a giant step for a company so stubbornly conservative that it had made only air-cooled engines for 100 years; its designers just couldn't bear the idea of hanging a radiator on the front of the bike.[23]

The V-Rod was Milwaukee-based Harley-Davison Inc.'s first truly new motorcycle in more than 50 years. A sleek machine in the making for more than six years, the V-Rod was

Exhibit 8

Selected United States and World Financial and Sales Information: Harley-Davidson, Inc.

A. Motor Company Revenue, 2001
(Dollar amounts in millions)

Harley-Davidson Motorcycles	$2.630.1
Parts and Accessories	507.3
General Merchandise	163.9
Buell Motorcycles	61.9
Other	0.2
Total	**$3,363.4**

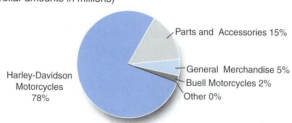

Parts and Accessories 15%
General Merchandise 5%
Buell Motorcycles 2%
Other 0%
Harley-Davidson Motorcycles 78%

B. Worldwide Motorcycle Shipments
(Units in thousands)

	1997	1998	1999	2000	2001
Exports	36.1	38.8	41.6	45.8	46.7
Total Motorcycle Shipments	132.3	150.5	177.2	204.6	234.5
Export Percentage	27.3%	25.8%	23.5%	22.4%	19.9%

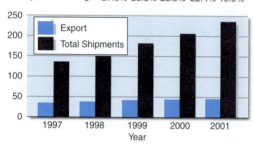

C. Worldwide Parts and Accessories and General Merchandise Revenue
(Dollar amounts in millions)

	1997	1998	1999	2000	2001
General Merchandise	95.1	114.5	132.7	151.4	163.9
Parts and Accessories	241.9	297.1	362.6	447.9	507.3

D. Operating Income
(Dollar amounts in millions)

1997	1998	1999	2000	2001
$270.0	$333.6	$415.8	$514.9	$662.5

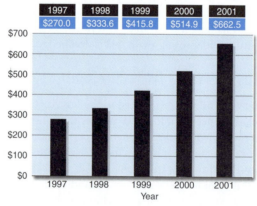

Source: Harley-Davidson, Inc., *2001 Annual Report* and *10-K*.

Exhibit 9

World Registrations: Harley-Davidson, Inc.

A. North American 651+CC Motorcycle Registrations
(Units in thousands)

	1992	1993	1994	1995	1996	1997	1998	1999	2000	2001
Total industry	112.0	132.8	150.4	163.1	182.7	206.1	246.2	297.9	365.4	422.8
Harley-Davidson	56.0	63.4	69.5	77.0	86.3	99.3	116.1	142.0	163.1	185.6
Harley-Davidson market share	50.0%	47.7%	46.2%	47.2%	47.2%	48.2%	47.2%	47.7%	44.6%	43.9%

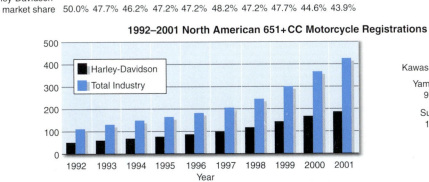

1992–2001 North American 651+CC Motorcycle Registrations

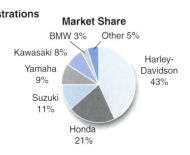

Market Share

BMW 3% · Other 5% · Kawasaki 8% · Yamaha 9% · Suzuki 11% · Honda 21% · Harley-Davidson 43%

B. European 651+CC Motorcycle Registrations
(Units in thousands)

	1992	1993	1994	1995	1996	1997	1998	1999	2000	2001
Total industry	212.1	218.6	201.9	207.2	224.7	250.3	270.2	306.7	293.4	293.6
Harley-Davidson	12.1	13.2	14.4	15.4	15.3	15.1	15.7	17.8	19.9	19.6
Harley-Davidson market share	5.7%	6.1%	7.1%	7.4%	6.8%	6.0%	5.8%	5.8%	6.8%	6.7%

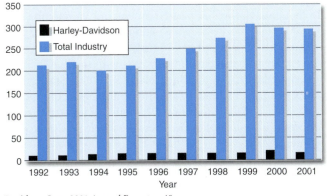

2001 European 651+CC Motorcycle Registrations

Market Share

Aprilia 3% · Other 5% · Triumph 5% · Ducati 6% · Harley-Davidson 7% · Kawasaki 9% · BMW 15% · Yamaha 16% · Suzuki 17% · Honda 17%

Source: Harley-Davidson, Inc., *2001 Annual Report*, p. 40.

Exhibit 9

World Registrations: Harley-Davidson, Inc. (*continued*)

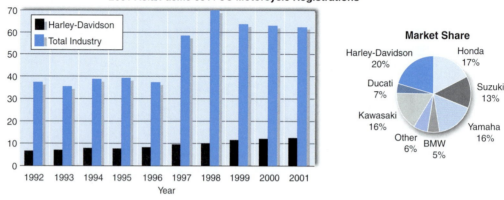

C. Asia/Pacific 651+CC Motorcycle Registrations
(Units in thousands)

	1992	1993	1994	1995	1996	1997	1998	1999	2000	2001
Total industry	37.5	35.7	39.1	39.4	37.4	58.9	69.2	63.1	62.7	62.1
Harley-Davidson	6.2	6.7	7.6	7.9	8.2	9.7	10.3	11.6	12.2	12.7
Harley-Davidson market share	16.1%	18.7%	19.4%	20.1%	21.9%	16.4%	14.8%	18.5%	19.5%	20.4%

2001 Asia/Pacific 651+CC Motorcycle Registrations

designed more for speed and handling, unlike the company's immensely popular touring bikes. The V-Rod was one factor behind Harley-Davidson's strong financial performance.

Harley-Davidson's Chief Executive Offer Jeffrey Bleustein, was well aware of the popularity. He was on a local dealer's list, eagerly awaiting the arrival of the V-Rod he ordered a few months ago.[24]

As the company ramped up production, premiums on many models disappeared. Chief Financial Offer James L. Ziemer says Harley wanted to "narrow the gap" between supply and demand in order to curb the long-standing—but fast-diminishing—practice of selling bikes at a premium.[25] The new V-Rod's $17,000 price tag had also failed to win younger buyers.[26] To that end, Harley has poured money into developing new, youth-oriented models. The $17,000 Harley V-Rod—a low-slung, high-powered number known formally as a sport performance vehicle and colloquially as a crotch rocket—was meant for hard-charging youths. Harley had also tried to go young with the Buell Firebolt ($10,000), its answer to Japanese sport bikes, and the Buell Blast ($4,400), a starter motorcycle. But Buell, a subsidiary Harley bought in 1988, has captured just 2% of the sport-bike market, and Harley would make only 10,000 V-Rods in 2002. Bleustein insisted that those numbers weren't the point: "These aren't one-shot deals. These are whole new platforms from which many models will proliferate."[27]

At the Detroit Harley-Davidson/Buell dealership in Center Line, owner Jim Loduca commented: "This is the first time in 10 years that I've actually had product on the floor available, but our sales are also up by 14 percent this year. The company has watched this demand curve very carefully. They are simply riding the wave. They know full well that it would be catastrophic to saturate the market." He was also encouraged by Harley's biggest product departure in recent decades—the V-Rod muscle bike.[28]

Clay Wilwert, whose family has owned a dealership in Dubuque since 1959, said, "But guess what, as they rode it, they loved it. They said, 'Hey, this is really cool that it doesn't shape my hands asleep.' "[29]

Some Harley traditionalists say the V-Rod, styled to compete with super-fast European bikes, strayed too far from the company's all-American roots, which tend to favor heavier cruising machines. Dealerships sold them for several thousand dollars over the $16,995 list price, and they're the talk of Bike Week.[30]

LICENSING[31]

Harley-Davidson endeavored to create an awareness of the "Harley-Davidson" brand among the nonriding public and provided a wide range of products for enthusiasts by licensing the name "Harley-Davidson" and numerous related trademarks. Harley-Davidson had licensed the production and sale of a broad range of consumer items, including t-shirts, jewelry, small leather goods, toys, and numerous other products (Licensed Products). They also licensed the use of the name in connection with a cafe located in Las Vegas. Although the majority of licensing activity occured in the United States, Harley-Davidson continued to expand these activities in international markets.

The licensing activity provided a valuable source of advertising and goodwill. Licensing also has proven to be an effective means for enhancing the corporate image with consumers, and it provided an important tool for policing the unauthorized use of the trademarks, thereby protecting the Harley-Davidson brand and its use. Royalty revenues from licensing, included in motorcycle segment net sales, were approximately $32 million, $31 million, and $26 million during 2001, 2000, and 1999, respectively. While royalty revenues from licensing activities were relatively small, the profitability of this business was relatively high.

INVENTORY

There was the question about the inventory lag. In the past, there was up to a two-year wait for a new Harley-Davidson bike. Current trends predicted that the lag will drop to nearly zero, potentially leaving inventory on the dealers' floor, a concept new to Harley-Davidson. "In the end, there's more inventory out there," says Dean Gianoukos, JP Morgan leisure-industry analyst. "The question is, is it because of the economy? Because of people waiting to get the 2003's so they're not buying the 2002 models? Or is it that, if you increase production every year by 15%, you're going to eventually hit a wall?" He has a "long-term buy" on the shares, JP Morgan's second-highest rating.[32] (See **Exhibit 10** for Motorcycle Unit Shipments and Unit Sales for 2000 and 2001.)

Critics saw deeper problems for Harley. They said sales had slowed and that Harley has tried to mask the slowdown by pushing dealers to buy bikes they don't need—known as channel stuffing—and allowing them to borrow to fund the purchases through Harley's financial arm. Dealers may feel the need to take on more inventory because their future allocations of hot models depend on past purchases, bears say. "There's no question there's a lot more inventory on the dealer floor and the parent company has basically shoved merchandise into the dealer network," says Doug Kass of Seabreeze Partners, a hedge fund, who has sold shares of Harley stock short. The company disagreed.[33]

MARKETING AND DISTRIBUTION[34]

It's hard to put into words," said Joanne Bischmann, Vice President of Marketing for Harley-Davidson. "We knew that kicking-off Harley-Davidson's next 100 years was going to call for something that couldn't easily be described in words, but would be an unforgettable Harley-Davidson experience for anyone who participated. We think the Open Road Tour fits the bill."[35]

Marketing efforts are divided among dealer promotions, customer events, magazine and direct-mail advertising, public relations, cooperative programs with Harley-Davidson/Buell

Exhibit 10

A. Motorcycle Unit Shipments and Net Sales: Harley-Davidson, Inc.

	2001	2000	Increase (Decrease)	Percentage Change
Motorcycle unit shipments				
Harley-Davidson motorcycle units	234,461	204,592	29,869	14.6
Buell motorcycle units	9,925	10,189	(264)	(2.6)
Total motorcycle units	244,386	214,781	29,605	13.8
Net Sales ($thousands)				
Harley-Davidson motorcycles	$2,630.1	$2,246.4	$383.7	17.1
Buell motorcycles	61.9	58.1	3.8	6.6
Total motorcycles	2,692.0	2,304.5	387.5	16.8
Motorcycle parts and accessories	507.3	447.9	59.4	13.3
General merchandise	163.9	151.4	12.5	8.2
Other	.2	2.6	(2.4)	(92.3)
Total motorcycles and related parts	$3,363.4	$2,906.4	$457.0	15.7

B. 2001 Quarterly Motorcycle Shipments: Harley-Davidson, Inc.

	Q1	Q2	Q3	Q4	2001
Shipping days	60	64	59	62	245
Harley-Davidson units					
Sportster	11,455	12,849	12,819	13,691	50,814
Custom	28,149	30,202	27,632	32,320	118,303
Touring	14,550	17,110	16,160	17,524	65,344
Total	54,154	60,161	56,611	63,535	234,461
Domestic	40,210	48,018	45,071	53,616	186,915
International	13,944	12,143	11,540	9,919	47,546
Total	54,154	60,161	56,611	63,535	234,461
Buell units					
Buell (excluding Blast)	1,593	1,757	1,878	1,208	6,436
Buell Blast	854	711	961	963	3,489
Total	2,447	2,468	2,839	2,171	9,925

Source: Harley-Davidson, Inc.

dealers and beginning in 2002, television advertising. In 1999, the Motor Company began a five-year strategic alliance with the Ford Motor Company that brought together resources to focus on a series of technical and marketing ventures. Harley-Davidson also sponsored racing activities and special promotional events and participated in all the major motorcycle consumer shows and rallies.

The Harley Owners Group®, or "H.O.G.®", had approximately 660,000 members worldwide in 2002 and was the industry's largest company-sponsored motorcycle enthusiast organization. Harley-Davidson formed this riders' club in 1983, in an effort to encourage Harley-Davidson owners to become more actively involved in the sport of motorcycling. The Buell Riders Adventure Group, or "BRAG®", was formed in recent years and had grown to approximately 10,000 members. BRAG sponsored events, including national rallies and rides, across the United States for Buell motorcycle enthusiasts.

Total expenditures on worldwide marketing, selling, and advertising were approximately $203.1 million, $189.8 million, and $164.3 million during 2001, 2000, and 1999, respectively.

E-COMMERCE[36]

Harley-Davidson's e-commerce capability had its first full year of operation in 2001. Its model was unique in the industry in that, while the online catalog was viewed from the Harley-Davidson Web site, orders were actually distributed to the participating authorized Harley-Davidson dealer that the customer selected. In turn, the dealer filled the order and handled any after-sale services that the customer may require. In addition to purchasing, customers actively browsed the site, created and shared product wish lists, and utilized the dealer locator.

INTERNATIONAL SALES[37]

International sales were approximately $597 million, $585 million, and $537 million, accounting for approximately 18%, 20%, and 22% of net sales of the Motorcycles segment, during 2001, 2000, and 1999, respectively. In 2001, Japan, Canada, and Germany, in that order, represented the largest international markets and together accounted for approximately 56% of international sales. Harley-Davidson ended 2001 with a 6.7% share of the European heavyweight (651cc+) market and a 20.4% share of the Asia-Pacific (Japan and Australia) heavyweight (651cc+) market.

DISTRIBUTION[38]

The basic channel of distribution in the United States for its motorcycles and related products consisted of approximately 633 independently owned full-service Harley-Davidson dealerships to which Harley-Davidson sold directly. This included 412 combined Harley-Davidson and Buell dealerships. There are no Buell-only dealerships. With respect to sales of new motorcycles, approximately 82% of the U.S. dealerships sold Harley-Davidson motorcycles exclusively. All dealerships stocked and sold genuine replacement parts, accessories, and MotorClothes™ apparel and collectibles, and performed service for the Harley-Davidson's motorcycles.

The company also sold a smaller portion of its parts and accessories and general merchandise through "non-traditional" retail outlets. The "non-traditional" outlets, which are extensions of the main dealership, consisted of Secondary Retail Locations (SRLs), Alternate Retail Outlets (AROs), and Seasonal Retail Outlets (SROs). SRLs, also known as Harley Shops, were satellites of the main dealership and were developed to meet the service needs of riding customers. Harley Shops also provide replacement parts and accessories and MotorClothes apparel and collectibles and were authorized to sell new motorcycles. AROs were located primarily in high-traffic areas such as malls, airports, or popular vacation destinations and focus on selling the MotorClothes apparel and collectibles and Licensed Products. SROs were located in similar high traffic areas, but operated on a seasonal basis out of temporary locations such as vendor kiosks. AROs and SROs were not authorized to sell new motorcycles. Presently, there were approximately 65 SRLs, 50 AROs, and under 20 SROs located in the United States.

RETAIL CUSTOMER AND DEALER FINANCING

Management believed HDFS and other financial services companies provided adequate retail and wholesale financing to Harley-Davidson's domestic and Canadian dealers and customers. In Europe, HDFS provided wholesale financing to dealers through a joint venture agreement with Transamerica Distribution Finance Corporation. HDFS had exercised its option to terminate the joint venture effective August 2002 and began serving the wholesale financing needs of Harley-Davidson's European dealers at that time.[39]

HARLEY-DAVIDSON CUSTOMER BASE

"Fads don't have 100th birthdays," boasts CEO Jeffery Bleustein[40]

Harley-Davidson's customers were not what some people expect. They expected rough and tumble riders and did not expect that a good proportion of Harley-Davidson riders were white-collar workers and executives who take weekend relaxation on their bikes. Selected quotes from customers follow:

"It's about an image—freedom of the road, hop on your bike and go, independent living, the loosing of the chains," said Dave Sarnowski, a teacher and Harley rider from La Farge, Wisconsin.[41]

"The Harley people I know go to church, have jobs, shop at the mall, just like everyone else." says Angie Robison, 68, of Daytona Beach, who helps her husband Joe run a motorcycle repair shop and Harley memorabilia/accessories store. "I can wear my silks over here and my leathers over there, and I'm still the same person."[42]

"I worked at a computer all day for the city, and for me it's pure relaxation. I wear the leathers because they're protective."[43]

IMPACT OF PRESIDENT BUSH'S STEEL TARIFFS

Steel tariffs put in place in 2002 posed a threat to Harley-Davidson and other users of steel. Sanctions were to "induce that party that would be subject to them to bring itself in line" with international trade rules, spokesman Anthony Gooch said. "The best way to avoid them is to compensate," he said, adding that the tariffs would take effect in May 2002. The 15-nation EU was protesting U.S. tariffs of as much as 30% on some steel imports, which it said broke World Trade Organization rules.[44] Domestic steel buyers eager to circumvent the three-year tariffs were sending lobbyists to make their case to the President's administration. Combine that with threats from Europe to retaliate against American steel and other goods—from Florida oranges to Harley-Davidson motorcycles—and the result could be loopholes big enough to drive a flatbed of cold-rolled sheet metal through.[45]

RECESSION RESISTANCE?

Harley had seen tremendous sales and stock price growth in spite of the recession. However, some analysts questioned whether Harley-Davidson would be hit by the deep recession the nation is facing, albeit later than most U.S. companies. "For years, Harley-Davidson and the analysts that cover the company have reported that the business is recession-resistant. Given the recent changes in the economic and political landscape, this assertion is being put to the test, and from what we can tell, is ringing true. . . . Among 17 Wall Street analysts tracked by Bloomberg who cover the stock, 16 rate it *buy* and one *hold*."[46] Harley's Ziemer: But if the recession persists, motorcycles, the critics say, are easily deferred purchases. "We always said we feel we are recession-resistant, not recession-proof."[47]

COMPETITION[48]

The heavyweight (651cc+) motorcycle market was highly competitive. Major competitors were based outside the United States and generally had more financial and marketing resources. They also had larger worldwide sales volumes and were more diversified. In addition to these larger, established competitors, a growing segment of competition had emerged in the United States. The new U.S. competitors generally offered heavyweight motorcycles with traditional styling that competed directly with many of Harley-Davidson's products. These competitors currently had production and sales volumes that were lower than Harley-Davidson's and did not hold significant market share (see **Exhibits 11, 12, 13**.)

Exhibit 11

Worldwide Heavyweight Motorcycle Registration Data (Engine Displacement of 651+cc)
(Units in thousands)

	2001 % Share	2001 Units	2000 % Share	2000 Units	1999 % Share	1999 Units
North America[1]						
Harley-Davidson new registrations	43.9%	185.6	44.6%	163.1	47.7%	142.1
Buell new registrations	.6%	2.7	1.2%	4.3	1.3%	4.0
Total company registrations	44.5%	188.3	45.8%	167.4	49.0%	146.1
Total market new registrations		422.8		365.4		297.9
Europe[2]						
Harley-Davidson new registrations	6.7%	19.6	6.8%	19.9	5.8%	17.8
Buell new registrations	0.7%	2.2	.6%	1.9	1.7%	2.1
Total company registrations	7.4%	21.8	7.4%	21.8	6.5%	19.9
Total market new registrations		293.6		293.4		306.7
Japan/Australia[3]						
Harley-Davidson new registrations	20.4%	12.7	19.5%	12.2	2.5%	11.6
Buell new registrations	1.0%	.7%	1.0	.7%	1.1	.7
Total company registrations	21.4%	13.4	20.5%	12.9	19.6%	12.3
Total market new registrations		62.1		62.7		63.1
Total						
Harley-Davidson new registrations	28.0%	217.9	27.1%	195.2	25.7%	171.5
Buell new registrations	0.7%	5.6	0.9%	6.9	1.0%	6.8
Total company registrations	28.7%	223.5	28.0%	202.1	26.7%	178.3
Total market new registrations		778.5		721.5		667.7

Notes:
1. Includes the United States and Canada. Data provided by the Motorcycle Industry Council (MIC). MIC has revised its data for 2000.
2. Includes Austria, Belgium, France, Germany, Italy, The Netherlands, Spain, Switzerland, and the United Kingdom. Data provided by Giral S.A.
3. Data provided by JAMA and ABS.
Source: Harley-Davidson, Inc., *Form 10-K*, p. 10.

Exhibit 12

Market Share of U.S. Heavyweight Motorcycles (Engine Displacement of 651+cc)[1]

	2001	2000	1999	1998
New U.S. registrations (thousands of units)				
Total market new registrations	394.3	340.0	275.6	227.1
Harley-Davidson new registrations	177.4	155.1	134.5	109.1
Buell new registrations	2.6	4.2	3.9	3.2
Total company new registrations	180.0	159.3	138.4	112.3
Percentage market share				
Harley-Davidson motorcycles	45.0%	45.6%	48.8%	48.1%
Buell motorcycles	0.7	1.2	1.4	1.4
Total company	45.7	46.8	50.2	49.5
Honda	20.5	18.5	16.4	20.3
Suzuki	10.8	9.3	9.4	10.0
Kawasaki	8.0	9.0	10.3	10.1
Yamaha	7.9	8.4	7.0	4.2
Other	7.1	8.0	6.7	5.9
Total	100.0%	100.0%	100.0%	100.0%

Note:
1. Motorcycle registration and market share information has been derived from data published by the Motorcycle Industry Council (MIC). MIC has revised its data for 1997 and 2000, and this table reflects the revised data.
Source: Harley-Davidson, Inc., *Form 10-K*, p. 9.

Exhibit 13

Motorcycle Industry Registration Statistics (Units): Harley-Davidson Inc.

U.S. and Canada	2001	2000	1999	1998	1997
651+cc volume	422,787	365,399	297,900	246,214	205,407
H-D volume	185,571	163,136	142,042	116,110	99,298
Buell volume	2,695	4,306	4,022	3,333	1,912
HDI total volume	188,266	167,442	146,064	119,443	101,210
% change 651+cc volume	15.7%	22.7%	21.0%	19.9%	15.1%
% change HDI total volume	12.4%	14.6%	22.3%	18.0%	16.6%
HDI market share	44.5%	45.8%	49.0%	48.5%	49.3%
Europe	**2001**	**2000**	**1999**	**1998**	**1997**
651+cc volume	293,554	293,424	306,748	270,212	250,293
H-D volume	19,563	19,870	17,836	15,650	15,286
Buell volume	2,171	1,912	2,079	1,600	771
HDI total volume	21,734	21,782	19,915	17,250	16,057
% change 651+cc volume	0.4%	-4.3%	13.5%	8.0%	11.4%
% change HDI total volume	-0.2%	9.4%	15.4%	7.4%	4.6%
HDI market share	7.4%	7.4%	6.5%	6.4%	6.4%
Japan and Australia	**2001**	**2000**	**1999**	**1998**	**1997**
651+cc volume	62,069	62,667	63,097	69,222	58,880
H-D volume	12,662	12,213	11,642	10,273	9,686
Buell volume	651	658	701	532	426
HDI total volume	13,313	12,871	12,343	10,805	10,112
% change 651+cc volume	-0.9%	-0.7%	-8.8%	17.6%	57.4%
% change HDI total volume	3.4%	4.3%	14.2%	6.9%	20.8%
HDI market share	21.4%	20.5%	19.6%	15.6%	17.2%
Total	**2001**	**2000**	**1999**	**1998**	**1997**
651+cc volume	778,410	721,490	667,694	585,648	514,580
H-D volume	217,796	195,219	171,520	142,033	124,270
Buell volume	5,517	6,876	6,802	5,465	3,109
HDI total volume	223,313	202,095	178,322	147,498	127,379
% change 651+cc volume	7.9%	8.1%	14.0%	13.8%	16.8%
% change HDI total volume	10.5%	13.3%	20.9%	15.8%	15.3%
HDI market share	28.7%	28.0%	26.7%	25.2%	24.8%

Notes:

1. Data provided by R.L. Polk & Company (1991–1996), Motorcycle Industry Council (1997–1998), Motorcycle and Moped Industry Council, Giral S.A., Australian Bureau of Statistics, and Japan Automobile Manufacturers Association.
2. Total HDI volume includes Portugal. Total 651+CC volume does not include Portugal.
3. These are actual registrations of motorcycles. The Harley-Davidson, Inc., registrations are typically lower than actual sales due to the timing differences.

Source: www.harley-davidson.com, accessed November 15, 2002.

Competition in the heavyweight motorcycle market was based on a number of factors, including price, quality, reliability, styling, product features, customer preference, and warranties. Harley-Davidson emphasized quality, reliability, and styling in its products and offered a one-year warranty for its motorcycles. They regard its support of the motorcycling lifestyle in the form of events, rides, rallies, H.O.G.®, and its financing through HDFS, as a competitive advantage. In general, resale prices for used Harley-Davidson motorcycles, as a percentage of prices when new, are significantly higher than resale prices for used motorcycles of competitors.

Domestically, Harley-Davidson competed most heavily in the touring and custom segments of the heavyweight motorcycle market, which together accounted for 79%, 78%, and 79% of total heavyweight retail unit sales in the United States during 2001, 2000, and 1999, respectively. The custom and touring motorcycles were generally the most expensive vehicles in the market and the most profitable. During 2001, the heavyweight segment including standard, performance, touring, and custom motorcycles represented approximately 50% of the total U.S. motorcycle market (on- and off-highway motorcycles and scooters) in terms of new units registered.

For the last 14 years, Harley-Davidson has led the industry in domestic (U.S.) unit sales of heavyweight motorcycles. The market share in the heavyweight market was 45.7% in 2001, compared to 46.8% in 2000. The market share decreased slightly in 2001 as a result of the ongoing capacity constraints, however, this share is still significantly greater than the largest competitor in the domestic market, which ended 2001 with a 20.5% market share.

RIDER TRAINING AND SAFETY

"Increasingly, the motorcycle riders who are getting killed are in their 40s, 50s, and 60s," says Susan Ferguson, vice president for research at the Insurance Institute for Highway Safety, which did the study.[49] Riders over 40 accounted for 40% of all fatalities in 2000, up from 14% in 1990. Part of the reason for the dramatic increase in older bikers' deaths is the growing number of men and women over 40 buying motorcycles, IIHS says.

In 2000, Harley-Davidson launched an instruction program called Rider's Edge, run through dealers. Rookies paid $225 or so for a 25-hour class. The program had grown to 42 dealers in 23 states and graduated 3,800 riders in 2002. Forty-five percent were women, 86% bought something, and a 25% bought a Harley-Davidson or a Buell within three months. "Going into a Harley dealership can be intimidating," says Lara Lee, who ran the program. "We give them a home base and get them riding."[50]

MOTORCYCLE MANUFACTURING[51]

The ongoing manufacturing strategy was designed to increase capacity, improve product quality, reduce costs and increase flexibility to respond to changes in the marketplace. Harley-Davidson incorporated manufacturing techniques focused on the continuous improvement of its operations designed to control costs and maintain quality. These techniques, which included employee involvement, just-in-time inventory principles, partnering agreements with the local unions, high-performance work organizations, and statistical process control, were designed to improve product quality, productivity, and asset utilization in the production of Harley-Davidson® motorcycles.

The use of just-in-time inventory principles allowed it to minimize its inventories of raw materials and work in process, as well as scrap and rework costs. This system also allowed quicker reaction to engineering design changes, quality improvements, and market demands. Harley-Davidson has trained the majority of its manufacturing employees in problem solving and statistical methods.

The company's management believe the worldwide heavyweight (651cc+) market would continue to grow and plans to continue to increase its Harley-Davidson motorcycle production to have the capacity to sustain its growth for units shipped. During 2001, Harley-Davidson began work on plans for capacity expansion that would take place at two of the existing manufacturing facilities. These plans included a 350,000-square-foot expansion at the York, Pennsylvania assembly facility and a 60,000-square-foot expansion at the Tomahawk, Wisconsin facility. The company began its investment in these plans during 2001 and continued to invest capital related to these plans during 2002 and 2003. Based on the results achieved in 2001, the 2002 annual production target increased to 258,000 Harley-Davidson units.

The manufacturing techniques employed at Buell, BMC, which were similar to those of the Motor Company, were designed to provide cost control and quality products in a lower-volume environment. Its product development staff was located in close proximity to the production facilities to ensure that new product and model-year change activities are coordinated prior to and during launch. The manufacturing techniques employed included employee involvement with an emphasis on a highly flexible and participative workforce. The new powertrain was produced at the manufacturing facility in Kansas City, Missouri through its joint venture with Porsche AG of Stuttgart, Germany, formed in 1997.

Finally, Harley-Davidson operated an assembly operation in Brazil that imported U.S.-made components and subassemblies for final assembly in Brazil. Assembling imported U.S.-made components increased the availability of Harley-Davidson motorcycles in Brazil and reduced duties and taxes, making them more affordable to a larger group of Brazilian customers. The facility, which had been operational since mid-1999, assembled select motorcycle models for the Brazilian market, with 2002 volumes less than 1,000 units per year.

RAW MATERIAL AND PURCHASE COMPONENTS[52]

Harley-Davidson has worked to establish long-term, mutually beneficial relationships with its suppliers. Through these relationships, Harley-Davidson gained access to technical and commercial resources for application directly to product design, development, and manufacturing initiatives. This strategy was resulting in improved product technical integrity, application of new features and innovations, reduced lead times for product development, and smoother/faster manufacturing ramp-up of new vehicle introductions.

Harley-Davidson purchased all its raw materials, principally steel and aluminum castings, forgings, sheets and bars, and certain motorcycle components, including carburetors, batteries, tires, seats, electrical components, and instruments. It hasn't anticipated significant difficulties in obtaining raw materials or components for which it relied on a limited source of supply.

As part of its strategic plan for sustainable growth, the Harley-Davidson Motor Company announced plans to move assembly of its Dyna Glide family of motorcycles to its facility in Kansas City, Missouri. All Dyna Glide models were currently assembled in York, Pennsylvania. "In our continuing efforts to narrow the gap between supply and demand, Harley-Davidson will relocate the Dyna line from York to Kansas City, Missouri," noted Motor Company President and Chief Operating Officer, Jim McCaslin. "The move is being made at this time to enable Harley-Davidson to more fully utilize these assets and increase capacity over time," said McCaslin. The Dyna Glide family was one of five families of motorcycles produced by Harley-Davidson: Sportster, Softail, Dyna, Touring, and the new VRSC family. Dyna models represented approximately 15% of their total production. [53]

Ultimately, Harley hoped to develop its supplier Web portal, www.H-dsn.com. Launched in July 2000, it had primarily been an accounts-payable network. Suppliers could log on and review their accounts and do their own reconciliation. Harley's payables department reported that since the portal was launched, it had seen a 90% drop in supplier phone calls from users. In 2001, 83 suppliers were using the portal. They clicked in to review shipping specifications or access forms for product testing. In 2002, the site posted 12 months' worth of forecasted volumes and schedules for all suppliers. Also H-dsn.com will be gaining transaction capabilities. This was especially helpful for smaller suppliers that had been unable to hook up to Harley's existing EDI system. "Our goal," said Cotteleer, "is to have the supplier doing their own replenishing, using the site. They can see what our consumption rates are, rather then trying to project based on historical information."[54]

RESEARCH AND DEVELOPMENT[55]

Harley-Davidson viewed research and development as significant in its ability to lead the market definition of touring and custom motorcycling and to develop products for the performance segment. In recent years, it has established a 218,000-square-foot Motor Company Product Development Center (PDC), which is currently in the process of receiving a 165,000-

square-foot addition. It also owned and operated a 43,000-square-foot Buell research and development facility. The innovative design of the PDC brought together employees from styling, purchasing, and manufacturing with regulatory professionals and supplier representatives to create a concurrent product and process development methodology. They incurred research and development expenses of approximately $80.7 million, $75.8 million, and $70.3 million during 2001, 2000, and 1999, respectively.

PATENTS AND TRADEMARKS[56]

Harley-Davidson owned patents that relate to its motorcycles and related products and processes for their production. It had increased its efforts to patent its technology and certain motorcycle-related designs and to enforce those patents. Management saw such actions as important as the money moves forward with new products, designs, and technologies.

Trademarks were important to Harley-Davidson's motorcycle business and licensing activities. It had a vigorous global program of trademark registration and enforcement to strengthen the value of the trademarks associated with its products and services, prevent the unauthorized use of those trademarks, and enhance its image and customer goodwill. Management believed the Harley-Davidson trademark and its Bar and Shield trademark were each highly recognizable by the public and were very valuable assets. The Buell trademark is well known in performance motorcycle circles, as is the associated Pegasus logo. Management was making efforts to ensure that each of these brands would become better known as the Buell business expanded. Additionally, the company uses numerous other trademarks, trade names, and logos, which are registered both in the United States and abroad. The following were among the trademarks of H-D Michigan, Inc.: Harley- Davidson, H-D, Harley, the Bar & Shield logo, MotorClothes, the MotorClothes logo, Rider's Edge, Harley Owners Group, H.O.G., the H.O.G. logo, Softail, Sportster, and V-Rod. The Harley-Davidson trademark had been used since 1903 and the Bar and Shield trademark since 1910. The following are among the trademarks of Buell Motorcycle Company: Buell, the Pegasus logo and BRAG. The Buell trademark had been used since 1984.

SEASONALITY[57]

In general, the Motor Company had not experienced significant seasonal fluctuations in its sales. This had been primarily the result of a strong demand for the Harley-Davidson motorcycles and related products, as well as the availability of floor plan financing arrangements for its North American and European independent dealers. Floor plan financing allowed dealers to build their inventory levels in anticipation of the spring and summer selling seasons.

REGULATIONS[58]

Federal, state, and local authorities had various environmental control requirements relating to air, water, and noise pollution that affect the business and operations. Harley-Davidson endeavored to ensure that its facilities and products complied with all applicable environmental regulations and standards.

The motorcycles were subject to certification by the U.S. Environmental Protection Agency (EPA) for compliance with applicable emissions and noise standards and by the State of California Air Resources Board (CARB) with respect to CARB's more stringent emissions standards. Motorcycles sold in California were also subject to certain tailpipe and evaporative emissions standards that were unique to California. Its motorcycle products had been certified to comply fully with all such applicable standards. CARB's motorcycle emissions standards would become more stringent in model year 2004 and 2008, respectively. Additionally, the European Union was considering making its motorcycle emissions standards more stringent and was considering making its motorcycle noise standards more stringent, which already were more stringent than those of the EPA. Similarly, motorcycle noise and emissions levels were becoming more stringent in Japan, as well as in certain emerging markets. Consequently, Harley-Davidson would continue to incur some level of research and development and production costs related to motorcycle emissions and noise in the foreseeable future.

Harley-Davidson, as a manufacturer of motorcycle products, was subject to the National Traffic and Motor Vehicle Safety Act, which were administered by the National Highway Traffic Safety Administration (NHTSA). It had certified to NHTSA that its motorcycle products complied fully with all applicable federal motor vehicle safety standards and related regulations. Harley-Davidson, has from time to time, initiated certain voluntary recalls. During the last three years, it initiated 24 voluntary recalls at a total cost of approximately $16.5 million. Management maintained reserves for all estimated costs associated with recalls in the period that the recalls were announced.

EMPLOYEES[59]

As of December 31, 2001, the Motorcycles segment had approximately 8,100 employees. Unionized employees at the motorcycle manufacturing and distribution facilities in Wauwatosa, Menomonee Falls, Franklin and Tomahawk, Wisconsin, and Kansas City, Missouri were represented principally by the Paper Allied-Industrial Chemical and Energy Workers International Union (PACE) of the AFL-CIO, as well as the International Association of Machinist and Aerospace Workers (IAM). Production workers at the motorcycle manufacturing facility in York, Pennsylvania, were represented principally by IAM. The collective bargaining agreement with the Wisconsin-PACE and IAM will expire on March 31, 2008, the collective bargaining agreement with the Kansas City-PACE and IAM will expire on August 1, 2007, and the collective bargaining agreement with the Pennsylvania-IAM will expire on February 2, 2007.

Approximately 50% of Harley-Davidson's 8,000 employees rode Harley-Davidsons. All employees, including Bleustein, went through a dealer to get their bikes. This way, the employees saw the customer experience firsthand.

COMMITMENTS AND CONTINGENCIES[60]

Harley-Davidson was subject to lawsuits and other claims related to environmental, product and other matters. In determining required reserves related to these items, management and legal counsel analyzed each individual case and considered the likelihood of adverse judgments or outcomes, as well as the potential range of probable loss. The required reserves were monitored on an ongoing basis and were updated based on new developments or new information in each matter.

LAWSUITS[61]

In January 2001, Harley-Davidson, on its own initiative, notified each owner of 1999 and early-2000 model year Harley-Davidson motorcycles equipped with Twin Cam 88 and Twin Cam 88B engines that Harley-Davidson was extending the warranty for a rear cam bearing to 5 years or 50,000 miles. Subsequently, on June 28, 2001, a putative nationwide class action suit was filed against Harley-Davidson in state court in Milwaukee County, Wisconsin; it was amended by a complaint filed September 28, 2001. The complaint alleged that this cam bearing was defective and asserted various legal theories. The complaint sought unspecified compensatory and punitive damages for affected owners, an order compelling Harley-Davidson to repair the engines, and other relief. Management believed that the warranty extension it announced in January 2001 adequately addressed the condition for affected owners. Management had established reserves for this extended warranty. Harley-Davidson filed a motion to dismiss the amended complaint, and on February 27, 2002, the motion was granted by the court, and the amended complaint was dismissed in its entirety.

In addition, Harley-Davidson was involved with government agencies in various environmental matters, including a matter involving soil and groundwater contamination at its York,

Pennsylvania, facility (the Facility). The Facility was formerly used by the U.S. Navy and AMF (the predecessor corporation of Minstar). Harley-Davidson purchased the Facility from AMF in 1981. Although management is not certain as to the extent of the environmental contamination at the Facility, it had been working with the Pennsylvania Department of Environmental Protection in undertaking certain investigation and remediation activities, including a sitewide remedial investigation/feasibility study. In January 1995, management entered into a settlement agreement (the Agreement) with the Navy. The Agreement called for the Navy and Harley-Davidson to contribute amounts into a trust equal to 53% and 47%, respectively, of future costs associated with investigation and remediation activities at the Facility (response costs). The trust administered the payment of the response costs at the Facility as covered by the Agreement. Recently, the U.S. Environmental Protection Agency (EPA) advised the management that it considered some of the Harley-Davidson's remediation activities at the Facility to be subject to the EPA's corrective action programs and had offered Harley-Davidson the option of addressing corrective action under a facility-lead agreement. The objectives and procedures for facility-lead corrective action were consistent with the investigation and remediation already conducted under the agreement with the Navy. Although substantial uncertainty existed concerning the nature and scope of the environmental remediation that will ultimately be required at the Facility, based on preliminary information currently available to management and taking into account Harley-Davidson's agreement with the Navy, the management estimated that it will incur approximately $5 million of future response costs at the Facility. The company had established reserves for this amount. Management's estimate of future response costs was based on reports of independent environmental consultants retained by the company, the actual costs incurred to date, and the estimated costs to complete the necessary investigation and remediation activities. Response costs were expected to be incurred over a period of several years, ending in 2009.

PROPERTIES[62]

The following is a summary of the principal operating properties of Harley-Davidson, as of March 15, 2002. Seven facilities performed manufacturing operations: Wauwatosa and Menomonee Falls, Wisconsin, suburbs of Milwaukee (motorcycle powertrain production); Tomahawk, Wisconsin (fiberglass parts production and painting); York, Pennsylvania (motorcycle parts fabrication, painting, and big-twin assembly); Kansas City, Missouri (Sportster assembly); East Troy, Wisconsin (Buell motorcycles assembly); Manaus, Brazil (assembly of select models for the Brazilian market) (see **Exhibit 14**).

Financial Services Segment[63]

The Financial Services segment consisted of Harley-Davidson's wholly owned subsidiary, Harley-Davidson Financial Services, Inc. (HDFS). HDFS was engaged in the business of financing and servicing wholesale inventory receivables, consumer retail installment sales contracts (primarily motorcycles and noncommercial aircraft). In addition, HDFS was an agency for certain unaffiliated insurance carriers providing property/casualty insurance and extended service contracts to motorcycle owners. HDFS conducts business in the United States, Canada, and Europe. The Financial Services segment had four office facilities: Chicago, Illinois (corporate headquarters); Carson City, Nevada and Reno, Nevada (retail operations); and Plano, Texas (wholesale operations).

HARLEY-DAVIDSON AND BUELL[64]

HDFS, operating under the trade name Harley-Davidson Credit and Insurance, provided wholesale financial services to Harley-Davidson and Buell dealers and retail financing to consumers. Wholesale financial services included floorplan and open account financing of

Exhibit 14

Principal Operating Facilities: Harley-Davidson, Inc.

Type of Facility	Location	Approximate Square Feet	Status
Corporate office	Milwaukee, WI	523,000	Owned
Product development Center	Wauwatosa, WI	218,000	Owned
Manufacturing	Wauwatosa, WI	422,000	Owned
Manufacturing	Menomonee Falls, WI	479,000	Owned
Manufacturing	Tomahawk, WI	179,000	Owned
Manufacturing	York, PA	1,033,000	Owned
Manufacturing	Kansas City, MO	330,000	Owned
Materials velocity center	Kansas City, MO	87,000	Lease expiring 2004
Manufacturing	East Troy, WI	40,000	Lease expiring 2003
Product development and office	East Troy, WI	48,000	Lease expiring 2003
Distribution center	Franklin, WI	250,000	Owned
Distribution center	York, PA	86,000	Lease expiring 2006
Motorcycle testing	Talladega, AL	24,000	Lease expiring 2004
Office	Ann Arbor, MI	3,000	Lease expiring 2004
Office	Morfelden-Waldorf, Germany	22,000	Lease expiring 2005
Office	Brackley, England	3,000	Lease expiring 2005
Warehouse	Brackley, England	1,000	Lease expiring 2005
Office	Windsor, England	10,000	Owned
Office	Liederdorp, The Netherlands	8,000	Lease expiring 2006
Office	Paris, France	6,000	Lease expiring 2004
Office	Arese, Italy	9,000	Lease expiring 2006
Warehouse	Arese, Italy	8,000	Lease expiring 2006
Office	Tokyo, Japan	14,000	Lease expiring 2004
Warehouse	Yokohama, Japan	15,000	Lease expiring 2004
Manufacturing and office	Manaus, Brazil	30,000	Lease expiring 2003

Source: Harley-Davidson, Inc., *Form 10-K*, p. 15.

motorcycles and motorcycle parts and accessories, real estate loans, computer loans, showroom remodeling loans, and the brokerage of a range of commercial insurance products. HDFS offered wholesale financial services to all Harley-Davidson dealers in the United States and Canada, and during 2001, approximately 96% of such dealers utilized those services. European dealers were currently serviced through a joint venture with another finance company. In August 2002, HDFS began serving the wholesale financing needs of Harley-Davidson's European dealers, as HDFS has exercised its option to terminate the joint venture effective August 2002. The wholesale finance operations of HDFS were located in Plano, Texas.

Retail financial services included installment lending for new and used Harley-Davidson and Buell motorcycles and the brokerage of a range of motorcycle insurance policies and extended service warranty agreements. HDFS acted as an insurance agent and did not assume underwriting risk with regard to insurance policies and extended service warranty agreements. Prior to the sale of Harley-Davidson Chrome Visa® Card business in March 2000, HDFS financed and serviced revolving charge receivables. HDFS's retail financial services were available through virtually all Harley-Davidson and Buell dealers in the United States and Canada. HDFS's retail finance operations were located in Carson City, Nevada and Reno, Nevada.

OTHER MANUFACTURERS[65]

HDFS's retail and wholesale aircraft financial service programs were similar to the programs for Harley-Davidson and Buell dealers and consumers described above. During 1999, HDFS ceased offering retail financial services to consumers of marine and recreational vehicles.

FUNDING[66]

HDFS has been financed by operating cash flow, advances and loans from Harley-Davidson, asset-backed securitizations, commercial paper, revolving credit facilities, senior subordinated debt, and redeemable preferred stock.

COMPETITION[67]

The ability to offer a package of wholesale and retail financial services was a significant competitive advantage of HDFS. Competitors competed for business based largely on price and, to a lesser extent, service. HDFS competed based on convenience, service, strong dealer relations, industry experience, terms, and price.

During 2001, HDFS financed 31% of new Harley-Davidson motorcycles retailed in the United States, as compared to 21% in 2000. HDFS faced minimal national competition for its retail motorcycle financing business. Competitors were primarily banks and other financial institutions that provided retail financing to local or regional markets. Competition to provide retail financial services to aircraft consumers include aircraft manufacturers' captive finance companies, such as Cessna Finance Corp., Debis Financial Services, and other financial entities, including MBNA and First Source Bank. Credit unions, banks, other financial institutions, and insurance agencies also competed for retail financial services business in segmented markets.

HDFS faced little national competition for Harley-Davidson's wholesale motorcycle financing business. Competitors were primarily regional and local banks and other financial institutions that provide wholesale financing to Harley-Davidson and Buell dealers in their local markets. Competition to provide wholesale financial services to aircraft dealers included aircraft manufacturers' captive finance companies.

TRADEMARKS

HDFS used several trademarks and trade names licensed from Harley-Davidson. In addition to the above-mentioned licenses, HDFS had a registered trademark for the "Eaglemark and Design logo" used in aircraft financing programs.

SEASONALITY[68]

In the northern United States and Canada, motorcycles were primarily used during warmer months, generally March through August. Accordingly, HDFS experienced significant seasonal variations. Retail customers typically did not buy motorcycles until they can ride them. From mid-March through August, retail financing volume increased and wholesale financing volume decreased as dealers depleted their inventories. From September through mid-March, there was a decrease in retail financing volume, while dealer inventories build and turn over more slowly, substantially increasing wholesale financing volume.

EMPLOYEES

At the end of 2001, the Financial Services segment had approximately 550 employees, none of which were unionized.

REGULATION[69]

The operations of HDFS were subject, in certain instances, to supervision and regulation by state, federal, and various foreign governmental authorities and may be subject to various laws and judicial and administrative decisions imposing various requirements and restrictions, which among other things (a) regulated credit-granting activities, including establishing licensing requirements, if any, in applicable jurisdictions; (b) established maximum interest rates, finance charges, and other charges; (c) regulated customers' insurance coverages; (d) required disclosure to customers; (e) governed secured transactions; (f) set collection, foreclosure, repossession, and claims handling procedures and other trade practices; (g) prohibited discrimination in the extension of credit and administration of loans; and (h) regulated the use and reporting of information related to a borrower's credit experience.

A subsidiary of HDFS, Eaglemark Savings Bank, formerly known as Eaglemark Bank, N.A., was a Nevada state thrift. Therefore, the activities of this subsidiary were restricted by federal and State of Nevada banking laws and were subject to examination by federal and state examiners.

Corporate Financial and Stock Price Performance

At a time when auto makers are whacking at their profit margins with 0% financing, Harley sold every bike it made, and dealers often charged $2,000 to $4,000 above the sticker price.[70] This has been fueled mainly by continued strong demand for most of Harley's bikes, including the Sportster (entry-level motorcycle), Custom (carried the highest margins), Touring (highest selling price, although also the costliest to manufacture), and the Buell lines. Further, management's focus on trimming costs, also with increased sales of parts and accessories, resulted in an improved operating margin for the quarter and the full year. The outlook was quite promising for Harley at the moment. (**Exhibits 15, 16, 17**, and **18** provide the company's summary of revenue, operating income, and assets, the balance sheet, the

Exhibit 15

Revenues, Operating Income, and Assets: Harley-Davidson, Inc. (Dollar amounts in thousands)

	Motorcycles and Related Products	Financial Services	Corporate	Consolidated
2001				
Revenue	$3,363,414	$181,545	—	$3,544,959
Operating income (loss)	$613,311	$61,273	$(12,083)	$662,501
Identifiable assets as of December 31	$1,385,932	$1,096,239	$636,324	$3,118,495
2000				
Revenue	$2,906,365	$140,135	—	$3,046,500
Operating income (loss)	$487,485	$37,178	$(9,691)	$514,972
Identifiable assets as of December 31	$1,158,813	$856,961	$420,630	$2,436,404
1999				
Revenue	$2,452,939	$132,741	—	$2,585,680
Operating income (loss)	$397,601	$27,685	$(9,427)	$415,859
Identifiable assets as of December 31	$1,058,934	$868,711	$184,432	$2,112,077

Source: Harley-Davidson, Inc., *2001 Annual Report*, pp. 55 and 81, and *2000 Form 10-K*, pp. 19 and 54.

Exhibit 16

Balance Sheet, 1997–2001: Harley-Davidson, Inc.
(Dollar amounts in thousands)

	2001	2000	1999	1998	1997
Assets					
Current assets					
Cash and cash equivalents	$ 439,438	$ 419,736	$ 183,415	$ 165,170	$ 147,462
Marketable securities	196,011	0	0	0	0
Account receivable, net	118,843	98,311	101,708	113,417	102,797
Current portion of finance receivables, net	656,421	530,859	440,951	360,341	293,329
Inventories	181,115	191,931	168,616	155,616	117,475
Deferred income taxes	38,993	28,280	29,434	29,076	24,941
Prepaid expenses and other current assets	34,443	28,147	24,870	21,343	18,017
Total current assets	1,665,264	1,297,264	948,994	844,963	704,021
Finance Receivables, net	379,335	234,091	354,888	319,427	249,346
Property, plant and equipment, net	891,820	754,115	681,741	627,759	528,869
Goodwill, net	49,711	54,331	55,408	51,197	38,707
Other assets	132,365	96,603	71,046	76,863	77,958
Total assets	$3,118,495	$2,436,404	$2,112,077	$1,920,209	$1,598,901
Liabilities & shareholders' equity					
Current liabilities					
Accounts payable	$ 194,683	$ 169,844	$ 137,660	$ 122,722	$ 106,112
Accrued expenses and other liabilities	304,376	238,390	199,331	199,051	164,938
Current portion of finance debt	217,051	89,509	181,163	146,742	90,638
Total current liabilities	716,110	497,743	518,154	468,515	361,688
Finance debt	380,000	355,000	280,000	280,000	280,000
Other long-term liabilities	158,374	81,707	65,093	67,376	62,131
Postretirement health care benefits	89,912	80,666	75,719	72,083	68,414
Deferred income taxes	17,816	15,633	12,031	2,324	0
Total liabilities	$1,362,212	$1,030,749	$950,997	$890,298	$772,233
Shareholders' equity					
Common stock	3,242	3,210	1,592	1,584	1,572
Additional PIC	359,165	285,390	236,540	211,960	187,180
Retained earnings	1,833,335	1,431,017	1,113,376	873,171	683,824
Accumulated other comprehensive income	(13,728)	308	(2,067)	1,128	(2,835)
Less					
Treasury stock	(425,546)	(313,994)	(187,992)	(57,133)	(41,959)
Unearned compensation	(185)	(276)	(369)	(799)	(1,114)
Total shareholders' equity	1,756,283	1,405,655	1,161,080	1,029,911	826,668
Total liabilities and shareholders' equity	$3,118,495	$2,436,404	$2,112,077	$1,920,209	$1,598,901

Source: Harley-Davidson, Inc., *2001 Annual Report*, pp. 56–57.

income statement, and the statement of cash flows. **Exhibit 19** provides a geographic breakdown of sales.)[71]

Since Harley went public, its shares had risen 15,000%. Harley-Davidson stock had remained strong, even when the general market has weakened. (**Exhibit 20** provides a comparison of Harley-Davidson stock and the Standard and Poor's 500 since the 1986 initial public offering and a second comparison from 1997–2002.) What does the future hold for Harley-

Exhibit 17

Income Statement, 1997–2001: Harley-Davidson, Inc.
(Dollar amounts in thousands)

	2001	2000	1999	1998	1997
Net sales	$3,363,414	$2,906,365	$2,452,939	$2,063,956	$1,762,569
Cost of goods sold	2,183,409	1,915,547	1,617,253	1,373,286	1,176,352
Gross profit	1,180,005	990,818	835,686	690,670	586,217
Financial services income	181,545	140,135	132,741	102,922	66,998
Financial services interest and operating expense	120,272	102,957	105,056	82,711	54,643
Operating income from financial services	61,237	37,178	27,685	20,211	$2,355
Selling, admin, and engineering expense	(578,777)	(513,024)	(447,512)	(377,265)	(328,569)
Income from operations	662,501	514,972	415,859	333,616	270,003
Gain on sale of credit card business	0	18,915	0	0	0
Interest income, net	17,478	17,583	8,014	3,828	7,871
Other, net	(6,524)	(2,914)	(3,080)	(1,215)	(1,572)
Income before provision for income taxes	673,455	548,556	420,793	336,229	276,302
Provision for income taxes	235,709	200,843	153,592	122,729	102,232
Net income	$ 437,746	$ 347,713	$ 267,201	$ 213,500	$ 174,070

Source: Harley-Davidson, Inc., *2001 Annual Report*, p. 41.

Davidson? It really depended on how one viewed the strengths, weaknesses, opportunities, and threats facing the company. Two analysts viewed the future prospects of Harley-Davidson's stock differently:

"It's an upper-middle-class toy," says Chad Hudson of the Prudent Bear fund, one of a number of prominent short-sellers convinced that Harley will skid. "As people run out of disposable income, that's going to hurt."[72]

Short-sellers—bearish investors who sell borrowed shares, hoping to replace them later with cheaper ones—"are banking on at some point the story cracking," says Chris Cox, a Goldman Sachs analyst who is bullish on Harley shares. "My point is that, if it does, it's not happening any time soon."[73]

How should Harley-Davidson ride out the recession? How should they maintain interest in the 2004 model bikes? How should they grapple with the aging baby boomers, who were generally the individuals who could afford a Harley-Davidson motorcycle? These were but a few of the questions in the minds of the 100th Anniversary Planning Committee as they strategized about the 2002–2003 celebration.

Exhibit 18

Statement of Cash Flows, 1997–2001: Harley-0Davidson, Inc. (Dollar amounts in thousands)

	2001	2000	1999	1998	1997
Cash flow from operating activities					
Net income	$ 437,746	$ 347,713	$ 267,201	$ 213,500	$ 174,070
Adjustments to reconcile net income to net cash provided by operating activities					
Depreciation and amortization	153,061	133,348	113,822	87,422	70,178
Gain on sale of credit card business	0	(18,915)	0	0	0
Tax benefit of stock options	44,968	35,876	15,504	0	0
Provision for finance credit losses	22,178	9,919	17,919	10,338	6,547
Deferred income taxes	(3,539)	1,363	11,393	1,190	2,748
Long-term employee benefits	21,588	4,631	(8,480)	5,302	1,275
Other	3,500	1,945	1,781	3,180	1,766
Net changes in current assets and current liabilities	77,761	49,609	12,502	(2,870)	53,151
Total adjustments	319,517	217,776	164,441	104,562	135,665
Net cash provided by operating activities	$ 757,263	$ 565,489	$ 431,642	$ 318,062	$ 309,735
Cash flow from investing activities:					
Net capital expenditures	$(290,381)	$(203,611)	$(165,786)	$(182,770)	$(186,171)
Finance receivables acquired or originated	(4,387,371)	(3,556,195)	(3,321,382)	(2,722,768)	(1,618,307)
Finance receivables collected	3,123,941	2,727,746	2,616,857	2,105,684	1,107,157
Finance receivables sold	987,676	723,928	574,997	469,653	300,000
Net proceeds from sale of credit card business	0		170,1460	0	0
Purchase of marketable securities	(247,989)	0	0	0	0
Sales and redemptions of marketable securities	51,978	0	0	0	0
Purchase of Italian distributor	(1,873)	(18,777)	0	0	0
Other, net	(7,943)	(14,269)	(4,308)	(9,952)	(9,189)
Net cash used in investing activities	$(771,962)	$(171,032)	$(299,622)	$(340,153)	$(406,510)
Cash flow from financing activities					
Net increase (decrease) in notes payable	0	0	0	(773)	(2,580)
Net increase (decrease) in finance debt	152,542	(16,654)	34,421	56,104	112,573
Dividends paid	(35,428)	(30,072)	(26,996)	(24,153)	(21,028)
Purchase of common stock for treasury	(111,552)	(126,002)	(130,284)	(15,175)	0
Issuance of common stock under employee stock plans	28,839	14,592	9,084	23,796	12,793
Net cash provided by (used in) financing activities	$ 34,401	$(158,136)	$(113,775)	$ 39,799	$ 101,758
Net increase in cash and cash equivalents	19,702	236,321	18,245	17,708	4,983
Cash and cash equivalents					
At beginning of year	419,736	183,415	165,170	147,462	142,479
At end of year	$ 439,438	$ 419,736	$ 183,415	$ 165,170	$ 147,462

Source: Harley-Davidson, Inc., *2001 Annual Report*, p. 47.

Exhibit 19

Geographic Information: Harley-Davidson, Inc. (Amounts in thousands)

	2001	2000	1999
Net Sales[1]			
United States	$2,766,391	$2,320,991	$1,915,631
Europe	301,729	285,372	274,737
Japan	141,181	148,684	135,589
Canada	96,928	93,352	80,271
Other foreign countries	57,185	57,966	46,711
Total	$3,363,414	$2,906,365	$2,452,939
Long-lived assets[2]			
United States	$1,021,946	$ 856,746	$ 775,764
Other foreign countries	33,234	27,844	8,948
Total	$1,055,180	$ 884,590	$ 784,712

Notes:
1. Net sales are attributed to geographic regions based on location of customer.
2. Long-lived assets include all long-term assets except those specifically excluded under SFAS Number 131, such as deferred income taxes and finance receivables.

Source: Harley-Davidson, Inc. *Form 10-K*, p. 59.

Exhibit 20

Comparison of the S&P 500 Annual Return and Harley-Davidson Annual Stock Return
at the Company's 1986 Initial Public Offering

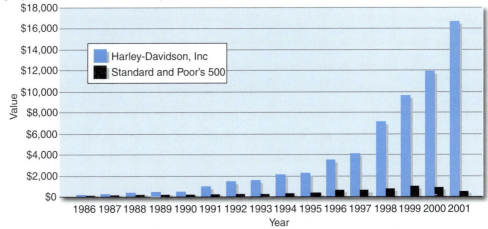

Source: www.harleydavidson.com, accessed November 3, 2002.

Recent Comparison of Harley-Davidson Stock Performance compared to S&P 500, 1997–2002

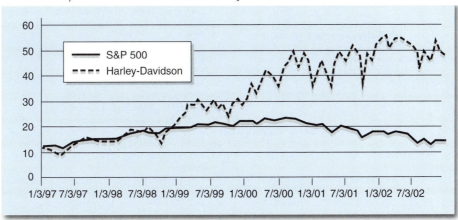

Source: www.yahoo.finance, accessed December 13, 2002.

Notes

1. Buell Motorcycle Press Release "Harley-Davidson Reports Record Fourth Quarter," January 17, 2002.
2. Thomas L. Wheelen, Kathryn E. Wheelen, Thomas L. Wheelen II, and Richard D. Wheelen, "Harley-Davidson: The 95th Anniversary," Case 16, *Strategic Management and Business Policy*, 8th Edition, (Upper Saddle River, NJ: Prentice Hall, 2002), pp. 16-1–16-31.
3. Jonathan Fahey, "Love into Money," *Forbes* (January 7, 2002), pp. 60–65.
4. Missy Sullivan. "High-Octane Hog," *Forbes* (September 10, 2002), pp. 8–10. The preceding two paragraphs are directly quoted, with minor editing.
5. "A Harley Takes an Engine From Porsche" *New York Times* (May 26, 2002). Accessed at www.nytimes.com. This paragraph is directly quoted, with minor editing.
6. Harley-Davidson, Inc., *2002 Proxy Statement*. This paragraph is directly quoted, with minor editing.
7. Harley-Davidson, Inc., *2002 Annual Report*, back cover.
8. Jonathan Fahey, pp. 60–65.
9. Harley-Davidson, Inc., *2001 Annual Report*, pp. 5–8.
10. Joseph Weber, "Harley Investors May Get a Wobbly Ride," *Business Week* (February 11, 2002), p. 65.
11. John Helyar, "Will Harley-Davidson Hit the Wall?" *Fortune* (August 12, 2002), pp. 120–124.
12. Harley-Davidson, *2001 Form 10-K*. The following four paragraphs are directly quoted, with minor editing.
13. Jonathan Fahey, pp. 60–65.
14. Joseph Weber, p. 65.
15. Jonathan Fahey, pp. 60–65.
16. Discover Today's Motorcycling, Press Release "Rockefeller Center Motorcycle Show Opens with 'Today Show' segment and Giant Preview Party" (April 6, 2002).
17. Harley-Davidson, Inc., *2001 Annual Report*, pp. 5–8. This section is directly quoted from President Bluestein's letter to the shareholders, with minor editing.
18. M. Schifrin, "100 Years Young," *Forbes* (September 10, 2001), p. 6.
19. Joseph Weber, p. 65.
20. John Helyar, pp. 120–124.
21. Missy Sullivan, "High-Octane Hog," *Forbes* (September 10, 2002), pp. 8–10.
22. Harley-Davidson, Inc. *2001 Form 10-K*.
23. Jonathan Fahey, pp. 60–65.
24. Rich Rovito, "No Revving Needed for Sales of Harley's V-Rod Motorcycle," *The Business Journal Serving Greater Milwaukee* (January 14, 2002). Accessed at http://milwaukee.bizjournals.com/milwaukee/stories/2002/01/14/story8.html.
25. Joseph Weber, p. 65.
26. "The Business Week 50 Ranking," *Business Week* (Spring 2002), p. 54.
27. John Helyar, pp. 120–124.
28. James V. Higgins, "All Hail, Harley-Davidson" *The Detroit News* (February 22, 2002). Accessed at http://detnews.com/2002.
29. Jonathan Fahey, pp. 60–65.
30. Jerry Shiver, "Richer, Older Harley Riders 'Like Everyone Else,'" *USA Today* (March 8, 2002) pp. 1A–2A.
31. Harley-Davidson, Inc., *2001 Form 10-K*. The following two paragraphs are directly quoted, with minor editing.
32. Ken Brown, "Heard on the Street: Harley-Davidson Growth Engine May Be Stalling," *Wall Street Journal* (February 12, 2002), p. C2.
33. Ken Brown, p. C2.
34. Harley-Davidson, Inc., *2001 Form 10-K*. The second, third, and fourth paragraphs are directly quoted, with minor editing.
35. Harley-Davidson, Inc., *Harley-Davidson 100th Anniversary Open Road Tour Is a Treat for Every Sense, Sound, and the Sense-sational*, Harley-Davidson Press Release (May 8, 2002).
36. Harley-Davidson, Inc., *2001 Form 10-K*. This paragraph is directly quoted, with minor editing.
37. *Ibid*. This paragraph is directly quoted, with minor editing.
38. *Ibid*. The following two paragraphs are directly quoted, with minor editing.
39. *Ibid*. Directly quoted, with minor editing.
40. Jerry Shiver, pp. 1A–2A.
41. "Harley Roars into Its Second Century," *The Tribune*, Ames Iowa (July 26, 2002), p. A2.
42. Jerry Shiver, pp. 1A–2A.
43. *Ibid*., pp. 1A–2A.
44. Adrian Cox, "Levi, Harley-Davidson May Face EU Retaliation Over U.S. Steel," Bloomberg.com (March 23, 2002).
45. Paul Magnusson, "Those Steel Tariffs Look Anything But Ironclad," *Business Week* (May 6, 2002), p. 45.
46. David Wells, "Lehman's Kantor Bets on Harley-Davidson: Call of Day, "Bloomberg.com (November 14, 2001).
47. *Ibid*.
48. Harley-Davidson, Inc., *2001 Form 10-K*. The following four paragraphs are directly quoted, with minor editing.
49. Earle Eldrige, "More Over-40 Motorcyclists Die in Crashes," *USA Today* (January 10, 2002), p. 1B.
50. Jonathan Fahey, pp. 60–65.
51. Harley-Davidson, Inc. *2001 Form 10-K*. The following five paragraphs are directly quoted, with minor editing.
52. *Ibid*. The first two paragraphs are directly quoted, with minor editing.
53. Harley-Davidson Web site press release, "Harley-Davidson Motor Company to move Dyna Assembly to Kansas City" (September 19, 2001).
54. Missy Sullivan, pp. 8–10.
55. Harley-Davidson, Inc., *2001 Form 10-K*. The following paragraph is directly quoted, with minor editing.
56. *Ibid*. The following two paragraphs are directly quoted, with minor editing.
57. *Ibid*. The following paragraph is directly quoted, with minor editing.
58. *Ibid*. The first three paragraphs are directly quoted, with minor editing.
59. *Ibid*. The first paragraph is directly quoted, with minor editing.
60. *Ibid*. The following paragraph is directly quoted, with minor editing.
61. *Ibid*. The following two paragraphs are directly quoted, with minor editing.
62. *Ibid*. The following paragraph is directly quoted, with minor editing.
63. *Ibid*. The following paragraph is directly quoted, with minor editing.
64. *Ibid*. The following two paragraphs are directly quoted, with minor editing.
65. *Ibid*. The following paragraph is directly quoted, with minor editing.
66. *Ibid*. The following paragraph is directly quoted, with minor editing.
67. *Ibid*. The following three paragraphs are directly quoted, with minor editing.
68. *Ibid*. The following paragraph is directly quoted, with minor editing.
69. *Ibid*. The following two paragraphs are directly quoted, with minor editing.
70. Jonathan Fahey, pp. 60–65.
71. Alan G. House, "Harley-Davidson," *ValueLine* 1830 (February 23, 2001).
72. John Helyar, pp. 120–124.
73. Ken Brown, p. C2.

case 16

Carnival Corporation: Acquiring Princess Cruise Line (2002)

Michael J. Keeffe, John K. Ross, III, and Bill J. Middlebrook

Carnival Corporation, in terms of passengers carried, revenues generated, and available capacity, was the largest cruise line in the world and considered the leader and innovator in the cruise travel industry. Carnival had grown from two converted ocean liners into an organization with multiple cruise brands to include Carnival Cruise Lines, Holland America Lines and Windstar Cruises, Costa Cruise Lines, Seabourn Cruise Lines, Cunard Lines Limited, along with a chain of Alaskan hotels and tour coaches to complement Alaska Cruises. Corporate revenues for fiscal 2001 reached $4.5 billion with net income from operations of $926 million. Carnival had several "firsts" in the cruise industry—with over one million passengers carried in a single year and the first cruise line to carry five million total passengers by fiscal 1994. In 2002, its market share of the cruise travel industry was approximately 32% overall.

Carnival Corporation CEO and Chairman, Micky Arison and the Carnival Corporation executive management team continually strove to maintain Carnival's reputation as the industry's leader and innovator. They had assembled one of the newest fleets catering to cruisers, with the introduction of several "superliners" built specifically for the Caribbean and Alaskan cruise markets. Management planned to invest over $6 billion in new ships by 2005 to be distributed among various cruise brands under the corporate umbrella.

In early December 2002, Arison reflected on the internal and external factors that impacted the firm since the terrorist events of September 11, 2001. After these events, cruise bookings were negatively impacted but started to recover late in the year, indicating that leisure travel could rebound in 2002. Still, Carnival Corporation had to offer deep discounts to lure back passengers and experienced a 10% performance decline with a net income of $129.6 million on revenues of $905.8 million in the first quarter of calendar 2002. Additionally, cumulative advanced bookings for 2002 were 7% behind bookings received in the previous year. Overall profitability for fiscal 2001 was down only $40 million from fiscal 2000 given an increase in revenues of almost $800 million.

On a high note, Carnival Corporation's offer for Princess Cruise Lines had been accepted by the stockholders of P&O, the parent of Princess Cruises. Carnival had been in a long battle with Royal Caribbean Cruises Ltd. to acquire Princess Cruises. Combining Royal Caribbean,

This case was prepared by Professors Michael J. Keeffe, John K. Ross, III, and Bill J. Middlebrook of South West Texas State University. This case was edited for SMBP-9th edition. Copyright © 2002 by Professors Michael J. Keeffe, John K. Ross, III, and Bill J. Middlebrook. Reprinted by permission.

second in cruise market share, with Princess, third in market share, would have created the largest cruise operator in the industry, displacing Carnival as the largest cruise operator in the world. Carnival's offer of approximately $5.67 billion was accepted by P&O stockholders and had passed regulatory approval in Germany and the United States, and was expected to be approved by other countries as well. The combination of Princess Cruises' market share of 11.9% with Carnival's 31.9% would create a dominant organization in the cruise segment of the leisure travel industry.

In addition to rebounding from the events of September 11 and the successful pursuit of Princess Cruises during 2001, Carnival Corporation received some negative publicity. In April 2002, for example, Carnival pleaded guilty to federal ocean pollution charges stemming from bilge water discharges from six ships under the Carnival brand. (Carnival had falsified records related to the dumping.) The company agreed to pay $18 million in fines and restitution as part of the settlement, but the most worrisome aspect to management was the negative publicity for the company and cruise vacations in general. During the summer of 2002, passengers on a Holland America ship contracted a virus and in November a virus struck passengers of Holland America, Carnival, and Disney Cruise Line ships. Labeled a "Norwalk-like" virus, some ships had to cancel sailings in order to clean the ships and many passengers had to be reimbursed or offered berths on other sailings. How the publicity of passengers getting sick on cruise outings would affect the industry and Carnival Corporation in particular was not yet known.

Management believed that cruises were taken by only a small amount of the North American vacation market, defined as persons who travel for leisure purposes on trips of three nights or longer, involving at least one night's stay in a hotel. The Boston Consulting Group, in a 1989 study, estimated that only 5% of persons in the North American target market had taken a cruise for leisure purposes and estimated the market potential to be in excess of $50 billion. Carnival Corporation's management believed that this percentage had increased to 12%–15% by 2002. Various cruise operators, including Carnival Corporation, had based their expansion and capital spending programs on the possibility of capturing part of the 85%–88% of the North American population who had yet to take a cruise vacation.

The Evolution of Cruising

With the replacement of ocean liners by aircraft in the 1960s as the primary means of transoceanic travel, the opportunity for developing the modern cruise industry was created. Ships no longer required to ferry passengers from destination to destination became available to investors with visions of a new vacation alternative to complement the increasing affluence of Americans. Cruising, once the purview of the rich and leisure class, was targeted to the middle class, with service and amenities similar to the grand days of first-class ocean travel.

According to Robert Meyers, Editor and Publisher of *Cruise Travel* magazine, the increasing popularity of taking a cruise as a vacation can be traced to two serendipitously timed events. First, television's *Love Boat* series dispelled many myths associated with cruising and depicted people of all ages and backgrounds enjoying the cruise experience. This show was among the top 10 shows on television for many years according to Nielsen ratings, and provided extensive publicity for cruise operators. Second, the increased affluence of Americans and the increased participation of women in the workforce gave couples and families more disposable income for discretionary purposes, especially vacations. As the myths were dispelled and disposable income grew, younger couples and families "turned on" to the benefits of cruising as a vacation alternative, creating a large new target market for the cruise product which accelerated the growth in the number of Americans taking cruises as a vacation.

Carnival History

In 1972 Ted Arison, backed by American Travel Services, Inc., (AITS), purchased an aging ocean liner from Canadian Pacific Empress Lines for $6.5 million. The new AITS subsidiary, Carnival Cruise Line, refurbished the vessel from bow to stern and renamed it the *Mardi Gras* to capture the party spirit. (Also included in the deal was another ship later renamed the *Carnivale*.) The company's start was not promising, however, as on the first voyage the *Mardi Gras*, with over 300 invited travel agents aboard, ran aground in Miami Harbor. The ship was slow and guzzled expensive fuel, limiting the number of ports of call and lengthening the minimum stay of passengers on the ship to reach break-even. Arison then bought another older vessel from Union Castle Lines to complement the *Mardi Gras* and the *Carnivale* and named it the *Festivale*. To attract customers, Arison began adding diversions on-board such as planned activities, a casino, nightclubs, discos, and other forms of entertainment designed to enhance the shipboard experience.

Carnival lost money for the next three years and in late 1974 Ted Arison bought out the Carnival Cruise subsidiary of AITS, Inc. for $1 cash and the assumption of $5 million in debt. One month later, the *Mardi Gras* began showing a profit and through the remainder of 1975 operated at more than 100% capacity. (Normal ship capacity was determined by the number of fixed berths available. Ships, like hotels, can operate beyond this fixed capacity by using roll-away beds, pullmans, and upper bunks.)

Ted Arison (then Chairman), along with Bob Dickinson (who was then Vice President of Sales and Marketing) and his son Micky Arison (then President of Carnival), began to alter the current approach to cruise vacations. Carnival went after first-time and younger cruisers with a moderately priced vacation package that included airfare to the port of embarkation and home after the cruise. Per diem rates were very competitive with other vacation packages and Carnival offered passage to multiple exotic Caribbean ports, several meals served daily with premier restaurant service, and all forms of entertainment and activities included in the base fare. The only things not included in the fare were items of a personal nature, liquor purchases, gambling and tips for the cabin steward, table waiter and busboy. Carnival continued to add to the shipboard experience with a greater variety of activities, nightclubs, and other forms of entertainment and varied ports of call to increase its attractiveness to potential customers. They were the first modern cruise operator to use multimedia-advertising promotions and established the theme of "Fun Ship" cruises, primarily promoting the ship as the destination and ports of call as secondary. Carnival told the public that it was throwing a shipboard party and everyone was invited. Today, the "Fun Ship" theme still permeates all Carnival Cruise brand ships.

Throughout the 1980s, Carnival was able to maintain a growth rate of approximately 30%, about three times that of the industry as a whole, and between 1982 and 1988 its ships sailed with an average capacity of 104%. Targeting younger, first-time passengers by promoting the ship as a destination proved to be extremely successful. Carnival's customer profile showed that approximately 30% of the passengers were between the ages of 25 and 39 with household incomes of $25,000 to $50,000.

In 1987, Ted Arison sold 20% of his shares in Carnival Cruise Lines and immediately generated over $400 million for further expansion. In 1988, Carnival acquired the Holland America Line, which had four cruise ships with 4,500 berths. Holland America was positioned to the higher-income travelers with cruise prices averaging 25%–35% more than similar Carnival cruises. The deal also included two Holland America subsidiaries, Windstar Sail Cruises and Holland America Westours. This purchase allowed Carnival to begin an aggressive "superliner" building campaign for their core subsidiary. By 1989, the cruise segments of Carnival Corporation carried over 750,000 passengers in one year, a "first" in the cruise industry.

Ted Arison relinquished the role of Chairman to his son Micky in 1990, a time when the explosive growth of the 1980's began to subside. Higher fuel prices and increased airline costs began to affect the industry as a whole. The Persian Gulf War caused many cruise operators to divert ships from European and Indian ports to the Caribbean area of operations, increasing the number of ships competing directly with Carnival. Carnival's stock price fell from $25 in June of 1990 to $13 late in that year. The company also incurred a $25.5 million loss during fiscal 1990 for the operation of the Crystal Palace Resort and Casino in the Bahamas. In 1991 Carnival reached a settlement with the Bahamian government (effective March 1, 1992) to surrender the 672-room Riveria Towers to the Hotel Corporation of the Bahamas in exchange for the cancellation of some debt incurred in constructing and developing the resort. The corporation took a $135 million write-down on the Crystal Palace for that year.

The early 1990s, even with industry-wide demand slowing, were still a very exciting time. Carnival took delivery of its first two "superliners", the *Fantasy* (1990) and the *Ecstasy* (1991), which were to further penetrate the three- and four-day cruise market and supplement the seven-day market. In early 1991, Carnival took delivery of the third "superliner," *Sensation* (inaugural sailing November 1, 1993), and later in the year contracted for the fourth "superliner" to be named the *Fascination* (inaugural sailing 1994).

In 1991, Carnival attempted to acquire Premier Cruise Lines, which was then the official cruise line for Walt Disney World in Orlando, Florida, for approximately $372 million. The deal was never consummated since the involved parties could not agree on price. In 1992, Carnival acquired 50% of Seabourn, gaining the cruise operations of K/S Seabourn Cruise Lines and formed a partnership with Atle Byrnestad. Seabourn served the ultra-luxury market with destinations in South America, the Mediterranean, Southeast Asia, and the Baltics.

The 1993 to 1995 period saw the addition of the "superliner" *Imagination* for Carnival Cruise Lines and the *Ryndam* for Holland America Lines. In 1994, the company discontinued operations of Fiestamarina Lines which attempted to serve Spanish-speaking clientele. Fiestamarina was beset with marketing and operational problems and never reached continuous operations. Many industry analysts and observers were surprised at the failure of Carnival to successfully develop this market. In 1995 Carnival sold a 49% interest in the Epirotiki Line, a Greek cruise operation, for $25 million and purchased $101 million (face amount) of senior secured notes of Kloster Cruise Limited, the parent of competitor Norwegian Cruise Lines, for $81 million.

Carnival Corporation also expanded through internally generated growth as evidenced by the number of new ships on order (see **Exhibit 1**). Additionally, Carnival seemed to be willing to continue with its external expansion through acquisitions if the right opportunity arose.

In June 1997, Royal Caribbean made a bid to buy Celebrity Cruise Lines for $500 million and assumption of $800 million in debt. Within a week, Carnival had responded by submitting a counter offer to Celebrity for $510 million and the assumption of debt. Two days later, Carnival raised the bid to $525 million. Nevertheless, Royal Caribbean announced on June 30, 1997 the final merger arrangements with Celebrity. The resulting company had 17 ships with over 30,000 berths.

Not to be thwarted in its attempts at continued expansion, Carnival announced in June 1997 the purchase of Costa, an Italian cruise company and the largest European cruise line, for $141 million. The purchase was finalized in September 2000. External expansion continued when Carnival announced the acquisition of Cunard Line for $500 million from Kvaerner ASA on May 28, 1998. Cunard was then operationally merged with Seabourn Cruise Line. Carnival owned 100% of the resulting Cunard Line in fiscal 2000. In an attempt at further expansion, Carnival announced on December 2, 1999 a hostile bid for NCL Holding ASA, the parent company of Norwegian Cruise Lines. Carnival was unsuccessful in this acquisition attempt. Its latest external acquisition would be the Princess Cruise Line once all approvals had been received.

Exhibit 1

Carnival Corporation Ships Under Construction

Vessel	Expected Delivery	Shipyard	Passenger Capacity[1]	Cost ($mils)
Carnival Cruise Lines				
Carnival Conquest	12/02	Fincantieri	2,974	$ 500
Carnival Glory	8/03	Fincantieri	2,974	500
Carnival Miracale	4/04	Masa-Yards	2,124	375
Carnival Valor	11/04	Fincantieri	2,974	500
Total Carnival Cruise Lines			11,046	$1,875
Holland America Line				
Zuiderdam	12/02	Fincantieri	1,848	410
Oosterdam	7/03	Fincantieri	1,848	410
Newbuilt	5/04	Fincantieri	1,848	410
Newbuilt	11/05	Fincantieri	1,848	410
Total Holland American Line			7,392	$1,640
Costa Cruise Lines				
Mediterranea	7/03	Masa-Yards	2,114	335
Fortuna	1/04	Fincantieri	2,720	390
Magica	12/04	Fincantieri	2,720	390
Total Costa Cruise Lines			7,554	$1,115
Cunard Line				
Queen Mary II	12/03	l'Alantique	2,620	780
Newbuilt	2/05	Fincantieri	1,968	410
Total Cunard Cruise Line			4,588	$1,190
Total all vessels			30,580	$5,820

Note:

1. In accordance with industry practice, all capacities indicated within this document are calculated based on two passengers per cabin, even though some cabins can accommodate three or four passengers.

The Cruise Product

Ted and Mickey Arison envisioned a product in which the classical cruise elegance, along with modern convenience, could be had at a price comparable to land-based vacation packages sold by travel agents. Carnival's all-inclusive package, when compared to resorts or a theme park, such as Walt Disney World, often was priced below these destinations; especially when the array of activities, entertainment, and meals were considered.

A typical vacation on a Carnival cruise ship began when the bags were tagged for the ship at the airport. Upon arriving at the port of embarkation, passengers were ferried by air-conditioned buses to the ship for boarding. Baggage was taken from the terminal to the cabin of the passenger by cruise/ship staff. Waiters on the ship offered tropical drinks to guests while the cruise staff oriented passengers to the various decks, cabins, and public rooms. In a few hours (most ships sail in the early evening), dinner was served in the main dining rooms where wine selection rivaled the finest restaurants and the variety of main dishes were designed to suit every palate. Diners could always order double portion if they decided not to save room for the variety of desserts and after-dinner specialties.

After dinner, cruisers could choose between many forms of entertainment, including live music, dancing, nightclubs, and a selection of movies; or they could sleep through the midnight buffet until breakfast. (Most ships had five or more distinct nightclubs.) During the night, a daily program for the next day of activities arrived at the passengers' cabins. The biggest decisions to be made for the duration of the vacation were what to do (or not to do), what to eat and when (usually eight separate serving times not including the 24-hour room service), and when to sleep. Service in all areas from dining to housekeeping was upscale and immediate. The service was so good that a common shipboard joke stated that if you leave your bed during the night to visit the head (sea talk for bathroom), your cabin steward will have made the bed and placed chocolates on the pillow by the time you return.

After the cruise, passengers were transported back to the airport in air-conditioned buses for the flight home. Representatives of the cruise line were on hand at the cruise terminal and airport to help cruisers in meeting their scheduled flights. When all amenities were considered, most vacation packages would be hard pressed to match Carnival's per diem prices that ranged from $125 to $300 per person/per day, depending on accommodations. (Holland America and Seaborn were higher, ranging from $157 to $725 person/per day.) Specials and discounts allowed for even lower prices. Special suite accommodations could be purchased for an additional payment.

Carnival Operations

Carnival Corporation, headquartered in Miami, was composed of Carnival Cruise Lines, Holland America Lines (which included Windstar Sail Cruises as a subsidiary, Holland America Westours, and Westmark Hotels), Costa Cruise Lines, Seabourn Cruise Lines, Gray Line of Alaska and Seattle, Cunard Line Limited, and, in the near future, Princess Cruise Line. Carnival Corporation was a Panamanian corporation and its subsidiaries were incorporated in Panama, the Netherlands Antilles, the British Virgin Islands, Liberia, and the Bahamas. The ships were subject to inspection by the U.S. Coast Guard for compliance with the Convention for the Safety of Life at Sea (SOLAS), which required specific structural requirements for safety of passengers at sea, and by the U.S. Public Health Service for sanitary standards. The company was also regulated in some aspects by the Federal Maritime Commission.

At its helm, Carnival Corporation was led by CEO and Chairman of the Board Micky Arison. Carnival Cruise Lines President and COO was Bob Dickinson and A. Kirk Lanterman was the President and CEO of the Holland America cruise division, which included Holland America Westours and Windstar Sail Cruises. (A listing of corporate officers is presented in **Exhibit 2**.)

Exhibit 2
Corporate Officers of Carnival Corporation

Micky Arison	**Howard S. Frank**
Chairman of the Board and Chief Executive Officer	Vice Chairman and Chief Operating Officer
Gerald R. Cahill	**Ian Gaunt**
Senior Vice President, Finance, and CFO	Senior Vice President, International
Lowell Zemnick	**Kenneth D. Dubbin**
Vice President and Treasurer	Vice President, Corporate Development
Richard D. Ames	**Arnaldo Perez**
Vice President, Audit Services	Vice President, General Counsel, and Secretary
Robert H. Dickinson	**A. Kirk Lanterman**
President and COO	Chairman of the Board and CEO
Carnival Cruise Lines	Holland America Line
Pier Luigi Foschi	**Pamela C. Conover**
Chairman and CEO	President and COO
Costa Cruise Lines	Cunard Line

Source: Carnival Corporation, 2002.

The company's product positioning stemmed from its belief that the cruise market was actually comprised of three primary segments with different passenger demographics, passenger characteristics, and growth requirements. The three segments were the contemporary, premium, and luxury segments. The contemporary segment was served by Carnival ships for cruises that were seven days or shorter in length and featured a casual ambiance. The premium segment, served by Holland America, served the seven-day and longer market and appealed to more affluent consumers, and Costa Cruises offered an Italian cruise experience in this segment. The luxury segment, while considerably smaller than the other segments, catered to experienced cruisers for seven-day and longer sailings and was served by Seabourn and Cunard. Specialty sailing cruises were provided by Windstar Sail Cruises, a subsidiary of Holland America.

Corporate structure was built around the profit center concept and was updated periodically when needed for control and coordination purposes. The cruise subsidiaries of Carnival Corporation had a presence in most of the major cruise segments and provided for worldwide operations.

Carnival always placed a high priority on marketing in an attempt to promote cruises as an alternative to land-based vacations. It wanted customers to know that the ship itself was the destination and the ports of call were important, but secondary, to the cruise experience. Education and the creation of awareness were critical to corporate marketing efforts. Carnival was the first cruise line to successfully break away from traditional print media and use television to reach a broader market. Even though other lines have followed Carnival's lead in selecting promotional media and were close to Carnival in total advertising expenditures, the organization still led all cruise competitors in advertising and marketing expenditures.

Carnival wanted to remain the leader and innovator in the cruise industry and intended to do this with sophisticated promotional efforts and by gaining loyalty from former cruisers, by refurbishing ships, varying activities and ports of call, and being innovative in all aspects of ship operations. Management intended to build on the theme of the ship as a destination given their historical success with this promotional effort.

Financial Performance

Carnival retained PricewaterhouseCoopers LLP as independent accountants and the First Union National Bank as its registrar and stock transfer agent. Its Class A Common stock traded on the New York Stock Exchange under the symbol CCL. The consolidated financial statements for Carnival Cruise Lines, Inc. are shown in **Exhibits 3** and **4** and selected financial data are presented in **Exhibit 5**.

Customer cruise deposits, which represent unearned revenue, were included in the balance sheet (current liability account) when received and recognized as cruise revenues on completion of the voyage. Customers also were required to pay the full cruise fare (minus deposit) 60 days in advance with the fares being recognized as cruise revenue on completion of the voyage.

Property and equipment on the financial statements was stated at cost. Depreciation and amortization was calculated using the straight-line method over the following estimated useful lives: vessels 25–30 years, buildings 20–40 years, equipment 2–20 years and leasehold improvements at the shorter of the "term of lease" or "related asset life". During 1995, Carnival received $40 million from the settlement of litigation with Metra Oy, the former parent company of Wartsila Marine Industries, related to losses suffered in connection with the construction of three cruise ships. (Wartsila declared bankruptcy in late 1994) Of this amount, $14.4 million was recorded as "other income" with the remainder used to pay legal fees and reduce the cost basis of the three ships.

Exhibit 3

Consolidated Statements of Operations: Carnival Corporation (Dollar amounts in thousands)

Year Ending November 30	2001	2000	1999	1998	1997	1996	1995	1994	1993	1992
Revenues	$4,535,751	$3,778,542	$3,497,470	$3,009,306	$2,447,468	$2,212,572	$1,998,150	$1,806,016	$1,556,919	$1,473,614
Costs and expenses										
Operating expense	2,468,730	2,058,342	1,862,636	1,619,377	1,322,669	1,241,269	1,131,113	1,028,475	907,925	865,587
Selling and administrative	618,664	487,403	447,235	369,469	296,533	274,855	248,566	223,272	207,995	194,298
Depreciation & amortization	372,224	287,667	243,658	200,668	167,287	144,987	128,433	110,595	93,333	88,833
Impairment charge	140,378									
	$3,599,996	$2,833,412	$2,553,529	$2,189,514	$1,786,489	$1,661,111	$1,508,112	$1,362,342	$1,209,253	$1,148,718
Operating income before affiliated	935,755	945,130	943,941	819,792	660,979	551,461				
Income from affiliated (loss)	(44,024)	37,828	75,758	76,732	53,091	45,967	—	—	—	—
Operating income	891,731	982,958	1,019,699	896,524	714,070	597,428	490,038	443,674	347,666	324,896
Other income (expense)										
Interest income	34,255	16,506	41,932	10,257	8,675	18,597	14,403	8,668	11,527	16,946
Interest expense, net of capitalized interest	(120,692)	(41,372)	(46,956)	(57,772)	(55,898)	(64,092)	(63,080)	(51,378)	(34,325)	(53,792)
Other income (expense)	108,649	8,460	29,357	1,793	5,436	23,414	19,104	(9,146)	(1,201)	2,731
Income tax benefit (expense)	12,257	(1,094)	(2,778)	(3,815)	(6,233)	(9,045)	(9,374)	(10,053)	(5,497)	(9,008)
Minority interest			(14,014)	(11,102)						
	34,469	(17,500)	7,541	(60,639)	(48,020)	(31,126)	(38,947)	(61,909)	(29,496)	(43,123)
Income before extraordinary item	926,200	965,458	1,027,240	835,885	666,050	566,302	451,091	381,765	318,170	281,773
Extraordinary item										
Loss on early extinguishment of debt										(5,189)
Net Income	$ 926,200	$ 965,458	$1,027,240	$ 835,885	$ 666,050	$ 566,302	$ 451,091	$ 381,765	$ 318,170	$ 276,584

Source: 1992–2001 Form 10-K and 10Q's.

Exhibit 4

Consolidated Balance Sheets: Carnival Corporation (Dollar amounts in thousands)

Year Ending November 30	2001	2000	1999	1998	1997	1996	1995	1994	1993
Assets									
Current assets									
Cash & cash equivalents	$ 1,421,300	$ 189,282	$ 521,771	$ 137,273	$ 139,989	$ 111,629	$ 53,365	$ 54,105	$ 60,243
Short-term investments	36,784			5,956	9,738	12,486	50,395	70,115	88,677
Accounts receivable	90,763	95,361	62,887	60,837	57,090	38,109	33,080	20,789	19,310
Consumable inventories [average cost]	91,996	100,451	84,019	75,449	54,970	53,281	48,820	45,122	37,245
Prepaid expenses & other	113,798	164,388	122,959	90,764	74,238	75,428	70,718	50,318	48,323
Fair value of hedged firm commitments	204,347								
Total current assets	$ 1,958,988	$ 549,482	$ 791,636	$ 370,279	$ 336,025	$ 290,933	$ 256,378	$ 240,449	$ 253,798
Property and Equipment [at cost]	8,390,230	8,001,318	6,410,527	5,768,114	4,327,413	4,099,038	3,414,823	3,071,431	2,588,009
Less accumulated depreciation & amortization									
Other assets									
Goodwill [less accumulated amortization]	651,814	701,385	462,340	437,464	212,607	219,589	226,571	233,553	237,327
Long-term notes receivable									29,136
Investment in affiliates & other assets	188,915	437,391	586,922	546,693	479,329	430,330	78,907	76,876	21,097
Other assets		141,744	34,930	56,773	71,401	61,998	128,808	47,514	89,553
Fair value of hedged firm commitments	373,605								
Total assets	$11,563,552	$9,831,320	$8,286,355	$7,179,323	$5,426,775	$5,101,888	$4,105,487	$3,669,823	$3,218,920
Liabilities and equity									
Current liabilities									
Current portion of long-term debt	21,764	248,219	206,267	67,626	59,620	66,369	72,752	84,644	91,621
Accounts payable	269,467	322,694	195,879	168,546	106,783	84,748	90,237	86,750	81,374
Accrued liabilities	298,032	302,585	262,170	206,968	154,253	126,511	113,483	114,868	94,830
Customer deposits	627,698	770,425	675,816	638,383	420,908	352,698	292,606	257,505	228,153
Dividends payable	61,548	61,371	64,781	53,590	44,578	32,416	25,632	21,190	19,763
Reserve for discontinued operations									34,253
Fair value of derivative contracts	201,731								
Total current liabilities	$ 1,480,240	$1,715,294	$1,404,913	$1,135,113	$ 786,142	$ 662,742	$ 594,710	$ 564,957	$ 549,994
Long-term debt	2,954,854	2,099,077	867,515	1,563,014	1,015,294	1,277,529	1,035,031	1,046,904	916,221
Convertible notes and						39,103	115,000	115,000	115,000
Other long-term liabilities	157,998	146,322	82,680	63,036	20,241	91,630	15,873	14,028	10,499
Fair value of derivative contracts									
Minority interest	379,683			132,684					
Shareholders' equity									
Class A common stock [1 vote share]	6,200	6,176	6,170	5,955	2,972	2,397	2,298	2,274	2,274
Class B common stock [5 votes share]					550	550	550	550	550
Paid in capital	1,805,248	1,772,897	1,757,408	880,488	866,097	819,610	594,811	544,947	541,194
Retained earnings	5,556,296	4,844,023	4,176,498	3,379,628	2,731,213	2,207,781	1,752,140	1,390,589	1,089,323
Unearned stock compensation	(12,398)								
Accumulated other comprehensive loss	(36,932)								
Treasury stock	(727,637)								
Other		(752,497)	(8,829)	19,405	4,816	546	(4,926)	(9,428)	(6,135)
Total shareholders' equity	6,590,777	5,870,617	5,931,247	4,285,476	3,605,098	3,030,884	2,344,873	1,928,934	1,627,206
Total liabilities	$11,563,552	$9,831,320	$8,286,355	$7,179,323	$5,426,775	$5,101,888	$4,105,487	$3,669,823	$3,218,920

Source: 1992–2001 Form 10K.

16-9

Exhibit 5

Selected Financial Data by Segment: Carnival Corporation
(Dollar amounts in thousands)

Year Ending November 30	2001	2000	1999[1]	1998[1]	1997	1996	1995	1994
Revenues								
Cruise	$4,357,942	$3,578,372	$3,286,701	$2,797,856	$2,257,567	$2,003,458	$1,800,775	$1,623,069
Tour	229,483	259,662	271,828	274,491	242,646	263,356	241,909	227,613
Intersegment elimination	(51,674)	(59,592)	(61,059)	(63,041)	(52,745)	(54,242)	(44,534)	(44,666)
Total	$4,535,751	$3,778,542	$3,497,470	$3,009,306	$2,447,468	$2,212,572	$1,998,150	$1,806,016
Depreciation & amortization								
Cruise	359,314	276,483	232,942	189,345	157,454	135,694	120,304	101,146
Tour	11,474	10,825	10,716	9,491	8,862	8,317	8,129	9,449
Corporate	1,436	359	—	—	971	976	—	—
Total	$ 372,224	$ 287,667	$ 243,658	$ 198,836	$ 167,287	$ 144,987	$ 128,433	$ 110,595
Operating income								
Cruise	958,273	957,226	947,452	822,242	656,009	535,814	465,870	425,590
Tour	(10,357)	7,664	10,403	9,248	13,262	21,252	24,168	18,084
Affiliated operations	(44,024)	37,828	75,758	—	—	—	—	—
Corporate	(12,161)	(19,760)	(13,914)	65,034	44,799	40,362	—	—
Total	$ 891,731	$ 982,958	$1,019,699	$ 896,524	$ 714,070	$ 597,428	$ 490,038	$ 443,674

Note:
1. Includes acquisitions.

Source: 1995–2001 Form 10-K.

On June 25, 1996, Carnival reached an agreement with the trustees of Wartsila and creditors for the bankruptcy, resulting in a cash payment of approximately $80 million. Of the $80 million received, $5 million was used to pay costs, $32 million was recorded as other income, and $43 million was used to reduce the cost basis of ships, which had been affected by the bankruptcy.

By the end of fiscal 2001, Carnival had outstanding long-term debt of almost $3 billion. According to the Internal Revenue Code of 1986, Carnival was considered a "Controlled Foreign Corporation" (CFC) since 50% of its stock was held by individuals who were residents of foreign countries and its countries of incorporation exempt shipping operations of U.S. persons from income tax. Because of its CFC status, Carnival expected that all of its income (with the exception of U.S. source income from the transportation, hotel, and tour businesses of Holland America) would be exempt from U.S. federal income taxes at the corporate level.

The primary financial consideration of importance to Carnival management involved the control of costs, both fixed and variable, for the maintenance of a healthy profit margin. Carnival had the lowest break-even point of any organization in the cruise industry (ships break-even at approximately 60% of capacity) due to operational experience and economies of scale. Unfortunately, fixed costs, including depreciation, fuel, insurance, port charges, and crew costs, represented more than 33% of the company's operating expenses. These costs could not be significantly reduced in relation to decreases in passenger loads and aggregate passenger ticket revenue. Major expense items were air fares (25%–30%), travel agent fees (10%), and labor (13%–15%) Increases in these costs could negatively affect the profitability of the organization.

Principle Subsidiaries

CARNIVAL CRUISE LINE

At the end of fiscal 2001, Carnival operated 16 ships (excluding the *Tropicale* which was transferred to Costa) with a total berth capacity of over 33,154. Carnival operated principally in the Caribbean and had an assortment of ships and ports of call serving the three-, four-, and seven-day cruise markets (see **Exhibit 6**).

Each ship was a floating resort including a full maritime staff, shopkeepers and casino operators, entertainers, and complete hotel staff. Approximately 14% of corporate revenue was generated from shipboard activities such as casino operations, liquor sales, and gift shop items. At various ports-of-call, passengers could also take advantage of tours, shore excursions, and duty-free shopping at their own expense.

Shipboard operations were designed to provide maximum entertainment, activities, and service. The size of the company and the similarity in design of the new cruise ships had allowed Carnival to achieve various economies of scale, and management was very cost-conscious.

Although the Carnival Cruise Lines division was increasing their presence in the shorter cruise markets, its general marketing strategy was to use three-, four-, or seven-day moderately price cruises to fit the time and budget constraints of the middle class. Shorter cruises cost less than $500 per person (depending on accommodations). Longer cruises cost up to $3,000 per person in a luxury suite on a seven-day cruise, including port charges. (Per diem rates for shorter cruises were slightly higher, on average, than per diem rates for seven-day cruises.) Average rates per day were approximately $180, excluding gambling, liquor and soft drinks, and items of a personal nature. Guests were expected to tip their cabin steward and waiter at a suggested rate of $3.50 per person/per day, and the bus boy at $2 per person/per day.

Some 97% of all Carnival cruises were sold through travel agents, who received a standard commission of 10% (15% in Florida). Carnival worked extensively with travel agents to help

Exhibit 6

The Ships of Carnival Corporation

Name	Registry	Built	First in Company	Service Capacity[1]	Areas of Operation
Carnival Cruise Lines					
Pride	Panama	2001	2001	2,124	Caribbean
Spirit	Panama	2001	2001	2,124	Caribbean
Victory	Panama	2000	2000	2,758	Caribbean
Triumph	Panama	1999	1999	2,758	East Coast, Caribbean
Paradise	Panama	1998	1998	2,040	Caribbean
Elation	Panama	1998	1998	2,040	Mexican Rivera
Destiny	Panama	1996	1997	2,642	Caribbean
Inspiration	Panama	1996	1996	2,040	Caribbean
Imagination	Panama	1995	1995	2,040	Caribbean
Fascination	Panama	1994	1994	2,040	Caribbean
Sensation	Panama	1993	1993	2,040	Caribbean
Ecstasy	Liberia	1991	1991	2,040	Caribbean
Fantasy	Liberia	1990	1990	2,044	Bahamas
Celebration	Liberia	1987	1987	1,486	Caribbean
Jubilee	Panama	1986	1986	1,486	Mexican Riviera
Holiday	Panama	1985	1985	1,452	Mexican Riviera
Tropicale	Liberia	1982	1982	1,022	Alaska, Caribbean

Total Carnival ship capacity = 34,196

Name	Registry	Built	First in Company	Service Capacity[1]	Areas of Operation
Holland America Line					
Zaandam	Netherlands	2000	2000	1,440	Worldwide
Amsterdam	Netherlands	2000	2000	1,380	Worldwide
Volendam	Netherlands	1999	1999	1,440	Europe, Worldwide
Rotterdam	Netherlands	1997	1997	1,316	Europe, Worldwide
Veendam	Bahamas	1996	1996	1,266	Alaska, Caribbean
Ryndam	Netherlands	1994	1994	1,266	Alaska, Caribbean
Maasdam	Netherlands	1993	1993	1,266	Europe, Caribbean
Statendam	Netherlands	1993	1993	1,266	Alaska, Caribbean
Westerdam	Netherlands	1986	1988	1,494	Canada, Caribbean
Noordam	Netherlands	1984	1984	1,214	Alaska, Caribbean

Total Holland America Line ship capacity = 13,348

Name	Registry	Built	First in Company	Service Capacity[1]	Areas of Operation
Windstar Cruises					
Wind Surf	Bahamas	1990	1990	312	Caribbean
Wind Spirit	Bahamas	1988	1988	148	Caribbean, Mediterranean
Wind Song	Bahamas	1987	1987	148	Costa Rica, Tahiti
Wind Star	Bahamas	1986	1986	148	Caribbean, Mediterranean

Total Windstar ship capacity = 756

Name	Registry	Built	First in Company	Service Capacity[1]	Areas of Operation
Cunard Line					
Caronia	England	1973	1973	24,500	Europe
Queen Elizabeth II	England	1969	1969	70,327	Worldwide

Total Cunard ship capacity = 94,827

Name	Registry	Built	First in Company	Service Capacity[1]	Areas of Operation
Seabourn Cruise Line					
Seabourn Legend	Norway	1992	1996	208	Pacific
Seabourn Spirit	Norway	1989	1989	208	Asia
Seabourn Pride	Norway	1988	1988	208	South America

Total Seabourn ship capacity = 624

Total capacity = 50,265

promote cruises as an alternative to a Disney or European vacation. In addition to training travel agents from nonaffiliated travel/vacation firms to sell cruises, a special group of employees regularly visited travel agents posing as prospective clients. If the travel agent specified a Carnival cruise before other options, they received $100 on the spot. In calendar 2000, Carnival took reservations from about 29,000 of the approximately 45,000 travel agencies in the United States and Canada, and no one travel agency accounted for more than 2% of Carnival revenues.

Onboard service was labor intensive, employing help from some 51 nations—mostly third world countries—with reasonable returns to employees. For example, waiters on the Jubilee could earn approximately $18,000 to $27,000 per year (base salary and tips), significantly greater than could be earned in their home country for similar employment. Waiters typically worked 10 hours per day with approximately one day off per week for a specified contract period (usually three to nine months). Carnival records showed that employees remained with the company for approximately eight years and that applicants exceeded demand for all cruise positions. Nonetheless, the American Maritime union had cited Carnival (and other cruise operators) several times for exploitation of its crew because of low wages.

HOLLAND AMERICA LINES

On January 17, 1989, Carnival acquired all the outstanding stock of HAL Antillen N.V. from Holland America Lines N.V. for $625 million in cash. Carnival financed the purchase through $250 million in retained earnings (cash account) and borrowed the other $375 million from banks at .25% over the prime rate. Carnival received the assets and operations of the Holland America Lines, Westours, Westmark Hotels, and Windstar Sail Cruises. Holland America in 2002 had 10 cruise ships with a capacity of 13,348 berths with new ships to be delivered in the future.

Founded in 1873, Holland America Lines was an upscale (it charged an average of 25% more than similar Carnival cruises) line with principal destinations in Alaska during the summer months and the Caribbean during the fall and winter, with some worldwide cruises of up to 98 days. Holland America targeted an older, more sophisticated cruiser with fewer youth-oriented activities. On Holland America ships, passengers can dance to the sounds of the Big Band era and avoid the more recent music played on Carnival ships. Passengers on Holland America ships enjoyed more service (a higher staff-to-passenger ratio than Carnival) and had more cabin and public space per person, and a "no tipping" shipboard policy. Holland America had not enjoyed the spectacular growth of Carnival cruise ships, but had sustained constant growth over the decade of the 1980s and 1990s with high occupancy. The operation of these ships and the structure of the crew were similar to the Carnival cruise ship model, and the acquisition of the line gave the Carnival Corporation a presence in the Alaskan market where it had none before.

Holland America Westours was the largest tour operator in Alaska and the Canadian Rockies and provided vacation synergy with Holland America cruises. The transportation division of Westours included motor coaches comprised of the Gray Line of Alaska, the Gray Line of Seattle, Westours motorcoaches, the McKinley Explorer railroad coaches, and three-day boats for tours to glaciers and other points of interest. Carnival management believed that Alaskan cruises and tours should increased in the future due to a number of factors. These included the aging population wanting relaxing vacations with scenic beauty coupled with the fact that Alaska was a U.S. destination.

Westmark Hotels consisted of 16 hotels in Alaska and the Yukon territories, and also provided synergy with cruise operations and Westours. Westmark was the largest group of hotels in the region providing moderately priced rooms for the vacationer.

Windstar Sail Cruises was acquired by Holland America Lines in 1988 and consisted of four computer-controlled sailing vessels with a berth capacity of 756. Windstar was very upscale and offered an alternative to traditional cruise liners with a more intimate, activity-oriented cruise. The ships operated primarily in the Mediterranean and the South Pacific, visiting ports not accessible to large cruise ships. Although catering to a small segment of the cruise vacation industry, Windstar helped with Carnival's commitment to participate in all segments of the cruise industry.

SEABOURN CRUISE LINES

In April 1992, the company acquired 25% of the capital stock of Seabourn. As part of the transaction, the company also made a subordinated secured 10-year loan of $15 million to Seabourn and a $10 million convertible loan to Seabourn. In December 1995, the $10 million convertible loan was converted by the company into an additional 25% equity interest in Seabourn. Full ownership was completed in 2000 with 100% ownership of Cunard Line Limited, which now operated both the Cunard and Seabourn brands.

Seabourn targeted the luxury market with three vessels providing 200 passengers per ship with all-suite accommodations. Seabourn was considered the "Rolls Royce" of the cruise industry and in 1992 was named the "World's Best Cruise Line" by the prestigious *Conde Nast Traveler's* fifth annual readers' choice poll. Seabourn cruised the Americas, Europe, Scandinavia, the Mediterranean, and the Far East.

COSTA CROCIERE S.P.A.

In June 1997, Carnival purchased the equity securities of Costa from the Costa family at a cost of approximately $141 million and completed the purchase of the remainder in September 2000. Costa was headquartered in Italy and was considered Europe's largest cruise line with eight ships and approximately 10,000 passenger capacity. Costa operated primarily in the Mediterranean, Northern Europe, the Caribbean, and South America. The major market for Costa in southern Europe, was mainly Italy, Spain, and France.

CUNARD LINE

Another Carnival acquisition was the Cunard Line, announced on May 28, 1998. Comprised of two ships, the Cunard Line was considered a luxury line with strong brand name recognition. Cunard had two ships (including the *Queen Elizabeth II*) in 2002 with two new ships on order.

Future Considerations

Carnival's management had to continue to monitor several strategic factors and issues for the next few years. The industry itself was expected to see further growth in passengers, consolidation through mergers, buyouts and smaller cruise operator failures, and the expansion of the industry worldwide. Another factor of concern to management was how to reach the large untapped North American market.

With the industry maturing, cruise competitors had become more sophisticated in their marketing efforts and price competition was the norm in most cruise segments. (For a partial listing of major industry competitors, see **Exhibit 7**) Royal Caribbean Cruise Lines had also instituted a major shipbuilding program and was successfully challenging Carnival Cruise Lines in the contemporary segment. The emergence of the Walt Disney Company in the cruise market with two 80,000-ton cruise liners in 1998 and the prospect of new ships on the horizon could significantly impact the "family" cruise vacation segment.

Exhibit 7

Major Industry Competitors

Celebrity Cruises, 5200 Blue Lagoon Drive, Miami, FL 33126

Celebrity Cruises operated six modern cruise ships on four-, seven-, and ten-day cruises to Bermuda, the Caribbean, the Panama Canal, and Alaska. Celebrity attracted first-time cruisers as well as seasoned cruisers. Purchased by Royal Caribbean on July 30, 1997.

Norwegian Cruise Lines, 95 Merrick Way, Coral Gables, FL 33134

Norwegian Cruise Lines (NCL), formally Norwegian Caribbean Lines, was the first company to base a modern fleet of cruise ships in the Port of Miami. It operated eight modern cruise liners on three-, four-, and seven-day Eastern and Western Caribbean cruises and cruises to Bermuda. A wide variety of activities and entertainment attracted a diverse array of customers. NCL had just completed reconstruction of two ships, and its newest ship, *Norwegian Sky*, a 2,000-passenger ship, was delivered in summer 1999.

Disney Cruise Line, 500 South Buena Vista Street, Burbank, CA 91521

Disney had just recently entered the cruise market, with the introduction of the *Disney Magic* and *Disney Wonder*. Both ships catered to both children and adults and feature 875 state-rooms each. Each cruise included a visit to Disney's private island, Castaway Cay. Although Disney had only two ships and the cruise portion of the vacation was small, its potential for future growth was substantial.

Princess Cruises, 10100 Santa Monica Boulevard, Los Angeles, CA 90067

Princess Cruises, with its fleet of ten *Love Boats*, offered seven-day and extended cruises to the Caribbean, Alaska, Canada, Africa, the Far East, South America, and Europe. Princess's primary market was the upscale 50-plus experienced traveler, according to Mike Hannan, Senior Vice President for Marketing Services. Princess ships had ambiance best described as casual elegance and were famous for their Italian-style dining rooms and onboard entertainment.

Royal Caribbean Cruise Lines, 1050 Caribbean Way, Miami, FL 33132

Royal Caribbean's ships had consistently been given high marks by passengers and travel agents over the past 21 years. Royal Caribbean's ships were built for the contemporary market, were large and modern, and offered three-, four-, and seven-day as well as extended cruises.

Source: Cruise Line International Association, 2001 and company 10k's and annual reports.

With competition intensifying, industry observers believed the wave of failures, mergers, buyouts, and strategic alliances would increase. Regency Cruises ceased operations on October 29, 1995, and filed for Chapter 11 bankruptcy. American Family Cruises, a spin-off from Costa Cruise Lines, failed to reach the family market and Carnival's *Fiestamarina* failed to reach the Spanish-speaking market. EffJohn International sold its Commodore Cruise subsidiary to a group of Miami-based investors, which then chartered one of its two ships to World Explorer Cruises/Semester At Sea. Commodore later folded and liquidated its ships. Sun Cruise Lines merged with Epirotiki Cruise Line under the name of Royal Olympic Cruises and Cunard bought the Royal Viking Line and its name from Kloster Cruise Ltd., with one ship of its fleet being transferred to Kloster's Royal Cruise Line.

The increasing industry capacity was also a source of concern to cruise operators. The slow growth in industry demand was occurring during a period when industry berth capacity continued to grow at a faster rate. The entry of Disney and the ships already on order by current operators should increase industry berth capacity by over 10,000 per year for the next four years, a significant increase. Combined with the lingering effects of September 11 and the recent negative publicity, the danger lies in cruise operators using the "price" weapon in their marketing campaigns to fill cabins, especially in the next few years. If cruise operators could make a reasonable return on investment, operating costs would have to be reduced (affecting quality of services) to remain profitable. This would increase the likelihood of further industry acquisitions, mergers, consolidations, and failures. Long-term implications concerned the addition of capacity faster than the growth in customer demand.

Carnival's management and board of directors (see **Exhibit 8**) believed that demand will continue to increase well into the future. Considering that only a small percentage of the North American market had taken a cruise vacation, reaching more of the North American target market would improve industry profitability. Industry analysts stated that the "assessment of market potential" was only an "educated guess." What if the current demand did not grow according to industry and cruise line projections?

Exhibit 8

Board of Directors of Carnival Corporation

Mickey Arison
Chairman of the Board and Chief
Executive Officer
Carnival Corporation

Maks L. Birnbach
Chairman of the Board
Fullcut Manufacturers, Inc.

Robert H. Dickinson
President and Chief Operating Officer
Carnival Cruise Lines

James M. Dublin
Senior Partner
Paul, Weiss, Rifkind, Wharton & Garrison

A. Kirk Lanterman
Chairman of the Board and Chief
Executive Officer
Holland American Line-Wastours Inc.

Stuart Subotnick
General Partner and Executive Vice President
Metromedia Company

Meshulam Zonis
Former Senior Vice President Operations
Carnival Cruise Lines

Shari Arison
Chairman
Arison Hildings (1998) Ltd.

Richard G. Capen, Jr.
Former United States
Ambassador to Spain

Arnold W. Donald
Chairman and Chief Executive Officer
Merisant Company

Howard S. Frank
Vice Chairman of the Board and Chief
Operating Officer
Carnival Corporation

Modesto A. Maidique
President
Florida International University

Sherwood M. Weiser
The Continental Companies, LLC
Chairman of the Board and Chief
Executive Officer

Uzi Zucker
Senior Managing Director
Bear Stearns & Co. Inc.

Source: Carnival Corporation, *2002 Annual Report*, p. 35.

case 17

Reebok International, Ltd. (2002)

Thomas L. Wheelen, Moustafa H. Abdelsamad, Richard D. Wheelen, and Thomas L. Wheelen II

Report of Chairman Fireman

Paul Fireman, Chairman and Chief Executive Officer (CEO) of Reebok, reviewed the accomplishments, highlights of 2001, and issues facing the company in his letter to shareholders in the *2001 Annual Report.*

2001 was another solid year for our company. Our profits increased 27% over the prior year despite some difficult economic declines in many of our key markets and a strong U.S. dollar which adversely impacted our margins in most foreign countries. Two years ago when I returned to managing the day-to-day operations of the company, I established several key objectives and committed to you that they would be achieved within two years. I committed to you that we would 1) establish a result-orientated culture, 2) strengthen our management team, 3) contemporize our products, 4) create relevant advertising and effective retail and consumer marketing campaigns, and as a result of these efforts, 5) grow quality market share. I am very pleased that we have made substantial progress on all of these fronts.

Our management team has been enhanced significantly with the promotions of Jay Margolis to the newly created position of President and Chief Operating Officer of Reebok International Ltd., and David Perdue as President and CEO of the Reebok Brand. Jay will be responsible for the day-to-day oversight of our company-wide operations. He has over 25 years of experience leading highly visible, fashion-oriented footwear and apparel brands. Jay has strong leadership skills and has already begun to provide invaluable product, marketing and operational support to our brand presidents. David has a wealth of international experience and understands the complexity of a global marketplace. He has earned the respect and trust of our retailers and employees.

In addition to enhancing our leadership team, we have significantly improved the style and fashionability of our products and the quality and effectiveness of our marketing platforms. These initiatives provide us with a solid foundation from which we can grow quality market share.

Our Reebok Brand management team had an excellent year in 2001 making solid progress in their quest to make the Brand more relevant and aspirational to young men and women. During 2001, we further strengthened the Reebok Brand management team by filing several key positions with industry veterans who are all well respected, seasoned professionals. In our largest market, the United States, the Reebok Brand grew market share in the key athletic specialty channel each month during 2001. This channel is very influential as it sets the fashion tone for the U.S. market, particularly among young men and women.

In order to generate even greater focus on our targeted consumer segments during 2001, we realigned and restructured our product creation teams. Under our new structure, individual teams design and develop products specifically geared toward the needs of each of our primary channels of distribution and each of our targeted consumer groups. As a result of this new structure, our product and marketing teams are much more connected with the ultimate consumer and are, therefore, more successful at creating product and marketing initiatives that are relevant to both the individual retailer and the specific consumer.

In order to support our product focus, we have launched three marketing campaigns to reach our core consumers. Our Classic campaign, which we began in 2000, has been very successful in growing this important segment of our business. Our new women's campaign called "It's a Woman's World," which we launched in October 2001, is centered around a contemporary and inspirational message designed to further attract young women to our Brand.

In January 2002 in New York City, we launched our newest marketing campaign, "The Sounds & Rhythm of Sport." This campaign has already begun to energize the Reebok Brand among the critically important fashion consumer, particularly young men. These campaigns provide us with a solid marketing platform for the Reebok Brand that will continue for the next several years.

In 2001 we began our exciting new business venture with the National Football League ("NFL"), by outfitting 26 NFL teams. Beginning with the 2002 season, and for the next 10 years, the Reebok Brand will be exclusively worn by all 32 NFL teams, on the field and on the sidelines. Each week, the NFL attracts more than 110 million spectators in the United States. During 2002 we will broaden our consumer reach by developing and bringing to market new performances and lifestyle product collections, such as "NFL Equipment" and "NFL Classics."

Also in 2001, we entered into a 10-year agreement with the National Basketball Association ("NBA") under which Reebok will design, manufacture, sell, and market licensed merchandise for the NBA, the Women's National Basketball Association ("WNBA") and the National Basketball Development League ("NBDL"), the NBA's new minor league. Over the next three years, we will expand our exclusive agreement with the NBA to include all 29 teams in the league.

Our partnerships with NFL and NBA are strategically aligned with our objective to build the most successful sports licensing business in the world. And, it appears that we are very timely in re-entering the sports licensing business. We have recently seen a return to fashionability for sports licensed apparel and retailers are currently enjoying improved profitability and sell-through for these product categories.

Our new NFL and NBA partnerships allow Reebok Brand to leverage its core competencies and significantly increase its Brand visibility and product sales. The increased visibility of the Reebok Brand on thousands of professional athletes is sending a very positive message to our consumers every day. To date, sales of these apparel licenses have exceeded our expectations and we are very optimistic about the long-term potential for growth.

Our Rockport, Ralph Lauren Footwear and Greg Norman brands had a somewhat difficult year due in large part to their dependency on the department store channel in the United States. This channel was very promotional and hard hit throughout 2001. We are optimistic that the performance of these brands will improve during 2002. The leadership at all of these brands was changed over the past year. We believe this new leadership is capable of driving future revenue growth by gaining quality market share. During 2002 these businesses will be launching several new initiatives in order to improve sales performances. These initiatives include the introduction of new product and segmentation strategies that are designed to maximize our opportunity in the various trade channels we serve. We believe that there is a long-term opportunity for revenue and profit growth for all of these brands and we intend to vigorously pursue these over the next several years.

Our multi-brand strategy continues to provide us with a strong foundation from which we can drive greater synergies and improve our operating performance. During 2001, we successfully integrated our Rockport and Ralph Lauren brands into our domestic shared service operation. We have now integrated all of our brands into this center. Our shared services philosophy enables us to leverage our core competencies and, as a result, we reduced our general and administrative type expenses for the year. This is the third consecutive year in which we have reduced these types of expenses by utilizing our shared services platform.

Our overall balance sheet remains strong. In 2001, we generated $176 million of cash flow from operations, and during the past four years we've generated approximately $800 million of operating cash flow. These are very solid cash flow results driven by the continual improvement of all our key balance sheet metrics. Our capital structure is sound and provides us with significant financial flexibility. Over the next several years we intend our free cash flow to grow our business and improve shareholder value.

*In all that we do, Reebok remains committed to corporate social responsibility, led by our stand for human rights. The most recent Reebok Human Rights Award ceremony was held as part of the Cultural Olympiad of the Salt Lake Olympic Winter games in February 2002. Over the last 14 years Reebok has honored 67 young men and women from around the world who have displayed uncommon courage and leadership. Our unwavering respect for individual human dignity guides the way we discharge our responsibilities to all our stakeholders, including our customers, business partners, employees and their families, suppliers, community neighbors and to our shareholders. This core value is expressed in our policies and our practices and is intrinsic to our company's identity. (See **Exhibit 1** for Reebok's Human Right's Production Standards). We believe that pursuing this philosophy is a prudent business decision that aids customer loyalty, enhances employee motivation and retention and helps protect our corporate image.*

Exhibit 1

Human Rights Production Standards: Reebok international, Ltd.

Nondiscrimination

Reebok will seek business partners that do not discriminate in hiring and employment practices on grounds of race, color, national origin, gender, religion, or political or other opinion.

Working Hours/Overtime

Reebok will seek business partners who do not require more than 60-hour workweeks on a regularly scheduled basis, except for appropriately compensated overtime in compliance with local laws, and we will favor business partners who use 48-hour workweeks as their maximum normal requirement.

Forced or Compulsory Labor

Reebok will not work with business partners that use forced or other compulsory labor, including labor that was required as a means of political coercion or as punishment for peacefully expressing political views, in the manufacture of its products. Reebok will not purchase materials that were produced by forced prison or other compulsory labor and will terminate business relationships with any sources found to utilize such labor.

Child Labor

Reebok will not work with business partners that use child labor. The term *child* generally refers to a person who was less than 14 years of age, or younger than the age for completing compulsory education if that age was higher than 14. In countries where the law defines *child* to include individuals who were older than 14, Reebok will apply that definition.

Freedom of Association

Reebok will seek business partners that share its commitment to the right of employees to establish and join organizations of their own choosing. Reebok will seek to assure that no employee was penalized because of his or her nonviolent exercise of that right. Reebok recognizes and respects the right of all employees to organize and bargain collectively.

Fair Wages

Reebok will seek business partners who share our commitment to the betterment of wage and benefit levels that address the basic needs of workers and their families.

Safe and Healthy Work Environment

Reebok will seek business partners that strive to assure employees a safe and healthy workplace and that do not expose workers to hazardous conditions.

Source: Reebok International, Ltd., "Reebok Human Rights Production Standards," company document.

In summary, I believe we have the management team in place that is capable of driving our brands forward by executing our long-term strategic plans. We will continue to create fashionable, high quality products that, at all times, meet and exceed our consumers' expectations. We will communicate marketing themes and relevant messages that speak directly to our various consumer segments thereby generating greater consumer demand for our products. We will work with all of our retail partners to ensure that our products are readily accessible at retail and that our brands are properly presented. Our goal is to grow quality market share for all our brands and to generate long-term improvement in the value we create for our shareholders. I look forward to meeting the challenges, which lie ahead, and delivering improved performance during 2002. I want to take this opportunity to thank our employees for their tireless efforts and unwavering commitment to our success. Our employees are our greatest assets and it is through their dedication to excellence that will continue to succeed.[1]

Background and History

The history of Reebok began in England in the 1890s. Athletes wanted to run faster. To meet this demand, Joseph William Foster developed cleated running shoes. By 1895, he had formed J.W. Foster and Sons, which made hand-stitched athletic shoes for many of the top athletes of that time.

In 1958, two of J. W. Foster's grandsons started a companion company that they named Reebok International after an African gazelle. In time this new company would absorb the parent company.

In 1979, Paul Fireman purchased an exclusive North American distribution license from Reebok. That year he marketed three running shoes in the United States, and at $60 a pair they were the most expensive on the market. Sales increased slowly, exceeding $1.3 million in 1981, and eventually outgrew the production capacity of the U.K. plant. In 1981, needing financing for expansion, Reebok USA swapped 56% of its stock for $77,500 with Pentland Industries, a British shoe distributor, and established production facilities in Korea. That year, in a move that was to characterize the company, Reebok noted the popularity of a new fitness craze called aerobic dancing. It also noted that no one was making a shoe for this purpose. Thus it was the first company to market an athletic shoe just for women. Shortly, the "Freestyle" line, a fashion-oriented aerobic shoe, was introduced and sales took off. Company sales increased from $3.5 million in 1982 to $3.6 billion in 1997.

In 1985, Reebok USA and Reebok International merged to become Reebok International, Ltd. Four million shares of stock were offered to the public, and Pentland became a large shareholder. Paul Fireman continued as CEO and Chairman. This share offering was used to finance the company's growth strategy.

Reebok pursued a strategy of line extensions and acquisitions. In 1986, it acquired the Rockport Company for $118.5 million in cash. In 1987, Reebok purchased the outstanding common stock of Avia Group International for $181.0 million in cash and 194,000 shares of Reebok common shares. It also acquired ESE Sports for $18 million in cash. Rockport purchased John A. Frye Co. for $10 million cash. In 1988 and 1989, it acquired Ellesse USA, Inc. (for $25 million in cash) and Boston Whaler, respectively. In 1981, it purchased a large portion of Pentland Group's holdings in Reebok (Pentland still had an ownership interest of about 13% after the Reebok purchase) and acquired the assets of Above the Rim International. The following year, Reebok acquired Perfection Sports Fashions, which marketed under the Tinley brand name. In 1993, Reebok sold Ellesse USA and Boston Whaler, Inc.

In the late 1980s, after five years of phenomenal growth in the United States, the decision was made to aggressively pursue expansion into overseas markets and achieve an objective of 50% sales internationally. In 1997, Reebok products were available in 140 countries, and about 45.1% of total sales were generated from international sales.

In 1992, Paul Fireman had set a bold goal for the company—to displace Nike as the top sports and fitness brand and become number one by 1995. By the end of 1994, Reebok's market share was 21.3%, a 3.4% increase over 1993. Nike's market share decreased by 6.3% from 31.7% to 29.7% during the same time. Since Fireman established this goal to be number one, public perceptions of the brand had noticeably changed. Reebok started out as a brand that focused on aerobics, walking, and women. Eventually, it began to receive real credence by serious athletes—but not to the extent received by Nike. "We've lost the Michael Jordan generation. That battle has been lost—Nike owns them,"[2] said Tom Carmody, Reebok's General Manager–North America. The next step was a two-year marketing offensive designed to bump Nike from number one. The project included more inspired and focused advertising, expansion of the apparel business, and more cross-promotion with other marketers, like Wheaties, to enhance Reebok's image as a leading sports brand.[3] Reebok intended to establish a worldwide reputation in sports as a supplier of innovative, high-performance athletic footwear, apparel, and equipment.

In late 1995, Reebok was facing an open revolt by a group of institutional shareholders who owned about 15% of Reebok's stock. This group included Warren Buffet's Government Employees Insurance Company (GEICO) and Chieftain Capital Management. These groups "were fed up with management missteps, rising costs, earning disappointments, and a sagging stock."[4] Some of the groups wanted Fireman to resign as CEO. Fireman said that he "isn't opposed to a new chief executive officer or chief operating officer." He further stated, "Titles don't mean anything."[5] Earlier in 1995, both joint presidents had resigned. Fireman announced that there had been "a consolidation of leadership and a focus."[6] Glenn Greenberg, Money Manager of Chieftain Capital, indicated that Chieftain had dumped 4.5 million shares of Reebok. Warburg Pincus Asset Management and GEICO had reportedly sold Reebok shares. Over the next year, the management team stabilized.

On June 7, 1996, Reebok sold its subsidiary, Avia Group International, Inc. The company recorded a special charge of $54,064,000 in the fourth quarter of 1995 for this sale. In 1987, Reebok had paid $181 million in cash and 194,000 shares of Reebok stock for Avia. The company sold the Avia Group to refocus the company's strategies back to its core brands. As part of this strategy, the company discontinued its Bok Division in November 1996. Bok products were aimed at four segments and targeting the 16- to 24-year-old market: "Freesport," characterized by activities such as skateboarding, surfing, snowboarding; "Clubsport," a fashion-oriented line; "Utility," with worker-boot influence; and "Classic," updated popular designs from earlier seasons.

On July 28, 1996, the Board of Directors authorized the repurchase of up to 24.0 million shares of the company's common stock. The offer to repurchase commenced on July 30, 1996, and expired on August 27, 1996, and the price range for repurchasing stock was $30.00 to $36.00 net per share in cash. The company repurchased approximately 17.0 million common stock at a price of $36.00. Reebok's Board of Directors also suspended the quarterly dividend.[7] An analyst felt these measures resulted from the earlier revolt by the institutional shareholders.

The mid-1990s until today has been characterized by 'Y' Generation revolt. The Y Generation moved from athletic shoes to brown shoes provided by companies like Van, Airwalk, Etonic, and DC. Both Reebok and Nike were caught flat footed on this change. Fireman said, "Consumers appear to be turning their backs on marketing type and superheroes. . . . Every 10 years or so, consumers get bored with the status quo. People change, fashions change, sports trends change. Without much warning a fundamental (Y Generation) market shift occurs. And things are never the same again."[8] The impact of the shift was still being felt. Intially, the Y generation revolt resulted in a "worldwide product glut."[9]

During this period, there was an Asian financial crisis, which caused serious decline in athletic shoes and apparel sales in this region of the world. This lasted for several years.

On March 9, 2001, the company purchased selected assets of LogoAthletic ("Logo") for $14.2 million. Included in the assets purchased were inventory, equipment, facility leases, and the rights to Logo's trademarks. The acquisition did not materially affect the company's consolidated financial statements. [10]

Effective January 1, 2001, the company increased its ownership in one of its European subsidiaries and acquired majority ownership in one of its Latin American distributors. The impact of these events was not material to the consolidated financial statements. Also effective January 1, 2001, the company sold its interest in its South African subsidiary to an independent distributor. The sale price and historical operating results of the company's South African subsidiary were not material to the consolidated financial results or consolidated financial position of the company. [11]

In fall of 2001, the company signed Allen Iverson, 2001 NBA Most Valuable Player and star guard of the Philadelphia 76ers, to a lifetime spokesperson contract for $50 million. On July 16, 2002, Iverson pleaded not guilty to 14 charges in a Philidelphia court. All charges were later dropped.

Corporate Governance

BOARD OF DIRECTORS

The Board of Directors of Reebok International, Ltd., as of December 31, 2001, were:[12]

Name	Company
Paul B. Fireman	Chairman, President, & Chief Operating Officer, & CEO Reebok International, Ltd.
Norman Axelrod	Chairman of the Board & Chief Executive Officer Linen 'N Things, Inc.
Paul R. Duncan	Retired Executive Vice President Reebok International, Ltd.
Mannie L. Jackson	Chairman of the Board & Chief Executive Officer Harlem Globetrotters International, Inc.
Richard G. Lesser	Senior Corporate Advisor & Director TJX Companies, Inc.
Jay Margolis	President & Chief Operating Officer Reebok International Ltd.
Geoffrey Nune	Retired Senior Vice President & General Counsel Millipore Corporation
David L. Patrick	Executive Vice President & General Counsel The Coca-Cola Compnay
Dorothy E. Puhy	Chief Financial Officer & Assistant Treasurer Dana-Farber Cancer Institute
Thomas M. Ryan	Chairman of the Board, President & Chief Executive Officer CVS Corporation

Exhibit 2 contains brief biographical sketches on each board member, lists the committees and membership, and describes compensation and stock options for the board members.

During 2001, each director who was not an officer or employee of the company received $25,000 annually plus $2,000 for each committee chairmanship held, $2,000 for each directors' meeting, and $1,000 for each committee meeting attended, plus expenses. Beginning in 1998, as a part of a new policy adopted by the Board of Directors that required each director to own Reebok Common Stock with a market value of at least four times the amount of the annual retainer within five years from the date of the director's first election to the Board, a minimum of 40% of the annual retainer was paid to the directors in Reebok's common stock. [13]

Exhibit 2
Board of Directors: Reebok International

A. BOARD MEMBERSHIP
1. Class I members whose terms will expire at the 2005 Annual Meeting of Shareholders:

Name	Business Experiences and Current Directorships	Age	Director Since
Paul B. Fireman	CEO and Chairman of the Board of Directors of the company; President of the company (1979 to March 1987 and December 1989 through December 2001); and Director of Abiomed, Inc., a manufacturer of medical devices.	58	1979
Dorothy E. Puhy	Chief Financial Officer and Assistant Treasurer, Dana-Farber Cancer Institute (since 1994), a leading health care provider and research concern; Chief Financial Officer, New England Medical Center Hospitals, Inc. (from 1989 to 1994), a major health care provider.	50	2000
Thomas M. Ryan	President and CEO (since May 1998) and Chairman of the Board (since April 1999) of CVS Corporation ("CVS"), a company in the chain drug store industry; President and Chief Executive Officer of CVS Pharmacy Inc. (since 1994); Director of FleetBoston Financial Corporation, a financial services company; and Directors, Tricon Global Restaurants, Inc., the world's largest quick-serve restaurant company.	49	1998

2. Class II members whose terms will expire at the 2003 Annual Meeting of the Shareholders:

Name	Business Experiences and Current Directorships	Age	Director Since
Norman Axelrod	Chief Executive Officer of Linens 'N Things, Inc. (LNT), a national retailer of home textiles, housewares, and home accessries (since 1988); Chairman of the Board of Directors for LNT (since 1996); President and CEO of LNT, a division of Melville Corp. (1998 to 1996); various senior management positions at Bloomingdale's, a national department store (1976 to 1988); and Director of Jaclyn, Inc., a handbags and apparel company.	49	1979
Paul R. Duncan	Retired Executive Vice President of the company (February 1990 to December 1998 and January 2000 to January 2001), with various executive responsibilities, including President of the company's Specialty Business Groups (October 1995 to November 1996 and January 2000 to January 2001); Chief Financial Officer of the company (1985 to June 1995); and Director of Entersays Networks, successor to Cabletron System, Inc., a computer networking company.	61	1989
Richard G. Lesser	Senior Corporate Advisor (since February 2002) and Director (since 1994) of TJX Companies, Inc., an off-price apparel and home furnishings retailer; Chief Operating Officer of TJX Companies (November 1994 to February 2000) and Executive Vice President (February 1991 through December 2001); Chairman, The Marmaxx Group, a division of TJX Companies that operates TJ Maxx and Marshalls (February 2001 to December 2001); President, The Marmaxx Group (February 1996 to February 2001); Director of A.C. Moore Arts & Crafts, Inc., an operator of arts and crafts stores; and Director of Dollar Tree Stores, Inc., a national chain of variety stores selling merchandise at $1.	67	1988
Deval L. Patrck	Executive Vice President and General Counsel, The Coca-Cola Company, a beverage sales company (since April 2001); Vice President and General Counsel, Texaco, Inc., an energy company (1999 to March 2001); Partner,	45	2001

(continued)

Exhibit 2

Board of Directors: Reebok International (*continued*)

Day, Berry & Howard (1997 to 1999), a law firm; Assistant Attorney General, Civil Rights Division of the U.S. Department of Justice (1994 to 1997); and Director, Coca-Cola Enterprises, Inc., which markets, distributes, and produces bottled and canned beverages.

3. Class I members whose terms will expire at the 2003 Annual Meeting of the Shareholders:

Name	Business Experiences and Current Directorships	Age	Director Since
Mannie L. Jackson	Chairman, CEO, and majority owner of Harlem Globertrotters International, Inc., a sports and entertainment entity (since August 1992); retired Senior Vice President, Corporate Marketing and Administration, Honeywell, Inc., a manufacturer of control systems, and prior to that served in various executive capacities for Honeywell, Inc., beginning in 1968; Director of Ashland Inc., a vertically intergrated petroleum and chemical company; and Director of The Stanley Works, a commerical, consumer, and specialty tools company.	62	1996
Jay Margolis	President and Chief Operating Officer of the company (since December 2001); Executive Vice President and President of the Specialty Business Groups of the company (December 2000 to December 2001); Chairman and CEO of E7th.com, a business-to-business supply solution for the footwear industry, linking wholesalers with retailers (August 2000 to November 2000); Chairman and CEO of Esprit de Corporation (June 1995 to January 1999); President and Vice Chairman of the Board of Tommy Hilfiger (January 1992 to June 1995); Vice Chairman of the Board of Liz Claiborne (January 1982 to January 1992).	53	2002
Geoffrey Nunes	Retired Senior Vice President and General Counsel for Millipore Corporation, a leader in the field of separation technology.	71	1986

B. BOARD COMMITTEES

During 2001 the Board of Directors held six meetings. All the directors attended at least 75% of the Board and relevant committee meetings during 2001, except for Mr. Ryan, who attended 63% of the meetings.

The Audit Committee, composed of Ms. Puhy (Chair), Mr. Lesser, and Mr. Nunes, held three meetings during 2001. The Audit Committee recommended to the Board of Directors the independent public auditors to be engaged by the company; reviewed with such auditors and management the company's internal accounting procedures and controls; and reviewed with such auditors the audit scope and results of their audit of the consolidated financial statements of the company.

The Compensation Committee, composed of Mr. Nunes (Chair), Mr. Ryan, and Mr. Axelrod (starting May 1, 2001), held four meetings during 2001 and acted once by unanimous written consent. The Compensation Committee administered the company's stock option and compensation plans, sets compensation for the CEO, reviewed the compensation of the other executive officers, and provided recommendations to the Board regarding compensation matters.

The Board Affairs Committee, composed of Mr. Lesser (Chair), Messrs. Jackson, Ryan, Nunes (until May 1, 2001), and Mr. Patrick (starting May 1, 2001), held two meetings during 2001. The Board Affairs Committee was responsible for considering Board governance issues. The Board Affairs Committee also recommended individuals to serve as Directors of the company and will consider nominees recommended by shareholders. Recommendations by shareholders should be submitted in writing to the Board Affairs Committee, in care of the President of the company.

The Executive Committee, composed of Mr. Fireman (Chair), Messrs. Duncan, and Nunes, did not meet during 2001. The Executive Committee may take certain action permitted by law and the bylaws in the intervals between meetings of the full Board, and in fact, it did take action once by unanimous written consent during 2001.

Exhibit 2

Board of Directors: Reebok International (*continued*)

C. BOARD COMPENSATION and STOCK OPTIONS

During 2001 each director who was not an officer or employee of the company received an annual retainer of $25,000, plus $2,000 for each committee chairmanship held and $2,000 for each directors' meeting and $1,000 for each committee meeting attended, plus expenses. As part of a policy adopted by the Board of Directors in 1998 that requires each director to own Reebok's common stock with a market value of at least four times the amount of the annual retainer within five years after the director's first election to the Board, a minimum of 40% of the annual retainer was paid to the directors in Reebok's common stock.

The company's Equity and Deferred Compensation Plan for Directors provided for the issuance of stock options to directors and provides a means by which directors may defer all or a portion of their directors' fees. In addition, the shareholders of Reebok approved the 2001 Equity Incentive and Director Deferred Compensation Plan at the 2001 Annual Meeting. These two plans shall be referred to as the "Directors' Plan" for purposes of this section.

Source: "2002 Notice of Annual Meeting of Shareholders," March 28, 2002, pp. 3–5.

TOP MANAGEMENT[14]

Paul B. Fireman (58) founded the company and served as its Chief Executive Officer and a Director since the company's founding in 1979 and its Chairman of the Board since 1986. With the exception of 1988, Fireman served as President of the company from 1979 until December 2001 with the appointment of Jay Margolis as President. In the mid and late 1980s, Fireman was one of the highest paid executives in the country. His salary package included base pay of $357,200 plus 5% of the amount by which Reebok's pretax earnings topped $20 million. He averaged $13.6 million a year. In 1990, the Board of Directors decided that Fireman's compensation should be more closely tied to increases in value for Reebok shareholders. Fireman had a new employment contract that determined his annual salary, plus an annual bonus based on the company's earnings, with a maximum of $1 million. He also was given a one-time grant of options to purchase 2.5 million Reebok common shares. The options become exercisable over a period of five years at exercise prices ranging from $17.32 to $18.37 per share and were exercisable until July 24, 2000. In 1991, Reebok paid a $513,601 premium on a $50 million life insurance policy for Fireman and his wife, Phyllis. This was reduced to only $46,162 in 1996. Fireman paid the remainder of the premiums. There had been some shareholder criticism of the high level of Fireman's compensation.

Paul Fireman and his wife Phyllis owned 8,298,377 (14.0%) and 6,412,000 (10.9%) shares, respectively. This represented about a 24.9% ownership interest. This left the company insiders and board members (excluding Fireman) with a 5.6% ownership interest.

Fireman was known to have a problem in delegation, which contributed to management turnover. A former executive who was highly recruited and lasted less than a year said that "Paul was the sort of fellow who would make a great neighbor . . . But he was absolutely convinced that no one can do a job better than he can."[15] The institution investment groups felt that this caused some of the turmoil in the company management team. Fireman was a strong advocate of "est training," the human-potential program founded by Werner Erhart in the 1970s. The Forum was the current version of est. His admiration for est was best summarized when he said, "I believe in anything that allows you to look at yourself and see what's possible."[16] A former Reebok executive said that "the company sometimes divides up between those who buy into the est message and those who don't." He further said, "Key employees, even top management, at times seem to be kept out of the loop, denied crucial new research or excluded from strategy meetings unless they accept the est outlook and methods. Fervent est adherents, meanwhile, form a sort of subculture with its own attitudes and jargon."[17]

On June 28, 2002, Paul Fireman and his wife announced that they had adopted a common stock trading contract plan under which they would sell up to two million shares of Reebok stock through variable common prepaid forward contracts at three pre-determined price levels. The Firemans had not sold any of their stock since 1994. These shares were to be sold over a three-year period under provisions of the contract. The contract provided flexibility to the Firemans in the timing of their transactions and allowed them to participate fully in the upscale potential of Reebok stock up to a level 40% above the pre-determined price level. The first million shares were sold in June 2002 at the current market price. Fireman said, "These contracts allow my wife and me to diversify our holdings and meet some long time estate planning goals. . . ." He further stated "We both remain committed to Reebok, as evidenced by our substantial stock interests. . . ."[18]

On August 9, 2002 Paul Fireman, Chairman and CEO, and Ken Watchmaker, CFO, both signed sworn statements and submitted the statements to the United States Securities and Exchange Commission (SEC), pursuant to Commission Order No. 4-460 (new legislation by Congress, in light of Enron, World Com, Tyco, and Global Crossing scandals requiring the personal signatures of top management on financial statements).

Jay M. Margolis (53) became President and Chief Operating Officer in December 2001. Margolis joined the company as Executive Vice President and President of the Specialty Business Groups in December 2000. Margolis was responsible for overseeing the management of the Reebok Brand (including its league licensing business), the Greg Norman Collection, Ralph Lauren Footwear Co., and the Rockport Company. Pior to joining the company, he served as the Chairman and CEO of E7th.com, a business-to-business supply solution for the footwear industry that linked wholesalers with retailers. Margolis also served as Chairman and CEO of Esprit de Corporation (1995–1999). From 1992–1994, he was President and Vice Chairman of the Board of Directors of Tommy Hilfiger. Margolis spent nine years at Liz Claiborne, Inc. where he held several positions including Vice Chairman of the Board of Directors (1989–1992), President of Liz Claiborne Sportswear (1986–1989) and President of Liz Claiborne Menswear (1983–1986).

Martin Cole was promoted from Executive Vice President to President and CEO of Reebok Brand on June 12, 2002. Cole joined the company in December, 2001. He previously was employed by Nike. He served five years as the Nike's general manager for Europe. He and his team were credited with increasing European sales from under $1 billion to over $2 billion during his five-year tenure. He replaced David Purdue, who accepted the postion of Chairman and CEO of Pillowtex Corporation.

Kenneth I. Watchmaker (59) has been an Executive Vice President of the company since February 1994 and was appointed Chief Financial Officer in June 1995. Prior to his appointment as Chief Financial Officer, he was Executive Vice President with responsibility for finance, footwear production, and management information systems. He joined the company in July 1992 as Executive Vice President, Operations and Finance, of the Reebok Brand. Prior to joining the company, Watchmaker was a Senior Partner of Ernst & Young LLP.

James R. Jones III (57) has been Senior Vice President of Human Resources for the company since May 1998. Jones joined the company as Senior Vice President of Human Resources for Reebok Brand in April 1997. Prior to that, Jones was Vice President of Inova Health System from May 1996 through April 1997. From July 1995 through May 1996, Jones was the Senior Vice President of Human Resources of Franciscan Health System. Prior to that, since 1991, Jones was the Vice President of Human Resources of Johns Hopkins University.

David A. Pace (41) became a Senior Vice President of the company in February 2001, having been appointed Vice President and General Counsel, and elected Clerk, in December 1999. From May 1999 until his promotion. Pace was Vice President, Global Alliances and Endorsements for the Reebok Brand. Prior to this position, Pace was Assistant General Counsel from January 1997 until May 1999. In June 1995, Pace joined the company's legal department as Counsel–Marketing. Prior to joining the company, Pace was Vice President and General Counsel of Applied Extrusion Technologies, Inc. from June 1994 to June 1995, prior to which he was an associate of the law firm of Ropes & Gray.

Richard Paterno (44) became Senior Vice President of the company and President of The Rockport Company in June 2001. Paterno was initially hired as Executive Vice President for Sales and General Merchandise Manager of Women's for Rockport in May 2001. Prior to joining Rockport, Paterno worked for Easy Spirit since its inception in 1987 in various capacities. Paterno was Executive Vice President of Sales and Marketing from 1996 until October 1999 when he was promoted to President of Easy Spirit. Paterno held this position until May 2001 when he joined Rockport.

Terry R. Pillow (48) became President and Chief Executive Officer of Ralph Lauren Footwear in June 2001. Pillow joined the company as Senior Vice President of the company and President and Chief Executive Officer of the Rockport Company in 1999. Prior to joining the company, Pillow was President of the apparel division of Coach Leatherware, a subsidiary of Sara Lee Corporation. From 1989 to 1994, Pillow served as President of A/X Armani Exchange, New York.[19]

EXECUTIVE COMPENSATION

Exhibits 3 and **4** show the aggregate compensation paid or accrued by the company for service rendered during the years ended December 1999, 2000, and 2001 for the Chief Executive Officer and the company's four other most highly compensated executive officers.

Exhibit 3

Summary Compensation Table: Reebok International, Ltd.

| Name and Principal Position | Year | Annual Compensation | | | Long-Term Compensation Awards | |
		Salary ($)	Bonus ($)	Restricted Stock Awards	Securities Underlying Options(#)(2)	All Other Compensation ($)
Paul B. Fireman	2001	$1,000,012	$2,075,000	None	None	$55,254
Chairman, President, and CEO	2000	1,000,012	2,100,000	None	2,000,000	55,254
	1999	1,000,012	None	None	500,000	81,539
Jay Margolis	2001	600,002	474,000	2,400,000	400,000	86,325
President and Chief Operating Officer	2000	23,077	200,000	None	150,000	None
Kenneth I. Watchmaker	2001	600,002	976,310	None	198,000	57,743
Executive Vice President and	2000	592,310	980,866	393,750	100,000	44,865
Chief Financial Officer	1999	542,308	457,542	None	101,000	44,062
David A. Perdue	2001	600,002	694,310	None	228,400	37,744
Executive Vice President and	2000	434,624	604,597	393,750	100,000	9,962
President & CEO, Reebok Division	1999	350,012	215,250	None	None	274,291
James R. Hones, III	2001	329,992	238,014	None	90,500	30,906
Senior Vice President and	2000	328,456	229,919	196,875	75,000	25,596
Chief Human Resources Officer	1999	316,928	145,333	None	70,000	13,077

Note: All notes were deleted

Source: Reebok International, Ltd., "2002 Notice of Annual Meeting of Shareholders," March 28, 2002, p. 10.

Exhibit 4

Aggregated Option Exercises in 2001 and Option Values as of December 31, 2001: Reebok International, Ltd.

Name	Acquired On Exercise	Shares Value Realized	Number of Unexercised Options at 12/31/01[1] Exercisable/Unexercisable	Value of Unexercised In-the-Money Options at 12/31/01[1] Exercisable/Unexercisable
Paul B. Fireman	—	—	611,150/2,000,000	4,245,000/17,250,000
Jay Margoolis	—	—	37,50/512,500	137,250/1,000,000
Kenneth I. Watchmaker	—	—	175,500/383,500	2,430,938/3,264,633
David A. Perdue	—	—	25,400/294,600	411,888/2,075/973
James R. Jones	—	—	66,250/174,250	963,047/1,586,366

Note:

1. Based on a fair market value as of December 31, 2001, of $26.50 per share. Values are stated on a pretax basis.

Source: Reebok International, Ltd., "2002 Notice of Annual Meeting of Shareholders," March 28, 2002, p. 13.

MANAGEMENTS' VIEWS ON THE FUTURE

Managements' views on 14 issues and uncertainties facing the company in 2002 are cited below:[20]

- *Issue 1*: **The company's business is subject to economic conditions in its major markets.** Such factors included without limitation, recession, inflation, general weakness in retail markets, and changes in consumer purchasing power and preferences. Adverse changes in such economic factors could have a negative effect on the company's business. In 2001, the company saw a considerable slowdown in worldwide growth, particularly following the September 11 terrorist attacks in the United States. Generally weak economic conditions have led to fluctuations in investor confidence, a softening in consumer demand, and a retrenchment in overall spending. It is anticipated that actions taken in the U.S. economy during 2002 will improve the situation. It is hoped that similar stimulus measures in Europe, the United Kingdom, and Asia/Pacific will energize the economies of those regions and contribute to a broader global recovery. However, such a recovery was contingent on a variety of factors and remains uncertain. Thus we expected the market for our business during 2002 to be challenging, at least in the near term.

- *Issue 2:* **The market for athletic footwear and apparel was intensely competitive and if we failed to compete effectively, we could lose our market position.** The athletic footwear and apparel industry was intensely competitive. The principal methods of competition in the industry include price, quality, product design, brand name, marketing and promotion, and our ability to meet delivery commitments to retailers. We competed against a number of domestic and international companies, some of which had greater financial resources than we do. A major marketing or promotional success or technological innovation by one of our competitors could adversely impact our competitive position. Additionally, in countries where the athletic footwear market was mature, our ability to maintain and increase our market share can principally come at the expense of our competitors, which may be difficult to accomplish. Our results of operations and market position may be adversely impacted by our competitors and the competitive pressure in the athletic footwear and apparel industries.

- *Issue 3:* **Our athletic footwear and apparel business was subject to consumer preferences and unanticipated shifts in consumer preferences could adversely affect our sales and results of operations.** The footwear and apparel industry is subject to rapid changes in consumer preferences. Consumer demand for athletic footwear and apparel is heavily influenced by brand image. Our initiatives to strengthen our brand image, which include conducting extensive market research, introducing new and innovative products that emphasize fashion, and initiating focused advertising campaigns, may not be successful. Additionally, consumers place an emphasis on the "performance" aspect of our athletic footwear. Consequently, we must utilize current and future technology to continue to offer performance-enhancing products. Our failure to anticipate, identify, and react to shifts in consumer preferences and maintain a strong brand image could have an adverse effect on our sales and results of operations.

- *Issue 4:* **If we fail to accurately forecast consumer demand, we may experience difficulties in handling customer orders or in liquidating excess inventories and our sales and brand image may be adversely affected.** The athletic footwear industry has relatively long lead times for the design and production of products. Consequently, we must commit to production tooling and in some cases to production, in advance of orders based on our forecasts of consumer demand. If we fail to forecast consumer demand accurately, we may under-produce or over-produce a product and encounter difficulty in handling customer orders or in liquidating excess inventory. Additionally, if we overproduce a product based on an aggressive forecast of consumer demand, retailers may not be able to sell the product and may return the unsold quantities and cancel future orders. These outcomes could have an adverse effect on our sales and brand image.

- *Issue 5:* **Our advertising and marketing expenditures are based on sales forecasts and our failure to achieve these sales forecasts could adversely affect our profitability.** Our advertising and marketing expenditures are based on sales forecasts. These expenditures are made in advance of actual sales. Because the markets in which we do business are highly competitive and our sales are affected by a variety of factors, including brand awareness, changing consumer preferences, and retail market conditions, we may be unable to achieve our sales forecasts. Our failure to achieve our sales forecasts would result in our advertising and marketing expenditures representing a higher percentage of revenues and we could experience higher inventory levels and associated carrying costs, all of which could adversely affect our profitability.

- *Issue 6:* **If we are required to decrease the price that we charge for our products, we may earn lower gross margins and our revenues and profitability may be adversely affected.** The prices that we are able to charge for our products depend on the type of product offered, the consumer and retailer response to the product, and the prices charged by our competitors. To the extent that we are forced to lower our prices, our gross margins will be lower and our revenues and profitability may be adversely affected.

- *Issue 7:* **Our report of our backlog of open orders may not be indicative of our level of future sales.** We report our backlog of open orders for our Reebok brand. Our backlog position may not be indicative of future sales because many customer orders are cancelable with little or no penalty. In addition, our backlog position does not reflect "at once" shipments, sales by retail stores that we own and sales made by independent distributors.

- *Issue 8:* **Our sales and profitability may be adversely affected if our investments in advertising and marketing and our athlete endorsements and athletic sponsorships do not have the effect of increasing retailer acceptance and consumer purchases of our products.** Because consumer demand for athletic footwear and apparel is heavily influenced by brand image, our business requires substantial investments in marketing and advertising, as well as athlete endorsements, athletic sponsorships, and retail presence. In the event that these investments do not achieve the desired effect of increasing consumer purchases and retailer acceptance of our products, our sales and profitability may be adversely affected.

■ *Issue 9:* **Our international sales and manufacturing operations are subject to the risks of doing business abroad, which could affect our ability to sell or manufacture our products in international markets, obtain products from foreign suppliers or control the cost of our products.** We operate facilities and sell products in numerous countries outside the United States. Additionally, a substantial portion of our products is manufactured abroad and we have suppliers located in China, Indonesia, Thailand, and the Philippines. Our athletic footwear and apparel sales and manufacturing operations are subject to the risks of doing business abroad. These risks include:

- fluctuations in currency exchange rates;
- political instability;
- limitations on conversion of foreign currencies into U.S. dollars;
- restrictions on dividend payments and other payments by our foreign subsidiaries;
- withholding and other taxes on dividend payments and other payments by our foreign subsidiaries;
- import duties, tariffs, quotas, and other restrictions on free trade, particularly as these regulations may affect our operations in China;
- hyperinflation in some foreign countries; and
- Investments regulation and other restrictions by foreign governments.

If these risks limit or prevent us from selling or manufacturing products in any significant international market, prevent us from acquiring products from our foreign suppliers, or significantly increase the cost of our products, our operations could be seriously disrupted until alternative suppliers are found or alternative markets are developed. Although we may enter into forward currency exchange contracts and options to hedge the risk of exchange rate fluctuations, these steps may not fully protect us against this risk and we may incur losses.

■ *Issue 10:* **Because we rely on independent manufacturers to produce most of our products, our sales and profitability may be adversely affected if our independent manufacturers fail to meet pricing, product quality and timeliness requirements or if we are unable to obtain some components used in our products from limited supply sources.** We depend upon independent manufacturers to manufacture our products in a timely and cost-efficient manner while maintaining specified quality standards. We also rely upon the availability of sufficient production capacity at our manufacturers. Additionally, it is essential that our manufacturers deliver our products in a timely manner because our orders are cancelable by customers if agreed-upon delivery windows are not met. A failure by one or more of our manufacturers to meet established criteria for pricing, product quality, or timely delivery could adversely impact our sales and profitability. In addition, some of the components used in our products are obtained from only one or two sources. A loss of one of these supply sources could disrupt and delay production and adversely affect our sales and profitability.

■ *Issue 11:* **We have substantial existing debt and may incur additional debt in the future.** We have substantial amounts of outstanding indebtedness. Our substantial level of indebtedness increases the possibility that we may be unable to generate cash sufficient to pay the principal of, interest on, and other amounts due in respect of our indebtedness when due. We may also obtain additional long-term debt and working capital lines of credit to meet future financing needs, which would have the effect of increasing our total leverage. Our substantial leverage could have significant negative consequences, including:

- increasing our vulnerability to general adverse economic and industry conditions:
- limiting our ability to obtain additional financing;
- requiring the dedication of a substantial portion of our cash flow from operations to service our indebtedness, thereby reducing the amount of our cash flow available for other purposes, including capital expenditures;

- limiting our flexibility in planning for, or reacting to, changes in our business and the industries in which we compete; and
- placing us at a possible competitive disadvantage with less leveraged competitors and competitors that may have better access to capital resources.

- *Issue 12:* **Our competitive position could be harmed if we are unable to protect our intellectual property rights.** We believe that our trademarks, patents technologies and designs are of great value. From time to time, third parties have challenged, and may in the future try to challenge, our ownership of our intellectual property. In addition, our business is subject to the risk of third parties counterfeiting our products or infringing on our intellectual property rights. We may need to resort to litigation in the future to enforce our intellectual property rights. The litigation could result in substantial costs and diversion of resources. Our failure to protect our intellectual property rights, and in particular, the loss of the Reebok, Rockport, Ralph Lauren, Greg Norman, or NFL and NBA trademark rights, could have an adverse impact on our business and our competitive position.

- *Issue 13:* **We may not be able to realize the full extent of our deferred tax assets.** We have approximately $120 million of net deferred tax assets, of which approximately $65 million is attributable to the expected utilization of tax net operating loss carry forwards and tax credit carry forwards. Our ability to realize the full value of the deferred tax assets will depend on several factors including the level of taxable income we generate, the countries in which taxable income is generated, and the effectiveness of our tax planning strategies. If our estimates of future taxable income are not realized in the near-term, the value of the deferred tax assets and our future net income could be reduced.

- *Issue 14:* **A strengthening U.S. dollar reduces our reported results of operations from our international business.** In 2001, we derived approximately 37.1% of our revenue from sales in foreign currencies. In our combined financial statements, we translate local currency financial results into U.S. dollars based on average exchange rates prevailing during a reporting period. During times of a strengthening U.S. dollar, our reported gross margins for merchandise purchased in U.S. dollars and sold in other currencies may be negatively impacted.

Corporate Organization

The four principal business group units of Reebok were Reebok Division, Rockport Company, Inc., Ralph Lauren Footwear Co., Inc., and Greg Norman Division.

The Reebok Brand

The Reebok brand designed, produced, and marketed sports, fitness, and casual footwear, apparel, and accessories that combined the attributes of athletic performance and style, as well as related sports and fitness products. Reebok's products included footwear for a variety of sports and fitness categories, lifestyle footwear marketed under the Reebok classic brand, and sports and fitness apparel and accessories. The products also included footwear and apparel for children sold under both the Reebok and Weebok® brands. Reebok continued to expand its product scope through a strategic licensing program, pursuant to which our technologies and/or trademarks were licensed to third parties for fitness equipment, sporting goods, accessories, sports and fitness videos, enhanced fitness water, and related products and services.

Reebok footwear products were designed to meet the demands of specific consumer types: image- and fashion-conscious athletes, sports and fitness enthusiasts, and casual athletic shoe buyers. In 2001, Reebok realigned the product creation teams to reflect this strategy—to focus more closely on consumers and the distribution channels that reach those consumers. Management's aim was to improve the product delivery cycle from design to delivery of the finished product by focusing on the consumers' needs. As part of this strategy, management had also aligned its product creation teams with the distribution channels that served those customer groups, such as athletic specialty stores and "urban" athletic outlets, sporting goods stores and independent speciality shops, as well as volume accounts. In 2002, management expected to drive the same strategy through Reebok's apparel product development cycles in order to achieve similar consumer and distribution alignments. Reebok's U.S. operations unit was responsible for all Reebok footwear and apparel products sold in the United States. Sales of footwear in the United States totaled approximately $930.5 million in 2001, compared to $925.1 million in 2000. Reebok brand apparel sales (including sales of Greg Norman Collection) in the United States in 2001 totaled approximately $395.1 million, compared to approximately $235.0 million in 2000. [21]

THE ROCKPORT COMPANY

Rockport designed, produced, and distributed specially engineered comfort footwear for men and women worldwide under the Rockport brand, and in 2001 produced, and distributed apparel through a licensee. In 2001, in furtherance of the company's shared services objective, Rockport cosolidated its corporate headquarters into Reebok's Canton facility and sold its former headquarters building in Marlborough, Massachusetts.

Rockport's net sales decreased to $399.6 million in 2001 from approximately $422.4 million in 2000, a reduction of approximately 5.4%. In 2001 Rockport's international revenues increased approximately 5.2% from its international revenues in 2000.

Designed to address the different aspects of consumers' lives, Rockport's product line included performance, casual, and dress shoes. In 2001, Rockport focused on contemporizing its men's product offerings with the introduction in spring 2001 of the Dressports® 2.0 collection, featuring updated, modern silhouettes while retaining the engineered comfort of its classic Dressports line, and the launch in fall 2001 of the premium "circle r" line, featuring sophisticated, fashion-forward styling. Rockport continued to use proprietary technologies to enhance comfort, incorporating into women's walking products its "Sole Identity" footbed, a microwaveable footbed that custom molds to a wearer's foot shape. Finally, in 2001 Rockport signed a license agreement for the development of a children's footwear line under the Rockport trademark, expected to launch in Fall 2002.

Rockport marketed its products to authorized retailers throughout the United States primarily through a locally-based employee sales staff, although Rockport utilized independent sales agencies in certain distribution channels. Internationally, Rockport marketed its products through approximately 30 distributors in approximately 50 foreign countries and territories. Many of the international distributors were subsidiaries of the company, the others were joint venture partners or independent distributors that also sold Reebok branded products. Rockport's direct consumer purchase program allowed consumers to purchase select Rockport products through Rockport's website located at rockport.com.

Rockport distributed its products in the United States predominantly through select higher-quality national and local shoe store chains, department stores, independent shoe stores, and outdoor outfitters, emphasizing retailers that provide substantial point-of-sale assistance and carry a full product line. Rockport also sold its products in Rockport concept or company stores in San Francisco (California), Newport (Rhode Island), King of Prussia (Pennsylvania), Boston (Massachusetts), New York City (New York), Santa Monica (California), Braintree (Massachusetts) and Las Vegas (Nevada). In addition there were a number of Rockport shops—independent stores that sold Rockport products exclusively—in and outside the United States. Rockport had not pursued mass merchandisers or discount outlets for the distribution of its products.[22]

RALPH LAUREN FOOTWEAR

Net sales for Ralph Lauren Footwear decreased to approximately $97.3 million in 2001 from approximately $106.7 million in 2000, a reduction of 8.8%. In 2001, a new management team was appointed to run the Ralph Lauren footwear business. Its product line featured traditional classics in addition to Polo Sport®, the Polo Jean Co.® line, a more fashion forward collection targeted to males between the ages of 16 and 25, and a children's line targeted to boys and girls between the ages of 5 and 12. Ralph Lauren Footwear also featured dress and casual silhouettes influenced by the Lauren® product line. Ralph Lauren Footwear sold Ralph Lauren® and Polo Ralph Lauren® products through top-tier retailers. The PoloJeans Co. and Polo Sport lines were sold through major department stores and through Polo Jean Co. and Polo Sport speciality stores, respectively.

Internationally, Ralph Lauren Footwear had distributors in Japan, Canada, and Central America that marketed Ralph Lauren Footwear products in approximately eight foreign countries and territories while products were distributed primarily through independent agents in Europe. Ralph Lauren Footwear marketed its products to authorized retailers principally through an employee staff. Products were also sold through space licensing arrangements at approximately 29 Ralph Lauren/Polo-owned retail stores. Ralph Lauren Footwear operated concept footwear departments in Polo Ralph Lauren stores in a number of locations in the United States, including New York City (New York), Beverly Hills (California), Chicago (Illinois), and Palm Beach (Florida). In addition, Ralph Lauren Footwear had footwear retail operations in approximately 17 Polo Ralph Lauren factory direct stores and operated four factory direct stores: Ellenton (Florida), Orlando (Florida), Freeport (Maine), and Wrentham (Massachusetts).[23]

GREG NORMAN DIVISION

The company's Greg Norman Collection produced a range of men's apparel and accessories marketed under the Greg Norman name and logo. Originally a golf apparel line, the Greg Norman Collection had grown its line of men's sportswear to include products ranging from leather jackets and sweaters to activewear and swimwear. In addition, the Greg Norman Collection offered Greg Norman belts, small leather goods, and hosiery products, which were sold through licensees of the company. Products were sold principally at upper-end price points in department and men's specialty stores, on-course pro shops and golf speciality stores, as well as in Greg Norman–dedicated shops.

In December 1999, the Greg Norman Collection expanded its line of products by assuming responsibility for the golf footwear business from Reebok. During 2001, the Greg Norman Collection continued its marketing on the DMX Trac technology used in Reebok golf shoes, accentuated by a new fixturing and point-of-sale introduced in spring 2001.

In 2001, the Greg Norman Collection further expanded it product offerings with the introduction of Reebok branded men's golf apparel for mid-tier distribution. Also during 2001, the Greg Norman Collection continued to offer a line of moisture management golf shirts marketed under the trademark Play Dry™. Additional Play Dry branded products, including shorts, socks, hats, and outerwear, were added throughout the course of 2001.

The Greg Norman Collection engaged in licensing arrangements for three categories of products: hat and accessories, leather goods and travel goods, and corporate sales. Licensing its corporate sales business offered the Greg Norman Collection an opportunity to gain royalties and increase brand exposure without incurring the risk of maintaining a large inventory, as would typically be required in this channel. Additionally, the Greg Norman Collection utilized a combination of distributors and licensees to market and distribute Greg Norman branded products internationally. The brand was represented in Australia, Singapore, Malaysia, and Indonesia in the Far East; in several Middle East countries; in England, Ireland, Scotland, Portugal, Germany, France, and the Benelux countries in Europe; in Canada; and in Mexico. During 2002, the Greg Norman Collection planned to further develop the Far East and Latin American markets.

During 2002, the Greg Norman Collection continued to offer a broad variety of lifestyle products and to expand into international markets, as well as corporate accounts, through various licensing and distribution arrangements.

The Greg Norman Collection was marketed through its endorsement by professional golfer Greg Norman, and a marketing and advertising campaign designed to reflect his multi-faceted, powerfully active and elegant lifestyle. Marketing activities included print advertising in consumer and trade periodicals, retail in-store promotions, trade shows, and worldwide merchandise fixturing program that ensures a consistent aesthetic presentation on a global basis. The Greg Norman Collection products were sold by a combination of independent sales representatives and employee account executives.[24]

INTERNATIONAL OPERATIONS

Reebok's international sales were coordinated from corporate headquarters in Canton, Massachusetts, which was also where its regional operations responsible for Latin America were located. There were also regional offices in Lancaster and London, England, which were responsible for operations in Europe, the Middle East and Africa, and in Hong Kong and Tokyo, which were responsible for Far East operations. Reebok's Canadian operations were managed through its wholly owned subsidiary headquartered outside of Toronto. Management marketed Reebok branded products internationally through wholly owned subsidiaries of the company in Austria, Belgium, France, Germany, Ireland, The Netherlands, Italy, Poland, Portugal, Sweden (covering Sweden, Denmark and Norway), the United Kingdom, Japan and South Korea; and through majority-owned subsidiaries in India, Mexico, and Spain. Reebok also marketed products internationally through 26 independent distributors and two joint ventures in which the company held a minority equity interest. Through this international distribution network, products bearing the Reebok brand were actively marketed in approximately 170 countries and territories.

Additionally, there were approximately 25 Reebok factory direct stores owned by the company, its subsidiaries, joint ventures, or independent distributors. Reebok management planned to continue opening retail stores, either directly or through our distributors, in numerous international markets, as such shops were an important means of presenting the brand in various international markets.

During 2001 the contribution of Reebok's international operations unit to overall sales of Reebok branded products (including the Greg Norman Collection) decreased to $1.170 billion from $1.176 billion in 2000. Reebok's 2001 international sales were adversely impacted by the weakening of various foreign currencies. Effective January 1, 2001, the company sold its South African subsidiary to an independent distributor and acquired a majority interest in its Mexico distributor. The sales figures noted above did not reflect the full wholesale value of all Reebok branded products sold outside the United States in 2001 and 2000 because some of the company's distributors were not subsidiaries and thus their sales to retailers were not included in the calculation of the company's international sales. If the full wholesale value of all international sales of Reebok branded products were included, total sales of Reebok branded products outside the United States represented approximately $1.267 billion in wholesale value, consisting of approximately 29.9 million pairs of shoes totaling approximately $728.0 million in wholesale value of footwear sold outside the United States in 2001 (compared with approximately 29.1 million pairs totaling approximately $719.6 million in 2000) and approximately $539.5 million in wholesale value of Reebok apparel (including the Greg Norman Collection) sold outside the United States in 2001 (compared with approximately $550.4 million in 2000).[25]

TRADE POLICY

With the recent admission of China into the World Trade Organization (WTO) the threat of U.S. restrictions on the import of shoes from China had receded substantially. Management did not believe import restrictions would be imposed during 2002. China remained the largest source of footwear for Reebok and its major competitors. Should trade between China and the United States be interrupted, Reebok, as well as its competitors would face similar challenges to locate alternative manufacturing sources for its products.

The United States had increased enforcement of apparel/textile import quotas, as well as surveillance of working conditions relating to the manufacture of apparel overseas. This has resulted in additional inspection and documentation requirements upon entry of the products into the United States, and in some cases, delays in delivery to customers. This was a concern of trade associations representing the entire U.S. apparel import industry. Management believed that due to Reebok's diversified apparel sourcing and careful selection of vendors and factories, consistent with Human Rights Production Standards (see **Exhibit 1**), import enforcement would not require its change in sourcing, although delivery delays could occur while documentation was processed. However, such delays should not impact the company to a greater extent than Reebok's major competitors.

The European Union ("EU") imposed import quotas on certain footwear from China in 1994. The effect of such quota scheme on the company had not been significant because the quota scheme provided an exemption for certain higher-priced special technology athletic footwear, which exemption was available for most Reebok branded products and some Rockport branded products. The EU and individual EU member states continued to review the athletic footwear exemption, which applied to both the quota scheme and antidumping duties discussed below. The company, on its own as well as through relevant trade associations, was working to prevent imposition of a more limited athletic footwear exception. Should revisions be adopted narrowing such exemption, certain of Reebok's product lines could be affected adversely, requiring sourcing from countries other than China or minor design modification. Should any narrowing of the exemption be imposed, management did not expect that its products would be more severely affected than those of major competitors.

In addition to the quotas on China-sourced footwear, the EU had imposed antidumping duties against certain textile-upper footwear from China and Indonesia. A broad exemption from the dumping duties was provided for athletic textile footwear, which covered most models sold under the Reebok brand. If the athletic footwear exemption remained in its current form, few Reebok branded product lines should be affected by the duties; however, Rockport branded products would be subject to these duties. Nevertheless, management believed that those products affected by the duties could generally be sourced from other countries not subject to such duties. If however, management was unable to implement such alternative sourcing arrangements, certain of Reebok's product lines could be adversely affected by these duties.

The EU also had imposed antidumping duties on certain leather-upper footwear from China, Thailand, and Indonesia. These duties applied only to low-cost footwear, below the import prices of most products sold under the Reebok and Rockport brands. Thus, the company's products had not been significantly impacted by such duties.

The EU continued to expand its list of restricted substances in consumer products. Reebok had taken aggressive steps to ensure that its suppliers and factories were in full compliance with

EU directives and the enforcement initiatives of EU member states. Despite these efforts, from time to time Reebok might have some product already in the distribution chain that did not comply with the most recent EU directives. This could cause some disruption to the delivery of product to the market. As a result, it may be necessary to substitute styles, to delay deliveries, or even to forgo sales. Management believed that Reebok's major competitors were similarly impacted by these EU restrictions.

Management was also aware of possible consumer rejection of products containing substances not restricted by the EU or any member state for environmental, health, and human rights concerns. Such consumer action, and the response of retailers, could disrupt distribution and cause withdrawal of the product from the market which would substantially impact its sales of those specific products. To date Reebok had not encountered rejection of any of its products, but management was aware of such consumer action against certain competitor's products, which had led to the voluntary recall of such products. While it was impossible to predict such consumer action, management was closely monitoring the demands of nongovernmental organizations active in Europe. Management believed that the company was no more exposed to such adverse action than its major competitors.[26]

Athletic Footwear Industry/Market Share and Competition

ATHLETIC FOOTWEAR

Industry retail sales are shown for men, women, and children for 2001, 2000, 1999, and 1998 in **Exhibit 5**.

ATHLETIC FOOTWEAR

Industry retail sales are shown by category for 2001, 2000 and 1999 in **Exhibit 6**.

Exhibit 7 shows the total number of pairs of shoes sold for men, women, and children for 2001, 2000, 1999, and 1998.

The average industry price of shoes for men declined by 10.6% between 1998 and 2001, and .007% for women, while increasing 5.0% for children. **Exhibit 8** shows the industry average price per pair of athletic shoes. The total number of pairs of shoes sold in 2001 was down by 1.4% from 2000, while total sales were up 2.0% from 2000 to 2001.

Greg Hartley, Vice President of the Sporting Goods Manufacturers Association, said, "The outlook is for a difficult year [2002] with modest growth at best." He further stated, "Manufacturers tell us that the mood of consumers and retail buyers in early 2002 remain extremely cautious."[27]

In 2001, the athletic shoe industry spent more than $5.9 billion on advertising and celebrity endorsements. New Balance had replaced Nike as the brand with the most loyal customers.

Exhibit 5

Industry Retail Sales, in Billions of Dollars

	1998	1999	2000	2001	Change 2000–2001
Men's	$ 8.470	$ 8.037	$8.236	$8.541	+3.7%
Women's	3.951	4.194	4.486	4.418	−1.5%
Children's	2.332	2.327	2.394	2.461	+2.8%
TOTAL	$14.753	$14.558	$15.115	$15.420	+2.0%

Note:
1. 2001 figures are estimated.

Exhibit 6

Industry Retail Sales by Category
(Dollar amounts in billions)

	1999	2000	2001[4]	Change, 2000–2001
Running	$4.076	$4.383	$4.549	+3.8%
Basketball	2.606	2.524	2.822	+11.8%
Cross-training	2.126	2.282	2.220	−2.7%
Walking	1.267	1.224	1.218	−0.5%
Athleisure[1]	1.121	0.937	0.971	+3.6%
Recreational boots[2]	0.466	0.922	0.802	−13.0%
Hiking	0.757	0.726	0.678	−6.6%
Tennis	0.524	0.469	0.571	+21.7%
Sports sandals	0.349	0.378	0.355	−6.1%
Aerobics	0.320	0.227	0.216	−4.8%
Other[3]	0.961	1.043	1.018	−2.4%

Notes:
1. Athleisure = Casual athletic styles, canvas, suede, etc.
2. Recreational boots = Hunting, fishing, waterproof, etc.
3. Other = Golf, baseball, football, soccer, etc.
4. 2001 figures are estimated.

Source: The NPD Group, Inc.

Exhibit 7

Industry Total Pairs, in Millions

	1998	1999	2000	2001[3]	Change, 2000–2001
Men's[1]	155.200	161.661	170.316	175.010	+2.8%
Women's[1]	106.486	115.755	125.999	119.973	−4.8%
Children's	106.508	102.986	111.676	106.961	−4.2%
Total[2]	368.194	380.402	407.990	401.943	−1.5%

Notes:
1. Men's and women's = age 13 and older.
2. Some totals affected by rounding.
3. 2001 figures are estimated.

Source: The NPD Group, Inc.

Exhibit 8

Industry Average Price Per Pair

	1998	1999	2000	2001[1]	Change, 2000–2001
Men's	$54.58	$49.72	$48.35	$48.80	+0.9%
Women's	37.10	36.24	35.60	36.83	+3.4%
Children's	21.90	22.60	21.43	23.00	+7.3%
Average	$40.07	$38.27	$37.05	$38.36	+3.5%

Note:
1. 2001 figures are estimated.

Source: The NPD Group, Inc.

Exhibit 9

Market Share of the U.S. Athletic Footwear Market

Manufacturer	2000	Manufacturer	1999
Nike	39.2%	Nike	48.9%
Adidas	15.1	Adidas	16.9
Reebok	10.9	Reebok	10.9
New Balance	9.4	New Balance	3.7
K-Swiss	3.6	K-Swiss	3.1
Timberland	2.9	Timberland	2.1
Asics	2.1	Asics	1.5
Saucony	1.4	Lugz	1.4
Skechers	1.4	And 1	0.9
And1	1.2	Saucony	0.9

Source: Sports Trend Info., *Business Wire*, April 7, 2000.

ATHLETIC FOOTWEAR MARKET SHARE

Exhibit 9 shows the market share for the first quarter of 2000 versus the first quarter of 1999. The major shift was in the sales of Nike, which had its market share decrease from 48.9% in 1999 to 39.2% in 2000. New Balance, which was in fourth place, had its market share increase from 3.7% in 1999 to 9.4% in 2000.

Competiton

NIKE

Nike's market share declined from 48.9% in 1999 to 39.2% in 2000 (see **Exhibit 9**). New Balance was the main winner (9.4% in 2000 versus 3.7% in 1999) of Nike's loss market share. Nike still had 8 out the top 10 basketball shoes while Adidas and Reebok each had one shoe in the top 10. Basketball (16.6%) was second to running shoes (25.1%) in sales by shoe category. The company's revenues were $9.9 billion, $9.5 billion, $9.0 billion, $8.8 billion, and $9.6 billion, and net income was $666.3 million, $580.7 million, $579.1 million, $451.4 million, and $399.6 million for 2002, 2001, 2000, 1999, and 1998, respectively. The sales were basically flat over these five years. Michael Jordan and Tiger Woods were Nike's two main spokespersons.

Nike acquired North Face for $240 million in 2001, which catapulted Nike into the top ranks of outdoor-gear (shoes and boots) maker. Gordon O. McFadden, Vice President for Outdoor Products, spent months courting North Face and fiercely lobbying for the acquisition. Phil Knight, CEO, and his top executives had favored Nike developing the business internally, instead of adding the problems of integrating another company. McFadden said, "The decision not to act stemmed from an insecurity of moving outside the Nike domain." Former Nike executives, analysts, and rivals said, "the company was in serious need of new blood and new ideas." They further believed that Nike's insular mindset was a major reason for current troubles. The company's inward decision-making culture caused highly recruited new outside talent to leave the company. They were recruited to bring new perception and views to assist the company to get out of its rut. Critics said Nike needed to revitalize its core U.S. footwear business, which was about 30% of the company's revenue, with new products and brands. Faye L. Landers, analyst, said Nike's culture will make it hard to do. He said, "The feeling is 'what we do is so special, no outsider can ever understand it.' . . . That's flawed thinking." Leslye L. Mundy, a Nike spokesperson, denied Nike's insularity by pointing out that nearly 40% of the Vice Presidents have been with Nike less than five years. In March 2001, Knight realigned Nike's top management.[28]

Adidas

Adidas–Solomon AG was the world's number two athletic footwear company (see **Exhibit 8**). Adidas' market share had grown steadily from 3.1% in 1993 to 15.1% in 2000. Adidas' sales were $5.5 billion and its net income was $188 million in 2001. Sales were up approximately 5%, which was the result of lowering costs, and net income was up 15% for 2001. Sales in Adidas' largest market, Europe, were $2.7 billion, which was an increase of 7%. Both Nike and Reebok traditionally outmarketed Adidas in Germany. Adidas was weakest in the United States, where sales dropped 5% to $1.6 billion in 2001. This decrease was expected since the company repositioned its products into the higher-end and sports specialty stores. Kobe Bryant, star basketball player for the Los Angeles Lakers, was the company's main endorser. Management expected increased sales in 2002.[29]

New Balance

New Balance Athletic Shoe, Inc., was a privately held corporation. The company's sales for 2001 were $1,160 million, which was 5.5% growth over 2000. The company's market share was 9.4% and 3.7% in 2000 and 1999, respectively (see **Exhibit 9**). This growth can be attributed to the company's differentiation strategy, which resulted in the most loyal customers in the athletic shoe industry.[30]

New Balance had no celebrity endorsers, did minimal advertising, and yet in the past five years had gained more customer loyalty than any other athletic shoe brand. Michael Jordan, Tiger Woods, and Mia Hamm held court for Nike (NKE). "NBA MVP Allen Iverson opined his hip-hop, straight-from-the-playground style for Reebok (RBK)." Jordan's air-apparent, L.A. Lakers wonderkid Kobe Bryant, dunks for Adidas. All told, athletic footwear makers spent more than $5.9 billion on advertising and celebrity endorsements last year. None of these companies however, commanded the most broad loyalty. The highest levels of customer devotion in one of the most volatile and hotly contested product categories on the planet belonged to a small New England company that was proudly endorsed by no one. According to market research firm Brand Keys, Boston-based New Balance Athletic Shoes hadn't simply replaced Nike as the footwear brand with the most loyal customers. It was also the only athletic shoe brand in the Brand Keys index's top 20, and during the past five years, its high-performance shoes had gained more loyalty than had any other competitive brand.

More remarkable, New Balance had accomplished all of this in a period during which brand loyalty in general had been eroding. To create the Brand Keys brand loyalty index, Robert Passikoff, Brand Keys President, surveyed 16,000 consumers twice a year about their level of satisfaction with nearly 150 U.S. companies. Since the index began in 1997, Passikoff had seen significant erosion not just in athletic footwear but also in financial services, telecommunications, and airlines, among other categories. He attributed this to the sheer volume of products on the market. There were nearly 10,000 athletic shoe models, filling every niche from $15 Keds to $200 Nike Air Jordan XVII basketball shoes. Measured by market share, New Balance was number four in this standing-room-only category, behind Nike, Adidas, and Reebok, but it had been gaining rapidly. Between 1999 and 2001, its domestic share climbed from 3.7% to 9.4%, while revenues jumped from $550 million to $813 million (see **Exhibit 9**). What's more, the growth came from only $13 million in national advertising in 2001. Nike, by comparison, spent $155 million and Reebok $49 million, according to Competitive Media Reporting.

How did New Balance do it? The company gave customers a truly unique product: athletic shoes in varying widths. No other athletic footwear manufacturer made shoes for wide or narrow feet, while New Balance covered all sizes from AA to extra-wide 6E. "I can't tell you how many people tell me that we make the only shoes they can wear," says Paul Heffernan, New Balance Vice President for Global Marketing. The company supported its product with a marketing strategy that emphasized consistency and subtlety and targeted serious athletes between the ages of 25 and 45. These customers spent less on sports shoes than teens did—

$2.3 billion compared with $3.5 billion—but according to Heffernan, they were far easier to keep. "Our customers are upwardly mobile, settled, very intense people," said New Balance marketing services manager John Donovan. "They're serious about fitness and their desire to achieve. Let me put it this way: Our customers don't really think they can win the Boston Marathon. But they believe they can beat last year's time."

New Balance ads featured unknown athletes and ran in niche magazines like *Outside*, *New England Runner*, and *Prevention* and on cable-TV channels favored by older viewers such as CNN, the Golf Channel, and A&E. New Balance's low-key slogan was "Achieve New Balance." It hadn't changed for five years. Even its ad tag lines go right after the Gen X and boomer mindset: "Life sucks, go for a run." Or "Turn off your phone and fax . . . achieve New Balance."

The company's advertising didn't always play it so quietly. In fact, New Balance was the first athletic footwear company to offer a multimillion-dollar endorsement deal, to L.A. Lakers star James Worthy, in the mid-1980s. But after sales of its basketball shoes did not increase with Worthy's endorsement, New Balance canceled its celebrity deals and has shied away from mass-market advertising ever since. "I don't have a poster of Michael Jordan in my bedroom anymore," Heffernan says, "and neither do our customers." [31]

K-Swiss

K-Swiss, Inc. designed, developed, and marketed a growing array of athletic footwear for high-performance sport use, fitness activities, and casual wear under the K-Swiss brand. During 2001, the company acquired two additional footwear brands: National Geographic (via license) and Royal Elastics. Sales of these two brands were insignificant during 2001. All footwear categories came in both men's (approximately 52% of 2001 revenues) and women's (approximately 27% of 2001 revenues). Most styles within each footwear category were offered in men's, women's, and children's.

In May 2001, the company formed a joint venture with Rugged Shark, a designer and manufacturer of young, active-oriented footwear, to license, produce, and market a men's, women's, and children's collection of National Geographic outdoor-oriented and casual footwear. The joint venture launched a full-scale line of outdoor and casual footwear in fall 2002. Under the terms of the joint venture, the company owned 75% of the new company and provided the infrastructure to design and develop, manufacture, distribute, and market the line of National Geographic footwear. Rugged Shark owned 25% of the venture.

In November 2001, the company acquired the worldwide rights and business of Royal Elastics (Royal), an Australian-based designer and manufacturer of elasticated footwear. The purchase excluded distribution rights in Australia, which were retained by Royal Management Pty, Ltd.

The company's product line through 1987 consisted primarily of the Classic. The Classic was originally developed in 1966 as a high-performance tennis shoe. In 2000, the company launched Classic Luxury Edition, which sold for slightly more than the original version. The Classic, fueled by new products, had evolved into a category of shoes referred to as the Classic category. The Classic category was comprised of the Classic originals, the K-Swiss Collection, the Limited Edition series, and the Davos Collection.

K-Swiss revenues were $236.1 million, $221.6 million, $285.5 million, and $161.5 million, and net income was $23.3 million, $21.1 million, $34.3 million, and $12.5 million for 2001, 2000, 1999, and 1998 respectively. Market share was 3.6% in 2000 and 3.1% in 1999 (see **Exhibit 9**).[32]

Fila

Fila Holding S.P.A. (Fila) was a holding company with direct or indirect control over 40 other companies in 24 different countries, active in the development, production, and distribution of activewear, sportswear and athletic footwear under the brands Fila, Ciesse, and Enyce. Fila's sports apparel, accessory, and footwear lines included gear for tennis, skiing, swimming, mountain climbing, sailing, soccer, basketball, golf, fitness, and running. The company's products were sold in approximately 60 countries and were manufactured by independent subcontractors in the Far East.

Fila's footwear collection offered a wide variety of products ranging from active sport styles designed for basketball, running, tennis, cross-training, fitness, and soccer, to sportswear products that were sports-inspired and fashion-oriented. The footwear lines, which blended design, performance, quality, and function, included designs and sizes for men, women, and children. The company's product range offered a combination of design and style (characteristics of a brand with an Italian stylistic sensibility) and performance, through its carbon-Kevlar and cushioning technologies. The company's two design and development centers, one in Italy and one in the United States, constantly incorporated new trends and innovations to create a footwear line that addressed market needs.

In 2001, Pininfarina, a manufacturer of high-performance sports cars, worked with the company to develop the Fila-Pininfarina shoe, which evokes the Italian design of one of its cars with Fila's expertise in footwear production. For 2001, the company's highest-volume footwear categories were sportswear, running, cross training, basketball, and tennis.[33]

Fila's revenues were $947.4 million, $976.3 million, $881.7 million, and $971.0 million, and losses were $135.9 million, $71.3 million, $57.3 million, and $125.5 million for 2001, 2000, 1999, and 1998, respectively.[34]

Puma

Puma, a venerable German athletic shoe manufacturer nearly collapsed in the 1990s. The company had suffered many years of losses. Nevertheless, Puma had recently returned to profitability. The company in 2002 expected sales to increase by 40% to $845 million, and pretax profits up 70% to more than $100 million. Puma signed Serena Williams, world-class tennis player, to an endorsement contract. Puma sales were 60% from Western Europe and needed to increase U.S. market sales to maintain growth and profitability. Puma was hedging its bets with product mix ranging from athletic products sold at traditional sports stores to upscale stores (Henri Bendel Ltd.) for its Platinum line of $250 leather shoes. Jochen Zeitz, CEO, said, "Puma's in no rush to expand." He further stated, "Growth is easy." Growth based on brand—that's the challenge." One analyst said, "The Company's revenue size could allow it to get lost in the pack of also-rans."[35]

Converse

On January 22, 2001, Converse, a 93-year old company, filed for Chapter 11 bankruptcy and closed three plants by March 31, 2001. The company was facing a January 31 deadline to creditors. The company missed a $25 million interest payment in June 2000, and had more than $183 million in debt due in July 2002. The company sold its products in 110 countries through about 5,500 stores. The company planned to become exclusively a licensor of Converse brand products.[36]

Marketing and Promotional Activity[37]

Reebok devoted significant resources to advertising its products to a variety of audiences through television, radio, print, and other media. The company also utilized relationships with major sports figures and leagues to enhance visibility for the Reebok-brand and created awareness of, and demand for, Reebok branded products. The marketing mix included advertising (television, print, radio, and outdoor), sports endorsements and sponsorships, public relations, in-store marketing, grassroots activities, and use of the Internet.

Reebok continued its sponsorship of the CBS television show *Survivor* with sponsorship of *Survivor 2—The Australian Outback* and *Survivor Africa*. As with the original *Survivor* series, Reebok was the official apparel supplier to contestants appearing on the series. During the second *Survivor* series, Reebok featured an advertising campaign entitled "Defy Convention," which was aimed at young men and women and consisted of a series of vignettes depicting various athletic and outdoor lifestyle situations set to the music of Rossini's "William Tell Overture." During *Survivor Africa*, Reebok created and launched a television campaign aimed at women, called "It's a Woman's World." This campaign, which *Time* magazine recognized as one of the "10 best" advertising campaigns of the year, featured women in stereotypically male contexts or roles and included participants from previous *Survivor* shows, as well as sports stars such as Venus Williams and Jennifer Azzi. The campaign also featured music from James Brown's 1960s Rhythm and Blues classic "It's a Man's World" and a specially recorded version of the song by current R&B singer Missy Elliot. Reebok continued its sponsorship of *Survivor* for the show's fourth season, which debuted at the end of February 2002.

In October 2001, Reebok announced its most aggressive women's advertising campaign, "It's a Women's World." Reebok's strategy was to leverage the enormous popularity of the hit CBS series, *Survivor*, which was the top-rated program among women in the U.S. Company spokespersons were some of the world's most dynamic and inspirational women hired to launch the company's most aggressive product and marketing women's program in the company's 22-year history.

Reebok built on past marketing success during 2001 with the continuation of its "Classics" print campaign, which showed Reebok Classic shoes in a striking black-and-white print campaign. The Classics campaign featured such music celebrities as Ice Cube, Iggy Pop, and Common and also tied into movies such as *Planet of the Apes*. The campaign appeared in magazines such as *Slam*, *Source*, *Vibe*, *In Style*, *GQ*, *Teen People*, and *Details*. A special promotion, featuring Common, was also run at the retailer Foot Action to launch the Arctic Ice range of Classic Footwear.

Consistent with its strategy of aligning product offerings with specific consumer preferences, Reebok continued in 2001 to focus its sports marketing efforts on key athletic icons who exemplified distinct lifestyles, other athletes who were either at the pinnacle of their profession or rising stars, and select team and league sponsorships.

Reebok's marquis athletes were:

■ *Allen Iverson*, charismatic Philadelphia 76ers point guard and 2001 National Basketball Association Most Valuable Player, with whom Reebok marketed a signature line of footwear and apparel. Reebok extended and restructured its endorsement arrangement with Iverson in 2001 and had the right to use his name and image both throughout his playing career and beyond.

■ *Venus Williams*, two-time winner of Wimbledon and U.S. Open, and an Olympic gold medallist in single and doubles, which Reebok featured as a lifestyle icon in its "Defy Convention" campaign during 2001.

To promote the sale of its basketball products in 2001, Reebok utilized athlete endorsements with:

■ *Steve Francis* of the Houston Rockets, co-winner of the 2000 Rookie of the Year award, whom Reebok featured in connection with its Blacktop® line of basketball shoes;

■ *Jalen Rose* of the Indiana Pacers, winner of the 2000 Most Improved Player award; and

■ The college basketball programs at the *University of Utah*, *University of Memphis*, and *Boston College*.

To promote the sale of cross-training cleated baseball and football shoes during 2001, Reebok maintained sponsorship arrangements with:

- NFL Pro Bowl players *Edgerrin James* and *Jevon Kearse*;
- Major League Baseball stars *Andy Pettite* and *Kevin Brown*, and six-time Cy Young winner *Roger Clemens*; and
- The college football programs at *Boston College* and the *Air Force Academy*.

In soccer, Reebok had a number of sponsorship agreements, both with individuals and teams, including those with:

- *Julie Foudy*, member of the U.S. national team;
- *Ryan Giggs* (of current English-league champion Manchester United);
- *Iker Casillas* (goalkeeper with Real Madrid and Spain);
- *Liverpool FC*, one of the world's best-known soccer teams;
- *Bolton Wanderers of England* (which includes the naming rights to the Wanderers' soccer arena, the "Reebok Stadium"); and
- The *Colombian national team*.

To promote its running and tennis footwear and apparel, Reebok had endorsement agreements with:

- Runner *Abel Anton* and *Christine Arron*; and
- Professional tennis players *Patrick Rafter* and *Andy Roddick*.

In addition to advertising and sports marketing, Reebok also used grassroots marketing and in-store merchandising to promote its products and enhance brand awareness, particularly among a younger and more urban audience. In 2002, Reebok was sponsoring events such as the Entertainers Basketball Classic tournament at Rucker Park, the largest street basketball competition in the United States, and continued to support various local running clubs and races. Beginning in March 2002, Reebok planned a series of product displays in more than 1,000 music stores across the United States. These displays gave customers an opportunity to preview new, innovative products before they become available at retail stores and also tell customers where they could buy the products when they arrived in stores.

NFL AND NBA BUSINESS VENTURES

During 2001, Reebok entered into an exclusive licensing agreement with the NFL for apparel, footwear, equipment, and certain accessories commencing in 2002. Beginning with the 2002–2003 season, Reebok supplied uniforms, sideline apparel, and coaches' wear for all 32 NFL teams. Reebok also developed a new line of performance apparel designed for young male athletes and marketed under the brand name "NFL Equipment," launched in April 2002. Additionally in 2002, Reebok introduced "Gridiron Classics," a line of lifestyle apparel evoking the history of the NFL. Reebok planned an integrated marketing campaign throughout the year in order to extend the selling season for its NFL-licensed products beyond the traditional NFL season. In connection with its marketing efforts, Reebok had the right to depict Reebok athletes in their NFL uniforms for advertising purposes and in point-of-purchase displays.

Also during 2001, Reebok entered into a license agreement with the NBA covering apparel, footwear, and certain accessories. Under the agreement, Reebok was the official supplier of uniforms to 12 teams during the 2001–2002 season, became the official supplier of uniforms to 19 teams for the 2002–2003 season, and became the semi-exclusive supplier to all teams in the league for the 2004–2005 season. In addition, Reebok had the right to depict Reebok athletes in their NBA uniforms for advertising purposes and in point-of-purchase displays. Reebok also provided player uniforms and footwear to the NBD (National Basketball Development League), the NBA's new minor league showcasing up-and-coming talent, and to all WNBA teams. During 2002, Reebok sponsored several NBA and WNBA events in order to leverage its new relationship with those leagues.[38]

OTHER MAJOR MARKETING EVENTS

In 2000, Reebok and Liverpool Football Club, a member of the English Premier League announced a multi-million dollar extension of its endorsement contract. Steve Barcewell, Reebok's global head of football, said, "Reebok is delighted to have extended our sponsorship (started 1996) of the Liverpool Football Club, which reaffirms Reebok's commitment to football and the club itself."[39]

In 2000, Reebok outfitted 2,500 athletes and coaches head-to-toe in training apparel and athletic shoes for the 2000 Summer Olympic Games. Reebok was the sponsor of several National Olympic Committees including Russia, Jamaica, Poland, New Zealand, South Africa, Trinidad, and Tobago.

In September 2001, the Reebok Sports Club opened at Canary Wharf complex in London. The club was the largest one in the United Kingdom (UK). It occupied 100,000 square feet.

In February 2002, the Indy Racing League (IRL) and Reebok announced a multi-year partnership naming Reebok the official outfitter of the IRL. Fireman said, "Auto racing continues to be one of the most popular and exciting spectator sports . . . . The partnership will further drive Reebok's growing sports licensing business. . . "[40]

SPORTS AND FITNESS EQUIPMENT

Reebok continued its promotional and educational efforts in 2001 in the fitness area, seeking to leverage and expand Reebok's position as a leading source of fitness programming and education. Reebok's multi-tiered Global Fitness Program, created by Reebok University® and driven by Reebok's website, encompassed strategic alliances, retail partnerships, interactive fitness programming, e-commerce, interactive marketing, consumer initiatives, and product offerings. Central to the development of the Global Fitness Program was the latest Reebok fitness program called Core Training. Core Training, which launched during the summer of 2000, was designed to improve cardiovascular performance and enhance functional strength, balance, and flexibility. The training utilized the Reebok Core Board, the first exercise board that tilted, twisted, torqued, and recoiled 360° in three dimensions in response to a user's movements. Reebok continued to promote Core Training by bringing Reebok Core Training and the Reebok Core Board to local facilities for the education of club owners, fitness instructors, personal trainers, and club members on the techniques and benefits of Core Training.

In addition, through Reebok University, its network of Master Trainers (including Gin Miller and Petra Kolber), and its Alliance fitness instructors, Reebok continued to develop and promote numerous other fitness programs. These programs were complemented by the marketing and sale of a line of Reebok fitness videos, as well as the marketing and sale of Reebok fitness equipment products such as the Step Reebok® exercise platform and the Reebok home exercise bike collection. Members of the Reebok Professional Alliance Program, a world-wide organization consisted of more than 200,000 fitness professionals, could access industry news, register for Reebok University seminars, and purchase Reebok products through Reebok's website, reebok.com. Reebok primarily used its website as a relationship building platform through the delivery of fitness-based information and services such as Reebok University programs and instructions. The unique content of the Reebok University site on reebok.com was developed in partnership with the American College of Sports Medicine.

Reebok also ran marketing promotions and brand extension programs on its website in order to drive sales to Reebok's retail partners. Planned initiatives for 2002 increased direct-to-consumer marketing, including e-mail direct marketing and posting a direct order catalog on its new site devoted exclusively to women, reebokwomen.com, which launched in late February 2002. Reebok was also the exclusive sponsor of the NBA "All Access Pass.com" on the NBA's website, NBA.com, through June 2002. [41]

Distribution

FOOT LOCKER

Foot Locker, Inc. (formerly Woolworth's athletic division) was the world's leading retailer of athletic footwear and apparel, operating retail stores and selling direct-to-customers through catalogs and the Internet. The company's approximate 3,600 retail stores comprised complementary formats under the brand names Foot Locker, Lady Foot Locker, Kid Foot Locker, and Champs Sports (the number one athletic footwear retailer in United States). The stores were primarily mall-based and were located in 14 countries in North America, Europe, and Australia. The company's direct-to-customer operation, Footlocker.com/Eastbay, was the largest Internet and catalog retailer of athletic footwear, apparel and equipment in the world. The company changed its name to Foot Locker to focus on athletic retailing and then sold its noncore interests (San Francisco Music Box Co. and more than a dozen Burger King and Popeye's fast-food franchises) after years of disappointing sales. Investment group Greenway Partners owned 9% of Foot Locker; FMR Corp owned 8%.[42]

The company's stores by global location were (1) 2,929 U.S. stores, (2) 323 European stores, (3) 158 Canadian stores, (4) 73 Puerto Rico and Virgin Island stores, (5) 73 Australian stores, (6) 21 Hawaiian stores and (7) 5 Guam. The Lady Foot Locker stores were the only national chain that specialized in women's athletic footwear, apparel, and accessories. The company planned to open 400 in-stores in Foot Lockers and Champs Stores. These boutiques were to sell Adidas merchandise endorsed by Tracy McGrady of the NBA's Orlando Magic.[43]

Sales had been flat over the past three fiscal years (FY). Sales were $4,379,000,000, $4,356,000,000 and, $4,647,000,000, respectively for FY 2002, 2001, and 2000. Net income was $92,000,000 for FY 2002, loss of $240,000,000 for FY 2001, and a profit of $48,000,000 for FY 2000. The company's profit margins were 2.1% and 1.0% for FY 2002 and FY 2000, respectively. The sales corresponded to the troubles the major athletic shoe companies had suffered over the previous five years. [44]

In August, 2002, management announced a re-alignment of shoes. The company reduced its inventory of shoes selling for over $120, the target market that Nike dominated. Customers were changing their preference from expensive to less expensive athletic shoes. The company could reduce its 2003 purchases from Nike by $150 million to $250 million, or about 23%.[45]

Reebok and Nike had been battling over dominance in sales in Foot Locker since the 1980s. At that time, Reebok's aerobic shoe sales were not in the stores. So, Foot Locker management asked Reebok to turn out a specialty line for Foot Locker. Josie Esquivel, an analyst at Morgan Stanley, said that "Reebok basically thumbed its nose" at the retailer. Reebok "was selling to whomever it wanted, including the discounter down the street from Foot Locker."[46] Foot Locker's strategy was to offer exclusive lines as a weapon against discounters and was receiving exclusive lines from other athletic shoe manufacturers. Nike agreed to make exclusive lines for Foot Locker. In 1996, Nike introduced Flight 65 and Flight 67, which were high-priced basketball shoes that sold only at Foot Locker. These shoes came in Nike's trademark black and white. Earlier in the year, Reebok had agreed to make shoes exclusively for Foot Locker, but none of the shoes had reached the store.

Fireman's views on the rocky relations with Foot Locker were that "Reebok wasn't as good a listener to [Foot Locker], which happens to have a good ear as to what's happening on the street and consumers."[47] Fireman tried to repair the relationship by spending a few days with buyers of Foot Locker. He said, we are "trying to discern their needs."

Over the past few years, "Reebok had hired an army of testers at [Foot Locker's] shoe chains . . . to find out whether Reebok was getting equal treatment with other brands." Reebok was disappointed with their findings. They found that Reebok had the most shoes on display in the stores but got little positive help from the stores' salespeople. A salesperson told one 17-year-old customer that "Nikes were hip."

Reebok recognized that Foot Locker's customers were not Reebok's core clients, who were older customers and preteens unable to spend $80 to $90 for shoes. Foot Locker's target market were teens and Generation X customers, who spent $80 to $90 for shoes. Fireman said, "There's no question Nike owns that market," and "there's no one really in that market to compete against them in the high-end niche."[48]

Nike had a special salesforce, Elkins, which called on stores and spread the gospel of Nike. They were enthusiastic sponsors of Nike's product lines. They provided the company with excellent information on market trends and competition.

William DeVrues, who headed Woolworth's footwear units, dismissed talk about bad relations with Reebok. He said, "We're only selling what the customer wants."[49]

Footlocker had 18% market share of U.S. sales of athletic shoes and 8% of European sales.

FOOTSTAR, INC.

Footstar, Inc. was a holding company, which directly or indirectly, through its wholly-owned subsidiaries; owned the capital stock of its subsidiaries. The retailer's Meldisco division, which accounted for about 60% of sales, operated leased footwear departments in about 5,800 U.S. stores, the majority of its sales came from about 1,800 Kmart stores. Meldisco offered shoes under private labels as well as licensed brands Everlast, Route 66, and Thom McAn. Footstar's athletic division, which sold shoes and apparel, included Footaction (about 500 stores, mostly in U.S. malls) and Just For Feet (about 90 stores in the southern half of the United States). Thom McAn will soon be sold in about 300 Wal-Mart stores.

On March 8, 2002, Kmart announced its intention to close 283 stores. Meldisco operated licensed footwear departments in all of those stores. The 283 stores had been removed from Meldisco's comparable store sales base as of April sales. The store closings were progressing in an orderly fashion, and all 283 stores were currently expected to be closed during June.

Footstar's sales had increased by $620,000,000 over the past three years. Sales were $2,460,000,000, $2,237,100,000, and $1,880,000,000, respectively for 2001, 2000, and 1999. The operating income decreased over the same three years from $153,900,000 in 1999, to $171,400,000 in 2000, to $97,000,000 in 2001. The operating margins were 3.9%, 7.7%, and 8.2%, respectively for 2001, 2000, and 1999.

On May 30, 2002, Footstar reported that comparable stores sales results for the four-week period ended May 25, 2002 decreased 9.6%.

Comparable store sales at Meldisco declined 16.1%, and comparable store sales for the athletic segment increased 2.1%.

For the month of May 2002, total sales were $178.4 million, a decrease of 11.7% from the $202.1 million posted in the same period last year. Total sales for the Meldisco division declined 17.7% to $107.9 million from $131.1 million, and total sales in the company's athletic segment decreased 0.6% to $70.5 million from $71.0 million.[50]

Mickey Robinson, Chairman and Chief Executive Officer, commented, "Our athletic segment posted a comparable store sales increase for May, however, Footstar's overall performance was impacted by disappointing results at Meldisco. Strong sales at both Footaction and

Just For Feet contributed to the athletic segment's gain for the month, although the overall environment continued to be very promotional. At Meldisco, the sales performance was negatively affected by lower sales of summer-related product, particularly sandals and canvas shoes, due to cooler than normal weather for most of the month. However, sales were less promotional than planned.[51]

The other major competitors were Wal-Mart and Target. An analyst said, "the slow down and consumer spending were likely to hurt mall-based retailers more than discounters such as Wal-Mart Stores and Target."

REEBOK'S RETAIL STORES

Reebok also operated approximately 201 factory direct store fronts in the United States (including Reebok, Rockport, Ralph Lauren Footwear, and Greg Norman stores and counting multiple store fronts in combination stores as separate store fronts) that sold a variety of footwear, apparel, and accessories marketed under our various brands. These factory direct stores were an extension of the firm's wholesale business that allowed Reebok to control the disposition of excess inventory without compromising our primary channels of distribution. Management did not anticipate any significant expansion in the number of factory direct stores in the United States.

In addition to these factory direct stores, Reebok operated a full-price "concept", or company retail, store in New York City, another at the company's Canton, Massachusetts headquarters, and approximately 10 Rockport concept stores. All of these concept stores showcased a wide selection of current, in-line Reebok or Rockport branded footwear, apparel, and accessories.[52]

REEBOK E-COMMERCE STORE

On July 9, 2002, Reebok management announced an alliance between Reebok and GSI Commerce. A leading outsource solution provider for e-commerce, to develop and operate an e-commerce store that would be accessible at www.reebok.com.

GSI Commerce was to develop and operate all facets of the online store, including website design, customer service, order processing, fulfillment, and merchandising, while Reebok featured a broad selection of Reebok's top-tier footwear, apparel, equipment, and accessories, including NFL, NBA, Classic, and Reebok merchandise. It was expected to launch in the United Sates during the third quarter of 2002.

"This online retail store reflects our desire to offer consumers our most exciting products and marketing initiatives in one place," said Reebok Chief Marketing Officer Micky Pant. "It will complement our traditional 'bricks and mortar' distribution with a virtual offering of key products that will enhance our brand images."[53]

Manufacturing and Production

Virtually all of the company's products were produced by independent manufacturers, almost all of which were outside the United States, except that some of the company's apparel and some of the component parts used in the company's footwear were sourced from independent manufacturers located in the United States. Each of the company's operating units generally contracted with its manufacturers on a purchase order basis, subject in most cases to the terms of a formal manufacturing agreement between the company and such manufacturers. All contract manufacturing was performed in accordance with detailed specifications furnished by the operating unit, subject to strict quality control standards, with a right to reject products that did not meet specifications. To date, the company had not encountered any significant problem with product rejection or customer returns. The company generally considered its relationships with its contract manufacturers to be good.

As part of Reebok's commitment to human rights, the management required agents and/or manufacturers of Reebok products to apply the Reebok Human Rights Standards, which set forth acceptable factory policies and procedures regarding workplace conditions (See **Exhibit 1**). The company used a global monitoring program to implement these standards. Through its human rights initiatives, Reebok had an ongoing program to provide technical assistance to improve air quality in factories producing its footwear, had implemented a worker communication system to resolve conflicts in such factories, and had taken other steps to improve workplace conditions consistent with the company's Human Rights Production Standards. In conjunction with its human rights program, Reebok required suppliers of soccer balls in Pakistan to end the use of child labor by centralizing all production, including ball stitching, so that the labor force could be adequately monitored to prevent the use of child labor. Reebok-branded soccer balls were sold with a guarantee that the balls were made without child labor.

Similarly, Reebok was cognizant of the need to monitor carefully the substances used in the manufacture of its products and to assure that the health of the consumer, as well as the overall environment, was protected. To this end, management maintained a comprehensive list of restricted substances, the use of which was either limited or prohibited in any product manufactured. Vendors whose materials were used in the production of Reebok's products, and factories that assembled the products, were required to certify that they were in compliance with *Reebok Restricted Substances Policy*. The company continued to monitor governmental restrictions worldwide, which were then incorporated into the Restricted Substances Policy. However, the Restricted Substances Policy exceeded the mandated governmental restrictions in many respects. For example, although not required to do so by any laws or governmental regulations, the company was in the final stages of eliminating PVC from its products, a process management anticipated would be substantially completed during 2002.

China, Indonesia, and Thailand were Reebok's primary sources for footwear, accounting for approximately 51%, 28%, and 15%, respectively, of total footwear production during 2001 (based on the number of units produced). The firm's largest manufacturer accounted for approximately 19% of total footwear production in 2001.

Reebok maintained a network of affiliates in China, Hong Kong, Indonesia, Thailand, Taiwan, and South Korea to inspect certain components and materials purchased by manufacturers for use in footwear production, facilitate the shipment of footwear from the shipping point to the point of destination, and to help arrange for the issuance of letters of credit or wire transfers, the primary means used to pay the footwear manufacturers for finished products. Reebok's apparel group utilized the services of independent third parties, as well as its Hong Kong subsidiary and its affiliates in the Far East, to assist in the placement, inspection, and shipment of apparel and accessories orders internationally. The apparel group retained and managed those independent contractors responsible for production of apparel in the United States. The remainder of Reebok's order placement, quality assurance, and inspection work was handled by a combination of employees and independent contractors for the various countries in which its products were made.[54]

RESEARCH AND DEVELOPMENT

In 2001, the company spent approximately $41.7 million on product research, development, and evaluation, compared to $49.8 million in 2000 and $55.4 million in 1999.[55]

The company placed a strong emphasis on technology and had continued to incorporate various proprietary performance technologies in its products, focusing on cushioning, stability, and lightweight features in its footwear and on comfort and moisture management in its apparel.

As part of its commitment to offer leading footwear technologies, Reebok engaged in product research, devlopment, and design activities in its headquarters, where state-of-the-art product development facility was dedicated to the design and development of technologically advanced athletic and fitness footwear. Reebok also had product development centers in Korea, China, and Taiwan to enable development activities to be more closely integrated with production.

The company's most signficant technologies were DMX®, the Pump®, and 3D Ultralite. The DMX technology provided cushioning utilizing a heel-to-forefoot, active airflow system that delivered cushioning when and where it was needed. Originally introduced in 1995, Reebok had enhanced and expanded this technology by developing multiple versions of DMX to meet the performance demanded of various activities, taking into account performance-attributed aesthetics and price among the various versions. Current versions included: a 6-pod system [the DMX (6)], a 10-pod system [the DMX (10)], two 2-pod systems [the DMX (2)], a DMX sockliner, and the DMX "Stimpak." Throughout 2001, Reebok continued to increase the range of products featuring DMX technology with the introduction of numerous new shoe models. The company also continued to incorporate 3D Ultralite, a proprietary material allowing midsole and outsole to be combined in a simple, injection-molded unit, in performance footwear. 3D Ultralite provided a unique blend of lighweight, flexible, and durable properties. In 2001 the company began to redevelop its proprietary inflatable shoe technology, the Pump®, exploring broader and more varied applications for this technology in its footwear. It was expected that new inflatable shoe products would be introduced in late 2002.

Reebok had also incorporated advanced technologies into certain of its apparel products with the Hydromove® and more advanced Play Dry™ moisture-management systems. These moisture-wicking technologies helped to keep athletes dry and thereby facilitate regulation of the wearer's body temperature. Management planned to expand the range of apparel products incorporating moisture-management technologies going forward.[56]

SOURCES OF SUPPLY

The principal materials used in the company's footwear products were leather, nylon, rubber, ethylvinyl acetate, and polyurethane. Most of these materials could be obtained from a number of sources, although a loss of supply could temporarily disrupt production. Some of the components used in the company's technologies were obtained from only one or two sources, and thus a loss of supply could disrupt production. The principal materials used in the company's apparel products were cotton, fleece, nylon, and spandex. These materials could be obtained from a number of sources.

The footwear products of the company that were manufactured overseas and shipped to the United States for sale were subject to U.S. Customs duties. Duties on the footwear products imported by the company ranged from 5.1% to 66% (plus a unit charge, in some cases, of $1.58), depending on whether the principal component was leather or some other material and depending on the construction.

As with its international sales operations, the company's footwear and apparel production operations were subject to the usual risks of doing business abroad, such as import duties, quotas and other threats to free trade, foreign currency fluctuations and restrictions, labor unrest, and political instability. Management believed that it had the ability to develop, over time, adequate substitute sources of supply for the products obtained from present foreign suppliers. If, however, events should prevent the company from acquiring products from its suppliers in China, Indonesia, Thailand, or the Philippines, or significantly increase the cost to the company of such products, the company's operations could be seriously disrupted until alternative suppliers were found, with a significant negative impact.[57]

BACKLOG

As of December 31, 2001, the backlog of orders that management believed to be firm (though cancelable by the purchaser) totaled approximately $979.4 million, compared to $967.4 million as of December 31, 2000. The backlog position was not necessarily indicative of future sales because the ratio of future orders to "at once" shipments and sales by company-owned retail stores varied from year to year. In addition, many markets in South America and Asia Pacific were not included in the backlog, since sales were made in those regions through Reebok's independent distributors.[58]

SEASONALITY

Sales by the company of athletic and casual footwear tended to be seasonal in nature, with the strongest sales occuring in the first and third quarters. Apparel sales also generally vary during the course of the year, with the greatest demand occurring during the spring and fall seasons.[59]

SINGLE CUSTOMER

There was no single customer of the company that accounted for 10% or more of overall net sales in 2001. Nevertheless, the company did have certain significant customers, the loss of any one of which could have an adverse effect on its business. There could also be a negative effect on business if any significant customer became insolvent or otherwise failed to pay its debts.[60]

Human Resource Management

As of December 31, 2001, the company had approximately 6,700 employees in all operating units. None of these employees were represented by a labor union, except for the approximately 200 employees in France who had a workers' committee. Reebok had never suffered a material interruption of business caused by labor disputes with employees, and it considered employee relations to be good.[61]

On July 1, 2002, Reebok and Bright Horizons Family Solutions announced the opening of a new child care center on the site of the 44-acre landscape surrounding Reebok's World Headquarters in Canton, Massachusetts. Designed, built, and owned by Reebok, Bright Horizons Family Solutions was to manage the center's day-to-day operations. Scheduled to open September 3, 2002, the center had the capacity to serve 14 infants, 18 toddlers, and 40 pre-school children. Demand for the center's 72 spots had been high since Reebok began accepting pre-enrollment registration forms in January.

"Many of our employees were having a difficult time finding quality child care, so we set out to find a solution," said Leslie Abrahamson, Reebok's Director of Compensation and Benefits. "Managed by Bright Horizons, Reebok's new center will provide our employees with consistent, reliable, quality child care in a safe and nuturing environment."[62]

Outsourcing HRM Problems

PROTESTS IN JAKARTA AGAINST FOOTWEAR COMPANIES FLEEING INDONESIA

Foreign footwear firms were scaling back their presence in Indonesia because of the country's deteriorating business environment and the lower labor costs offered by its neighbors. As an indication of this trend, Indonesia's footwear exports declined to $1.5 billion last year from nearly $2.2 billion in 1996, when the country accounted for 38% of Nike's production volume.

Indonesia's share of the footwear giant's output is now at 30%. In contrast, Vietnam, which offered lower wages and a more stable business climate, had seen its share of Nike's production volume grow to 15% from 2%. The exodus of footwear firms to other countries had grave implications for the "flying geese" theory of development, which was followed by Indonesia. The theory stated that less-developed countries go up the production hierarchy as they pursue industrialzation. According to Hal Hill, an expert on Indonesia at Australian National University, if the country "can't do it in footwear, you've have got to wonder whether it can do it in similar industries" like electronics and garments.[63]

PROTESTS AGAINST REEBOK

On June 29, 2002, around 1,200 workers of PT Primarindo Asia Infrastructure, the local supplier of U.S. shoe manufacturer Reebok, staged rallies near the U.S. embassy. The demonstrators protested the unprovoked halt of purchasing order by the Reebook Trading International (RTI) without a tolerable period for Primarindo to find substitute buyers. They also demanded RTI to hold negotiations with Primarindo, located in Bandung, capital of West Java province, around 150 kilometers south of Jakarta. At around 13:00 local time (0600 GMT) the rally moved to Monas square and started to burn down a six-meter-long shoe replica and dozens of Reebok shoes while shouting simultaneously "expel Reebok out from here." Around 5,400 Primarindo workers faced the threat of losing their jobs since 100% of their products were sold only to Reebok. Two weeks ago a local newspaper reported some representatives of Primarindo's labor union met Reebok's country manager to Indonesia, Chris Barnett, but apparently failed to achieve any important deal. Indonesia was among other developing countries where Reebok sets up factories. It had five Reebok companies but all are sub-contracted, mostly by South Korean companies. Labor activists, however, criticized Reebok for its low standard wage implemented on local workers. Dita Sari, an organizer with the National Front for Workers Struggle in Indonesia, rejected in January this year the 13th Annual Human Rights Award hosted by Reebok in Salt Lake City of the United States, because in her country Reebok workers get only around $1.5 U.S. dollars a day.[64]

PROTEST AGAINST NIKE

On August 20, 2002, around 3,000 workers of PT Doson Indonesia, subcontractor of U.S. sportswear company Nike, packed onto the major street of Sudirman to protest against the withdrawal order by Nike.

The mob's main target was the BRI building where Nike leases its representative office in Jakarta. An employee even threatened to lead the others to the U.S. embassy. They claimed to have been laid off by the company due to the absence of purchase orders. The angry workers carried a banner that said "Nike runs uncivilized business, clear evidence of capitalism and liberalism."

Earlier Monday, the labor union of PT Doson failed to reach an agreement with the management over the amount of separation pay.

The union demanded a five-month separation pay for around 6,800 workers following the mass layoff at PT Donson, which has served Nike since 1993. Nike's General Manager to Indonesia, Jeff DuMont, announced on August 7 the discontinuance of orders from PT Doson, on grounds that the company's performance had been the poorest among other subcontractors here.

Nike began full production in Indonesia in 1988, and by 1996 one third of its shoes were produced here. In 2001, the sportswear giant bought shoes and sportswear from a total of 25 factories in Indonesia.

Similar to the Nike case, U.S. athletic apparel giant Reebok also halted orders from one of its subcontractors in West Java, forcing around 5,400 workers out of their jobs.[65]

Human Rights

REEBOK HISTORY

In 1988, Amnesty International invited Reebok to be the sponsor of its Human Rights Now! World Tour. That tour, which featured artists Peter Gabriel, Bruce Springsteen, Sting, Tracy Chapman, and Youssou N'Dour, carried messages of freedom and justice to millions of people in 23 cities on four continents. That experience inspired Reebok to place human rights at the center of its corporate culture. That same year, it established the Reebok Human Rights Award program. Since then, it has become a leader in incorporating human rights into its business practices and making it an integral part of its corporate identity.

UNDERSTANDING HUMAN RIGHTS

The following human rights information is directly from Reebok's Web site.

- On December 10, 1948, the General Assembly of the United Nations adopted and proclaimed the UNIVERSAL DECLARATION OF HUMAN RIGHTS as the common standard of achievement for all peoples and all nations. At Reebok, we believe that as individuals we all have the responsibility to understand what human rights are and to GET INVOLVED with the critical issues that impact our fellow human beings across the globe as well as in our own neighborhoods.

- Please familiarize yourself with the Universal Declaration of Human Rights, learn about the extraordinary efforts of the Reebok Human Rights Awards recipients, and find ways to get involved with the many organizations that work to ensure dignity and rights of all human beings.

OUR BUSINESS PRACTICES

We believe that the incorporation of internationally recognized human rights standards into our business practice improves worker morale and results in a higher quality working environment and higher quality products.

—Reebok Human Rights Production Standards

- A commitment to human rights is an integral part of Reebok's corporate culture and identity. As a company operating in a global marketplace, we believe we have an obligation to act in a socially responsible way. In 1986, we were the first in our industry to pull out of South Africa in support of the anti-apartheid movement. Since then, we have implemented a number of programs and policies aimed at IMPROVING CONDITIONS for workers involved in making Reebok products. Some of these key initiatives include: the adoption of STANDARDS for production to protect the rights of workers who produce Reebok products; a comprehensive program to ensure that NO CHILD LABOR is used in the production of soccer balls; and an innovative WORKER COMMUNICATION SYSTEM that provides employees with a safe way to voice concerns or report violations. In addition, Reebok sponsored an independent assessment of working conditions in Indonesia and released a report entitled PEDULI HAK/CARING FOR RIGHTS. As a result of this report, many improvements in the factories have been implemented.

- Such actions have helped to define Reebok as a corporation that is willing to follow its conscience. To learn more about current human rights programs, please visit NEWS AD NOTES. (www.reebok.com)

REEBOK HUMAN RIGHTS AWARD

Standing up for human rights is a REEBOK hallmark—as much a part of our corporate culture and identity as our products. We believe that we all have a responsibility to UNDERSTAND HUMAN RIGHTS, to expose injustice, and to support efforts that ensure dignity and rights for all human beings. The BUSINESS PRACTICES we have developed and implemented around the world and OUR HISTORY, are a reflection of our commitment. Grants provided by the REEBOK HUMAN RIGHTS FOUNDATION help support human rights initiatives around the globe. The REEBOK HUMAN RIGHTS AWARD gives recognition and financial support to young activists who have made significant contributions to human rights through non-violent means. For more information about the REEBOK HUMAN RIGHTS PROGRAM please explore this website, or CONTACT US.[66]

2002 HUMAN RIGHTS RECIPIENTS

The four winners are women, the first time all winners were women. The winners were: Kavwumbu Hakachima (age 27) of Zambia was ardent spokesperson and advocate for victims of child abuse in Zambia, a country ravaged by poverty and AIDS. Ms. Hakachima now heads Children in Crisis, an organization dedicated to helping abused children.

Over the past eight years, Dita Sari (age 29) has been harassed, arrested, imprisoned, and tortured for her efforts to improve the deplorable labor conditions for thousands of factory workers, primarily women, in Indonesia. Today, Ms. Sari leads a union that is 22,000 strong and growing. She refused to accept the award because Reebok workers earned only around $1.5 U.S. dollars per day. She rejected her award. (See Protests Against Reebok.)

Babita Maili Lama (age 25) was a young mother who was abducted from her village in Nepal and sold into forced prostitution in Bombay. After surviving two years of unspeakable horrors, she escaped and now risks her own life to rescue other girls who suffer a similar fate.

A second-generation civil rights activist, Malika Asha Sanders (age 27) is Executive Director of the 21st Century Youth Leadership Movement, an innovative organization dedicated to developing leadership and community building skills for young African-Americans.

Award recipients received a $50,000 grant from the Reebok Human Rights Foundation to help further their work. They also became members of Forefront, a network of former recipients that helps each other gain skills and resources, share strategies and opportunities, communicate with the international community, and respond to cries.[67]

Financial Performance

MANAGEMENT REPORT ON 2001 OPERATING RESULTS[68]

During calendar year 2001, net income for the company increased to $102.7 million, or $1.66 per diluted share, from $80.9 million, or $1.40 per diluted share, for the calendar year 2000. Net sales for the company increased by 4.5%, from $2.865 billion in 2000 to $2.993 billion in 2001.

Net sales for the year ended December 31, 2001 were $2.993 billion (see **Exhibit 10**), a 4.5% increase from the year ended December 31, 2000 sales of $2.865 billion. Sales comparisons were adversely affected by the weakening of most foreign currencies against the U.S. dollar. On a constant-dollar basis, net Reebok brand sales (including the sales of the Greg Norman Collection) were $2.496 billion in 2001 an increase of 6.8% from the year ended

Exhibit 10

Consolidated Statements of Income: Reebok International, Ltd.
(Dollar amounts in thousands, except per share data)

Year Ending December 31	2001	2000	1999
Net Sales	$2,992,878	2,865,240	$2,899,872
Costs and expenses			
Cost of sales	1,894,497	1,799,686	1,783,914
Selling, general and administrative expenses	913,941	915,387	971,945
Special charges	(532)	3,289	61,625
Interest expense, net	17,630	22,126	40,532
Other expenses, net	11,536	8,947	13,818
Total costs and expenses	$2,837,072	$2,729,435	$2,871,834
Income before income taxes and minority interest	155,806	135,805	28,038
Income taxes	48,300	49,000	10,093
Income before minority interest	107,506	86,805	17,945
Minority interest	4,780	5,927	6,900
Net income	$ 102,726	$ 80,878	$ 11,045
Basic earnings per share	$ 1.75	$ 1.42	$ 0.20
Diluted earnings per share	$ 1.66	$ 1.40	$ 0.20
Dividends per common share	$ 0.00	$ 0.00	$ 0.00
Common shares	98,049,605	96,208,558	92,985,737

Source: Reebok International, Ltd., *2001 Annual Report.*

December 31, 2000 sales of $2.336 billion. On a constant-dollar basis, the Reebok brand's worldwide sales increased $219.5 million or 9.6%.

U.S. footwear sales of the Reebok brand increased 0.6% to $930.5 million in 2001 from $925.1 million in 2000. During the year, U.S. footwear sales to the athletic specialty channel of distribution increased 11%. The company believed its retail presence in this channel had improved compared to the prior year and that this improvement was strategically important to its long-term objective of growing quality market share in the United States. Sales increased 33% in the key strategic category of basketball. The company believed that its basketball increase was being fueled by a general resurgence in this category in the United States and by the strong presence of its endorsed athletes led by last season's MVP, Allen Iverson. U.S. sales of the company's Classic product line increased approximately 10% for the year. The company believed this increase was partially attributable to a strong positive consumer response to its Classic advertising campaign. During 2001, U.S. footwear sales in the children's category also increased, whereas sales in the cross-training and running categories declined. U.S. apparel sales of the Reebok brand (including the sales of the Greg Norman Collection) increased by 68.1% to $395.1 million from $235.0 million in 2000. During 2001, the company entered into new licensing agreements with the National Football League ("NFL") and the National Basketball Association ("NBA"). In order to support its new sports licensing business, in February 2001 the company purchased selected assets of LogoAthletic ("Logo"). Included in the assets purchased were inventory, equipment, the assumption of certain facility leases, and the rights to Logo's trademarks. The total purchase price was $14.2 million. Much of the increase in U.S. apparel sales was from sales of this licensed product, however, wholesale sales of Reebok branded apparel also increased by 13.3% during the year as the result of some new apparel silhouettes with a strategic focus on women's fitness, Allen Iverson–inspired street wear, and Classics.

International sales of the Reebok brand (including footwear and apparel) were $1.170 billion in 2001, a decrease of 0.5% from sales of $1.176 billion in 2000. On a constant-dollar basis, international sales of the Reebok brand increased $54.0 million or 4.8%. On a reported-dollar basis, net sales in Europe increased 1.3% and net sales in Asia Pacific region decreased 10.3% for the year. On a constant-dollar basis, net sales in Europe increased $48.7 million or 6.1% for the year, and sales in the Asia Pacific region increased 1.2%. In Latin America, the company's sales to its independent distributors increased approximately 7.0% for the year. In constant dollars, international footwear sales increased approximately 6.8%, and international apparel sales increased by approximately 2.5%. Effective January 1, 2001, the company sold its South African subsidiary to an independent distributor and purchased a majority interest in its Mexican distributor. These changes did not have a material impact on sales or earnings during 2001.

Rockport's sales for 2001 decreased by 5.4% to $399.6 million from sales of $422.4 million in 2000. Domestic sales for the Rockport brand decreased by 9.0%. A significant portion of this decline occurred post-9/11 as a result of a decline in Rockport's business in the department store channel of distribution, as well as with the independent shoe stores. In the fourth quarter of 2001, Rockport's domestic business declined by 25%. The company believed that some of the decline was attributable to retailers adjusting down their model stock positions post 9/11 and that the decline was not indicative of a major deterioration in Rockport's U.S. market share. The company estimated that Rockport's market share in the United States declined by only 50–75 basis points in the fourth quarter. International revenues, which grew by 5.2%, accounted for approximately 28.4% of Rockport's sales in 2001 as compared to 25.5% in 2000. During 2002, Rockport was launching several new initiatives in order to improve sales performance, including a focused product strategy to enhance Rockport's women's business and a new product segmentation strategy to address the needs of its retailers and consumers.

Ralph Lauren Footwear had sales of $97.3 million in 2001, a decrease of 8.8% from $106.7 million in 2000. The decline was partially attributable to the weak department store business during most of 2001 and partially due to the re-aligning of the company's product strategy to conform with that of Polo Ralph Lauren corporate.

The company's overall gross margin was 36.7% of sales for 2001, as compared to 37.9% for 2000, a decrease of 120 basis points. The company's margins were adversely affected by currency, the promotional retail climate in certain key markets, particularly in United States, and by the general slowdown in business that occurred post-9/11. Business had gradually rebounded from post-9/11 lows. Based on foreign currency exchange rates on December 31, 2001 and the company's hedging strategy, currency should continue to adversely impact margins throughout 2002. The company believed that 2002 gross margins should improve from fourth quarter 2001 levels. This improvement was based on the company's belief that this along with an assumed stabilization of foreign exchange rates should cause margins to improve from those experienced in the fourth quarter of 2001.

Selling, general, and administrative expenses for the year ended December 31, 2001 were $913.9 million, or 30.5% of sales, as compared to $915.4 million, or 31.9% of sales for 2000, a decline of $1.5 million or 140 basis points as a percentage of sales. The company continued to improve its expense leverage while at the same time increasing its Reebok Brand advertising and marketing investments. The company's shared service operation, which supported its multiple-brand strategy, continued to generate improved expense leverage as core services are implemented across all brands. As a result the company was able to reduce general and administrative type expenses by approximately 7% during 2001.

Net interest expense was $17.6 million for the year ended December 31, 2001, a decrease of $4.5 million as compared to 2000, as a result of strong cash flow generation and the refinancing of the company's long-term debt. In the first quarter of 2001, the company refinanced its term loan, which was due August 31, 2002 with the sale of $250 million in 20-year convertible debentures.

For the year ended December 31, 2001, other expenses, net was $11.5 million. During the year, the company identified an under accrual of buying agent's commissions of approximately $10.6 million was recorded in other expense during the second quarter of 2001. Also included in other expenses, net, are the gains from the sale of certain real estate assets of $8.2 million, the amortization of intangibles of $4.0, the write-off of $5.2 million of unamortized debt costs associated with the early extinguishment of the company's term loan, foreign currency losses, and other non-operating income and expenses.

Exhibit 11 shows Reebok's consolidated balance sheet.

Exhibit 11

Consolidated Balance Sheets: Reebok International, Ltd.
(Dollar amounts in thousands, except per share data)

Year Ending December 31	2001	2000
Assets		
Current assets		
Cash and cash equivalents	$ 413,281	$ 268,665
Accounts receivable, net of allowance for doubtful accounts		
(2001, $55,240; 2000, $48,016)	383,372	423,830
Inventory	362,927	393,599
Deferred income taxes	104,280	101,715
Prepaid expenses and other current assets	30,835	37,396
Total current assets	1,294,695	1,225,205
Property and equipment, net	133,952	141,835
Other noncurrent assets		
Intangibles, net of amortization	76,686	64,288
Deferred income taxes	16,094	18,110
Other	21,746	13,608
Total assets	$1,543,173	$1,463,046
Liabilities and stockholders' equity		
Current liabilities		
Notes payable to banks	$ 11,779	$ 8,878
Current portion of long-term debt	97	13,813
Accounts payable	127,286	172,035
Accrued expenses	269,738	272,076
Income taxes payable	40,506	21,337
Total current liabilities	449,406	488,139
Long-term debt, net of current portion	351,210	345,015
Minority interest and other long-term liabilities	22,619	22,029
Commitments and contingencies		
Stockholders' equity		
Common stock, par value $.01; authorized 250,000,000 shares;		
issued shares: 98,049,605 in 2001; 96,208,558 in 2000	981	962
Retained earnings	1,453,348	1,301,269
Less 39,010,827 shares in 2001 and 38,716,227 shares in		
2000 in treasury at cost	(660,422)	(653,370)
Unearned compensation	(2,736)	(1,402)
Accumulated other comprehensive income (expense)	(71,233)	(39,596)
Total stockholders' equity	719,938	607,863
Total liabilities and stockholders' equity	$1,543,173	$1,463,046

Source: Reebok International, Ltd., *2001 Annual Report.*

ACQUISITION OF COMMON STOCK

Under various share repurchase programs from 1992 to 1995, the Board of Directors authorized the repurchase of up to $800,000 of the company's common stock in the open market or privately negotiated transactions. During the year ended December 31, 2001 the company acquired 294,600 shares of treasury stock for approximately $7,100. During the year ended December 31, 2000, the company acquired 2,000,000 shares of treasury stock in a noncash exchange pursuant to a stock option exercise by a major shareholder. As of December 31, 2001, the company had approximately $119,500 available for future repurchases of common stock under these programs.

Exhibit 12 shows sales of Reebok products by geographic regions. Exhibit 13 shows sales by product type.

Exhibit 12

Geographical Sales: Reebok International, Ltd.
(Dollar amounts in thousands)

Net Sales	2001	%	2000	%	1999	%
United States	$1,721,834	57.53	$1,599,406	55.82	$1,609,697	55.51
United Kingdom	511,426	17.09	514,722	17.96	545,562	18.81
Europe	467,207	15.61	462,342	16.15	476,695	16.44
Other countries	292,411	9.77	288,770	10.08	267,918	9.24
Total net sales	$2,992,878	100.00	$2,865,240	100.00	$2,899,872	100.00

Source: Reebok International, Ltd., *2001 Annual Report*, p. 63.

Exhibit 13

Net Sales by Product Type: Reebok International, Ltd.
(Dollar amounts in thousands)

Net Sales	2001	%	2000	%	1999	%
Footwear	$2,081,393	69.54	$2,098,028	73.22	$2,071,768	71.44
Apparel	911,485	30.46	767,212	26.78	828,104	28.56
Total net sales	$2,992,878	100.00	$2,865,240	100.00	$2,899,872	100.00

Source: Reebok International, Ltd., *2001 Annual Report*, p. 61.

Notes

1. Reebok International, Ltd., Form–10K, (December 31, 2001), pp. i–iv. This letter was directly quoted.
2. *Footwear News*, May 8, 1995.
3. *Ibid.*
4. Joseph Perira, "In Reebok-Nike War, Big Woolworth Chain Was a Major Battle Ground," *Wall Street Journal*, (September 22, 1995), p. A-1
5. *Ibid.*
6. *Ibid.*
7. Reebok International Ltd., *1996 Annual Report*, p. 16.
8. *Ibid.*, p. i.
9. *Ibid.*
10. *Ibid.*, p. 62.
11. *Ibid.*
12. *Ibid.*, p.67.
13. Reebok International Ltd., "2001 Notice of Annual Meeting of Shareholders," p. 5. This was directly quoted.
14. "Form 10-K, "(December 31, 2001), 18–19.
15. Kenneth Labich, "Nike vs. Reebok," *Fortune* (September 18, 1995), p. 104.
16. *Ibid.*
17. *Ibid.*
18. "Reebok Press Release" (June 28, 2002).
19. Form 10-K (December 31, 2001), pp. 30–34.
20. *Ibid.*, p. 4. This was directly quoted.
21. *Ibid.*, pp. 8–9. These six paragraphs were directly quoted.
22. *Ibid.*, pp. 10–11. These two paragraphs were directly quoted.
23. *Ibid.*, pp. 11–12. These six paragraphs were directly quoted.
24. *Ibid.*, pp. 12–13. These six paragraphs were directly quoted.
25. *Ibid.*, pp. 8–9. These three paragraphs were directly quoted.

26. *Ibid.*, pp. 17–18. These seven paragraphs were directly quoted.
27. *Ibid.*
28. *Ibid.*
29. www.forbes.com–consumer goods:adidas.
30. www.hoovers.com and www.yahoo.com/bw.
31. Douglas Robson, "Just Do Something," *Business Week,* July 2, 2001, pp. 70–71. "Form 10-K," pp. 2–5. This section was directly quoted.
32. www.yahoo.com/bw.
33. www.theonlineinvestor.com and www.yahoomarketing.com.
34. www.biz.yahoo.com/bw.
35. Carol Matlack, "Puma Sharpens Its Elaws," *Business Week* (September 16, 2002), p. 46.
36. www.espn.go.com/moresports/news and www.itochu.co.jp/main/news.
37. Form 10-K, pp. 4–7. This entire section was directly quoted.
38. *Ibid*, p. 9–14. These two paragraphs were directly quoted.
39. Reebok Press Release (May 4, 2000).
40. *Ibid* (February 22, 2002).
41. Form 10-K, p. 7. These 3 paragraphs were directly quoted.
42. www.footlocker_inc.com.
43. www.hoovers.com.
44. www.footlocker_inc.com.
45. www.hoover.com.
46. Pereina, p. A-1.
47. *Ibid.*
48. Lasbick, p. 104.
49. Pereina, p. A-1.
50. http://biz.yzhoo.com.
51. *Ibid.*
52. www.hoovers.com.
53. Reebok Press Release, (July 9, 2002).
54. Form 10-K, pp.13–14. These five paragraphs were quoted directly.
55. Form 10-K, p. 13. These two paragraphs were directly quoted.
56. *Ibid.*, pp. 11–12. These four paragraphs were directly quoted.
57. *Ibid.*, pp. 14–15. These three paragraphs were directly quoted.
58. *Ibid.*, p. 16.
59. *Ibid.*, p. 12. This paragraph was directly quoted.
60. *Ibid.*, This paragraph was directly quoted.
61. *Ibid.*, This paragraph was directly quoted.
62. Reebok Press Release (July 1, 2002).
63. www.WSNR.com/apps/art.
64. *Ibid.*
65. *Ibid.*
66. www.reebok.com/Reebok/US/Humanrights/text-only. The above five paragraphs were directly quoted.
67. www.reebok.com/US/Reebok/InvestorRelations/PressRelease.
68. Form 10-K, pp. 24–26. This entire section was directly quoted.

case 18

U.S. Major Home Appliance Industry in 2002: Competition Becomes Global

J. David Hunger

The U.S. major home appliance industry in 2002 was an example of a very successful industry. Contrasted with the U.S. automobile and consumer electronics industries, U.S. major appliance manufacturers had been able to successfully ward off strong foreign competition and were actually on the offensive internationally. The industry had been very successful in keeping prices low and in improving the value of its products. Compared to 1982, major home appliance prices had increased more slowly than the increase in U.S. earnings and the Consumer Price Index. Thus, the average American consumer in 2002 could earn a new appliance in fewer hours on the job than a half-century ago. From 1991 to 2001, after adjusting for inflation, retail prices actually declined—washers fell 12.7%, dryers dropped 9.8%, cooking equipment dropped .4%, and refrigerators/freezers fell 9.2%.[1] In addition, the energy efficiency of the most common major appliances had increased every year since 1972. Sales had also been increasing. More appliances were made and sold in the United States in 2001 than in any preceding year (see **Exhibit 1** for U.S. shipments of major home appliances). The Association of Home Appliance Manufacturers were predicting slight increases during 2002 in each category of "white goods"—refrigerators, freezers, washing machines, dryers, ranges, microwave ovens, and dishwashers.[2]

The major home appliance industry faced some significant threats as well as opportunities. After more than 50 years of rising sales, both in units and dollars, the U.S. and Canadian market had reached maturity. (Annual unit shipments of appliances in the United States were a little over 70 million compared to 4.3 million units in Canada.) Aside from some normal short-term fluctuations, future unit sales were expected to grow only 1.9% annually from 2000 to 2005 in the U.S. and Canadian markets. Operating margins had been dropping as appliance manufacturers were forced to keep prices low to be competitive even though costs kept increasing. The situation was the same in Western Europe, a market 25% larger than the U.S. major home appliance market, where unit sales were expected to grow only 1.7% annually during the same period. Markets in Asia, Eastern Europe, and Latin America had become more important to world trade as more countries changed to a free market economy. Industry analysts expected appliance markets in these areas to grow at a rate of 5%–6% annually between 2000 and 2005.[3] The industry was under pressure from governments around the world to make environmentally safe products plus significantly improve appliance efficiency in terms of energy usage and water consumption.

This case was prepared by Professor J. David Hunger of Iowa State University for SMBP-9th edition. All rights reserved by the author. Copyright © 2002 by J. David Hunger.

Exhibit 1

U.S. Manufacturers' Unit Shipments of Major Home Appliances[1]
(Amounts in thousands)

PRODUCT	2001	2000	1999	1995	1990	1980
Compactors	117	118	115	98	185	235
Dishwashers, built-in	5,478	5,663	5,542	4,327	3,419	2,354
Dishwashers, portable	149	164	170	226	217	384
Disposers	5,547	5,485	5,369	4,519	4,137	2,962
Dryers, compact	NA	NA	170[2]	160[2]	275	207
Dryers, electric	5,117	5,095	4,865	4,020	3,318	2,287
Dryers, gas	1,384	1,480	1,443	1,205	1,002	682
Freezers, chest	1,285	1,075	1,058	934	723	963
Freezers, compact[2]	490	473	433	357	351	310
Freezers, upright	930	888	929	757	573	789
Microwave ovens, in ranges[2]	82	82	81	80	146	265
Microwave ovens, countertop	10,220	10,114	9,264	7,760	8,193	3,320
Microwave/convection ovens	200	196	155	115	303	N/A
Microwave ovens, over range	2,946	2,334	2,162	1,100	780	N/A
Range/oven hoods	3,200	3,150	3,000	2,740	2,450	2,400
Ranges, electric, built-in	723	706	704	619	631	555
Ranges, electric, freestanding	3,842	3,826	3,785	3,004	2,358	1,975
Ranges, electric, surface cooking	498	494	493	425	455	N/A
Ranges, electric, glass/ceramic[2]	2,314	2,057	2,035	955	85	155
Ranges, gas, built-in	71	70	72	86	106	102
Ranges, gas, freestanding	2,850	2,729	2,698	2,490	2,061	1,437
Ranges, gas, surface cooking	384	377	367	278	262	N/A
Ranges, gas, glass/ceramic[2]	58	34	—	—	—	—
Refrigerators, built-in	137	133	116	83	—	N/A
Refrigerators, compact[2]	1,355	1,530	1,497	1,032	932	543
Refrigerators, standard	9,305	9,217	9,099	8,670	7,101	5,124
Washers, automatic	7,362	7,495	7,313	6,901	6,192	4,426
Washers, compact	N/A	N/A	195[2]	200[2]	344	266
Water heaters, electric	4,333	4,257	4,281	3,917	3,226	2,451
Water heaters, gas	4,931	4,907	4,934	4,453	3,906	2,818
Water softeners	935	989	951	718	574	N/A
Total	73,300	72,492	70,381	60,476	53,726	37,010

Notes:
1. Exports not included.
2. Figures not included in industry total.

Source: "Statistical Review," *Appliance*, April, 2002, 1998, and 1990, p. 50.

Development of the U.S. Major Home Appliance Industry

In 1945, there were approximately 300 U.S. major appliance manufacturers in the United States. By 2002, however, the "big four"—Whirlpool, General Electric, Maytag, and AB Electrolux—controlled 99% of the U.S. market. Although the German-based Bosch-Siemens entered the U.S. major home appliance industry in 1996, it had yet to earn a significant market share in any appliance category. The consolidation of the industry over the period was a result of fierce domestic competition. Emphasis on quality and durability coupled with strong price competition drove the surviving firms to increased efficiencies and a strong concern for customer satisfaction.

INDUSTRY HISTORY

All of the major U.S. automobile firms except Chrysler had participated at one time in the major home appliance industry. Giants in the consumer electronics industry had also been involved heavily in appliances. Some of the major auto, electronics, and diversified companies active at one time in the appliance industry were General Motors (Frigidaire), Ford (Philco), American Motors (Kelvinator), Studebacker (Franklin), Bendix, International Harvester, General Electric, RCA, Emerson Electric, Westinghouse, McGraw Edison, Rockwell, United Technologies, Raytheon, Litton, Borg-Warner, and Dart & Kraft. Only General Electric and Emerson Electric remained in major home appliances in 2002. Emerson Electric continued through its In-Sink-Erator line of disposers as well as being a major supplier of electronic parts (primarily motors) to the remaining appliance makers. Most of the other firms divested their appliance business units, many of which were acquired by White Consolidated Industries, which itself was acquired by the Swedish firm AB Electrolux in 1986 and subsequently renamed Frigidaire as its North American Division.

Prior to World War II, most appliance manufacturers produced a limited line of appliances derived from one successful product. General Electric made refrigerators. Maytag focused on washing machines. Hotpoint produced electric ranges. Each offered variations of its basic product, but not until 1945 did firms begin to offer full lines of various appliances. By 1955, the major appliance industry began experiencing overcapacity, leading to mergers and acquisitions and a proliferation of national and private brands.

The industry almost doubled in size during the 1960s, as sales of several products grew rapidly. Dishwasher unit sales almost quadrupled. Unit sales of clothes dryers more than tripled. Product reliability improved even though real prices (adjusted for inflation) declined around 10%.

Although the 1970s were a time of high inflation and high interest rates, the major home appliance industry continued to increase its unit sales. Profit margins were squeezed even more, and the industry continued to consolidate around fewer firms. Although antitrust considerations prevented GE and Whirlpool from acquiring other appliance units, White was able to buy the troubled appliance divisions of all the automobile manufacturers, along with Westinghouse's, as they were put up for sale.

The market continued to expand in the 1980s, thanks partially to the acceptance by the U.S. consumer of the microwave oven. By the 1990s, U.S. appliance manufacturers offered a full range of products even if they did not make the item themselves. A company would fill the gaps in its line by putting its own brand name on products it purchased from another manufacturer. For example, Whirlpool made trash compactors for Frigidaire (AB Electrolux), In-Sink-Erator (Emerson Electric), Jenn-Air, Magic Chef (Maytag), and Sears. Caloric (Amana) not only made gas ranges for its in-house Amana brand, but also for Whirlpool. General Electric made some microwave ovens for Caloric (Amana), Jenn-Air (Maytag), Magic Chef (Maytag), and its own Hotpoint and RCA brands.

PRODUCT AND PROCESS DESIGN

Innovations in the industry tended to be of four types: (1) new products that expanded the appliance market, (2) new technologies and designs to increase efficiency and effectiveness, (3) new customer-oriented features, and (4) process improvements to reduce manufacturing costs.

New products historically drove the growth of major home appliances. The washing machine and the refrigerator were the founding products of the industry. A survey by the Harris Corporation in 1999 revealed that the top technological achievements of the 20th century were the computer and television, followed closely by the refrigerator, microwave oven, and washing machine.[4] New home appliances that had strongly increased industry unit sales were dishwashers in the 1960s and microwave ovens in the 1980s.

New technologies and designs were being introduced into major home appliances. Due to governmental pressure, appliance manufacturers were introducing energy-efficient versions of refrigerators and washing machines at the dawn of the 21st century. Examples of these were Maytag's Neptune front-loading clothes washer and Whirlpool's top-loading Calypso washing machine. Both of these used less energy and water and resulted in more effective cleaning action than traditional washers. Research was being conducted to replace current technologies with more efficient ones. One example was the use of microwave energy in clothes dryers so that clothes could be dried faster, at a lower temperature (thus less shrinkage and damage), with less energy use than a conventional dryer. Unfortunately, the technology needed further development before it could be marketed: Microwaves had a tendency to heat metal objects to such a point that they caused fabric damage. In another example, researchers at Iowa State University, in cooperation with Astronautics Corporation of America, were developing a refrigerator using magnets. The cooling apparatus consisted of a wheel containing gadolinium powder moving through a high-powered, rare earth permanent magnet. The result was a virtually silent, vibration-free refrigerator instead of the traditional ozone-depleting refrigerant and noisy, energy-consuming compressor.[5] Other researchers were experimenting with sound waves to clean clothes.

Customer-oriented features included the self-cleaning oven, pilot-less gas range, automatic ice-cube-making refrigerator, warming drawers in ranges, and dishwashers with half-load washing capability. In most cases, features were introduced on top-of-the-line models and made available on lower-priced models later. Manufacturers' own brands usually had the newest and most elaborate features, followed by national retailers such as Sears Roebuck, whose offerings usually copied the most successful features from the previous year. In this competitive industry, aside from patented features, no one producer could successfully keep a new innovation to itself for more than a year.

In 2002, three trends continued to be evident in customer-oriented features. First, design aesthetics were becoming more important in product development and marketing. Appliances were being given a more prominent place in the home. For example, washers and dryers were increasingly being placed not in the basement, but on the main floor. As a result, the washer and dryer were expected to be quieter and more aesthetically pleasing, complementing the decor of the room in which they resided. As the kitchen evolved into a hub of household activity, the refrigerator and range began to take on a greater importance in the household. European visual product design was having a strong impact on appliance design worldwide. Stainless steel was used like a color in high-end appliances to connote quality—especially to those people desiring ranges similar to those used by professional cooks. Refrigerators could be built in to various parts of the kitchen as drawers for distinct uses instead of as a large box with a door.

Second, manufacturers were introducing "smart" appliances with increasingly sophisticated electronic controls and self-diagnostic features. The Japanese firms Matsushita, Hitachi, Toshiba, and Mitsubishi had pioneered the use of "fuzzy logic" computer software in the 1980s to replace the many selector switches on an appliance with one start button. By 2000 all of the U.S. major home appliance manufacturers were using fuzzy logic to some extent in the making and marketing of their products. Whirlpool's "Sixth Sense" oven could determine the necessary settings for reheating or defrosting food, with no guesswork from the cook. The user simply pressed a single button for defrost—the oven then calculated on its own the correct time and power output. By 2002, these "smart appliances" were being connected to the Internet. For example, Haier, a Chinese appliance maker, demonstrated Internet-enabled refrigerators, washing machines, dishwashers, microwave ovens, air conditioners, and water heaters at the 2001 Domotechnica trade show in Cologne, Germany. These appliances could call for service, download programs, contact security providers in case of gas leaks or fire, pay utility bills, and be programmed remotely to start and stop when needed.

Third, there was an increasing global emphasis on environmentally safe products, such as the use of CFC-free refrigerant, and on greater efficiency in the use of water and energy. Since 1980, U.S. appliance makers have invested more than $1 billion to improve refrigerator energy efficiency. For the average home appliance customer, the appliance would cost less to operate and be better for the environment.

Process improvements for more efficient manufacturing of current products (compared to new-product development) tended to dominate research and development efforts in the U.S. major home appliance industry. Although modern appliances were much more effective and efficient, a refrigerator or a stove in 2002 still looked and acted very much the same as it did in the 1950s. It was built in a far different manner, however. The appliance industry historically had been characterized by low intensity in product research and development because of intense cost competition and demand for higher reliability. Until the late 1990s, the basis for effective competition had been producing the fewest basic components necessary in the most efficient plants. Although individual designs might vary, the components inside the appliances were becoming more universal and were being produced in highly automated plants, using computer-integrated manufacturing processes. Examples of this emphasis on product simplification were Maytag's "Dependable Drive" and Whirlpool's frame fabrication for its "Eye Level" ranges. Maytag's washer transmission was designed to have 40.6% fewer parts than the transmission it replaced. Fewer parts meant simplified manufacturing and less chance of breakdown. The result was lower manufacturing costs and higher product quality.

Most industry analysts agreed that continual process improvements had kept U.S. major home appliance manufacturers dominant in their market and competitive globally. The emphasis on quality and durability, coupled with a reluctance to make major design changes simply for the sake of change, resulted in products with long average life expectancy. The average useful life of a refrigerator or range was 15 to 20 years and those of washers, dryers, and dishwashers were around 12 to 14 years. (see **Exhibit 2** for life expectancy by appliance.)

Exhibit 2

Average Life Expectancy of Major Home Appliances

Appliance	Life Expectancy (Years)
Compactor	10
Dishwasher	12
Disposer	10
Dryer, electric	14
Dryer, gas	13
Freezer	16
Microwave oven	11
Range, electric	15
Range, gas	21
Range hood	14
Refrigerator, compact	7
Refrigerator, standard	15
Washer	12
Vacuum cleaner	8
Shampooer/steam cleaner	11
Water heater, electric	11
Water heater, gas	9

Source: "20th Annual Portrait of the U.S. Appliance Industry," *Appliance*, September 2001, Special Insert, pp. 5–6.

MANUFACTURING AND PURCHASING

Although many manufacturing operations took place in an appliance factory, much of the process focused on proper preparation of the metal frame within which the washing, drying, or cooking components and elements would be attached. Consequently, appliance manufacturers could be characterized as "metal benders" who fabricated different shapes of metal boxes out of long coils of metal. As a result, the U.S. major home appliance industry purchased 22% of total coated-coil metals, second only to the building and construction industry.[6] Sophisticated machines would form and even weld the frames, and automated assembly lines and robots would add porcelain to protect the metal and add color to the finish. People were usually still needed to install the internal components in the frame and to wire sophisticated electronic controls. Quality control was often a combination of electronic diagnostics and personal inspection by employees.

Manufacturing costs were generally in the range of 65%–75% of total operating costs. Although direct labor costs were still an important part of the cost of completed goods (around 10%), most companies were carefully examining material costs, general administration, and overhead for cost reduction. Traditionally, the optimal size of an assembly plant was considered to be an annual capacity of 500,000 units for refrigerators, ranges, washers, dryers, and dishwashers. Even though production costs were believed to be 10%–40% higher in smaller-sized plants, the use of robots suggested that the optimal plant could be even smaller than previously believed.[7]

The trend continued toward "dedicated" manufacturing facilities combining product line production in fewer larger plants to gain economies of scale. Although a plant's production line dedicated to the production of washing machines could be adjusted to make many different models, it could still only be used to make washing machines. Each product category required its own specialized manufacturing equipment.

All of the major home appliance manufacturers were heavily engaged in renovating and building production facilities to gain economies of scale, improve quality, and reduce labor and materials costs. For example, Electrolux's Frigidaire division in the United States spent over $600 million upgrading its current factories and building new refrigerator and dishwasher plants. It then invested $100 million each in its Anderson, South Carolina, and Greenville, Michigan, plants in 2001 to manufacturer its new Next Generation line of refrigerators. The General Electric Appliance (GEA) division spent around $1 billion over a four-year period (1994–1998) in product development and capital equipment (a 50% increase over previous spending levels) to upgrade its 40-year-old "appliance park" in Louisville, Kentucky. It then invested over $800 million during 2001 and 2002 in its 42 manufacturing plants in Mexico.[8] To ensure global quality standards, appliance manufactures have been going through the process of International Organization for Standards (ISO) 9000 series certification.

Key materials purchased by the U.S. appliance industry were steel (primarily in sheets and coils), plastics, coatings (paint and porcelain), motors, glass, insulation, wiring, and fasteners. By weight, major appliances consisted of about 75% steel. Sales to the major home appliance industry of steel and aluminum together accounted for 10% of total industry sales.[9]

As the major home appliance industry had consolidated, so too had its suppliers. A. O. Smith, best known in the United States for its water heaters, acquired MagneTek's worldwide electric motor operations in 1999. Siebe and BTR merged in 2000 to form Invensys Appliance Controls and Invensys Climate Controls. Siebe had already purchased Eaton Corporation's worldwide controls business, Robertshaw Controls, Paragon Electric, and Ranco. The purchasing function and relationship with suppliers had changed considerably from the 1980s as more companies used fewer suppliers and more long-term contracts to improve quality and ensure JIT (just-in-time) delivery.

The 2000 update to the ISO 9000 series pushed appliance manufacturers to further integrate their supply chains to ensure total quality management. Along with its increasing global orientation, Whirlpool was putting emphasis on working with global suppliers. Appliance companies used certification programs to ensure that their smaller supplier bases were able to supply both the needed quantity and quality of materials, parts, and subassemblies when they were needed. Full-line, full-service suppliers had an advantage over one-dimensional suppliers. Appliance makers continued to put pressure on their suppliers to institute cost-saving productivity improvements. On the other hand, they were much more willing to involve suppliers earlier in the design stage of a product or process improvement.

Alliances between appliance makers and their suppliers were one way to speed up the application of new technology into new products and processes. For example, Maytag Corporation was approached by Honeywell, one of its suppliers, which offered its expertise in fuzzy logic technology—a technology Maytag did not have at that time. The resulting partnership in product development resulted in Maytag's new IntelliSense dishwasher. Unlike previous dishwashers, which had to be set by the user, Maytag's fuzzy logic dishwasher automatically selected the proper cycle to get the dishes clean based on a series of factors, including the amount of dirt and presence of detergent.

Although most U.S. appliance makers used both the Internet and extranets to communicate with their suppliers and distributors, there was no overall electronic marketplace between appliance makers and their suppliers (as there was in the auto industry) currently in existence in the United States.

MARKETING AND DISTRIBUTION CHANNELS

Due to relatively high levels of saturation in the United States, the market for major home appliances was driven primarily by the demand for replacements. Washers, ranges, refrigerators, and even microwave ovens were in more than 90% of U.S. households. (see **Exhibit 3** for saturation by product category.) Generally speaking, replacements accounted for 75% of sales, new housing for 20%, and new household formation for about 5% of sales of major home appliances. Replacement demand was usually driven by existing housing turnover, remodeling,

Exhibit 3

Saturation of Selected Major Home Appliances in the United States, Western Europe, and Japan[1]
(Percentage of households with at least one of a particular appliance)

Appliance	United States	Western Europe	Japan
Compactor	5	N/A	N/A
Cooker	N/A	95	N/A
Dishwasher	59	39	N/A
Disposer	46	N/A	N/A
Dryer	59 (E), 20 (G)	28	22
Freezer	44	51	N/A
Microwave oven	96	60	N/A
Range	60 (E), 40 (G)	N/A	N/A
Refrigerator	99	98	98
Vacuum cleaner	99	N/A	98
Washer	93	94	99

Note:
1. (E) = electric, (G) = natural gas.

Source: "24th Annual Portrait of the U.S. Appliance Industry," *Appliance*, September 2001, Special Insert; "Portrait of the European Appliance Industry," *Appliance*, November 2001, p. 50; "Portrait of the Japanese Appliance Industry," *Appliance*, March 2002, p. 50.

changes in living arrangement trends, introduction of new features, and price levels in the economy. Although each new house had the potential to add four to six new appliances, the sale of an existing house also had an impact. According to J. Richard Stonesifer, President and CEO of GE Appliances, "About 4 million existing homes are sold each year, and approximately one new appliance is sold for every existing home that changes hands."[10] The National Kitchen and Bath Association estimated that about $4 billion of the total $25 billion spent annually on kitchen remodeling was for home appliances.

Both the new housing and remodeling markets currently tended to emphasize more upscale appliances in contrast to the previous tendency for builders to economize by buying the cheapest national brand appliances. A study by Simmons Market Research Bureau for *New Home* magazine revealed that more than $13 billion was spent annually by new-home owners on household goods, especially appliances. In order of importance, the appliances typically bought within the first 3 months of owning a new home were the refrigerator, washer, dryer, microwave oven, vacuum cleaner, dishwasher, coffeemaker, and range.[11] This phenomenon provided sales opportunities for well-positioned appliance makers because brand loyalty in the appliance industry was only 35%.[12]

Changes in U.S. demographics favored the highly profitable, high-end, high-profile segment of the business. This trend was detrimental to the mass-market business, which emphasized cost over features. The aging of the baby boomers and the increase of two-income families had increased the upscale market, which demanded more style and costly features. According to Ken Gronbach, president of KGA Advertising, appliance manufacturers should continue to court the 80 million aging baby boomers because generation X contains only 50 million people. "[Baby boomers] want the high-end appliances and that's why companies that cater to that generation are doing well."[13] Appliance manufacturers responded by expanding product lines that emphasized quality and features. Those brands most identified in customers' minds with high product quality, such as Maytag and KitchenAid, were achieving good sales. (See **Exhibit 4** for ratings of brands by perceived quality.) Gronbach further proposed that the best way for appliance makers to appeal to the younger generation X was to offer new and unique products. "If your product is neither unique nor new it will be sold only on price because the demand will be pale compared to the supply."

Exporting was reasonably strong for high-quality U.S.-made refrigerators, vacuum cleaners, and laundry appliances but was much less than the importing of microwave ovens from Asia. For a number of reasons, exporting was not a significant factor for the U.S. major home appliance industry. The weight of most of these appliances meant high transportation costs, which translated into higher prices to the consumer. In addition, U.S.-made major appliances tended to be fairly large, whereas European and Asian markets preferred smaller appliances. As a result, most people around the world tended to buy appliances made locally, if they were available. Thus, those appliance companies wanting a significant presence in other parts of the world were either acquiring local companies, engaging in joint ventures, or building new manufacturing facilities in those regions in order to have a local presence.

There were two major distribution channels for major home appliances in the United States: contract and retail. A third, but less important, distribution channel was the commercial market, comprising laundromats and institutions.

Contract sales were made to large home builders and to other appliance manufacturers. Direct sales accounted for around 80% of contract sales. Firms sold appliances to the contract segment both directly to the large builders and indirectly through local builder suppliers. Since builders were very cost conscious, they liked to buy at the middle to low end of a well-known appliance brand. Consequently, appliance manufacturers with strong offerings in this range, such as General Electric, Whirlpool, and Frigidaire, tended to do very well in this market. (See **Exhibit 5** for appliance sales by market segment.) In contrast, companies such as Maytag (except for the lower-priced Magic Chef brand) and Bosch-Siemens, which tradition-

Exhibit 4

Ratings of Brands in Terms of Consumer Perception of Quality According to U.S. Dealers
(Percentage of responses by 300 appliance dealers from excellent to poor quality)

Appliance Brand[1]	Dealers Stocking Brand (%)	Excellent (%)	Poor (%)
Maytag	50	77	1
KitchenAid (Whirlpool)	45	76	2
Jenn-Air (Maytag)	45	66	3
Whirlpool	59	41	2
Amana (Maytag)	38	32	4
Profile (GE)	28	39	13
GE	44	24	3
Monogram (GE)	4	36	17
Frigidaire (Electrolux)	45	13	7
Magic Chef (Maytag)	36	8	10
RCA (GE)	28	6	10
Speed Queen [inactive]	8	6	1
Tappan (Electrolux)	29	5	15
White-Westinghouse (Electrolux)	28	6	15
Hotpoint (GE)	22	4	13
Gibson (Electrolux)	18	2	22
Roper (Whirlpool)	34	1	19
Kelvinator (Electrolux)	14	5	29
Caloric [inactive]	11	3	26
Admiral (Maytag)	7	0	30

Note:
1. Owners of brands shown in parentheses.

Source: J. Jancsurak, "What Retailers and Consumers Want Most," *Appliance Manufacturer*, May 1998, pp. 39–40.

ally emphasized high-end products, sold little to builders. Whirlpool and GE designed whole kitchen concepts and sold the entire package—including their appliances—to builders. To further its advantage, Whirlpool opened a 35,000-square-foot customer center at its Benton Harbor, Michigan, headquarters in 1993 to demonstrate its offerings to retailers and contractors—the first such customer center in the industry.

Retail sales in the United States were made to three major kinds of outlets: (1) national chain stores and mass merchandisers; (2) department, furniture, and discount stores; and (3) independent appliance dealers.

Exhibit 5

Revenue by Market Segment of Major White Goods Producers
(Dollar amounts in billions)

Appliance Manufacturer	Discount Segment	Middle Segment	Premium Segment	Super Premium Segment
Electrolux	$1.7	$2.9	1.3	—
Whirlpool	0.4	5.3	0.8	—
General Electric	0.2	1.1	1.4	—
Bosch-Siemens	—	0.5	3.7	$0.9
Maytag	—	0.3	2.5	0.1

Source: Goldman Sachs, "Brand Challenge," *The Economist*, April 6, 2002, p. 54.

National chain stores and mass merchandisers usually sold the most well-known brands and private brands promoted by the retailers. For example, Whirlpool has traditionally been the sole supplier of Sears and Kenmore washers and dryers to Sears Roebuck. Magic Chef sold similar private brand appliances to Montgomery Ward until Ward's bankruptcy in 1998. Almost half of U.S. white goods were traditionally sold through this mass merchandiser channel. Sears Roebuck has been so strong in major home appliance sales that it alone sold nearly two out of every five major appliances sold in the United States.[14]

Department stores, furniture stores, and discount stores were another important channel for major appliances, selling about 25% of white goods sold in the United States. These stores usually purchased well-known brands to offer their customers. As department stores tended to alter their product offerings to more soft goods (clothing items) and fewer hard goods (furniture and appliances) during the 1980s, discount stores became more important in major home appliance sales. Their concern with price, however, put even more pressure on manufacturers to sell in large quantity at low price. Lowe's, Home Depot, and Best Buy were becoming important outlets for appliances. Home Depot, for example, sold appliances not only from in-stock products, but also by using Internet-connected kiosks on the sales floor. Although Circuit City decided in 2001 to no longer sell major appliances, Wal-Mart's decision to offer selected GE appliances in a low-cost format suggests that appliance sales through discount and home improvement stores should continue to increase.

Independent appliance dealers had traditionally been an important retail outlet for white goods. Around 25% of major home appliances continued to be sold through this channel, although the amount was steadily declining. Many locally owned stores were being replaced by national chains and discount stores. By 2000, the so-called "power retailers"—Sears, national chains, and discount stores—were selling over 60% of all retail appliances in the United States.

Commercial sales were through an additional distribution channel. Never as important to manufacturers as the contract and retail channels, this channel nevertheless provided an important set of customers for sales of washing machines and dryers. Laundromats and institutions, such as colleges for their dormitories, typically bought the most durable appliances made for the home market. Manufacturers simply added coin meters to the tops of the washers and dryers destined for use in these commercial or public establishments. Although these home laundry appliances adapted for the commercial market comprised over 50% of sales to this channel, there were some indications that this market might be moving to commercial washers built to last two to three times longer than would a home washer used commercially. With regard to the makers of freezers, refrigerators, and ranges for use in business establishments such as restaurants, these were usually a different group of U.S. manufacturers (for example, Welbilt, Traulsen, Hobart, and Glenco) from those manufacturing home appliances. Contrasted with home appliances, commercial appliances were typically larger and more durable, with fewer convenience features. They were sold through different marketing channels. In addition, the commercial market was far smaller than the home market. Unit shipments of commercial major appliances in 2001 totaled only 2.6 million in the United States, compared to 73.3 million major home appliances.

By 2002, all of the major U.S. appliance makers used their own Web sites to market their products and provide consumer-related information via whirlpool.com, maytag.com, ge.com, and frigidaire.com. The independent applianceadvisor.com provided industry information regarding individual brands for potential buyers, with links to manufacturer Web sites. Maytag introduced online appliance shopping in 2001 to enable consumers to purchase Maytag appliances online from local dealers. Sears was said to have the busiest appliance e-commerce site at sears.com.[15] In 2001, Bosch Siemens Hausgerate, AB Electrolux, and Whirlpool formed a business-to-business (B2B) electronics marketplace for European household appliance makers, distributors, and retailers called *Tradeplace*. For the convenience of the dealers, *Tradeplace* provided one common access point connected to the manufacturers' existing portals without having to log in every time.[16] BuildNet, Inc., offered Internet commerce for homebuilders in the United States. General Electric, the top supplier of major home appliances to builders, owned a part of BuildNet and sold its appliances through that Web site.[17] Nevertheless, a true B2B electronic marketplace similar to *Tradeplace* had yet to be established in North America.

Appliance manufacturing shifted in the 1990s from its primary emphasis on quality and reliability to speed and agility. (See **Exhibit 6** for reliability data by appliance brand.) This

Exhibit 6
Reliability Ratings of Selected Major U.S. Home Appliance Brands
(Listed in order of frequency, from fewest to most repairs by percentage of appliances purchased)

Washers (Top Loaders)	Dryers (Electric)	Dryers (Gas)
Roper (7%)	Whirlpool (6%)	Whirlpool (7%)
Whirlpool—tied for 2nd	Roper	Kenmore
Maytag—tied for 2nd	Maytag	KitchenAid
Kenmore	Kenmore	Maytag
Hotpoint—tied for 5th	KitchenAid	Amana
Frigidaire—tied for 5th	Hotpoint	General Electric (10%)
Amana	Amana	
KitchenAid	Frigidaire	
General Electric (14%)	General Electric (9%)	

Refrigerator (Top Freezer/No Ice Maker or Dispenser)	Refrigerator (Top Freezer/Ice Maker Only)	Refrigerator (Side-By Side/Icemaker & Dispenser)
Hotpoint—tied for 1st (4%)	Kenmore (7%)	Whirlpool (9%)
KitchenAid—tied for 1st	Whirlpool	KitchenAid
Whirlpool—tied for 1st	KitchenAid	Kenmore
Kenmore—tied for 1st	General Electric	General Electric
General Electric	Amana	Amana
Amana: bottom freezer	Maytag	Frigidaire
Maytag	Amana: bottom freezer	Maytag (33%)
Frigidaire	Frigidaire	
Amana (7%)	Sub-Zero: built-in bottom freezer (26%)	

Ranges (Gas)	Ranges (Electric)	Dishwashers
General Electric—tied for 1st (8%)	General Electric (5%)	Whirlpool (7%)
Hotpoint—tie for 1st	Hotpoint	Kenmore
Kenmore	Kenmore—tied for 3rd	KitchenAid
Frigidaire	Whirlpool—tied for 3rd	Maytag
Whirlpool	Frigidaire	Hotpoint
Tappan	Magic Chef—tied for 6th	GE Monogram—tied for 6th
Magic Chef	Amana—tied for 6th	Bosch—tied for 6th
KitchenAid	Maytag	Magic Chef
Maytag	KitchenAid	General Electric
Jenn-Air	Jenn-Air (15%)	Jenn-Air—tied for 10th
Amana (21%)		Amana—tied for 10th
		Asko—tied for last
		Frigidaire—tied for last (18%)

Sources: "Washing Machines and Dryers," *Consumer Reports*, July 2002, pp. 42, 44; "Refrigerators," *Consumer Reports*, January 2002, p. 47; "Ranges," *Consumer Reports*, February 2002, p. 34.

meant that manufacturers worked to improve their use of logistics in order to provide better service to their distributors. Concepts similar to JIT had been applied in the 1990s to distribution and marketing. For example, Whirlpool introduced "Quality Express" in 1992 as part of its revamped distribution system. Quality Express used dedicated trucks, personnel, and warehousing to deliver Whirlpool appliances to 90% of all dealer and builder customers within 24 hours and 100% within 48 hours. As part of the service, drivers delivering product unloaded units from the truck and put them where the customer wanted them. This service even included uncrating, customizing, and installation if desired. Other appliance companies soon followed Whirlpool's lead. A 1998 survey of 2,000 North American appliance dealers ranked appliance manufacturers in terms of how well they serviced retailers:

1. Whirlpool Corporation
2. Maytag Corporation
3. GEA
4. Frigidaire (AB Electrolux's U.S. appliance unit)
5. Goodman (Amana; subsequently sold to Maytag)[18]

In the early years of the 21st century, U.S. appliance manufacturers were moving toward a stronger product-market orientation. Appliance makers had long known that their emphasis on quality and reliability meant that people replaced their appliances only when the appliances wore out or when they changed houses.

By 2002, a survey of 500 residential U.S. households found that energy efficiency had replaced price as the top appliance-purchasing consideration. Roughly 25% of the population said that they would be willing to pay 15%–25% above the standard price for higher-energy-saving appliances.[19]

Uniquely differentiated products, such as Maytag's Neptune washer, Gemini double oven, and Accellis range, Whirlpool's Calypso washer, and GE's Advantium oven, were successfully motivating people to replace their current working appliances. To continue to compete successfully in the 21st century, it had become essential to invest heavily in product development (not just process R&D) and in more sophisticated marketing. This meant that appliance makers could no longer rely on their traditional engineering orientation to create a competitive advantage. When the Wolf Appliance Company, an affiliate of Sub-Zero Freezer Company (a niche manufacturer of premium, built-in refrigerators and freezers), launched a new upscale built-in cooking appliance line, it conducted significant market research, using focus groups and conjoint analysis, to determine which combination of attributes and features would be most attractive to a specific market segment. To build its competence in marketing, Whirlpool had begun to hire brand management people from consumer products firms such as Kraft and General Foods to oversee the development of new brands.

ENVIRONMENTAL ISSUES AND GOVERNMENT REGULATION

Home appliance manufacturers around the world faced increasing regulation regarding their products. One example was refrigerators and freezers. On the one hand, governments were requiring less use of refrigerants, which might cause global warming. On the other hand, the U.S. Department of Energy (DOE) was requiring energy conservation improvements for refrigerators and freezers. These appliances had traditionally been notorious energy hogs—consuming about 20% of the electricity used in the American home. The appliance industry had worked significantly to make products more energy efficient over the decades. For example, from 1972 to 1990 for a typical top-mount, automatic-defrost refrigerator (the most popular U.S. refrigerator), the amount of energy consumed declined from 1,986 kilowatt hours per year to 950 kilowatt hours per year (kwh/yr). Chest freezer energy consumption dropped during the same period, from 1,268 kwh/yr to 575 kwh/yr. Nevertheless, the U.S. DOE standard in effect on July 1, 2001, required that the amount of energy used by a typical refrigerator equal no more than that used by a 55-watt light bulb.[20] According to a 2001 DOE minimum energy efficiency standard, U.S. clothes washers manufactured in 2004 were to be 22% more efficient than those in 2001 and 35% more efficient by 2007.[21] Units imported into the United States were also required to meet the regulations.

Another issue facing appliance manufacturers was the presence of widely different standards for major appliances in countries around the world. The emergence of a true global market in major home appliances required the development of common world standards. There were at least three categories of standards: safety/environmental, energy efficiency, and testing procedures. Existing standards had been drafted by such bodies as the British Standards Institute (BSI) in the United Kingdom, Japanese Industrial Standards Committee (JISC), AFNOR in France, DIN in Germany, CSA in Canada, and UL in the United States. These standards had traditionally created entry barriers that served to fragment the major home appliance industry by country. The International Electotechnical Commission (IEC) standards were created to harmonize standards in the European Union and eventually to serve as worldwide standards, with some national deviations to satisfy specific needs. In addition, the International Organization for Standardization (ISO) was tasked with preparing and publishing international standards. These standards provided a foundation for regional associations to build upon. CANENA, the Council for Harmonization of Electrotechnical Standards of the Nations of the Americas, was created in 1992 to further coordinate the harmonization of standards in North and South America. Efforts were also under way in Asia to harmonize standards. By 2002, it appeared that the industry was working toward achieving international standards with some allowance being made for regional differences.[22]

With the dawn of the 21st century, major home appliance manufacturers faced a new set of certification standards beyond the ISO 9000 series. While ISO 9000 standards dealt with quality management systems, ISO 14001 covered environmental management systems (EMS) and addressed the need for one international environmental management standard. Some international markets, such as the European Union, could require certification as a prerequisite for doing business.

Products

Major home appliances, or white goods, as they were commonly called, were generally classified as laundry (washers and dryers), refrigeration (refrigerators and freezers), cooking (ranges and ovens), and other (dishwashers, disposals, and trash compactors) appliances. (See **Exhibit 7** for U.S. market share by appliance category.) In addition to making white goods, some appliance manufacturers also made and sold floor care appliances (Maytag), room air conditioners (Whirlpool and Electrolux), or lawn and garden equipment (Electrolux). The majority of U.S. heating and cooling appliances (water heaters, furnaces, and central air conditioning) were made by other manufacturers, such as Rheem, A.O. Smith, Lennox, and Carrier.

Competitors

Four major home appliance manufacturers controlled around 99% of the U.S. market for white goods. In order of 2001 market share, Whirlpool led, with 39.2%; followed by General Electric, with 23.2%; Maytag, with 21.6%; and A.B. Electrolux (Frigidaire), with 15.0%. The remaining 1% belonged to the foreign firms of Bosch-Siemens and Haier, which had recently begun to produce in North America, and to various manufacturers of a single type or category

Exhibit 7

U.S. Major Home Appliance Market Shares by Category
(By percentage of total U.S. sales)

Appliance	2001	1996[1]	Appliance	2001	1996[1]
Compactor			**Microwave oven**		
Whirlpool	88%	90%	Samsung	26	18
Broan NuTone	11	10	Sharp	24	29
Others	1	0	LG Electronics (Goldstar)	11.5	12
Dishwasher			Matsushita	10	15
Whirlpool	48	37	Whirlpool	7.5	5
Maytag	21	19	Sanyo Fisher	6.5	7
GEA	19	40	Daewoo	4.5	3
Electrolux	11	4	Maytag	3	3
Others	1	0	Others	7	8
Disposer			**Range Hood**		
In-Sink-Erator	75	70	Broan NuTone	85	65
Anaheim/Watertown/WKing	25	30	Watertown Metal Prod.	6	11
Dryer			Vent Line	5	—
Whirlpool	50.5	54	Others	4	5
Maytag	24	20	**Range (gas)**		
GEA	19	19	GEA	31	40
Electrolux	5.5	6	Electrolux	27	19
Others	1	1	Whirlpool	24	—
Freezer			Maytag	17	34
Whirlpool	63	60	Others	1	7
W.C. Wood	24	35	**Range (electric)**		
Haier	8	—	GEA	41	49
Sanyo Fisher	1	3	Whirlpool	26	19
Others	4	2	Electrolux	18	9
Refrigerator			Maytag	14	20
Whirlpool	28.5	27	Others	1	3
Electrolux	24.5	14	**Washer**		
GEA	23	37	Whirlpool	51.5	52
Maytag	23	20	Maytag	25	24
Others	1	2	GEA	15	17
			Electrolux	7.5	7
			Others	1	0

Note:

1. Raytheon's 1996 Amana appliance share totals included with Maytag share totals.

Source: "Special Report: 2002 Market Profile," *Appliance Manufacturer,* April 2002, p. 11.

of appliance, such as Sub-Zero (built-in refrigerators and freezers and Wolf's professional ranges) and Emerson Electric (garbage disposals). (See **Exhibit 8** for overall U.S. and Western European market shares by company.) The strongest competitors in the United States during the five-year period from 1996 to 2001 were Whirlpool, Maytag, and Electrolux. Whirlpool had increased its market share by almost five points, from 34.9% five years earlier. Maytag had been steadily increasing its market share (about 1% per year), from 15.2% in 1996 to 20.8% in 2000. Its purchase of Amana's home appliances from Goodman in 2001 raised Maytag's total market share an additional point, to 21.6% in 2001. Frigidaire, AB Electrolux's North American home appliance division, increased its market share over five points from 9.6% in 1996. In contrast, General Electric had lost about nine points of market share (almost 2% each year!), from 32.0% in 1996. By the time Maytag bought Amana home appliances, Amana's market share had been 2.9% in 2000, down from 6.7% in 1996.

Exhibit 8

Shares of U.S. and Western European Market in White Goods
(Including dishwashers, dryers, ranges, refrigerators, and washers)

U.S. Combined Market Share by Company			
Company	**2001**	**1996**	**Brands**
Whirlpool	39.2%	34.9%	Estate, Inglis, KitchenAid, Roper, Whirlpool
GEA	23.2%	32.0%	GE, Hotpoint, Monogram, Profile, RCA
Maytag[1]	21.6%	15.2%	Admiral, Amana, Jenn-Air, Magic Chef, Maytag
Electrolux	15.0%	9.6%	Frigidaire, Gibson, Kelvinator, Tappan, White-Westinghouse
Raytheon	—	6.7%	Amana, Caloric, Speed Queen
Others	1.0%	1.6%	

Western European Combined Market Share by Company			
Company	**Home Country**	**2000**	**1996**
Electrolux	Sweden	16.2%	22.3%
Bosch-Siemens	Germany	14.4%	15.9%
Whirlpool	U.S.	9.4%	10.5%
Merloni Bonferraro	Italy	9.4%	6.0%
Groupe Brandt	France	4.1%	6.0%
Miele	Germany	4.0%	6.0%
Arcelik	Turkey	4.0%	6.0%
Ardo Merloni	Italy	4.0%	—
GDA	UK	3.6%	3.8%
Candy	Italy	3.4%	4.8%
Fagor	Spain	3.4%	—
Others		24.1%	18.7%

Note:
1. Includes Amana.

Source: "Special Report: 2002 Market Profile," *Appliance Manufacturer*, April 2002 and 1997, Special Insert; "Portrait of the European Appliance Industry," *Appliance*, November 2001, pp. 49–53, and November 1997, pp. 59–64.

When viewed in terms of total world sales, the U.S. major home appliance manufacturers were major contributors. The top 10 global appliance makers, in order of units sold worldwide, were Whirlpool (U.S.), AB Electrolux (Sweden), General Electric (U.S.), Matsushita (Japan), Bosch-Siemens (Germany), Maytag (U.S.), Sharp (Japan), Toshiba (Japan), Haier (China), and Hitachi (Japan).[23] Of these 10, only Whirlpool and AB Electrolux had strong positions in all the key world markets of North America, Western Europe, Latin America, and Asia (particularly China and India). For example, AB Electrolux was first in market share in Western Europe, with 16.2% in 2000. Whirlpool was third, with 9.4% share, following Bosch-Siemens, with 14.4%. General Electric placed ninth, with 3.6% market share, before it sold its half ownership of the British joint venture General Domestic Appliances (GDA) to the Italian appliance maker Merloni Electrodomestici in 2002. The GDA joint venture had been successful in the United Kingdom but had achieved only minimal sales to the European continent.

The Japanese appliance firms were well entrenched in Asia but had no real competitive presence (outside of microwave ovens) in the rest of the world. This was similar to Maytag's being strong only in North America. Earlier Maytag had purchased Hoover to obtain Hoover's major appliance facilities in the United Kingdom (thus gaining access to the European market), but the enormous cost of upgrading the plants combined with Hoover's low sales outside Britain caused Maytag to sell Hoover's European operations to Candy, the Italian appliance firm. Although Bosch-Siemens was attempting to grow its presence throughout the world, it was overshadowed outside Europe by Whirlpool and Electrolux and by various strong regional competitors, such as Maytag in the United States and Haier in China. Nevertheless, Bosch-Siemens's recent investments in the Americas was likely to soon move it to fourth place in global unit sales. Haier, the dominant appliance maker of China, followed the Bosch-Siemens strategy by working diligently to establish itself in Europe and the Americas. Since 1987, Haier's sales had increased faster than those of any other home appliance company in the world.

In terms of their competitive orientation in 2002, major home appliance manufacturers could be placed in one of the following categories:

Global Players

Whirlpool (U.S.)
AB Electrolux (Sweden)
General Electric (U.S.)

Global Aspirants

Bosch-Siemens (Germany)
Haier (China)
LG Electronics (Korea)

Strong Regional Players

Matsushita, Sharp, Toshiba, and Hitachi (Japan) in Asia
Maytag (U.S.) in North America
Candy and Merloni (Italy) in Western Europe
Miele (Germany) in Western Europe
Samsung and Daewoo (Korea) in Asia

Strong Local Players with Some Regional Presence

Arcelik (Turkey)
Mabe (Mexico)
Multibras (Brazil)
Fisher & Paykel (New Zealand)

Domestic and Niche Players

Sub-Zero/Wolf (U.S.)
Guangdong Midea Group (China)
Many others

Many of the major home appliance manufacturers, such as Whirlpool and Maytag, had fairly narrow product lines, concentrating on home appliances. Some, like Electrolux and Haier, also sold related appliances such as air conditioning and commercial appliances. Other competitors were part of a larger, highly diversified corporation. General Electric Appliances, for example, was a division of the General Electric Company. Bosch-Siemens Hausgerate was a joint subsidiary of Robert Bosch GmbH and Siemens AG. Matsushita, Sharp, Toshiba, and Hitachi of Japan and Samsung and Daewoo of Korea were appliance units of larger, much diversified, global corporations. Even though the Japanese and Korean appliance firms did not have strong positions in major home appliances in every key world market in 2002, they were broadly diversified and well established globally in brown goods (consumer electronics) and other product lines.

As the major home appliance industry became increasingly global, industry analysts wondered if regional and domestic major home appliance companies concentrating on white goods, such as Maytag in North America and Miele in Western Europe, would continue to be successful as independent firms. Appliance expert Paul Roggema wondered if such a company was big enough to play the global game, in terms of purchasing and advertising power. Would Miele's technological leadership and quality brands allow it to survive, despite globalization, or would it be the perfect fit for Electrolux's brand portfolio?[24]

The construction in 1997 of a 200,000-unit-capacity dishwasher plant in New Bern, North Carolina, by the powerful German-based Bosch-Siemens Hausgerate to serve the North American market signaled that the U.S. major home appliance industry was changing significantly. This aggressive move was soon followed by Haier, the number-one Chinese appliance manufacturer. Haier's construction of a refrigerator plant in Camden, South Carolina (with plenty of room for expansion), in 2000 was one indication of the company's desire to join Bosch-Siemens as a major player in the U.S. market.[25]

Until the entry of Bosch-Siemens, the only foreign home appliance manufacturing presence had been in floor care. Whirlpool Corporation had arranged a joint venture in 1990 with Matsushita Electric Industrial Company, Ltd., to own and operate Whirlpool's current manufacturing plant in Danville, Kentucky, to provide vacuum cleaners for Sears.

WHIRLPOOL

Whirlpool and General Electric had traditionally dominated the U.S. major home appliance industry. (In 1991, Whirlpool's U.S. market share had been 33.8%; GE's had been 28.2 %.) Unlike General Electric, major home appliances were Whirlpool's primary business. Whirlpool's market share had been steadily increasing to almost 40% in 2001, whereas GE's share had recently fallen to 23%. Whirlpool owed its leadership position to its 50-plus-year relationship with Sears, to which it has been the sole supplier of Kenmore (Sears's own brand label) washers and dryers, the principal supplier of trash compactors and microwave/hood combinations, and a major supplier of dishwashers, ranges, refrigerators, and freezers. Sears's movement away from a heavy reliance on its Kenmore brands toward offering all lines of major home appliances had serious implications for Whirlpool. Nevertheless, even though it no longer dominated Whirlpool's sales, Sears continued to be the firm's largest single customer in 2002 and accounted for around 21% of Whirlpool's sales.

With the completion of its purchase of Dutch-based Philips Electronics's appliance operations in 1991, Whirlpool became a serious competitor in the emerging global major home appliance industry. Sales and market share consistently increased annually in every geographic section of the company—North America, Europe, Latin America, and Asia. It was first in North America and third in Western Europe in terms of market share. The company's marketing strategy was to focus on making the Whirlpool name a global brand. (Even though the company ranked only third in Europe in terms of overall market share of its Philips, Whirlpool, Backnecht, and Ignis brands, management liked to point out that the Whirlpool brand alone had the highest share of any brand in Europe.) In 2002, Whirlpool purchased Polar SA, a leading appliance maker in Poland, and was in the process of bidding for the washing machine and cooking appliance plants of the bankrupt French appliance maker Moulinex-Brandt.[26]

Whirlpool manufactured appliances in 44 locations, 34 of which were outside the United States, in 12 countries. Whirlpool had developed a series of joint ventures and equity arrangements with appliance manufacturers throughout Asia and South America. Although its share of the Asian market was still fairly small, Whirlpool, together with its affiliates in Argentina and Brazil, had the largest manufacturing base and market share in South America. (Whirlpool owned 94% of the Brazilian appliance companies Brasmotor and Multibras.) In cooperation with its affiliates in Brazil and joint venture partners in India and Mexico, Whirlpool built facilities in those countries to produce what the company called the "world washer." Five years after acquiring Kelvinator of India in 1995 to gain entry into the Indian market, Whirlpool had established itself as the market leader in refrigerators and washing machines.[27]

Fifty-nine percent of Whirlpool's 2001 sales were in North America. The company's top management believed that the firm's global position provided a competitive advantage "by reason of its ability to leverage engineering capabilities across regions, transfer best practices, and economically purchase raw materials and component parts in large volumes."[28]

Whirlpool's global expansion carried a significant cost in efficiency. It posted losses of $70 million in 1996 and $55 million in 1997 in Asia. Consequently, the company undertook a global restructuring program in 1997 to revive its sagging European and Asia operations. It cut 10% of its 46,000-person workforce, increased its presence in South America, pulled out of two troubled joint ventures in China (leaving it with two remaining joint ventures), and sold its financing business.[29]

Whirlpool revealed its excellence in product development when it successfully built a prototype to win the Super Efficient Refrigerator Program (SERP) award. Another example of new product development was in washing machines—the category in which Whirlpool owned over half of the U.S. market. Even when Frigidaire and Maytag announced that they were developing radically new front-loading washing machines to meet tightening energy and water usage requirements, Whirlpool chose to build a new type of top-loading machine. The resulting washing machine, to reach the market in late 2000, was a huge success, both as the Whirlpool Calypso and the Kenmore Elite. Like Maytag's front-loading Neptune washer, the Calypso/Elite used less energy and water and was gentler on clothes than traditional top loaders.[30]

Even though Whirlpool continued to expand throughout the world, it was also diversifying into other products. Whirlpool began this process with the introduction in 2000 of its Cielo brand plumbing and bath appliance line, including jetted and soaking spas. According to Kelley Akre, National Accounts Manager for the Cielo brand, "The vision for Whirlpool Corporation is to be in 'Every Home, Everywhere' on the appliance side of the business. . . . We're taking on rooms in every home, everywhere."[31] It was rumored that the company would soon be introducing a line of products for the garage, such as workbenches, sinks, and storage systems. (See **Exhibit 9** for operating financial results for primary U.S. competitors.)

Exhibit 9

Major Home Appliance Operating Results for Primary U.S. Competitors[1]
(Dollar and Swedish krona amounts in millions)

Company[2]	Category	2001	2000	1999
A.B. Electrolux	Revenue	SEK108,990	SEK98,488	SEK91,689
	Operating income	4,629	5,779	4,997
	Assets	30,510	27,444	26,224
General Electric	Revenue	$5,810	$5,887	$5,671
	Operating income	643	684	655
	Assets	3,100	2,775	2,463
Maytag	Revenue	4,093	3,713	3,706
	Operating income	324	478	562
	Assets	2,264	1,794	1,792
Whirlpool	Revenue	10,343	10,325	10,511
	Operating income	306	807	875
	Assets	6,967	6,902	6,826

Notes:
1. Figures for Electrolux given in Swedish kronor (SEK). U.S.$1 roughly equals SEK9.
2. Results for Electrolux's consumer durables area, GE's appliance business unit, and Maytag's home appliances segment. Above results include worldwide sales, profits, and assets in home appliances area.

Source: 10-K reports of companies.

GENERAL ELECTRIC APPLIANCES

General Electric, with a U.S. major home appliance market share of 23.2% in 2001, was a strong and profitable competitor in many industries but was failing to keep up with the industry in major home appliances. As a business unit, GE Appliances accounted for 4.6% of the corporation's total sales in 2001, down from 14% in 1996. General Electric had a powerful name and brand image and was the most vertically integrated of the major home appliance manufacturers. For example, General Electric Plastics was an important supplier to the industry. GEA was the only appliance producer to own its entire distribution and service facilities.

Realizing that GE's manufacturing facilities at its 40-year-old Appliance Park near Louisville, Kentucky, were slowly losing their competitiveness, management spent $100 million in the mid-1990s to modernize the washing machine plant. The Park's refrigerator plant was next in line for a $70 million makeover. Overall, the company invested around $1 billion over a four-year period in appliance product development and capital equipment—a 50% increase over previous spending levels. It then invested over $800 million during 2001 and 2002 in its 42 plants in Mexico. Committed to performing its own research, the company invested $100 million in 2002 to modernize its corporate research and development center in Niskayuna, New York.

Thirty percent of GE's appliance sales were currently outside the United States.[32] In 1989, GE paid $580 million for a joint appliance venture and other ventures with the UK's General Electric Corporation (GEC). Perhaps frustrated by the venture's inability to make significant sales inroads in the rest of Europe and by the growing saturation of the Western Europe appliance market, General Electric sold its half interest in the venture to Merloni Electrodomestici in 2002. Nevertheless, the company was heavily involved with international partners in Mexico (48% of MABE), Venezuela (Madosa), Brazil (majority interest in DAKO S.A.), India (40% of joint venture with Godrej & Boyce), the Philippines (Philacor), and Japan (Toshiba). These ventures have generally been successful. Although most appliances manufactured by the joint ventures were planned originally for sale in the country of origin, MABE gas stoves had been heavily exported into the United States, significantly cutting into Magic Chef's (a Maytag unit) dominance in this product line. More than one-third of all gas ranges and mini-refrigerators sold in the United States were being manufactured in MABE plants in northern Mexico.[33]

Since 1995, GE Appliances had been actively implementing a Six Sigma quality initiative throughout its many operations. Partly as a consequence of this program, GE refrigerators were rated in 1999 by U.S. property management personnel as being number one in quality compared to all other brands.[34] This rating further reinforced GE's reputation as the appliance sales leader to the North American builder market.

MAYTAG

Maytag Corporation, with a U.S. market share of 21.6% in 2002, had been steadily growing its share from 14.2% in 1991. It had moved past Electrolux into third place in the industry in 1995 and was now nipping at the heels of GE for second place in the North American home appliance market.

Realizing that the company could not successfully compete in the major home appliance industry as just a manufacturer of high-quality laundry products, the company embarked during the 1980s on the acquisition of Hardwick Stoves, Magic Chef, and Jenn-Air. These acquisitions provided Maytag the full line of laundry, cooking, and refrigeration appliances it needed to compete effectively in the U.S. market. Realizing that the industry was going global as well, Maytag purchased Hoover Company, a successful floor care company in the United States and a strong white goods producer in the United Kingdom and Australia. Increased debt from the acquisition, coupled with the heavy amount of investment needed to upgrade and integrate its newly acquired facilities and operations, put a big strain on Maytag's profitability. Consequently, Maytag sold as losses Hoover Australia in 1994 and Hoover Europe in 1995. Maytag then undertook a joint venture with the Rongshida appliance company of China in 1996 but ended its involvement in 2001, after continuous losses.

In 1995, Maytag invested $13.7 million to expand its recently completed state-of-the art dishwasher plant in Tennessee. At that time dishwasher sales were increasing at twice the rate of the rest of the industry.[35] This investment plus the corporation's decisions to spend $160 million upgrading its Admiral refrigerator plant (part of the Magic Chef purchase) and $50 million to build a new plant for its front-loading, horizontal-axis Neptune washer plant indicated that Maytag had no intention of being out-maneuvered by others in North America. The company finally decided in 1998 to offer its full line of Maytag brand appliances through Sears. (It was the last major U.S appliance maker to do so.) Maytag also established 10 Maytag retail stores in the late 1990s for the purpose of allowing consumers to use Maytag's appliances before buying them. The stores were independently owned but supplied by Maytag and were larger on average than the 550 independently owned Maytag dealers. Management decided to open 16 more stores in 2002. These stores were to also offer brands from other manufacturers.

Uninterested in being a takeover target, Maytag spent $325 million in 2001 to acquire Amana, a respected major home appliance brand noted for its excellence in refrigeration technology. Amana had earlier been the major home appliance unit of Raytheon before being sold to the Goodman Global Holding Company, a Texas heating and air conditioning company, in 1997. As a unit of Raytheon, the Amana appliance unit had been composed of the Amana, Speed Queen, and Caloric brands. (Speed Queen's commercial appliance unit was sold separately.) Goodman's Amana and Caloric brands posted a market share of 5.2% in 1998 but dropped to only 2.9% in 2000.

Maytag had purchased in 1997 the G. S. Blodgett Company, a leading commercial food service equipment maker in Burlington, Vermont. Blodgett made ovens, fryers, and char-broilers for restaurants and hotels. After the acquisition of Amana, Maytag sold Blodgett in order to reduce its debt and to concentrate on North American major home appliances. As part of its consolidation of Amana and Maytag operations, management sold the firm's components parts business in Jefferson City, Missouri, and moved limited refrigeration manufacturing to Amana's refrigeration plant in Amana, Iowa, in 2002. To further reduce manufacturing costs, management invested $2 million in a new subassembly plant in Mexico in 2002. Until this decision, subassembly work had either been done at Maytag's U.S. facilities or by outside suppliers.

According to William Beer, President of Maytag Appliances, Maytag's strategy was to focus on delivering a constant stream of innovative products, such as the Neptune washer, Gemini oven, and Wide-by-Side refrigerator. Although CEO Ralph Hake agreed that innovative products were very important, he felt that for the company to return to sustainable and attractive levels of profitability would require shoring up channels of distribution and even thinking beyond the "Core 5" major appliance product categories: dishwashers, dryers, ranges, refrigerators, and washers. "We're not going to have product hits each and every year like Neptune and Gemini," warned Hake.[36]

AB ELECTROLUX

Along with Whirlpool, AB Electrolux of Sweden was an established global competitor. With its purchase of White Consolidated Industries in 1986, Electrolux became a major part of the U.S. major home appliance industry. Electrolux sold approximately 17 million appliances with over 40 brand names in countries around the world. Electrolux had a strong presence in every

European country from Finland to Portugal and extended eastward with production facilities in Hungary, Estonia, and Russia. With Electrolux's purchase of Brazil's second largest appliance maker, Refrigeracao Parana (Refripar); Email, Ltd., the largest producer of appliances in Australia; and the Indian appliance firm Voltas, the company had a solid presence in Latin America and Asia.

In 1991, the WCI Major Appliance Group was renamed Frigidaire Company in order to provide AB Electrolux's U.S. subsidiary the recognition earned by its pioneering namesake brand. Previously, the company's brands had competed against one another and had not been designed for automated manufacturing. Consequently, the quality of many of its well-known branded products had deteriorated over time. Its share of the U.S. market dropped significantly from 16.9% in 1994 to 13.5% in 1995 and had caused the company to drop from its traditional third place in the U.S. market to fourth place, behind Maytag. To reverse this situation, the company invested more than $600 million to upgrade its existing plants and build new refrigerator and dishwasher plants. Top management also introduced benchmarking and total quality management to boost production quality and efficiency. The company aggressively advertised its products and was successful in regaining some of the market share it had earlier lost.

Electrolux was heavily involved in restructuring its many activities. For example, it cut 2,800 jobs worldwide in 2001 and closed or relocated four plants in Europe and Asia as a way to cut costs and boost productivity. This brought the total cuts to 4,900 jobs, roughly 5.6% of the company's total workforce. It also sold its three motor operations plants in Europe and its compressor plant in Mexico.

The Electrolux Group was divided into two business areas: consumer durables and professional products. The consumer durables business unit included American Yard Products, Frigidaire, and Poulan/Weed Eater and was composed of white goods (including room air conditioners) plus floor care, sewing machines, garden equipment, and light-duty chain saws. White goods composed 75% of sales in the consumer durables area. Management indicated that the marked decline in U.S. white goods operating income was due to retail stock-outs and to the phase-in of a new generation of refrigerators—costing the firm SEK (Swedish krona) 1,050 million (US$100 million).[37]

In 2002, Electrolux was first in white goods market share in Western Europe, with a 16.2% market share (down from 23.9% in 1994), and fourth in North America, with a 15.0% market share (up from 13.5% in 1995). Europe accounted for about 50% of its major home appliance sales. North America accounted for approximately 35%. The rest was scattered throughout Asia, Latin America (especially Brazil), Oceania, and Africa.

Careful planning was needed by Electrolux to properly take advantage of a proliferation of brands worldwide without getting bogged down with competing internal demands for attention to each brand. After noticing Whirlpool's success with one brand across all of Europe, the company began the introduction of its own pan-European brand using the Electrolux name. The company spent SEK 600 million over a five-year period to market the Electrolux products throughout Europe. It also invested $50 million in Southeast Asia, with an objective of becoming one of the top three suppliers of white goods in the region. The company then acquired the Electrolux name and trademark in North America in 2000 from Electrolux LLC, maker of canister vacuum cleaners. AB Electrolux had given up the name when it had sold its share of the U.S. vacuum manufacturer in 1968. The much-smaller American vacuum cleaner company changed its name to Aerus, and the Swedish firm once again had full worldwide control of the company name and brand. Rumors had circulated in 2000 that Electrolux pursued Maytag as an acquisition in order to add a high-quality brand to its stable of mid- to low-quality brands in the United States. Electrolux's commitment to use the Electrolux name throughout the world suggested that the company would likely introduce the Electrolux brand as its premium line of home appliances in North America.

OTHER COMPETITORS

The remaining 1% of U.S. market share in major home appliances was accounted for by a number of other competitors. Two of these, Bosch-Siemens and Haier, were large, global competitors recently establishing themselves in North America. Others were smaller firms manufacturing one or more unique products sold to a premium niche in the market.

GLOBAL COMPETITORS

Although not new to North America, Bosch-Siemens and Haier had recently switched from importing to manufacturing in North America.

Bosch-Siemens Hausgerate GmbH (BSH)

BSH was an equally held joint venture of Robert Bosch GmbH and Siemens AG. Like Whirlpool and Maytag, it concentrated on manufacturing and selling major home appliances. With 32,000 employees distributed among 90 companies around the world, BSH viewed itself as a global competitor marketing 15 brands. Although its market share in North America was very small in 2002, it had the second largest market share (14.4%) in Western Europe. Over the past 20 years, BSH has acquired 400 companies, some of which have since been sold or closed. The company earned around 60% of its profits outside of its base in Germany. According to Dr. Herbert Worner, Chairman of BSH, "Right from its inception, with just four German production facilities, BSH pledged itself to the path of internationalization."[38]

The construction in 1997 of a 200,000-unit-capacity dishwasher plant in New Bern, North Carolina, initiated Bosch-Siemens's entry into the North American market. As the European market leader in dishwashers, BSH intended to expand sales of its high-end dishwashers from the 40,000 units it was exporting to North America in 1995 to a 5% dishwasher market share.[39] The company optimistically expanded its New Bern location with a washing machine plant in 2000, even though it not yet accomplished its share objective in dishwashers.

BSH management claimed in 2001 that the company had achieved third position in the world rankings of major home appliance manufacturers since 2000. (A report in 2000 placed Bosch-Siemens fifth, after GE and Matsushita.) According to company sources, BSH claimed to be behind Electrolux and Whirlpool but just ahead of General Electric. The company also intended to be the market leader in Europe.[40] BSH reported total net earnings for 2001 had leaped by 47.3%, from 311.8 million € to 459.4 €. The company posted a total sales figure for 2001 of 6.1 billion €.

Haier Electrical Appliance International

Ranked China's number-one consumer electronics maker, Haier accounted for nearly 40% of China's refrigerator sales and one-third of its washing machine and air conditioner sales. According to President Zhang Ruimin, it wanted to become "a famous global brand like Japan's Matsushita." During the period from 1987 to 2001, Haier's sales had increased faster than those of any other home appliance company in the world. By 1997, the company was selling washing machines to Japan, air conditioners to France, and refrigerators to the United States.[41] A poll of Chinese executives revealed Haier to be the domestic company most respected by Chinese executives. Respondents admired the company's business globalization, advanced management methodologies and systems, brand recognition, and consistent business strategy.[42]

In 2000, Haier built a brand new refrigerator plant in Camden, South Carolina, followed by its purchase of an Italian refrigerator manufacturing plant. Previously, it had established a research center in Los Angeles and a U.S. sales network. It had also formed an alliance with India's Bestavision to manufacture and market clothes washers in India. As a result of these and other actions, Haier operated 48 manufacturing plants and sold products in more than 160 countries. Haier took the lead in China by establishing a B2B service and selling Haier products on the Internet. In 2002, Haier opened its $15 million U.S. headquarters in New York City. The offices housed corporate offices, R&D labs, a restaurant, and showrooms.

Haier announced that profits for 2001 were more than 50% higher than in 2000. As part of CEO Zhang Ruimin's strategy to join the *Fortune* Global 500, Haier has continuously expanded its business scope. Growing from a small regional refrigerator factory in China through a series of joint ventures, it had expanded to appliances in every category and had a strong presence throughout China. It was not only expanding globally, it was diversifying into other products, such as kitchen cabinets, life insurance, personal computers, and mobile phones.[43] The company attempted to transfer some of the technology used in one part of its organization to another. For example, it was the first major home appliance company to introduce a complete line of Internet-enabled appliances at the 2001 Domotechnica trade show.

NICHE COMPETITORS

There were a number of smaller major home appliance companies operating in North America, such as Sub-Zero, Viking Range, W.C. Wood, and Brown Stove Works. Most of them manufactured and sold one category of appliance, such as specialized ranges or freezers.

Sub-Zero Freezer Company

Founded in Madison, Wisconsin, in 1945, the company made high-end built-in refrigerator and freezers. It offered a comprehensive line of built-in refrigerators and freezers, including under-the-counter models and wine storage drawers. In 2000, it bought Wolf Gourmet, premier maker of residential ranges, cook tops, grills, and ventilation equipment. Wolf stated that its products were hand-built for exceptional quality. Like Sub-Zero, Wolf's products appealed to the super-premium niche of the home appliance market.

Viking Range Corporation

Founded in 1984 to manufacture a commercial-type range for the home, Viking Range offered a complete line of super-premium, professional-type kitchen appliances, including ranges, ventilation equipment, and dishwashers. The company added refrigerators in 2000, with the purchase of Amana's built-in refrigeration unit. Viking owned a cooking products plant, a ventilation products plant, and a newly opened refrigeration plant in Greenwood, Mississippi.

A Global Future?

According to an analysis by The Freedonia Group, world demand for major home appliances was expected to increase 3.6% annually through 2005, reaching 337 million units. Particularly favorable prospects would be in the Asia/Pacific region, where there would be above-average urban population growth and increasing personal incomes. Latin America should also provide growth opportunities because of continuing industrialization and urbanization of the region. Above-average growth was also expected in the Africa/Middle East region and in most of Eastern Europe. Gains in the developed nations should result more from consumer demand for more convenient and energy-efficient appliances. Rising consumption expenditures in Europe should boost demand. The gains in the developed nations should be modest because of the increasingly saturated market and because demographics should not result in a high level of new household formation. Microwave ovens should post strong sales gains through 2005 due to untapped market potential in the developing regions. Conventional ranges were expected to post only modest gains due to market saturation. Dishwashers and clothes dryers should also exhibit growth, although price, size, and cultural considerations should prevent these items from becoming commonplace in areas where they were not already established. Because of rising industrialization and personal income levels in the developing nations, refrigerators and freezers should experience above-average sales gains.[44] (See **Exhibit 10** for forecasted major home appliance demand by region and by product line.)

According to Robert Holding, president of the Association of Home Appliance Manufacturers (AHAM), several industry trends were defining the industry's future in North America:

- Industry consolidation was raising the competitive stakes.
- Market maturity was leaving limited avenues for home market growth. A greater emphasis on new products was emerging.
- Free trade opened market opportunities but brought new competition. International standards and nontariff trade barriers were becoming more important.
- Globalization by some manufacturers created significant differences in strategic situations.
- Stronger niche producers were emerging in traditional product categories.

Exhibit 10

Actual (1998) and Forecasted (2008) Major Home Appliance Demand by Region and by Product

World Demand by Region (In millions of units)		
Region	**1998**	**2008**
World	256.3	354.9
North America	58.4	64.4
United States	49.3	51.8
Canada & Mexico	9.1	12.6
Latin American	18.0	25.4
Western Europe	64.9	73.9
Eastern Europe	18.1	31.9
Africa/Mideast	16.9	24.2
Asia/Pacific	80.1	135.1
Japan	18.6	19.1
China	35.1	75.2
Other Asia/Pacific	26.4	40.9

World Demand by Product (In thousands of units)		
Product	**1998**	**2008**
Households	1,474	1,728
World demand	256,300	354,900
Refrigerators & freezers	77,530	110,350
Clothes washers & dryers	66,595	89,850
Washers	55,005	73,600
Dryers	11,590	16,250
Cooking	98,135	134,150
Ranges & ovens	61,540	78,050
Microwave ovens	36,595	56,100
Dishwashers	14,040	20,550

Source: J. Jancsurak, "Majors: Good (Not Great) Times Ahead Worldwide," *Appliance Manufacturer,* February 2001, p. G–15.

■ Much faster product development times and the need to have unique features accelerated time frames for industry decision making when government regulations or product standards were involved.[45]

Even though the major home appliance industry continued to become more global, cultural differences should continue to make it impossible to create one type of appliance for all markets. Whirlpool's concept of one "world washer" that it could make and sell around the world collapsed when not only did the manufacturing processes have to be changed to suite local conditions, but also local preferences demanded a differentiated product. In cooking appliances, for example, over 90% of the ranges purchased in Germany were electric, whereas gas prevailed through the rest of Europe. Also, 65% of German ranges were built-in, while the percentage of built-ins outside Germany was considerably less. Top-loading washers dominated North American, but front-loaders dominated Europe, where washers and dryers must fit into a kitchen under a work surface or in a bathroom. Although built-in refrigerators formed only a small part of refrigerator sales in most of Europe, they comprised over 50% of the German market. The large, freestanding home appliances preferred by Americans were much less popular in Europe and Asia, where smaller, energy-efficient units were generally preferred. The Japanese market was most interested in appliances that minimized water usage. Top-loading washers using agitators to clean the clothes were not preferred in India because they tended to tear the long saris preferred by women. The cooking habits in Asia, Africa, and many other parts of the world dictated that the distance between burners be larger and the control knobs be put on the same surface as the burners.[46]

Hans G. Backman, President of Frigidaire Company and Vice-President of AB Electrolux commented on industry globalization:

Globalization of the product and globalization of the company are two different things. The appliance industry is becoming global, but the products and the consumers are still local. The more the world comes together, the more national differences get emphasized.[47]

Notes

1. U.S. Department of Labor, as reported by D. Delano, "It's Official; Now What?" *Appliance Manufacturer* (January, 2002), p. 82.
2. J. Jancsurak, "It's All Good," *Appliance Manufacturer* (July 2002), p. 5. "White goods" is the traditional term used for major home appliances. The contrasting term "brown goods" refers to home electronics products, such as radios and televisions.
3. Freedonia Group, *World Major Household Appliances*, summarized in *Appliance* (April 2002), p. 19.
4. Harris Web site, at harris.com (July 11, 2002).
5. "Ames Laboratory Testing First Magnetic Refrigerator," *Appliance* (February 2002), p. 14.
6. N. C. Remich, Jr., "Appliances Use About 20% of Coated Coil," *Appliance Manufacturer* (December 1996), p. 14.
7. C. R. Christensen, K. R. Andrews, J. L. Bower, R. G. Hamermesh, and M. Porter, "Note on the Major Home Appliance Industry in 1984 (Condensed)," *Business Policy*, 6th ed. (Homewood, IL: Irwin, 1987), p. 340.
8. "GE to Invest in Mexico," *Appliance* (November 2001), p. 13.
9. D. Ritchey, "Recycle America?" *Appliance* (July 2002), p. 9; "For Appliances, Coated Coil Grows by 14.6%," *Appliance Manufacturer* (June 1993), p. 10.
10. D. Davis, "1996: A Soft Landing," *Appliance* (January 1996), p. 52.
11. "Buying Power—Home Purchase Triggers Sales of Appliances," *Appliance Manufacturer* (February 1989), p. 31.
12. C. Miller, Vice President of Marketing, North American Appliance Group, Whirlpool Corporation, quoted by R. J. Babyak and J. Jancsurak in "Product Design & Manufacturing Process for

the 21st Century," *Appliance Manufacturer* (November 1994), p. 59.
13. D. Ritchey, "The Worst Consumer?" *Appliance* (May 2002), p. 11.
14. D. Ritchey, "Appliance Retail Speaks," *Appliance* (March 2001), p. 11. Kenmore is Sears's private-label appliance brand.
15. *Ibid.*, p. 11.
16. L. Bonnema, "Tradeplace—A Retailer's Dream Come True," *Appliance* (April 2002), p. 49.
17. "GE to Begin Selling Appliances Online," *Daily (Ames, IA) Tribune* (June 22, 1999), p. C8.
18. J. Jancsurak, "What Retailers and Consumers Want Most," *Appliance Manufacturer* (May 1998), pp. 39–44.
19. D. Ritchey, "Craving for Energy," *Appliance* (February 2002), p. 9.
20. J. M. McGuire, "Energy Use an AHAM Priority," *Appliance Manufacturer* (August 2001), p. 14.
21. "Manager's Update," *Appliance Manufacturer* (March 2001), p. 13.
22. L. Swatkowski, "Building Towards International Standards," *Appliance* (December 1999), p. 30.
23. J. Jancsurak, "Majors: Good (Not Great) Times Ahead Worldwide," *Appliance Manufacturer* (February 2001), p. G-13.
24. P. Roggema, "European Consolidation," *Appliance* (June 2001), p. 30.
25. D. Ritchey, "Aiming Haier and Haier . . . ," *Appliance* (November 2001), p. 8.
26. "Whirlpool Corporation Bids for Parts of Brandt," *Appliance* (January 2002), p. 13, and "Whirlpool News," *Appliance* (May 2002), p. 15.

27. A. Chatterjee, "Whirlpool's Market Leadership Gameplan," *Appliance* (May 2000), p. 24.

28. Whirlpool Corporation, *2001 Form 10-K*, p. 3.

29. C. Quintanilla and J. Carlton, "Whirlpool Unveils Global Restructuring Effort," *Wall Street Journal* (September 19, 1997), pp. A3, A6.

30. R. J. Babyak, "The Sway of Calypso," *Appliance Manufacturer* (February 2001), pp. 35–40.

31. L. Bonnema, "The Luxury Appliance," *Appliance* (July 2002), p. 32.

32. S. Stevens, "Executing Stretch," *Appliance* (June 1997), pp. GE-1–GE-6.

33. H. W. Lane, M. B. Brechu, and D. T. A. Wesley, "MABE's President Luis Berrondo Avalos on Teams and Industry Competitiveness," *Academy of Management Executive* (August 1999), pp. 8–14.

34. "GE Refrigerators Rated Highest Quality in U.S.," *Appliance* (January 2000), p. 19.

35. "Maytag to Expand Dishwasher Plant," *Appliance* (December 1994), p. 29.

36. J. Jancsurak, "New CEO; New Agenda Signal Changes Ahead," *Appliance Manufacturer* (November 2001).

37. AB Electrolux, *2001 Annual Report*, pp. 23–25.

38. H. Worner, "Newsquotes," *Appliance* (May 1998), p. 32.

39. "BSH to Build U.S. Plant," *Appliance* (January 1996), p. 17; "Bosch Targets U.S. Niche," *Appliance Manufacturer* (April 1996), p. 26.

40. "Bosch-Siemens Hausgerate: Saturated? Innovate!" *Appliance* (August 2001), p. 24.

41. K. Chen, "Global Cooling: Would America Buy a Refrigerator Labeled 'Made in Qingdao'?" *Wall Street Journal* (September 17, 1997), pp. A1, A14.

42. D. Ritchey, "Aiming Haier and Haier . . . ," p. 8.

43. C. Stevens, "Top of the Pile and Going Haier in China," *Appliance* (April 2002), p. 22.

44. The Fredonia Group, *World Major Household Appliances* (January 2002), as reported in "World Major Household Appliances," *Appliance* (April 2002), p. 19.

45. R. L. Holding, "30th Anniversary Reflections," *Appliance Manufacturer* (April 1997), p. 16.

46. M. Ashjaee, "Newsquotes," *Appliance* (November 1999), p. 34.

47. J. Jancsurak, "Global Trend for 1995–2005," *Appliance Manufacturer* (June 1995), p. A-3.

case 19

Maytag Corporation 2002: Focus on North America

J. David Hunger

D riving 30 miles east from Des Moines on Interstate 80 through bright sunshine, a traveler nears the Newton exit. It has been a mild winter in the upper Midwest, and by mid-April the surrounding fields already appear ready for the plow. It is easy to visualize the rich black soil of the rolling Iowa countryside in its future summer abundance of ripening corn and soybean plants. Motoring north from the I80 exit for a mile and then east on U.S. route 6, one enters the quiet town of Newton—population 16,000 and location of the headquarters for Maytag Corporation. Approaching the town square, a left turn puts the visitor on course for the Sodexho Marriott Conference Center, site of this year's annual shareholders' meeting. Even though the Center adjoins company facilities, it is on a street lined with the well-kept houses and flower gardens typical of small-town Iowa. A right turn followed by a quick left into the Conference Center's spacious parking lot locates the visitor only a few feet from the entrance. Walking from cars into the building, people exude an air of anticipation. Another beautiful spring day is predicted for May 9, 2002. It is 8:15 A.M. The meeting is scheduled to begin at 8:30 A.M.

Notices at the door direct people to a large stairway leading to the second floor. The foyer at the top of the stairs is filled with people chatting and munching on coffee and pastries. Women sitting at the "proxy station" table at the far side of the foyer provide copies of annual reports (each including the 10-K report) to any shareholder wishing one. Maytag executives, with their distinctive blue nametags, mingle with the crowd. The mood is relatively friendly but anticipatory of Ralph Hake's chairing his first shareholders' meeting since becoming CEO and Chairman of the board. Although the company seems to have stabilized after much executive turnover and some confusion over Maytag's future, shareholders want some reassurance that their investment is in good hands. Anticipating an interesting meeting, people move toward the auditorium entrance, hoping to get a "good" seat. A group of visiting high school students is ushered to the back of the auditorium as a combination of young and old, known and unknown, wander into the room in their coats and ties and heels and hose. From their comments and age, a significant number of the stockholders appear to be retired Maytag employees living in the area. Seated in the first row are the members of Maytag Corporation's board of directors. Immediately behind them are the company's top managers. The auditorium is filled to capacity but hushes respectfully as Ralph Hake makes the short climb to the stage, walks to the podium, and begins to speak.

This case was prepared by Professor J. David Hunger of Iowa State University for SMBP-9th edition. All rights reserved by the author. Copyright © 2002 by J. David Hunger.

Corporate Governance

One by one, Chairman Hake introduces the nine other members of the board of directors and briefly describes each person's background. Each stands briefly as his or her name is announced. The present board had shrunk in size to 10, from 17 members in 1989 and 14 members in 1996. One-third of the board is elected every year for a three-year term. The audience notes the presence of Lester Crown and Neele Stearns, previous directors of the former Chicago Pacific Corporation who had joined Maytag's board when Maytag acquired Chicago Pacific (for Hoover's appliance business) in 1989. Lester Crown personally owns 3.9% of Maytag's stock, but through holdings by associates and family members effectively controls 7% of the stock (5,486,850 shares)—far more than any other member of the board. Although more than 60% of Maytag's 77,122,582 shares of common stock is owned by individual shareowners, 14.9% of the stock is owned by FMR Corporation (an investment company) and 5.9% by the State Street Bank and Trust Company (as trustee).

The board is a mixture of long-term members and more recent arrivals. (See **Exhibit 1** for a listing of the board of directors.) Counting only personally owned shares (including Crown's), all officers and directors owned only 6.1% of Maytag's outstanding shares. The board meets quarterly, with additional meetings as needed (plus committee meetings). Non-

Exhibit 1

Board of Directors: Maytag Corporation (2002)
(Listed in order of time served)

Director	Age	Joined Board	Fix Position	Term Expires	Shares Owned[1]
Howard L. Clark[3]	58	1986	Vice Chairman, Lehman Brothers, Inc.	2002[2]	39,836
W. Ann Reynolds[4]	64	1988	President, U. of Alabama, Birmingham	2004	18,619
Lester Crown[4]	76	1989	Chairman, Material Services Corporation	2002[2]	3,064,403
Neele E. Stearns, Jr.[3]	66	1989	Chairman, Financial Investments Corp	2003	28,801
Fred G. Steingraber[4]	63	1989	Chairman Emeritus, CC Industries, Inc.	2004	26,000
Wayland R. Hicks	59	1994	Vice Chair & CEO, United Rentals, Inc.	2004	25,000
Bernard G. Rethore[5]	60	1994	Chairman Emeritus, Flowserve Corporation	2003	16,000
Barbara R. Allen[3,5]	49	1995	Past CEO, Women's United Soccer Assoc.	2002[2]	14,845
William T. Kerr[3,5]	60	1998	Chair & CEO, Meredith Corporation	2002	9,100
Ralph F. Hake	60	2001	Chair & CEO, Maytag Corporation	2003	470,168

Notes:
1. Includes stock options not yet exercised.
2. Up for reelection May 9, 2002.
3. Members of Audit Committee.
4. Members of Governance & Nominating Committee.
5. Members of Compensation Committee.

Source: Maytag Corporation, *Notice of Annual Meeting and Proxy Statement*, April 2, 2002, pp. 4–7.

Maytag directors receive $30,000 per year and $1,250 plus expenses for each board and committee meeting attended. Non-Maytag directors also receive an annual option to purchase 3,000 shares of common stock.

Chairman Hake introduces the executive officers seated next to and behind the board members in the first two rows of the auditorium. (See **Exhibit 2** for a listing of corporate officers.) Each stands briefly as he or she is presented. Ralph Hake, Craig Breese, Ernest Park, and Thomas Piersa joined Maytag during the past two years. Hake had previously served as Executive Vice President and CFO for Whirlpool until 1999, when he failed to be named President of Whirlpool. Hake then joined Fluor Corporation as its Executive VP and CFO until being offered the top position at Maytag in June 2001. The audience was pleased to acknowledge the presence of William Beer, the President of Maytag Appliances, the second-most-important position after CEO. Beer had been with Maytag since 1974 but had resigned in 1998, when Lloyd Ward, Maytag's previous CEO, had replaced him with Lawrence Blanford as President of the Major Appliance Division. Upon Ward's departure from Maytag in 2000, Beer had been rehired in his old position.

Once the introductions are completed, Corporate Secretary Patricia Martin, sitting at a table next to the podium, reports that a quorum is present and that the minutes of last year's meeting are available at the proxy station in the auditorium foyer. A quorum requires the presence either in person or by proxy of a majority of the 77,122,582 shares of common stock, not

Exhibit 2

Executive Officers: Maytag Corporation (2002)

Officer	Age	Position	Year Became Maytag Officer	Shares Owned[1]
Ralph F. Hake	53	Chairman & CEO	2001	470,168
William L. Beer	49	President, Maytag Appliances	1993	48,715
Craig Breese	49	President, Maytag International	2001	N/A
Thomas A. Briatico	54	President, Dixie-Narco	1985	N/A
Steven J. Klyn	36	VP & Treasurer	2000	N/A
Keith G. Minton	54	President, Hoover Company	1989	61,989
Jon O. Nicholas	62	Senior VP, HRM	1993	N/A
Ernest Park	49	Senior VP & CIO	2000	N/A
Thomas J. Piersa	50	VP, Global Procurement	2000	N/A
Roger K. Scholten	47	Senior VP & General Counsel	2000	15,286
Vitas A. Stukes	48	VP & Controller	1989	N/A
Steven H. Wood	44	Executive VP & CFO	1992	66,833

Note:
1. Includes options not yet exercised.

Source: Maytag Corporation, *2001 Annual Report*, p. 5, and *Notice of Annual Meeting and Proxy Statement*, April 2, 2002, p. 8.

including 40,028,011 shares of treasury stock. Martin then turns to Hake, who reads the first three shareholder proposals. The first proposal deals with the election of the nominated slate of four directors. Since the board of directors is a staggered board elected for renewable three-year terms, the four directors whose term is up in 2002 (Allen, Clark, Crown, and Kerr) are the nominees to be elected. The second proposal deals with ratifying the selection of Ernst & Young as the corporation's auditors for 2002. The third proposal is to approve the Maytag 2002 Employee and Director Stock Incentive Plan. (Among other things, the proposal gives each director the right to annually purchase 10,000 shares of Maytag common stock, 7,000 more shares than was allowed currently.)

The audience leans forward in their seats as Hake introduces the last three stockholder proposals: elect each director annually, replace the super-majority provisions with simple majority shareholder voting, and allow shareholders to vote on poison pills proposed by the board of directors. A person in the audience who represents the initiating shareholders is recognized and stands to read the rationale for each proposal. It is clear to the audience that the proposals are attempts to eliminate some of the anti-takeover devices put in place over the years by the board of directors. Maytag had introduced a classified board in 1977, a super-majority provision in 1984, and a share purchase rights plan (poison pill) in 1986. The current super-majority voting provision requires an 80% vote of outstanding shares when a potential acquirer offers a premium price only to some shareholders. Interestingly, similar proposals had been approved by a majority vote at past shareholders' meetings but had never been implemented by the board. The board of directors had earlier presented its rationale why the passed proposals had not been implemented in the 2002 proxy statement. According to the board, although the first proposal received 55.7% of the shares voting in 2001, those shares represented only 38.7% of all shares outstanding. Even though the third proposal had received 61.6% of shares voted at the 2001 meeting, the votes only accounted for 42.8% of shares outstanding, according to the board statement. Although similar proposals to the second proposal had been approved in 2000 and 2001, the board had not chosen to implement them. According to the board, "super-majority provisions assure that carefully considered corporate governance rules are not replaced without a substantial consensus majority for change." The board has strongly argued that these provisions continue to be necessary "to protect the share-owners against takeover tactics that do not treat all shareholders fairly and equally, such as partial and two-tiered tender offers and creeping stock accumulation programs." The results of this year's votes are to be announced later in the meeting.

With the completion of the introductions and the reading of the shareholder proposals, Chairman and CEO Ralph Hake looks over the packed auditorium and presents his report on the state of the corporation. He first presents two goals that he has set for himself during his time as CEO:

1. Return the corporation to the historic earnings levels under Leonard Hadley.

2. Exceed those earnings results.

His remarks echo his Letter to the Shareholders in Maytag's *2001 Annual Report*:

In June of 2001, the Maytag board of directors entrusted me with the leadership of this company. After 12 years in the household appliance industry, I was extremely excited about joining a company with a multitude of opportunities. Although I was cognizant of the challenges, I was enamored by Maytag's powerful group of brands and distinguished heritage of quality, innovation, and achievement.

My first nine months at Maytag have only increased my enthusiasm. After meeting with my co-workers, visiting our manufacturing facilities, interacting with customers, and developing our business plans, I am confident we will attain our corporate goals of delivering sustainable profitable growth, achieving operational excellence, and creating value for our shareholders in 2002 and beyond.

We have challenges ahead of us, however. In terms of financial performance, 2001 was disappointing. We sold more and earned less than we did in 2000. Our sales grew 8.2% to $4.3 billion due to our acquisition of Amana in August and good volume in our major appliance lines.

During the year, we took a number of special charges against income, including those for discontinuing some operations and a restructuring that primarily involved a salaried workforce reduction. However, even when you exclude those charges, our comparative net income still fell 45% to $139 million, and comparative earnings per share were down 42% to $1.77.

There were a number of reasons for this performance: On the major appliance front, a combination of low price points and increased marketing, distribution and support costs had an adverse effect. Our floor care business suffered from reduced volume, and income from our vending business failed to meet expectations. We fully understand that this is not acceptable performance, and we have been addressing the issues before us.[1]

As Hake continues his speech, it becomes increasingly apparent that Maytag Corporation has come a long way from the days when F. L. Maytag sold agricultural machinery to local farmers.

History of the Company

Fred L. Maytag (or F. L., as he was commonly called), who came to Newton, Iowa, as a farm boy in a covered wagon, joined three other men in 1893 to found the Parsons Band Cutter and Self Feeder Company. The firm produced attachments invented by one of the founders to improve the performance of threshing machines. The company built its first washing machine, the Pastime, in 1907 as a sideline to its farm equipment. The founders hoped that this product would fill the seasonal slumps in the farm equipment business and enable the company to have year-round production.

In 1909, F. L. Maytag became sole owner of the firm and changed its name to The Maytag Company. Farm machinery was soon phased out as the company began to focus its efforts on washing machines. With the aid of Howard Snyder, a former mechanic whose inventive genius had led him to head Maytag's development department, the company generated a series of product and process improvements. Its gasoline-powered washer (pioneered by Maytag), for example, became so popular with rural customers without electricity that Maytag soon dominated the small town and farm markets in the United States.

Under the leadership of Lewis B. Maytag, a son of the founder, the company expanded from 1920 to 1926 into a national company. Using a radically new gyrator to move clothes within its tub, the Model 80 was introduced in 1922. F. L. Maytag, then serving as Chairman of the Board, was so impressed with the new product that he personally took one of the first four washers on a western sales trip. Sales of the Model 80 jumped from 16,000 units in 1922 to more than 258,000 units in 1926! The company went from a $280,000 loss in 1921 to profits exceeding $6.8 million in 1926. Throughout the 1920s and 1930s, Maytag Company had an average U.S. market share of 40%–45% in washing machines. During the Great Depression of the 1930s, Maytag never suffered a loss.

FROM MARKET LEADER TO NICHE MANAGER

Unfortunately, the innovative genius and entrepreneurial drive of the company's early years seemed to fade after the death of its founder. Top management became less interested in innovation and marketing than it was with quality and cost control practices. Bendix, a newcomer to the industry, introduced an automatic washing machine at the end of World War II that used a spin cycle instead of a wringer to squeeze excess rinse water out of the clothes. Maytag, however, was slow to convert to automatic washers. Management felt that the automatic washer needed more research before it could meet Maytag quality standards. The company still had a backlog of orders for its wringer washer, and management was reluctant to go into debt to finance new manufacturing facilities. This reluctance cost the company its leadership of the industry. Even with its own automatic washers, Maytag's share of the U.S. washer market fell to only 8% in 1954. Nevertheless, the company continued to be a profitable manufacturer of high-quality, high-price home laundry appliances.

During the 1960s and 1970s, Maytag reaped the benefits of its heavy orientation on quality products and cost control. *Consumer Reports* annually ranked Maytag washers and dryers as the most dependable in the U.S. market. Maytag washers lasted longer, needed fewer repairs, and had lower service costs when they did require service. The Leo Burnett advertising agency dramatized the concept of Maytag brand dependability by showing that Maytag products were so good, repairmen had nothing to do and were thus "lonely." The company's *Ol' Lonely* ads, which first aired in 1967 and featured the lonely Maytag repairman, were consistently ranked among the most effective on television. Profit margins were the highest in the industry. The company invested in building capacity, improved its dishwasher line, and changed the design of its clothes dryers. Maytag's plants were perceived at that time to be the most efficient in the industry. By the end of the 1970s, Maytag's share of the market had increased to approximately 15% in both washers and dryers.

REVITALIZATION: GROWTH THROUGH ACQUISITIONS

In 1978 top management, under the leadership of CEO Daniel Krumm, decided that the company could no longer continue as a specialty manufacturer operating only in the higher-priced end of the laundry market. Consequently, Maytag adopted a strategy to become a full-line manufacturer and develop a stronger position in the U.S. appliance industry. Up to this point the company had been able to finance its growth internally. The strategic decision was made to grow by acquisition within the appliance industry through debt and the sale of stock.

In 1981, Maytag purchased Hardwick Stove Company, a low-priced manufacturer of gas and electric ranges with an estimated 5% share of the range market. In 1982, the company acquired Jenn-Air, a niche manufacturer of high-quality built-in electric grill ranges. In 1986, Maytag purchased Magic Chef, Inc., a successful manufacturer of mass-marketed appliances in the mid-price segment of the market. The acquisition included not only Magic Chef's best-selling ranges and other products but also appliances sold under the Admiral, Norge, and Warwick labels, plus Dixie-Narco, a leading manufacturer of soft-drink vending equipment. Maytag Company and the Magic Chef family of companies were then merged under a parent Maytag Corporation on May 30, 1986, headed by Chairman and CEO Daniel Krumm. Maytag-brand products continued to be produced by Maytag Company, now just a part of the larger Maytag Corporation.

In 1988, realizing that the U.S. major home appliance market had reached maturity, the top management of the new Maytag Corporation decided to extend the corporation's growth strategy to the international arena. Maytag offered close to $1 billion in cash and Maytag stock for Chicago Pacific Corporation (CP), the owner of Hoover Company. In this one step, Maytag Corporation moved into the international home appliance marketplace, with nine manufacturing operations in the United Kingdom, France, Australia, Mexico, Colombia, and Portugal. Hoover was known worldwide for its floor care products and throughout Europe and Australia for its washers, dryers, dishwashers, microwave ovens, and refrigerators. Prior to the acquisition, Maytag's international revenues had been too small to even report.

RELUCTANT RETRENCHMENT

By 1995, Maytag Corporation had achieved its goal of becoming an internationally oriented, full-line major home appliance manufacturer. However, its profits had deteriorated significantly. Although Hoover's North American operations had always been very profitable,

Hoover Europe had not shown a profit since being acquired by Maytag, until 1994, when it earned a modest one. Hoover Australia had also incurred significant losses during this time. Unknown to Maytag Corporation's top management before the acquisition, Hoover's U.K. facilities had been in desperate need of renovation, and the product line badly needed upgrading. Some weaknesses at the South Wales facility were apparent before the purchase but had been discounted. CEO Leonard Hadley, who had served earlier as COO under CEO Daniel Krumm, later admitted that the corporation's top management had been too preoccupied with learning about the vacuum cleaner business to investigate further into Hoover's major home appliance business. Once it realized the need to modernize the U.K. facilities, Maytag's top management committed many millions of dollars to renovate the laundry and dishwasher plant in South Wales and its floor care plant in Scotland.

Although some former executives talked of a culture clash between the collegial Hoover and the more rigid Maytag executives, CEO Leonard Hadley blamed Hoover's woes purely on the poor U.K. business environment. However, industry analysts concluded that the Hoover acquisition had been a strategic error. To pay for the acquisition, management had not only increased long-term debt to its highest level in the company's history, it also had to sell more stock. These actions combined with a high level of investment in the unprofitable overseas facilities to result in lower corporate profits and decreasing earnings per share. Since other major home appliance companies continued to operate profitably during this time period, some analysts were beginning to question management's ability to run an international corporation.

After concluding that there was no way the corporation could recoup its overseas investments, Maytag sold its Hoover operations in Australia and New Zealand in December 1994 and Hoover Europe in May 1995. The sale of the Australian/New Zealand operations for $82 million resulted in a 1994 after-tax loss of $16.4 million. The sale of Hoover Europe to Candy S.p.a of Monza, Italy for $180 million resulted in a more significant 1995 after-tax loss of $135.4 million. In evaluating the strength of both Hoover Europe and Hoover Australia, Chairman Hadley commented, "Each lacked the critical mass alone to be strong players in their respective global theaters. As a result, we sold both businesses to focus on growth from our North American–based businesses." The sales enabled the corporation to reduce the long-term debt it had acquired in the Chicago Pacific purchase.

CAUTIOUS EXPANSION

Although the corporation continued to focus on North America, the firm's entry into the 21st century was characterized by several new product initiatives and by the acquisitions of Blodgett, Jade Range, and Amana. With the retirement of Leonard Hadley in 1998 as CEO, the company was led first by Lloyd Ward and subsequently by Ralph Hake.

Consistent with its commitment to North America, Maytag's top management decided in 2001 to end its 1996 joint venture with China's Hefei Rongshida (RSD). Although the joint venture to make washers and dryers had been originally considered an opportunity to be in "one of the greatest growth markets in the world,"[2] the venture had not been profitable, and its market share had failed to grow.

Maytag successfully introduced its revolutionary Neptune front-loading washer and dryer, followed by other well-received new products, such as the Maytag Gemini double-oven range and lower-price Maytag Performa and Atlantis laundry lines. According to Chairman and CEO Hake, Maytag had become the industry's most innovative maker of household appliances. The firm's Wide-by-Side refrigerator earned a New Product *Best of Show* award at the 2001 Kitchen and Bath Industry Show.

In a strategic move to diversify into the commercial side of major appliances, Maytag Corporation acquired G. S. Blodgett Corporation in 1997 for $148.3 million. Blodgett had

1997 sales of $135 million. Headquartered in Burlington, Vermont, Blodgett was a profitable manufacturer of commercial ovens, fryers, charbroilers, and other food service equipment. Its customers included major hotel and restaurant chains and institutions. Following CEO Ward's statement in early 1998 that Maytag intended to use Blodgett to increase its presence in commercial major appliances, Maytag purchased Jade Range in January 1999 for a little over $20 million. Jade made ultra-premium commercial ranges and outdoor grills. In addition, Maytag began buying a line of premium-quality commercial clothes washers from Primus, a Belgian family-owned appliance company. In August 2001, however, Maytag sold Blodgett to Middleby Corporation for $95 million. According to Hake, the sale of Blodgett reflected a strategic decision to focus on the basics. "Our core home appliance and vending businesses will be the focus of our growth strategy going forward. Activities and operations that don't directly support and complement this foundation will be de-emphasized, if not eliminated."[3] The company used the proceeds of the sale to reduce corporate debt. Although management was quiet on the subject, Lawrence Horan, an analyst at Parker Hunter, Inc., commented that Maytag had not been able to grow the commercial side of the business because it had more competence in household appliances. This was exasperated by the poorer economy of 2001.[4]

In July 2001, Maytag purchased Amana Appliances (including its major home appliance and commercial microwave businesses) for $325 million. Approximately 95% of the purchase was in cash and the remainder in Maytag stock. The Amana purchase added about $900 million to Maytag's total annual sales. Maytag's acquisition of Amana announced to the industry that, although Maytag had withdrawn from international operations, it intended to be aggressive in its home base in North America. Hake explained the rationale for the Amana purchase:

> We acquired Amana Appliances, a company with a premium brand strategy remarkably similar to Maytag's. This move not only strengthened our major appliance business by adding a leading refrigeration brand, it also has provided the basis for greater cost efficiencies throughout the organization. The integration of Amana into Maytag's major appliance division went well, and we entered 2002 with a single, successful major appliance business unit, operating under one leadership team. We are taking major appliance orders on one system, and one national sales force is handling all of our brands. Additionally, we are implementing an integrated brand strategy that will better position us in the kitchen using both the Jenn-Air and Amana brands, along with Maytag. This will lead to enhanced profits for both our company and our dealers.[5]

The U.S. Major Home Appliance Industry

The U.S. major home appliance industry in 2002 was a very successful industry. More appliances were made and sold in the United States in 2001 than in any preceding year. The Association of Home Appliance Manufacturers was predicting slight increases during 2002 in each category of "white goods"—refrigerators, freezers, washing machines, dryers, ranges, microwave ovens, and dishwashers.[6]

The major home appliance industry faced some significant threats as well as opportunities. After more than 50 years of rising sales, both in units and dollars, the U.S. and Canadian market had reached maturity. (Total unit shipments of appliances in the U.S. were a little over 70 million compared to 4.3 million units in Canada.) Aside from some normal short-term fluctuations, future unit sales were expected to grow only 1.9% annually from 2000 to 2005 in the U.S. and Canadian market. Operating margins had been dropping as appliance manufacturers had been forced to keep prices low to be competitive even though costs kept increasing. The situation was the same in Western Europe, a market 25% larger than the U.S. major home appliance market, where unit sales were expected to grow only 1.7% annually during the same period. Markets in Asia, Eastern Europe, and Latin America had become more important to world trade as more countries had changed to a free market economy. Industry analysts expected appliance markets in these areas to grow at a rate of 5%–6% annually between 2000 and 2005.[7] The industry was under pressure from governments around the world to make environmentally safe products plus significantly improve appliance efficiency in terms of energy usage and water consumption.

The U.S. major home appliance industry had consolidated from around 300 manufacturers in 1945 to only a few major players in 2002. This consolidation of the industry over the period was a result of fierce domestic competition. Emphasis on quality and durability coupled with strong price competition drove the surviving firms to increased efficiencies and a strong concern for customer satisfaction. Four major home appliance manufacturers controlled around 99% of the U.S. market for white goods. In order of 2001 market share, Whirlpool led, with 39.2%; followed by General Electric, with 23.2%; Maytag, with 21.6%; and AB Electrolux (Frigidaire), with 15.0%. The remaining 1% belonged to the foreign firms Bosch-Siemens and Haier, which had recently begun to produce in North America, and to various manufacturers of a single type or category of appliance, such as Sub-Zero (built-in refrigerators and freezers and Wolf professional ranges) and Emerson Electric (garbage disposals).

The strongest competitors in the United States during the five-year period from 1996 to 2001 were Whirlpool, Maytag, and Electrolux. Whirlpool had increased its market share by almost five points, from 34.9% five years earlier, in 1996. Maytag had been steadily increasing its market share (about 1% per year), from 15.2% in 1996 to 20.8% in 2000. Its purchase of Amana's home appliances from Goodman Global Holdings of Houston in 2001 raised Maytag's total market share an additional point, to 21.6% in 2001. Frigidaire, AB Electrolux's North American home appliance division, increased its market share over five points, from 9.6% in 1996. In contrast, General Electric had lost about nine points of market share (almost 2% each year!), from 32.0% in 1996. By the time Maytag bought Amana home appliances, Amana's market share had been 2.9% in 2000, down from 6.7% in 1996.

Both Whirlpool and AB Electrolux were global competitors, with strong positions in the Americas, Europe, and Asia. General Electric was also strong in North and South America but was much weaker in Europe and Asia. Bosch-Siemens was a newcomer to the Americas but was second in European market share and a very aggressive competitor. Haier, the largest appliance maker in China, was expanding rapidly—with new manufacturing facilities in Europe and North America. The major home appliance industry was clearly changing from a purely domestic industry with each country having its own appliance makers to one in which global competitors were engaging in battles for market share and economies of scale. Although Maytag was the only major competitor without any operations outside of North America, there were similar geographically focused companies in Europe, such as Candy and Merloni of Italy and Miele of Germany. The Asian appliance industry was still fragmented, with multiple domestic appliance manufacturers (especially Japanese) exporting to other countries within the region.

(For additional industry information, see Case 18, "U.S. Major Home Appliance Industry in 2002: Competition Becomes Global.")

Maytag Corporation Business Segments and Products

In 2002, Maytag Corporation was organized for official reporting purposes into two business segments: home appliances and commercial appliances. Home appliances constituted 94.7% of consolidated net sales in 2001. For practical purposes, however, Maytag Corporation was managed as three distinct businesses: major home appliances (Maytag, Jenn-Air, Amana, and Magic Chef brands), floor care appliances (Hoover), and commercial appliances (Dixie-Narco and Jade Range).

MAJOR HOME APPLIANCES

Compared to its primary competitors, Maytag's home appliances ranked third, with a total U.S. market share of 21.6%. Washers and dryers were Maytag's traditional strength. Market surveys consistently found Maytag brand laundry appliances to be not only the brand most desired by consumers (when price was not considered) but also the most reliable. Refrigeration was a traditional strength of Amana. Gas ranges had always been a particular strength of Magic Chef and were perceived to be very reliable in surveys.

Exhibit 3 lists Maytag's 2001 share of the U.S. market by home appliance category compared to that of the market leader. Contrasted with 1996, Maytag's share had increased in dishwashers, washing machines, clothes dryers, and refrigerators but had dropped in electric and gas ranges.

Headquartered in Newton, Iowa, the original Maytag Company was the flagship of the corporation and manufactured Maytag brand washing machines and dryers in its Newton plant. It also marketed Maytag brand cooking products made in the Cleveland, Tennessee, Magic Chef plant, a refrigerator line manufactured in the Galesburg, Illinois, Admiral plant, and dishwashers manufactured at the Jackson, Tennessee, manufacturing facility. Market emphasis was on the premium price segment and the upscale builder market. A survey of Americans found the Maytag brand to be 15th in a list of the strongest brand names, based on consumer recognition and perception of quality.

Located in Galesburg, Illinois, the Admiral plant manufactured refrigerators for Maytag, Jenn-Air, Admiral, and Magic Chef brands. The corporation had originally invested $60 million in the Galesburg plant to improve production efficiencies, enhance product quality, and increase capacity, plus another $160 in 1995 to further upgrade the facility.

Jenn-Air specialized in electric and gas downdraft grill ranges and cooktops. The brand also marketed Jenn-Air brand refrigerators, freezers, dishwashers, and disposers manufactured by the Admiral plant, the corporation's Jackson plant, and other non-Maytag appliance manufacturers, such as Emerson Electric. Jenn-Air billed itself as "The Kitchen Equipment Expert" and believed that its high-quality cooking expertise complemented Maytag Company's high-quality image in laundry appliances. Jenn-Air's Indianapolis manufacturing plant had been closed when production of ranges was concentrated at Magic Chef's Cleveland, Tennessee, facilities.

Magic Chef manufactured gas and electric ranges for the Admiral, Magic Chef, Jenn-Air, and Maytag brands in its Cleveland, Tennessee, facilities. It also marketed refrigerators, dish-

Exhibit 3

Maytag Corporation's 2001 Share of U.S. Market Compared to Market Leaders' Shares by Home Appliance Category[1]

Appliance Category	Market Leader	Leader Share	Maytag Share	Maytag Rank
Dishwashers	Whirlpool	48%	21%	2
Dryers	Whirlpool	50.5%	24%	2
Refrigerators	Whirlpool	28.5%	23%	3 (tied with GE)
Microwave ovens	Samsung	26%	3%	8
Ranges (gas)	GE	31%	17%	4
Ranges (electric)	GE	41%	14%	4
Washers	Whirlpool	51.5%	25%	2

Note:

1. Data for compactors, disposers, freezers, and range hoods not given because Maytag does not participate significantly in these appliance categories.

Source: "Special Report: 2002 Market Profile," *Appliance Manufacturer*, April 2002, p. 11.

washers, laundry equipment, and microwave ovens under the Magic Chef brand to the mid-price segment and to certain private-label businesses. Prior to its purchase by Maytag, Magic Chef had been a small, family-run business. Its product development strategy had been to be a very fast follower. Maytag Corporation had invested $50 million in the Cleveland facilities. From this investment came new lines of Magic Chef and Maytag brand ranges. The medium-to low-price orientation of the Magic Chef and Admiral brands had enabled them to be successfully sold to builders.

Located in Jackson, Tennessee, Jackson Dishwashing Products was a $43 million, 400,000-square-foot state-of-the-art manufacturing facility dedicated to producing dishwashers for the Maytag, Admiral, Jenn-Air, and Magic Chef brands. It was designed as a "team plant," with little distinction made between hierarchical levels. Upon the completion of this plant in 1992, dishwasher production was phased out at Maytag's Newton plant, and the company no longer had to purchase dishwashers from General Electric for Magic Chef or Jenn-Air.

FLOOR CARE APPLIANCES

Headquartered in North Canton, Ohio, The Hoover Company manufactured and marketed to all price segments upright and canister vacuum cleaners, stick and handheld vacuum cleaners, disposable vacuum cleaner bags, floor polishers and shampooers, central cleaning systems, commercial vacuum cleaners, and washing machines in Mexico. It heavily advertised to the consumer. The company was almost totally vertically integrated. In addition to the North Canton headquarters and three Stark County, Ohio, manufacturing plants, Hoover North America controlled four other facilities, in El Paso, Texas; Ciudad Juarez, Mexico (a maquiladora assembly plant); Burlington, Ontario (Hoover Canada); and Industrial Vallejo, Mexico (Hoover Mexicana). Praised by industry experts in 1990 as one of the best manufacturing facilities in the United States, the new North Canton "factory within a factory" was designed by an interdisciplinary team to reduce costs and improve quality. In 1996, Hoover invested $7 million in two of its Ohio plants to increase manufacturing capacity for its Steam Vac line of extractors. At the same time, Hoover also spent $44 million to double the capacity of its El Paso and Ciudad Juarez vacuum cleaner maquiladora production plants.

Hoover held a 26.5% share of the very competitive U.S. market for residential full-size vacuum cleaners and 72% of the floor polisher market in 2001. It was in first place in both categories. Nevertheless, its share of the market for full-size vacuum cleaners had significantly dropped from 40% in 1983 when it led the industry. Eureka (part of AB Electrolux of Sweden) was a close second in 2001 full-sized cleaner sales, with a U.S. market share of 26%. Royal was third in full-sized cleaner sales in 2001, with a declining market share of 17%. Hoover only held 4% of the handheld market, compared to Black & Decker's 39% and Royal's 30%. Hoover's share of the extractor market was 39.5%, down from 49% in 1996. See **Exhibit 4** for details.

Growth in the U.S. floor care market generally exceeded that of many other appliance segments. Close to 20 million vacuum cleaners (upright, canister, and stick), 3.4 million extractors, and 162 thousand polishers were sold in the United States in 2001. Compared to the 10%–12% sales increases of 1999 and 2000, only moderate growth was predicted for the near future. Although 99% of U.S. households had at least one vacuum cleaner, many had two to three full-sized vacuums plus handheld vacuums. The average life expectancy of full-size vacuum cleaners was eight years.

COMMERCIAL APPLIANCES

Maytag's commercial appliances were composed of Jade Range's commercial cooking and refrigeration equipment, Dynasty's commercial washers and dryers, and Dixie-Narco's vending equipment. The primary product lines of Jade Range were ultra-premium commercial

Exhibit 4

U.S. Floor Care Market Shares by Category
(By percentage of total U.S. sales)

Appliance	2001	1996	Appliance	2001	1996
Vacuum cleaners (upright, canister, stick)			**Vacuum cleaners (handheld)**		
Hoover	26.5	37	Applica (Black & Decker)	39	30
Eureka	26	24	Royal	30	42
Royal	17	11	EuroPro	14.5	—
Matsushita	9	12	Eureka	7.5	5
Bissell	6.5	4	Hoover	4	11
Oreck	5	—	Bissell	2	8
Iona	3	2	Others	3	4
Kirby	2.5	5	**Extractors**		
Aerus (Electrolux)	2	2	Bissell	44.5	41
Rexaire	1.5	2	Hoover	39.5	49
Others	1	1	Royal	15	—
Floor polishers			Others	1	10
Hoover	72	70			
Thorne Electic	19	20			
Electrolux	9	10			

Source: "Special Report: 2002 Market Profile," *Appliance Manufacturer*, April 2002, p. 12.

ranges sold under the Jade brand and outdoor grills sold for residential use under the Dynasty brand. The Jade and Dynasty appliances were made in a plant in Commerce, California. When Jade Range was purchased in 1999, then-CEO Hadley stated that he expected Jade to add to Maytag's cooking product knowledge in both residential and commercial appliances.[8]

Dixie-Narco, Inc., made canned and bottled soft drink and juice vending machines sold to soft drink syrup bottlers and distributors, canteen owners, and others. Headquartered in Williston, South Carolina, Dixie-Narco manufactured vending machines in its factory there. The unit sold vending equipment directly to independent bottlers and full-service operators who installed banks of vending machines in offices and factories. It also marketed through bottlers directly to syrup company-owned bottlers. Sales of vending machines continued to be relatively flat in the United States, but due to strong demand for Dixie-Narco products, the company was able to hold its solid share of the U.S. market. International sales had been increasing, thanks to the introduction in 1994 of its glass-front merchandiser without coin slots. Traditional coin-fed vending machines had not been well accepted outside North America. In 2001, Dixie-Narco expanded beyond Coke and Pepsi products to market Eastman Kodak film and cameras and to test-market milk vending machines in schools. It also formed an alliance with Nippon Conlux, Ltd., to be the exclusive distributor of electronic payment systems for vending machines in the United States and Canada.

When asked why Dixie-Narco remained a part of Maytag Corporation, past-CEO Hadley had responded:

> *Mechanically, a vending machine is a refrigerator, and we build thousands of refrigerators per day at our plant in Galesburg, Illinois. . . . As a marketing assignment, our Dixie-Narco customers have the same needs as our Maytag commercial laundry customers. . . . Dixie-Narco's great value to us is that it has a different set of competitors than the major home appliance business or the floor care indus-try. It allows us an important earnings stream from a business that our largest two major appliance competitors don't have. . . . It provides us with an important supplement to our U.S. business by allowing us an international export opportunity.[9]*

Role of Strategic Planning

Strategic planning had led to many of the recent changes in Maytag Corporation. In 1978, when Leonard Hadley was working as Maytag Company's Assistant Controller, CEO Daniel Krumm asked him and two others from manufacturing and marketing to serve as a strategic planning task force. Krumm asked the three people the question "If we keep doing what we're now doing, what will the Maytag Company look like in five years?" The question posed a challenge—considering that the company had never done financial modeling and none of the three knew much of strategic planning. Hadley worked with a programmer in his MIS section to develop "what if" scenarios. The task force presented its conclusion to the board of directors: A large part of Maytag's profits (the company had the best profit margin in the industry) was coming from products and services with no future: repair parts, portable washers and dryers, and wringer washing machines.

Looking back to 1978, Hadley felt that this was a crucial time for the company. The Board of Directors was becoming less conservative as more outside directors came from companies that were growing through acquisitions. With the support of the board, Krumm promoted Hadley to the new position of Vice President of Corporate Planning. Hadley was given the task of analyzing the industry to search for acquisition candidates. Until that time, most planning had been oriented internally, with little external analysis. From that time forward, the job of the Director of Corporate Strategy has been to work closely with the company's business units to coordinate and facilitate strategic planning throughout the company. Maytag's current President of Maytag Appliances, William Beer, had served in this position earlier in his career.

Marketing

Of the four major home appliance brands—Maytag, Amana, Magic Chef, and Jenn-Air—only the Maytag and Amana brands had been heavily advertised to consumers. The Magic Chef and Jenn-Air brands usually received cooperative advertising, promotions through the dealers, and some print advertising. Both sold well to house and apartment builders, in contrast to the relatively poorer sales to this channel by Maytag and Amana. The lower-priced Admiral brand received little advertising. Norge and Hardwick were low-end brands used for special opportunities and received little to no marketing effort. Advertising expenses were $164 million in 1999, $158.5 in 2000, and $187.2 in 2001. Corporate selling, general, and administrative expenses (of which advertising expenses were a part) had risen from $609.3 million in 2000 to $704.6 million in 2001.[10] A single corporate sales force handled the Maytag, Amana, Jenn-Air, Magic Chef, and Admiral brands.

According to William Beer, President of Maytag Appliances, Maytag had three "power" brands—Maytag, Amana, and Jenn-Air—and two "value" brands—Magic Chef and Admiral. The acquisition of Amana in 2001 created a challenge in positioning the brands. "Jenn-Air is at one end (upscale) and is sold through select distribution channels. Maytag is broadly distributed and will continue to be. And Amana is somewhere between those two guideposts." Beginning in mid-2002, the ad/marketing campaigns were to play to the strengths of these power brands. "For Maytag, it will be dependability and performance. For Amana, it will be clever conveniences and styling. And for Jenn-Air, innovation, elegance, and high-end performance," explained Beer.[11]

Chris Wignall, Vice President of Marketing, further explained how advertising was being used to differentiate the power brands. The Maytag brand ads featured the Ol' Lonely repairman and his younger sidekick in humorous situations. Some print ads were used in addition to the usual heavy television ads. Amana's campaign emphasized print ads in the home-and-shelter magazines but also used television. Humor was also used. One example was for the

Amana Messenger refrigerator, with message-record capabilities in which the message said, "Touch the cake and you're toast.—Love, Mom." Jenn-Air's ad campaign targeted an upscale audience through print ads in city magazines and special interest publications.

Maytag and the Leo Burnett USA advertising agency (originator of the Ol' Lonely ad) were honored by the New York chapter of the American Marketing Association in 1998, with a gold EFFIE award for the "Keeping Your Cool" advertising campaign featuring "I Scream" and "U.F.O." (Unidentified Frozen Objects). The campaign was designed to let consumers know that the food they were throwing out prematurely would have stayed fresh longer if they had a Maytag refrigerator. This award was Maytag's fourth gold EFFIE in eight years.[12] The 1995 award was for the campaign featuring the Maytag repairman, Ol' Lonely, and included TV commercials, print advertising, and point-of-purchase materials.[13] Few people realized that appliance manufacturers such as Maytag did not do their own repair work. It was contracted out to independent dealers. According to Dale Reeder, Vice President of Customer Service at Maytag Appliances, "For Maytag, effective customer service is absolutely critical, not just to our retail partners, but to our customers." Reeder pointed out that research indicated that if the level of service was strong when a product failed, consumer loyalty was actually higher than before the sale[14] (see **Exhibit 5**).

Distribution channels were another challenge for Maytag, especially for the company's power brands. According to Wignall, "Maytag is broad-based (Maytag Home Appliance Centers, Lowe's, Home Depot, Sears, etc.). Amana is less so, and tends to be distributed through more of the independent retailers. Jenn-Air is more tightly focused, with builders and upscale retailers being the main channels." The Maytag brand sponsored the Women's United Soccer Association (WUSA) and the uniforms of the Atlanta Beat soccer team. Management hoped to use the WUSA sponsorship to gain greater access to a key target market: affluent women. Although the corporation was currently satisfied with its interim brand positioning/distribution strategy, longer-term marketing strategies needed to be developed. "We need a higher degree of precision around the consumers we are targeting, in terms of demographics, psycho-graphics, and societal trends," stated Wignall.[15]

Through the 1990s, the Maytag brand sales slowly changed from being distributed only through its 725 independent dealers to being heavily sold through the "power retailers" of Sears, Best Buy, Circuit City, Sam's Club, Home Depot, and Lowe's. Although this change antagonized the independent dealers, it significantly boosted sales. For example, sales to Sears alone increased from 11% in 1999 to 18% in 2001 of the corporation's consolidated annual net sales. Part of these sales included providing Kenmore brand appliances to Sears. Michael Headley, a veteran Maytag appliance dealer, expressed the views of most appliance dealers when he stated that the prices charged by super-sized competitors pushed down profit margins, making it difficult for the small dealer to survive. For example, Headley's largest store had 4,000 square feet of space, compared to the giant electronics or home improvement stores that can have more than 100,000 square feet. "You'll see independent dealers dropping like flies in the next couple of years," commented Headley. "They can't compete against the super-stores."[16]

In 1999, the corporation opened in Des Moines, Iowa, a new style of Maytag brand appliance store designed to be more inviting to customers who want to "test drive" the equipment. The concept was developed by Maytag in conjunction with Maytag appliance dealer Michael Headley. According the Steve Anderson, Maytag's Manager of Survey Research, the old approach to selling appliances was to fill the store with appliances lined up in rows. The new approach, in contrast, involved setting up appliances in a more home-like setting. "It's more of a come and look at me type atmosphere," commented Patti Beatty of West Des Moines. Although Headley later closed his two test stores, the company by 2001 had successfully opened 11 "Maytag Stores" in other states.[17]

Some industry analysts argued that the company strategy for the Maytag brand was confusing. Efraim Levy, an analyst with S&P Equity Group, said that the Maytag brand was posi-

Exhibit 5

The Real Maytag Repairman

> The "Ol' Lonely" Maytag repairman created for television ads in 1967 had little to do with the actual daily life of a real Maytag repairman. Michael Headlee of Michael's Maytag Home Appliance Center in Des Moines, Iowa, repaired approximately 40 malfunctioning machines per week. On average, only three of them were Maytags. Although Headlee sold only Maytag, he serviced all brands. No one exclusively repaired Maytag-brand appliances. "You won't find one because he would starve," explained Headlee. Headlee had been working as an independent service contractor until 1991, when Maytag Company asked him to open a Maytag store.
>
> Headlee enjoyed doing stunts to show off the quality built into Maytag-brand appliances. In 1992 he started a Maytag and a Kenmore washer after rigging both to run continuously. Although Maytag officials weren't too excited about this project, Headlee went ahead to see for himself which product would last longer. The Kenmore died in six months; the Maytag continued for two years.
>
> When a customer walked into Headlee's store one day to look at refrigerators, Headlee showed him the fine points of a floor model. According to Headlee, Maytag built for the "what ifs." For example, what if a neighbor boy used the door as a step ladder and knocked out one of the storage bins? No problem, said Headlee. The bins were removable and adjustable. No need to replace the $180 liner or the $35 bin—only a $2 breakaway clip. "The hinges are heavier than any other in the industry. . . . Rollers? We've got the fattest rollers in the industry." To demonstrate, Headlee took out the meat-cheese drawer, turned it over on the floor, and jumped on it. According to Headlee, a person could do aerobics on the meat-cheese drawer!
>
> Competition from "super stores" kept profit margins low, so Headlee depended on repair work to stay in business. "We got a deck of cards. We got a cribbage board. And that keeps us pretty well occupied when we're not working on . . . a Kenmore or a Whirlpool," joked Headlee.

Source: M. A. Lickteig, "A Real Repairman Juggles Calls and Sales," *Des Moines Register* (November 1, 1994), p. M1.

tioned as a higher-end line, but the brand was also being sold through discounters, such as Sam's Club and Home Depot. He contended that higher-end brands should be limited to independent dealers and mass merchandisers, like Sears, and lower-priced models, such as the Maytag Proforma line, should be sold through discount stores.[18]

Hoover floor care products had traditionally received strong advertising in all the media. The business unit continued its successful "Nobody Does It Like Hoover" consumer-oriented advertising. After noting that 70 dealers accounted for approximately 80% of Hoover's North American floor care sales, management restructured the sales organization in 1992 to better serve these "power retailers."

Corporate Culture

Much of Maytag Corporation's corporate culture derived from F. L. Maytag's personal philosophy and from lessons the founder learned when starting the Maytag Company at the turn of the century. His greatest impact was still felt in Maytag's (1) commitment to quality, (2) concern for employees, (3) concern for the community, (4) concern for innovation, (5) promotion from within, (6) dedication to hard work, and (7) emphasis on performance:

- **Commitment to quality.** Concerned when almost half the farm implements sold were defective in some way, F. L. Maytag vowed to eliminate all defects. Maytag's employees over the years had taken great pride in the company's reputation for high-quality products and being a part of "the dependability company."

- **Concern for employees.** Long before it was required to do so by law, Maytag Company established safety standards in the workplace and offered its employees accident and life insurance policies. Wages have traditionally been some of the highest in the industry.

- **Concern for the community.** Following F. L. Maytag's example, Maytag management has been active in community affairs and concerned about pollution. The decision to build its new automatic washer plant in Newton after World War II indicated the company's loyalty to the town.

- **Concern for innovation.** From its earliest years, the company was not interested in cosmetic changes for the sake of sales, but in internal improvements related to quality, durability, and safety.

- **Promotion from within.** F. L. Maytag was very concerned about building company loyalty and trust. The corporation's policy of promoting from within was an extension of that concern.

- **Dedication to hard work.** In tune with the strong work ethic permeating the Midwestern United States, F. L. Maytag put in huge amounts of time to establish and maintain the company. His fabled trip west, while chairman of the board, to sell personally a train-car load of washers set an example to his sales force and became a permanent part of company lore.

- **Emphasis on performance.** Preferring to be judged by his work rather than by his words, F. L. Maytag was widely regarded as a good example of the Midwestern work ethic.

This intense Maytag corporate culture had traditionally been one of the company's key strengths. It was seen by many to be an important contributor to the company's reputation and ability to make and sell high-quality products. This devotion to quality was exemplified by a corporate policy that no cost reduction proposal would be approved if it reduced product quality in any way. A 2000 survey of 26,000 people from all walks of life ranked Maytag second in corporate reputation (after Johnson & Johnson) of all U.S. firms.[19]

Maytag management expected any acquired company to adopt Maytag's culture. This first became an issue when Maytag acquired Admiral's refrigeration plant as part of its Magic Chef purchase in 1986. A prime reason for the acquisition had been to obtain the expertise and facilities to make a Maytag brand refrigerator. Unfortunately, the Admiral plant had been allowed by previous management to deteriorate. The employees had little pride in what they were doing, and refrigerators rolled off the line with screws driven in crooked and temperature balances askew.[20] Worried about their jobs, Admiral employees were very pleased when the company became part of Maytag. Nevertheless, they weren't sure how they would be treated by new management. When Leonard Hadley, then serving as Maytag Company President, first visited Admiral's plant in Galesburg, he was concerned that the Admiral plant would not be able to produce the level of quality needed for Maytag products. During the discussion, Admiral personnel asked Hadley when the name on the plant water tower would be changed from Admiral to Maytag. Hadley responded, "When you earn it." It was very clear to all that the Admiral plant needed to adopt the values of the Maytag culture if it was to have any future. Admiral's labor union worked closely with Maytag management to help ensure the future of the plant and its employees. The refrigerator resulting from the Maytag-Admiral collaboration was a huge success. The project crystallized corporate management's philosophy for forging synergies among the Maytag companies, while simultaneously allowing the expertise among those units to flourish.

The successful integration of Jenn-Air and Magic Chef (including Admiral) into the Maytag corporate culture did not prepare Maytag's management for dealing with its acquisition of Hoover in 1989. There was little difficulty with Hoover North America since the company had always been the leader in the vacuum cleaner business. Its management and employees had pride in their work and endorsed many of Maytag's core values (such as being involved in its local community and making quality products). Since Maytag's management had little knowledge of the floor care business, it allowed Hoover North America to operate fairly autonomously. Hoover's European operations were, however, a very different matter. Visiting

Maytag executives were perceived by their British counterparts as being too rigid and uptight. The Maytag executives, for their part, saw the British managers as being "laid back" and too collegial. Even after pouring millions of dollars into the U.K. plants to make them more competitive, Maytag was unable to adequately deal with the Hoover Europe culture (among other things) and sold Hoover's European holdings in 1995.

Maytag's management hoped that the integration of Amana with Maytag would go smoothly. According to Arthur Learmonth, Vice President of Manufacturing and Engineering of Maytag Appliances, "The Amana acquisition has been more of a blending than it has been an assimilation. The cultures are very much the same and the strengths of Maytag and Amana complement each other, with Amana's strengths tending to be in refrigeration and Maytag being more focused on laundry and wet products."[21] Even though Amana had been losing market share recently, Maytag management and employees generally respected this appliance maker—located less than 50 miles from Newton, in Amana, Iowa. Founded in 1934, Amana pioneered the side-by-side refrigerator freezer and the counter-top microwave oven—the Radarange. Amana's overall market share had been dropping since the mid-1990s. Soon after Maytag's purchase of Amana's home appliance business in June 2001, 22 top executives left Amana because of job duplication with Maytag management. Although the typical Amana employees had some concern for their jobs, they accepted Maytag as being a good company.[22]

Executive Succession

Until the mid-1990s, most of the Maytag Corporation executive officers had worked their way up through the corporation and had spent most their careers immersed in the Maytag Company culture. This had certainly been the case for Leonard Hadley, Chair and CEO, who since joining the company as a cost accountant, had served the company continuously until his retirement in 1999. Hadley came out of retirement in 2000 and served an additional year during the search for a new Maytag CEO. Once Ralph Hake was hired as CEO, Hadley retired for the second time but remained on the board until January 2002.

In a move to diversify top management backgrounds in 1993, then-CEO Leonard Hadley hired John Cunningham to serve as Corporate Executive Vice President and Chief Financial Officer (CFO) and Joseph Fogliano to serve as Corporate Executive Vice President and President of North American Operations. These were the second and third, respectively, most powerful corporate executive officers after Hadley. Cunningham had previously been Vice President and Assistant General Manager of IBM's Main Frame Division. Fogliano previously had served as President and CEO of Thomson Electronics.

In a surprise move, North American President Fogliano resigned from the corporation in August 1995. In an interview, Fogliano (age 55) stated that he had joined the corporation with the understanding that he would be a leading candidate to replace Leonard Hadley. As time went by, according to Fogliano, it became apparent that this was not to be. He further explained that there may have been a lack of fit between himself and the Maytag culture.[23] Four months later, John Cunningham announced that he was leaving the corporation to take a similar position with Whirlpool Corporation.

The corporation hired Lloyd D. Ward in 1996 to serve as Executive Vice President and President of Maytag Appliances. Ward had previously served as president of PepsiCo's western and central Frito-Lay sales divisions. Armed with a strong background in marketing, Ward was instrumental in creating the successful introduction extravaganza for Maytag's innovative front-loading Neptune washer in 1997. Heralded by the press as the top U.S. African-American executive, Ward replaced Leonard Hadley as CEO and Chair of Maytag Corporation in 1999. Ward was a charismatic speaker who stood in stark contrast to the quiet-spoken style of Leonard Hadley. Ward worked to speed up the corporation's traditionally slow product development efforts in order to get new products more quickly to the market. He also proposed that corporate headquarters might be moved out of Iowa and that many corporate administrative jobs be outsourced. He also added a group president structure so that division presidents would no longer report directly to the CEO. He replaced veteran executives, such as William Beer, with people he had worked with earlier at PepsiCo and Procter & Gamble. These actions, among others, served to antagonize the workforce and the Newton community. Newton assembly line workers complained that the emphasis on getting to market faster meant that quality production standards were being unnecessarily lowered. Some in the community had been disturbed that Ward had chosen to live in Des Moines instead of in Newton—even after becoming CEO and Chair of the corporation. When combined with the rumor circulating in the summer of 2000 that AB Electrolux was thinking of purchasing Maytag, employees, shareholders, and the local community were emotionally shaken and uncertain of the company's future. The average share of Maytag stock had fallen from its high of $70 in mid-1999 to under $30 during the fourth quarter of 2000. Concerned about differences over strategy and the direction of the company, the board of directors asked for Ward's resignation at its November 2000 meeting. The board also asked Leonard Hadley to return to the CEO and Chair position while they searched for Ward's replacement.

Immediately dismantling Ward's group structure, Hadley stated, "The group president structure duplicated many of the functions and expenses that exist already at the business unit level. A structure that has division presidents reporting directly to the CEO is one that has worked well in the past and, I believe, is a proven model for a corporation our size." Hadley also reversed centralized research and development in favor of handling it within business units. Ward's outsourcing plan was also canceled. According to Hadley, "We must prudently, but smartly, measure our resources and deploy those resources against the core businesses in our most critical areas. This is also a model that has worked for us in the past."[24] Hadley also stated that Maytag would be staying in Newton. Said Hadley, "I'm disappointed that so much time, money, and effort were devoted to the project, that so many people were distracted, and that so much work in our business was disrupted by it."[25] With Hadley's return to power, three executives hired by Ward also tendered their resignations. In February 2001, Hadley announced the return of William Beer, the former head of the Maytag Appliance Group, to his former position as President of Major Appliances.

Maytag employees at all levels were pleased to have Beer back with the company. Beer had joined Maytag in 1974 as a market analyst. He then served as Director of Corporate Strategy in 1991. In 1993 he was named Vice President of Marketing for Maytag and Admiral products. In 1996 he was promoted to Senior Vice President for Product Supply for Maytag Appliances. Beer first served as President of Maytag Appliances from 1998 to 2000. He had a bachelor's degree in business administration from University of Nebraska, Lincoln, and had done graduate work at Drake University.

With the arrival of Ralph F. Hake as the new CEO and Chairman of the board, Leonard Hadley retired once again. Most employees and shareholders seemed to be pleased that the board had found someone like Hake who had significant experience in the major home appliance industry. While at Whirlpool, Hake had led the company's North American region operations, served as President of Whirlpool's Bauknecht Appliance Group, Vice President of Whirlpool Europe, and Whirlpool's CFO, before being passed over for the CEO position. Hake was a business and economics graduate of the University of Cincinnati and held an MBA from the University of Chicago. In early 2002, Hake reiterated Hadley's earlier announcement that Maytag's headquarters would remain in Newton. The local community was pleased to note that Hake was building a $750,00 home within Newton. "We love that," said Bill Jensen, a retired "Maytager," the local term for anyone who works or has worked for the company. Hake stated that he looked forward to walking home for lunch once his new home was finished sometime in late 2002. Hake and his wife, Robin, quickly involved themselves in the local community. They donated several thousand dollars to a downtown beautification project. Hake's wife volunteered to chair a Chamber of Commerce committee. Newton's Mayor David Aldridge stated that Ralph Hake has been readily accessible to city officials, businesses, and community leaders. "He gives you time to sit and visit. He's a very open, easy person to converse with," commented Aldridge.[26]

R&D and Purchasing

Research and Development (R&D) at Maytag Company (long before it acquired other firms to become Maytag Corporation) had always been interested in internal improvements related to quality, durability, and safety. This orientation traditionally dominated the company's view of product development. One example was the careful way the company chose to replace in 1989 the venerable Helical Drive transmission with a new Dependable Drive transmission for its automatic washers. The new drive was delivered in 1975, patented in 1983, and put into test markets in 1985, after it was demonstrated that the drive would contribute to a 20-year product life. The Dependable Drive contained only 40 parts, as compared to the previous drive's 65, and allowed the agitator to move 153 strokes a minute compared to only 64 previously.

However, this methodical approach to R&D meant that Maytag Corporation might miss out on potential innovations. Realizing this dilemma, the corporation began to emphasize closer relationships with its key suppliers in both product development and process engineering. Joe Thomson, Vice President of Purchasing at Galesburg Refrigeration Products (Admiral), provided one example:

> We made an arrangement with a large steel supplier that led to a team effort to establish hardness specifications on our cabinet and door steel to improve fabrication. This team was very successful and the quality improvement and reduction in cost reached all our expectations. The company is now supplying all of our steel requirement.[27]

These strategic alliances between appliance makers and their suppliers were one way to speed up the application of new technology to new products and processes. For example, Maytag Company was approached by one of its suppliers, Honeywell's Microswitch Division, offering its expertise in fuzzy logic technology—a technology Maytag did not have at that time. The resulting partnership in product development resulted in Maytag's new IntelliSense dishwasher. Unlike previous dishwashers, which had to be set by the user, Maytag's fuzzy logic dishwasher automatically selected the proper cycle to get the dishes clean based on a series of factors such as the amount of dirt, presence of detergent, and other factors.[28] Terry Carlson, Vice President of Procurement for Maytag Corporation, stressed the importance of close relationships with suppliers:

> Strategic partnerships are a developing reality in our organization. . . . By paring our supplier base down by more than 50% in the past three years, we are encouraging greater supplier participation in our product design and production-planning processes. We're making choices to establish preferred supplier directions for our technical groups. These groups interact with their supplier counterparts. We are assigning joint task teams to specific projects, be they new-product-design oriented or continuous improvement of current products or processes.[29]

Prior to 1996, the various Maytag manufacturing plants acted independently and autonomously in their sourcing of components and materials. Since that time, corporate headquarters coordinated purchasing decisions to reach higher efficiencies but has allowed the plants significant leeway. According to Carlson, purchasing "signaled" the preferred suppliers to the engineering groups but didn't issue directives. The groups then worked together with the suppliers on new designs.[30] According to Doug Ringger, Director of Product Planning for Admiral and Maytag products, the use of cross-functional teams has helped cut development time in half from what it used to be. He states, "By having input from all areas early in the development cycle, issues are resolved before becoming problems."[31]

During the second half of the 1990s, the corporation poured significant money and effort into new technology and product development. In 1998, for example, the company spent $28 million to develop innovations in its traditional line of clothes washers and dryers and to upgrade its laundry manufacturing operations in Newton. In September 1999, Maytag announced the formation of its World Innovation Network, an integrated set of strategic partnerships, alliances, and engineering resources focused on delivering continuous discovery, invention, and rapid deployment of innovation. Through relationships with Arthur D. Little, Rhode Island School of Design, and the Battelle Institute, the company was attempting to further new technology development and application.[32] In early 2000, Maytag acquired an ownership position in e-Vend.net, a company making technology to control vending machines and appliances over the Internet. The company also formed an agreement with Microsoft to develop "smart" appliances that can interact with each other and the Internet. Representatives of Maytag served on a special committee with Microsoft to define how refrigerators, microwaves, and ovens will communicate with one another.

The corporation's R&D expenses were $58.3 million in 1999, $71.8 million in 2000, and $84.8 million in 2001. In 2001, the company announced that it was investing $8 million to expand three laundry products' R&D laboratories in Newton. Referring to the company's recent successful stream of new product introductions, William Beer stated that Maytag would launch a product in 2003 "that will rival Neptune in terms of innovation and success." Other recent successful new products were the Maytag Jetclean II Dishwasher (the first dishwasher with three full racks), the Jenn-Air Luxury Series Built-in Refrigerator (capable of being personalized for the buyer), and the Maytag Gemini Gas and Electric Ranges (containing twin ovens that operate independently). Beer said that Maytag will focus its efforts on designing in technology that improves the quality of life without complicating daily living. Such features, he stated, included turbidity sensors in dishwashers, adaptive defrost control systems in refrigerators, or, perhaps, a "smart" dryer that would be interconnected with a washer, thus enabling it to know what types of clothing were washed. The dryer could then set itself based on this information.[33]

Maytag applied new market research methodologies to define the benefits most desired by the consumer. In the past Maytag would prototype a new appliance or new features and ask the consumer, "What do you think?" Maytag recently applied the science of ethnography, literally having researchers live in a consumer's home to understand his or her lifestyle, then designing products to serve that lifestyle. "Before, all we cared about was how consumers used their dishwasher," said Beer. "Today we are just as interested in knowing they have to pick up Suzi for soccer and deliver Tommy to piano lessons. We weren't putting the refrigerator or dishwasher in a wide enough context to drive pure innovation. We could drive product development, but we couldn't truly change the game."[34] In recognition for its efforts, Maytag received the 1999 Outstanding Corporate Innovator Award by the Product and Development Association. The award, which recognizes firms for sustained success in the introduction of new products, was the first in its 12-year history to be awarded to an appliance manufacturer.[35]

According to T. Brent Freese, Director of Industrial Design at Maytag, it takes 4 to 12 ideas to get to one that can be developed into a new product. "Ideas are confirmed through consumer research, with some value assigned to them as they line up in a business model. Then that model would be reviewed for execution of resources before moving forward." One example, said Freese, was "the zig-zag configuration of the Maytag Wide-by-Side Refrigerator which was designed around how people want to store party trays, pizza boxes, etc." One task that faced Freese and his staff was to create a "family look" for each of the different brands. "We need to differentiate our Jenn-Air, Maytag, and Amana brands so that they aren't competing."[36]

Although President Beer envisioned Maytag's future as having a continuous stream of innovative new products, CEO Hake was more reserved. "We're not going to have product hits each and every year like Neptune and Gemini," cautioned Hake. "Therefore we have to look at what we can do from a channel standpoint, from an individual dealer standpoint, and what we can do outside the Core five products that is tangential or similar, and that will enable us to grow." In a recession, Hake was concerned about trimming costs to stay competitive. "Right now we're running at about 17% SGA [selling, general, and administrative expenses as a percentage of sales], and we want that at 15%."[37]

Manufacturing

The Maytag Appliances unit contained the original Maytag Company plus the manufacturing plants of Admiral, Magic Chef, and Amana, in addition to the Jackson dishwasher plant, for a total of nine plants. (Jenn-Air's Indianapolis plant was not included since it had recently been closed and consolidated with Magic Chef's Cleveland facilities.) Four of the nine current manufacturing plants served as "Centers of Excellence," in which engineering and R&D activities were centralized. These were:

- Refrigeration—Amana, Iowa (Amana plant)
- Laundry—Newton, Iowa (Maytag plant)
- Cooking—Cleveland, Tennessee (Magic Chef plant)
- Dishwashers—Jackson, Tennessee

Additional manufacturing plants were in Galesburg, Illinios (Admiral refrigeration); Herrin, Illinios (Magic Chef laundry); Searcy, Arkansas (Amana laundry); Florence, Kentucky (Amana cooking); and Jefferson City, Missouri (components). Given the corporation's interest in obtaining synergy in production and marketing among the various products, there was no attempt to identify or isolate Admiral, Jenn-Air, Magic Chef, or Amana as separate profit centers. The Admiral Galesberg plant made refrigerators for all the brands. Magic Chef's Cleveland facilities made cooking products for Maytag, and so on.

Like other major home appliance manufacturers, Maytag Corporation had been investing millions of dollars in upgrading its plants and other facilities. Once considered to be the most efficient in the nation, Maytag's Newton, Iowa, plant had shown its age by the late 1980s. Consequently, top management made a controversial decision to move dishwasher production from its Newton plant to a new plant in Jackson, Tennessee. This new plant was dedicated to the manufacturing of dishwashers for all the corporation's brands. This was in line with the industry trend to build "dedicated" highly efficient plants to produce only one product line, with variations for multiple brands and price levels. Previously, only Maytag brand dishwashers had been made in Newton. Dishwashers had been purchased from General Electric for the Jenn-Air and Magic Chef brands. After only two years of operation, Maytag spent $13.7 million to add two more assembly lines to its successful Jackson dishwasher plant. The corporation also invested $160 million to further update the old Admiral refrigeration plant in Galesburg, Illinois, from 1995 to 1998. It also invested $12 million in 1998 plus $3 million in 2001 to upgrade and increase production capacity in its Herrin, Illinois, plant. In addition to making washing machines, the Herrin plant made transmissions used in the Newton and Herrin laundry plants.

Community leaders and union officials who had been discouraged by the corporation's dishwasher decision were jubilant in January 1994, when top management announced that it had chosen Newton as the production site for its new line of horizontal-axis (H-axis) clothes washing machines. (The Iowa Department of Economic Development had offered Maytag a $1 million forgivable loan if it built the plant in Newton.[38]) A front-loader, the new Neptune washer used 40% less water than comparable top-loaders (vertical axis) and significantly less electricity. Like Frigidaire, Maytag concluded that only a horizontal axis washer would meet future U.S. Department of Energy (DOE) standards. In contrast, GE and Whirlpool were unsure about the superiority of this design and instead designed more efficient vertical-axis washers. According to John Jansen, Vice President and General Manager of Newton Laundry Products, "We had to make the critical investment decision without knowing how the DOE would decide. It was an environment of tremendous uncertainty. We didn't know whether the washer would be a niche product or a dominant product. So we had to develop a strategy from an investment and manufacturing standpoint that offered us the flexibility to support a range of scenarios, from the H-axis being a niche product all the way to 100% conversion."[39] The company had invested another $11 million to add a second assembly line for increased manufacturing capacity of the Neptune washers and dryers.

The plan for centralizing the engineering and R&D activities within each of the appliance division's four product categories (cooking, laundry, refrigeration, and dishwashers) was implemented once Amana became a part of Maytag Corporation. According to Arthur Learmonth, Vice President of Manufacturing and Engineering of Maytag Appliances, "We had to make a choice between a decentralized or centralized approach, and to a certain extent we came up with a middle approach with the four Centers of Excellence and with key individuals sprinkled around at all the plants." Each of the core businesses, explained Learmonth, had a vice president and general manager headquartered at the Centers, to whom engineering reported. Maytag also had two senior directors of R&D and manufacturing for overall coordination of these areas. "This approach gives us the advantages of having decentralized engineering, while the strategists are able to tie everything together."[40]

Maytag Corporation launched a Lean Sigma initiative in 1998. The program combined "lean" manufacturing with the Six Sigma process utilized by Motorola. The focus of Lean Manufacturing was on reducing waste, managing shorter lead times, and increasing flexibility. The emphasis in Six Sigma was on process improvement—that is, defining, measuring, analyzing, improving, and controlling results. During the first quarter of 2002, the company held 800 training programs, each involving groups of 10–12 hourly and salaried employees for as much as a week in length. According to Vice President Learmonth, the program had resulted in 20%–30% productivity cost savings. The use of the program at the Jackson dishwasher plant increased productivity by 22% an hour and improved quality by 55%.[41] By simply reducing the work flow in the Cleveland, Tennessee, plant, more than $25 million was saved.

Management hoped that the Lean Sigma initiative would enable the company to provide consumers with made-to-order appliances delivered within a week of the initial order. The corporation hired TBM Consulting Group in early 2000 to help link the manufacturing process via computer, allowing for changes to be made at each step. "Once lean manufacturing systems are in place, linking various parts of the supply chain electronically is relatively easy," stated Anand Sharma, President and CEO of TBM. "It will lead directly to improved responsiveness to the market and reduced lead times, and virtually eliminate unsold physical inventories."[42]

Human Resources and Labor Relations

Throughout the corporation, employees were organized into various labor unions. The bargaining unit representing Maytag's unionized employees in Newton, Iowa, was the United Auto Workers. The unions representing employees at other Maytag Corporation companies were the International Brotherhood of Electrical Workers (Hoover North America) and the International Association of Machinists and Aerospace Workers (Magic Chef and Amana facilities). All the presidents of local unions belonged to the Maytag Council, which met once a year to discuss union issues.

Traditionally, the Maytag Company had had cordial relations with its local union, but the change to a large corporation seemed to alter that union relationship. Nevertheless, until 2000, the corporation had not had any strikes by any of its unions since a 1974 one-day walkout at Maytag Company. This was worthy of note considering that during the three-year period 1990–1992 the corporation reduced employment by 4,500 people.

In June 2000, 1,200 members of the International Association of Machinist and Aerospace Workers at Maytag's Herrin, Illinois, washing machine plant went on strike for nine days while disagreements with a proposed five-year contact were settled. In September 2001, the International Association of Machinists and Aerospace Workers Local 1526 went on a two-month strike after its Amana, Iowa, refrigeration plant workers rejected a new three-year contract. The union disagreed with mandatory overtime provisions, increasing insurance costs, and a two-tier wage system in which new hires would make $1.50 less than the current employees. Workers at the Amana, Iowa, plant had previously gone on strike for four days in 1995, in response to threats of company relocation, and for 16 days in 1992 for health insurance issues.

Following the Amana acquisition, Maytag eliminated 225 salaried jobs nationwide as part of integrating Amana Appliances into its major appliances division. Maytag's major appliance division had 4,600 salaried employees nationwide.[43] Some concern had been expressed among Maytag employees in Newton with the manner in which some long-time white-collar workers were being laid off. They were being escorted from the building shortly after they were informed that they were losing their jobs. When Ralph Hake was asked about this new procedure, he responded that he didn't know where the idea came from but that layoff procedures would be modified.[44]

Financial Situation

By the time of the shareholders' meeting on May 9, 2002, most of the corporation's shareholders knew how much the company had changed since the days when Maytag sold washing machines only as a sideline. Most appreciated management's attempts to build the company but were concerned with how executives were managing such a large company. Sales had steadily grown from $3 billion in 1991 to $4.3 billion in 2001, but profits had often fluctuated. Maytag Corporation showed a net loss in both 1992 and 1995 but had been profitable since then. Excluding special items, operating income had increased from $79 million in 1991 to $572.5 million in 1999 but then dropped to $479.6 in 2000 and to $289 million in 2001. Return on assets increased from 7.4% in 1997 to 13.8% in 1999 but then fell to 10.5% in 2000 and 5.4% in 2001. Maytag's stock price had dropped from a high of $70 in mid-1999 to under $30 during the fourth quarter of 2000 and was selling at $46.07 on May 9, 2002. (See **Exhibits 6–10** for Maytag's financial information.) After admitting the disappointing financial results of 2001, Hake stated that first quarter 2002 operating income was up and that earning per share was up 63% since last quarter.

The Shareholders' Meeting

Chairman Hake continues his speech on the state of the corporation. He points to last year's strategic acquisition of Amana Appliances as a key part of Maytag's growth strategy. The corporation is currently following three key initiatives to better position itself in the industry:

1. Quality
2. Product development
3. Cost reduction

As part of the product development initiative, the company has established a cross-functional new product development team for innovation. To show examples of some of the

Exhibit 6

Consolidated Statements of Income: Maytag Corporation (Dollar amounts in thousands)

Year Ended December 31	2001	2000	1999	1998	1997
Net sales	$4,323,713	$3,994,918	$4,053,185	$4,069,290	$3,407,911
Cost of sales	3,320,209	2,906,019	2,870,739	2,887,663	2,471,623
Gross profit	1,003,504	1,088,899	1,182,446	1,181,627	936,288
Selling, general and administrative expenses	704,596	609,284	609,958	658,889	578,015
Special charges	9,756	39,900	—	—	—
Operating income	289,152	439,715	572,488	522,738	358,273
Interest expense	(64,828)	(60,309)	(48,329)	(62,765)	(58,995)
Loss on securities	(7,230)	(17,600)	—	—	—
Other, net	(5,010)	(5,152)	8,193	10,912	1,277
Income from continuing operations before income taxes, minority interests, extraordinary item, and cumulative effect of accounting change	212,084	356,654	532,352	470,885	300,555
Income taxes	30,089	119,719	192,520	176,100	109,800
Income from continuing operations before minority interests, extraordinary item, and cumulative effect of accounting change	181,995	236,935	339,832	294,785	190,755
Minority interests	(14,457)	(20,568)	(11,250)	(8,275)	(7,265)
Incomes from continuing operations before extraordinary item and cumulative effect of accounting change	167,538	216,367	328,582	286,510	183,490
Discontinued operations:					
Income (loss) from operations of discontinued Blodgett and China joint venture	(7,987)	(19,919)	2,526	—	—
Income tax (benefit) on discontinued operations	1,113	(4,519)	2,580	—	—
Provision for impairment of China joint venture	42,304	—	—	—	—
Loss on sale of Blodgett	59,500	—	—	—	—
Loss from discontinued operations.	(110,904)	(15,400)	(54)	—	—
Income before extraordinary item and cumulative effect of accounting change	56,634	200,967	328,528	—	—
Extraordinary item—loss on early retirement of debt	(5,171)	—	—	(5,900)	(3,200)
Cumulative effect of accounting change	(3,727)	—	—	—	—
Net income	$ 47,736	$ 200,967	$ 328,528	$ 280,610	$ 180,290

Source: Maytag Corporation, *2001 Annual Report*, p. 19, and *1999 Annual Report*, p. 39.

corporation's new products, Hake gives the signal to turn down the lights. Videos are shown of the company's latest television commercials. They show the new "sidekick" of the Maytag repairman carrying the Maytag Wide-by-Side refrigerator through a grocery store, Hoover's commercials for the Windtunnel vacuum and for its wet machine Floor MATE, and for The Maytag Store.

Hake also describes the formation of a quality improvement team whose job is to check all plants and make recommendations. After mentioning the introduction of a "strategic sourcing initiative" to complement the current Lean Sigma program, Hake contends that Maytag Corporation is well positioned versus the competition. Through new product innovation, the company's ultimate goal is to "Own the Kitchen." "Demographics are with us. The baby boomers are in their peak spending years. We have confidence in our ability to execute well. We enter 2002 with a stronger company."

Hake then introduces Maytag Appliances President Bill Beer, who steps up to the stage to present his new products. According to Beer, "2001 was a rebuilding year for Maytag

Exhibit 7

Consolidated Balance Sheet: Maytag Corporation
(Dollar amounts in thousands)

	December 31				
Year Ending December 31	**2001**	**2000**	**1999**	**1998**	**1997**
ASSETS					
Current Assets					
Cash & cash equivalents	$ 109,370	$ 6,073	$ 28,815	$ 28,642	$ 27,991
Accounts receivable, less allowance for doubtful accounts (2001—$24,121; 2000—$15,583; 1999—$22,327; 1998—$22,305)	618,101	476,211	494,747	472,979	473,741
Inventories	447,866	325,313	404,120	383,753	350,209
Deferred income taxes	63,557	45,616	35,484	39,014	46,073
Other current assets	40,750	51,895	58,350	44,474	36,703
Discontinued current assets	89,900	171,451	—	—	—
Total current assets	1,369,544	1,076,559	1,021,516	968,862	934,717
Noncurrent assets					
Deferred income taxes	227,967	110,393	106,600	120,273	118,931
Prepaid pension cost	1,532	1,526	1,487	1,399	2,160
Intangible pension assets	101,915	49,889	48,668	62,811	33,819
Other intangibles, less allowance for amortization (2001—$123,395; 2000—$112,790; 1999—$112,006; 1998—$98,106; 1997—$85,071)	296,909	272,431	427,212	424,312	433,595
Other noncurrent assets	62,548	42,910	54,896	44,412	49,660
Discontinued noncurrent assets	60,001	251,154	—	—	—
Total noncurrent assets	750,872	728,303	638,863	653,207	638,165
Property, plant, and equipment					
Land	20,854	19,616	19,660	19,317	19,597
Buildings and improvements	352,447	320,545	349,369	333,032	309,960
Machinery and equipment	1,812,446	1,607,006	1,622,764	1,499,872	1,427,276
Construction in progress	146,335	84,980	74,057	102,042	59,376
	2,332,082	2,032,147	2,065,850	1,954,263	1,816,209
Less accumulated depreciation	1,296,347	1,168,085	1,089,742	988,669	874,937
Total property, plant, and equipment	1,035,735	864,062	976,108	965,594	941,272
Total assets	$3,156,151	$2,668,924	$2,636,487	$2,587,663	$2,514,154

Year Ending December 31	**2001**	**2000**	**1999**	**1998**	**1997**
Liabilities and shareowners' equity					
Current liabilities					
Notes payable	$ 148,247	$ 299,603	$ 133,041	$ 112,898	$ 112,843
Accounts payable	316,050	229,998	277,780	279,086	221,417
Compensation to employees	78,281	56,439	77,655	81,836	62,758
Accrued liabilities	285,627	176,289	194,074	176,701	161,344
Current portion of long-term debt	133,586	64,181	170,473	140,176	8,276
Discontinued current liabilities	112,702	145,177	—	—	—
Total current liabilities	1,074,493	971,687	853,023	790,697	566,638
Noncurrent liabilities					
Deferred income taxes	25,100	21,463	22,842	21,191	23,666
Long-term debt, less current portion	932,065	444,652	337,764	446,505	549,524
Postretirement benefit liabilities	497,182	479,452	467,386	460,599	454,390
Accrued pension costs	352,861	50,265	56,528	69,660	31,308

(*continued*)

Exhibit 7

Consolidated Balance Sheet: Maytag Corporation (*continued*)
(Dollar amounts in thousands)

Year Ending December 31	2001	2000	1999	1998	1997
Other noncurrent liabilities	128,084	107,614	101,776	117,392	99,096
Discontinued noncurrent liability	22,678	72,018	—	—	—
Total noncurrent liabilities	1,957,970	1,175,464	986,296	1,115,347	1,157,984
Company obligated manditorily redeemable preferred capital securities of subsidiary trust holding solely the company's debentures	—	200,000	200,000	—	173,723
Minority interests	100,142	100,097	169,788	174,055	—
Temporary equity: Put options	—	200,000	—	—	—
Shareowners' equity					
Preferred stock					
Authorized—24,000,000 shares (par value $1.00)					
Issued—none	—	—	—	—	—
Common stock:					
Authorized—200,000,000 shares (par value $1.25)					
Issued—117,150,593 shares, including shares in treasury	146,438	146,438	146,438	146,438	146,438
Additional paid-in capital	450,683	285,924	503,346	467,192	494,646
Retained earnings	1,164,021	1,171,364	1,026,288	760,115	542,118
Cost of common stock in treasury (2001—40,286,575 shares; 2000—40,910,458 shares; 1999—34,626,316 shares; 1998—27,932,506 shares; 1997—22,465,256 shares)	(1,527,777)	(1,539,163)	(1,190,894)	(805,802)	(508,115)
Employee stock plans	(23,522)	(31,487)	(38,836)	(45,331)	(48,416)
Accumulated other comprehensive income (losses)	(186,297)	(11,400)	(18,962)	(15,048)	(10,862)
Total shareowners' equity	23,546	21,676	427,380	507,564	615,809
Total liabilities and shareowners' equity	$3,156,151	$2,668,924	$2,636,487	$2,587,663	$2,514,154

Source: Maytag Corporation, *2001 Annual Report*, pp. 20–21, *1999 Annual Report*, pp. 40–41, and *1997 Annual Report*, pp. 36–37.

Exhibit 8

Business Segment Financial Information: Maytag Corporation
(Dollar amounts in thousands)

	2001	2000	1999
Net sales			
Home appliances	$4,093,552	$3,712,708	$3,706,357
Commercial appliances	230,161	282,210	346,828
Operating income			
Home appliances	$324,646	$478,137	$562,288
Commercial appliances	5,755	29,532	51,891
Capital expenditures			
Home appliances	$131,777	$133,809	$117,765
Commercial appliances	7,919	3,665	2,826
Total assets			
Home appliances	$2,264,575	$1,793,626	$1,792,185
Commercial appliances	103,034	104,964	106,870

Source: Maytag Corporation, *2001 Annual Report*, p. 46.

Exhibit 9

Common Stock Data: Maytag Corporation
(Amounts in dollars)

Year	High	Low	Annual Dividends per Share
2001	$37.40	$22.25	$0.72
2000	47.75	25.00	0.72
1999	74.81	31.25	0.72
1998	64.50	35.44	0.66
1997	37.50	19.75	0.64

Source: Maytag Corporation annual reports.

Corporation." He goes on to say that we are in a "wear out" industry. People have traditionally not purchased a new appliance until it wears out. We must change to a "want in" industry in which people buy a new appliance before the old wears out. He points to the Neptune washer and dryer as one example. "We have sold over 2.5 million Neptune washers—saving enough energy to light Des Moines for eleven years! We successfully established a $1095 retail price for the new Neptune and were able to attain a 1000 rpm spin cycle." Beer then describes the new Gemini range, with two ovens, and the new three-rack dishwasher. Jenn-Air has just developed a built-in refrigerator to compete with Sub-Zero. It has a stainless steel front, and its interior is completely customizable, says Beer. It is being built in the Amana, Iowa, facility.

Beer then introduces the President of Hoover Floor Care, Keith Minton, who takes over center stage to describe Hoover's new products. According to Minton, "Hoover is a strong name, one synonymous with floor care. Hoover has been identified as one of the 100 brands that changed America in the 20th century. It has the highest brand awareness in the industry, a dependable reputation, and its upright vacuum is rated as requiring the least repair." To point out the importance of innovation to Hoover, Minton tells the audience of the company's new central vacuum system, its WindTunnel bagless upright, and its replacement of belts with a new gear-train drive system. "For any price point, we deliver better performance than the competition." He describes Hoover's new extractor line, the Floor MATE, for hard surface cleaning, and its experimentation with a robotic vacuum cleaner.

Minton relinquishes the stage to Ralph Hake. Hake moves to the podium to present the results of the voting. "The four nominees for a three-year term (expiring 2005) on the board of directors, Barbara Allen, Howard Clark, Lester Crown, and William Kerr, have been elected." The audience politely applauds. Hake continues. "Ernst & Young has been ratified as the independent auditors to audit the 2002 financial results." The Chairman then announces that the proposed 2002 employee and director stock incentive plan has been approved. After a slight

Exhibit 10

Inventory Data: Maytag Corporation
(Dollar amounts in thousands)

	2001	2000	1999	1998	1997
Raw materials	$ 62,587	$ 42,393	$ 66,731	$ 69,039	$ 61,740
Work in progress	76,524	60,588	72,162	66,578	53,069
Finished goods	382,925	303,249	325,844	317,331	229,450
Supplies	9,659	7,451	9,615	8,856	5,950
Total FIFO cost	$531,695	$413,681	$484,352	$461,804	$350,209

Source: Maytag Corporation annual reports.

pause, he states that propositions 4, 5, and 6 have passed. Hake then states that the board will review the results and determine the best course of action. (Maytag management had always contended that the shareholder votes were advisory only. That is why past votes had never been implemented.)

Hake than opens the meeting for questions from the audience. A shareholder in the back of the auditorium stands and moves to the aisle. An usher with a microphone joins him. He asks, "Has Maytag outsourced its internal audit function to Ernst & Young?" Hake responds in the affirmative, but states that the company intends to hire another firm to handle the internal part of the job so that the functions will have separate oversight. Another shareholder, seated in the front of the auditorium, stands to ask two questions: "We know that economies of scale through large, dedicated manufacturing plants help to cut costs. Now that Maytag has purchased Amana with its various plants, what is the future of Maytag's manufacturing facilities? Will you be building large, dedicated plants to replace the current plants, or will you be consolidating the manufacturing of each type of appliance, like refrigerators, in one existing plant? As a second question, we know that the big appliance manufacturers like Whirlpool and Electrolux are becoming internationally oriented, just at a time when Maytag seems to be retreating to North America. Will Maytag continue to be economically viable as a domestic maker of appliances in an increasingly global industry?" The Chairman ponders the questions for a moment and then responds: "We know that cost competitiveness is key at the retail level. We must have highly efficient factories to compete. It is important to note, however, that 50% to 70% of our manufacturing costs are from purchased materials. To reduce some of these costs, we are opening a component plant in Mexico." Hake states that the company has already announced plans to sell its Jefferson City, Missouri, parts business to a leading powdered metal manufacturer. The parts assembly for major appliances that will be moving to Reynosa, Mexico, is now being performed in Maytag plants or by outside suppliers. Planned to open late in 2002, the Mexican plant will enable the company's appliance manufacturing operations to focus more on parts fabrication and final assembly. Operating a plant in Mexico will save the company money because of lower labor costs and lower costs of some materials. Hake then moves his attention to the second question. "Our focus will continue to be in North America. We do have an international subsidiary that exports our top-end products. That will continue." (For the years 1999, 2000, and 2001, net sales to countries outside the United States by Maytag Corporation ranged from 9.3% to 10.1% of consolidated total net sales.[45])

With no more questions from the audience, Chairman Hake declares this year's annual shareholders' meeting to be adjourned. He then motions to the members of the board of directors to join him leaving the auditorium. It is 9:30 A.M. when the board walks out the front side door for its quarterly meeting a block away at Maytag Corporation headquarters.

As the shareholders and visitors wend their way out of the auditorium, down the stairs, and into the parking lot, a number of them comment on the meeting. Shareholder Lewis Rowles of West Des Moines gives Hake good marks for his performance thus far. "He's been here a short time, but I think he's going to make a good CEO." Shareholder John Chevedden, a self-described shareholder activist from Los Angeles, explains to a reporter from the *Des Moines Register* why he had submitted the proposal for the annual election of directors. He wants "better corporate governance, which should translate into better management." Shareholder Bob Koch voices a concern that Maytag has had three CEOs in the past three years.

Financial analysts were still cautious in their judgment of Maytag's recent performance. Lawrence Horan, an analyst with Parker/Hunter, says that Maytag hasn't turned the corner yet, noting that the Amana acquisition largely contributed to the increased sales in 2001. According to Horan, the company needs to get more products in the pipeline, improve efficiency, and grow in the high-end business. Pointing out that Amana's figures for April though December 2001 had been included in Maytag's 2001 financial statements, Horan added, "They're basically admitting that they're losing market share." Doug West, a vice president at the Urbandale, Iowa office of A. G. Edwards & Sons, comments that Maytag is back on track, but that it could take a few years for the company to return to record earnings levels and stock prices.[46]

One shareholder wonders: Does Maytag Corporation have what it takes to succeed in this increasingly competitive industry? Is this a good time to buy or to sell Maytag stock?

Notes

1. R. F. Hake, "Letter to Shareholders," Maytag Corporation *2001 Annual Report*, p. 2.
2. L. A. Hadley, "Letter to Shareholders," Maytag Corporation *1996 Annual Report*, p. 6.
3. R. F. Hake, p. 5.
4. C. Schlisserman, "Maytag Agrees to Sell Commercial Cooking Unit," *Des Moines Register* (September 1, 2001), p. D1.
5. R. F. Hake, p. 2.
6. J. Jancsurak, "It's All Good," *Appliance Manufacturer* (July 2002), p. 5. "White goods" is the traditional term used for major home appliances. The contrasting term "brown goods" refers to home electronics products, such as radios and televisions.
7. Freedonia Group, *World Major Household Appliances*, summarized in *Appliance* (April 2002), p. 19.
8. W. Ryberg, "Maytag Will Buy Jade Range," *Des Moines Register* (January 16, 1999), p. 10S.
9. Maytag Corporation, "Interview with Leonard Hadley," *1994 Annual Report*, p. 10.
10. Maytag Corporation, *2001 Annual Report*, p. 43.
11. J. Jancsurak, "Maytag Revs Up Innovation, Execution Engines," *Appliance Manufacturer* (August 2002).
12. "Maytag Honors," *Appliance Manufacturer* (September 1998), p. 19.
13. Maytag Corporation News Release, 1995.
14. D. Ritchey, "Service Friendly Appliances," *Appliance* (April 2002), p. 11.
15. J. Jancsurak, "Marketing Challenges," *Appliance Manufacturer* (August 2002), pp. Maytag-15 to 17.
16. W. Ryberg, "2nd Maytag Store Expects to Close," *Des Moines Register* (September 30, 2000), p. 1D.
17. W. Ryberg, p. 1D, and W. Ryberg, "Maytag Invites Customers to Take Hands-on Approach," *Des Moines Register* (March 14, 1999), pp. 1G, 2G.
18. W. Ryberg, "Maytag Urged to Review Retail Focus," *Des Moines Register* (November 11, 2000), p. D1.
19. "You've Got a Corporate Reputation—Now Don't Blow It," *U.S. News & World Report* (February 19, 2001), p. 12.
20. R. L. Rose, "Maytag's Acquisitions Don't Wear as Well as Washers and Dryers," *Wall Street Journal* (January 31, 1991), p. A6.
21. J. Jancsurak, "Excellence in Manufacturing," *Appliance Manufacturer* (August 2002), pp. Maytag-10 to 11.
22. P. Johnson and T. Meeser, "Maytag to Purchase Amana: Workers Weigh Effect on Jobs," *Des Moines Register* (June 6, 2001), pp. 1D, 6D.
23. W. Ryberg, "Maytag's No. 2 Officer Resigns," *Des Moines Register* (August 12, 1995), p. 10S.
24. "Maytag Announces Changes," *The (Ames, IA) Tribune* (December 9, 2000), p. B3.
25. "Hadley: Maytag Will Stay in Newton," *The (Ames, IA) Tribune* (December 7, 2000), p. B9.
26. W. Ryberg, "Maytag Chief Happy to Call Newton Home," *Des Moines Register* (April 11, 2002), pp. 1D, 6D.
27. M. Sanders, "Purchasing Power," *Appliance* (June 1993), pp. 45–46.
28. A. Baker, "Intelligent Dishwasher Outsmarts Dirt," *Design News* (April 10, 1995), pp. 69–73.
29. N. C. Remich, Jr., "The Power of Partnering," *Appliance Manufacturer* (August 1994), p. A-1.
30. R. J. Babyak, "The Power of One," *Appliance Manufacturer* (August 1997), pp. M-29–M-30.
31. R. Dzierwa, "The Permanent Press," *Appliance* (September 1995), p. 48.
32. D. Topping, "Innovation and the Internet," *Appliance* (January 2001), p. 87.
33. J. Jancsurak, "Maytag Revs Up Innovation, Execution Engines," *Appliance Manufacturer* (August 2002), pp. Maytag-3 to 6.
34. T. Stevens, "From Reliable to 'Wow,'" *Industry Week* (June 22, 1998).
35. "Maytag Wins Innovator Award," *Appliance Manufacturer* (October 1999), p. 18.
36. J. Jancsurak, "Multifaceted Industrial Design," *Appliance Manufacturer* (August 2002), pp. Maytag-12 to 13.
37. J. Jancsurak, "New CEO; New Agenda Signal Changes Ahead," *Appliance Manufacturer* (November 2001), pp. Maytag-5 to 9.
38. "Maytag, Fawn, Lennox, Parsons Get State Aid," *The (Ames, Iowa) Daily Tribune* (June 23, 1995), p. 1A.
39. R. J. Babyak, "The Washer Watch," *Appliance Manufacturer* (August 1997), p. M-11.
40. J. Jancsurak, "Excellence in Manufacturing," *Appliance Manufacturer* (August 2002), pp. Maytag-8 to 12.
41. P. Johnson, "Quality Counts," *Des Moines Register* (November 5, 2001), pp. 1D, 4D.
42. "Maytag to Customize Service," *Des Moines Register* (March 22, 2000), p. 1D.
43. W. Ryberg, "Maytag to Cut Salaried Jobs," *Des Moines Register* (October 11, 2001), p. 1D.
44. W. Ryberg, "Maytag Chief Happy to Call Newton Home," *Des Moines Register* (April 11, 2002), pp. 1D, 6D.
45. Maytag Corporation, *2001 Annual Report*, p. 47.
46. W. Ryberg, "Maytag Sees Turning Point," *Des Moines Register* (April 17, 2002), pp. 1D, 6D.

Kmart Corporation: Seeking Survival in a Changing Marketplace (2002)

James W. Camerius

On January 22, 2002, Troy, Michigan–based Kmart Corporation became the largest retailer in the history of the United States to seek bankruptcy protection. In its voluntary petition for reorganization under Chapter 11 of the U.S. Bankruptcy Code, Kmart management announced that it would outline a plan for repaying its creditors, reducing its size, restructuring its business, and emerging from court protection in July 2003. "After considering a wide range of alternatives, it became clear that this course of action was the only way to truly resolve the company's most challenging problems," Kmart Chief Executive Charles C. Conway said in a prepared statement. He promised that the nation's third-largest discount retailer would reemerge "as a stronger, more dynamic, more profitable enterprise with a well-defined position in the discount retail sector."

On March 11, 2002, Kmart announced that Charles Conway had resigned. He was replaced as Chief Executive Officer (CEO) by James B. Adamson, who also would continue as Chairman of the Board of Kmart, a position he was elevated to just prior to the bankruptcy. Upon assuming the position, Adamson indicated that Kmart would emerge from bankruptcy protection "as a strong and healthy competitor, with a clearly defined place in the discount retail sector." On his first day as CEO, Adamson said he would initially be focusing on basics, such as cleaning up stores and making sure shelves were full of merchandise. He knew that he must develop a strategic plan of action that would guide the long-run performance of the organization following bankruptcy protection.

The early years of the 21st century were problematic and difficult ones for Kmart and the entire retail industry. Sluggish consumer spending, rising unemployment, the energy crisis, increased competitive pressures, battle for market share, a dismal holiday season, halts in shipments from wary vendors, problems in the securities and bond market, liquidity issues, and the events of September 11, 2001, all came together to make this period a very challenging time in which to operate. Several historic retail chains had also filed for bankruptcy protection and had either been reorganized or liquidated. Some analysts doubted if Kmart could survive in a changing marketplace and felt it would face eventual liquidation. Others felt that the firm needed an entirely new strategy that would reorganize and reposition the company in an extremely competitive marketplace. Retail analysts agreed that Kmart management had a huge task to undertake in the immediate future and the years ahead.

This case was prepared by Professor James W. Camerius, Northern Michigan University. All rights reserved by the author. Copyright © 2002 by James W. Camerius. This case was edited for SMBP-9th edition. Reprinted by permission.

Kmart Corporation was one of the world's largest mass merchandise retailers. After several years of restructuring, it was composed largely of general merchandise businesses in the form of Kmart discount department stores (general merchandise and convenience items) and large Kmart Supercenters (food and general merchandise). It also merchandised though an e-commerce site, www.bluelight.com. It operated in all 50 of the United States and in Puerto Rico, Guam, and the U.S. Virgin Islands. It had equity interests as well in Meldisco subsidiaries of Footstar, Inc., that operated Kmart footwear departments. Measured in sales volume in 2001, it was the third largest retailer and the second largest discount department store chain in the United States. Kmart financial summaries are shown in **Exhibits 1, 2,** and **3.**

Exhibit 1

Consolidated Balance Sheet: Kmart Corporation[1]
(Dollar amounts in millions except per share data)

Fiscal Year Ending January[1]	2001	2000
Assets		
Current assets		
Cash and cash equivalents	$ 1,245	$ 401
Merchandise inventories	5,822	6,412
Other current assets	817	939
Total current assets	7,884	7,752
Property and equipment, net	6,161	6,557
Other assets and deferred charges	253	523
Total assets	$14,298	$14,832
Liabilities and Shareholders' Equity		
Current liabilities		
Long-term debt due within 1 year	$ —	$ 68
Accounts payable	103	2,159
Accrued payroll and other liabilities	378	1,587
Taxes other than income taxes	143	187
Total current liabilities	624	4,001
Long-term debt and notes payable	330	2,084
Capital lease obligations	857	943
Other long-term liabilities	79	834
Total liabilities not subject to compromise	1,890	7,862
Liabilities subject to compromise	8,060	—
Company obligated mandatorily redeemable convertible preferred securities of a subsidiary trust holding solely 7 ¾ convertible junior subordinated debentures of Kmart (redemption value of $898 and $898, respectively)	889	887
Common stock, $1 par value, 1,500,000,000 shares authorized: 503,294,515 and 486,509,736 shares issued, respectively	503	487
Capital in excess of par value	1,695	1,578
Retained earnings	1,261	4,018
Total liabilities and shareholders' equity	$14,298	$14,832

Note:
1. Fiscal year is February to January.
2. FY2001 ended on January 31, 2002 and FY2000 ended on January 31, 2001.

Source: Kmart Corporation, *10-K Report*, May 1, 2002.

Exhibit 2

Consolidated Statement of Operations: Kmart Corporation[1]
(Dollar amounts in millions, except per share data)

Fiscal year Ending January[1]	2001[2]	2000[2]	1999[2]
Sales	$36,151	$37,028	$35,925
Cost of sales, buying, and occupancy	29,936	29,658	28,111
Gross margin	6,215	7,370	7,814
Selling, general, and administrative expenses	7,588	7,402	6,558
Equity income (loss) in unconsolidated subsidiaries	—	(13)	44
Restructuring, impairment, and other charges	1,099	—	—
Continuing income (loss) before interest, income taxes, reorganization items, and dividends on convertible preferred securities of subsidiary trust	(2,472)	(45)	1,300
Interest expense, net (contractual interest for fiscal year 2001 was $352)	344	287	280
Reorganization items	(184)	—	—
Income tax provision (benefit)	(115)	(134)	337
Dividends on convertible preferred securities of subsidiary trust, net of income taxes of $0, $25, and $27, respectively (contractual dividend for fiscal year 2001 was $72)	70	46	50
Net income (loss) from continuing operations	(2,587)	(244)	633
Discontinued operations, net of income taxes of $0 and $124	169	—	(230)
Net income (loss)	$ (2,418)	$ (244)	$ 403
Basic earnings (loss) per common share			
Net income (loss) from continuing operations	$ (5.23)	$ (0.48)	$ 1.29
Discontinued operations	0.34	—	(0.47)
Net income (loss)	$ (4.89)	$ (0.48)	$ 0.82
Diluted earnings (loss) per common share			
Net income (loss) from continuing operations	$ (5.23)	$ (0.48)	$ 1.22
Discontinued operations	0.34	—	(0.41)
Net income (loss)	$ (4.89)	$ (0.48)	$ 0.81
Basic weighted average shares (millions)	494.1	482.8	491.7
Diluted weighted average share (millions)	494.1	482.8	561.7

Note:
1. The company's fiscal year is January through February.
2. FY2001 ended on January 31, 2002; FY2000 ended on January 31, 2001; and FY1999 ended on January 26, 2000.

Source: Kmart Corporation, *10-K Report*, May 1, 2002.

The discount department store industry was perceived by many to have reached maturity. Kmart, as part of that industry, had a retail management strategy that was developed in the late 1950s and revised several times in the 1990s. The firm was in a dilemma in terms of corporate strategy. The problem was how to lay a foundation to provide a new direction that would reposition the firm in a fiercely competitive environment. Analysts had noted, however, that the firm was without a definable niche in discount retailing. Studies had shown that number one ranked Wal-Mart, originally a rural retailer, had continued to be known for lower prices. Target Corporation, number three in sales, had staked out a niche as a merchandiser of discounted stylish upscale products. Kmart was left without a feature that would give it competitive distinction in the marketplace.

Exhibit 3

Selected Financial Data: Kmart Corporation
(Dollar amounts in million, except per share data)

Fiscal year Ending	2001[2]	2000[2]	1999[2]	1998[2]	1997[2]
Summary of operations[2]					
Total sales	$36,151	$37,028	$35,925	$33,674	$32,183
Comparable sales %	(0.1%)	1.1%	4.8%	4.8%	4.8%
Total sales %	(2.4%)	3.1%	6.6%	4.6%	2.4%
U.S. Kmart total sales %	(2.4%)	3.1%	6.6%	5.6%	5.0%
Cost of sales, buying, and occupancy	29,936	29,658	28,111	26,319	25,152
Selling, general, and administrative expenses	7,588	7,402	6,558	6,283	6,178
Restructuring, impairment, and other charges	1,099	—	—	19	114
Interest expense, net	344	287	280	293	363
Continuing income (loss) before income taxes, preferred dividend, and reorganization items	(2,816)	(332)	1,020	798	418
Chapter 11 reorganization items	184	—	—	—	—
Net income (loss) from continuing operations(3)	(2,587)	(244)	633	518	249
Discontinued operations	169	—	(230)	—	—
Net income (loss)	(2,418)	(244)	403	518	249
Per common share					
Basic					
Continuing income (loss)	$ (5.23)	$ (0.48)	$ 1.29	$ 1.05	$ 0.51
Discontinued operations	$ 0.34	$ —	$ (0.47)	$ —	$ —
Net income (loss)	$ (4.89)	$ (0.48)	$ 0.82	$ 1.05	$ 0.51
Diluted					
Continuing income (loss)	$ (5.23)	$ (0.48)	$ 1.22	$ 1.01	$ 0.51
Discontinued operations	$ 0.34	$ —	$ (0.41)	$ —	$ —
Net income (loss)	$ (4.89)	$ (0.48)	$ 0.81	$ 1.01	$ 0.51
Book value	$ 6.87	$ 12.50	$ 13.10	$ 12.12	$ 11.15
Financial data:					
Working capital	$ 7,260	$ 3,751	$ 4,083	$ 4,174	$ 4,237
Total assets	14,298	14,832	15,208	14,255	13,625
Liabilities subject to compromise	8,060	—	—	—	—
Long-term debt	330	2,084	1,759	1,538	1,725
Long-term capital lease obligations	857	943	1,014	1,091	1,179
Trust convertible preferred securities	889	887	986	984	981
Capital expenditures	1,456	1,089	1,277	981	678
Depreciation and amortization	824	777	770	671	660
Current ratio	12.6	1.9	2.0	2.1	2.3
Basic weighted average shares outstanding (millions)	494	483	492	492	487
Diluted weighted average shares outstanding (millions)	494	483	562	565	492
Number of stores	2,114	2,105	2,171	2,161	2,136
U.S. Kmart store sales per comparable selling square footage	$ 235	$ 236	$ 233	$ 222	$ 211
U.S. Kmart total selling square footage (millions)	154	153	155	154	151

Note:

1. The company's fiscal year is February through January.

2. FY2001 ended on January 31, 2002; FY2000 ended on January 31, 2001; FY1999 ended on January 26, 2000, FY1998 ended on January 27, 1999; and FY1997 ended on January 28, 1998.

3. Notes were deleted.

Source: Kmart Corporation, *10-K Report*, May 1, 2002.

Corporate Governance

CHARLES C. CONAWAY

June 1, 2000, the search for the new chairman and CEO of Kmart Corporation was over. Charles C. Conaway, a 39-year-old drugstore chain executive, was selected to fill the position vacated by retiring Chief Executive Floyd Hall. His appointment meant that the strategic direction of Kmart would come from a man who was previously unknown outside of the drugstore industry. He would have to provide an answer to a crucial question: How can Kmart respond to the challenges of industry leader Wal-Mart Stores, Inc., in the extremely competitive arena of discount retailing?

As President and Chief Operating Officer (COO) of CVS Corporation, Conaway was the number-two executive at the nation's largest drugstore chain, whose annual sales were about half those of Kmart's annual revenue of $36 billion. By all accounts, Conaway had made a sizable contribution in sales, earnings, and market value at CVS, Inc., headquartered in Woonsocket, Rhode Island. CVS had 1999 sales of $18 billion with 4,100 stores. Conaway, who became president and COO of CVS in 1998, was responsible for merchandising, advertising, store operations, and logistics. After joining the firm in 1992, he helped engineer the restructuring of the then-parent Melville Corporation, a diversified retailer, into a successful drugstore chain. Conaway said in an interview upon assuming his new position with Kmart that his primary task would be to improve customer service, productivity of resources, and problems with out-of-stock merchandise. Setting the stage for a new direction, Conaway said, "Customer service is going to be at the top. We're going to measure it and we're going to tie incentives around it," he noted. Following the implementation of this part of the comeback plan, he made big investments in computerized inventory systems and logistics to make the company more efficient. He revived Kmart's old trademark Blue Light Special that promoted an instant markdown on a particular item and at the same time cut back on weekly circulars that always had drawn traffic into stores.

Conaway also challenged Wal-Mart directly by lowering prices on 50,000 items as part of a "BlueLight Always" program and introduced an ill-fated "Dare to Compare" advertising campaign. The campaign contrasted Kmart prices on selected items with Target and Wal-Mart prices. Target sued for false advertising. Wal-Mart cut prices some more. Kmart dropped the "Dare to Compare" campaign.

Some industry analysts concluded that the Kmart Board of Directors held Charles Conway and President Mark S. Schwartz, who left the company on January 17, 2002, largely responsible for the lack of clearly defined turnaround plans and a number of strategic missteps that drained the company of cash and left it millions of dollars in debt and unable to pay its vendors, precipitating the bankruptcy. Some speculated that Conway would leave Kmart with at least $9.5 million. This included a severance package three times his base salary, which was $4.5 million. It also included forgiving a $5 million loan made to him in 2001 and, subject to court approval, one-third of previously promised bonuses worth $6.5 million and some stock options. An internal review in 2002, which initially focused in accounting irregularities at Kmart, was later extended to include a variety of issues, including executive loans, misuse of company funds by executives, and whether these employees performed any illegal acts or violated Kmart's policies during their tenure with the company.

NEW LEADERSHIP

James B. Adamson, 54, an outside Kmart director with firsthand experience in managing distressed companies, was appointed Chairman of the Board of Directors of Kmart on January 18, 2002. He was Appointed CEO, as well, on March 11, 2002. Adamson was CEO of Advantica

Exhibit 4

Corporate Directors and Officers, May 1, 2002: Kmart Corporation

Directors

James B. Adamson, Chair and CEO
Kmart Corporation
Director since 1996

Robert D. Kennedy, Past CEO
Union Carbide Corporation
Director since 1996

Lilyan H. Affinito, Past Vice Chair
Maxxam Group, Inc.
Director since 1990

Robin B. Smith, Chair and CEO
Publishers Clearing House
Director since 1996

Richard G. Cline, Chairman
Hawthorne Investors, Inc.
Director since 1995

Thomas T. Stallkamp, CEO
MSX International
Director since 1999

Willie D. Davis, President
All Pro Broadcasting, Inc.
Director since 1986

Richard J. Statuto, CEO
St. Joseph Health System
Director since 2001

Joseph P. Flannery, Chair and CEO
Uniroyal Holding, Inc.
Director since 1985

Executive and Senior Corporate Officers

James B. Adamson
Chairman of the Board and CEO

James E. Defebaugh, IV
SVP Chief Compliance Officer and Secretary

Julian D. Day
President and Chief Operating Officer

Steve Feuling
SVP Operations Administration

Albert A. Koch
Chief Financial Officer

Paul J. Hueber
SVP Operations Administration

Randy L. Allen
EVP Strategic Initiatives and
Chief Diversity Officer

Keith A. Jelinek
SVP Inventory Management

Ronald B. Hutchison
EVP Chief Restructuring Officer

Nicholas J. Just
SVP GMM Apparel

Cecil B. Kearse
EVP Merchandising

Lori McTavish
SVP Communications

Janet G. Kelley
EVP General Counsel

James P. Mixon
SVP Logistics

Michael T. Macik
EVP Human Resources

Paula Paquette
SVP GMM Home

Karen A. Austin
SVP Chief Information Officer

Steve Ryman
SVP Global Operations

Richard Blunck
SVP and CEO, Bluelight.com

Source: Kmart Corporation, *2001-10K Annual Report*, May 1, 2002.

Restaurant Group, Inc., which operated 2,400 Denny's, CoCo's, and Carrow's franchises, when he joined Kmart's board in 1996. During his tenure at Advantica, then known as Flagstar Cos., the firm filed for Chapter 11 protection to relieve debt from a leveraged buyout. The company emerged in 1998, after eliminating more than $1 billion in debt.

Adamson had previously served as Executive Vice President of Marketing at drugstore chain Revco, Inc., and was instrumental in bringing it out of bankruptcy. He also served as Executive Vice President of Merchandising at Target Stores, as a Senior Executive at B. Dalton Bookseller, and as the Chief Executive of Burger King Corporation.

To signal the beginning of a new era at Kmart, Julian Day, 49, former Executive Vice President and Chief Executive Operating Officer of Sears, Roebuck and Co. was named President and COO of Kmart on March 11, 2002. Albert A. Koch, 59, Chairman of the turnover firm Jay Alix & Co. became CFO, replacing John McDonald. Edward Stenger, 44, a principal of Jay Alix, was named the new Kmart Treasurer. In an earlier announcement, Kmart said it hired Ronald B. Hutchison, 51, to fill the new position of Chief Restructuring Officer. Mr. Hutchison was considered "one of the key architects" of an earlier reorganization at Advantica Restaurant Group, Inc. Since the filing of bankruptcy at the beginning of 2002, several other executives had either left the firm voluntarily or had been dismissed and replaced as part of the reorganization. A list of the Board of Directors, Executive Vice Presidents, and Senior Vice Presidents on May 1, 2002, is shown in **Exhibit 4**.

The Early Years

Kmart was the outgrowth of an organization founded in 1899 in Detroit by Sebastian S. Kresge. The first S.S. Kresge store represented a new type of retailing that featured low-priced merchandise for cash in low-budget, relatively small (4,000- to 6,000-square-foot) buildings with sparse furnishings. The adoption of the "5 and 10 cents" or "variety store" concept, pioneered by F.W. Woolworth Company in 1879, led to the rapid and profitable development of what was then the S.S. Kresge Company.

Kresge believed it could substantially increase its retail business through centralized buying and control, developing standardized store operating procedures, and expanding with new stores in heavy traffic areas. In 1912, the firm was incorporated in Delaware. It had 85 stores, with sales of $10,325,000, and, next to Woolworth's, was the largest variety chain in the world. In 1916 it was reincorporated in Michigan. Over the next 40 years, the firm experimented with mail-order catalogues, full-line department stores, self-service, a number of price lines, and the opening of stores in planned shopping centers. It continued its emphasis, however, on variety stores.

By 1957, corporate management became aware that the development of supermarkets and the expansion of drug store chains into general merchandise lines had made inroads into market categories previously dominated by variety stores. It also became clear that a new form of store with a discount merchandising strategy was emerging.

The Cunningham Connection

In 1957, in an effort to regain competitiveness and possibly save the company, Frank Williams, then President of Kresge, nominated Harry B. Cunningham as General Vice President. This maneuver was undertaken to free Mr. Cunningham, who had worked his way up the ranks in the organization, from operating responsibility. He was being groomed for the presidency and was given the assignment to study existing retailing businesses and recommend marketing changes.

In his visits to Kresge stores, and those of the competition, Cunningham became interested in discounting—particularly in new operation in Garden City, Long Island. Eugene Ferkauf had recently opened large discount department stores called E.J. Korvette. The stores had a discount mass-merchandising emphasis that featured low prices and margins, high turnover, large freestanding departmentalized units, ample parking space, and a location typically in the suburbs.

Cunningham was impressed with the discount concept, but he knew he had to first convince the Kresge Board of Directors, whose support would be necessary for any new strategy to succeed. He studied the company for two years and presented it with the following recommendation:

> We can't beat the discounters operating under the physical constraints and the self-imposed merchandise limitations of variety stores. We can join them—and not only join them, but with our people, procedures, and organization, we can become a leader in the discount industry.

In a speech delivered at the University of Michigan, Cunningham made his management approach clear by concluding with an admonition from the British author Sir Hugh Walpole: "Don't play for safety; it's the most dangerous game in the world."

The Board of Directors had a difficult job. Change is never easy, especially when the company had established procedures in place and a proud heritage. Before the first presentation to the Board could be made, rumors were circulating that one shocked senior executive had said:

> We have been in the variety business for 60 years—we know everything there is to know about it, and we're not doing very well in that, and you want to get us into a business we don't know anything about.

The Board of Directors accepted Cunningham's recommendations. When President Frank Williams retired, Cunningham became the new President and CEO and was directed to proceed with his recommendations.

The Birth of Kmart

Management conceived the original Kmart as a conveniently located one-stop-shopping unit where customers could buy a wide variety of quality merchandise at discount prices. The typical Kmart had 75,000 square feet, all on one floor. It generally stood by itself in a high-traffic, suburban area, with plenty of parking space. All stores had a similar floor plan.

The firm made an $80 million commitment in leases and merchandise for 33 stores before the first Kmart opened in 1962 in Garden City, Michigan. As part of this strategy, management decided to rely on the strengths and abilities of its own people to make decisions rather than employing outside experts for advice.

The original Kresge 5 & 10 variety store operation was characterized by low gross margins, high turnover, and concentration on return on investment. The main difference in the Kmart strategy would be the offering of a much wider merchandise mix.

The company had the knowledge and ability to merchandise 50% of the departments in the planned Kmart merchandise mix and contracted for operation of the remaining departments. In the following years, Kmart took over most of those departments originally contracted to licensees. Eventually all departments, except shoes, were operated by Kmart.

By 1987, the 25th anniversary year of the opening of the first Kmart store in America, sales and earnings of Kmart Corporation were at all-time highs. The company was the world's largest discount retailer, with sales of $25.6 billion, and operated 3,934 general merchandise and specialty stores.

On April 6, 1987, Kmart Corporation announced that it agreed to sell most of its remaining Kresge variety stores in the United States to McCrory Corporation, a unit of the closely held Rapid American Corporation of New York.

The Nature of the Competitive Environment

A CHANGING MARKETPLACE

The retail sector of the U.S. economy went through a number of dramatic and turbulent changes during the 1980s and 1990s. Retail analysts concluded that many retail firms were negatively affected by increased competitive pressures, sluggish consumer spending, slower-than-anticipated economic growth in North America, and recessions abroad. As one retail consultant noted:

> The structure of distribution in advanced economies was currently undergoing a series of changes that are as profound in their impact and as pervasive in their influence as those that occurred in manufacturing during the 19th century.

This changing environment affected the discount department store industry. Nearly a dozen firms, such as E.J. Korvette, W.T. Grant, Arlans, Atlantic Mills, Bradlees, and Ames, passed into bankruptcy or reorganization. Some firms, such as Woolworth (Woolco Division), had withdrawn from the field entirely after years of disappointment. St. Louis-based May Department Stores sold its Caldor and Venture discount divisions, each with annual sales of more than $1 billion. Venture announced liquidation in early 1998. After declaring bankruptcy twice, New England regional discounter Ames Department Stores, Inc., announced in the summer of 2002 that it was closing all 237 of its stores, dismissing all of its employees, and liquidating its inventory. Many historic retailers, such as Chicago-based Montgomery Ward and Company and Jackson, Michigan–based Jacobson's Stores, Inc., also went out of business during this period.

Senior management at Kmart felt that most of the firms that had difficulty in the industry faced the same situation. First, they had been very successful 5 or 10 years ago but had not changed and, therefore, had become somewhat dated. Management that had a historically successful formula, particularly in retailing, was perceived as having difficulty adapting to change, especially at the peak of success. Management would wait too long when faced with a threat in the environment and then would have to scramble to regain competitiveness.

Wal-Mart Stores, Inc., based in Bentonville, Arkansas, was an exception. It was especially growth oriented and had emerged in 1991 and continued in that position through 2002 as the nation's largest retailer as well as largest discount department store chain in sales volume. Operating under a variety of names and formats, nationally and internationally, it included Wal-Mart stores, Wal-Mart Supercenters, Sam's Warehouse Clubs, and Neighborhood Markets. The firm found early strength in cultivating rural markets, merchandise restocking programs, "everyday low-pricing," and the control of operations through companywide computer programs that linked cash registers to corporate headquarters. In early 2002, Wal-Mart became the largest company in the world, as measured by annual revenue.

Sears, Roebuck, and Co., in a state of stagnated growth for several years, completed a return to its retailing roots by spinning off to shareholders its $9 billion controlling stake in its Allstate Corporation insurance unit and the divestment of financial services. After unsuccessfully experimenting with an "everyday low-price" strategy, management chose to refine its merchandising program to meet the needs of middle-market customers, who were primarily women, by focusing on product lines in apparel, home, and automotive. In 2001, Sears again revised this strategy to "position Sears in the retail marketplace as not a department store, not a discount store, but a broad line retailer with outstanding credit and service capabilities."

Many retailers, such as Target Corporation (formerly Dayton Hudson), that adopted the discount concept, attempted to go generally after an upscale customer by emphasizing stylish merchandise. The upscale customer tended to have a household income of $25,000 to $44,000 annually. Other segments of the population were served by firms like Ames Department

Stores, (Rocky Hill, Connecticut), which appealed to outsize, older, and lower-income workers, and by Shopko Stores, Inc. (Green Bay, Wisconsin), which attempted to serve the upscale rural consumer. Kohl's Corporation, a relatively new firm based in Menominee Falls, Wisconsin, which operated 420 family-focused, value-oriented department stores in 32 states in 2002 and the J.C. Penney Company, which operated 1,075 value-based department stores in all 50 states, were also considered competitors of Kmart in most markets.

Kmart executives found that discount department stores were being challenged by several other retail formats. Some retailers were assortment oriented, with a much greater depth of assortment within a given product category. To illustrate, Toys "R" Us was an example of a firm that operated 20,000-square-foot toy supermarkets. Toys "R" Us prices were very competitive within an industry that was very competitive. When the consumers entered a Toys "R" Us facility, there was usually no doubt in their minds if the product wasn't there no one else had it. In the late 1990s, Toys "R" Us was challenged by Wal-Mart and other firms that offered higher service levels, more aggressive pricing practices, and more focused merchandise selections. In 2001, Toys "R" Us introduced a new strategy designed to update its stores to make them more convenient, open, and fun to shop.

Some retailers, such as Value City, were experimenting with the "off price" apparel concept, where name brands and designer goods were sold at 20%–70% discounts. Others, such as Home Depot, Lowe's, and Menards, operated home improvement centers that were warehouse-style stores with a wide range of hard-line merchandise for both do-it-yourselfers and professionals. Still others opened drug supermarkets that offered a wide variety of high-turnover merchandise in a convenient location. In these cases, competition was becoming more risk oriented by putting $3 or $4 million in merchandise at retail value in an 80,000-square-foot facility and offering genuinely low prices. Jewel-Osco stores in the Midwest, Rite Aid, CVS, Eckerd, and a series of independents were examples of organizations employing the entirely new concept of the drug supermarket. The Walgreen Company maintained its position as number one in drug sales by emphasizing prescription and general merchandise and by building its own stores in prime, high-traffic locations.

The competition was offering something that was new and different in terms of depth of assortment, competitive price image, and format. Kmart management perceived this as a threat because these were viable businesses and hindered the firm in its ability to improve and maintain share of market in specific merchandise categories. An industry competitive analysis is shown in **Exhibit 5**.

Expansion and Contraction

When Joseph E. Antonini was appointed Chairman of Kmart Corporation in October 1987, he was charged with the responsibility of maintaining and eventually accelerating the chain's record of growth, despite a mature retail marketplace.

He moved to string experimental formats into profitable chains. He noted:

Our vision calls for the constant and never-ceasing exploration of new modes of retailing, so that our core business of U.S. Kmart stores can be constantly renewed and reinvigorated by what we learn from our other businesses.

In the mid-1970s and throughout the 1980s, Kmart became involved in the acquisition or development of several smaller new operations. Kmart Insurance Services, Inc., acquired as Planned Marketing Associates in 1974, offered a full line of life, health, and accident insurance centers located in 27 Kmart stores, primarily in the South and Southwest.

In 1982, Kmart initiated its own off-price specialty apparel concept called Designer Depot. A total of 28 Designer Depot stores were opened in 1982, to appeal to customers who wanted quality upscale clothing at a budget price. A variation of this concept, called Garment

Exhibit 5

An Industry Competitive Analysis, 2001[1] (Dollar amounts in millions)

	Kmart	Wal-Mart	Sears	Target	Kohl's
Sales	$36,151	$217,799	$41,078	$39,888	$7,489
Net income	($2,418)	$6,671	$735	$1,368	$496
Sales growth	(0.1%)	14%	.99%	8%	22.0%
Profit margin	N/A	3.1%	1.78%	3.4%	6.6%
Sales/sq.ft.	$235	$455	$319	$247	$262
Return/equity	N/A	19.0%	12.0%	17.4%	17.1%
Number of stores:					

Kmart Corporation
   Kmart discount stores—2,114
   Kmart Supercenters—105

Wal-Mart Stores, Inc.
   Wal-Mart discount stores—1,647
   Supercenters—1,066
   SAM'S Clubs—500
   Neighborhood Markets—31
   International Stores—1,170

Sears, Roebuck and Company
   Full-line department stores—867
   Hardware Stores—248
   Sears dealer stores—793
   Home supply stores (The Great Indoors)—13
   National Tire & Battery stores—223
   Outlet stores—35

Target Corporation
   Target—1,053
   Mervyn's—264
   Marshall Field's department stores—64

Kohl's Corporation
   Kohl's department stores—382

Note: The company's Fiscal Year (FY) is February through January.

Source: Company annual reports.

Rack, was opened to sell apparel that normally would not be sold in Designer Depot. A distribution center was added in 1983, to supplement them. Neither venture was successful.

Kmart also attempted an unsuccessful joint venture with the Hechinger Company of Washington, DC, a warehouse home center retailer. However, after much deliberation, Kmart chose instead to acquire, in 1984, Home Centers of America of San Antonio, Texas, which operated 80,000-square-foot warehouse home centers. The new division, renamed Builders Square, had grown to 167 units by 1996. It capitalized on Kmart's real estate, construction, and management expertise and on Home Centers of America's merchandising expertise. Builders Square was sold in 1997 to the Hechinger Company. On June 11, 1999, Hechinger filed for Chapter 11 bankruptcy protection. As a result, Kmart recorded a noncash charge of $354 million that reflected the impact of lease obligations for former Builders Square locations that were guaranteed by Kmart.

Waldenbooks, a chain of 877 bookstores, was acquired by Kmart from Carter, Hawley, Hale, Inc., in 1984. It was part of a strategy to capture a greater share of the market with a product category that Kmart already had in its stores. Kmart management had been interested in the book business for some time and took advantage of an opportunity in the marketplace to build on its common knowledge base. Borders Books and Music, an operator of 50 large-format superstores, became part of Kmart in 1992, to form the "Borders Group," a division that would include Waldenbooks. The Borders Group, Inc., was sold during 1995.

The Bruno's, Inc., joint venture in 1987 formed a partnership to develop large combination grocery and general merchandise stores, or "hypermarkets," called American Fare. The giant, one-stop-shopping facilities of 225,000 square feet, traded on the grocery expertise of Bruno's and the general merchandise of Kmart to offer a wide selection of products and services at discount prices. A similar venture, called Super Kmart Center, represented later thinking on combination stores with a smaller size and format. In 2001, these stores were renamed Kmart Supercenters.

In 1988, the company acquired a controlling interest in Makro, Inc., a Cincinnati-based operator of warehouse club stores. Makro, with annual sales of about $300 million, operated member-only stores that were stocked with low-priced fresh and frozen groceries, apparel, and durable goods in suburbs of Atlanta, Cincinnati, Washington, and Philadelphia. PACE Membership Warehouse, Inc., a similar operation, was acquired in 1989. The club stores were sold in 1994.

PayLess Drug Stores, a chain that operated super drugstores in a number of western states, was sold in 1994 to Thrifty PayLess Holdings, Inc., an entity in which Kmart maintained a significant investment. Interests in The Sports Authority, an operator of large-format sporting goods stores, which Kmart acquired in 1990, were disposed of during 1995.

On the international level, an interest in Coles Myer, Ltd., Australia's largest retailer, was sold in November 1994. Interests in 13 Kmart general merchandise stores in the Czech and Slovak Republics were sold at the beginning of 1996 to Tesco PLC, one of the United Kingdom's largest retailers. In February 1998, Kmart stores in Canada were sold to Hudson's Bay Co., a Canadian chain of historic full-service department stores. The interest in Kmart Mexico, S.A. de C.V. was disposed of in fiscal year 1997.

Founded in 1988, OfficeMax, with 328 stores, was one of the largest operators of high-volume, deep-discount office products superstores in the United States. It became a greater than 90% owned Kmart unit in 1991. Kmart's interest in OfficeMax was sold during 1995.

In November 1995, Kmart also sold its auto service center business to a new corporation controlled by Penske Corporation. In connection with the sale, Kmart and Penske entered into a sublease arrangement concerning the operation of Penske Auto Service Centers.

During 1999, Kmart signed agreements with SuperValu, Inc., and Fleming Companies, Inc., under which they would assume responsibility for the distribution and replenishment of grocery-related products to all Kmart stores. Kmart also maintained an equity interest in Meldisco subsidiaries of Footstar, Inc., operators of footwear departments in Kmart stores.

The Maturation of Kmart

Early corporate research revealed that on the basis of convenience, Kmart served 80% of the population. One study concluded that one out of every two adults in the United States shopped at a Kmart at least once a month. Despite this popular appeal, strategies that had allowed the firm to have something for everybody were no longer felt to be appropriate for the new millennium. Kmart found that it had a broad customer base because it operated on a national basis. Its early strategies had assumed that the firm was serving everyone in the markets where it was established. The financial community believed the Kmart customer was blue-collar, low-income, and upper lower class.

Although Kmart had made a major commitment in more recent years to secondary or rural markets, these were areas that had previously not been cultivated. The firm, in its initial strategies, perceived the rural consumer as different from the urban or suburban customer. In re-addressing the situation, it discovered that its assortments in rural areas were too limited, and there were too many preconceived notions regarding what the rural customer really wanted. The firm discovered that the typical farmer didn't always shop for bib overalls and shovels, but shopped for microwave ovens and the same things everyone else did.

One goal was not to attract more customers but to get the customer coming in the door to spend more. Once in the store, the customer was thought to demonstrate more divergent tastes. The upper-income consumer would buy more health and beauty aids, cameras, and sporting goods. The lower-income consumer would buy toys and clothing.

In the process of trying to capture a larger share of the market and get people to spend more, the firm began to recognize a market that was more upscale. When consumer research was conducted and management examined the profile of the trade area and the profile of the person who shopped at Kmart in the past month, they were found to be identical. Kmart was predominately serving the suburban consumer in suburban locations. In 1997, Kmart's primary target customers were women, between the ages of 25 and 45 years old, with children at home and with household incomes between $20,000 and $50,000 per year. The core Kmart shopper averaged 4.3 visits to a Kmart store per month. The purchase amount per visit was $40. The purchase rate was 95% during a store visit. The firm estimated that 180 million people shopped at Kmart in an average year.

In "lifestyle" research in markets served by the firm, Kmart determined there were more two-income families, families were having fewer children, there were more working wives, and customers tended to be homeowners. Customers were very careful how they spent their money and were perceived as wanting quality. This was a distinct contrast to the 1960s and early 1970s, which tended to have the orientation of a "throwaway" society. Customers wanted better-quality products but still demanded competitive prices. According to a Kmart *Annual Report*, "Consumers today are well educated and informed. They want good value and they know it when they see it. Price remains a key consideration, but the consumers' new definition of value includes quality as well as price."

Corporate management at Kmart considered the discount department store to be a mature idea. Although maturity was sometimes looked on with disfavor, Kmart executives felt that this did not mean a lack of profitability or lack of opportunity to increase sales. The industry was perceived as having been "reborn." It was in this context, in the 1990s, that a series of new retailing strategies, designed to upgrade the Kmart image, were developed.

The 1990 Renewal Program

The strategies that emerged to confront the changing environment were the result of an overall reexamination of existing corporate strategies. This program included accelerated store expansion and refurbishing, capitalizing on dominant lifestyle departments, centralized merchandising, more capital investment in retail automation, an aggressive and focused advertising program, and continued growth through new specialty retail formats.

The initial 1990, five-year, $2.3 billion program involved virtually all Kmart discount stores. There would be approximately 250 new full-size Kmart stores, 620 enlargements, 280 relocations, and 30 closings. In addition 1,260 stores would be refurbished to bring their layout and fixtures up to new store standards. Another program, introduced in 1996, resulted in an additional $1.1 billion being spent to upgrade Kmart stores. By year-end 1999, 1,860 new Big Kmart stores offered more pleasant shopping experiences, thanks to the updated and easy-to-shop departmental adjacencies, better signing and lighting, wider aisles, and more attractive in-store presentation.

One area receiving initial attention was improvement in the way products were displayed. The traditional Kmart layout was by product category. Often these locations for departments were holdovers from the variety store. Many departments would not give up prime locations.

As part of the new marketing strategy, the shop concept was introduced. Management recognized that it had a sizable do-it-yourself store. As planning management discussed the issue, "nobody was aware of the opportunity. The hardware department was right smack in the center of the store because it was always there. The paint department was over here and the electrical department was over there." "All we had to do," management contended, "was put them all in one spot and everyone could see that we had a very respectable 'do-it-yourself' department." The concept resulted in a variety of new departments, such as Soft Goods for the Home, Kitchen Korners, and Home Electronic Centers. The goal behind each department was to sell an entire lifestyle-orientated concept to consumers, making goods complementary so shoppers would want to buy several interrelated products rather than just one item.

Name brands were added in soft and hard goods as management recognized that the customer transferred the product quality of branded goods to perceptions of private-label merchandise. In the eyes of Kmart management, "If you sell Wrangler, there is good quality. Then the private label must be good quality."

The company increased its emphasis on trusted national brands such as Rubbermaid, Procter & Gamble, and Kodak, and put emphasis of major strategic vendor relationships. In addition, it enhanced its private label brands such as Kathy Ireland, Jaclyn Smith, Route 66, and Sesame Street in apparel. Additional private label merchandise included K Gro in home gardening, American Fare in grocery and consumables, White-Westinghouse in appliances and Penske Auto Centers in automotive services. Some private labels were discontinued following review.

Kmart hired Martha Stewart, an upscale Connecticut author of lavish best-selling books on cooking and home entertaining, as its "life-style spokesperson and consultant." Martha Stewart was featured as a corporate symbol for housewares and associated products in advertising and in-store displays. Management visualized her as the next Betty Crocker, a fictional character created some years ago by General Mills, Inc., and a representative of its interest in "life-style" trends. The "Martha Stewart Everyday" home fashion product line was introduced in 1995 and expanded in 1996 and 1997. A separate division was established to manage strategy for all Martha Stewart label goods and programs. Merchandise was featured in the redesigned once-a-week Kmart newspaper circular that carried the advertising theme: "The quality you need, the price you want."

Several thousand prices were reduced to maintain "price leadership across America." As management noted, "it is absolutely essential that we provide our customers with good value—quality products at low prices." Although lowering of prices hurt margins and contributed importantly to an earnings decline, management felt that unit turnover of items with lowered prices increased significantly to "enable Kmart to maintain its pricing leadership that will have a most positive impact on our business in the years ahead."

A centralized merchandising system was introduced to improve communication. A computerized, highly automated replenishment system tracked how quickly merchandise sold and just as quickly, put fast moving items back on the shelves. Satellite capability and a point-of-sale (POS) scanning system were introduced as part of the program. Regular, live satellite communication from Kmart headquarters to the stores would allow senior management to communicate with store managers and allow for questions and answers. The POS scanning system allowed a record of every sale and transmission of the data to headquarters. This enabled Kmart to respond quickly to what's new, what's in demand, and what would keep customers coming back.

The company opened its first Kmart Supercenter (originally called Super Kmart Centers) in 1992. The format combined general merchandise and food with emphasis upon customer service and convenience and ranged in size from 135,000 to 190,000 square feet, with more than 40,000 grocery items. The typical Supercenter operated 7 days a week, 24 hours a day and generated high traffic and sales volume. The centers also featured wider shopping aisles, appealing displays, and pleasant lighting to enrich the shopping experience. Kmart Supercenters featured in-house bakeries, USDA fresh meats, fresh seafood, delicatessens, cookie kiosks, cappuccino bars, in-store eateries and food courts, and fresh carry-out salad bars. In many locations, the center provided customer services like video rental, dry cleaning, shoe repair, beauty salons, optical shops, express shipping services, and a full line of traditional Kmart merchandise. To enhance the appeal of the merchandise assortment, emphasis was placed on "cross-merchandising." For example, toasters were featured above the fresh baked breads, kitchen gadgets were positioned across the aisle from produce, and baby centers featured everything from baby food to toys. At the end of 2001, the company operated 105 Supercenter stores.

The Planning Function

Corporate planning at Kmart during the 1980s and 1990s was the result of executives, primarily the senior executive, recognizing change. The role played by the senior executive was to get others to recognize that nothing is good forever. "Good planning" was perceived as the result of those who recognized that at some point they would have to get involved. "Poor planning" was done by those who didn't recognize the need for it. When they did, it was too late to survive. Good planning, if done on a regular and timely basis, was assumed to result in improved performance. Kmart's Michael Wellman, then Director of Planning and Research, contended, "Planning, as we like to stress, is making decisions now to improve performance tomorrow. Everyone looks at what may happen tomorrow, but the planners are the ones who make decisions today. That's where I think too many firms go wrong. They think they are planning because they are writing reports and are aware of changes. They don't say, 'because of this, we must decide today to spend this money to do this to accomplish this goal in the future.'"

Kmart management believed that the firm had been very successful in the area of strategic planning. "When it became necessary to make significant changes in the way we were doing business," Michael Wellman suggested, "that was accomplished on a fairly timely basis." When the organization made changes in the 1960s, it recognized there was a very powerful investment opportunity and capitalized on it—far beyond what anyone else would have done. "We just opened stores," he continued, "at a great, great pace. Management, when confronted with a crisis, would state, 'It's the economy, or it's this, or that, but it's not the essential way we are doing business.'" He noted, "Suddenly management would recognize that the economy may stay like this forever. We need to improve the situation and then do it." Strategic planning was thought to arise out of some difficult times for the organization.

Kmart had developed a reasonably formal planning organization that involved a constant evaluation of what was happening in the marketplace, what competition was doing, and what kinds of opportunities were available. Management felt a need to diversify because it would not be a viable company unless it was growing. Management felt it was not going to grow with the Kmart format forever. It needed growth and opportunity, particularly for a company that was able to open 200 stores on a regular basis. Michael Wellman, Director of Planning and Research, noted, "Given a 'corporate culture' that was accustomed to challenges, management would have to find ways to expend that energy. A corporation that is successful," he argued, "has to continue to be successful. It has to have a basic understanding of corporate needs and be augmented by a much more rigorous effort to be aware of what's going on in the external environment."

A planning group at Kmart represented a number of functional areas of the organization. Management described it as an "in-house consulting group" with some independence. It was made up of financial planning, economic and consumer analysis, and operations research. The CEO was identified as the primary planner of the organization.

Early Reorganization and Restructuring

Kmart financial performance for 1993 was clearly disappointing. The company announced a loss of $974 million on sales of $34,156,000 for the fiscal year ended January 26, 1994. Chairman Antonini, noting the deficit, felt it occurred primarily because of lower margins in the U.S. Kmart stores division. "Margin erosion," he said, "stemmed in part from intense industry-wide pricing pressure throughout 1993." He was confident, however, that Kmart was on track with its renewal program to make the more than 2,350 U.S. Kmart stores more "competitive, on-trend, and cutting-edge merchandisers." Tactical Retail Solutions, Inc., estimated that during Antonini's seven-year tenure with the company, Kmart's market share in the discount arena fell to 23% from 35%. Other retail experts suggested that because the company had struggled for so long to have the right merchandise in the stores at the right time, it had lost customers to competitors. An aging customer base was also cited.

In early 1995, following the posting of its eighth consecutive quarter of disappointing earnings, Kmart's Board of Directors announced that Joseph Antonini would be replaced as chairman. It named Donald S. Perkins, former Chairman of Jewel Companies, Inc., and a Kmart director, to the position. Antonini relinquished his position as President and CEO in March. After a nationwide search, Floyd Hall, 57, former Chairman and CEO of the Target discount store division of the Dayton Hudson Corporation, was appointed Chairman, President, and CEO of Kmart in June 1995.

The company concluded the disposition of many noncore assets in 1996, including the sale of the Borders group, OfficeMax, The Sports Authority, and Coles Myer. During the 1990s, it also closed a large number of underperforming stores in the United States and cleared out $700 million in aged and discontinued inventory in the remaining stores.

In 1996, Kmart converted 152 of its traditional stores to feature a new design that was referred to as the "high-frequency format." These stores were named Big Kmart. The stores emphasized those departments that were deemed the most important to core customers and offered an increased mix of high-frequency, everyday basics and consumables in the pantry area located at the front of each store. These items were typically priced at a one- to three-percentage differential from the leading competitors in each market and served to increase inventory turnover and gross margin dollars. In addition to the pantry area, Big Kmart stores featured improved lighting, new signage that was easier to see and read, and adjacencies that created a smoother traffic flow. In 1999, 588 stores were converted to the new Big Kmart format, bringing the total to 1,860. Other, smaller stores were updated to a "best of Big Kmart" prototype, as resources permitted.

Kmart launched its first e-commerce site in 1998. The initial Kmart.com offered a few products and was not considered a successful venture. In 1999, it partnered with SOFTBANK Venture Capital, which provided technical expertise, experienced personnel, and initial capital to create an Internet site 60% owned by Kmart. BlueLight.com increased the number of Kmart products it offered online to about 65,000 from 1,250. It planned to boost the number to 100,000 by year end 2000 and possibly to millions of items in the future. The name was changed to Kmart.com in 2002.

At the end of his tenure, Floyd Hall announced in 2000 that the company mandate in the year and century ahead was to create sustained growth that would profitably leverage all of the core strengths of the firm. The corporate mission was "to become the discount store of choice for low- and middle-income households by satisfying their routine and seasonal shopping needs as well as or better than the competition." Management believed that the actions taken by Charles Conaway during his tenure as CEO, would have a dramatic impact on how customers perceived Kmart, how frequently they shopped in the stores, and how much they would buy on each visit. Increasing customers' frequency and the amount they purchased each visit were seen as having a dramatic impact on the company's efforts to increase its profitability.

Restructuring and Repositioning a Bankrupt Company

The major objective of Kmart management in 2002 was to eventually emerge from bankruptcy protection as a strong and healthy competitor with a clearly defined place in the discount retail sector.

The bankruptcy filing had the immediate effect of stopping the loss of goods from suppliers no longer confident of Kmart's ability to pay. Dallas, Texas–based Fleming Companies, Inc., had announced that it was discontinuing shipments of groceries and other types of products to Kmart stores. Fleming resumed shipments once the bankruptcy court assured it of payment of bills outstanding.

On March 20, 2002, the bankruptcy court approved the closure of 283 Kmart stores, or approximately 13% of the 2,114 stores operating at the end of 2001. The closures included 270 Kmart discount stores and 12 Kmart Supercenters in 40 states and one Kmart store in Puerto Rico. Stores were selected by evaluating the market and financial performance of every store and the terms of every lease. Candidates for closure were stores that did not meet management's financial requirements for ongoing operations. In some cases, lease terms were renegotiated to attempt to improve store profitability and avoid the need for closure. Approximately 22,000 employees were affected by the store closures. The move also involved terminating leases on 350 Kmart stores that were closed prior to the bankruptcy.

On April 9, 2002, management announced that it had reached an agreement with Penske Corporation to close all of its auto service centers at more than 563 Kmart stores in 44 states.

Kmart management earlier announced that it would work on a marketing strategy to become "the authority for what moms value" and also be "the store that understands what really matters in life." This was later changed to suggest that Kmart featured "The stuff of life," in an attempt to focus on family values. A key component of this strategy was to invest in merchandise and marketing initiatives to enhance the firm's strategic positioning by offering exclusive brands that would differentiate it from competition. These exclusive brands included Martha Stewart Everyday home, garden, colors, baby, kitchen, keeping, and decorating products, along with candles and accessories; Jaclyn Smith women's apparel, jewelry, and accessories; Kathy Ireland apparel for infants and children; Route 66 men's and women's apparel and accessories; and Joe Boxer apparel, accessories, and home furnishings. As part of the new brand emphasis, displays of Disney, Sesame Street, and Joe Boxer were moved to the front of stores, where parents might be more tempted to browse. In 2002, Martha Stewart was in court fighting accusations of insider trading, a scandal that some analysts said could affect sales of the brand.

Management concluded that the "BlueLight Always" campaign had significantly affected Kmart's gross margin. The campaign, which had initially lowered prices on over 30,000 items, was therefore scaled back to approximately 18,000 items. Several other changes were made in an attempt to reduce gross margin erosion.

In October 2002, Kmart unveiled a store in White Lake, Michigan, that would serve as a prototype while management decided on a final strategy on how to move forward in repositioning itself in the marketplace. The prototype store featured a new logo, sleekly designed signs, brighter lighting, lower shelves, and wider aisles to encourage shoppers to buy more. A new color scheme was a key to the new design. The fire-engine-red Kmart logo, which had graced the outside of all the chain's stores since 1990, was replaced by a lime-green K logo. The new green, which Kmart management said suggested growth and nature, was also used on employee aprons and color decorating accents in the stores. Mr. Adamson said that the company would study the prototype and focus on changes that increase sales the most.

In addition to developing a new look for stores, management also experimented with how it controlled store operations and merchandising in an attempt to position Kmart as the "store of the neighborhood." Store operations traditionally were decisions made by Kmart management at corporate headquarters in Troy, Michigan. Inventory and merchandise were ordered centrally for the stores, and managers were told how to arrange the goods. In a pilot program involving about 40 stores in the Chicago metropolitan area, store managers were given the freedom to customize inventory, store hours, and displays based on customer preferences. During the first 10 weeks, sales at the stores in the test program outperformed the overall company by 12%.

Kmart's financial results reported in the fiscal second quarter of 2002 noted that it lost $377 million as spending cuts and layoffs failed to offset declines in sales and shrinking profit margins. Sales fell 15.7%, or nearly $1.4 billion, for the 13-week period ended July 31, 2002. The company lost an additional $126 million in August, the seventh consecutive month of losses at the company since it filed for bankruptcy protection. Kmart posted net sales of $7.2 billion for the second quarter, down from $8.92 billion during the same quarter of 2001. Same-store sales, a measurement that factors out stores that had been opened or closed and other changes, were down 11.9%. The profit margin dropped to 17.6% from 18.7% in the second quarter of 2001.

Kmart's ongoing financial losses, combined with its failure to sustain any kind of sales momentum, had many retail experts speculating on whether the company could successfully emerge from bankruptcy. "Kmart appears to be directionless," indicated one retail consultant. "What we're seeing is a bunch of tactical moves that don't have much substance to them, which is why they don't resonate with consumers for very long," he noted.

Most retail analysts believed that in addition to closing stores, lowering costs, and improving efficiency while in bankruptcy, Kmart management needed to develop a strategy for differentiating itself from Wal-Mart, Target, and other major competitors in the marketplace. In addition, some suggested that a leaner, more efficient Kmart should seek a buyer such as a general merchandiser and/or food distributor. Others proposed that Kmart merge with an international retailer eager to enter the U.S. market.

FINANCIAL SITUATION AND ISSUES

Kmart's financial position is shown in **Exhibits 1, 2, 3,** and **6.** A 12-year (1990–2001) record of Kmart's financial performance is shown in **Exhibit 6.** In fiscal year 1990, Kmart's sales were $32,070,000,000, and Wal-Mart's sales were $32,601,594,000. In fiscal year 2001, Kmart's sales were $36,151,000,000 (an increase of $4,081,000,000 or 12.72%), while Wal-Mart's sales increased to $217,799,000,000 (an increase of $185,197,406,000 or 568.1%). Wal-Mart's fiscal year 2001 net income was $6,671,000,000 compared with Kmart's net loss of $2,418,000,000. Kmart had 105 Super Kmart Centers and 2,114 discount stores, for a total of 2,219. Wal-Mart had 2,295 Wal-Mart stores, 564 SAM's Clubs, 1,521 Supercenters, and 34 Neighborhood Markets, for a total of 4,414 stores.

Toward the end of 2002, Kmart's management announced that it was restating the company's financial statements for three prior fiscal years and for the first two quarters of 2002. Problems had been discovered as part of the company's review of its accounting practices. The adjustments were likely to reduce the company's net loss for the first two quarters of the year by less than $100 million. For fiscal years 1999–2001, it was likely to reduce total earnings during the period by nearly $100 million. (These adjustments are *not* reflected in case exhibits.) The adjustments derived from a software programming error in Kmart's accounts payable system, an understatement of historical accruals for certain leases with varying rent payments, and a related understatement of historical rent expenses.

Exhibit 6

Financial Performance: Wal-Mart and Kmart, 1990–2001
(Dollar amounts in thousands)

A. Kmart Financial Performance

Fiscal Year[1]	Sales	Assets	Net Income[2]	Stores[3]
2001	$ 36,151,000	$14,298.000	($2,418,000)	$2,114
2000	37,028,000	14,832,000	(244,000)	2,105
1999	35,925,000	15,104,000	403,000	2,171
1998	33,674,000	14,166,000	518,000	2,161
1997[3]	32,183,000	13,558,000	249,000	2,136
1996[3]	31,437,000	14,286,000	(220,000)	2,201
1995[3]	31,713,000	15,033,000	(571,000)	2,161
1994	34,025,000	17,029,000	296,000	2,481
1993	34,156,000	17,504,000	(974,000)	2,486
1992	37,724,000	18,931,000	941,000	2,435
1991	34,580,000	15,999,000	859,000	2,391
1990	$ 32,070,000	$13,899,000	$756,000	2,350

B. Wal-Mart Financial Performance

Fiscal Year[1]	Sales	Assets	Net Income	Stores[4]
2001	$217,799,000	$83,451,000	$6,671,000	$4,414
2000	191,329,000	78,130,000	6,295,000	4,189
1999	165,013,000	70,349,000	5,377,000	3,996
1998	137,634,000	49,996,000	4,430,000	3,999
1997	117,958,000	45,384,000	3,526,000	3,406
1996	104,859,000	39,604,000	3,056,000	3,054
1995	93,627,000	37,541,000	2,740,000	2,943
1994	82,494,000	32,819,000	2,681,000	2,684
1993	67,344,000	26,441,000	2,333,000	2,400
1992	55,484,000	20,565,000	1,995,000	2,136
1991	43,886,900	15,443,400	1,608,500	1,928
1990	$ 32,601,594	$11,388,915	$1,291,024	1,721

Notes:
1. The company's fiscal year is February through January.
2. Net income from discontinued operations.
3. Kmart 2,114 discount stores (not including Supercenters).
4. Wal-Mart all category of stores.

Source: Fortune financial analysis, Wal-Mart annual reports.

One financial analyst (Konicki–1/28/02–Information Week.com) cited specific facts and his perception of the issues facing Kmart:

Facts:
  A. *The average customer spends 17 minutes in Kmart store vs. 36 minutes in a Wal-Mart.*
  B. *Half the U.S. population has been inside a Kmart in the past three months.*
  C. *Someone from 45% of U.S. households was in a Kmart in the past week.*
  D. *Asians, blacks and Hispanics represent 31% of the population but 36% of Kmart traffic and 39% of Kmart sales.*

Perception:
Formula: A discount store uses the lure of lower prices to sell huge volumes of the most popular items of general merchandise. Chains pull this off by wrangling volume discounts from suppli-

ers, narrowing the selection of a product only to best sellers and operating on a skinnier profit margin. If the most popular brand won't supply products to a discount chain, the chain produces its own. The big discount chains are getting into the grocery business to increase customer frequency.

Recent Troubles: Kmart's bargain-basement image hit bottom when Dustin Hoffman's autistic character in the 1988 movie Rain Man learned how to say "Kmart sucks." That pop culture moment confirmed Kmart had became synonymous with cheapness, not value. An unwillingness to invest in technology made Kmart less competitive while its stores developed a reputation for listless clerks. Kmart gave up on its warehouse clubs and its venture in grocery-laden supercenters remains stuck in first gear.

Governance Issues: Regulators and the U.S. Attorney's Office are investigating the previous management group for forgiving tens of millions of dollars in loans to keep a dozen key executives who resigned anyway. Also probing accounting irregularities, including one that restated 2001 earnings because of $500-million accounting error that had artificially inflated results. Current CEO James Adamson, then an outside director, was head of the audit committee at the time.

Compared to Wal-Mart, Kmart's distribution and inventory system was inefficient and outdated. CEO Conaway tried to remedy this by unveiling an IT project based on Manhattan Associates' software, estimated at $600 million, to manage the flow of goods. In the process, he wrote off two distribution centers and IT assets, reportedly including some supply-chain and warehouse management software purchased the previous year, worth $130 million. A Kmart spokesperson stated that the software was so heavily modified that it cost too much to maintain. Due to problems with the system, inventory planners were unable to learn what was selling. Thus, many items were left on clearance racks and not enough of the items that customers wanted were available. Store clerks were forced to spend time dealing with paperwork in the back room instead of working with customers. The average store clerk only spent 22% of his/her time interacting with customers—leading customers to perceive Kmart as being less helpful and out-of-date. According to ex-CEO Charles Conaway, "That number should be 60% or 70%." In addition, Kmart was no longer able to effectively compete on price. A March 2001 survey by the *Minneapolis Star Tribune* of 21 identical items in Minneapolis discount stores found Kmart's total price to be $5.00 above Target's and $10.00 above Wal-Mart's.

References

Albright, Mark (December 1, 2002) "Kmart Bank on a Happy Holiday," *St. Petersburg Times* pp. 1H, 11H.

Albright, Mark (January 23, 2002), "Kmart's Effort to Compete a Case of Too Little, Too Late," *St. Petersburg Times*, 1A.

Bussey, John (April 6, 1987), "Kmart Is Set To Sell Many of Its Roots to Rapid-American Corp's McCrory," *Wall Street Journal*, 24.

Carruth, Eleanore (July 1977), "Kmart Has To Open Some New Doors On The Future," *Fortune*, 143–150, 153–154.

Coleman, Calmetta (June 19, 2000), "BlueLight.com Aims to Coax Kmart Shoppers Online," *Wall Street Journal*, B4.

Coleman, Calmetta (July 27, 2000), "Kmart's New CEO Outlines Plans for Fast Changes," *Wall Street Journal*, B4.

Coleman, Calmetta (July 26, 2000), "Kmart Sees $740 Million Pretax Charge from Closing 72 Stores, Other Changes," *Wall Street Journal*, B10.

Coleman, Calmetta (June 1, 2000), "Kmart Selects CVS President to Be Its CEO," *Wall Street Journal*, June 1, 2000.

Cuneo, Alice (July 29, 2002), "Kmart Still Struggles to Find Its Way out of Darkness," *Advertising Age*, 13.

Dewar, Robert E. (July 2, 1975), "The Kresge Company and the Retail Revolution," *University of Michigan Business Review*, 2.

Dixon, Jennifer (March 20, 2002), "Martha Stewart Talks, Kmart Boss Listens," *Detroit Free Press*, E1.

Elmer, Vickie, and Joann Muller (March 22, 1995), "Retailer Needs Leader, Vision," *Detroit Free Press*, 1A, 9A.

Ewoldt, J. (March 1, 2001), "Discounter Encounter: Comparing Target, Wal-Mart, and Kmart," *Minneapolis Star Tribune*.

Grant, Lorrie (January 23, 2002), "Sticking by Kmart," *USA Today*, 5B.

Grant, Lorrie (January 25, 2002), "Kmart Food Supplier Resumes Shipments," *USA Today*, 7B.

Grant, Lorrie (March 12, 2002), "Kmart Cleans Its Executive House," *USA Today*, B1.

Grant, Lorrie (March 11, 2002), "Kmart Takes Aim at 284 Underperforming Stores," *USA Today*, 4B.

Guiles, Melinda G. (September 8, 1987), "Kmart, Bruno's Join to Develop 'Hypermarkets'", *Wall Street Journal*, 17.

Horovitz, Bruce (January 23, 2002), "With Image Crumbling, Kmart Files Chapter 11," *USA Today*, B1.

Ingrassia, Paul (October 6, 1987), "Attention Non-Kmart Shoppers: A Blue-Light Special Just for You", *Wall Street Journal*, 42.

"Kmart Adjustments," *Des Moines Register* (December 10, 2002), 3D.

Kmart Corporation, *Annual Report*, Troy, Michigan, 1999.

Kmart Corporation, *Annual Report*, Troy, Michigan, 2000.

Kmart Corporation, *Annual Report (10-K)*, Troy, Michigan, 2001.

Kmart Corporation, *Kmart Fact Book*, Troy, Michigan, 1997

"Kmart Board Weighs Bankruptcy-Court Filing" (January 22, 2002), *Wall Street Journal*, A3.

"Kmart Declares Bankruptcy," *St. Petersburg Times* (January 23, 2002), E1.

"Kmart Runs Out of Money Options" (February 22, 2002), *St. Petersburg Times*, 1A, 11A.

Konicki, S. (January 28, 2002), "Now in Bankruptcy, Kmart Struggled with Supply Chain," *Information Week.com*.

Kranhold, Kathryn (July 27, 2000), "Kmart Hopes to Steer Teens to Route 66," *Wall Street Journal*, B14.

Main, Jerry (September 21, 1981), "Kmart's Plan to Be Born Again," *Fortune*, 74–77, 84–85.

Merrick, Amy (January 23, 2002), "Kmart Lays Out Plans to Trim Its Size, Increase Efficiency in Bankruptcy Filing," *Wall Street Journal*, A3.

Merrick, Amy (February 6, 2002), "Kmart, Seeking Focus, Demotes Chief of Store Operations, Reorganizes Units," *Wall Street Journal*, B13.

Merrick, Amy (March 12, 2002) "Kmart Says CEO Conaway Resigned, Adds Post to Plate of Chairman Adamson," *Wall Street Journal*, A3.

Merrick, Amy (April 5, 2002) "Kmart Store Closures Will Include Many of Its New Ones," *Wall Street Journal*, B4.

Merrick, Amy (June 20, 2002) "Kmart, Turned Off by BlueLight.com, Renames Web Site," *Wall Street Journal*, B8.

Merrick, Amy (October 8, 2002), "Can Martha Deliver Merry?" *Wall Street Journal*, B1.

Merrick, Amy (October 15, 2002), "Turning Red Ink to Green," *Wall Street Journal*, B1.

Merrick, Amy (May 2, 2002), "Kmart Announces It May Restate Financial Results," *Wall Street Journal*, B2.

Muller, J. (September 4, 2002), "A Kmart Special: Better Service," *Business Week Online*.

Rice, Faye (October 9, 1989), "Why Kmart Has Stalled," *Fortune*, 79.

Saporito, Bill (May 6, 1991), "Is Wal-Mart Unstoppable?," *Fortune*, 50–59.

Sellers, Patricia (February 4, 2002), "First It's (Not) a Good Thing," *Fortune*, 22–23.

Smith, Joel J. (June 11, 2002), "Kmart Widens Corruption Investigation," detnews.com.

Talaski, Karen (January 11, 2002), "Kmart Reorganizes as Troubles Mount," *The Detroit News*, 2A.

Talaski, Karen (August 11, 2000), "Kmart to Invest $2 Billion," *The Detroit News*, 1C.

Talaski, Karen (May 12, 2000), "Kmart Profits Plunge Sharply," *The Detroit News*, 1B.

Yue, Lorene (May 16, 2002), "Kmart Reports Its Biggest Loss," *Detroit Free Press*, 1E.

Wellman, Michael (August 6, 1984), Interview with Director of Planning and Research, Kmart Corporation.

Woodruff, David (January 22, 1990), "Will Kmart Ever Be a Silk Purse?" *Business Week*, 46.

case 21

Wal-Mart Stores, Inc.: On Becoming the World's Largest Company (2002)

James W. Camerius

Reflecting on the events of 2001, Lee Scott, President and CEO of Wal-Mart Stores, Inc., was struck not only by how disappointing a year it was, but also how positively the company had responded to one of the most challenging times in its history. The year began after one of the worst holiday seasons (end-2000) in recent memory. Sluggish consumer spending, rising unemployment, the energy crisis, and the terrorist events of September 11, 2001 all had converged to make the year a very difficult time in retailing.

Lee Scott was only the third CEO in the entire history of Wal-Mart when he was elected to the position in 2000. Its first CEO, Sam Walton, had built the company from the ground up. During the 12 years that David Glass, the previous CEO, held the position, sales grew from $16 billion to $165 billion. Lee Scott had been personally recruited by David Glass 21 years before, from a Springdale, Arkansas, trucking company to come to Wal-Mart as the manager of the truck fleet. In his years at Wal-Mart, Glass had established himself as a leader, an innovator, and a team player. He had served as Chief Operating Officer (COO) and Vice Chairman of the company. He was aware that there were tremendous opportunities to serve new markets with the company's stores. His management mandate was to drive the company to a new level of success in domestic and international markets. David Glass continued to be active in the firm as Chairman of the firm's executive committee.

Wal-Mart: A Maturing Organization

In 2002, Wal-Mart Stores, Inc., of Bentonville, Arkansas, operated mass merchandising retail stores under a variety of names and retail formats, including Wal-Mart discount department stores; Sam's Wholesale Clubs, wholesale/retail membership warehouses; Neighborhood Markets, small grocery/drug store formats; and Wal-Mart Supercenters, large combination grocery and general merchandise stores in all 50 states. In the International Division, it operated its own stores in Canada, Mexico, Argentina, Brazil, Germany, South Korea, United Kingdom, and Puerto Rico, plus stores in China operated through joint ventures. It was not only the nation's largest discount department store chain but also had surpassed the retail division of Sears, Roebuck, and Co. in sales volume as the largest retail firm in the United States. It was also considered the largest retailer in the world, with sales of $217.8 billion in 2001. The McLane

Company, Inc., a Wal-Mart subsidiary, sold a wide variety of groceries, nongrocery products, and institutional food services to a variety of retailers, including selected Wal-Marts, Sam's Clubs, and Supercenters. In 1999, *Discount Store News* honored Wal-Mart as "Retailer of the Century." In 2000, *Fortune* magazine named it as one of the "100 Best Places to Work." In 2001, it was ranked number three in *Fortune*'s annual list of "America's Most Admired Companies" and fifth on the list of *Fortune*'s "Global Most Admired Companies." Sales for the year ending January 31, 2002, were approximately $218 billion, making Wal-Mart Stores, Inc., the largest company in the world, as measured by annual revenue.

A financial summary of Wal-Mart Stores, Inc., for the fiscal years ended January 31, 2002, and January 31, 2001, is shown in **Exhibits 1** and **2**. An 11-year financial summary for the fiscal years ended January 31, 1992, to January 31, 2002, is shown in **Exhibit 3**.

Exhibit 1

Consolidated Income Statements: Wal-Mart Stores, Inc.
(Dollar amounts in millions except per share data)

Fiscal Years Ending January 31[1]	2002	2001	2000
Revenues			
Net sales	$217,799	$191,329	$165,013
Other income, net	2,013	1,966	1,796
	219,812	193,295	166,809
Costs and expenses			
Cost of sales	171,562	150,255	129,664
Operating, selling, and general and administrative expenses	36,173	31,550	27,040
Interest costs			
Debt	1,052	1,095	756
Capital leases	274	279	266
	209,061	183,179	157,726
Income before income taxes, minority interest, and			
cumulative effect of accounting change	10,751	10,116	9,083
Provision for income taxes			
Current	3,712	3,350	3,476
Deferred	185	342	(138)
	3,897	3,692	3,338
Income before minority interest and			
cumulative effect of accounting change	6,854	6,424	5,745
Minority interest	(183)	(129)	(170)
Income before cumulative effect of accounting change	6,671	6,295	5,575
Cumulative effect of accounting change, net tax benefit of $119	—	—	(198)
Net income	$ 6,671	$ 6,295	$ 5,377
Net income per common share			
Basic net income per common share			
Income before cumulative effect of accounting change	$ 1.49	$ 1.41	$ 1.25
Cumulative effect of accounting change, net of tax	—	—	(0.04)
Net income per common share	$ 1.49	$ 1.41	$ 1.21
Average number of common shares	4,465	4,465	4,451
Diluted net income per common share			
Income before cumulative effect of accounting change	$ 1.49	$ 1.40	$ 1.25
Cumulative effect of accounting change, net of tax	—	—	(0.04)
Net income per common share	$ 1.49	$ 1.40	$ 1.20
Average number of common shares (millions)	4,481	4,484	4,474

Note:
1. The company's fiscal year is February through January.

Source: Wal-Mart annual reports.

Exhibit 2

Consolidated Balance Sheets: Wal-Mart Stores, Inc. (Dollar amounts in millions)

Fiscal Year Ending January 31[1]	2002	2001
Assets		
Current assets		
Cash and cash equivalents	**$2,161**	$2,054
Receivables	**2,000**	1,768
Inventories		
At replacement cost	**22,749**	21,644
Less LIFO reserve	**135**	202
Inventories at LIFO cost	**22,614**	21,442
Prepaid expenses and other	**1,471**	1,291
Total current assets	**28,246**	26,555
Property, plant, and equipment, at cost		
Land	**10,241**	9,433
Building and improvements	**28,527**	24,537
Fixtures and equipment	**14,135**	12,964
Transportation equipment	**1,089**	879
	53,992	47,813
Less accumulated depreciation	**11,436**	10,196
Net property, plant, and equipment	**42,556**	37,617
Property under capital lease		
Property under capital lease	**4,626**	4,620
Less accumulated amortization	**1,432**	1,303
Net property under capital leases	**3,194**	3,317
Other assets and deferred charges		
Net goodwill and other acquired intangible assets	**8,595**	9,059
Other assets and deferred charges	**860**	1,582
Total assets	**$83,451**	$78,130
Liabilities and shareholders' equity		
Current Liabilities		
Commercial paper	**$743**	$2,286
Accounts payable	**15,617**	15,092
Accrued liabilities	**7,174**	6,355
Accrued income taxes	**1,343**	841
Long-term debt due within 1 year	**2,257**	4,234
Obligations under capital leases due within 1 year	**148**	141
Total current liabilities	**27,282**	28,949
Long-term debt	**15,687**	12,501
Long-term obligations under capital leases	**3,045**	3,154
Deferred income taxes and other	**1,128**	1,043
Minority interest	**1,207**	1,140
Shareholders' equity		
Preferred stock ($0.10 par value; 100 shares authorized, none issued)		
Common stock ($0.10 par value; 11,000 shares authorized, 4,453 and 4.470 issued and outstanding in 2002 and 2003, respectively)	**445**	447
Capital in excess of par value	**1,484**	1,411
Retained earnings	**34,441**	30,169
Other accumulated comprehensive income	**(1,268)**	(684)
Total shareholders' equity	**35,102**	31,343
Total liabilities and shareholders' equity	**$83,451**	$78,130

Note:

1. The company's fiscal year is February through January.

Source: Wal-Mart Stores, Inc., *2002 Annual Report.*

Exhibit 3

Financial Summary: Wal-Mart Stores, Inc.
(Dollar amounts in millions except per share data)

11-Year Financial Summary

Fiscal Year Ending January 31	2002	2001	2000
Net sales[1]	$217,799	$191,329	$165,013
Net sales increase	14%	16%	20%
Domestic comparative store sales increase	6%	5%	8%
Other income, net	2,013	1,966	1,796
Cast of sales	171,562	150,255	129,664
Operating, selling, and general and administrative expenses	36,173	31,550	27,040
Interest costs			
Debt	1,052	1,095	756
Capital leases	274	279	266
Provision for income taxes	3,897	3,692	3,338
Minority interest and equity in unconsolidated subsidiaries	(183)	(129)	(170)
Cumulative effect of accounting change, net of tax	—	—	(198)
Net income	6,671	6,295	5,377
Per share of common stock			
Basic net income	1.49	1.41	1.21
Diluted net income	1.49	1.40	1.20
Dividends	0.28	0.24	0.20
Financial position			
Current assets	$ 28,246	$ 26,555	$ 24,356
Inventories at replacement cost	22,749	21,644	20,171
Less LIFO reserve	135	202	378
Inventories at LIFO cost	22,614	21,442	19,793
Net property, plant, and equipment and capital leases	45,750	40,934	35,969
Total assets	83,451	78,130	70,349
Current liabilities	27,282	28,949	25,803
Long-term debt	15,687	12,501	13,672
Long-term obligations under capital leases	3,045	3,154	3,002
Shareholders' equity	35,102	31,343	25,834
Financial ratios			
Current ratio	1.0	0.9	0.9
Inventories/working capital	23.5	(9.0)	(13.7)
Return on assets	8.5%	8.7%	9.5%
Return on shareholders' equity	20.1%	22.0%	22.9%
Other year-end data			
Number of U.S. Wal-Mart stores	1,647	1,736	1,801
Number of U.S. Supercenters	1,066	888	721
Number of U.S. SAM'S Clubs	500	475	463
Number of U.S. Neighborhood Markets	31	19	7
International units	1,170	1,071	1,004
Number of associates	1,383,000	1,244,000	1,140,000
Number of shareholders of record (as of March 31)	324,000	317,000	307,000

Exhibit 3

Financial Summary: Wal-Mart Stores, Inc. (*continued*)
(Dollar amounts in millions except per share data)

1999	1998	1997	1996	1995	1994	1993	1992
$137,634	$117,958	$104,859	$93,627	$82,494	$67,344	$55,484	$43,887
17%	12%	12%	13%	22%	21%	26%	35%
9%	6%	5%	4%	7%	6%	11%	10%
1,574	1,341	1,319	1,146	914	645	497	404
108,725	93,438	83,510	74,505	65,586	53,444	44,175	34,786
22,363	19,358	16,946	15,021	12,858	10,333	8,321	6,684
529	555	629	692	520	331	143	113
268	229	216	196	186	186	180	153
2,740	2,115	1,794	1,606	1,581	1,358	1,171	945
(153)	(78)	(27)	(13)	4	(4)	4	(1)
4,430	3,526	3,056	2,740	2,681	2,333	1,995	1,609
0.99	0.78	0.67	0.60	0.59	0.51	0.44	0.35
0.99	0.78	0.67	0.60	0.59	0.51	0.44	0.35
0.16	0.14	0.11	0.10	0.09	0.07	0.05	0.04
$ 21,132	$ 19,352	$ 17,993	$17,331	$15,338	$12,114	$10,198	$ 8,575
17,549	16,845	16,193	16,300	14,415	11,483	9,780	7,857
473	348	296	311	351	469	512	473
17,076	16,497	15,897	15,989	14,064	11,014	9,268	7,384
25,973	23,606	20,324	18,894	15,874	13,176	9,793	6,434
49,996	45,384	39,604	37,541	32,819	26,441	20,565	15,443
16,762	14,460	10,957	11,454	9,973	7,406	6,754	5,004
6,908	7,191	7,709	8,508	7,871	6,156	3,073	1,722
2,699	2,483	2,307	2,092	1,838	1,804	1,772	1,556
21,112	18,503	17,143	14,756	12,726	10,753	8,759	6,990
1.3	1.3	1.6	1.5	1.5	1.6	1.5	1.7
3.9	3.4	2.3	2.7	2.6	2.3	2.7	2.1
9.6%	8.5%	7.9%	7.8%	9.0%	9.9%	11.1%	12.0%
22.4%	19.8%	19.2%	19.9%	22.8%	23.9%	25.3%	26.0%
1,869	1,921	1,960	1,995	1,985	1,950	1,848	1,714
564	441	344	239	147	72	34	10
451	443	436	433	426	417	256	208
4	—	—	—	—	—	—	—
715	601	314	276	226	24	10	—
901,000	825,000	728,000	675,000	622,000	528,000	434,000	371,000
261,000	246,000	257,000	244,000	259,000	258,000	181,000	150,000

Note:
1. Notes were deleted.

Source: Wal-Mart annual reports.

The Sam Walton Spirit

Much of the success of Wal-Mart was attributed to the entrepreneurial spirit of its founder and Chairman of the Board, Samuel Moore Walton (1918–1992). Many considered him one of the most influential retailers of the century.

Sam Walton, or "Mr. Sam," as some referred to him, traced his down-to earth, old-fashioned, home-spun, evangelical ways to growing up in rural Oklahoma, Missouri, and Arkansas. Although he appeared to be remarkably unconcerned about his roots, some suggested that it was his simple belief in hard work and ambition that had "unlocked countless doors and showered upon him, his customers, and his employees . . . the fruits of . . . years of labor in building [this] highly successful company."

"Our goal has always been in our business to be the very best," Sam Walton said in an interview, "and, along with that, we believe that in order to do that, you've got to make a good situation and put the interests of your associates first. If we really do that consistently, they in turn will cause . . . our business to be successful, which is what we've talked about and espoused and practiced." "The reason for our success," he said, "is our people and the way that they're treated and the way they feel about their company." Many have suggested it was this "people first" philosophy, that guided the company through the challenges and setbacks of its early years and allowed the company to maintain its consistent record of growth and expansion in later years.

A unique, enthusiastic, and positive individual, Sam Walton was "just your basic home-spun billionaire," a columnist once suggested. "Mr. Sam is a life-long small-town resident who didn't change much as he got richer than his neighbors," he noted. Walton had tremendous energy, enjoyed bird hunting with his dogs, and flew a corporate plane. When the company was much smaller, he could boast that he personally visited every Wal-Mart store at least once a year. A store visit usually included Walton leading Wal-Mart cheers that began, "Give me a W, give me an A . . ." To many employees, he had the air of a fiery Baptist preacher. Paul R. Carter, a Wal-Mart Executive Vice President, was quoted as saying, "Mr. Walton has a calling." He became the richest man in America, and by 1991 had created a personal fortune for his family in excess of $21 billion. In 1999, despite a division of wealth, five family members were still ranked among the richest individuals in the United States.

In late 1989 Sam Walton was diagnosed as having multiple myeloma, or cancer of the bone marrow. He remained active in the firm as Chairman of the Board of Directors until his death in 1992. A son, S. Robson Walton, held the position of Chairman of the Board of Directors in 2002.

Corporate Governance

Exhibit 4 lists the 16 members of Wal-Mart's board of directors. Four are internal members: (1) S. Robson Walton, Chairman, (2) David D. Glass, Chairman, Executive Committee of the Board, (3) Thomas M. Coughlin, Executive Vice President and President & CEO of Wal-Mart Store Division, and (4) H. Lee Scott, President and CEO.

The Marketing Concept

GENESIS OF AN IDEA

Sam Walton started his retail career in 1940 as a management trainee with the J.C. Penney Co. in Des Moines, Iowa. He was impressed with the Penney method of doing business and later modeled the Wal-Mart chain on "The Penney Idea" as reviewed in **Exhibit 5**. The Penney

Exhibit 4

Board of Directors and Executive Officers: Wal-Mart Stores, Inc. January 31, 2002

Directors

James W. Breyer, Managing Partner
Accel Partners
Director since 2001

John T. Chambers, CEO
Cisco Systems
Director since 2000

Thomas M. Coughlin, CEO
Wal-Mart Stores, Inc.
Director since 2001

Stephen Friedman, Past Chair
Goldman Sachs & Company
Director since 1996

Stanley C. Gault, Past CEO
Goodyear Tire & Rubber Co.
Director since 1996

David D. Glass, Past CEO
Wal-Mart Stores, Inc.
Director since 1977

Roland Hernandez, Past CEO
Telemundo Group, Inc.
Director since 1998

Dawn G. Lepore, Vice Chair
Charles Schwab Corporation
Director since 2001

J. Paul Reason, CEO
Metro Machine Corporation
Director since 2001

Elizabeth A. Sanders, Past VP
Nordstrom, Inc.
Director since 1992

H. Lee Scott, President and COO
Wal-Mart Stores, Inc.
Director since 1999

Jack C. Shewmaker, Past Executive
Wal-Mart Stores, Inc.
Director since 1977

Donald G. Soderquist, Past COO
Wal-Mart Stores, Inc.
Director since 1980

Jose Villarreal, Law Partner
Akin, Gump, Struass, Hauer and Fled
Director since 1998

John T. Walton, Chairman[1]
True North Partners
Director since 1992

S. Robson Walton, Chairman[1]
Wal-Mart Stores, Inc.
Director since 1978

Officers

S. Robson Walton
Chairman of the Board

H. Lee Scott
President and CEO

David D. Glass
Chairman, Executive
Committee of the Board

Thomas M. Coughlin
Executive Vice President;
President and CEO,
Wal-Mart Stores Division

Michael Duke
Executive Vice President, Administration

Thomas Grimm
Executive Vice President;
President and CEO,
SAM'S Club Division

Thomas Hyde
Executive Vice President,
Legal and Corporate Affairs

John B. Menzer
Executive Vice President;
President and CEO,
International Division

Coleman Peterson
Executive Vice President,
People Division

Thomas M. Schoewe
Executive Vice President and CFO

Note:
1. Sons of founder, Sam Walton.

Source: Wal-Mart Stores, Inc., *2002 Annual Report* January 31, 2002.

Exhibit 5

The Penney Idea (1913)

> 1. To serve the public, as nearly as we can, to its complete satisfaction.
> 2. To expect for the service we render a fair remuneration and not all the profit the traffic will bear.
> 3. To do all in our power to pack the customer's dollar full of value, quality, and satisfaction.
> 4. To continue to train ourselves and our associates so that the service we give will be more and more intelligently performed.
> 5. To improve constantly the human factor in our business.
> 6. To reward men and women in our organization through participation in what the business produces.
> 7. To test our every policy, method, and act in this way: "Does it square with what is right and just?"

Source: Trimble, Vance H., *Sam Walton: The Inside Story of America's Richest Man*, (New York: Dutton), 1990.

Company found strength in calling employees "associates" rather than clerks. Penney's, founded in Kemerer, Wyoming, in 1902, located stores on the main streets of small towns and cities throughout the United States.

Following service in the U.S. Army during World War II, Sam Walton acquired a Ben Franklin variety store franchise in Newport, Arkansas. He operated this store successfully with his brother, James L. "Bud" Walton (1921–1995), until losing the lease in 1950.

The early retail stores owned by Sam Walton in Newport and Bentonville, Arkansas, and later in other small towns in adjoining southern states, were variety store operations. They were relatively small operations of 6,000 square feet, were located on "main streets," and displayed merchandise on plain wooden tables and counters. Operated under the Ben Franklin name and supplied by Butler Brothers of Chicago and St. Louis, they were characterized by a limited price line, low gross margins, high merchandise turnover, and concentration on return on investment. The firm, operating under the Walton 5 & 10 name with 15 stores, was the largest Ben Franklin franchisee in the country in 1962. The variety stores were phased out by 1976 to allow the company to concentrate on the growth of Wal-Mart discount department stores.

FOUNDATIONS OF GROWTH

The original Wal-Mart discount concept was not a unique idea. Sam Walton became convinced in the late 1950s that discounting would transform retailing. He traveled extensively in New England, the cradle of "off-pricing." After he had visited just about every discounter in the United States, he tried to interest Butler Brothers executives in the discount store concept. The first Kmart, as a "conveniently located one-stop shopping unit where customers could buy a wide variety of quality merchandise at discount prices" had just opened in Garden City, Michigan. Walton's theory was to operate a similar discount store in a small community and in that setting, he would offer name brand merchandise at low prices and would add friendly service. Butler Brothers executives rejected the idea. Undeterred, Walton opened the first "Wal-Mart Discount City" in late 1962 in Rogers, Arkansas.

Wal-Mart stores sold nationally advertised, well-known-brand merchandise at low prices in austere surroundings. As corporate policy, Wal-Mart cheerfully gave refunds, credits, and rain checks. Management conceived the firm as a "discount department store chain offering a wide variety of general merchandise to the customer." Early emphasis was placed upon opportunistic purchases of merchandise from whatever sources were available. Heavy emphasis was placed upon health and beauty aids (H&BA) in the product line and "stacking it high" in a manner of merchandise presentation. By the end of 1979, there were 276 Wal-Mart stores located in 11 states.

The firm developed an aggressive expansion strategy. New stores were located primarily in communities of 5,000 to 25,000 in population. The stores' sizes ranged from 30,000 to 60,000 square feet, with 45,000 being the average. The firm also expanded by locating stores in contiguous geographic areas. When its discount operations came to dominate a market area, it moved to an adjoining area. While other retailers built warehouses to serve existing outlets, Wal-Mart built the distribution center first and then spotted stores all around it, pooling advertising and distribution overhead. Most stores were less than a six-hour drive from one of the company's warehouses. The first major distribution center, a 390,000-square-foot facility, opened in Searcy, Arkansas, outside Bentonville in 1978.

BECOMING NATIONAL

At the beginning of 1991, the firm had 1,573 Wal-Mart stores in 35 states, with expansion planned for adjacent states. Wal-Mart had become the largest retailer and the largest discount department store in the United States.

As a national discount department store chain, Wal-Mart Stores, Inc., offered a wide variety of general merchandise to the customer. The stores were designed to offer one-stop shopping with 40 departments that included family apparel, health and beauty aids, household needs, electronics, toys, fabric and crafts, automotive supplies, lawn and patio, jewelry, and shoes. A pharmacy, automotive supply and service center, garden center, or snack bar were also operated at certain locations. The firm operated its stores with "everyday low prices" as opposed to putting heavy emphasis on special promotions, that called for multiple newspaper advertising circulars. Stores were expected to "provide the customer with a clean, pleasant, and friendly shopping experience."

Although Wal-Mart carried much the same merchandise, offered similar prices, and operated stores that looked much like the competition, there were many differences. In the typical Wal-Mart store, employees wore blue vests to identify themselves, aisles were wide, apparel departments were carpeted in warm colors, store employees followed customers to their cars to pick up their shopping carts, and the customer was welcomed at the door by a "people greeter" who gave directions and struck up conversation. In some cases, merchandise was bagged in brown paper sacks rather than plastic bags because customers seemed to prefer them. The "Wal-Mart" and the slogan "Always Low Prices" on the front of the store served to identify the firm. Yellow smiley faces were used on in-store displays along with the slogan "Watch for Falling Prices." In consumer studies it was determined that the chain was particularly adept at striking the delicate balance needed to convince customers its prices were low without making people feel that its stores were too cheap. In many ways, competitors like Kmart sought to emulate Wal-Mart by introducing people greeters, by upgrading interiors, by developing new logos and signage, and by introducing new inventory response systems.

A "satisfaction guaranteed" refund and exchange policy was introduced to allow customers to be confident of Wal-Mart's merchandise and quality. Technological advancements like scanner cash registers, handheld computers for the ordering of merchandise, and computer linkages of stores with the general office and distribution centers improved communications and merchandise replenishment. Each store was encouraged to initiate programs that would make it an integral part of the community in which it operated. Associates were encouraged to "maintain the highest standards of honesty, morality, and business ethics" in dealing with the public.

The External Environment

In 2002, Wal-Mart management was aware that its business operations on a national and international level were subject to a number of factors outside of its control. Any one, or a combination, of these factors could materially affect the financial performance of the firm.

These factors included the costs of goods, the cost of electricity and other energy requirements, competitive pressures, inflation, consumer debt levels, interest rate levels, and unemployment levels. They also included currency exchange fluctuations, trade restrictions, changes in tariff and freight rates, and other capital market and economic conditions.

Industry analysts labeled the 1980s and the 1990s as eras of economic uncertainty for retailers. Although the United States had experienced one of the longest periods of economic expansion in its history during this period, increased competitive pressures, sluggish consumer spending, the energy crisis, lack of worldwide economic growth, and the terrorist events of September 11, 2001, all converged to create a very challenging environment for all retailers at the beginning of the new century.

Many retail enterprises confronted heavy competitive pressure by restructuring. Sears was one example. Sears, Roebuck and Company, based in Chicago, became a more focused retailer by divesting itself of Allstate Insurance Company and its real estate subsidiaries. In 1993, the company announced it would close 118 unprofitable stores and discontinue the unprofitable Sears general merchandise catalog. It eliminated 50,000 jobs and began a $4 billion, five-year remodeling plan for its remaining multiline department stores. After unsuccessfully experimenting with an "everyday low-price" strategy, management chose to realign its merchandise strategy to meet the needs of middle-market customers, who were primarily women, by focusing on product lines in apparel, home, and automotive. The new focus on apparel was supported with the advertising campaign "The Softer Side of Sears." A later companywide campaign broadened the appeal: "The many sides of Sears fit the many sides of your life." Sears completed its return to its retailing roots by selling off its ownership in Dean Witter Financial Services, Discover Card, Coldwell Banker Real Estate, and Sears mortgage banking operations. In 1999, Sears refocused its marketing strategy with a new program that was designed to communicate a stronger whole-house and event message. A new advertising campaign introduced the slogan "The good life at a great price. Guaranteed." In 2000, a new store format was introduced that concentrated on five focal areas: appliances, home fashions, tools, kids', and electronics. Other departments, including men's and women's apparel, assumed a support role in these stores. In 2001, Sears developed another plan to reposition and restructure its core business: The full-line stores. Alan J. Lacy, Chairman and CEO, announced that this strategy would position Sears in the retail marketplace as "not a department store, not a discount store, but a broad-line retailer with outstanding credit and service capabilities."

The discount department store industry by the late 1990s had changed in a number of ways and was thought by many analysts to have reached maturity. Several formerly successful firms like E.J. Korvette, W.T. Grant, Atlantic Mills, Arlans, Federals, Zayre, Heck's, and Ames had declared bankruptcy and as a result either liquidated or reorganized. Venture announced liquidation in early 1998. Firms like Target and Shopko began carrying more fashionable merchandise in more attractive facilities and shifted their emphasis to more national markets. Specialty retailers, such as Toys "R" Us, Pier 1 Imports, and Oshman's had matured and were no longer making big inroads in toys, home furnishing, and sporting goods. The "superstores" of drug and food chains were rapidly discounting increasing amounts of general merchandise. Some firms like May Department Stores Company with Caldor and Venture and Woolworth Corporation with Woolco had withdrawn from the field by either selling their discount divisions or closing them down entirely. Woolworth's remaining 122 Woolco stores in Canada were sold to Wal-Mart in 1994. All remaining Woolworth variety stores in the United States were closed in 1997.

Several new retail formats had emerged in the marketplace to challenge the traditional discount department store format. The superstore, a 100,000 to 300,000-square-foot operation, combined a large supermarket with a discount general-merchandise store. Originally a European retailing concept, these outlets where known as "malls without walls." Kmart's Super

Kmart, Target's SuperTarget, and Wal-Mart's Supercenter stores were examples of this trend toward large operations. Warehouse retailing, which involved some combination of warehouse and showroom facilities, used warehouse principles to reduce operating expenses and thereby offer discount prices as a primary customer appeal. Home Depot combined the traditional hardware store and lumberyard with a self-service home improvement center to become the largest home center operator in the nation.

Some retailers responded to changes in the marketplace by selling goods at price levels 20%–60% below regular retail prices. These off-price operations appeared as two general types: (1) factory outlet stores, like Burlington Coat Factory Warehouse, Bass Shoes, and Manhattan's Brand Name Fashion Outlet, and (2) independents, like Loehmann's, T.J. Maxx, Marshall's, and Clothestime, which bought seconds, overages, closeouts, or leftover goods from manufacturers and other retailers. Other retailers chose to dominate a product classification. Some super specialists, like Sock Appeal, Little Piggie, Ltd., and Sock Market, offered a single narrowly defined classification of merchandise with an extensive assortment of brands, colors, and sizes. Others, as niche specialists, like Kids Foot Locker and Champs Sports, a division of Foot Locker, Inc. (formerly Woolworth Corporation), targeted an identified market with carefully selected merchandise and appropriately designed stores.

Some retailers, like Silk Greenhouse (silk plants and flowers), Office Club (office supplies and equipment), and Toys "R" Us (toys), were called "category killers" because they had achieved merchandise dominance in their respective product categories. Stores like The Limited, Limited Express, Victoria's Secret, and Banana Republic became mini-department specialists by showcasing new lines and accessories alongside traditional merchandise lines.

Kohl's Corporation, a relatively new firm based in Menominee Falls, Wisconsin, operated 420 family-focused, value-oriented department stores in 32 states as of April 2002. The company's stores offered moderately priced national brand-name apparel, shoes, accessories, and home products targeted to middle-income consumers in convenient neighborhood locations. During the period 1992–2001, Kohl's operation grew from 76 stores to 382 stores; its net sales increased nearly seven-fold, from $1.1 billion in 1992 to $7.5 billion in 2001.

Kmart Corporation, headquartered in Troy, Michigan, had been in 1990 the industry's third largest retailer and second largest discount department store chain in the United States. By 2001, Kmart operated 2,114 stores and had sales of $36,151 million in sales but had fallen to fourth largest retailer and third largest discounter. (See **Exhibit 6**.) The firm was perceived by many industry analysts and consumers in several independent studies as a laggard. In the same studies, Wal-Mart was perceived as the industry leader, even though according to the *Wall Street Journal*: "They carry much the same merchandise, offer prices that are pennies apart and operate stores that look almost exactly alike." "Even their names are similar," noted the newspaper. The original Kmart concept of a "conveniently located, one-stop shopping unit where customers could buy a wide variety of quality merchandise at discount prices," had lost its competitive edge in a changing market. As one analyst noted in an industry newsletter: "They had done so well for the past 20 years without paying attention to market changes, now they have to." Kmart acquired a new President and CEO in 2000. The firm filed for bankruptcy under Chapter 11 of the federal bankruptcy laws on January 22, 2002, but continued to operate as an ongoing business while reorganizing.

Wal-Mart and Kmart sales over the period 1990–2001 are reviewed in **Exhibit 7**.

Some retailers, like Kmart, had initially focused on appealing to professional, middle-class consumers who lived in suburban areas and who were likely to be price sensitive. Other firms, like Target, which had adopted the discount concept early, attempted to go generally after an upscale consumer. Some firms, such as Fleet Farm and Pamida, served the rural consumer, while firms like Value City and Ames Department Stores chose to serve the urban consumer.

Exhibit 6

An Industry Comparative Analysis, 2001
(Dollar amounts in millions, except per share data)

	Wal-Mart	Sears	Kmart	Target	Kohl's
Sales	$217,799	$41,078	$ 36,151	$39,888	$7,489
Net income	$ 6,671	$ 735	$ (2,418)	$ 1,368	$ 496
Sales/sq. ft	$ 455	$ 319	$ (235)	$ 247	$ 262
Profit margin	3.1%	1.78%	$ N/A	3.4%	6.6%
% sales change	14.0%	.99%	(0.1)%	8.0%	22.0%

Number of stores:

Wal-Mart United States
   Discount stores—1,647
   SAM'S Clubs—500
   Supercenters—1,066
   Neighborhood Markets—31

Wal-Mart International
   Discount stores—648
   SAM'S Clubs—64
   Supercenters—455
   Neighborhood Markets—3

Sears, Roebuck and Company (all divisions)
   Sears Merchandise Group
      Full-line department stores—867
      Hardware Stores—248
      Sears dealer stores—793
      Home supply stores—13
      NTB National Tire & Battery stores—223
      Outlet stores—35

Kmart Corporation
   Kmart discount stores—2,114
   Kmart Supercenters—105

Target Corporation
   Target—1,053
   Mervyn's—264
   Marshall Field's department stores—64

Kohl's Corporation
   Kohl's department stores—382

Source: Corporate annual reports.

In rural communities Wal-Mart success often came at the expense of established local merchants and units of regional discount store chains. Hardware stores, family department stores, building supply outlets, and stores featuring fabrics, sporting goods, and shoes were among the first to either close or relocate elsewhere. Regional discount retailers in the Sunbelt states, like Roses, Howard's, T.G.&Y., and Duckwall-ALCO, which had once enjoyed solid sales and earnings, were forced to reposition themselves by renovating stores, opening bigger and more modern units, and re-merchandising. In many cases, stores like Coast-to-Coast and Ben Franklin closed upon a Wal-Mart announcement that it was planning to build in a specific community. "Just the word that Wal-Mart was coming made some stores close up," indicated one local newspaper editor. Ames Department Stores, Inc., which sought bankruptcy protection in 2001, announced in the summer of 2002 that it would close all 237 of its stores and liquidate inventory.

Exhibit 7

Competitive Sales and Store Comparison, 1990–2001 (Dollar amounts in thousands)

	Kmart			Wal-Mart		
Fiscal Year[1]	Sales	Net Income[2]	Stores[3]	Sales	Net Income	Stores[4]
2001	$36,151,000	($2,418,000)	2,114	$217,799,000	$,6,671,000	4,414
2000	37,028,000	(244,000)	2,105	191,329,000	6,295,000	4,189
1999	35,925,000	403,000	2,171	165,013,000	5,377,000	3,996
1998	33,674,000	518,000	2,161	137,634,000	4,430,000	3,999
1997	32,183,000	249,000	2,136	117,958,000	3,526,000	3,406
1996	31,437,000	(220,000)	2,261	104,859,000	3,056,000	3,054
1995	31,713,000	(521,000)	2,161	93,627,000	2,740,000	2,943
1994	34,025,000	296,000	2,481	82,494,000	2,681,000	2,684
1993	34,156,000	(974,000)	2,486	67,344,000	2,333,000	2,400
1992	37,724,000	941,000	2,435	55,484,000	1,995,000	2,136
1991	34,580,000	859,000	2,391	43,886,900	1,608,000	1,928
1990	32,070,000	756,000	2,350	32,601,594	1,291,000	1,721

Note:
1. Fiscal year is February through January.
2. Net income from discontinued operations.
3. Number of general merchandise stores (excludes Super Center).
4. Total Wal-Mart Stores.

Source: Corporate annual reports.

Domestic Corporate Strategies

The corporate and marketing strategies that emerged at Wal-Mart were based upon a set of two main goals that had guided the firm through its growth years. In the first goal the customer was featured: "customers would be provided what they want, when they want it, all at a value." In the second objective team spirit was emphasized: "treating each other as we would hope to be treated, acknowledging our total dependency on our Associate-partners to sustain our success." The approach included aggressive plans for new store openings; expansion to additional states; upgrading, relocation, refurbishing, and remodeling of existing stores; and opening of new distribution centers. For Wal-Mart management, the 1990s were considered an era in which the firm grew to become a truly nationwide retailer that operated in all 50 states. At the beginning of 2000, Wal-Mart management predicted that over the next five years, 60%–70% of sales and earnings growth would come from domestic markets with Wal-Mart stores and Supercenters and another 10%–15% from Sam's Club and McLane. The remaining 20% of the growth would come from planned growth in international markets. As David Glass once noted, "We'll be fine as long as we never lose our responsiveness to the customer."

During the 1980s, Wal-Mart developed a number of new retail formats. The first SAM'S Club opened in Oklahoma City, Oklahoma, in 1983. The wholesale club was an idea which had been developed by other firms earlier, but that found its greatest success and growth in acceptability at Wal-Mart. Sam's Clubs featured a vast array of product categories with limited selection of brand and model; cash-and-carry business with limited hours; large (100,000-square-foot), bare-bones facilities; rock-bottom wholesale prices; and minimal promotion. The limited membership plan permitted wholesale members who bought membership and others who usually paid a percentage above the ticket price of the merchandise. A revision in merchandising strategy resulted in fewer items in the inventory mix, with more emphasis on lower prices. A later acquisition of 100 PACE warehouse clubs, which were converted into Sam's Clubs, increased that division's units by more than one-third. At the beginning of 2002, there were 500 Sam's Clubs in operation in the United States and 64 in other countries. A new Sam's Club format was introduced with the opening of a 154,000-square-foot store in 2001 in East Plano, Texas. The store featured an expanded product line with emphasis on fresh food, an open layout, a café, and an Internet kiosk where customers were invited to shop at the www.sams.com Web site. A new Sam's Club slogan, "It's a Big Deal!" referred to the size of the facility and the features of the prototype store.

Wal-Mart Supercenters were large combination stores. They were first opened in 1988 as Hypermarket*USA, a 222,000-square-foot superstore that combined a full general merchandise discount store with a large full-line grocery supermarket, a food court of restaurants, and other service businesses, such as banks or videotape rental stores. A scaled-down version of Hypermarket*USA was called Wal-Mart Supercenter, and was similar in merchandise offerings, but with about 180,000 to 200,000 square feet of space. The company proceeded slowly with these plans and later suspended its plans for building any more hypermarkets in favor of the Supercenter concept. At the beginning of 2002, Wal-Mart operated 1,066 Supercenters.

Wal-Mart also tested a new concept called the Neighborhood Market in a number of locations in Arkansas. Identified by the company as "small-marts," these green-and-white stores were stocked with fresh fruits and vegetables, a drive-up pharmacy, a 24-hour photo shop, and a selection of classic Wal-Mart hard goods. Management elected to move slowly on this concept, planning to open no more than 10 a year. The goal was to ring the Superstores with these smaller stores to attract customers who were in hurry and wanted only a few items. At the end of 2001, the firm operated 31 Neighborhood Markets.

The McLane Company, Inc., a provider of retail and grocery distribution services for retail stores, was acquired by Wal-Mart in 1991. It was not considered a major segment of the total Wal-Mart operation.

Several programs were launched in Wal-Mart stores to highlight popular social causes. The "Buy American" program was a Wal-Mart retail program initiated in 1985. The theme was "Bring It Home to the USA," and its purpose was to communicate Wal-Mart's support for American manufacturing. In the program, the firm directed substantial influence to encourage manufacturers to produce goods in the United States rather than import them from other countries. Vendors were attracted into the program by encouraging manufacturers to initiate the process by contacting the company directly with proposals to sell goods that were made in the United States. Buyers also targeted specific import items in their assortments on a state-by-state basis to encourage domestic manufacturing. According to Haim Dabah, president of Gitano Group, Inc., a maker of fashion discount clothing that imported 95% of its clothing and now makes about 20% of its products in the United States: "Wal-Mart let it be known loud and clear that if you're going to grow with them, you sure better have some products made in the U.S.A." Farris Fashion, Inc. (flannel shirts), Roadmaster Corporation (exercise bicycles), Flanders Industries, Inc. (lawn chairs), and Magic Chef (microwave ovens) were examples of vendors that chose to participate in the program.

From the Wal-Mart standpoint, the "Buy American" program centered around value—producing and selling quality merchandise at a competitive price. The promotion included television advertisements featuring factory workers, a soaring American eagle, and the slogan "We buy American whenever we can, so you can too." Prominent in-store signage and store circulars were also included. One store poster read: "Success Stories—These items, formerly imported, are now being purchased by Wal-Mart in the U.S.A."

Wal-Mart was one of the first retailers to embrace the concept of "green" marketing. The program offered shoppers the option of purchasing products that are better for the environment in three respects: manufacturing, use, and disposal. It was introduced through full-page advertisements in the *Wall Street Journal* and *USA Today*. In-store signage identified those products that were environmentally safe. As Wal-Mart executives saw it, "customers are concerned about the quality of land, air, and water, and would like the opportunity to do something positive." To initiate the program, 7,000 vendors were notified that Wal-Mart had a corporate concern for the environment and asked for their support in a variety of ways. Wal-Mart television advertising showed children on swings, fields of grain blowing in the wind, and roses. Green and white store signs, printed on recycled paper, marked products or packaging that had been developed or redesigned to be more environmentally sound.

The Wal-Mart private brand program began with the "Ol' Roy" brand, the private-label dog food named for Sam Walton's favorite hunting companion. Introduced to Wal-Mart stores in 1982 as a low-price alterative to national brands, Ol' Roy became the biggest seller of all dog-food brands in the United States. "We are a (national) brand-oriented company first," noted Bob Connolly, Executive Vice President of merchandising of Wal-Mart. "But we also use private label to fill value or pricing voids that, for whatever reason, the brands left behind." Wal-Mart's private-label program included thousands of products that had brand names, such as Sam's Choice, Great Value, Equate, and Spring Valley.

With almost $40 billion in "soft good" sales in 2001, Wal-Mart was the largest clothing seller in the world. Although most of the sales of its clothing business were in basics such as socks, underwear, t-shirts, and blue jeans, the firm developed a 100-member development team to begin to focus its clothing lines on fashion and style in all sizes. Claire Watts was hired from Limited, Inc., to become the first Director of Product Development. The company also made a significant investment in technology so that all the factors of the development process, from design to production, were coordinated online among Wal-Mart, its suppliers, and factories. Rather than wait for suppliers to bring products to Wal-Mart, merchandise teams traveled to Europe four times a year to visit trendy boutiques and fashion shows and bring back racks of clothes to be evaluated at corporate headquarters on the basis of quality, fashion, and style. In 2002, Wal-Mart introduced a contemporary brand nationwide called George. George, a stylish line of clothing for women and men, had been sold exclusively for 10 years in England's ASDA supermarkets, which Wal-Mart acquired in 1999.

In 2000, according to DSR Marketing Systems, Wal-Mart became the largest retailer of groceries in the United States, surpassing traditional grocery retailers such as Cincinnati, Ohio–based Kroger, Boise, Idaho–based Albertsons, and Pleasanton, California–based Safeway. Wal-Mart's 2001 discount store grocery sales, which included candy, paper towels, dog food, and tobacco, were estimated at $30.6 billion and amounted to 22% of overall store sales. Food sales, in 2001, at Sam's Club were $8.8 billion or 30% of sales.

Wal-Mart had become the channel commander in the distribution of many brand name items. As the nation's largest retailer and in many geographic areas the dominant distributor, it exerted considerable influence in negotiation for the best price, delivery terms, promotion allowances, and continuity of supply. Many of these benefits could be passed on to consumers in the form of quality name brand items available at lower-than-competitive prices. As a matter of corporate policy, management often insisted on doing business only with producers' top sales executives rather than going through a manufacturer's representative. Wal-Mart had been accused of threatening to buy from other producers if firms refused to sell directly to it. In the ensuing power struggle, Wal-Mart executives refused to talk about the controversial policy or admit that it existed. As a representative of an industry association representing a group of sales agencies representatives suggested, "In the Southwest, Wal-Mart's the only show in town." An industry analyst added, "They're extremely aggressive. Their approach has always been to give the customer the benefit of a corporate saving. That builds up customer loyalty and market share."

Another key factor in the mix was an inventory control system that was recognized as the most sophisticated in retailing. A high-speed computer system linked virtually all the stores to headquarters and the company's distribution centers. It electronically logged every item sold at the checkout counter, automatically kept the warehouses informed of merchandise to be ordered, and directed the flow of goods to the stores and even to the proper shelves. Most importantly for management, it helped detect sales trends quickly and sped up market reaction time substantially. According to Bob Connolly, Executive Vice President of Merchandising, "Wal-Mart has used the data gathered by technology to make more inventory available in the key items that customers want most, while reducing inventories overall."

At the beginning of 2000, Wal-Mart set up a separate company for its Web site, with plans to go public. Wal-Mart.com, Inc., based in Palo Alto, California, was jointly owned by Wal-Mart and Accel Partners, a Silicon Valley venture-capital firm. The site included a wide range of products and services that ranged from shampoo to clothing to lawn mowers, as well as airline, hotel, and rental car bookings. After launching and then closing a SAM'S Club Web site, Wal-Mart reopened the site in mid-June 2000, with an emphasis on upscale items such as jewelry, housewares, and electronics and full product lines for small business owners. SamsClub.com was operated by Wal-Mart from the company's Bentonville, Arkansas, headquarters.

International Corporate Strategies

In 1994, Wal-Mart entered the Canadian market with the acquisition of 122 Woolco discount stores from Woolworth Corporation. When acquired, the Woolco stores were losing millions of dollars annually, but operations became profitable within three years. At the end of 2001, the company had 196 Wal-Mart discount stores in Canada. The company's operations in Canada were considered as a model for Wal-Mart's expansion into other international markets. With 35% of the Canadian discount and department store market, Wal-Mart was the largest retailer in that country.

With a tender offer for shares and mergers of joint ventures in Mexico, the company in 1997 acquired a controlling interest in Cifra, Mexico's largest retailer. Cifra, later identified as Wal-Mart de Mexico, operated stores with a variety of concepts in every region of Mexico, ranging from the nation's largest chain of sit-down restaurants to a softline department store. Retail analysts noted that the initial venture involved many costly mistakes. Time after time it sold the wrong products, including tennis balls that wouldn't bounce in high-altitude Mexico City. Large parking lots at some stores made access difficult as many people arrived by bus. In 2002, Wal-Mart operated 443 discount stores, 62 Supercenters, and 46 Sam's Clubs in Mexico. The Cifra outlets in Mexico included 106 Bodegas, 51 Suburbias, 44 Superamas, and 242 VIPS stores.

When Wal-Mart entered Argentina in 1995, it also initially faced challenges adapting its U.S.-based retail mix and store layouts to the local culture. Although globalization and U.S. cultural influences had swept through the country in the early 1990s, the Argentine market did not accept U.S. cuts of meat, bright-colored cosmetics, and jewelry that gave prominent placement to emeralds, sapphires, and diamonds, even though most Argentine women preferred wearing gold and silver. The first stores even had hardware departments full of tools wired for 110-volt electric power; the standard throughout Argentina was 220. Compounding the challenges was store layout that featured narrow aisles; stores appeared crowded and dirty. In 2002, Wal-Mart operated 11 Supercenters in Argentina.

Wal-Mart management concluded that Brazil offered great opportunities for Wal-Mart because it had the fifth largest population in the world and a population that had a tendency to follow U.S. cultural cues. Although financial data were not broken out on South American operations, retail analysts cited the accounts of Wal-Mart's Brazilian partner, Lojas Americanas SA, to suggest that Wal-Mart lost $100 million in start-up costs for the initial 16 stores. Customer acceptance of Wal-Mart stores was mixed. In Canada and Mexico, many customers were familiar with the company from cross-border shopping trips. Many Brazilian customers were not familiar with the Wal-Mart name. In addition, local Brazilian markets were already dominated by savvy local and foreign competitors, such as Grupo Pao de Acucar SA of Brazil and Carrefour SA of France. Wal-Mart's insistence on doing things "the Wal-Mart way" initially alienated many local suppliers and employees. The country's continuing economic problems also presented a challenge. In 2002, Wal-Mart operated 12 Supercenters and 8 Sam's Clubs in Brazil and planned to expand its presence in that country.

Wal-Mart entered the European market by acquiring three retail chains. Because of stubborn local regulations, management felt it would be easier for Wal-Mart to buy existing stores in Europe than to build new ones. Wal-Mart moved into Germany at the end of 1997 by acquiring 21 stores from hypermarket operator Wertkauf. Also as part of its expansion efforts in Germany, Wal-Mart acquired 74 stores that were a part of the Interspar chain. Soon after the takeover, Wal-Mart quickly filled the top management positions with U.S. expatriates. Within weeks of the purchase, most of the top German managers left the company. Management also discovered that these stores were either cramped, unattractive, or poorly located and needed to be entirely renovated.

All of these German stores were identified with the Wal-Mart name and restocked with a new and revamped selection of merchandise. In response to local laws that forced early store closings and forbid Sunday sales, the company simply opened stores earlier, to allow shopping to begin at 7 a.m. In January 2000, the company launched its first big "rollback" by cutting prices on several hundred items by up to 23%. Germany was well populated with discounters such as Aldi and Lidl, which ran no-frills, cheap supermarkets. These discounters responded fiercely to price challenge by cutting their prices by up to 25%. As a result, price cuts did not have a dramatic impact on sales. A decrease in the International segment's operating income as a percentage of sales in 2001 resulted primarily from the continued negative impact of store remodeling cost, costs related to the start-up of a new distribution system to serve the stores, excess inventory, and related expenses in the company's German units. Despite Wal-Mart's lackluster performance in Germany, management remained positive and committed to serving this market.

Wal-Mart acquired ASDA, Britain's third largest supermarket group, for $10.8 billion in July 1999. With its own price rollbacks, people greeter, "permanently low prices," and even "smiley" faces, ASDA had emulated Wal-Mart's store culture for many years. Based in Leeds, England, the firm had 232 stores in England, Scotland, and Wales. While the culture and pricing strategies of the two companies were nearly identical, there were differences, primarily the size and product mix of the stores. The average Wal-Mart Supercenter was 180,000 square feet in size and had about 30% of its sales in groceries. In contrast, the average ASDA store had only 65,000 square feet and did 60% of sales in grocery items.

The response in Europe to Wal-Mart was immediate and dramatic. Competitors scrambled to match Wal-Mart's low prices, long hours, and friendly service. Some firms combined to strengthen their operations. For example, France's Carrefour SA chain of hypermarkets combined forces with competitor Promodes in a $16.5 billion deal. In 2002, Carrefour dominated the European market with three leading formats: hypermarket, supermarket, and hard discount (small food stores with low prices). It was also one of the world's largest retailers, with more than 9,200 stores not only in Europe, but in Latin America and Asia as well. It was widely speculated that Wal-Mart might eventually target other European retailers, such as Metro of Germany, Jernimo Martins of Portugal, Casino or Auchan of France, and Safeway of the United Kingdom for acquisition. Wal-Mart's decision to expand to Europe had been widely considered to be a catalyst for the defensive merger between Carrefour and Promodes.

Wal-Mart's initial effort to enter China fell apart in 1996, when Wal-Mart and Thailand's Charoen Pokphand Group terminated an 18-month old joint venture because of management differences. Wal-Mart decided to consolidate its operations with five stores in the Hong Kong border city of Shenzhen, one in Dalian, and another in Kumming. Analysts concluded that the

Exhibit 8

Wal-Mart International Division, 2002

Country	Stores
Mexico	551
United Kingdom	250
Canada	196
Germany	95
Brazil	22
Puerto Rico	17
Argentina	11
China	19
South Korea	9

Source: Wal-Mart *2002 Annual Report.*

company was taking a low-profile approach because of possible competitive response and government restrictions. Beijing restricted the operations of foreign retailers in China, requiring them, for instance, to have government-backed partners. In Shenzhen, it limited the number of stores Wal-Mart could open. Planned expansion in the China market came as China prepared to enter the World Trade Organization and its economy showed signs of accelerating. At the beginning of 2002, the company operated 15 Supercenters, three Sam's Clubs, and one Neighborhood Market in China. It also operated nine Supercenters in South Korea.

The international expansion accelerated management's plans for the development of Wal-Mart as a global brand along the lines of Coca-Cola, Disney, and McDonald's. "We are a global brand name," said Bobby Martin, an early President of the International Division of Wal-Mart. "To customers everywhere it means low cost, best value, greatest selection of quality merchandise and highest standards of customer service," he noted. Some changes were mandated in Wal-Mart's international operations to meet local tastes and intense competitive conditions. "We're building companies out there," said Martin. "That's like starting Wal-Mart all over again in South America or Indonesia or China." Although stores in different international markets would coordinate purchasing to gain leverage with suppliers, developing new technology and planning overall strategy would be done from Wal-Mart headquarters in Bentonville, Arkansas. At the beginning of 2002, the International Division of Wal-Mart operated 648 discount stores, 455 Supercenters, 64 Sam's Clubs, and three Neighborhood Markets.

Wal-Mart's international unit accounted for $35.5 billion in sales in 2001. **Exhibit 8** shows the countries in which stores were operated and the number of units in each country at the beginning of 2002.

Decision Making in a Market-Orientated Firm

One principle that distinguished Wal-Mart was the unusual depth of employee involvement in company affairs. Corporate strategies put emphasis on human resource management. Employees of Wal-Mart became "associates," a name borrowed from Sam Walton's early association with the J.C. Penney Co.

Input was encouraged at meetings at the store and corporate levels. The firm hired employees locally, provided training programs, and through a "Letter to the President" program, management encouraged employees to ask questions and made words like "we," "us," and "our" a part of the corporate language. A number of special award programs recognized individual, department, and division achievement. Stock ownership and profit-sharing programs were introduced as part of a "partnership" concept.

The corporate culture was recognized by the editors of the trade publication *Mass Market Retailers*, when it recognized all 275,000 associates collectively as the "Mass Market Retailers of the Year." "The Wal-Mart associate," the editors noted, "has come to symbolize all that is right with the American worker, particularly in the retailing environment and most particularly at Wal-Mart." The "store within a store" concept, as a Wal-Mart corporate policy, trained individuals to be merchants by being responsible for the performance of their own departments as if they were running their own businesses. Seminars and training programs afforded them opportunities to grow within the company. "People development is not just a good 'program' for any growing company but a must to secure our future," was how Suzanne Allford, Vice President of the Wal-Mart People Division explained the firm's decentralized approach to retail management development.

"The Wal-Mart Way" was a phase that was used by management to summarize the firm's unconventional approach to business and the development of the corporate culture. As noted in a report referring to a recent development program: "We stepped outside our retailing world to examine the best managed companies in the United States in an effort to determine the fundamentals of their success and to 'benchmark' our own performances. The name "Total Quality Management" (TQM) was used to identify this vehicle for proliferating the very best things we do while incorporating the new ideas our people have that will assure our future." In 1999, *Discount Store News* honored Wal-Mart Stores, Inc., as *Retailer of the Century*, with a commemorative 200-page issue of the magazine.

The Growth Challenge

H. Lee Scott indicated that he would never forget his first meeting with Sam Walton. "How old are you?" Walton asked the then 30-year-old Scott, who had just taken a job managing Wal-Mart's trucking fleet. "Do you think you can do this job?" asked Walton. When Scott said yes, Walton agreed and said "I reckon you can." More than 20 years later, as Wal-Mart's new CEO, Scott was facing his toughest challenge yet: keeping the world's biggest retailer on its phenomenal roll and delivering the huge sales and earnings increases that investors had come to expect from Wal-Mart over the years. Analysts had correctly projected that Wal-Mart would surpass General Motors to be ranked number one in revenue on the *Fortune* 500 list in 2000. The combination of growth and acquisition had caused revenue increases every year. In 2001, it increased 14%, from $191 billion in 2000 to $218 billion. Earnings also increased in 2001 by 9%, to nearly $6.67 billion. Industry analysts noted that this growth was on top of an 18% compound annual growth rate over the past decade.

Wal-Mart Stores, Inc., revolutionized American retailing with its focus on low costs, high customer service, and everyday low pricing to drive sales. Although the company had suffered through some years of lagging performance, it experienced big gains from its move into the grocery business with one-stop Supercenters and into international markets with acquisitions and new ventures. To keep it all going and growing was a major challenge. As the largest retailer and firm in the world, the company and its leadership were challenged to find new areas to continue to grow sales and profits into the future. Lee Scott knew that an ambitious expansion program was called for to allow the company to meet these objectives.

Continued growth could exasperate some problems Wal-Mart was facing. For example, Wal-Mart has always suffered from annual employee-turnover of approximately 65%. To deal with this problem, management initiated a program called People Asset Review (PAR) in which senior management and division presidents reviewed areas in the firm where development was needed, tracked promotable individuals, and developed specific succession plans. In addition, critics contend that Wal-Mart discriminated against women, underpaid workers, and used illegal tactics to stop unionization efforts. Some 40 lawsuits have been filed by employees who said that they had been forced to work overtime for no pay. The company was also facing a sexual discrimination lawsuit in California that could become the largest case in U.S. history. Although more than 70% of Wal-Mart's sales associates were women, less than one third were in management positions. Men held 90% of Wal-Mart store manager positions and only one woman was among the company's 20 top officers. Even after accounting for seniority, store location, and other factors, women earned from 5% to 15% less than men in each year from 1996 to 2001. Since Wal-Mart's 1.3 million employees made it the world's largest private employer, both its reputation and profits were at stake. Overtime and sexual bias lawsuits could cost the company millions of dollars. These came at a time when the company was planning to hire more than one million employees between 2002 and 2007. Although none of Wal-Mart's employees were unionized in 2002, Wal-Mart was a defendant in 28 complaints brought by the U.S. National Labor Relations Board citing anti-union activities such as threats, interrogations, or disciplining. Critics contend that the company moved quickly to block organizing. For example, when a majority of meat cutters at a store in Jacksonville, Texas, voted to organize, the company closed its butcher departments at Jackson and other stores.

FINANCIAL SITUATION

In fiscal year 1990, Kmart's sales were $32,070,000,000, and Wal-Mart's sales were $32,601,594,000. In fiscal year 2001, Kmart's sales were $36,151,000,000 (an increase of $4,081,000,000, or 12.72%, while Wal-Mart's sales increased to $217,799,000,000 (an increase $185,197,406,000, or 568.1%). Wal-Mart's fiscal year 2001 net income was $6,671,000, compared with Kmart's net loss of $2,418,000,000. Kmart had 105 Super Kmart Centers and 2,114 discount stores, for a total of 2,219 stores. Wal-Mart had 2,295 Wal-Mart stores, 564 SAM's Clubs, 1,521 Supercenters, and 34 Neighborhood Markets, for total of 4,414 stores.

References

Albright, Mark, "Changes in Store," *New York Times* (May 17, 1999) pp. 10, 12.

Armour, S. "Wal-Mart Takes Hits on Worker Treatment," *USA Today* (February 10, 2003), p. B1.

Bergman, Joan, "Saga of Sam Walton," *Stores* (January 1988), pp. 129–130.

Berner, Robert, and Stephanie Anderson Forest, "Wal-Mart is Eating Everybody's Lunch," *Business Week* (April 15, 2002), p. 43.

Boudette, Neil E., "Wal-Mart Plans Major Expansion in Germany," *The Wall Street Journal* (July 20, 2000), p. A21.

Cummins, Chip, "Wal-Mart's Net Income Increases 28%, but Accounting Change Worries Investors," *Wall Street Journal* (August 10, 2000), p. A6.

"David Glass's Biggest Job Is Filling Sam's Shoes," *Business Month* (December 1988), p. 42.

Feldman, Amy, "How Big Can It Get?" *Money* (December 1999), pp. 158+.

Friedland, Johnathan and Louise Lee, "The Wal-Mart Way Sometimes Gets Lost in Translation Overseas," *Wall Street Journal* (October 8, 1997), pp. A1, A12.

Gimein, Mark, "Sam Walton Made Us a Promise," *Fortune* (March 18, 2002), pp. 121–130.

Grant, Lorrie, "Wal-Mart Bagging Success as Grocer," *USA Today* (June 6, 2002), p. 3B.

Gustke, Constance, "Smooth Operator," *Worth* (March 2000), pp. 41+.

Helliker, Kevin, "Wal-Mart's Store of the Future Blends Discount Prices, Department-Store Feel," *Wall Street Journal* (May 17, 1991), pp. B1, B8.

"How the Stores Did," *Wall Street Journal* (May 5, 2000), p. B4.

Huey, John, "America's Most Successful Merchant," *Fortune* (September 23, 1991) pp. 46–48+.

Johnson, Jay L., "The Supercenter Challenge," *Discount Merchandiser* (August 1989), pp. 70+.

Kmart Corporation, *Annual Report*, Troy, Michigan, 2001.

Kohl's Corporation, *Annual Report*, Menominee Falls, Wisconsin, 2001.

Komarow, Steven, "Wal-Mart Takes Slow Road in Germany," *USA Today*, (May 5, 2000), p. 3B.

Krauss, Clifford, "Wal-Mart Learns a Hard Lesson," *International Herald Tribune* (December 6, 1999), p. 15.

Larrabee, John, "Wal-Mart Ends Vermont's Holdout," *USA Today* (September 19, 1995), p. 4B.

Lee, Louise, "Discounter Wal-Mart Is Catering to Affluent to Maintain Growth," *Wall Street Journal* (February 7, 1996), p. A1.

Lee, Louise, and Joel Millman, "Wal-Mart to Buy Majority Stake in Cifra," *Wall Street Journal* (June 4, 1997), pp. A3+.

Loomis, Carol J., "Sam Would Be Proud," *Fortune* (April 17, 2000), pp 131+.

"Management Style: Sam Moore Walton," *Business Month* (May 1989), p. 38.

Marsch, Barbara, "The Challenge: Merchants Mobilize to Battle Wal-Mart in a Small Community," *Wall Street Journal* (June 5, 1991), pp. A1, A4.

Mason, Todd, "Sam Walton of Wal-Mart: Just Your Basic Homespun Billionaire," *Business Week* (October 14, 1985), pp. 142–143+.

Mitchener, Brandon, and David Woodruff, "French Merger of Hypermarkets Gets a Go-Ahead," *Wall Street Journal* (January 26, 2000), p. A19.

Murphy, Cait, "Now That Wal-Mart Is America"s Largest Corporation, the Service Economy Wears the Crown," (April 15, 2002), pp. 95–98.

Nelson, Emily, "Wal-Mart to Build a Test Supermarket in Bid to Boost Grocery-Industry Share," *Wall Street Journal* (June 19, 1998), p. A4.

Nelson, Emily, and Kara Swisher, "Wal-Mart Eyes Public Sale of Web Unit," *Wall Street Journal* (January 7, 2000), p. A3.

O'Keefe, Brian, "Meet Your New Neighborhood Grocer," *Fortune* (May 13, 2002) pp. 93–96.

"Our People Make the Difference: The History of Wal-Mart," Videocassette, (Bentonville, Arkansas: Wal-Mart Video Productions, 1991).

Peters, Tom J., and Nancy Austin, *A Passion for Excellence* (New York: Random House), pp. 266–267.

Rawn, Cynthia Dunn, "Wal-Mart vs. Main Street," *American Demographics* (June 1990), pp. 58–59.

"Retailer Completes Purchase of Wertkauf of Germany," *Wall Street Journal* (December 31, 1997), p. B3.

Rudnitsky, Howard, "How Sam Walton Does It," *Forbes* (August 16, 1982), pp. 42–44.

"Sam Moore Walton," *Business Month* (May 1989), p. 38.

Schwadel, Francine, "Little Touches Spur Wal-Mart's Rise," *Wall Street Journal* (September 22, 1989), p. B1.

Sears, Roebuck and Co., *Annual Report*, Chicago, Illinois, 2001.

Sheets, Kenneth R., "How Wal-Mart Hits Main St.," *U.S. News & World Report* (March 13, 1989), pp. 53–55.

Target Corporation, *Annual Report*, Minneapolis, Minnesota, 2001.

"The Early Days: Walton Kept Adding 'a Few More' Stores," *Discount Store News* (December 9, 1985), p. 61.

Tomlinson, Richard, "Who's Afraid of Wal-Mart?" *Fortune* (June 26, 2000), p. 186.

Trimble, Vance H., *Sam Walton: The Inside Story of America's Richest Man* (New York: Dutton), 1990.

Troy, M., "Finding Successors to the Dynasty Starts by Winning the Turnover War," *DSN Retailing Today* (June 5, 2000).

Voyle, Susanna, "ASDA Criticised for Price Claims," *Financial Times* (December 8, 1999), p. 3.

"Wal-Mart Spoken Here," *Business Week* (June 23, 1997), pp. 138+.

Wal-Mart Stores, Inc., *Annual Report*, Bentonville, Arkansas, 2000.

Wal-Mart Stores, Inc., *Annual Report*, Bentonville, Arkansas, 2001.

Wal-Mart Stores, Inc., *Annual Report*, Bentonville, Arkansas, 2002

Wal-Mart's ASDA Says CEO to Head Europe Expansion," *Wall Street Journal Europe* (December 3, 1999), p. 6.

"Wal-Mart Takes a Stand," *The Economist* (May 22, 1999), p. 31.

"Wal-Mart: The Model Discounter," *Dun's Business Month* (December 1982), pp. 60–61.

"Wal-Mart Wins Again," *The Economist* (October 2, 1999), p. 33.

Walton, Sam, with John Huey, *Sam Walton: Made in America* (New York: Doubleday Publishing Company), 1992.

Wonacott, Peter, "Wal-Mart Finds Market Footing in China," *Wall Street Journal* (July 17, 2000), p. A31.

"Work, Ambition—Sam Walton," Press Release, Corporate and Public Affairs, Wal-Mart Stores, Inc.

Zellner, W., "No Way to Treat a Lady," *Business Week* (March 3, 2003), pp. 63–66.

Zellner, Wendy, "Someday, Lee, This May All Be Yours," *Business Week* (November 15, 1999), pp. 84+.

Zimmerman, Ann, and Teri Agins, "Pinstripes and Motor Oil: Wal-Mart Attempts Chic Although Still on the Cheap, with Fresh, Hipper Apparel," *Wall Street Journal* (September 3, 2002), p. B1.

Zimmerman, Ann, "Wal-Mart to Open Reworked Web Site for SamsClub.com," (June 6, 2000), p. B8.

case 22

The Home Depot, Inc.: Growing the Professional Market (Revised)

*Thomas L. Wheelen, Hitesh (John) P. Adhia,
Thomas H. Cangley, and Paul M. Swiercz*

O n April 23, 1988, Arthur M. Blank, President and Chief Executive Officer (CEO) was presiding over a strategic planning session for new strategies for each of Home Depot's six regional divisions (see "Organizational Structure") for the professional contractor market. Home Depot's management estimated this market to be $215 billion in 1997. Home Depot has been concentrating on the Do-It-Yourself/Buy-It-Yourself market sector, which Home Depot management had estimated to be $100 billion in 1997. Home Depot sales were $24.1 billion in 1997. **Exhibit 1** shows the combined sales for the Do-It-Yourself/Buy-It-Yourself sector and the professional sector to be $365 billion. The heavy industry sector was treated as a separate market sector. In 1998, Home Depot had less than 4% of the $215 billion professional sector.

In early April 1998, the company's management announced a new store format. In 1998, the company planned to build four new smaller stores with about 25% (25,000 square feet) of the existing store size. These stores would be similar to local hardware stores or Ace Hardware stores.

The Home Depot, Inc.

Founded in Atlanta, Georgia, in 1978, Home Depot was the world's largest home improvement retailer and ranked among the 10 largest retailers in the United States. At the close of fiscal year 1997, the company was operating 624 full-service, warehouse-styled stores—555 stores in 44 states and 5 EXPO Design Center stores in the United States, plus 32 in four Canadian provinces (See **Exhibit 2**).

The average Home Depot store had approximately 106,300 square feet of indoor selling space and an additional 16,000–28,000 square feet of outside garden center, including house-plant enclosures. The stores stocked approximately 40,000–50,000 different kinds of building materials, home improvement products, and lawn and garden supplies. In addition, Home

This case was prepared by Professor Thomas L. Wheelen of the University of South Florida, Hitesh (John) P. Adhia, CPA, Founder of mutual fund, Adhia Funds, Inc., Thomas H. Cangley, Manager, of Raytheon Corporation and Professor Paul M. Swiercz of the George Washington University. The authors would like to thank the research assistants, Carla N. Mortellaro and Vincent E. Mortellaro, for their support. This case may not be reproduced in any form without written permission of the copyright holder, Thomas L. Wheelen. This case was edited for SMBP-9th Edition. Copyright © 1999 by Thomas L Wheelen. Reprinted by permission.

Exhibit 1

Total Market for Do-It-Yourself/Buy-It-Yourself Sector, Professional Sector, and Heavy Industry Sector

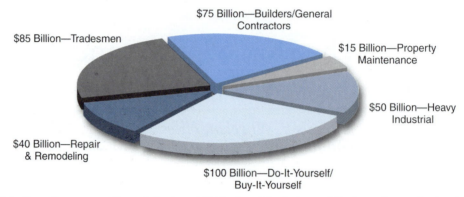

$365 Billion Market

$75 Billion—Builders/General Contractors

$85 Billion—Tradesmen

$15 Billion—Property Maintenance

$50 Billion—Heavy Industrial

$40 Billion—Repair & Remodeling

$100 Billion—Do-It-Yourself/ Buy-It-Yourself

Note: Home Improvement Research Institute, 1997 Product Sales Estimates; U.S. Census Bureau Product Sales Estimates.

Source: The Home Depot, Inc., *1997 Annual Report*, p. 3.

Depot stores offered installation services for many products. The company employed approximately 125,000 associates, of whom approximately 7,900 were salaried, and the remainder of the employees were paid on an hourly basis.

Retail industry analysts had credited Home Depot with being a leading innovator in retailing, by combining the economies of warehouse-format stores with a high level of customer service. The company augmented that concept with a corporate culture that valued decentralized management and decision making, entrepreneurial innovation and risk taking, and high levels of employee commitment and enthusiasm.

The stores served primarily the Do-It-Yourself (DIY) repair person, although home improvement contractors, building maintenance professionals, interior designers, and other professionals have become increasingly important customers.

Home Depot also owned two wholly owned subsidiaries, Maintenance Warehouse and National Blind & Wallpaper Factory. The company also owned Load 'N Go™, an exclusive rental truck service for their customers.

History[1]

Home Depot's Chairman, Bernard Marcus, began his career in the retail industry in a small pharmacy in Millburn, New Jersey. He later joined the Two Guys Discount Chain to manage its drug and cosmetics departments and eventually became the Vice President of Merchandising and Advertising for the parent company, Vornado, Inc. In 1972 he moved into the Do-It-Yourself home improvement sector as President and Chairman of the Board at Handy Dan/Handy City. The parent company, Daylin, Inc., was chaired by Sanford Sigoloff. He and Marcus had a strong difference of opinion over control, and one Friday at 5:00 P.M. in 1978, Marcus and two other Handy Dan top executives were discharged.

That weekend, Home Depot was born when the three men—Bernard Marcus, Arthur Blank, and Kenneth G. Langone—laid out plans for the Do-It-Yourself chain. Venture capital was provided by investment firms that included Inverned of New York as well as private investors. Two key investors were Joseph Flom, a takeover lawyer, and Frank Borman, then Chairman of Eastern Airlines.

Exhibit 2
Store Locations: Home Depot, Inc.

The Home Depot Canada
32 stores

Western Division
153 stores

Midwest Division
63 stores

Northeast Division
137 stores

Southwest Division
86 stores

Southeast Division
148 stores

Western Division	153
	Number
Location	**of Stores**
Arizona	**18**
Phoenix	14
Prescott	1
Tucson	3
California	**96**
Bakersfield	1
Fresno	3
Los Angeles	51
Modesto	1
Sacramento	5
San Diego	11
San Francisco	23
Stockton	1
Colorado	**10**
Colorado Springs	2
Denver	7
Pueblo	1
Idaho	**1**
Boise	1
Nevada	**5**
Las Vegas	3
Reno	2
Oregon	**7**
Eugene	1
Portland	6
Utah	**4**
Salt Lake City	4
Washington	**12**
Seattle/Tacoma	11
Spokane	1

Southeast Division	148
	Number
Location	**of Stores**
Alabama	**6**
Birmingham	3
Huntsville	1
Mobile	1
Montgomery	1
Florida	**63**
Daytona Beach/	
Melbourne/	
Orlando	10
Ft. Lauderdale/Miami/	
West Palm Beach	25
Ft. Myers, Naples	6

Ft. Walton	1
Gainesville/Ocala	3
Jacksonville	4
Pensacola	1
Tallahassee	1
Tampa/	
St. Petersburg	12
Georgia	**32**
Athens	1
Atlanta	24
Augusta	1
Columbus	1
Dalton	1
Macon	1
Rome	1
Savannah	1
Valdosta	1
Indiana	**1**
Clarksville	1
Kentucky	**3**
Lexington	1
Louisville	2
Mississippi	**1**
Horn Lake	1
North Carolina	**18**
Asheville	1
Charlotte	6
Fayetteville	1
Greensboro/	
Winston-Salem	3
Hickory	1
Raleigh	5
Wilmington	1
South Carolina	**7**
Charleston	1
Columbia	2
Greenville/	
Spartanburg	4
Tennessee	**17**
Chattanooga	2
Johnson City/	
Kingsport	2
Knoxville	3
Memphis	3
Nashville	7

Northeast Division	137
	Number
Location	**of Stores**
Connecticut	**13**
Hartford	6

New Haven	3
Danbury/Fairfield	
Norwalk	4
Delaware	**1**
Christana	1
Maine	**2**
Bangor	1
Portland	1
Maryland	**14**
Baltimore	8
Washington,	
DC area	**6**
Massachusetts	**17**
Boston	13
Southern Mass.	3
Springfield	1
New Hampshire	**4**
Manchester	1
Nashua	1
Portsmouth	1
Salem	1
New Jersey	**25**
Northern	
New Jersey	19
Southern	
New Jersey	6
New York	**32**
Albany	2
Buffalo	4
Hudson Valley	4
Johnson City	1
New York City/	
Long Island	16
Rochester	3
Syracuse	2
Pennsylvania	**20**
Allentown/	
Bethlehem	2
Harrisburg/	
Reading	3
Philadelphia	10
Pittsburgh	3
Scranton/	
Wilkes Barre	2
Rhode Island	**1**
Warwick	1
Vermont	**1**
Williston	1
Virginia	**7**
Washington,	
DC area	7

Southwest Division	86
	Number
Location	**of Stores**
Arkansas	**2**
Little Rock	2
O'Fallon	1
Kansas	**1**
Kansas City	1
Louisiana	**9**
Baton Rouge	1
Lafayette	1
Lake Charles	1
New Orleans	5
Shreveport	1
Mississippi	**3**
Gulfport	1
Jackson	2
Missouri	**7**
Columbia	1
Kansas City	2
St. Louis	4
New Mexico	**3**
Albuquerque	3
Oklahoma	**6**
Oklahoma City	4
Tulsa	2
Texas	**54**
Auston	5
Beaumont	1
Corpus Christi	1
Dallas/Ft. Worth	21
El Paso	2
Houston	16
Lubbock	1
Midland	1
San Antonio	6

Midwest Division	63
	Number
Location	**of Stores**
Illinois	**24**
Chicago	23
Quincy	1
Indiana	**2**
Evansville	1
Hobart	1
Iowa	**1**
Waterloo	1

Michigan	**22**
Detroit	14
Flint/Saginaw	3
Grand Rapids	2
Kalamazoo	1
Lansing	1
Traverse City	1
Minnesota	**10**
Minneapolis/	10
St. Paul	
Ohio	**4**
Boardman	1
Cleveland	2
Toledo	1

Home Depot Canada	32
	Number
Location	**of Stores**
Alberta	**4**
Calgary	2
Edmonton	2
British Columbia	**8**
Vancouver	8
Manitoba	**1**
Winnipeg	1
Ontario	**19**
Kitchener	1
London	1
Ottawa	2
Toronto	14
Windsor	1

EXPO Design Center	5
	Number
Location	**of Stores**
Atlanta	1
Dallas	1
Long Island	1
Miami	1
San Diego	1

Total Stores	**624**

Source: Home Depot, Inc., *1994 Annual Report*, p. 32, and *1997 Annual Report*, p. 36.

When the first stores opened in Atlanta in 1979, the company leased space in three former Treasury Discount Stores with 60,000 square feet each. All three were suburban locations in the northern half of the city. Industry experts gave Home Depot 10-to-1 odds it would fail.

In 1980, a fourth Atlanta stored opened, and the company had annual sales of $22.3 million. The following year, Home Depot ventured beyond Atlanta to open four stores in South Florida and also had its first public offering at $12 a share. By early 1990, its stock had soared by 7,019% and split eight times. In May 1995, an original share was worth $26,300.

In the early 1980s, inflation rose over 13%, and unemployment was as high as 9.5%. These were rough times for most start-up companies, but Home Depot prospered as hard-pressed shoppers sought out the best buy. The company was voted the Retailer of the Year in the home center industry in 1982 and had its first stock splits.

By 1983, Marcus was a nationally recognized leader in the Do-It-Yourself industry. New Orleans was a strong market with many homeowners and young people, so Home Depot moved in with three stores. Other additions were in Arizona and Florida. Two stores opened in Orlando, in the backyard of the Winter Haven–based Scotty's, and one more opened in South Florida. Home Depot's strong drawing power became evident as customers passively waited in long checkout lines.

In 1984, Home Depot's common stock was listed on the New York Stock Exchange. It was traded under the symbol "HD" and was included in the Standard & Poor's 500 Index. Marcus believed about the only restraint Home Depot faced that year was its ability to recruit and train new staff fast enough. However, Home Depot was soon to face other problems. In December, things briefly turned sour when Home Depot bought the nine-store Bowater Warehouse chain with stores in Texas, Louisiana, and Alabama. Bowater had a dismal reputation. Its merchandise didn't match Home Depot's, and nearly all its employees had to be dismissed because they were unable to fit into the company's strong customer service orientation.

Of the 22 stores opened in 1985, most were in eight new markets. Going into Houston and Detroit were moves into less hospitable terrain. The company lost money with promotional pricing and advertising costs. This rapid expansion into unknown territories also took management's attention away from the other stores. The media quickly noted that Home Depot was having problems and suggested that its troubles could be related to rapid expansion into the already crowded home center business. Home Depot's earnings dropped 40% in 1985.

Marcus had to regroup in 1986. He slowed Home Depot's growth to 10 stores in existing markets, including the first supersized store with 140,000 square feet. Home Depot withdrew from the Detroit market, selling its five new stores. By 1987, six California stores and two Tennessee stores had opened, and the company had sales of $1 billion. In that same year, Home Depot introduced an advanced inventory management system; as a result, inventory was turned 5.4 times a year instead of the 4.5 times for 1986. The company also paid its first quarterly dividend.

In 1988, 21 stores opened, with heavy emphasis in California. For the second time, Home Depot was voted the Retailer of the Year in the home center industry.

Home Depot expanded its market beyond the Sunbelt in early 1989 by opening two stores in the northeast—East Hanover, New Jersey, and North Haven, Connecticut. By the end of the year, there were five stores in the Northeast.

The year 1989 was also a benchmark year for technological developments. All stores began using Universal Product Code (UPC) scanning systems to speed checkout time.

The Company's satellite data communications network installation improved management communication and training. Sales of the year totaled $2.76 billion, and plans were made to open its initial contribution of $6 million to the Employee Stock Ownership Plan (ESOP). On its tenth anniversary, Home Depot opened its 100th store (in Atlanta) and by the year's end had become the nation's largest home center chain.

Thirty stores opened in 1990, bringing the total to 147, with sales of $3.8 billion. The largest store—140,000 square feet—was in San Diego. To handle more volume per store,

Home Depot developed and tested a new store productivity improvement (SPI) program designed to make more effective use of existing and new store space and to allow for more rapid replenishment of merchandise on the sales floor. The SPI program involved the renovation of portions of certain existing stores and an improved design for new stores with the goal of enhanced customer access, reducing customer shopping time, and streamlining merchandise stocking and delivery. As part of SPI, the company also experimented with modified store layouts, materials handling techniques, and operations.

Home Depot continued its expansion by opening an additional 29 stores to bring the total number of stores to 174 in 1991, which generated total sales of $5.1 billion. In addition, the company's SPI program proved successful and was implemented in substantially all new stores and in selected existing stores. Home Depot also continued to introduce or refine a number of merchandising programs during fiscal 1991. Included among such programs were the introduction of full-service, in-store interior decorating centers staffed by designers and an expanded assortment in its lighting department. In 1991, management created a new division, EXPO Design Centers. The first store was opened in San Diego. EXPO Design Centers' niche was the extensive use of computer-aided design technology that the store's creative coordination used. It was targeted to upscale homeowners. These features were of assistance to customers remodeling their bathrooms and kitchens. To assist this strategy further, Home Depot offered a selection of major kitchen appliances. The product line offered was the top of the line. This allowed Home Depot to remain a leading-edge merchandiser.

From 1991 through 1995, many of the new merchandising techniques developed for the Home Depot EXPO were transferred to the entire chain. In 1994, the second EXPO store opened in Atlanta and was mostly dedicated to offering design services. The Atlanta store was 117,000 square feet, and the San Diego store was 105,000 square feet. In 1995 these stores were expanded in California, New York, and Texas. This division was expected to grow to 200 to 400 stores.

By the end of fiscal year 1992 Home Depot had increased its total number of stores to 214, with annual sales of $7.1 billion. Earlier that year, the company had begun a companywide rollout of an enlarged garden center prototype, which had been successfully tested in 1991. These centers, which were as large as 28,000 square feet, featured 6,000- to 8,000-square-foot greenhouses or covered selling areas, providing year-round selling opportunities and significantly expanded product assortment. Also during 1992, the company's "installed sales program," which it began testing in three selected markets in 1990, became available in 122 stores in 10 markets. This program targeted the buy-it-yourself customer (BIY), who would purchase an item but either did not have the desire or the ability to install the item. Finally, the company announced its national sponsorship of the 1994 and 1996 U.S. teams at the Winter and Summer Olympics.

During 1993, Home Depot introduced Depot Diners on a test basis in Atlanta, Seattle, and various locations in South Florida. Depot Diners were an extension of the company's commitment to total customer satisfaction and were designed to provide customers and employees with a convenient place to eat. The company continued to develop innovative merchandising programs that helped to grow the business further. The installed sales program became available in 251 stores in 26 markets, with approximately 2,370 installed sales vendors who, as independent, licensed contractors, were authorized to provide service to customers. By the end of fiscal year 1993, Home Depot had opened an additional 50 stores and sales were $9.2 billion, up by 30% from 1992.

From the end of fiscal year 1989 to the end of fiscal year 1994, the company increased its store count by an average of 24% per year (from 118 to 340) and increased the total store square footage by 28% per year (from 10,424,000 to 35,133,000). Home Depot entered the Canadian market on February 28, 1994. The company entered into a partnership with and, as a result, acquired 75% of Aikenhead's Home Improvement Warehouse. At any time after the sixth anniversary of the purchase, the company had the option to purchase, or the other partner had the right to cause the company to purchase, the remaining 25% of the Canadian company. Home Depot Canada commenced operations with seven stores previously operated by

Aikenhead's. Five additional stores were built during fiscal 1994, for a total of 12 stores at fiscal year end. Approximately nine additional new Canadian stores were planned for a total of 21 by the end of fiscal year 1995.

The company also made its initial entry into the Midwest by opening 11 stores in the region's two largest markets: Chicago, Illinois, and Detroit, Michigan. Approximately 16 new stores were scheduled for 1995, and by the end of 1998, the company expected approximately 112 stores to open.

During fiscal year 1994, Home Depot began developing plans to open stores in Mexico. The first store was scheduled to open in 1998. Although the company was already building relationships with key suppliers in Mexico, entry into the market was to be cautious and slow, paying special attention to Mexico's volatile economy. On a long-term basis, however, the company anticipated that success in Mexico could lead to more opportunities throughout Central and South America. Home Depot planned to expand its total domestic stores by about 25% per year, on average, over the foreseeable future. The international openings were to be above and beyond this figure. Management felt that its growth was optimal, given its financial and management resources.

In 1995, the company offered more private-label products. The company used the "Homer" character on all its private products and its advertisements. The first 24-hour store was opened in Flushing, New York. Ben Sharon of *Value Line* said, "[Home Depot's] ability to adopt different characteristics among regions and markets should keep Home Depot ahead of the industry in the years ahead."[2] By the end of 1995, the company had a total of 423 stores, of which 400 were Home Depot stores, 19 were Canadian stores in 3 provinces, and 4 EXPO stores.

In March 1995, *Fortune* announced that Home Depot had made its list of America's Most Admired Corporations. Home Depot ranked 8.24, or fifth overall in the competition. In 1996, Home Depot ranked second. The company ranked first for rate of return (39.0%) for the past 10 years. The top four companies were Rubbermaid (8.65), Microsoft (8.42), Coca-Cola (8.39), and Motorola (8.38). *Fortune* stated, "The winners chart a course of constant renewal and work to sustain culture that produces the very best products and people."[3] Over 1,000 senior executives, outside directors, and financial analysts were surveyed. Each corporation was rated in 10 separate areas.

Home Depot had encountered local opposition to locating one of its stores in a small community in Pequannock Township, New Jersey. A group called "Concerned Citizens for Community Preservation" mobilized to prevent Home Depot from opening a store in the town. Members of the group posted flyers and signs throughout the township. These flyers documented Home Depot's alleged "legacy of crime, traffic, and safety violations." The flyers stated, "Our kids will be crossing through this death trap," referring to Home Depot's proposed parking lot. Another flyer asked, "How will we be protected?"[4]

In July 1995, Home Depot filed a lawsuit against Rickel Home Centers, a closely held competitor based in South Plainfield, New Jersey, claiming that "[Rickel] used smear tactics in a concerted effort to block Home Depot from opening stores in Pequannock and Bloomfield, about 25 miles to the south."[5] The suit stated that Rickel had published false statements "impugning Home Depot's name, reputation, products, and services." The suit named Rickel and Bloomfield citizens' groups as defendants.

This was not the first time that citizens' groups had tried to stop a new store or development. Wal-Mart had a severe challenge when it was trying to open a new store in Bennington, Vermont. In 1997, the company opened its first store in Williston, Vermont.

On July 20, 1995, Dennis Ryan, President of CrossRoads, announced the opening of the first of Home Depot's new rural chain, CrossRoads, in Quincy, Illinois. A second store was planned to be opened in Columbus, Missouri, in January or February 1996. The target market for this chain was farmers and ranchers who shopped in smaller, rural towns across America. At that time, there were about 100 farm and home retailers, with about 850 stores and annual sales of $6 billion. A typical CrossRoads store would have about 117,000 square feet of inside retail space, plus a 100,000-square-foot lumberyard. In contrast, the average size of a Tractor Supply Company (a competitor) store was about one tenth the size of a CrossRoads store and did not have a lumberyard. Dennis Ryan said, "This really is a Home Depot just tailored to this [Quincy] community."[6]

The store carried the typical products of Home Depot. In addition, CrossRoads carried pet supplies, truck and tractor tires and parts, work clothing, farm animal medicines, feed, and storage tanks, barbed wire, books (such as *Raising Sheep the Modern Way*), and other items. Employees would install engines and tires and go to the farm to fix a flat tractor tire.[7] The company soon terminated this strategy because the stores did not generate sales and profits that Home Depot expected. The existing CrossRoads stores were renamed Home Depot stores.

By year-end 1996, the company acquired Maintenance Warehouse/America Corporation, which was the leading direct mail marketer of maintenance, repair, and operating products to the United States building and facilities in management market. The company's 1996 sales were approximately $130 million in an estimated $10 billion market. Home Depot management felt this was "an important step towards strengthening our position with professional business customers."[8] The company's long-term goal was to capture 10% of this market.

At the end of 1996, the company had 512 stores, including 483 Home Depot stores and five EXPO Design Centers in 38 states, and 24 stores in Canada.

In 1997, the company added 112 stores for a total of 624 stores in 41 states. Stores in the United States were 587 Home Depot stores and 5 EXPO Design Center stores plus 32 stores in 4 Canadian provinces. This was a 22% increase in stores over 1996. Two thirds of the new stores in fiscal 1997 were in existing markets. The company "continues to add stores to even its most mature markets to further penetrate and increase its presence in the market."[9]

The company planned to add new stores at a 21 to 22% annual growth rate, which would increase stores from 624 at the end of 1997 to 1,300 stores at the end of fiscal 2001. This meant the company would have to increase its associates from approximately 125,000 at the end of 1997 to 315,000 in four years (2001).

During 1998, Home Depot planned to open approximately 137 new stores, which would be a 22% increase in stores. The company planned to enter new markets—Anchorage, Alaska; Cincinnati and Columbus, Ohio; Milwaukee, Wisconsin; Norfolk and Richmond, Virginia; San Juan, Puerto Rico; Regina, Saskatchewan, and Kingston, Ontario in Canada; and Santiago, Chile. The company intended to open two stores in Santiago during fiscal 1998. To facilitate its entry into Chile, Home Depot entered into a joint venture agreement, in fiscal 1997, with S.A.C.I. Falabella, which was the largest department store retailer in Chile. The company's position on the joint venture was that it "was proving to be beneficial in expediting The Home Depot's startup in areas such as systems, logistics, real estate, and credit programs."[10]

This global expansion fit the company's stated vision to be one of the most successful retailers in the next millennium. According to management, "the most successful retailers . . . will be those who, among other things, can effectively profitably extend their reach to global markets."[11] Home Depot management "plans to employ a focused, regional strategy, establishing platform markets for growth into other markets."[12]

Corporate Culture

The culture at Home Depot was characterized by the phrase, "Guess what happened to me at Home Depot?" This phrase showed Home Depot's bond with its customers and the communities in which it had stores and was a recognition of superb service. Home Depot called this its "orange-blooded culture."

The orange-blooded culture emphasized individuality, informality, nonconformity, growth, and pride. These traits reflected those of the founders of the company, who within hours of being fired from Handy Dan, were busily planning the Home Depot stores to go into competition with the company from which they had just been summarily dismissed. The culture was "really a reflection of Bernie and me[sic]," said Blank. "We're not formal, stuffy folks. We hang pretty loose. We've got a lot of young people. We want them to feel comfortable."[13]

The importance of the individual to the success of the whole venture was consistently emphasized at Home Depot. Marcus's statements bear this out: "We know that one person can make a difference, and that is what is so unique about The Home Depot. It doesn't matter where our associates work in our company, they can all make a difference."[14] While emphasizing the opportunities for advancement at Home Depot, Marcus decried the kind of "cradle to grave" job that used to be the ideal in America and is the norm in Japan. To him, this was "a kind of serfdom."[15] Home Depot attempted to provide excellent wages and benefits, and superior training and advancement opportunities, while encouraging independent thinking and initiative.

Informality was always in order at Home Depot—"spitballs fly at board meetings"—and there was always someone around to make sure that ties got properly trimmed. When executives visited stores, they went alone, not with an entourage. Most worked on the floors in the beginning and knew the business from the ground up. They were approachable and employees frequently came forward with ideas and suggestions.

Nonconformity was evident in many different areas of the company—from the initial warehouse concept to the size and variety of merchandise to human resource practices. Both Marcus and Blank "flout conventional corporate rules that foil innovation." Training employees at all levels was one of the most powerful means of transmitting corporate culture, and Home Depot used it extensively. One analyst noted that Home Depot (in a reverse of the "top-to-bottom" training sequence in most organizations) trained the carryout people first: "The logic is that the guy who helps you to your car is the last employee you come in contact with, and they want that contact to be positive."[16]

Company management perception of what the customer finds on a visit to a Home Depot store is a "feel good" store. The company defined a feel good store as "a place where they *feel good* about walking in our doors, *feel good* about consulting our knowledgeable associates, *feel good* about paying a low price, and *feel good* about returning time after time."[17]

The Home Depot was built on a set of values that fostered strong relationships with its key constituencies. The company's management embraced the values of taking care of its people, encouraging an entrepreneurial spirit, treating each other with respect, and being committed to the highest standards. For the customers, management believed that excellent customer service was the key to company success, and that giving back to the communities it served was part of its commitment to the customer. Importantly, management believed that if all employees lived all of these values, they would also create shareholder value.

The Home Depot's long-term growth planning was taking place with full recognition of the importance of the company's culture to its future success. Its goal was for each associate to not only be able to explain the company's culture of respect, trust, ownership, and entrepreneurial spirit, but most importantly, to believe it and live it.

The management of Home Depot was often asked how the company had managed to grow so fast for as long as it had and still be successful, both financially and with its customers. They responded that aggressive growth required adapting to change, but continued success required holding fast to the culture and values of the company as the company grew.[18]

In addition, Home Depot recognized its role in the community, and strove to be known as a good "corporate citizen." In one community, a woman lost her uninsured home and teen-aged son to a fire. Home Depot's management responded, along with other residents, by providing thousands of dollars of free materials and supplies to assist in the rebuilding effort. In another incident, a community organization sponsored a graffiti cleanup, and the Home Depot store in the area donated paint and supplies to assist in the project. These were just a few of the stories that communities told about Home Depot, which also participated in

Habitat for Humanity and Christmas in April, and had provided over $10 million to help fund many community projects in the United States and Canada. The company also was active in environmental activities and promoted environmentally healthy building and home improvement practices.

Merrill Lynch stated about Home Depot's culture that its "entrepreneurial culture and heavy dedication toward customer service, combined with its large merchandise selection, has resulted in a retailer that leads its industry by almost every performance measure."[19]

Corporate Governance

BOARD OF DIRECTORS

The Board of Directors of Home Depot were as follows.[20]

Bernard Marcus (68) had been Cofounder, Chairman, and Chief Executive Officer since the inception of the company in 1978 until 1997, when he passed the title of CEO to Arthur M. Blank, and remained as Chairman. He had served on many other boards. He owned 21,842,890 shares (2.98%) of the company's stock.

Arthur M. Blank (55) had been Cofounder, President, Chief Operating Officer, and Director since the company's inception, and was named Chief Executive Officer in 1997. He had served on many other boards. He owned 12,182,614 shares (1.66%).

Ronald M. Brill (54) had been Executive Vice President and Chief Financial Officer since March 1993. He joined the company in 1978 and was elected Treasurer in 1980. He owned 872,392 shares of the company's stock.

Frank Borman (70) had been a Director since 1983. He had been a NASA astronaut and retired U.S. Air Force colonel. He was the retired Chairman and Chief Operating Officer of Eastern Airlines and presently was the Chairman of Patlex Corporation. He was a major investor in 1983 and owned 265,782 shares of the company's stock. He served on many other boards.

Barry R. Cox (44) had been a Director since 1978. For the past 20 years, he had been a private investor. He owned 1,650,243 shares of stock.

Milledge A. Hart, III (64) had been a Director since 1978. He served as Chairman of the Hart Group, Chairman of Rmax Inc., and Chairman of Axon, Inc. He served on many other boards. He owned 1,733,185 shares of the company's stock.

Donald R. Keough (71) had been a Director since April 1993. He was President and Chief Operating Officer and Director of Coca-Cola Company until his retirement in April 1993. He owned 20,304 shares of the company's stock. He served on many other boards.

John I. Clendenin (63) had been a Director since 1996. He had been Chairman and Chief Executive Officer of BellSouth Corporation for the last five years until his retirement in 1996 and remained Chairman until 1997. He owned 5,477 shares of the company's stock.

Johnnetta B. Cole (61) had been a Director since 1995. Dr. Cole served as President of Spelman College in Atlanta, Georgia, from 1987 until July 1997. She served on many other boards and foundations. She owned 4,803 shares of the company's stock.

Kenneth G. Langone (62) had been Cofounder and Director since the company's inception. He had served as Chairman, President, Chief Executive Officer, and Managing Director of Invened Associates, Inc., an investment banking and brokerage firm. He served on many other boards. He owned 6,850,243 shares of the company's stock.

M. Faye Wilson (60) had been a Director since 1992. She had been Executive Vice President of Bank of America NT&SA since 1992. She owned 16,743 shares of the company's stock.

The Directors were paid $40,000 per annum, of which $10,000 was in the form of restricted shares of common stock, and an additional $1,000 fee and expenses for each meeting. The Executive Committee included Messrs. Marcus, Blank, and Langone. The Audit

Committee included Messrs. Borman, Cox, Hart, and Keough. The Compensation Committee included Messrs. Borman, Clendenin, Cox, and Keough. The Human Resource Committee included Dr. Cole, Mr. Langone, and Ms. Wilson.

FRM (Fidelity) Corporation owned 55,991,937 (7.65%) shares of common stock.

TOP MANAGEMENT

Key executive officers of Home Depot, besides Bernard Marcus, Arthur M. Blank, and Ronald M. Brill, who served on the Board, were as follows:[21]

Mark R. Baker (40) has been President of the Midwest Division since December 1997. Mr. Baker first joined the company in 1996 as Vice President—Merchandising for the Midwest Division. Prior to joining Home Depot, from 1992 until 1996, Mr. Baker was an Executive Vice President for HomeBase in Fullerton, California.

Bruce W. Berg (49) has been President—Southeast Division since 1991. Mr. Berg joined the company in 1984 as Vice President—Merchandising (East Coast) and was promoted to Senior Vice President (East Coast) in 1988.

Marshall L. Day (54) has been Senior Vice President—Chief Financial Officer since 1995. Mr. Day previously served as Senior Vice President—Finance from 1993 until his promotion to his current position.

Bill Hamlin (45) was recently named Group President and continues to serve as Executive Vice President—Merchandising. Prior to being named Executive Vice President—Merchandising, Mr. Hamlin served as President—Western Division from 1990 until 1994.

Vernon Joslyn (46) has been President—Northeast Division since 1996. Mr. Joslyn previously served as Vice President—Operations for the Northeast Division from 1993 until his promotion to his current position.

W. Andrew McKenna (52) was named Senior Vice President—Strategic Business Development in December 1997. Mr. McKenna joined Home Depot as Senior Vice President—Corporate Information Systems in 1990. In 1994 he was named President of the Midwest Division and served in that capacity until he assumed the duties of his current position.

Lynn Martineau (41) has been President—Western Division since 1996. Mr. Martineau most recently served as Vice President—Merchandising for the company's Southeast Division from 1989 until his promotion to his current position.

Larry M. Mercer (51) was recently named Group President and has been Executive Vice President—Operations since 1996. Mr. Mercer previously served as President—Northeast Division from 1991 until his promotion to his current position.

Barry L. Silverman (39) has been President of the Southwest Division since July 1997. Mr. Silverman previously served as Vice President—Merchandising of the Northeast Division from 1991 until his promotion to his current position.

Bryant W. Scott (42) has been President of the EXPO Design Center Division since 1995. Since 1980, Mr. Scott has served in a variety of positions, including Vice President—Merchandising for the Southeast Division.

David Suliteanu (45) was named Group President—Diversified Businesses in April 1998. Mr. Suliteanu previously served as Vice Chairman and Director of Stores for Macy's East, a position he held from 1993 until he joined Home Depot in April 1998.

Annette M. Verschuren (41) has been President of The Home Depot Canada since 1996. In 1992, Ms. Verschuren formed Verschuren Ventures Inc. and remained there until joining Michaels of Canada Inc. in 1993 where she served as President until joining the company.

In 1997, Bernard Marcus, who had been CEO since the company's inception in 1978, passed the title to Arthur M. Blank. Mr. Blank now served as President and CEO.

Exhibit 3 shows all the officers of Home Depot.

Exhibit 3

Officers: Home Depot, Inc.

Corporate

Bernard Marcus
Chairman of the Board

Arthur M. Blank
President and Chief Executive Officer

Ronald M. Brill
Executive Vice President and
Chief Administrative Officer

Bill Hamlin
Executive Vice President
Merchandising and Group President

Larry M. Mercer
Executive Vice President
Operations and Group President

David Suliteanu
Group President, Diversified Services

Alan Barnaby
Senior Vice President, Store
Operations

Marshall L. Day
Senior Vice President,
Chief Financial Officer

Pat Farrah
Senior Vice President, Merchandising

Bryan J. Fields
Senior Vice President, Real Estate

Ronald B. Griffin
Senior Vice President
Information Services

Richard A. Hammill
Senior Vice President, Marketing

W. Andrew McKenna
Senior Vice President
Strategic Business Development

Stephen R. Messana
Senior Vice President, Human
Resources

Dennis Ryan
Senior Vice President, Merchandising

Lawrence A. Smith
Senior Vice President, Legal and
Secretary

Terence L. Smith
Senior Vice President, Imports/
Logistics

Richard L. Sullivan
Senior Vice President, Advertising

Robert J. Wittman
Senior Vice President, Merchandising

Mike Anderson
Vice President, Information Services

Ben A. Barone
Vice President, Credit Marketing

Dave Bogage
Vice President, Management and
Organization Development

Patrick Cataldo
Vice President, Training

Gary C. Cochran
Vice President, Information Services

Charles D. Crowell
Vice President, Distribution Services

Kerrie R. Flanagan
Vice President, Merchandise Accounting

Mike Folio
Vice President, Real Estate

Frank Gennaccaro
Vice President, Merchandising

Paul Hoedeman
Vice President, Information Services

Ted Kaczmarowski
Vice President
Construction/Store Planning

Bill Peña
Vice President/General Manager
International Development

William K. Schlegal
Vice President, Imports

Kim Shreckengost
Vice President, Investor Relations

Don Singletary
Vice President, Human Resources—
North American Stores

Grady Stewart
Vice President, Operations

Carol B. Tome
Vice President, Treasurer

DeWayne Truitt
Vice President
Compensation and Benefits

Gregg Vickery
Vice President, Controller

Edward A. Wolfe
Vice President, Loss Prevention

Ken Young
Vice President, Internal Audit

Midwest Division

Mark Baker
President

H. George Collins
Vice President, Store Operations

Robert Gilbreth
Vice President, Store Operations

Steven L. Mahurin
Vice President, Merchandising

Michael J. Williams
Vice President, Human Resources

Northeast Division

Vern Joslyn
President

Jeff Birren
Vice President, Store Operations

Carol A. Freitag
Vice President, Human Resources

William G. Lennie
Vice President, Merchandising

Michael McCabe
Vice President, Store Operations

Pedro Mendiguren
Vice President, Store Operations

Southeast Division

Bruce Berg
President

Tony Brown
Vice President, Store Operations

Dennis Johnson
Vice President, Merchandising

Eric Johnson
Vice President, Store Operations

H. Gregory Turner
Vice President, Store Operations

John Wicks
Vice President, Merchandising

(continued)

Exhibit 3 Officers: Home Depot, Inc. *(continued)*

Southwest Division	**The Home Depot Canada**	**Steven L. Neeley**
Barry L. Silverman	**Annette M. Verschuren**	Vice President, Sales
President	President	**Kevin Peters**
Jerry Edwards	**John Hayes**	Vice President, Logistics
Vice President, Merchandising	Vice President, Merchandising	**Ron Turk**
Frank Rosi	**Dennis Kennedy**	Vice President
Vice President, Human Resources	Vice President, Store Operations	Chief Financial Officer
Tom Taylor		**Jeffrey R. Wenham**
Vice President, Store Operations	**EXPO Design Center Division**	Vice President, Human Resources
	Bryant Scott	
Western Division	President	**National Blind & Wallpaper Factory**
Lynn Martineau	**Christopher A. McLoughlin**	**David Katzman**
President	Vice President, Division Controller	President
Terry Hopper	**Steve Smith**	**Rick Kovacs**
Vice President, Store Operations	Vice President, Merchandising	Senior Vice President, Merchandising
Ethan Klausner		**David Littleson**
Vice President, Merchandising	**Maintenance Warehouse**	Chief Financial Officer
Bruce Merino	**Jonathan Neeley**	**Steve Kaip**
Vice President, Merchandising	President	Vice President, Information Systems
Timothy J. Pfeiffer	**Jim Ardell**	**Debra Russell**
Vice President, Store Operations	Vice President, Merchandising	Vice President, Operations
Thomas "Buz Smith	**Mike Brown**	**Bob Shepard**
Vice President, Store Operations	Vice President, Information Systems	Vice President
Greg Lewis	**Bill Luth**	Installation/Retail Development
Division Controller	Vice President, Marketing	

Source: The Home Depot, Inc., *1997 Annual Report*, p. 36.

Organizational Structure

The official organizational structure of Home Depot (see **Exhibit 4**) was much like that of other retail organizations, but according to a human resources spokesperson, the environment was so relaxed and casual people felt like they could report to anyone. Marcus and Blank presided at the top of Home Depot's organizational chart and were supported by Executive Vice Presidents: Executive Vice President and Chief Administrative Officer; Executive Vice President of Merchandising and Group President; and Executive Vice President of Operations and Group President.

There were three Group Presidents, of which two were also Executive Vice Presidents. The other was the Group President of Diversified Businesses. These executives were supported by 13 Senior Vice Presidents (see **Exhibit 4**). The company had 21 Vice Presidents at the corporate level.

The organization was divided into seven divisions:

1. Southeast Division,
2. Western Division,
3. Northeast Division,
4. Midwest Division,
5. Home Depot Canada Division,
6. Southwest Division, and
7. EXPO Design Centers.

Exhibit 4

Organizational Chart: Home Depot, Inc.

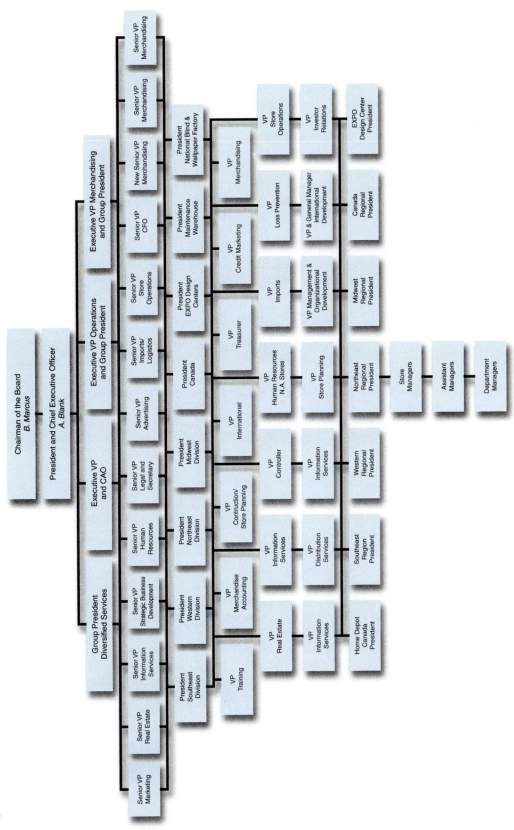

Note: This does not include the company's wholly-owned subsidiaries (1) National Blind & Wallpaper Factory and (2) Maintenance Warehouse.

Source: Company records.

22-13

Each division was headed by a President, who was supported by Vice Presidents of Merchandising and Store Operations. Under each Vice President in a division was a group of regional managers responsible for a number of stores. There were a number of Vice Presidents at the division level, some of which included Legal, Information Services, Logistics, Advertising, the Controller, and Human Resources.

At the store level, Home Depot was set up much as would be expected—with a Manager, Assistant Managers, and Department Managers. The average Home Depot store had one Manager whose primary responsibility was to be the master delegator. Four to six Assistants usually presided over the store's 10 departments. Each Assistant Manager was responsible for one to three departments. One Assistant Manager was responsible for receiving and the "back end" (stock storage area), in addition to his or her departments. The Assistant Managers were supported by Department Managers who were each responsible for one department. The Department Managers reported directly to the Assistant Managers and had no firing/hiring capabilities. Assistant Managers normally handled ordering and work schedules, and so on. Department Managers handled employees' questions and job assignments. In a recent change, human resource officers were made responsible for recruiting, staffing, employee relations, and management development for each division.[22]

HOME DEPOT CANADA (AIKENHEAD'S)

On February 28, 1994, Home Depot acquired a 75% interest in Aikenhead's Home Improvements Warehouse chain of seven warehouses in Canada for approximately $161,584,000. It was a joint venture with Molson Companies, Ltd.; Home Depot served as the general partner. Stephen Bebis, a former Home Depot officer, developed the chain along the Home Depot concept. He initially served as President of this unit and was replaced by Annette M. Verschuren in 1995.

Operations[23]

The stores and their merchandise were set up so that all of the stores were very similar. The company's corporate headquarters was responsible for the "look," but individual managers could change a display or order more or less of a product if they could justify the change. The Managers within individual stores made decisions regarding their employees, such as firing and hiring, but they looked to headquarters in areas such as training. One Manager of a store in Georgia said that if he did not like a particular display or promotion, it was at his discretion to change it or drop it. The Manager went on to say that he and other store managers work hand in hand with corporate headquarters, and that if he wanted to make "major" changes or had a significant store or personnel problem, he would deal with headquarters.

During 1994, Home Depot introduced a prototype store format, which offered about 32,000 more square feet of selling space and a significantly broader and deeper selection of products and services, as well as a more convenient layout than the traditional stores. These "Type V" stores were designed around a design center, which grouped complementary product categories.

Operational efficiency had been a crucial part of achieving low prices while still offering a high level of customer service. The company was assessing and upgrading its information to support its growth, reduce and control costs, and enable better decision making. From the installation of computerized checkout systems to the implementation of satellite communications systems in most of the stores, the company had shown that it had been and would continue to be innovative in its operating strategy.

By fiscal year 1994, each store was equipped with a computerized point-of-sale system (POS), electronic bar code scanning systems, and a minicomputer. These systems provided efficient customer checkout with approximately 90% scannable products, store-based inventory management, rapid order replenishment, labor planning support, and item movement information. In fiscal year 1994, faster registers were introduced along with new check approval systems and a new receipt format to expedite credit care transactions.

Home Depot's attitude of complete customer satisfaction has led the company to constantly seek ways to improve customer service. When the company was faced with clogged aisles, endless checkout lines, and too few salespeople, it sought creative ways to improve customer service. Workers were added to the sales floor. Shelfstocking and price tagging were shifted to nighttime, when the aisles are empty. The changes were worth the expense because now employees were free to sell during the day. In an effort to ease customer crowding, Home Depot used a "clustering" strategy to locate new stores closer to existing ones.

The company also operated its own television network (HDTV). This money-saving device allowed Home Depot's top executives to get instant feedback from local managers and also allowed training and communications programs to be viewed in the stores. Management's operating philosophies and policies were more effectively communicated because information presented by top management could be targeted at a large audience. This addition had increased employee motivation and saved many dollars by making information available in a timely manner.

Home Depot was firmly committed to energy conservation and had installed reflectors to lower the amount of lighting required in a store. The reflectors darkened the ceiling but saved thousands of dollars a year in energy bills. Further, the company had pursued a computerized system to maintain comfortable temperatures, a challenge due to the stores' concrete floors, exposed ceilings, and open oversized doors for forklift deliveries. The system also had an automated feedback capability that could be used for equipment maintenance.

The adoption of the Point-of-Sale (POS) technology had improved each store's ability to identify and adapt to trends quickly. The information provided by this technology was transferred to computer centers in Atlanta and Fullerton, California, where consumer buying trends were traced. This allowed Home Depot to adjust its merchandising mix and track both buyer trends and inventory.

In 1987, the company had introduced an advanced inventory management system that allowed it to increase inventory turnover significantly, from 4.1 in 1985 to 5.7 in 1994. This let Home Depot carry $40 million less in inventory, tying up less working capital to finance it. This efficiency allowed a cost structure that was significantly lower than the competition's.

In 1994, the company introduced phone centers to serve its customers who called to inquire about pricing and availability of merchandise. Adding experienced salespeople to a phone bank to answer calls quickly and efficiently had increased weekly phone sales. Without having to respond to phone calls, the sales staff could better concentrate on serving in-store customers.

The company continued to see greater efficiency as a result of its Electronic Data Interchange (EDI) program. Currently over 400 of the company's highest volume vendors were participating in the EDI program. A paperless system, EDI electronically processed orders from stores to vendors, alerted the store when the merchandise was to arrive, and transmitted vendor invoice data.

In fiscal year 1994, stores were outfitted with Electronic Article Surveillance (EAS) detectors, which triggered an alarm if a person exited the store with merchandise that had been affixed with an EAS label that had not been desensitized at the cash register. The system was proving to be a deterrent to theft, with many stores reporting reductions in shoplifting offenses.

Home Depot continuously experimented with new operating concepts, such as CrossRoads and EXPO Design Centers. Its investment in new retail technology and its willingness to streamline operations for the benefit of the customer and employees had paid off in areas such as inventory turnover, in-stock turnover, in-stock inventory positions, querying problems, employee motivation, and information flow from the company's buyers to its store-level managers and employees.

MERCHANDISING[24]

If Home Depot's advertising strategy of creating awareness of the company's stores and encouraging do-it-yourselfers (DIYs) to tackle more at-home projects was getting people into the stores, the merchandising mix was aimed at getting people to buy. According to Marcus, "We could sell them anything . . . but we don't. We don't want the customer to think we're a discounter, food store, a toy store, or anything else, because it would confuse [them]."[25] Home Depot wanted to be thought of as the DIY warehouse, nothing less.

Advertising

The company maintained an aggressive campaign, using various media for both price and institutional policy. Print advertising, usually emphasizing price, was prepared by an in-house staff to control context, layout, media placement, and cost. Broadcast media advertisements were generally institutional and promoted Home Depot "the company," not just pricing strategy. These advertisements focused on the "You'll feel right at home" and "Everyday Low Pricing" ad slogans, name recognition, and the value of Home Depot's customer service. Although the company had grown over the years, the goal of its advertising was still to project a local flavor. The Western Division maintained its own creative department because of its different time zone and unique product mix. The company attempted to use information for the field in the various markets and put together an effective advertising campaign. The company still relied heavily on print media.

Home Depot sponsored the 1996 U.S. Summer Olympic Games in Atlanta. Through the sponsorship, Home Depot had hoped to further its ties with the home improvement customer, create sales opportunities, further differentiate itself from competitors, maintain its corporate culture, and support key businesses in the community. Home Depot began 1994 by unveiling a program to help pave the Olympic Park in Atlanta with engraved bricks, hiring athletes to work in the stores and office while they trained for the Games, and continuing a cooperative partnership with vendors in the Home Depot Olympic Family. This partnership had grown to include 29 key suppliers in the United States and 26 in Canada. Each member of the "Family" represented a specific home improvement product category and could participate in many of Home Depot's Olympic Games promotions.

The company participated in the Olympic Job Opportunities Program, in which Home Depot provided part-time jobs for 100 hopeful Olympic athletes as they trained for the Olympics. Twenty-six of the American and Canadian athletes participated in the Olympic Games and 6 earned medals. The company planned to remain a sponsor for at least the next six years for the Olympic Games in 2000, 2002, and 2004. The company also acted as a sponsor for the 1998 Winter Olympic Games.

Customer Target Market

Home Depot stores served primarily do-it-yourselfers, although home improvement contractors, building maintenance professionals, interior designers, and other professionals had become increasingly important customers. DIY customers continued to be the core business and made up approximately two thirds of the total home improvement segment. DIY customers bought materials for the home and installed them personally.

Due to the increasing home improvement activity, buy-it-yourself (BIY) customers began to emerge. BIY customers chose products, made the purchase, and contracted with others to complete the project or install the furnishings. Home Depot was catering to this segment by expanding its installed sales program companywide.

Home Depot also continued to target the professional business customer. It had set up a commercial credit program, provided commercial checkout lines in the stores, and had hired additional associates with experience in various professional fields.

The typical DIY customer was a married male homeowner, aged 25 to 34, with a high school diploma or some college, and had an annual income of $20,000 to $40,000. Projections through 1999 indicated that households headed by 25- to 35-year-olds with earnings over $30,000 would increase 34% to 38% by 1999. The 45 to 54 age group was earning over $30,000 and was expected to increase by 40%.

Economics

The DIY industry exhibited a demand pattern that was largely recession-proof. Because a mere 15% of Home Depot's business came from contractors, a downturn in home construction had only a modest impact on Home Depot sales. In addition, analysts pointed out that, during hard times, consumers could not afford to buy new or bigger homes; instead they maintained or upgraded their existing homes. Home improvement spending had declined in one recession during the past 20 years. The new strategy to penetrate the professional market might affect the company's sales more in future recessions.

Merchandising Strategy

The company's *1994 Annual Report* stated that Home Depot's goal was to be "The Do-It-Yourself Retailer." Merchandising included all activities involved in the buying and selling of goods for a profit. It involved long-range planning to ensure that the right merchandise was available at the right place, at the right time, in the right quantity, and at the right price. Success depended on the firm's ability to act and react with speed, spot changes, and catch trends early.

During 1994, Home Depot refined its merchandising function to be more efficient and responsive to customers. The new structure gave Division Managers responsibility for specific product categories, and specialists in each of these categories made sure the business lines were kept current. There were also field merchants who worked with the stores to ensure proper implementation of new programs as well as the maintenance of any ongoing programs. This approach strengthened product lines, got the right merchandise to the customers, reduced administration costs, and prepared Home Depot to expand into additional product lines.

The merchandising strategy of Home Depot followed a three-pronged approach: (1) excellent customer service, (2) everyday low pricing, and (3) wide breadth of products.

Each Home Depot store served 100,000 households with a median income of $45,000. Of those households, 75% were owner-occupied. In 1997, Home Depot responded to the demographics of certain markets by expanding its service hours to 24 hours a day in 15 store locations.

Home Depot continued to introduce or refine several merchandising programs during fiscal 1997. Key among them was the company's ongoing commitment to becoming the supplier of choice to a variety of professional customers, including remodelers, carpenters, plumbers, electricians, building maintenance professionals, and designers. According to management, the company had reacted to the needs of this group by enhancing and increasing quantities of key products for professional customers. In addition, the company was testing additional products and service-related programs designed to increase sales to professional customers, including expanded commercial credit programs, delivery services, and incremental dedicated staff.

The company's installed sales program was available, with varying services offered, in all of the company's stores. The company authorized approximately 3,500 installed sales vendors who, as independent licensed contractors, provide services to customers. This program targeted the BIY customer, who would purchase a product but did not have the desire or ability to install it.

Construction on the company's new Import Distribution Center (IDC), located in Savannah, Georgia, was completed in fiscal 1997. Built with the intention of servicing the company's stores located east of the Rocky Mountains, the IDC began shipments in April

1997, and by the end of fiscal 1997 was servicing all targeted stores. The 1.4-million-square-foot facility was staffed with approximately 600 associates. The IDC enabled the company to directly import products not currently available to customers or offer products currently sourced domestically from third-party importers. Other benefits included quicker turnaround deliveries to stores, lower costs, and improved quality control than would be possible if the products were purchased through third-party importers.

The company sponsored the "1997 National Home and Garden Show Series." Bringing together 16 of the nation's most successful consumer shows under one national sponsorship provided maximum exposure and support to the shows. Through this sponsorship, the company played a key role in bringing the most innovative lawn and garden, interior design, and home improvement products and services to the attention of the general public.

Home TLC, Inc., an indirect, wholly owned subsidiary of The Home Depot, Inc., owned the trademarks, "The Home Depot," and "EXPO," as well as the "Homer" advertising symbol and various private label brand names that the company uses. The company's operating subsidiaries licensed from Homer TLC, Inc., the right to use this intellectual property. Management believed that the company's rights in this intellectual property were an important asset of the company.

Home Depot was the only big-box retailer to offer a number of other exclusive, high-quality products such as Pergo® laminate flooring, Ralph Lauren® paints, and Vigoro® fertilizer. Each of these products made The Home Depot unique from its competitors and provided its customers with a better selection of products. Home Depot's proprietary products included Behr Premium Plus paints, Hampton Bay ceiling fans and lighting products, Husky tools, and Scott's lawnmowers. These proprietary products provided Home Depot customers with a quality product at a value price and often filled a needed void in the product offerings.

Following the success of Home Depot's best-selling *Home Improvement 1-2-3*™ book, the company recently released *Outdoor Projects 1-2-3*™, the company's latest how-to book sold in Home Depot stores and bookstores. For the past three years, Home Depot has sponsored *HouseSmart with Lynette Jennings*™, one of the highest-rated shows on The Discovery Channel®. The company planned to extend its reach to tomorrow's homeowners in 1998 through *Homer's Workshop*™, the first how-to, project-oriented television program for children.

Clustering Strategy

The clustering strategy had been employed to allow Home Depot's aggressive expansion program. Home Depot had intentionally cannibalized sales of existing stores by opening two other stores in a single market area. The short-run effect was to lower same-store sales, but a strategic advantage was created by raising the barrier of entry to competitors. It reduced overcrowding in the existing stores. It also allowed the company to spread its advertising and distribution costs over a larger store base, thereby lowering selling, general, and administrative costs. The company's 1997 gross margin was 28.1%.

Customer Service

The availability of sales personnel to attend to customer needs was one clear objective of the Home Depot customer service strategy.

Customer service differentiated Home Depot from its competitors. The provision of highly qualified and helpful employees, professional clinics, and in-store displays had developed into a customer service approach referred to as "customer cultivation." It gave DIY customers the support and confidence that no home project was beyond their capabilities with Home Depot personnel close at hand.

Home Depot employees went beyond simply recommending appropriate products, tools, and materials. Sales personnel cultivated the customer by demonstrating methods and techniques of performing a job safely and efficiently. This unique aspect of the company's service also served as a feedback mechanism—employees helping the next customer learn from the problems and successes of the last one.

All of the stores offered hands-on workshops on projects such as kitchen remodeling, basic plumbing, ceramic tile installation, and other activities in which customers in a particular locality had expressed interest. Offered mainly on weekends, the workshops varied in length, depending on complexity. Only the most experienced staff members, many of them former skilled craftsmen, taught at these workshops. Promotion of the workshops was done through direct mail advertising and in-store promotion.

At many Home Depot stores, customers could rent trucks by the hour through Load 'N Go™, Home Depot's exclusive truck rental service. The company also expanded a tool rental service to more stores during fiscal 1998. In addition, the company's special order capabilities should improve, due in part to the acquisition in November 1997 of National Blind & Wallpaper Factory and Habitat Wallpaper & Blinds stores, which became wholly owned subsidiaries of Home Depot. When integrated with the stores beginning in fiscal 1998, the innovative ordering systems of these companies should give Home Depot the capability to handle wallpaper and window covering special orders in a more efficient, cost-effective, and convenient manner for customers.

Pricing Strategy

Home Depot stressed its commitment to "Everyday Low Pricing." This concept meant across-the-board lower prices and fewer deep-cutting sales. To ensure this, Home Depot employed professional shoppers to check competitors' prices regularly.

One of the major reasons that Home Depot was able to undercut the competition by as much as 25% was a dependable relationship with its suppliers. The company conducted business with approximately 5,700 vendors, the majority of which were manufacturers. A confidential survey of manufacturers conducted by Shapiro and Associates found that Home Depot was "far and away the most demanding of customers." Home Depot was most vocal about holding to shipping dates. Manufacturers agreed that increased sales volume had offset concessions made to Home Depot.

Products

A typical Home Depot store stocked approximately 40,000 to 50,000 products, including variations in color and size. The products included different kinds of building materials, home improvement products, and lawn and garden supplies. In addition, Home Depot stores offered installation services for many products. Each store carried a wide selection of quality and nationally advertised brand name merchandise. The contribution of each product group was as follows.[26]

	Percentage of Sales		
Product Group	Year Ending February 1, 1998	Year Ending February 2, 1997	Year Ending January 28, 1996
Plumbing, heating, lighting, and electrical supplies	27.1%	27.4%	27.7%
Building materials, lumber, floor, and wall coverings	34.2	34.0	33.9
Hardware and tools	13.5	13.4	13.2
Season and specialty items	14.8	14.7	14.8
Paint and others	10.4	10.5	10.4
	100.0%	100.0%	100.0%

The company sourced its store merchandise from approximately 5,700 vendors worldwide, and no single vendor accounted for more than 5% of total purchases.

Average Store Profile

According to Bob Evans in the Store Planning Division of Home Depot, all of the stores were company-owned, not franchised, and most were freestanding, built to Home Depot's standards.

Home Depot owned 74% of its buildings in 1997, leasing the remainder. Marcus planned to increase that percentage. In 1989, the company had owned only about 40% of its stores. Although the company preferred locations surrounded by shopping centers, Marcus insisted that the company was not interested in being attached to a shopping center or mall. Stores were placed in suburban areas populated by members of the Home Depot target market. Ownership provided Home Depot with greater operational control and flexibility, generally lower occupancy loss, and certain other economic advantages. Construction time depended on site conditions, special local requirements, and related factors. According to Evans, depending on "if we have to move a mountain, fill a canyon, level a forest, or how many gopher turtles are in the ground that we have to relocate," building a store can take up to a year.

Current building standards were 108,000 square feet for each store itself and 16,000 to 28,000 square feet of outside selling space for the garden department. Stores did vary, however, because the company "will make the store fit the land," and many of the original stores were located in leased strip-center space. Home Depot had increased its average store size from about 97,000 to 108,000 square feet, with an additional 20,000 to 28,000 square feet of outside (garden) selling space. The average weighted sales per square foot was $406, $398, $390, $404, and $398 for 1997, 1996, 1995, 1994, and 1993, respectively. The weighted average weekly sales per operational store was $829,000; $803,000; $787,000; $802,000; and $764,000 for 1997, 1996, 1995, 1994, and 1993, respectively. Although Marcus would like to see stores averaging 120,000 square feet, Evans said that "the hundred [thousand square-foot size] is what we're building most of [sic]." Some stores had thousands of customers a week and "just get too crowded," according to Evans. Marcus had estimated that "in some cases, we have 25,000 to 30,000 people walking through a store per week."

Because of the large number of customers, older stores were being gradually remodeled or replaced with new ones to add room for new merchandise, to increase selling space for what is already there, and sometimes even to add more walking room on the inside—and more parking space.

Because merchandising and inventory were centrally organized, product mix varied slightly from store to store. Each, however, sported the Home Depot look: warehouse style shelves, wide concrete-floored aisles, end-displays pushing sale items, and the ever-present orange banners indicating the store's departments. Most stores had banners on each aisle to help customers locate what they're looking for. Regional purchasing departments were used to keep the stores well stocked and were preferred to a single, strong corporate department "since home improvement materials needed in the Southwest would differ somewhat from those needed in the Northeast."

Information Systems

Each store was equipped with a computerized point-of-sale system, electronic bar code scanning system, and a UNIX server. Management believed these systems provided efficient customer check-out (with an approximately 90% rate of scannable products), store-based inventory management, rapid order replenishment, labor planning support, and item movement information. Faster registers as well as a new check approval system and a new receipt format had expedited transactions. To better serve the increasing number of customers applying for credit, the charge card approval process time had been reduced to less than 30 seconds. Store information was communicated to the Store Support Center's computers via a land-based frame relay network. These computers provided corporate, financial, merchandising, and other back-office function support.

The company was continuously assessing and upgrading its information systems to support its growth, reduce and control costs, and enable better decision making. The company continued to realize greater efficiency as a result of its electronic data interchange (EDI) program. Most of the company's highest volume vendors were participating in the EDI program. A paperless system, EDI electronically processed orders from buying offices to vendors, alerted the stores when the merchandise was to arrive, and transmitted invoice data from the vendors and motor carriers to the Store Support Center. In addition, during fiscal 1997 the company continued to develop new computer systems to facilitate and improve product order replenishment in Home Depot stores.[27]

The Year 2000 Problem

The company was currently addressing a universal situation commonly referred to as the "year 2000 problem." The year 2000 problem related to the inability of certain computer software programs to properly recognize and process date-sensitive information relative to the year 2000 and beyond. During fiscal 1997, the company developed a plan to devote the necessary resources to identify and modify systems impacted by the year 2000 problem, or implement new systems to become year 2000 compliant in a timely manner. The cost of executing this plan was not expected to have a material impact on the company's results of operations or financial condition. In addition, the company had contacted its major suppliers and vendors to ensure their awareness of the year 2000 problem. If the company, its suppliers, or vendors were unable to resolve issues related to the year 2000 on a timely basis, it could result in a material financial risk.[28]

HUMAN RESOURCES[29]

Home Depot was noted for its progressive human resources policies, which emphasized the importance of the individual to the success of the company's operations.

Recruitment/Selection

Throughout its entire recruiting process, Home Depot looked for people who shared a commitment to excellence. Also, management recognized that having the right number of people, in the right jobs, at the right time was critical. Employee population varied greatly among stores, depending on store size, sales volume, and the season of the year. In the winter, a store could have had fewer than 75 employees and in the spring would add another 25 to 40 employees. Some of the larger northeastern stores had as many as 280 employees. Full-time employees filled approximately 90% of the positions.

When a store first opened, it attracted applications through advertisements in local newspapers and trade journals such as *Home Center News*. A new store would usually receive several thousand applications. When seasonal workers and replacements were needed, help-wanted signs were displayed at store entrances. Walk-in candidates were another source, and applications were available at the customer service desk at all times. There was no formal program to encourage employees to refer their friends for employment. At the management level, the company preferred to hire people at the Assistant Manager level, requiring them to work their way up to store Manager and beyond. Historically the company often hired outside talent for senior positions. Now that the company had grown, Home Depot believed that, whenever possible, executives should come up through the ranks, although management from the outside was occasionally brought in. To support its growing infrastructure, Steven Messana served as Senior Vice President for Human Resources.

Interviews were scheduled one per day per week; however, if someone with trade experience applied, an on-the-spot interview might be conducted. "Trade" experience included retail, construction, do-it-yourself, or hardware. The company tended to look for older people who brought a high level of knowledge and maturity to the position. In addition to related experience, Home Depot looked for people with a stable work history who had a positive attitude, were excited, outgoing, and hard workers.

The selection process included preemployment tests (honesty, math, and drugs). The stores displayed signs in the windows that said that anyone who used drugs need not apply. Interviews were conducted with three or four people—an initial qualifier, the Administrative Assistant in operations, an Assistant Manager, and the store Manager. Reference checks were completed prior to a job offer. More in-depth background checks (financial, criminal) were conducted on management-level candidates.

To help ensure that Home Depot selected the best qualified people, during fiscal 1997 the company designed a proprietary automated system for identifying the best candidates for store sales associate positions. This system, which had been through extensive validation testing, screened candidates for competencies and characteristics inherent to Home Depot's best sales associates. The company planned to use this system to evaluate additional positions in the future.

Retention

Employee turnover varied from store to store. In the first year of operations, turnover could run 60% to 70% but would fall below 30% in future years. The company's goal was to reduce turnover to below 20%. The major causes of turnover were students who returned to school, employees who were terminated for poor performance, and tradespeople who considered Home Depot an interim position (often returning to their trade for a position paying as much as $50,000 per year). Very few people left the organization looking for "greener pastures" in the retail industry.

Career development was formally addressed during semiannual performance reviews, with goals and development plans mutually set by employees and managers. The company was committed to promotions from within and had a formal job-posting program. Vacancy lists were prepared at the regional level and distributed to the stores. Store managers were promoted from within. Affirmative action plans were used to increase female and minority representation.

Compensation

Employees were paid a straight salary. Bernard Marcus said, "The day I'm laid out dead with an apple in my mouth is the day we'll pay commissions. If you pay commissions, you imply that the small customer isn't worth anything." Most management-level employees were eligible for bonuses that were based on such factors as a store's return on assets and sales versus budget. Assistant Managers could receive up to 25% of their base salary in bonuses, and store Managers could earn up to 50% if their stores' performance warranted. Store managers could earn $50,000 to $120,000. The typical employee earned $10 to $14 per hour.

During fiscal year 1988, the company established a leveraged Employee Stock Ownership Plan (ESOP), covering substantially all full-time employees. In 1989, the company made its initial contribution to the ESOP of $6 million, which represented about $0.05 per share. Fully funded by the company, the ESOP was established to provide additional retirement security for the employees, while simultaneously reducing taxable income and discouraging hostile takeover attempts. At February 1, 1998, the ESOP held a total of 10,161,272 shares of the company's common stock in trust for plan participants. The company made annual contributions to the ESOP at the discretion of the Board of Directors. All employees eligible for the ESOP were entitled to receive a substantial portion of their annual salary in profit sharing. Tim Sparks, 31, who started out loading customers' cars in the lot at the age of 19 and managed a store in Jacksonville, Florida, said, "My father was a peanut farmer in Alabama. Dirt poor. Where else could a son go from that to being a millionaire?"

Recognition programs emphasized good customer service, increased sales, safety, cost savings, and length of service. Badges, cash awards, and other prizes were distributed in monthly group meetings.

Communication was the key by which Home Depot perpetuated its culture and retained its people. That culture included an environment in which employees were happy and where they felt productive and secure. The company sold employees on their role in Home Depot's success—they were giving the company a return on its assets. The environment avoided bureaucracy, was informal and intense, and encouraged honesty and risk taking. Each store maintained a strong open-door policy, and a Manager would spend two or three hours discussing a concern with an employee.

Top management was equally accessible to employees through frequent visits to the stores. An in-house TV broadcast, "Breakfast with Bernie and Arthur," was held quarterly. Impromptu questions were solicited from the employees. Department Managers met with employees weekly to provide new information and solicit feedback. Worker opinions also mattered at the top. When the company planned to open on New Year's Day, the employees voted to close and prevailed. When the company wrote a check-out training manual, a store cashier from Jacksonville helped write it. Internal sales charts were posted on bulletin boards so that employees would know how their store compared with others in the area.

Training

Home Depot believed that knowledgeable salespeople were one of the keys to the company's success and spent a great deal of time training them to "bleed orange." Callers to the home office found that corporate executives spent most of their time in the stores training employees. "We teach from the top down, and those who can't teach don't become executives," said one top executive. Training costs to open a new store were about $400,000 to $500,000.

Regular employees went through both formal and on-the-job training. Classes were held on product knowledge (giving the employee "total product knowledge . . . including all the skills a trade person might have"); merchandising concepts, and salesmanship (so that they could be sure that a customer has available, and would purchase, everything needed to complete a project); time management; personnel matters; safety and security; and how to interpret the company's various internally generated reports.

Each new employee was required to go through a rigorous week-long orientation, which introduced new hires to Home Depot's culture. To ensure that employees were convinced of the company's commitment, Bernard Marcus, Arthur Blank, and Ron Brill conducted many of the management training sessions. New employees were then paired with experienced associates in the stores to gain first-hand knowledge of customer service and general store operations. They trained an average of four weeks before working on their own. Even then, when there were no other customers in the department, newer employees would watch more experienced employees interact with customers to learn more about products, sales, and customer service. Employees were cross-trained to work in various departments, and even the cashiers learned how to work the sales floor.

The Home Depot Television Network allowed the company to disseminate policies and philosophies, product upgrades, and so on. With the ability to target special or mass audiences, the training possibilities were endless. The fact that the programs were broadcast live, with telephone call-ins, enhanced their immediacy and made interaction possible.

According to management, Home Depot's training programs were key to arming associates with the knowledge they needed to serve customers. During fiscal 1997, the company made several changes to its human resources and training programs to prepare for and support Home Depot's future growth plans. To address the unique growth needs of its divisions, new human resources officers were responsible for areas such as recruiting, staffing, employee relations, and management development in their divisions. They were also responsible for areas such as recruiting, staffing, employee relations and management development in their divisions. They were also responsible for implementing the store training programs that take entry-level sales associates from the basics to becoming project experts and, ultimately, masters in their respective departments.

Employees

As of the end of January 1998, the company employed approximately 125,000 people, of whom approximately 7,900 were salaried and the remainder were on an hourly basis. Approximately 76% of the company's employees were employed on a full-time basis. There were no unions. The company has never suffered a work stoppage.

Industry and Competitors

RETAIL BUILDING AND SUPPLY INDUSTRY

The retail building supply industry was moving rapidly from one characterized by small, independently run establishments to one dominated by regional and national chains of vast superstores. Home Depot developed the concept of the all-in-one discount warehouse home improvement superstore, designed to be all things to all people. The main rival to Home Depot was Lowe's, which had been replacing its older, smaller stores with new superstores. Other companies in the industry were facing the challenge by reconfiguring their stores and by targeting niche segments, but some were being forced to close stores in the face of increased competition.

In 1997, the retail building supply industry showed mixed results. The stronger companies (Home Depot and Lowe's) got stronger, and the weak struggled. The largest two operators, Lowe's and Home Depot, extended their dominance, especially in the Do-It-Yourself (DIY) segment of the market (see **Exhibit 5**). Small regional operators such as Grossman in the Northeast were liquidated.

In 1997, Leonard Green & Partners bought out both Hechinger and Builders Square, formerly owned and started by Kmart, in an effort to turn the two struggling chains into one profitable chain.[30]

The retail building supply industry served two distinct clients—the professional building contractor and the DIY homeowner. The DIY customer had grown in importance over the past few years. Home Depot's main competitors were:

- **Hechinger** was located in the mid-Atlantic states and was recently acquired by Leonard Green & Partners. Hechinger had financial problems for several years before it was acquired.

- **Lowe's** was located in 22 states with 442 stores and had recently moved into large metropolitan areas—Dallas and Atlanta. The company had developed regional distribution centers to better serve its growing markets. Lowe's 1997 sales were estimated to be $10,190,000,000 and second to Home Depot with sales of $24,156,000,000 for 1997 (see **Exhibit 5**).

- **BMC** was renamed Building Materials Holding Corporation. The company had over 50 stores in 10 western states and was focusing on the professional/contractor market segment.

- **Hughes Supply** had 310 stores, principally in Florida, Georgia, and other southeastern states. The 1997 sales were estimated to be $1,810,000,000. The company made 13 acquisitions in 1996, which added about $340 million to its sales base. After these acquisitions, Hughes was in new territories—upper New York and California. The company focused on the professional/contractor market segment (see **Exhibit 5**).

- **Wolohan Lumber** had 58 stores located in Illinois, Indiana, Kentucky, Ohio, and Wisconsin. The company strategy was to focus on the professional/contractor market segment. The 1997 sales were estimated to be $425,000,000 (see **Exhibit 5**).

Exhibit 5 provides a summary of the key information on these companies.

The industry did not have barriers to entry in the form of patents or special technology. There was a major learning curve on efficiently managing a 100,000-square-foot store. The superstore warehouses tried to serve all market segments, but they had become increasingly consumer-oriented. Because of this, smaller competitors were focusing their strategies on the professional constructor segment of the market.[31]

Exhibit 5
Retail Building Supply Industry

A. Competitors

Company	Number of Stores 2000-2002	1997	Sales in Millions ($) 2000-2002	1998	1997	1996
Homebase, Inc.	105	84	$ 1,900.0	$ 1,500.0	$ 1,465.0	$ 1,448.8
Home Depot	**1,050**	**624**	**54,000.0**	**30,100.0**	**24,600.0**	**19,535.0**
Hughes Supply	362	310	2,500.0	1,960.0	1,810.0	1,516.1
Lowe's Companies	620	442	17,500.0	11,900.0	10,190.0	8,600.2
Woloham Lumber	75	58	620.0	410.0	425.0	430.4
Industry totals and averages			$66,000.0	$42,000.0	$38,050.0	$33,287.0

Company	Net Profit in Millions ($) 2000-2002	1998	1997	1996	Net Profit Margins % 2000-2002	1998	1997	1996
Homebase, Inc.	$ 38.0	$ 24.0	$ 21.0	$ 21.4	2.0%	1.6%	1.4%	1.5%
Home Depot	**2,790.0**	**1,455.0**	**1,160.0**	**937.7**	**5.2**	**4.8**	**4.7**	**4.8**
Hughes Supply	70.0	50.0	40.0	32.5	—	2.6	2.2	2.1
Lowe's Companies	645.0	405.0	345.0	292.2	3.7	3.4	3.4	3.4
Woloham Lumber	12.5	6.0	5.0	6.7	—	1.5	1.2	1.6
Industry totals and averages	$2,310.0	$1,510.0	$1,330.0	$1,287.2	3.6%	3.6%	3.5%	3.5%

B. Industry Indicators

	2000-2002	1998	1997	1996
Sales in millions ($)	$66,000.0	$38,050.0	$33,287.0	$27,152.0
Number of stores	2,350	1,980	1,860	1,922
Net profits in millions ($)	$ 2,310.0	$ 1,510.0	$ 1,330.0	$ 1,287.0
Net profit margin (%)	3.6%	3.6%	3.5%	3.6%

Note: Figures for 1998–2002 are projections.

Source: Value Line, January 16, 1998, pp. 884, 888–892.

Eagle Hardware & Garden of Seattle, Washington, operated 24 home improvement stores. Its founder, David Heerensperger, viewed Home Depot's entry into Seattle as a "war." He said, "They are aiming for us, but we're a thorn in their side. Eagle is the first home center they haven't completely run over."[32]

Eagle's stores averaged 128,000 square feet, compared to Home Depot's 103,000 square feet. Eagle offered other services, namely, a custom-design section, free chain-cutting station, fences, and an idea center where customers could watch videotapes and live demonstrations of home improvement techniques. Heerensperger began preparing for Home Depot's onslaught six years ago. He came up with a design for new stores that were brighter and more elegant than Home Depot's stores. He took into consideration women customers by reducing rack-type displays.[33] Eagle was building the largest stores in the industry in the West Coast and Northwest markets. Eagle planned to maintain a managed-growth strategy.

According to Ronald Pastore, real estate expert, "Between 1992 and 1994, 55% of all new retail square footage was built by big-box retailers (like Wal-Mart and Home Depot)."[34] In 1994, these retailers accounted for 80% of all new stores.

There had been a rampant construction of new retail space over the past 20 years. The supply of retail space nationally was 19 square feet for each person, and this was more than double the level of 20 years ago. The supply had far exceeded the population in growth for the same period. Christopher Niehaus, real estate investment banker, said, "That number is too high. It needs to come down."[35] He predicts that the discount sector is heading for the "'biggest shake-out' in retailing because of overbuilding."[36] Don McCrory, real estate expert, said, "Our question is, if the big-box tenants go out of business, what do you do with the enormous box?"[37]

THE PROFESSIONAL BUSINESS SEGMENT[38]

Early in fiscal 1997, Home Depot began a formal study of the professional business customer market. The findings of this study clearly indicated that there were many opportunities to grow its presence in the pro market that fit within the company's core business. The study also indicated that many of these opportunities could be captured inside its stores.

Estimated professional business customer sales across all channels in the United States were approximately $265 billion in 1997, substantially higher than the $100 billion Do-It-Yourself market. Excluding the heavy industrial sector, the majority of which was outside Home Depot's core business, the pro market opportunities for the company totaled approximately $215 billion. Home Depot's share of this market was less than 4% in 1998.

The initial focus for growing sales in the professional market was on the professional business customer who already shopped in Home Depot stores, but also made purchases at other retail and wholesale outlets. By listening and responding to his or her needs, the company intended to make Home Depot this customer's supplier of choice.

Late in fiscal 1997, Home Depot began a test in its stores in the Austin, Texas, market designed to increase professional customer sales while continuing to serve the strong and growing Do-It-Yourself customer market.

The test in Austin included incremental associates primarily responsible for serving and building relationships with the professional business customer. Professional business customers in these stores were assisted at a Pro Service Desk to more quickly meet their product and service needs. In addition, customized services, such as enhanced ordering and credit programs and a menu of product delivery options were available to the pro customer. The test, which was to be expanded to additional stores in fiscal 1998, was helping the company to successfully develop and refine its formula for serving the professional business customer inside its stores.

There were other ways to reach the professional customer, too. During fiscal 1997, Home Depot distributed its ProBook™ professional equipment and supply catalog to professional customers across North America. The ProBook contained over 15,000 products from its stores

Exhibit 6

Professional Business Customer Market

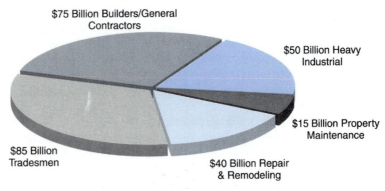

Source: The Home Depot, *1997 Annual Report*, p. 4.

chosen especially for facility maintenance managers and the building trades. In addition, the company's longer term growth initiatives included exploring opportunities for serving professional customers with more specialized needs through distribution channels outside Home Depot stores.

The total professional business customer market was estimated to be $265 billion in 1997 (see **Exhibit 6**). The heavy industry with an estimated $50 billion in sales was treated as a separate sector. The professional business market ($215 billion) consisted of four subsectors: (1) tradesmen ($85 billion), (2) builders/general contractors ($75 billion), (3) repair and remodeling ($40 billion), and (4) property maintenance ($15 billion).

In 1996, the $215 billion professional business customer target market can be further separated by volume of expenditures. The typical Home Depot pro customer was a repair and remodel professional who purchased up to $200,000 of products annually, but tended to buy less than 10% of this amount from the company. The Home Depot planned to capture more of this customer's sales by responding to the distinct product and service needs of this professional. (See **Exhibit 7**.)

The company purchased Maintenance Warehouse as part of Home Depot's strategy to penetrate the professional market.

Exhibit 7

U.S. Professional Business Customer Profile—$215 Billion Total Target Market

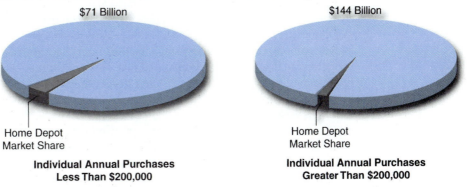

Source: The Home Depot, Inc., *1997 Annual Report*, p. 7.

DO-IT-YOURSELF (DIY) INDUSTRY

The Home Depot occupied the number one position in the DIY industry with sales of $24.1 billion, more than twice its nearest competitor, Lowe's Companies. Home Depot had approximately 24% market share. Clearly the $100 billion industry was extremely fragmented. The industry remained dominated by small- to mid-sized stores, with only a handful of the top retailers operating stores about 100,000 square feet in size. The trend was clearly moving in the direction of bigger stores, however, as companies such as Lowe's and Home Depot enjoyed success with their large-store formats. As these companies continued to roll out their superstores at an aggressive rate, industry analysts expected the industry to consolidate over time, with the major retailers gaining their share at the expense of the smaller, less efficient DIY chains.

Home Depot was regarded as the premier operator in the DIY industry. The following list shows the six top competitors in 1996. However, based on competitors' announced expansion plans, Home Depot believed that the level of direct competition would increase to 22% of its total store base. The largest and most formidable foe facing Home Depot was the North Carolina chain, Lowe's. Since 1995, Lowe's had gone into more direct competition with Home Depot in more cities as both companies expanded. As Home Depot added more stores in Lowe's market, analysts believed that Lowe's could face increased margin pressure. Lowe's had been able to maintain its profit margin at 3.4% since 1996. Because Home Depot was more geographically dispersed than Lowe's and had a more balanced portfolio of stores, Home Depot was better able to be price competitive in these markets. The top six retail building supply companies in 1996 were as follows:

1. Home Depot
2. Lowe's Companies
3. Payless Cashways
4. Builders Square
5. Menard's
6. Hechinger's

Other competitors were Sutherland Lumber, Wickes Lumber, and Scotty's.

America's do-it-yourselfers spent approximately $100 billion in home improvement products in 1997, up more than 6% from the previous year. This all-important customer group was getting larger in number and more confident and capable to take on home improvement projects every year. In addition, demographic changes were taking place within the Do-It-Yourself customer group that had important implications for the future of the home improvement industry. Home Depot was positioning itself to continue to grow its share of this industry segment as these changes took place.

The rate of home ownership in the United States continued to grow as first-time buyers entered the housing market at a rapid pace and baby-boomers moved in force to more expensive homes and second homes. During 1997, existing single-family home sales reached their highest point on record, and new single-family home sales showed strong increases from the previous year. In addition, studies showed that the average age of existing homes continued to increase, and people were staying in their homes later in life. All of these trends enhanced Home Depot's opportunities to add new stores across North America as well as to increase sales in its existing stores.[39]

The $100 billion DIY market breaks into five market segments: (1) lumber and building materials, (2) lawn and garden, (3) plumbing and electrical, (4) hardware and tools, (5) paint and supplies, and (6) hard surface flooring. **Exhibit 8** shows their market segment shares.

HomeBase, formerly HomeClub, was acquired by Zayre Corporation, a discount retail chain, in 1986. It was consolidated with BJ's Wholesale Club and renamed Waban, Inc. Zayre spun the company off to shareholders on June 14, 1989. In July 1997, Waban spun off the com-

Exhibit 8

$100 Billion Do-It-Yourself Market

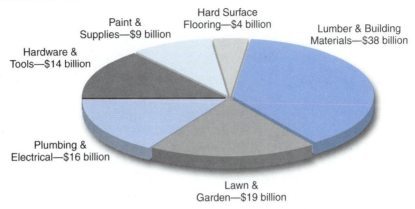

Source: The Home Depot, Inc., *1997 Annual Report*, p. 8.

pany to shareholders and was renamed HomeBase. In 1997, the company had to write off $27 million to cover store closings. The company was changing its strategy from being defensive to a more aggressive stance, such as accelerating store remodeling program. Analysts said, "This is an extremely competitive industry, and profit margins are small, so only the well-managed companies prosper and survive." He went on to say, "Look at Kmart; the company could not effectively manage Builders Square. They had to sell it off."[39]

Finance

The 10-year performance of Home Depot in selected key growth financial indicators is as follows:

	Compound Growth Rate	
Financial Indicator	**5-year Annual**	**10-year Annual**
Net sales	27.6%	32.5%
Earnings before taxes	28.3	35.6
Net earnings	27.5	36.6
Total assets	23.4	35.8
Working capital	19.9	33.6
Merchandise inventory	30.8	32.8
Net property and equipment	32.3	38.8
Long-term debt	9.1	37.9
Shareholders' equity	25.2	36.3
Capital expenditures	28.4	32.8
Number of stores	23.9	23.6
Average total company weekly sales	27.6	32.5
Number of customer transactions	23.8	27.6
Average sale per transaction	$3.00	$3.70
Weighted average sales per square foot	$1.00	$4.40

These compound growth rates had provided Home Depot shareholders with 48 consecutive quarters of growth in sales and earnings. Fiscal year (FY) 1997 was from February 3, 1997, to February 1, 1998.

Exhibit 9 shows that the average sale per transaction had increased from $33.92 in 1990 to $43.63 in 1997, or 28.7%. During the same period, average total company weekly sales had

Exhibit 9

Ten-Year Selected Financial and Operating Highlights: Home Depot, Inc.
(Dollar amounts in thousands, except where noted)

	5-Year Annual Compound Growth Rate	10-Year Annual Compound Growth Rate	Fiscal Years[3]									
			1997	1996[1]	1995	1994	1993	1992	1991	1990[1]	1989	1988
Statement of Earnings Data												
Net sales	27.6%	32.5%	$24,156	$19,535	$15,470	$12,477	$9,239	$7,148	$5,137	$3,815	$2,759	$2,000
Net sales increase—%	—	—	23.7	26.3	24.0	35.0	29.2	39.2	34.6	38.3	38.0	37.6
Earnings before taxes[2]	28.3	35.6	2,002	1,535	1,195	980	737	576	396	260	182	126
Net earnings[2]	27.5	38.6	1,224	938	732	605	457	363	249	163	112	77
Net earnings increase—%[2]	—	—	30.5	28.2	21.0	32.2	26.1	45.6	52.5	46.0	45.9	41.9
Diluted earnings per share ($)[2,3,4,5]	24.4	31.0	1.64	1.29	1.02	0.88	0.67	0.55	0.39	0.30	0.21	0.15
Diluted earnings per share increase—%[2]	—	—	27.1	26.5	15.9	31.3	21.8	41.0	30.0	42.9	40.0	36.4
Weighted average number of common shares outstanding assuming dilution[3,4]	1.7	4.6	762	732	717	714	711	699	662	608	574	519
Gross margin—% of sales			28.1	27.8	27.7	27.9	27.7	27.6	28.1	27.9	27.8	27.0
Store selling and operating—% of sales			17.8	18.0	18.0	17.8	17.6	17.4	18.1	18.2	18.3	17.8
Pre-opening expense—% of sales			0.3	0.3	0.4	0.4	0.4	0.4	0.3	0.4	0.3	0.4
General and administrative expense—% of sales			1.7	1.7	1.7	1.8	2.0	2.1	2.3	2.4	2.5	2.4
Net interest income (expense)—% of sales			—	0.1	0.1	(0.1)	0.3	0.4	0.3	(0.1)	(0.1)	(0.1)
Earnings before taxes—% of sales[2]			8.3	7.9	7.7	7.8	8.0	8.1	7.7	6.8	6.6	6.3
Net earnings—% of sales[2]			5.1	4.8	4.7	4.8	5.0	5.1	4.8	4.3	4.1	3.8
Balance Sheet Data and Financial Ratios												
Total assets	23.4%	35.8%	$11,229	$9,342	$7,354	$5,778	$4,701	$3,932	$2,510	$1,640	$1,118	$699
Working capital	19.9	33.6	2,004	1,867	1,255	919	994	807	624	301	274	143
Merchandise inventories	30.8	32.8	3,602	2,708	2,180	1,749	1,293	940	662	509	381	294
Net property and equipment	32.3	38.8	6,509	5,437	4,461	3,397	2,371	1,608	1,255	879	514	332
Long-term debt	9.1	37.9	1,303	1,247	720	983	874	844	271	531	303	108
Shareholders' equity	25.2	36.3	7,098	5,955	4,988	3,442	2,814	2,304	1,691	683	512	383
Book value per share ($)[3]	22.9	31.2	9.70	8.26	6.97	5.06	4.17	3.46	2.67	1.29	0.99	0.75
Long-term debt to equity—%			18.4	20.9	14.4	28.6	31.1	36.6	16.0	77.7	59.1	28.1
Current ratio			1.82:1	2.01:1	1.89:1	1.76:1	2.02:1	2.07:1	2.17:1	1.73:1	1.94:1	1.74:1
Inventory turnover			5.4x	5.6x	5.5x	5.7x	5.9x	6.3x	6.1x	6.0x	5.9x	5.8x
Return on beginning equity—%			19.5	18.8	21.3	21.5	19.9	21.5	36.5	31.9	29.2	23.9

Statement of Cash Flows Data

Depreciation and amortization	32.4%	38.8%	$283	$232	$181	$130	$90	$70	$52	$34	$21	$15
Capital expenditures	28.4	32.8	1,525	1,248	1,308	1,220	900	437	432	400	205	105
Cash dividends per share ($)[3]	28.6	43.5	0.19	0.15	0.13	0.10	0.07	0.05	0.04	0.02	0.02	0.01
Store Data[6]												
Number of stores	23.9%	23.6%	624	512	423	340	264	214	174	145	118	96
Number of states	16.6	17.8	41	38	31	28	23	19	15	12	12	10
Number of Canadian provinces	—	—	4	3	3	3	—	—	—	—	—	—
Square footage at year-end	26.0	26.8	66	54	44	35	26	21	16	13	10	8
Increase in square footage (%)	—	—	23.1	21.6	26.3	33.2	26.3	26.8	24.1	27.4	26.9	33.4
Average square footage per store (in thousands)	1.6	2.6	106	105	105	103	100	98	95	92	88	86
Store Sales and Other Data[6]												
Comparable stores sales increase—%[7]	—	—	7	7	3	8	7	15	11	10	13	13
Average total company weekly sales	27.6%	32.5%	$465	$369	$298	$240	$178	$137	$99	$72	$53	$38
Weighted average weekly sales per operating store (in thousands)	2.7	7.1	829	803	787	802	764	724	633	566	515	464
Weighted average sales per square foot ($)[7]	1.0	4.4	406	398	390	404	398	387	348	322	303	282
Number of customer transactions	23.8	27.6	550	464	370	302	236	189	146	112	84	64
Average sale per transaction ($)	3.0	3.7	43.63	42.09	41.78	41.29	39.13	37.72	35.13	33.92	32.65	31.13
Number of associates at year end (actual)	26.2	29.9	124,400	98,100	80,800	67,300	50,600	38,900	28,000	21,500	17,500	13,000

Notes:
1. Fiscal years 1996 and 1990 consisted of 53 weeks; all other years reported consisted of 52 weeks.
2. Excludes the effect of the $104 million nonrecurring charge in fiscal 1997.
3. All share and per-share data have been adjusted for a 3-for-2 stock split on July 3, 1997.
4. Share and per-share data have been restated for the adoption of SFAS 128 "Earnings per Share."
5. Diluted earnings per share for fiscal 1997, including the $104 million nonrecurring charge, were $1.55.
6. Excludes Maintenance Warehouse and National Blind and Wallpaper Factory.
7. Adjusted to reflect the first 52 weeks of the 53-week fiscal years in 1996 and 1990.

Source: Home Depot, Inc. *1997 Annual Report,* first page fold-out.

increased from $72,000 to $465,000, or 545.8%. The weighted average weekly sales per operating store had increased from $566,000 in 1990 to $829,000 in 1997, or 464%. The weighted average sale per square foot had increased from $322 in 1990 to $406 in 1997, or 25.5%.

If someone had invested $1,000 on June 30, 1982, in Home Depot, on June 28, 1997, the investment would have been worth $152,479. Only two stocks surpassed Home Depot's performance: Keane ($321,022) and Mark IV Industries ($269,265).

Exhibits 9, **10**, and **11** provide the company's 10-year selected financial and operating income highlights, consolidated statement of earnings, and balance sheet.

Exhibit 10

Consolidated Statement of Earnings: Home Depot, Inc.
(Dollar amounts in millions, except per share data)

Fiscal Year Ending[1]	February 1, 1998	February 2, 1997	January 28, 1996
Net sales	$24,156	$19,535	$15,470
Cost of merchandise sold	17,375	14,101	11,184
Gross profit	6,781	5,434	4,286
Operating expenses			
Selling and store operating	4,287	3,521	2,784
Pre-opening	65	55	52
General and administrative	413	324	270
Nonrecurring charge	104	—	—
Total operating expenses	4,869	3,900	3,106
Operating income	1,912	1,534	1,180
Interest income (expense)			
Interest and investment income	44	25	19
Interest expense	(42)	(16)	(4)
Interest, net	2	9	15
Minority interest	(16)	(8)	—
Earnings before income taxes	1,898	1,535	1,195
Income taxes	738	597	463
Net earnings	$1,160	$938	$732
Basic earnings per share	$1.59	$1.30	$1.03
Weighted average number of common shares outstanding	729	719	709
Diluted earnings per share	$1.55	$1.29	$1.02
Weighted average number of common shares outstanding assuming dilution	762	732	717

Notes:
1. Fiscal year (FY) 1997 was February 3, 1997 to February 1, 1998.
2. Notes were deleted.

Source: Home Depot, Inc. *1997 Annual Report*, p. 21.

Exhibit 2
Balance Sheet: Gardner Distributing Co.

Year Ending December 31	1998	1997	1996	1995	1994
Assets					
Accounts receivable	$ 693	$ 595	$ 996	$1,077	$ 860
Inventory					
Iams—Billings	289	276	250	181	141
Spokane	184	199	280	168	165
Pet supplies	290	447	572	589	497
Lawn and garden	222	192	267	229	372
Total inventory	985	1,114	1,369	1,167	1,175
Current assets	1,678	1,709	2,365	2,244	2,035
Fixed assets (net)	74	195	208	203	46
Total assets	$1,752	$1,904	$2,573	$2,447	$2,081
Liabilities and equity					
Accounts payable	$ 287	$ 230	$ 335	$ 290	$ 186
Notes payable					
Bank		71	300	200	120
Officers[1]	383	618	826	568	294
Other	55	60	97	102	102
Current liabilities	725	979	1,558	1,160	702
Long-term liabilities		78	212	327	358
Stockholders' equity					
Common stock	104	104	104	104	104
Retained earnings					
C corporation	82	82	82	82	82
S corporation	245	257	257	257	257
Accumulated S corp. net income	596	404	360	517	578
Total equity	1,027	847	803	960	1,021
Total liabilities and shareholders' equity	$1,752	$1,904	$2,573	$2,447	$2,081

Note:
1. The note payable to officers is money that Butch lent the corporation.

Source: Company records.

Most Iams distributors sold only Iams products. Gardner was the only Iams distributor that sold lawn and garden supplies. The pet supplies and lawn and garden businesses gave Gardner options and created synergies.

As Butch headed for the baggage claim area, he met Rob Chouinard, General Manager of Gardner Distributing Co. (**Exhibit 3**). Rob had worked for Colgate-Palmolive and Supervalu. Supervalu was a large wholesaler and retailer of grocery products. When he arrived in December 1996, there was no strategic planning and minimal budgeting. By 1998, the team was operating to a budget. By 1999, the team had developed a statement of purpose, mission, and objectives (**Exhibit 4**). The team members worked well together and shared common expectations about the business, but they had yet to define Gardner's strategies.

Rob's greeting was enthusiastic. In March 1999, he and Butch had attended the Iams distributors meeting in Cancun, Mexico; and Rob had fond memories of that trip. Rob was also enthusiastic because he had been getting calls from other distributors. They had heard from Iams about Gardner's success in opening new accounts, and they wanted to know how Gardner was doing it.

At the Iams meeting in Cancun, Butch had told the Iams people, "We are aggressively looking for more volume in our region. We also want to expand our business territory, and we hope Iams will support this." The Iams people were very receptive to these comments.

Background

Butch grew up in the small town of Aberdeen, South Dakota. He graduated from the University of North Dakota in 1967 with a degree in marketing, and he worked part-time for Sears, Roebuck and Co. while he was at the university. His father was the store manager for Sears in Aberdeen.

After graduation, Butch went to work for Sears as a management trainee in Grand Forks, North Dakota. In 1970, he was promoted to Assistant Store Manager in Butte, Montana. In 1972, he was promoted to Merchandise Manager in Great Falls, Montana. By 1976, the Sears culture was changing. The store managers were losing their autonomy, so Butch left Sears. As he explained, "I was single. I toured the western U.S. for three months and sort of lived like a hobo."

Exhibit 3

Gardner Distributing Co., Organizational Chart and Biographies

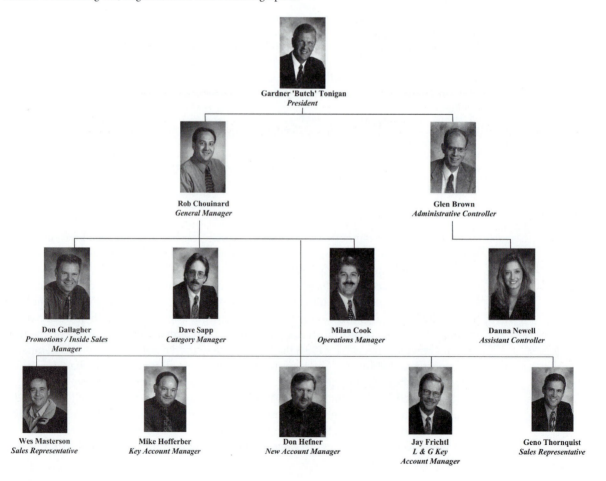

Exhibit 3

Gardner Distributing Co., Organizational Chart and Biographies (*continued*)

Butch Tonigan – President

After 14 years in management with Sears, Roebuck & Co. followed by several years as a managing partner of a predecessor company, Graham and Ross, Butch started Gardner Distributing Co. with the aid of "smoke and mirrors" and very little liquid capital. Butch graduated from the University of North Dakota in 1967 with a Bachelor of Science in Business Administration (BSBA) degree. Butch likes to think of himself as a good judge of people and recognizes that his employees are the most valuable asset of Gardner Distributing Co. Focusing his efforts on developing the capacity of the company's management and capital resources in preparation for triggering Gardner's next growth stage is his primary current objective, all while planning for the succession of his company.

Rob Chouinard – General Manager

Hired in 1996 as a key candidate in the company's succession planning strategy, Rob brings to the company those leadership skills important to directing the company's management toward meeting the company's strategic plans. Rob graduated from Eastern Montana College in 1987 while learning the distribution business from the bottom up by working part-time in the Supervalu distribution warehouse. In 1988 Rob began his career as a Territory Sales Manager for Colgate Palmolive followed by a position as a Sales Consultant for the Supervalu Corporation. In 1990 Rob was promoted to a management position with Supervalu as a Category Buyer, which led to yet another promotion to that of Category Merchandise Manager. Rob works closely with Butch as President and Glen as Administrative Controller developing and executing the company's strategic plans.

Glen Brown – Administrative Controller

Glen truly created his own position with Gardner. Joining Gardner in 1988 while still a student at Eastern Montana College, Glen juggled his work and student time to earn a Bachelor of Science in Business Administration (BSBA) degree in 1990 and then go on to receive his CPA certification in 1994. Starting as an invoicing clerk, Glen proved his prowess at number crunching and computer skills to advance to Controller and eventually to Administrative Controller. Self taught in RPG computer programming, Glen creates in-house software to provide the company management with information to excel at their work. Glen works closely with Butch as President and Rob as General Manager in developing company strategy and planning.

Milan Cook – Operations Manager

A graduate of North Dakota State University with an Urban Forestry Degree, it didn't take long for Milan to realize that there weren't many trees in North Dakota. Milan started his career as a warehouse manager in a lawn and garden distributor's branch warehouse in Fargo, ND and then moved to Montana as a retail store manager of a lawn and garden, and pet supplies center. Recruited by Gardner in 1994 to manage its new branch distribution facility in Spokane, WA, Milan quickly demonstrated his ability to squeeze a dime out of a nickel and his management and personnel skills. In the newly created position as Operations Manager, Milan is transferring to the Billings headquarters where he will be responsible for meeting and exceeding vendor and industry standards of the company's operations in its present and future locations.

Don Gallagher – Promotions / Inside Sales Manager

Approaching the challenge of his job with the "can do" attitude from his training as an Army MP, Don supervises the inside sales team and develops marketing programs to grow incremental sales for the company. Joining Gardner in 1995, it didn't take long to see Don's "take no enemies" approach. Don works with vendors, inside and outside sales people and buyers to develop and administer sales promotions that work.

Danna Newell – Assistant Controller

The newest member to the Gardner team, Danna joined the company in 1998. After earning a degree in Finance from the University of Montana in 1991, Danna continued balancing a full-time job and school to pass the uniform CPA exam soon after joining Gardner. Danna quickly demonstrated her ability to collect past due receivables while keeping satisfied customers. As the Assistant Controller, Danna is training in all functions of the Administrative Controller position including accounting and information systems.

(*continued*)

Exhibit 3

Gardner Distributing Co., Organizational Chart and Biographies (*continued*)

Dave Sapp – Category Manager

Determined never to lose a sale because of an out of stock, Dave is responsible for buying more than 200 vendor lines and maintaining the best fill-rate and inventory turn-over ratios in our industries and throughout the history of the company. Dave joined Gardner in 1984 serving his stint in the warehouse and delivery before his promotion as a category buyer. With a Forestry Technician degree from the Montana University System and his customer service skills, Dave is responsible for much of the company's sales growth of professional horticultural products to commercial growers.

Jay Frichtl – L & G Key Account Manager

A true professional sales consultant to the professional horticultural customer, Jay joined Gardner in 1990 after over nine years experience in retail lawn and garden center sales where he supervised the landscape division and learned garden center, nursery, and greenhouse management. Jay has been largely responsible for Gardner's dominating the horticulture grower and garden center market in the geographical markets Gardner serves.

Don Hefner – New Account Manager

Considered "bullet-proof" in his ability to win over new customers, Don's position as New Account Manager focuses nearly exclusively on adding retail distribution for the company by seeking and opening new independent retail dealers. Don grew up in retail sales, selling pet supplies before he was old enough to drive a car and going on to work in retail pet supplies sales until he joined Gardner in 1987. He draws on his retail experience, enthusiasm, and warm personality necessary to develop the rapport with a retail owner or manager and open them as a Gardner account.

Mike Hofferber – Key Account Manager

Mike and Butch first became acquainted when Butch hired Mike as a high school student to work his first job as part-time sales at Sears. Their careers parted and Mike went on to earn a B. S. degree in Business Management from Montana State University in 1978. Mike was hired as a Key Account Manager to assist Gardner's entry into serving the grocery, drug, and hardware multiple store chain accounts. Mike's past employment and management experience with Osco Drug, Coast to Coast Hardware, and over 10 years as Retail Sales Manager and General Manager of a regional food brokerage firm bring the insight, skills and knowledge required to enter this class of retailer customer trade.

Geno Thornquist – Sales Representative

Give him a program to sell and he draws on his previous training as a Pitney Bowes salesman to close the sale time after time. Geno is responsible for developing sales growth with assigned existing customers by increasing the number of product lines they purchase from Gardner and by creating enthusiasm for, and the execution of sales promotions and programs. After earning his BSBA degree from Eastern Montana College in 1991, Geno gained valuable experience in merchandising, promotional execution, and retail shelf management as a Retail Account Manager for Hershey. Geno joined Gardner in 1993 as a sales representative based out of Billings for Iams pet foods and pet supplies.

Wes Masterson – Sales Representative

Wes joined Gardner in 1994 as a distributor sales representative responsible for the new Iams territory served by the Spokane, WA branch facility. Graduating with both a B. A. in Business Administration and a B. A. in Psychology from the University of Washington, Wes has the educational background to assist the future growth of Gardner. With his sales and merchandising training from previous employment as a sales representative with Gallo Wine, Wes demonstrates his training by repeatedly gaining choice merchandise positioning and incremental shelf space in retail dealer locations. Never afraid to get his hands dirty, Wes is quick to reset retail shelf racks and displays to grow visibility and retail shelf position.

Exhibit 4

Purpose, Mission, and Objectives, May 1999: Gardner Distributing Co.

Purpose: The purpose of Gardner Distributing Co. is the distribution of premium pet foods, pet supplies, and horticultural supplies while improving the economic well being and quality of life of all stakeholders.

Mission: We will be the leading regional marketing and distributing company of premium pet foods, pet supplies, and horticultural products.

We will achieve a growth rate consistent with the expectations of our vendors and shareholders.

We will continuously improve employee performance and company processes.

We will earn the loyalty of our customers by consistently meeting their performance expectations.

We will create a sense of pride and long-term commitment for everyone associated with our company.

In all we do, we will be guided by the following principles:

    We will act professionally and with integrity in all circumstances.
    We will honor the intent of all our commitments, contracts, and governing laws.
    We will build an environment of individual trust and respect.
    We will provide an environment for employees to realize professional growth and development.
    We will expect and reward excellence in all aspects of our business.

Objectives:

1. Achieve a minimum 15% increase each year in cash flow from company operations.

   (This objective was set in 1999. The reductions in accounts receivable and incentory increased Gardner's cash flow from operations, but this was a 1-time-only increase. As of May 1999, Gardner had not established a measure of historical cash flows against which it could measure the future cash flow performance of the management team.)

2. Expand retail distribution by achieving no less than a 15% annual increase each year in the number of A, B, and C class customer locations.

3. Develop and maintain to the satisfaction of the stockholder, contingent plans of action which assure the company's future viability is independent of any individual owner, employee, vendor, or customer.

Source: Company records.

In 1976, Butch returned to Great Falls and went to work for Graham and Ross, a family-owned retailer and wholesaler of farm supplies, pet supplies, and lawn and garden supplies in Montana and Wyoming. The company's sales grew from $2.5 million in 1976 to $4.6 million in 1980. Butch received stock options and purchased stock in the company. In 1980, he had the opportunity to spin off the pet supplies and lawn and garden businesses.

In the spin off, Butch received a small warehouse in Billings that was worth $40,000. Billings was growing much faster than Great Falls, so Butch decided to locate in Billings. Graham and Ross's Norwest Bank manager in Great Falls introduced Butch to the Norwest manager in Billings. As Butch explained:

> In August 1980, I presented my business plan. I asked for a $330,000 credit line to finance sales of $1 million. I had $64,000 in inventory and trucks, but it was the $40,000 of real estate that the bank wanted for collateral. The oil and gas industry was booming in Billings. The banks had money, and I got the $330,000.
>
> I used the loan to finance the spring lawn and garden inventory. We moved into the warehouse with six employees from Graham and Ross and started ordering merchandise for the spring. Then Ortho, my largest supplier, decided my financing wasn't good enough. They jerked the contract and gave it to another local distributor. Then I faced the possibility of losing other lines. Ortho was the key player in lawn and garden and an entry into many of the retailers. If you didn't have Ortho, you weren't a full-line lawn and garden distributor.

My plan was unraveling, but I didn't tell the bank. I convinced an Ortho distributor in Denver to sell to me at 3% over cost, and for five years I supplied my retailers with Ortho products from Denver and kept my business alive. Ortho gained market coverage with no credit risk. The other local distributor didn't like it. In 1986, they gave up the Ortho line, and we got it.

We plugged along in the first six years. In 1980, my equity was $104,000. The first year we lost $100,000. The second year we lost $30,000. I was afraid the bank was going to call the loan; but they stuck with me. In the third year, we made a profit. It was the sixth year before my equity was back where I started!

In 1987, we were in the right place at the right time. We got the Iams distributorship for eastern Montana. Iams had a distributor in Missoula that went belly-up, and they came to us. In the spring of 1994, we took on the distribution of Iams products in northern Idaho and eastern Washington with a warehouse and eight people in Spokane.

By 1996, I was thinking about reducing my time involvement in the company. But I felt that Iams seemed to want distributors who managed the day-to-day operations, 50 weeks a year. A lot of guys were trying to do succession planning. They were nervous about it because Iams didn't seem to reinforce it. Yet all of us realized that for the survival of our companies that was what we had to do. We didn't want to be managing our businesses day-to-day all of our lives.

Everyone always came to me with his or her problems. What should I do about the flat tire on the truck? Can I have Friday off? What should I do about this customer's order? I loved to make these decisions, but it was becoming overwhelming, so I began to appoint some managers from within the company. Then, my biggest problem was learning to let the managers solve the problems!

In 1996, I decided to hire a Chief Operating Officer. I developed a case study of the company and asked the best candidates to analyze it. A local man talked to my customers and employees and carefully analyzed the business. I offered him the job in December, but he didn't want to move until after his March bonus was paid.

Then, as I thought about it, I realized I was not ready to make the move. In March, I withdrew the offer. I was nervous about turning the business over to someone else. Ironically, Rob had joined us in December 1996; and it was soon evident that he had the leadership skills we needed. I feel so fortunate! Rob came in and earned the respect of the employees!

In May 1999, Gardner's Iams territory spanned a sparsely settled area of rolling grasslands and mountains that included Montana (population 860,000), northern Idaho, eastern Washington, northern Wyoming, and western North and South Dakota. The other two businesses operated within this area. Billings was the largest city in Montana, and the largest city in the market was Spokane, Washington (population 200,000). The Continental Divide bisected the region. The summers were warm and pleasant, but the winters could be formidable, with temperatures ranging to 30 or 50 degrees below zero Fahrenheit. In the winter of 1996–1997, Billings received a record snowfall of 8.5 feet. As Butch noted:

Part of our success is attributable to the fact that we operate in a part of the country that until recently hasn't been attractive to the competition. Most distributors don't like it here, it's too vast, there's too little business, and it's too hard to operate.

Gardner leased a 41,000-square-foot warehouse in Billings and a small warehouse in Spokane. The office facilities in the Billings warehouse were functional. The atmosphere was friendly and casual. The people were variously dressed—shorts, bib overalls, jeans, sports casual, and the occasional tie. The fixed assets included office and warehouse equipment. The trucks were leased from a company owned by Butch. The statements, "Gardner Distributing Co." and "Providing Products for Plants & Pets" were positioned prominently on the sides of the trailers.

Gardner was Subchapter S corporation. Originally, it was incorporated as an S corporation. It was then changed to a C corporation and then back to an S corporation. Butch later attributed the firm's stint as a C corporation to bad advice.

An S corporation did not pay income taxes. Pre-tax net income and losses were allocated to the shareowners based on the number of shares held. The pre-tax net income was taxed as personal income in the year it was incurred, even if it was not withdrawn from the business. Thus, the pre-tax net income from Gardner was combined with Butch's personal income and losses from other sources, and the total was taxed at the personal income tax rates.

Societal Forces

Gardner operated in two industries: (1) the pet supplies industry and (2) the lawn and garden industry. Several societal forces were affecting these industries in North America:

1. In 1999, economic conditions were supporting business development and consumer spending. The economy was growing; interest rates, unemployment rates, and inflation rates were relatively low; and personal discretionary income was rising. However, acquisitions, alliances, and mergers on a global scale were leading to consolidation and economies of scale in many industries.

2. Computer and communications technology was enabling small firms to compete effectively against larger rivals.

3. The rising level of discretionary income was enabling people to give their pets a better lifestyle and to improve their lawns and gardens.

4. The pet industry and particularly the lawn and garden industry were benefiting from the increasing number of retired people who had the money and the time to have and to pamper pets, lawns, and gardens. Marketing strategies recognized pets, lawns, and gardens created rewarding experiences for retired people.

5. The premium pet food industry was benefiting from people's desire to eat healthier foods, which carried over into pet foods. Some people wanted their pets to eat healthier foods too, and the premium pet food industry promoted an increasing awareness of this need.

6. Environmental consciousness had established a "green is good" mentality that benefited the lawn and garden industry. People expected firms and institutions to attractively landscape their facilities.

7. The increasing number of institutions that catered to retired people (e.g., country clubs, golf courses, retirement communities, etc.) were expected to be attractively landscaped and appropriately maintained.

8. Innovations in gardening (e.g., hydroponics, personal greenhouses, patio gardens, etc.) were increasing the size of the lawn and garden market.

9. The "1-stop-shopping" strategies of the mass retailers were making lawn and garden products more accessible to buyers. Special trips to a nursery were often unnecessary and more expensive than going to, say, a Wal-Mart or Home Depot.

The Competition

PREMIUM PET FOOD MANUFACTURERS

The Iams Company was a private firm located in Dayton, Ohio. Iams's annual sales were about $800 million. Iams targeted the premium dog and cat food markets with its Iams and Eukanuba (pronounced "you-caa-new-baa") brands. Iams had about 27% of the market.

Iams's primary competitor was Hill's Pet Nutrition, Inc., with its Science Diet brand. Hill's had about 33% of the market. Hill's was a subsidiary of Colgate-Palmolive. The Ralston Purina Co., the leader in mass-market pet-food sales, had about 15% of the premium pet food business. There were about six smaller competitors in the premium market. While all of the competitors promoted their products, Hill's in particular invested heavily in developing early brand loyalty among veterinarian students; and the retail profit margins on premium pet foods were significant. As Parker-Pope (1997) explained:

> *Borrowing a page from pharmaceuticals companies, which routinely woo doctors to prescribe their drugs, Hill's has spent a generation cultivating its professional following. It spends hundreds of thousands of dollars a year funding university research and nutrition courses at every one of the 27 U.S. veterinary colleges. Once in practice, vets who sell Science Diet and other premium foods directly from their offices pocket profits of as much as 40%.*

Iams had tried to establish its brands in the veterinary schools but had been only moderately successful. Butch felt that Hill's did a better job of marketing its "prescription diet" specialty products to veterinarians than Iams did.

Iams and Hill's monitored each other's actions closely. Hill's owned its distribution channels. Iams's policy was to use independent distributors, but its actions suggested that this policy might be changing. Iams had recently acquired the operations of a bankrupt distributor in California and Arizona. Iams's operating expenses in these operations were less than 10% of sales, and it was pressuring its distributors to reduce their operating expenses accordingly. However, as Rob pointed out, "The figures [operating expenses] weren't directly comparable."

Iams's strategy toward its distributors was unclear. As Butch explained:

> *This is the mystery to us. We [the distributors] sensed that Iams sees a further consolidation of distributors, and maybe Iams is purposely leaving an environment where only the strongest will survive. I'm not sure we know where they're going. The market is changing so fast.*

PET FOOD & PET SUPPLIES RETAILERS

The competition in premium pet foods and pet supplies was intensifying. For example, in Gardner's market, PETsMART, a specialty retailer of premium pet foods and animal supplies, was opening stores in Billings and Missoula, Montana. PETCO, a similar competitor, was opening a store in Great Falls, Montana. Both companies had recently opened stores in Spokane, Washington.

Iams sold direct to the "national accounts" (e.g., PETsMART and PETCO), and its distributors were paid a delivery fee to deliver the products. The national accounts were large-volume accounts, and there were no associated sales expenses for Gardner. So in this sense the accounts were attractive. However, Iams's sales to PETsMART and PETCO in Montana would reduce Gardner's gross profit percentage in the Iams business because the PETsMART and PETCO sales were low-margin volumes. Moreover, the entry of the specialty retailers was expected to reduce the number of independent pet stores who were currently Gardner's relatively higher-margin Iams customers. The margin on Iams sales was generally lower than in pet supplies and lawn and garden.

The independent pet store faced increasing competition from the specialty retailers—also known as "big box" stores—and the mass merchandisers (e.g., Wal-Mart was the largest pet food retailer). The independent pet store averaged 1,000–3,000 square feet and carried 1,000 to 2,000 stock keeping units (SKUs). The specialty retailers carried 10,000 to 12,000 SKUs. The mass merchandisers carried about 500 high-volume SKUs.

PETsMART—"where pets are family"—had about 550 stores in the U.S., Canada, and the U.K. Its stores averaged 25,000 square feet and carried about 12,000 SKUs. Pet owners were encouraged to shop with their pets. PETsMART was aggressively acquiring competitors and opening new stores.

PETCO had over 482 stores in 37 states and the District of Columbia. Most of its stores averaged 13,000 square feet, carried more than 10,000 SKUs, and were located in sites coanchored by strong consumer-oriented retailers. PETCO was also aggressively acquiring competitors and opening new stores.

PETsMART and PETCO were the largest survivors of a decade of consolidation in the pet supplies industry. Both companies had experienced difficulties absorbing some of their acquisitions; and by May 1999, their common shares were trading well below their 1996–1997 highs.

LAWN AND GARDEN RETAILERS

In the lawn and garden industry, independent retailers, such as flower and gift retailers and nurseries, specialty retailers, and mass merchandisers sold lawn and garden supplies. The buyers included individuals and organizations, such as golf courses, government agencies, hospitals, landscaping firms, and universities.

CENTRAL GARDEN & PET

Central Garden & Pet was Gardner's primary competitor and the leading U.S. distributor of lawn and garden and pet supplies. It offered 45,000 brand-name products from 1,000 manufacturers to mass merchants, warehouse clubs, nurseries, and grocery store chains through its 41 distribution centers and affiliated distributors. About 32% of its revenues came from sales of the Solaris Group's Ortho, Round-Up, and Green Sweep lawn products. (In 1994, Gardner once again lost the Ortho line when Ortho signed a national contract with Central Garden & Pet.)

Gardner's Operations Strategy

By 1996, it was apparent that the company's financial performance was slipping; and Butch and his managers were groping for an explanation. As Butch explained:

> We'd been going along for 16 years making our numbers and growing about as fast as I could afford to. Suddenly, we were leveling out. We had to find out what forces were driving us. We had to find out what was going to work for us in the future.

Gardner's information system provided some of the answers. It was developed by Glen Brown, the administrative controller, and it was used to manage accounts payable and receivable, billing, the general ledger (i.e., income statements, balance sheets, and cash flow statements), inventory, order entry, payroll, purchasing, and warehousing. EDI (electronic data interchange) was used for credit checks and some supplier transactions.

As the system came online in 1997, Butch was surprised at the response of his employees:

> It was amazing! As people realized they could access information, they'd download it to their PCs from the mainframe and use it to help them manage their part of the business. They became empowered, and they loved it!

Most of the North American Iams distributors (about 25 in early 1999) participated in an annual data exchange that was facilitated by an independent firm. The data exchange gave Butch benchmark data, but they were aggregated, so the identity of the distributors was unknown (**Exhibits 5** and **6**). The data reflected a median sales level of $14 million and a median return on assets of 22% (i.e., pre-tax profit divided by total assets). Given the time lags inherent in data collection and dissemination, the data were from the 1996–1997 period.

ACCOUNTS RECEIVABLE

By early 1997, accounts receivable were under scrutiny. Gardner's billing cycle closed on the 25th of each month so all credit sales from the 26th of one month through the 25th of the next month were due on the 10th of the following month. Thus, purchases on the 26th of the prior

Exhibit 5

Survey Sample, Common-Size Income Statement (percent)

	Median[1]
Total net sales	100.0
Cost of goods sold	81.4
Gross profit	18.6
Operating expenses	
Wages	5.5
Salaries—owners	0.8
Payroll taxes, benefits, etc.	1.0
Total labor	8.6
Advertising and promotion	0.4
Bad debts	0.1
Building rent	0.9
Depreciation and amortization	0.6
Freight	0.1
Insurance	0.4
Legal and professional fees	0.2
Office and postage expense	0.3
Repairs and maintenance	0.4
Supplies (warehouse & delivery)	0.2
Taxes and licenses	0.2
Telephone and utilities	0.4
Travel and entertainment	0.3
Delivery truck expense (rental, fuel, maintenance)	1.2
Other	0.2
Total operating expenses	15.7
Operating profit	3.0
Interest expense	0.2
Other income	0.1
Net income before taxes	2.9

Note:

1. Due to the proprietary nature of the data, the data are approximate and generally representative of the 1996–1997 period. Median values do not add to 100%.

Source: Company records.

month were outstanding for 45 days; purchases on the 25th of the current month were outstanding for 15 days. If people paid on the 10th, the average age of the receivables would be 30 days. Glen charted the collections and found they peaked around the 13th—extending the receivables by 10%.

Glen also monitored the seasonal pattern in receivables and aged them. The receivables ranged from a high of 40 days in April and May to a low of 25–30 days in July. On the average, 24% of the receivables were 30–90+ days in arrears. Given his knowledge of other distributors' operations, Butch knew that Gardner's credit terms were relatively liberal. The benchmark data showed accounts receivable averaging 30.2% of current assets (**Exhibit 6**). Gardner's accounts receivable were a significantly higher proportion of current assets (e.g., 42% in 1996). Butch was concerned that reducing the availability of credit would reduce sales, but the

Exhibit 6

Survey Sample, Common-Size Balance Sheet (percent)

	Median[1]
Current assets	
Accounts receivable	30.2%
Inventory	42.1
Prepaid expenses, etc.	0.8
Total current assets	84.1
Fixed assets	
Buildings	0.0
Furniture, fixtures, and equipment	27.0
Leasehold improvements	0.6
(−) Accumulated depreciation	−14.8
Total fixed assets	13.2
Other assets	1.7
Total assets	100.0%
Liabilities and shareholders' equity	
Accounts payable	17.6%
Accrued liabilities	3.0
Notes payable	2.3
Other current liabilities	1.0
Total current liabilities	43.4
Long-term debt (less current portion)	10.5
Total liabilities	58.3
Shareholders' equity	
Common stock	0.4
Retained earnings	36.4
Total shareholders' equity	41.7
Total liabilities and shareholders' equity	100.0%

Note:
1. Due to the proprietary nature of the data, the data are approximate and generally representative of the 1996–1997 period. Median values do not add to 100%.

Source: Company records.

reduction in net income had reduced the cash flow from operations. With cash flows contracting, Butch had to act. As Glen explained:

> We implemented delivery-to-delivery terms. The customer pays the driver for the prior week's delivery before the new delivery is off-loaded. This avoids delays for mail time, and it gives us closer control over the customer because we can hold the delivery hostage. There are still some delays because the driver may be on the road for a week, and chains with multiple stores and central disbursement won't pay until they receive the invoice from the store.

INVENTORY

In early 1997, inventory levels also came under scrutiny. As Rob explained:

> Iams sets the buying configurations. They tell me where to buy from, what kinds of configurations to buy in, and things like that. It's not a problem. The Iams inventory turns quickly.
>   When I arrived, we carried about 10,000 items in pet supplies. When the items were ranked in descending order of sales, we found the top 1,000 items accounted for 67% of the sales and

*32% of the inventory value [**Exhibit 7**]. The last 3,500 items accounted for 34% of the inventory and 1% of the sales. We set aggressive targets, closed out a lot of inventory, and freed up a lot of cash.*

The strategy is to limit the number of lines and optimize the SKUs. The pet retailers need to carry products that turn quicker, or they won't be competitive with PETsMART and PETCO.

When I started, the average fill rate in pet supplies was 82%. Now we're at 92 to 94% in pet. (The fill rate was the average percent of customers' orders that was filled at the time the orders were placed.) As we shrink our SKUs, we may be able to raise the fill rate. On Iams it is 99%, and our lawn and garden fill rate is 96 to 97%.

NOTES PAYABLE AND LONG-TERM LIABILITIES

In 1997, action was also taken to reduce notes payable and long-term liabilities. By October 1998, the debt/equity ratios had improved. As Glen stated, "We want to be positioned to take advantage of the opportunities."

TRUCKING AND WAREHOUSE EQUIPMENT

In April 1999, the management team decided to move Milan Cook, the Spokane branch manager, to Billings and make him Operations Manager for all of Gardner's operations. Rob in particular felt this was an important move and noted, "When Milan was in Spokane, we didn't have any problems! Milan took care of things. Milan is extremely important to the future of this company." As Milan explained:

I'll be taking some of the day-to-day work off Rob, so he can concentrate on marketing. We need to develop a real efficient warehouse and order picking system. I also need to get a program going for buying new trucks and replacing warehouse equipment.

Exhibit 7

Comparison of April 8, 1997, Inventory and January–March Sales for Pet Supplies: Gardner Distributing Co.

Item Ranking Descending Order of Sales	Sales	Percent of Sales %	Inventory	Percent of Inventory %
0–1000	$315,959	67	$174,364	32
1001–1500	46,612	10	40,264	7
1501–2000	31,533	7	28,756	5
2001–2500	23,547	5	24,955	5
2501–3000	17,348	4	23,035	4
3001–3500	9,502	2	20,619	4
3501–4000	8,898	2	21,415	4
4001–4500	7,052	1	15,642	3
4501–5000	5,358	1	13,720	2
5001–8491	6,902	1	185,749	34
Totals	$472,711	100	$548,519	100

Additional Closeout Items	Sales		Inventory	
2,634	$ 20,348		$132,970	

Source: Company records.

GARDNER'S MARKETING STRATEGY

In the early 1990s, Iams began to take over the marketing and sales for the distributors' high-volume accounts. Gardner turned over 31 accounts (42% of its Iams business) and reduced its staff. It delivered the product, but the gross profit percentage was much lower than on the smaller Iams accounts. The role of the distributor changed accordingly. As Butch explained:

> Recently, I visited three distributors' operations. They sold only Iams products. Their warehouse and delivery operations were very efficient. There was very little sales, service, or marketing.
>
> What I like best is the buying and selling. Even when I was a kid, I was buying and selling things. Dad would bring home old lawn mowers he'd taken in on trade at Sears; and I'd clean them up, paint them, and get them running good. Then, I'd take them door-to-door and sell them. When I was in high school, I'd buy and sell cars. I don't like the office work. I like to be out in the field finding business opportunities!

In 1996, Gardner segmented its customers by contribution to gross profit (**Exhibit 8**) and, as Butch explained, focused on four issues:

> How can we get more products into each store? How can we increase our share of each store's purchases? How do we grow each customer's business? How do we grow our customer base?
>
> We separated our customer accounts into four categories according to each account's annual contribution to gross profit. Then, we identified about 250 key accounts with potential for growth, given their resources and attitudes. A key account might be a C account, but we'd treat them as a B account to help them grow.
>
> It was costing us about $100 to make a sales call. We couldn't afford to call on a C or D account, so inside sales serviced them by telephone. C accounts that had the potential to become B accounts within one year were serviced by outside sales. (Inside sales people operated from Gardner's office. Outside sales people traveled the region and called on existing and potential customers.) We're finding that the big accounts are getting bigger and the small accounts are holding their own or getting smaller, and we can't change the small account mentality.
>
> We have five outside sales people. We assigned them 40 to 50 accounts and are holding them accountable for the growth of those accounts. The inside sales people are also accountable for their accounts.
>
> We have other customers that are not regular customers; but they are key accounts, for example, a nursery that needs a new green house or a landscaper that is putting in a golf course.
>
> Most of our customers don't know how to stock their stores. They don't have good inventory controls. They can't identify their best-selling items. And their floor and shelf space management concepts are rudimentary. It's scary! But it also creates an opportunity for us. We are becoming more of a consultant to our customers, and this may help us promote our products and build our customer base.

Exhibit 8

Classification of Customer Accounts: Gardner Distributing Co.

Customer Accounts	Annual Contribution To Gross Profit	Personal Sales Contacts
A (40)	$15,000–$100,000	Two–four personal visits/month
B (93)	$ 5,000–$ 14,999	One–two personal visits/month
C (202)	$ 1,000–$ 4,999	One telephone call/week
D (162)	$<1,000	Two+ telephone calls/month

Source: Company records.

In September 1998, Butch hired a key account manager, Mike Hofferber, to develop large volume accounts through the central purchasing operations of multistore businesses. Heretofore, the strategy had been to sell to one store at a time. Mike had the knowledge and interpersonal skills to bundle and sell multiple products and lines (e.g., in lawn and garden) to knowledgeable buyers.

Mike arrived in November 1998. He began his career in retail management with OSCO Drug after college, and he worked for OSCO for six years. During this time, he worked with Gardner who was supplying Ortho to the OSCO store. After that, he managed a Coast-to-Coast store in Billings for three years. Then, he worked for a food broker for 11 years where he worked with clients such as Albertsons, Buttreys, Smiths, and Supervalu. As he explained in May 1999:

> I sold to Rob when he was at Supervalu. He contacted me in the summer of 1998. Gardner didn't have the know-how to develop the drug, hardware, and mass customers. The goal was to make Gardner the everyday supplier to some of the key multioutlet retailers, like Albertsons, OSCO Drug, Smiths, Costco, Tidymans, County Market, and owners of multiple Ace Hardware stores. We wanted to be the go-to distributor for these major players!
>
> In pet supplies and lawn and garden, we are putting programs in place, so we can get the stores doing the same thing. For example, the average hardware store doesn't understand pet, so we show them how to set it up. We have also designed systems for them, so they can fax their orders, and we can deliver every week.
>
> That was the real key for us at Albertsons! We put a program in front of them, and all the buyer had to do was sign his name to it. At Albertsons, we started with 12 SKUs. Now we're looking at putting whole lines in there! Robinson Pottery is a good example. We tested this in 2 of their stores in Great Falls. When this settles in, and it varies by season, we'll have about 50 SKUs in 10 stores! Next year I want Albertsons to come to us and say, "Okay, design our program for us."
>
> We have hydraulic lifts on all of our semitruck trailers. The lifts cost about $12,000 each, but this allows us to off-load pallets at the store and put them where the store wants them. The store's labor is nonexistent. Albertsons loves it!
>
> This strategy is going to put us into a hundred accounts that we weren't in a year ago, and a third of those might be Albertsons! There are so many opportunities; we physically can't get to all of them! Our trucks are full, and that's becoming a bottleneck for us, even though this is our busy time of year.
>
> Shortly after I came to Gardner, Iams made a policy change that has really helped us, although it has received a negative reaction from some of the independents and PETsMART. For years, Iams had been telling its buyers, "You'll never see Iams in grocery or mass." They built their business on this! But in the last 3 years, Iams has lost 5,000 independent accounts with the entry of PETsMART and PETCO. It's been a brutal eye-opener for Iams!
>
> We now have Iams's permission, on a case-by-case basis, to sell Iams products to "rural and upscale" [Iams's terms] grocery stores in areas where Iams products are not available. Traditionally, the premium pet foods have not been available in grocery stores. Iams still does not want to sell direct to the chains other than PETsMART and PETCO.
>
> We are one of the lead distributors doing this, and it opens up tremendous opportunities for us! Rural grocers are trying to keep people from driving to larger places to shop. For example, Columbus is 40 miles from Billings; and we now have an agreement to put Iams products in the IGA grocery in Columbus. I can open 60 grocery stores in the next 6 months! Moreover, when we go in with our Iams presentations, we do pet supplies and lawn and garden presentations too. The Iams products pull the other product lines and underwrite the cost of developing them!

Butch felt Hill's would not follow Iams's "rural and upscale" grocery store strategy. He felt Hill's and the other competitors in premium pet foods would exploit the opportunity and tell their independent pet store customers that, unlike Iams, they weren't going to abandon them!

In May 1999, a presentation of Gardner's marketing strategy to the Iams people emphasized three objectives:

1. Expand retail availability and increase product exposure to more consumers.
   a. Focus Don Hefner, our senior sales representative, on opening new independent retail accounts.
   b. Utilize the extensive talent and experience of Mike Hofferber and Rob Chouinard in grocery, hardware, and mass merchants to aggressively develop our pet supplies, premium pet foods, and lawn and garden categories in those industries.

2. Dominate retail store presence with store resets, e.g.:
   a. Planograms (product display layouts).
   b. Backtagging (This was an adhesive shelf tag in a plastic clip that was supplied by Gardner. It had an item description and a bar code for reordering.)
   c. Promotional and seasonal displays.
   d. Merchandising aids, e.g., clipstrips (cross-merchandising displays, e.g., chew toys hung in the pet food section).

3. Execute vendor and in-house promotions, e.g., Iams national promotions, Iams regional promotions, monthly sales flyers, inside sales specials, and seasonal promotions.

Expanding Gardner's Territory

On separate occasions, two U.S. distributors had told Butch they were concerned about the future of their businesses. This led Butch to think about acquiring more territory. As he explained:

> Do I make the investment and have a $35 to $45 million company in the next four to five years? Or do I take the conservative approach and be happy with a $20 million company in four to five years?
>
> One distributor has annual sales of about $12 million. Like us, they have a primary distribution center and a branch warehouse, but their business is virtually all Iams. One of their markets is dominated by national accounts with relatively low margins. So they've had to become very efficient. We might, for example, acquire a part or all of the distributor's territory.
>
> What will an acquisition do for us? I know Rob feels there may be synergies in distribution (e.g., back-haul opportunities from major markets), information systems, and management.

Butch knew the distributors did not have to sell, thus a buyer would have to pay a premium for the business. Also, Iams would have to agree to transfer the territory to Gardner.

> Iams has been reluctant to let buyers pay premiums of more than 5% of sales. Thus, I'd buy the assets at market value plus a 5% premium, which is about two years of net profit.

Butch could raise the acquisition capital. The prime rate was 8%, and he was paying 1½% over prime for working capital. Equity financing could be arranged, but Butch had reservations about this.

> The bank said they'd lend me up to $1.5 million. The next option would be a private placement through D. A. Davidson (a regional investment and underwriting firm). The problem with going public is that I'd be more of an administrator, and that doesn't appeal to me. It'd take away the freedom of entrepreneurship.

Gardner's Strategic Alternatives

In April 1999, Iams retained a consulting firm to help the distributors develop their strategic planning capabilities. Iams agreed to pay half of the cost or up to $10,000 per distributor.

Gardner was the fourth distributor selected to participate. The first meeting with the consultant was scheduled for late May. As Butch explained:

> This is an opportunity for us to get a better understanding of Iams's strategy and to build our partnership with Iams. I asked the consultants to sign a confidentiality agreement promising not to disclose the contents of our discussions with Iams. They agreed.

In May 1999, as Butch and Rob were waiting for Butch's luggage to be off-loaded from the Delta flight on his return from Puerto Vallarta, Butch said:

> I'm seriously thinking about retiring to Puerto Vallarta, maybe next year. I'm okay with our mission and objectives, but we must define our strategies. I want to be able to leave for, say, six months and be confident that there will be no unpleasant surprises when I return. Where are you at on that?

Rob said, "We're meeting on Friday morning to discuss strategy." Butch decided not to attend the meeting. The management team had performed well in his absence, and he wanted to maintain the continuity of Rob's leadership. He also felt it was time for the management team to develop and implement its own strategies. The Iams consultant would not be at the meeting.

At the Friday morning meeting, several of the managers arrived with their laptop computers, giving them easy access to the corporate data. As the meeting proceeded, it was apparent that there were various views of how Gardner should position itself for the future. Rob and Glen were on performance-based compensation plans, and other members of the management team looked forward to being on similar plans. Hence, some of the views were fairly forcefully stated. Typical of many such meetings, the ideas developed spontaneously, and the managers had difficulty staying on task (**Exhibit 9**).

Just before noon Rob brought the meeting to a close with the suggestion that he and Glen develop a written statement of Gardner's strategies. The statement would be distributed to the managers before the next meeting, which was scheduled for next Friday morning. As the meeting was breaking up, Rob reiterated Butch's concerns about clearly defining the company's strategies in each of its three businesses. In response, someone noted how Butch's management style had changed in the last few years; and that triggered a parting discussion.

> I can remember how he used to react if he thought we were having fun. If he heard music or someone laughing, he'd come out of his office with a frown on his face. . . . He still has his desk from Sears. . . . His old office had a window that looked out over the warehouse floor. Over the years the racks gradually blocked off his view. . . . When we began the recent office renovation, he asked for an office with an outside view. . . .
>
>   Butch has changed from a manager to a leader. . . . His management style has become more professional. He knew what he wanted, but he needed the assistance of someone who knew how to get it done. . . . Hiring Rob was very important. . . . He's had trouble letting others manage, but that's changing. He realizes that to pass over the management he has to pass the whole thing, and that's been difficult for him to do. . . .
>
>   He isn't as involved in the day-to-day. He likes working with Don Gallagher on the catalogues and flyers. . . . He goes out and visits the customers. When the owner of the business stops to visit, that really helps us. He doesn't distinguish between the customers. He stops to talk to all of them. . . .
>
>   He's been gone more lately. When he went to Mexico recently, we didn't hear anything from him. Finally, we got an e-mail saying, "I haven't heard from you guys. Is the building still there?" . . . Even though he doesn't want to talk about the business, he wants us to say: "Everything is okay, and we're still here!" . . . We even got a call from his sister in Arizona saying, "Butch hasn't heard from you guys for a while." . . .

Exhibit 9

Excerpts from the May 1999 Meeting of Gardner's Managers to Discuss Gardner's Strategic Alternatives

The May 1999, Friday morning meeting to discuss the company's strategies was held in a meeting room at the Gardner Distributing Co.'s office in Billings, Montana. Most of Gardner's managers were at the meeting. The following excerpts are from comments made by Rob Chouinard, the General Manager; Glen Brown, the Administrative Controller; Milan Cook, the Operations Manager; and Mike Hofferber, the Key Account Manager.

Rob: Our strategy this year has been to increase our pet supplies and lawn and garden sales. We've identified classes of trade, like hardware and even farm-type operations, that we've been selling Iams to but nothing else. We've started to develop programs for them so that we can take over their pet supplies departments. We customize the programs based on the type of trade. For example, we've just set three Ace Hardware stores with Iams and pet supplies.

At the same time, Iams is allowing us to sell to "rural and upscale" grocery stores in areas where Iams products are not available. Once we are selling Iams to the store, we can afford to develop programs for the store in pet supplies and lawn and garden. Iams has to approve each store, and we have to move carefully. Our independents don't like this, and we've lost 2 accounts.

Glen: Lawn and garden is the future of our business! In green goods there are always going to be growers, retailers, and distributors. It won't be like pet supplies where there are big-box stores, like PETsMART and PETCO. Also there are the demographics—the aging of the population. Then, there is the institutional business—the golf courses, municipalities, hospitals, and schools. There's lots of market there!

Rob: It's getting so people will pay to have someone care for their lawn. Also there are patio gardens. We need to reach out to those small but growing markets.

Right now we're not selling lawn and garden products in the Spokane market. We need to think about that! Do we buy an existing competitor or develop our own operation there?

When you talk about soils and pots, there aren't a lot of dollars in that. It's hard to market. Everyone is talking about developing a Web page and selling from that, but getting the product in here would kill them. We're looking at using a Web page for order entry, product promotion, etc.

The rumor is that Scotts is buying Ortho. We deal with Scotts, so this should help us.

Mike: Central is not going to put a distribution center in Montana. There's not enough business. Central is closing its distribution center in Denver and consolidating its Salt Lake City distribution center. I doubt if anyone is looking at opening a lawn and garden business in Montana. There are better places to invest. If we do a good job, we won't give someone an opportunity to open up in Montana!

Rob: We are well positioned in Billings to service a very large area. We're also well positioned to defend it!

Glen: Our geography is an advantage! We can go north into Canada, which we haven't done. We can go east to Minneapolis, west to Seattle, and south to Denver and Salt Lake City. We can go into their markets more easily than they can come into ours. Our central location plus our experience with delivery in that geography gives us an advantage.

Mike: For us, the nearest regional distribution centers are located in Denver, Salt Lake City, Seattle, and Portland. Manufacturers prepay the freight to the distribution center. Thus, some products aren't profitable to truck into our area. This creates opportunities for us! An example is rock salt. Rock salt is heavy, and it is only worth $2 a bag. Albertsons doesn't want to ship it from Salt Lake City. If we can convince the manufacturer to prepay the freight to our warehouse, then it may be profitable for us to distribute it.

Rob: We are poised to buy more Iams geography. The opportunity may arise in the next three to five years. Buying more Iams geography is not that simple.

In February, we received a three-year commitment from Iams with two one-year renewal options. Some distributors only got one-year renewals. That's positive!

Milan: We should be able to double our size in the next five years. We can do this by expanding our territory and developing a new class of dealer, which we've started to do in lawn and garden. I think we know how to go into a new market and how to develop a class of trade that wouldn't be there initially.

(continued)

Exhibit 9

Excerpts from the May 1999 Meeting of Gardner's Managers to Discuss Gardner's Strategic Alternatives (*continued*)

Glen: For me, the issue is this: Where does the company want to be longer term? We need to grow to be a viable distributor for a manufacturer—so we can be viable with Iams, Ortho, or someone else. Iams wants to be working with players who can dominate their markets, and they are realizing that takes someone like us who has some marketing competencies in their geography and some synergies that they get from some other products rather than being just a distributor.

The Iams business creates opportunities in lawn and garden and pet supplies. Lawn and garden and pet provide a lot more gross profit! If we could fill our trucks with lawn and garden and pet supplies like we do with Iams and roll them down the road, we'd be fat cats. But we can't do that, so we need Iams.

Longer term we must get the gravy business with lawn and garden and pet supplies and get our foot in the door to those markets with Iams! Iams will get us to breakeven. From there, we can expand into the lawn and garden and pet businesses.

Milan: In the last two years we have developed real management synergy. Three years ago everyone did a little bit of something. Now, everyone knows exactly where they're at and where the company wants to be.

Glen: Rob has taken over the marketing very effectively. That's the one piece we didn't have—a proactive marketing approach. Marketing is now much more a part of our business, and that ties in with our long-term strategy of combining Iams with the lawn and garden and pet businesses.

We're also developing a second layer of management and management succession.

We're putting down infrastructure! We're looking at two questions: What do we want to be? What does it take to do that? That's a big shift. We're preparing for what we want to be. We've done a lot of that this year.

Rob: We're changing from micromanagement to empowerment! Mike created this position. He's out working with the customers getting new business! I really feel we have the pieces in place, and we're financially sound. Our year-to-date net income is over $200,000!

Glen: That's great! But our year-to-date net cash flow is only $30,000! We need to watch that too! At this time of year we're extending our receivables and building inventory. Cash flow is more important than net income.

The Future

As Butch was leaving the office that Friday, he was reflecting on Rob's recap of the meeting.

Rob's enthusiasm is contagious! He and Mike are sure pushing Iams's "rural and upscale" grocery store strategy. It's opening opportunities in premium pet foods, pet supplies, and lawn and garden supplies. But this may be a relatively short-run opportunity, given the region's vast expanse and limited population. Moreover, Hill's is going to respond! And they're a tough competitor!

Apparently, Mike also favors purchasing, selling, and distributing products that the large, multistore retailers don't want to ship from their distribution centers (e.g., rock salt). But we must also service and expand the existing customer base.

Glen is our long-range thinker. He believes the future of the business is in lawn and garden supplies. Rob says Glen wants to develop acquisition strategies, new markets and marketing strategies, and new supplier linkages (e.g., with desirable brand names).

We have a good working relationship with Iams. We need to develop the relationship and the synergies the partnership creates across our other businesses without losing our ability to pursue new opportunities! This may be our biggest challenge!

In sum, we need to decide what businesses to grow and how to grow them. We also need to examine the possibility that one or more of our businesses may have reached maturity or may be declining. If so, then we need to decide how to retrench!

Note

T. Parker-Pope, "For You, My Pet: Why the Veterinarian Really Recommends That 'Designer' Chow," *Wall Street Journal* (November 3, 1997), p. A1.

case 24

Adrenaline Air Sports: Where the Speed Limit Is 120 Miles per Hour . . . or More

Larry D. Alexander, Billy Cockrell, and Jonathan Charlton

Billy Cockrell graduated from Botetourt High School in Roanoke, Virginia, on a Saturday in June 1990. His family had a small party for him later that day at their home to celebrate his graduation. At that gathering, his uncle J. C. Cockrell approached Billy and told him of the unique present he was giving Billy for graduation. He invited Billy to come to his parachute drop zone and take a tandem parachute jump free of charge. Billy's instant response to his uncle was, "No way I'm jumping out of a plane!"

After High School

Billy did not feel mature enough to go on to college after high school. Instead, he enlisted for six years in the Navy in December 1990, six months after graduating from high school. In the Navy, he was trained and worked as a fire-control technician, radar operator, and, occasionally, search-and-rescue swimmer.

At times in the Navy, he would be out to sea on a cruise for three months at a stretch. In August 1992, he was stationed in Charleston, South Carolina. While many other sailors spent much of their spare time drinking in bars, Billy was looking for something different. One day while visiting on the telephone with his grandmother, Grosejean, she reminded him of the free tandem parachute jump that J. C., his uncle, had offered Billy two years before. This time Billy moved fast on the offer and made the jump the next Saturday at his uncle's drop zone in Greensboro, North Carolina.

Parachute industry statistics show that only a few people who take a first parachute jump ever jump again. This was not the case with Billy Cockrell. He took his second jump the very next day, on Sunday. He became hooked on parachuting and thought he would like to someday work full time at his own parachute drop zone.

Billy was transferred to various land and sea locations during his six-year Navy stint. In 1993, he was sent to San Diego, California, for three months to go through more advanced naval training. While there, he parachuted at Air Adventure, which was a fairly large drop zone operation, also located in San Diego. Billy was so enthused with his newfound sport that he recruited between 40 and 50 people to take their first jump at that drop zone.

This case was prepared by Larry D. Alexander of Virginia Tech, Billy Cockrell of Adrenaline Air Sports, and Jonathan Charlton, student at Virginia Tech. This case was edited for SMBP-9th edition. Copyright © 2002 by Larry D. Alexander. Reprinted by permission.

According to the U.S. Parachute Association, about 540,000 parachutists worldwide made 5,563,000 jumps in 1998 alone. In the United States, 317,741 people made 3,500,000, as shown in **Exhibit 1**, combined jumps in the year 2000, and 34,217 people were members of the U.S. Parachute Association (www.uspa.org), headquartered in Alexandria, Virginia, near Washington, DC.

While approximately 300,000 people in the United States took a once-in-a-lifetime jump during 2000, other parachutists made multiple jumps in just one weekend. These veterans of the sport often took up to 5 or even 10 jumps in a single day. At the extreme, Mike Zang made an amazing 500 parachute jumps in a 24-hour period in April 2001. This amounted to one jump from a Porter-type airplane at just 2,100 feet elevation every 2 minutes, 53 seconds.

A typical parachute jump by experienced jumpers can be described as follows. Four parachuters took off with a pilot in a small Cessna-type airplane. It took about 20 to 25 minutes to reach 10,000 feet, where the pilot positioned the plane so that the jumpers could parachute and maneuver themselves back to the drop zone. When ready, the parachutists opened the Cessna's passenger door and briefly stood on a step outside the plane or jumped right out from inside the plane.

Exhibit 1

U.S. Parachute Association Skydiving Statistics

Number of skydivers worldwide (last reported in 1998 by FAI):
540,000

Number of skydives worldwide (last reported in 1998 by FAI):
5,563,000

Number of people making a skydive in the U.S., 2000:
317,741 [1999: 311,511]

Number of skydives in the U.S., 2000:
3,500,000

USPA members, end of 2000:
34,217

Number of student jumps:

Student Method	2000	1999
AFF	32,410	31,775
Tandem	185,410	181,775
Static line	60,338	59,155
Total	278,158	272,705

Members by Age Group:

Age	Percentage of Members
0–29	21.0%
30–39	34.4%
40–49	25.7%
50–59	11.2%
60+	3.3%
Unknown	4.4%
	100.0%

Gender:	
Male	82.0%
Female	14.7%
Unknown	3.3%
	100.0%

Source: U.S. Parachute Association, "Skydive Stats," March 5, 2002, www.uspa.org.

The parachutist initially did a freefall—from 10,000 down to 3,000 feet—with the main chute closed. The jumper's speed quickly accelerated to about 120 miles per hour. On average, a skydiver fell the first 1,000 feet in about 10 seconds and then accelerated, falling each additional 1,000 feet in about 6 seconds. Thus, to freefall from 10,000 to 3,000 feet, it took only about 46 seconds. At 3,000 feet the jumper pulled a ripcord, which opened first the small pilot chute and then the large main parachute. At that point, the parachutist was "under canopy," slowly descending from the "adrenaline high" of freefall, enjoying the view, and pulling various steering cords to maneuver his parachute back to the drop zone landing area.

All parachute gear was required to have a separate reserve chute in case the main chute did not open or opened incorrectly. Many jumpers paid $500 or more to have an optional automatic activation device attached to their packs so that their second, or reserve, chute opened at a preset altitude. The industry was so safety conscious that all reserve chutes had to be repacked by a rigger, a professional parachute packer, every four months, even if they had not been used. This person also checked the two chutes for wear and tear and made any necessary repairs.

During freefall, some parachutists did what was called *relative work* with other parachutists before opening their parachutes. If four people were jumping together and doing relative work, they might start off in a star formation or point (all holding hands in a square with their feet farthest out), then go to a diamond for a second point, and then to a donut for a third point; if time permitted, they might form an open accordion for a fourth point.

The record number of skydivers to join hands and legs in a freefall pattern was 286 people, accomplished over Ottawa, Illinois, in 1998. These very experienced skydivers jumped out of several different planes very quickly and then joined up in one huge preplanned pattern. It was planned months in advance and rehearsed to accomplish it and to do it safely.

Other parachutists did free flying before they opened their parachutes. This was similar to the standard technique of "belly flying" except that the skydiver typically rotated through three positions: head down, feet first, and sitting. These skydivers often did relative work with other free flyers as they moved from one position to another in a choreographed plan. They might come together in a formation or spin and turn relative to each other without touching.

Free flyers going head first with their arms at their sides could at times exceed 200 miles an hour. These speeds were measured by a Pro-Track helmet computer, which calculates the jumper's statistics, such as his elevation when jumping out of the plane, time in freefall, average speed in freefall, maximum speed in freefall, total elapsed time, and altitude at which the parachute opened.

Another activity performed by a parachutist was canopy relative work. In this exercise, the parachutists opened their canopies (also called parachutes) quickly after exiting the airplane. Then they came together and hooked their feet into the lines of the parachute immediately beneath them. Thus, the parachuters were stacked on top of each other's canopy, with the top parachutist controlling the direction of all those below him. This activity was risky and was done at only a few drop zones throughout the United States, Adrenaline Air Sports not included.

Occasionally, some parachutists requested a "hop and pop" jump. This involved a shorter, and therefore cheaper airplane ride to just 3,000 or 4,000 feet. The parachutists opened their chute in a very short time after exiting the plane to test out equipment or to keep down the costs per jump.

The highest parachute jump ever made was by Captain Joseph Kittinger on August 16, 1960. He jumped using bottled oxygen from a balloon at an altitude of 102,800 feet, approximately 20 miles high. As he free-fell down past about 80,000 feet in very thin air, he was traveling in excess of 600 miles an hour. Thus, he almost became the first person to break the speed of sound barrier without flying a plane or space vehicle. He also set another record for freefalling 84,700 feet, some 16 miles, before opening his chute. As of 2002, Kittinger's records had never been broken, although recently several people had considered trying to break them.

Perhaps more amazing was the highest fall without a parachute and surviving by Vessna Vulovic on January 26, 1972. She was a stewardess on a DC-9 jet that blew up at 33,330 feet over Czechoslovakia. Everyone else on the plane died. She was thrown free of the plane, fell some six miles, hit a snow drift, and lived.

Adrenaline Air Sports Opens for Business in November 1999

In the fall of 1999, Billy Cockrell signed a five-year lease to open his Adrenaline Air Sports drop zone at Smith Mountain Lake Airport. His rent paid for a hangar, a business office, an adjacent grassy area for parachutists to land on, and rights to take off and land on an unlimited basis from the airport, which was owned and operated by Joe Borgess.

The airport had an elevation of 940 feet and was located about a half mile from the beautiful and large Smith Mountain Lake, which offered boating, sailing, water skiing, swimming, fishing, golf, and parasailing. According to one statistic, up to 10,000 boats could be found on the lake on a busy weekend day. Billy Cockrell had heard from the local realtors that 10,000 new people came to stay at the lake each week during the busy warm months.

Adrenaline Air Sports's scenic drop zone was located 35 miles southeast of Roanoke, Virginia, a city of 94,911 people that was adjacent to Salem to the west. Salem had a population of 24,747 people. Some 43 miles west of downtown Roanoke (and further west of Salem) was Blacksburg, a college town of 39,573 people. It was the home of Virginia Tech, with an enrollment of 25,000 students.

Billy started getting his drop zone under way in fall 1999. A major goal was to acquire an airplane to take jumpers up. In December 1999, he purchased a 1959 Cessna 182 for $45,000. He arranged to pay for it over a 10-year period with a loan from the Navy Credit Union, which he was eligible to borrow from as a Navy veteran. **Exhibit 2** shows Billy's first plane, parked right outside his hanger at the Smith Mountain Lake Airport.

Billy used eBay and other Internet sources to get most of the equipment he needed to start up his operation. This included helmets and jump suits, which were both fairly expensive. From a Las Vegas supplier on the Internet, he purchased two tandem chutes and two student chutes, larger-sized parachutes used by parachutists starting to jump by themselves. In all, he paid some $15,000 for most of his equipment.

As the year 2000 approached, Billy gradually prepared to open for business and waited for the warm weather in March and April, during which, he hoped, he would attract more customers. As the number of customers increased, Billy realized he needed more equipment. In May 2000, he bought a third tandem chute, and then in August a fourth one.

In calendar 2000, Adrenaline Air Sports's total sales amounted to about $90,000—a surprisingly good start for the first year of operations.

Adrenaline Air Sports in Summer 2001

The year 2001 was even better than 2000, particularly from April through October. Total sales for the year were $154,000.

Adrenaline Air Sports used part-time employees exclusively. Even Billy worked part-time for Adrenaline, even though he might average 40 hours a week. And that was on top of his regular full-time job at Luna Innovations in Blacksburg.

In addition, Billy did weekend work at the Adrenaline Air Sports drop zone. During the many bad-weather weekends from late fall to early spring, Billy often went down to his drop

Exhibit 2

Billy Cockrell's First Cessna 182 and Rented Hanger at Smith
Mountain Lake Airport

zone to get work done, even if no customers were likely to come by. Once the good weather arrived, he would put in a 40-hour weekend, beginning Friday night and ending Sunday night.

After work ended at 5 P.M. on Friday, Billy went home for a short time and then drove or flew the 70 miles to his drop zone at Smith Mountain Lake, usually arriving there between 7 and 8 P.M. He usually went first to Adrenaline's office building, which had lights, water, heat, lounge chairs, a bathroom, and some office space. As of March 2002, it also had a shower with hot and cold water, which Billy and some customers helped install. The term "customer" probably sounded strange to him because these people were fellow skydivers who were as committed to the sport as Billy.

The manifest on the computer listed all people who had reserved tandem-jump slots for Saturday or Sunday. Tandem jumps were made by the first-time parachuters hooked to experienced and certified tandem instructors, using one large canopy, or parachute.

Most of these people made reservations with Billy during the week, calling him either at his full-time job or at night at his home. Billy said that he got the most telephone calls on Mondays for parachuting the following weekend. He speculated that first-time jumpers convinced themselves and/or their friends the prior weekend to jump on something of a dare. Then they would call on Monday because if they waited beyond that day, they would often decide not to do it after all.

At Billy's office, he made sure that the various forms jumpers would have to complete were assembled. This included five pages of waivers of liability the jumpers would have to fill out before they were permitted to skydive.

Billy then went to the hangar. There was no heat in the hangar, but it did have lights. He cleaned the hangar and moved items to the wall so that parachuters could repack their chutes on the floor over the weekend or pay a packer to do it. Friday night Billy often repacked any parachutes that his customers would need for Saturday morning.

He owned eight parachutes, which he stored at Adrenaline Air Sports. In addition, some customers stored their own chutes in Billy's hangar when they were not using them. Billy's chutes included four tandem canopies, used for beginners who were attached to their instructor or tandem master, two for accelerated free fall for the next level of skydiving, and two used by just Billy himself. By late Sunday afternoon, nearly everyone was tired, so often nobody would pack these parachutes for the next weekend. Billy would therefore pack them Friday night, if necessary. He would then sleep in his office, along with any parachuting customers and/or employees who had arrived early for the weekend. During warm months, they would sleep in the hangar. Everyone slept in sleeping bags, often on air mattresses for some added comfort.

Billy usually started working on Saturday morning by 7 A.M. The manifest was again rechecked and any additional paperwork for that day's jumpers assembled. Training aids were made available. First-time tandem jumpers started arriving by 8 A.M. or soon thereafter for their 8:30 jumps. As first-time jumpers arrived, they filled out forms and paid their $189 fee. They then met their instructor, who gave them ground training, and were asked if they wanted a videotape of their jump, which cost $60. The majority of first-time jumpers purchased the videotape so that they would have a souvenir of their skydiving adventure.

Marketing

Billy used a variety of strategies to get customers to try parachuting at his drop zone. They all helped, though it was hard to pinpoint which marketing approaches were the most effective.

One very helpful advertising technique involved using 8 ½ × 11 inch posters with the headline "Skydive Adrenaline Air Sports," as shown in **Exhibit 3**. The posters contained such statements as "Skydive at Virginia's Most Scenic Skydiving Center," "Specializing in Tandem and Accelerated Freefall," and "Your SAFETY is our FIRST PRIORITY!"

At the bottom of each sheet were tear-off strips of paper that had the name of Adrenaline Air Sports, a telephone number, and a Web address. The posters were put up on bulletin boards, walls, and doors at colleges, grocery stores, strip shopping centers, and other places where likely first-time parachuters might see them. Billy also gave them to his loyal customers, asking them to put them up where they worked or near where they lived.

Exhibit 3
Paper Poster Ad with Tear-Off Phone Numbers

Another marketing strategy was advertising in the Yellow Pages of area telephone directories. Adrenaline Air Sports's ad in Verizon's November 2000 Yellow Pages for Montgomery County of Virginia, whose center was 70 miles from Billy's drop zone, read as follows:

SKYDIVE AT VIRGINIA'S MOST

SCENIC DROP ZONE

Located at Smith Mtn Lake Airport

LEARN TO SKYDIVE

WITH PROFESSIONALS

YOUR SAFETY

IS OUR #1 PRIORITY

Tandem AFF, Video

www.air-sports.com

Smith Mountain Lake . . . 296-1100

The problem with this was that since telephone directories covered such small geographic areas, a business had to spend a lot of money for ads if it was going to cover a large region. Billy paid approximately $18,000 for his numerous Yellow Pages ads per year.

Also appearing in this telephone directory were ads for two of Billy's main competitors, Skydive Orange and Skydive Virginia, both located northeast of Smith Mountain Lake and Charlottesville, approximately 140 miles away from his drop zone.

Billy had tried radio advertising briefly but never had run a television commercial. Because he had only used radio occasionally, he was not sure of its effectiveness.

Adrenaline Air Sports also placed a small monthly ad in *Parachutist: Official Publication of the United States Parachute Association.* Adrenaline's three-line monthly ad usually read as follows:

Adrenaline Air Sports/Skydive Blue Ridge

Smith Mountain Lake Airport, Moneta, 30 minutes

Southeast of Roanoke, (540) 296-1100; www.air-sports.com

Like all ads, this appeared along with six others from parachute drop zones in Virginia. Both Skydive Orange and Skydive Virginia were listed. Members of the U.S. Parachute Association automatically got this monthly magazine as part of their yearly membership dues. Over 400 drop zones were listed in it, by state and country.

Adrenaline Air Sports also had eye-catching bumper stickers. They contained one large A for both Adrenaline and Air. The stickers also said "SKYDIVE BLUE RIDGE" and gave a telephone number and Web site address. They were given out free of charge to Billy's customers, their friends, and anyone who wanted them.

For first-time parachutists, another form of advertising was the videotape they could purchase as a souvenir of their adventure. Billy was convinced that these jumpers showed their videotapes to many of their friends, helping to stimulate an interest in parachuting. The cost of the advertising was free to Adrenaline Air Sports because beginners paid $60 to get their jumps videotaped.

Tracy Harris did almost all of the skydiving photography at Adrenaline Air Sports. He was about 35 years old and ran his own construction business during the week. On the weekends, he worked part-time for Billy with his video camcorder affixed to the top of his helmet. He would go up with every first-time jumper who wanted a videotape, and exited the plane just before the jumper and his tandem instructor. Tracy would record their exit, their freefall, the opening of the parachute (also called canopy), and some of their descent. He then quickly landed so that he could record the pair when they came in for their landing.

So popular were the videotapes that of Tracy Harris's 400 jumps in 2001, about 300 were made taking videos. Since Tracy was Adrenaline's sole skydive photographer, Adrenaline could only handle one videotaping at a time.

Once Tracy finished recording one jumper's landing, he went up almost immediately in another plane with the next jumper. He stored his tapes and worked on them between jumps, on Saturday evenings and on Sundays. Billy tried to deliver the finished videotapes by the end of Sunday night, if at all possible. Often, Billy or someone else would deliver the videotape to the jumper's home on Sunday night so he or she could have it almost immediately. Billy felt that the videotape was an effective marketing tool because the proud first-time parachuter would want to show it to everyone he or she knew.

Flight Operations

Billy purchased his second Cessna 182 in April 2001 to handle the increased number of customers coming to his drop zone. Both planes were purchased with bank loans he obtained from the Navy Credit Union and a local bank in southwest Virginia. With an average purchase price in excess of $40,000, these two small, single-engine propeller planes were a major investment.

Aviation fuel was another significant cost. During 2001, he purchased 11,000 gallons of aviation fuel, which cost almost $26,000, or $2.34 a gallon. On a busy weekend, each plane would consume about $400 in aviation fuel, or one refill every three flights.

Some simple airplane maintenance Billy did on his own. For example, he replaced the oil on each plane frequently, every 25 hours. Billy felt it was a cheap investment considering the age of the planes.

However, he had a problem getting his planes maintained on a regular basis. No one at his small airport did maintenance, so his planes had to be taken elsewhere to get maintenance. He couldn't ask his three pilots to fly his planes in the middle of the week because they all had regular jobs. One day in February 2001, Billy called the airport in Harrisonburg, Virginia. He said he needed to learn to fly for his business. He got started that day, and just seven days later, he had soloed and received his pilot's license. This changed one aspect of Billy's Adrenaline Air Sports operations.

At the end of a weekend of running his drop zone, Billy often flew one of his planes back to the Virginia Tech airport in Blacksburg, near where he lived and worked during the week. He left the plane there, got into his car, which was parked there for the weekend, and drove a few miles to his home. Then during the week, Billy would fly his plane late in the afternoon 100 miles to Greensboro, North Carolina. There, his mechanic did routine maintenance on the plane and checked its airworthiness.

That same evening, Billy would fly the plane back to either Blacksburg or his drop zone. If he dropped it off at Adrenaline Air Sports, then someone—often one of his customers—would pick him up and take him back to the Blacksburg area. In this way, Billy's planes received regular maintenance checks in North Carolina during the week. While maintaining the planes took time, Billy was committed to running a very safe skydiving operation, and this started with safe airplanes.

On a busy weekend of good weather, both planes were used all day long. Each plane could handle a maximum of four skydivers (or parachuters) and the pilot. Seats were removed from the planes, except for the pilot's seat, to accommodate the jumpers and their parachutes.

Billy recently changed the maximum altitude at which his planes would release skydives. The new policy was that jumpers would be taken to a maximum of 10,000 feet. The Smith Mountain Airport was at an elevation of 1,130 feet, so jumpers could skydive and parachute a total of 8,870 feet. Previously, Billy had taken jumpers up to 12,000 feet, charging them more. But he realized that it was not worth it because of the extra 10 to 15 minutes it took to climb to 12,000 feet. The new fee schedule was simple: $6 for a plane ride, plus $1 for each 1,000 feet. Thus, a ride to 10,000 feet cost $16, and a low-level "hop and pop" (hop out of the plane and pop the parachute) at, say, 4,000 feet, would cost $10.

By 8 A.M., the two pilots had arrived to fly the jumpers. The strategy was to keep taking jumpers up as quickly as possible. Adrenaline Air Sports was lucky to have three competent part-time pilots: J. D. Shumate was a 22-year-old full-time flight instructor at Averett College in Danville, Virginia. He had been a pilot at Adrenaline since it opened in 1999 and had approximately 40 parachute jumps himself. Jeff "Maverick" Perkins was a 26-year-old UPS (United Parcel Service) truck driver had previously been a scheduler for U.S. Air Express. He also served as a paramedic in his hometown. Bobby Bruch was a 42-year-old electrician who worked for Norfolk Southern railroad. He had been a pilot for Billy for one year.

After the first-time tandem jumpers, other parachuters went up. This was based on the order in which they had signed up during the preceding week. Experienced jumpers usually had their own parachutes, gear, and clothing, so all they needed was a plane ride, which cost $16 and which took from 20 to 25 minutes. Some of these experienced jumpers had been in the sport for 10, 20, or more years and had several thousand jumps to their credit.

This routine of taking jumpers up, letting them exit the plane, landing the plane, refueling when needed, and taking the next group up continued all morning. At 1 P.M., another set of first-time parachuters arrived.

Billy Cockrell paid approximately $8,000 for insurance each year. This covered his two Cessna planes and provided protection for lawsuits from customers who might get hurt.

Skydiving Instruction

Another key element of Billy's operations was skydiving instruction. **Exhibit 4** shows Billy Cockrell right after landing, talking with a student jumper still in the air with a walkie-talkie to help him maneuver safely to the landing area. Billy had several part-time instructors who supported him.

Richard Wagner was his lead instructor. He was an interesting person, like most of the people in the sport. He was 42 years old, first started parachuting at age 19, and had done over 2,500 jumps. He was vice president of a company in Mount Airy, North Carolina, that made steel reinforcing wire used in building construction.

Exhibit 4
Billy Cockrell Using a Walkie Talkie to Help a Student Make
a Safe Landing

Exhibit 5
Student with Richard Wagner, Lead Instructor,
Practicing How to Exit the Plane and Get
Stabilized by Arching his Back

He had been a friend of Billy's since 1993 and usually came to the drop zone one day of the weekend. He was willing to do whatever Billy asked him to do, such as doing tandem jumps with beginners or coaching others doing accelerated freefall jumps. **Exhibit 5** shows Richard Wagner, in white, instructing a fairly new jumper how to hold his body upon exiting the plane.

If Richard was not needed as a paid instructor, he would rehearse with other skydivers some four-way skydive patterns, and then jump them. This so-called relative work was done during the 50 seconds or so that four jumpers were in freefall.

Billy had other part-time flight instructors. They included Miles Peters, age 35, who instructed tandem and accelerated freefall jumpers. Miles had done over 1,900 jumps and had been skydiving for 10 years. Randy Fields, age 33, also instructed jumpers. Randy had over 2,000 jumps and had been with the sport over 10 years. Finally, Tracy Gasperini, age 36, instructed just tandem jumpers.

Beginning jumpers paid $189 for their tandem jump with an instructor. If they continued, the prices for the next set of jumps were as follows:

2nd jump	$189	with tandem instructor
before 3rd jump	$100	for six-hour ground school
3rd jump	$189	student with own chute but two instructors jumping holding on to the student's sides until the student opens chute
4th jump	$189	same as jumps 1 and 2
5th jump	$189	jump with own chute with one coach with his own chute nearby
6th jump	$179	jump with own chute with one coach nearby
7th jump	$179	jump with own chute with one coach nearby
8th jump	$179	jump with own chute with one coach nearby

9th jump	$0	free jump for completing basic set of jumps; own chute and one coach nearby
	$1,582	total price for basic instructional jump
10th jump	$41	$16 to be taken to 10,000 feet and $25 to rent one parachute per jump; no charge for instructor or instructor's helper
11th–14th jump	$41	same as jump 10
15th jump	$41	first solo jump; one-way walkie-talkie provided so instructor on the ground can communicate with parachuting student and help him maneuver and land

If a beginning jumper who was enthusiastic about the sport wanted to get his own equipment, he would probably purchase used equipment. Prices for good used parachute equipment might fall in the following range:

$750–$1,000	for main parachute
$750–$1,000	for reserve second chute
$750–$1,000	for pack containing both chutes
$750–$1,000	for automatic-activation device to open second parachute automatically (optional, but good to have)
$3,000–$4,000	total price

If the skydiver wanted all new equipment, then the price range would be $4,000 to $6,000, depending on the quality of the parachute gear. Thus, if a parachuter made a significant investment in used or new equipment and packed his own chutes as well, the price per jump would be just $16, like veteran jumpers paid.

After taking basic jumps, a parachuter would have taken a solo jump and be looking forward to getting an A license. After that, a jumper could work toward getting B, C, and D licenses and then perhaps a coaching rating and an instructor's rating. How long it took to get these various licenses varied widely. Karen Alexander, age 18, got all four licenses plus her coaching certificate in just 10 months. Other jumpers might take several years to obtain their A and B licenses.

Another type of very unique parachuting was BASE jumping, which could not be done at Adrenaline Air Sports. BASE jumping involved parachuting off a building for *B*, off an antenna (radio tower or antenna on top of a building) for *A*, off a span of a bridge for *S*, and off the earth for *E*. A person who had parachuted off all four was a true BASE jumper. Since many of these challenges were from low elevations, the jumper had no time to use a reserve chute if the first one failed. For example, on "Bridge Day" in October on the New River Valley Gorge Bridge, BASE jumpers can jump legally all day from the bridge, which is just 876 feet above the river. A higher location of BASE jumps was the Great Trango Tower, in Pakistan, which was BASE jumped by two people, Nicholas Feteris and Glenn Singleman, from an elevation of 19,300. This mountain, shaped like a pickle standing on its end, required more vertical and difficult climbing than going up Mt. Everest. While BASE jumping could not be practiced at Billy's drop zone, one regular customer, Johnny Woody, was a qualified BASE jumper and was getting ready to jump into a 1,200-foot vertical cave in Mexico in the next few months.

Packing Parachutes

Another support operation at Billy's drop zone was the packing of parachutes so that someone else, or the same person, could make another jump. Experienced parachutists often packed their own parachutes, called the main chutes.

For $5, they could have Karen Alexander or someone else at Adrenaline Air Sports pack their chutes. Packing of the larger tandem chute that all beginners used cost $10. Karen had

Exhibit 6
Karen Alexander Landing at Adrenaline Air Sports

learned to pack chutes from Billy and Billy's rigger, Buzz Conner, so she could earn enough money to take more jumps herself to pay for her new hobby. Other people were available to pack chutes if the demand was high enough. **Exhibit 6** shows the reward for Karen Alexander, a part-time employee, taking another parachute jump earned by packing parachutes.

It must be emphasized that each parachute pack had two chutes: the main chute and the backup chute. Only the main chute was packed by an experienced parachuter or by a trained person, usually for a fee. The backup, or reserve, chute was packed only by a "rigger" who was certified by the Federal Aviation Administration to do this important backup safety proce-dure. A malfunction with the main chute constituted an emergency situation; the parachutist would then cut away that chute, allowing it to drift down by itself, and open the backup chute. The U.S. Parachute Association standards required that only a rigger pack the life-saving backup chute.

Human Resources

As briefly mentioned, all people who worked at Adrenaline Air Sports worked part time. Furthermore, that work was done primarily on weekends when weather conditions made parachuting possible and enjoyable. Billy, as the owner, was the only one who came close to being a full-time employee.

The pilots and some of the instructors worked regularly for Billy. Most of the other employees came out to Adrenaline Air Sports not knowing if they would pay to jump for fun or if they would pack parachutes, coach, or fly planes. Because they loved skydiving, like Billy, and enjoyed the people at the drop zone, they would instantly switch from being a customer to an employee if asked to do so.

Competition

SKYDIVE ORANGE

Located in Orange, Virginia, Skydive Orange was probably the largest parachute operation in the state of Virginia, which had seven major drop zones. Skydive Orange, which was about three hours from Billy's Adrenaline Air Sports, was usually open Friday, Saturday, and Sunday during the season. It also was open on Wednesdays from late April to midfall. During the colder months, it was only open on Saturday and Sunday, weather permitting. Some young, committed skydivers were there seven days a week, however, living in school buses that the drop zone rented out.

This drop zone operated two Cessna 182s and a Twin Otter (a twin-engine propeller plane). The Otter took approximately 14 skydivers as high as 14,000 feet in just 20 minutes. More jumpers in less time generated much higher revenues per hour of operation. While Skydive Orange had this bigger plane, it also had higher prices for beginners and experienced jumpers. Videotapes were available but also cost more than Adrenaline.

SKYDIVE VIRGINIA

Near to Skydive Orange's operation was Skydive Virginia. It was located between Fredericksburg and Charlottesville, near Lake Anna, and was about three hours from Adrenaline Air Sports. It was somewhat larger than Billy's operation and smaller than Skydive Orange. It was usually open four days a week during the season: Friday, Saturday, Sunday, and Monday. During the colder months, it was open just on Saturday and Sunday.

Like Skydive Orange, Skydive Virginia had a couple of Cessnas capable of taking up four parachuters at once. This operation also used a King Air twin-engine plane (similar to Skydive Orange's Twin Otter) that could carry 12 jumpers up at a time.

SKYDIVE THE POINT

Skydive the Point was located in West Point, Virginia, 40 miles east of Richmond, the state's capitol. It was open Saturday and Sunday 12 months a year. For key weekends like Memorial Day, Skydive the Point would be open Thursday through Monday. It used a Twin Otter plane that fit 22 jumpers and flew up to between 13,500 and 14,500 feet. The cost per jump for parachutists who owned their own gear was $20, or $19 if they were club members. Since Skydive the Point was between Richmond and the greater Virginia Beach coastal area, and south of the Washington, DC–northern Virginia area, it drew on a huge population base.

SKYDIVE SUFFOLK

Skydive Suffolk was located at the Suffolk Airport, 25 miles west of Norfolk and near the Atlantic Ocean. Like Skydive the Point, this drop zone was near a number of populated areas, particularly the Norfolk–Virginia Beach area. Open Friday, Saturday, and Sunday year round, Skydive Suffolk used a King Air, which took 14 jumpers with their own parachute gear up to 14,000 feet for a price of $19. The company also had a Cessna, which took five jumpers up to 10,500 feet for $13.

Strategic Issues Facing Adrenaline Air Sports

A major issue facing Billy and all other parachute drop zones was getting first-time jumpers to come back. According to statistics, only 3% of all first-time jumpers ever took a second jump, even though most first-time jumpers had favorable experiences. The first jump cost $189 at Adrenaline Air Sports and somewhat more at other drop zones. Furthermore, the cost for jump two was also $189, but there was a $100 additional charge for ground school before jump three is made. By jump six, the price reduced a little to $179. The ninth jump was thrown in for free by Billy. Thus the cost of the first nine jumps was about $1,582, or $175 per jump. After that, the price fell to $41 if the jumper was taken to 10,000 feet and rented a parachute.

Jared Campbell's first jump was taken in March 2001 and was somewhat typical of many first-time jumpers' experiences. Jared had once told his friends that he wanted to take a parachute jump someday. His friend and past roommate Chris Sides therefore picked up one of Adrenaline Air Sports's cards from a poster on a bulletin board at Virginia Tech, where Jared was a student, 80 miles from Billy's drop zone. Chris then privately collected about $200 from Jared's friends to pay for one jump. Then on the Saturday after his 22nd birthday, Chris and several of these "paying" friends told Jared they were taking him to see an air show that would include a flyby of the B2 Stealth Bomber.

Jared became suspicious after being driven for 1½ hours. Finally, when they turned onto a dirt road miles past Roanoke, he began to doubt that they were going to the air show.

His friend Chris said, "I guess by now you've guessed that there is no air show." Jared, while still puzzled, agreed. Chris then said, "The air show is you, Jared. We came here to see you parachute." So Jared received some training and went on a tandem jump attached to an instructor.

Most of the friends who had paid for Jared's jump came along to watch. While this meant a lot to him, little did he know that some of them had made informal bets on whether or not he would follow through. Chris chipped in the extra $60 to have the jump videotaped and then gave Jared the tape of his jump—before, during, and after—set to music. A year after the jump, Jared was still interested in jumping again. However, he lacked funds to do so.

An unusual example of someone taking a second and third jump is former President George Bush. During World War II, he was a fighter pilot whose plane was shot down. Fortunately, he was able to parachute to safety and later get picked up by U.S. troops. Amazingly, after being president from 1989 to 1993, at age 71 he took his second parachute jump in March 1995 with the Golden Knights, the Army elite parachute team. Several years later, Bush did another jump, in 1999, at age 75. Still older is the record setter for age, Edwin Townsend, who parachuted with his own chute in 1987 at age 89.

Another strategic issue was determining how best to market this sport. What type of customer group should Adrenaline Air Sports target? What form of advertising would best reach these daredevils? Should Billy go after other sports enthusiasts, such as winter and summer skiers, skateboarders, bicyclists, scuba divers, and cavers? Should he pursue more first-time jumpers, who often were young people in college, even though they almost never jumped again? People had to be at least 18 to parachute unless the drop zone allowed them to jump younger with their parents' written permission, in which case they had to be at least 16. Adrenaline Air Sports did not allow anyone under 18 to jump at its drop zone.

Other possible market segments existed. He could target married, childless men and women who were looking for some new excitement and challenge in their lives. Another possible target was men in their mid-30s to 50s facing midlife crises, wanting a challenge to prove themselves. These and other groups continually came to mind when Billy considered which customer segments to focus on. Irrespective of the particular target, which marketing media would best reach them still needed to be determined.

A third issue facing Adrenaline Sports was what could be done, if anything, to make the sport more affordable for new skydivers. Once a person had an A license, after 20 or so jumps, the cost dropped considerably, but it was still an expensive sport. Billy's students paid for the first eight jumps, then received the ninth one free. One parachutist at Billy's drop zone commented that people who had already taken eight jumps would undoubtedly pay for the ninth one. Billy had considered offering a free jump earlier to encourage a person to continue.

At $189, Adrenaline Air Sports's fee for first-time jumpers was a little cheaper than most other drop zones. And while the first jumps were expensive, Billy made money from these people, who often never jumped again; he claimed that he didn't make money off the veteran jumpers, who owned their own gear and paid just $16 a jump. Perhaps there was some way for Billy to lower the price of the instructors' jumps with new parachutists and increase rates for veteran jumpers. However, if rates were raised too much for the experienced jumpers, they might go elsewhere.

Another strategic issue was whether Billy could make Adrenaline Air Sports his full-time job. While Billy clearly was off to a good start with his drop zone, his location was not as suitable to year-round operations as locations in California or Florida, where mild winters made this possible. Still, some of the mid-Atlantic drop zones like Skydive Virginia were full-time businesses for the owners, even if they were open just on weekends during cold months.

What Billy needed to do was get more customers to come to his drop zone, which was beautiful when viewed from the air, during good weather periods. Unfortunately, Billy had two small planes, Cessna 182s, which could only take up four jumpers at a time. Billy also lacked enough parachutes to rent if he were to get more customers during prime weekends and months. Finally, his location was far away from major metropolitan areas, such as Richmond, northern Virginia, and the Tidewater–Virginia Beach area. And while the Greensboro area of North Carolina was only 80 miles away, larger North Carolina cities like Durham, Raleigh, Winston-Salem, and Charlotte were farther.

A final issue was safety. For most people, the thought of "jumping out of a perfectly good airplane," as military pilots like to put it, sends chills down their spine. The sport was, out of necessity, very safety conscious, but with speeds exceeding 120 miles an hour and no safety device resembling a seat belt, accidents were often fatal. Most nonjumpers felt parachuting was extremely dangerous. The type of people who were attracted to the sport were often outdoor types oriented to extreme sports. Jim Crouch, the safety and training coordinator for the U.S. Parachute Association, has noted that jumpers are "lacking in emergency canopy procedures, which causes accidents." He added that parachutists should not "downsize too quickly" to smaller-sized, higher-performance parachutes as this also increases risk.

Overall, expert opinion and industry statistics showed that skydiving was a safe, wholesome sport that had very loyal customers.

case 25

Inner-City Paint Corporation (Revised)

Donald F. Kuratko and Norman J. Gierlasinski

History

Stanley Walsh began Inner-City Paint Corporation in a run-down warehouse, which he rented, on the fringe of Chicago's "downtown" business area. The company is still located at its original site.

Inner-City is a small company that manufactures wall paint. It does not compete with giants such as Glidden and DuPont. There are small paint manufacturers in Chicago that supply the immediate area. The proliferation of paint manufacturers is due to the fact that the weight of the product (52½ pounds per five-gallon container) makes the cost of shipping great distances prohibitive. Inner-City's chief product is flat white wall paint sold in five-gallon plastic cans. It also produces colors on request in 55-gallon containers.

The primary market of Inner-City is the small- to medium-sized decorating company. Pricing must be competitive; until recently, Inner-City had shown steady growth in this market. The slowdown in the housing market combined with a slowdown in the overall economy caused financial difficulty for Inner-City Paint Corporation. Inner-City's reputation had been built on fast service: it frequently supplied paint to contractors within 24 hours. Speedy delivery to customers became difficult when Inner-City was required to pay cash on delivery (C.O.D.) for its raw materials.

Inner-City had been operating without management controls or financial controls. It had grown from a very small two-person company with sales of $60,000 annually five years ago, to sales of $1,800,000 and 38 employees this year. Stanley Walsh realized that tighter controls within his organization would be necessary if the company was to survive.

Equipment

Five mixers are used in the manufacturing process. Three large mixers can produce a maximum of 400 gallons, per batch, per mixer. The two smaller mixers can produce a maximum of 100 gallons, per batch, per mixer.

This case was prepared by Professor Donald F. Kuratko of Ball State University and Professor Norman J. Gierlasinski of Central Washington University. This case was edited and revised for SMBP-9th Edition. Copyright © 1984 by Donald F. Kuratko and Norman J. Gierlasinski. Reprinted by permission.

Two lift trucks are used for moving raw materials. The materials are packed in 100-pound bags. The lift trucks also move finished goods, which are stacked on pallets.

A small testing lab ensures the quality of materials received and the consistent quality of their finished product. The equipment in the lab is sufficient to handle the current volume of product manufactured.

Transportation equipment consists of two 24-foot delivery trucks and two vans. This small fleet is more than sufficient because many customers pick up their orders to save delivery costs.

Facilities

Inner-City performs all operations from one building consisting of 16,400 square feet. The majority of the space is devoted to manufacturing and storage; only 850 square feet is assigned as office space. The building is 45 years old and in disrepair. It is being leased in three-year increments. The current monthly rent on this lease is $2,700. The rent is low in consideration of the poor condition of the building and its undesirable location in a run-down neighborhood (south side of Chicago). These conditions are suitable to Inner-City because of the dusty, dirty nature of the manufacturing process and the small contribution of the rent to overhead costs.

Product

Flat white paint is made with pigment (titanium dioxide and silicates), vehicle (resin), and water. The water makes up 72% of the contents of the product. To produce a color, the necessary pigment is added to the flat white paint. The pigment used to produce the color has been previously tested in the lab to ensure consistent quality of texture. Essentially, the process is the mixing of powders with water, then tapping off of the result into 5- or 55-gallon containers. Color overruns are tapped off into two-gallon containers.

Inventory records are not kept. The warehouse manager keeps a mental count of what is in stock. He documents (on a lined yellow pad) what has been shipped for the day and to whom. That list is given to the billing clerk at the end of each day.

The cost of the materials to produce flat white paint is $2.40 per gallon. The cost per gallon for colors is approximately 40% to 50% higher. The 5-gallon covered plastic pails cost Inner-City $1.72 each. The 55-gallon drums (with lids) are $8.35 each (see **Exhibit 1**).

Selling price varies with the quantity purchased. To the average customer, flat white sells at $27.45 for 5 gallons and $182.75 for 55 gallons. Colors vary in selling price because of the

Exhibit 1

Paint Cost Sheet: Inner-City Paint Corporation

	5 Gallons	55 Gallons
Sales price	$ 27.45	$ 182.75
Direct material	(12.00)	(132.00)
Pail and lid	(1.72)	(8.35)
Direct labor	(2.50)	(13.75)
Manufacturing overheard ($1/gallon)	(5.00)	(5.00)
Gross margin	$ 6.23	$ 23.65
Gross profit ratio	22.7%	19.9%

variety in pigment cost and quantity ordered. Customers purchase on credit and usually pay their invoices in 30 to 60 days. Inner-City telephones the customer after 60 days of nonpayment and inquires when payment will be made.

Management

The President and majority stockholder is Stanley Walsh. He began his career as a house painter and advanced to become a painter for a large decorating company. Walsh painted mostly walls in large commercial buildings and hospitals. Eventually, he came to believe that he could produce a paint that was less expensive and of higher quality than what was being used. A keen desire to open his own business resulted in the creation of Inner-City Paint Corporation.

Walsh manages the corporation today in much the same way that he did when the business began. He personally must open *all* the mail, approve *all* payments, and inspect *all* customer billings before they are mailed. He has been unable to detach himself from any detail of the operation and cannot properly delegate authority. As the company has grown, the time element alone has aggravated the situation. Frequently, these tasks are performed days after transactions occur and mail is received.

The office is managed by Mary Walsh (Walsh's mother). Two part-time clerks assist her, and all records are processed manually.

The plant is managed by a man in his twenties, whom Walsh hired from one of his customers. Walsh became acquainted with him when the man picked up paint from Inner-City for his previous employer. Prior to the eight months he has been employed by Walsh as Plant Manager, his only other experience has been that of a painter.

Employees

Thirty-five employees (20 workers are part-time) work in various phases of the manufacturing process. The employees are nonunion, and most are unskilled laborers. They take turns making paint and driving the delivery trucks.

Stanley Walsh does all of the sales work and public relations work. He spends approximately one half of every day making sales calls and answering complaints about defective paint. He is the only salesman. Other salesmen had been employed in the past, but Walsh felt that they "could not be trusted."

Customer Perception

Customers view Inner-City as a company that provides fast service and negotiates on price and payment out of desperation. Walsh is seen as a disorganized man who may not be able to keep Inner-City afloat much longer. Paint contractors are reluctant to give Inner-City large orders out of fear that the paint may not be ready on a continuous, reliable basis. Larger orders usually go to larger companies that have demonstrated their reliability and solvency.

Rumors abound that Inner-City is in difficult financial straits, that it is unable to pay suppliers, and that it owes a considerable sum for payment on back taxes. All of the above contribute to the customers' serious lack of confidence in the corporation.

Financial Structure

Exhibits 2 and **3** are the most current financial statements for Inner-City Paint Corporation. They have been prepared by the company's accounting service. No audit has been performed because Walsh did not want to incur the expense it would have required.

Exhibit 2

Balance Sheet for the Current Year Ending June 30: Inner-City Paint Corporation

Current assets		
Cash	$ 1,535	
Accounts receivable (net of allowance for bad debts of $63,400)	242,320	
Inventory	18,660	
Total current assets		$262,515
Machinery and transportation equipment	47,550	
Less accumulated depreciation	15,500	
Net fixed assets		32,050
Total assets		$294,565
Current liabilities		
Accounts payable	$217,820	
Salaries payable	22,480	
Notes payable	6,220	
Taxes payable	38,510	
Total current liabilities		$285,030
Long-term notes payable		15,000
Owners' equity		
Common stock, no par, 1,824 shares outstanding		12,400
Deficit		(17,865)
Total liabilities and owners' equity		$294,565

Future

Stanley Walsh wishes to improve the financial situation and reputation of Inner-City Paint Corporation. He is considering the purchase of a computer to organize the business and reduce needless paperwork. He has read about consultants who are able to quickly spot problems in businesses, but he will not spend more than $300 on such a consultant.

The solution that Walsh favors most is one that requires him to borrow money from the bank, which he will then use to pay his current bills. He feels that as soon as business conditions improve, he will be able to pay back the loans. He believes that the problems Inner-City is experiencing are due to the overall poor economy and are only temporary.

Exhibit 3

Income Statement for the Current Year Ending June 30:
Inner-City Paint Corporation

Sales		$1,784,080
Cost of goods sold		1,428,730
Gross margin		$ 355,350
Selling expenses	$ 72,460	
Administrative expenses	67,280	
President's salary	132,000	
Office Manager's salary	66,000	
Total expenses		337,740
Net income		$ 17,610

case 26

Guajilote Cooperativo Forestal, Honduras

Nathan Nebbe and J. David Hunger

Guajilote (pronounced wa-hee-low-tay) Cooperativo Forestal was a forestry cooperative that operated out of Chaparral, a small village located in the buffer zone of La Muralla National Park in Honduras' Olancho province. Olancho was one of 18 Honduran provinces and was located inland bordering Nicaragua. The cooperative was one result of a relatively new movement among international donor agencies promoting sustainable economic development of developing countries' natural resources.[1] A cooperative in Honduras was similar to a cooperative in the United States. It was an enterprise jointly owned and operated by members who used its facilities and services.

Guajilote was founded in 1991 as a component of a USAID (United States Agency for International Development) project. The project attempted to develop La Muralla National Park as an administrative and socioeconomic model that COHDEFOR (the Honduran forestry development service) could transfer to Honduras' other national parks. The Guajilote Cooperativo Forestal was given the right to exploit naturally fallen (not chopped down) mahogany trees in La Muralla's buffer zone. Thus far, it was the only venture in Honduras with this right. A buffer zone was the designated area within a park's boundaries, but outside its core protected zone. People were allowed to live and engage in economically sustainable activities within this buffer zone.

Guajilote in 1998 was facing some important issues and concerns that could effect not only its future growth, but also its very survival. For one thing, the amount of mahogany wood was limited and was increasingly threatened by forest fires, illegal logging, and slash and burn agriculture. If the total number of mahogany trees continued to decline, trade in its wood could be restricted internationally. For another, the cooperative had no way to transport its wood to market and was thus forced to accept low prices for its wood from the only distributor in the area. What could be done to guarantee the survival of the cooperative?

Operations

Guajilote's work activities included three operations using very simple technologies. First, members searched the area to locate appropriate fallen trees. This, in itself, could be very difficult since mahogany trees were naturally rare. These trees were found at elevations up to 1,800

This case was prepared by Nathan Nebbe and Professor J. David Hunger of Iowa State University. Copyright ©1999 by Nathan Nebbe and J. David Hunger. This case was edited for SMBP-9th Edition. Reprinted by permission. Presented to the Society for Case Research and published in *Annual Advances in Business Cases 1999*. Reprinted by permission.

meters (5,400 feet) and normally were found singly or in small clusters of no more than four to eight trees per hectare (2.2 acres).[2]

Finding fallen mahogany in La Muralla's buffer zone was hampered due to the area's steep and sometimes treacherous terrain. (La Muralla means "steep wall of rock" in Spanish.) The work was affected by the weather. For example, more downed trees were available during the wet season due to storms and higher soil moisture—leading to the uprooting of trees.

Second, the cooperative set up a temporary hand-sawmill as close as possible to a fallen tree. Due to the steep terrain, it was often difficult to find a suitable location nearby to operate the hand-sawmill. Once a suitable work location was found, men used a large cross-cut saw to disassemble the tree into various components. The disassembling process was a long and arduous process that could take weeks for an especially large tree. The length of time it took to process a tree depended on a tree's size—mature mahogany trees could be gigantic. Tree size thus affected how many trees Guajilote was able to process in a year.

Third, after a tree was disassembled, the wood was either carried out of the forest using a combination of mule and human power, or floated down a stream or river. Even if a stream happened to be near a fallen tree, it was typically only usable during the wet season. The wood was then sold to a distributor who, in turn, transported it via trucks to the cities to sell to furniture makers for a profit.

Guajilote's permit to use fallen mahogany was originally granted in 1991 for a 10-year period by COHDEFOR. The permit was simply written, and stated that if Guajilote restricted itself to downed mahogany, its permit renewal should be granted automatically. The administrator of the area's COHDEFOR office indicated that if things remained as they were, Guajilote should not have any problem obtaining renewal in 2001. Given the nature of Honduran politics, however, nothing could be completely assured.

In 1998, Guajilote's mahogany was still sold as a commodity. The cooperative did very little to add value to its product. Nevertheless, the continuing depletion of mahogany trees around the world meant that the remaining wood should increase in value over time.

Management and Human Resources

Santos Munguia, 29 years old, had been Guajilote's leader since 1995. Although Munguia had only a primary school education, he was energetic, intelligent, and had proven to be a very skillful politician. In addition to directing Guajilote, Mr. Munguia farmed a small parcel of land and raised a few head of cattle. He was also involved in local politics.

Munguia had joined the cooperative in 1994. Although he had not been one of Guajilote's original members, he quickly became its de facto leader in 1995, when he renegotiated a better price for the sale of the cooperative's wood.

Before Munguia joined the cooperative, Guajilote had been receiving between three and four lempiras ($0.37 or 11 lempiras to the dollar) per foot of cut mahogany from its sole distributor, Juan Suazo. No other distributors were available in this remote location. The distributor transported the wood to Tegucigalpa or San Pedro Sula and sold it for 16 to 18 lempiras per foot. Believing that Suazo was taking advantage of the cooperative, Munguia negotiated a price increase to seven to eight lempiras per foot ($0.60 to $0.62 per foot at the July 15, 1998 exchange rate) by putting political pressure on Suazo. The distributor agreed to the price increase only after a police investigation had been launched to investigate his business dealings. (Rumors circulated that Suazo was transporting and selling illegally logged mahogany by mixing it with that purchased from Guajilote.)

Munguia: El Caudillo

After renegotiating successfully with the cooperative's distributor, Santos Munguia quickly became the group's caudillo (strong man). The caudillo was a Latin American political and social institution. A caudillo was a (typically male) purveyor of patronage. All decisions went through, and were usually made by, him. A caudillo was often revered, feared, and hated at the same time because of the power he wielded. Munguia was viewed by many in the area as an ascending caudillo because of his leadership of Guajilote.

Guajilote did not operate in a democratic fashion. Munguia made all of the decisions—sometimes with input from his second in command and nephew, Miguel Flores Munguia—and handled all of Guajilote's financial matters. Guajilote's members did not seem to have a problem with this management style. The prevailing opinion seemed to be that Guajilote was a lot better off with Munguia running the show by himself than with more involvement by the members. One man put the members' view very succinctly: "Santos, he saved us (from Suazo, from COHDEFOR, from ourselves)."

Guajilote's organizational structure emphasized Munguia's importance. He was alone at the top in his role as decision maker. If, in the future, Munguia became more involved in politics and other ventures that could take him out of Chaparral (possibly for long periods of time), he would very likely be forced to spend less time with Guajilote's operations. Munguia's leadership has been of key importance to Guajilote's maturing as both a work group and as a business. In 1998, there did not seem to be another person in the cooperative that could take Munguia's place.

Guajilote's Members

When founded, the cooperative had been composed of 15 members. Members were initially selected for the cooperative by employees of USAID and COHDEFOR. The number of employees has held steady over time. Since the cooperative's founding, three original members have quit; four others were allowed to join. Although no specific reasons were given for members leaving, they appeared to be because of personality differences, family problems, or differences of opinion. No money had been paid to them when they left the cooperative. In 1998 there were 16 members in the cooperative.

None of Guajilote's members had any education beyond primary school. Many of the members had no schooling at all and were illiterate. As a whole, the group knew little of markets or business practices.

Guajilote's existence has had an important impact on its members. One member stated that before he had joined Guajilote, he was lucky to have made 2,000 lempiras in a year; whereas, he made around 1,000 to 1,500 in one month as a member of the cooperative. He stated that all five of his children were in school, something that he could not have afforded previously. Before joining the cooperative, he had been involved in subsistence farming and other activities that brought in a small amount of money and food. He said that his children had been required previously to work as soon as they were able. As a simple farmer, he often had to leave his family to find work, mostly migrant farm work, to help his family survive. Because of Guajilote, his family now had enough to eat and he was able to be home with his family.

This was a common story among Guajilote's members. The general improvement in its members' quality of life also appeared to have strengthened the cooperative members' personal bonds with each other.

Financial Situation

No formal public financial records were available. As head of the cooperative, Santos Munguia kept informal records. Guajilote's 1997 revenues were approximately 288,000 lempiras (US $22,153). (Revenues for 1996 were not available.) Guajilote processed around 36,000 feet of wood during 1997. Very little of the money was held back for capital improvement purchases due to the operation's simple material needs. Capital expenditures for 1997 included a mule plus materials needed to maintain Guajilote's large cross-cut saws.

Each of Guajilote's 16 members was paid an average of about 1,500 lempiras (US $113) per month in 1997 and 1,300 lempiras (US $100) per month in 1996. 1998 payments per month had been similar to 1997's payments, according to Guajilote's members. Money was paid to members based on their participation in Guajilote's operations.

There was conjecture, among some workers, that Santos Munguia and his second in charge were paying themselves more than the other members were receiving. When Munguia was asked if he received a higher wage than the others because of his administrative position in the group, he responded that everything was distributed evenly. An employee of COHDEFOR indicated, however, that Munguia had purchased a house in La Union—the largest town in the area. That person conjectured, based on this evidence, that Munguia was likely receiving more from the cooperative than were the other members.

Issues Facing the Cooperative

Guajilote's size and growth potential was limited by the amount of mahogany it could produce in a year. Mahogany was fairly rare in the forest and Guajilote was legally restricted to downed trees. Moreover, with the difficulties of finding, processing by hand, and then moving the wood out of the forest, Guajilote was further restricted in the quantity of wood it could handle.

Lack of transportation was a major problem for Guajilote. The cooperative had been unable to secure the capital needed to buy its own truck; lending through legitimate sources was very tight in Honduras and enterprises like Guajilote did not typically have access to lines of credit. Although the prices the cooperative was receiving for its wood had improved, the men still thought that the distributor, Juan Suazo, was not paying them what the wood was worth. It was argued that when demand was high for mahogany, the cooperative gave up as much as 10 lempiras per foot in sales to Suazo. Guajilote could conceivably double its revenues if it could somehow haul its wood to Honduras' major market centers and sell it without use of a distributor. The closest market center was Tegucigalpa—three to four hours from Chaparral on dangerous, often rain soaked, mountain roads.

A Possibility

Some of the members of Guajilote wondered if the cooperative could do better financially by skipping the distributor completely. It was possible that some specialty shops (chains and independents) and catalogs, throughout the world, might be interested in selling high quality mahogany furniture, i.e., chests or chairs, that were produced in an environmentally friendly manner. Guajilote, unfortunately, had no highly skilled carpenters or furniture makers in its membership. There were, however, a couple towns in Honduras with highly skilled furniture makers who worked on a contract basis.

A U.S. citizen with a furniture export business in Honduras worked with a number of independent furniture makers on contract to make miniature ornamental chairs. This exporter reviewed Guajilote's situation and concluded that the cooperative might be able to make and market furniture very profitably—even if it had to go through an exporter to find suitable markets. Upon studying Guajilote's operations, he estimated that Guajilote might be able to more than treble its revenues. In order to do this, however, the exporter felt that Guajilote would have to overcome problems with transportation and upgrade its administrative competence. Guajilote would need to utilize the talents of its members more if it were to widen its operational scope. It would have to purchase trucks and hire drivers to transport the wood over treacherous mountain roads. The role of administrator would become much more demanding, thus forcing Munguia to delegate some authority to others in the cooperative.

Concerns

In spite of Guajilote's improved outlook, there were many concerns that could affect the cooperative's future. A serious concern was the threat of deforestation through fires, illegal logging (i.e., poaching of mahogany as well as clear cutting), and slash and burn agriculture.

Small fires were typically set to prepare soils for planting and to help clear new areas for cultivation. Often these fires were either not well supervised or burned out of the control of the people starting them. Due to the 1998 drought, the number of out-of-control forest fires had been far greater than normal. There seemed to be a consensus among Hondurans that 1998 would be one of the worst years for forest fires. Mahogany and tropical deciduous forests are not fire resistant. Fires not only kill adult and young mahogany trees, but also destroy their seeds.[3] Mahogany could therefore be quickly eliminated from a site. Each year, Guajilote lost more area from which it could take mahogany.

To make matters worse, many Hondurans considered the area around La Muralla National Park to be a frontier open to settlement by landless campesinos (peasant farmers). In fleeing poverty and desertification, people were migrating to the Olancho province in large numbers.[4] Not only did they clear the forests for cultivation, but they also cut wood for fuel and for use in building their homes. Most of the new settlements were being established in the area's best mahogany growing habitats.

Another concern was that of potential restrictions by CITIES (the international convention on trade in endangered species). Although trade in mahogany was still permitted, it was supposed to be monitored very closely. If the populations of the 12 mahogany species continued to decrease, it was possible that mahogany would be given even greater protection under the CITIES framework. This could include even tighter restrictions on the trade in mahogany, or could even result in an outright ban similar to the worldwide ban on ivory trading.

Notes

1. Kent Norsworthy, *Inside Honduras* (Albuquerque: Inter-Hemispheric Education Resource, 1993), pp. 133–138.
2. Hans Lamprecht, *Silviculture in the Tropics* (Hamburg: Verlag, 1989), pp. 245–246.
3. Lamprecht.
4. Norsworthy.

The Vermont Teddy Bear Co., Inc.: Challenges Facing a New CEO (Revised)

Joyce P. Vincelette, Ellie A. Fogarty, Thomas M. Patrick, and Thomas L. Wheelen

"A teddy bear is almost a 100-year-old product that has been made in every conceivable size, style, fabric, and price combined with a saturated market. Yet the teddy bear industry stands as a model of strength and durability. Every year, bear makers create and market hundreds of original models."[1]

Vermont Teddy Bear Company was founded in 1981 by John Sortino selling handsewn teddy bears out of a pushcart in the streets of Burlington, Vermont. Since this time, the company's focus has been to design, manufacture, and direct market the best teddy bears made in America using quality American materials and labor.

Until 1994, Vermont Teddy Bear experienced a great deal of success and profitability. Problems arose in 1995. Since 1995, the company has had two CEOs. It changed its name to The Great American Teddy Bear Company and then changed it back to The Vermont Teddy Bear Company when customers got confused. From its inception, Vermont Teddy Bear had been known for its Bear-Gram delivery service. In 1996, the company decided to shift emphasis away from Bear-Grams to other distribution channels. By 1998, the company decided to renew its emphasis on Bear-Grams. Vermont Teddy has always been proud of the fact that its teddy bears were made in America with American materials and craftsmanship. In 1998, the company changed this philosophy by exploring the offshore sourcing of materials, outfits, and manufacturing in an effort to lower costs.

Elisabeth Robert assumed the titles of President and Chief Executive Officer in October 1997 and began to cut costs and position the company for future growth. According to Robert, there were many reasons to invest in The Vermont Teddy Bear Company. "I believe that there is growth potential in this company. We are going to regain our balance this year. This is a rebuilding year. We are taking key steps to reposition the company. The move offshore is going to provide this company an opportunity to become more profitable. We will gain additional flexibility with price points. There is opportunity for us to expand from a regional brand to a national brand. While we continue to emphasize the premium teddy bear gift business, we intend to expand into larger markets. There is now a whole new opportunity for us in the corporate incentives and promotions market as well as the wholesale market. We have weekly inquiries from companies who recognize our brands. These companies would love to buy and resell our product or use our product as a corporate gift. Our growth will come not only from

This case was prepared by Professor Joyce P. Vincelette, Ellie A. Fogarty, Business Librarian, and Professor Thomas M. Patrick of the College of New Jersey, and Professor Thomas L. Wheelen of the University of South Florida. They would also like to thank Matthew Tardougno for his assistance on this project. This case was edited for SMBP-9th Edition. This case may not be reproduced in any form without written permission of the copyright holder, Thomas L. Wheelen. Copyright © 1998 by Thomas L. Wheelen. Reprinted by permission.

expansion of our radio markets but in the corporate and wholesale markets as we use offshore manufacturing alternatives to move to broader price points."[2]

According to Robert, "our competitors are the people who sell chocolates, flowers, and greeting cards. We target the last minute shopper who wants almost instant delivery."[3] Gift purchases account for 90% of the Company's sales.[4] "We thought we were in the teddy bear business," said Robert. "In fact we are in the gift and personal communications business. Our competition isn't Steiff [the German toy manufacturer]: it's 1-800 Flowers."[5]

On one beautiful June day in Vermont, Elisabeth Robert reflected on the enormous tasks to be accomplished. She wondered if she could successfully reposition her company and return it to profitability. Was she making the correct strategic decisions?

History: Why a Bear Company?

The Vermont Teddy Bear Co., Inc., was founded in 1981 by John Sortino. John got the inspiration for the teddy bear business shortly after his son Graham was born. While playing with his son, he noticed that Graham had many stuffed animals, but they were all made in other countries. Sortino "decided that there should be a bear made in the United States."[6]

He decided to design and manufacture his own premium-quality teddy bears. To turn his concept into reality, Sortino taught himself to sew and enrolled in drawing classes. In 1981, his first creation, Bearcho, was a bear whose thick black eyebrows and mustache resembled those of Groucho Marx. His first bear line included Buggy, Fuzzy, Wuzzy, and Bearazar, the bear with super powers. In 1982, Vermont Teddy Bear Company began limited production of Sortino's early designs using five Vermont homesewers. In 1983, Sortino took his operation to the streets where he sold his handmade bears from a pushcart on the Church Street Marketplace in downtown Burlington, Vermont. Four days later he sold his first bear. By the end of 1983, 200 bears were sold. He concluded from his selling experiences that customers "want bears that are machine washable and dryable. They want bears with joints. They want bears that are cuddly and safe for children. They want bears with personality."[7]

In 1984, Vermont Teddy was incorporated under the laws of the State of New York and Sortino's pushcart business had turned into a full-time job. To facilitate bear manufacturing, local homeworkers were contracted to produce an assortment of the founder's original designs. Even though the company opened a retail store in Burlington, Vermont, in 1985, the majority of the company's products were sold through department stores such as Macy's and Nieman Marcus during the 1980s. As the retail industry consolidated through mergers and store closings during the late 1980s, Sortino realized that a new market needed to be found for his bears. In search of a new customer base, Sortino turned to a local radio station and began advertising the company's products. This advertising strategy paved the way for the "Bear-Gram," where customers could send the gift of a Vermont Teddy Bear by placing an order through the company's 800 number.

The company initiated its Bear-Gram marketing strategy in 1985 in the Burlington, Vermont area. Local radio advertisements aired on WXXX in Burlington and customers called an 800 number to order the product. It was not until shortly before Valentine's Day in 1990 that the company introduced radio advertising of its Bear-Gram product on radio station WHTZ ("Z-100") in New York City, positioning the Bear-Gram as a novel gift for Valentine's Day and offering listeners a toll-free number to order from the company's facility in Vermont. The test proved to be successful, and the Bear-Gram concept was expanded to other major radio markets across the country. These radio advertisements were generally read live by popular radio personalities. John Sortino believed that the radio had been a successful medium for the Bear-Gram for several reasons. He believed that the use of popular radio personalities lent credibility to the product. In addition, because the disk jockey could give away a few bears, more air-time was spent on the product than the paid "60 seconds."[8] He also believed that radio advertising allowed for flexibility in the use of advertising copy, which could be adjusted as the company changed its marketing focus.

Due to the success of the Bear-Gram concept, Vermont Teddy's total sales of $400,000 in 1989 rose to $1.7 million in 1990 and over $5 million in 1991.[9] As sales increased, a larger manufacturing facility was needed. In 1991, the company leased and moved into a new factory space and guided factory tours began. The larger production facilities made it possible for Vermont Teddy Bear to begin producing bears in bulk and to enter into larger sales agreements with retail establishments. In 1992, *Inc.* magazine listed Vermont Teddy as the eightieth fastest growing company in the United States with sales totaling $10.6 million.[10]

Vermont Teddy Bear went public on November 23, 1993. By this time, sales totaled $17 million.[11] In 1993, the company was named the first national winner of the Dun & Bradstreet "Best of America" Small Business Award and was ranked as the fifty-eighth fastest growing company in the United States by *Inc.* magazine.[12] Also in 1993, the company was the recipient of the Heritage of New England Customer Service Award. Previous recipients of the award included L.L. Bean, Inc., Boston Beer Company, and Ben & Jerry's Homemade, Inc.[13]

In 1994, construction began on a new factory and retail store in Shelburne, Vermont, which opened for business in the summer of 1995. In 1994, *Inc.* magazine listed Vermont Teddy Bear, with sales totaling $20.5 million, as the twenty-first fastest growing small, publicly owned company in the United States and named the company "Small Business of the Year."[14]

Prior to 1994, Vermont Teddy Bear had experienced a great deal of success and profitability, with sales growth in excess of 50% for three consecutive years.[15] However, 1994 marked the beginning of the company's financial troubles. The company's expenses increased in accordance with its anticipated growth, but sales did not increase as rapidly.

Vermont Teddy Bear's rapid growth during the 1990s taxed the organizational structure and efficiency of the company's operations. Due to the company's declining financial situation, on June 20, 1995, the company's Founder, President, and Chief Executive Officer, John Sortino, resigned. Sortino recognized that the future success of the company "depends on the transition from an entrepreneurial company to a professionally managed organization." He further stated, "I wanted to assist the company in positioning itself for the arrival of a new CEO. I will provide guidance to the company in a consulting role, and I will retain my position on the Board of Directors."[16]

On August 2, 1995, R. Patrick Burns was appointed as President and CEO. Also in 1995 Elisabeth Robert joined the company as Chief Financial Officer. Outside observers wondered if the company could successfully make the transition to a new CEO and generate enough sales to pull itself out of debt and remain profitable.

In its attempts to turn the company around, the new management team eliminated several unprofitable marketing ventures (such as its sponsorship of a NASCAR circuit race car and driver) and reduced general and administrative cost. By 1996, the new team had generated a profit of $152,000.[17]

During the later part of 1996, Vermont Teddy Bear took on a new trademarked name, "The Great American Teddy Bear Company," in an attempt to broaden brand appeal and take advantage of national and international distribution opportunities. Even though the "Vermont" name gave good name recognition in the Northeast, the company felt that it had less impact in other parts of the country. They were wrong. Customers became confused, and Disney's entry into the personalized teddy bear gift market with their "Pooh-Grams" added to the confusion. The confusion contributed to a decrease in Bear-Gram sales. By Valentine's Day, the company returned to its established mark, The Vermont Teddy Bear Company.

Late in 1996, the new management team began to explore opportunities for growth. They believed that the emphasis of the company should shift from the Bear-Gram business to other distribution channels. Their new five-year plan included opening new retail stores and expanding the catalog.

By 1997, retail sales were the fastest growing part of Vermont Teddy's business. Sales for the factory retail store in Shelburne for the fiscal year ending June 30, 1996, were 19% ahead of 1995.[18] It appeared obvious to top management that retail was a growing profit center for the company. The company's factory store had become a major Vermont tourist destination and had averaged 130,000 visitors a year since opening in July 1995.[19] As a result, the company became interested in high tourist traffic areas for retail expansion, hoping to duplicate this success at other retail locations.[20]

The location for the company's second retail store was North Conway, New Hampshire, a major tourist destination in both winter and summer months. The store opened in July 1996. The third retail location opened at 538 Madison Avenue in New York City in February 1997. The New York City location was chosen because it had been the number one market for Bear-Grams since the company began advertising on radio in 1990. The company believed that the New York store would benefit from the millions of dollars of radio advertising that the company had invested in this market. The fourth store opened in Freeport, Maine, on August 16, 1997, two doors down from L.L. Bean.

Fiscal 1997 was a disappointing year for Vermont Teddy. After a year of controlling costs and a return to profitability in 1996, they had set out in pursuit of revenue growth in 1997. The 1997 initiatives included an expanded catalog and the new retail stores. As part of the shift away from Bear-Grams, the company downsized their radio media buying department. The company lost money on their catalog programs, and the new retail stores were not as profitable as expected. Resources diverted to expanding secondary marketing channels, coupled with accelerating changes in the radio industry, contributed to a decline in Bear-Gram sales. The end result was a loss of $1,901,795 in fiscal 1997.[21]

Because of Vermont Teddy Bear's declining performance, R. Patrick Burns chose to step down as President and CEO in October 1997. Elisabeth Robert assumed the title of President and CEO and retained the title of Chief Financial Officer.

According to CEO Robert, "When we made the decision to expand our distribution channels in the areas of retail and catalog, our focus was on being a teddy bear category killer. We thought we were in the teddy bear business. Now what I believe is that we are in the Bear-Gram business, the gift business, and the impulse business. This is a completely different marketplace. Our competitors are the people who sell chocolates, flowers, and greeting cards. We target the last-minute shopper who wants almost instant delivery."[22] She further stated that "the primary focus of the company would return to maximizing returns in the radio Bear-Gram business, which constituted the majority of the company's annual revenue."[23]

In 1998, the management team began seriously looking at the profitability of their various retail locations. They also began looking at the catalog, intending to optimize its size and product offerings to ensure its future profitability.

Corporate Governance

As of June 30, 1998, The Vermont Teddy Bear Co., Inc., had a total of seven Board members and two Executive Officers, both of whom were also members of the Board of Directors.

BOARD OF DIRECTORS AND EXECUTIVE OFFICERS[24]

The Board members, Executive Officers, and their experience and qualifications were as follows.

R. Patrick Burns (53) had been President and CEO of Vermont Teddy Bear from 1995 until 1997. He had been a Director of the company since 1995. He planned to remain active as a consultant to the company focusing on developing strategic marketing partnerships for the next two years. Prior to joining the company, he was the Chief Executive Officer of Disney Direct Marketing. He had also held senior management positions at J. Crew, Inc., and at L.L. Bean, Inc.

Joan H. Martin (74) was a private investor who had been a Director of the company since 1991. Martin had no business experience during the past eight years apart from managing her private investment portfolio.

Fred Marks (70) became a Director of the company in 1987 and became its Treasurer and Chairman of the Board in 1989. He served as the company's Chief Financial Officer until January 1995 and Treasurer until 1996. Previously Marks had served as Chairman of the Board of two privately held companies: Selection, Ltd., a manufacturer of remote controls for computers and televisions; and Contaq Technologies, a manufacturer of ultrasonic instruments.

Elisabeth B. Robert (43), Director, Chief Executive Officer, President, Treasurer and Chief Financial Officer, joined the company in 1995 as the Chief Financial Officer replacing Stephen Milford. She was appointed a Director of the company in January 1996 and Treasurer of the company in April 1996. She assumed the titles of CEO and President from R. Patrick Burns who stepped down from the positions in October 1997. Before joining Vermont Teddy, Robert served as the Chief Financial Officer for a high-tech start-up company specializing in remote control devices, where she was also a founding partner.

Spencer C. Putnam (52), Director, Vice President, and Secretary, joined the company as its Chief Operating Officer in June 1987 and continued in this role. He had been a Director of the company and Secretary of its Board since 1989. Before joining the company, Putnam was the director of the Cooperative Education Program at the University of Vermont.

David W. Garrett (55) had been a Director of the company since 1987. He was a Vice President of First Albany Corporation, an investment banking and brokerage firm. Garrett was also President of the Garrett Hotel Group, a private hotel development and management firm and President of The Black Willow Group, Ltd., a private company which owned and operated The Point, a luxury hotel in Saranac Lake, New York.

Jason Bacon (64) became a Director of the company in 1997. He was a consultant to nonprofit organizations and a private investor focusing on real estate and securities with international perspective. Prior to his involvement with Vermont Teddy Bear, he served as a Managing Director at Kidder, Peabody & Company.

OWNERSHIP

As of June 30, 1998, there were 5,183,733 shares of the company's common stock outstanding held by 1,553 shareholders.[25] Approximately 2,551,300 shares or approximately 49.2% of the stock was owned beneficially by the current directors and officers of the company. These figures did not include options or warrants held by current directors and officers, their spouses or minor children to purchase shares of the company's Common Stock or Series B Preferred Stock.[26]

In November 1993, the company made an Initial Public Offering (IPO) of 5,172,500 shares of common stock. The stock ranged from $17.19 to $11.44 from offering to December 31, 1993. Prior to the IPO, 4,000,000 shares of common stock were outstanding and held by nine shareholders. Ninety shares of nonvoting Series A Preferred Stock were held by shareholder Joan H. Martin. This preferred stock had an 8% cumulative dividend and liquidation value of $10,000 per share. On July 12, 1996, the company privately placed 204,912 share of Series B preferred stock. This stock was held by 12 shareholders and was not entitled to any dividends or voting rights. The 204,912 Series B shares were convertible into 482,441 shares of common stock.[27]

The following individuals owned more than 5% of the company's stock as of June 30, 1998.[28]

Beneficial Owner	Number of Shares	Percent Owned
Joan H. Martin	1,840,975	35.5
Fred Marks	600,500	11.6
Margaret H. Martin	267,000	5.2
Spencer C. Putnam	84,000	1.6
R. Patrick Burns	17,625	0.3
Jason Bacon	5,500	0.1
Elisabeth B. Robert	2,700	0.1

Notes were deleted.

Vermont Teddy has never paid cash dividends on any of its shares of common stock. The high and low stock prices for 1998 were[29]

Quarter Ending	High	Low
June 30, 1998	$1.63	$1.06
March 31, 1998	$1.63	$0.75
December 31, 1997	$2.13	$0.88
September 30, 1997	$2.56	$1.06

Company Philosophy

From its founding by John Sortino in the early 1980s until 1998, the company's focus has been to design and manufacture the best teddy bears made in America, using American materials and labor. The company believed that apart from its own products, most of the teddy bears sold in the United States were manufactured in foreign countries, and that the company was the largest manufacturer of teddy bears made in the United States. The company's Mission Statement can be seen in **Exhibit 1**.

This philosophy was modified significantly in 1998 with the company's decision to explore the offshore sourcing of materials and manufacturing alternatives in an effort to lower the company's cost of goods sold and to broaden its available sources of supply. Company customer surveys revealed that price was more important to potential customers than the "Made in America" label.[30] During 1998, the company began purchasing raw materials for bear production and some teddy bear outfits from offshore manufacturers. Vermont Teddy felt that plush materials from offshore were of better quality and less costly than those produced in the United States. They felt that importing these materials would enable them to produce a better, lower cost product and would provide the flexibility to meet a broader range of price points in response to customer needs.[31] The company planned to continue to handcraft the 15-inch "classic" teddy bear in Vermont for those customers interested in an American-made product. The new label read, "Made in America, of domestic and foreign materials."[32] The company also planned to explore opportunities to introduce new teddy bear products made offshore to their design specifications at significantly lower cost points for sale initially into the wholesale and corporate channels.

With this change in philosophy, the company was committed to understanding its potential offshore partners and to ensuring that its partners provided decent, lawful working conditions. It required that all offshore vendors sign a written statement to this effect prior to any business dealings.[33]

Exhibit 1
Mission Statement: The Vermont Teddy Bear Co., Inc.

The Vermont Teddy Bear provides our customers with a tangible expression of their best feelings for their families, friends, and associates. We facilitate, communicate, and therefore participate in caring events and special occasions that celebrate and enrich our customers' life experiences.

Our products will represent unmatchable craftsmanship balanced with optimal quality and value. We will strive to wholesomely entertain our guests while consistently exceeding our external and internal customer service expectations.

The Vermont Teddy Bear brand represents the rich heritage of the "Great American Teddy Bear" begun in 1902. We are the stewards of a uniquely American tradition based on the best American virtues including compassion, generosity, friendship, and a zesty sense of whimsy and fun.

Exhibit 2

Stakeholder Beliefs: The Vermont Teddy Bear Co., Inc.

Our customers are the foundation of our business. Exceeding their expectations *everyday* will form the backbone of our corporate culture. Zealous pursuit of "world class" customer service will build a self-fulfilling cycle of pride, partnership, team spirit, and personal commitment in every player in our company.

Our employees are our internal customers. The philosophy that applies to our external customers extends also to our internal associates. We will cultivate a results-oriented environment that encourages fairness, collaboration, mutual respect, and pride in our organization. Pro-active, positive, open-minded confrontation among well-intentioned colleagues will ensure innovation, reject complacency, and stimulate individual growth. Our company supports employee diversity and provides clear opportunities for each of us to reach our full personal and professional potential.

Our investors provide capital in good faith, and we are accountable for creating a realistic return while protecting the assets of our company. Our financial strength and profitability are essential to fulfilling all of our stakeholder commitments.

Our vendors provide a partnership opportunity for innovative product development, unsurpassed external customer service, and mutual prosperity. This is based on exceeding our customers' expectations for unique, innovative, high-quality communications and products delivered to our customers where and when they want them at a price that reinforces our reputation for perceived value.

Our community deserves our commitment to being ethically, legally, and environmentally responsible while remaining fiscally sound. We will support organizations and individuals with values similar to ours and participate actively in those enterprises that seek to improve local and world conditions for future generations. We will seek to maintain a dynamic balance between meeting our commitment to our community and maintaining the viability of our own enterprise.

Exhibit 2 details Vermont Teddy's statement of Stakeholder Beliefs. The company believed that the quality, variety, and creativity of the company's products, and its commitment to customer service, were essential to its business. Its manufacturing practices were environmentally sound. The company sought to use the best available materials for its bears. Customer service policies rivaled those of L.L. Bean. Each bear was sold with a "Guarantee for Life," under which the company undertook to repair or replace any damaged or defective bear at any time even if eaten by the family dog or destroyed by a lawn mower.[34]

Products and Services

Vermont Teddy Bear made old-fashioned, handmade, jointed teddy bears ranging from 11 to 72 inches tall, in 6 standard color selections including tan, honey, brown, and black. More than 100 different bear outfits were available for customers to outfit and individualize their bears or to emphasize certain relevant characteristics of the receiver such as policewoman, gardener, doctor, or racing car driver. Some of the more popular outfits included tutus, wedding gowns, tuxedos, business suits, and sports uniforms. Bears could also be dressed in a wide variety of outfits that personalized the bear for significant life events, such as a new baby, get well, birthdays, graduations, weddings, and "I love you." A collection of bears could also be designed for schools, sports teams, businesses, and other organizations. New "edgier" products were added in 1997 such as "Shredder, the Snowboarder Bear," targeted primarily at radio customers. As of June 30, 1998, 40% of the outfits were outsourced to overseas contractors.[35] Prices for the bears in standard outfits ranged from $40 to more than $200. Custom-made clothing was available at an additional cost.

Until 1997, bear materials were mostly American made, though mohair fur used for the premium bears came from Europe. All other fur was hypoallergenic, plush polyester. Bears were stuffed with virgin Dacron 91, a fire retardant filler for safety. Vermont teddy bears had movable joints, a feature associated with traditional, high-quality teddy bears. These joints were made from recycled Ben & Jerry's ice cream containers. In keeping with the company's attempt to produce the bears with domestic materials, the bears' eyes had come from the only eye maker left in America. Noses and paw pads were ultrasuede, also 100% American made.[36] Using American-made materials had been one of the methods by which Vermont Teddy Bear differentiated its products from those of its competitors. The company's 1998 move to the off-shore sourcing of raw materials represented a significant departure from the company's historical position as an American manufacturer using almost exclusively American materials.[37]

In addition to the products it manufactured, Vermont Teddy Bear sold items related to teddy bears, as well as merchandise from other manufacturers featuring the logo of Vermont Teddy Bear. It did a small amount of licensing with Tyco, Landmark, and a manufacturer of children's and women's sleepwear. Some items such as clothing, jewelry, and accessory ornaments were available primarily at the company's retail stores and through its direct mail catalog. The company also sold stuffed toys that had been manufactured by other companies, such as Gund and Steiff.[38] Vermont Teddy Bear planned to alter this strategy in 1999 to focus more attention on the sale of the company's own manufactured products, including those manufactured offshore.

In addition to manufacturing and selling bears and bear-related merchandise to individual consumers, the company's Corporate Division provided unique and original customized products for corporations. Vermont Teddy also silk-screened or embroidered bears on clothing with the customer's logo, slogan, or team name. In 1998, the company planned to offer a line of offshore-manufactured ancillary products for corporate customers and outlets such as QVC.[39] Information about products offered through the company's Corporate and Wholesale Programs could be found on the company's Web site.

Marketing Strategies and Distribution Methods

Vice President of Sales was Katie Camardo. Robert D. Delsandro was appointed Vice President of Marketing and Design in May 1998. He had been employed by The Vermont Teddy Bear Company as Creative Director since 1996 and had been responsible for developing a completely new look for the company's products, retail stores, printed promotional materials, and catalog. He was credited with creating the new "edgier" look of Vermont Teddy Bear.[40]

Although many teddy bear producers defined their product as a toy and marketed solely to children, Vermont Teddy Bear marketed its bears as an attractive gift or collectible for both children and adults. The company defined its target market as "children between the ages of 1 to 100."[41]

The company was primarily known for its Bear-Gram delivery service. Bear-Grams were personalized teddy bears that were delivered directly to recipients as gifts for holidays and special occasions. Bear-Grams were gift boxed in unique containers complete with "air-holes" for the bear. The bears were accompanied by a personal greeting from the sender.

Orders for Bear-Grams were generally placed by calling a toll-free number (1-800-829-BEAR) and speaking with company sales representatives called "Bear Counselors." Customers could also visit the company's Web site <**www.vtbear.com**> and place their orders online. "Bear Counselors" entered an order on a computer, which was part of the company's computer network of approximately 250 workstations that linked order entry with sales and accounting systems. The company had plans to upgrade, expand, and integrate its computer systems, including the purchase of an inventory control system. In 1994, the company installed a new telephone system, which improved its telemarketing operations and was designed to accommodate future growth in telephone call volume. The company strove to provide rapid response to customer orders. Orders placed by 4 P.M. EST (3 P.M. on the Internet) could be shipped the same day. Packages were delivered primarily by UPS and other carriers by next day air or ground delivery service.[42] The company also sought to respond promptly to customer complaints. The company believed that, as a result of the quality of its products and service, it had established a loyal customer base.

The company attributed its success to this direct-marketing strategy. Since 1990, when the Bear-Gram was introduced to prime-time and rush-hour audiences in the New York City market, the company had continued to rely primarily on Bear-Gram advertising. It had also continued to focus its advertising on morning rush-hour radio spots, with well-known personalities such as Don Imus and Howard Stern, promoting the bears.

For the fiscal year ending June 30, 1998, Bear-Grams accounted for 70.2% of net revenues of $17.2 million. The percent of net revenues for the company's primary distribution methods can be seen in **Exhibit 3**. Included in Bear-Gram revenues were sales from the company's Internet Web site. Other principal avenues of distribution included company-owned retail stores, direct mail catalogs, and licensing and wholesale agreements. The company's sales were heavily seasonal, with Valentine's Day, Christmas, and Mother's Day as the company's largest sales seasons.[43] For Valentine's Day 1998, more than 47,000 bears were sent out by people across the country who wished to say "I love you."[44]

During the summer of 1997, Vermont Teddy Bear Company began doing business on the Internet with a new Web site designed to inform and entertain Internet subscribers. The Web site provided a low-cost visual presence and was developed for the purpose of supporting the radio advertising of Bear-Grams. Pictures of the product and other information could be accessed. A total of 396, 000 hits to the Web site were recorded during fiscal 1998, more than double the 195,000 hits recorded during fiscal 1997.[45] By August 1998, 10 to 20% of Vermont Teddy's business was being handled online.[46] All radio advertisements were tagged with a reference to the Web site, which, in turn, provided visual support for the radio advertising and the opportunity for customers to place orders online.[47]

Since 1990, the company had extended its Bear-Gram marketing strategy beyond New York City to include other metropolitan areas and syndicated radio programs across the United States. During the fiscal year 1998, the company regularly placed advertising on a total of 44 radio stations in 12 of the 20 largest market areas in the United States.[48] **Exhibit 4** shows the company's largest markets. **Exhibit 5** shows the most frequent reasons given by customers for purchasing a Vermont Teddy Bear-Gram. The company was featured on Dateline NBC, Tuesday, December 17, 1996. Newsbroadcaster Stone Phillips interviewed R. Patrick Burns, President and CEO, on the subject of American companies that manufactured products in the United States.[49]

Exhibit 3

Primary Distribution Methods: The Vermont Teddy Bear Co., Inc.

Year Ending June 30	1998	1997	1996	1995
Bear-Grams[1]	72.0%	70.0%	75.8%	78.7%
Retail Operations	18.0%	17.7%	12.9%	9.2%
Direct Mail	9.2%	10.9%	7.2%	8.8%
Other	0.8%	1.4%	4.1%	3.3%

Note:
1. Excludes Bear-Gram revenues from retail operations.

Source: The Vermont Teddy Bear Co., Inc., *1998 Annual Report*, p. 3.

Exhibit 4

Vermont Teddy Bear's Largest Markets
(Percentage of Bear-Grams for the 12 months ending June 30)

Markets	1998	1997	1996	1995
New York City	37.8%	40.8%	35.5%	38.6%
Boston	13.4%	13.2%	9.5%	9.5%
Philadelphia	8.9%	11.6%	8.9%	7.3%
Chicago	6.5%	8.9%	7.3%	8.5%
Los Angeles	6.3%	5.8%	4.0%	3.8%

Source: The Vermont Teddy Bear Company, Inc., *1998 Annual Report*, p. 4.

In 1998, the company was planning to expand its radio advertisements into new markets including Minneapolis, Dallas, and Milwaukee and to examine opportunities to consolidate radio advertising buys through annual contracts with major stations.[50]

The company had explored additional methods to market Bear-Grams and to publicize its toll-free telephone number. In June 1993, the company's toll-free number was listed for the first time in the AT&T toll-free telephone directory. Before then, the toll-free number was not readily available to customers, except in radio advertisements. Vermont Teddy Bear also expanded its listings in metropolitan phone book Yellow Pages and initiated the use of print advertising in magazines and newspapers, as well as advertising on billboards and mass transit panels.

Vermont Teddy Bear believed that the popularity of Bear-Grams created an opportunity for catalog sales. For the fiscal year ending June 30, 1998, direct mail accounted for 9.2% of net revenues.[51] In addition, repeat buyers represented 33% of sales, giving the company an opportunity to use its customer database in excess of 1,500,000 names.[52] The company introduced its first catalog for Christmas in 1992. By 1994, catalog sales accounted for 16.7% of sales.[53] Vermont Teddy planned to prepare three catalogs in 1995, but the management shakeup that resulted in Patrick Burns's becoming CEO caused the company to scale back its plans. Instead it mailed just 165,000 copies of an eight-page book to previous customers. The small-size book kept up the company's presence but did not have the pages nor the product range to boost holiday sales. Quarterly sales dropped 24% below December 1994 levels.[54]

In 1996, to compensate for the decline in radio advertisement effectiveness, the company increased December 1996 catalog circulation to approximately one million. To increase its catalog circulation, Vermont Teddy Bear acquired additional mailing lists from prominent catalog companies, including Disney, FAO Schwarz, Hammacher-Schlemmer, Saks Fifth Avenue,

Exhibit 5

Most Frequent Reasons for Purchasing Bear-Grams: Vermont Teddy Bear Co., Inc.
(Percentage of Bear-Grams for the 12 months ending June 30)

Reasons for Purchases	1998	1997	1996	1995
Valentine's Day	27.7%	22.1%	20.8%	19.2%
Birthdays	11.8%	11.6%	13.4%	15.9%
New Births	11.6%	10.3%	12.8%	9.9%
Get Wells	11.0%	9.7%	12.0%	10.4%
Christmas	8.4%	5.6%	8.6%	10.4%

Source: The Vermont Teddy Bear Company, Inc., *1998 Annual Report*, p. 4.

and Harry & David. To strengthen its retail and catalog offerings, Vermont Teddy broadened the scope of its product line. New items included lower priced teddy bears, company-designed apparel, toys, books, and jewelry, as well as plush animals from other manufacturers such as Gund and Steiff.

Its Valentine mailing in 1997 amounted to 600,000 catalogs. Direct mail revenues increased from 1996, but they did not meet expectations due to the poor performance of rented mailing lists. In addition, the company incurred higher than anticipated costs due to the outsourcing of the order fulfillment process and was left with inflated inventories due to lower than expected sales.

During fiscal 1998, more than 15 million circulated pages were mailed to prospective customers. CEO Robert believed that Vermont Teddy's in-house list, which stood at 1.4 million names, would be a profitable future source of business. The company planned to increase the number of circulated pages during 1999, primarily though renting and exchanging of additional names from other catalogs and mailing to more names on the in-house mailing list.[55] It planned to handle all catalog fulfillment at company facilities in Shelburne. It also planned to continue to develop its own internal systems to adapt to the requirements of its catalog customers as the catalog business grew.[56]

During fiscal 1998, sales from retail operations accounted for 18.0% of net revenues.[57] Due to the continued unprofitability in its retail stores, the company reversed its retail expansion strategy in fiscal 1998. Vermont Teddy Bear's New York City retail outlet was closed to the public on December 7, 1997, due to structural problems. A sales profile for the store reaffirmed the company's core market. Bear-Grams accounted for 60 to 70% of the store's purchases—the same product that was being sold through the radio advertisements, without the overhead of New York rents.[58]

The company planned to close its retail location in Freeport, Maine, in August 1998 and its North Conway, New Hampshire, store in October 1998. CEO Robert commented, "After two successful holidays at Valentine's Day and Mother's Day, it is more clear than ever, that focusing on radio Bear-Grams is the right strategy. Retail apart from our highly successful factory store here in Shelburne, is not a distribution channel that fits our current business. We are in the Bear-Gram business, offering a convenient, creative and expressive gift delivery service. It makes no sense to ship out a Bear-Gram from an expensive retail store front."[59]

The Shelburne factory store had continued to be successful as the company added new merchandise. To make the store more entertaining and interactive, the company invested $100,000 in its renovation in 1996.[60] Programs such as "Make a Friend for Life," which enabled customers to stuff, dress, and personalize their own bear and "virtual" factory tours, using video and theatrical demonstrations of teddy bear making received favorable responses from customers.[61]

In November 1996, the company announced that it had joined forces with Gary Burghoff to produce a video that promoted the company's new "Make a Friend for Life" products.[62] Burghoff was known for playing the character Radar O'Reilly in the *M*A*S*H* television show and was famous for his relationship with his teddy bear.

Vermont Teddy Bear had also targeted children's literature as a way of generating name recognition. A children's book, *How Teddy Bears Are Made: A Visit to the Vermont Teddy Bear Factory,* was available for purchase and could be found at libraries. The company also began to publish other children's books in order to develop characters for their teddy bears.

Beginning September 1, 1997, The Vermont Teddy Bear Co., Inc., introduced nationally a line of officially licensed NFL Teddy Bears. The NFL Bear was offered in 14 different teams and wore NFL Properties' uniforms and gear, including officially licensed jerseys, pants, and Riddell helmets.[63] NFL Properties, Inc., was the licensing and publishing arm of the National

Football League. To advertise this new product, Vermont Teddy enlisted Wayne Chrebet, wide receiver for the NY Jets, and Mark Chmura, tight end for the Green Bay Packers, to be spokespeople for the NFL Teddy Bears. Chrebet and Chmura were featured in radio and print advertisements in New York and Milwaukee, respectively. The company believed that officially licensed NFL Bears would be a popular choice for sports fans, especially during the football and Christmas seasons. The company advertised the bear on sports-talk radio in metropolitan areas around the country.[64]

Vermont Teddy Bear conducted business almost exclusively in the United States. Bears could be shipped abroad, but it was very expensive. Some bears were shipped into Canada, and some radio advertising was done in Montreal. The added shipping charges, along with unfavorable exchange rates, caused price resistance to the products in Canada. In 1995, the company test marketed both the Bear-Gram and the use of the 800 number via radio advertising in the United Kingdom. Test results indicated that both were successful, but the program had to be eliminated because the company did not have the corporate infrastructure or the financial resources to support it.[65] The company had some trademarks registered in Great Britain and Japan and had discussions with companies in both of these countries. According to Robert, "These are the two countries that seem to have the most interest in Vermont Teddy's products."[66]

Vermont Teddy Bear's management believed that there were a number of opportunities to increase company sales. The company's strategy for future growth included increasing sales of Bear-Grams in existing markets, expanding sales of Bear-Grams in new market areas, increasing direct-mail marketing of teddy bears through mail-order catalogs and similar marketing techniques, increasing sales of premium teddy bears through wholesale channels to unaffiliated retail stores, and increasing the company's retail store sales through increased factory tours and visits.[67] Management was also interested in expanding sales through its Corporate Division.

Facilities and Operations

In the summer of 1995, in an effort to consolidate locations and improve manufacturing efficiency, the company relocated its offices, retail store, and manufacturing, sales, and distribution facilities to a newly constructed 62,000-square-foot building on 57 acres in Shelburne, Vermont. The new site was approximately 10 miles south of Burlington, the state's largest city. The new buildings were designed as a small village, the Teddy Bear Common, to promote a warm and friendly atmosphere for customers as well as employees. The new facility was estimated to have cost $7,900,00.[68] The company intended to minimize lease costs by subleasing any unused space. On September 26,1995, the company had entered into a $3.5 million commercial loan with the Vermont National Bank. Repayment of the mortgage loan was based on a 30-year fixed-principal payment schedule, with a balloon payment due on September 26, 1997.[69]

On July 18, 1997, Vermont Teddy completed a sale-leaseback transaction with W. P. Carey and Co., Inc., a New York–based investment banking firm, involving its factory headquarters and a portion of its property located in Shelburne. W. P. Carey bought the 62,000-square-foot headquarters facility and its 15-acre site, leaving the company with ownership of the additional land. W. P. Carey was not interested in acquiring the other building lots on the site due to their zoning restrictions. This financing replaced the company's mortgage and line of credit, which was about to come due on September 26, 1997.[70]

The company had a three-year lease on 10,000 square feet of inventory space at a separate location in Shelburne for $56,000 annually.[71] The company also had the following lease agreements for its retail stores:[72]

Location	Square Footage	Annual Rent	1999 Rent Obligation	End of Lease Obligation
North Conway, NH	6,000	$ 49,608	$ 28,938	1/31/1999
New York City, NY	2,600	$300,000	$300,000	10/23/2006
Freeport, ME	6,000	$240,000	$ 25,644	8/6/1998

For in-house manufacturers, all production occurred in the Shelburne manufacturing space, which included state-of-the-art packing and shipping equipment. The plant manager was Brad Allen. Visitors and guests were given the opportunity to take guided or self-directed tours that encompassed the entire teddy bear making process. The factory tour had become such a popular tourist attraction that approximately 129,000 visitors toured the factory and retail store in fiscal 1998. Since moving to its new location in 1995, more than 390,000 visitors had toured the facilities.[73]

In 1994, when the company was looking for a new location, it purchased only the 15-acre parcel it built on in Shelburne. Then the company bought the surrounding property because it wanted some control in the kind of neighbors it would have. As of June 30, 1998, plans to sell or lease the other lots had not been successful due to stringent zoning restrictions on the site. The zoning restrictions required that less than a quarter of the space be devoted to retail, effectively ruling out any kind of direct retail or outlet mall approach, which is the kind of business that could take advantage of the visitor traffic to the teddy bear factory. The company proposed a project for this unused space involving an attempt to bring together up to 50 Vermont manufacturers in a cooperative manufacturing, demonstration, and marketing setting—a made-in-Vermont manufacturing/exhibition park. Investors expressed concerns about the capital investment requirement.[74]

Vermont Teddy Bear began using Sealed Air Corp's Rapid Fill air-filled packaging (air bags) system to protect its teddy bears from damage during shipping in 1997. Previously it had used corrugated cardboard seat belt inserts to package the bears during shipping, but found that there were drawbacks, including minor damage to the products and the high cost of postage. Sealed Air's inflatable plastic bags were lighter than the corrugated inserts resulting in savings in postage costs and the plastic bags did not damage the bears with plush fur. Vermont Teddy Bear saved $150,000 in postage costs in 1997 and could realize $30,000 to $40,000 in additional savings in 1998.[75]

Vice President of Data Processing was Bonnie West. According to CEO Robert, Vermont Teddy Bear's desktop computers were in need of updating. However, West believed the company's call centers had state-of-the-art technologies, including PC terminals and very-high-tech telephone switching equipment that allowed the company to handle significant call volume. The company also had a high-tech shipping system, including state-of-the-art multicarrier software so that if a major carrier like UPS went on strike, it could immediately make adjustments.

Human Resource Management

Vermont Teddy Bear employees were known as the "Bear People," a term that expressed management's appreciation and respect for their dedication. Beth Peters was Vice President of Human Resources. As of June 30, 1998, the company employed 181 individuals, of whom 94 were employed in production-related functions, 67 were employed in sales and marketing positions, and 20 were employed in administrative and management positions.[76] None of the employees belonged to a union. Overall, the company believed that favorable relations existed with all employees.[77]

The company supplemented its regular in-house workforce with homeworkers who performed production functions at their homes. The level of outsourced work fluctuated with company production targets. As of June 30, 1998, there were 21 homeworkers producing product for the company. Homeworkers were treated as independent contractors for all purposes, except for withholding of federal employment taxes. As independent contractors, homeworkers were free to reject or accept any work offered by the company.[78] Independent contractors allowed the company flexibility in meeting heavy demand at holiday periods such as Christmas, Valentine's Day, and Mother's Day. This relationship also allowed the homeworkers flexibility in scheduling their hours of work.

Bear Market

The teddy bear was first created in the United States in 1902. The Steiff Company of Grengen/Brenz, Germany, displayed one at a fair in Leipzig in 1903. Thomas Michton of Brooklyn, New York, was credited with creating the name "Teddy Bear" in honor of President Theodore Roosevelt. At the time of the naming, President Roosevelt had been on a well-publicized hunting trip in Mississippi while negotiating a border dispute with Louisiana. When he came up empty-handed from his hunting, his aides rounded up a bear cub for the President to shoot. His granddaughter, Sarah Alden "Aldie" Gannett, said, "I think he felt he could never face his children again if he shot anything so small. So he let it go."[79]

The incident was popularized in cartoons by Clifford Berryman of the *Washington Post*. Michton and his wife stitched up a couple of honey-colored bears and then displayed them in their novelty store window along with a copy of Berryman's cartoon.

The bears sold in a day. Michton made another stuffed bear and sent it to President Roosevelt requesting his permission to use his name. Roosevelt replied with a handwritten note: "I doubt if my name will mean much in the bear business, but you may use it if you wish." It was simply signed "T. R."[80]

Teddy bears today fall into one of two broad categories: either to a subsegment of the toy industry, plush dolls and animals, or are part of the collectibles industry. Although no one knows exactly how many teddy bears are sold each year, it is known that teddy bears accounted for 70 to 80% of the $1 billion plush toy industry in 1997.[81] "Bears sell across every season, occasion, and holiday," said Del Clark, Director of Merchandising for Fiesta, a Verona, California, maker of stuffed animals.[82] Not only have bears historically been a steady seller, but returns of teddy bears are almost nonexistent.[83]

The U.S. toy industry (including teddy bears, dolls, puzzles, games, action figures and vehicles, and preschool activity toys) was estimated to be worth $25 billion in sales and had been growing at an annual rate of more than 3%.[84] With its combination of a large demographic base of children and a population with a high level of disposable income, the U.S. toy market was larger than those of Japan (the number two market) and Western Europe combined.[85] Most toys that are sold in the United States were made in foreign countries. Chinese-produced toys represented about 30% of all U.S. toy sales due to inexpensive labor and favorable duty rates on imports.[86] The big toy manufacturers were buying each other's operations and those of smaller toy makers. In 1997, the number one toy manufacturer, Mattel (maker of Fisher-Price toys and Barbie dolls), bought Tyco Toys, formerly ranked number three. Hasbro (maker of G.I. Joe, Monopoly, and Milton Bradley toys) was the number two toy maker. Some games and toys maintained popularity over time, others were passing fads. It was difficult to predict which would remain popular over time. In the 1990s, marketing appeared to be the key to success. Toy production and marketing were regularly integrated with movies and television programs. For example, Star Wars action figures and other merchandise accounted for about one third of number 3 toy make Galoob Toys' 1997 sales of $360 million.[87] Small toy makers found it difficult to compete with the multimillion-dollar marketing campaigns and the in-depth market research of companies like Mattel, although there was always an exception such as Beanie Babies.

During 1997, manufacturers' shipments of plush products rose 37.5%, from $984 million to $1.4 billion, largely as a result of the Beanie Baby craze.[88] Designed by Ty Warner, the owner of Ty, Inc., Beanie Babies had been the big sales item since 1996 when they generated sales of $250 million. The $5 toys were produced in limited numbers and sold through specialty toy stores rather than through mass-market retailers. Beanie Baby characters no longer in production fetched up to $3,000 among collectors. Some retailers reported a decline in the sales of other plush toys due to the demand for Beanie Babies.[89]

Competitors of Vermont Teddy Bear were of various types. Major plush doll manufacturers such as Mattel and Hasbro were considered competition in this subsegment of the toy industry. More direct competition for Vermont Teddy came from other bear manufacturers including Steiff of Germany, Dakin, Applause, Fiesta, North American Bear, and Gund, the leading maker of toy bears. Information about some of these direct competitors is presented in **Exhibit 6**.

In general, these competitors relied on sales though retail outlets and had much greater financial resources to drive sales and marketing efforts than did Vermont Teddy Bear. Unlike Vermont Teddy Bear, these companies depended on foreign manufacturing and sources of raw materials, enabling them to sell comparable products at retail prices below those currently offered by Vermont Teddy. In addition, small craft stores had begun to sell locally produced all-American-made teddy bears, and publications had been developed to teach people to craft their own bears.

The collectible market in bears had recently been booming with people seeking bears as financial investments. Collectible bears are those that are meant to be displayed, not drooled or spit up on by their owners. "In the past 5 to 10 years we've seen a tremendous growth in the

Exhibit 6

Competition: The Vermont Teddy Bear Co., Inc.

Steiff
High-quality bears are manufactured in Germany and the Far East. The bears are not individually customized. The company's trademark is a button sewn into the ear of each bear. Prices of Steiff bears range from $50 for a 6-inch-tall bear to several thousand dollars for a life-size model. The bears are sold in a variety of outlets from discount stores and supermarkets to high-end specialty shops and antique stores.

Gund
This mass producer of a wide range of plush animals established an Internet Web site, allowing users to view and purchase products. Bears are manufactured overseas, primarily in Korea. Appearance of the bears is different from Vermont Teddy Bears', with shorter noses and limbs. They offer a broad range of styles and prices.

Teddy Bear Factory
This is the only other American manufacturer of teddy bears. The company is located in San Francisco and highly regional in its sales and marketing efforts. Vermont Teddy Bear advertises in the San Francisco Bay area but does not consider the Teddy Bear Factory to be strong competition because of the size and because its market is so regional.

North American Bear Company
This middle-sized company manufactures all of its bears in the Orient, primarily in Korea. Appearance of the bears is different from Vermont Teddy Bears, with shorter noses and limbs. The company advertises in trade magazines and has begun to do consumer advertising. It sells to retailers in Europe and Japan and collectors and gift shops in the United States.

Applause Enterprises, Inc.
This company focuses on manufacturing plush toy versions of Sesame Street, Looney Tunes, Star Wars, Muppets, and Disney characters as well as nonplush toys. Company was formed by the 1995 merger of plush toy maker Dakin and a company founded by Wallace Berrie.

upscale bear, the limited editions, and the artist-designed bears," said George B. Black, Jr., director of the Teddy Bear Museum in Naples, Florida.[90] The "collectible" segment of the plush market generated $441 million in consumer sales for 1996, up from $354 million in 1995. Collectible plush sales for 1997 were expected to reach nearly $700 million. This would make plush one of the fastest growing categories in the $9.2 billion collectibles industry.[91] Collectible bears started at about $25 but could cost $1,000 or more. This number was somewhat misleading, considering that the value of a collectible bear can be in excess of $50,000. A 1904 Steiff "Teddy Girl" bear sold at a Christie's auction in 1994 for a record $171,380.[92]

Two trade magazines, *Teddy Bear and Friends* and *Teddy Bear Review*, targeted the collectibles market. These magazines tell bear collectors where they can buy and sell old bears. In 1998, major bear shows and jamborees were held in at least 25 states, as well as hundreds of bear-making retreats and workshops.[93]

The concept of Bear-Grams lent itself to two distinct groups of competitors. Vermont Teddy Bear competed not only with soft plush stuffed animals, especially teddy bears, but also with a variety of other special occasion greetings such as flowers, candy, balloons, cakes, and other gift items that could be ordered by phone for special occasions and delivered the next day. Many of these competitors had greater financial, sales, and marketing resources than Vermont Teddy Bear.[94]

Patents, Trademarks, and Licenses

The company's name in combination with its original logo was a registered trademark in the United States. In addition, the company owned the registered trademarks in the United States for "The Vermont Teddy Bear Company," "Bear-Gram," "Teddy Bear-Gram," and "Make A Friend For Life." The company also owned the registered service marks "Bear Counselor," "Vermont Bear-Gram," and "Racer Ted," and had applications pending to register the company's second and third company logos, "Bearanimal," "Coffee Cub," "Vermont Bear-Gram," "Vermont Baby Bear," "The Great American Teddy Bear," "All-American Teddy Bear," "Beau and Beebee," "Teddy-Grams," and "Vermont Teddy Wear."[95]

Vermont Teddy Bear also owned the registered trademark "Vermont Teddy Bear" in Japan and had an application pending to register "The Great American Teddy Bear" in Japan.[96]

Although the company had continuously used the "Bear-Gram" trademark since April 1985, its initial application to register the mark on June 13, 1990, was rejected by the U.S. Patent and Trademark Office due to prior registration of the mark "Bear-A-Grams," by another company on June 7, 1988. The company reapplied to register "Bear-Gram," and its application was approved on November 5, 1996.

The company also claimed copyright, service mark, or trademark protection for its teddy bear designs, its marketing slogans, and its advertising copy and promotional literature.

On May 16, 1997, Vermont Teddy Bear sued Disney Enterprises, Inc., for injunctive relief and unspecified damages claiming that Disney copied its bear-by-mail concept with Pooh-Grams based on Disney's Winnie the Pooh character. The complaint accused Disney of unfair competition and trademark infringement saying the Pooh-Gram is "confusingly similar" to Bear-Grams in name, logo, how it is personalized, how it is delivered, and even how it is marketed.[97] Disney introduced Pooh-Grams in its fall 1996 catalog and escalated its promotion of the product using the Internet, print, and radio advertising. Disney disagreed saying that the Vermont Teddy lawsuit was without merit because Winnie the Pooh has been a well-known Disney character for 25 years and there are all kinds of grams—mail-grams, candy-grams, money-grams, telegrams, flower-grams—not just Bear-Grams.

On September 9, 1997, Vermont Teddy announced that it had entered into an agreement to resolve its dispute with Walt Disney Co. Under the agreement, Disney will continue to offer its Pooh-Gram products and services but will voluntarily limit its use of the Pooh-Gram mark in certain advertising and will adequately distinguish its trademarks and service marks from those of Vermont Teddy Bear. Vermont Teddy in turn will be allowed to offer certain Winnie-the-Pooh merchandise for sale in its mail order catalogs but cannot offer the merchandise with its Bear-Gram program.[98]

Finance

On November 23, 1993, Vermont Teddy Bear Co., Inc., sold 1.15 million shares of stock at $10 a share through an underwriting group led by Barrington Capital Group L.P. The stock rose as high as $19 before closing the day at $16.75, an increase of 67.5% in its first day of trading. The market's reaction to the IPO signaled that investors thought the stock was undervalued at $10 and that the company had a great deal of growth potential. During fiscal 1998, the company's stock price fluctuated between $2.56 and $0.75 a share. This was an indication that investors reconsidered the growth potential of Vermont Teddy Bear.

Vice President of Finance was Mark Sleeper. **Exhibits 7** and **8** detail Vermont Teddy Bear's financial situation. Prior to 1994, Vermont Teddy Bear had experienced a great deal of success and profitability. The company's net sales increased 61% from $10,569,017 in 1992 to $17,025,856 in 1993, while the cost of goods sold decreased from 43.1% of sales to 41.8% during the same time period. Net income increased 314% from $202,601 in 1992 to $838,955 in 1993.

Sales reached a peak in 1994 at $20,560,566. This represented a 21% growth over 1993. Unfortunately profits did not experience similar growth. Had it not been for an almost $70,000 tax refund, the company would have experienced a net loss in 1994. The company's net profit fell to $17,523 after taxes in 1994 due to a substantial increase in both selling expense and general and administrative expenses. These two items combined for an increase of 35% over comparable figures for 1993.

In 1995, sales fell to $20,044,796. Although this represented only a 2.5% decline, this decline in sales painted a picture for the next two years. While sales were decreasing, selling and general and administrative expenses continued to climb. These expenses grew by 10% to $13,463,631 in 1995. These two items represented 67% of sales in 1996, whereas they were 53% of sales in 1993.

After three years of declining sales, Vermont Teddy Bear's sales grew by 4.4% in 1998 to $17,207,543. Vermont Teddy Bear experienced a loss of $2,422,477 in 1995. It returned to profitability in 1996, earning $151,953. Unfortunately that was the last profitable year for the company. Losses were $1,901,745 in 1997 and $1,683,669 in 1998. Interest expense had risen dramatically for the company from $35,002 in 1995 to $608,844 in 1998.

The company included in its quarterly report to the SEC (Filing Date: 5/14/98) that it had been operating without a working capital line of credit since July 18, 1997. On that date, the company completed a sale-leaseback transaction involving its factory headquarters and a portion of its property located in Shelburne, Vermont. This financing replaced the company's mortgage and line of credit. The company received $5.9 million from this transaction. Of this amount, $3.3 million was used to pay off the mortgage and $600,000 was used to pay off the line of credit. A $591,000 transactions cost was associated with the sale-leaseback. The lease obligation was repayable on a 20-year amortization schedule through July 2017.

On October 10, 1997, Vermont Teddy received a commitment from Green Mountain Capital L.P. whereby it agreed to lend the company up to $200,000 for up to five years at 12% interest. The loan was secured by security interest in the company's real and personal property. Green Mountain Capital also received warrants to purchase 100,000 shares of common stock at an exercise price of $1.00. The warrants could be exercised any time from two years from the date of the loan to seven years from the date of the loan.

Exhibit 7

Consolidated Balance Sheets: The Vermont Teddy Bear Co., Inc.

Year Ending June 30	1998	1997	1996	1995	1994[1]	1993[1]	1992[1]
Assets							
Current assets							
Cash and marketable securities	$ 1,527,052	$ 441,573	$ 1,121,500	$ 1,070,862	$ 2,379,760	$ 8,561,525	$ —
Accounts receivable, trade	51,538	46,304	131,550	122,679	142,029	103,762	77,815
Inventories	2,396,245	3,302,313	1,974,731	3,042,484	4,024,247	2,425,233	1,135,940
Prepaid expenses	444,229	386,947	277,502	213,236	568,680	123,886	10,681
Due from officer	—	—	—	—	565,714	—	—
Deferred income taxes	233,203	259,016	240,585	126,393	322,106	194,082	—
Total current assets	4,652,267	4,436,153	3,745,868	4,575,654	8,002,536	11,408,488	1,224,436
Property and equipment	8,844,475	9,845,935	10,300,318	10,493,214	3,052,002	861,419	589,196
Construction in progress	—	—	—	—	3,275,527	—	—
Due from officer	—	—	—	—	128,008	128,008	102,480
Deposits and other assets	903,110	272,348	98,086	102,676	121,640	97,400	14,356
Notes receivable	87,500	95,000	95,000	190,000	190,000	—	—
Total assets	$14,487,352	$14,649,436	$14,239,272	$15,361,544	$14,769,713	$12,495,315	$1,930,468
Liabilities and shareholders' equity							
Current liabilities							
Cash overdraft	$ —	$ —	$ —	$ —	$ —	$ —	$ 148,048
Line of credit	—	550,000	—	—	—	—	—
Notes payable, bank	45,603	—	—	—	36,748	108,748	180,748
Current installments of							
Long-term debt	231,133	3,443,096	187,095	27,805	21,981	22,793	19,075
Capital lease obligations	225,738	103,759	104,146	126,306	99,901	45,604	41,795
Accounts payable	1,846,042	2,562,536	1,353,698	2,513,468	3,336,558	1,319,499	1,604,066
Accrued expenses	916,191	657,347	449,048	860,440	442,467	381,146	156,777

Income taxes payable	—	—	37,365	90,889	117,810	117,810	—
Total current liabilities	3,264,707	7,316,738	2,131,352	3,618,908	4,055,465	1,995,600	2,150,509
Construction loan payable							
Long-term debt	338,317	372,999	3,505,812	3,252,379	60,408	82,411	81,401
Capital lease obligations	5,748,182	209,054	312,814	347,874	398,220	58,883	61,350
Other liabilities	—	—	84,430	204,430	—	—	—
Accrued interest payable, debentures	—	—	—	—	—	—	958,219
Deferred income taxes	233,203	259,016	240,585	126,393	105,992	47,492	—
Total liabilities	9,584,409	8,157,807	6,274,993	7,549,984	4,620,085	2,184,386	3,251,479
Shareholders' equity							
Preferred stock $.05 par value:							
Authorized 1,000,000 shares							
Series A	1,044,000	900,000	900,000	900,000	900,000	900,000	—
Cumulative dividends at 8%							
Preferred stock $.05 par value:							
Authorized 375,000 shares							
Series B	10,245	10,245	—	—	—	—	—
Common stock, $.05 par value:							
Authorized 20,000,000 shares	259,787	258,638	258,638	258,625	258,625	258,625	200,000
Additional paid-in capital	10,587,316	10,565,482	10,074,595	10,073,842	10,073,842	10,073,842	185,868
Treasury stock at cost							
(12,000 shares)	(106,824)	(106,824)	(106,824)	(106,824)	(106,824)		
Accumulated deficit	(6,891,581)	(5,135,912)	(3,162,130)	(3,314,083)	(976,015)	(921,538)	(1,706,879)
Total shareholders' equity	4,902,943	6,491,629	7,964,279	7,811,560	10,149,628	10,310,929	(1,321,011)
Total liabilities and shareholders' equity	$14,487,352	$14,649,436	$14,239,272	$15,361,544	$14,769,713	$12,495,315	$1,930,468

Note:
1. Fiscal year ending December 31.

Source: The Vermont Teddy Bear Company, Inc., *1998 Annual Report.*

Exhibit 8

Statement of Operations: The Vermont Teddy Bear Co., Inc.

Year Ending June 30	1998	1997	1996	1995	1994[1]	1993[1]	1992[1]
Net sales	$17,207,543	$16,489,482	$17,039,618	$20,044,796	$20,560,566	$17,025,856	$10,569,017
Cost of goods sold	7,397,450	7,068,549	7,309,038	9,101,028	8,619,580	7,123,930	4,555,424
Gross margin	9,810,093	9,420,933	9,730,580	10,943,768	11,940,986	9,901,926	6,013,593
Selling expenses	7,866,843	7,961,003	6,287,208	9,121,023	8,907,440	6,862,328	4,454,891
General and administrative expenses	3,031,716	2,938,251	2,954,601	4,342,608	3,311,306	2,184,500	1,266,770
Total expenses	10,898,559	10,899,254	9,241,809	13,463,631	12,218,746	9,046,828	5,721,661
Operating income (loss)	(1,088,466)	(1,478,321)	488,771	(2,519,863)	(277,760)	855,098	291,932
Interest income	26,126	53,267	41,092	192,156	248,987	27,887	2,152
Miscellaneous income	29,243	(11,973)	63,236	1,620	1,620	25,000	—
Interest expense	(650,572)	(464,768)	(441,146)	(35,002)	(24,848)	(97,810)	(91,483)
Income (loss) before taxes	(1,683,669)	(1,901,795)	151,953	(2,361,089)	(52,001)	810,175	202,601
Income tax provision (benefit)	—	—	—	61,388	(69,524)	(28,780)	—
Net income (loss)	$(1,683,669)	$(1,901,795)	$ 151,953	$(2,422,477)	$ 17,523	$ 838,955	$ 202,601
Preferred stock dividends	(72,000)	(72,000)	—	(72,000)	(72,000)	(53,614)	—
Net earnings (loss) common shareholders	(1,611,669)	(1,829,795)	151,953	(2,350,477)	89,523	892,569	202,601
Net earnings (loss) per common share	(0.34)	(0.38)	0.03	(0.48)	(0.10)	0.19	0.05
Weighted average number of shares outstanding	5,172,475	5,160,750	5,160,583	5,160,500	5,164,057	4,210,070	4,024,140

Note:
1. Fiscal year ending December 31.

Source: The Vermont Teddy Bear Company, Inc., *1998 Annual Report.*

To reduce costs, the company closed its retail store in New York City and planned to close the Freeport, Maine, and North Conway, New Hampshire, stores before the end of 1998 because the revenue increases necessary to support the annual lease obligations would not be achievable in the short run. The company's lease obligation of $300,000 per year on the New York City store would continue until a replacement tenant was found.

On May 22, 1998, it was announced that The Vermont Teddy Bear Co., Inc., had signed a letter of intent with the Shepherd Group, a Boston-based private equity investment firm, for a proposed $600,000 equity investment with the company. The Shepherd Group invested in venture and existing small- to middle-market companies focusing on companies with high-growth potential and unique market-ready quality products and services. In return for the $600,000 investment, the Shepherd Group received 60 shares of Series C Preferred Stock as well as warrants to purchase 495,868 shares of Common Stock at $1.21 per share. The transaction was subject to final agreements and various approvals and conditions.

The Series C Convertible Redeemable Stock carried a 6% coupon, and each share was convertible into 8,264,467 shares of the company's Common Stock. The Preferred had voting rights, and the Shepherd Group was entitled to two seats on the company's Board of Directors.

Elisabeth Robert noted, "The additional funds will provide working capital for the company to pursue growth in the Bear-Gram channel and to maximize the benefits of importing raw materials. Additionally Tom Shepherd has strong financial and operations experience and will bring a valuable perspective to the Board of Directors. Tom's strong suit has been working with companies that have not yet realized the full potential of their brand."[99]

According to some analysts, the survival of this company was going to depend on maintaining a source of working capital, cost containment, and a rebound in sales back to their 1995 level. The company had taken an aggressive approach to ensuring survival, but this was not done cheaply. High interest rates were paid and warrants to purchase stock, at what might turn out to be a bargain price, had been issued.

Notes

1. Cynthia Crossen, "Isn't It Funny How a Bear Makes Money, Year After Year?" *Wall Street Journal* (February 17, 1998), p. B-1.
2. "Vermont Teddy President and CEO Interview," *The Wall Street Journal Corporate Reporter, Inc.* (January 21, 1998).
3. *Ibid.*
4. The Vermont Teddy Bear Co., Inc., *1997 Annual Report.*
5. Richard H. Levy, "Ursine of the Times: Vermont Teddy Bear Company Pulls Back from Catalog Sales," *Direct Marketing* (February 1998), p. 16.
6. Maria Lisa Calta, "Cub Scout," *Detroit News* (March 5, 1995), pp. 22-D, 23-D.
7. *Ibid.*
8. Phaedra Hise, "Making Fans on Talk Radio," *Inc.* (December 1993), p. 62.
9. The Vermont Teddy Bear Co., Inc., *1994 Annual Report*, p. 3.
10. The Vermont Teddy Bear Co., Inc., *Company Time Line,* Information Packet, p. 2.
11. *Ibid.*
12. *Ibid.*
13. The Vermont Teddy Bear Co., Inc., *Form 10-KSB* (June 30, 1995), p. 1.
14. *Company Time Line,* p. 2.
15. The Vermont Teddy Bear Co., Inc., Press Release (April 17, 1995).
16. The Vermont Teddy Bear Co., Inc., *1994 Annual Report* (Letter to Shareholders), p. 2.
17. *The Wall Street Journal Corporate Reporter, Inc.* (January 21, 1998).
18. "The Vermont Teddy Bear Company Roars into New York City," Vermont Teddy Bear Co., Inc., Press Release (October 9, 1996).
19. "The Vermont Teddy Posts Year-End Results, Closes Equity Deal," Vermont Teddy Bear Co., Inc., Press Release (September 29, 1998), p. 1.
20. "The Vermont Teddy Bear Company Expands Retail Activities," Vermont Teddy Bear Co., Inc., Press Release (June 20, 1996).
21. The Vermont Teddy Bear Co., Inc., *1997 Annual Report* (Letter to Shareholders), p. 3.
22. *The Wall Street Journal Corporate Reporter, Inc.* (January 21, 1998).
23. The Vermont Teddy Bear Co., Inc., *1997 Annual Report* (Letter to Shareholders), p. 3.
24. The Vermont Teddy Bear Co., Inc., *1997 Annual Report*, p. 22, and *1997 Proxy Statement* (October 28, 1997), pp. 6, 10, 21–23.
25. The Vermont Teddy Bear Co., Inc., *Form 10-KSB* (September 28, 1998), p. 10.
26. The Vermont Teddy Bear Co., Inc., *1997 Proxy Statement* (October 28, 1997), pp. 4–5.
27. The Vermont Teddy Bear Co., Inc., *Form 10-KSB* (September 28, 1998), p. 10.
28. The Vermont Teddy Bear Co., Inc., *1998 Proxy Statement* (July 23, 1998), p. 5.
29. The Vermont Teddy Bear Co., Inc., *Form 10-KSB* (September 28, 1998), pp. 9–10.
30. The Vermont Teddy Bear Co., Inc., *1997 Annual Report*, p. 4.
31. *Ibid.*

32. *Ibid.*

33. The Vermont Teddy Bear Co., Inc., *Form 10-KSB* (September 28, 1998), p. 6.

34. Calta, p. 22-D.

35. The Vermont Teddy Bear Co., Inc., *Form 10-KSB* (September 28, 1998), p. 6.

36. The Vermont Teddy Bear *Gazette* (summer 1995 edition), p. 7.

37. The Vermont Teddy Bear Co., Inc., *Form 10-KSB* (September 28, 1998), p. 6.

38. *Ibid.*

39. Levy, p. 16.

40. "Vermont Teddy Bear Appoints Vice President of Marketing and Design," The Vermont Teddy Bear Co., Inc., Press Release (May 5, 1998).

41. Calta, p. 22-D.

42. The Vermont Teddy Bear Co., Inc., *Form 10-KSB* (September 28, 1998), p. 3.

43. *Ibid.*

44. The Vermont Teddy Bear Co., Inc., "Vermont Teddy Bear Posts Quarterly Profit on Increased Revenues," Press Release (May 14, 1998), p. 1.

45. The Vermont Teddy Bear Co., Inc., *Form 10-KSB* (September 28, 1998), p. 4.

46. Jim Kerstetter, "Setting Up Mom and Pop," *PC Week On-Line* (August 24, 1998), p. 1.

47. The Vermont Teddy Bear Co., Inc., *Form 10-KSB* (September 28, 1998), p. 4.

48. *Ibid.*

49. "Vermont Teddy Bear Company to be Featured on Dateline NBC, December 17, 1996," The Vermont Teddy Bear Co., Inc., Press Release (December 17, 1996).

50. The Vermont Teddy Bear Co., Inc., *1997 Annual Report*, p. 10.

51. The Vermont Teddy Bear Co., Inc., *Form 10-KSB* (September 28, 1998), p. 3.

52. *Ibid.*, p. 5

53. The Vermont Teddy Bear Co., Inc., *1994 Annual Report*, p. 3.

54. Melissa Dowling, "Vermont Teddy Bears the Pressure," *Catalog Age* (May 1996), p. 12.

55. The Vermont Teddy Bear Co., Inc., *Form 10-KSB* (September 28, 1998), p. 5.

56. The Vermont Teddy Bear Co., Inc., *1997 Annual Report* (Letter to Shareholders), p. 4.

57. The Vermont Teddy Bear Co., Inc., *Form 10-KSB* (September 28, 1998), p. 3.

58. Levy, p. 16.

59. "Vermont Teddy Bear Announces Second-Quarter Results," Press Release (February 13, 1998).

60. The Vermont Teddy Bear Co., Inc., *1997 Annual Report*.

61. The Vermont Teddy Bear Co., Inc., *1997 Annual Report* (Letter to Shareholders), p. 4.

62. "Vermont Teddy Bear Company Joins Forces with America's Most Famous Teddy Bear Person," The Vermont Teddy Bear Co., Inc., Press Release (November 5, 1996).

63. "NFL Football Soft and Cuddly? The Vermont Teddy Bear Company Introduces Officially Licensed NFL Teddy Bears," The Vermont Teddy Bear Co., Inc., Press Release (August 27, 1997).

64. "The Vermont Teddy Bear Company Kicks Off NFL Bear-Grams," The Vermont Teddy Bear Co., Inc., Press Release (September 30, 1996).

65. *The Wall Street Journal Corporate Reporter* (January 21, 1998).

66. *Ibid.*

67. *Ibid.*

68. The Vermont Teddy Bear Co., Inc., *1997 Annual Report*, p. 13.

69. The Vermont Teddy Bear Co., Inc., *Form 10-KSB* (September 28, 1998), p. 8.

70. "Vermont Teddy Bear Refinances Factory Headquarters," The Vermont Teddy Bear Co., Inc., Press Release (July 21, 1997).

71. The Vermont Teddy Bear Co., Inc., *Form 10-KSB* (September 28, 1998), p. 5.

72. *Ibid.*

73. *Ibid.*

74. Edna Tenney, "A Teddy Bear's Modest Proposal," *Business Digest*, <webmaster@vermontguides.com> (October 10, 1997), pp. 1–3.

75. Bernard Abrams, "Switch to Air Bags Bears Watching," *Packaging Digest* (March 1998), pp. 50–52.

76. The Vermont Teddy Bear Co., Inc., *Form 10-KSB* (September 28, 1998), p. 7.

77. "Bear Necessities," *Direct Marketing Magazine* (July 1998), p. 18.

78. *Ibid.*

79. Calta, p. 23-D.

80. *Ibid.*

81. Crossen, p. B-1.

82. *Ibid.*

83. "Bullish for Bears," *The Times* (Tampa) (February 18, 1998), pp. E1–2.

84. Stuart Hampton, *Hoovers Online: Toys and Games Industry Snapshot*, 1998, p. 1.

85. J. S. Krutick, et al., "Salomon Smith Barney Toy Industry Update," *Investext Report*, number: 2715626 (June 23, 1998), p. 6.

86. Hampton, p. 2.

87. Donna Leccese, "Growth at a Price," *Playthings* (June 1998), p. 30.

88. *Ibid.*

89. The Vermont Teddy Bear Co., Inc., *1997 Annual Report*, p. 11.

90. Leccese, p. 30.

91. Calta, p. 23-D.

92. Crossen, p. B-1.

93. The Vermont Teddy Bear Co., Inc., *1997 Annual Report*, p. 11.

94. The Vermont Teddy Bear Co., Inc., *Form 10-KSB* (September 28, 1998), p. 7.

95. *Ibid.*

96. Bruce Horovitz, *USA Today* (May 27, 1997), p. B-2.

97. "Vermont Teddy Bear and Disney Settle Suit," The Vermont Teddy Bear Co., Inc., Press Release (September 9, 1997).

98. The Vermont Teddy Bear Co., Inc., *1994, 1995, 1996, 1997 Annual Reports* and *Form 10-KSB* (September 28, 1998).

99. The Vermont Teddy Bear Co., Inc., Press Release (May 22, 1998), pp. 1–3.

case 28

The Carey Plant

Thomas L. Wheelen and J. David Hunger

The Gardner Company was a respected New England manufacturer of machines and machine tools purchased by furniture makers for use in their manufacturing process. As a means of growing the firm, the Gardner Company acquired Carey Manufacturing three years ago from James Carey for $3,500,000. Carey Manufacturing was a high quality maker of specialized machine parts. Ralph Brown, Gardner's Vice President of Finance, had been the driving force behind the acquisition. Except for Andy Doyle and Rod Davis, all of Gardner's Vice Presidents (**Exhibit 1**) had been opposed to expansion through acquisition. They preferred internal growth for Gardner because they felt that the company would be more able to control both the rate and direction of its growth. Nevertheless, since both Peter Finch, President, and R. C. Smith, Executive Vice President, agreed with Brown's strong recommendation, Carey Manufacturing was acquired. Its primary asset was an aging manufacturing plant located 400 miles away from the Gardner Company's current headquarters and manufacturing facility. The Gardner Company was known for its manufacturing competency. Management hoped to add value to its new acquisition by transferring Gardner's manufacturing skills to the Carey Plant through significant process improvements.

James Carey, previous owner of Carey Manufacturing, agreed to continue serving as Plant Manager of what was now called the Carey Plant. He reported directly to the Gardner Company Executive Vice President, R. C. Smith. All functional activities of Carey Manufacturing had remained the same after the acquisition, except for sales activities being moved under Andy Doyle, Gardner's Vice President of Marketing. The five Carey Manufacturing salesmen were retained and allowed to keep their same sales territories. They exclusively sold only products made in the Carey Plant. The other Carey Plant functional departments (Human Resources, Engineering, Finance, Materials, Quality Assurance, and Operations) were supervised by Managers who directly reported to the Carey Plant Manager. The Managers of the Human Resources, Engineering, Materials, and Operations Departments also reported indirectly (shown by dotted lines in **Exhibit 1**) to the Vice Presidents in charge of their respective function at Gardner Company headquarters.

Until its acquisition, Carey Manufacturing (now the Carey Plant) had been a successful firm with few problems. Following its purchase, however, the plant had been plagued by labor

---

This case was prepared by Professors Thomas L. Wheelen of the University of South Florida and J. David Hunger of the Iowa State University. Names and dates in the case have been disguised. An earlier version of this case was presented to the 2000 annual meeting of the North American Case Research Association. This case may not be reproduced in any form without written permission of the two copyright holders. This case was edited for SMBP-9th Edition. Copyright © 2001 by Thomas L. Wheelen and J. David Hunger. Reprinted by permission.

Exhibit 1
Gardner Company Organization Chart

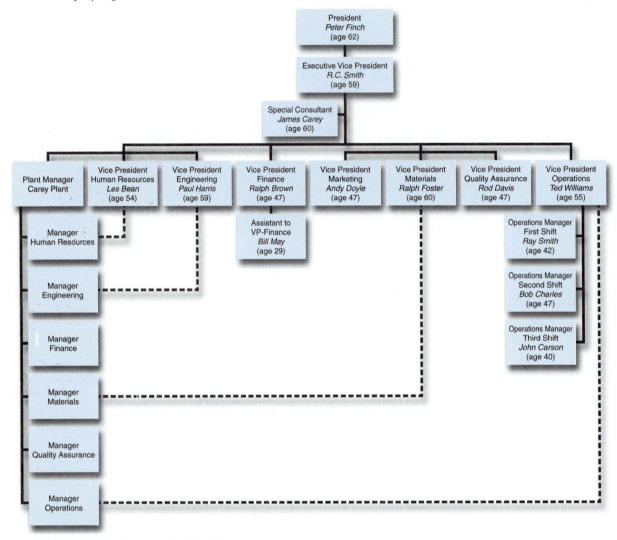

Note: Dotted lines show an indirect reporting relationship.

problems, increasing costs, a leveling of sales, and a decline in profits (**Exhibit 2**). Two years ago, the Carey Plant suffered a 10-week strike called by its union in response to demands from the new management (Gardner Company) for increased production without a corresponding increase in pay. (Although Gardner Company was also unionized, its employees were represented by a different union than were the Carey Plant employees.) Concerned by both the strike and the poor performance of the Carey Plant since its purchase two years earlier, Ralph Brown initiated a study last year to identify what was wrong. He discovered that the poor performance of the Carey Plant resulted not only from its outdated and overcrowded manufacturing facility, but also from James Carey's passive role as Plant Manager. Gardner's Executive Committee (composed of the President and eight Vice Presidents) had been aware of the poor condition of the Carey Plant when it had agreed to the acquisition. It had therefore initiated plans to replace the aging plant. A new state-of-the-art manufacturing facility was being built on available property adjacent to the current plant and should be completed within a few months. The information regarding James Carey was, however, quite surprising to the

Exhibit 2

Carey Plant: Recent Sales and Profit Figures

Year	Sales	Profits
5 Years Ago	$12,430,002	$697,042
4 Years Ago	13,223,804	778,050
3 Years Ago	14,700,178	836,028
2 Years Ago	10,300,000	(220,000)*
Last Year	13,950,000	446,812

*Ten-week strike during October, November, December.

Committee. Before Gardner's purchase of Carey Manufacturing, James Carey had been actively involved in every phase of his company's operations. Since selling the company, however, Carey had delegated the running of the plant to his staff, the Department Managers. One of his Managers admitted that "He was the driving force of the company, but since he sold out, he has withdrawn completely from the management of the plant."

After hearing Brown's report, the Executive Committee decided that the Carey Plant needed a new Plant Manager. Consequently, James Carey was relieved of his duties as Plant Manager in early January this year and appointed special consultant to the Executive Vice President, R. C. Smith. The current staff of the Carey Plant was asked to continue operating the plant until a new Plant Manager could be named. Vice Presidents Brown and Williams were put in charge of finding a new Manager for the Carey Plant. They recommended several internal candidates to the Executive Vice President, R. C. Smith.

The Offer

On January 31 of this year, Smith offered the Plant Manager position of the Carey Plant to Bill May, current Assistant to Ralph Brown. May had spent six years in various specialist capacities within Gardner's Finance Department after being hired with an MBA. He had been in his current position for the past two years. Brown supported the offer to May with praise for his subordinate. "He has outstanding analytical abilities, drive, general administrative skills and is cost conscious. He is the type of man we need at the Carey Plant." The other executives viewed May not only as the company's efficiency expert, but also as a person who would see any job through to completion. Nevertheless, several of the Vice Presidents expressed opposition to placing a staff person in charge of the new plant. They felt the Plant Manager should have a strong technical background and line management experience. Brown, in contrast, stressed the necessity of a control-conscious person to get the new plant underway. Smith agreed that Gardner needed a person with a strong finance background heading the new plant.

Smith offered May the opportunity to visit the Carey Plant to have a private talk with each of his future staff. Each of the six Department Managers had been with the Carey Plant for a minimum of 18 years. They were frank in their discussions of past problems in the plant and in its future prospects. They generally agreed that the plant's labor problems should decline in the new plant, even though it was going to employ the same 405 employees (half the size of Gardner) with the same union. Four of them were concerned, however, with how they were being supervised. Ever since the acquisition by the Gardner Company, the Managers of the Operations, Materials, Human Resources, and Engineering Departments reported not only to James Carey as Plant Manager, but also to their respective functional Vice Presidents and staff at Gardner headquarters. Suggestions from the various Vice Presidents and staff assistants often conflicted with orders from the Plant Manager. When they confronted James Carey about the situation, he had merely shrugged. Carey told them to expect this sort of thing after an acquisition. "It's important that you get along with your new bosses, since they are the ones who will decide your future in this firm," advised Carey.

Bill May then met in mid-February with Ralph Brown, his current supervisor, to discuss the job offer over morning coffee. Turning to Brown, he said, "I'm worried about this Plant Manager's position. I will be in a whole new environment. I'm a complete stranger to those Department Managers, except for the Finance Manager. I will be the first member of the Gardner Company to be assigned to the Carey Plant. I will be functioning in a line position without any previous experience and no technical background in machine operations. I also honestly feel that several of the Vice Presidents would like to see me fail. I'm not sure if I should accept the job. I have a lot of questions, but I don't know where to get the answers." Looking over his coffee cup as he took a drink, Brown responded, "Bill, this is a great opportunity for you. What's the problem?" Adjusting himself in his chair, May looked directly at his mentor. "The specific details of the offer are very vague in terms of salary, responsibilities, and authority. What is expected of me and when? Do I have to keep the current staff? Do I have to hire future staff members from internal sources or can I go outside the company? Finally, I'm concerned about the lack of an actual job description." Brown was surprised by his protégé's many concerns. "Bill, I'm hoping that all of these questions, except for salary, will soon be answered at a meeting Smith is scheduling for you tomorrow with the Vice Presidents. He wants it to be an open forum."

The Meeting

The next morning, May took the elevator to the third floor. As he walked down the hall to the Gardner Company Executive Committee conference room, he bumped into Ted Williams, Vice President of Manufacturing, who was just coming out of his office. Looking at Bill, Ted offered, "I want to let you know that I'm behind you 100%. I wasn't at first, but I do think you may have what it takes to turn that place around. I don't care what the others think." As the two of them entered the conference room, May looked at the eight Gardner Vice Presidents. Some were sitting at the conference table and working on their lap tops while others were getting some coffee from the decanter in the corner. R. C. Smith was already seated at the head of the table. Ralph Brown, sitting on one side of the table, motioned to May to come sit in an empty chair beside him. "Want some coffee?" Brown asked. "Good idea," responded May as he walked over to the decanter. Pouring cream into his coffee, May wondered, "What am I getting myself into?"

case 29

Arm & Hammer: Church & Dwight Grows Up (2002)

Roy A. Cook

As management stepped firmly into another new century, an exciting new chapter in the company's history was opened. "2001 was an exciting and eventful year for Church & Dwight Co., Inc., during which major consumer brands and businesses were acquired, directly and through our new Armkel affiliate, creating a $1.5 billion consumer packaged goods and specialty chemicals company."[1] Had the pieces finally been put in place for the company to compete in the consumer products arena successfully?

Background

For over 156 years, Church & Dwight Co., Inc., worked to build market share on a brand name that is rarely associated with the company. This brand name became so pervasive that it can now be found on a variety of consumer products in 95% of all U.S. households. As the world's largest producer and marketer of sodium bicarbonate–based products, Church & Dwight had achieved fairly consistent growth in both sales and earnings as new and expanded uses were found for sodium bicarbonate. Although Church & Dwight may not be a household name, the name on the company's ubiquitous yellow box of baking soda was: ARM & HAMMER.

Shortly after its introduction in 1878, ARM & HAMMER Baking Soda became a fundamental item on the pantry shelf as homemakers found many uses for it other than baking, such as cleaning and deodorizing. It could also be used as a dentrifice, a chemical agent to absorb or neutralize odors and acidity, a kidney dialysis element, a blast media, an environmentally friendly cleaning agent, and a pollution control agent. It also showed promise in the area of odor control/elimination.

From the 1980s through the early 1990s, average company sales increased almost 15% annually. However, the stated strategy of "selling related products in different markets all linked by common carbonate and bicarbonate technology"[2] faltered and sales growth plateaued. As the chairman of one investment company said, "The only thing they had going for them [was] their uniqueness and they lost it. They made poor marketing and operating decisions that cost them a lot of money."[3] These decisions proved to be a mistake as consumer products were launched in major competitors' markets when the company was operating from a much smaller financial base.

This case was prepared by Professor Roy A. Cook of Fort Lewis College. This case was edited for SMBP-9th edition. Copyright © 2002 by Roy Cook. Reprinted by permission.

Exhibit 1

Consolidated Statements of Income: Church & Dwight Co., Inc.
(Dollar amounts in thousands, except per share data)

Year Ending December 31	2001	2000	1999
Net sales	$1,080,864	$795,725	$740,181
Cost of sales	680,211	450,321	414,486
Gross profit	400,653	345,404	325,695
Advertising, consumer, and trade promotion expenses	195,960	178,614	176,123
Selling, general, and administrative expenses	111,832	92,718	87,047
Impairment and other items	(660)	21,911	6,617
Gain on sale of mineral rights	—	—	(11,772)
Income from operations	93,521	52,161	67,680
Equity in earnings (loss) of affiliates	(6,195)	3,011	6,366
Investment earnings	2,224	2,032	1,216
Other income (expense)	(269)	(187)	201
Interest expense	(11,537)	(4,856)	(2,760)
Income from minority interest and taxes	77,744	52,161	72,703
Minority interest	3,889	287	525
Income before taxes	73,885	51,874	72,178
Income taxes	26,871	18,315	26,821
Net income	$ 46,984	$ 33,559	$ 45,357

Source: Church & Dwight Co., Inc., *2001 Annual Report*, and "SEC 10-K," 3/28/2002, p. 12 of 14. Entire Document
(EX-99).

Faced with investment community concerns and a string of disappointing financial results, Robert A. Davies III was brought in as President and chief executive officer (CEO). His primary goals were to reshape the company while raising sales and operating profit margins. The results of his efforts can be seen in the financial statements shown in **Exhibits 1** and **2**. In six years, he reshaped the company from a $500 million into an $1.08 billion business entity with an objective of achieving earnings growth of 12% to 15% per year through 2005.

Management

The historically slow but steady course Church & Dwight had traveled over the decades reflected top management's efforts to focus the company's activities. The ability to remain focused may be attributable to the fact that about 25% of the outstanding shares of common stock are owned by descendants of the company's co-founders. Dwight C. Minton, a direct descendant of Austin Church, actively directed the company as CEO from 1969 through 1995 and remained on the Board as Chairman Emeritus. He passed on the duties of CEO to the first non-family member in the company's history, Robert A. Davies III, in 1995. Davies assumed the additional duties of Chairman of the Board from Minton in 2001.

Although Davies was a non-family member, he had a long history of service with Church & Dwight. He served as Vice President, General Manager of the Arm & Hammer Division and then as President/Chief Operating Officer from 1969 through 1984. Davies continued to expand his experiences by serving as President and CEO of California Home Brands (a group of canning companies). In 1995, he returned to Church & Dwight as President of the Arm & Hammer Division to put the division "back on track."[4] According to Davies, future growth would be accomplished with "a well-balanced portfolio of household, personal care, and specialty products."[5]

Exhibit 2

Consolidated Balance Sheets: Church & Dwight Co., Inc. (Dollar amounts in thousands)

Year Ending December 31	2001	2000	1999
Assets			
Current assets			
Cash and cash equivalents	$ 52,446	$ 21,573	$ 19,765
Short term investments	—	2,990	4,000
Accounts receivable	106,291	64,958	64,505
Inventories	101,214	55,165	72,670
Deferred income taxes	19,849	11,679	8,221
Note receivable and portion of long-term note receivable	5,803	—	—
Prepaid expenses	7,604	4,136	6,622
Total current assets	293,207	160,501	175,783
Property, plant, and equipment, net	231,449	168,570	182,219
Notes receivable	11,951	—	3,000
Equity investment in affiliates	115,121	19,416	20,177
Long-term supply contract	7,695	8,152	4,105
Trade names	136,934	29,699	—
Goodwill and other intangibles	127,320	53,140	83,744
Other assets	25,408	16,154	7,278
Total assets	$949,085	$455,632	$476,306

Year Ending December 31	2001	2000	1999
Liabilities and stockholder's equity			
Current liabilities			
Short-term borrowings	$ 3,220	$ 13,178	$ 25,574
Accounts payable and accrued expenses	176,176	129,268	106,109
Current portion of long-term debt	8,360	685	685
Income taxes payable	8,260	6,007	8,240
Total current liabilities	196,016	149,138	140,608
Long-term debt	406,564	20,136	58,107
Deferred income taxes	27,032	17,852	20,416
Deferred and other long-term liabilities	19,164	15,009	11,860
Nonpension postretirement & postemployment benefits	15,880	15,392	15,145
Minority interest	2,126	3,455	3,437
Stockholders' equity			
Common stock—$1 par value	46,661	46,661	46,661
Additional paid-in capital	28,414	22,514	18,356
Retained earnings	312,409	276,700	253,885
Accumulated other comprehensive income (loss)	(9,728)	(9,389)	(4,599)
	377,756	336,486	314,303
Less common stock in treasury, at cost	(95,453)	(101,836)	(87,021)
Due from shareholder	—	—	(549)
Total stockholders' equity	282,303	234,650	226,733
Total liabilities and stockholders' equity	$949,085	$455,632	$476,306

Source: Church & Dwight Co., Inc., *2002 Annual Report.*

Many companies with strong brand names in the consumer products field have been susceptible to leveraged buy-outs and hostile takeovers. However, a series of calculated actions spared Church & Dwight's management from having to make last-minute decisions to ward off unwelcome suitors. Besides maintaining majority control of the outstanding common stock, the Board amended the company's charter, giving current shareholders four votes per share, but required future shareholders to buy and hold shares for four years before receiving the same privilege. The Board of Directors was also structured into three classes, with four directors in each class serving staggered three-year terms. According to Minton, the objective of these moves was to "give the Board control so as to provide the best results for shareholders."[6]

As a further deterrent to would-be suitors or unwelcome advances, the company entered into an employee severance agreement with key officials. This agreement provided severance pay of up to three times the individual's highest annual salary and bonus plus benefits for three years if the individual was terminated within one year after a change in control of the company. Change of control was defined as "the acquisition by a person or group of 25% or more of Company Common Stock; a change in the majority of the board of directors not approved by the pre-change board of directors; or the approval by the stockholders of the Company or a merger, consolidation, liquidation, dissolution, or sale of all the assets of the Company."[7]

As Church & Dwight pushed more aggressively into the consumer products field, several changes were made in key management positions. **Exhibit 3** shows the company's directors and executive officers. Several of these individuals, including Davies, Henry Kornhauser, and Larry Koslow, brought extensive marketing experience to the top management team. The marketing team has continued to be strengthened with the addition of Bradley Casper and Joseph Sipia. With over 40 years of combined domestic and international experience ranging from Procter & Gamble to FMC Corporation, Casper and Sipia brought extensive experience in marketing a variety of consumer and industrial products to the top management team.[8]

In addition to the many changes that had taken place in key management positions, changes have also begun to be made in the composition of the Board of Directors. Although 7 of the 11-member board had served for 20 years or more, 3 have served for 5 years or less. One woman serves on the board, and ages of the current members ranged from 52 to 70. Although in a less active role as Chairman Emeritus, Dwight Minton continued to provide leadership and a long legacy of "corporate memory."

A Change in Direction

Entering the 21st century, management recognized a major challenge to overcome the company's small size compared to its competitors in basic product lines of household and personal care. They also recognized the value of a major asset, the company's pristine Balance Sheet, and made the decision to grow the business with two decisive transformational moves:

1. On April 2, 2001, a tender offer was made to acquire USA Detergents, Inc. (NASDAQ:USAD), its partner in the Armus joint venture. With this acquisition, and Church & Dwight's laundry business became the third largest in the $7 billion retail U. S. laundry category. XTRA and NICE'N FLUFFY brands were part of the acquisition and Church & Dwight acquired the consumer products business of Carter-Wallace, Inc., purchasing outright the ARRID Anti-Perspirant and the LAMBERT KAY Pet Care businesses. Armkel, LLC, Church & Dwight's 50-50 joint venture with the private equity group Kelso & Company, acquired the remainder of Carter-Wallace consumer products businesses, including such brands as TROJAN Condoms, NAIR Depilatories and FIRST RESPONSE Home Pregnancy and Ovulation test kits. Combining these products with the company's

Exhibit 3
Key Officers and Their Management Positions: Church & Dwight Co., Inc.

Corporate Governance: Church & Dwight Co. Inc.

A. Directors

William R. Becklean
Managing Director
SunTrust Equitable Securities
Director since 1980

Robert A. Davies, III
Chairman and CEO
Church & Dwight Co., Inc.
Director since 1995

J. Richard Leaman, Jr.
Retired President and CEO
S.D. Warren Company
Director since 1985

John D. Leggett III, Ph.D.
President
Sensor Instruments Co., Inc.
Director since 1979

Robert A. McCabe
Chairman
Pilot Capital Corporation
Director since 1987

Burton B. Staniar
Chairman and CEO
Knoll, Inc.
Director since 1999

Robert H. Beeby
Retired President and CEO
Frito-Lay, Inc.
Director since 1992

Rosina B. Dixon, M.D.
Physician and Consultant
Director since 1979

Richard D. LeBlanc
President and CEO
Handy & Harman
Director since 1998

John F. Maypole
Managing Partner
Peach State Real Estate Holding Co.
Director since 1999

Dwight C. Minton
Chairman Emeritus
Church & Dwight Co., Inc.
Director since 1965

John O. Whitney
Professor and Executive Director
The Deming Center for Quality Management,
Columbia Business School
Director since 1992

B. Executive Officers

Robert A. Davies, III
Chairman and CEO

Raymond L. Bendure, Ph.D.
Vice President, Research & Development

Mark A. Bilawsky
Vice President, General Counsel, and Secretary

Mark G. Conish
Vice President, Operations

Steven P. Cugine
Vice President, Human Resources,
Acting President and Chief Operating Officer,
Specialty Products Division

Zvi Eiref
Vice President, Finance, and Chief Financial
Officer

Henry Kornhauser
Vice President, Advertising

Dennis M. Moore
President, ARMUS, LLC
Vice President, Sales,
Arm & Hammer Division

C. Principal Accounting Officers

Gary P. Halker
Vice President, Controller, and Chief Information Officer

Steven J. Katz
Assistant Controller

Source: Church & Dwight Co., Inc., *Notice of Annual Meeting of Stockholders and Proxy Statement*, 2002, p. 5.

existing product lines makes Church & Dwight one of the leading consumer packaged goods companies in the United States.

2. On September 28, 2001, the company completed the acquisition of the consumer products business of Carter-Wallace, Inc. in a partnership called Armkel, LLC with the private equity group, Kelso & Company. These two acquisitions doubled the Company's size and almost tripled the number of employees, and set the stage for several years of growth.[9]

This change led to a restructuring of the company. What had once been a small company focusing on a few consumer and specialty products had emerged as a much larger competitor. Consumer products now encompassed a broad array of personal care, deodorizing and cleaning, and laundry products, while specialty products offerings were expanded to specialty chemicals, animal nutrition, and specialty cleaners.

Consumer Products

Prior to its acquisition spree, the company's growth strategy had been based on finding new uses for sodium bicarbonate. Using an overall family branding strategy to further penetrate the consumer products market in the United States and Canada, additional products were introduced displaying the ARM & HAMMER logo. This logoed footprint remains significant as the ARM & HAMMER brand controlled a commanding 85% of the baking soda market. By capitalizing on its easily recognizable brand name, logo, and established marketing channels, Church & Dwight moved into such products as laundry detergent, carpet cleaners and deodorizers, air deodorizers, toothpaste, and deodorant/antiperspirants. This strategy worked well, allowing the company to promote multiple products using only one brand name.

From the company's founding until 1970, it produced and sold only two consumer products: ARM & HAMMER Baking Soda and a laundry product marketed under the name Super Washing Soda. In 1970 under Minton, Church & Dwight began testing the consumer products market by introducing a phosphate-free, powdered laundry detergent. Several other products, including a liquid laundry detergent, fabric softener sheets, an all-fabric bleach, tooth powder and toothpaste, baking soda chewing gum, deodorant/antiperspirants, deodorizers (carpet, room, and pet), and clumping cat litter have been added to the expanding list of ARM & HAMMER brands. However, simply relying on baking soda extensions and focusing on niche markets to avoid a head-on attack from competitors with more financial and marketing clout limited growth opportunities.[10] So, in the late 1990s, the company departed from its previous strategy of developing new product offerings in-house and bought several well-known consumer brands such as Brillo, Parsons Ammonia, Cameo Aluminum & Stainless Steel Cleaner, Rain Drops water softener, SNO BOWL toilet bowl cleaner, and TOSS 'N SOFT dryer sheets from one of its competitors, The Dial Corporation. (See **Exhibit 4**.)

Church & Dwight faced the same dilemma as other competitors in a mature domestic market for consumer products. New consumer products had to muscle their way into markets by taking market share from current offerings. With the majority of company sales in the United States and Canada, it was well-equipped to gain market share with its low-cost strategy. However, in the international arena, where growth was more product driven and less marketing sensitive, the company did not posses the in-house expertise to capture market share.[11] To compensate for this weakness, Church & Dwight relied on acquisitions to improve its international footprint and reach. The breadth of its expanded consumer product offerings can be seen in **Exhibit 4**.

According to Minton, as the company had grown, "We have made every effort to keep costs under control and manage frugally."[12] A good example of this approach to doing business can be seen in the Armkel partnership. "Armkel borrowed money on a non-recourse basis so a failure would have no impact on Church & Dwight, taking any risk away from shareholders."[13]

Exhibit 4

Consumer Product Breakdown

CONSUMER PRODUCTS - DOMESTIC - CHURCH & DWIGHT*

Laundry Products*	Deodorizing & Household Cleaning Products*
ARM & HAMMER FABRICARE Powder Laundry Detergent	ARM & HAMMER Pure Baking Soda
ARM & HAMMER Liquid Laundry Detergent	ARM & HAMMER Carpet & Room Deodorizer
XTRA Liquid Laundry Detergent	ARM & HAMMER VACUUM-FREE Foam Carpet Deodorizer
XTRA Powder Laundry Detergent	ARM & HAMMER Cat Litter Deodorizer
NICE'N FLUFFY Liquid Fabric Softener	ARM & HAMMER SUPER SCOOP Clumping Cat Litter
ARM & HAMMER FRESH'N SOFT Fabric Softener Sheets	ARM & HAMMER SUPER CLAY Cat Litter
	ARM & HAMMER CRYSTAL BLEND Cat Litter
DELICARE Fine Fabric Wash	ARM & HAMMER Super Puppy Pads
	ARM & HAMMER HOME ALONE Floor Protection Pads
ARM & HAMMER Super Washing Soda	LAMBERT KAY Pet Care Products
	BRILLO Soap Pads
	SCRUB FREE Bathroom Cleaners
	CLEAN SHOWER Daily Shower Cleaner
	CAMEO Aluminum & Stainless Steel Cleaner
	SNO BOL Toilet Bowl Cleaner
	PARSONS' Ammonia

CONSUMER PRODUCTS - DOMESTIC - CHURCH & DWIGHT* and ARMKEL, LLC**

Personal Care Products - Church & Dwight*	Personal Care Products - Armkel, LLC**
ARM & HAMMER-ULTRAMAX Deodorants & Anti-Perspirants	TROJAN Condoms
	NATURALAMB Condoms
ARRID Anti-Perspirants	CLASS-ACT Condoms
LADY'S CHOICE Anti-Perspirants	NAIR Depilatories Lotions, Creams and Waxes
ARM & HAMMER DENTAL CARE Toothpaste, Gum, Kids' Gum, Powder	FIRST RESPONSE Home Pregnancy and Ovulation Test Kits
ARM & HAMMER PEROXICARE Toothpaste	ANSWER Home Pregnancy and Ovulation Test Kits
ARM & HAMMER ADVANCE WHITE Toothpaste, Gum	PEARL DROPS Toothpolish and Toothpaste
ARM & HAMMER P.M. Toothpaste	RIGIDENT Denture Adhesive
ARM & HAMMER ADVANCE BREATH CARE Toothpaste, Gum, Mouthwash, Breathmints	CARTER'S LITTLE PILLS Laxative

CONSUMER PRODUCTS - INTERNATIONAL - CHURCH & DWIGHT and ARMKEL, LLC

International Products

CANADA	UNITED KINGDOM	FRANCE
Baking Soda	Toothpaste	Skin Care
Anti-Perspirants	Toothpolish	Toothpaste
Toothpaste	Anti-Perspirants	Depilatories
Bathroom Cleaners	Depilatories	OTC Products
Carpet & Room Deodorizer	Pregnancy Kits	Diagnostics
	Skin Care	
Condoms		ITALY
Depilatories	SPAIN	Toothpolish
Pregnancy Kits		Pregnancy Kits
OTC Products	Depilatories	Denture Adhesive
	Skin Care	OTC Products
MEXICO		Diagnostics
Condoms		
Depilatories		AUSTRALIA
Toothpaste		Baby Powder
Pregnancy Kits		Depilatories
OTC Products		Toothpaste
		Pregnancy Kits
		OTC Products

SPECIALTY PRODUCTS - DOMESTIC AND INTERNATIONAL - CHURCH & DWIGHT*

Specialty Chemicals*	Animal Nutrition Products*	Specialty Cleaners*
ARM & HAMMER Performance Grade Sodium Bicarbonate	ARM & HAMMER Feed Grade Sodium Bicarbonate	ARMEX Blast Media
ARM & HAMMER TORTILLA BLEND Leavening Mix	MEGALAC Rumen Bypass Fat	ARMAKLEEN Aqueous Cleaner
ARMAND PRODUCTS Potassium Carbonate Potassium Bicarbonate	SQ-810 Natural Sodium Sesquicarbonate	AQUAWORKS Aqueous Cleaner
	S-CARB Feed Grade Sodium Sesquicarbonate	**International**
ARMICARB 100 Fungicide	DCAD Plus Feed Grade Potassium Carbonate	QUIMICA GERAL DO NORDESTE, BRAZIL Sodium Bicarbonate Barium Carbonate
ARMAGRIP Anti-Slip Floor Treatment		
SORB-N-C Pollution Control	BIO-CHLOR and FERMENTEN Rumen Fermentation Enhancers	BROTHERTON SPECIALITY PRODUCTS, LTD. - UNITED KINGDOM Specialty Chemicals Specialty Cleaners

Notes:

**All trademarks are owned by Church & Dwight Co., Inc. or by one of its wholly-owned subsidiaries or affiliates.

***All trademarks are owned by Armkel, LLC, a 50-50 joint venture between Church & Dwight Co., Inc. and Kelso & Company.

Source: Church & Dwight Co., Inc., 2001 Annual Report, pp. 8–9.

With its new stable of products and expanded laundry detergent offerings, Church & Dwight found itself competing head-on with consumer product giants such as Procter & Gamble, Clorox, Lever Brothers, and Dial. Church & Dwight's market share positions in key product categories can be found in **Exhibit 5**.

As more and more products were added to Church & Dwight's consumer line-up, the need for additional marketing expertise had grown. Along with the addition of Henry Kornhauser to the top management team in 1997, Church & Dwight brought many of its marketing tasks in-house. Kornhauser brought 17 years of senior management and advertising agency experience with him to Church & Dwight.

The first major project undertaken by this new in-house function was the $15 million launch of ARM & HAMMER Dental Care Gum.[14] Although it entered a crowded field of specialty products, Church & Dwight planned to ride the crest of increasing interest of both dentists and hygienists in baking soda as an important element in a regimen for maintaining dental health.[15] Church & Dwight was able to sneak up on the giants in the industry and moved rapidly from the position of a niche player in the toothpaste market (along with products such as Topol, Viadent, Check-Up, Zact, and Tom's of Maine) to that of a major competitor.

For the most part, Church & Dwight's entries into the consumer products market have met with success. However, a potential marketing problem may be looming on the horizon for its ARM & HAMMER line of consumer products. The company could be falling into the

Exhibit 5

U. S. Market Share Position

Product Category	Position
Laundry Detergent	#3
Cat Litter	#2
Bathroom Cleaner	#1
Antiperspirants	#5
Condoms	#1
Depilatories	#1
Home Pregnancy Test Kits	#2

precarious line-extension snare. Placing a well-known brand name on a wide variety of products could cloud its position and cause it to lose marketing pull.[16] Will the addition of such well-known brand names as XTRA, Nair, Trojan, and First Response provide sufficient avenues for growth?

Specialty Products

The stated strategy for the Specialty Products division was "to solidify worldwide leadership in sodium bicarbonate and potassium carbonate, while broadening our product offerings to other related chemicals . . . to build a specialized high-margin specialty cleaning business, allying carbonate technology, the ARM & HAMMER trademark and environmental position."[17] Management's apparent increased focus on consumer products had somewhat affected the growth of specialty products, as is shown in the company's product mix in **Exhibit 6**.

Church & Dwight was in an enviable position to profit from its dominant niche in the sodium bicarbonate products market since it controlled the primary raw material used in its production. The primary ingredient in sodium bicarbonate was produced from the mineral trona, which was extracted from the company's mines in southwestern Wyoming. The other ingredient, carbon dioxide, was a readily available chemical that could be obtained from a variety of sources.

The company maintained a dominant position in the production of the required raw materials for both its consumer and industrial products. It manufacturered almost two-thirds of the sodium bicarbonate sold in the United States and, until recently, was the only U.S. producer of ammonium bicarbonate and potassium carbonate. The company in 2002 had the largest share (approximately 75%) of the sodium bicarbonate capacity in the United States and was the largest consumer of baking soda as it filled its own needs for company-produced consumer and industrial products.[18]

To meet these needs and solidify market dominance, product capacity had been raised by 80,000 tons, to 520,000 tons, in 2000.[19–21] Even though it was the dominant player in the field, additional competition was on the horizon. "The playing field in the sodium bicarbonate industry is broadening with two nahcolite solution mining producers on the horizon. This alternative to trona processing involves extracting nahcoite, or naturally occurring sodium

Exhibit 6

Percentage of Net Sales: Church & Dwight Co., Inc.

	2001	2000	1999	1998	1997
Consumer Products	82	77	77	79	80
Specialty Products	18	23	23	21	20

ried one or more imported brands such as Becks, Corona, Heineken, Labatts, Moosehead, Guinness, and San Miguel. The majority of beers imported into the U.S. were bottled in Mexico, Europe, and Canada. Extent of advertising varied from importer to importer but was generally intensive using such media as radio spots, print, and outdoor signage.

CRAFT BEERS

Craft beer, with 2.9% of the beer market, was the newest growth segment of the industry.[3] During the 1980s and 1990s, ever increasing numbers of craft brewers both created and filled a demand for distinctive flavorful beers, using high-quality ingredients brewed with European-style recipes. Some craft beers featured flavors of fruit, honey, spices, oatmeal, coffee, pumpkin, or other additives.

The market was increasingly fragmented with 1,306 craft brewers across the nation as of January 1998, up from 1,042, 803, and 540 at the end of 1996, 1995, and 1994, respectively.[4] While the number of firms was continuing to grow, the craft beer market had reached a time in its development where total demand had ceased to grow at double-digit rates. After growth in demand of about 50% in 1994 and 1995, 1996 saw 25% growth, and, in 1997, total sales only increased 5%.[5]

There were four categories of brewers producing craft beer. Microbreweries produced less than 15,000 barrels per year and served limited markets, usually through independent distributors and direct sales. Brewpubs were the smallest volume producers, usually brewing 2,500 barrels or less per year for consumption in the pub. Regional specialty brewers produced over 15,000 barrels per year and distributed through independent distributors both locally and in one or more regional markets. Contract brewers developed beer recipes and contracted with larger national or regional breweries, e.g., Strohs and Pittsburgh Brewing, for the actual brewing. Contract brewers usually marketed their branded beers regionally or nationally using independent distributors and their own advertising and promotion.

In 1997, 48 brewers each produced over 10,000 barrels of craft beer. Five contract brewers led by Boston Beer and Pete's Brewing Company each produced 15,000 or more barrels. Twenty-five regional specialty brewers produced at least 15,000 barrels. Another 10 microbrewies each produced between 10,000 and 15,000 barrels. Boston Beer Company, Pete's Brewing Company, Sierra Nevada Brewing Company, Redhook Ale Brewery, Pyramid Brewing Company, and Widmer Brewing Company all topped 100,000 barrels in 1997.[6] The relative craft beer market shares among the top 10 craft brewers in 1996 are presented in **Exhibit 1**.

Exhibit 1
Craft Brewer Market Shares

Brewer	1996 Market Share
Boston Beer	25.1 %
Pete's Brewing	8.8 %
Sierra Nevada Brewing	5.5 %
Redhook Ale Brewery	4.7 %
Pyramid Brewing	2.6 %
Widmer Brewing	2.6 %
Anchor Brewing	2.2 %
Full Sail Brewing	1.7 %
Portland Brewing	1.4 %
Spanish Peaks Brewery	1.2 %

Source: Adapted from Sarah Theodore, "Domestic Specialty Suffers Growing Pains in '97," *Beverage Industry*, January 1998, pp. 9–18.

THE MARKET FOR BEER

Adult per-capita consumption of beer declined from the early 1980s to about 30 gallons in 1997 as federal beer taxes were doubled, blue-collar jobs declined, health and fitness became fashionable, and the population aged.[7] This per-capita decline was offset by growth in the total adult population so total U.S. beer sales were relatively constant at between 185 and 190 million barrels per year. However, major differences existed among the 3 segments. Since 1995, sales of national brands declined about 5%, popular brands declined 9%; imported beer sales increased 25% to 14 million barrels; and craft beer sales increased 32% to 5.2 million barrels.[8] Taste, demand for greater variety, and a "trading-up phenomenon" were offered as reasons for the continuing growth in demand for craft and imported beer.[9] While craft beer sales were expected to continue growing, the rate of growth was expected to be lower as the market matured, and importers used larger advertising budgets and marketing skills to increase their share.

A national survey found that beer consumers who drank craft beer were more likely to be young (less than 45 years of age), to be college educated, and to have above-average incomes (greater than $50,000). Greater numbers of men than women were drawn to craft beer, although a greater share of beer-drinking women had an interest in craft beers than did beer-drinking men. Craft beer drinkers also tended to drink more than the average drinker. However, 80% of those who drank craft beer consumed less craft beer than other types of beer.[10] In addition, there were regional differences in craft beer consumption. Craft beer was most popular in the West, followed by the Northeast and Midwest. While craft beer was most popular in the upscale segment of the population, it had seen increasing popularity in middle-income households. This increased acceptance was reflected in a study that showed 19% of surveyed adults had tried craft beer in 1996, up from 13% a year earlier.[11]

COMPETITIVE PRACTICES

Imported and craft beers were aimed at beer drinkers who sought prestige products and who desired superior flavor. However, a high level of substitutability existed among the three classes of beer. Consequently, national brand, import, and craft beer companies competed and attempted to get the beer drinking populace to switch to their types of beer and thus increase their market share. Imported and craft beers competed head to head since both were at the premium price, distinctive flavor end of the beer spectrum.

The national brewers used extensive advertising, often through costly mass media. However, they faced the threat of restrictions on what, how, and where they could advertise as a result of political and news media concerns that drinking was harmful. They developed and relied on wide distribution through networks of wholesale distributors. These distributors sought to saturate the market by placing their products in bars, restaurants, grocery stores, convenience stores, and other outlets. They provided regularly scheduled deliveries with secured and stocked shelf space and rotated retailers' inventory to insure freshness.

Imported beers, with a much smaller market share, used selective targeted advertising and relied more on their distributors to push their higher margin product through on-site consumption and consumer retail channels. Distribution was the key for craft brewers as well, but actual methods of distribution varied depending on size of the company. For example, brewpubs selling only for consumption in their own establishments, relied on creating a pleasant atmosphere, complementary foods, and the idea that the pub itself was something special. Many of the microbreweries, regional specialty brewers, and contract brewers also had their own pubs and attempted to create a local identity using similar methods. Smaller microbreweries often distributed only kegged beer to local restaurants and bars and tried to instill a local pride in their premium beers. Larger microbreweries usually sold both kegged and bottled products by using independent distributors in a broader local or regional area. Across all craft brewers, the split between packaged (bottled) and draft (kegged) beer was 72 to 28%.[12]

Microbrewery advertising and promotion were limited and most often took the form of displays in drinking establishments; giveaways such as glasses, mugs, and coasters; and sponsorship of concerts, festivals, or seasonal events. Most regional specialty brewers and contract brewers used the same distribution and promotion strategy as the large microbreweries. Boston Beer and Pete's Brewing Company became the first exceptions when they introduced local TV advertising.

Growth of the craft beer market was noted by the large national brewers and they entered the craft segment with their own specialty beer products. Anheuser-Busch sought to have 60% of the craft beer market by 2005[13] while Miller's objective was 25% by 2000.[14] Anheuser-Busch, Adolph Coors, Miller, and Strohs all set up specialty units with separate staff to manage their new brands.[15] By the end of 1996, Miller and Strohs each had acquired control or an interest in two microbreweries, while Coors had one. Anheuser-Busch had a 25% interest in Redhook and distribution alliances with both Redhook and Widmer Brewing. Brand names offered by the majors included Augsburger, Blue Moon, Celis, Elk Mountain, George Killian, Icehouse, J. W. Dundee, J. J. Wainwright, Jacob Leinenkugel, Michael Shea's, Red Dog, Red River Valley, and Red Wolf. In most cases the brands were marketed under a name other than the controlling company's name, e.g., Northern Plains Brewing (Strohs), Plank Road Brewery (Miller), and Blue Moon Brewing Company (Coors). In 1995 Anheuser-Busch alone had seven craft-type beers that sold 650,000 barrels.[16] In addition, in 1996, Anheuser-Busch initiated a program to increase its exclusive distributor force from 40% of the total Anheuser-Busch distributors to 70%. This would reduce the incidence of competitors benefiting from the services of Anheuser-Busch distributors. While Anheuser-Busch could not use punitive measures because they could be considered to be in restraint of trade, it could encourage its distributors to voluntarily carry Anheuser-Busch products, including Redhook, exclusively. Incentives were provided to reward this exclusive distribution. Some speculated that eventually pressures would be placed on distributors to cause them to volunteer.[17] Miller and Coors also appeared to be interested in getting their distributors to devote more effort on their own specialty beers and less on microbrewery beers.[18]

In addition to pressures from major national brewers on their distributors to reduce product lines to a narrower spectrum of selected brands, the sheer number of craft and other brands in the United States overwhelmed distributors. With about 4,500 brands and ever increasing numbers of craft brewers seeking to add their brands to the market, distributors began to cull less popular brands and restrict themselves to the higher volume brands for which they could reasonably expect to secure shelf space.

Growth was a widely sought goal among craft brewers. The large contract and regional specialty brewers were moving toward national distribution. By 1996, Boston Beer had already reached all 50 states and Redhook sold in 47 states, Pete's in 40 states, and Pyramid Brewing in 27 states. A number of microbreweries were operating more than one brewery and several brewpubs had started chains. Starting in 1995, seven of the largest craft brewers went public or announced a public offering to raise funds for growth; these included Boston Beer, Brandevor Enterprises, Pyramid Breweries, Pete's Brewing, Portland Brewing Company, Redhook, and Widmer Brewing.

Redhook's Objective and Business Strategy

Redhook had set an objective to be the leading craft brewer through market development into unserved regions of the nation and continued market penetration once established in a region. The company articulated a business strategy in its 1995 annual report and prospectus with six key elements:

1. Production of high-quality craft beers
2. Control of production in company-owned breweries

3. Operation of regional brewing facilities

4. Production economies through technologically advanced equipment

5. Strategic distribution alliance with Anheuser-Busch

6. Promotion of products within local markets[19]

Products and Production

Redhook did not pasteurize its craft beers. Not pasteurizing ensured that the flavor was not degraded, but it reduced shelf life to about three months.

In 1997, Redhook produced nine different branded products and from time to time produced small batches of experimental brews that it test marketed under its Redhook Blueline label. These products were brewed and packaged in both kegs and bottles at its own operating breweries. The Fremont brewery in Seattle had a capacity of 75,000 barrels per year. The brewery was installed in an old trolley car barn under a lease with an option to buy. The company also owned and leased adjacent properties for kegging, warehousing, and other uses. This brewery was temporarily closed early in 1998. The Woodinville, Washington, brewery, constructed on 22 acres owned by the company, started with a capacity of 60,000 barrels, reached 170,000 barrels in 1995, and 250,000 in 1996. The Portsmouth, New Hampshire, brewery constructed on 23 acres of subleased land started with a capacity of 100,000 barrels to be increased in stages to 250,000. Portsmouth was chosen as a site because of its central location in a large market and the high cost of transporting kegged and bottled beer from the Northwest.

Only the highest quality malts, grains, hops, and other ingredients were purchased from a few regular suppliers at competitive prices. Alternative sources were available, if needed. The ingredients were processed in state-of-the-art automated brewing equipment designed in Europe for efficient production of small batches. The bottling line was fully integrated and automated with fast changeover capability.

As a producer of premium craft beers, Redhook emphasized quality in product formulation, brewing, and bottling. Each brewery had its own laboratory for testing product quality. In addition, the Woodinville brewery served as the focal point for quality, monitoring all breweries' production and product quality control.

Distribution

In 1994, Redhook formed a distribution alliance with Anheuser-Busch.[20] The alliance was to run for 20 years but could be terminated after 10 years under certain conditions. Under the alliance, Anheuser-Busch invested in Redhook, gaining a 25% stake in the company's equity, and made its nationwide network of some 700 wholesale distributors (44% of the nation's wholesalers) available for distribution of Redhook products. Redhook retained full control over production and marketing. Anheuser-Busch distributors in the U.S. and Mexico participating in the alliance were to be given exclusive distribution rights in their territories. Distribution agreements with Redhook's current distributors remained in effect until they expired, at which time Anheuser-Busch distributors could take over. When an Anheuser-Busch distributor for an area declined to carry Redhook products, Redhook could use a non-alliance distributor.

In accordance with the agreement, Redhook sold its beer to Anheuser-Busch and shipped the beer to the latter's distribution centers. Anheuser-Busch distributors then ordered from and paid Anheuser-Busch for the Redhook beer they received for retail distribution. While Anheuser-Busch was paid a per-barrel fee for use of the distribution network, Redhook believed that the added cost was more than offset by efficiencies in shipping, billing, and paperwork. In addition, distributor acceptance of Redhook and its products was good.

The Redhook and Anheuser-Busch alliance was controversial. Critics found fault with the alliance, citing the belief that it would heat up the fight for shelf space and wondering if small brewers could remain independent once they became dependent on a large brewer. Jim Koch, CEO of Boston Beer Company, referred to Redhook as Budhook (a takeoff from Anheuser-Busch's Budweiser brand) after the alliance. He implied his views concerning the threat of national brewers gaining control over craft brewers in the statement:

> In the long run, the big brewers would like to dominate this part of the beer business the way they do every other part—why shouldn't they? Anheuser-Busch has stated they want to control half the beer industry. Microbreweries are naive to think that doesn't mean half the microbrew business.[21]

An even stronger statement came from another executive who said "as soon as they put you into their distribution network, they control your inventory, pricing, and own you lock, stock, and barrel."[22]

Others believed that major brewers entry into the craft beer market benefited the industry because they increased awareness of craft beer. Pete Slosberg of Pete's Brewing Company reflected this view in his statement:

> I believe any vehicle that will introduce more Americans to different beers, even if it's not our brand is a good thing. It lets drinkers know there is an alternative.[23]

Marketing and Sales

Redhook's marketing strategy emphasized distribution and didn't rely on costly media advertising. The company focused its efforts on distributor training, retailer education and support, and spread of word-of-mouth awareness through various consumer promotions. Redhook coached its distributors, worked with distributor salespeople to get greater attention for Redhook products during their sales calls, and, in cooperation with the distributors, offered incentives for the salespeople to develop new accounts. The 44 member (as of March 1, 1998) sales and marketing staff[24] conducted a number of other education and promotion programs such as

1. Distributor Tours
2. Community Gatherings
3. Marketing On-Site
4. Price Discounting
5. Company-Owned Pubs
6. Visitor Tours
7. Homepage

DISTRIBUTOR TOURS

Redhook offered distributors tours of the breweries, conducted on-site sales training, and provided sales support. The latter included providing point-of-sale materials; assistance in designing grocery store displays, stacking, and merchandising inventory; and company sales representative contact with restaurant and grocery buyers. In addition, Redhook often helped distributors in new markets by hiring a local sales representative prior to first distribution to help generate product awareness.

COMMUNITY GATHERINGS

Redhook sponsored and participated in local community gatherings such as craft beer festivals, food events, sporting events, and music and other entertainment programs.

MARKETING ON-SITE

The company promoted its products on-premises at pubs and restaurants. This included providing samples of Redhook products, consumer and retailer education, tap handles, neon signs, banners, coasters, table tents, and glassware. In addition, limited quantities of the company's Blueline label products were placed in selected establishments, providing consumers the chance to try something different and exclusive.

PRICE DISCOUNTING

Redhook selectively discounted prices to distributors and, through them, retailers. Price discounts were a direct response to price cuts by rivals in intensely competitive markets.

COMPANY-OWNED PUBS

There were three company-owned and operated pubs: Trolleyman Pub at the Fremont brewery, Forecaster's Public House at Woodinville, and Cataqua Public House at Portsmouth. A pleasant atmosphere with scheduled live music, a complete selection of Redhook beers, and a food menu to complement the beers were used as ways of increasing awareness of and identification with Redhook and its beer. In addition, the pubs were used as sources of consumer feedback on its Blueline and other beers.

VISITOR TOURS

Brewery tours were also used as a means of educating the public about Redhook. Tours took visitors through the brewery, showing key activities in the brewing process. More than 50,000 visitors toured the company's operating breweries in 1997.

HOMEPAGE

Redhook provided a homepage on the World Wide Web and offered classes on brewing through a program called Redhook University.[25] The homepage contained information about the company, its breweries and brewing process; its products, including Blueline offerings; live music schedules for its pubs; news about company progress; a schedule of events; and brewery tours. Redhook University classes available to the public included subjects such as homebrewing, commercial production, brewing science, and brewing history.

Human Resources

The company had 210 employees; 69 in production, 44 in marketing and sales, 15 in administration, and 82 in pubs. Fifty-seven of these worked part time. The company's salesforce was large enough to service the nationwide distributor network.

The executive group consisted of Shipman as President and Chief Executive Officer; Brad Berg, Executive Vice President and Chief Financial Officer; David Mickelson, Executive Vice President and Chief Operating Officer; Pamela Hinkley, Vice President, Sales and Marketing; and Allen Triplett, Vice President, Brewing. Berg, with a bachelor's degree in accounting from the University of Northern Iowa, had experience as a Partner in the Coopers & Lybrand accounting firm and had served in executive positions in Burlington Resources, Inc., and Holly Residential Properties, Inc. Mickelson graduated with a bachelor's degree in business from the University of Washington. He had served as a loan officer for Barclays Bank PLC and as Controller for Certified Foods, Inc., prior to joining Redhook in 1987. Hinckley joined Redhook in 1988 with a bachelor's degree in psychology from Suffolk University and several years' experience in the wine industry, first with Stevenot Winery and later as a wine buyer for a specialty food and wine retailer. Prior to joining Redhook in 1985, Triplett had earned a degree from the University of Wyoming and had studied at the Siebel Institute of Brewing and University of California at Davis. Shipman was considered to be strong in delegation to these executives and encouraged subordinates to develop their own ideas and act on them. His strategy specialist, Anthony Grasst, summed it up as follows:

> You have to be completely independent and willing to do something instinctively rather than by order. Paul believes everybody finds their niche. You either bloom or you die. It's an extraordinarily dynamic environment. You have to take risks. His attitude is: Let's do it.[26]

The management team worked in an open office where collegiality and collaboration were part of the culture. Staff participation in major decisions was common. Even the hiring process was collegial—everyone in a department had a say in who was hired.

Ownership

Anheuser-Busch was the largest Redhook stockholder with a 25% equity interest. GE Capital Redhook Investment Corporation owned 9.3% of the stock while the three original Co-owners, Paul Shipman, Jerry Jones, and Gordon Bowker owned 6.4, 3.2, and 2.1%, respectively. The Board of Directors consisted of Shipman and eight outside directors, including two Anheuser-Busch representatives.

Anheuser-Busch's investment in Redhook was subject to a standstill agreement until November 16, 2001. Under the standstill, Anheuser-Busch and its affiliates could not own more than 25% of the common stock prior to November 16, 1999 and not more than 30% after that until November 16, 2001. Anheuser-Busch could terminate the standstill before November 16, 2001, if another individual or organization acquired or attempted to acquire 25% or more of the company's common stock before November 16, 1999, or 30% before November 16, 2001. The standstill could also be terminated in the event of a merger or consolidation agreement between Redhook and a third party.

In September 1995, Redhook's board approved a "poison pill" agreement to protect against any unwanted takeover. In the event of an uninvited takeover bid or the acquisition of 20% or more of the common stock in the open market, stockholders, other than the acquirer, could exercise one shareholder right per share held. Each right would allow the holder to buy $240 worth of stock for $120. In the case of a takeover attempt by Anheuser-Busch prior to November 11, 2001, the rights would not be exercisable until Anheuser-Busch bought shares to exceed the limits specified in the standstill agreement.

Financial Performance

Redhook experienced continuous growth in sales through 1996 and income through 1995. Most sales were to distributors although beer, food, and other items sold through the company's pubs contributed to total sales. Pub sales grew to $3,406,000 in 1997 from $3,372,000, $3,347,000, and $1,739,000 in 1996, 1995, and 1994, respectively. **Exhibit 2** shows that while profits were up in each year between 1991 and 1995, the profit growth in 1994 and 1995 was less than the increase in net sales and units sold. Profit in 1996 declined despite a 38% increase in sales. A net loss along

Exhibit 2
Capacity, Units Sold, Sales Revenue, and Net Income

Year	Usable Capacity (barrels)	Barrels Shipped	Change (%)	Net Sales	Change (%)	Net Income (in millions)	Change (%)
1997	425,000	214,600	(4.5%)	$34,286	(8.9%)	($1,399)	(145.3%)
1996	425,000	224,700	42.0%	$35,678	38.0%	$3,086	(3.0%)
1995	245,000	158,700	69.0%	$25,894	73.0%	$3,182	50.0%
1994	135,000	93,700	27.0%	$14,929	30.0%	$2,125	6.0%
1993	75,000	73,900	49.0%	$11,484	42.0%	$2,005	59.0%
1992	75,000	49,500	46.0%	$ 8,086	34.0%	$1,260	74.0%
1991		34,000		$ 5,797		$ 724	

Source: Redhook Ale Brewery, *1995, 1996, and 1997 Annual Reports.*

with a decline in sales was incurred in 1997. Redhook attributed the reduced profits to increased competition from more craft brewers with more brands and price cutting, particularly in the saturated western states' market starting in the second half of 1996. In addition, 1996 and 1997 saw higher costs in establishing national sales and distribution along with the higher depreciation and operating costs associated with the new Portsmouth brewery. The stock market reacted to the company's growth and profit problems with a reduction in Redhook's stock price to about $6 compared to its initial public offering price of $17 and a high of over $34. **Exhibit 3** shows comparative income statements for the years 1993 through 1997.

The growth and profit slump was continued into 1998. In the first quarter of 1998, Redhook reported a net loss of $715,000. Sales volume declined 4.9% from the 1997 first quarter. On the other hand, reductions in sales, marketing, and administration resulted in a decline in selling, general, and administrative expenses of 3.8% over first quarter 1997 figures.

Exhibit 3
Income Statement: Redhook Ale Brewery
(Dollar amounts in thousands, except income per share)

Year Ending December 31	1997	1996	1995	1994	1993
Gross sales	$37,894	$39,410	$28,426	$16,209	$12,331
Less excise taxes	3,608	3,732	2,532	1,280	847
Net sales	34,286	35,678	25,894	14,929	11,484
Cost of sales	25,963	23,581	16,970	8,686	6,163
Gross profit	8,323	12,097	8,924	6,243	5,321
S, G, & A expenses	9,981	7,853	4,606	2,801	2,000
Operating income	(1,658)	4,244	4,318	3,442	3,321
Interest expense	378	—	23	130	158
Other income (expense)	93	615	678	9	40
Income before taxes	(1,943)	4,859	4,973	3,321	3,203
Income taxes	544	1,773	1,791	1,196	1,099
Income before accounting change	(1,399)	3,086	3,182	2,125	2,104
Effect of change in accounting					99
Net income	$(1,399)	$ 3,086	$ 3,182	$ 2,125	$ 2,005
Net income per diluted share	$ (.18)	$ .34	$ .44	$ .43	$ .53

Source: Redhook Ale Brewery, *1996 and 1997 Annual Reports.*

Prior to the 1995 public offering, Redhook had been largely dependent on the use of debt to finance growth. After Anheuser-Busch's 25% investment in Redhook and the company's initial public offering, use of debt decreased. **Exhibit 4** displays leverage ratios prior to and after Anheuser-Busch's investment and the initial public offering in 1995. **Exhibit 5** provides balance sheet data for 1995 through 1997.

At the end of 1997, the company had 7,687,486 shares of common and 1,289,872 shares of convertible redeemable preferred stock outstanding. All of the preferred stock was owned by Anheuser-Busch and was credited as though converted to common stock in calculating that company's share of common stock. Redhook declared an extraordinary dividend of $2.00 per share in 1994 but otherwise had not declared dividends.

The Future?

By late 1996, several conditions had intensified competition and price cutting for craft and specialty beers, including imports. First, the number of craft brewers had continued to grow rapidly. Second, the major beer companies, with their financial, marketing, and distribution strengths had gone on the offensive to try to reach a dominant position in specialty beers. Third, importers had wakened to the increased demand for flavorful, high quality beer and had marketed their well-known brands to consumers who were confused by a myriad of craft beers. Fourth, some regional markets had become saturated and others were approaching saturation. Under these conditions, some craft brewers had grown while others had lost sales. Redhook and several other brewers in the saturated Northwest market were among the latter.

Knowledgeable people, including Redhook's Shipman, suggested the craft beer segment had entered a shakeout period.[27] An increase in closures and consolidation among weaker firms was expected. Other strategic responses to the increased competition included further market development and market penetration on one hand and concentration on a focused market on the other. Some craft brewers were continuing their move toward regional and national distribution. A few, including Boston Beer and Pete's Brewing Company and several microbreweries were exporting beer for sale in foreign nations. Smaller microbreweries that had expanded regionally were, in some cases, retrenching and reconcentrating on their home territories where they were better known and had stronger distribution. Major brewers had added to their lines of specialty beers and were aggressively marketing them.

Exhibit 4

Redhook Ale Brewery Use of Debt

Year Ended December 31	Total Debt to Equity	Long-Term Debt to Equity	Total Debt to Total Assets
1997	.58/.25	.16/.13	.37/.20
1996	.52/.21	.10/.08	.34/.17
1995	.45/.15	.03/.02	.31/.13
1994	26.34/.33	2.99/.15	.96/.25
1993	2.0/.33	.31/.14	.67/.25

Note: Convertible redeemable preferred stock is like a debt in that it can be redeemed at its original price under certain conditions. On the other hand, the stock is fully convertible to common and has the same voting rights as common. Because of these features, each ratio is calculated in two ways. The first ratio treats preferred stock as a short-term liability (debt) and the second ratio treats it as equity.

Source: Redhook Ale Brewery, 1995, 1996, and 1997 Annual Reports.

Exhibit 5

Balance Sheet: Redhook Ale Brewery

Year Ending December 31	1997	1996	1995
Current assets			
Cash (& equivalent)	$ 892,165	$ 1,162,352	$24,676,600
Receivables	1,588,368	2,051,591	2,027,454
Inventory	2,815,782	2,229,376	1,340,444
Tax receivable & other	1,644,328	2,153,017	272,849
total current assets	6,940,643	7,596,336	28,317,347
Fixed assets (net)	88,761,436	86,357,559	57,799,694
Other assets	1,067,264	1,170,144	521,395
Total assets	96,769,343	95,124,039	86,638,436
Liabilities and equity			
Current liabilities			
Accounts payable	2,290,012	4,075,699	4,828,902
Accrued payroll & taxes	1,322,966	1,220,212	695,645
Refundable deposits	1,166,070	950,926	972,957
Other accrued expenses	231,816	367,025	312,948
Current long-term debt	591,759	132,554	121,659
Total current liabilities	5,602,623	6,746,416	6,932,111
Long-term debt, less current portion	9,873,973	6,190,764	1,825,339
Deferred income taxes	3,987,519	3,582,692	2,389,588
Other	40,546	52,461	35,348
Convertible redeemable Preferred stock	15,966,255	15,921,855	15,877,455
Stockholders equity			
Common stock	38,438	38,428	38,417
Paid-in capital	56,805,633	56,652,764	56,642,663
Retained earnings	4,454,356	5,938,659	2,897,515
Total stockholders equity	61,298,427	62,629,851	59,578,595
Total liabilities and equity	$96,769,343	$95,124,039	$86,638,436

Source: Redhook Ale Brewery, *1995, 1996, and 1997 Annual Reports.*

In spite of the maturity of the beer market, saturation or near saturation in the craft beer segment, and competition-induced lower prices and profit margins, some saw continued growth prospects in craft beer of up to 8% of the national market.[28] With the Anheuser-Busch distribution alliance, Redhook was well positioned to develop new markets, especially the northeast, close to its new brewery in New Hampshire. Earlier, in a 1994 meeting with August Busch III, Shipman was given a rough map of the United States and asked to "put X's where you want to build breweries."[29] Shipman was reported to have put five X's on the map. While only one new brewery had been built by the end of 1996, in an interview with the author Shipman stated

> I'm convinced that we are going to figure out the keys to success in this industry and act on them in a way that delivers the kind of success that's going to lead to building more breweries.[30]

In 1997, Paul Shipman stated his goals as

1. Continued market development and penetration in the East and other parts of the nation

2. Addressing the shortfall of growth in the West and, particularly, the Pacific Northwest by working with distributors and retailers, introducing new products, and salesmanship

3. In the longer run, growth in international markets, e.g., Japan where Redhook products were being sold through 7-Eleven convenience stores[31]

Into 1998, Redhook had not deviated from the goals and strategy developed when the industry was in a rapid growth phase in spite of the company's sales decline and overall poor performance in 1997. The only strategic change was to cut costs by temporarily closing the Fremont brewery, transferring all Western production to the Woodinville brewery. For Paul Shipman, 1998 was a time for reevaluation. Were Redhook's goals and strategy still valid and, if so, what should be done to implement them in view of the changes in growth and competition affecting the craft beer segment?

Notes

1. Sarah Theodore, "Domestic Specialty Suffers Growing Pains in 97," *Beverage Industry*, January 1998, pp. 9–18.
2. "Specialty and Microbrewery Report," *Modern Brewery Age*, May 18, 1998, pp. 12–17.
3. *Ibid.*
4. Lee Moriwaki, "Shakeout brewing," *The Seattle Times*, November 3, 1996, pp. F1, 4; David Edgar, "Craft Brewing: Fastest Growth in the Industry," *The New Brewer*, May–June 1995, p. 13; and M. Sharon Baker, "Yakima Brewing Defies Industry," *Puget Sound Business Journal*, March 27–April 2, 1998, p. 15.
5. Richard A. Melcher, "Those New Brews Have the Blues," *Business Week*, March 9, 1998, p. 40.
6. "Specialty and Microbrewery Report," pp. 12–17.
7. Sarah Theodore, pp. 9–18.
8. *Ibid.*
9. Eric Sfiligoj, "Small Wonder," *Beverage World*, May 1996, p. 72.
10. John Student, "True Brew," *American Demographics*, May 1995, pp. 32–39.
11. John P. Robinson, "Microbrews Going Mainstream," *American Demographics*, December 1996, pp. 25–26.
12. Eric Sfiligoj, p. 72.
13. Melanie Wells, "Pete's Gut-Instinct Marketing Push," *USA Today*, October 7, 1996, p. 2B.
14. Gene Muller, "Message in a Bottle," *The New Brewer*, July–August 1995, p. 13.
15. Richard A. Melcher, Sandra Dallas, and David Woodruff, "From the Microbrewers Who Brought You Bud, Coors . . . ," *Business Week*, April 24, 1995, pp. 66, 70.
16. Steve Kaufman, "Microbrewery Stocks Look to Full-Bodied Future," *The News Tribune*, April 4, 1996.
17. Maxim Lenderman, "Mind Games," *Beverage World*, September 1996, pp. 70, 72, 74.
18. Jerry Kherouch, "Even as A_B Backs Off, Small Brews Still Face Distribution Bottleneck," *Brandweek*, September 30, 1996, p. 9.
19. *Redhook Ale Brewery 1995 Annual Report.*
20. Redhook Ale Brewery, *Prospectus*, April 16, 1995.
21. Gordon Young, "Attack of the Microbreweries," <http://www.metroactive.com/features/breweries.html>.
22. Gerry Khermouch, "Micros on Majors' Menu at Taste Fest," *Brandweek*, October 31, 1994, p. 12.
23. Gordon Young.
24. *Redhook Ale Brewery 1997 Annual Report.*
25. Redhook Ale Brewery, <http://www.redhook.com>.
26. Leslie Holdcroft, "Going Public a Rebirth for Northwest Brewer," *Washington CEO*, November 1995, p. 15.
27. Lee Moriwaki, "Forecast Sinks Redhook Stock," *The Seattle Times*, December 20, 1996, p. D1.
28. Lee Moriwaki, p. F1, 4.
29. Patricia Sellers, "A Whole New Ball Game In Beer," *Fortune*, September 19, 1994, p. 86.
30. Paul Shipman, Personal Interview, May 16, 1997.
31. *Ibid.*

American Airlines' Dilemma: 2002

Richard C. Scamehorn

It was Tuesday morning, September 17, 2002, when Anne Currie asked, "Is this just a bail-out?" Currie was asking the question during the second hour of NBC's *Today* program, and she was asking it of Leo F. Mullin, Chairman and CEO of Delta Air Lines, one of the United States's seven major airlines. Mullin was advocating a multi-billion-dollar subsidy for the airlines of the United States.

He testified the next day before the Congressional subcommittee on aviation, along with Richard H. Anderson, Chairman and CEO of Northwest Airlines, Joseph B. Leonard, Chairman and CEO of AirTran Airways, and Donald Carty, Chairman and CEO of American Airlines, the world's largest. During this testimony, Carty said the economic pressures on airlines were so severe that they could "inevitably sink several carriers."

Birth of Commercial Aviation

Just as the United States entered combat in World War I in 1917, the U.S. Post Office received a federal grant of $100,000 to experiment with air mail service. This experiment proved worthwhile, and in May 1918, a regular U.S. Air Mail Service started using single-engine JN-4 "Jenny" biplanes with service between Washington, DC, and New York City. Typical of the confusion that would become characteristic of the airline industry, the pilot of the inaugural flight flew the wrong way from Washington, DC, and after correcting his heading ran out of fuel and was forced to land in Maryland. America's first air mail was actually delivered to New York City by train.

The cost of an air mail letter in 1918 was 34 cents (constant dollar of about $4.00 in 2002). The Jenny could only accommodate 140 pounds of mail, stuffed into the front of the plane's two open cockpits. In 1921, service between New York and Los Angeles cut the delivery time from 3 days (by train) to just 33 hours.

Although the U.S. Army flew the inaugural flight, private companies were quickly awarded routes across the United States, forming an embryo of an airline industry.

This case was prepared by Richard C. Scamehorn, Executive-in-Residence at Ohio University. This case was edited for SMBP-9th edition. Copyright © 2002 by Richard C. Scamehorn. Reprinted by permission.

Passenger Air Travel

These private companies found the military aircraft of World War I unreliable and unprofitable. Responding to the need, The Ford Motor Company produced the famous Ford 5 "Tri-Motor" airplane in 1926, which could accommodate up to 13 passengers at a speed of 113 miles per hour. Using the new Tri-Motor, Western Air Express (later to become part of TWA) started regularly scheduled passenger service between Detroit and Chicago and Chicago–Cleveland–New York.

Government control over the fledgling airline industry was established by the Waters Act of 1930, giving U.S. Postmaster General Walter Brown control over which airlines received lucrative air mail contracts. Brown forced mergers of the small airlines into larger, and what he believed more stable, airlines.

The Big Four

These series of acquisitions resulted in what the industry then called "The Major Carriers": TWA, Pan American, United Airlines, Eastern Airlines, and American Airlines. The competition for coast-to-coast passenger travel between these five "majors" resulted in price discounting. These majors could afford to cut passenger prices with "subsidies" from the lucrative air mail contracts. Thus, the infant industry was born into price competition. Other firms (Continental, Delta, Northwest, and U.S. Airways) eventually entered the industry while others, (Eastern and Pan American) left it. TWA was acquired by American Airlines in 2001.

Continental Airlines flew air mail in west Texas, New Mexico, Colorado, and Nevada in 1934. As was the case of other airlines, several acquisitions, particularly that of Texas International Airlines in 1982, turned Continental into an international airline, flying from North America to South America, Asia, and Australia.

But there were troubles, and Continental filed bankruptcy under Chapter 11 in 1983, returned to profitability in 1984, and came out of bankruptcy in 1986. It started flights to Europe in 1985, acquired Frontier Airlines, People Express, and New York Air by 1987, and then again filed bankruptcy under Chapter 11 in 1990. Out of bankruptcy in 1993, by 2001 it had produced 24 consecutive profitable quarters of operation. Continental's hubs were located in Houston, New York, and Los Angeles.

Delta Airlines, started in 1928, grew through the acquisition of Chicago and Southern Airlines in 1953 and Pan American Airlines in 1991, securing Pan Am's routes and aircraft (except to London's Heathrow airport). In 1955, Delta pioneered the hub-and-spoke system in which passengers would be flown from regional airports to a central hub for long-distance transit to another hub. Delta established hubs in Atlanta, Cincinnati, and Dallas.

Northwest Airlines commenced operations in 1926 as Northwest Airways and adopted the name Northwest Orient in 1947 to promote its DC-4 long-haul polar flights to Asia. Its hubs were established in Minneapolis, Detroit, and Memphis.

United Airlines chose its name as a result of a half-dozen acquisitions, truly uniting into an airline. United pioneered the San Francisco to New York route in the 1930s, but its busiest route developed between Chicago and New York, putting United into head-to-head competition on this route against American Airlines. In 1991, United acquired Pan Am's valued route and landing rights at London's Heathrow airport, again placing it in direct competition with American Airlines.

U.S. Airways started as a regional freight carrier in the towns of western Pennsylvania and the Ohio Valley, under the name of All American Aviation, but did not start passenger service until 1949 and subsequently changed its name to Allegheny Airlines, indicating its regional character. Subsequent acquisitions of Mohawk Airlines (1972) and Piedmont Airlines (1989) expanded its north-central regional, short-haul character. It grew into a national carrier with the acquisition of Pacific Southwest Airlines in 1988. It changed its name to U.S. Airways and developed more hubs than any other airline, in Washington, DC, Baltimore, Pittsburgh, Philadelphia, Indianapolis, Dayton, and Charlotte.

American Airlines, the world's largest, started operations as American Airways in 1934. Although American's growth followed the pattern of the other majors, it pioneered many concepts that were, sooner or later, copied by most of its competitors. In 1934, American created the Admiral's Club, an honorary courtesy airport lounge for use by VIP customers.

In 1942, it created Sky Chef catering for airline food service and sold its service to many competitors. Immediately following the cessation of World War II, it started transatlantic service to Europe, and in 1953 nonstop coast-to-coast service, which became nonstop jet service in 1959 using Boeing 707 jets.

American inaugurated the industry's *super-saver* ticket pricing in 1977 for fares from New York to Los Angeles. The concept required an advance purchase and an over-the-weekend stay at the destination before returning. The strategy was called *yield management*, intended to fill up what would otherwise be empty seats with non-business passengers at highly discounted fares.

In 1978, the airline industry changed forever. President Carter's administration deregulated the airline industry in a sweeping move that allowed market forces to determine both routes and fares. While regulation forced some unprofitable routes on the airlines, their overall operations were virtually guaranteed profitability by the FAA, almost the same as public utilities. Deregulation removed all protection, and competition quickly escalated to a fever pitch.

Although the new wide-open competition forced down the price for a passenger-seat-mile flown (what the airlines call *yield*), the lower ticket prices stimulated increased demand (what the airlines call *load-factor*), and the overall profitability of the industry was not greatly affected.

Six of the now seven majors (not including Southwest) continued their basic strategy of being everything to everybody (see **Exhibit 1**). They all flew both coast-to-coast and transoceanic, most over both oceans. They all offered full service, meals, snacks, drinks, and three levels of seating: first class, business, and economy. They all offered the super-saver tickets started by American Airlines in 1977. Competition was fierce. The only saving factor was the continued growth of passenger traffic.

In 1981, a maverick airline called People Express initiated a completely different strategy. It offered highly discounted tickets for a no-frills flight. The prices were discounted far below the major's super-savers, but the passenger had to accept some compensating trade-offs. To begin with, People Express had only one hub: Newark, NJ, airport. Maintaining only one hub cut People's costs to the bone, but it also required a passenger flying from Detroit to Chicago to fly to Newark and then board a plane to Chicago. Nevertheless, the cost savings to People Express allowed it to undercut all of the majors. In addition, passengers had to carry their own luggage out to the airplane, and after landing were required to lug it back into the terminal. Other similar cost-cutting tactics made People Express the low cost airline in the United States.

People Express, in a 1985 change of strategy, started to offer numerous routes across the highly competitive North Atlantic. The losses incurred with this strategy caused People Express to file for bankruptcy, and it was acquired in 1986 by Continental Airlines. In variations of People Express's strategy, other low-cost, no-frills airlines entered the industry: AirTran, Frontier, JetBlue, Midway Airlines, Southwest Airlines, Spirit Airlines, and Western Airlines. The result of this cost cutting allowed Southwest to fly at a cost of 7.5 cents per air seat mile (ASM), compared to 11.33 cents per ASM for American Airlines, 12.06 cents for United Airlines, and 13.4 cents for US Airways. Overall, however, the U.S. airline industry was profitable during the 1980s and 1990s. (See **Exhibit 2**.)

Exhibit 1

U.S. Airlines Market Shares in 2002

Airline	Market Share
American	21.0%
United	17.6%
Delta	16.1%
Northwest	11.4%
Continental	9.7%
U S Airways	9.3%
Southwest	6.9%
All others	7.9%

Things Change

With its entry into the 21st century, the airline industry experienced a change. The almost steady growth in demand started to level off. Each of the majors (except Southwest) had formed an alliance with another international carrier. The expectation was that an alliance would provide revenue for at least a portion of an international flight—perhaps only to the gateway city, but something was better than nothing. So, United, which did not fly to Singapore, teamed with Singapore Airlines and then obtained revenues to the West Coast, from which Singapore Airlines provided the trans-Pacific route.

The appearance of a moderate recession in late 2000 and early 2001 resulted in a downturn in airline industry demand. By the summer of 2001, airlines were starting to announce quarterly losses. The terrorist acts at the World Trade Center and the Pentagon on September 11, 2001, had a severe impact on the airlines.

The U.S. federal government shut down all domestic flights for four days, during which most airlines' costs continued, but with zero revenue. International carriers had airplanes and crews overseas, which required not only salaries, but food and lodging expenses. The scare of terrorism caused a spike in crude oil prices and a resultant increase in jet fuel prices.

Many passengers decided not to fly for an indefinite period until the situation was stabilized. Airline demand dropped, and losses piled up. The industry was predicted to lose $4 billion in 2001, but the 9/11 tragedy increased that loss to $7 billion. US Airways filed for bankruptcy in August 2002, along with Midway and Vanguard Airlines. It was feared that United Airlines, the nation's second largest, might also file. American Airlines lost $1,013,000,000 on revenues of $8.0 billion during the first half of 2002, whereas Southwest generated a profit of $183,700,000 on revenues of $2.7 billion during the same period.

In response to the earnings differential, the stock market rewarded Southwest's shareholders by placing a market value on Southwest's stock greater than that of all the other six majors combined.

The U.S. Airline Industry in 2002

One analyst provided the following analysis of the airline industry:[1]

- Pummeled by poor profits and scarred from a terrorist attack against the United States, the airline industry finds itself on a bumpy course. In an effort to head off a drop in the number of passengers and rising costs for security, companies laid off staff and trimmed services. In an already intensely competitive market, the inevitable industrywide shakedown will have far-reaching effects on the industry's trend towards expanding domestic and international services. (See **Exhibit 1** for market share information.)

- Many airlines are still partly owned by their respective nations, and treaties between nations determine which airlines can land where. To get around national laws and regulatory problems, airlines have formed global alliances such as Star (United Airline and Lufthansa), Oneworld (American Airlines and British Airways), and SkyTeam (Delta Air Lines, Air France, and AeroMéxico). Through such alliances, airlines benefit from each other's resources, which include additional routes and marketing strategies as well as code-sharing agreements, without incurring the high costs of expansion. The costs involved with increased security precautions and route changes will force the airlines to examine their agreements. For customers, airline alliances offer broader frequent flyer programs, streamlined travel, and simplified systems for purchasing tickets, but those benefits may do little to allay passenger concerns regarding safety.

- Even as airlines stake out their positions in the global market, they are not immune to competition in their own backyard. Regional airlines have gained new ground with the development of newer, smaller jets that are faster than turboprop planes and have greater ranges. The new regional jets have also made operating in previously underserved markets more cost-efficient.

- Recognizing their potential, major U.S. carriers Delta Air Lines (which owns regional carriers Delta Express, Atlantic Southeast, and Comair) and American Airlines (with its American Eagle) have sought to control all or part of the upstart regionals. There is a similar trend in Europe, where regional airlines are seeking partnerships with major airlines to more effectively gain access to certain hubs.

- Major carriers hoping to merge—such as United Airlines and US Airways—have been rebuffed by a headwind of regulators scrutinizing competition issues. An operating partnership established by KLM/Royal Dutch Airlines and Alitalia has fallen apart amid disputes.

- As the world's airlines struggle to rise above regulators and each other in efforts to grow bigger and better, they are finding themselves in a struggle on other fronts. Airport capacity, route structures, weather, technology, and, most significantly, rising fuel and labor costs have cut into airline profits. Carriers have sought refuge in higher prices, primarily for business customers, who during the thriving economic times of the late 1990s were willing to pay more in exchange for better services and scheduling freedom. The move worked until corporate belt-tightening became the norm in 2000 and 2001 and companies began to reevaluate their travel budgets.

- Increasingly, business travelers are looking to various alternatives to high ticket prices: using software to streamline travel expenses, scouring the Net for cheaper fares that leisure

Exhibit 2

Airline Industry Net Income
(Dollars amounts in billions)

Year	Net Income
1993	$1.4
1994	$2.5
1995	$5.3
1996	$3.5
1997	$6.0
1998	$4.5
1999	$3.5
2000	$7.0

travelers enjoy, and relying increasingly on video- and teleconferencing technologies. The results have left airlines struggling to come up with ways of attracting more premium passengers.

- Exacerbating that struggle further are the tragedies at the World Trade Center in New York and the Pentagon in Washington, DC, where two American Airlines jets and two United Airlines jets were hijacked and crashed as part of apparent terrorist attacks in 2001. The catastrophe led to a first-time shutdown of all U.S. air traffic by the Federal Aviation Administration (FAA). The shutdown not only halted all domestic traffic, it prevented all international traffic from entering the United States.

- Effects from the shutdown have already surfaced. Midway Airlines decided to permanently halt its operations but later resumed limited operations with the help of $10 million in federal aid. Of the major carriers, Continental Airlines and US Airways were the first to react by cutting back their flights and laying off workers (about 20% each). Other carriers soon followed, which brought the number of layoffs to about 100,000 in the United States. European carriers, such as British Airways and Lufthansa, also began cutting services and workers.

- In a panic over anticipated financial losses, major U.S. carriers requested government help and received $15 billion worth in direct aid and guaranteed loans. (The EU has so far discouraged state bailouts.) The forces buffeting the industry, however, practically guarantee that there won't be any smooth take-offs back into profitability; most U.S. carriers still anticipate heavy losses.

Another analyst provided the following comments on the industry:[2]

- In recent years, the major U.S. airlines have formed marketing alliances with other U.S. and foreign airlines. Such alliances generally provide for code-sharing, frequent flyer program reciprocity, coordinated scheduling of flights to permit convenient connections, and other joint marketing activities. These arrangements permit an airline to market flights operated by other alliance members as its own. This increases the destinations, connections, and frequencies offered by the airline, which provide an opportunity to increase traffic on that airline's segment of flights connecting with alliance partners.

- The airline industry is both cyclical and seasonal in nature. For example, the second- and third-quarter operating results of Northwest Air Lines have historically been more favorable due to increased leisure travel on domestic and international routes during the spring and summer months.

- In addition, the industry may undergo consolidation. Any business combination could significantly alter the conditions and competition within the airline industry.

- Increased government regulations may impose additional requirements and restrictions. Airlines are subject to extensive regulatory requirements. In the last several years, Congress has passed laws and the FAA has issued a number of maintenance directives and other regulations. These requirements impose substantial costs on airlines.

- On November 19, 2001, Congress passed, and the president signed into law, the Aviation and Transportation Security Act. This law federalizes substantially all aspects of civil aviation security and requires, among other things, the implementation of certain security measures by airlines and airports, such as the requirement that all passenger bags be screened for explosives. Funding for airline and airport security under the law is primarily provided by a new $2.50 per enplanement ticket tax; however, airlines are responsible for costs in excess of this fee, which may not exceed 2000 security expense levels through 2004. Implementation of the requirements of the Aviation Security Act will result in increased costs for the airlines and their passengers.

■ Additional laws, regulations, taxes, and airport rates and charges have been proposed from time to time that could significantly increase the cost of airline operations or reduce revenues. Congress and the DOT have also proposed the regulation of airlines' responses to their competitors' activities. The ability of U.S. carriers to operate international routes is subject to change because the applicable arrangements between the United States and foreign governments may be amended from time to time or because appropriate slots or facilities may not be available.

AMR Corporation

AMR Corporation (AMR, or the Corporation) was incorporated in October 1982. AMR's principal subsidiary, American Airlines, Inc., was founded in 1934. On April 9, 2001, American Airlines, Inc., purchased substantially all of the assets and assumed certain liabilities of Trans World Airlines, Inc. (TWA). Accordingly, the operating results of TWA since the date of acquisition were included in the consolidated financial statements for the year ended December 31, 2001. American Airlines, Inc., including TWA (collectively, American), was the largest scheduled passenger airline in the world in 2002. AMR's operations were almost entirely in the airline industry.[3]

CORPORATE GOVERNANCE

Exhibit 3 lists the directors of AMR Corporation and the board committees. **Exhibit 4** provides the executive management team of American Airlines and American Eagle Airlines.

CEO'S LETTER TO SHAREHOLDERS:[4]

■ As everyone knows, 2001 was not just another year. It was a year that brought enormous pain and unprecedented challenges to our country, to our industry, and certainly to AMR Corporation. For American Airlines, every accomplishment, indeed every other event, was overshadowed by the twin calamities of the September 11 attacks and the loss of Flight 587 in Queens, New York, on November 12.

■ Prior to September 11, our company's greatest obstacle had been the slowing U.S. economy, which triggered a substantial decline in air travel generally and business travel in particular. The previously stable relationship between industry supply and demand deteriorated badly, and as revenues fell, many of our costs continued to rise. As a consequence, AMR posted significant losses in the first half of the year.

■ The September 11 attacks turned a difficult year into a down year for several days. And though we were able to handle a slew of new security-related operational demands and get our airline up and running again, passenger traffic for the entire industry was dramatically lower. In the days and weeks following the attacks, we acted quickly by reducing our capacity to get supply and demand better aligned.

■ When we fly less, we need fewer aircraft, so we also hastened the retirement of many older aircraft, while eliminating others through lease returns. All told, we removed about 70 aircraft from our fleet. (See **Exhibit 5**.) And as we ratcheted down capacity, we also focused very hard on reducing both capital spending and operating expenses. Earlier in the year, in response to the weakening revenue environment, we removed close to $1 billion from our 2001–2002 capital plan. In the post-9/11 environment, we took that initiative quite a bit further by drastically reducing capital spending for aircraft and nonaircraft items.

■ In terms of our fleet, we deferred 35 of the 45 firm 2002 deliveries until sometime beyond 2003. We also made significant cutbacks in our nonessential aircraft modifications, scaled

Exhibit 3

Board of Directors: AMR Corporation

John W. Bachmann
Managing Partner
Edward Jones
(financial services)
St. Louis, Missouri
Named a Director in 2001

David L. Boren
President
University of Oklahoma
(educational institution)
Norman, Oklahoma
Elected in 1994

Edward A. Brennan
Retired Chairman,
President, and CEO
Sears, Roebuck and Co.
(merchandising)
Chicago, Illinois
Elected in 1987

Donald J. Carty
Chairman, President,
and CEO
AMR Corporation/
American Airlines, Inc.
(air transportation)
Fort Worth, Texas
Elected in 1998

Armando M. Codina
Chairman and CEO
Codina Group, Inc.
(real estate investments,
development and
construction, property
management, and
brokerage services)
Coral Gables, Florida
Elected in 1995

Ann McLaughlin Korologos
Chairman Emeritus
The Aspen Institute
(educational and public
policy organization)
Aspen, Colorado
Elected in 1990

Michael A. Miles
Special Limited Partner
Forstmann Little & Co.
(investment banking)
New York, New York
Elected in 2000

Charles H. Pistor, Jr.
Retired Vice Chair
Southern Methodist University
(educational institution)
Dallas, Texas
Elected in 1982
Retired in March 2001

Phillip J. Purcell
Chairman and Chief Executive
Morgan Stanley Dean Witter & Co.
(financial services)
New York, New York
Elected in 2000

Joe M. Rodgers
Chairman
The JMR Group
(investment company)
Nashville, Tennessee
Elected in 1989

Judith Rodin
President
University of Pennsylvania
(educational institution)
Philadelphia, Pennsylvania
Elected in 1997

Roger Staubach
Chairman and CEO
The Staubach Group
(real estate services)
Addison, Texas
Named a Director in 2001

Earl G. Graves
Chairman and CEO
Earl G. Graves, Limited
(communications
and publishing)
Publisher and CEO
Black Enterprise Magazine
General Partner
Black Enterprise/
Greenwich Street
Corporate Growth
Partners, L.P.
New York, New York
Elected in 1995

back facilities projects in a number of cities, cut our information technology development budget, and drastically cut spending on ground equipment and training simulators. All told, we were able to remove another $2.5 billion from our capital plan—on top of the $1 billion we cut earlier.

- 2001 was a painful year for all three of our major constituency groups. We lost many valued customers, friends, and colleagues on both September 11 and November 12. For many others, the joy of flight has been dampened, at least temporarily. Thousands of AMR employees lost their jobs, and all of us were deeply troubled by the attacks on our country. Customers and employees alike have had to make some dramatic adjustments to deal with the new security requirements of the post-9/11 world. And of course, our shareholders

Exhibit 4

Management—Divisions and Subsidiaries: AMR Corporation

A. American Airlines, Inc.

Donald J. Carty[1]
Chairman, President, and
CEO

Robert W. Baker[1]
Vice Chairman

Gerald J. Arpey[1]
Executive Vice President,
Operations

Daniel P. Garton[1]
Executive Vice President,
Customer Service

Michael W. Gunn[1]
Executive Vice President,
Marketing and Planning

Peter J. Dolara
Senior Vice President,
Miami, Caribbean, and
Latin America

Monte E. Ford
Senior Vice President,
Information Technology,
and Chief Information
Officer

Thomas W. Horton[1]
Senior Vice President,
Finance, and Chief
Financial Officer

Dan P. Huffman
Senior Vice President
Maintenance and
Engineering

Henry C. Joyner
Senior Vice President,
Planning

Timothy J. Ahern
Vice President,
Safety, Security and
Environmental

Jane G. Allen
Vice President,
Flight Service

Walter J. Aue
Vice President,
Capacity Planning

James A. Beer
Vice President,
Corporate Development,
and Treasurer

David R. Brooks
President,
American Airlines
Cargo Division

Jeffrey J. Brundage
Vice President,
Employee Policy and
Relations

David L. Campbell
Vice President,
Alliance Base
Maintenance

Jeffrey C. Campbell
Vice President,
Europe

John A. Carpenter
Vice President,
Corporate Affairs

Robert C. Cordes
Vice President,
St. Louis

Timothy J. Doke
Vice President,
Corporate Communications

Bella D. Goren
Vice President,
Customer Services Planning

William T. Greene
Vice President,
Finance and Planning
for Maintenance
and Engineering

Gregory F. Hall
Vice President,
Line Maintenance

Douglas G. Herring
Vice President and
Controller

Gary F. Kennedy
Vice President,
Corporate Real Estate

Craig S. Kreeger
Vice President and
General Sales Manager

Robert P. Kudwa
Vice President,
Flight

Dennis LeBright
Vice President,
Miami

John R. MacLean
Vice President,
Purchasing

Charles D. MarLett[1]
Corporate Secretary

Exhibit 4 (*continued*)
Management—Divisions and Subsidiaries: AMR Corporation

Anne H. McNamara[1]
Senior Vice President and
General Counsel

Susan M. Oliver
Senior Vice President,
Human Resources

William K. Ris, Jr.
Senior Vice President,
Government Affairs

Benard J. DeSena
Vice President, Chicago

John R. Samuel
Vice President,
Customer Technology

Andrew O. Watson
Vice President,
e-Business

Carolyn E. Wright
Vice President,
Human Resources
Strategic Partnerships

Lauri L. Curtis
Vice President,
Reservations and eTDS

C. David Cush
Vice President,
International Planning
and Alliances

Thomas R. Del Valle
Vice President,
Customer Service

Ralph L. Richardi
Vice President,
Operations Planning
and Performance

Di Ann Sanchez
Vice President,
Diversity and Talent
Management

Scott D. Nason
Vice President,
Operations Technology,
Research, and Analysis

Robert E. Olson
Vice President,
Revenue Management

Randy H. Phillips
Vice President,
Engineering and
Quality Assurance

Carmine J. Romano
Vice President,
Tulsa Base Maintenance

Peggy E. Sterling
Vice President,
Dallas/Fort Worth

Kenneth D. Wilcox
Vice President,
Technology Services

B. Amercian Eagle Airlines, Inc.

Peter M. Bowler
President

Robert W. Reding
Chief Operations

Thomas Bacon
Senior Vice President,
Marketing and Planning

R. Stan Henderson
Senior Vice President,
Customer Services

C. AMR Investment Services, Inc.

William F. Quinn
President

Note:
1. AMR Corporation Officers

Source: American Airlines, Inc., *2001 Annual Report*, p. 43.

have taken a tremendous hit, as AMR shares fell significantly in the aftermath of the September attacks.

And yet, despite all the bad news, 2001—which, among other things, marked our company's 75th anniversary—did contain a number of important highlights and milestones.

MANAGEMENTS' COMMENTS ON 2001 OPERATING RESULTS[5]

AMR's net loss in 2001 was $1.8 billion, or $11.43 loss per share. AMR's net earnings in 2000 were $813 million, or $5.43 per share ($5.03 diluted). On September 11, 2001, two American Airlines aircraft were hijacked and destroyed in terrorist attacks on the World Trade Center in New York City and the Pentagon in northern Virginia. On the same day, two United Air Lines

Exhibit 5

Operating Aircraft Fleets: AMR Corporation

As of December 31, 2001	Seating Capacity	Owned	Capital Leased	Operating Leased	Total	Average Age (Years)
American Airlines aircraft						
Airbus A300-600R	178/250/251	10	—	24	34	12
Boeing 727-200[1]	138	33			33	23
Boeing 727-800	134	67	—	10	77	1
Boeing 757-200	176	75	11	31	117	8
Boeing 767-200	160	8	—	—	8	19
Boeing 767-200 Extended Range	158	9	12	—	21	16
Boeing 767-300 Extended Range	190/228	32	7	10	49	9
Boeing 777-200 Extended Range	223/245/252	40	—	—	40	2
Fokker 100	87	67	3	4	74	9
McDonnell Douglass MD-80	129	130	20	109	259	14
Total		471	53	188	712	10
TWA LLC aircraft						
Boeing 717-200[2]	100	—	—	30	30	1
Boeing 757-200	168	—	—	27	27	4
Boeing 767-300 Extended Range	215/233	—	—	9	9	7
McDonnell Douglas MD-80	131	19	23	61	103	9
Total		19	23	127	169	7
AMR Eagle aircraft						
ATR 42	46	20	—	10	30	11
Bombardier CRJ-700	70	1	—	—	1	—
Embraer 135	37	40	—	—	40	2
Embraer 140	44	15	—	—	15	—
Embraer 145	50	56	—	—	56	3
Super ATR	64/66	40	—	3	43	7
Saab 340B	34	17	49	—	66	10
Saab 340B Plus	34	—	—	25	25	6
Total		189	49	38	276	7

Notes:
1. The Boeing 727-200 fleet will be removed from service by May 2002.
2. The Boeing 717-200 fleet will be removed from service by June 2002.

Source: AMR Corporation, *2001 Annual Report,* p. 41.

aircraft were also hijacked and used in terrorist attacks, the Federal Aviation Administration (FAA) issued a federal ground stop order on September 11, 2001, prohibiting all flights to, from, and within the United States. Airports did not reopen until September 13, 2001 (except for Washington Reagan Airport, which was partially reopened on October 4, 2001). The company was able to operate only a portion of its scheduled flights for several days thereafter. When flights were permitted to resume, passenger traffic and yields on the company's flights were significantly lower than prior to the attacks. As a result, the company reduced its operating schedule to approximately 80% of the schedule it flew prior to September 11, 2001. Somewhat offsetting the impact of the September 11 events, the company recorded $856 million in reimbursement from the U.S. government under the Air Transportation Safety and System Stabilization Act. **Exhibit 6** shows the consolidated operating statement, and **Exhibit 7** shows the balance sheet.

Exhibit 6

Consolidated Statements of Operations: AMR Corporation
(Dollar amounts in millions, except per share data)

Year Ending December 31	2001	2000	1999
Revenues			
Passenger			
American Airlines	$ 15,780	$16,394	$14,724
AMR Eagle	1,378	1,452	1,294
Cargo	662	721	643
Other revenues	1,143	1,136	1,069
Total operating revenues	18,963	19,703	17,730
Expenses			
Wages, salaries, and benefits	8,032	6,783	6,120
Aircraft fuel	2,888	2,495	1,696
Depreciation and amortization	1,404	1,202	1,092
Other rentals and landing fees	1,197	999	942
Maintenance, materials, and repairs	1,165	1,095	1,003
Commissions to agents	835	1,037	1,162
Aircraft rentals	829	607	630
Food service	778	777	740
Other operating expenses	3,695	3,327	3,189
Special charges, net of U.S. government grant	610	—	—
Total operating expenses	21,433	18,322	16,574
Operating income (loss)	(2,470)	1,381	1,156
Operating income (expense)			
Interest income	110	154	95
Interest expense	(538)	(467)	(393)
Interest capitalized	144	151	118
Miscellaneous, net	(2)	68	30
	(286)	(94)	(150)
Income (loss) from continuing operations before income taxes and extraordinary loss	(2,756)	1,287	1,006
Income tax provision (benefit)	(994)	508	350
Income (loss) from continuing operations before extraordinary loss	(1,762)	779	656
Income from discontinued operations, net of applicable income taxes and minority interest	—	43	265
Gain on sale of discontinued operations, net of applicable income taxes	—	—	64
Income (loss) before extraordinary loss	(1,762)	822	985
Extraordinary loss, net of applicable income taxes	—	(9)	—
Net earning (loss)	$(1,762)	$ 813	$ 985
Earnings (loss) per share			
Basic			
Income (loss) from continuing operations	$ (11.43)	$ 5.20	$ 4.30
Discontinued operations	—	0.30	2.16
Extraordinary loss	—	(0.07)	—
Net earnings (loss)	$ (11.43)	$ 5.43	$ 6.46
Diluted			
Income (loss) from continuing operations	$ (11.43)	$ 4.81	$ 4.17
Discontinued operations	—	0.27	2.09
Extraordinary loss	—	(0.05)	—
Net earnings (loss)	$ (11.43)	$ 5.03	$ 6.26

Source: AMR Corporation, *2001 Annual Report,* p.141.

Exhibit 7

Consolidated Balance Sheet: American Airlines
(Dollar amounts in millions, except per share data)

Year Ending December 31	2001	2000
Assets		
Current assets		
Cash	$ 120	$ 89
Short-term investments	2,872	2,144
Receivables, less allowance for uncollectable accounts (2001—$52; 2000—$27)	1,414	1,303
Inventories, less allowance for obsolescence (2001—$383; 2000—$332)	822	757
Deferred income taxes	790	695
Other current assets	522	191
Total current assets	6,540	5,179
Equipment and property		
Flight equipment, at cost	21,707	20,041
Less accumulated depreciation	6,727	6,320
	14,980	13,721
Purchase deposits for flight equipment	929	1,700
Other equipment and property, at cost	4,202	3,639
Less accumulated depreciation	2,123	1,968
	2,079	1,671
	17,988	17,092
Equipment and property under capital leases		
Flight equipment	2,658	2,618
Other equipment and property	163	159
	2,821	2,777
Less accumulated amortization	1,154	1,233
	1,667	1,544
Other assets		
Route acquisition costs and airport operating and gate lease rights, less accumulated amortization (2001—$556; 2000—$498)	1,325	1,143
Goodwill, less accumulated amortization (2001—$110; 2000—$83)	1,392	385
Other	3,929	870
	6,646	2,398
Total assets	$32,841	$26,213
Liabilities and stockholders' equity		
Current liabilities		
Accounts payable	$ 1,785	$ 1,267
Accrued salaries and wages	721	955
Accrued liabilities	1,471	1,276
Air traffic liability	2,763	2,696
Current maturities of long-term debt	556	569
Current obligations under capital leases	216	227
Total current liabilities	7,512	6,990
Long-Term Debt, Less Current Maturities	8,310	4,151
Obligations Under Capital Leases, Less Current Obligations	1,524	1,323
Other Liabilities and Credits		
Deferred income taxes	1,627	2,385
Deferred gains	520	508
Postretirement benefits	2,538	1,706
Other liabilities and deferred credits	5,437	1,974
	10,122	6,573

(*continued*)

Exhibit 7 (*continued*)
Consolidated Balance Sheet: American Airlines
(Dollars amounts in millions, except per share data)

Year Ending December 31	2001	2000
Commitments and Contingencies		
Stockholders' Equity		
Preferred stock—20,000,000 shares authorized; None issued		
Common stock—$1 par value; 750,000,000 shares authorized; 182,278,766 shares issued	182	182
Additional paid-in capital	2,865	2,911
Treasury shares at cost: 2001—27,794,380; 2000—30,216,218	(1,716)	(1,865)
Accumulated other comprehensive loss	(146)	(2)
Retained earnings	4,188	5,950
	5,373	7,176
Total Liabilities and Stockholders' Equity	$32,841	$26,213

Source: AMR Corporation, *2001 Annual Report*, p. 17.

The company's 2001 revenues, yield, passenger miles (RPMs), and available seat miles (ASMs) were severely impacted by the September 11, 2001, terrorist attacks, the company's reduced operating schedule, a worsening of the U.S. economy that had already been dampening the demand for travel both domestically and internationally prior to the September 11, 2001, events, business travel declines as a result of the September 11, 2001, attacks, and increased fare sale activity occurring subsequent to the September 11 attacks to encourage passengers to resume flying. The company's revenues decreased approximately $740 million, or 3.8%, versus 2000. However, excluding TWA's revenues for the period April 10, 2001, through December 31, 2001, the company's revenues would have decreased approximately $2.6 billion versus 2000[6].

For comparability purposes, the following discussion does not combine American's and TWA's results of operations or related statistics for 2001. American's passenger revenues decreased by 14%, or $2.3 billion. In 2001, American derived approximately 68% of its passenger revenues from domestic operations and approximately 32% from international operations. American's domestic revenue per available seat mile (RASM) decreased 11.3%, to 9.28 cents, on a capacity decrease of 5%, or 104 billion ASMs. International RASM decreased to 9.07 cents, or 5.2%, on a capacity decrease of 4.9%. The decrease in international RASM was led by an 11.8% and 10.8% decrease in Pacific and European RASM, respectively, slightly offset by a 0.9% increase in Latin American RASM. The decrease in international capacity was driven by a 6.5% and 4.7% reduction in Latin American and European ASMs, respectively, partially offset by an increase in Pacific capacity of 2.8%.

TWA's passenger revenues were approximately $1.7 billion for the period April 10, 2001, through December 31, 2001. TWA's RASM was 7.74 cents on capacity of 21.7 billion ASMs.

AMR Eagle's passenger revenues decreased $74 million, or 5.1%. AMR Eagle's traffic remained flat compared to 2000, at 3.7 billion RPMs, while capacity increased to 6.5 billion ASMs, or 3.4%. Similar to American, the decrease in AMR Eagle's revenues was due primarily to the September 11, 2001, terrorist attacks and a worsening of the U.S. economy that had already been dampening the demand for air travel prior to that date.

Cargo revenues decreased 8.2%, or $59 million, for the same reasons as noted earlier. Selected financial information table (stated in millions of dollars, except per-share data) for AMR (excluding TWA) and AMR Eagle are shown below:[7]

Year Ended December 31,	2001	2000	1999
American Airlines			
Revenue passenger miles (millions) (RPM)	106,224	116,594	112,067
Available seat miles (millions) (ASM)	153,035	161,030	161,211
Cargo ton miles (millions)	2,058	2,280	2,068

Year Ended December 31,	2001	2000	1999
Passenger load factor	69.4%	72.4%	69.5%
Breakdown load factor	78.1%	65.9%	63.8%
Passenger revenue yield per passenger mile (cents)	13.28	14.06	13.14
Passenger revenue per available seat mile (cents) (RASM)	9.22	10.18	9.13
Cargo revenue yield per ton mile (cents)	30.24	31.31	30.70
Operating expenses per available seat mile (cents)	11.14	10.48	9.50
Operating aircraft at year end	712	717	697
AMR Eagle			
Revenue passenger miles (millions) (RPM)	3,725	3,731	3,371
Available seat miles (millions) (ASM)	6,471	6,256	5,640
Passenger load factor	59.6%	59.6%	59.8%
Operating aircraft at year end	276	261	268

Competition

UAL CORPORATION[8]

UAL's main subsidiary, United Airlines, was the world's number-one air carrier, based on revenue passenger miles. United flew some 540 jets to more than 130 destinations in the United States and 27 other countries, from hubs in Chicago, Denver, Los Angeles, San Francisco, and Washington, DC. It led the Star Alliance, a global marketing partnership with Lufthansa and others. The carrier had hoped to expand by acquiring US Airways, but the companies called off the deal after antitrust regulators at the U.S. Department of Justice moved to block it. UAL low-fare carrier United Shuttle offered about 455 short-haul flights daily to 23 western U.S. cities. Employees controlled 55% of UAL's voting stock.

Selected financial information (stated in millions of dollars, except per-share data) is shown below:

Year ending December 31	2001	2000	1999
A. Income Statement[9]			
Revenue	$16,138.0	$19,352.0	$18,027.0
Cost of goods sold	6,989.0	7,926.0	6,445.0
Gross profit	9,149.0	11,426.0	11,582.0
Gross profit margin	56.7%	59.0%	64.2%
SG&A expenses	9,626.0	9,780.0	9,390.0
Depreciation & amortization	1,866.0	992.0	801.0
Operating income	(2,343.0)	654.0	1,391.0
Operating margin	—	3.4%	7.7%
Total net income	(2,145.0)	50.0	1,235.0
Net profit margin	—	0.3%	6.9%
Diluted EPS ($)	(40.04)	0.04	9.94
B. Selected information[10]			
Revenue passengers	75	85	87
Revenue passenger miles (millions) (RPM)	116,635	126,933	125,465
Available seat miles (millions) (ASM)	164,849	175,485	176,686
Passenger load factor	70.8%	72.3%	71.0%
Breakeven passenger load factor	90.1%	69.4%	64.9%
Passenger revenue per passenger mile	11.7¢	13.3¢	12.5¢
Operating revenue per available seat mile (RASM)	9.8¢	11.0¢	10.2¢
Operating expense per available seat mile	12.0¢	10.6¢	9.4¢
Fuel gallons consumed of jet	2,861	3,101	3,065
Average price per gallon of jet fuel, including tax	86.5¢	81.0¢	57.9¢

Exhibit 8

Operating Revenues by Geographic Regions: AMR Corporation

Year Ending December 31	2001	2000	1999
Domestic	$13,657	$13,881	$12,563
Latin America	2,732	2,907	2,697
Europe	2,076	2,338	1,984
Pacific	498	577	486
Total consolidated revenues	**$18,963**	**$19,703**	**$17,730**

Source: AMR Corporation, *2001 Annual Report*, p. 41.

DELTA AIR LINES, INC.[11]

Delta Air Lines, the number-three U.S. carrier (behind UAL's United and AMR's American), was expanding its U.S. regional operations while building a global alliance. With hubs in Atlanta, Dallas/Fort Worth, Cincinnati, New York City (Kennedy), and Salt Lake City, Delta flew to nearly 210 U.S. cities and about 45 foreign destinations. It also served 220 U.S. cities and nearly 120 destinations abroad through code-sharing agreements. In the United States, Delta owned regional carriers Delta Express, Atlantic Southeast Airlines, and Comair. It had formed the SkyTeam alliance with Air France, Cintra's AeroMéxico, and Korean Air Lines, to compete with rival alliances Star and Oneworld. Delta also owned 40% of computer reservation service Worldspan.

Selected financial information (stated in millions of dollars, except per-share data) is shown below:

Year ending December 31	2001	2000	1999
A. Income statement[12]			
Revenue	$13,879.0	$16,741.0	$15,888.0
Cost of goods sold	4,100.0	4,128.0	4,500.0
Gross profit	9,779.0	12,613.0	11,388.0
Gross profit margin	70.5%	75.3%	71.7%
SG&A expenses	8,797.0	8,832.0	8,399.0
Depreciation & amortization	1,283.0	1,187.0	1,146.0
Operating income	(301.0)	2,594.0	1,843.0
Operating margin	—	15.5%	11.6%
Total net income	(1,216.0)	828.0	1,303.0
Net profit margin	—	4.9%	8.2%
Diluted EPS ($)	(9.99)	6.28	9.42
B. Selected information[13]			
Revenue passengers enplaned (thousands)	104,943	119,930	110,304
Revenue passenger miles (millions) (RPM)	101,717	112,998	106,165
Available seat miles (millions) (ASM)	147,837	154,974	147,073
Passenger load factor	68.8%	72.9%	72.6%
Breakeven passenger load factor	74.7%	64.8%	62.7%
Cargo ton miles (millions)	1,583	1,855	—
Cargo ton mile yield	31.95¢	31.46¢	—
Fuel gallons consumed (millions)	2,649	2,922	2,730
Average aircraft fuel price per gallon, Net of hedging gains	68.60¢	67.38¢	49.83¢
Number of aircraft in fleet at year end	814	831	809
Average age of aircraft fleet at years end (years)	9.1	9.6	—
Average aircraft utilization (hours per day)	7.3	8.0	—
End of year full-time equivalent employees	73,273	83,952	81,000

NORTHWEST AIRLINES CORPORATION[14]

Northwest Airlines, the number-four U.S. airline (UAL's United was number one), flew to more than 145 cities worldwide, with hubs in Detroit, Memphis, Minneapolis/St. Paul, Osaka, and Tokyo. It also owned Memphis regional carrier Express Airlines. Through code-sharing agreements with other carriers, the airline served about 750 destinations in 120 countries. It had extensive alliances with Continental Airlines and Dutch airline KLM. Northwest was one of the world's top air cargo carriers. Facing reduced demand for air travel, Northwest cut both its flight schedule and its workforce in 2001.

Selected financial information (stated in millions of dollars, except per-share data) is shown below:

Year ending December 31	2001	2000	1999
A. Income statement[15]			
Revenue	$9,905.0	$11,415.0	$10,276.0
Cost of goods sold	4,640.0	5,020.0	4,114.0
Gross profit	5,265.0	6,395.0	6,162.0
Gross profit margin	53.2%	56.0%	60.0%
SG&A expenses	5,443.0	5,209.0	4,970.0
Depreciation & amortization	690.0	617.0	478.0
Operating income	(868.0)	569.0	714.0
Operating margin	—	5.0%	6.9%
Total net income	(423.0)	256.0	300.0
Net profit margin	—	2.2%	2.9%
Diluted EPS ($)	(5.03)	2.77	3.26
B. Selected information[16]			
Available seat miles (millions) (ASM)	98,356	103,256	98,446
Revenue passenger miles (millions) (RPM)	73,126	79,128	74,168
Passenger load factor	74.3%	76.6%	74.6%
Revenue passengers (millions)	54.1	58.7	56.1
Revenue yield per passenger mile (RASM)	11.24¢	12.04¢	11.58¢
Passenger revenue per scheduled ASM	8.36¢	9.21¢	8.64¢
Operating revenue per total ASM	9.17¢	10.01¢	9.44¢
Operating expense per total ASM	9.78¢	9.33¢	8.71¢
Cargo ton miles (millions)	2,161	2,502	2,336
Cargo revenue per ton mile	33.28¢	34.25¢	31.31¢
Fuel gallons consumed (millions)	2,029	2,113	2,039
Average fuel per gallon	79.26¢	82.99¢	53.55¢
Number of aircraft in fleet at year end	428	424	410
Full-time equivalent employees at year end	45,708	53,491	51,823

SOUTHWEST AIRLINES[17]

Southwest Airlines (the number-seven U.S. carrier) will fly any plane, as long as it's a Boeing 737, and let passengers sit anywhere they like, as long as they get there first. Sticking with what works, Southwest has expanded its low-cost, no-frills, no-reserved-seats approach to air travel throughout the United States to serve about 60 cities in 30 states. To curb maintenance and training costs, the airline used only Boeing 737s; it operated about 360. Southwest offered ticketless travel to trim back-office costs and operated its own reservation system. The airline boasted a highly participative corporate culture and only one strike during its 30-year history. It had also enjoyed 29 straight profitable years. Southwest was expanding service to the eastern United States.

Southwest currently operated 366 Boeing 737 jets:

Type	Number	Seats
737-200	27	122
737-300	194	137
737-500	25	122
737-700	120	137

Selected financial information (stated in millions of dollars, except per-share data) is shown:

Year Ending December 31	2001	2000	1999
A. Income statement[18]			
Revenue	$5,555.2	$5,649.6	$4,735.6
Cost of goods sold	2,115.9	2,021.6	1,638.2
Gross profit	3,439.3	3,628.0	3,097.4
Gross profit margin	61.9%	64.2%	65.4%
SG&A expenses	2,462.4	2,304.4	2,053.3
Depreciation & amortization	345.8	302.4	262.4
Operating income	631.1	1,021.2	781.7
Operating margin	11.4%	18.1%	16.5%
Total net income	511.1	603.1	474.4
Net profit margin	9.2%	10.7%	10.0%
Diluted EPS ($)	0.63	0.76	0.59
B. Selected information[19]			
Revenue passengers carried (millions)	64,446	63,678	57,500
Revenue passenger miles (millions) (RPM)	44,493	42,215	36,479
Available seat miles (millions) (ASM)	65,295	59,909	52,855
Load factor	68.1%	70.5%	69.0%
Average length of passenger haul (miles)	690	663	634
Trips flown	940,426	903,754	846,823
Average passenger fare	83.46	85.87	79.35
Passenger revenue yield per RPM	12.09¢	12.95¢	12.51¢
Operating revenue yield per ASM (RASM)	8.51¢	9.43¢	8.96¢
Operating expenses per ASM	7.54¢	7.73¢	7.48¢
Fuel cost per gallon (average)	70.86¢	78.69¢	52.71¢
Number of employees at year-end	31,580	29,274	27,653
Size of fleet at year-end (2)	355	344	312

Rivalry Intensifies

The intense rivalry of the airline industry was raised to a new height on August 22, 2002, when Southwest Airlines announced it was slashing its fares by an astounding 25%. Southwest Airlines (although in fourth place in domestic market share) commanded less than 10% of the domestic airline industry's market share, but, in the regions where Southwest operated, it held a share of about 65% following the cutbacks by the other majors. The combined low-cost carriers accumulated a 19% domestic market share.

The industry's mainstay during the 1990s was the last-minute full-fare business traveler, but by 2002 this category had fallen to only 20% of passengers. The industry's new mainstay had become the discount-fare leisure and vacation traveler.

What to Do?

American Airlines was the industry's proverbial 800-pound gorilla, offering domestic and international full service across an incredible network of hubs and spokes, incorporating jumbo and small regional jet aircraft. In contrast, Southwest Airlines was a niche player, offering almost no service other than transport to a select number of point-to-point destinations.

As the 2002 year came to an end, the two-year-long recession continued, with little optimism for either a rapid or significant recovery. The major stock market indices were at five year lows and struggling to avoid further slippage. Although the Federal Reserve had set the Federal Funds rate at the lowest level ever recorded (1.75%), the action failed to act as an economic stimulus.

Amid this gloomy outlook, American Airlines still needed to return to profitability and maintain its industry dominance. Several strategies had to be considered:

- **Major market retrenchment:** Eliminate all nonprofitable routes along with the closing of the facilities at those destinations. This would significantly reduce its market share, but would result in cost reductions greater than the revenue reductions.

- **Major union concessions:** Renegotiate all union contracts, starting with the pilots, using Southwest's 70 hours per month as a benchmark. Demand similar reductions from the International Association of Machinists (ground-crew personnel) as well as the Flight Attendants Union and ticket and gate personnel.

- **Abandon the hub and spoke model:** Shift to mostly point-to-point flights, using the existing five hubs as much as possible. Eliminate the spokes and allow other regional airlines to handle the low-revenue, short-haul flights to the hubs. Ticket offices and flight and ground crews would be eliminated.

- **Downsize the spoke model:** Retain the hub and spoke model, but significantly downsize service at the regional spokes through the use of small, regional jet aircraft. This could create a high load-factor in the smaller planes and reduce the current losses on the partly full large aircraft now serving the spokes.

- **Eliminate services:** Stop meal service, snacks, baggage transfers, and all other "frills." Significantly reduce employees now performing any and all labor-intensive activities other than the actual flight operations. Require e-ticketing to reduce check-in counter personnel.

- **Stay the course:** Keep up the pressure on Congress for an industry subsidy. Maintain all existing routes to avoid market share loss just to achieve a quick profitability turnaround. As the U.S. economy rebounds, staying the course will retain American's route structure and industry dominance.

- **Tighten up everything:** Significantly reduce the availability of cheap, super-saver seats. Make all tickets nonrefundable and add a surcharge for a change of itinerary. Increase the requirements for free frequent flyer tickets. Charge for more than one carry-on bag and for checked luggage over 40 pounds.

Notes

1. Danny Cummings, "Airlines," www.hoovers.com/industry/snapshot/profile. The following 10 paragraphs are directly quoted, with minor editing.
2. www.hoovers.com. The following five paragraphs are directly quoted, with minor editing.
3. AMR Corporation, *2002 Annual Report* p. 8. This is directly quoted, with minor editing.
4. *Ibid*, pp. 1–4. The following six paragraphs are directly quoted, with minor editing.
5. *Ibid*, p. 6. This paragraph is directly quoted, with minor editing.

6. *Ibid.* These following five paragraphs are directly quoted, with minor editing.
7. AMR Corporation, *SEC 10-K 405*, 02/28/2002, p. 25.
8. www.Hoovers.com/co./capsule, "UAL Corporation." This paragraph is directly quoted, with minor editing.
9. *Ibid*, financials.
10. UAL Corporation, *SEC 10-K 405*, 08/08/2002, Item 6.
11. www.Hoovers.com/co./capsule, "Delta AirLines, Inc." This paragraph is directly quoted, with minor editing.
12. *Ibid*, financials.
13. Delta Air Lines, Inc., *SEC 10-K 405*, 03/2/2008, p. 9. This paragraph is directly quoted, with minor editing.
14. www.Hoovers.com/co./capsule, "Northwest Airlines Corporation." This paragraph is directly quoted, with minor editing.
15. *Ibid*, financials.
16. Northwest Airlines Corporation, *SEC 10-K 405*, 04/01/2002, p. 19.
17. www.Hoovers.com/co./capsule, "Southwest Airlines Co." This paragraph is directly quoted, with minor editing.
18. *Ibid*, financials.
19. Southwest Airlines, Co., *SEC 10K 405*, 02/04/2002, p. 11.

case 32

The Boeing Commercial Airplanes Group: Decision 2001

Richard C. Scamehorn

How It All Started—The Boeing Company

With the advent of World War I, Bill Boeing started The Boeing Company in 1916 in response to the military's growing interest in air power. Their first big success, during the peace between World War I and World War II, was the B-9 bomber, called the "Death Angel."

In the mid-1930s Boeing developed Project "X," later called the XB-15. Although not a success, its technology led to the development of the B-17. This heavy bomber, when viewed by the press in 1940, had so many machine guns as protective armament that one reporter called it, a "Flying Fortress." The name stuck and it was produced in greater numbers than any other large aircraft during World War II.

Boeing's further advancements came with jet-powered aircraft: The B-47 "Stratojet," The KC-135 "Tanker," and the B-52. The B-52 was first used by the United States Air Force during the 1950s and it remains today as the workhorse heavy bomber of the U.S. Air Force.

However, Boeing's greatest claim to fame was in commercial aircraft. Utilizing the KC-135 technology, Boeing developed the world's first successful long-range commercial jet transport—the B-707. This airplane created the "jet set." Passengers could now fly overnight from Europe to Asia or North America, or with a refueling stop, from Asia to North America. It cut the travel from Europe to North America from five days (by ship) to eight hours, and across the Pacific from 10 days to 17 hours. It obsoleted entire fleets of steamships and made international travel so economical that it became a common event for both pleasure and business.

Boeing quickly followed this success with a mid-range B-727, followed by a short-range B-737. Then, in 1969, Boeing launched the era of the jumbo jets with the maiden flight of the B-747 jumbo jet from New York to Los Angeles carrying 385 passengers. With this stable of safe, reliable aircraft, Boeing dominated the world's aircraft market. McDonnell Douglas developed its jumbo jet DC-10 and Lockheed had its L-1011, but neither could challenge the B-747.

Boeing then increased its competitive advantage by "stretching" the B-747 into a B-747-SUD (Stretched-Upper-Deck) allowing 40 first-class passengers to sit in the upper level in isolated quiet. They further developed the 747-SP for ultra-long-range flights, nonstop from Sydney to Los Angeles. This was accomplished by shortening the body, removing 35 rows of

This case was prepared by Richard C. Scamehorn, Executive in-Residence Emeritus, at Ohio University. This case was edited for SMBP-9th Edition. Copyright © 2001 by Richard C. Scamehorn. Reprinted by permission.

seats, and using the resultant savings of weight to add additional fuel tanks for the increased range. The most recent design is the B-747-400, a high performance, fuel-efficient, long-range version that became the standard for long-haul, intercontinental flights. **Exhibit 1** shows the major products manufactured and sold by Boeing's three strategic business segments—(1) Boeing Commercial Aircraft, (2) Boeing Military Aircraft and Missile Systems, and (3) Boeing Space and Communications and (4) other units. The 2000 sales and other operating revenues for these segments were $31,171,000,000 (60.7%), $12,197,000,000 (23.8%) $8,039,000,000 (15.7%) and $758,000,000 (1.4%),[1] respectively (less accounting adjustments of $844,000,000).

A Late Entrant into the Industry

Airbus Industrie was formed on December 18, 1970 as a *Groupement d'Interet Economique* (the French term for a grouping of economic interests), with the governments of France, Germany, and Britain as partners. The private companies involved represented some of the world's best aircraft technology. They were Aerospatile (of France) with 37.9% ownership, Daimler-Benz Aerospace Airbus (of Germany) also with 37.9% ownership, British Aerospace Ltd. with 20%, and Construcciones Aeronauticas SA (CASA of Spain) with 4.2%.

With this consortium of noteworthy firms, the most advanced economies of Europe became stakeholders in Airbus Industrie, giving it commercial advantage within the European Common Market (later to become the European Union). However, the organization, or more explicitly, the lack of an organization, was dysfunctional. The partners were continuously required to agree on each business decision since the organization lacked a CEO or Managing Director who, under a corporate structure, would make such management decisions.

Airbus Industrie developed innovative features in their aircraft which were offered by neither Boeing nor McDonnell Douglas. They included:

1. A large reduction in the number of mechanical parts
2. Comprehensive built-in diagnostic test equipment
3. Reduction of maintenance
4. Reduced airframe weight
5. Better aircraft handling
6. Easier introduction of active controls
7. Simpler autoflight system interface
8. Better optimization of control functions
9. The first inflatable passenger evacuation slide with in-fuselage storage
10. The first extended twin operations (ETOPS) with airborne auxiliary power units for high-altitude engine restarts

These features were important to airlines for both safety and operational economies. In addition, Airbus Industrie created virtually identical flight decks, handling characteristics, and procedures that were shared by the A-320 family and the A-330/340 family. This commonality, covering aircraft from 120 seats to 400 seats, is possible only with the similar handling that can be achieved from a fly-by-wire control system. It leads to Cross Crew Qualification (CCQ) and Mixed Fleet Flying (MFF) and the resultant cost benefits.

CCQ enables a pilot to train for a new aircraft type with "Difference Training" instead of a new full type rating training course because the flight decks, handling characteristics, and operational procedures of CCQ-capable aircraft are so similar. Difference Training is 70% shorter than training for a completely dissimilar aircraft. As an example, when adding four A-330s to an exist-

---

1. This adds to 101.6%. The accounting differences and eliminations were $844,000,000 (1.6%) so with this subtracted— the four would equal 100.0%

Exhibit 1

Strategic Business Unit Products: Boeing Company

A. Boeing Commercial Airplanes   Alan Mulany, President / Renton, Washington

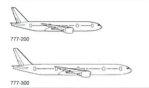
747-400

The Boeing 747-400

The 747-400 seats 416 to 568 passengers, depending on seating configuration and, with the recent launch of the Longer-Range 747-400, has a range of 8,850 miles. With its huge capacity, long range and fuel efficiency, the 747 offers the lowest operating cost per seat of any twin-aisle commercial jetliner. The 747-400 is available in an all-cargo freighter version as well as a combi model for passengers and cargo. Boeing continues to study 747 derivatives that will fly farther or carry more passengers to continue the 747 leadership in meeting the world's need for high-capacity, long-range airplanes.

Orders: 1,338[1] Deliveries: 1,261

777-200

777-300

The Boeing 777-200 and 777-300

The 777-200, which seats 305 to 440 passengers depending on configuration, has a range of up to 5,925 miles. The 777-200ER (extended range) can fly the same number of passengers up to 8,861 miles. The 777-300 is about 33 feet longer than the -200 and can carry from 368 to 550 passengers, depending on seating configuration, with a range of 6,854 miles. The company recently introduced two longer-range 777s.

Orders: 563[1] Deliveries: 316

767-200

767-300

767-400

The Boeing 767-200, 767-300, and 767-400

The 767-200 will typically fly 181 to 224 passengers up to 7,618 miles in its extended-range version. The 767-300, also offered in an extended-range version, offers 20 percent more passenger seating. A freighter version of the 767-300 is available. The first extended-range 767-400ERs were delivered to Delta Air Lines and Continental Airlines in August 2000. The airplane typically will carry between 245 and 304 passengers up to 6,501 miles. In a high-density inclusive tour arrangement, the 767-400ER can carry up to 375 passengers. Boeing committed to production in September 2000 a longer-range 767-400ER. This longer-range version is the same size as the 767-400ER, but has the equivalent range of the 767-300ER.

Orders: 901[1] Deliveries: 817

757-200

757-300

The Boeing 757-200 and 757-300

Seating 194 passengers in two classes, the 757-200 is ideal for high-demand, short-to-medium-range operations and can fly nonstop intercontinental routes up to 4,500 miles. It is also available in a freighter version. The 757-300 can carry 240 to 289 passengers on routes of up to 3,990 miles.

Orders: 1,027[1] Deliveries: 948

737-600

737-700

737-800

737-900

The Boeing 737-600, 737-700, 737-800 and 737-900

The Boeing 737 is the best-selling commercial jetliner of all time. The Next-Generation 737-600/-700/-800/-900 have outsold all other airplanes in their market segment. These new 737s incorporate advanced technology and design features that translate into cost-efficient, high-reliability operations and outstanding passenger comfort. The 737 is the only airplane family to span the entire 100-to-189-seat market, with maximum ranges from 3,159 (the -900) to 3,752 (the -700) miles. The 737 family also includes two Boeing Business Jets, derivatives of the 737-700 and -800.

Orders: 4,873[1] Deliveries: 3,857

717-200

The Boeing 717-200

The 717 twinjet meets the growing need worldwide for a 100-seat, high-frequency, short-range jet, flying a maximum range of 1,647 miles. The durable, simple, ultra-quiet and clean twinjet's effective use of technology results in the lowest operating costs.

Orders: 151[1] Deliveries: 44

Boeing Commercial Aviation Services

Boeing Commercial Aviation Services

Boeing Commercial Aviation Services provides the most complete portfolio of commercial aviation support products and services in the industry. This organization is an important component in the company's total solutions approach, and offers a wide range of products and services aimed at bringing even more value to our customers. This includes spare parts, airplane modification and engineering support, and a comprehensive worldwide customer support network. Commercial Aviation Services also oversees a number of joint ventures such as FlightSafetyBoeing Training International and wholly owned subsidiaries Jeppesen Sanderson Inc., Continental Graphics and The Preston Group.

---

1. Orders and deliveries as of December 31, 2000.
2. Order numbers do not include options.
3. For Section D--Other Units title added by authors.

(continues)

Exhibit 1

Strategic Business Unit Products: Boeing Company (*continued*)

B. Boeing Military Aircraft and Missile Systems   Jerry Daniels, President / St. Louis, Missouri

C-17 Globemaster III

The C-17 Globemaster III is the most advanced, versatile airlifter ever made. It is capable of flying long distances, carrying 169,000 pounds of payload and landing on short, austere runways close to front lines. Since entering operational service in 1995, the C-17 has become the U.S. Air Force's premier airlifter. The United Kingdom is the C-17's first international customer.

C-17 Globemaster III

F/A-18E/F Super Hornet

The F/A-18E/F Super Hornet is the nation's newest, most advanced strike fighter, designed from its inception to perform both fighter (air-to-air) and attack (air-to-surface) missions. During 2000, deliveries continued ahead of schedule. The Super Hornet also received the 1999 Collier Trophy, and the U.S. Navy's highest possible grade for operational evaluation.

F/A-18E/F Super Hornet

Joint Strike Fighter

Boeing and the JSF One Team have developed an affordable multirole strike fighter to meet the tactical aircraft modernization needs of the U.S. Air Force, Navy and Marine Corps, and also the United Kingdom Royal Air Force and Royal Navy. Boeing is building and flight-testing two concept demonstration aircraft while also designing the operational JSF. During design and build of the aircraft, Boeing demonstrated the lean design and manufacturing processes that will keep JSF affordable for all military services. Selection of a single contractor to build as many as 3,000 of the multiservice fighters is scheduled for 2001.

JSF Preferred Weapon
System Concept

F-22 Raptor

Boeing and Lockheed Martin are developing the U.S. Air Force's next-generation air superiority fighter. The team is building nine flight-test and two ground-test aircraft, and eight production-representative test vehicles. The Raptor is meeting all performance requirements.

F-22 Raptor

F-15 Eagle

The F-15E Eagle is the world's most capable multirole fighter and the backbone of the U.S. Air Force fleet. The F-15E carries payloads larger than any other tactical fighter but retains the air-to-air capability of the F-15C. It can operate around the clock and in any weather. Since entering operational service, the F-15 has a perfect air combat record with more than 100 victories and no losses. Three other nations fly the F-15.

F-15 Eagle

AV-8B Harrier II Plus

The newest upgraded variant of the AV-8 Harrier family, the multimission Harrier II Plus adds the APG-65 radar system to the aircraft's proven vertical/short-takeoff-and-landing capabilities. A Boeing, BAE Systems and Rolls-Royce team produces the AV-8B. The Harrier II Plus was developed through a three-nation agreement among the United States, Spain and Italy.

AV-8B Harrier II Plus

T-45 Goshawk

The T-45 Goshawk aircraft is the key component of the U.S. Navy's T-45 Training System. The system includes advanced flight simulators, a computer-assisted instructional program, a computerized training integration system, and a contractor logistics support package. U.S. Navy and Marine Corps student naval aviators train in the T-45 at Naval Air Stations Meridian, Mississippi, and Kingsville, Texas.

T-45 Goshawk

V-22 Osprey

In partnership with Bell Helicopter Textron, Boeing has developed the V-22 Osprey tiltrotor aircraft. Low-rate initial production and flight testing have begun. Initial deliveries of 360 aircraft to the U.S. Marine Corps began in 1999. The U.S. Special Operations Command has 50 CV-22s on order.

V-22 Osprey

CH-47 Chinook

Preparation is under way for a new modernization program for the U.S. Army's CH-47 Chinook. The CH-47F is scheduled to enter the fleet in 2003 with several major system improvements. Under this program, Chinooks will remain in Army service at least until 2033 and will achieve an unprecedented 71-year service life. Boeing is also manufacturing CH-47SD Chinooks for international customers.

CH-47 Chinook

RAH-66 Comanche

The Boeing-Sikorsky team is developing the RAH-66 Comanche, the U.S. Army's 21st century combat helicopter. Two prototypes are in flight test. In the year 2001, the program will validate aircraft systems and prepare for development of 13 production-representative aircraft for operational test, evaluation and training.

RAH-66 Comanche

Exhibit 1

Strategic Business Unit Products: Boeing Company (*continued*)

B. Boeing Military Aircraft and Missile Systems (continued)

AH-64D Apache Longbow

AH-64D Apache Longbow

The AH-64D Apache Longbow, an advanced version of the combat-proven AH-64A Apache, is the most lethal, survivable, deployable and maintainable multimission combat helicopter in the world. In addition to multiyear contracts from the U.S. Army for 501 Apache Longbow aircraft, Boeing is under contract to deliver advanced Apache aircraft to the Netherlands, Singapore and the United Kingdom. Egypt and Israel are finalizing agreements for new or remanufactured AH-64Ds, and several other nations are considering the Apache Longbow for their defense forces.

SLAM-ER

JDAM

CALCM

SLAM-ER, JDAM, CALCM

A world leader in all-weather precision munitions, Boeing covers a wide spectrum of attack weapon capabilities. These include the Standoff Land Attack Missile Expanded Response (SLAM-ER), the Joint Direct Attack Munition (JDAM), the Conventional Air Launched Cruise Missile (CALCM), the Air-to-Ground Missile (AGM-130), and Brimstone and Harpoon missiles. Customers include all U.S. military services and the armed forces of 27 other nations. Export sales are approved by the U.S. government.

Military Aerospace Support

Military Aerospace Support

Military Aerospace Support is developing and delivering innovative products and services to reduce life-cycle costs and increase the effectiveness of aircraft and missile systems fielded around the globe. The business has a comprehensive support portfolio that includes upgrade, modification and maintenance programs; a full range of training systems and services; support systems; domestic and international logistics support services; and sustainment data and supply chain management support competencies.

C. Boeing Space and Communications   Jim Albaugh, President / Seal Beach, California

Space Shuttle

Space Shuttle

The Space Shuttle is the world's only operational, reusable and human-rated launch vehicle. Boeing builds, maintains, modifies and, as a United Space Alliance partner, operates the Shuttle system. Boeing also builds, tests and performs flight processing for the Shuttle's main engines – the world's only reusable liquid-fueled large rocket engines. Boeing-developed upgrades could enable the Shuttle to fly to 2030 and beyond.

Delta II

Delta II

Delta II has become the industry standard for reliability, on-time delivery of payloads to orbit, and customer satisfaction since its introduction in 1989. Delta II enjoys a 97-percent success rate for more than 90 launches.

Delta III

Delta III

With the successful launch of Delta III on August 23, 2000, the performance of operational Delta vehicles has nearly doubled, with demonstrated ability to place up to 3,810-kg class commercial satellites into geo-synchronous transfer orbit.

Medium, Medium-Plus, Heavy – Delta IV

Delta IV

The Boeing Delta family of rockets continues to evolve to meet launch market needs and will offer a family of launch vehicles, beginning in 2002, for nearly every payload class from 900 kg to more than 13,000 kg to geosynchronous transfer orbit. The Delta IV will bring assured and affordable access to space while lowering the per-kilogram cost of launch to orbit by up to 50 percent.

Sea Launch

Sea Launch

Boeing is part of an international consortium, including firms from Russia, Ukraine and Norway, that conducts commercial satellite launches from a mobile sea-based platform. Sea Launch successfully launched its first commercial payload in October 1999 from the equatorial Pacific. Home port is Long Beach, California.

International Space Station

International Space Station

Boeing is prime contractor to NASA for the design, development and on-orbit performance of the International Space Station. The first components were joined in orbit in 1998. In 2000 the station began hosting humans and by 2005 will permanently house up to seven crew members. Station assembly will require more than 40 U.S. and Russian launches.

(continues)

Exhibit 1

Strategic Business Unit Products: Boeing Company (*continued*)

C. Boeing Space and Communications (continued)

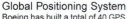

NMD Prime Contractor

Boeing is prime contractor for the National Missile Defense (NMD) program, which is designed to defend the United States from a limited ICBM attack. The multiyear, multibillion-dollar effort calls for the company to develop, test and integrate all NMD elements. The program has enjoyed several successful integrated flight demonstrations. Current plans include developing and demonstrating the system to a point at which a decision to deploy can be made within the next several years.

NMD Prime Contractor

Future Imagery Architecture

In 1999, a Boeing-led team was awarded the FIA contract from the National Reconnaissance Office (NRO) – a key element of the NRO's space-based architecture. This significant contract, which extends through 2010, confirms the leadership position of Boeing in the area of space imaging.

Future Imagery Architecture

Global Positioning System

Boeing has built a total of 40 GPS satellites. Currently, Boeing is under contract to build six follow-on Block IIF satellites with a possibility of 27 additional vehicles. Additionally, Boeing is under U.S. Air Force contract to lead the ground control segment of the GPS constellation and is competing to build the next-generation GPS Block III.

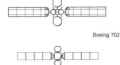

Global Positioning System

Airborne Laser

Boeing is prime contractor on the Airborne Laser program and leads a team with a $1.3-billion contract to conduct the program definition and risk reduction phase of the ABL program. This U.S. Air Force effort is intended to explore the feasibility of an airborne laser system for defense against tactical theater ballistic missiles during their boost phase. Boeing is also leading a national team on the Space-Based Laser program.

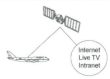

Airborne Laser

737-700 Airborne Early Warning & Control System

In 2000, a Boeing-led team was selected to develop an AEW&C system for Turkey and Australia. The program, which in Australia is known as Project Wedgetail, will utilize 737-700 aircraft to provide airborne electronic and communications systems for the Turkish and Australian defense forces. Boeing has gained significant experience on such systems through 30 years of successfully designing, developing and managing 707 AWACS and 767 AWACS systems and upgrades.

737-700 Airborne Early Warning & Control System

Boeing 376, Boeing 601, Boeing 702

With the October 2000 acquisition of Hughes Electronics' space and communications businesses, Boeing Satellite Systems is the world's largest manufacturer of commercial communications satellites. Core products include: the versatile Boeing 376 spacecraft; the Boeing 601 satellite, the world's best-selling large spacecraft; and the Boeing 702, the world's highest power satellite. Boeing Satellite Systems has launched over 190 satellites since 1963, including 12 in 2000.

Boeing 702

Boeing 376

Boeing 601

D. Other Units

| Boeing Capital Corporation | Jim Palmer, President / Renton, Washington |

An asset-based leasing and lending organization, Boeing Capital Corporation manages a portfolio of more than $6 billion in assets, an amount that could grow significantly in the next five years. For more than 30 years, it has been a worldwide provider of lease and loan financing for all types of commercial and business aircraft and a wide range of commercial equipment.

| Connexion by Boeing | Scott Carson, President / Kent, Washington |

Connexion by Boeing℠ will effectively change the way people travel by providing high-speed, two-way Internet and live television services to aircraft in flight. Through the service, two-way, broadband (or high-data-rate) connectivity is delivered directly to airline seats, providing passengers with personalized and secure access to the Internet, company intranets and live television and audio content. Connexion by Boeing will also provide airline personnel with information that will enhance operational efficiency on the ground and in the air.

Internet
Live TV
Intranet

Connexion by Boeing

| Air Traffic Management | John Hayhurst, President / Kent, Washington |

Many of the world's air traffic systems are straining today to maintain efficient, reliable and convenient service, much less support the anticipated growth. Boeing is developing an air traffic management system that will dramatically increase capacity, improve safety and remain affordable for those who use the system. It will require a fundamental change to how the system operates. The Boeing approach involves defining system requirements, applying an operational concept that supports those requirements and selecting the right technology set.

Air Traffic Management

Source: The Boeing Company, *2000 Annual Report*, pp 100–103.

ing fleet of 20 A-320s, CCQ can reduce training costs by $500,000 per additional aircraft per year. This gets pilots out of the retraining program and back on flight duty faster, increasing crew productivity up to 20%. It results in total savings of over $1,000,000 per additional aircraft per year.

The Boeing 777

In the late 1980s, Airbus Industrie had launched two new 300-seat aircraft—the twin engine A-330 and the longer range, four-engine A-340. The economies of Airbus' twin-engine, wide-body jumbo jet interested the world's airlines. Boeing considered the concept of introducing a double-deck version of Boeing's successful B-767, but discussions with airline executives caused them to shelve this idea.

Instead, in December, 1989, Boeing announced the B-777 project: a totally new twin-engine design with 310 to 395 seats (depending on multiple or single class configuration). This program would become Boeing's largest project since the highly successful B-747 program of the 1960s. The staggering development cost of the B-777 was budgeted at more than $6 billion.

Boeing put Philip Condit (later to become Boeing's Chairman and CEO) in charge of the exciting program. Condit utilized the previously proven concept of sharing the risk of the development costs with the major subcontractors and also introduced new features in the development of the B-777. Foremost was the inclusion of airline executive's inputs, which Boeing called "working together," into the features of the B-777. United Airlines, the first buyer of the new plane, had the largest role along with executives from seven of the other world's airlines.

In addition, the B-777 was Boeing's first plane designed completely by computer, without the usual full-scale mock-ups to identify interferences of either mechanical or electronic components. Further, the design would also be Boeing's first to utilize state-of-the-art fly-by-wire controls instead of mechanical linkages to move the airplane's control surfaces.

By June 1995 the B-777s were operating at the world's airlines and its acceptance was typified in a British Airways report that, "It's been the most successful new aircraft ever to enter the fleet."

Unfortunately, not every aspect of the B-777 program was hailed as successful. The implementation of the computer-design program's cost was at least 50% more than Boeing's traditional hard-copy, blueprint approach.

Although a stand-alone success, critics of the B-777 program argued that it cannibalized sales from Boeing's biggest profit generator, the B-747-400. The B-747-400's nominal seating capacity was 416; about 20% larger than the B-777. These critics argued that some amount (the exact percentage had a wide range) of B-747-400s would have been sold to these customers instead without the $6 billion development cost.

From the standpoint of strategic market mix, the B-777 allowed Boeing to catch up with Airbus' A-330, but not surpass the Airbus product line (the creators of state-of-the-art fly-by-wire controls in commercial jets). As Boeing was making deliveries of the B-777s, Airbus was talking with the world's airlines about a "super-jumbo" airliner, a step beyond any existing design.

Boeing Buys Big

In December, 1996, Philip Condit announced that Boeing would acquire McDonnell Douglas Corporation. The news shocked the world's aerospace industry, wondering why Boeing would want to buy the manufacturer of the MD-11 jumbo and the smaller MD-80 jet. Pundits thought the deal would have a difficult time obtaining approval from the U.S. Justice Department and an even more difficult process obtaining approval from the European Union's Competition Commission, who had already stalled a proposed merger between American Airlines and British Airways.

After these critics examined the deal further, they realized that McDonnell Douglas' strong position in defense market products would complement Boeing's weak position. Correspondingly, Boeing's strong position in commercial airliners would complement McDonnell Douglas' weak position.

With this conclusion, approvals followed by both U.S. Justice Department and EU Competition Commission. Harry Stonecipher, McDonnell Douglas' Chairman and CEO, became Boeing's Vice Chair and Chief Operating Officer. Many thought this also was a synergistic outcome, since Stonecipher was a hands-on operational specialist, whereas Condit gave more attention to strategic events. *Fortune*, describing the relationship in Condit's own words, "He [Stonecipher] can see a hole in an operational plan from 50 yards. I, for whatever reason, can see around corners."

The acquisition was successfully completed in 1997.

A Change in the Product Line

Following the successful launch of the B-777, it became clear that the MD-11 jumbo jet was redundant and was dropped from the enlarged Boeing product line. For some time, the future of the much smaller MD-80, now restyled as the MD-95, was unclear. The MD-95 was close in seating capacity to the B-737 (although smaller), and was therefore considered as a possible competitor to the B-737, therefore, many thought that it would follow the MD-11 to oblivion.

However, as private business jets were becoming larger and more customized, Boeing announced the B-717 during the summer of 1997, a shortened version of the MD-95. It was the only business jet offering well over 100 seats, and many observers felt a business jet with such a large seating capacity would serve only a tiny niche segment. Others concluded that the only reason Boeing made this move was out of loyalty to the major risk-sharing subcontractors who had invested to keep the MD-95 program alive.

The Summer of 1997

The successful acquisition of McDonnell Douglas was good reason to break out the champagne, and there was reason to break out a second bottle! Boeing had been booking orders at a pace that elevated their backlog to a record altitude. There were two reasons for this.

First, the airline industry was upgrading their fleets of aircraft. With the availability of the B-767 and B-777 along with the A-330 and A-340, no airline wanted to be labeled as having an "old" fleet. They all wanted to brag to the market that they fly the most modern equipment in the industry.

Second, the price was right. Boeing's President of commercial aircraft, Ron Wooddard, believed that a newly instituted production system, called DCAC/MRM would reduce costs by as much as 25%. Based upon this, Boeing began discounting prices to customers in an attempt to achieve a publicly stated goal of 67% market share. Although it looked like the right thing at the time, it would soon develop into a classic "Hurry Up and Wait" scenario.

The Hurry Up

The onslaught of orders raised Boeing's contractual backlog to record levels (see **Exhibit 1**), and by the summer of 1997 it appeared necessary to double production output. The plan for the hot-selling B-737 was to ramp up production from 10 planes per month to 24 per month by the spring of 1998. The leviathan B-747-400, currently at two planes per month, was scheduled to increase to five per month by 1998.

In an interview with the *Wall Street Journal*, Wooddard said, "There's no doubt we are intentionally driving the system right to the ragged edge [to achieve market share]. We're nervous about everything, but we're not panicked and we're not going to miss our schedules." He further forecast that the company's total output would rise from the 1996 level of 18 planes per month to 43 per month by the spring of 1998 (the previous record output was 39 per month in 1992).

The Wait

Unfortunately, this attempt ran head-on into the unsuccessful implementation of DCAC/MRM and the result was chaos. Shortages of thousands of parts developed from Boeing's 3,000 parts suppliers. By the fall of 1997, Boeing managers said that parts shortages ranged at times from 2,000 parts up to 7,000 parts. On September 15, Boeing announced it would miss deliveries for 12 of the 36 aircraft scheduled for September delivery, including 4 of its most profitable B-747-400s.

As the situation worsened, production personnel were averaging 20% overtime each week (some were working seven days per week). The company was planning to hire 400 workers from the McDonnell Douglas plant in Long Beach, California, some from rival Lockheed Martin Corporation, and even some from the airlines. The situation finally got so bad that production of the two hot sellers—the B-737 and the B-747-400—actually had to be halted for three weeks in October, 1997.

The outcome from this chaos was a third-quarter loss of $696,000,000. This news was followed by the announcement on October 22 that Boeing would sustain a "production disruption" charge of $2,600,000,000 against earnings. As a result, 1997 performance showed a loss.

These losses were only part of the picture. Boeing rescheduled two of the four B-737-700s for Southwest Airlines from late 1997 into 1998. In addition, deliveries of 21 B-737-700s would slip by at least one month. Southwest, the nation's eighth largest carrier, was the "launch" customer for Boeing's new B-737-700. This news caused Southwest Airlines, a highly successful low-cost (but high profit) airline to delay its plans to expand service to a new city by as much as three months.

With the exit of 1997, a flu bug was making an entrance—the Asian economic flu. Although it showed signs of development in 1997, it wasn't until 1998 that the effects started to translate into events at Boeing. The company felt its first hit when Philippine Airlines announced in January 1998 that it could not accept delivery of four B-747-400s, valued at about $600 million. About the same time, Thai Airlines asked for a delay in 1998 deliveries and Asiana Airlines asked that a B-777 delivery be delayed from 1998 to 1999.

The economic flu showed some additional and unusual symptoms in the Asian airline industry. Singapore Airlines, one of the world's most respected, asked Northwest Airlines to purchase some of their (then) surplus used aircraft. It was later determined that Asiana Airlines took the same approach. The impact on Boeing was nearly overwhelming. Just as Boeing was ramping up for a huge production expansion, airlines in Asia wanted substantial delays. At the start of 1998, 30% of Boeing's backlog was for planes bound for Asia. Industry analysts estimated that 70 to 80 aircraft scheduled for 1998 shipment could be delayed or even cancelled.

On January 23, 1998, Boeing was forced to announce that their plan to raise production (developed just two months earlier) to 47 planes per month was now being scaled back to about 43 per month. The difference between 47 and 43 per month would amount to about $1.5 billion in lost revenue for 1998.

Like an unwelcome nightmare, delays and cancellations increased just as Boeing was trying to increase production. By March, 1998, Boeing announced a downsizing of 8,200 jobs due to the closing of former McDonnell Douglas defense plants. This was in addition to 12,000 cuts announced the prior December.

Adding to problems was a ruling from Europe's Joint Aviation Authority. Because of the larger seating capacity of the B-737-700, the Authority had ruled the Boeing must redesign the plane's over-the-wing emergency exits. By the time Boeing came up with the necessary changes, two dozen B-737-700s had already been produced; it would be necessary to retrofit these planes. An additional 35 planes being built would need to be put on hold until the necessary parts were available. Boeing eked out a profit in the first quarter of 1998, but that was all. More important, because of price discounting, product margins had dropped from 11% to 4.8%.

In 1999, the cancellations and delays continued and caused a major reduction in Boeing's contractual backlog of orders. From the end of 1998 to the end of 1999, the contractual backlog shrank by $13,688,000,000 even though shipments had increased during the period by only $1,839,000,000, roughly a quarter of a year's production (see **Exhibit 2**).

The Bad News Continues

In March, 1999, the National Transportation Safety Board started considering a demand that Boeing implement extensive and expensive modifications to its B-737, the world's most popular jet aircraft. This issue stemmed from the 1994 crash of a U.S. Airways jet in which problems with the rudder controls were the prime suspect. A United Airlines B-737 crash in Colorado added to these concerns.

As Boeing developed successive generations of the B-737, they were allowed to "grandfather-in" most of the basic design concepts of the original version. The rudder control mechanism was one of those design concepts that was grandfathered. What was suspect was known as "rudder reversal": a phenomenon when the pilot pushed on the right rudder pedal the rudder would shift, not to the right (as expected) but to the left. As a result, the plane responded just the opposite of what was expected, so the pilot tended to push harder on the right rudder pedal, causing the rudder to shift further to the left. This could cause the pilot to lose control of the plane (and this was suspected to be the cause of at least one crash). Although the NTSB had not yet made any final directive, the preliminary conclusion did not bode well for Boeing.

In September 2000, Boeing agreed to replace the rudder control systems on all 4,000 of its B-737 aircraft. After years of opposing such a retrofit, Boeing agreed to spend an estimated $200 million to design and install a redundant, dual-valve rudder control system to replace the single hydraulic valve system originally supplied. Boeing refused to supply an additional feature of a rudder position indicator (requested by pilots), which would show the position of the rudder on the cockpit's panel.

Exhibit 2

Financial Highlights: Boeing Company
(Dollar amounts in millions, except per share data)

	2000	1999	1998	1997	1996	1995
Sales & other operating revenues	$51,321	$57,993	$56,154	$45,800	$35,453	$32,960
Net earnings (loss)	2,128	2,309	1,120	(178)	1,818	(36)
Earnings per share: diluted	2.44	2.49	1.15	(.18)	1.85	(.04)
Contractual backlog	120,600	99,248	112,896	121,640	114,173	95,448
Research & development	1,441	1,341	1,895	1,924	1,633	1,674
Capital expenditures	932	1,236	1,665	1,391	971	747
Cash & short-term investments	1,010	3,454	2,462	5,149	6,352	4,527
Customer financing assets	6,959	6,004	5,711	4,600	3,888	4,212
Total debt	8,799	6,732	6,972	6,854	7,489	5,401
Cash dividends	504	537	564	557	480	537

Source: The Boeing Company.

Strike 1

As if this were not enough, in February 2000, Boeing's white-collared engineers union, which had affiliated with the AFL-CIO, launched the first major strike in its 56-year history. The union held out for more than a month and caused the shipping delay of at least 50 aircraft. The union leader told *Fortune*, "We weren't fighting against Boeing, we were fighting to save Boeing." All this concern stemmed from the Boeing Company's culture as an engineering driven company. With no new designs slated for production, engineers were becoming redundant, and Harry Stonecipher was determined to cut costs to enhance profitability. The engineers decided to formalize their protest.

It was clear that the culture at Boeing was changing. Wall Street thought it was for the better. The engineers thought otherwise.

Strike 2

In October 2000, the Federal Aviation Administration announced the results of "special [quality] audit," held early that year of seven of Boeing's aircraft engineering and manufacturing facilities. It found "deep-rooted" and "systemic" problems in the company's design and manufacturing systems.

The FAA conducted the audit after what it called a "series of high-visibility production breakdowns" during the fall of 1999. It included everything from aircraft engineering to the manufacturing process at Boeing plants in Seattle, Everett, Renton, Auburn, Fredrickson and Spokane, Washington, and in Portland, Oregon.

Some of the specific incidents included:

- An airline told Boeing that 2 of 16 bolts holding the vertical stabilizer onto the tail of a B-767 were not sufficiently tightened.

- Assembly line mechanics at Boeing's Everett plant (where B-747s, B-767s and B-777s are built) reported that fuel tank repairs were being made after the tanks had been inspected and that debris, such as sealant tubes and rivet guns, was occasionally left behind.

- An adhesive was applied improperly to a condensation barrier that keeps moisture from dripping onto cockpit electronics.

These, and other specifics, led the FAA to conclude that:

- Some production processes were "incomplete or overly complex."
- Work instructions were "inadequate."
- Inspections, to ensure products conformed with design, were "inadequate."
- Some rank-and-file workers were "not knowledgeable" of approved processes and procedures.

At a news conference, John Hickey of the FAA stated that, "The findings show that these were not isolated events. What we found were very deep-rooted systemic problems that, if uncorrected, could result in noncompliance [with federal regulations]."

Liz Otis, Boeing's Commercial Airplanes Groups Vice President for Quality, agreed with the audit findings. As a result, Boeing agreed to add at least 370 new positions to its own inspection system while the company and the FAA are jointly evaluating whether increased maintenance efforts are required for certain production operations.

Officials of both Boeing and the government said they expected that millions of dollars of fines and penalties might be assessed against Boeing.

Airbus Catches Up

Early in January 1998, Airbus Industrie decided to brag a little bit, announcing that they had booked 671 aircraft orders and commitments in 1997, valued at $44.2 billion. This included a record 460 firm orders valued at $29.6 billion (see **Exhibit 3**). Although Boeing was ready to announce firm orders for 524 aircraft, Airbus still saw this high level of bookings as the airline industry's endorsement of their products. Managing Director Jean Pierson said they were, "Now well on course to achieving our objective of a consistent 50% market share early in the next century."

There were inconsistencies in these calculations, as evidenced by the claims for 1996 market share: Airbus claimed 42% while Boeing was claiming 64% share. Notwithstanding this difference, it was now clear that Airbus Industrie had arrived as Boeing's equal in the aircraft manufacturing industry (see **Exhibit 3**).

Results

During the past five years, revenues continued to increase, but organizational difficulties caused erratic profitability and the engineers strike would limit earnings in 2000 (see **Exhibit 2**). Other trends, such as shrinking research and development expenditures demonstrated Boeing's capability to manage for improved profitability.

In addition, Boeing had the capability to support their customer's financing needs and continued to show increases in this asset on its balance sheet.

The Airbus Industrie Organization

As late as the summer of 1999, the various Airbus partners declared that, ". . . too many obstacles stand in the way of quick moves toward that goal [of incorporation]." There were reports of a major spate in 1999, when one partner planned to acquire a business which would impinge on another partner, and when the actions of one firm's government acted to the detriment of another's government. In particular, the French Government refused to relinquish its ownership stake.

This stalemate was unfortunate, since all the partners (as well as all the analysts of the industry) saw incorporation as a more effective structure to compete with Boeing. Other

Exhibit 3

Boeing vs. Airbus: Aircraft Orders
(9 months—2000)

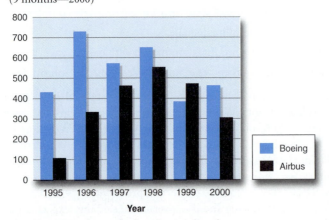

Note: Year 2000 orders are for first nine months only.

Source: USA Today, October 19, 2000.

expected advantages were the streamlining of redundant costs. It was at this point, in the late spring of 2000, that Jurgen Schrempp, the CEO of DaimlerChrysler who had engineered the major acquisition of Chrysler by Daimler A.G., stepped into the fray. In a matter of weeks Schrempp had brought the four business partners to agreement. Then he achieved the master stroke by obtaining agreement from the governments of these four that only the French Government be allowed to retain a small stake in the new corporation.

With that agreement, on July 10, 2000, European Aeronautic Defence & Space Company—EADS for short—became a reality. As a defense contractor, EADS was repositioned to become a huge rival to Boeing and Lockheed Martin Corporation. In addition, it became a more efficient and effective competitor to Boeing's Commercial Airplanes Group.

Airbus Industrie had previously matured as a technological manufacturing consortium. Now it had matured as an organization as well, and as such was ready to break new ground.

2 Weeks Later

With the aeronautical equivalent of the "shot heard 'round the world," EADS announced it was accepting orders for the new A3XX Super Jumbo Aircraft. EADS expected such a plane to seat about 650 passengers, although a 100% coach-class configuration would well exceed 700 passengers. It would be able to carry these passengers nonstop on such popular routes as Singapore to London and Tokyo to London. Finally, the A3XX would accomplish this at a (per passenger) cost 20% less than Boeing's B-747-400.

However, this concept was not without controversy. Much of the controversy concerned the ultimate market for such an aircraft. EADS, after extensive discussions with the world's leading airlines, determined the market would be at least 1,500 aircraft. Boeing, having equally extensive discussions with many of the same airlines, concluded the market would be less than 350 aircraft. An independent analyst, Richard Aboulafia of the Teal Group, said the market would more likely be about 927 aircraft by 2019.

Furthermore, there is widespread disagreement as to the A3XX's design cost. EADS says its development will cost $10.7 billion through 2006. Independent analysts peg the cost as high as $16 billion. Many agree that even with development costs at $10.7 billion and a selling price of $225 million per aircraft, EADS would need to sell 528 planes by 2019 to break even. Sales at the Teal Group's estimate of 927 would certainly make it profitable. Sales of 1,500 would make it a bonanza (see **Exhibit 4**). Sales of 350 would make it a disaster.

Exhibit 4

A3XX Estimated Profits

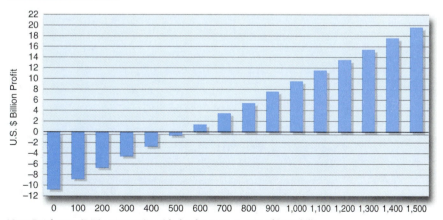

Note: Break even (B/E) at 528 units with development at costs of $10.7 billion.

To design and start construction of the A3XX, EADS would need to borrow heavily, thereby mortgaging the company against the success of the A3XX. If Boeing's market analysis was correct, EADS would probably become bankrupt. On the other hand, there was the possibility for EADS to reap a fortune in profits as well as becoming the world's premier jumbo jet manufacturer. From EADS perspective, it was a super jumbo win/lose.

On the Other Hand

Boeing's perspective was quite different. If EADS market estimates held true, it would certainly represent a major loss to Boeing. Each A3XX would represent at least one B-747-400 lost sale by Boeing. If Boeing's market assessment was correct, they would lose the sale of 350 B-747-400s, but then, following EADS bankruptcy, would again be the premier jet airliner manufacturer. They might even be in a position to acquire EADS (perhaps at a bargain) and thus have their cake and eat it too.

There was another possible outcome that Boeing had been studying for some time—the production of an enhanced B-747X. Such a plane would increase Boeing's seating to 522 and represent a compromise between the B-747-400 and the A3XX. The cost to develop a B-747X might be "only" $4 billion. This would lower the number required to reach breakeven as well as lower the plane's selling price to around $200 million each (see **Exhibit 5**).

Some analysts declared that Boeing had no choice but to jump in with the B-747X and compete as well as it could against the A3XX. Others claim that if Boeing's market estimate is correct, doing nothing is the correct choice. These pundits feared that EADS might achieve, more or less, sales around the A3XX breakeven. This would keep EADS in the industry as a competitor, but would probably limit sales of the B-747X to no more than its break-even point, perhaps less.

Strike 3?

In September 2000, prestigious Singapore Airlines ordered 10 A3XXs with options for an additional 15 aircraft. The list price for the A3XX might run as high as $230 million each. Although the price for this order was not announced, people close to such transactions have said that large discounts are applied for initial "launch" customers. Conventional wis-

Exhibit 5

B-747X Estimated Profit: Boeing Corporation

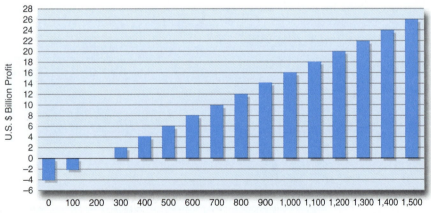

Note: Developmental cost of $4 billion.

dom estimated that the Singapore Airlines order might have been in the neighborhood of $160 million each: less than the price for Boeing's latest 416-seat current-generation B-747-400.

In November 2000, Singapore Airline's arch-rival, Qantas Airways Ltd., of Australia, announced the purchase of 18 A3XXs, valued at $3.5 billion. Although quick math calculates a unit price of $194 million each, it was not announced what, if any, spare parts, ground support equipment, or other extras were part of the Qantas order. Conventional wisdom held to the possibility of "launch" prices around $160 million.

Decision 2001

Along with the Qantas, Air France, and other orders, EADS had firm orders for 50 A3XX aircraft and had achieved the "critical mass" for a go/no-go decision. On December 19, 2000, the EADS Board of Directors formally approved the plans to develop the new super-jumbo, which was designated the A380. Specifications provided seating from 481 to 656 passengers along with a cargo version with a 150 metric ton payload. EADS announced that the A380 would take to the skies in 2006.

Notwithstanding that the stakes were extremely high and the outcome uncertain, Boeing must decide what to do about the development of a B-747X.

Financial Information

Exhibit 6 shows the consolidated statement of operations. **Exhibit 7** shows the consolidated balance sheet. Cash flows are shown in **Exhibit 8**.

Exhibit 6

Consolidated Statements of Operations: Boeing Company
(Dollar amounts in millions, except per share data)

Year Ending December 31	2000	1999	1998	1997
Sales and other operating revenues	$51,321	$57,993	$56,154	$45,800
Cost of products and services	43,712	51,320	50,492	42,001
	7,609	6,673	5,662	3,799
Equity in income (loss) from joint ventures	64	4	(67)	(43)
General and administrative expense	2,335	2,044	1,993	2,187
Research and development expense	1,998	1,341	1,895	1,924
Gain on dispositions	34	87	13	—
Net				
Share-based plans expense	316	209	153	(99)
Operating earnings (loss)	3,058	3,170	1,567	(256)
Other income (principally interest)	386	585	283	428
Interest and debt expense	(445)	(431)	(453)	(513)
Earning (loss) before income taxes	2,999	3,324	1,397	(341)
Income taxes (benefit)	871	1,015	277	(163)
Net earnings (loss)	$ 2,128	$ 2,309	$ 1,120	$ (178)
Basic earnings (loss) per share	2.48	2.52	1.16	(.18)
Diluted earnings (loss) per share	2.44	2.49	1.15	(.18)
Cash dividends per share	.59	.56	.56	.56

Exhibit 7

Consolidated Balance Sheet: Boeing Company
(Dollar amounts in millions, except per share data)

Year Ending December 31	2000	1999	1998
Assets			
Cash and cash equivalents	$ 1,010	$ 3,354	$ 2,183
Short-term investments	—	100	279
Accounts receivable	4,928	3,453	3,288
Current portion of customer and commercial financing	995	799	781
Deferred income taxes	2,137	1,467	1,495
Inventories, net of advances and progress billings	6,794	6,539	8,584
Total current assets	15,864	15,712	16,610
Customer and commercial financing	5,964	5,205	4,930
Property, plant and equipment, net	8,814	8,245	8,589
Deferred income taxes	60	—	411
Goodwill	5,214	2,233	2,312
Prepaid pension expense	4,845	3,845	3,513
Other assets	1,267	907	659
Total assets	42,028	36,147	37,024
Liabilities and shareholders' equity			
Accounts payable and other liabilities	11,979	11,269	11,085
Advances in excess of related costs	3,517	1,215	1,251
Income taxes payable	1,561	420	569
Short-term debt and current portion of long-term debt	1,232	752	869
Total current liabilities	18,189	13,656	13,774
Deferred income taxes	—	172	—
Accrued retiree health care	5,152	4,877	4,831
Long-term debt	7,567	5,980	6,103
Shareholders' equity			
Common shares, par value $5.00			
1,200,000,000 shares authorized	5,059	5,059	5,059
Additional paid-in capital	2,693	1,684	1,147
Treasury shares at cost	(6,221)	(4,161)	(1,321)
Retained earnings	12,090	10,487	8,706
Accumulated other comprehensive income	(2)	6	(23)
Unearned compensation	(7)	(12)	(17)
ShareValue			
Trust shares	(2,592)	(1,601)	(1,235)
Total shareholders' equity	11,020	11,462	—
Total shareholders' equity and liabilities	$42,018	$36,147	$37,024

Source: The Boeing Company.

Exhibit 8

Consolidated Statements of Cash Flows: Boeing Company
(Dollar amounts in millions)

Year Ending December 31	2000	1999	1998	1997
Cash flows—operating activities				
Net earnings (loss)	$2,128	$2,309	$1,120	$(178)
Adjustments to reconcile net earnings (loss)				
Share-based plans	316	209	153	(99)
Depreciation	1,317	1,538	1,517	1,354
Amortization of goodwill	162	107	105	104
In process R&D	557	—	—	—
Customer & commercial financing provision	13	72	61	64
Gain on dispositions, net	(34)	(87)	(13)	—
Changes in assets and liabilities				
Short-term investments	100	179	450	154
Accounts receivable	(768)	(225)	(167)	(240)
Inventories, net of progress billings	1,097	2,030	652	(96)
Accounts payable and other liabilities	(311)	217	(840)	1,908
Advances in excess of related costs	1,387	(36)	(324)	(139)
Income taxes payable and deferred	421	462	145	(451)
Other items	(712)	(579)	(479)	(272)
Accrued retiree health care	269	46	35	(4)
Net cash provided by operating activities	5,942	6,224	2,415	2,105
Cash flows—investing activities				
Customer & commercial financing (additions)	(2,571)	(2,398)	(2,603)	(1,889)
Customer & commercial financing (reductions)	1,433	1,842	1,357	1,025
Property, plant and equipment, net adds	(932)	(1,236)	(1,665)	(1,391)
Acquisitions, net of cash acquired	(5,727)	—	—	—
Proceeds from dispositions	169	359	37	—
Net cash used by investing	(7,628)	(1,433)	(2,874)	(2,255)
Cash flows—financing activities				
New borrowings	2,687	437	811	232
Debt repayments	(620)	(676)	(693)	(867)
Common shares purchased	(2,357)	(2,937)	(1,397)	(141)
Common shares issued				268
Stock options exercised	136	93	65	166
Dividends paid	(504)	(537)	(564)	(557)
Net cash used by financing activities	(658)	(3,620)	(1,778)	(899)
Net increase (decrease) in cash and equivalents	(2,344)	1,171	(2,237)	(1,049)
Cash & cash equivalents at beginning of year	3,354	2,183	4,420	5,469
Cash & cash equivalents at end of year	$1,010	$3,354	$2,183	$4,420

Source: The Boeing Company.

case 33

Mercedes-Benz and Swatch: Inventing the 'smart' and the Networked Organization

Eric Pfaffmann and Ben M. Bensaou

I n April 1998, just a few months before the start of volume production of the new 'smart,' Mr. Meyer came out of a difficult meeting with Mr. Hoffmann, his counterpart at one of the key partners in the Micro Compact Car (MCC) venture. He was pacing up and down in his office overlooking a row of 'smart' prototypes brought in for testing to Renningen, Germany. In light of the evolution of his relationship with Mr. Hoffmann, he started to wonder whether cooperation with system partners in general were really working. 'Would systems partners be able to deliver in the end? What should we do if one system partner happened to fail us at the last minute?' What are the implications for the whole concept of a modular car and networked organization that Mercedes-Benz created jointly with the Swatch company?

Micro Compact Car: The Joint Venture

The whole adventure of the company MCC started in 1994. It was in April that Helmut Werner, then CEO of the Mercedes-Benz, and Nicolas Hayek, the CEO of SMH (Société Suisse de Microélectronique et d'Horlogerie SA), the company that made the world famous "Swatch" line of products, agreed on a rather unconventional joint venture in the automobile industry. Mercedes-Benz initially held 51% of the capital and SMH the remaining 49%. In the summer of 1997, the German partner increased its stake by SFr 75 million, now holding up to 81% of the joint venture's capital. The headquarters of MCC were located in Biel, Switzerland, the development premises in Renningen, Germany, and the production plant in Hambach, France. The marketing, sales, finance and control functions were centralized in Biel. MCC Renningen started developing the car in March 1994, the site for the plant was selected in early 1995 and inaugurated in October 1997. Volume production was scheduled for July 1998.

Mercedes-Benz owned 38.5% of MCC France, SMH 36.5%, and the French association SOFIREM (Société Financière pour Favoriser l'Industrialisation des Régions Minières) owned the remaining 25%. While MCC France invested up to FF 1.5 billion for the buildings and factory infrastructure, it was the suppliers who invested up to FF 1.3 billion for machines and tools (see **Exhibit 1**). The plant also received FF 450 million in subsidies from the European

This case was written by Eric Pfaffmann, Visiting Research Fellow at INSEAD, Doctoral Candidate at Hohenheim University, Stuttgart, Germany, under the supervision of Professor Ben M. Bensaou, Associate Professor at INSEAD. It is intended to be used as a basis for class discussion rather than to illustrate either effective or ineffective handling of an administrative situation. All names except those of senior corporate officers have been disguised. Detail financial data are not disclosed by MCC. This case may not be reproduced in any form without written permission of the two copyright holders. This case was edited for SMBP-9th Edition. Copyright © 1998 by INSEAD, Fountainebleau, France. Reprinted by permission.

Exhibit 1
Financial Structure of MCC

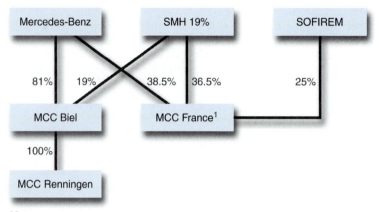

Note:
1. MCC France reports to MCC Biel.

Union as a recognition for (1) its environment-friendly production system, (2) creating a new market segment, and (3) inventiveness of the concept.

'smart' was the name chosen for the new car, where *S* stands for Swatch, *M* for Mercedes, and *ART* to highlight the inventiveness of the total concept. Micro Compact Car was the name chosen for the company to evoke the revolutionary notion of a small city car. The joint venture was given extremely limited resources to carry out this experimental, yet rather ambitious, project. Under stiff financial and human capital constraints, MCC was forced from the very beginning to concentrate on the essential. "Reduce to the max" was the claim the company used to explain MCC's outsourcing strategy. What he meant was to create a new organizational form, where MCC would sit in the center and coordinate a group of key suppliers who would effectively provide more than 85% of the value-added of the 'smart.'

Mercedes-Benz

Until 1997, Mercedes-Benz AG was a wholly owned company of the Daimler-Benz group. It was the automotive division covering all vehicle segments. Following a major restructuring of the group, Mercedes-Benz as a company was dismantled. The passenger car division and the commercial vehicle division reported directly to the board of Daimler-Benz group, now comprising five divisions: Passenger Cars, Commercial Vehicles, Aerospace, Services, and Directly Managed Business (Rail Systems, Microelectronics, MTU/Diesel Engines). Daimler-Benz remained Germany's largest industrial company, and its vehicle divisions represent the largest divisions in terms of employees, revenues, and even profits.

Daimler-Benz was created in 1926 by two German automobile pioneers, Gottlieb Daimler and Karl Benz, who decided to merge their companies after World War I. Highly prosperous in the 1930s, Daimler-Benz established a strong reputation for high quality and superior engineering products. It was at the beginning of the 1960s that the company developed its image for engineering and manufacturing high quality, prestigious, and safe cars for the premium segment. This has been a key asset of the company ever since.

It was under Helmut Werner's leadership that Mercedes-Benz heavily invested in developing new passenger car models, shortening development time and significantly cutting costs. As an indication, in 1997 the company managed to launch three major new models: the M-Class launched first in the U.S. market, the A-Class, and the CLK. The A-Class represented for

Mercedes-Benz its first attempt to diversify away from the high end market and enter the mass market segment. These efforts in streamlining operations and strengthening innovation seemed to have paid off. In 1997, the passenger car division boasted DM 53.9 billion in revenues (up from DM 46.7 billion in 1996) and 715,000 cars in sales (up from 645,000). The car division grew by 15% when average market growth was barely 5%. The German market remained by far the most important one for Daimler-Benz taking up to 39% of total sales with 277,000 units a year, against 122,000 units for the U.S. market and 477,000 units for the whole of Europe (see **Exhibit 2**).

SMH

The SMH group was founded in 1983 as a merger between Switzerland's two largest companies, ASU AG (Allgemeine Schweizer Uhrenindustrie) and the SSIH (Société Suisse pour l'Industrie Horlogère). The Swiss watch industry went through a severe crisis with the entry of Japanese watchmakers and their technological innovations in quartz technology and LCD screens. Within a few years, a company like Seiko became the largest watch producers in the world. SMH response to the Japanese challenge was a technological and marketing innovation known as the Swatch. This was a tremendous success. In addition to the Swatch, SMH carries other brand names, such as Omega, Longines, and Tissot. Development and production were mainly done by ETA SA Fabriques d'Ebauche, a company established at the end of the 19th century, the technological backbone of the group's watch division (see **Exhibit 3**).

Nicholas G. Hayek was the craftsman of the company's turnaround. He was the mastermind behind the new lifestyle concept behind the Swatch. SMH was now respected as a provocative and innovative company. Check the Web page for Swatch <www.swatch.com> and you will be welcomed by the Swatch slogan: "Provocation, Innovation, Fun. Forever." In 1996, SMH sold nearly 102.5 million watches (all brand names included). It achieved CHF 2,789 million in revenues with a headcount of 16,459 employees. It has become the world's largest watchmaker.

Nicholas Hayek started to look for ways to further leverage the marketing success of the Swatch concept and the unique competence his company had in marketing and distribution. In this diversification effort, he created an automobile division. He wanted to leverage SMH's proven expertise in designing and building microelectronic propulsion systems and apply it to the automobile sector. Hayek also felt they could make a contribution toward developing environmentally friendly propulsion systems with low fuel consumption. Aware that SMH lacked the automobile expertise, he had approached a few of the key automobile

Exhibit 2
Revenues of the Daimler-Benz Passenger Cars Division by Regions

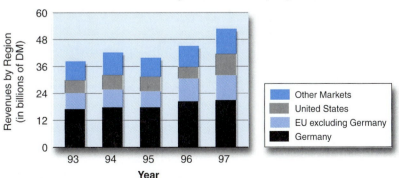

Source: Daimler-Benz Web page.

Exhibit 3
The SMH Group

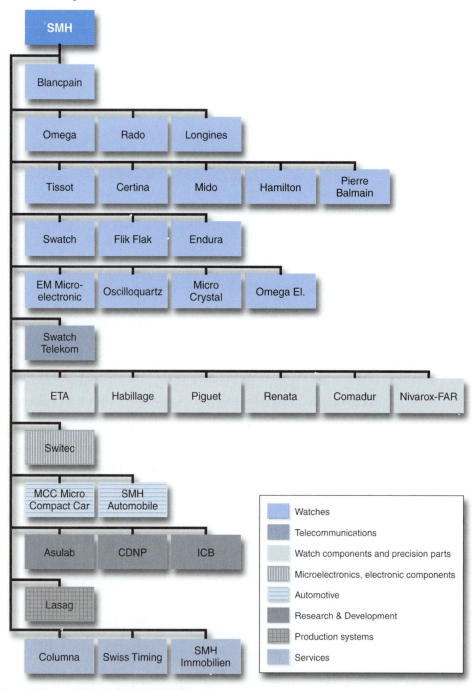

Source: Web page ETA SA Fabriques d'Ebauches.

competitors. Renault and Volkswagen declined the offer to join efforts, but Johann Tomforde, an early advocate of the city car concept within Mercedes-Benz was the one with a very receptive ear. The joint venture was signed in 1994, and SMH was expected to contribute its marketing savoir-faire to attract the younger consumer segments and to develop innovative sales concepts.

The Background of the 'smart' Concept

Two major developments triggered the search for a new car concept. First, in Germany, consumers had, since the early 1980s, become increasingly sensitive to the societal costs of individual transportation, e.g., air pollution, and energy and materials consumption. Second, individual car use was on the increase and the total number of registered cars, as well as the average number of kilometers per capita, had risen to alarming levels. In particular, the highly concentrated car park in urban areas was held responsible for negative effects on the quality of life, e.g., daily traffic jams, air pollution, living space taken by highways, shortage of parking space, and of course noise levels. There definitely was a potential market for a car that could alleviate these problems in congested urban areas. Under the strong pressure from consumer and environmentalist lobbies, governments were considering measures to restrict car pollution, control emissions, and increase taxation on fuel.

In 1990, Johann Tomforde, then heading the Mercedes-Benz strategic design and car concept department in Sindelfingen, Germany, had been working on a new concept to address these growing consumer concerns. The objective was to create a car with the following features: small size, yet maintaining a high level of passenger comfort and safety; low fuel consumption, using nontoxic, easy-to-recycle materials; and environmentally friendly production process (**Exhibit 4**). However, further market research pointed out that consumers were not ready to acquire such a city car unless it offered additional qualitative and emotional utility. Tomforde repeatedly insisted:

> *The reduction of fuel consumption and emissions does not guarantee success. For potential customers, a qualitative leap must be visible, an increased utility.*[1]

He pushed for a stronger marketing statement for the car, in particular an original external appearance to attract attention, a "navigation system" and customized design. The car needed to provide the customer enhanced total driving experience in order to earn acceptance of this new technology and concept of a city car. To deliver a distinct qualitative advantage, Tomforde pushed his engineers to focus on three concepts: the "pleasure to drive," the "mobility concept," and the concept of a customized design.

The 'smart'

What kind of car would people buy and how could you make money out of a venture like this? These were key questions for MCC. The 'smart' resulted in a significant departure from the usual product offerings from Mercedes-Benz, traditionally focused on luxury cars. The car was supposed to create its own new market in the city car segment niche. It was revolutionary in its technological innovations and the way it was designed and produced. Only 2.50 meters in length, 1.51 meters in width, but 1.53 meters high, the car was definitely designed to attract attention. The car had only two seats and customers could choose between two engines. To be on the market by October 1998, with a price tag ranging from DM 16,000 to DM 20,000, the 'smart' would be first distributed in Austria, Belgium, France, Germany, Italy, Luxembourg, the Netherlands, Spain, and Switzerland. Projected sales amounted to 130,000 units for 1999 and nearly 200,000 per year starting in 2000.

Exhibit 4
Innovations of the 'smart'

Fields of innovation	Major implementations
(1) Energy consumption	Reduced fuel consumption to below 5 liters per 100 km and reduced weight to 720 kg is achieved by innovations in the drive module; application of advanced lightweight materials; integration of functions inside technical components (e.g., the car engine).
(2) Passenger safety	Passenger safety is addressed by the interaction of the: *Tridion-frame:* Steel-faced body of the car, around which the entire vehicle is built; *Power unit:* The engine and gearbox are designed as an integrated power unit that is decoupled from the passenger compartment; *Sandwich construction:* The engine lies at the rear and underneath the passenger compartment. In event of an accident this power unit absorbs the likely return shocks to which particularly small cars are prone; *Crash box:* Security boxes that are installed in the front and in the back of the car and are able to fully absorb crashes at speeds of up to 15 km/h; *Traction and stability system (TRUST):* Electronic power management that acts on the engine and gearbox control units to keep the speed transferred to the driven wheels under surveillance and diffuse critical situations.
(3) Passenger comfort	Tridion-frame and sandwich construction maximize the available space and visibility for two passengers. Seats and control panels are designed according to ergonomic principles.
(4) Customized design	Modular car design allows a variety of parts that vary in color and/or material, Parts can be easily replaced. In particular Exterior "Customized Body Panel System" (CBS) consists of plastic bodywork components that cover the Tridion-frame. CBS parts can be replaced within two hours; Elements of the car interior such as trim panels, fittings and upholstered parts including seat upholstery.
(5) Environmental compatibility	Low emissions due to its low fuel consumption; Car parts can be recycled to a degree of 95%; Nontoxic and regenerating materials are used; Environmental friendly production methods are applied such as the powder coating of the Tridion-frame.
(6) Mobility-related services	Delivery of individualized mobility packages that go beyond the actual vehicle. Major components are the "Mobility Box" of the vehicle that offers help functions, traffic information, or assistance in finding the best way to the destination as well as a mobile phone; Decoupling of car usage and car ownership: The 'smart' is meant to be a city car for short distances. MCC therefore plans to provide 'smart' cars at airports and train stations in major European cities, as well as larger Mercedes-Benz vehicles for holiday trips.

The 'smart' would not have been a viable product in the market without some major technological innovations (see **Exhibit 4**) such as its use of new advanced light weight materials in the engine (only 59 kg, a third of the weight of comparable engines) and the body panels to improve on fuel consumption (the whole car weighs 720 kg compared to 815 kg for the Renault Twingo). In addition, the number of components in the engine turbocharger were brought down to eight instead of the normal 18.

The 'smart' was a tiny passenger car and safety was an even more important factor. MCC wanted it to be superior to other cars of this size. Its engineers were able to use Tridion-frame technology invented by Mercedes-Benz—a steel-faced body for the car, around which the entire vehicle was designed. They also came up with the "sandwich" design where the engine is located in the rear underneath the passenger compartment. The engine and the gearbox were designed as an integrated power unit decoupled from the passenger compartment. In the event of an accident the power unit would absorb the likely return shocks to which small cars are particularly prone. Crash boxes were installed in the front and in the back of the car and were able to fully absorb crashes at speeds of up to 15 kilometers per hour.

Another key feature of the 'smart,' likely to make it a market success, was its customized design and its "mobility box" concept. Tomforde used to complain that car design has traditionally been an engineers' monologue where the only time the customer could express himself or herself was at the time of purchase. He preferred to have a dialogue and wanted to bring back the customer into the conversation. He aggressively pushed for shorter development time to allow for faster customer feedback and championed a "modular" design that would allow complete customization. Miss Dessain, for instance, would walk into a 'smart' dealership or visit the smart homepage and custom design her own vehicle. She could independently choose from four colors from the body panels, two colors from the Tridion frame, or select one of the special colors and many other options. In addition, she could at any time after her purchase change any of these features very quickly (e.g., body panel changes take only two hours) and at low cost. The "mobility box" offers individualized "mobility" packages to include car navigation services, such as help functions, traffic information and assistance, and a mobile phone.

The Networked Organization

MCC was under very tough constraints to develop and make the 'smart.' Mercedes-Benz took almost six years to develop the new A-Class. There was no way MCC could afford this luxury, since volume production was already scheduled to start four years down the road. The low target price necessary for the 'smart' to make it in the marketplace was also a fundamental challenge for the organization. Notwithstanding the fact that MCC had a limited set of financial resources provided by its two parent companies. The task clearly required a novel approach to product development and production, and an organizational innovation was necessary to follow suit on the innovation in the product concept. This meant developing two things: (1) a "modular" car design and (2) a corresponding networked organization where MCC would act as a central coordinator of a network of system partners.

THE MODULAR ARCHITECTURE OF THE SMART

The architecture of a car's design can be defined as a set of the modules and systems. A module would refer to a spatial area of the car, e.g., the cockpit, the doors, the seats, or the drivetrain. Modules are then determined in a way to facilitate the assembly process and minimize assembly and logistics costs and time. MCC defined large modules of the 'smart' that could be outsourced to system partners for development and production. The target of MCC was to optimize logistics and minimize final assembly time to a world-best of 4.5 hours.

Within the spatial modules you would find systems, e.g., the air management system, the brake system, or the wiper system. They are determined by the function they have to fulfill and the components that execute this function. As such, systems are defined by the development process. Conflicts are bound to occur between the needs of the development process and the requirements of the assembly process each time some physical component, executing a given function, is shared by multiple spatial modules. Finally, modules and systems are made of parts and components. Parts are typically technologically simple, generic, with a standardized interface and execute a standardized function, e.g., screws or oil seal rings. Components are made of parts and usually would have a distinct, stand-alone functionality.

THE MODULAR ORGANIZATIONAL DESIGN

An important consequence of the modular architecture of the 'smart' was the possibility of designing an organization where boundaries would set exactly around the technical modules. At the outset, there were five organizational modules: (1) the bodywork and fittings, (2) the cockpit and front-end module, (3) the chassis, (4) the drive module, and (5) the doors, flaps and roof (see **Exhibit 5**). **Exhibit 6** in addition illustrates the parallelism between the technical architecture of the 'smart' chassis and the organizational structure highlighting the interfaces between MCC and its partner suppliers.

The modular organizational design could not, however, eliminate the impact of some inconsistencies in the product architecture. For instance, to heat the interior of a car, the engine blows warm air into the passenger compartment at different temperatures depending on its own heat level. This warm airflow is also affected by other factors, e.g., the speed of the vehicle or the local weather conditions. In other words, the heating system is a cross-modular function. This implies the need for some incremental and interactive redesigns, which affect function design and module boundaries during the development process. The design of the organizational model was based on the premise of perfect modularity, whereby each system neatly fitted into its allotted module and no system cut across technical module boundaries. In

Exhibit 5
Organizational Modules of the 'smart'

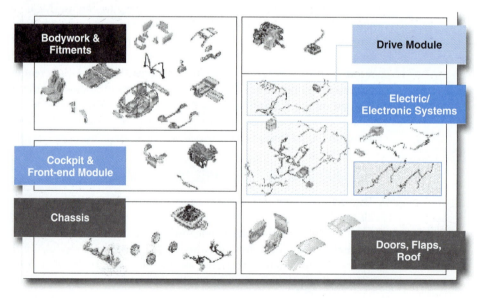

Exhibit 6
Illustration of the Isomorphic Interfirm Modular Organization for the Chassis Development and Production

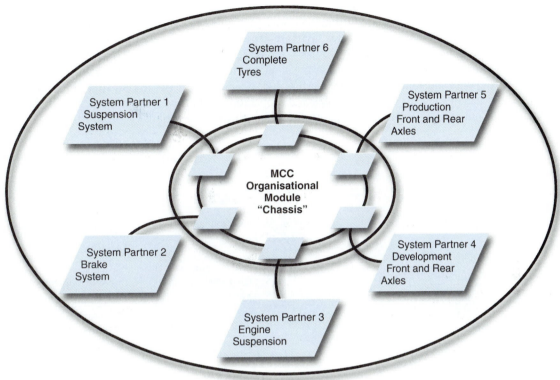

fact, perfect modularity is quasi-impossible for a car, since systems such as air-management, acoustics, or wire harnessing are inevitably cross-modular.

The integration across modules was difficult, as the technical interaction between the modules was ill defined and fuzzy. It also revealed another problem with the modular organization: cross-unit responsibility. Looking at how the "heating" function was managed showed that nobody was really responsible for the overall integration across modules. Engineers and managers, at MCC, as well as the suppliers, were more preoccupied with their modules and naturally suboptimized. Mr. Meyer explained: "I was working with Mr. Hoffmann on a consistent tolerances concept within the doors module. Of course, I did not oversee what was going on in the drive module."

After some incidents, MCC realized that given the modular design of the organization, the cross-modular functions of the 'smart' would not receive enough attention and care during the development phase. Furthermore, the organizational modularity in itself masked the danger that optimization of the entire vehicle was not promoted with the necessary rigor. The solution was to add a sixth organizational model, called "electrical connections/electronic systems" that would specifically focus on cross-modular issues. As an overlay structure, MCC also established another cross-module organization, "total vehicle optimization/vehicle testing" that would look after the systematic coordination of cross-module information flows. The managers in charge were made responsible for testing and the optimization of the entire vehicle and had the same hierarchical level as functional managers within the other organizational modules. They were to settle conflicts within MCC across the various modules.

System Partner Integration

MCC heavily relied on outsourcing from legally independent suppliers. The successful execution of the 'smart' project was therefore dependent on the level of mutual cooperation and agreement about the division of tasks and responsibilities between MCC and its system partners. Precise process definitions were developed to clarify mutual targets and facilitate coordination and adjustments between MCC and system partners. At the same time, these processes had to allow for greater flexibility and cooperation at the buyer-supplier interfaces. **Exhibit 7** summarizes the guiding principles for system partner integration.

Exhibit 7

Principles of System Partner Integration

Measures	Agreements
(1) Supplier contracts	(1) Single sourcing (2) Lifetime-contracts (3) Minimum purchasing volumes (4) Profit margins per unit (5) Obligatory target costs of each product developed by a system partner
(2) Intellectual property management	(1) MCC acquired ownership of the design concepts contained in rejected suppliers' proposals (2) MCC claimed ownership rights for patents where the underlying innovations concern the security and the competitive advantage of the 'smart,' regardless of whether they were developed by suppliers or by MCC (3) Patents that are based on generic product and process innovations are registered by the supplier who developed them. The property rights remain exclusively theirs
(3) Fundamental guidelines	(1) MCC controls the entire process chain (2) Supplier companies invest in production equipment, machines, and tools and operate their business on their own behalf according to the development and production contracts (3) MCC provides plant surfaces and industrial services (4) MCC is responsible for the general context conditions that ensure that suppliers could smoothly execute their tasks
(4) Organizational structure	(1) System partners should set up and maintain a project organization that mirrors the organization of MCC. (2) System partners must assign function managers and project managers for the duration of the entire project. (3) System partners locate their offices on the development premises of MCC during particular development stages
(5) Control of information flows	(1) Open-books calculation (2) Development protocol (3) Conflict management

CONTRACTUAL ARRANGEMENTS

The relationships between MCC and its system partners were based on contracts and rules to which all participants had to agree. The contracts spelled out the rights and duties of system partners and the formal agreements on intellectual property management. The rules defined the fundamental project guidelines, the project organization, and transparency between MCC and system partners. Contracts were separately negotiated with each system partner and were not based on the standard contract schemes provided by the Association of German Automobile Industry (VDA). The contracts stipulated exclusivity rights for the suppliers, e.g., single sourcing principle for MCC, but also expected system partners to assume some of the project's business risk, for instance, by prefinancing of system and module development as well as tools. Contracts also stipulated an obligatory target price that served as the reference for the assessment of any cost deviations likely to occur in later stages of the development process.

INTELLECTUAL PROPERTY RIGHTS AGREEMENTS

Intellectual property rights was a critical issue for both sides. MCC wanted to avoid supplier companies exploiting innovations developed for 'smart' with other customers. This would clearly affect the market attractiveness of the 'smart.' MCC therefore decided in some cases to acquire all ownership of the design concepts, even for rejected suppliers' proposals. Rejected suppliers would receive a lump sum compensation upon demand. MCC did not engage in any joint patent registration with any system partner. It would quickly become a source of dispute.

PROJECT ORGANIZATION

The fundamental guidelines were called "smart alliance" and in simple terms allocated the basic responsibilities and obligations between MCC and the suppliers. MCC was the smart project leader and played the role of the focal company in a broad network of tight buyer–supplier relationships (even though suppliers assumed part of the risk of the project). Modifications brought to components during the development phase or completion of the quality control of the assembled vehicle needed approval and supervision from MCC.

System partners should develop a three-layer project hierarchy for development and production parallel to the hierarchical structure within MCC, with its function managers, then project managers and finally the board of directors on top. In addition, system partners had to assign function managers and project managers for the duration of the entire project. This should provide the channel for lateral communication between MCC and system partners and clearly identified who would be the contact person responsible for the 'smart' project within each organization. Furthermore, suppliers had temporary desks in Renningen and were asked to produce/assemble their systems at the very assembly plant MCC built in France for the 'smart.'

CONFLICT MANAGEMENT MECHANISMS

Conflicts during the project were anticipated and unavoidable. The basic channel for interfirm conflict resolution was provided by the project organization and its lateral communication bridges. For example, Mr. Meyer of MCC was not quite satisfied with some tolerance calculations for the doors' module that his system partner counterpart, Mr. Hoffmann, had just sent him. He went to talk to him directly. "If I had talked directly to his boss, the project manager, Mr. Hoffmann would have felt bad and thought the customer was complaining to his boss about him personally." The procedure prescribed by MCC required that conflicts should be resolved at the level they occur.

Transparency, also conceded by MCC, was instrumental in reducing conflict and supported smooth interactions and trust building in the relationships. Mr. Meyer explained: "We agreed with most system partners on 'open-book calculations' to provide each other with the most relevant data." MCC guaranteed purchasing volumes to the suppliers and gave them access to its market research data from which they could gain confidence in estimated sales volumes themselves. The same applied for the composition of the target price to which system partners were committed.

THE ROLE OF DEVELOPMENT PROTOCOLS

A major tool to control the information flows between MCC and system partners was the so-called "development protocols." These included all product-relevant data and were interactively updated during the course of the 'smart' development. A system partner would get access only to the data relevant to their own development responsibilities and could not see the protocol for other suppliers. In fact, knowledge about the smart was distributed between MCC and the system partners according to the predetermined task assignments and responsibilities. On the other hand, system partners would disclose only 'smart'-related knowledge to MCC, which was, of course, only a fraction of their own knowledge base.

Nevertheless, it was still not possible to force mutual transparency with contracts. Mr. Meyer's experience was that: "Transparency on the side of system partners depends very much on the supplier you deal with. It also depends on the personal relationships you have built with component managers at the suppliers." He also admitted that the degree of transparency varied during the different stages of the project.

Partner Integration During the Development Process for the 'smart'

The concept of the 'smart' and of the organization of MCC were quite revolutionary ideas in the car business and required a fundamental departure from the traditional ways of designing and producing a car. It was critical to develop the proper management processes to deal with the unique aspects of the technical architecture of the 'smart'—the internal modular project organization as well as the external network of system partners. The smart project was broken down into three phases: (1) concept development, (2) concept realization, and (3) full production (see **Exhibit 8**). Not surprisingly, the most time-consuming phases of the project were concept realization and production. Each phase consisted of a set of subprocesses that dictated "what to do when" and how to reach the planned targets. Each phase corresponded to a different team composition within MCC's modular organization. The teams reflected the nature of the major tasks to be accomplished at each development stage and the corresponding domains of expertise required.

CONCEPT DEVELOPMENT

There were distinct phases during the concept development of the 'smart': (1) strategic product planning, (2) procurement marketing, and (3) concept competition.

Strategic Product Planning

Some strategic product planning activities had been carried out by Mercedes-Benz and SMH prior to the foundation of MCC. However, the major work load was carried out when MCC took up its work around April 1994. The main objective was to develop an initial definition of the development protocols. These protocols were to reflect the basic concept requirements of the 'smart,' of which the most important one was to determine how much customers were ready to pay for the car.

Exhibit 8

Structure of the Development Process

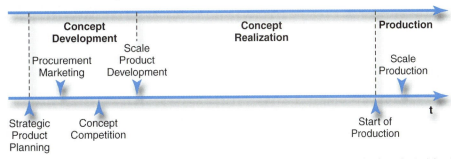

Note: Exhibit 8 indicates the time duration of each phase (except for strategic product planning and scale production), but should not be interpreted as an exact time schedule. Also, the starting and termination times of distinct development phases tend to overlap. Therefore, Exhibit 8 should be seen as an approximate representation of the development process structure.

This target price was the basis for the calculation of the cost structure for the whole vehicle and for prospective system partners. The procedure estimated how much customers were willing to pay for the key functionalities of the 'smart' value proposition to the market. Each key utility was given a price tag, then each function was translated in terms of its constituent physical components. The result gave the maximum cost allowed for each component. This latter task was typically delicate, as most key functions can be implemented in different ways, with different combinations of components, and required the participation of the most experienced component managers, purchasing specialists as well as benchmarking experts.

In the first half of 1994, Mr. Meyer was heavily solicited for his long experience in door design and his knowledge of the related upstream component markets. This analysis represented the very first contact newly founded MCC had with external supplier and in particular the first contact Mr. Meyer had with Mr. Hoffmann.

Procurement Marketing

The procurement marketing phase also started in spring 1994 and partly overlapped with strategic product planning. During this phase, MCC preselected up to six to eight potential system suppliers. Those who passed this initial screening were invited to take part in a concept competition and were asked to propose concept studies for their specialty system, or module, on the basis of the customer price targets defined during the strategic planning phase. This was the first time in the 'smart' project that MCC tapped suppliers' creativity and the specialized knowledge they had developed in the domain of their expertise. The quality of a supplier's concept study, even though very important, was not the only key factor in MCC's evaluation. MCC also looked at other factors related to the supplier's general performance, e.g., company size, turnover, plant locations, certificates, and references.

Benchmarking and purchasing specialists and component managers supported by controllers would be working together to determine which companies could deliver on the creativity required in their new roles within the MCC networked organization. Suppliers were indeed expected to develop from scratch feasible and innovative product concepts within the domain of their expertise. The burden on them in terms of conceptual complexity and creativity was different from what was usually expected in the traditional way of making cars. They were used to developing products around preexisting blueprints or physical components. The system partner's financial stability was also essential to guarantee that it could make the needed investments.

Mr. Meyer admitted:

Mr. Hoffmann's company was very promising. They had an excellent reputation for quality in processes and products. Their financial foundation was solid. My colleagues in the doors selection team were also very positive. I have to say that in the beginning I was not sure they would be able to deliver feasible door solutions without receiving precise specifications from us. This was a sensitive issue for us because door development had always been done inside. One of my former colleagues in the Mercedes-Benz purchasing department knew this supplier and strongly recommended them to us. This made a difference, and finally Mr. Hoffmann's company was invited to join the concept competition.

CONCEPT COMPETITION

In June 1994, MCC began the concept competition phase to determine who would be their "dancing partners." MCC gave those companies invited to the competition a first development protocol, which provided them with the basic description of the product they were asked to deliver. The specifications included the external measurements of the item, its design, the interfaces with other physical components as well as its functional and crash-resistance requirements. In addition, suppliers received the detailed target costs for their parts and the outline of the development contract.

Each candidate was required to present its concept proposal to MCC within a couple of months. Once all proposals were received, MCC started the most critical task, i.e., the evaluation and final selection of system partners and their concepts. The evaluation team included component managers, benchmarking specialists, purchasing agents, and controllers.

The evaluation scheme developed by MCC assessed the product concepts with respect to their technical and economic aspects and included both quantitative and qualitative dimensions. In particular, they were assessed against the original marketing and technological targets of the 'smart.' The "weight reduction" target, for instance, was assessed by converting the manufacturing costs of a module into a price-per-kilogram factor and then estimating the weight of the total car. A concept solution with a lower manufacturing price but a heavier weight than competing solutions would be handicapped by its price-per-kilogram factor. Mr. Meyer was pleased:

Mr. Hoffmann and his colleagues did very well in this respect. Their door concept had the lowest price per kilogram and seemed to be the most appropriate solution for the complex doors of the smart. This further confirmed my trust in them. After the final assessment was completed, they were given a contract offer.

CONCEPT REALIZATION

When this phase started in April 1995, the 'smart' project significantly increased in size and cost. System partners had allocated human and financial resources to the project and were actively involved in implementation. The first peak in the interaction between MCC and its system partners took place at the beginning of the concept realization phase when concepts had to be translated into products and when MCC asked its partners to locate their project teams at MCC's development facilities in Renningen.

Engineers from both sides were starting to cooperate. First of all, they had to learn how to interact and coordinate across their firm boundaries. This was not easy for them. They had to develop and get accustomed to new rules of conduct. It took about one year for MCC to get people inside and outside on the same wavelength. Their cooperation centered around the sequential fulfillment of all functions and the related target costs agreed upon. Neither the system partners nor MCC had earlier blueprints to work from. Components and the production equipment, e.g., dies and tools, had to be built from scratch. The main documents on which system partners and MCC-module teams based their development activities were the development protocols.

Optimization of product functions at the concept realization phase often implied some design changes for supplier components. Yet agreeing on design changes was one of the most difficult parts of managing relationships in the network. Design changes opened the door to price negotiations. All system partners had signed a contract in which target prices and function execution were set in writing, and suppliers were entitled to demand a price increase only when they delivered a functionality at a higher level of performance than the contracted target value. Conversely, if they underperformed in a functionality, their price would drop below the stipulated target costs.

Conflicts were common as it was difficult to determine whether a design change would bring an increase or decrease in function performance. Typically system partners would insist that the design changes provided some improvement in functionality.

This was where the organization structures and conflict management mechanisms were put into action, as experienced by Mr. Meyer and Mr. Hoffmann when they had to develop consistent tolerances. As Mr. Meyer explained:

> Tolerances have to be defined for the doors and the frame into which the doors will be installed in such a way that these tolerances compensate each other and guarantee integration. At the beginning, the tolerances worked out by Mr. Hoffmann and his team did not fit. I already got on quite well with him, and found him to be a nice person, but I had difficulty explaining to him what I really needed from him. I would make suggestions but he would come up with his own proposals.

Clearly, managing coordination and conflicts within the network required some elaborate and transparent evaluation scheme. MCC used the concept of "value-analysis," similar to the process used for the determination of customer target prices. With this technique MCC would examine whether supplier solutions deviated from stipulated target values. This would apply to supplier products as well as development and production processes.

As indicated in **Exhibit 9**, design changes could be initiated by either a system partner or an MCC module team, but the supplier had to work out an appropriate solution. MCC com-

Exhibit 9

The Interface between MCC and System Partners during Concept Realization

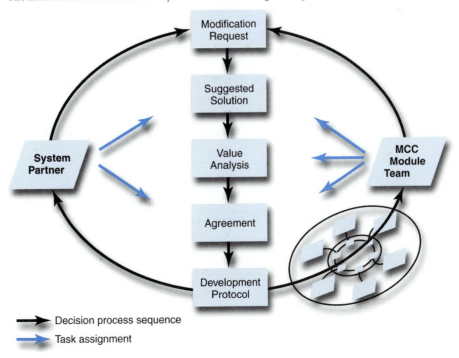

ponent managers could nevertheless make suggestions, the supplier had the discretion to accept or refuse. If no agreement could be reached, MCC would conduct detailed value analyses on costs and functions and eventually system partners and MCC had to agree upon a solution (which could also imply further changes). The changes were then included in the development protocols with which both MCC and its partners had to comply. Any revisions would become the basis for the next phase of improvements and changes.

PRODUCTION

The production phase was scheduled to start in July 1998. The manufacturing and assembly process at the Hambach plant in France was characterized by a quasi-dissolution of the boundaries between MCC and its system partners (see **Exhibit 10**). There was a risk for MCC components managers, for example, experiencing some conflict in their role. They had been in direct contact with the supplier on a daily basis, they knew most about the supplier problems, and they could identify with the interest of the supplier instead of enforcing MCC positions.

Which supplier would be asked to manufacture at the new Hambach plant and which ones would be asked to produce and ship from their existing factories? Determining factors included the specificity of the deliveries to the 'smart,' the potential for economies of scale, the

Exhibit 10
Organization of the Collaborative Production Process

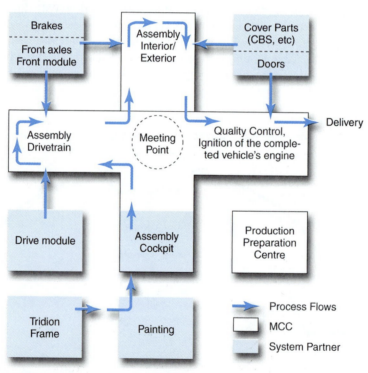

Note: The organization of the final assembly process corresponded to the modular product and organization architecture of the 'smart.' As Exhibit 10 indicates, MCC performed the core assembly that took the form of a cross, or in the term of MCC, a "plus." The core assembly of MCC was the focal point of the production plant. The cross was surrounded by the system partners who were self-dependent for the manufacturing and assembly of the modules. The cross shape of the assembly line allowed the system partners to be correctly located on the assembly line for the installation of their modules. As can be seen in Exhibit 10, "the assembly process followed the product," beginning with the welding of the car body, and moving on to the painting of the frame. The next assembly steps were "engagement" of the car body and cockpit, the installation of the drive module, front module, brake system, and exterior as well as interior system-modules. The assembly process of the 'smart' was completed by quality control and the ignition of the completed vehicle's engine.

level of additional investments required, and the complexity of the logistics. For instance, the body of the 'smart' and the Customized Body Panel System (CBS) were completely 'smart'-specific, so no prior manufacturing facilities existed. Manufacturing the car body and the CBS-parts away from Hambach and delivering them JIT to the final assembly plant would have significantly increased the complexity of the logistics and costs. Conversely, system partners for engines, axles, and seats had no intention of setting up new manufacturing facilities at Hambach. They integrated the additional production volumes into their existing facilities and could realize scale economies.

Full production was to start in a few months, but for Mr. Meyer there were some fundamental questions left to answer, in particular if the 'smart' project is a financial success. Does the approach really achieve the desired results in terms of innovativeness, lead times, and costs? In the long run, wouldn't the networked organization approach destroy an automobile company's ability to initiate and integrate innovation? Would MCC be able to maintain its focal position in the network even without the backing of Mercedes-Benz? In fact, MCC as system integrator did not build and maintain technical knowledge about products and processes. This was done by supplier companies. What could and what should Mr. Meyer do if Mr. Hoffmann does not deliver?

Note

1. Johann Tomforde, "smart—Vom Designkonzept eines urbanen Kompaktfahrzeugs bis zum Aufbau eines Unternehmens für individuelle Mobilität." Lecture at the conference "Automobil-Design—Visionen für die Zukunft des Automobils" (Essen, Germany: November 28/29, 1996), p. 7 (Translation by the authors).

A.W.A.R.E.

John K. Ross III and Eric G. Kirby

I t was a typically beautiful morning in central Texas as Sherry stood at the office door watching the bustle of activity in the arena. It was just before the first client arrived and Bobby, the Lead Instructor, and several volunteers were getting Duke ready for Cindy. Duke was a 1,000-pound horse that would be led from his stall, groomed, tacked, and then would provide Cindy an hour of physical and emotional therapy. Cindy was a beautiful nine-year-old girl with cerebral palsy who used a small walker and leg braces to walk and would, for a short time, allow Duke to be her legs—and her friend.

With a grin and a bang, Cindy opened the screen door to the office and entered as fast as she could. Sherry turned to help her put on her helmet, and within minutes Cindy was being assisted into the arena and onto the mounting blocks where Bobby and Duke waited. Cindy's smile grew wider as she approached Duke and carefully climbed the mounting blocks. With the help of Bobby and the volunteers, Cindy lifted one leg up and over the saddle, and she was ready to ride. After carefully leaving the mounting blocks Cindy excitedly said "Walk on" and Duke, Cindy, Bobby, and the volunteers began an hour of intense physical therapy, which for Cindy would seem to pass like minutes and would be the highlight of her week.

History

This was A.W.A.R.E. (Always Wanted A Riding Experience). Located in San Marcos, Texas (30 miles south of Austin), A.W.A.R.E. was a not-for-profit therapeutic horseback riding center under the provisions of Section 501(c)3 of the U.S. Internal Revenue Service. Cathy Morgan founded A.W.A.R.E. in October of 1986 using her personal horse, four horses borrowed from friends, and a small arena borrowed from another friend. Cathy was a certified special education teacher and horse-riding expert. For years she had dreamed of combining her love for special children and horseback riding. There was a ready clientele for her specialized type of therapy and growth occurred quickly.

The authors wish to thank the fine people at A.W.A.R.E. for their cooperation and assistance. Although A.W.A.R.E. is real, the names used in this case have been changed. This case was prepared by Professors John K. Ross III and Eric G. Kirby of Southwest Texas State University. This case was edited for SMBP-9th Edition. Copyright © 2000 by John K. Ross III and Eric G. Kirby.

Horseback riding as physical and emotional therapy began in Europe, probably in the 1600s. The modern therapeutic benefits were not realized until Liz Hartel of Denmark won the silver medal for dressage at the 1952 Helsinki Olympic Games—despite having paralysis from polio. Within a short period of time, medical and equine professionals had begun riding centers for rehabilitation purposes in England and then in North America by the 1960s. The first professional organization, North American Riding for the Handicapped Association (NARHA), was formed in 1969 for educational purposes and later to accredit active centers. Today, the number of NARHA-affiliated centers totals more than 550, providing more than 30,000 individuals with riding experiences <www.narha.org>.

Within two years of founding A.W.A.R.E., Cathy had moved to a larger outdoor arena with nine stalls and lights for night riding. By then she had found three additional riding experts to become instructors and was soon "riding" clients from 9:00 A.M. until 9:00 P.M. She was charging $10 for a one-hour riding lesson and providing scholarships (discounted rates or free-of-charge) for some clients. A small Board of Directors, comprised of Cathy's acquaintances, had been formed and they provided some assistance. For the most part they were not a strong Board, being comprised of well-meaning individuals who were not members of the community's "movers and shakers" and not particularly savvy at running a business. Cathy was able to continue offering the therapeutic riding services, but, as in many small not-for-profits, cash flow was a continual problem. In fact, some weeks her instructors did not get paid until a client paid.

In 1992 Cathy began a letter-writing campaign for donations to help support A.W.A.R.E. with operating expenses, to provide scholarships, and to move to a covered arena. Their facilities were unusable when it rained, at which time the arena turned into a quagmire. Additionally, riders and volunteers were suffering from the heat and sun during the long Texas summers when afternoon temperatures in the 100s were not uncommon. The fund-raising campaign paid off when two locally owned corporations joined together and donated 20 acres with a covered arena, worth about $250,000. For the next year Cathy and a group of volunteers worked to refurbish the land and arena to meet NARHA accreditation standards.

During that same time A.W.A.R.E. put on a successful fundraiser dinner-dance-auction which netted approximately $19,000, and Cathy decided to return to teaching. The Board searched to replace Cathy but was unable to successfully find a long-term Executive Director. After two Executive Directors left within a short time because of the long hours, hard work, and meager salary, one of the volunteers, Sherry Ross (a local CPA who was working as a full-time volunteer), took over the functions of Executive Director and began exercising tight fiscal control of the operation.

Current Situation

A.W.A.R.E. was located on the donated property seven miles south of San Marcos, approximately one-quarter mile off of an interstate highway, and directly behind one of the country's largest outlet malls. Recently the property across the street had begun to be developed into an upscale residential community. A.W.A.R.E. had 13 horses, over 100 clients per session (a 16-week period of time equivalent to a university semester), an unpaid Executive Director, two full-time paid instructors, four part-time paid instructors, and over 200 volunteers per session. A typical day began when Yvonne (who lived in a mobile home on the A.W.A.R.E. property as part of her salary) fed the horses at 7:00 A.M. Classes then began sometime after 8:00 A.M. and continued throughout the day, ending around 9:00 P.M.

For a typical lesson, the instructor began preparations 30 minutes prior to its start by reviewing previous lessons and goals for that client, organized aids (toys for fine motor skills, etc.), then assisted the volunteers as they groomed and tacked the horse. Once the client arrived they donned a helmet and mounted their horse. During the lesson, one volunteer would be the "horse handler" and also had responsibility for observing and controlling the horse. One or two other volunteers would walk beside the horse as "sidewalkers" (spotters) for safety reasons and to interact with the client. The instructor then guided the class, leading the client through a series of activities designed to focus on verbal, gross or fine motor skills, balance, flexibility, or some other specific goal. Frequently these activities were disguised as games or play and may have included singing, interactions with other riders, and other "fun" activities. All of this was accomplished while the client was sitting, lying, or standing on the horse's back. At the conclusion of the hour lesson, the client was dismounted and returned with the instructor to the office area, returned his or her helmet, and talked briefly with the instructor. The volunteers untacked the horse and returned it to its stall. The instructor would then make notes about the current lesson in the client's file for future reference. Up to six clients may have ridden in a group lesson and been supervised by one instructor.

The Executive Director was also an instructor and, with the help of the Lead Instructor, performed all of the office work necessary to keep A.W.A.R.E. operating. This included preparing financial records, correspondence, payroll, schedule preparation, and the like. To begin a typical semester session, A.W.A.R.E. must contact previous riders to confirm continuing riding, select others who might want to ride from a waiting list, advertise for volunteers and conduct volunteer training, schedule lesson times that match both rider and instructor needs, perform routine maintenance on the facilities, and so forth. The workload was very heavy and the Executive Director generally worked 60 to 70 hours per week. **Exhibit 1** shows the current organizational structure for A.W.A.R.E.

The Lead Instructor typically worked 40 to 50 hours per week and the one other full-time instructor worked a 40-hour week (both were paid about $10/hour). All other instructors were part time and were paid $8.00 per hour. Instructors had to be trained in the dual disciplines of horsemanship and physical therapy. A.W.A.R.E. would not ride a client unless a physician had approved horse riding as a beneficial therapy and the instructors had been able to provide not just a pony ride, but a therapeutic riding experience. The instructors continuously supported each other with ideas to improve their lessons and the sharing of knowledge about instructional pedagogy. Additionally, A.W.A.R.E. supported instructors attending specialized conferences on therapeutic horseback riding. However none of the instructors were certified physical therapists.

Exhibit 1
Organizational Structure

The Board of Directors for A.W.A.R.E was comprised of six volunteers from the local community and included two physicians, a university business professor, the wife of the local newspaper editor, the spouse of a local prominent lawyer, and a local businessperson. Although the Board members were good, well-intentioned individuals, the Board, as a whole, was not strong. They had put on two successful fund-raising events and seemed prepared to attempt another. However, the average tenure of the current Board member was well over five years, which was much too long to remain effective in a not-for-profit such as A.W.A.R.E. With only six members, the work of the Board could be demanding, and burnout could occur.

A.W.A.R.E. had a very good reputation in the local community as a well-run, efficient, and caring organization. The staff and volunteers were active in community affairs, A.W.A.R.E. received funds from the United Way, participated in local and state equestrian Special Olympics (where their riders generally took home most of the gold medals), and cooperated with other not-for-profits in local events. A.W.A.R.E. also had an excellent reputation amongst the equestrian community throughout the state.

Financials

When A.W.A.R.E. was located in a small arena, the majority of the expenses concerned involved payroll and horses. These were still the two largest expense items, however, maintenance and upkeep on the much larger facility had increased expenses dramatically. Additionally, expenses from several other items, like insurance, taxes, and veterinary care, had also increased drastically. Revenues came almost entirely from client fees, supplemented by donations. (See **Exhibits 2** and **3**.)

The contributors of the land placed a stipulation that for the first five years, only therapeutic horseback riding was to be allowed on the property. That time had now expired; how-

Exhibit 2
Balance Sheet: A.W.A.R.E.

Year Ending December 31	1999	1998	1997	1996	1995
Assets					
Current assets					
Checking and savings	$ 17,336	$ 20,229	$ 20,312	$ 8,608	$ 19,961
Accounts receivable	(864)	(1,189)	(659)	(362)	(187)
Total current assets	16,472	19,040	19,653	8,246	19,774
Fixed assets					
Buildings and land	265,419	265,000	265,000	265,000	265,000
Horses	10,551	10,850	7,550	4,401	4,400
Equipment	32,486	31,485	18,622	27,195	28,073
Accumulated depreciation	(85,195)	(70,622)	(24,087)	(22,034)	(11,329)
Total fixed assets	223,261	236,713	267,085	274,561	286,144
Total Assets	$239,733	$255,753	$295,738	$282,808	$305,918
Liabilities and equity					
Liabilities					
Current liabilities	$ 157	$ 0	$ 0	$ 0	$ 124
Total liabilities	157	0	0	0	124
Equity					
Retained earnings	239,576	255,753	295,738	282,808	305,794
Total equity	239,576	255,753	295,738	282,808	305,794
Total liabilities and equity	$239,733	$255,753	$295,738	$282,808	$305,918

Note: Rounding errors on total.

Exhibit 3
Profit and Loss Statement: A.W.A.R.E.

Year Ending December 31	1999	1998	1997	1996	1995
Ordinary income/expenses					
Income					
Rider fees	$ 50,097	$49,703	$44,894	$28,863	$42,184
Donations	10,670	12,716	8,056	4,051	6,579
United Way	7,653	423	5,550	3,982	3,924
Other income	4,095	1,451	3,275	4,367	25,089
Total income	72,515	64,293	61,775	41,263	77,767
Expenses					
Hay and feed	5,097	5,832	6,094	8,866	1,685
Facility maintenance	2,555	2,015	1,229	1,214	1,602
Insurance	3,294	1,875	1,900	1,864	1,265
Payroll	38,381	29,615	22,780	26,194	31,057
Other expenses	37,938	25,034	26,053	17,074	27,156
Total expenses	87,265	64,371	58,056	55,212	62,765
Net ordinary income	(14,750)	(78)	3,719	(13,949)	15,002
Other income/expenses					
In-kind donations	3,960	2,500	7,400	0	350
Net other income	3,960	2,500	7,400	0	350
Net income	$(10,790)	$ 2,422	$11,119	$13,696	$15,352

ever, no other revenue sources had been attempted. Clients were charged $25.00 for a one-hour riding session with one of A.W.A.R.E.'s instructors. A modified fee could be charged for group lessons and some clients were given scholarships. Hippotherapy, horseback riding with a certified physical therapist (PT), billed out as physical therapy and is covered by insurance. Currently, a local physical therapist brings a group of her clients to A.W.A.R.E. once a week. A.W.A.R.E. charges only their regular riding fees and the PT bills the insurance companies at her regular rates.

Decision Time

Sherry, still standing at the door to the arena, frowned as she began to ponder several recent events that had placed A.W.A.R.E. in a precarious position. She was worried about, and unsure of, both the short-term and long-term viability of the organization. Over the past several years, the summer session had been very profitable for A.W.A.R.E. During the summer, a diagnostic camp for children was run by a national social organization that had brought 12 to 14 riders per day as part of their planned activities. This cash flow paid the summer salaries for the instructors, bought a year's supply of hay for the horses, and allowed A.W.A.R.E. to net around $7,000 for the summer. The camp informed A.W.A.R.E. only weeks before the summer session was to begin that they were not participating this summer. The loss of cash flow could severely impact both the summer and fall programs. The loss of additional future revenues could force A.W.A.R.E. to scale back operation significantly.

Cash flow will also be impacted when Sherry steps down as Executive Director. Sherry had been the volunteer Executive Director for over six years and a medical condition was forcing her to retire. It would be expensive to replace her with a paid Executive Director (a typical salary range might be $36,000 per year) and an additional full-time instructor.

While these problems can be overcome, Sherry was worried about the future. What will A.W.A.R.E. be in 5 to 10 years? Will it even be in existence, operating as it does now, or be something completely different? What was best for the short- and long-term viability of A.W.A.R.E.? As volunteer Executive Director, Sherry realized there was a number of alternatives ranging from closing A.W.A.R.E. to the creation of a nationwide network of similar programs. More realistically, A.W.A.R.E. could offer profit-generating activities such as riding camps for well children or perhaps hold another fund-raiser and hire a new Executive Director. Other options might include partnering with the local hospital or other not-for-profits in the surrounding area. Sherry did realize that due to the success and proximity of the outlet mall, the current property could be sold for about $750,000.

When Cathy Morgan first began A.W.A.R.E., she envisioned the eventual development of an entire therapy complex with staff physicians, live-in clients, and extensive therapy programs. However, Cathy was no longer with the program, and Sherry was unsure what direction A.W.A.R.E. should take or how to get there.

References and Sources for Additional Information

North American Riding for the Handicapped Association: <www.narha.org>

San Marcos Home Page: <ci.san-marcos.tx.us>

San Marcos Chamber of Commerce: <www.sanmarcostexas.com>

case 35

eBay

Maryanne M. Rouse

J une 2, 2002—WASHINGTON: *The U.S. Air Force is looking into the Internet auction of sensitive government aircraft-communications equipment. The sales on eBay Inc.'s online auction site, which were reported by* Newsweek *magazine, were of parts used in aircraft like the SR-71 spy plane and F-16 fighter. "It is actively under investigation by the Air Force Office of Special Investigations," an Air Force spokesman, Capt. David L. Englin, said Sunday. Antiques dealer Norb Novocin told the magazine he bought the parts in Jacksonville, Fla., for $244 in an unclaimed property sale. The seller was a shipping company which had been hired to take the parts in 1989 from Dover Air Force Base in Delaware to Warner Robins in Georgia, the magazine reported. Mr. Novocin said that he initially called the Georgia base about buying the goods but was turned away. After he was contacted by the Air Force, Mr. Novocin said he turned over the names and addresses of purchasers and agreed to stop selling the equipment.*

—Copyright (c) 2002 Dow Jones & Company, Inc.

Seven years ago, eBay pioneered online personal trading by creating a Web-based platform to bring buyers and sellers together in an efficient, entertaining auction format to buy and sell items ranging from antiques, high-end artwork, automobiles, electronics and jewelry to the practical, arcane, pure kitsch, and downright bizarre—as demonstrated by *Newsweek*'s report of the sale of sensitive aircraft communications equipment on the site.

eBay began as a no-registration, no-fee grassroots trading company, called "Auction Web", in September 1995. After its listing on the National Center for Supercomputing Application's "What's Cool" list, the site's popularity soared. Minimal fees were introduced, and by March 1996, the company turned its first profit. eBay was incorporated in California in May 1996 and reincorporated in Delaware in 1998; the company went public in 1998.

The eBay dynamic pricing (auction-style) format permits sellers to list items for sale, buyers to bid on items of interest, and all eBay users to browse through listed items. Through wholly and partially owned subsidiaries, the company operates trading platforms targeted to the United States, Australia, Austria, Belgium, Canada, France, Germany, Ireland, Italy, The Netherlands, New Zealand, Singapore, Spain, South Korea, Sweden, Switzerland, and the United Kingdom. (eBay recently exited the market in Japan.) The company's consumer base has grown from individual consumers to include merchants, small to medium-size businesses, global corporations, and government agencies. eBay also provides offline, traditional auction

This case was prepared by Professor Maryanne M. Rouse of The University of South Florida. Copyright © 2002 by Maryanne M. Rouse. This case was edited for SMBP-9th edition. Reprinted by permission.

services for fine arts, antiques, collectibles, and collector cars. Online services accounted for 95% of 2001 revenues, with offline auctions accounting for 5%.

Online Services

eBay defines this segment to include U.S. and international online trading platforms as well as key features offered through those platforms, including electronic payments, photo hosting, Buy It Now, and third-party advertising.

The eBay trading platform is a fully automated, topically arranged, easy-to-use online service that is available 24 hours a day. Anyone can visit eBay and browse through the items for sale; however, only registered users can bid on and list items for sale. The registration process is both easy and quick, allowing users to bid on and list items immediately. Registered sellers can list an item for sale by completing a short online form, selecting a minimum price for opening bids, and choosing whether the listing will expire after 3, 5, 7, or 10 days. The seller may also indicate a "reserve" price. A reserve price is the minimum price at which the seller would be willing to sell the item; the reserve price is not disclosed to bidders. At the time of listing, sellers can also chose to use the Buy It Now feature, which allows the seller to set a price at which he or she would be willing to sell without waiting for the auction to end. Sellers with multiple identical items to sell can take advantage of eBay's Dutch auction feature, which allows the highest bidders (number of bidders equal to the number of items) to all receive the item at the same price. Only sellers with sufficiently high feedback ratings may use the reserve and Dutch auction features.

eBay's core business model is still person-to-person selling, which accounts for the largest percentage of its revenue. The company generates revenue from listing fees, feature fees, and final value fees. There is no charge to buyers; however, sellers pay a small placement fee to list an item:

Minimum Bid, Opening Value or Reserve Price	Listing Fee
$ 0.01–$ 9.99	$0.30
$10.00–$ 24.99	0.55
$25.00–$ 49.99	1.10
$50.00–$199.99	2.20
$200.00 and up	3.20

eBay generates additional revenue by offering sellers opportunities to enhance their listings by adding features to attract buyers:

Seller Feature	Description	Fee
Featured on home page	Item is listed in a special featured section and is also rotated on the eBay home page	$99.95
Featured Plus!	Item appears in the category's featured item section and in the bidder's search results	$19.95
Highlight	Listing is emphasized with a colored band	$ 5.00
Bold	Item title is listed in bold type	$ 2.00
Buy It Now	Allows the seller to close an auction instantly For a specified price	$ 0.05

Final value fees are based on the selling price. The fee for items sold at up to $25 is 5.25% of the sale price. For items sold at between $25.01 and $1,000, the fee is 5.25% of the first $25 plus 2.75% of the amount over $25. For items sold at over $1,000, the fee for the first $1,000 is as above, with an additional 1.75% of the amount over $1,000.

When an auction ends, the eBay system validates whether a bid has exceeded the minimum or reserve price. If so (or, if the buyer elected to Buy It Now), eBay automatically notifies the buyer and seller via email. The company never takes possession of the item; it's up to the buyer and seller to arrange for shipment and payment; the buyer typically pays for shipping. Although eBay has no power to force a buyer or seller to complete a transaction, it can ban repeat offenders from trading on the site.

Platform enhancements include "Trust and Safety Programs" such as the Feedback Forum, SafeHarbor, as well as such differentiating features as My eBay. The Feedback Forum encourages users to record comments, both favorable and unfavorable, about their trading partners. The company organizes feedback to create user profiles that contain complaints, criticisms, and positive comments and include ratings. Users who develop good reputations have color-coded star symbols placed next to their user names to indicate the number of positive feedback ratings received. eBay users are encouraged to review a seller's feedback profile before bidding on an item. The company's SafeHarbor staff investigates users' complaints of possible misuse of the site and may take actions ranging from issuing warnings to suspending users from bidding or listing items for sale. My eBay gives users a report of their recent activity, including bidding, selling, items bidders are watching, account balances, favorite categories, and recent feedback. Users who have their own Web pages can create links to their home pages; those without home pages can use About Me to create one free of charge.

eBay monitors the trading activity in existing categories and, when it sees sales of merchandise picking up in an area, it creates a new trading category. In late 1998, for example, eBay noticed that users were beginning to sell full-size cars in an area of the site devoted to toy and collectible cars. The company formed a separate auto category, and within two years the annualized value of cars and car parts sold through the site exceeded $1 billion.

Business and Industrial Sales

In early June 2001, eBay announced that it would create stores on its Web site featuring goods from retailers. Recognizing the significant revenue growth opportunities offered by large businesses, eBay began successfully cultivating such corporate sellers as IBM, Xerox, Dell, Home Depot, Motorola, the U.S. Post Office, ReturnBuy (a closely held merchandise liquidator), and eValueville (one of the largest liquidators of apparel for Bloomingdales). By early September 2002, at least 71 large companies were selling outdated merchandise, from laptops to tractors on eBay, up from just a dozen a year earlier. The key reason driving growth in eBay's business and industrial sales segment is that sellers can recoup $.45 on the dollar for excess inventory rather than the $.15–$.20 they could expect from traditional liquidators. For example, Motorola, which started Net auctions in April 2002, now sells $1 million of outdated phones a month. While many items are sold in lots, individual items, such as high-end photo equipment, also sell well. Such sellers are contributing to a shift in the composition of goods sold on eBay from "collectibles" to "practicals." ("Practicals" include everything from computers and sporting goods to power drills and athletic socks.) All told, eBay estimates that big companies now make up 5% of its sales—roughly $500 million a year.

Some small sellers have not welcomed the corporate merchants and have expressed concern about the site becoming the QVC of the Internet. However, eBay management insists the company has not lost sight of small sellers, and an analysis of transactions shows that eBay auctions are, on average, bringing higher prices than ever before. The company does concede that it provides special promotional benefits and discounts to some corporate sellers but notes that those concessions also drive added buyer traffic to eBay, adding to the legitimacy of the site and benefiting all sellers. The challenge for eBay will be to find a balance between preserving the eBay experience that small sellers and seasoned buyers find compelling while growing new revenue sources.

Offline Businesses

eBay's offline businesses include Butterfields Auctioneers Corporation and Kruse International, both of which provide traditional auction services. Butterfields, established in 1865, is the largest auction house headquartered on the west coast of the United States. With galleries in San Francisco and Los Angeles and representatives throughout the West and Midwest, it specializes in fine art, antiques, and collectibles. Kruse International, established in Indiana in 1971, is one of the world's leading collector car auction companies.

The PayPal Acquisition

In early July 2002, eBay agreed to acquire Internet-payment provider PayPal, Inc., for $1.4 billion in stock. PayPal, an increasingly popular electronic payment mechanism with a "viral" effect (the more people who sign up, the more attractive the system becomes to potential new users), is widely used to transact business by buyers and sellers on eBay, a situation that, before the announced merger, created both interdependency and rivalry between the two businesses. eBay had attempted to build its own electronic-payment service, Billpoint, but PayPal's earlier entry into the market and superior technology created entry barriers eBay found difficult to overcome. (Of electronic payments that occur among eBay users, 70% are handled by PayPal.) eBay plans to shut down Billpoint once the acquisition is completed. Industry analysts note that the acquisition makes strategic sense for eBay, giving it a chance to capture payment fees on top of the 7%–8% of total merchandise sales it currently collects from sellers.

Although the biggest chunk of PayPal's business (67%) comes from eBay users, PayPal is also used in thousands of other transactions, including person-to-person money transfers, and is accepted at many e-commerce Web sites, including pornography sites and small online businesses that do not accept credit cards. Highly popular among online casinos (estimated to currently account for 10%–15% of the company's revenue), PayPal will no longer facilitate gambling transactions once the acquisition is complete because of the murky legal and regulatory issues eBay believes are involved.

Site Operations and Technology

The eBay site operates on an internally developed software platform that comprises a scalable user interface and transaction processing system that supports the trading cycle, including email notifications and confirmations, and sends daily status updates to active buyers and sellers. The system also stores registration, billing, and credit card information for traders who use an open account balance. Although the company uses multiple, redundant host sites and emergency power backup, its systems are vulnerable to damage or interruption resulting from weather, hardware/software problems, and telecommunication failures. Systems are also vulnerable to break-ins, sabotage, and intentional acts of violence. eBay constantly adds to its infrastructure (hardware, software, engineers, support staff) to meet the demands of exponential growth.

Marketing

eBay uses market penetration and product and market development to support aggressive growth. To build brand awareness and interest, the company relies on word of mouth, public relations, and participation in trade shows and other events. To attract new users, eBay makes strategic purchases of online advertising as well as engaging in more traditional promotional activities, including radio, television, and print media. To retain existing users and increase their online activity, eBay emphasizes effective merchandising of users' product offerings, new features, and communication via direct messaging. The *New York Times* monthly analysis of Web site hits, appearing in the newspaper's business section on September 9, 2002, provides insight into eBay's popularity and market share:

Web Sites/Retail

At Home		At Work	
Property	**Visitors**	**Property**	**Visitors**
1. eBay.com	24.3 million	1. eBay.com	11.1 million
2. Amazon.com sites	21.6	2. Amazon.com sites	11.0
3. Yahoo.com Shopping	17.5	3. Yahoo.com Shopping	8.9
4. AmericanGreetings.com	10.5	4. AmericanGreetings.com	4.6
5. ColumbiaHouse.com	6.7	5. Dell.com	4.0

Finance

eBay's net revenue from both online and offline activities grew from $41.37 million for fiscal 1997 to $748.82 million for fiscal 2001, a five-year revenue growth significantly higher than the industry average. The successive year-over-year growth is primarily the result of increased online auction transaction activity, reflected in the growth of the number of registered users (42.4 million at the end of 2001), listings (423.1 million for 2001), and gross merchandise sales ($9.3 billion for 2001) but has also been fueled by acquisitions. The company has taken advantage of its economies of scale to drive cost of sales from 26% in 1999 to 18% in 2001. Although sales and marketing have increased on an absolute basis, as a percentage of sales, these below-the-line costs decreased from 43% of sales in 1999 to 34% in 2001. Product development and General & Administrative (G&A) costs have followed a similar pattern. eBay is less leveraged and more profitable that industry competitors. Cash provided by operations in 2001 was $252.1 million. (Complete annual and quarterly SEC filings are available via www.sec.gov, www.ebay.com, and www.wsj.com.)

Internet Fraud and Negative Publicity

Current laws regarding liability are still evolving and remain vague; however, because of the growing popularity of the Internet and online services, many potential new laws that would address issues from taxation to privacy, freedom of expression, pricing, fraud, and intellectual property rights are currently being debated at both the state and federal levels. Several states have proposed laws that would limit the ways in which personal information is collected and provided to third parties. Although eBay provides only the platform for exchange, it has still been the subject of suits by individuals who believe they have been defrauded on the eBay site. Because it is unable to prevent fraudulent activity on its site, eBay may face potential liability for misuse of its site by users. Negative publicity from deceptive sellers can also harm the company. Concerns about fraud could serve as a damper on eBay's rapid growth via new user acquisition. Owning PayPal will open eBay up to new risks, including payment fraud.

Competition

eBay's competitive space is characterized by rapidly changing technology, evolving industry standards, frequent new service and product announcements and enhancements, and changing customer demands. The company encounters aggressive competition from numerous sources, including online and offline retailers, distributors, liquidators, auctioneers, catalog and mail order companies, and virtually all online and offline commerce venues and participants. Direct competitors in the auction trading via the e-commerce subsegment include Yahoo!, Amazon, C/NET, and uBid. In a surprising move in late May 2002, Yahoo! withdrew from the online auction business in most European markets after negotiating a 2½-year marketing pact with eBay. Under the terms of the agreement, eBay will advertise throughout Yahoo! in the United Kingdom, Ireland, France, Germany, Italy, and Spain, and eBay will be featured as the preferred auction service on Yahoo! in the region. Earlier in the year, eBay had withdrawn from the market in Japan, but it still actively pursues other Asian markets. Marketing strategies pursued by eBay and its online competitors to attract large businesses are likely to shift the power of buyers/suppliers in the industry.

case 36

Hershey Foods Corporation

Maryanne M. Rouse

Hershey Foods, principally through its Hershey Chocolate U.S.A., Hershey International, and Hershey Canada, Inc., produces and distributes a broad line of quality chocolate, confectionary, and grocery products. In a related diversification move it hoped would help overcome the seasonality of the chocolate/confectionary segment, Hershey acquired San Giorgio Macaroni and Delmonico foods, both pasta manufacturers, in 1968. Acquired brands included San Giorgio, Ronzoni, Skinner, P&R, Light 'n Fluffy, and American Beauty. In January 1999, Hershey completed the sale of 94% of its U.S. pasta business to New World Pasta for $450 million in cash. The divestiture was intended to allow Hershey to focus on its core businesses. Hershey also divested its two main European businesses, Gubor in Germany and Spelari in Italy, and its Canadian Planters business, as well as its Luden's throat drops business. Although the company's products are distributed in over 90 countries, almost 90% of Hershey's sales are currently in the United States, Mexico, and Canada. The company appears uncommitted to markets outside North America, even in the face of evidence that the confectionary industry has globalized.

Products and Brands

Hershey grew from a small, one-product company in 1894 to a global company with fiscal year 2001 sales of $4.56 billion. The company's products include chocolate and nonchocolate confectionary products consisting of bar goods, bagged items, and boxed items; grocery products include baking items, peanut butter, chocolate chips, chocolate syrup, cocoa drink mixes, dessert toppings, and beverages. Hershey's chocolate milk is produced by independent dairies throughout the United States, using chocolate milk mix manufactured by Hershey. Chocolate and confectionary products are marketed under more than 50 brands, including Hershey, Kit Kat, Mr. Goodbar, Reese's, Kisses, Mounds, Almond Joy, Skor, Twizzlers, and Amazin' Fruit gummy bears fruit candy. Hershey significantly increased its participation in the nonchocolate side of the confectionary industry through its late 1996 acquisition of Leaf North America, whose major brands include Jolly Rancher, Whoppers, Milk Duds, and Good & Plenty. In December 2000, the company purchased the intense and breath freshener mints and gum businesses of Nabisco for $135 million. The acquired brands include Breath Savers mints and Ice Breakers, Carefree, Stickfree, Bubble Yum, and Fruit Stripe gums.

Marketing Strategies

Hershey's marketing strategies are based on the consistently superior quality of its products, mass distribution, and the best possible consumer value in terms of price and weight. Hershey devotes considerable resources to the development, manufacturing, and distribution of new products. Because the significant power of buyers, intense competition, and low inflation make it difficult to raise prices, the company has sought to adjust the prices and weights of its products to accommodate changes in manufacturing costs and profit objectives while at the same time maintaining consumer value. Recent product strategies include focusing on big brands and improving marketing mix, with a stronger emphasis on promotion.

The company's products are distributed in over two million retail outlets in the United States, including grocery wholesalers, chain stores, convenience stores, mass merchandisers, drugstores, vending companies, wholesale clubs, and food distributors. In recent months, Hershey has stepped up its focus on the convenience and vending channels, two channels in which its primary competitor Mars has traditionally done well. A single customer, Wal-Mart, accounts for approximately 18% of Hershey's total sales.

Labor Relations

Approximately half of Hershey's full- and part-time employees are covered by collective bargaining agreements. On April 27, 2002, nearly 3,000 workers at two Hershey Foods plants went on strike two days after negotiations between the company and a union broke down. The workers, who make chocolate and other confections in Hershey, Pennsylvania, began picketing about 9 A.M. in the first strike at the company in 22 years. The chocolate workers' Local 464 had been at odds with the company, which is based in Hershey, over wages and health care costs. The striking workers represent about one-fifth of the company's employees. Hershey said about 25% of its production comes from the two plants, but it had made contingency plans to meet its customers' needs during the strike.

A Summer of Discontent

In an unexpectedly swift reversal of its plans to diversify its holdings of Hershey Foods Corporation stock, by a vote of 10–7, the Hershey Trust Company, which is legally responsible for overseeing the Milton Hershey School, rejected Wrigley's $12.5 billion offer and announced that its 77% stake in Hershey was no longer for sale. The next morning, September 19, the Commonwealth Court upheld 4–1 an earlier injunction against any sale conducted without full public hearings.

The school, created for orphans but now serving a wide array of 1,200 disadvantaged youngsters, has been the sole beneficiary of Mr. Hershey's charitable trust as it has grown into the multibillions on the success of Hershey Foods. The 17 trustees, who ultimately control Hershey Foods, the school, and other Hershey entities, maintain that their concern for the school and community as well as advice from Pennsylvania Attorney General Michael Fisher led to the trust's initial decision to put the company up for sale. Trustees maintained that because more than half its $5.4 billion portfolio was in Hershey stock, the trust and school were quite vulnerable to business downturns.

When the town and alumni heard of the possible sale of the highly profitable candy company, they were aghast. Despite assurances that jobs would be protected and that the company would maintain its presence in the town, Hershey employees and school alumni banded together in a "Derail the Sale" campaign that ultimately had the Attorney General filing an injunction in Orphan's Court to overturn the very sale he had counseled. The rift between the trust and other Hershey stakeholders will be difficult to heal: A petition with 6,500 signatures was hand-delivered to Attorney General Fisher on Monday, September 23, calling for the removal of the 17 trustees.

Finance

Hershey's financial results have strengthened over the past two years, driven by divestitures, the elimination of marginal product lines, Hershey's ability to integrate a number of complementary acquisitions, and an extraordinarily high rate of new product success. The company also appears to have recovered from the flawed implementation of an enterprise wide information system that led to an inability to meet demand during Halloween and Christmas 1999 (increased order cycle time, decreased fill rates.) However, while cost of goods sold showed a slight decrease, selling and administrative expenses have increased as a percentage of sales, reflecting increased promotional spending. Hershey's annual and quarterly reports and SEC filings are available via www.hersheys.com, www.freeEdgar.com, and www.wsj.com.

The Industry

The $10+ billion U.S. confectionery industry is dominated by five major competitors that control over 70% of the market: Hershey, M&M Mars (Mars), Brach and Brock, Nestle, and RJR Nabisco; the remaining 30% is shared by local and regional candy manufacturers. The U.S. market leader for many years, Hershey slipped to number two, behind Mars, in 1999. Hershey dominates the U.S. chocolate segment, with a 43% share, followed by M&M Mars, with 27%, and Nestle, with just 12%.

Nestle, which acquired Carnation in the late 1990s, is the largest food company in the world and the strongest global competitor in the chocolate and confectionery segment, with 98% of its sales outside its home country, Switzerland. Nestle manufactures in 23 countries in highly automated plants. Although Mars is privately held and family controlled, analysts estimate the company's sales to be in excess of $7.5 billion. Mars has a much stronger presence outside the United States than Hershey and was able to gain over 12% market share in Mexico only one year after entering that market. In its grocery products segment, Hershey competes against such processed foods giants as Kraft, ConAgra, Heinz, General Mills, and Kellogg.

The confectionery segment of the processed foods industry is characterized by manufacturing economies of scale and high transportation costs for moving milk and sugar, the principal raw materials. Cocoa beans, the primary ingredient in chocolate, are imported from West Africa, South America, and equatorial regions in Asia. West Africa accounts for about 70% of the world crop. Over the past three years, cocoa prices have been subject to wide fluctuations attributable to the effect of weather on crop yield, imbalances between supply and demand, political unrest, currency exchange rates, and speculative influences. Hershey uses commodities futures contracts to hedge the prices of cocoa, sugar, corn sweeteners, and dairy products. U.S. import quotas and import duties to support the price of domestic sugar have resulted in domestic sugar prices that are substantially higher than those in the world market.

Industry analysts expect the mature, competitive confectionery segment of the global processed food industry to grow at 5%–8% per year. Consumption of chocolate appears to be closely correlated with national income; however, Asia is an exception to this rule as Asian consumers at all income levels have shown a preference for nonchocolate confections. Americans consume about 22 pounds of candy per person per year, while Europeans consume approximately 27 pounds. Chocolate accounts for approximately 54% of all candy consumption. Among European countries, Switzerland, Norway, and the United Kingdom consume the most chocolate.

case 37

AirTran Holdings, Inc.

Maryanne M. Rouse

AirTran Airways's ability to grow in what is arguably the worst environment in years for airlines adds an unexpected new chapter to one of the most unlikely turnaround stories in the airline industry. In 1996, when the carrier was known as ValuJet, it grounded all flights for three months after the crash of its Flight 592 in the Florida Everglades killed all 110 people on board. Fortunately, the carrier had floated a package of $150 million in junk bonds just prior to the Everglades crash, cash resources that proved critical as the company addressed safety concerns during the shutdown and the 11 successive loss quarters that followed. In 1997, ValuJet merged with AirTran Airways Corporation to form AirTran Holdings, Inc. (AAI).

At the end of October 2002, AirTran operated 388 daily flights to 40 destinations, primarily in the eastern United States, making it the second-largest "affordable-fare" scheduled airline in the United States in terms of departures and number three among discounters (behind Southwest and Jet Blue) in profitability. The company's operating cost per available seat mile (ASM) dropped 8.8% to 8.21 cents for third quarter 2002, below competitor Southwest's 8.37 cents. AirTran's reduction in units costs is all the more impressive because the carrier experienced a 179% increase in security and insurance costs compared to the same quarter a year earlier.

Although the company moved its headquarters from Atlanta to Orlando, Florida, after the 1996 crash, it still flies most of its flights to and from Atlanta, providing both point-to-point and one-stop flights through its Hartsfield hub. AirTran offers a business class any business can afford, all-assigned seating, a generous frequent-flyer program, and a corporate program dubbed "A2B." Unlike its competitors, the carrier never requires a roundtrip purchase or a Saturday night stay.

On September 26, 2002, AirTran announced that it would launch a regional jet operation, AirTran JetConnect, on November 15. AirTran JetConnect, which is operated by joint venture partner Air Wisconsin, flies 50-seat Canadair regional jets in short-haul markets to and from the airline's hub at Hartsfield Atlanta International Airport. AirTran JetConnect initially served Greensboro, North Carolina, Pensacola, Florida, and Savannah, Georgia—all of which were served by AirTran. The new service allows the company to redeploy its 717s to increase frequencies in longer-haul, more profitable markets and facilitate growth in larger markets not previously served. In addition, AirTran JetConnect allows the airline to expand into other short-haul markets as well as increase frequencies in underserved markets.

This case was prepared by Professor Maryanne M. Rouse of The University of South Florida. Copyright © 2002 by Maryanne M. Rouse. This case was edited for SMBP-9th edition. Reprinted by permission.

Marketing and Operations

AirTran's marketing strategy is to develop an innovative brand identity that sets it apart from its low-fare and full-service competitors. The company targets two primary segments: price-sensitive business travelers and leisure travelers, primarily in the eastern United States. To attract business travelers, the carrier launched a business class product that is, in terms of comfort, the equivalent of the first-class service offered by its full-service rivals. The business class cabin is configured with two-by-two oversized seats providing considerably more leg and seat room than the typical coach cabin. Targeted to the price-sensitive business flyer, upgrades to business class from coach are just $25.

AirTran offers a range of fares based on advance purchases of 14 days, seven days, three days, and "walk-up" fares. All fares are one-way and most are nonrefundable; however, reservations can be changed prior to departure with a service charge. The company also offers a unique frequent-flyer program called "A-Plus Awards" that allows members to earn free travel more quickly than its competitors and, for twice the number of flight credits, will even buy members a free domestic ticket on any other major carrier. However, while most major airlines keep track of member points electronically, members of A-Plus Awards must collect and save "flight credit" certificates in order to obtain award seats.

In addition to targeting individual business travelers, AirTran has focused on developing travel partnerships with companies of all sizes, from one- and two-person small businesses to such large corporations as BellSouth, State Farm, and John Deere. Under the terms of its A2B corporate travel program, employees of registered companies get free confirmed upgrades to business class when paying full coach fares, fee waivers for ticket refunds or changes, and advance seat assignment. Unlike rival Southwest, AirTran has established interline ticketing and baggage agreements with Delta, United, US Airways, and American Trans Air and has ticketing arrangements with major online travel services such as Orbitz, Priceline, Expedia, and Travelocity.

AirTran has been aggressive in lining up corporate and community support via public–private partnerships that allow the carrier to shift more of the risk of expansion to communities and businesses expected to benefit from overall lower fares in their markets. The "public" part comprises revenue guarantees by cities, counties, or other municipal entities to protect AirTran against losses during the initial phase of operations; the "private" part builds "travel banks" in which businesses pledge to spend a specified amount on tickets. Both elements help to build a loyal following and serve as a cushion against the early losses of expanding into a new city and the invariable backlash from bigger competitors, which often respond by slashing their own fares and expanding service. Because AirTran's arrival in a market typically drives fares down by as much as 50%, both cities and businesses view the partnership guarantees as money well spent. For example, when AirTran began service to Wichita in May 2002, the average full fare on the Wichita–Washington flight dropped from $1,667 to $460. Wichita, which was competing with other cities to lure AirTran, estimates that the entry of the low-fare carrier could lead to annual airfare savings of $43 million for business and leisure travelers.

Named "Best Low-Fare Airline" for 2001 and 2002 by *Entrepreneur* magazine, AirTran's cost structure is among the lowest in the domestic airline industry in terms of cost per ASM. The company's low-cost position is supported by an emphasis on cost controls, lower distribution costs (reservations, ticketing), and high employee productivity. The company's labor costs are equivalent to approximately 25% of revenue—the same percentage as Frontier's and JetBlue's—below Southwest's 30% and significantly below the full-service carriers' 40+%. An award-winning Web site that makes it easy to book flights online has helped AirTran shift 54.5% of its sales to the site—one of the highest percentages in the industry. The company estimates its cost per booking online at less than $1—a significant saving over the $8.50 average cost of booking through a travel agent.

In September 1999, the company became the launch customer for the new Boeing 717, an innovative, cost-efficient, and environmentally friendly commercial aircraft that should reduce both fuel and maintenance costs. As AirTran continues to replace its less efficient DC9s with Boeing 717s (the company's current fleet comprises 44 Boeing 717s and 20 DC9s), it has forged closer ties with Boeing and Boeing Capital Corporation, a full-service provider of financial services, including asset-based lending and leasing. Boeing Capital, an indirect wholly owned subsidiary of the Boeing Company, refinanced $201 million of AirTran's junk bonds in 2001 and also agreed to finance the 20 Boeing 717s to be delivered in 2002 and 22 used and 1 new 717 in 2003, enabling AirTran to continue its rapid fleet modernization.

Finance

AirTran struggled in 2001, posting a net loss of $2.8 million on revenue of $665.1 million. Although the carrier reported a full year loss, revenue was up from 2000. And, while the company posted a $3 million loss for first quarter 2002, earnings for both quarters two and three were in positive territory. Total quarter three 2002 operating revenues of $178 million reflected a 21.2% increase over the same quarter in the previous year, while quarter three 2002 net income of $1.18 million was a dramatic improvement over quarter three 2001 $10.6 million loss. Complete annual and quarterly financial information is available from the company's Web site (www.airtran.com), the *Wall Street Journal* (www.wsj.com), and FreeEdgar (www.edgar.gov).

The Industry

On the morning of September 11, 2001, terrorist attacks shut down the U.S. airline industry. The Federal Aviation Administration (FAA) suspended all commercial flights within hours after the attacks on the World Trade Center's Twin Towers and the Pentagon. Although some flights resumed three days later, on September 14, the industry still had not recovered nine months later. Continuing concerns about the safety of flying, a weaker-than-expected economic recovery, and delays resulting both from tighter security and fewer flights led to a passenger traffic year-over-year decline of approximately 12% among the nine major U.S. airlines in the first three quarters of 2002.

Major airlines, many of which deferred or canceled new aircraft deliveries, pared down flight schedules and furloughed employees in the wake of 9/11, have been slow to increase capacity to previous levels. Some majors have permanently retired up to 5% of their total capacity, mostly large, older, gas-guzzling planes such as the DC-10 and 727. And, while analysts and airline financial officers agree that retiring inefficient aircraft is a positive step toward profitability in an industry that had suffered from overcapacity, a great deal of that capacity is being replaced by low-fare start-ups, most of which are still growing, and by small-jet regional carriers. For example, New York–based Jet Blue Airways (JBLU), while still small (500 million revenue passenger miles in April 2002, about 10% of what Continental carried in the same period), has won over a significant number of business travelers on the long-haul routes that have been the province of big, full-service carriers for years. Strongly capitalized and well run, analysts predict that Jet Blue can grow at an aggressive 25% per year for the next five years by taking market share from the majors. Similarly, both Frontier Airlines (FRNT) and American Trans Air (AMTR) have made traffic gains at the expense of UAL's United Airlines in Denver and other western cities.

The airline industry is highly competitive as to fares, frequent-flyer benefits, routes, and service. Profit levels in the industry are highly sensitive to changes in operating and capital costs and the extent to which competitors attempt to "match" each other's fares and services as well as to general economic trends. Energy prices continue to be unpredictable: Favorable prices in the first quarter of 2002 were followed by sharp increases in April and May. The airlines have racked up higher costs for the security tax assessed on tickets; for the monthly security fees paid to the Transportation Department; for a war-risk insurance premium; for federally mandated directives such as stronger cockpit doors; and for the first class seats dedicated to federal air marshals. Testifying recently before a congressional committee, airline executives noted that if the United States does strike Iraq, the results will be disastrous for the industry because travel, particularly international travel, will fall off sharply at the same time that oil prices surge.

Of increasing concern to carriers is the number of business travelers who are practicing what one industry analyst calls "Airline Avoidance." Poor service and complex pricing, further exacerbated by arcane rules, regulations, and restrictions on reservation changes, have created an environment in which companies and individuals are purchasing planes, purchasing fractional ownership in planes, or choosing to drive. So many travelers are choosing the latter that Delta Air Lines (DAL) launched a "fare sale" at the end of March 2002 specifically to provide additional customer incentive to fly rather than drive. The short-haul market is crucial to profitability for full-service carriers because, in general, travelers pay more per mile to fly short trips.

Increasing numbers of travelers are using Web sites to book airline tickets, hotel rooms, and car rentals. According to the Internet analysis group Jupiter Media Metrix, consumers are expected to spend about $30.8 billion on travel sites in 2002, up from $24 billion in 2001. Concerned about prices and practices of online travel services, Congress created a nine-member commission to investigate the pricing, practices, and exclusive marketing agreements of various airline and independent sites.

The industry is subject to regulation by a number of federal, state, and local departments and agencies. The Department of Transportation (DOT) has regulatory jurisdiction over passenger airlines, with the FAA regulating aircraft maintenance and operations, including equipment, ground facilities, licensing, and communications. The Aviation and Transportation Security Act of 2001 established a new Transportation Security Administration (within the DOT) with responsibility for aviation security functions including passenger and baggage screening.

AirTran's key direct competitors include US Airways, Delta, and Southwest, in addition to regional and commuter lines. AirTran was ranked 18th among the largest global competitors in market capitalization (number of shares outstanding multiplied by market price), 19th in trailing 12-month (TTM) revenue, and 12th in TTM net income as of November 1, 2002 (see table below):

Company	Market Capitalization	TTM Revenue	Net Margin
Southwest Airlines Co. (LUV)	$11,310	$ 5,359	4.9%
Delta (DAL)	1,242	12,860	(12.18)
AirTran (AAI)	688	688	(1.60)

case 38

Tyson Foods, Inc.

Maryanne M. Rouse

Tyson Foods, Inc., produces, distributes, and markets beef, chicken, and pork products, including prepared foods and related allied products. The company's products are marketed and sold to national and regional grocery chains, regional grocery wholesalers, meat distributors, clubs, and warehouse stores. Institutional customers include military commissaries, industrial food processing companies, and national and regional chain restaurants. Tyson also distributes via international export companies and domestic distributors. The company's major export markets include Canada, China, Japan, Mexico, Puerto Rico, Russia, and South Korea.

The IBP Acquisition

In August 2001, Tyson acquired IBP, Inc., a major supplier of processed, minimally processed, and prepared beef and pork products. The combined company comprises two primary marketing groups: a food service and international group and a fresh meats and retail group. Operations are conducted in five segments: beef, chicken, pork, prepared foods, and other. Tyson holds about 28% of the U.S. beef market, 23% of the chicken market, and 18% of the pork market. Chicken accounted for 67% of fiscal 2001 revenues; beef, 19%; prepared foods, 8%; and pork, 6%; other sources of revenue were nominal. Tyson expects both increased revenue and decreased costs associated with purchasing, logistics, and administration once the integration of IBP is complete.

Prior to the acquisition, IBP had begun developing the first national retail brand of both case-ready red meat and quick-frozen steaks and pork chops under the Thomas E. Wilson brand. The IBP acquisition also allowed Tyson to extend its line of branded convenience foods to beef and pork via the Thomas E. Wilson brand of fully cooked family dinner meats. Found in the refrigerated meat case, these products can be prepared in as little as five minutes. Varieties under this brand include beef pot roast, seasoned pork roast, seasoned beef meatloaf, and seasoned beef sirloin roast. Although Tyson initially embraced the Thomas E. Wilson brand as a means of gaining market share in the fast-growing ready-to-eat segment, the company announced only a year later—to the surprise of industry analysts—that it would drop the Thomas E. Wilson brand and replace it with the Tyson name on some beef and pork

This case was prepared by Professor Maryanne M. Rouse of The University of South Florida. Copyright © 2002 by Maryanne M. Rouse. This case was edited for SMBP-9th edition. Reprinted by permission.

products while temporarily offering unbranded fresh meat to stores wishing to use their own labels.

Continued Restructuring

In August 2002, Tyson announced that it would close its company-owned and leased hog farms and end contracts with 132 contract hog producers in Arkansas and eastern Oklahoma. The company noted that transportation costs were a big factor in the decision to exit the pork processing business: Competing companies have pork-processing operations closer to packing facilities and consequently can avoid higher transportation costs for both finished hogs and grain.

As part of a continuing restructuring, both to integrate IBP into Tyson and to reposition the combined company as a provider of high-quality protein, the company announced in mid-September 2002 that it had reached a definitive agreement to sell its Specialty Brands, Inc., subsidiary to Fremont Partners, a San Francisco–based private equity firm. Specialty Brands is a leading producer of frozen food products, including frozen handheld Mexican appetizers and entrees, frozen filled pasta, and coated appetizers under the Jose Ole, Fred's for Starters, Rotanelli, Marquez, Posada, Little Juan, and Butcher Boy brands. The former Tyson subsidiary, which is headquartered in Ontario, California, has manufacturing sites in New York, Missouri, Texas, New Mexico, and California. With approximately 1,650 employees, Specialty Brands had sales of approximately $300 million in fiscal 2001. The sale is expected to result in a pretax gain of up to $25 million; Tyson expects to use the proceeds to pay down debt.

Finance

Tyson has had several difficult years. Reported earnings in 2001, although bolstered by the inclusion of nine weeks of postacquisition operating results of IBP, were negatively affected by an oversupply of chickens for most of the year and increases in operating costs: both cost of goods sold and operating expenses as a percentage of sales increased for the year. In early September 2002, Tyson lowered its fourth quarter projections for 2002 (fiscal year ended September 28, 2002) as a result of exiting the pork-processing business (estimated at $20–$30 million, pretax) and conversion from the Thomas E. Wilson brand (estimated at $27 million pretax). Annual reports and SEC filings are available via www.tyson.com, www.freeEdgar.com, www.wsj.com, and www.sec.gov.

Competitors and the Industry

Key competitors in the subindustry group of poultry, meats, and seafood processing include Pilgrim's Pride, a vertically integrated poultry processor offering a broad range of 600+ value-added products, Hormel, and Smithfield Foods. Smithfield Foods' principal activities include hog production and meat processing. The meat-processing group produces (domestically and internationally) a variety of fresh pork and processed meat products and markets them nationwide. This group has seven domestic processing subsidiaries and four international meat-processing entities. The hog production group provides the meat-processing group with approximately 50% of its live hog requirements. Meat processing accounted for 95% of Smithfield's fiscal 2001 revenues; hog production accounted for 5%.

Hormel Foods Corporation is a multinational manufacturer and marketer of consumer-branded meat and food products. The company is into processing of meat and poultry products and the production of prepared foods. The company markets its products to food wholesalers, retailers, and food service distributors.

Chicken has experienced greater growth in per capita consumption in U.S. markets than most other meat categories over the past 25 years. During that time, chicken consumption has increased 110%, while beef consumption has decreased approximately 41%. Consumption rates have been influenced by consumer awareness of the health and nutritional characteristics of chicken, the price advantage of chicken relative to red meat, the convenience of processed and prepared chicken products, and concerns about BCE (bovine spongiform encephalopathy, or "mad cow disease"). Recently, however, meatpackers have begun to invest hundreds of millions of dollars in a campaign to reverse a decades-long decline in red meat consumption. IBP, Hormel, Smithfield, and others are developing and aggressively marketing high-quality, prepackaged steaks, roasts, and chops under their company's own logos.

Key competitors in the broader food processing industry (consumer noncyclical sector) include ConAgra Foods, Kraft, Unilever, and Sara Lee. The mature, intensely competitive poultry and meat-processing industries are vulnerable to weather, demand shifts, and global political events. For example, in anticipation of the Bush administration's decision to impose steel tariffs, Russia announced that it would prohibit the import of chickens from the United States. (Russia noted that the ban would address concerns about the use of antibiotics by U.S. processors; however, Russia is expected to export approximately $1.2 billion worth of steel to the United States in the next two years—about the same dollar value of poultry U.S. processors expect to export during the same period.)

Negative Publicity

The entire industry has suffered some bad publicity relating to the unsanitary conditions of plants, high illness and injury rates for poultry and meatpacking workers, and heavy-handed tactics with growers and other suppliers, Tyson has been the subject of more negative news stories than its competitors, including wage and hour suits filed by current and former employees; EPA suits alleging violations of various environmental laws, including the Clean Air Act, the Clean Water Act, and the Resource Conservation and Recovery Act; a suit alleging violation of securities laws with respect to the IBP merger; and various patent infringement actions. In addition, Tyson has been targeted for investigation of influence peddling and charged with conspiracy to smuggle illegal aliens to work at a handful of the company's poultry plants.

The Challenge

How should Tyson position the company to gain and sustain competitive advantage in an industry characterized by increasing consolidation and intense competition? What strategies could the company pursue to effectively integrate the IBP acquisition while responding to competitive changes and a new emphasis on branding and value-added products in the beef and pork segments of the industry. What actions can Tyson take to overcome the perception that it is ethically challenged in its dealings with stakeholders?

case 39

Eli Lilly and Company

Maryanne M. Rouse

A leading U.S. pharmaceutical company, Eli Lilly and Company produces a wide variety of ethical drugs (approximately 94% of 2001 revenues) and animal health products (just under 6% of 2001 revenues). The company traces its history to Colonel Eli Lilly, a Union officer in the Civil War, who invented a process for coating pills with gelatin. Lilly's principal activities are to discover, develop, manufacture, and market pharmaceutical-based health care solutions. The company's pharmaceutical product lines comprise Neuroscience, Endocrine, Anti-infective, Cardiovascular agents, Oncology, and Animal Health. Lilly manufactures and distributes its products through owned or leased facilities in the United States, Puerto Rico, and 26 other countries; the company's products are sold in approximately 160 countries.

In the United States, Lilly's pharmaceutical products are distributed through approximately 35 independent wholesalers that serve physicians, pharmacies, hospitals, and other health care professionals. Three wholesalers in the United States—AmeriSource Bergen Corporation, Cardinal Health, and McKesson—each accounted for between 19% and 23% of 2001 consolidated net sales. Products are promoted through sales representatives who call on physicians, wholesalers, hospitals, managed-care organizations, retail pharmacists, and other health care professionals. The company supports sales representatives' efforts with advertising in medical and drug journals and distributes literature and samples of products to physicians at medical meetings. Like its competitors, Lilly also advertises certain products directly to consumers, a practice coming under increased criticism from public health and cost-containment advocates. Marketing methods and product emphasis is adapted to meet local needs and regulations in markets outside the United States. Lilly's patents are critical to maintaining its competitive position. Current patents include Zyprexa, Prozac, Permax, Darvon, Humulin, Evista, Humalog, Actos, Humatrope, Ceclor, Vancocin, Keflex, Nebcin, Lorabid, Gemzar, Tylan, Rumensin, Micotil, Surmax, Coban, ReoPro, Xigris, Dobutrex, and Axid. For a number of these products, in addition to the compound patent, the company holds patents on the manufacturing process, formulation, or uses that may extend beyond the expiration of the product patent.

Despite an array of new products that were on schedule to be introduced during 2002 and 2003, industry analysts have concerns for Lilly's performance as it moved beyond the "Prozac era." The company lost patent protection for its blockbuster antidepressant in August 2001, after a Federal Circuit Court reversed a part of a Federal Court decision upholding Lilly's

This case was prepared by Professor Maryanne M. Rouse of The University of South Florida. Copyright © 2002 by Maryanne M. Rouse. This case was edited for SMBP-9th edition. Reprinted by permission.

patents. Aggressive competition from generics resulted in a sales decline for Prozac of 66% in fourth Quarter 2001 and a decline of 23% for the year. The loss of Prozac revenues was partially offset by sales increases for five new drugs: the anti-psychotic *Zyprexa*; cancer agent *Gemzar*, a drug of choice for small-cell lung cancer; hormone replacement *Evista*, which is currently marketed as a preventive treatment for osteoporosis; *Humalog*, a synthetic insulin analog; and *Actos*, an oral type 2 diabetes treatment developed by one of Lilly's partners, Takeda Chemical Industries. Collectively, these five drugs posted a sales increase of 36% from 2000 to 2001 and accounted for 47% of the company's 2001 revenues.

As part of an inspection related to regulatory reviews of Lilly's Zyprexa intramuscular and Forteo products in 2001, the Federal Drug Administration (FDA) found quality problems at several of the company's manufacturing sites. Although Lilly appears to be moving in the right direction in resolving these quality issues, some observers doubt whether the company will be ready for a planned reinspection in early 2003. The bottom-line implication from this manufacturing mess is that several new product approvals could be delayed since a number of Lilly's near-term pipeline products are manufactured at two Indianapolis facilities scheduled for reinspection. The company's recent announcement that regulators may require a new trial for Strattera prior to granting approval may further derail the time table for this particular product. Lilly's margins are likely to remain under pressure from lower volumes and costs associated with resolving its manufacturing problems.

In early October 2002, Lilly and Bristol-Meyers Squibb settled over 300 lawsuits accusing them of failing to stop Kansas City pharmacist Robert Courtney from diluting cancer drugs over a period of years. Plaintiffs had maintained that both companies were complicit in the pharmacists' actions based on internal documents showing they knew as early as 1998, three years before the arrest, that cancer drugs were being diluted but failed to act. Lilly still faces a number of consumer lawsuits related to Prozac and is involved in patent litigation involving both Prozac and Zyprexa. Lilly may also face charges of deceptive marketing in connection with its osteoporosis drug, Evista. Critics have noted that Lilly has attempted to position Evista as a means of lowering the risk of cardiovascular (heart attack, heart-related chest pain, and other coronary events) based on data gathered in a study designed solely to assess Evista's effects on osteoporosis. There have also been questions raised about financial support provided by Lilly to the authors of the study.

The Industry

Despite near-term uncertainties with respect to pricing and patent expirations, the pharmaceutical industry is still one of the healthiest and widest-margin industries in the United States. U.S. prospects for the longer term are enhanced by demographic growth in the elderly segment of the population (accounting for about one-third of industry sales), as well as by new therapeutic products resulting from discoveries in genomics and biotechnology. However, drugs generating over $40 billion of industrywide sales in 2001 have lost or will lose patent protection over the next four years. The flood of patent expirations offers major opportunities for the generic manufacturers, especially for those obtaining 180 days of "first to file" marketing exclusivity.

On the regulatory front, the FDA has become much tougher on new drug approvals: Regulatory compliance is costly in both in- out-of-pocket application, establishment, and product fees and in time required to gain approval. The agency is also cracking down on drug manufacturing, with some plants closed as a result of quality problems.

Three key developments are expected to act as a ceiling on profits for pharmaceutical firms: (1) managed care plan buyers, which account for 65% of prescription drug purchases, have made drug cost containment a priority; (2) the likely passage of some type of prescription drug benefit for Medicare beneficiaries, would result in steep discounts; and (3) states have become very aggressive in pushing for new legislation aimed at obtaining greater drug discounts for Medicaid and other state-run programs.

Recent Developments

A growing challenge to U.S. pharmaceutical firms comes from increased out-of-country purchases. On October 12, 2002, the largest U.S. health insurer informed members of the senior citizens lobbying group, AARP, that it would reimburse them for prescriptions filled in Canada and elsewhere abroad. UnitedHealth Group, Inc., sent a letter to 97,000 people who bought insurance with a drug benefit through AARP about the coverage. Although buying prescription drugs outside the United States for use in the United States violates federal regulations, it is a growing practice among older Americans seeking relief from high-priced name-brand drugs. UnitedHealth and AARP appeared to want to keep the announcement low key; however, thousands of AARP members, as well as other senior citizens, regularly purchase their drugs in Canada and Mexico, where they are significantly cheaper—even if not reimbursed.

In early October 2002, the U.S. Office of the Inspector General warned drug companies that offering incentives, such as concert tickets and vacations, to physicians could lead to civil or criminal charges. The draft policy comes after years of concern about drug industry marketing practices that critics say influence doctors to prescribe certain drugs that lead to higher costs for consumers. The draft, which was open for 60 days of public comment, would not bar nominal-cost gifts. However, golf balls or bags emblazoned with company logos, meals other than those in conjunction with medical education, concert and other entertainment tickets, cash payments, and a wide range of other incentives would not be allowed.

The draft policy also prohibits drug companies from reporting average wholesale prices that differ substantially from what is actually charged—and touting those prices in marketing. The government's concern stems from the use of average wholesale prices in determining reimbursement for the drugs Medicare currently covers. There has been some concern that if drugs are sold to doctors for less, doctors can bill for the higher amount and keep the difference. Critics say it's a tactic drug makers use to lure doctors to their products and further inflate consumer drug costs by more than $1 billion annually.

Case Index

Glossary

80/20 rule A rule stating that one should monitor those 20% of the factors that determine 80% of the results. p. 259

absorptive capacity A firm's ability to value, assimilate, and utilize new external knowledge. p. 288

action plan A plan that states what actions are going to be taken, by whom, during what time frame, and with what expected results. p. 229

activity-based costing (ABC) An accounting method for allocating indirect and fixed costs to individual products or product lines based on the value-added activities going into that product. p. 245

adaptive mode A decision-making mode characterized by reactive solutions to existing problems rather than a proactive search for new opportunities. p. 19

advisory board A group of external business people who voluntarily meet periodically with the owners/managers of the firm to discuss strategic and other issues. p. 308

agency theory A theory which states that problems arise in corporations because the agents (top management) are not willing to bear responsibility for their decisions unless they own a substantial amount of stock in the corporation. p. 29

assessment center An approach to evaluate the suitability of a person for a position. p. 222

autonomous work teams A group of people who work together without a supervisor to plan, coordinate, and evaluate their own work. p. 97

balanced scorecard A measure that combines financial measures with operational measures of customer satisfaction, internal processes, and the corporation's innovation and improvement activities. p. 250

basic research and development (R&D) Research and development with focus on theoretical problem areas. p. 93

behavior control A control that specifies how something is to be done through policies, rules, standard operating procedures, and orders from a superior. p. 243

behavior substitution A phenomenon that occurs when people substitute activities that do not lead to goal accomplishment for activities that do lead to goal accomplishment because the wrong activities are being rewarded. p. 258

benchmarking The process of measuring products, services, and practices against those of competitors or companies recognized as industry leaders. p. 254

brainstorming The process of proposing ideas in a group without first mentally screening them. p. 72

budget A statement of a corporation's programs in terms of money required. p. 15

business model The mix of activities a company performs to deliver goods and services to customers. p. 304

business plan A written strategic plan for a new entrepreneurial venture. p. 306

Business Policy A previous name for strategic management; has a general management orientation and tends to look inward with concern for integrating the corporation's many functional activities. p. 2

Business Strategy A competitive and cooperative strategy at the business unit or product level that emphasizes improvement of the competitive position of a corporation's products or services in the specific industry or market segment served by that business unit. p. 13

cannibalize To replace popular products before they reach the end of their life cycle and become cash cows. p. 68

capability Something that a corporation can do exceedingly well, a key strength, a constituent skill. p. 165

capital budgeting The process of analyzing and ranking possible investments in terms of the additional outlays and additional receipts that will result from each investment. p. 92

cash cow A product that brings in far more money than is needed to maintain its market share. p. 152

categorical imperatives Kant's two principles to guide actions: A person's action is ethical only if that person is willing for that same action to be taken by everyone who is in a similar situation and a person should never treat another human being simply as a means but always as an end. p. 44

cellular organization A structure composed of cells (self-managing teams, autonomous business units, etc.) that can operate alone but can interact with other cells to produce a more potent and competent business mechanism. p. 207

center of gravity The part of the industry value chain that is most important to the company and the point where the company's greatest expertise and capabilities lay. p. 85

code of ethics A code that specifies how an organization expects its employees to behave while on the job. p. 43

codetermination The inclusion of a corporation's workers on its board of directors. p. 32

collusion The active cooperation of firms within an industry to reduce output and raise prices in order to get around the normal economic law of supply and demand. This practice is usually illegal. p. 126

common-size statements Income statements and balance sheets in which the dollar figures have been converted into percentages. p. 346

competitive intelligence A formal program of gathering information about a company's competitors. p. 70

competitive scope The breadth of a company's or a business unit's target market. p. 118

competitive strategy A strategy that states how a company or a business unit will compete in an industry. p. 117

complementor A company or an industry whose product works well with another industry's or firm's product and without which a product would lose much of its value. p. 64

concurrent engineering A process in which specialists from various functional areas work side-by-side rather than sequentially in an effort to design new products. p. 97

conglomerate structure A variant of the divisional structure, sometimes called a holding company. A conglomerate structure is typically an assemblage of legally independent firms (subsidiaries) operating under one corporate umbrella but controlled through the subsidiaries' boards of directors. p. 88

consolidated industry An industry in which a few large companies dominate. p. 122

constant dollars Dollars adjusted for inflation. p. 347

constraints on strategic management Characteristics peculiar to a not-for-profit organization that constrain its behavior and affect its strategic management. p. 329

continuous improvement A system developed by Japanese firms in which teams strive constantly to improve manufacturing processes. p. 172

cooperative strategies Strategies that involve working with other firms to gain competitive advantage within an industry. p. 126

core competency A corporate capability, something that a corporation can do exceedingly well. p. 82

corporate culture A collection of beliefs, expectations, and values learned and shared by a corporation's members and transmitted from one generation of employees to another. p. 89

corporate entrepreneurship Also called intrapreneurship; the creation of a new business within an existing organization. p. 291

corporate governance The relationship among the board of directors, top management, and shareholders in determining the direction and performance of a corporation. p. 26

corporate scenarios Pro forma balance sheets and income statements that forecast the effect that each alternative strategy will likely have on return on investment. p. 178

corporate stakeholders Groups that affect or are affected by the achievement of a firm's objectives. p. 40

corporate strategy A strategy that states a company's overall direction in terms of its general attitude toward growth and the management of its various business and product lines. p. 13

corporation A mechanism established to allow different parties to contribute capital, expertise, and labor for their mutual benefit. p. 26

cost focus A low-cost competitive strategy that concentrates on a particular buyer group or geographic market and attempts to serve only that niche. p. 119

cost leadership A low-cost competitive strategy that aims at the broad mass market. p. 118

cost proximity A process that involves keeping the higher price a company charges for higher quality close enough to that of the competition so that customers will see the extra quality as being worth the extra cost. p. 120

crisis of autonomy A time when people managing diversified product lines need more decision-making freedom than top management is willing to delegate to them. p. 200

crisis of control A time when business units act to optimize their own sales and profits without regard to the overall corporation. p. 200 *See also* suboptimization.

crisis of leadership A time when an entrepreneur is personally unable to manage a growing company. p. 200

cross-functional work team A work team composed of people from multiple functions. p. 97

defensive centralization A process in which top management of a not-for-profit retains all decision-making authority so that lower-level managers cannot take any actions to which the sponsors may object. p. 331

defensive tactic A tactic in which a company defends its current market. p. 125

Delphi technique A forecasting technique in which experts independently assess the probabilities of specified events. These assessments are combined and sent back to each expert for fine-tuning until agreement is reached. p. 72

devil's advocate An individual or a group assigned to identify the potential pitfalls and problems of a proposal. p. 183

dialectical inquiry A decision-making technique which requires that two proposals using different assumptions be generated for each alternative under consideration. p. 184

differentiation focus A differentiation competitive strategy that concentrates on a particular buyer group, product line segment, or geographic market. p. 119

differentiation strategy A strategy that involves providing unique and superior value to the buyer in terms of product quality, special features, or after-sale service. p. 118

distinctive competencies Capabilities of a firm that are superior to those of competitors. p. 82

divisional structure An organizational structure in which employees tend to be functional specialists organized according to product/market distinctions. p. 87

domain The suffix to a URL, such as .com, .gov, or .edu. p. 351

downsizing Planned elimination of positions or jobs. p. 222

due care The obligation of board members to closely monitor and evaluate top management. p. 27

durability The rate at which a firm's underlying resources and capabilities depreciate or become obsolete. p. 82

earnings per share (EPS) A calculation dividing net earnings by the number of shares of common stock issued. p. 246

EBITDA An acronym standing for earnings before interest, taxes, depreciation, and amortization. p. 347

economic value added (EVA) A shareholder value method of measuring corporate and divisional performance. EVA measures after-tax operating income minus the total annual cost of capital. p. 249

economies of scale A process in which unit costs are reduced by making large numbers of the same product. p. 97

economies of scope A process in which unit costs are reduced when the value chains of two separate products or services share activities, such as the same marketing channels or manufacturing facilities. p. 87

EFAS table External Factors Analysis Summary table, a table that organizes external factors into opportunities and threats and how well management is responding to these specific factors. p. 73

enterprise resource planning (ERP) **software** Software that unites all of a company's major business activities, from order processing to production, within a single family of software modules. p. 256

entrepreneur A person who initiates and manages a business undertaking and who assumes risk for the sake of a profit. p. 303

entrepreneurial mode A strategy made by one powerful individual in which the focus is on opportunities and problems are secondary. p. 18

entrepreneurial venture A new business whose primary goals are profitability and growth and that can be characterized by innovative strategic practices. p. 303

entry barrier An obstruction that makes it difficult for a company to enter an industry. p. 61

environmental scanning The monitoring, evaluation, and dissemination of information from the external and internal environments to key people within the corporation. p. 52

environmental uncertainty The degree of complexity plus the degree of change existing in an organization's external environment. p. 52

ethics The consensually accepted standards of behavior for an occupation, a trade, or a profession. p. 43

evaluation and control A process in which corporate activities and performance results are monitored so that actual performance can be compared with desired performance. p. 16

executive leadership The directing of activities toward the accomplishment of corporate objectives. p. 36

executive succession The process of grooming and replacing a key top manager. p. 221

executive type An individual with a particular mix of skills and experiences. p. 220

exit barrier An obstruction that keeps a company from leaving an industry. p. 62

experience curve A conceptual framework which states that unit production costs decline by some fixed percentage each time the total accumulated volume of production in units doubles. p. 96

expert opinion A nonquantitative forecasting technique in which experts in a particular area attempt to forecast likely developments. p. 72

explicit knowledge Knowledge that can be easily articulated and communicated. p. 83

external environment Forces outside an organization that are not typically within the short-run control of top management. p. 9

external strategic factors Environmental trends with both high probability of occurrence and high probability of impact on the corporation. p. 60

extranet An information network within an organization that is available to key suppliers and customers. p. 100

extrapolation A forecasting technique that extends present trends into the future. p. 72

financial leverage The ratio of total debt to total assets. p. 92

financial strategy A functional strategy to make the best use of corporate monetary assets. p. 169

first mover The first company to manufacture and sell a new product or service. p. 124

flexible manufacturing A type of manufacturing that permits the low-volume output of custom-tailored products at relatively low unit costs through economies of scope. p. 97

fragmented industry An industry in which no firm has large market share and each firm serves only a small piece of the total market. p. 64

free cash flow The amount of money a new owner can take out of a firm without harming the business. p. 347

functional strategy An approach taken by a functional area to achieve corporate and business unit objectives and strategies by maximizing resource productivity. This approach is concerned with developing and nurturing a distinctive competence to provide a company or business unit with a competitive advantage. p. 13

functional structure An organizational structure in which employees tend to be specialists in the business functions important to that industry, such as manufacturing, sales, or finance. p. 87

geographic-area structure A structure that allows a multinational corporation to tailor products to regional differences and to achieve regional coordination. p. 211

global industry An industry in which a company manufactures and sells the same products, with only minor adjustments for individual countries around the world. p. 65

goal An open-ended statement of what one wants to accomplish, with no quantification of what is to be achieved and no time criteria for completion. p. 12

goal displacement Confusion of means with ends, which occurs when activities originally intended to help managers attain corporate objectives become ends in themselves or are adapted to meet ends other than those for which they were intended. p. 258

gross domestic product (GDP) A measure of the total output of goods and services within a country's borders. p. 347

hierarchy of strategies A nesting of strategies by level from corporate to business to functional, so that they complement and support one another. p. 13

horizontal growth A corporate growth concentration strategy that involves expanding the firm's products into other geographic locations and/or increasing the range of products and services offered to current markets. p. 142

horizontal integration The degree to which a firm operates in multiple geographic locations at the same point in an industry's value chain. p. 142

horizontal strategy A corporate parenting strategy that cuts across business unit boundaries to build synergy across business units and to improve the competitive position of one or more business units. p. 159

human resource management (HRM) strategy A functional strategy that makes the best use of corporate human assets. p. 175

hypercompetition An industry situation in which the frequency, boldness, and aggressiveness of dynamic movement by the players accelerates to create a condition of constant disequilibrium and change. p. 68

IFAS table Internal Factor Analysis Summary table, a table that organizes internal factors into strengths and weaknesses and how well management is responding to these specific factors. p. 101

imitability The rate at which a firm's underlying resources and capabilities can be duplicated by others. p. 82

index of R&D effectiveness An index that is calculated by dividing the percentage of total revenue spent on research and development into new product profitability. p. 294

index of sustainable growth A calculation that shows how much of the growth rate of sales can be sustained by internally generated funds. p. 346

individual rights approach An approach which proposes that human beings have certain fundamental rights that should be respected in all decisions. p. 44

industry A group of firms that produce a similar product or service. p. 60

industry analysis An in-depth examination of key factors within a corporation's task environment. p. 53

industry matrix A chart that summarizes the key success factors within a particular industry. p. 69

industry scenario A forecasted description of an industry's likely future. p. 72

information systems strategy A functional strategy that uses information systems technology to provide competitive advantage. p. 176

input control A control that specifies resources, such as knowledge, skills, abilities, values, and motives of employees. p. 243

inside director An officer or executive employed by a corporation who serves on that company's board of directors; also called management director. p. 29

institution theory A theory which proposes that organizations adapt to changing conditions by imitating other successful organizations. p. 7

integration A process that involves a relatively balanced give-and-take of cultural and managerial practices between merger partners, with no strong imposition of cultural change on either company. p. 227

interlocking directorate A conditions that occurs when two firms share a director or when an executive of one firm sits on the board of a second firm. p. 33

internal environment Variables within an organization that are not usually within the short-run control of top management. p. 9

internal strategic factors Strengths (core competencies) and weaknesses that are likely to determine whether a firm will be able to take advantage of opportunities while avoiding threats. p. 81

intranet An information network within an organization that also has access to the Internet. p. 100

investment center A unit in which performance is measured in terms of the difference between the unit's resources and its services or products. p. 253

issues priority matrix A chart that ranks the probability of occurrence versus the probable impact on the corporation of developments in the external environment. p. 59

job characteristics model An approach to job design that is based on the belief that tasks can be described in terms of certain objective characteristics and that those characteristics affect employee motivation. p. 209

job design The design of individual tasks in an attempt to make them more relevant to the company and to the employee. p. 208

job enlargement Combining tasks to give a worker more of the same type of duties to perform. p. 208

job enrichment Altering jobs by giving the worker more autonomy and control over activities. p. 208

job rotation Moving workers through several jobs to increase variety. p. 208

joint venture An independent business entity created by two or more companies in a strategic alliance. p. 128

justice approach An approach which proposes that decision makers be equitable, fair, and impartial in the distribution of costs and benefits to individuals and groups. p. 44

just-in-time (JIT) A purchasing concept in which parts arrive at the plant just when they are needed rather than being kept in inventories. p. 174

key performance measures Essential measures for achieving a desired strategic option. p. 251

key success factors Variables that significantly affect the overall competitive position of a company within a particular industry. p. 69

late movers The later companies to manufacture and sell a new product or service. p. 124

law A formal code that permits or forbids certain behaviors. p. 43

lead director An outside director who coordinates the annual evaluation of the CEO. p. 34

lead user A customer who is ahead of market trends and has needs that go beyond those of the average user. p. 281

lead To provide direction to employees to use their abilities and skills most effectively and efficiently to achieve organizational objectives. p. 225

learning organization An organization that is skilled at creating, acquiring, and transferring knowledge and at modifying its behavior to reflect new knowledge and insights. p. 8

level of moral development One of Kohlberg's proposed three levels of moral development through which a person progresses: the preconventional level, the conventional level, and the principled level. p. 42

leveraged buy out An acquisition in which a company is acquired in a transaction financed largely by debt—usually obtained from a third party, such as an insurance company or an investment banker. p. 170

licensing arrangement An agreement in which the licensing firm grants rights to another firm in another country or market to produce and/or sell a product. p. 129

lifestyle company A small business in which the firm is purely an extension of the owner's lifestyle. p. 314

liquidation The termination of a firm in which all its assets are sold. p. 150

logical incrementalism A decision-making mode that can be viewed as a synthesis of planning, adaptive, and entrepreneurial modes. p. 19

logistics strategy A functional strategy that deals with the flow of products into and out of the manufacturing process. p. 174

long-term evaluation method A method in which managers are compensated for achieving objectives set over a multiyear period. p. 260

long-term orientation The extent to which society is oriented toward the long term versus the short term. p. 233

lower cost strategy A strategy in which a company or business unit designs, produces, and markets a comparable product more efficiently than its competitors. p. 118

management audit A technique used to evaluate corporate activities. p. 252

management by objectives (MBO) An organizationwide approach to ensuring purposeful action toward desired objectives. p. 231

management contracts Agreements through which a corporation uses some of its personnel to assist a firm in another country for a specified fee and period of time. p. 146

market development A marketing functional strategy in which a company or business unit captures a larger share of an existing market for current products through market penetration or develops new markets for current products. p. 168

market location tactics Tactics that determine where a company or business unit will compete. p. 125

market position Refers to the selection of specific areas for marketing concentration and can be expressed in terms of market, product, and geographical locations. p. 90

market research A means of obtaining new product ideas by surveying current or potential users regarding what they would like in a new product. p. 282

market segmentation The division of a market into segments to identify available niches. p. 90

market value added (MVA) The difference between the market value of a corporation and the capital contributed by shareholders and lenders. p. 250

marketing mix The particular combination of key variables (product, place, promotion, and price) that can be used to affect demand and to gain competitive advantage. p. 90

marketing strategy A functional strategy that deals with pricing, selling, and distributing a product. p. 168

mass customization The low-cost production of individually customized goods and services. p. 97

mass production A system in which employees work on narrowly defined, repetitive tasks under close supervision in a bureaucratic and hierarchical structure to produce a large amount of low-cost, standard goods and services. p. 172

matrix of change A chart that compares target practices (new programs) with existing practices (current activities). p. 194

matrix structure A structure in which functional and product forms are combined simultaneously at the same level of the organization. p. 204

mission The purpose or reason for an organization's existence. p. 10

mission statement A statement that defines the fundamental, unique purpose that sets a company apart from other firms of its type and identifies the scope of the company's operations in terms of products offered and markets served. pp. 10–11

modular manufacturing A system in which pre-assembled subassemblies are delivered as they are needed to a company's assembly-line workers, who quickly piece the modules together into finished products. p. 173

moral relativism A theory which proposes that morality is relative to some personal, social, or cultural standard, that there is no method for deciding whether one decision is better than another. p. 42

morality Precepts of personal behavior that are based on religious or philosophical grounds. p. 43

multidomestic industry An industry in which companies tailor their products to the specific needs of consumers in a particular country. p. 64

multinational corporation (MNC) A company that has significant assets and activities in multiple countries. p. 56

multiple sourcing A purchasing strategy in which a company orders a particular part from several vendors. p. 173

mutual service consortium A partnership of similar companies in similar industries that pool their resources to gain a benefit that is too expensive to develop alone. p. 128

net present value A calculation of the value of a project that is made by predicting the project's payouts, adjusting them for risk, and subtracting the amount invested. p. 181

network structure An organization (virtual organization) that outsources most of its business functions. p. 206

new entrants Businesses entering an industry that typically bring new capacity to an industry, a desire to gain market share, and substantial resources. p. 61

no-change strategy A decision to do nothing new, to continue current operations and policies for the foreseeable future. p. 147

not-for-profit organizations Private nonprofit corporations and public governmental units or agencies. p. 325

objectives The end results of planned activity, which are quantified and have time horizons. p. 12

offensive tactic A tactic that calls for competing in an established competitor's current market location. p. 125

operating budget A budget for a business unit that is approved by top management during strategy formulation and implementation. p. 252

operating cash flow The amount of money generated by a company before the costs of financing and taxes are figured. p. 347

operating leverage The impact of a specific change in sales volume on net operating income. p. 96

operations strategy A functional strategy that determines how and where a product or service is to be manufactured, the level of vertical integration in the production process, and the deployment of physical resources. p. 171

organization slack Unused resources within an organization. p. 139

organizational analysis Internal scanning concerned with identifying an organization's strengths and weaknesses. p. 81

organizational life cycle How organizations grow, develop, and eventually decline. p. 201

organizational structure The formal setup of a business corporation's value chain components in terms of work flow, communication channels, and hierarchy. p. 87

output control A control that specifies what is to be accomplished by focusing on the end result of the behaviors through the use of objectives and performance targets. p. 243

outside directors Members of a board of directors who are not employees of the board's corporation; also called nonmanagement directors. p. 29

outsourcing A process in which resources are purchased from others through long-term contracts instead of being made within the company. p. 142

parallel sourcing A process in which two suppliers are the sole suppliers of two different parts, but they are also backup suppliers for each other's parts. p. 174

parenting-fit matrix A summary of various judgments regarding corporate/business unit fit for a corporation as a whole. p. 157

patterns of influence A concept stating that influence in strategic management derives from a not-for-profit organization's sources of revenue. p. 327

pause/proceed with caution strategy A corporate strategy in which nothing new is attempted; an opportunity to rest before continuing a growth or retrenchment strategy. p. 147

penetration pricing A marketing strategy to hasten market development that offers a pioneer the opportunity to use the experience curve to gain market share. p. 169

performance The end result of activities, actual outcomes of a strategic management process. p. 16

performance appraisal system A system to systematically evaluate employee performance and promotion potential. p. 221

periodic statistical reports Reports summarizing data on key factors such as the number of new customer contracts, volume of received orders, and productivity figures. p. 252

pioneer p. 124 *See* first mover.

piracy The making and selling counterfeit copies of well-known name-brand products. p. 255

planning mode A decision-making mode that involves the systematic gathering of appropriate information for situation analysis, the generation of feasible alternative strategies, and the rational selection of the most appropriate strategy. p. 19

policy A broad guideline for decision making that links the formulation of strategy with its implementation. p. 14

political strategy A strategy to influence a corporation's stakeholders. p. 181

population ecology A theory which proposes that once an organization is successfully established in a particular environmental niche, it is unable to adapt to changing conditions. p. 7

portfolio analysis An approach to corporate strategy in which top management views its product lines and business units as a series of investments from which it expects a profitable return. p. 151

pressure-cooker crisis A situation that exists when employees in collaborative organizations eventually grow emotionally and physically exhausted from the intensity of teamwork and the heavy pressure for innovative solutions. p. 201

prime interest rate The rate of interest banks charge on their lowest-risk loans. p. 347

privatization The selling of state-owned enterprises to private individuals or corporations or the hiring of a private business to provide services previously offered by a state agency. p. 326

pro forma financial statements Financial statements projected into the future. p. 178

procedures A list of sequential steps or techniques that describe in detail how a particular task or job is to be done. Procedures detail the various activities that must be carried out in order to complete a corporation's programs. p. 15

process innovations Improvements to the making and selling of current products. p. 287

product champion A person who generates a new idea and supports it through many organizational obstacles. p. 291

product development A marketing strategy in which a company or unit develops new products for existing markets or develops new products for new markets. p. 169

product life cycle A graph showing time plotted against dollar sales of a product as it moves from introduction through growth and maturity to decline. p. 90

product R&D Research and development concerned with product or product-packaging improvements. p. 93

product/market evolution matrix A table in which products are plotted in terms of their competitive positions and their stages of product/market evolution. p. 289

product-group structure A structure of a multinational corporation that enables the company to introduce and manage a similar line of products around the world. p. 211

production sharing The process of combining the higher labor skills and technology available in developed countries with the lower-cost labor available in developing countries. p. 145

profit center A unit's performance, measured in terms of the difference between revenues and expenditures. p. 253

profit strategy A strategy that artificially supports profits by reducing investment and short-term discretionary expenditures. p. 147

program A statement of the activities or steps needed to accomplish a single-use plan in strategy implementation. p. 15

propitious niche A portion of a market that is so well suited to a firm's internal and external environment that other corporations are not likely to challenge or dislodge it. p. 112

public or collective goods Certain goods that are available to all in a society that profit-making firms cannot or will not provide. p. 325

pull strategy A marketing strategy in which advertising pulls the products through the distribution channels. p. 169

purchasing power parity (PPP) A measure of the cost, in dollars, of the U.S.-produced equivalent volume of goods that another nation's economy produces. p. 58

purchasing strategy A functional strategy that deals with obtaining the raw materials, parts, and supplies needed to perform the operations function. p. 173

push strategy A marketing strategy in which a large amount of money is spent on trade promotion in order to gain or hold shelf space in retail outlets. p. 169

quality of work life A concept that emphasizes improving the human dimension of work to improve employee satisfaction and existing union relations. p. 98

quasi-integration A type of vertical growth/integration in which a company does not make any of its key supplies but purchases most of its requirements from outside suppliers that are under its partial control. p. 141

question marks New products that have the potential for success and need a lot of cash for development. Also called problem children or wildcats. p. 151

R&D intensity A company's spending on research and development as a percentage of sales revenue. p. 92

R&D mix The balance of basic, product, and process research and development. p. 93

R&D strategy A functional strategy that deals with product and process innovation. p. 170

ratio analysis The calculation of ratios from data in financial statements to identify possible strengths or weaknesses. p. 342

real options An approach to new project investment when the future is highly uncertain. p. 181

red tape crisis A crisis that occurs when a corporation has grown too large and complex to be managed through formal programs. p. 201

reengineering The radical redesign of business processes to achieve major gains in cost, service, or time. p. 207

repatriation of profits The transfer of profits from a foreign subsidiary to a corporation's headquarters. p. 53

replicability The ability of competitors to duplicate resources and imitate another firm's success. p. 83

resource An asset, a competency, a process, a skill, or knowledge that is controlled by a corporation. p. 81

responsibility center A unit that is isolated so that it can be evaluated separately from the rest of the corporation. p. 252

retrenchment strategies Corporate strategies to reduce a company's level of activities and to return it to profitability. p. 138

return on equity (ROE) A measure of performance that is calculated by dividing net income by total equity. p. 247

return on investment (ROI) A measure of performance that is calculated by dividing net income before taxes by total assets. p. 246

revenue center A responsibility center in which production, usually in terms of unit or dollar sales, is measured without consideration of resource costs (e.g., salaries). p. 252

reverse engineering Taking apart a competitor's product in order to find out how it works. p. 82

risk A measure of the probability that one strategy will be effective, the amount of assets the corporation must allocate to that strategy, and the length of time the assets will be unavailable. p. 180

scenario writing A forecasting technique in which focused descriptions of different likely futures are presented in a narrative fashion. p. 72

SFAS matrix Strategic Factors Analysis Summary matrix, a chart that summarizes an organization's strategic factors by combining the external factors from an EFAS table with the internal factors from an IFAS table. p. 110

shareholder value The present value of the anticipated future stream of cash flows from a business plus the value of the company if it were liquidated. p. 248

simple structure A structure for new entrepreneurial firms in which the employees tend to be generalists and jacks-of-all-trades. p. 87

skim pricing A marketing strategy in which a company charges a high price while a product is novel and competitors are few. p. 169

social responsibility The ethical and discretionary responsibilities a corporation owes its stakeholders. p. 39

societal environment Economic, technological, political–legal, and sociocultural environmental forces that do not directly touch on the short-run activities of an organization but influence its long-run decisions. p. 52

sole sourcing Relying on only one supplier for a particular part. p. 174

sources of innovation Drucker's proposed seven sources of new ideas that should be monitored by those interested in starting entrepreneurial ventures. p. 310

sponsor A department manager who recognizes the value of a new idea, helps obtain funding to develop the innovation, and facilitates the implementation of the innovation. p. 291

stability strategies Corporate strategies to make no change to the company's current direction or activities. p. 138

staffing Human resource management priorities and use of personnel. p. 218

stages of corporate development A pattern of structural development that corporations follow as they grow and expand. p. 198

stages of international development The stages through which international corporations evolve in their relationships with widely dispersed geographic markets and the manner in which they structure their operations and programs. p. 210

stages of new product development The stages of getting a new innovation into the marketplace. p. 290

staggered board A board on which directors serve terms of more than one year so that only a portion of the board of directors stands for election each year. p. 34

stakeholders *See* corporate stakeholders.

stakeholder measures Various criteria used by each stakeholder category to determine how well a corporation is performing. p. 247

stakeholder priority matrix A chart that categorizes stakeholders in terms of their interest in a corporation's activities and their relative power to influence the corporation's activities. p. 181

standard cost center A responsibility center that is primarily used to evaluate the performance of manufacturing facilities. p. 252

standard operating procedures (SOPs) Plans that detail the various activities that must be carried out to complete a corporation's programs. p. 196

stars Market leaders that are able to generate enough cash to maintain their high shares of the market. p. 151

statistical modeling A quantitative technique that attempts to discover causal or explanatory factors that link two or more time series together. p. 72

steering controls Measures of variables that influence future profitability. p. 243

stewardship theory A theory which suggests that executives tend to be more motivated to act in the best interests of the corporation than for their own self-interests. p. 30

strategic alliance A partnership of two or more corporations or business units to achieve strategically significant objectives that are mutually beneficial. p. 127

strategic audit A checklist of questions by area or issue that enables a systematic analysis of various corporate functions and activities. pp. 252, 262

strategic business unit (SBU) A division or group of divisions composed of independent product-market segments that are given primary authority for the management of their own functions. p. 87

strategic choice The evaluation of strategies and selection of the best alternative. p. 183

strategic choice perspective A theory which proposes that organizations adapt to a changing environment and have the opportunity and power to reshape their environment. p. 8

strategic decisions Decisions that deal with the long-run future of an entire organization and are rare, consequential, and directive. p. 18

strategic factors External and internal factors that determine the future of a corporation. p. 9

strategic group A set of business units or firms that pursue similar strategies and have similar resources. p. 66

strategic inflection point A point in time when a major change takes place in an industry due to the introduction of new technologies, a change in regulatory environment, a change in customer's values, or a change in what customers prefer. p. 17

strategic management A set of managerial decisions and actions that determine the long-run performance of a corporation. p. 2

strategic myopia The willingness to reject unfamiliar as well as negative information. p. 59

strategic piggybacking The development of a new activity for a not-for-profit organization that would generate the funds needed to make up the difference between revenues and expenses. p. 332

strategic planning staff A group of people charged with supporting both top management and business units in the strategic planning process. p. 37

strategic rollup A means of consolidating a fragmented industry in which an entrepreneur acquires hundreds of owner-operated small businesses, resulting in a large firm with economies of scale. p. 122

strategic type A category of firms based on a common strategic orientation and a combination of structure, culture, and processes that are consistent with that strategy. p. 66

strategic vision A description of what a company is capable of becoming. p. 36

strategic window A unique market opportunity that is available only for a particular time. p. 112

strategic-funds method An evaluation method that encourages executives to look at development expenses as being different from expenses required for current operations. p. 260

strategy A comprehensive plan that states how a corporation will achieve its mission and objectives. p. 13

strategy formulation Development of long-range plans for the effective management of environmental opportunities and threats in light of corporate strengths and weaknesses. p. 10

strategy implementation A process by which strategies and policies are put into action through the development of programs, budgets, and procedures. p. 15

strategy shadow committee An approach for generating a series of strategic alternatives via a committee that is composed of employees at least two echelons below the executive-level strategy committee. p. 184

structure *See* organizational structure.

stuck in the middle A term that refers to a situation in which a company or business unit has not achieved a generic competitive strategy and has no competitive advantage and is therefore doomed to below-average performance. p. 120

suboptimization A phenomenon in which a unit optimizes its goal accomplishment to the detriment of the organization as a whole. p. 259

substitute products Products that appear to be different but can satisfy the same need as other products. p. 62

supply chain management The formation of networks for sourcing raw materials, manufacturing products or creating services, storing and distributing goods, and delivering goods or services to customers and consumers. p. 102

support activities Activities which ensure that the primary value-chain activities operate effectively and efficiently. p. 86

SWOT analysis Analysis that involves the strengths, weaknesses, opportunities, and threats that may be strategic factors for a specific company. p. 9

synergy A concept which states that the whole is greater than the sum of its parts, that two units will achieve more together than they could separately. p. 143

tacit knowledge Knowledge that is not easily communicated because it is deeply rooted in employee experience or in a corporation's culture. p. 83

taper integration A type of vertical integration in which a firm internally produces less than half of its own requirements and buys the rest from outside suppliers. p. 141

task environment The part of the business environment that includes the elements or groups that directly affect the corporation and, in turn, are affected by it. p. 53

technological competence A corporation's proficiency in managing research personnel and integrating their innovations into its day-to-day operations. p. 92

technological discontinuity The displacement of one technology by another. p. 94

technology transfer The process of taking a new technology from the laboratory to the marketplace. p. 93

time to market The time from inception to profitability of a new product. p. 284

timing tactic A tactic that determines when a business will enter a market with a new product. p. 124

total quality management (TQM) An operational philosophy that is committed to customer satisfaction and continuous improvement. p. 232

TOWS matrix A chart that illustrates how the external opportunities and threats facing a corporation can be matched with that company's internal strengths and weaknesses to result in four sets of strategic alternatives. p. 114

tracking stock A type of common stock that is tied to one portion of a corporation's business. p. 170

transaction cost economics A theory which proposes that vertical integration is more efficient than contracting for goods and services in the marketplace when the transaction costs of buying goods on the open market become too great. p. 140

transfer pricing A practice in which one unit can charge a transfer price for each product it sells to a different unit within a company. p. 253

transfer pricing, international A practice that involves selling goods from one unit to another unit (in a different country) within the same multinational corporation in order to minimize taxes. p. 255

transferability The ability of competitors to gather the resources and capabilities necessary to support a competitive challenge. p. 83

transparency The speed with which other firms can understand the relationship of resources and capabilities supporting a successful firm's strategy. p. 82

Triad The three developed markets of Japan, North America, and Western Europe, which form a single market with common needs. p. 56

triggering event Something that acts as a stimulus for a change in strategy. p. 17

turnaround specialist A manager who is brought into a weak company to salvage that company in a relatively attractive industry. p. 220

turnaround strategy A plan that emphasizes the improvement of operational efficiency when a corporation's problems are pervasive but not yet critical. p. 148

turnkey operations Contracts for the construction of operating facilities in exchange for a fee. p. 145

utilitarian approach A theory which proposes that actions and plans should be judged by their consequences. p. 43

value chain A linked set of value-creating activities that begins with basic raw materials coming from suppliers and ends with distributors getting the final goods into the hands of the ultimate consumer. p. 84

value trap businesses Units that fit well with parenting opportunities but are misfits with the parent's understanding of the units' strategic factors. p. 158

value-chain partnership A strategic alliance in which one company or unit forms a long-term arrangement with a key supplier or distributor for mutual advantage. p. 129

vertical growth A corporate growth strategy in which a firm takes over a function previously provided by a supplier or distributor. p. 139

vertical integration The degree to which a firm operates in multiple locations on an industry's value chain, from extracting raw materials to retailing. p. 140

virtual organization An organizational structure that is composed of a series of project groups or collaborations linked by changing nonhierarchical, cobweb-like networks. p. 206

virtual teams Groups of geographically and/or organizationally dispersed co-workers that are assembled using a combination of telecommunications and information technologies to accomplish an organizational task. p. 103

VRIO framework Barney's proposed analysis to evaluate a firm's key resources in terms of value, rareness, imitability, and organization. p. 81

weighted-factor method A method that is appropriate for measuring and rewarding the performance of top SBU managers and group-level executives when performance factors and their importance vary from one SBU to another. p. 260

whistleblower An employee who reports questionable behavior by other employees of the same company to a higher authority or to the media. p. 43

z-value A formula that combines five ratios by weighting them according to their importance to a corporation's financial strength to predict the likelihood of bankruptcy. p. 346

Name Index

Subject Index